The Handbook of Global Communication and Media Ethics

Volume I

Handbooks in Communication and Media

This series aims to provide theoretically ambitious but accessible volumes devoted to the major fields and subfields within communication and media studies. Each volume sets out to ground and orientate the student through a broad range of specially commissioned chapters, while also providing the more experienced scholar and teacher with a convenient and comprehensive overview of the latest trends and critical directions.

The Handbook of Children, Media, and Development, *edited by Sandra L. Calvert and Barbara J. Wilson*
The Handbook of Crisis Communication, *edited by W. Timothy Coombs and Sherry J. Holladay*
The Handbook of Internet Studies, *edited by Mia Consalvo and Charles Ess*
The Handbook of Rhetoric and Public Address, *edited by Shawn J. Parry-Giles and J. Michael Hogan*
The Handbook of Critical Intercultural Communication, *edited by Thomas K. Nakayama and Rona Tamiko Halualani*
The Handbook of Global Communication and Media Ethics, *Robert S. Fortner and P. Mark Fackler*

Forthcoming
The Handbook of Global Research Methods, *edited by Ingrid Volkmer*
The Handbook of International Advertising Research, *edited by Hong Cheng*
The Handbook of Communication and Corporate Social Responsibility, *edited by Oyvind Ihlen, Jennifer Bartlett and Steve May*
The Handbook of Gender and Sexualities in the Media, *edited by Karen Ross*
The Handbook of Global Health Communication and Development, *edited by Rafael Obregon and Silvio Waisbord*
The Handbook of Global Online Journalism, *edited by Eugenia Siapera and Andreas Veglis*

The Handbook of Global Communication and Media Ethics

Volume I

Edited by

Robert S. Fortner and P. Mark Fackler

A John Wiley & Sons, Ltd., Publication

This edition first published 2011
© 2011 Blackwell Publishing Ltd

Blackwell Publishing was acquired by John Wiley & Sons in February 2007. Blackwell's publishing program has been merged with Wiley's global Scientific, Technical, and Medical business to form Wiley-Blackwell.

Registered Office
John Wiley & Sons Ltd, The Atrium, Southern Gate, Chichester, West Sussex, PO19 8SQ, United Kingdom

Editorial Offices
350 Main Street, Malden, MA 02148-5020, USA
9600 Garsington Road, Oxford, OX4 2DQ, UK
The Atrium, Southern Gate, Chichester, West Sussex, PO19 8SQ, UK

For details of our global editorial offices, for customer services, and for information about how to apply for permission to reuse the copyright material in this book please see our website at www.wiley.com/wiley-blackwell.

The right of Robert S. Fortner and P. Mark Fackler to be identified as the authors of the editorial material in this work has been asserted in accordance with the UK Copyright, Designs and Patents Act 1988.

All rights reserved. No part of this publication may be reproduced, stored in a retrieval system, or transmitted, in any form or by any means, electronic, mechanical, photocopying, recording or otherwise, except as permitted by the UK Copyright, Designs and Patents Act 1988, without the prior permission of the publisher.

Wiley also publishes its books in a variety of electronic formats. Some content that appears in print may not be available in electronic books.

Designations used by companies to distinguish their products are often claimed as trademarks. All brand names and product names used in this book are trade names, service marks, trademarks or registered trademarks of their respective owners. The publisher is not associated with any product or vendor mentioned in this book. This publication is designed to provide accurate and authoritative information in regard to the subject matter covered. It is sold on the understanding that the publisher is not engaged in rendering professional services. If professional advice or other expert assistance is required, the services of a competent professional should be sought.

Library of Congress Cataloging-in-Publication Data
The handbook of global communication and media ethics / edited by Robert S. Fortner and P. Mark Fackler.
  p.   cm. – (Handbooks in communication and media; 7)
  Includes bibliographical references and index.
  ISBN 978-1-4051-8812-8 (hardback)
  1. Communication–Moral and ethical aspects.   2. Mass media–Moral and ethical aspects.
I. Fortner, Robert S.   II. Fackler, Mark P.
  P94.H354 2011
  175–dc22

                                                        2010043496
A catalogue record for this book is available from the British Library.

This book is published in the following electronic formats: ePDFs 9781444390605; Wiley Online Library 9781444390629; ePub 9781444390612

Set in 10/13pt Galliard, SPi Publisher Services, Pondicherry, India
Printed and bound in Singapore by Markono Print Media Pte Ltd

1   2011

Contents

Volume I

Notes on Contributors	ix
Preface	xix

1 Primordial Issues in Communication Ethics   1
Clifford G. Christians

2 Communication Ethics: The Wonder of Metanarratives
in a Postmodern Age   20
Ronald C. Arnett

3 Information, Communication, and Planetary Citizenship   41
Luiz Martins da Silva

4 Global Communication and Cultural Particularisms: The Place
of Values in the Simultaneity of Structural Globalization
and Cultural Fragmentation – The Case of Islamic Civilization   54
Bassam Tibi

5 The Ethics of Privacy in High versus Low Technology Societies   79
Robert S. Fortner

6 Social Responsibility Theory and Media Monopolies   98
P. Mark Fackler

7 Ethics and Ideology: Moving from Labels to Analysis   119
Lee Wilkins

8 Fragments of Truth: The Right to Communication
as a Universal Value   133
Philip Lee

9 Glocal Media Ethics   154
Shakuntala Rao

10	Feminist Ethics and Global Media *Linda Steiner*	171
11	Words as Weapons: A History of War Reporting – 1945 to the Present *Richard Lance Keeble*	193
12	Multidimensional Objectivity for Global Journalism *Stephen J.A. Ward*	215
13	New Media and an Old Problem: Promoting Democracy *Deni Elliott and Amanda Decker*	234
14	The Dilemma of Trust *Ian Richards*	247
15	The Ethical Case for a Blasphemy Law *Neville Cox*	263
16	The Medium is the Moral *Michael Bugeja*	298
17	Development Ethics: The Audacious Agenda *Chloe Schwenke*	317
18	Indigenous Media Values: Cultural and Ethical Implications *Joe Grixti*	342
19	Media Ethics as Panoptic Discourse: A Foucauldian View *Ed McLuskie*	364
20	Ethical Anxieties in the Global Public Sphere *Robert S. Fortner*	376
21	Universalism versus Communitarianism in Media Ethics *Clifford G. Christians*	393
22	Responsibility of Net Users *Raphael Cohen-Almagor*	415
23	Media Ethics and International Organizations *Cees J. Hamelink*	434
24	Making the Case for What Can and Should Be Published *Bruce C. Swaffield*	452
25	Ungrievable Lives: Global Terror and the Media *Giovanna Borradori*	461
26	Journalism Ethics in the Moral Infrastructure of a Global Civil Society *Robert S. Fortner*	481

Volume II

27 Problems of Application   501
    P. Mark Fackler

28 Disenfranchised and Disempowered: How the Globalized
    Media Treat Their Audiences – A Case from India   516
    Anita Dighe

29 Questioning Journalism Ethics in the Global Age:
    How Japanese News Media Report and Support
    Immigrant Law Revision   534
    Kaori Hayashi

30 Ancient Roots and Contemporary Challenges:
    Asian Journalists Try to Find the Balance   554
    Jiafei Yin

31 Understanding Bollywood   577
    Vijay Mishra

32 Peace Communication in Sudan: Toward Infusing
    a New Islamic Perspective   602
    Haydar Badawi Sadig and Hala Asmina Guta

33 Media and Post-Election Violence in Kenya   626
    *P. Mark Fackler, Levi Obonyo, Mitchell Terpstra,
    and Emmanuel Okaalet*

34 Ethics of Survival: Media, Palestinians,
    and Israelis in Conflict   655
    Oliver Witte

35 Voiceless Glasnost: Responding to Government Pressures
    and Lack of a Free Press Tradition in Russia   677
    Victor Akhterov

36 Media Use and Abuse in Ethiopia   700
    Zenebe Beyene

37 Collective Guilt as a Response to Evil: The Case of Arabs
    and Muslims in the Western Media   735
    Rasha A. Abdulla and Mervat Abou Oaf

38 Journalists as Witnesses to Violence and Suffering   752
    Amy Richards and Jolyon Mitchell

39 Reporting on Religious Authority Complicit
    with Atrocity   774
    Paul A. Soukup, S.J.

40 The Ethics of Representation and the Internet   785
    Boniface Omachonu Omatta

41	Authors, Authority, Ownership, and Ethics in Digital Media and News *Jarice Hanson*	803
42	Ethical Implications of Blogging *Bernhard Debatin*	823
43	Journalism Ethics in a Digital Network *Jane B. Singer*	845
44	Now Look What You Made Me Do: Violence and Media Accountability *Peter Hulm*	864
45	Protecting Children from Harmful Influences of Media through Formal and Nonformal Media Education *Asbjørn Simonnes and Gudmund Gjelsten*	891
46	Ethics and International Propaganda *Philip M. Taylor*	912
47	Modernization and Its Discontents: Ethics, Development, and the Diffusion of Innovations *Robert S. Fortner*	933
48	Communication Technologies in the Arsenal of Al Qaeda and Taliban: Why the West Is Not Winning the War on Terror *Haydar Badawi Sadig, Roshan Noorzai, and Hala Asmina Guta*	953
49	The Ethics of a Very Public Sphere: Differential Soundscapes and the Discourse of the Streets *Robert S. Fortner*	973

Index   992

Notes on Contributors

Rasha A. Abdulla (PhD University of Miami, 2003) is Associate Professor and Chair of the Journalism and Mass Communication Department of the American University in Cairo. Dr Abdulla's research interests include the uses and effects of mass media, new media, intercultural communication, and media diversity and ethics. She is the author of three books and several articles on the Internet and mass media in the Arab world, including *The Internet in the Arab World: Egypt and Beyond* and *Policing the Internet in the Arab World*. A native of Egypt, Dr Abdulla is the recipient of several local and international research awards.

Victor Akhterov (DLitt et Phil) is the program director of Radio TEOS, a network of radio stations in Moscow, St Petersburg, and other key cities of Russia. He now resides in the United States and shares his time between Los Angeles and Moscow. His scholarly interests include media studies, Bakhtin's ideas of dialog and carnival, and questions of media freedom in Russia.

Ronald C. Arnett (USA, PhD, Ohio University, 1978) is chair and professor of the Department of Communication & Rhetorical Studies at Duquesne University, and is also the university's Henry Koren, C.S.Sp., Endowed Chair for Scholarly Excellence. He is the author/co-author of six books and three edited books, including *Dialogic Confession: Bonhoeffer's Rhetoric of Responsibility*, for which he received the 2006 Everett Lee Hunt Award for Outstanding Scholarship. Dr Arnett is the editor of the *Review of Communication* and executive director of the Eastern Communication Association. His scholarly interests include philosophy of communication, communication ethics, and interpersonal communication.

Zenebe Beyene is a former Assistant Dean of the Graduate School of Journalism and Communications at Addis Ababa University (Ethiopia). He is currently studying for his PhD at the University of Nebraska, Lincoln. He would like to express his heartfelt gratitude to Will Norton, Charlyne Berens, and John Bender for their insightful comments on the manuscript.

Giovanna Borradori is Professor of Philosophy at Vassar College. She is a specialist of Continental philosophy, the aesthetics of architecture, and the philosophy of terrorism. She is the editor of *Recoding Metaphysics: The New Italian Philosophy* and the author of dozens of essays and two books: *The American Philosopher* and *Philosophy in a Time of Terror: Dialogues with Jürgen Habermas and Jacques Derrida*, a "philosophy best-seller" that appeared in 18 languages.

Michael Bugeja, a dual national of Malta and the United States, is an internationally known ethicist and author of 22 books, including *Living Ethics Across Media Platforms* and *Interpersonal Divide: The Search for Community in a Technological Age*, both awarded the Clifford G. Christians Award for Research in Media Ethics. He is the director of the Greenlee School of Journalism and Communication at Iowa State University of Science and Technology.

Clifford G. Christians is Research Professor of Communications Emeritus, University of Illinois at Urbana-Champaign, USA. He is the editor of *The Ellul Forum* and executive publisher of *Media Ethics Magazine*. He is co-author of these recent books: *Key Concepts in Critical Cultural Studies; Moral Engagement in Public Life: Theorists for Contemporary Ethics, Normative Theories of the Media; The Media, Ethical Communication: Moral Stances in Human Dialogue;* and *The Handbook of Mass Media Ethics*. The 9th edition of his co-authored text, *Media Ethics: Cases and Moral Reasoning* is in press.

Raphael Cohen-Almagor is an Israeli educator, researcher, human rights activist and Chair in Politics, University of Hull. He has published extensively in the fields of political science, philosophy, law, media ethics, medical ethics, sociology, history and education. He was Visiting Professor at UCLA and Johns Hopkins, Fellow at the Woodrow Wilson Center for Scholars, Founder and Director of the Center for Democratic Studies, University of Haifa, and Member of The Israel Press Council. Among his recent books are *Speech, Media and Ethics, The Scope of Tolerance, The Democratic Catch*, and his second poetry book *Voyages*. His sixteenth book is scheduled to be published in 2011, dealing with public responsibility in Israel.

Neville Cox (Ireland) is a practising barrister at the Irish bar and senior lecturer in Law in the law school of Trinity College Dublin where he is the Director of Postgraduate Studies. He is the author amongst other books of *Blasphemy and the Law* and *Defamation Law* as well as numerous law review articles on topics related to the manner in which the law balances the competing claims of free speech and religion.

Luiz Martins da Silva (Brazil) is a Journalist and Professor of Journalism (University of Brasilia – UnB); and a researcher (National Council of Scientific and

Technological Development). He holds an MA in communications and a PhD in Sociology. His current research deals with "The idea of the postjournalism." In addition he is both a poet and philatelist.

Bernhard Debatin (Germany) is a Professor of Multimedia Policy at Ohio University's School of Journalism (USA) and director of the honors tutorial program in journalism. His research and teaching interests are media ethics, multimedia/online journalism, science/environmental journalism, media theory and diversity. Before coming to Ohio University in 2000, he taught in Germany at Leipzig University and Berlin's University of Fine Arts, Technical University and Free University. He holds a PhD in Philosophy from the Technical University Berlin (1994). He has edited or co-edited six books, authored a book on the *Rationality of Metaphor*, and published over 70 scholarly articles.

Amanda Decker is an MA Candidate for Journalism and Media Studies at the University of South Florida, St. Petersburg. She holds a BA from the State University of New York at Binghamton where she studied philosophy, politics, and law. Her research interests include communication and cultural studies.

Anita Dighe After retiring from the University of Delhi as Director, Campus of Open Learning, she worked with Himgiri Nabh Vishwavidyalaya, Dehradun, and is presently a guest faculty at the School of Mass Communication at the Doon University, Dehradun. She has co-edited two books, *Mass Media and Village Life: An Indian Experience and Affirmation* and *Denial: Construction of Femininity on Indian Television*. Her areas of academic interest include adult and non-formal education, continuing education, extension education, distance- and open learning. She has a large number of national and international publications to her credit. Beside participating and presenting papers at international conferences, she has done short-term consultancy work for UNESCO on several occasions.

Deni Elliott holds the Eleanor Poynter Jamison Chair in Media Ethics and Press Policy at the University of South Florida. She is a US citizen who seeks cultural diversity within the US boundaries on Native American reservations and through international travel. She has published in a broad range of practical ethics topics including animals, bioethics, business, government, philanthropy, research, and teaching, with most of her publications relating to media.

P. Mark Fackler (USA) is Professor of Communications at Calvin College, Grand Rapids, Michigan. He is co-author of *Media Ethics: Cases and Moral Reasoning* (9th edition), co-editor of *Ethics and Evil in the Public Sphere*, and other works. He regularly teaches and conducts research in East Africa.

Robert S. Fortner (USA) is a Research Scholar in the Institute of Communications Research at the University of Illinois at Urbana-Champaign, Executive Director of the International Center for Media Studies and Senior Consultant to Media Research International. These two volumes which he co-edited follow on *Ethics and Evil in the Public Sphere*. He has published four other books on international communication and communication theory, contributed essays on ethics, research methodology, history, technology and theory to several other books, handbooks and encyclopedias (including five essays in these two volumes), and published nearly 50 other scholarly articles.

Gudmund Gjelsten (Norwegian) is Director of Bergbo Media. He does research and writing on media ethics, and on children and the media together with Dr Asbjørn Simonnes. The Research Council of Norway endorsed and financed a four year research project on "The Child in the Interaction between Intentional and Functional Education" concluded in 2004. He holds a CandTheol, STM from Yale Divinity School. Has been Director of Studies at the Department of Media, Volda University College, Program Editor at Radio Voice of the Gospel, Addis Adaba, and Editor and Literature Secretary at the Norwegian Missionary Society. Has written and edited several books and articles on media ethics and media education. He has also served as a pastor in The Church of Norway.

Joe Grixti is senior lecturer and coordinator of the media studies programme at the Auckland campus of Massey University, New Zealand. He is of Maltese origin and has held university teaching appointments in Malta, the United Kingdom and Australia. His teaching and research interests are interdisciplinary and focus on the intersections between cultural, literary, film, and media studies. Previous publications include two field-based monographs on young people's use of the media in Malta, as well as several journal articles and book chapters on popular culture, youth media, cultural identity and globalization.

Hala Asmina Guta is a doctoral candidate at the School of Media Arts and Studies, Scripps College of Communication at Ohio University. Her research interests include communication for social change and peace communication in societies emerging from conflict, with special emphasis on Africa.

Cees J. Hamelink (Dutch) is currently Professor for Globalization, Health and Human Rights at the Vrije Universiteit in Amsterdam, Professor for Knowledge Management in Development at the University of Aruba and Professor Emeritus of International Communication at the University of Amsterdam. Professor Hamelink is the editor-in-chief of the *International Communication Gazette* and honorary president of the International Association for Media and Communication Research. He has authored 17 books, published numerous edited books and articles on communication and human rights, and is the recipient of several life-time achievement awards.

Jarice Hanson (USA), is Professor of Communication at the University of Massachusetts, Amherst, and Verizon Chair in Telecommunications at Temple

University, in Philadelphia. She has published widely in the areas of telecommunications policy, ethics, and public opinion formation. Author, editor, and co-editor of over 20 books, including *24/7: How Cell Phones and The Internet Change the Way We Live, Work, and Play*, and *The Unconnected: Social Justice and Marginalized Individuals in the Information Society* (with Paul M.A. Baker and Jeremy Hunsinger, (eds).

Kaori Hayashi (Japan) is Professor of Media and Journalism Studies at the Graduate School of Interdisciplinary Information Studies/Interfaculty Initiative in Information Studies of the University of Tokyo. Her scholarly interests are in comparative media studies and journalism ethics.

Peter Hulm is a British-Swiss citizen based near Geneva, and a journalist and communications consultant as well as Advisor on Innovative Journalism to the European Graduate School (www.egs.edu). He has a PhD in communication from EGS (2004), an MA in mass communications from Leicester University in the UK, and a BSc from the UK's Open University. His research interests are the implications of postmodernism/poststructuralism/posthumanism for liberatory media practice.

Richard Lance Keeble (UK) is professor of journalism at the University of Lincoln. Born in Nottingham, he previously taught in the journalism department at City University, London, for 19 years. He has written and edited 18 publications including *The Newspapers Handbook* and *Ethics for Journalists*. He edited *Print Journalism: A Critical Introduction*, co-edited *The Journalistic Imagination: Literary Journalists from Defoe to Capote and Carter* and *Communicating War: Memory, Media and Military*. He is also the joint editor of *Ethical Space: The International Journal of Communication Ethics*.

Philip Lee (UK) joined the staff of the World Association for Christian Communication in 1975, where he is currently Deputy Director of Programs and Editor of the international journal *Media Development*. His current work revolves around communication rights, the democratization of communication, and the right to memory. His publications include *The Democratization of Communication* (ed.), *Requiem: Here's Another Fine Mass You've Gotten Me Into*; *Many Voices, One Vision: The Right to Communicate in Practice* (ed.); and *Communicating Peace: Entertaining Angels Unawares* (ed.).

Ed McLuskie is Professor of Communication, Boise State University, USA. He was a Fulbright Professor at the University of Vienna, Austria (1997), and T'bilisi State University, Georgia (2005). His research and teaching foci include critical theory, postmodernist debates, and their intersections with communication theory and social inquiry. Journal articles are published in *Javnost – The Public, Journal of Communication, Journal of Communication Inquiry*, and *Journalism: Theory, Practice and Criticism*. Other essays appear in *Communication Yearbook* and the

International Encyclopedia of Communication Theory. Current work includes a book about the reception of Jürgen Habermas's communication theory of society within communication and media theory.

Vijay Mishra is Professor of English Literature and Australian (ARC) Professorial Fellow at Murdoch University, Perth, Australia. Born in Fiji he holds doctorates from the Australian National University and Oxford. Among his publications are: *Dark Side of the Dream: Australian Literature and the Postcolonial Mind* (with Bob Hodge), *The Gothic Sublime, Devotional Poetics and the Indian Sublime, Bollywood Cinema: Temples of Desire*, and *The Literature of the Indian Diaspora: Theorizing the Diasporic Imaginary*. He plays the Indian harmonium, is a Beatles fan, and reads Sanskrit.

Jolyon Mitchell (UK) is Director of the Centre for Theology and Public Issues at the University of Edinburgh. A former BBC World Service producer and journalist his publications include: *Media Violence and Christian Ethics, The Religion and Film Reader, Mediating Religion: Conversations in Media, Religion and Culture*, and *Visually Speaking*. He is currently completing *Promoting Peace: Inciting Violence*.

Roshan Noorzai is a doctoral candidate in the School of Media Arts and Studies, Ohio University. A native of Afghanistan, Roshan's research interests include peace and conflict studies, political communication and ICTs for development. Currently he works on the role of media in post-Taliban conflict in Afghanistan.

Mervat Abou Oaf (doctoral candidate, Autonomous University of Barcelona) is Associate Professor of Practice and Associate Chair of the Journalism and Mass Communication Department of the American University in Cairo. Her research interests include media policies, uses and effects of mass media, media law and ethics, as well as studies in film industry. She is a native of Egypt.

Levi Obonyo (PhD, Temple) is Professor of Communications at Daystar University in Nairobi, Kenya. He has worked as a journalist in Kenya's leading media, and as an academic consultant throughout Africa.

Emmanuel Okaalet is a graduate of Calvin College. He works presently as an associate producer at Mandala TV in Nairobi, Kenya.

Boniface Omachonu Omatta is a Nigerian doctoral student at the Universiteit Gent in Belgium. His areas of scholarly interest are religion and politics, religion and media, the sociology of religion, cultural studies, and interreligious dialogue and ecumenism. He is married and has three children.

Shakuntala Rao is Professor of Communication Studies at State University of New York, Plattsburgh. She was born in India and is a dual citizen of India and

Notes on Contributors

United States. She received her PhD from University of Massachusetts, Amherst, USA. Her research interests are in the areas of postcolonial theory, media ethics, and globalization. Her articles in media ethics have appeared in *Journalism Studies, Journal of Global Media and Communication, Asian Journal of Communication*, and *Mass Media Ethics*. Her most recent work in media ethics focuses on South Asian journalism and social responsibility.

Amy Richards (USA) is a 2010 PhD graduate from New College School of Divinity, University of Edinburgh. Her interdisciplinary research is focused on the concept of "bearing witness" as it is understood in Communication, Media, and Journalism Studies as well as in Holocaust and Religious Studies. In Media Studies in particular, this research topic opens ethical inquiry into the modern concern of witnessing distant suffering.

Ian Richards is Professor of Journalism at the University of South Australia in Adelaide, Australia. His research interests include journalism and communication ethics and he has published widely in this field. He is the author of *Quagmires and Quandaries: Exploring Journalism Ethics* and since 2003 has been editor of *Australian Journalism Review*, Australia's leading refereed journal in the academic field of journalism. A former newspaper journalist, he has worked and studied in Australia and the United Kingdom.

Chloe Schwenke is an American development practitioner and academic, currently serving as an independent consultant on projects of the World Bank, USAID, and DFID. Her scholarly interests include international development ethics, gender & development, and leadership ethics. As a practitioner, she has over three decades of comprehensive international experience in the design, management and implementation of a wide range of gender, transgender/LGBT, local governance & decentralization, civil society capacity building, conflict, and leadership programming. Among her most recent work is *Reclaiming Value in International Development: The Moral Dimensions of Development Policy and Practice in Poor Countries*.

Haydar Badawi Sadig is a Sudanese-American professor and scholar who taught in the United States, Africa, and the Middle East. He earned his PhD from Ohio University. Currently, he is Associate Professor of Sociology of Communication at King Fahd University of Petroleum and Minerals, Dhahran, Saudi Arabia. As a progressive scholar/activist, he is engaged in advocating Islamic reform, peace, democracy and human rights in his native Sudan and the larger Muslim World. His activism is mainly channeled through new communication technologies. His publications and research interests, in English and Arabic, include topics on peace communication, sociology of communication, global communication ethics and intercultural communication.

Asbjørn Simonnes (Norwegian) is Professor at Volda University College. He holds the Doctor of Ministry (1996) and PhD (2004) from Fuller Theological

Seminary, Pasadena, CA. He has been a lecturer since 1980 in general teaching of philosophy and ethics, and leader of a four year research project, "The Child in the Interaction between Intentional and Functional Education," within The Research Council of Norway. Has written several books and articles, especially about media ethics, media education and children at risk. Asbjørn lives in Volda on the west-coast of Norway, is married to Inger-Tove and they have six children.

Jane B. Singer teaches conceptual and hands-on classes in digital journalism, as well as undergraduate courses in editing, journalism ethics and political coverage, and graduate courses in communication technology and theory at the University of Iowa. She is also a Visiting Professor at the University of Central Lancashire in the UK, where she taught for three years as the Johnston Press Chair in Digital Journalism. She holds a PhD in journalism from the University of Missouri, Columbia, an MA in liberal studies from New York University and a bachelor's degree in journalism from the University of Georgia. She also spent 10 years in the editorial department of what evolved into the Prodigy interactive service and was Prodigy's first news manager. She also has five years experience as a reporter and editor at three East Coast newspapers. She is co-author of *Online Journalism Ethics: Traditions and Transitions*, published in 2007, and of *Participatory Journalism in Online Newspapers: Guarding the Internet's Open Gates*, due for publication in 2011. She also has published widely in scholarly journals and is the 2007 recipient of the Clifford G. Christians Ethics Research Award.

Paul A. Soukup, S.J. (USA) is the holder of the Pedro Arrupe Chair at Santa Clara University and teaches in the Communication Department there. He has explored the connections between communication and theology since 1982 and, more recently, orality-literacy studies, particularly as applied to religious contexts such as Bible translation. His publications include *Communication and Theology, Christian Communication: A Bibliographical Survey, Media, Culture, and Catholicism*, and *Fidelity and Translation: Communicating the Bible in New Media* (with Robert Hodgson). He and Thomas J. Farrell are editing the collected works of Walter J. Ong, SJ.

Linda Steiner(PhD) studies how and when gender matters in news and news-rooms and how feminist groups use media. Other research areas include: media ethics; journalism history; and public journalism. Steiner is editor of *Critical Studies in Media Communication* and serves on six editorial boards. Before coming to Maryland she taught at Rutgers University, where she served as Department Chair and coordinator of the PhD program's Media Studies track. She has written, co-authored, or edited several books, book chapters, and refereed articles. Steiner has chaired several task forces for the Association for Education in Journalism and Mass Communication, for which she is now drafting a code of ethics.

Bruce C. Swaffield is Professor in the School of Communication and the Arts, Regent University (Virginia Beach, US), and founder and director of the *Worldwide*

Forum on Education and Culture, which meets annually in Rome, Italy. He writes a bimonthly commentary on international issues in the media for *Quill* magazine, published by the Society of Professional Journalists. His most recent publications include *Education Landscapes in the 21st Century: Cross-Cultural Challenges and Multi-Disciplinary Perspectives* and *Rising from the Ruins: Roman Antiquities in Neoclassic Literature*.

Philip M. Taylor is Professor of International Communications at the University of Leeds, UK. A British national, he has spent almost 40 years researching governmental propaganda, military-media relations and psychological operations. In that capacity he has been invited to lecture all over the world, especially to military organizations, and he holds academic positions from Southern California to Malaysia. His many publications include *Munitions of the Mind: A History of Propaganda from the Ancient World to the Present Day*. His latest books are *The Routledge Handbook of Public Diplomacy* (co-edited with Nancy Snow) and *Shooting the Messenger: The Political Impact of War Reporting* (co-authored with Paul Moorcraft).

Mitchell Terpstra is a graduate of Calvin College and was awarded a McGregor Fellowship by the college to help conduct this research. He is presently writing for multiple publications in Michigan while trying to find a way back to Nairobi.

Bassam Tibi is a political scientist and German citizen, who was born in 1944 in Damascus and migrated in 1962 to Germany, thus he combines Arab-Muslim and European education in a background most pertinent to intercultural communication. Between 1973 and 2009 he was the Georgia Augusta Professor for International Relations at Göttingen University alongside 18 prestigious visiting appointments he had in four continents (including Harvard, Princeton, Yale, Yaoundé/ Cameroon, Jakarta/ Indonesia and NUS-Singapore). Between 1969 and 2009 he published 28 books written in German and 8 written in English, the most recent of which is: *Islam's Predicament with Modernity*. His book: *Islam and Islamism* will be published in 2011. In 1995 the President of the Federal Republic of Germany awarded Professor Tibi the German Cross of Merits/ First Class for his contribution to a better intercivilizational communication between Islam and the West.

Stephen J.A. Ward is Burgess Professor of Journalism Ethics in the School of Journalism and Mass Communication at the University of Wisconsin-Madison. He is director of the school's Center for Journalism Ethics. He is author of two books, the award-winning *The Invention of Journalism Ethics* and *Global Journalism Ethics*, and co-editor of *Media Ethics Beyond Borders*. He is associate editor of the *Journal of Mass Media Ethics*. He has a PhD in philosophy and, previously, was director of the journalism school at the University of British Columbia in Vancouver. He was a reporter, war correspondent, and newsroom manager for 14 years.

Lee Wilkins (USA) is a Curator's Teaching Professor at the School of Journalism at the University of Missouri. Her research interests are in media ethics and focus more specifically on moral decision making and the influences on it. She is the editor of the *Journal of Mass Media Ethics*, co-editor with Clifford Christians of the *Handbook of Mass Media Ethics*, and co-author with Philip Patterson of the undergraduate media ethics text, *Media Ethics: Issues and Cases*, which is now in its 7th edition. She is a former newspaper reporter and editor and, for the past 16 years, has been a regular panel member on a weekly radio show, "Views of the News," that critiques media performance and is broadcast on the public radio station KBIA in Columbia, Missouri. Her current research focuses on neuroscience and what it can contribute to understanding ethical decision making. She holds a doctorate in political science from the University of Oregon.

Oliver Witte (USA) is a doctoral candidate in Mass Communication and Media Arts at Southern Illinois University in Carbondale. He previously taught at Loyola University Chicago and Toccoa Falls College and has worked in both the magazine and newspaper publishing industries. His scholarly interests include the business and management of news media, especially new media, media effects, the ethnic press in the United States and media in the Middle East.

Jiafei Yin, a Chinese-American and Professor of Journalism at Central Michigan University, is interested in international communication and explored a new model for the Asian and the world press. Her work in that regard was published in the *Journalism & Communication Monographs*. Yin also published in the *Journal of Advertising Research* and the *Asian Journal of Communication*, and contributed book chapters in the *Issues and Challenges in Asian Journalism, Emerging Issues in Contemporary Journalism, Terrorism, Globalization & Mass Communication, Cultural Identity and New Communication Technologies: Political, Ethnic and Ideological* Implications, and *Global Journalism*.

Preface

Robert S. Fortner and P. Mark Fackler

"It was the best of times, it was the worst of times." With this sentence, probably one of the best known in the English language, Charles Dickens begins his novel on the French Revolution, *A Tale of Two Cities*. I thought of this sentence while compiling the final list of authors for this two-volume Handbook. On the one hand, it was the best of times: Mark Fackler and I were able to recruit 60 very fine scholars from across the planet to contribute original – and lengthy – essays on a topic that has had little written about it – ethics as they apply to global communication and media practices.

Other ethics books in the fields of communication or journalism cover the same terrain – privacy, fairness, attribution, portrayal, interviewing, reputation, and so forth, as it applies within the professional practices of journalists, film-makers, TV producers, editors, and like occupations. However, with this book we were able to stand back and look at the global dimensions of these problems, such as how the Internet, which cannot be regulated or controlled by a single state, should be evaluated when ethics are applied. Where should these ethics be grounded in a world of fragmented ideologies, conflicting religious perspectives, and historical traditions? Are the ethics that would be applied in this case different to those that should be applied when a film is physically shipped across a border? Or take the problem of representation of adversaries, or groups believed to have perpetrated atrocities hundreds of years ago when oral traditions constructed myths of sometimes awesome proportions. Such myths can now be perpetuated, not by word of mouth or storytelling around a bonfire, but by recreations and reinterpretations on television, or film, that can reconstruct events, which can themselves be deconstructed, with various powerful ideologies used as extracontextual explanations. How does the truth of events compare to the truth of lore, of retelling, of reconstruction and deconstruction? Can truth itself be a value in such an environment? – as a postmodernist might well ask. These volumes are compleat with such issues that cannot be easily contained or understood within the narrower framework of professional practice.

Preface

It was also the worst of times. Despite having 60 stellar authors, there are topics that even they could not cover. There are simply too many problems that, unless you sit down and try to imagine creatively what they could be, would probably never be considered. There were also topics that we could not get an author to address and others that, because of pregnancies, new responsibilities or preexisting commitments, appropriate authors could not commit to write about. We could easily have filled a third volume in this handbook if everyone we contacted had been able to write. Instead of 49 essays, we might have been able to tackle as many as 100. However, this is academe in the age of publish or perish.

What these two volumes did do – and we trust will do for a reader – is expand our collective understanding of ethics in the new global environment. Globalism does not merely make problems more complicated than they were in the days of isolated political ideologies, more restricted technologies, or independent media practices, it also introduces entirely new issues. The nations of the world have been committed for several decades now to the idea of communication as a human right. It is clear that these same nations do not necessarily practice what they preach. Sovereignty interferes with the ability of collectivities of nations to demand adherence to international agreements. What, then, is the most ethical position to take in this matter? Is it more ethical to demand that a right to communicate be practiced despite changes in political climates, the rise of hate parties, and the development of indigenous frameworks for ethics? Or must the principles developed during the Enlightenment and beyond within Western political traditions grounded in a Judeo-Christian ethic be applied universally? Does ethics trump faith, or is the other way around? Within a given nation, even when demographics change, there are usually ethical, political, or legal traditions that survive. But not always. The demand of Muslims for the application of Sharia in their communities, for instance, has upset traditions within nonreligious regimes. Does Sharia put non-Muslims at risk when their ethical practices may not accord with it?

What happens, too, when globalization makes multinational corporations more significant in many people's lives than their own domestic governments? What are the ethics that should be applied in a situation where financial institutions in one country have made commitments in another that they suffer a monetary meltdown? Does the recipient nation "owe" protection to institutions outside its own borders? Is it ethical that the citizens of one rich nation live lifestyles that are dependent on the underpaid labor of another – even if the labor now has work and more income than it ever had before? What are the ethics that should apply to the public discourse about global warming when it is clearly a few nations that are the primary culprits in the phenomenon?

What are the ethics that should apply in the information distribution arena where some intelligence is provided by news organizations exercising editorial discretion (or even bias) and some provided by entrepreneurial bloggers or "citizen journalists?" Do the ethics of a profession prevail, must different ethical standards be accepted due to the differential status of these new competitors, or is ethics out the window entirely? Do both types of news gathering and dissemination "owe" the

Preface

public that access their material the same standards? Where does the so-called "public's right to know" begin and end in such an environment?

We could go on for pages with sets of these questions. Rather than do that, however, we took on the task of recruiting the best minds that we could find – and we are sure there are many others out there that we did not locate – to tackle many of the significant issues raised by the new international context within which ethics must be practiced – insofar as it applies to the activities that collectively make up communication work. Our hope is that each reader will find the essays we have collected here to be enlightening and challenging.

1

Primordial Issues
in Communication Ethics

Clifford G. Christians

In order to organize the primordial issues in communication ethics, and give them their correct scope and character, a standard typology should be useful. The study of ethics is normally divided into three parts: metaethics, normative ethics, and descriptive ethics.

Descriptive ethics reports on the moral behavior of specific persons or groups and studies the way ethical decision-making functions *de facto*. In terms of communication, descriptive ethics gives an account of failures and successes in journalism practice, locates the problems, and identifies specific dilemmas facing media workers. Metaethics addresses issues about normative theories and philosophically examines, among other things, the nature of the good and right, the problem of evil, and the validity of ethical theories. Normative ethics fuses actual morality with principles, concentrating on the justice or injustice of societies and institutions. Most broadly, normative ethics concerns the best ways for professionals to lead their lives and the principles to be promoted. Normative ethics seeks to establish norms and guidelines, not merely to describe details or deal with abstractions.

The normative category has received the greatest scholarly attention in media ethics, so five of the eight primordial issues presented below are from that domain: social justice, truth, non-violence, human dignity, and privacy. The need to retheorize classical theory and relativism are the two major issues in metaethics. Given the dramatic innovations in global media technology, instrumentalism is the premiere issue when conducting research into the morality of communication professionals and institutions.

The Handbook of Global Communication and Media Ethics, First Edition. Edited by Robert S. Fortner and P. Mark Fackler.
© 2011 Blackwell Publishing Ltd. Published 2011 by Blackwell Publishing Ltd.

Metaethics

1   Moral theory

Ethical theory always needs attention, and with a special urgency today. The classical canon – centered on virtue or consequences or duty – has opened the pathway to sophisticated work in media ethics. However, a new generation of media ethics in the multicultural and transnational mode requires that we retheorize existing theory (see Christians, 2009). Rather than ethical theories rooted in rationalism that are rule-ordered and gendered masculine, beliefs and worldviews should be made more central in theory-making. Rather than a rule-based system, theory should empower the imagination to give us moral discernment and an inside perspective on reality. Even though we make an epistemologically acceptable move to more dynamic theory, a crucial challenge is whether it answers the question, "Why should I be moral?" This is a summary of the first primordial issue; what follows is an elaboration.

Presuppositional thinking

Mainstream ethical theory, grounded in rationalism, produces moral principles that are unconditioned by circumstances. For ethical rationalists, the truth of all legitimate claims about moral obligation can be settled by formally examining their logical structure. Humans act against moral obligations only if they are willing to be irrational.

This kind of media ethics, rooted in classical moral philosophy, is unidimensional. Autonomous moral agents are presumed to apply rules consistently and self-consciously to every choice. Through rational processes, basic rules of morality are created that everyone is obliged to follow and against which all actions can be evaluated. In communication ethics, neutral principles operate by the conventions of impartiality and formality. This is an ethics of moral reasoning that arranges principles in hierarchical fashion and rigorously follows logic in coming to conclusions. Journalism ethics that follows this approach, therefore, is based on standards and doctrines that guide professional practice. In mainstream professional ethics, codes of ethics are the typical format.

Utilitarianism is a single consideration theory, for example. It does not simply demand that we maximize general happiness, but renders irrelevant all other moral imperatives that are in conflict with it. Moral reasoning is equivalent to calculating the consequences for human happiness. Utilitarianism presumes there is one domain that determines what we ought morally to do. The exactness of this one-factor model is appealing, but gains its validity by leaving out whatever cannot be calculated. Kant is another example. He assimilated ethics into logic. Moral laws to be universally applicable must be free from inner contradiction. Through the mental calculus of willing an action to be universalized, imperatives emerge unconditioned by circumstances. Moral absolutes are identified in the same rational way that syllogisms are identified as valid or invalid.

A new generation of media ethics that is both intercultural and international needs to go beyond one-dimensional models by incorporating presuppositions into its theories. Human beings are committed to presuppositions inescapably. All human knowledge must take something as given. A faith commitment is the condition through which human cognition universally is intelligible. Theories of morality do not arise from an objectivist rationalism, but from our fundamental beliefs about the world. Worldviews are the gyroscope around which our thinking and experience revolve. They are the home of our ultimate commitments at the core of our being. Worldviews give meaning to our consciousness. They represent a set of basic beliefs about human destiny. Presuppositions are therefore *sine qua non* in rethinking moral theory

Why be moral?

Even if we broaden the boundaries of our moral theory to include the presuppositional, does this retheorizing answer the question, "Why should I be moral?" When theoretical models center on decision-makers who are accountable to a principle, then why I should be moral is pertinent and answerable. However, when transnational and intercultural beliefs and values are the target and beginning point, the issue seems obscure and tenuous.

An inescapable contribution of classical theory is that they were serious about addressing the question, "Why be moral?" The only presuppositional theory that is acceptable is one that answers it also. The moral domain by its very character entails the question. Like a magnetic force, the good compels me as a moral agent. Should no such imperative exist, morality as a whole is incoherent. "Why should I be moral?" is understood not as a prudential question ("Why is morality in my interest?"), but as a question about justification: "Why should I accept the moral demand as a demand upon me?" (cf. Hare, 2001).

The virtue ethics of Aristotle and Confucius both assumed that moral obligations have authority from the community to which we belong. For Aristotle, the city is like a parent; it has made us what we are. Membership in a community reaches beyond our values and sentiments to engage our identity itself. To be true to ourselves, we have to acknowledge the authority of the moral demand our community instills into us.

Another alternative from the classics is to locate the authority of morality in human nature, specifically in the organic human inclinations. In this perspective, we can tell what is good for us by looking at what we are naturally inclined to act upon. Doing the good benefits our human flourishing. For Jeremy Bentham, for example, the chief good is satisfaction, and for all humans the source of their true happiness is experiencing pleasure and avoiding pain.

For Kant, reason demands moral action. It is the nature of reason to will universal law, and it demands this not only in theories of science, but in practical thinking about what we do. Hence, we ought to base morality on reason. Reason is my authority for acting morally.

If our motivation is only self-interest, psychoanalysis is needed, not morality. If I decide to seek a Provost's position because of my own career and without altruism, then the moral domain has no validity. Forty-six million Americans are without health insurance. Why should I care about health care reform if it means higher rates or poorer quality for me? Politics or economics could explain my position – health care is currently out of control and providing it more extensively hurts my small business. Or politically, for the sake of our international reputation and attracting foreign investment, our country should be able to match or exceed national health care anywhere in the world.

Regarding the biological turn, why should I be held accountable if the moral arena is subsumed by sociobiology or neuroscience? James Q. Wilson's *The Moral Sense* (1993) faces the critique that morality and sense perception are two different domains. Morality is not like other human arenas, in this case, perception. I am reading Charles Taylor's *The Secular Age* and too preoccupied with it to lay it down. I feel a moral compulsion to attend a university workshop on Palestinian refugee camps, but decide in this instance to keep reading. But, I have no choice regarding perception. I'm at my desk and the desk exists. The moral sense is inescapable, but where is the moral demand in it?

For those of us committed to ethics, we insist on moral obligations as crucial, over the long term, to human action. It is obvious in family life that self interest, politics and economics do not exhaust our motivations. Regarding the environment, a vocabulary of moral obligation is taking shape that will help ensure social and cultural change. However, psychoanalytic, economic, and political explanations are so powerful that the moral domain is typically rendered impotent. Once again the urgent question – will a new generation of presuppositional theory be able to answer convincingly, "What should I be moral?" To be intellectually legitimate, resolving this issue is essential as media ethics theory is retheorized.

2 Relativism

Another premiere challenge in metaethics is relativism, and unless we deal with it philosophically, the future of the news media is limited (see Christians, 2009). Relativism is a longstanding problem since Friedrich Nietzsche made it inescapable. However, in this first decade of the twenty-first century, relativism has reached maturity, and has taken on a comprehensiveness that threatens our conceptual progress in media ethics.

Friedrich Nietzsche

Obviously relativism has been a prominent issue since the nineteenth century's Friedrich Nietzsche (1844–1900). In his terms, in a world where God has died and everything lacks meaning, morality makes no sense. We live in an era beyond good and evil ([1886]1966). Since there is no transcendent answer to the why of human existence, we face the demise of moral interpretation altogether. For Nietzsche, morality had reached the end of the line. In its contemporary version, defending a good beyond the senses is not beneficent, but imperialism over the moral judgments of diverse communities.

For relativists in the Nietzschean tradition, the right and valid are only known in local space and native languages. Judgments of right and wrong are accepted as such by their adherents' internal criteria. Therefore, these concepts and propositions are considered to have no validity elsewhere. For cultural relativism, morality is a social product. Whatever the majority in a given culture approve is a social good. Since all cultures are presumed to be equal in principle, all value systems are equally valid. Cultural relativity now typically means moral relativism. Contrary to an ethnocentrism of judging other groups against a dominant Western model other cultures are not considered inferior only different.

All forms of public communication tend to exacerbate the problem of relativism – journalism's emphasis on particulars, for instance. Reporters work at the juncture of globalization and local identities – both of them happening simultaneously. They are caught in the contradictory trends of cultural homogeneity and resistance. The integration of globalization and ethnic self-consciousness is a major necessity. The news media's penchant for everyday affairs makes integration difficult. In their passion for ethnography, for diversity, for the local – media academics and practitioners typically allow cultural relativity to slide into philosophical relativism.

The preoccupation in communication studies with narrative usually leaves relativism unattended. Through stories we constitute ways of living in common. Moral commitments are embedded in the practices of particular social groups and they are communicated through a community's stories. However, narrative ethics is conflicted in its own terms about which value-driven stories ought to be valued. What in narrative itself distinguishes good stories from destructive ones? On what grounds precisely does narrative require fundamental changes in existing cultural and political practices? Because some customs are relative, it does not follow that all are relative. While there are disagreements over details, policies, and interpretations, these differences do not themselves mean that no moral judgments can be made about major historical events – The Holocaust, Stalinism, genital mutilation, the slave trade, apartheid in South Africa, and so forth. The challenge for journalism ethics in a global age is honoring cultural diversity, while simultaneously rejecting moral relativism.

When cultural pluralism slides into moral relativism, we usually have not faced up to the pernicious politics that insists on the prerogatives of a nation, caste, religion or tribe. Cultural relativism turned into a moral claim is disingenuous. If we argue that moral action depends on a society's norms, then "one must obey the norms of one's society and to diverge from those norms is to act immorally ... Such a view promotes conformity and leaves no room for moral reform or improvement" (Velasquez *et al.*, 2009). Ordinarily social consensus does not indicate the wrongness of a society's practices and beliefs. While continuing to critique relativism on its own terms, another need in metaethics is defending the credibility of realism. A valid realism is the antidote to philosophical relativism, and the next section establishes its possibility.

Realism

Our creative ability works within the limits of a given animate order, creativity within a shared cosmos. People shape their own view of reality. This fact however, does not presume that reality as a whole is inherently formless until it is defined by human language. A natural world that exists as a given totality is the presupposition of historical existence. Reality is not merely raw material, but is ordered vertically and through an internal ordering among its parts. Some kinds are hierarchical, subspecies within species, and species within genus; but relations among humans are horizontal, that is, no inferior race to serve a superior one. This coherent whole is history's source, an intelligible order that makes history itself intelligible. From a realist perspective, we discover truths about the world that exist within it.

This is ontological realism, inscribed in our very humanness. It does not appeal to an objective sphere outside our subjectivity. Among human beings are common understandings entailed by their creatureliness as lingual beings. All human languages are intertranslatable. In fact, some human beings in all languages are bilingual. All languages enable their users to make abstractions, draw inferences, deduce and induce when solving problems. All human languages serve cultural formation, not merely social function. All humans know the distinction between raw food and cooked. Of major importance in our philosophical work is a legitimate realism on this side of Einstein, Freud, and Darwin, and realism grounded in human language qualifies.

In terms of ontological realism, norms can be embedded successfully within culture and history, East and West. As an indicator of its distinctiveness, the sociologist Robert Wuthnow (1987) argues that as the human species generates symbolic systems it maintains boundaries between moral norms and actual behavior. Through natural language, *homo sapiens* establishes the differences and similarities of people's worldviews. In an ironic twist on conventional skepticism, normative claims that presume realism are not a medieval remnant but the catalyst for innovation. Given the ambiguities within relativism itself, and the possibility of a constructive response through realism, theorizing in media ethics can move forward constructively.

Normative Ethics

3   Social justice

The bulk of the work in communication ethics is normative, where principles are established for media institutions and practitioners. Of the five normative principles requiring the most attention, justice is first. To insure the effectiveness of new media technologies for the long term, a number of moral issues have become transparent within the global information system. Some are new moral problems and others are being transformed. The centerpiece is social justice. Especially in these days of the information revolution, the venerable concept of justice should be at

Primordial Issues in Communication Ethics 7

the forefront of normative media ethics. Only a sophisticated view of social justice can respond adequately to the new world information order. Justice is the normative foundation on which to base regulatory standards and professional guidelines for the convergence of information and computer technologies (ICTs).

The major question for social justice as a primordial issue is accessibility. In terms of the principle of just distribution of products and services, media access ought to be allocated to everyone according to essential needs, regardless of income or geographical location. Comprehensive information ought to be assured to all parties without discrimination.

In contrast, the standard conception among privately owned media is allocating to each according to the ability to pay. The open marketplace of supply and demand determines who obtains the service. The assumption is that decisions about the consumers' money belong to them alone as a logical consequence of their right to exercise their own social values and property rights without coercion from others. From this perspective, media businesses are not considered charitable organizations and therefore have no obligation to subsidize the information poor.

An ethics of justice in which distribution is based on need defines fundamental human needs as those related to survival or subsistence. They are not frivolous wants or individual whims or desires. As a matter of fact, there is rather uniform agreement on a list of most human necessities – food, housing, clothing, safety, and medical care. If we cannot provide them for ourselves because of the limitations of our circumstances, they nonetheless remain as essential goods. Everyone is entitled without regard for individual success to that which permits them to live humanely.

The electronically convergent superworld cannot be envisioned except as a necessity. Media networks make the global economy run, they give us access to agricultural and health care information, they organize world trade, and they are the channels through which the United Nations and political discussion flow; through them, we monitor both war and peace. Therefore, as a necessity of life in a global order, the ICT system ought to be distributed impartially, regardless of income, race, geography, or merit.

However, there is no reasonable likelihood that need-based distribution will ever be fulfilled by the marketplace itself. Technological societies have high levels of computer penetration and nonindustrial societies do not. Digital technology is disproportionately concentrated in the developed world, and under the principle of supply-and-demand there are no structural reasons for changing these disproportions. Even in wired societies, the existence of Internet technology does not guarantee it will reach its potential as a democratic medium. There is a direct correlation between per capita Gross National Product and Internet distribution. In the United States, for example, 80% of those households with incomes of $75 000 have computers; only 6% do of those with incomes of $15 000 or less. "Socio-cultural barriers, such as income, gender, age, education, and ethnic status still prevail worldwide despite countervailing trends in industrialized countries. New media and the Internet do not just perpetuate social inequalities, but often multiply them. In reality the global village is a gated community" (Debatin, 2008, p. 260; cf. Chester, 2007).

What is most important about convergent media technology is not so much the availability of the computing device or the Internet line, but rather the ability to make use of both the device and conduit for meaningful social practice. Those who cannot read, who have never learned to use a computer, and who do not know the major languages of software and digital content will have difficulty getting online, much less using the information system productively.

There are no grounds for supposing that the geography of the digital world will be fundamentally different from that of the offline world. There is no technological solution for universal diffusion. This history of the communications media indicates that they follow existing political and economic patterns; inequities in society lead to inequities in technology. The normative principle of social justice requires that we intervene through legislation, government policy, technology practice, and public ownership to implement open access. Our thinking about media institutions should be modeled after schools, which we accept as our common responsibility, rather than determined by engineers or profits alone.

In the age of convergent media – rooted in computers, fiber optics, the Internet, satellites, and the World Wide Web – ideally all types of persons will use all types of media services for all types of audiences. But universal service is the Achilles heel of new technologies driven by invention, engineering, and markets. Without intervention into the commercial system on behalf of distributive justice, we will continue to divide the world into the technologically elite and those without adequate means to participate. Therefore, the normative guideline ought to be universal access, based on need.

However, the concept of social justice is not limited to fairness in present circumstances. Under the conditions of globalized media technology, unintended consequences cannot be ignored. Any consideration of new media technologies must include an assessment of possible negative consequences, particularly in light of the complexity and sophistication of networked media. Social justice insists on "the regulatory idea that development must meet the needs of the present without compromising the ability of future generations to meet their own needs" (Debatin, 2008, p. 258). In policy decisions regarding convergent media, technological and societal development are assured while making certain that this growth will not be achieved at the expense of the future. The emphasis is not only on equity within generations but also between generations, including equitable distribution and democratic participation. Sustainable development of communication technology should therefore ensure that both present and future media foster an informed citizenry and a democratic polity.

4 Truth

Truth is not only a primordial issue, but a perennial one in normative media ethics. Nearly all codes of ethics begin with the reporter's duty to tell the truth under all circumstances. Credible language has long been considered pivotal to the media enterprise as a whole – accuracy in news, no deception in advertising, authenticity

Primordial Issues in Communication Ethics 9

in entertainment. Media professionals have tended to agree, at least in a low-level sense, with philosopher Karl Jaspers (1955): "The moment of communication," he said, "is at one and the same time the preservation of, and a search for, the truth." Though interpreted in various ways, media ethics as a scholarly field and professional practice recognizes the wheel imagery of the Buddhist tradition – truth is the immovable axle.

Historically the mainstream media have defined themselves in terms of an objectivist worldview. Centered on human rationality and armed with the scientific method, the facts in news have been said to mirror reality. The aim has been true and incontrovertible accounts of a domain separate from human consciousness. Truth is understood in elementary epistemological terms as accurate representation and precision with data. News corresponds to context-free algorithms, and professionalism is equated with impartiality.

During a formative period for the media in the 1920s, a dichotomy between facts and values dominated Western thinking. Genuine knowledge was identified with the physical sciences, and the objectivity of physics and mathematics set the standard for all forms of knowing. Journalistic morality became equivalent to unbiased reporting or neutral data. Presenting unvarnished facts was heralded as the standard of good reporting. Objective reporting was not merely a technique, but withholding value judgments was considered a moral imperative (Ward, 2004, ch. 6).

James Carey has observed correctly that the commitment to objectivism is rooted in both academia and the profession. Objectivity emerged in journalism out of the struggle within the press for a legitimate place to stand within the complexities of rapid industrialization. "Journalists, capitalizing on the growing prestige of science, positioned themselves outside the system of politics, as observers stationed on an Archimedean point above the fray of social life" (Carey, 1997b, p. 207). Originally this form of journalism – beginning most prominently with the wire services – was rooted "in a purely commercial motive: the need of the mass newspaper to serve politically heterogeneous audiences without alienating a significant segment" of them. Subsequently this strategy of reporting "was rationalized into a canon of professional competence and the ideology of professional responsibility" (Carey, 1997b, p. 208). With scientific naturalism the ruling paradigm in the academy, universities institutionalized the conventions of objective reporting in journalism curricula.

Seeking the truth in newsgathering and producing the truth in newswriting have been complicated by budget constraints, deadlines, editorial conventions, and self-serving sources. Agreeing on visual accuracy in a digital world has been almost impossible, even among competent professionals of good will. Even if we could get our thinking straight, sophisticated electronics bury us with unceasing information and little time to sift through the intricacies of truth-telling.

The prevailing view of truth as accurate information is now seen as too narrow for today's social and political complexities. Objectivity has become increasingly controversial as the working press' professional standard, though it remains entrenched in various forms in our ordinary practices of news production and dissemination. In Carey's dramatic terms,

> The conventions of objective reporting were developed as part of an essentially utilitarian-capitalist-scientific orientation toward events. ... Yet despite their obsolescence, we continue to live with these conventions as if a silent conspiracy had been undertaken between government, the reporter, and the audience to keep the house locked up tight even though all the windows have been blown out (Carey 1997a, p. 208).

As Ward describes it, "the traditional notion of journalistic objectivity, articulated about a century ago, is indefensible philosophically, weakened by criticism inside and outside of journalism" (Ward, 2004, p. 4). "Traditional news objectivity is, by all accounts, a spent ethical force, doubted by journalists and academe" (p.261).

With the dominant scheme no longer tenable for this primordial principle, philosophical work on it is critically needed. Instead of abandoning the idea or appealing to coherence versions, the concept of truth needs to be transformed intellectually. In Descartes' mathematical reasoning, it is the mind alone that knows. However, in a fuller understanding, there is no propositional truth independent of human beings as a whole. Truthtelling is not considered a problem of cognition per se, but is integrated into human consciousness and social formation. In Dietrich Bonhoeffer's *Ethics*, a truthful account takes hold of the context, motives, and presuppositions involved" (Bonhoeffer, 1995, ch. 5). Truth means, in other words, to strike gold, to get at "the core, the essence, the nub, the heart of the matter" (Pippert, 1989, p. 11). To replace newsgathering rooted in the methods of the natural sciences, rigorous qualitative procedures must be followed instead. Reporters aiming to inform the public adequately will seek what might be called interpretive sufficiency, or in Clifford Geertz's terms, thick description. This paradigm opens up the social world in all its dynamic dimensions.

The thick notion of sufficiency supplants the thinness of the technical, exterior, and statistically precise received view. No hard line exists between fact and interpretation; therefore, truthful accounts entail adequate and credible interpretations rather than first impressions. The best journalists weave a tapestry of truth from inside the attitudes, culture, and language of the people and events they are actually reporting. The reporters' frame of reference is not derived from free-floating data, but from an inside picture that gets to the heart of the matter. Rather than reducing social issues to the financial and administrative problems defined by politicians, the media disclose the subtlety and nuance that enable readers and viewers to identify fundamental issues themselves. Telling the truth is not aimed at informing a majority audience of racial injustice, for example, but offers a form of representation that fosters participatory democracy. Interpretive sufficiency in its multicultural dimension locates persons in a noncompetitive, nonhierarchical relationship to the larger moral universe. It imagines new modes of human transformation and emancipation, while nurturing those transformations through dialogue among citizens. The nature of truth as the larger context requires continuing debate so that this cornerstone of communication ethics continues to have credibility.

Primordial Issues in Communication Ethics

5 Nonviolence

Nonviolence is also an important ethical principle at present, and how to implement it a major challenge. Mahatma Ghandi and Martin Luther King, Jr., developed this principle beyond a political strategy into a philosophy of life. Vaclev Havel and Nelson Mandella were totally committed to it. In Emmanuel Levinas, interaction between the self and the Other makes peace normative. "The first word from the Other's face is 'Thou shalt not kill.' It is an order. There is a commandment in the appearance of the face, as if a master spoke to me" (Levinas, 1985, p. 89). In the dialogic, face-to-face encounter, the infinite is revealed. The Other's presence involves an obligation to which I owe my immediate attention. In communalistic and indigenous cultures, care of the weak and vulnerable (children, sick, and elderly), and sharing material resources are a matter of course. Along with *dharma*, *ahimsa* (nonviolence) forms the basis of the Hindu worldview. For St Augustine, peace is natural to human relationships. The public's general revulsion against physical abuse in intimate settings and its consternation over brutal crimes and savage wars, are glimmers of hope reflecting this principle's validity.

The golden rule is the ethical principle for dealing nonviolently with unrest, protest, and civil disobedience (Battles, 1996). In fact, almost all discussion of ethics in a violent context refers to the golden rule as the best guide for morally appropriate action. It can function effectively as an ethical principle without borders, that is, as an expression of the common moral wisdom of humanity worldwide. "Do unto others as you would have them do unto you" is fully practicable in the face of the extremely complex situations in which individuals or groups must often act. Its brevity and simplicity obscure its radical implications (Kang, 2006).

The golden rule when understood generally as a rule of reciprocity between others and oneself seems unarguable, the natural way to live harmoniously in human community. It proceeds from the assumption of human equality; in thinking about and living the golden rule we regard others as basically like ourselves. For media institutions internally and externally, the golden rule leads away from hostile actions and verbal abuse toward respect and goodwill.

Peace journalism is an illustration of how this principle works itself out for the news in violent conflicts worldwide. As a form of reporting, peace journalism is an interpretive process, and the principle of nonviolence gives the foundation and direction by which the interpretation ought to be done.

The Norwegian scholar, Johan Galtung, has developed and applied the principle systematically through peace studies, concerned not simply with the standards of war reporting, but positive peace – creative, nonviolent resolution of all cultural, social, and political conflicts (e.g., 2000, 2004). As with Galtung, Jake Lynch recognizes that military coverage feeds the very violence it reports, and therefore he has developed an on-the-ground theory and practice of peace initiatives and conflict resolution (e.g. Lynch and McGoldrick, 2005; Lynch, 2008).

Conflict has significant news value. Peace journalism is a self-conscious, working concept which denies that premise. Galtung (1998) has sought to reroute journalism on the "high road to peace," instead of the "low road" often taken by news media, when they fixate on "a win-lose outcome, and simplify the parties to two combatants slugging it out in a sports arena." In his literature review of war and peace journalism, Seow Ting Lee (2009) sees three contrasting features of each.

The three characteristics of mainstream war journalism are: (1) Focus on the here and now, on military action, equipment, tangible casualties and material damage; (2) An elite orientation: use official sources, follow military strategy, quote political leaders, be accurate with the military command perspective; and (3) A dichotomy of good and bad. Simplifying the parties to two combatants, them versus us, in a zero sum game – binaries such as Arab intransigence and Israeli militarism (Lee, 2009).

There are three salient features of peace journalism, grounded in the principle of nonviolence (Lee, 2009). (1) Present context, background, historical perspective following the golden rule. Use linguistic accuracy – not generic Muslim rebels but rebels identified as dissidents of a particular political group. (2) Take an advocacy stance editorially for peace, and focus in news on common values rather than on vengeance, retaliation, and differences. Emphasis on people's perspective – not just organized violence between nations, but patterns of cooperation and integration among people. 3) Multiplicity orientation. Represent all sides and all parties. Create opportunities for society at large to consider and value nonviolent responses to conflict. Include ways the conflict can be resolved without violence (e.g. as in Dayton and Kriesberg, 2009). Consensus building efforts are considered newsworthy.

Peace journalism is typically understood as an innovation in mainstream news-gathering – along with developmental and public journalism. If these three, and perhaps others, offer new paradigms for reporting then a detailed comparative analysis is needed of their histories, demographics, achievements, and structure (e.g., see Hackett and Zhao, 2005). In order to advance this demanding agenda, journalism needs to give up its utilitarian neutrality and detachment, and adopt the principle of nonviolence. Humans are moral beings and this ethical principle, implemented through the golden rule, can inspire journalists to report on a violent world and act peaceably at the same time.

6   Human dignity

The principle of human dignity is also of primordial importance to communication ethics across the globe. Different cultural traditions affirm human dignity in a variety of ways, but together they insist that all human beings have sacred status without exception. Native American discourse is steeped in reverence for life, an interconnectedness among all living forms so that we live in solidarity with others as equal constituents in the web of life. In communalistic societies, *likute* is loyalty to the community's reputation, to tribal honor. In Latin-American societies, insistence on cultural identity is an affirmation of the unique worth of human beings. In Islam, every person has the right to honor and a good reputation. In Confucius, veneration of authority is necessary because authorities are human beings of dignity. Humans are a unique species, requiring from within itself regard for its members as a whole.

From this perspective, one understands the ongoing vitality of the Universal Declaration of Human Rights issued by the United Nations General Assembly in 1948. As the preamble states: "Recognition of the inherent dignity and of the equal and inalienable rights of all members of the human family is the foundation of freedom, justice and peace in the world" (Universal Declaration of Human Rights, 1988, p. 1). Every child, woman, and man has sacred status, with no exceptions for religion, class, gender, age, or ethnicity. The common sacredness of all human beings regardless of merit or achievement is not only considered a fact but is a shared commitment.

For two decades now, media ethicists have emphasized human dignity in working on ethnic diversity, racist language in news, and sexism in advertising. Gender equality in hiring and eliminating racism in organizational culture are no longer dismissed as political correctness, but seen as moral imperatives. Human dignity takes seriously the decisive contexts of gender, race, class, and religion. A community's polychromatic voices are understood to be essential for a healthy democracy.

Ethnic self-consciousness these days is considered essential to cultural vitality. The world's cultures each have a distinctive beauty. Indigenous languages and ethnicity have come into their own. Culture is more salient at present than countries. Rather than the melting-pot Americanization of the past century, immigrants now insist on maintaining their culture, religion, and language. With identity politics arising as the dominant issue in world affairs following the end of the cold war, social institutions, including the media, are challenged to develop a healthy cultural pluralism. Human dignity pushes us to comprehend the demands of cultural diversity, and give up an individualistic morality of rights. The public sphere is conceived as a mosaic of distinguishable communities, a plurality of ethnic identities intersecting to form a social bond, but each seriously held and competitive as well.

Putting the principle of human dignity to work, Robert Entman and Andrew Rojecki (2000) indicate how the race dimension of cultural pluralism ought to move forward in the media. Race in twenty-first century United States remains a preeminent issue, and their research indicates a broad array of White racial sentiments toward African Americans as a group. They emphasize not the minority of outright racists but the perplexed majority. On a continuum from comity (acceptance) to ambivalence and then racism, a complex ambivalence most frequently characterizes the majority (p. 21). Correcting White ignorance and dealing with ambiguities appear to hold "considerable promise for enhancing racial comity" (p. 21). The reality is, however, that ambivalence shades off into animosity most easily and frequently. In Entman and Rojecki's interviews, personal experiences of Black effort and achievement tend to be discounted "in favor of television images, often vague, of welfare cheats and Black violence. ... The habits of local news – for example, the rituals in covering crime – facilitate the construction of menacing imagery" (p. 34). Rather than actively following human dignity and enhancing racial understanding among those most open to it, the media tend to tip "the balance toward suspicion and even animosity among the ambivalent majority of Americans" (p. 44). When the normative principle of human dignity becomes a priority in the media, this important swing group would be enabled to move forward and cultural pluralism would be enhanced.

7   Privacy as a moral good

Privacy is another fundamental issue, especially with the dramatic growth of digital technologies for gathering and storing personal information. Privacy is not merely a legal right but a condition or status in which humans, by virtue of their humanness, control the time, place, and circumstances of information about themselves. A private domain gives people their own identity and unique self-consciousness within the human species. Democracies as a system of rule by the people distinguish themselves in these terms. Legally it means that citizens have freedom from government control over what they themselves control. Totalitarian societies use the near absence of privacy to produce a servile populace. Those with no privacy lose their sense of human dignity. Government surveillance may demand personal records outside owner controls, but human dignity requires absolute protection. Security measures that intrude upon personal information without notification in the process of securing a nation state deny its democratic character.

Instead of a bevy of rules and constraints to determine whether privacy is being invaded by the press or the government, the question is whether the people themselves consider the information or action invasive. Protection of privacy is basically a citizen's ethics, understood and implemented by policy makers and media professionals who see themselves first of all as human beings, not as professionals. The human dignity of the citizenry, rather than legalities, is the alpha and omega, the beginning and end. Hence the formal criterion for privacy as a moral good: Since human dignity entails control of private life space, information is communicated about human beings to others if and only if a reasonable public considers it permissible.

Public opinion polls indicate that the invasion of privacy ought to be a premier issue in journalism ethics. Intruding on privacy creates resentment and damages the credibility of the information providers. Legal definitions by themselves are an inadequate foundation. How can the legally crucial difference between newsworthy material and gossip or voyeurism be reasonably determined? Privacy is not a legal right only but a moral good. For all of the sophistication of case law and tort law in protecting privacy, legal safeguards do not match the challenges of powerful new media technologies for storing data and disseminating information.

Therefore, while acknowledging legal distinctions and boundaries, the protection of privacy must be constructed and defended as a normative principle. Privacy is a moral good since it is a condition for developing a healthy sense of personhood. Violating it, therefore, violates human dignity. However, privacy cannot be made absolute because people are cultural beings with responsibility in the social and political arena. People are individuals and therefore need privacy. People are social

Primordial Issues in Communication Ethics 15

beings and therefore need public information about others. Since people are individuals, eliminating privacy would eliminate human existence as they know it; since people are social, elevating privacy to absolute status would likewise render human existence impossible. These considerations lead to the formal criterion that the intimate life space of individuals cannot be invaded without permission unless the revelation averts a public crisis or is of overriding public significance and all other means to deal with the issue have been exhausted.

ICTs have greatly facilitated data collection, privacy invasion, and surveillance. And with the "War on Terrorism", ICT-based surveillance policies and practices have increased dramatically.

> Invasion of privacy and abuse of personal data by third parties, as well as harassment and identity theft are oft-criticized side effects of data networks and new communication technologies. Popular Web 2.0 applications such as social networking sites, provide a convenient socializing tool for its users who often carelessly reveal detailed personal information in their profiles. This makes social networking sites gigantic data collection agencies that allow highly individualized forms of marketing and advertising through the combination of user profiles and user behaviors (Debatin, 2008, p. 261).

Small micromedia, such as podcasts, blogs, mobile phones, and social networking sites are increasingly used to publicize personal and intimate information within the so-called anonymity of the digital environment. It can be assumed that the threats to privacy will only be aggravated as new smart communication technologies pervade industrial societies. This type of technology tends to become invisible because it is so widely adapted that it is readily taken for granted. "In the not-too-distant future, ubiquitous computer technology will be embedded in every aspect of our everyday environment. It is obvious that this new pervasive technology will inevitably lead to unintended consequences with ethical implications due to its invisibility, definitional power and deep impact on existing social structures" (Debatin, 2008, p. 261).

In fostering an ethics of privacy, the vitality of education becomes our preoccupation rather than focusing on the violations of privacy one-by-one. The question is not first of all policy makers and media professionals dealing with privacy issues case-by-case, but their commitment to privacy as normative for a healthy democracy. To the extent that privacy as a moral good is known and appreciated, the details of privacy protection in law and professional practice will be interpreted correctly.

Descriptive Ethics

8   Instrumentalism

As with metaethics and the normative, academic work in the third category of media ethics has a worldwide scope. Descriptive ethics is only now turning to the developing world to account for its media use and social values. Robert Fortner's Center for International Media has become a world leader in systematically researching media technologies in nonindustrial societies. This handbook pays special attention to ethical issues under the conditions of low-level technology, with advanced media only available for the elite few. As this research multiplies, primordial issues will become transparent.

The focus here is on instrumentalism as the major challenge for doing descriptive ethics in technologically sophisticated countries. The prevailing worldview in industrial societies is instrumentalism – the view that technology is neutral and does not condition our thinking and social organization.

The French social philosopher, Jacques Ellul, developed the argument that technology is decisive in defining contemporary culture (Ellul, 1964). A society is instrumental, he argues, not because of its machines, but from the pursuit of efficient techniques in every area of human endeavor. Unlike previous eras where techniques are constrained within a larger complex of social values, the pervasiveness and sophistication of modern ICTs reorganize society to conform to the demand for efficiency.

In Ellul's (1969) framework, the media represent the meaning-edge of the technological system. Convergence media technologies, for example, incarnate the properties of technology while serving as agents for interpreting the meaning of the very phenomenon they embody. Though exhibiting the structural elements of all technical artifacts, their particular identity comes from their function as bearers of symbols. Scientific techniques are applied not just to nature, but to social organizations and our understanding of personhood. Civilizations across history have engaged in technical activities and produced technological products, but modern society has sacralized the genius behind machines and uncritically allowed its power to infect not just industry, engineering, and business, but also politics, education, the church, labor unions, health, and international relations.

The problem for technological societies is not technologies per se, but the mystique of efficiency that underlies them. Like heatness in red hot iron, the spirit of machineness permeates everywhere. The world of means expands in size and speed; human ends shrivel and become mysterious. Human values are replaced by the machine-like imperative of efficiency. Human goals are buried under a preoccupation with means. The new electronic media exacerbate the problem. While ICTs amplify, store, and distribute information as do books and television, ICTs specialize in the processing and connecting of information. Bernhard Debatin of Ohio University describes the contemporary situation this way:

> As technology advances from mere use of tools to the employment of machines and then to the implementation of complex technical systems, technology depends more and more on its own mediating capacities, since technicization introduces greater complexity into the human realm of action and perception. In other words, the technologically created sphere requires increasingly technical mediation for its own operations. This is the birth of homeostatic machines, cybernetic systems, control technology, and user interfaces. In the technical-scientific world, the focus of technology changes from merely controlling the forces of nature to controlling increasingly intransparent technologies and compensating for their unintended and unforeseen consequences (2008, p. 258).

Primordial Issues in Communication Ethics

The average end-user is reduced to participating in a largely predetermined system through the computer/browser interface.

In an instrumental age enamored of machines, life becomes amoral, without moral bearings, devoid of moral categories. Moral vocabulary is not understood. Moral distinctions have little meaning. In the process of fabricating expert mechanical systems such as the digital order, the world is sanitized of the moral dimension. In a technological era, the social fashion is to be emancipated from moral standards and to disavow moral responsibility.

Several social analysts have noted that basic human values have deteriorated in today's technological world. Disrespect for others, lack of civility, crude and offensive language, selfishness and greed – all of these are increasing dramatically on the Internet and in popular culture. Politicians show little concern for ethical standards. Opportunism through the financial system created a massive worldwide collapse. Children are increasingly defiant at home and school. When efficiency, speed, and productivity dominate, morality based in human life becomes alien to us. Moral purpose is sacrificed to technical excellence.

Under these conditions, in order to do research on descriptive ethics credibly, we need to reconceive technology itself. A fundamentally different approach to technology is needed instead of the instrumentalist one. The technological enterprise is a human process, value-laden throughout. Valuing penetrates all technological activity, from selecting the needs to address and which materials to use, through the processes of design and fabrication, to the resulting tools and products. Although valuing is surely involved in the uses to which people put technological objects, valuing saturates every phase prior to usage as well. There can be no isolated, neutral understanding of technology as though it exists in a presupposition-less vacuum. The problems of one group are addressed but not all. Certain resources are used and not others.

True to the character of machineness, the values of productivity, power, and efficiency direct the technological process when societies are characterized by instrumentalism. The principle of self-augmentation begins to rule, pushing the global media toward greater speed and larger size, marginalizing small-scale activities, and taking on a life of its own, no longer subject to human control. This instrumentalist worldview must be reversed. The whole phenomenon ought to be called into question, not just some of its features. Policy-makers, academics, business executives, and media professionals face a double challenge – developing a noninstrumental perspective on convergent media and a deep understanding of the global technological revolution that is concentrated in the electronic giant nations of the world.

The opposition is not to technological products, but to technicism. We need to desacralize technology and free our academic and professional language from technological metaphors. Against an overweening technocratic mystique, a culture needs to be developed in which questions of meaning, life's purpose, and moral values predominate.

Instead of the elementary view that technologies are value-free, the reality is that they are caught in ever-expanding means that tend to overwhelm all ideals worthy of human allegiance. In the instrumental view, technology is static – products, machines, laptops, iPods, communication satellites. In a more adequate human-centered model, technology is not a noun but a verb, the arena in which human existence is established. We need a new paradigm. The instrumental worldview must be turned on its head and inside out.

There is no magic answer. The only solution is long term. Through education, beliefs about media technology can change, and when our values are transformed, technologies will follow in their wake. Rather than emphasize computers for their own sake in a mechanized society, the humanities ought to be emphasized instead. The arts, music, philosophy and literature should prosper, not just engineering and electronic gadgetry. Beliefs about instrumental progress, consumerism, expertise and magnitude must be replaced with values rooted in the sacredness of human life.

Summary

Primordial issues in communication ethics can never be solved once-and-for-all. The dynamic and continually changing world of media technology makes permanent resolution impossible. Given the complexity of communication ethics across the three categories, no one academic or media professional is competent to address these issues singlehandedly. Scholarship on primordial issues is a shared enterprise, and this collaboration must be decisively international and multicultural.

References

Battles, J. (1996) *The Golden Rule*, Oxford University Press, New York.

Bonhoeffer, D. (1995) *Ethics*, (trans. N.H. Smith), Macmillan, New York.

Carey, J.W. (1997a) The communications revolution and the professional communicator, in *James Carey: A Critical Reader*, (eds E.S. Munson and C. Warren), University of Minnesota Press, Minneapolis, pp. 128–143.

Carey, J.W. (1997b) Afterword: The culture in question, in *James Carey: A Critical Reader*, (eds E.S. Munson and C. Warren), University of Minnesota Press, Minneapolis, pp. 308–339.

Chester, J. (2007) *Digital Destiny: New Media and the Future of Democracy*, New Press, New York.

Christians, C. (2009) Theoretical frontiers in international media ethics. *Australian Journalism Review*, 31 (2), 5–18.

Dayton, B.W., and Kriesberg, L. (2009) *Conflict Transformation and Peacebuilding: Moving from Violence to Sustainable Peace*, Routledge, London.

Debatin, B. (2008) The future of new media ethics, in *An ethics trajectory: Visions of the Media Past, Present, and Yet to Come*, (eds. T.W. Cooper, C.G. Christians and A.S. Babbili), University of Illinois – Institute of Communications Research, Urbana, pp. 257–264.

Ellul, J. (1964) *The Technological Society* (trans. J. Wilkinson), original publication 1954, Random Vintage, New York.

Ellul, J. (1969) *Propaganda: The Formation of Men's Attitudes*, (trans. K. Kellen and J. Lerner), original publication 1962, Alfred A. Knopf, New York.

Entman, R.M., and Rojecki, A. (2000) *The Black Image in the White Mind: Media and Race in America*, Chicago University Press, Chicago.

Galtung, J. (1998) High road, low road: Charting the course for peace journalism. *Track two*, 7 (4), December 1, www.ccr.uct.ac.za/archive/two/7_4/p07_highroad_lowroad.html (accessed June 17, 2010).

Galtung, J. (2000) *Conflict Transformation by Peaceful Means: A Participants' and Trainers' Manual*, UNDP, Geneva.

Galtung, J. (2004) *Transcend and Transform: An Introduction to Conflict Work (Peace by Peaceful Means)*, Pluto Press, London.

Hackett, R., and Zhao, Y. (eds) (2005) *Democratizing Global Media*, Rowman & Littlefield, Lanham, MD.

Hare, J.E. (2001) *God's Call: Moral realism, God's Commands, and Human Autonomy*, Eerdmans, Grand Rapids, MI.

Jaspers, K. (1955) *Reason and Existenz*, (trans. W. Earle), Routledge and Kegan Paul, New York.

Kang, Y.A. (2006) Global ethics and a common morality. *Philosophia reformata*, 71, 79–95.

Lee, S.T. (2009) Peace journalism, in (eds L. Wilkins and C. Christians), *The Handbook of Mass Media Ethics*, Routledge, New York and London, pp. 258–275.

Levinas, E. (1985) *Ethics and Infinity: Conversations with Philippe Nemo*, Duquesne University Press, Pittsburgh, PN.

Lynch, J. (2008) *Debates in Peace Journalism*, University of Sydney Press, Sydney.

Lynch, J., and McGoldrick, A. (2005) *Peace Journalism*, Hawthorn Press Glasgow, UK.

Nietzsche, F. ([1886]1966) *Beyond Good and Evil*, (trans. W. Kaufmann), Random House, New York.

Pippert, W. (1989) *An Ethics of News: A Reporter's Search for Truth*, Georgetown University Press, Washington, DC.

Universal Declaration of Human Rights (1988) *Human Rights: A Compilation of International Instruments*, Centre for Human Rights, Geneva, pp. 1–7.

Velasquez, M., Andre, C., Shanks, T. *et al.* (2009) *Ethical Relativism*, Markkula Center for Applied Ethics, www.scu.edu/ethics/practicing/decision/ethicalrelativism.html (accessed June 18, 2010).

Ward, S.J.A. (2004) *The Invention of Journalism Ethics: The Path to Objectivity and Beyond*, McGill-Queen's University Press, Montreal and Kingston, Canada.

Wilson, J.Q. (1993) *The Moral Sense*, Free Press, New York.

Wuthnow, R. (1987) *Meaning and Moral Order*, University of California Press, Berkeley.

2

Communication Ethics
The Wonder of Metanarratives in a Postmodern Age

Ronald C. Arnett

I will be making a continuing polemic against what I call "subtraction stories."
Concisely put, I mean by this stories of modernity in general, and secularity
in particular, which explain them by human beings having lost, or sloughed
off, or liberated themselves from certain earlier, confining horizons, or illusions,
or limitations of knowledge. What emerges from this process – modernity or
secularity – is to be understood in terms of underlying features of human nature
which were there all along, but had been impeded by what is now set aside.

(Taylor, 2007, p. 22)

This essay follows the lead of Charles Taylor, forgoing the ongoing temptation of
"subtraction stories." The task of this essay is two-fold: (1) to unite a story about
communication ethics around the term *wonder*; and (2) to frame the use of this
word within postmodern pragmatism. It is the meeting and delight of *wonder* that
propels this essay; it is not out of conviction that we must appreciate existence, but
rather out of *pragmatic surprise*. The pragmatic acknowledgment of wonder welcomes a postmodern communication ethics paradox – what postmodernity deconstructs, it cannot destroy. This essay outlines the wonder of the continuing reality
of metanarratives in communication ethics in an age defined by deconstruction of
metanarrative reality.

Introduction

Philosophically and practically, one can assert that we live in a time of commonality
under attack. The fervent call to challenge anything that attempts to make a
metanarrative claim defines our age. One can suggest that postmodernity, under-

The Handbook of Global Communication and Media Ethics, First Edition. Edited by Robert S. Fortner
and P. Mark Fackler.
© 2011 Blackwell Publishing Ltd. Published 2011 by Blackwell Publishing Ltd.

stood as narrative and virtue contention (MacIntyre, 1981), is a practical call for deconstruction. Yet, in the continuing reality of some living and dying for a given metanarrative, we discover the recalcitrance of existence and our inability to theorize away that which continues to have currency in what Arendt called public opinion (Arendt, 1963, p. 225).

The persistent reality of multiple metanarratives continues to compete for communication ethics consideration. This essay functions in a theoretical and practical paradox, accommodating the theoretical veracity of a postmodern understanding of communication ethics centered on the importance of *difference* (Arnett, Fritz, and Bell, 2009) and accepting the practical acknowledgement that communication ethics does not live within a world of theoretical truth, but within a world of existential public opinion.

Arendt (1958) reminded us that it is not the *pristine pursuit of theory* that ultimately guides communities, but the interplay of human beings in conversation propelled *by opinion*. Following this logic, one cannot use theory alone or discussion of a singular interpretation of a given historical moment to displace opinions that people continue to embrace, even when that belief manifests itself as a metanarrative. Postmodernity is an accepted theoretical reality from the perspective of this author. The tricky admission of postmodern work is that postmodernity is an age of difference, of rhetoric, of opinion, even those we cannot embrace, endorse, condone, or believe. Ironically, in this case, opinion, not postmodern theory, places metanarrative truth within a genre similar to that of Mark Twain's famous quotation, "the report of my death was an exaggeration" (Robinson, 1995, p. 7).[1] This essay examines metanarrative and communication ethics, not as pristine theory, but as an acknowledgement of the premature announcement of metanarrative's death, while metanarrative is kept alive and, in many cases, healthy by the recalcitrance of public opinion. This essay assumes that we live in a postmodern moment that cannot eliminate the nagging opinion that metanarratives matter.

The task of this essay is to tell a story about a position that refuses to die and why, in a postmodern age, we cannot offer a final "taps" for its demise. The telling of this story begins at a number of different entrances and revisits the reality of communication ethics in a postmodern age. Central ideas function as characters in this story: (1) the importance of wonder, (2) framing the connection between the unexpected and protecting the good, (3) a brief history of communication ethics, and (4) a statement of change from tradition to universal to difference, (5) the reclamation of existentialism, and (6) the wonder of communication ethics in a era defined by difference. Communication ethics must continue to grapple with an idea that will not die – metanarrative. The remainder of this essay outlines this communication story about an idea, a conviction, which refused to die.

Difference and Wonder

This historical moment rests firmly within a postmodern vocabulary of difference with a focus upon small bits of land upon which we can stand, called "petite narratives" by one of the architects of a postmodern pragmatism (Rorty, 1989). Working within the spirit of postmodernity's affirmation of difference, we must acknowledge that major communication ethics differences exist as one version of a metanarrative vies for supremacy over another; it is at this point that the theory of metanarrative declines and contention assists. Yet, the pragmatic reality is that there are still communication ethics propelled by metanarrative conviction. This essay examines with wonder the reality of metanarratives in a postmodern age of supposed metanarrative collapse.

The notion of wonder elicits a confession; it brings forth a form of *Dialogic Confession* (Arnett, 2005), as a necessary and pragmatic starting point for this inquiry. Discussion of the reality of metanarratives does not roll easily off a postmodern tongue; such admission leads this author to the existential reality of the continuing life of metanarratives. This view is more responsive to the demands of existence than to the demands for theoretical postmodern fit. This confessional admission recognizes the importance of Burke's proclamation about the "recalcitrance of existence" (Burke, 1973, p. 131). He gives us a handle on the existential why for the inability of authors like me to claim the doom of metanarrative convictions that dominate human existence. The strife in the global community is akin to the fight of ideas unwilling to "go gently into that good night" (Thomas, 1952, p. 116). Existence indicates otherwise than quick agreement.

As we watch events in the global community, we have our clear positions of right and wrong, good and evil. With this clarity, however, comes the rude reminder that we assume that all will and do agree with us. There are human beings willing to fight and die for a given position that opposes our own. The theoretical celebration of difference and diversity shapes our time, but the practical reality is that much suffering and death come from such clashes. It is often the conviction of our correctness or that of the "enemy" that openly displays a metanarrative dispute that guides conflicting sides in conflict and/or crisis. The reality of our world does not rest simply with extreme positions, but in truth guides that opposing sides consider metanarrative descriptions of existence.

This task of bringing together communication ethics and postmodernity with attentiveness to the "recalcitrance of existence" requires reluctant admission of metanarrative convictions that guide us and others if any peace is to be found around a global discourse table functionally defined by difference. The wonder of this postmodern moment is that the rejection of metanarrative inherent within a postmodern perspective makes it impossible to displace that which our theory considers no longer valid – a metanarrative. The ironic nature of a postmodern understanding of difference is that we cannot displace all the opposition, even when we consider such positions "wrong." Indeed, this is perhaps an acknowledged moment of existential wonder.

The understanding of wonder that fames this essay finds its meaning in terms such as awe and marvel. From the *Merriam-Webster's Collegiate Dictionary*, one finds wonder associated with the following definitions: "1. a) a cause of astonishment or admiration, b) MIRACLE; 2. The quality of exciting amazed admiration; 3) rapt attention or astonishment at something awesomely mysterious or new to one's experience" (Merriam-Webster, 1997, p. 1361). This view of wonder assumes that as we meet with the unexpected, we encounter a state close to awe that evokes a wide range of responses, including the one that shapes this essay – can you believe that existence seems to house or harbor an idea in contrast with our best theory? This essay ties the unexpected to existential wonder. Like it or not, the good of difference exists – *voilà*, we are on our way to wonder about the pragmatic reality of metanarrative stubbornness.

This is the reality of a communication ethics moment of wonder – a moment in which a communication ethics author who writes from a postmodern perspective cannot take off the table that with which he disagrees – metanarratives. I have proclaimed postmodernity as a given and the accompanying reality of metanarrative decline and collapse a fixture of our time (Arnett and Arneson, 1999). This essay reflects a practice engaged in many of life's pursuits; as one understands something increasingly well, the learning is followed by further complexity and ambiguity and, once again, I must examine this same ground, but differently. We seem to move from a lack of clarity to unduly confident clarity to clarity that shares space with ambiguity and fuzziness of insight. It is as if we end up in a place similar to where we started, lack of understanding, but in reality, when one works with an idea for a long enough period of time, the return to ambiguity might better be defined as wonder (Taylor, 1989). We cannot take such a beginning without an unusual assertion that fundamentally shapes the study and practice of communication ethics in our time – the reality of metanarrative conviction remains a large part of the human fabric in a postmodern age. The study of and agreement with the existence of an age called postmodernity does not presuppose that the arguments of modernity are now anachronistic. Postmodernity is best understood as a historical juncture, not as a moment unto itself. Postmodernity is a dwelling composed of many rooms, each of which is considered a defining sense of home by differing constituencies. This essay examines the ironic place that the notion of metanarrative has at the table of communication ethics, which is played out, not in abstract theory, but in the way and manner in which human beings live their lives.

We do not get to this place of wonder quickly. First, there is the stage of confusion and not knowing. Then there is the stage of unknowing self-deceit. We work with a degree of conviction that propels us into stances of telling, expecting that all others will listen to us and find the error of their ways. Finally, there is a nagging sense of questioning that begins to disrupt our clarity, finally yielding to an initially unwanted recognition, wonder that begins to unite what we do not know and a confession of what we do not understand, and we are likely to end up recognizing that we know even less than we did when we started. In actuality, we know much more in this latter stage, but the relative comparison between that which we know and that which we do not understand is far greater. Such is the mystery of wonder. This essay lives in the space of clarity and ambiguity or, in communication ethics terms, in the space of conviction and doubt (Arnett, 2005), which this essay offers as a metaphor for postmodernity properly understood as a dwelling of wonder. In a dwelling of wonder it is difficult to eradicate that with which one does not agree if it continues to manifest itself in our communicative lives. Thus, this essay begins a reflection of wonder upon the notion of metanarrative in a postmodern age. In this returning examination that recognizes the unreality of complete clarity, an idea previously understood takes on a texture and complexity previously unseen.

The remainder of this essay is dedicated to a working out of a story of wonder that outlines why, in a postmodern age so keenly unresponsive to the notions of metanarrative and universal, we cannot escape the reality of their durability and contribution to communicative life. This argument is similar to that of those wanting to revisit books previously termed as central to an English canon (Kramnick, 1997; Friedman, 1993). Once the notion of canon can no longer carry the full weight of argument, its argument must be taken seriously once again – now with new eyes, guided more by wonder than by divisive rhetoric propelled by undue self-assurance.

Meeting the Unexpected and the Good

In a classical age, when one met the unexpected, which Socrates (Plato, 1987) delivered with regularity, the action and the person were stopped – for the good of the polis. When the unexpected was met in a medieval era, as land deemed "the Holy Land" of the birth of Christianity was considered potentially lost as the Byzantine Empire began to decline, Pope Urban II then permitted mercenaries to join the fight against Muslim forces. The Crusades began in an effort to assist the Christian Church in an unexpected change in power in the East (*Encyclopaedia Britannica*, 2005). In the classical era, the unexpected that was fought was challenge against the polis, and in a medieval Western age, the effort was to protect the sacred places of the Church.

In the Renaissance, we find another version of the unexpected in the ongoing emergence of science, which was met with claims of blasphemy and opposition. One of the most celebrated cases was that of Galileo and his insistence upon a Copernican rather than a Ptolemaic view of the world and its place in the universe (Drake, 1978). In modernity, we have met the unexpected with acts of colonization, imperialism, totalitarianism, and one global conflict after another (Arendt, 1958). The unexpected was met with force and efforts of control and domination (Toulmin, 1992). As one reflects upon the progression from a classical world to a medieval world to the Renaissance to modernity, one sees first the protection of the polis, then the church, then belief, then nation, and one's own group. In each case of meeting the unexpected, we find a response of reaction and protection of something. Whether we would approve of that protection or not, it has guided human life century after century.

One can understand one of the functions of communication ethics as a form of protection in response to the unexpected. In the work *Communication Ethics Literacy: Dialogue and Difference*, the following definition of communication ethics guides the inquiry: "The good is the valued center of a given communication ethic – what is most important and held in highest regard finds protection and promotion in our communicative practices" (Arnett, Fritz, and Bell, 2009, p. 3). The notion of the "good" traced to its classical roots reminds us that the issue of the good was a central question. It is from the inquiry that we come to the question about the "good life." From the classical era forward there was a difference in lives; not each life was of the same worth. What made one life more fundamental than another in Greek culture was the pursuit of a "good life." The good life was virtuous with the trinity of bravery, honor, and justice (Plutarch, 1935). The central feature of the good life was its contrast with pleasure. Acts of pleasure were considered the most vulgar of virtues. This odd description of pleasure that unites the words "vulgar" and "virtue" is illustrative of the fact that pleasure was part of Classical culture and was not rejected, but nevertheless understood with extreme caution. Life was understood to have within it acts and moments of pleasure, but it was not the avenue through which one could and should pursue the good life.

The notion of the good life was tied to happiness in contrast to pleasure. This happiness required labor worthy of being done in the public domain (Arendt, 1958). It was the public element of happiness tied to labor that was of importance; therefore, there is a reason that the great Greek historians recorded the "deeds" of war and public action. Homer was the great recorder of deeds that could move mortal man into immortality of story. The historian classically was a "witness" to deeds that require remembering. This is the key to Arendt's differentiation between behavior and action, with the latter situated within a story that is worthy of remembering (Arendt, 1958). The public domain is central to this understanding of the pursuit of happiness.

There is an ongoing competitor to this stress of public happiness tied to deeds; it is the Epicurean pursuit of pleasure and enjoyment that avoids the public limelight (Hyde, 1980). We have multiple persons who keep this philosophy alive, including Erasmus, whom many consider the first major proponent of humanism (Erasmus, 1965). This humanistic model of the importance of the person and a celebration of pleasure and enjoyment drives much of what Philip Rieff (1966) calls a therapeutic culture. The enjoyment of the self, the self's enjoyment of "enjoying oneself," becomes the standard from which one would judge whether or not something is of value and worth.

In short, this postmodern assumption that we have difference between and among dwellings/understandings of the good is not new. The works of Plato and Aristotle reflect understandings of the good at odds with Epicurus. From the beginning of classical thought, we have difference in the dwellings from which what this essay calls communication ethics is played out. Thus, from the beginning of what we term Western culture the understanding of the "good" was not housed within a single dwelling. Arnett, Fritz, and Bell (2009) use this assumption of difference in the framing of *Communication Ethics Literacy: Dialogue and Difference*. In that work, communication ethics is understood as having multiple dwellings of the good. What we now consider the "good life" is not uniform; we live in a time of multiplicity. Communication ethics becomes the protecting and promoting of a given dwelling or sense of the good that is played out in the interplay of opinion, theory, and the particular. Communication ethics is the engagement of multiplicity of dwellings of understandings of the good that we seek to protect and promote; the irony is that in this multiplicity, we fold practically back into the reality of the metanarrative. Indeed, it is a wonder, but we still live in a time in which metanarrative is alive; this time punctuated by the plural(s).

This work frames a postmodern understanding of communication ethics around the pragmatic importance of protection; the point here is that the union of communication ethics and protection may be as old as human civilization. Protection occurs when one has a good that one wants to endure. The idea of the good, tied to Aristotle and later to Aquinas, is not something that is the opposite of bad. A good is a presupposition or sense of ground upon which all depends. When Aquinas states that God is good, he is stating that God is a presupposition upon which all must rest and depend (Aquinas, 1945).

Goods are presuppositions that give our ongoing lives meaning. We can view communication ethics as practices put into place to protect these goods. In a classical time, one had to find practices to protect the polis. In the medieval age, one found practices to protect the Church. In the Renaissance, we begin to witness clear competing goods between the faith of the Church and the faith of science. Where one enters this conversation determines what one will attempt to protect. In modernity, one attempts to protect one's place in the world with expansion, aggression, or defensive engagement. The more powerful one's neighbor becomes, the more one must find ways to address that power, from the beginning of the colonial movement to the United States takeover from the French in Vietnam in 1955 (Karnow, 1983). This rendering of an impressionistic picture of communication ethics assumes a familial connection among ideas such as the unexpected, protection, and the good.

The importance of intercultural communication ethics must now drive our inquiry (Chesebro, 1969; pers. com. 2009). The reality of intercultural communication is that it assumes the importance of difference. As we move to any global question in communication, understood as intercultural communication, the ongoing difference between cultures needs to propel the inquiry. Intercultural communication finds its existence from the reality of difference. The shift made by postmodern scholarship is to move beyond the claim of the reality of difference into a qualitatively different scholarly position. For postmodern scholars, difference becomes the defining good. The irony is that in a time of supposed disjunctures, we find ourselves ironically meeting commonality – the commonality of protection. Our current era is engaged in the protection of the postmodern good of difference.

The naming of this moment as postmodern and driven by difference is not accomplished by a modern imposition of a term upon the human landscape. The naming emerges in attentive reaction to the world before us. We find scholars on both the left and the right offering such descriptions. For instance, Alasdair MacIntyre engages in a description of the world before him that does not meet

Metanarratives in a Postmodern Age 27

with his approval. In book after book MacIntyre has articulated what he deems the crisis of this age, the clashing of differences without a standpoint from which to render a judgment that will assure all of justice. In particular, four of his works address this question directly: *After Virtue: A Study in Moral Inquiry* (1981); *Three Rival Versions of Moral Enquiry: Encyclopaedia, Genealogy, and Tradition* (1991); *Whose Justice? Which Rationality?* (1988); and *Dependent Rational Animals: Why Human Beings Need the Virtues* (1999). It is as if the scholarship of MacIntyre is a reluctant description of the recalcitrance of existence. He cannot ignore the power and the reality of difference in this era. At the conclusion of *Whose Justice? Which Rationality?*, MacIntyre (1988) pens the description of existence before him:

> There is thus a deep incompatibility between the standpoint of any rational tradition of enquiry and the dominant modes of contemporary teaching, discussion, and debate, both academic and nonacademic. Where the standpoint of a tradition requires a recognition of the different types of language-in-use through which different types of argument will have to be carried on, the standpoint of the forums of modern liberal culture presupposes the possibility of a common language for all speakers or at the very least of the translatability of any one language into any other. Where the standpoint of a tradition involves an acknowledgement that fundamental debate is between competing and conflicting understandings of rationality, the standpoint of the forums of modern liberal culture presupposes the fiction of shared, even if unformulable, universal standards of rationality. Where the standpoint of a tradition cannot be presented except in a way which takes account of the history and the historical situatedness, both of traditions themselves and of those individuals who engage in dialogue with them, the standpoint of the forums of modern liberal culture presupposes the irrelevance of one's history to one's status as a participant in debate. We confront one another in such forums abstracted from and deprived of the particularities of our histories (p. 400).

Of course, there are more eager postmodern voices in this conversation, including Derrida (2002), Foucault (1973), Lyotard (1999), and Rorty (1989). The point is that in a postmodern era, it is not the person that protects all goods, but existence itself. Therefore, it does not matter whether one approves or not of the good of difference.

Communication Ethics

The notion of the good shapes the study of communication ethics (Arnett, Arneson, and Bell, 2006); this communicative ethics carriage of the good is in contrast with a philosophical discussion of ethics. Those of us studying communication ethics are indebted to philosophers who have historically given us traction in the study and understanding of ethics; therefore, this essay begins with a philosopher who offers important ideas for the study of ethics. This essay begins with the insight of Alasdair MacIntyre (1998) in his *Short History of Ethics: A History of Moral Philosophy from the Homeric Age to the Twentieth Century*. MacIntyre provides a thoughtful historical examination of the interplay between ethics and philosophy. MacIntyre states that philosophy is a subversive enterprise; it gives people different, contrasting, and, at times, quite contentious ways of thinking and conceptualizing, moving persons from unknowing enslavement to questioning and choice with the notion of choice emerging as central to a Western engagement of ethics.

Ethics within the genre of choice requires the exercise of *free will*; without such a possibility, we are left to following the "herd" (Nietzsche, 1989, p. 26) without consideration and reflection. Choice makes primary and fundamental the availability of options. Philosophy makes possible the reality of options; with the existence of competing philosophies from the time of the pre-Socratics to the later writings of Plato and Aristotle to scholarship today, philosophical options abound. The question of ethics follows this historical sense of philosophical diversity; it is a safe pragmatic position to state that the reality of contrasting theories requires one to choose.

MacIntyre functions as a storyteller informing us about the ongoing historical shifts in philosophy and ethics. He does what Arendt (1978) considers essential; he gives life to ideas within narrative form, offering us access to how different philosophies lend themselves to contrasting views of ethics and contrasting views of the good. MacIntyre suggests that the prephilosophical view of the "good" lives within human practices without a sense of reflective choice. Both Socrates and the Sophistics offer access to a world of contrary and alternative positions that challenge the status quo and Socrates dying for the right to deconstruct the "natural attitude" (Husserl, 1970) of conventional perception. This movement of contention propels Plato more than typical assumption would suggest.

Plato's *Republic* sought to stabilize the classical world with discussion of the importance of roles and the necessity of working within the limits of those roles, the importance of the *a priori* and obligation of a few to bring forth universal truths into the light. Plato offers a clear counter to the relativism of the Sophists, with Aristotle following the train of thought by connecting virtues that become expected – in fact, these virtues are demanded public practices expected within the life of the polis. For Plato the answer rests in the *a priori* and for Aristotle within the *polis*, and in each case, what is missing overtly is an explicit understanding of choice. The implicit choice to refuse one's role in the polis would leave one on the outside, a form of self-imposed exclusion.

At this juncture, we can sense two emerging presuppositions about ethics that emerge out of MacIntyre's story about the Greeks. The first is that ethics was clearly skewed to an aristocratic population. If one was a woman, slave, or without some wealth, the story of ethics had little to do with one's life, unless, of course, one followed Plato's admonition for all to attend to their roles and work within them. For MacIntyre, the next major step in philosophy and ethics is Christianity, understood as a philosophy, with its concern for the disadvantaged and those without resources. Christianity becomes the philosophy of those on the margins. The major elements of choice emerge with acts of Luther and all the ramifications of

Metanarratives in a Postmodern Age

such thinking, which begin to shape four quite different homes or dwellings: (1) Plato's *a priori*, (2) Aristotle's *polis*, and (3) Christianity's eventual institutional commitments outlined most fully by Augustine, to (4) increasing attentiveness to the *individual*. The eighteenth century is a major modern marker of ethics. The French Revolution and the writers that support such a view connect the notion of the individual to universal rights with a contrasting British position that connects the individual to contractual rights assured by the nation state – in the words of Edmund Burke, "Englishmen therefore obey a natural and instinctive sentiment in cherishing their liberties as an inheritance; and, in so doing, they guarantee them more effectually than they would do by any contrivances which reason or reflection could suggest" (Burke and Selby, 1890, p. 316). At this stage in MacIntyre's story we find ethics located in the *a priori*, the polis, the Church, and in the individual connected either to universal rights or to the nation. It is then Kant (1987), working as a major author of Enlightenment ethics, who takes us into what is a genuinely modern understanding of ethics, which assumes the inevitability of *progress*. (Kant offers a textured view of progress differentiating the new from progress, with the latter species specific and a propeller of an "enlarged mentality" in the public domain.)

This form of irony offers an example of Arendt's differentiation between reason and judgment discussed above and, more importantly, her discussion of the difference between philosophy and political science (Arendt, 1978). Philosophy lives in the land of reason and the realm of the pristine. However, political science lives in the "mud of everyday life" (Buber, 2002). In this less than ideal situation opinion guides our interaction with one another in the public domain. Now here is the rub of the irony: between the philosophy of reason and political life of opinion in the public domain, it is not the former, but the latter that brings forth courage to sacrifice and die for another and for a cause. Opinions matter, no matter how we try to wish them away with the philosophy of reason. Granted, it is possible for philosophy of reason to test and challenge opinion. One of the more famous cases of the philosophy of reason challenging opinion is that that of Galileo and the Catholic Church. Galileo is often referred to the "father of modern science." He was a major supporter of Copernicus's deconstruction of a Ptolemaic Universe. The earth was moved from the center in the shift from Ptolemy's worldview to that of Copernicus. The opinion at that time left Galileo under house arrest for the last few years of his life. The conflict between the philosophy of reason and opinion was not an easy one for many, particularly Galileo. In this case opinion was challenged and eventually shifted by the philosophy of reason. The emerging world from the seventeenth century onward found opinion increasingly challenged, informed, and changed by the philosophy of reason.

Unsubstantiated opinion began to lose to an increasingly attentive world to the pursuit of truth in an open and public fashion. Opinions and beliefs that could not stand public examination and verification with a philosophy of reason were simply called into question. In the movement from the seventeenth to the eighteenth century, the philosophy of reason played out in the form of Enlightenment conviction that one can pursue truth in the public domain. One can understand the struggle between Galileo and the Church as the tension between a new competing narrative understood as the Enlightenment fueled by the philosophy of reason and the metanarrative of the Church. One can understand the seventeenth century as the century of challenge of an emerging narrative against an established metanarrative. The eighteenth century finds increasing parity between the philosophy of reason and the Church. The eighteenth century is the era of the Scottish Enlightenment. The work of Adam Ferguson (1995), David Hume (1976), and Adam Smith (1977) depend upon the philosophy of reason instead of the Church; the eighteenth century is the era of increasing narrative parity between the philosophy of reason and the Church. The nineteenth century, however, is the year in which parity is no longer pursued and the philosophical foundations of religion, itself, come under attack with the principle voice being that of Nietzsche. In the West, the nineteenth century engages a paradigmatically different stance toward religion – this century is the era of deconstruction.

The deconstructive move toward religion in the nineteenth century does not curtail the importance of science tied to an illusive Enlightenment assumption of progress. Science becomes the extended form of the philosophy of religion. This union of progress united with an emerging scientific metanarrative is played out in public life. This combination shapes the work of Hegel (1837) in the philosophy of history, Darwin (1859) and the *Origin of Species*, and Karl Marx's (Marx and Engels, 1848) commitment to scientific materialism in the nineteenth century. Major social movements depend upon the emerging metanarrative of progress played out in various forms of scientific language. The irony is that the philosophy of reason no longer challenges, or is on par, or deconstructs religion, it begins to become the metanarrative of the twentieth century. This language of progress is used in the introduction of new technologies, new ways to teach, and new ways to understand war, as the "domino theory" of the fall of one country after another would inevitably occur without intervention and victory in Vietnam. The twentieth century is the century of the clear victory – progress has won. Yet, as soon as this assumption is considered a given, the world begins to rebel against the metanarrative of progress.

If all technological change is progress, then why does the world feel less safe in its nuclear capacity? Why is it that the new fabric of plastic seems to lessen the value of furniture? What is it that Pete Seeger sings about "little boxes [houses] made of ticky-tacky" that are in safe places? Why is the *company man* beginning to take on a negative persona? The 1960s, for all their entire oddities and excesses, signaled an emerging refusal to accept the metanarrative of progress, given birth in the Enlightenment's commitment to a philosophy of reason that spurs science that spurs technology on which all depends – the metanarrative of progress. Understanding the 1960s philosophically opens us to an era that openly questioning progress while still immersed within the phenomenon. The progress of the industrial complex is questioned by the movement of the 1960s with a sense of innocence more akin to the actions of Billy Budd, Melville's reminder of the danger

Metanarratives in a Postmodern Age

that lurks within innocence itself. Thus, as the notion of progress meets with challenge in the streets, there is yet another form of optimism fueled by the metanarrative of progress that continues to abide with the social movements of the 1960s. Again, we witness irony at work. The very issue under fire is the energy propelling social movements of the 1960s. We find ourselves not just with the power of progress, but with the seemingly indestructible nature of metanarratives still before us. Even the "Jesus movement" is an example of the revival of a metanarrative that the Enlightenment sought to neuter long ago.

We seem to live in a time of the rising of the phoenix, with that which we thought was dead or at least socially tempered rising again in power and significance. Just as the 1960s seem to announce the return to a world less defined by progress, the 1970s became the era of self-actualization. The work of Abraham Maslow (1987) and the term, originally defined by Kurt Goldstein (1939), of self-actualization began with a hierarchy of needs and the assumption of progress. Such an emphasis taken to an extreme led Christopher Lasch to pen three major works that questioned the shape of that historical moment – *The True and Only Heaven: Progress and Its Critics* (1991), *The Culture of Narcissism: American Life in an Age of Diminishing Expectations* (1979), and *The Minimal Self: Psychic Survival in Troubled Times* (1984). It is not surprising that this movement gave way to something claims of the "death of the author" (Barthes, 1968) and the focus on "embedded agency" (Arnett, Fritz, and Holba 2007). The postmodern move was a turn from a point of exhaustion that relied on the individual alone. This focus on the individual did not emerge out of a vacuum; it was the untutored extension of seventeenth and eighteenth century scholarship on ethics.

It is this metaphor of progress that additionally shapes the philosophy of history framed by Hegel (1837) and eventually the scientific materialism of Marx (1939). Hegel provides the last grand view of the continuity of ideas in which Marx offers us a rationale for the inevitability of change. The work of Kierkegaard (1946) and Nietzsche (1989) take us more deeply into questions of existence and what is known as a "hermeneutic of suspicion" (Ricoeur, 1970). This story of ethics and philosophy reveals a move from grand schemes for the human being and the progression of human history to living with existence without definitive clarity. It is this turn to a hermeneutic of suspicion that begins to vie for the place of primacy as our guide in knowing.

MacIntyre's story of ethics takes us from ethics situated with the *a priori*, the polis, the Church, the individual armed with universal rights or contractual national commitments to grand theories of human progress, and finally to the human finding that, indeed, this is a moment in which there is no "ethics Eden," with suspicion taking on pragmatic characteristics. Within existence we must struggle for what seems to be a good in a time in which life seems unclear and without a final answer. Indeed, this is where we are in a moment described by this author as the collapse of modernity (Arnett, Fritz, and Holba 2007) as we observe the global meltdown that is going on before our eyes in financial and social life at the end of the first decade and into the second of the twenty-first century. We are now in a major moment of challenge to the modern view of progress. In reflection, the existential and suspicious contenders against modernity begin to look more like philosopher prophets who were shouting loudly as the world was losing its way.

MacIntyre's story of philosophy and ethics offers the study of communication ethics a practice of situating or locating ethics in a place, framing that place as a driving force that functions as a dwelling for the study of communication ethics. The *similarity* between the philosophy of ethics and communication ethics begins with the importance of location. The *difference* between a philosophical view of ethics and communication ethics is that the place or location of communication ethics is never enough; this sense of place must engage the particulars of a given situation. Communication ethics simply understood is a conversation between a dwelling of ethics or the good and the particulars that must be met and addressed. Communication ethics cannot impose a dwelling on particulars; there must be a conversation between them. A review of Kant will assist an understanding of the focus upon the particular.

Kant (1998) differentiated *reason* from *judgment* with the latter ever attentive to the *particular*. Communication ethics is not pristine; it seems unwise to connect it to reason alone. Communication ethics is an act of communication engagement involving the ongoing interplay of the ethical and the good, dwelling, persons, context, and the particular. (Note: the notion of particular can be understood as including persons, context, and historical moment; for communication, fleshing out these assumptions has significant utility.) Different communication ethics find themselves situated within a theory or narrative that functions as a dwelling protecting a given view of the good that then makes a conversational turn to the particulars in the realm of everyday living. Communication ethics looks more like judgment than like pristine reason. Judgment rests in opinion, conversing otherwise than the pristine hope of reason tied to universals. Communication ethics walks in the mud of judgment and in the problematic of the particulars.

Arendt (1992), in using the work of Kant, informs us of the importance of opinion in the public domain. With communication ethics being outside the realm of pristine reason, but within the coordinates of the particular as it meets theory, communication ethics is akin to a derivative creation emerging from opinion in the public domain (Arendt, 1992). Communication ethics has kinship with Kant's and Arendt's view of judgment in that the ambiguity of opinion presupposes the messy meeting of theory and particulars, which lend themselves to communicative engagement with another or with some organizational structure.

It is this dwelling composed of ambiguity and the interplay of theory and particular played out in everyday life that makes possible Arendt's view of judgment and what this essay deems as communication ethics. The theory holds the good that a given communication ethic seeks to protect and promote. The particular requires the unique use of a given understanding of the good. Ambiguity suggests that before, during, and after the delivery of a given communication ethic, there are consequences and changes that must be made sometimes on the spur of the moment and at others times after greater reflection. This constant adding to and changing a theory is not novel; its best known description is hypodeductive theory (Popper, 1968). In essence, that which makes a difference in the narrative construct is what guides us. A communication ethic, thus understood, is the manner in which a position or theory is taken into public action as a guide without reifying into an inflexible ideology. A communication ethic working from this perspective brings a given theory to the particular and then is transformed by the meeting, ever changing, ever responsive to the interplay of opinion, theory, and the particular.

This three-fold interaction of opinion, theory, and the particular works in creative tension. The framers of the constitution worked with the insights of Montesquieu (1698–1755) (Bederman, 2008), who was one of the first to discuss separation of powers in government. One can understand a communication ethic as a governing structure with each of the parts (opinion, theory, and the particular) working in creative tension. One can understand the notion of theory contribution as the legislative branch, public opinion shaping as the judicial branch, and the executive ever attentive to the particular in actual governing. The interaction of these three dimensions renders a judgment akin to what this essay could name a communication ethic in action.

In addition to the trinity stated above, a dwelling or home within which this three-fold construct can function with a pragmatic and appropriate sense of tension is necessary. As pointed to earlier, MacIntyre framed the historic understanding of different dwellings that can house what is understood as the construct of communication ethics – opinion, theory, and the particular, which give birth to communication ethics judgment in action in the *a priori*, the polis, the Church, and the individual armed with universal rights or contractual national commitments to grand theories of human progress. In the actual study of communication ethics within the discipline of communication, we find that the importance of location, the home, the dwelling, and the place that offers a standard from which to understand what is good has driven the study of communication ethics.

There are over 200 essays on communication ethics, with the first major review work framed by James Chesebro, who offers us categories that serve as dwellings for the protection of a given sense of the good (Arnett, Arneson, and Bell, 2006, p. 71). Through scholarship in the communication discipline, begun in 1914 (Cohen, 1994), we find an outline of diversity of dwellings for the protected sense of the good in communication ethics.

A summary of the scholarly placements of the good in a particular dwelling anchors communication ethics in discourse arenas that shape a human community. The work of Chesebro (1969), Arnett (2008), and Arnett, Arneson, and Bell (2006) point to six different categories or dwellings: (1) universal, (2) democracy, (3) codes and procedures, (4) contextual, (5) narrative, and (6) dialogic. The works of Chesebro (1969) and Arnett, Fritz, and Bell (2009) detail the perspectives within the discipline that frame the contrasting theories of communication ethics, with each situated within an understanding of choice; it is the latest work of Arnett (2010), "Embeddedness/Embedded Identity," that frames the connecting links between narrative and "tainted ground" (Arnett, 2008). Leading with the metaphor

of choice, the work of Chesebro can be understood as the following: (1) a democratic ethic of choice, (2) a contextual ethic of choice, (3) a universal ethic that permits choice through reason, and (4) codes and procedures which outline what
choices are viable within a given organization. The work of Arnett (2005) and then
of Arnett, Fritz, and Bell (2009) offer two additional understandings of communication ethics: (5) a narrative ethic that suggests the choice of a narrative or ground
from which one stands makes a difference in a communication ethic, and (6) a dialogic ethic that permits both parties an opportunity to discern necessary direction
and action from the framework of a given communication ethic. The dwellings of
communication ethics are not as intuitional in nature as those of the philosophy of
ethics, but are ideas in action. These active ideas call forth choice in judgment with
the dwellings offering a biased frame from which to begin the interplay of opinion,
theory, and the particular. The authors above suggest that choice then happens
within six major dwellings: the democratic, the universal, the contextual, codes and
procedures, and finally in narrative and dialogic elements of human life.

When conversation about *democracy* is central, the dwelling of communication
ethics becomes some form of one person, one vote. When the *universal* was central
in the development of communication science (Berger and Chaffee, 1987) communication ethics found another home, in the public use of reason and method in
the pursuit of universal precepts and enduring truths that must bear the test of
reasoned public examination. When organizations discovered the importance of
public accountability, *codes and procedures* became yet another place from which to
start a conversation about communication ethics. Then the movement toward *contextual* opened another door to another home of communication ethics, which
began to take the particulars seriously. Yet, as the field discovered *narrative* as an
important way to describe the temporal ground upon which we stand embedded-
ness within a story became salient. Fisher gave the discipline of communication a
warrant for investigating the work of MacIntyre, Taylor, Arendt, and Hauerwas;
Fisher's work permitted the discipline of communication to join a conversation,
situating ethics in a given place. The latest sense of dwelling that has emerged in
that of *dialogic* ethics, which continues long after the introduction of Martin Buber
into the discipline of communication. Communication ethics in dialogue has a
dwelling in what Buber (1955) called "the ontology of the between" (pp. 161–181).
Each realm of scholarship in communication ethics lives within different dwellings:
democracy, the universal, codes and procedures, the context, narrative, and dialogue between persons.

At this postmodern juncture, we need to offer another dwelling of *difference*.
Joining this conversation, communication ethics has a home in a postmodern age
– in the dwelling of *difference*. One could even go so far as to suggest that in this
dwelling of difference lives something akin to a metanarrative, bound ever so
tightly to the metaphor of difference. This is our first inkling that the notion of
metanarrative is not simply a part of philosophical and sociological history. The
theme of metanarrative, a connecting link that helps us in making sense of the
world, just seems hard to vanquish – even within postmodernity itself.

Metanarratives in a Postmodern Age

In the discipline of communication, this mantra of difference has played its way out within multiple theories, each driven by the notion of choice. Thomas Nilsen (1974) penned the notion of "significant choice," a metaphor that sums up work within the discipline of communication. Of course, there is a contrast between this view of *choice* and a postmodern understanding of *difference*. The latter term suggests that difference among theories and paradigms requires understanding that choice within the discipline of communication is confined within a given theory or perspective. The point of this essay thus far can be summarized as follows: (1) the protection of some form of good gives pragmatic currency to the construction of a communication ethic; (2) communication ethics cannot impose upon existence, but must work in the interplay of theory and particular (including persons, context, and historical moment); (3) communication ethics in a postmodern age acknowledges the reality of multiple dwellings of the good; (4) a communication ethic has more family resemblance to judgment than to the Enlightenment hope of reason; and (5) we are now are a point in which the notion of choice is not a strong enough communicative action for decision-making in the doing of communication ethics.

With all the movement of location and place of the dwelling of the good there is a linkage between and among eras, including our own. This essay does not conceptualize an unbridgeable chasm in the movement from a classical to a postmodern understanding of a communication ethic from a macro level of discussion. The question is no longer a choice among different dwellings, but rather the necessity of recognizing and acknowledging (Hyde, 2006) the unique differences among dwellings that house the interplay of opinion, theory, and particular. *Identity* driven by difference is a defining postmodern contribution to communication ethics. The fundamental change is not actually difference, but the manner in which we engage difference. Choice, central to modernity, understands a hierarchy of dwellings with the task of communication ethics as a guide in making a choice and defending the decision. Identity meets difference in the acknowledgement of singular uniqueness.

Difference at the macrolevel of dwelling can be understood as the uniting theme of communication ethics. What separates this moment from other historical eras is the acknowledgment of identity. The differentiation between choice and identity in the meeting of all goods differentiates the position of this essay from that of MacIntyre, who calls this moment a "moral crisis" (MacIntyre, 1981). In the words of Taylor, however, we are still in disagreement about the notion of the "good" (Taylor, 1992; Aristotle, 2002). The "good" from a macrolevel perspective of the study of communication ethics renders itself as *difference/choice* and in the particular of a postmodern era, *difference/identity*. In both cases, at the macrolevel and at the levels of the particulars of living in today's era, a good still guides us, with difference connecting us at the theoretical and particular levels of human existence. The agreement upon difference and the disagreement on choice and identity leads to a single conclusion: the focus on acknowledging difference and recognizing identity does not permit me to do that which I, like many scholars working from a postmodern perspective, would have wanted – to take the notion of metanarrative off the table of conversation and opinion as a shaper of identity. The conclusion of this essay leads not to a winning postmodern communication ethic, but to a radically Other-centered communication ethic.

An Other-Centered Communication Ethic: From Identity to Metanarrative(s)

Identity and the acknowledgement of identity require recognition of difference and, more fundamentally, attentiveness to Otherness from which insight into genuine difference emerges. What emerges as this part of our conceptual journey is an irony. I do not think – and I use that term in concurrence with Kant (1987) and Arendt (1978) – that a postmodern commitment to difference and identity that understands Otherness can take the reality of metanarratives off the table of communication ethics conversation.

Irony emerges when there is discrepancy between what is perceived and what exists. The term "irony" has a long history and was first used by Aristotle (1987, p. 53). Throughout history, the term implies disconnection or a form of discordance between a surface reading and the underlying meaning of a given phenomenon. Irony often leads us to a moment of pause or contemplation. For instance, it is ironic that that the person who worries less about a given task may actually do it better.

Irony related to communication ethics permits a bold claim: in a postmodern culture, metanarrative is alive and well. To take this irony off the table, we must stand above history and claim a universal theory that casts a dismissive eye upon public opinion of metanarratives connected with particular views of good. To make such a dismissive claim is to adhere to a hierarchy of goods, violating a postmodern presupposition. One senses an irony as one reflects upon metanarrative and the fact that *meta* means one above – and that unless one is to take this stance, one cannot take a metanarrative off the table of communication ethics conversation. The irony of this moment requires one to stand above all other positions and make a proclamation of truth against an ethic that does just that. Irony demands that one recognize that the very issue that is fought against must be used to complete the battle to take a metanarrative off the table of possibilities.

Therefore, we find ourselves at a strange point in human history. Philosophically, there is almost a consensus that that the era of the metanarrative is dead. When there is anything that even resembles consensus in philosophical discourse, one must listen. Works from Nietzsche (1989) to Levinas (1981) to Derrida (2002) to Foucault (1973) to Rorty (1989) outline the demise of the notion of the metanarrative; they make it clear that it is no longer possible to stand above history and make a single proclamation. To a person these writers take the notion of metanarrative off the table. Yet, ironically, they cannot – the only way to eliminate the notion of metanarrative is to stand above history and render a verdict that all lesser minds must follow.

It is this disconnect between our expectation and the emergent reality that unites irony and wonder. The cliché that drives such a union is simply, "It is a wonder..." Communication ethics, from a postmodern perspective, privileges understanding (Gadamer, 2004), not debate. Understanding does not permit us to discern the deeply ignorant from the newly enlightened. In short, I end this postmodern communication ethics lament with the realization that I cannot take metanarrative off the table of communication ethics conversation. I must seek to understand identities, opinions, and difference without the assurance of hierarchy. Communication ethics thus understood gives us few definitive answers, but such a rendering does require us to think, to meet, to learn, and ultimately to have the courage to follow a theory to its end – unwilling to stand above history and claim erasure of a metanarrative position that stubbornly continues to join our conversation. Communication ethics attentive to Otherness ends in irony: one cannot assume that one's position is supreme, and such a confession ends with an acknowledgment that for many, metanarrative lives. Communication ethics is informed by pristine theory, but ultimately lives in a world of Otherness and difference leading us back to wonder, to recalcitrant opinion that keeps the notion of metanarrative alive in a postmodern world.

Note

1   In 1897, after reading his own obituary in the *New York Journal*, Twain wrote this to a reporter who had confused him with his cousin whose last name was Clemens.

References

Aquinas, T. (1945) *The Basic Writings of Saint Thomas Aquinas*, (trans. A.C. Pegis), Random House, New York.

Arendt, H. (1958) *The Human Condition*, University of Chicago Press, Chicago.

Arendt, H. (1963) *On Revolution*, New York, Penguin Books.

Arendt, H. (1978) *The Life of the Mind*, Harcourt Brace and Company, New York.

Arendt, H. (1992) *Lectures on Kant's Political Philosophy* (ed. R. Beiner), University of Chicago Press, Chicago.

Aristotle (1987) *Poetics*, (ed. R. Janko), Hackett Publishing, Indianapolis.

Aristotle (2002) *Nichomachean Ethics*, (ed. C. Rowe), Oxford University Press, Oxford.

Arnett, R.C. (2005) *Dialogic Confession: Bonhoeffer's Rhetoric of Responsibility*, Southern Illinois University Press, Carbondale.

Arnett, R.C. (2008) The rhetoric of communication ethics, in *International Encyclopedia of Communication*, (ed. W. Donsbach), New York, Wiley-Blackwell/International Communication Association.

Arnett, R.C. (2010) Embeddedness/embedded identity, in *Encyclopedia of Identity*, (ed. R.L. Jackson), Sage, Thousand Oaks, CA.

Arnett, R.C., and Arneson, P. (1999) *Dialogic Civility in a Cynical Age: Community, Hope, and Interpersonal Relationships*, SUNY, Albany, NY.

Arnett, R.C., Arneson, P., and Bell, L.M. (2006) Communication ethics: The dialogic turn. *Review of Communication*, 6 (1–2), 62–92.

Arnett, R.C., Fritz, J.H., and Bell, L.M. (2009) *Communication Ethics Literacy: Dialogue and Difference*, Sage, Thousand Oaks, CA.

Arnett, R.C., Fritz, J.H., and Holba, A. (2007) The rhetorical turn to otherness: Otherwise than humanism. *Cosmos and History: The Journal of Natural and Social Philosophy*, 3, 115–133.

Barthes, R. (1968) The death of the author, in (ed./trans. S. Heath) *Image – Music – Text*, Hill and Wang, New York, pp.142–148.

Bederman, D.J. (2008) *The Classical Foundations of the American Constitution*, Cambridge University Press, Cambridge.

Berger, C.R. and Chaffee, S.H. (1987) *The Handbook of Communication Science*, Sage, Thousand Oaks, CA.

Buber, M. (1955) *Between Man and Man*, (trans. R.G. Smith), Beacon Press, Boston, MA.

Buber, M. (2002) *Between Man and Man*, (trans. R.G. Smith), Routledge, New York.

Burke, K. (1973) *The Philosophy of Literary Form: Studies in Symbolic Action*, University of California Press, Berkeley.

Burke, E., and Selby, F.G. (1890) *Reflections on the Revolution in France*, Macmillan, New York.

Chesebro, J.W. (1969) A construct for assessing ethics in communication. *Central States Speech Journal*, 20, 104–114.

Cohen, H. (1994) *The History of Speech Communication: The Emergence of a Discipline, 1914–1945*, Speech Communication Association, Annandale, VA.

Darwin, C. (1859) *On the Origin of Species by Means of Natural Selection, or the Preservation of Favoured Races in the Struggle for Life*, John Murray, London.

Derrida, J. (2002) *Ethics, Institutions and the Right to Philosophy*, (trans. P. P. Trifonas), Rowman & Littlefield, Lanham, MD.

Drake, S. (1978) *Galileo at Work: His Scientific Biography*, Dover, New York.

Encyclopaedia Britannica (2005) *Encyclopaedia Britannica*, vol. 3, Encyclopaedia Britannica, Chicago, p. 764.

Erasmus, D. (1965) *Christian Humanism and the Reformation*, (ed. J.C. Olin), Harper and Row, New York.

Ferguson, A. (1995) *An Essay on the History of Civil Society*, Cambridge University Press, Cambridge.

Foucault, M. (1973) *The Order of Things: An Archaeology of the Human Sciences*, Vintage Books, New York.

Friedman, E.G. (1993) Where are the missing contents: (Post)modernism, gender, and the canon. *Publications of the Modern Language Association of America*, 108, 240–252.

Gadamer, H.G. (2004) *Truth and Method*, (trans. J. Weinsheimer and D.G. Marshall), Continuum, New York.

Goldstein, K. (1939) *The Organism: A Holistic Approach to Biology Derived from Pathological Data in Man*, American Book Company, New York.

Hegel, G.W.F. (1837) *The Philosophy of History*, (ed. E. Gans).

Hume, D. (1976) *The Natural History of Religion*, (ed. A.W. Colver), Clarendon Press, Oxford.

Husserl, E. (1970) *The Crisis of European Sciences and Transcendental Phenomenology: An Introduction to Phenomenological Philosophy*, (trans. D. Carr, Trans.), Northwestern University Press, Evanston, IL.

Hyde, M. J. (2006) *The Life-Giving Gift of Acknowledgement: A Philosophical and Rhetorical Inquiry*, Purdue University Press, West Lafayette.

Hyde, W. (1980) *The Epicurean Pursuit of Pleasure*, Macmillan, New York.

Kant, I. (1987) *Critique of Judgment*, (trans. W.S. Pluhar), Hackett Publishing, Indianapolis.

Kant, I. (1998) *Critique of Pure Reason*, (trans. P. Guyer and A.W. Wood), Cambridge University Press, Cambridge.

Karnow, S. (1983) *Vietnam: A History*, Penguin, New York.

Kierkegaard, S. (1946) *Fear and Trembling*, (trans. R. Payne), Oxford University Press, Oxford.

Kramnick, J.B. (1997) The making of the English canon. *Publications of the Modern Language Association of America*, 112, 1087–1101.

Lasch, C. (1979) *The Culture of Narcissism: American Life in an Age of Diminishing Expectations*, Warner Books, New York.

Lasch, C. (1984) *The Minimal Self: Psychic Survival in Troubled Times*, WW. Norton, New York.

Lasch, C. (1991) *The True and Only Heaven: Progress and its Critics*, W.W. Norton, New York.

Levinas, E. (1981) *Otherwise than Being or Beyond Essence*, (trans. A. Lingis), Kluwer Academic, Dordrecht, Boston, London.

Lyotard, J.F. (1999) *Toward the Postmodern*, Humanity Books, Amherst, NY.

MacIntyre, A. (1981) *After Virtue: A Study in Moral Theory*, Notre Dame University Press, Notre Dame, IN.

MacIntyre, A. (1988) *Whose Justice? Which Rationality?*, Notre Dame University Press, Notre Dame, IN.

MacIntyre, A. (1991) *Three Rival Versions of Moral Enquiry: Encyclopaedia, Genealogy, and Tradition*, Notre Dame University Press, Notre Dame, IN.

MacIntyre, A. (1998) *A Short History of Ethics: A History of Moral Philosophy from the Homeric Age to the Twentieth Century*, Notre Dame University Press, Notre Dame, IN.

MacIntyre, A. (1999) *Dependent Rational Animals: Why Human Beings Need the Virtues*, Open Court, Chicago.

Marx, K. (1939) *Economic and Philosophic Manuscripts of 1844*, (trans. M. Milligan), International Books, New York.

Marx, K., and Engels, F. (1848) *The Communist Manifesto*, Communist League, London.

Maslow, A. (1987) *Motivation and Personality*, Harper Collins, New York.

Merriam-Webster (1997) *Merriam-Webster's Collegiate Dictionary* 10th edn, Merriam-Webster, Springfield, MA.

Nietzsche, F.W. (1989) *The Genealogy of Morals*, (trans. W.A. Kaufmann), Vintage Books.

Nilsen, T. (1974) *Ethics of Speech Communication*, 2nd edn, Merriam-Webster, Springfield, MA.

Plato (1987) *The Republic*, (trans, D. Lee), Penguin, New York.

Plutarch (1935) *Plutarch's Lives*, (ed. R.T. Bond), Tudor Publishing Company, New York.

Popper, K. (1968) *The Logic of Scientific Discovery*, Hutchinson, London.

Ricoeur, P. (1970) *Freud and Philosophy: An Essay on Interpretation*, Yale University Press, New Haven, CT.

Rieff, P. (1966) *The Triumph of the Therapeutic: Uses of Faith after Freud*, Harper & Row, New York.

Robinson, F.G. (1995) *The Cambridge Companion to Mark Twain*, Cambridge University Press, Cambridge.

Rorty, R. (1989) *Contingency, Irony, and Solidarity*, Cambridge University Press, Cambridge.

Smith, A. (1977) *The Wealth of Nations*, (eds. W. Letwin and E.R.A. Seligman), J.M. Dent and Sons Ltd, London.

Taylor, C. (1989) *Sources of the Self: The Making of the Modern Identity*, Harvard University Press, Cambridge.

Taylor, C. (1992) *Sources of the Self: The Making of the Modern Identity*, Cambridge University Press, Cambridge.

Taylor, C. (2007) *A Secular Age*, Harvard University Press, Cambridge.

Thomas, D. (1952) *Collected Poems, 1934–1952*, J.M. Dent and Sons, Ltd, London.

Toulmin, S. (1992) *Cosmopolis: The Hidden Agenda of Modernity*, University of Chicago Press, Chicago.

3

Information, Communication, and Planetary Citizenship

Luiz Martins da Silva

Human beings are members of a whole,
In creation of one essence and soul.
If one member is afflicted with pain,
Other members uneasy will remain.
If you have no sympathy for human pain,
The name of human you cannot retain

(Sa'di de Shiraz[1])

There will be no survival without a world ethics.

(Hans Kung[2])

Introduction

I come back, in this opportunity,[3] to the analysis of the recurrent counter point between *information* and *communication*, particularly as we verify that it continues to be important in the present technological environment and, above all, in the ethics panorama, if we contemplate another topic of today's life, that is, *globalization* and *universalization*, the latter concept being related to such questions as: human rights; education with autonomy; development with justice; and information at the service of a communication is in fact deserving its name, that is, dialogic.

Is There a Humanity?

The answer is ambiguous, as it wobbles between two visions, one pessimistic, the other optimistic. First, affirmation of a humanity synonymous to the gathering of all human populations; second, the recognition of it as a processing, dynamic, and

The Handbook of Global Communication and Media Ethics, First Edition. Edited by Robert S. Fortner and P. Mark Fackler.
© 2011 Blackwell Publishing Ltd. Published 2011 by Blackwell Publishing Ltd.

constructive idea, without a horizon for completeness. So, what is this something that exists but is not ready yet? This paradox not only applies to humanity but also to the human being himself, as both are self constructive beings.

Human beings are naturally begotten; what in fact makes them human is another generating procedure: the interactive life in the social space. Humanity, on the other hand, is gradually processed as universal rights and obligations are consolidated. Therefore, both are two ontological beings in an incessant becoming: the human being and the nation-beings on the path towards an ethical horizon. There is a difficulty in attributing to them totality and completeness, although stages of maturity and stability may be contemplated, for example in matters of development and peace. Advancements and retrocession however would be peristaltic movements inherent to civilization processes, in a new context.

In the past – given that major cohesions were the ones of clan, tribe, nation, and frontier – ascendancies and decendancies were encapsulated to a certain extent, decreases that sometimes brought about the disappearance of once splendid nations reduced to ruins or enigmatic monuments, under open skies or entangled in dense jungles.

Economic and technological factors prevailing in today's world, model the conditions for the consolidation of the idea that the experiences of the societies, either in advance or recession, be shared, on account of the planet's reticulation, although the repercussions are still excessively vitiated in the North-South direction.

The evolution of the idea that development standards do not conform to disparities, either endogenous or relating to the abyss that separates rich and poor countries in the matter of quality of life is impressive. In view of the complexity of the structure of the Human Development Index (HDI), it is possible to forecast that future components of the HDI will have to take into account the correlation between development and justice. In other words, the HDI may become a Moral Development Index (MDI), inasmuch as development without justice does not conform with the notion of *sustainability* and *legitimacy*.

Planetary Citizenship

The morality of development indicators could be elaborated starting with two concepts previously explored, the *psychogenesis* and the *sociogenesis*, the first well developed by the psychology of moral development (Piaget and Kohlberg), but the latter considered, an analogic inference directly formulated by Jürgen Habermas (1929–),[4] and indirectly by some of his contemporary peers: Karl-Oto Apel (1922–) and Edgar Morin (1921–), in their reference to a "universal and planetary macroethics"(Apel) or a "planetary citizenship," both corresponding to an "antropoethics" (Morin). We further reference John Rawls' (1993) *A Theory of Justice*, a first magnitude theoretic, about a new principle of equity, precisely the one where the "institutions are just when there is no arbitrary discrimination in the attribution of basic rights and duties"[5] that is, a principle that overcomes the implicit fallacy in the maxim of liberty, equality, and fraternity, since, in view of the challenges to be faced in the world, to put on the same level of "equality" a European child and one from Moçambique, or, in another context, a handicapped citizen and another without any disability (natural or acquired). Therefore, Rawls takes into account factors that make individuals "different" (gender, among them) and/or lacking "compensations," without which institutions would not be apt to administer justice.

Apel's ideas,[6] which we try to summarize, were presented in his article "The necessity, the apparent difficulty and the effective possibility of a planetary macroethics for the humanity", published in Portugal.[7] In this regard, we concentrate on examining how Apel circumvents the skepticism and proposes his macroethics of coresponsibility of the humanity and to the humanity. Apel agrees that eighteenth century philosophers' ideas were realized in respect of the *unity of human history*, but not in the Marxist sense of a unity of the scientific theory and praxis in regard to the known and controlled "necessary course of history," but as a required and partially existent *unity of cooperation*, in reference to the modeling, preservation and remodeling or reformulation of the general conditions of the present world civilization.

A universal ethics? Too optimistic when we take into consideration the most traumatic episode of this young century, the 9/11 events in 2001 and their political and military aftermath; the wars in Afghanistan, Iraq, and Lebanon.

Technologically, the world consolidates a globalization scenery where a *global village* map is drawn in terms of telecommunication and, therefore, of connectivity and interactivity, making possible the existence of a world *polis*; Humanity, nevertheless, has not yet put together the conditions for a global *civitas*, a world with universal human, political, economic, and social rights.[8] Possibly because in the communicational sense the ethical conditions for a global society have not yet been built, although, as we have already seen, one can discern on the horizon the technology for a functional *informational society*. There is a lack of equality in the communication flow, even in the marketing environment. Frei Betto, a Brazilian intellectual, says:

> The fashion now is globalization. It is good that the planet has been transformed into a village. What worries me is, for instance, something I came across in the countryside of China, where I visit a record store and saw posters of Michael Jackson decorating the walls; however, I never encountered, in the US heartland, any Chinese singer's poster! This globalization is the imposition of a cultural model, with only one paradigm of behavior: globecolonization![9]

Apel is one of the first contemporary philosophers who endorses the "argumentative speech as a reflexive form of human communication." He goes beyond that, when he gathers together elements to try to demonstrate that it is possible to imagine a universal macro ethics *of the humanity* and *to the humanity*.

First, Apel aims to demonstrate the "urgent necessity" of a macro ethics that, in his opinion, must cosubstantiate the new and eminent philosophical ethical task of our time. Second, he comments about the "apparent difficulties" that, in the past decades, have led to the supposition that the problem with "rational fundamentality" of a universal macroethics is that it has no solution, or sense whatsoever. Third, he proposes a "possible solution" from the view point of a "transcendental pragmatism of human communication."

Apel believes that there are few aspects of today's civilization where a "desynchronization" occurs in the same magnitude as the one in the *conventional moral*. This noncontemporaneousness demands attention in view of the requirements for a common and solid responsibility due to the planetary effects of human activities. For this reason, its advent would entail a new stage in the civilization process.

In all cultures, observes Apel, the *conventional moral* is still essentially restricted to human relationships established in small groups (*microethics*) or, in a bigger picture, to the fulfillment of duties inherent to professional roles in a social system of rules as it happens in a country (*mesoethics*).

Therefore, the set of requirements relating to roles and rules defined in a social system (of law and order), in the same way as it goes through sympathy, charity, and loyalty relations, which constitute the social basis of small groups, families and clans, mobilizes national, religious, and parareligious (war or revolutions) sentiments, although not carrying the same efficiency when imposed by public acceptance and the sanction of the laws. It is common that nations and moral rules of social systems lose authority and efficiency. Their functions may then revert to families and clans.

In revising cultural evolution using *homo faber* (invention of utensils and particularly weapons) as a starting point, Apel splits cultural evolution into two stages: the first, soon after man overcame the stage of instinctive behavior and differentiated himself from animals with the war phenomenon (figuratively Abel's assassination by Cain); and the second, with the creation of moral rules for human actions, which created *social institutions*.

Until today, therefore, humanity has not developed beyond the two stages (*microethics and mesoethics*) of *homo faber*. In the twentieth century, according to Apel, it is not possible to envision a global situation of humanity, for two reasons:

1   The development of social institutions went beyond the sphere of the State during Hegel's time. Hegel considered it the most integrated form of regulation of human activities and the most elevated moral authority which became differentiated through subsystems, where the *social subsystem of the international economy* (interaction at a distance and through anonymous relations) constitutes its better example. At the same time, this circumstance points towards a new and until now unanswered challenge to humanity's moral responsibility. Economic actions may have an unthinkable effect on the daily life of people, countries, and continents.

2   The repercussion of human actions on the ecology – as is the case with economic actions – affects the human *ecosphere*, whose resources are not inexhaustible and invulnerable anymore and come to determine a "new relationship between humanity and nature."

Therefore, from economic and ecologic standpoints, the *microethics* and *mesoethics* inherited from *homo faber* are not satisfied anymore, as the consequences of man's technical success always were ahead of *homo sapiens* moral responsibilities. In the twentieth century, however, it became clear that a *collective responsibility* must be organized, given the effects and repercussions of our activities in science and technology. It is thus necessary that everyone "at least" accepts his share of responsibility for pollutant discharges, as well as in the concern of citizenship (at least as a participant in the public opinion and election process). "So, it seems to be evident that, in both dimensions of the cultural evolution – the technological interventions in nature and the social interaction – a global situation has been outlined in our time, claiming a new *ethics of corespon-sibility*, that is, a kind of ethics that, in contraposition to the traditional or conventional form of ethics, may be designated by the name of *macroethics*.[10]

If people, individually, cannot take responsibility for something outside the role and function they perform in the social system, what does coresponsibility mean? After examining the thoughts of two Nobel prize laureate – Konrad Lorenz and Friedrich August von Hayed – Apel derives the conclusion that a new ethics, whether it ever becomes possible, requires a "rational foundation transcending all traditions," since a *macroethics* "cannot be based upon either in the predispositions or in the para-instinctive loyalty feelings that exist in the interior of small groups or in the conventional morals represented by the present social institutions, including the spirit of the prevailing lawfully constitute state."[11]

Apel also questions the mentality, somewhat still prevailing, in the sense of a nonvalue science (Max Eber) based on a "neutral value rationality of the science." According to Apel's thinking, scientific investigation is not only a "subject–object relationship" question of the cognitive act but also, simultaneously and always, a question of the "relationship between subjects" proper to the communication and interaction among members of a scientific community:

> It then becomes clear that even, or precisely, the science of non-value nature – i.e., the objective of the neutral nature in terms of values, in the line of subject-object relationship – has to presuppose an ethics for an *ideal community of communication* in respect to the relationship between subjects, which complements the relationship *subject–object*. It becomes immediately evident that the ethics of an ideal community of communication, presupposed by science, cannot be reduced to something irrational, fraught with mere emotions and private and subjective decisions. Because it is precisely the objective of deciding on the requirements of the inter-subjective validity employing rational arguments that presupposes, in principle, a community ethics which implies equal rights and equal responsibilities at argumentation level.[12]

Contrary to several trends leading to ethical solutions in terms of a good life only in a local *polis* environment (so waiving the search for an universal ethics), Apel defines his postulation as follows:

> Nowadays we live in semi-autarchic societies or "polises," like in the classic era of the Greek Civilization. … Today, for the first time in history, we find ourselves living in a planetary civilization where, at least in some culture vital aspects – as, for example,

science, technology and economy, – found itself so unified that we have become members of a truly communication community or, put in another way, crew members of the same ship, as in regard to ecological crisis problems.[13]

Apel points out that his proposal for an universally valid ethics for all humanity "does not mean we need an ethics which prescribes a *good life* style for all human beings, or for all different socio-cultural forms of life." Much to the contrary, "we may accept and even mandate that we protect the *pluralism* of individual forms of life, provided it is warranted that a universally valid ethics for equal rights and equal co-responsibility in resolving the problems shared by humanity is respected in any and each form of life."

Apel stresses as a fatal mistake of the philosophical thinking the assumption of a fundamental antagonism, or even a contradiction, between the requested *universalism* of a post-Kant ethics and the pluralism of a para-Aristotle ethics of good life. Apel, in the same line, also does not assume that a person may stop relying on one's prenotions of good, originated in the historical fundament of one's cultural tradition, although recognizes that the *argumentative discourse* is not "contingent nor accidental," that is, presupposes that the ones involved are not in a situation (common purpose) to "find out, by means of rational argumentation, who is right about the subject under consideration" (when controversial) and not through "acts of discussion self based on performance means." This does not let him ignore that "in all human controversies at a level of a pre-discoursive communication, the participants spontaneously come forward with universally valid requests provided they do not interrupt or restrict communication."

Apel, nevertheless, does not present a ready formula to achieve the *macroethics* he proposes. However, he indicates what he considers to be the "the main problem of our days: the difficulty to somehow organize the collective co-responsibility of all members in the human communication community in regard to the effects of our collective actions. It is evident," Apel concludes, "that this issue goes much beyond the simple pragmatic-transcendental foundation of a universally valid principle of co-responsibility."

Kant, cited by Apel, had already postulated an *international lawful order*, that, in fact, would fulfill the requirements for the aspired *macroethics*. Apel, on the other hand, identifies his own philosophical community skepticism and waivers in the search for a universal ethics. He regrets that everyday all over the world "public statements" are made with a view to attain acceptable solutions to all affected individuals, although many are not compatible with the *media*'s manipulative humanitarian language. Apel recognizes, nevertheless, that they "at least evidence that today is possible a conscience conforming to the requirements of a macroethics of co-responsibility."

Globalization and Macroethics

Apel refers to economy and ecology as two great areas wherein human actions bring about consequences not only collective – anonymous and from a distance – but planetary, implying, from a moral standpoint, problems that the ethical dimensions of groups (microethics) and institutions (mesoethics) are not sufficient anymore to deal with, thus justifying the emergence of a macroethics of coresponsibility. Apel places his proposal in the communication and intersubjectivity fields, but does not put into context problems and solutions in the sphere of a field where, in the present, human actions take place on a global level, overcoming the barriers of distance: the media field.

Although Apel recognizes that there already exists a conscience agreeing with the demands for a *macroethics of coresponsibility* – notwithstanding more declaratory and strategic than inter-subjective – Apel does not directly refer to the argumentative conditions on a planetary level, so to speak, when human actions take place by means of the media or through the media.

The developments in telecommunication bring about an even more problematic question formulated by Apel whereby the *homo sapiens* still behave according to the ethical stages created starting from the *homo faber*, that is, the *microethics* and the *mesoethics*. Apel acknowledges that human actions have always been ahead of their capacity, or willingness, to measure and avoid the consequences. In sum, the human being has not yet developed effective principles of responsibility whenever the emergency to be dealt with demands the necessity of coresponsibility.

A dialogue between Apel, Piaget, Kohlberg and Habermas,[14] would be: human actions have not kept pace with man's capacity for empathy and altruism, that is, in regard of moral evolution he still lags behind the facts he produces. In terms of the psychogenesis conceived by Piaget and Kohlberg, man still behaves in a selfish way, without cooperation and altruism; he has *autonomy* for heteronomous actions, but lacks an autonomous moral to judge his own acts. In a hypothetical dialogue, Apel could agree with Durkheim that, in times claiming for the emergence of an *organic solidarity* (restituting right), the answers still happen in terms of a *mechanical solidarity* and may not be so even when we consider that many of his acts do not get a mechanical answer and, therefore, in terms of punitive right; except from the economy and the ecology themselves inasmuch as they are, ultimately, two sides of the same nature: economy (*oikos + nomia* = administration of the house) and ecology (*oikos + logos* = conscience of the house). Both converge at the same house and at the same cause, since economic actions impact natural resources.

Despite distance and language barriers, the media has prepared itself to transform the world into McLuhan's *global village*. As verified by Apel, the problem is that the actions become global, but ethically what still predominates is the village ethics, the *microethics* or, at most, the *mesoethics* of the nations (states). McLuhan's *global village* expression is thus appropriate, but what Apel advocates is in fact a cosmopolitan world ruled by an ethics of coresponsibility and, therefore, from humanity for humanity.

In such a context the media's role may be described in five points:

1   The media may perform an integrated role, which consists of divulging human actions (economic and environmental) and reducing the gap between such actions and their knowledge on the part of the participants in the global

community. In other worlds, the aspects of distance and anonymity of actions are reduced and allow for a discussion and collective argumentation about them. In this case the media renders a service in favor of an ethics of corespon-sibility and therefore, in favor of a *communicative reason*.

2   In view of a context of *systematically distorted communication*, the media per-forms a role inserted in the reproduction system of the conditions that allow for human actions' irresponsibility in terms of global community. In this instance, the media performs a nonintegrating role but an alienating one and, therefore, of supporting a *strategic and instrumental reason* at the service of domination.

3   We may say that the media gives with one hand and takes back with the other, but we have to acknowledge it was worse in the past. At least facts are instantly and globally divulged, allowing for global discussion, that is, they have a global repercussion, never mind they do not beget enough reaction and control, nei-ther in terms of *punitive right* (mechanic solidarity), nor of *restituting right* (organic solidarity) but, as Apel acknowledges, and create a conscience that a *macroethics* is necessary. It is always important to point out the moral autonomy character of the proposals of Piaget, Kohlberg, Habermas and Apel, that is, it does not mean to control the world from a starting point of control emanating from a heteronomous and imperial (coming from outside) moral authority, but through a collective consensus concerning a world collectivity, which may be achieved according to institutional mechanisms comprising the villages micro-cosm up to the global village macrocosm: parliaments, regional organizations and the United Nations. Naturally it is not a perfect system, since in such insti-tutional mechanisms we perceive the weight of existing niches of domination.

4   The media may contribute to the dissemination of moral and ethical values and even to awareness appeals in regard of human actions carrying a collective and global resonance. It would be the case of divulging institutional messages with an international reach and, therefore, of international impact. This would not be difficult, were it not for the fact that the world of conveying information via telecommunication did not work according to the exclusive market dimension. Information is merchandise. We buy/sell it, speculate with it. It is the imperial power of sponsorship. It is the answer to the question someone on the other side of the counter is always posing: "Who pays?" The world of information is also colonized by the systemic spheres of Power and Money.

5   Besides the need for a macroethics of corespalibility, it is necessary to have institutional mechanisms capable of rendering *visibility* to human actions, including communicative actions; otherwise the phenomenon pointed out by Habermas, *of a systematically distorted communication*, may remain insoluble, in a self-reproducing process. Human actions *publicity* should not be depend-ent only upon *interested sponsors*, but on a sponsorship whose interest is, in fact, *globally public*, inasmuch as the present context is of a *global public sphere*.

Edgar Morin (2001), on the other hand, presupposes the possibility of a "human kind's ethics," or "anthropoethics," blueprinted by comprehension and solidarity among human beings.[15] According to the French author, this new paradigm should be thought of in three dimensions – the individual, the society, and the species – and "undertake the human condition individual/society/species in the complexity of our being; to reach for humanity in ourselves, in our personal conscience, and undertake human destiny in its antinomies and wholeness." A correct formulation of this anthropoethics would be, therefore, "to work for the humanization of humanity; to carry out the dual pilotage of the planet: obey life, guide life; reach planetary unity in the diversity; respect in the other, at the same time, difference and identity as in regard of yourself; develop the ethics of solidarity; develop the ethics of understanding; teach the ethics of human kind."[16]

As already pointed out,[17] if, unfortunately, wars (Cold War inclusive) were a great communication propelling factor, maybe peace would come to be the divine grace able to give impulse to a new time of the universalization (and not only globalization) of human beings in their prerogatives, rights, duties as well as in their possibilities to share assets and conquests. Morin advocates exactly this: the humanization of the human being and the realization of humanity. Were they not for this purpose, what is the use of communication and all the knowledge accumulated in the field of communication? A fragmented Humanity with first and second rate human beings would be absurd.

Informational Sphere

Information is an essential factor in exercising human rights, citizenship and, consequently, world citizenship. As stated in the Declaration of Human Rights, Article XIX, any person is entitled to the right to inform and be informed, in any place, by any means, independent of censorship. This precept is coherent with a philosophical conception that language is the basis of humanism and of the human being's own essentialness.

Heidegger conceives the human being as the clearing of the Being (*Dasein* = Being-in-the-world), but such "clearance" cannot be realized other than by the coexisting. Coexistence, on the other hand, will only happen through the mutual and plural production of sense. That is, there is no way to conceive the human being, and humanity, other than by means of their discursive condition, therefore dialogic. Human *beings*, thus, would only humanize themselves beginning with their capacity (while *being*) of thinking about themselves, the world, and others. Today, however, a new paradigm, a new cogitation, is even more presupposed:[18] "We think, then I am," instead of the old "I think, then I am," as already recommended by Paulo Freire. Maybe we should not substitute one for the other but put them in an orderly sequence of subjectivity: "I think, then I am"; "We think, then we are." It should be contextualized, however, that, according to the "information order" put on the Planet since the expansion process of "communications" (whose rudiments belong to Marconi, at the beginning of the twentieth century), there has been a characterization of a linear, unilateral and unidimensional diffusion of information, so compounding an *immense informational sphere*, but still a reduced *communicational* sphere.[19] This implies a revision of the international information flow, still heavily concentrated in a specific ethnocentrism: the North-American information production, traded all over the world, followed by Western Europe as the second most important transmitter pole for news, entertainment, and advertisement content.

In Brazil, for instance, the chance that information about Lebanon may come directly from a Lebanese news agency is close to zero. The same also applies to great powers like India and China. Has anybody in Brazil, while reading a Brazilian newspaper, listening to the radio or watching news on television ever remembered some reporter mention something like: "According to a dispatch we received from such Chinese news agency", complemented by details given by such and such an Indian news agency? The worst is that we have grown so used to this situation that it would be strange to get information from the sources of origin, that is, from autochthonous sources on local, regional, or national matters in a certain country.

Communicational Sphere

The considerations insofar expressed allow for an understanding that even under ideal situations for the circulation of information (without distortions, manipulations, omissions), we will only overcome the *informational sphere* and come into the *communicational sphere* when it models an ethics according to which people, groups, movements, governments, and societies envision a context of cooperation for the wellbeing of all. This implies in granting communication a more noble status other than simply sending and receiving information. Today, in most cases, we do not even have a flow and counter flow of information. In general, we have a continuous and unilateral flow of information. Nevertheless, the progress made by a plurality of characters in regard to the use of information as a fundamental element in the planning and execution of actions promoting the human being and human wellbeing is notable while, at the same time, it has allowed a worldwide spread of a notion of human values about the human being and universal being as one but not necessarily equal. I adopt here Portuguese Professor Boaventura de Sousa Santos' ontological finding, in his speech on Human Rights,[20] whereby it should be taken into account the need that human beings be equal (in rights), as they are different (in conditions): "The two principles do not overlap necessarily and for that reason not all equalities are identical and not all differences mean inequality." The Coimbra professor considers then that individuals and social groups are entitled to be equal when difference diminishes them and are entitled to be different when equality makes them uncharacteristic. We also incorporate Habermas' theoretic foundation that permeates this Frankfurt School philosopher's literature produced in the past two decades about a communicative reason (counterpointed to ethnical/functional/instrumental reason), as well as the contextualization he has brought about in proposing knowledge as

Information, Communication, and Planetary Citizenship

a social theory of emancipating character. Habermas–Apel's dialogues are frequent and, although we have herein privileged more of Apel's views (because he deals more directly with a discursive ethics universally projected), we have to recognize Habermas' idea of a Erkenntnistheorie (critical theory of knowledge) whereby, ultimately, it has the "function of detecting the possibilities to utilize knowledge in favor of the interest (postulated as general for all humanity, or better said, as inherent reason for human kind's self constituting process) in the emancipation of individual and society."[21]

In Habermas' vision,[22] "emancipation in the good use of man's external nature for a full realization of his inner nature," added to which is the assertion that: "human kind's self constitution is conceived by Habermas as humanity's conscious formation process 'Bildungsprozess'." Such process, in turn, has its basis in the field of language and therefore, on communication but within a context of the *argumentative sphere* wherein "systematically distorted communication" has given place to a context capable of putting together "the ideal conditions of speaking," in which the better argument wins, regardless of others, and in which the use of *communicative reason* is predominant over *strategic reason* and *communicative action* (based on noncoercion and consensus) over *strategic action* (not exempt from domination and violence).

Seven Conclusions, Seven Hypotheses

Given the contingencies, but also the possibilities herein brought forth, I have formulated seven hypotheses which take into account the environment under analysis. They are summarized in the following: the connectivity and interactivity conditions prevailing in the world of today, in spite of disparities and "pathologies of modernity", are sufficient to assert that:

1 There is no longer an isolated process of civilization.
2 The idea of a decadence of civilizations no longer makes sense.
3 There is an advanced stage of humanity that incorporates a virtual planetary civil society conceived as an "argumentative community" – and not just of independent nationstates under the umbrella of one organization (e.g. United Nations).
4 There is an advanced process of implanting a planetary citizenship and ethics.
5 There is an advanced stage of implanting a *macroethics*, that is, a universal *ethos*, as a counterpoint to a global *ethos* (markedly occidental, markedly North-American and supposedly dominant).
6 In spite of remaining pockets of exclusion, apartheid and discrimination, the predominant idea today is one where the human being is one being and universal.
7 There exists, to a considerable level, the thought that citizenship, besides being planetary, is no longer solely anthropocentric, that is, humankind are no longer the center nor the only measure of all things; they have to be viewed as equally important to the idea of an earth cosmos as a penguin or any other species.

Notes

1 Reference to Mushrif-ud-Din Abdullah (1184–1283/1291). Saadi or Sadi (in Farsee) a poet born in Shiraz (Persia); Matsuura (2004, p. 466).
2 cf Küng (1993, p. 7).
3 This chapter derives from my yet unpublished doctorate work *State, Advertisement, and Society*. I have put forward some theoretical thoughts collected at the time of research (thesis presented in 1995), which I believe are still plausible.
4 Habermas refers to a "hermeneutic utopia of a universal and unrestricted dialogue in the world of life inhabited for all" Cf. Habermas (1988).
5 cf Rawls (1993, p. 29).
6 Professor at Johann Wolfgang Göethe-Universität (now retired).
7 Apel (1992, pp. 11–26).
8 The most eloquent criticism in this regard came from the famous *McBride Report*, so called in tribute to the Scottish scientist who supervised UNESCO's diagnostic work on the disparities of the flux of information in the world which proposed a New International Order of Information (did not materialize). The main conclusions of this document are described and analyzed in UNESCO (1983).
9 cf Betto (2000, p. 38).
10 Apel (1992, p. 11–26).
11 Apel (1992, p. 106).
12 Apel (1992, p. 11–26).
13 Apel (1992, p. 11–26).
14 A reference to the three models of morality conceived by Piaget (1977), which are: *preconventional* (ego-centric moral centered in an external authoritarian control); *conventional* (abiding to the norm, but without giving in for the sake of justice); and the *postconventional* (abiding to the norm but allowing justice to prevail when the norm reveals itself unjust).
15 cf Morin (2001).
16 Apel (1992, p. 106).
17 cf Silva (2005, pp. 10–11).
18 cf Freire (2001, p. 63). "There is not in the strict sense, an 'I think,' but rather a 'We think.' It's not the 'I think' that constitutes the 'We think,' but on the contrary, it is the 'We think' that makes it possible for one to think" (Lima 2001, p. 63).
19 The antinomy informational sphere/communicational sphere is dealt with in a matrix form in Rodrigues (1990).
20 Santos (1997, p. 115).
21 Freitag (2005, pp. 12–13).
22 cf Freitag (2005, p. 12).

References

Apel, K. (1992) A necessidade, a aparente dificuldade e a efectiva possibilidade de uma macroética planetária da (para a) humanidade, in *Revista de Comunicação e Linguagens*, Centro de Estudos da Comunicação e Linguagens (CECL), Universidade Nova de Lisboa, Lisboa, 15/16, julhoe, pp. 11–26.

Information, Communication, and Planetary Citizenship   53

Betto, F. (2000) Crise da Modernidade e Espiritualidade, in *O desafio ético*, (ed. A. Roitman), Garamond, Rio de Janeiro, p. 38.

Freire, P. (1992) *Extensão ou comunicação?* 10th edn, Paz e Terra, São Paulo, (originally published 1971).

Freitag, B. (2005) *Dialogando com Habermas*, Tempo Brasileiro, Rio de Janeiro.

Habermas, J. (1988) *Teoria de la acción comunicativa*, Vols, I & II, Taurus, Madrid.

Küng, H. (1993) *Projeto de ética mundial: uma moral em vista da sobrevivência humana*, Paulinas, São Paulo.

Lima, V.A. de. (2001) *Mídia, teoria e política*, (ed. Fundação Perseu Abramo), São Paulo, Brasília.

Matsuura, K. (2004) *La Unesco y la idea de Humanidad*, UNESCO, Brasília.

Morin, E. da Silva, C.E.F., and Sawaya, J. (2001) *Os sete Saberes Necessários à Educação do Futuro*, 3rd edn, Cortez, São Paulo.

Piaget, J. (1977) *O julgamento moral na criança*, Mestre Jou, São Paulo.

Rawls, J. (1993) *Uma Teoria da Justiça*, Editorial Presença, Lisboa.

Rodrigues, A.D. (1990) *O campo dos media*, in *Estratégias da comunicação, questão comunicacional e formas de sociabilidade*, (ed) Lisboa, Presença.

Roitman, A. (ed.) (2000) (Org.). *O desafio ético*, Rio de Janeiro, Garamond.

Santos, B. de Sousa. (1997) Por uma concepção multicultural de direitos humanos. São Paulo, *Lua Nova – Revista de Cultura e Política*, 39, 105–124.

Silva, L.M. da (2005) *Teorias da Comunicação*, Casa das Musas, Brasília.

UNESCO (1983) International Commission for the Study of Communication Problems. *One World and Many Voices: Communication and Information in our Time*, FGV, Rio de Janeiro.

4

Global Communication and Cultural Particularisms

The Place of Values in the Simultaneity of Structural Globalization and Cultural Fragmentation – The Case of Islamic Civilization

Bassam Tibi

There is an ideal view of global communication[1] that sees it as a dialogic platform for interaction among nations for the promotion of mutual cultural understanding and borrowing. This interaction takes place among peoples of different cultures and civilizations. In this intercultural understanding global communication would serve as a contribution to crosscultural fertilization. Understood in this sense, global communication is supposed to take place in the context of shared knowledge and a common discourse. It is certain that intercultural communication of this kind would provide a better understanding of the cultural other and thus be placed in the pursuit of world peace. How close is this model to reality?

Today, the commonalities supposed to underlay global communication are contested with a reference to an assumed contradiction between cultural diversity and universality in regard to moral values. This chapter is committed to the ideal view of intercultural communication as outlined. Nonetheless, I do not let wishful thinking drive my reasoning and argue throughout in realist terms. The cited contestation is well-taken and the model referred to is juxtaposed to reality. This juxtaposition is pursued in the case of Islamic civilization and its place in international society with the assumption of an intercivilizational value-based conflict (*not* a "clash"). This conflict emerges from simultaneity of structural globalization and cultural fragmentation. The idea of this simultaneity stands at the core of the present chapter.

The Handbook of Global Communication and Media Ethics, First Edition. Edited by Robert S. Fortner and P. Mark Fackler.
© 2011 Blackwell Publishing Ltd. Published 2011 by Blackwell Publishing Ltd.

Introduction

Under conditions of globalization some have expected to see the emergence of a global village of peace, but the reality of tensions, conflicts and wars runs counter to this expectation. As the late Oxford scholar Hedley Bull once maintained,

> The shrinking of the world ... has brought societies to a degree of mutual awareness and interaction that they never had before ... [It] does not in itself create a unity of outlook and has not in fact done ... [so] ... humanity is becoming simultaneously more unified and more fragmented.[2]

Here Bull acknowledges an existing cultural fragmentation along with the reality of structural globalization and he dismisses the argument of standardization. On these grounds the validity of the so-called "global village" is questioned. In a way, this is the theme of the present chapter that aims to achieve two tasks:

- First, to provide an analysis of the existing cultural fragmentation which not only accompanies – as a preexisting setup – the processes of structural globalization, but is also intensified through its side-effects;
- Second, to conduct an inquiry into the tensions that emanate from the disparity between individual cultures and an overall globalization.[3] This would be grounds for further inquiry into the potential of global communication to mend fences between cultures under the outlined conditions. It is concerned with how bridging between different local cultures, as well as between rival crosscultural civilizations with the assistance of an intercultural communication, could be accomplished. The focus is on Islam and the West as a case in point.

Having outlined the theme under scrutiny, and determined the point of departure, this introduction continues the line of reasoning in maintaining that contemporary global communication has not yet contributed to a better state of mutual understanding. It has been supposed that modern communication technologies bring people closer to one another. In contrast, existing interaction has been contributing to more cultural fragmentation and thus to tensions and conflicts. In other words, contemporary global communication generates an assertive and defensive cultural identity politics.[4]

The mechanism of a defensive culture determines global communication and promotes an awareness of the cultural other in the negative sense. There are two channels for communication. One is virtual, that is, the Internet and the exposure to global media, while the other is physical. The latter happens through encounters and interactions related to traveling across the borders of cultures. The first channel of global communication is modern while the latter is as old as civilizations.[5] Today, both channels have become a major avenue for the unfolding patterns of identity politics not always favorable to acknowledging the other as an equal partner.

Travelling today is bound to global migration.[6] This kind of interaction among cultures takes place in most big cities in the world. How do involved people then communicate? One may at first respond with a reference to the facts by stating: Not so well.

Today, even the common discourse of reason-based thinking (rationality) needed for intercultural communication is rebuffed as an "epistemological imperialism."[7] Ziauddin Sardar – a British Muslim academic with a migratory background – maintains this while he implicitly pretends to speak also for diaspora Muslims. In response one may argue: There is a need for a balance between diversity and universality. The rampant globalization did not contribute to this end, but instead furthered identity politics resulting in the stated cultural fragmentation. This is a major assumption of the present study. Contemporary communication is pursued by the modern means of technology and its channels. These are instruments that do not in themselves bridge. One should beware of confusing a discourse that facilitates substantive communication with the instruments employed. Values can bridge, but they are not shared. What happens under these conditions? What can one do to mend fences?

The present analysis includes first an effort to identify the pending issues to specify what we are talking about. Hereafter, this essay engages in a search for a better conceptual grasp of the place of cultural values and discourse in global communication. It asks how culturally different people define the self and also the other. In this context, the assumption of the bridging function of global communication is juxtaposed to the reality of conflict. Here one faces a puzzle. On the one hand there is the locality of cultures and on the other the global structural framework in which these cultures are embedded. This puzzle points out the most intriguing aspect in the present. This issue is addressed in terms of a simultaneity of more globalized, as well as more globalizing structures and fragmenting cultural particularisms. The structures are global, while cultures are more localized, that is, embedded in a culturally fragmented global entity. This is the substance of the idea of a simultaneity of structural globalization and cultural fragmentation. This reality is the hallmark of the present world and it is therefore the theme of the present chapter. The addressed simultaneity also affects the pendulum between culture and politics. This insight is illustrated by references to the contemporary Islamic civilization referred to as a case in point in the pursuit of a study of global communication aimed at reaching general insights.

The Inquiry

Global communication takes place in the context of culture, but it is affected by economic and political constraints in the global age of the twenty-first century. This reference to "The Global Age" is combined with the contention that the unifying structures on a global scale do not generate cultural commonalities, nor speak of a homogeneous and standardized international society. In contrast, culture divides, resulting in fragmentation. Cultural divides are expressed in identity politics of we versus them.[8] No doubt, globalization is a real process, but it never includes a cultural standardization of the world. Instead, global communication under these circumstances leads to an intensified divisive awareness of the self and of the other. Cultural diversity is a blessing, if it is combined with ways to bridge. Cultural diversity is also a reality. The perceptual imagery of the self contrasted to an imagery of the cultural other exacerbates existing problems. This happens for instance in the imagery confrontation of what is called "*gharb*/West" confronted with "*dar al-Islam*/the abode of Islam." The growing networks of interaction on global grounds do not promote values generally shared by peoples of different cultures. Could this reality be changed for the better?

Of course, values do change over time, as do cultures. The interplay between cultural and social change is embedded in politics and happens in a broader context. The argument of change acknowledges that cultural values are not to be essentialized, but it also challenges the unexamined assumption that cultures – in a process of change – automatically – or even mechanically – accommodate to the patterns of social change. This adjustment is assumed to be an effect of structural globalization. In contrast to this unexamined assumption, we must acknowledge that there are tensions between the local and the global which can affect their mutual development and can even hobble cultural accommodation. In my research in Islamic civilization I encountered this outcome.[9] Under such adverse global conditions one may ask whether civilizational bridging can be accomplished through global communication. Could the discourse of cultural modernity be shared as a means for global communication?

My assumption is that if people of different civilizations were to agree to engage in establishing a crosscultural consensus on core values based on a universal morality, then they would all have to accept a prerequisite of mutual respect. The reference to inequalities, lack of justice and to power asymmetries often serves as a pretext. Communication presupposes a consent to a shared discourse and also a willingness to endorse intercivilizational pluralism. Diversity has to be related to acknowledging the other as equal. This is a problem in Islam. If Islam were to become a significant part of an avowedly plural world – instead of being the source of a "geocivil war", as it is at present[10] – Muslim people would have to abandon the neoabsolutism of their cultural system that is revived in a political shape by contemporary Islamism and orthodoxy. In a global communication with the cultural other the notion of Islamic supremacism "*siyadat al-Islam*" has to be reconsidered.

A non-Muslim may not have the liberty to address the issue as candidly as I do as a liberal Muslim. It would be most helpful for Muslims, and the rest of the world, to engage in global communication as an honest intercultural dialogue. However, not in the form of an event management as it often happens at present, for instance in Saudi Arabia in 2008 in the interfaith dialogue, using an UN umbrella for this insincerity. Wahhabi Saudi Arabia neither recognized basic human rights (e.g., freedom of faith) nor the pluralism of cultures and religions on an equal footing. So what it the rationale of this global communication?

The needed dialogue in contemporary global communication is hampered by the politicization of religious beliefs. This happens in a revival of the related cultural symbols in which tradition is invented. This phenomenon gives rise to these questions: Is the current crossregional repoliticization of the sacred a positive indication? Is it justified to unfold patterns of an assertive identity being the expression of a revolt against West? Is the target of the return of the sacred[11] only Western hegemony? Or is it more, that is, a desecularization? Is a reversing of the disenchantment of the world at stake? These questions are the drivers of the present inquiry.

Manuel Castells coins the term "resistance identity" for depicting the response of people "stigmatized by the logic of domination."[12] In this context one may also ask whether this revolt is purely and simply an expression of a nostalgic romanticism as a kind of regressive and defensive-cultural resistance to the ongoing rapid change on a global scale. Two Muslim scholars speak in this context of nativism and of cultural schizophrenia.[13] This debate gives rise to another question: Could people stigmatized by inequality and domination engage in a global communication with those perceived as dominators? In other words, is global communication only possible when injustice and asymmetries generated by globalization are overcome?

If this were the case, then we might have to wait for a century or so, and thus accept the defensive-cultural response of an Islamization. This is an example for a response to real or perceptual domination. It turns the tables. In contrast, the vision of a democratic peace seems to be more promising in the search for a conflict resolution. The Peace of Westphalia went along with a process of secularization. For a global communication there must be secular grounds for the interaction, because religion generally divides and leads to conflict, not resolution. What is an absolute truth for the one party – as is the case in any religion – is a threat to the other. Therefore, the secularism of the Peace of Westphalia is worth considering,[14] despite all of its acknowledged shortcomings.

Despite the focus in the present inquiry on culture, this chapter dissociates all of its arguments from culturalism. In acknowledging that the existing worldviews are embedded in an interplay[15] between cultural values, economics and politics, it is made clear that their relations are reciprocal and that all constraints – including culture – are subject to chance; hence the dissociation from all kinds of essentialism. The chapter suggests the necessity of upgrading culture and placing it next to economic development and political factors. These issues are to be related to one another, however, in an interplay, not in a reductionist manner that places economy on the top of the constraints. It is deplorable that many Western scholars have great difficulties in adequately understanding the hardships growing from the tensions and discrepancies between social and cultural change and thus fail to place these in an interplay between the constraints. In short, culture is equated with economy with the result of admitting the notion of "developing cultures" analogous to the one of developing countries.[16] Those who underestimate the place of values in a process of global cultural communication, while they discard culture and overestimate

Global Communication and Cultural Particularisms 59

structural constraints, fail to understand how people with different cultural values could communicate with one another.

It is often not understood that reductionism prevails in the dominant research to the extent that general analyses overlook the politicization of religion and ethnicity that results in religious or ethnofundamentalism. In all religions and ethnicities ethnofundamentalists fail to communicate with the culturally ethnic other due to their exclusivist mindset, not due to structural obstacles. It is therefore not helpful to deal with processes of modernization as Roland Inglehart[17] does with the unspecific term of "postmodernization" without specifically pondering the substance of the issue. How could premodern, not yet industrialized societies be postmodern and postindustrial? Inglehart believes that these processes lead straight to secularization, but why is it not so in reality? Today, the issue is rather desecularization. Inglehart down plays the fact of the present processes of desecularization arising from the current modernization crisis, as a crisis of development by suggesting that this issue is simply an "impression" that the "mass media tend to convey." This phrasing not only reflects a very poor conclusion, but also an entirely wrong analysis. Desecularization and the revival of religions in world affairs are cultural phenomena that need to be taken most seriously. They matter in the present context, because they charge global communication and undermine the positive aspects of it outlined earlier.

In the context of the return of the sacred we can see a global trend toward fundamentalism. There is solid research on this subject. Inglehart ignores this research and contends that this phenomenon is represented by "a dwindling segment of the population"[18] and fails to explain the fundamentalist challenge. The available data provide evidence for identifying fundamentalism as a major issue in contemporary Islamic civilization and in the world at large. Fundamentalists cannot talk to one another and thus create an obstacle to global communication. They intensify existing cultural fragmentation.

In short, this contribution rests on the hypothesis of a reciprocal relationship between socioeconomic and cultural change. The assumed reciprocity shapes the arguments of the present study. Those who virtually reduce culture to "economy" and, most disturbingly, Islamic revival to "oil-wealth" – as Roland Inglehart does – fall into the trap of reductionism. He most mistakenly states:

> Islamic fundamentalism remains an alternative model insofar as oil revenues make it possible to obtain many of the advantages of modernization without industrializing; but we would not expect this model's credibility and mass appeal to outlast oil reserves."[19]

The present analysis suggests we go beyond this kind of simplistic and reductionist thinking. Serious scholars need to dissociate global communication from what is named "oil wealth" and so forth. The detailed reference made to the work of Inglehart is justified due to its exemplary character. In other words, the reference serves as a facilitator for moving on in the analysis of global communication as it is embedded in globalization as well as in the modernization process. We also need to note that it is advisable to free the subject matter from the "impression" that Western media are the source of existing images. This would be too simplistic. Instead, an effort is needed for looking at Islam from the inside as it manifests within local cultures. Without this effort we cannot understand the issue properly. A preoccupation with identifying the Islamic revival with media, oil, and with the impact of petro-dollars leads to nowhere. This crude reductionism of modernization and what is labeled postmodernization is not a theory, but an "impression" on the surface that overlooks the place of global communication in the twenty-first century and its critical importance for bridging in a situation of intercivilizational conflict.[20]

Islam and Global Communication

It is the civilizational worldview of people, and not "oil" that affects their discourse; they may change their behavior in a pragmatic manner, but not their cultural views. In stating this, I avoid essentialism and maintain that the Islamic worldview changes, but not automatically along with social and economic change. True, this worldview is based on principles (e.g. divine revelation) believed by the people in point to be immutable. However, the world of Islam and its values are always subject to change, even if "believers" do not allow this kind of thinking. In their worldview these "essential" beliefs (*al-usul*) claim universality that presents itself as the ultimate and immutable divine revelation based on verbal inspiration and valid for all humankind. Islamic values claim to stand above time and space. Orthodox Muslims and Islamists themselves through such thinking essentialize Islam in this manner. They refer to the quoted doctrine of *usul*/essentials believed to be immutable. If this setup is presented as grounds for the communication of people of Islamic faith among themselves and with the non-Muslim other, then obstacles for global communication among equals are inevitable. We should not avoid making this statement in the name of political correctness. The statement refers to an understanding of the "essentials" of the Islamic doctrine as a matter of fact. Then one needs to ask: How do today's Muslims view global communication?

The *umma* (community) is in Islam the unit for communication; it recognizes neither limitations nor exclusivity. Any person who converts to Islam becomes a member of this *umma*, while Christians and Jews are allowed to live as *dhimmi* (protected minorities) under Islamic supremacy. The tolerance of Islam is that it admits Christian and Jewish monotheists, but the problem is that it denounces all nonmonotheist others as *kafirun*/unbelievers. The tensions between these religious precepts and the idea of pluralist equality charge all aspects of life as Muslims interact with the non-Muslim other. The revival of holistic and parochial worldviews (e.g., the splitting of the world in *dar al-Islam* and *dar al-harb*) is based on these addressed *usul*/essentials. This revival creates great obstacles for a mutual understanding in a global communication between peoples of different faiths.

Global Communication and Cultural Particularisms 61

In reality, the Islamic civilizational model of an *umma*-based community of *dar al-Islam* versus the rest of the world is no longer of any significance in the contemporary world. The model of *umma*-unity was not even reflected in classical Islamic history.[21] Nonetheless, the scriptural doctrine, as Najib Armanazi[22] informs us, has never been revised as reality has changed. The inherited Islamic worldview continues to be entangled in this tradition, even twisted in its constructed dichotomy. Even though it is not in line with reality, the binary remains binding for more than 1.6 billion Muslims living as the majority in 57 states and as minorities all over the world. Of course, there have been some adjustments to changed circumstances, in particular to legitimate the adoptions of science and technology.[23] The Islamic *Weltanschauung* represents the cultural commitment of many religiopolitical groups in this period of the repoliticization of Islam. In the ideology of political Islam, the structure of disparity in the existing worldwide North–South gap is referred to in religiopolitical terms to present the call for the awaited *sahwa Islamiyya*,[24] that is the awakening of Muslims as the "underdogs" of a world order dominated by the West (i.e. by Europe and the United States). Global communication promotes this awakening, as it happens among Muslims across continents. It is justified to be critical of Western hegemony as an obstacle to a comprehensive global communication among equals.

The problem with political Islam is, however, the mentality of self-ghettoization that cannot be reduced to existing asymmetries. The exposure of the people of Islam to global structures is a reality and self-ethnicization, as a sentiment, is also real. To avoid a severe misunderstanding it has to be noted that Muslims in their history had a rich tradition of cultural borrowing and interaction with non-Muslims. The worldview of Islamic rationalism facilitated this opening in the past. Islamic *fiqh* – orthodoxy in the past, and political Islam at present have never demonstrated such open-mindedness.

For the greatest Muslim revivalist of the nineteenth century, Afghani, the primary characteristic of Islam consists of its claim to "dominance and superiority."[25] It follows that the leaders of Islamic movements criticize the Western dominance from a civilizational, not a political, viewpoint. In general, they are not committed to any egalitarian and pluralist concept of global communication. Their concern is rather to reverse the current hegemonic power situation in favor of Islam. At issue is not the "End of History" as Fukuyama once maintained, but rather "the return of history." There is a "hopeless dream"[26] for shifting the center of power in a process of decentring the West in order to to pave the way for a global dominance of Islam. Islamist internationalism is engaged in this hopeless dream. The envisioned Islamic order cannot be achieved. Instead world disorder occurs.[27]

Seen from a point of view of global communication that requires the acceptance of religious and cultural pluralism, the Islamists' claim to dominance not only indicates an anachronism and a lack of intercultural openmindedness, it also creates obstacles. I do share the criticism of Western hegemony, but reject any drive to substitute one hegemonic structure for another one, regardless of whether it is Islamic or not.

Without being apologetic, it is safe to state that, in the past the dominance of Muslims over other civilizations established in the course of Islamic expansion, had less disruptive effects than the devastating outcome of the European conquests of the world. Moreover, it is fair to say that Islamic conquests did not imply a kind of racism or any related views comparable to those of Europe. This is not to excuse the Islamic conquests, but merely to state historical realities. These facts are pertinent to the subject-matter of global communication. In their history, Muslims were able in the past to interact with the non-Muslim other. Muslims of today could learn from their own past for proper responses, among which would be an abandoning of their neoabsolutism to be able to embrace pluralism. I reiterate: in the pursuit of global communication between people of different cultures on equal grounds, secular commonalities based on a consensus are required to facilitate intercultural interaction.

The most popular public choice in the contemporary world of Islam seems to be the Islamist option labeled as *al-hall al-Islami/*the Islamic solution. In fact, Islamism is but one variety of the global phenomenon of religious fundamentalism qualified as an obstacle to intercultural communication.

The acceptance of equality among people of different cultures undergoing processes of modernization is hampered by the crisis of development. In the Western civilization, specifically in heartland Europe, the industrial revolution took place within a cultural and structural context in which modern science and technology have determined a radical change in the worldview of the European people. The mastery over nature, which is no longer explained in religious terms, is one of the essential features of industrial societies. Hence, rationalization is a process addressed by Max Weber (1964) as "the disenchantment of the world" (*Entzauberung der Welt*). The pervasive rationalization of all spheres of society has been facilitated by a shift in the European worldview from a medieval to a modern, rational, and secular one. This secularization analyzed by Franz Borkenau had great effects on the modern Western worldview.[28] In contrast, the Islamic *Weltanschauung* (see note 23) continues to be defined in preindustrial, religious, and theocentric (*tawhid-*) terms. This feature both of Islamic and other non-Western civilizations affects the intercultural communication and other interactions that take place in our globalized world. Is the interfaith dialogue an exit strategy? Is it a substitute to secular-rational global communication? The one launched by Saudi-Arabia first in Madrid, then at the UN was a ceremonial event management, a nonstarter!

In contrast, the project "Encountering the Stranger"[29] pursued in a trialogue is among the important and serious ventures. The point of departure should be, however, the international system that is truly global. It is diverse and not as homogenous as a national social system is. Nonetheless, its components are bound together structurally despite existing cultural fragmentation. The global system embraces segmented structures and cultures of various levels of development and, of course, it brings people of different norms, values, and worldviews to interact with one another more closely. In view of the existing cultural fragmentation a global communication on equal footing between peoples of radically divergent values and worldviews would be a contribution to peace. However, people are currently forced into one structure where an inequality exists between the center cultures that are technological-scientific and the periphery nonindustrial cultures that lack these means of power. Despite this acknowledgement I refuse to place the emergence of fundamentalism in this context and prefer to lean on Hedley Bull with whom this chapter started. Bull states a distinction between "international system" and "international society". The contemporary international system is "a system composed of states that are sovereign." Due to the "interaction between them sufficient ... we may speak of their forming a system."[30] In contrast to this system, a society of states is more than an interaction.

An international society would only exist "when a group of states, conscious of certain common interests and common values form a society in the sense that they conceive themselves to be bound by a common set of rules in their relations with one another."[31]

In another publication Bull deals with the non-Western revolt against the West and distinguishes between just antihegemonial decolonization and a revolt against European values: "the struggle of non-Western peoples to throw off the intellectual or cultural ascendancy of the Western world as to assert their own identity" is not only "against Western dominance", it is also "a revolt against Western values as such."[32]

This is my understanding of value-based intercivilizational conflict.

This section pointed out the structural and normative problems of Islam with global communication in the past and at present. In the contemporary "Revolt against the West" (Bull) that occurs in the shape of a repoliticization of the sacred, a process takes place that brings Muslim societies into conflict with modernization in a drive towards a desecularization. This process hampers discursive global communication. For certain, contemporary desecularization does even more: It also becomes an obstacle to interfaith dialogue. The global system technically promotes communication, but not a mutual understanding. The existing international environment exacerbates Islam's predicament with cultural modernity. This reference is not an excuse for Muslims in their underachievement to embrace pluralism and should not serve as a justification for what is named the postsecular society.[33]

Culture, Communication and Development in a Global Context

The contemporary politicization of faith and of religion – here interpreted as a cultural system – is normative, but it also emanates from the existing structural setup. There is a development crisis, also leading to a conflict between secularization and desecularization. In this context it becomes clear that the study of international conflicts needs to be supplemented by a new approach that considers the study of civilizations. I distinguish between local cultures and crosscultural civilizations. The latter assemble and relate these cultures to one another. Development and communication need to be discussed within this framework. The intermingling of religious culture and of secular politics on global grounds requires an integration of the study of culture and intercultural conflict into international studies. Communication could be viewed in this context as a means for peacefully negotiating conflicts. Therefore, the terms negotiation and communication are related to one another in this study.

In addition to the methodological needs mentioned, one has to respond to the Eurocentric bias, where development is conceived as a transfer of the model of European social systems to the non-Western world. However, the attitude of a particular ethnocultural authenticity that emerges among non-Westerners in response to Eurocentric bias is questionable as well. The illusion of a restoration of the precolonial past involves a romanticizing of development. The communication between those affected by Eurocentric bias and others dominated by the perception or an imagery that prevails in anti-Western ideologies of *tiers-mondisme* (third-worldism) is not promising at all. Eurocentrism and *tiers-mondisme* opposed to one another are obstacles in the way of establishing the rational knowledge required for global communication. One example of this is the mindset of Orientalism that reverses the prejudice, that is, by an "Orientalism in reverse."[34] The reference to cultural constraints of underdevelopment in the world of Islam and elsewhere is not an expression of Orientalism in development studies. Any dismissing of cultural analysis in favor of the flourishing discipline of political economy is counterproductive, for culture matters.

There are two misconceptions, one of which relates to the interpretation of intercultural conflicts within the global setup. These are conflicts between industrial (i.e., modern) and nonindustrial (i.e., premodern) civilizations and cultures. Certainly, the terms "premodern" and "preindustrial" are used free from the implications of evolutionist and "culturalist" bias. The suspicion of an evolutionist determination of the concept of modernity ought to be defused. Industrialization and rationalization are related to historical choices and they are not determined in an evolutionary unilinear development. Global communication can be affected by tensions that arise from this setup. For instance, Islamic–Western tensions hobble efforts at mutual understanding between the related civilizations.

The second misconception concerns the focus on the sociocultural dimension of underdevelopment that could give rise to the criticism that any study with such a focus is charged with culturalism. This criticism implies that cultural analysis overlooks the structural constraints that political economy could unravel. I do not replace the monocausality of economism by the one of culturalism. This one-dimensional cultural analysis is dismissed as a mere "culturalist" approach. The argument is, that any attempt to interpret reality needs to be multidimensional and able to cover all aspects in society. An interdisciplinary approach facilitates dealing with economics and politics interconnected with culture and social structures. Given the focus of the present chapter on global communication, the structure of underdevelopment is seen to have political, sociocultural and economic dimensions. These are not to be reduced to one another. The focus on culture is chosen, because the discourse of communication is a cultural one. However, the cultural analysis is not pursued in its own terms, but instead is integrated into a more general framework. The focus on culture is not charged by explaining everything through reference to culture. In short, culture is only one level of the analysis. Cultural analysis is an effort to bring this domain back, however, in a new design, into international studies and the study of global communication. In other words: Despite the narrowing of the scope of my analysis to focus on cultural issues, I continue to keep the overall context of global communication in mind. Therefore, I view the European expansion as a global conquest of the world restructuring it into an entity dominated by the European center. This is the structural context of global communication. Eurocentrism, which is a combination of an imagery and the realities of a domination, is dismissed as much as the romanticizing third-worldist responses to it. Global communication requires an open-mindedness of the involved parties and an unbiased acknowledging of the other.

With a reference to the case in point, the politicization of Islam is equally a value-related phenomenon and also relates to the existing global disparities that give rise to Islamist movements. The spokesmen of these movements always communicate to Western audiences in a discourse of self-victimization, the reference to these developmental disparities to promote a Christian–Western feeling of guilt. In their inner circle they proceed differently; they focus on civilizational tensions imbued with normative outlooks. The different worldviews embedded in structural realities are difficult for Westerners to understand. This displays the increasing significance of culture that affects the method of global communication. Cultures and civilizations are, however, – as argued above – not the same. Cultures are local, civilizations are crosscultural. I repeat the major premise of this chapter: People of different cultures need a common discourse to be shared in a global communication, not a platform for blame and accusation.

Civilizations, Dialogue and Global Communication

Today, global communication is often referred to as dialogue between civilizations. This venture has become a lucrative business of event management. Therefore, conflictual issues and the potential for their resolution go out of the window. For the understanding of civilizations the theory developed by Norbert Elias in his work *The Civilizing Process*[35] is highly pertinent. The European conquest of the world was possible, because it was based on a highly developed civilization. This process of European expansion affected other civilizations tremendously. The "civilizing process" identified by Norbert Elias creates global standards, but tensions as well. This insight touches on communication about civilizational standards that can be shared in contrast to being dismissed.

There has been another model of civilization not well understood in the West. The universalism of Islamic civilization legitimated the related *futuhat*/expansion, once bound to a vision of Islamizing the world. That expansion was successful and took place from the seventh to the seventeenth centuries,[36] but stopped short of achieving its goal on a global scale as did the expansion of Europe. Elias does not deal with Islam, but gives the following explanation why Europe was more successful than others in its endeavor to establish its own "civilizing process."

> What lends the civilizing process in the West its special and unique character is the fact that here the division of functions has attained a level, the monopolies of force and taxation a solidity, and interdependence and competition an extent, both in terms of physical space and of numbers of people involved, unequalled in world history.[37]

In the context of the European colonial expansion, the processes addressed by Elias were "exported" not only as a structure from Europe to the rest of the world. This pattern of socioeconomic complexity and competition was associated with cultural components. In the view of Elias this process was "the last wave of the continuing civilizing movement that we are able to observe,"[38] and he adds: "[T]he contrasts in conduct ... are reduced with the spread of civilization; the varieties of nuances of civilized conduct are increased."[39] With a reference to this globalization of the civilizing process I discuss differing variants of cultural patterns to establish the distinction between globalization and universalization which is missing in the literature.[40] Globalization relates to structures, while values spread via universalization. This is not the same. A communication between people of different cultures is affected by both processes. To be sure, the reference to Norbert Elias for pointing out the universalizing and globalizing effects of the European expansion in a civilizing process is also accompanied with the critique that there is not one single civilization, but rather multiple civilizations. The mindset of one civilization could be good or bad. Those who identify "civilization" with the West[41] are charged with Eurocentric bias, others who use civilization to denote one humanity that respects one standard of ethics have good will, but are naïve.[42] Both parties are wrong. There are multiple civilizations.[43]

Under conditions of globalization all cultures and civilizations are related to one another by global communication. The diversity compels tolerance within the socio-cultural sphere in view of contrasts, be they normative (Islam vs. Europe) or structural between industrial and nonindustrial societies. At this point one is reminded of the need to beware of a "Clash of Civilizations" as a rhetoric, however, without overlooking the pending conflicts. These are also related to a politicization of the sacred and Islam is the most prominent case in point.

Identity Politics as a Civilizational Awareness of the Self: Sources of Fragmentation in Global Communication

Globalization not only refers to the process of linking the diverse parts of the world to one another, but also to the mapping of the world into one system originating in Europe that becomes global. The cultures embedded into this process are characterized by diversity. How could global communication function?

Global Communication and Cultural Particularisms

Today, there is a "Revolt against the West" exemplified best by political Islam which is based on a repoliticization of religion. Each civilization has also its own pattern of communication. In the contemporary return of the sacred one makes instrumental use of one's own cultural symbols in pursuit of political ends. This is the current expression of the "Revolt against the West" carried out by political Islam. It happens in a global context. It is not only an articulation of an upheaval against Western dominance, but is also enhanced to a dismissal of European values and challenges their claim to universality. This articulation of a civilizational awareness of the self directed against the West enforces a specific politicization of Islam. Globalization and the modern means of communication contribute to upholding an imagined Islamic *umma* rebelling against the West.[44] Identity politics[45] is the framework of the assertive articulation of a civilizational awareness of the self which contributes to cultural fragmentation. These articulations are placed in global communication in situations in which people are challenged. In their response they become challengers themselves. They turn the tables.

The present chapter adheres to the concept that dismissing responses to prejudice can simply be reversed. The reader is reminded of the example of Orientalism and the response to it of an Orientalism in reverse (see note 34). As a scholar who migrated from West Asia (the term the Middle East – east of Europe – expresses Eurocentric geography) to Europe I was always skeptical of "tiers-mondisme" in all of its variations and continue to admire Frantz Fanon's critique.[46] For instance, Fanon did not like the ideology of négritude as a response to European racism. Fanon dismissed the glorification of "blackness" as a response to the dehumanization of Africans as "negro". Fanon argued that the response of négritude remains entangled in racist logic, or better "unlogic". This issue continues to be topical and it matters to identity politics entangled in a defensive culture that does the same as négritude did. This kind of global communication ends up with the parties shouting out at one another.

With the exception of a few illuminating works on the subject under issue, there exists within a myriad of Western authors the tendency to reduce all issues related to political Islam to "Western security." Other misleading interpretations go to the other extreme of praising Islamic identity politics as a "liberation." In contrast to both, my point of departure is the fact that Islamism religionizes politics in the conflict. Religion serves as a vehicle for the pursuit of nonreligious ends. It is wrong to reduce the Islamic value system to a mere means of articulation of economic and political demands. For those social scientists who are preoccupied with political economy – but mostly who are not professional economists – Islam remains a puzzle difficult to understand. Hence, the reduction of the cultural system of meaning that shapes the worldview of most Muslims to structural constraints in Western writings on the subject whose authors miss a major point: The meaning of religion in processes of global communication. The unaccomplished task remains to investigate the politicization of Islam in the process of cultural and social change without reducing its system of meaning to social realities and without the bias of scholars obsessed with academic word games anthropologists who dominate the field. The interrelationship between the cultural system and the particular societal structure – not only structurally and in terms of a critique of ideology, but also in the context of cultural analysis – needs to be subjected to a careful scrutiny in order to enable oneself to arrive at viable statements on the subject pertinent to all issues of contemporary communication.

Could Cultural Modernity be Shared as a Discourse for Global Communication? Modernization and Secularization

The notion of cultural modernity is European.[47] In the context of cultural and social "change" not only social structures, but also belief systems are supposed to change. In Islam, one faces the peculiarity that any talk about change raises the suspicion of an involvement in heresy, because "belief" is believed to be immutable, as it is based on a "*wahi*/verbal inspiration" that emanates from Allah. In fairness, one has to state in a general manner that change is problematic for every religion, not only Islam. Underlying this attitude is the idea that religion – being the incorporation of the absolute – should not be subjected to change because the result would be in itself a heresy. In going beyond this scriptural understanding one sees religion is embedded into social reality. All societies are subject to social change. And how about cultural change? Religion is a cultural system embedded in social realities. Religious symbols expose meaning and are not simply reflections of these realities. These symbols are fixed in the scriptures of the particular religion. Therefore, it is as wrong to see in religion merely an ideological form of articulation of reality, as it is wrong to look at religion as untouched by change in the realities.

If these premises are right, one has to concede a role for religion in sociocultural change in the context of global modernization. What about secularization? Is it not a requirement for a global communication among peoples of different religions and cultures? How could they communicate with one another?

In this section a discourse of cultural modernity is proposed. It presupposes secularization to facilitate communication with the cultural and religious other. Earlier, Westernized intellectual elites were particularly affected by the acculturative contact and, despite all dissatisfactions arising out of the existing social tensions, shared means of communication and its ordering channels. The contemporary counter-elites tend to de-Westernize their views and to ideologize religion by resorting to the imputed "moral order" that is believed to have existed prior to this situation of Westernization. Is it right to turn down these counter-elites and their identity politics aimed at exclusionary authenticity? It is not Eurocentric to characterize these protest movements in non-Western civilizations in Western social-scientific terms as nativist or as embued with "cultural schizophrenia" as Muslim-Iranians, and Europeans (see note 13) do this. The concern is the quest for objective knowledge that underpins inter-cultural communication. This runs counter to an agenda of an "Islamization of knowledge".[48] I argue for a universal

human knowledge in the pursuit of cultural borrowing, interaction and communication between people of different cultures. The grounds, therefore, have to be
secular, because no religion can be shared by all humanity, not even Islam that
presents itself as the sole religion for all humans. To establish secular grounds is to
dismiss Islam's missionary claim as well as any identification of global communication with *da'wa*, that is, Islamic proselytization.

The preference for a secular discourse based in cultural modernity is not a support for outdated modernization theories. In his comparative social historical studies, Reinhard Bendix has overcome this problem and gone beyond the old, almost
scholasticized debate on the dichotomy of traditionality and modernity to impressively demonstrate that the concept of "modernization" is vague, but still useful.
This usefulness is retained only if one manages to know how to avoid "confusion
between scientific constructions and actual development."[49] On these grounds the
insight is established

> that modernization does not necessarily lead to modernity. Moreover the moderniza-
> tion process itself is neither uniform nor universal, for the economic and political
> breakthrough made at the end of the eighteenth century in England and France has
> put every other country in the world in a situation of relative backwardness.[50]

The introduction of cultural modernity cannot be understood in evolutionist terms
nor, of course, in ways of reducing cultural or social and economic change to one
another. The transition at issue is not a repetition of the process that has already
taken place in Europe. It is true that the distortive rapid social change in non-
Western societies, as exemplified on Muslim societies, was triggered by European
expansion and the Western mapping of the world. But the solution to the problems
cannot be a ghettoization. Again, one is asked not to confuse reality with scholarly
constructs (e.g., dependency theory) manufactured at the desks of the academe.
For dealing with processes of rapid social change taking place in Muslim societies
since their mapping into the global system, one needs proper knowledge about the
political and cultural conflicts created by that change in these societies. As Bendix
tells us, each of these is faced with

> the problem of fusing its historically handed-down structure and typical tensions ...
> with the effects of ideas and techniques coming from outside ... Each one must bring
> the gravitational pull of the developed societies into harmony with the values con-
> tained in its own traditions.[51]

Bendix made this statement in a paper presented at an international sociological
congress back in 1966. At that time, it was still believed that evolutionary modernization consisted of the wholesale adoption of basically Western structures. The
collapse of the Shah's Iranian modernization experiment and also the failure of
other experiments contributed to questioning the approach of Westernization.[52]
The learning processes were very flawed and went into the other extreme of

postmodernism that questions any objective knowledge and herewith the discourse of cultural modernity needed for global communication.

Parallel to the move from the bias of modernization theory to that of postmodernism there has been a turn from evolutionism to globalism, thus replacing one general concept by another. As earlier evolutionists believed that change leads to modernity, globalists believe that the effects of globalization are irresistible and shall result in a kind of standardization emanating from global structures. This wisdom is challenged in this chapter by presenting the fact of a cultural fragmentation simultaneous to the other fact of a structural globalization.

The contemporary counter-elites are the drivers of the challenge of desecularization that generates cultural fragmentation. Acting on the premise of cultural modernity that there is an objective and universal knowledge I subscribe to Max Weber's notion of *Entzauberung der Welt*, that is, to secularization and ask: Is this process possible in Islam? There is no escape from this perennial question! Among the escapes are the references to the authenticity and particularism of Islam. Factually, Islamic civilization is torn in the twenty-first century between secularization and desecularization. This chapter argues that this competition matters to the needs of global communication. The introduction of secularism and modernity to the world of Islam took place in a historical process of the dissolution of Islamic order and the forceful mapping of Islamic civilization into a world order created by Europe. This is a historical context different from the one of Weberian rationalization of culture and politics. In the classical heritage of Islam there is a synthesis with rationalism established by Islamic medieval philosophers who combined Islam with the Hellenism of Aristotle and Plato. This Hellenized Islam promoted an Islamic rationalism as a promising, but not lasting sign in Islamic history.[53] This reference runs counter to overstretching the notion of Islamic peculiarities. In the past, Muslim rational philosophers set an example for intercultural communication and for rationalization in the context of cultural borrowing. In contrast, Muslim *ulema* scribes have always been reluctant to admit the notion of change into Islamic doctrine. Muslims were and continue to deal with changed conditions within the adherence to a cultural system that is viewed to be unchangeable.

Among the premises of the present study is the idea that in intercultural global communication people not only communicate messages, but also learn and change. People have their own cultural system that underpins their cultural beliefs and the related worldview. What happens when rapid change takes place in society? Would the respective cultural system promote or hinder changes and learning from the other in a process of global communication? There is a predicament. On the one hand reality is in flux, but on the other religion claims to be immutable! This predicament gives rise to the question: How do Muslims perceive this predicament and how do they accommodate social change culturally?

The struggle over these issues is often silenced. Because I ask freely and because I establish a linkage between secularization, modernity, and industrialization I have been blamed for embracing modernity and of "self-Orientalization" by US scholars who are outsiders to the Islamic civilization in which I was born and socialized.

The present inquiry on global communication in the context of modernization and secularization distinguishes between secularism, being an ideology (e.g., Kemalism), and secularization, being a social process that could take place in any society. The Muslim Westernized elites were not successful because they espoused secularism with no parallel efforts at secularization in society.

As a Muslim, I do not think that it is the job of Muslims to pursue *da'wa* when they engage in global communication. If this insight is accepted, then intercultural, global communication has to be secular. The acceptance of a crosscultural morality shared by all could contribute to overcoming the cultural fragmentation stated in this study. The discourse of cultural modernity could be at present acceptable to Muslims as was Hellenism to their ancestors.

Conclusion

The contemporary politicization of religion embedded in a process of desecularization is a reality of the twenty-first century no one can afford to overlook. Those Westerners distancing themselves from "the secularization" that has so far been regarded as universal seem to abandon cultural modernity altogether in an illusion to accommodate the Islamic revival. I disagree with this approach, because it is not the proper response to cultural fragmentation. One may criticize modernity, but the outcome needs not to be a denial of the existence of what is being criticized. To point out the limitations is not to abandon secularity for the favor of a post-secular society. In an earlier book, *The Crisis of Modern Islam* (1988), I interpreted secularization as a by-product of a process of functional differentiation of society affecting the religious system. This approach is not areligious, as radical secularism is; it simply reduces religion to a part-system within a given society as a whole. In spite of all the reservations conceded here, I continue to hold firm to this interpretation. In the course of my continued research, I have been able to further differentiate this concept and to enrich it with some nuances and to think anew two thematic spheres. These are:

First, the correspondence between the sacred and the political viewed by political Islam as central to Islam. In contrast, I argue for the necessity for desacralizing politics in an effort at rationalization in a broad sense in order to decrease cultural fragmentation.

Second, one needs to address the potential of an Islamic accommodation of technological-scientific accomplishments in a way that goes beyond adopting items of modernity, that is, instruments decoupled from their context. In a process of coming to terms with Islam's predicament with cultural modernity the notion "Islamic" would then be reduced to the ethical and cultural implications embedded in a process of desacralization.

One of the sources of cultural fragmentation is the Islamic claim to superiority/ *siyadat al-Islam*. It appears inevitable that conflict would be – seen from the perspective of cultural pluralism – the outcome. The claim is based on a doctrine that today has no material underpinning. As a source of ideological intolerance it stands in the way of establishing true cultural pluralism. Therefore, cultural change is required to allow Muslims to embrace secularization and pluralism.[54] This would contribute to a better condition of Muslim's relations to others, not only to the West, but also to Asia and Africa, where non-Muslims are affected by cultural fragmentation.

In the past, Muslims were open to learn from the history of others. Today they need to learn from their ancestors in medieval Islam, who set great records in this regard. With reference to modern European social history, it is possible to point out that the secularization of Christianity has resulted from the unfolding of cultural modernity. It did not contribute to the abolition of religion as most Islamists wrongly conclude. It is sad to see these authors, being anxious for their religion, identify secularization with atheism and some even view it as a result of a "Jewish conspiracy."[55] The Islamists' awareness of secularization is overly polemical and it is based on a misconception of the issue. Islamists do not honor the fact that this process is a by-product of change and related to differentiation within society itself. Instead, they equate secularization with "Westernization" to discard the issue in a cultural atmosphere of anti-Westernism altogether. The critique of religion-based cultural fragmentation is in no way an argument against religious culture per se, it is rather a plea for a desacralization of politics in Islamic civilization. The solution that some Muslims like A. An-Na'im present as a synthesis between shari'a and secularity could never work. It is simply a misconception of the issue when An-Na'im embraces the idea of the secular state, but argues at the same time against secularization in society. This is an inconsistent reasoning.[56]

A better way of thinking would be to distinguish between secularization and profanation. Earlier I referred to Daniel Bell who proposes a restriction of the meaning of the term secularization to its original content (see note 11). At one time, secularization meant simply a separation of religion from political life. In the course of the last two centuries, however, the concept has acquired a further dimension in Western societies – that of profanation. In Bell's view, underlying this idea is the belief that man can penetrate and master everything with the aid of science and his own instrumental reason. For Bell, total modernism thus implies nihilism.[57] In fact, postmodernism, not cultural modernity, is a nihilism. Cultural modernity[58] is based on norms, values, and a rational view of the world. In contrast, postmodernity is a nihilism, because it deconstructs every reality to end up in rubble. In line with Bell, this chapter seeks not to restrict the concept of culture to its anthropological implications, that is, to how people live and cope with their lives, but to go further and argue that culture means the: "modalities of response by sentient men to the core questions that confront all human groups in the consciousness of existence".[59]

Modern science and technology are means; they contribute to the mastery of man over nature, but culture is meaning. In this sense religion is understood in terms of religious ethics as providing meaning within a cultural system.[60] It is important to add that Bell has no specific religion, and definitely no exclusive

Global Communication and Cultural Particularisms   73

religion in mind here. Above all we are not talking about a political religion. Political Islam is a variety of exactly this kind of politicized religion. Therefore, Islamists are not favorable to global communication in a secular context of pluralism. When they talk of religion, they mean Islam, specifically their understanding of it. Such understanding stands in the way of a universal religious ethics providing answers to the fundamental questions of humanity. Global communication pursued in interfaith dialogue should not be abused for proselytization as often pursued in Saudi-sponsored event management. The critique of secularization should be limited to its by-product of profanation which is – professedly – areligious. In short, a secularization would not do away with religion, but profanation does.

For global communication desacralizing politics in decoupling religious symbols from political legitimation is a contribution to a disenchantment of the world. Religion should be preserved as an ethical answer to the questions of human existence. Diversity should be honored in any intercultural communication, however, under conditions of pluralism. In other words, cultural diversity has to be based on religious pluralism. The appeal for cultural and civilizational pluralism on a global-democratic basis does not absolve the discrete cultures from their outstanding internal social tasks. These include embracing reforms leading to a better cultural accommodation of change and to decoupling religion, as a belief and a cultural system, from politics. In its oscillation between culture and politics Islam needs a cutting edge of a secularity combined with democracy and civil society. This is a challenge to Islamic civilization in the new millennium in its predicament with cultural modernity. This challenge shapes the communication of Muslims with the non-Muslim other.

The conclusion here on the dichotomy of structural globalization and the kind of cultural self-assertion that leads to cultural fragmentation is that secularization and the challenge of desecularization affect global communication. There is a real modernization crisis that relates to more than the lack of industrialization. At issue is the need for cultural secularization in non-Western civilizations to make them embrace pluralism.

The analysis of cultural change has to cover, further, two issues/areas of development. One of them is political development (institution building) and the other is cultural analysis as an analysis of value systems. In this regard, there are significant links between cultural change and the resilience of tradition. To be sure, an invention of tradition is not yet a sign of cultural change. There exists no automatic mechanism between modernization and secularization. The interplay between social, political and cultural change is by all means reciprocal, and really reciprocal! It is not enough to pay lip service to this reciprocity parallel to pursuing mechanic reductionism.

The study of structural globalization and cultural fragmentation requires a proper understanding of how cultural systems work in the interplay mentioned. In a postbipolar world, efforts at *Preventing the Clash of Civilizations*[61] are the needed strategy for the new millennium. This job is not done by replacing the rhetoric of "clash" with the rhetoric of "convergence" between civilizations, and not to speak of the nonsense of maintaining a Christian-Islamic civilization.[62]

An interaction between civilizations based on the separation between religion and politics (secularity) and pluralism (diversity supported by a basic consensus over core values) would ensure peaceful resolution of conflicts which are not an expression of an intractable clash. The plea for crosscultural morality to guide global communication cannot be sustained if the parties involved resort to a mix of politics and religion.

In the past times of Hellenized Islam and during the Islamic impact on European Renaissance – both civilizations of Islam and Europe had their best records of mutual respect and fascination. Rationality and secular tolerance are the foremost bridges between the civilizations, in contrast political religions create frontiers! Along with a crosscultural morality[63] there can be a shared crosscultural discourse for a global communication that promotes bridging instead of cultural trenches.

Notes

1 See Asante and Gudykunst (1989).
2 Bull (1977, p. 273).
3 See Anheier and Raj Isar (2007).
4 See Tibi (2007b).
5 For an inquiry into this issue in Islamic history see Euben (2006).
6 Weiner (1995).
7 The nonsensical term "epistemological imperialism" was coined by (1985) in his pursuit of "postcolonial studies" taught at British universities.
8 See Kenny (2004) and Tibi (2007b).
9 Tibi (1990).
10 "Islam's geo-civil war" is a formula coined by Brenkman (2007), pp. 165–169. To prevent this war scenario from happening and to do this in Islamic terms liberal Muslims need to establish the culture of pluralism in Islam. The whole world is concerned, but Asia is an important case in point as shown in the contributions to Reid and Gilseman (2007), see chapter by Tibi (2007a, pp. 28–52).
11 On this issue see the essay by Daniel Bell (1980). Bell questions the Weberian formula of a disenchantment of the world/*Entzauberung der Welt* understood as a secular rationalization. This classical debate has been resumed in the light of the post-9/11 developments in the new chapter 11 added to the enlarged edition of *Islam between Culture and Politics* (Tibi, 2005).
12 Castells (1997, p. 8).
13 See the work of the Iranian scholars Shoyegan (1992) and Boroujerdi (1996).
14 Philpott (2002, pp. 66–95).
15 Tibi (1988).
16 This work was accomplished at The Culture Matters Research Project/CMRP that was conducted at the Fletcher School/Tufts University 2003–2006. The project was chaired by Lawrence Harrison (2006) in which the research papers of the project are published.
17 Inglehart (1997).
18 Inglehart (1997).

Global Communication and Cultural Particularisms 75

19 Inglehart (1997).
20 To be sure, a conflict and a clash are not the same. I dissociate myself and this analysis from the Huntingtonian clash rhetoric. See Tibi (2007c, pp. 39–64).
21 Bernard Lewis points at three caliphates which existed in an inner-Islamic rivalry next to one another in the tenth century (Schacht and Bosworth, 1974, p. 168).
22 Armanazi (1990) first published in Damascus 1930.
23 Tibi (1993, pp. 73–102).
24 Imara (1991).
25 al-Afghani (1968, p. 328).
26 See Kagan (2008) in particular pp. 80–85. On the debate on the end of history, or reversely the return of history see Tibi (2008) Introduction and chapter five.
27 On the place of Islam in order and disorder in postbipolar world politics see Tibi (1998, updated 2002).
28 Borkenau (1980) belonged to the scholar community of the Frankfurt School established by Max Horkheimer who fled Nazi Germany in 1933.
29 See the contributions by Roth and Gelb (2010).
30 Bull (1977, pp. 10, 11).
31 Bull (1977, p. 13).
32 Bull's "The Revolt against the West" (1984).
33 Tibi (2009) in particular Chapter 7 on pluralism. On the notion of "post-secular society" coined in the aftermath of 9/11 by Jürgen Habermas (2001), see Tibi (2002, pp. 265–296). See also Bell (1980) and Tibi (2005).
34 On this issue see Said (1979). Said was accused of engaging in "an Orientalism in reverse" by S. al-Azm (1992). For an overview on this debate see Tibi (2001, chapter 4).
35 Elias (1978).
36 On this Islamic expansion between the seventh and the seventeenth centuries see Tibi (1999). The authoritative work on the history of Islamic civilization is Hodgson (1977).
37 Elias (1978).
38 Elias (1978).
39 Elias (1978), p. 255. On the groundbreaking work of Elias (1978), see Mennell, (1989).
40 The argument that a universalization of values does not match with globalization of structures is elaborated upon by Tibi (2005).
41 McNeill (1963).
42 An example for this flawed thinking is the illusion of Weltethos based on a misconception of the realities on the grounds. This wishful thinking is propagated by Hans Küng in his numerous books full of repetitions not worth being listed in detail.
43 Braudel (1994).
44 Lubeck (2002, pp. 69–90), Lubeck states "ironically globalization … increased communication … for the … Muslim communities of the global umma", p. 79. See also the chapter on "Islamic Radicalization in the European Union" by M. Laskier (Frisch and Inbar, 2008, pp. 93–120).
45 See Kenny (2004) and Tibi (2007b).
46 Fanon (1961).
47 Habermas (1987).

48 Tibi (1995, pp. 1–24), see also chapter two Tibi (2009) on knowledge.
49 Bendix (1970, pp. 505ff.), particularly p. 506.
50 Bendix (1970, p. 507).
51 Bendix (1970, p. 511).
52 On Westernization see der Laue (1987).
53 On Hellenism and its adoption by Islamic rationalism see chapter eight Tibi (2009). There the reader finds multiple references on this theme.
54 See chapters 6 and 7 in Tibi (2009).
55 See Jarisha and Zaibaq (1987, pp. 37ff., 92ff)., who view secularization as a "Jewish conspiracy directed against Islam."
56 An-Na'im (2007).
57 Bell (1980, pp. 324ff. particularly p. 332).
58 Habermas (1987).
59 Bell (1980, p. 333).
60 On Geertz views on religion as a cultural system see Tibi (2005) chapter 1.
61 Herzog and Schmiegelow (1999). On this issue there are two rhetorics opposed to one another, one is of a clash by Huntington (1993), and the other is of convergence, see Adler, Crawford and Bicchi (2006). In a proper global communication one is advised to write-off both.
62 See the wishful thinking by Bullet (2004). In history there never existed such a thing.
63 See Tibi in Herzog and Schmiegelow (1999).

References

Adler, E., Crawford, B., and Bicchi, F. (eds) (2006) *The Convergence of Civilizations*, University of Toronto Press, Toronto.

al-Afghani, J.a-D. (1968) *al-A'mal al-Kamilah* [Collected Works], Dar al-Katib al-Arabi, Cairo.

al-Azm, S. (1992) *Dhihniyyat al-Tahrim* [The Mentality of Taboos], Riad El-Rayyes, London.

Anheier, H., and Raj Isar, Y. (eds) (2007) *Conflicts and Tensions*, Sage, London.

An-Na'im, A. (2007) *Islam and the Secular State. Negotiating the Future of Shari'a*, Harvard University Press, Cambridge.

Armanazi, N. (1990/1930) *al-Shar' al-Duwali fi al-Islam* [International Law in Islam], Riad E. Rayyes, London.

Asante, M., and Gudykunst, W.B. (eds) (1989) *Handbook of International and Intercultural Communication*, Sage, London.

Bell, D. (1980) *The Winding Passage. Essays 1960 - 1980*, Basic Books, New York, pp. 324-354.

Bendix, R. (1970) Modernisierung in internationaler Perspektive, in *Theorien des sozialen Wandels*, (ed. W. Zapf), Kiepenheuer & Witsch, Cologne and Berlin, pp. 505ff.

Borkenau, F. (1980) *Der Übergang vom feudalen zum bürgerlichen Weltbild*, Wissenschaftliche Buchgesellschaft, Darmstadt.

Boroujerdi, M. (1996) *Iranian Intellectuals and the West*, Syracuse University Press, Syracuse, NY.

Braudel, F. (1994) *A History of Civilizations*, Harmondsworth, Penguin.

Brenkman, J. (2007) *The Cultural Contradictions of Democracy. Political Thought since September 11*, Princeton University Press, Princeton/NJ, pp. 165–169.

Bull, H. (1977) *The Anarchical Society. A Study of Order in World Politics*, Columbia University Press, New York.

Bull, H. (1984) The revolt against the West, in *The Expansion of International Society*, (eds H. Bull and A. Watson), Clarendon Press, London, pp. 217–228.

Bullet, R. (2004) *Islamo-Christian Civilization*, Columbia University Press, New York.

Castells, M. (1997) *The Power of Identity*, Blackwell, Oxford.

der Laue, T.V. (1987) *The World Revolution of Westernization*, Oxford University Press, New York.

Elias, N. (1978) *The Civilizing Process*, 2 vols, Pantheon Books, New York.

Euben, R. (2006) *Journeys to the Other Shore. Muslim and Western Travellers in Search for Knowledge*, Princeton University Press, Princeton, NJ.

Fanon, F. (1961) *Les Damnés de la Terre*, Maspero, Paris.

Habermas, J. (1987) *The Philosophical Discourse of Modernity*, MIT Press, Cambridge, MA.

Habermas, J. (2001) *Glauben und Wissen*, Suhrkamp, Frankfurt.

Harrison, L. (2006) *Developing Cultures*, 2 vols, Routledge, New York.

Herzog, R., and Schmiegelow, H. (1999) *Preventing the Clash of Civilizations*, St. Martin's Press, New York.

Hodgson, M. (1977) *The Venture of Islam. Conscience and History in a World Civilization*, 3 vols, University of Chicago Press, Chicago.

Huntington, S.P. (1993) *The Clash of Civilizations*, Schuman and Schuster, New York.

Imara, M. (1991) *al-Sahwa al-Islamiyya wa al-tahaddi al-hadari* [Islamic Awakening and the Civilizational Challenge], Dar al-Shruq, Cairo.

Inglehart, R. (1997) *Modernization and Postmodernization*, Princeton University Press, Princeton, NJ.

Jarisha, A.M., and Zaibaq, M.Sh. (1987) *Asalib al-ghazu al-fikri li al-alam al-Islami* [Methods of Intellectual Invasion of the Islamic World], Dar al-Shruq, Cairo.

Kagan, R. (2008) *The Return of History and the End of Dreams*, Alfred Knopf, New York.

Kenny, M. (2004) *The Politics of Identity*, Polity, Cambridge.

Laskier, M. (2008) Islamic radicalization in the European Union, in *Radical Islam and International Security*, (eds H. Frisch and E. Inbar), Routledge, New York, pp. 93–120.

Lewis, B. (1974) Politics and War, in *The Legacy of Islam*, (eds J. Schacht and C.E. Bosworth), Clarendon Press, Oxford, pp. 156–209.

Lubeck, P. (2002) The challenge of Islamic networks, in *Muslim Europe or Euro-Islam*, (eds N. AlSayyad and M. Castells), Lexington Books, Lanham, MD.

McNeill, W. *The Rise of the West. A History of the Human Community*, University of Chicago Press, Chicago.

Mennell, S. (1989) *Norbert Elias: An Introduction*, Blackwell, Oxford.

Philpott, D. (2002) The challenge of September 11 to secularism in international relations, *World Politics*, 55 (1), 66–95.

Reid, A., and Gilseman, M. (eds) (2007) *Islamic Legitimacy in a Plural Asia*, Routledge, New York.

Roth, J., and Gelb, L. (eds) (2010) *Encountering the Stranger*, University of Washington Press, Seattle, WA.

Said, E. (1979) *Orientalism*, Random House, New York.

Sardar, Z. ed. (1985) *Islamic Futures. The Shape of Ideas to Come*, Mansell, London.

Shoyegan, D. (1992) *Cultural Schizophrenia*, Saqi, London.

Tibi, B. (1988) The interplay between social and cultural change, in *Arab Civilization*, (eds G. Atiyeh and I. Oweis), SUNY, Albany, NY, pp. 166–182.

Tibi, B. (1990) *Islam and the Cultural Accommodation of Social Change*, Westview, Boulder, CO.

Tibi, B. (1993) The worldview of Sunni-Arab fundamentalists, in *Fundamentalisms and Society*, (eds M. Marty and S. Appleby), Chicago University Press, Chicago, pp. 73–102.

Tibi, B. (1995) Culture and knowledge: The Islamization of knowledge as a postmodern project?, *Theory, Culture & Society*, 12 (1), 1–24.

Tibi, B. (1998) *The Challenge of Fundamentalism. Political Islam and the New World Disorder*, University of California Press, Berkeley, CA.

Tibi, B. (1999) *Kreuzzug und Djihad. Der Islam und die christliche Welt*, Bertelsmann, Munich.

Tibi, B. (2001) *Einladung in die islamische Geschichte*, Primus, Darmstadt.

Tibi, B. (2002) Habermas and the return of the sacred, *Religion-Staat-Gesellschaft*, 3, 265–296.

Tibi, B. (2005) *Islam between Culture and Politics*, 2nd edn, Palgrave, New York.

Tibi, B. (2007a) Islam and cultural modernity, *Islamic Legitimacy in a Plural Asia*, (eds A. Reid and M. Gilseman), Routledge, New York, pp. 28–52.

Tibi, B. (2007b) Islam: Between religious-cultural practice and identity politics, in *Conflicts and Tensions*, (eds H. Anheier and Y. Raj Isar), Sage, London, pp. 221–231.

Tibi, B. (2007c) Jihadism and inter-civilizational conflict. Conflicting images of the self and of the other, in *Islam and Political Violence*, (eds S. Akbarzadeh and F. Mansouri, Taures), London, pp. 39–64.

Tibi, B. (2008) *Political Islam, World Politics and Europe*, Routledge, New York.

Tibi, B. (2009) *Islam's Predicament with Modernity. Religious Reform and Cultural Change*, Routledge, New York.

Weber, M. (1964) Soziologie – Weltgeschichtliche Analysen – Politik, Kröner, Stuttgart.

Weiner, M. (1995) *The Global Migration Crisis*, Harper Collins, New York.

5

The Ethics of Privacy in High versus Low Technology Societies

Robert S. Fortner

The protection of privacy from government, corporate, and individual intrusion is a major legal issue in the United States. As Alderman and Kennedy (1995) explain it in the introduction to their book on the subject (p. xiii), privacy "covers many things. It protects the solitude necessary for creative thought. It allows us the independence that is part of raising a family. It protects our right to be secure in our own homes and possessions, assured that government cannot come barging in. Privacy also encompasses our right to self-determination and to define who we are. Although we live in a world of noisy self-confession, privacy allows us to keep certain facts to ourselves if we so choose. The right to privacy, it seems, is what makes us civilized." Legal cases that attempt to enforce these rights, often after they have been violated by the state (and especially its exercise of police powers), corporations (that often "appropriate" a person's identity without permission), or individuals (often as the result of surveillance activities or surreptitious recording or photography), keep thousands of attorneys in business.

What is troublesome about the concept as Alderman and Kennedy explain it, is that so much of the world – by their definition – would not be "civilized." This conclusion also applies as well to the myriad of legal cases and rulings that have delineated this "right to be left alone," as eventual US Supreme Court Justice Louis Brandeis put it in an essay in 1890 (along with fellow author Samuel D. Warren). Most people in the developing world have no real privacy. If there is someone standing between an individual and a camera, it's usually a chief or local district official with his open palm extended for a bribe. If a family is to survive in many places, it will be through the efforts of its community or nongovernmental organizations (NGOs). If people are to ground their identities, it will not be through rationality in which people define themselves, but through the sense of moral responsibility for parentage, clan, tribe, community and place of origin, often with a significant dose of myth thrown in.

The Handbook of Global Communication and Media Ethics, First Edition. Edited by Robert S. Fortner and P. Mark Fackler.
© 2011 Blackwell Publishing Ltd. Published 2011 by Blackwell Publishing Ltd.

As a member of the Western Enlightenment tradition, I can say at least two things about privacy without too much fear of contradiction. First, I would not want to do without the privacy protections that have developed within this tradition. Second, there is nothing globally sacred about such protections. The issue of privacy seems to those in the West as a necessary protection for the self. It makes people who have embraced this "right to be left alone," feel secure, especially those of us within the American individualistically-inclined culture that posits that each of us is responsible for our own actions and can be held accountable for them by community pressure, shame, or – if all else fails – legal demands. Over the past few decades people have become increasingly subject to surveillance, identity theft, and "embarrassment" as the connections between individual databases have been increased. Since 9/11, 2001, people have felt their privacy violated by searches of their reading habits at libraries, tapping of their email and perusal of telephone records, theft of credit card numbers and mortgage loan data, and various data mining activities that have attempted to "personalize" Internet advertising, based on information from surfing habits, bar code scans in grocery stores, and various other collection points. "New technology has not only increased the amount of information circulating about individuals, but also the ease of retrieving virtually anything one wants to know about someone. This information comes from several sources. Anytime one provides information for credit card applications, medical records, insurance applications, driver's applications and renewals [sic], on-line purchases, or visits to Web sites, information is gathered and stored. ... [S]uch information is a hot commodity and is for sale" (Buchholz and Rosenthal, 2002, p. 34).

Most of this, however, has little to do with the lives of most of the world's population. One reason for this is that at least two-thirds of the people on the planet live day-to-day based on necessity. That is, they do what is necessary to accomplish the tasks of the day, from earning a living to raising children and voting for political candidates. In my experience in the developing world, little effort is put into protecting privacy if doing so would result in making it more difficult to get done what needs to be done.

We might ask ourselves, then, whether the so-called right of privacy is a concept that results merely from a context of abundance, or leisure, and thus cannot legitimately be considered a universal. We might also ask ourselves whether this notion can really be considered a right, or necessity, when so much of the world seems to get along without it, or even whether it is grounded more in convenience than in ethics. These are the issues that this essay will explore.

What does it mean to say that people have a right to be left alone? The clearest sense of this may be that people have a right to make public what they will make public, and to keep from the public all else. We tend to think that others have no right to know what books we purchase or check out from the library, or to know the titles of the videos we rent at Blockbuster – although those of us who do these things do them *in* public. They have no right to know who we choose to vote for, or what sexual proclivities we practice, or our activities in the toilet, even though, generally speaking, everyone engages in such activities in more or less the same way

Ethics of Privacy in High versus Low Technology Societies 81

("deviant" practices notwithstanding). Having said that, if sexual activities include forcible intercourse, or dalliance with a child, people are not allowed to claim a right to engage in such activities. There are sometimes exceptions for the exceptions to the exceptions.

Much of what passes for necessary privacy rights in any society is itself the result of social convention. These rights do not inhere to the human frame as inviolable individual rights so much as they legitimize society's definitions of what is permissible and what is not. Mostly they are unquestioned within one society, even as they are absent in another. Even in the industrialized West that was the birthplace of the Enlightenment and its subsequent definitions of human rights, different societies define their mores and taboos differently. Tolerance for both male and female nudity, either in public venues or mediated representations thereof, differ. In the United States, it is given that the sexes will not mingle in public toilet facilities. In parts of Europe this is not the case. Prostitution is both illegal and legal in Western societies. Gay or lesbian relationships (and the sexual practices this implies) are both legally prohibited and acceptable. In Uganda the legislature debates whether sexual orientation itself may be a crime, while in some states of the United States, it is legal for same-sex couples to marry. In some cases acceptance of practices that would be condemned (or at least discouraged) by orthodox faiths have been trumped by moves toward secular (i.e., physiological or psychological) understandings. In other cases squeamishness alone is enough to define exposure to practices as "pornographic." Sex is porn in one context; violence is porn in another. In either case porn is not to be viewed in public. In neither case are the practices that result in the porn to be tolerated in the public sphere.

Other aspects of "fundamental" privacy rights, such as the protection of personal records of various kinds, are basic due to their instrumentality. Protection of personal records protects financial independence, the ability to obtain insurance, or to escape punishment (at least temporarily) by law enforcement. All such protections provide a measure of control over one's own destiny, but are themselves protections resulting from necessities created by societal capacities that are not shared across all societies. Americans sometimes gripe about invasions occasioned by decennial census reports, when many countries have been unable to conduct a census for 30 years or more. People in those societies do not share the American hand-wringing over exposure to government functionaries. However, they are conscious of the watchful eyes of those around them. Often they live in much closer proximity than those in industrialized and high technology countries. They have more interchange with neighbors. They have little choice in where to shop, worship, or chat. They do not have the individual freedom afforded by the automobile. Surveillance exists, although it is less organized and purposive. It however, can be equally intrusive.

Perhaps the most basic question to ask is "why privacy?" What is its value within either type of society – high or low technology? Warren and Brandeis, in their famous essay on privacy published in 1890, argued that, "The intensity and complexity of life, attendant upon advancing civilization, have rendered necessary some retreat from the world, and man, under the refining influence of culture, has become more sensitive to publicity, so that solitude and privacy have become more essential to the individual; but modern enterprise and invention have, through invasions upon his privacy, subjected him to mental pain and distress, far greater than could be inflicted by mere bodily injury."

This argument has several components worth highlighting. First, it is modernity, or progress, generally, the authors argue, that has resulted in the necessity to protect privacy. In other words, this necessity is of rather recent origin, or a recent necessity. Second, privacy has to do with a person's ability to absent himself from public life. Privacy is a retreat. Third, a "refining culture" has made people "more sensitive to publicity." People are more easily embarrassed, perhaps, or more squeamish, about what they may reveal in public, or what may be revealed about them by others – and in the context of this famous essay, it was the press (particularly photojournalists) that came in for criticism about its policies of reporting about private matters. Finally, the harm that came from any invasion of the "retreat from the world", or exposure of behavior or language that might be condemned in more refined society was that it created mental distress. The harm, in other words, was internal – it was not the change in the esteem with which others hold a person that is the fundamental problem – it is the change in the esteem with which a person holds himself.

This essay became one of the most famous legal essays in American history, establishing a tort (wrong) that was subsequently cited in state, appellate, and U.S Supreme Court decisions (Bratman, 2002, pp. 638–643). It also established the four separate wrongs that would constitute an invasion of privacy.

Privacy in High Technology Societies

The difficulty with trying to discuss privacy in high technology societies is that the issue has become a legal issue and it is easy for any discussion to quickly become an exploration of the laws that attempt to protect privacy rather than an exploration of the ethical dimensions of privacy. Also, once outside the legal realm, the issues can quickly become sociological, with attention to various methods of surveillance and their intrusive characteristics. The question, however, that I will address in this essay is more basic: is intrusive technology ethically wrong? If so, why?

To reiterate, the difficulty with assuming that intrusiveness is wrong is that so much of the world seems to live day to day in environments where intrusiveness is not an issue (despite the lack of privacy that often exists in communities), or where there is, simply speaking, no privacy at all. These societies survive, and often thrive. So we cannot assume that the need for, or the protection of, privacy is essential to the human condition, or the social need for it universal. Why, then, is it an ethical issue – unless that issue is merely a function of technology itself, or of a peculiar take on what is required in a rationally-based society in post-Enlightenment history. As Manfred Stanley (1978, p. 8) puts it, "technological norms and values can erode other norms and values."

Much concern has been raised with the rapid development of social networking, personal web pages, and the arrival of multi-media messaging systems (MMS), and especially their use by teenagers, that "sexting," posting of personal information, photos, and videos on the web, as well as potentially embarrassing comments on Facebook "walls," could harm a young person's future prospects in applying to college or seeking employment (See Ahmed, 2009; Irvine, 2007; Schrotenboer, 2006; Wright, 2009). Sexting even led to the arrest of six high school students for distributing child pornography when three girls sent nude photos of themselves to their boyfriends who saved the images, thus making the girls both "victims" and perpetrators in this crime.[1] "The issue is so toxic that a week of phone calls did not get this columnist a single response, not from the Westmoreland County DA's office, not from the school district, and not from state police or Greensburg [Pennsylvania] city police" (Seate, 2009).

From an ethical perspective the application of communications and imaging technologies in such situations is a quagmire. It is not a crime in most localities for a teen male to see a teen female naked, or even to have sex with her provided both are "under age," but it is a crime for her to take a photo of herself nude and send it to that boyfriend, or for him to do more than merely glance at it before deleting it from his phone or email. We must ask the question of whether this is an example of Stanley's contention that a new technology-based norm has replaced earlier more restrictive norms, or whether such a situation is the more "normal" ethical posture (nudity itself not being unethical) rather than the more "prudish" one that would make such behavior unethical. In these cases the tort was the distribution of child pornography, not invasion of privacy. Andrea Slane (2009) has argued, however, that it may be more appropriate to use privacy as the basis for legal action, especially when such photos are circulated maliciously, intending to humiliate or to incite bullying behavior among peers. She writes that "an additional benefit of such an offence is that it emphasizes the dignity-based privacy values which underlie the harms caused by these actions."

What is most useful about Slane's point here is her recognition that "dignity-based privacy values" precede the torts that may result from violating them. Ethics trumps law. So it is worth exploring these dignity-based privacy values apart from the legal repercussions that may follow their application.

To return to Stanley (1978, pp. 58–59): "dignity is a code word for whatever is considered to be intrinsically inviolable or 'sacred' about the human status. Dignity-talk is talk about the limits of permissible profanation of the human." Although Stanley admits that to use "dignity-talk" is to use "categories of Western discourse," as opposed to universal discourse (p. 62), he also argues that the problem or issue of human dignity must be seen as universal because the " 'destiny' of the human is everywhere considered (and institutionally treated) as a serious, not a trivial or profane, question" (p. 63). (I will consider the implications of this statement for low technology societies later.)

Stanley thinks that, in counterposition to the way that we understand animals – who we might respect for their power, beauty, or grace – that we understand humans as having capacities beyond the merely material or "'secular' (i.e., biological, physical, or other definitive) limitations" (p. 67). Of course, we should admit that admiring the "majesty" of a lion also goes beyond such definitives. Stanley's position is, however, that "the dignity of the human status, then, resides in the extraordinary human capacity for intentional creativity (and, of course, destruction). ... Human dignity as respect-worthiness rests on the sheer factuality of human potency and on the assumption that to *be* human is somehow to share in this power for agency *regardless* of one's personal desires or merit" (Stanley, 1978, pp. 67). In other words, we respect a person because of his ontological status, the mere fact of his existence as human, regardless of whether or not he has done anything worthy of respect (Fortner, 2007, p. 86). "Without dignity," Stanley concludes, "man would be man as purely biological object. He would not, in some important traditional and mythic sense, be human any longer" (Stanley, 1978, p. 86).

I find this a powerful argument, but it by no means stands without objection. The debates occurring within the field of bioethics are a case in point. The President's Council on Bioethics (appointed under former President Bush), published a series of essays on this topic in March 2008. F. Daniel Davis quotes the "American medical ethicist Ruth Macklin, who bluntly asserted four years ago that 'dignity is a useless concept in medical ethics and can be eliminated without any loss of content'" (2008, p. 19). We may read this remark as only applying to bioethical discussions, of course, but to do so would be to trivialize it unfairly. Macklin's remark could equally apply to any issue concerning the nature of humanity's ontological status – and especially to Stanley's claims. In this same volume Daniel C. Dennett (2008a), a self-described naturalist, while denying the idea of a divine foundation for a human soul, nonetheless agrees that "science and technology are encroaching on domains of life in a way that undermines human dignity," and that what is required is vigorous resistance.

Robert P. Kraynak's essay (2008a) claims that when people discuss the violation of human dignity they are referring to "the powerful moral intuition that certain practices are wrong because they treat people as sub-humans or even as non- humans" (p. 62). Taking on scientific materialism's assumption that "man is a complex machine without soul or special moral status," he claims that most who espouse such a view "ultimately find this view untenable and restore the soul in some fashion to account for morality and their own scientific activities" (p. 63). In Dennett's commentary on Kraynak's essay he admits that human beings have souls, but that they're made up of "lots of tiny robots," including cells, motor proteins, and neurotransmitter molecules (2008b, p. 84). Kraynak will have none of this. He responds to Dennett (2008): "He is a Darwinian materialist in his cosmology and metaphysics while also strongly affirming human dignity as well as a progressive brand of liberalism in his ethics and politics. Herein lies the massive contradiction of his system of thought" (pp. 90–91).

I will let the last word on this dispute rest with Alfonso Gómez-Lobo (2008). "No scientific progress is sufficient to make us abandon the rational moral conviction that it would be wrong intentionally to kill an innocent adult human being.

Ethics of Privacy in High versus Low Technology Societies 85

If we reject dualism as part of the old myths and accept the basic, commonsense conviction that we are unified human animals, then we should accept that as long as we are alive we are the same being, and if an adult is endowed with dignity then it follows that he or she also was endowed with dignity in earlier phases of his or her life, back to the beginning. I submit that this conception of the acknowledgement of dignity deserves the respect of all because in principle no human being is excluded."

Clearly there are differences of opinion as to whether or not human dignity is a viable (or useful) ethical concept, and if it is, upon the basis that it rests. If we follow Gómez-Lobo's argument, which is the one most in accord with Stanley's, then human dignity does not develop within human beings as they mature, it is there from the beginning. It inheres at the time the zygote is created by the merger of egg and sperm. It lasts until the death of the human being, regardless of his consciousness or retention of mental faculties. It is thus a radical notion, one that can only be refuted by denial of dignity per se.

If Kraynak and Gómez-Lobo are correct (which I find little reason to doubt), then dignity is the basis for humankind's ontological status (what makes us "distinctively human") and "a core concept getting at what is distinctively human, first at basic levels, where dignity is inalienable and common to us all, and further at developmental levels, where dignity can be achieved or lost, recognized or withheld" (Rolston, 2008, p. 129). However, dignity is problematic because, even if it is inherent – and recognized as such – (which is in no way guaranteed), its application in everyday life is by no means certain. A person probably has to learn the implications of this dignity much as a small child must be taught to recognize her image in a photograph or a mirror.

Most parents are probably reluctant to give their nine or ten-year-old child a 9mm Glock semi-automatic pistol for his or her birthday, especially if the child had not been trained to use such a firearm. The parents would be understandably concerned that the child might injure or kill another person. (It does not follow, of course, that even such reluctant parents will take the steps necessary to assure their children do not gain access to firearms – even those in their own home – as evidenced by the number of times teens and preteens have managed to secure them to take to school – and sometimes to slaughter classmates and teachers.) Just as parents may be unlikely providers of firearms, however, they are likely to be providers of mobile telephones. While these are not typically used as weapons, the examples of malicious use of photos shows that they can be used in this way.

The answer to this problem does not seem to lie in the passage of new laws – such as the one proposed in Ohio that would make sexting a misdemeanor rather than a felony for teens – or more attention to the ethical issues that flow from technological innovations. It may lie, however, in attending to the development of the understanding of the human self as one with the dignity outlined by Kraynak, Gómez-Lobo, and Stanley. Parents and teachers may try to teach the "golden rule," and use it as the basis for fostering understanding or benign treatment of others, but by the time children begin puberty, hormones overwhelm all.

A preteen may not understand the vulnerability she opens up with sexting, or how this vulnerability may be exploited to deny her dignity in schools full of competitive sexual urges, but attending to the nature of the "self," its needs, tenuous identity creation, and vulnerability to criticism and exploitation, seems more responsive to existential conditions than the more abstract attention to the ethical use of technology. Admittedly, however, there are no guaranteed solutions.

Communication always entails an element of risk if trust is to be achieved between people. As the old aphorism puts it, "nothing ventured, nothing gained." But risk, by definition, does not always pay off. Young people need to understand risk assessment as it relates to their fragile identities and human dignity.

This attention to the ethics of risk-taking does not merely apply to this single phenomenon of sexting, or even to the wider environment of social networking. Using any technology can have implications for self-definition and understanding. Young people distinguish, for instance, between "skaters" and "skateboarders," each with a distinct identity (and websites to match). Young people also define themselves by the contents of their iPods, becoming "Goths," "Punks," or "thugs/gangstas," depending on their choices (see Connell and Gibson, 2004; McCarthy, Hudak, Miklaucic and Saukko, 1999; Roe, 1999). Even video games, whether played in arcades or on home systems, can influence a person's self understanding, particularly since they rely on immersive simulations with alternative symbolic constructs allowing the "gamer" to take on alternative persona rather than merely engaging with a narrative of someone else's story (Frasca, 2003). One of the most successful computer simulation games, which actually invited gamers to violate set narratives, and has been heavily criticized for its violent content, is Grand Theft Auto, now in its fourth incarnation and second iteration in three-dimensional cyberspace (See Bailey, 2006; Higgin, 2006).

The more risks are taken in interpersonal communication or in the use of the means of technological mediation for communication – such as using social networking sites or SMS – the more questions of ethics – of both the original connection and its potential downstream results – are brought into play. It is not the technology itself that raises ethical issues, but the uses made of the technology for connecting or sharing that it enables to occur. The difficulty for teens using such means of connection is that often considerations other than rational evaluations of potential uses or repercussions are paramount. (This can also be the case for post-teens, of course, but they are generally supposed to know better in the societies within which they connect.) Developing interpersonal relationships, the need to for acceptance, developing romances, expectations of peer groups, rebellion against parental control, and so on, are often more significant to teens developing their identities than is the case for postteen individuals. Risk-taking, as necessary as it is in the communication process that leads to deeper connections and long-term relationships, is greatly facilitated by new technological means, some of which have the ability to "teach" risky behavior – at least virtually-speaking.

All societies have minimum ages at which people can engage in certain activities. There are minimum ages for obtaining a driver's license, ordering an alcoholic beverage, voting, or enlisting in the military, for instance. These ages vary from society to society and, even within societies, are usually not the same "magic" age. Each of these activities is seen as problematic for both the individual concerned and the society at large. Maturity is required so age restrictions apply.

In this restrictive world it would be unethical to allow a young person to possibly injure another through reckless behavior in a car, with a weapon, through drunkenness, or from inadequate civic indoctrination. Societies are not willing to run the risk that a young driver might take a life through inexperience behind the wheel of a car before he or she has developed the maturity necessary to understand the moral implications of a license. Similarly, it is unethical to ask a young person to shoulder a rifle and possibly take a life before he or she is "ready" to do so, that is, to understand morally what purposely taking a life might mean psychologically. As odd as it might sound, allowing young people access to communications technologies before they are able to cope with the moral implications of using them may fall into this same category.

The ethical issue then becomes that of whether it is right for society not to restrict access, or use, of technology in a way that could result in lifelong damage to identity, self-esteem, education or job prospects, marriage opportunities and the like. Before these technologies were widely deployed and put to use by young people (who often lead the way when it comes to their use), youthful indiscretions or peccadilloes could be conveniently forgotten (except, perhaps, by parents). There were even laws that prevented crimes committed by juveniles to be carried forward into adult lives. But the ability to communicate, however one chooses to do so, and about whatever topic, or using whatever images, one chooses to use in that communication, is not seen as an obvious candidate for restriction.

In some places there are explicit or implicit guarantees that no restrictions on communication are legitimate (such as assumptions about guarantees within the US First Amendment guaranteeing free speech despite the many cases where such rights have been abridged). In many societies without such guarantees, the expectations of such documents as the Universal Declaration of Human Rights, Article 19 of which declares that "Everyone has the right to freedom of opinion and expression; this right includes freedom to hold opinions without interference and to seek, receive and impart information and idea through any media and regardless of frontiers." Two other articles of this Declaration, however, demonstrate how problematic this right can be. Article 1 declares that "All human beings are born free and equal in dignity and rights." Article 12 declares that "No one shall be subjected to arbitrary interference with his privacy, family, home or correspondence, nor to attacks upon his honour and reputation. Everyone has the right to the protection of the law against such interference or attacks."

What a tangled web we weave. This Universal Declaration obliges states to protect persons from attacks upon honor and reputation to preserve the universal dignity and rights of all human beings. Does this call for restrictions to be placed upon young people who may damage their own rights and dignity as a result of postings using communications technologies that themselves carry the kernel of such damage? Is this "arbitrary interference" with privacy or inappropriate restriction of the right of free expression? What is the most "universal" of these universal rights? When might they legitimately and ethically be abridged in the interests of privacy? This Declaration was signed in 1948, long before communications technologies had developed to the extent that they, which at one time might have enhanced Article 19 alone, became concurrently a threat to Articles 1 and 12.

Privacy in Low Technology Countries

What of Stanley's comment that the " 'destiny' of the human is everywhere considered (and institutionally treated) as a serious, not a trivial or profane, question" (quoted earlier)? Is it true? In the main, I would argue that it's not. We have experienced, or heard about, many examples of where human destiny is – at least for some people – treated as a trivial matter. The Nazis appeared to think of the destiny of the Jews as trivial – not really worth troubling oneself about. The same appears to have been the case for the Turks' treatment of the Armenians, the radical Hutus' treatment of Tutsis and moderate Hutus, Pol Pot's regime's treatment of "intellectuals," the Serbs' treatment of Bosnians and Kosovars, Saddam Hussein's treatment of the Kurds, Israel's treatment of Palestinians, or Palestinians' treatment of Israelis, Bin Laden's treatment of the victims in the World Trade Center, and so on. In most of these cases the victims were dehumanized (or trivialized) so that they could be slaughtered (see Fortner, 2006, 2008). In other cases, they were simply "collateral damage," casualties occasioned by a wider conflict. In no case, at least to my mind, were they treated seriously.

One of the legacies of colonialism in many parts of the world has to be at least some of the continuing conflicts within countries. For instance, although the East Timorese speak virtually the same language as the West Timorese (those in Indonesia) and share culture with them, their *Weltanschauung* developed under Portuguese rule was quite different from that developed under Dutch rule. Vietnam is full of quite different tribal groups, as is most of sub-Saharan Africa (see Broche-Due, 2000). Tito's cobbled-together Yugoslavia is another. The South African situation is perhaps the most egregious example of "strange bedfellows." In these or similar circumstances it can often be difficult to see the "other" as part of one's responsibility to protect. People often restrict – especially in situations of deprivation that do not seem to be universally shared – their concerns for the other to more manageable proportions – family, clan, community or tribe.

Human dignity as a universal ethical concern in such circumstances can easily be ignored or forgotten. Perhaps it should not be, but that is the truth of it. "When individuals feel their particular needs and opinions are not being recognized or their opportunity to exercise their basic capabilities is being denied, they experience humiliation and anger and often resort to covert or open acts of rebellion to demand recognition, or in other words, they counter unsociable treatment with more of the same" (Engster, nd p. 29). In addition the lure of wealth through the

Ethics of Privacy in High versus Low Technology Societies 89

exploitation of others can be a powerful incentive for demeaning others through sexual exploitation, slavery, servitude or creating child soldiers, with many such practices rampant in Africa and southeast Asia (see Ariyo, 2001). In South Africa the necessity for many married men and married couples to migrate to major centers such as Johannesburg to find work has meant that what were once men-only hostels have gradually become "integrated." "The reality of physical space constraints in the hostel environment places a lot of strain on the marital relationship. Spouses are in some cases unable to discuss private matters without being overheard by the other occupants of the hostel room. Couples are furthermore compelled to have sexual intercourse in rooms filled with other people due to the fact that privacy is in most cases non-existent" (Smit, 2001).

In many countries of Africa and Asia (especially those with significant traditional religion or Muslim populations) polygamy is still practiced. This form of marriage also raises significant privacy issues in these contexts, particularly for women who may have to "share" a husband with women who she does not know. Although in some cases different wives do know and assist one another, in many cases (one-third of cases in field research I conducted in East Africa in 2007) the wives have never met one another. In an age and area where HIV/AIDS is a significant concern, where medical facilities are often scarce, and families often live on the edge of starvation (with polygamous families more prone to this condition), the inability to control the sexual behavior of a spouse inextricably demeans the dignity of a woman, mocks any concern for individual privacy for intimacy, and limits the recourse she may have to know whether she is infected or how to plan for her children's future.[2] In Indonesia, although economic conditions were not as severe, the same situation prevailed in the results of fieldwork conducted in 2008. In South Africa the HIV/AIDS epidemic led to conflict "between the right to privacy and the right to information. It is generally accepted that HIV status is a private matter. … In the administration of justice a conflict may emerge involving the relation between the right to privacy and the right to information, and the security of a person and the health risk of others (e.g., health workers)" (Vorster, 2003).

Housing is also an issue in many parts of the low technology world (see Konadu-Agyemang, 2001, especially chapter 2). Families often live in cramped quarters, whether in urban or rural environments, and many rooms not meant for habitation have been converted to dwellings due to the rapid population increases in some urban centers (see Jacobsen, Khan, and Alexander, 2002; Last, 2008). Anyone who has seen the films *The Constant Gardner*, that showed the slums of Nairobi, or *Slum Dog Millionaire*, portraying the slums of Mumbai, can have some appreciation of the privacy issues and other difficulties faced by families in such circumstances.

Working on an ethnography of life in internally displaced persons (IDP) camps in northern Uganda in 2004, I had the opportunity to hear from people themselves what their lives were like. In one urban camp, on the grounds of a former starch factory in Lira that had been destroyed by Idi Amin's rebel forces, one of the camp leaders told me that rape was a major issue in the camp, usually within the younger age groups. When visiting the interior of the plant in the company of a member of Parliament, I could see why rape was an issue. There was no privacy to speak of. Families had staked out small areas of the plant in and around the rusted machinery to live, cooking on charcoal fires inside the building itself (thus creating the danger of carbon monoxide poisoning). There was no light in the building, so it was in a state of perpetual gloom, with odd shadows cast from cooking fires. No family had much more than 100 square feet of space to itself. Another older woman who was raising 11 children (eight of them her own), lived on a verandah of another building without any privacy at all. Even those who had their own tukels (mud and straw thatched houses) were living in much closer proximity to one another than would typically be the case in a normal village. Often the thatch from one house would touch, or even intermingle, with the thatch of its neighboring dwelling. All cooking in the areas of the camps was done outdoors. People bathed in "bath shelters" and used "toilet shelters," both were round unroofed woven structures about four feet in diameter that were shared among several tukels. The toilet shelters had a pit while the bath shelters had clay floors. Both were situated in public areas of the camp for easy access. There was no sense of a man's or woman's home as being his or her castle. These were shelters to tolerate until people could return home – and most of the inhabitants had been in them for 20 years.

The situation is little better in the poverty-stricken areas of Asia. In the squatter settlements alongside the rebuilding "Smokey Mountain" in Manila, although houses are constructed of concrete, often they are no larger than 150 square feet, they house as many as twelve people, are patched with cardboard or splintered plywood, and people can see from the inside of one home to another. Bathing is often done in the street and toilets are communal. In areas of the terraced rice paddies, although the houses are further apart, the lack of everyday privacy is also evident, with cooking, bathing, and toilet activities occurring out of doors or in small shelters. People share communal life whether they are comfortable with it or not, and the necessities of everyday life dictate that they have little choice in the matter.

Still another intrusive characteristic of life in low technology environments is the necessity to seek help from others – family members, local political or tribal leaders, NGOs – to deal with problems that individuals have no ability to solve themselves. In research I have conducted in several countries in Africa and Asia, 80% or more of people said they did have problems they could not solve themselves. In addition to consulting spouses, parents, or siblings on these issues (presumably keeping disclosure more private), they also reported consulting with best friends, religious leaders, chiefs or elders, clan leaders, other friends and teachers. All of these consultations would require a willingness to give up at least some measure of privacy to seek assistance. They consulted with these people on both personal and family matters. Many even reported discussing the most important issues of their lives with neighbors.

Such decisions to consult are necessary, I suspect, when so little professional help with children's sickness or death (over 43% of Africans interviewed said they had lost at least one child), financial needs (including payment of school fees), personal health and medical issues, family conflict, and hunger. In such cases privacy matters far less than survival.

In terms of the use of technology, too, privacy is far less important. Mobile telephones are routinely shared in families and with friends. Much radio listening or television viewing is done in group settings. Many older Filipinos and Indonesians interviewed in 2009 said they depended on children or even grand-children to stay connected with distant family members, as the younger genera-tions understood the use of telephones far better than they did. This reminded me of my own experience as a sponsor of a Lao family in Iowa in the early 1980s. Since the parents had difficulty learning English, they always needed a translator handy. Gradually their own children became the translator. When it fell to me to discuss birth control with the parents – at the insistence of other members of the sponsoring committee – I discovered that the parents wanted to use their 11-year-old daughter as the translator. Clearly they did not see the privacy issues in the same context as I did.

The Universality of Privacy

All attempts to justify the existence of a right to privacy revolve around the "fact" that the desire for privacy is an innate aspect of human nature. For that reason, many have found that the most productive and credible way of justifying privacy is as a natural right aspect of human dignity (Winch, 1996, p. 198).

Given the different privacy issues that apply in high versus low technology coun-tries, it is a fair question to ask whether Winch is right in thinking that a "desire for privacy is an innate aspect of human nature." Of course such an abstract claim is difficult to affirm or deny. Perhaps the desire is there. The reality, however, often is not. However, as this essay has explored, there are different reasons for the lack of privacy. Some intrusions are the result of circumstances. They are likely to continue until circumstances change. Some are self-inflicted. This may be due to immaturity, hormonally-overwhelmed common sense, simple desire, or failure to rationally consider possible consequences of taking particular actions. There are, of course, the intrusions on privacy occasioned by government actions, usually justified under its police powers to stop crime or protect national security. There are likewise those of corporate interests' intent on mining information for commercial gain. Some breaches of privacy, in either high or low technology societies are likely to result, too, from overwhelming curiosity – the basis of many intrusions by paparazzi. This can also occur anytime someone peeks in a window, too.

If Winch is right, we should be able to see some common threads in both types of societies, regardless of their enormous contextual differences. The problem emerges about what assumptions should be made about the rationale for privacy itself. As the introduction suggested, the Western philosophical tradition of the post-Enlightenment period informs most discussion about privacy, although its applicability in low technology societies is suspect. Kwame Anthony Appiah (2005) points out another difficulty, too. He argues that there are two rival "pictures" of individuality in Western thinking. Since it is the privacy of the individual that is at issue, it is worth highlighting these two pictures.

The first picture is the romantic one: it assumes that individuality is present at birth and all that a person needs do is discover his *authentic* self. This is the perspective informed by the Judeo-Christian take on the creation of humankind. The second picture is the existential one: it assumes that people construct their individuality *ex nihilo*, from nothing (Appiah, 2005, p. 17). Basing his analysis on the works of John Stuart Mill and Charles Taylor, Appiah denies the validity of both of these pictures. He argues (p. 20) that "an identity is always articulated through concepts (and practices) made available to you by religion, society, school, and state, mediated by family, peers, friends. ... It follows that the self whose choices liberalism celebrates is not a presocial thing – not some authentic inner essence independent of the human world into which we have grown – but rather the product of our interaction from our earliest years with others. As a result, individuality presupposes sociability, not just a grudging respect for the individuality of others."

The question is – having presupposed a society of liberalism here – whether this analysis would equally apply to both high and low technology societies (or at least those societies that are not part of the liberal tradition). If it does, then the real issue is the nature of the dialogic context (Taylor's formulation) within which people construct their individual identities (or selves). Clearly the nature of the dialog that occurs within low technology societies is quite different than that which occurs in the high technology ones. The issue, then, is how the dialog that occurs within each context assists or retards the development of the self and thus privacy as a moral dimension of self-construction. Of course, the social ethics of privacy that are part of the context within which people develop their moral postures on privacy.

While Appiah's primary concern in his work (2005) has to do with the development of identity and individuality in counter-distinction to others, including the state, some of what he has to say is useful as a way to get into the ethics of privacy, particularly when intrusion is self-induced. According to Appiah (p. 21), people draw on the models of individuals available in their society to construct their identities. They do this (p. 23) by constructing narrative arcs through which they make sense of their experiences and responses to those experiences. This self-development, involving creative responses to social contexts, "puts identity at the heart of human life" (p. 26).

Any identity, however, has to be created within a social context in which other individual identities also function. This means that any identity constructed is both an affirmation of the constructed self and a repudiation of others' constructs – in whole or in part. So there is always the question about legitimate choices – could an individual make a choice in the construction of his identity that would result in harm to another's identity or choices in his construction? And what would be the role, then, of the state (in Mill's and Appiah's analysis) or of tribe, clan, and community (in this analysis)?

Appiah does argue that governments often do provide public goods (such as education). It is not enough merely to say that such education is a parental responsibility

Ethics of Privacy in High versus Low Technology Societies 93

with no role for the state. He asks, "suppose they won't or can't? Shouldn't society step in, in the name of individuality, to insist that children be prepared for life as free adults?" (p. 29) We might ask if his response – the necessity for literacy, for knowledge of language, the ability to assess arguments and interpret traditions – might not also usefully include the technological literacy and moral foundations to understand the consequences of employing the means of communication to construct virtual identities on social networking sites? Whose responsibility is it? A person harming him or herself is, in most cases, not harmful to others. A brother might be embarrassed by his sister's posting, or parents by a child's, but more usually the harm that accrues from use of technology is to the individual him or herself. Does this mean that society has no stake in helping these individuals avoid such harms?

If we answer this question affirmatively, then the social ethics of identity construction, the self, and privacy have been delineated: you are on your own. Is such a posture defensible within high technology societies, many of which are far more corporate in sharing responsibility than the more individualistically-oriented United States? Yet, even in the United States, some states have declared that parents are responsible for the crimes of their children. They can be prosecuted if children do not attend school regularly, or damage another's property. Although the doctrine of *en loco parentis* has largely been abandoned in American education, the ever-present threat of lawsuits for negligence are always at the ready. The United States is not always as individualistic as its rhetoric suggests.

In corporatively-oriented societies – encompassing many communities in low technology countries – the social ethics that delimit privacy must function within a context of scarcity – not merely material scarcity but what we might call psychic scarcity. This type of scarcity emerges in contexts within which individuals have delimited choices created by material scarcity, social organization to respond thereto, and systems of inclusion/exclusion that limits responsibility for others to a manageable level. This seems to be one function of extended family connections, clans and tribes, among others. The system both limits the possibilities for personal individuation and assures a more congruous self within the existing social context, and establishes clear responsibilities for care. People do not always follow the social expectations, of course, but everyone seems to know what they are. Scarcity has so far prevented the privacy problems of high technology societies, and in the limited amount of access currently available in these societies, the social constraints (one might even say social control implicitly exercised) have so far been effective. However, they have also failed to solve the issues within the societies that have made the concept of privacy far more problematic than they are, at least foundationally, in high technology contexts.

It is thus difficult to argue that there is a universal right to privacy, even if there is a universal "desire." We also have to admit that even the "desire" would not be defined universally across different societies separated by the so-called "digital divide."

What does seem applicable in these disparate cases, insofar as it relates to privacy, is the developing moral consensus that responsibility for one another's welfare is a legitimate concern. Charles Taylor (1991, p. 55), responding to individualistically-oriented high technology societies, says that what has emerged there is a "culture of narcissism," that is defined by its outlook "that makes self-fulfillment the major value in life and that seems to recognize few external moral demands or serious commitments to others."

This is the context for what we might call an atomistic privacy ethic – and it's every man/woman for him/herself. This is the perspective taken – and applauded by postmodern ethics as explained by Zygmunt Bauman (1993). As no universal ethical code has as yet been devised, and because modernism has demonstrated the inherent contradictions in trying to respond in nonambiguous ethical ways (thus creating what he calls an 'aporetic' situation (p. 8), he makes seven claims to justify this post-modern position. These are (1) humans are morally ambivalent; (2) moral phenomena are inherently "nonrational"; (3) morality is incurably aporetic (is based on an unresolvable conflict); (4) morality is nonuniversalizable; (5) morality (moral choice) is irrational; (6) moral responsibility is the first reality of the self; and (7) "ethical codes… are plagued with relativism, that plague being but a reflection or a sediment of tribal parochialism of institutional powers that usurp ethical authority" (pp. 10–14, quotation on p. 14).

This is descriptive of the modern human condition and has some heuristic value in establishing the current condition of high technology societies – perhaps even to a degree low technology ones – but it posits a human condition that is too atomistic to be credible. Bauman says, for instance (1993, p. 20), that "we miss responsibility badly when it is denied to us, but once we get it back it feels like a burden too heavy to carry alone. And so now we miss what we resented before: an authority stronger than us, one which we can trust or must obey, one which can vouch for the propriety of our choices, and thus, at least, share some of our 'excessive' responsibility. Without it, we may feel lonely, abandoned, helpless. … In so many situations in which the choice of what to do is ours and apparently ours alone, we look in vain for the firm and trusty rules which may reassure us that once we followed them, we could be sure to be in the right."

This analysis is both fatalistic (and thus despairing) and excessive. Although Bauman's rejection of codes and imperatives (or post-Kantian ethics) is understandable given the postmodern emphasis on the value and necessity of individual interpretation – and thus responsibility – his claims assume too much. People as a matter of practice group themselves and take responsibility for one another. Even as developing teens this occurs (with many groups mentioned earlier in this essay) and this is in high technology societies. In low technology societies people are often utterly dependent on one another for survival or for some vestige of communal happiness. However, in neither case do they fully take responsibility for the other (which Bauman complains can lead to the annihilation of the autonomy of the other, to domination and oppression, p. 11).

In the main, people do the best they can. Sometimes they fail in determining the right thing for themselves and for others. Sometimes everyone breathes a sigh of relief. Sometimes, "all hell breaks loose." These are realities. People need perspectives, if not rules or universals, so that they have some basis to choose for themselves, or advise others. As Charles Taylor explains (1991), for each individual human being

Ethics of Privacy in High versus Low Technology Societies   95

to be what Bauman proposes (and which Taylor defines as "authenticity"), he must be engaged with others in dialog (p. 33). It is only by comparing oneself with others that a person can know what is truly original or unique about himself (see p. 34).

Bauman's despair that an individual will see-saw between taking responsibility himself and then throwing it on his community, with neither option being fully satisfying, is unnecessary. People do, as Taylor suggests, live in communities. They are engaged in conversation both internally (struggling perhaps with what they see as the social ethics of their community) and externally, partly with those in author-ity and partly with those with whom they have chosen to congregate in the con-struction of their own selves. This dialogical relationship applies both to the low technology context, where most external dialog occurs face-to-face, and to the high technology context where dialog increasingly happens via SMS, Twitter, Facebook postings and wall writings, as well as by mediated and unmediated (F2F) conversa-tion. It is through this process that people learn, but it is also through this process that they can damage the very self that they are in the process of constructing. It is here then that they need community, both those who can point out the folly of posting oneself nude (or flaming, mocking, or commenting inappropriately) because once in cyberspace always in cyberspace, and those who can offer advice on the reasons that such activities might backfire within a peer context of one sort or another. Although this approach to ethics can be unsatisfying or even fail to prevent activities that are destructive to self, relationship, or communal life, it is the best that social ethics can offer. Atomistic ethics is no substitute for the community that gathers around an individual to assist them in moral development.

Notes

1 In another case a 14 year old girl was arrested for possessing and distributing child por-nography because she posted 30 nude photos of herself on her MySpace page (NCAC, 2009).
2 Married women in Africa may do without the protection of condoms either because they do not control the sexual encounter itself or because they see the practices of clinics where they could go for contraceptives to be privacy-invasive (see Caldwell and Caldwell, 2002).

References

Ahmed, M. (2009) Teen 'sexting' craze leading to child porn arrests in US, http://technology.timesonline.co.uk/tol/news/tech_and_web/article5516511.ece (accessed June 21, 2010).
Alderman, E. and Kennedy, C. (1995) *The Right to Privacy*, Alfred A. Knopf, New York.
Appiah, K.A. (2005) *The Ethics of Identity*, Princeton University Press, Princeton, NJ.
Ariyo, D. (2001) The future lost: The economic and social consequences of child abuse in Africa. *Africa Economic Analysis*, www.afbis.com/analysis/child_abuse.htm (accessed June 21, 2010).

Bailey, W.R. (2006) Inviting subversion: Metalepses and tmesis in rockstar games' grand theft auto series, in *The Meaning and Culture of Grand Theft Auto*, (ed. N. Garrelts), McFarland & Company, Inc., New York, pp. 210–225.

Bauman, Z. (1993) *Post-Modern Ethics*. Oxford, UK: Blackwell.

Bratman, B. (2002) Brandeis and Warren's "The Right to Privacy and the Birth of the Right to Privacy." University of Pittsburgh Legal Studies Research Paper, *Tennessee Law Review*, 69, 623–651

Broche-Due, V. (2000) *A Proper Cultivation of Peoples: The Colonial Reconfiguration of Pastoral Tribes and Places in Kenya*, Nordic Africa Institute, Uppsala.

Buchholz, R.A. and Rosenthal, S.B. (2002) Internet privacy: Individual rights and the common good. *SAM Advanced Management Journal*, 67 (1), 34ff.

Caldwell, J.C., and Caldwell, Pt. (2002) Is integration the answer for Africa? *International Family Planning Perspectives*, 28, available on subscription at: www.questia.com.

Connell, J., and Gibson, C. (2004) World music: Deterritorializing place and identity. *Progress in Human Geography*, 28, 342–361.

Davis, F.D. (2008) Human dignity and respect for persons: A historical perspective on public bioethics. *Human Dignity and Bioethics: Essays Commissioned by the President's Council on Bioethics*, Washington, DC, pp. 19–36, www.bioethics.gov (last accessed August 31, 2009).

Dennett, D.C. (2008a) Commentary on Kraynak. *Human Dignity and Bioethics: Essays Commissioned by the President's Council on Bioethics*. Washington, DC, pp. 84–88, www.bioethics.gov (last accessed August 31, 2009).

Dennett, D.C. (2008b) How to protect human dignity from science. *Human Dignity and Bioethics: Essays Commissioned by the President's Council on Bioethics*. Washington, DC, pp. 39–60, www.bioethics.gov (last accessed August 31, 2009).

Engster, D. (nd) Can care ethics be institutionalized: Toward a caring natural law theory. www.csus.edu/ORG/WPSA/pisigmaalphaaward.pdf (accessed June 21, 2010).

Fortner, R.S. (2006) Markers of evil: The Identification and prevention of genocide and ethnic cleansing. *International Journal of Interdisciplinary Social Sciences*, 1 (2), 149–157.

Fortner, R.S. (2007) *Communication, Media, and Identity: A Christian Theory of Communication*, Rowman & Littlefield, New York.

Fortner, R.S. (2008) The media in evil circumstances, in *The Handbook of Mass Media Ethics*. (eds. L. Wilkins and C.G. Christians), Lawrence Erlbaum, Mahwah, NJ, pp. 340–352.

Frasca, G. (2003) Simulation versus narrative: Introduction to ludology, in *Video/Game/Theory*. Routledge, New York www.ludology.org/aarticles/VCT_final.pdf (last accessed September 1, 2009).

Gómez-Lobo, A. (2008) Commentary on Dennett. *Human Dignity and Bioethics: Essays Commissioned by the President's Council on Bioethics*. Washington, DC, pp. 95–98.

Higgin, T. (2006) Play-Fighting: Understanding Violence in Grand Theft Auto III, in *The Meaning and Culture of Grand Theft Auto*, (ed. N. Garrelts), McFarland & Company, Inc., New York, pp. 70–87.

Irvine, M. (2007) Web of embarrassment, *The Ledger*, January 1, FL, Lakeland, www.theledger.com/article/20070101/NEWS/701010311?Title=Web-of-Embarrassment (accessed June 21, 2010).

Jacobsen, K., Khan, S.H., and Alexander, A. (2002) Building a foundation: Poverty development, and housing in Pakistan. *Harvard International Review*, 23, available on subscription at: www.questia.com.

Konadu-Agyemang, K. (2001) *The Political Economy of Housing and Urban Development in Africa: Ghana's Experience from Colonial Times to 1998*. Praeger, Westport, CT.

Kraynak, Robert P. (2008a) Human dignity and the mystery of the human soul. *Human Dignity and Bioethics: Essays Commissioned by the President's Council on Bioethics.* Washington, DC, pp. 61–82, www.bioethics.gov (last accessed August 31, 2009). Kraynak, Robert P. (2008b) Commentary on Dennett. *Human Dignity and Bioethics: Essays Commissioned by the President's Council on Bioethics,* Washington, DC, pp. 89–94, www.bioethics.gov (last accessed August 31, 2009).

Last, M. (2008) The search for security in Muslim Northern Nigeria. *Africa,* 78 available on subscription at: www.questia.com.

McCarthy, C., Hudak, G., Miklaucic, S. *et al.* (eds) (1999) *Sound Identities: Popular Music and the Cultural Politics of Education,* Peter Lang, New York.

NCAC (2009) National Coalition against Censorship. Sexting Roundup: The Anxiety Surrounding Teens Sharing Naked Pictures of themselves Continues to Make News. Ncacblog.wordpress.com/2009/04/01/sexting-roundup-the-anxiety-surrounding-teens-sharing-naked-photos-of-themselves-continues-to-make-news/ (last accessed August 31, 2009).

Roe, K. (1999) Music and Identity among European Youth. *Soundscapes,* (2), www.icce.rug.nl/`soundscapes/DATABASES/MIE/Part2_chapter03.shtml (last accessed August 31, 2009).

Rolston, Holmes III. (2008) Human uniqueness and human dignity: Persons in nature and the nature of persons. *Human Dignity and Bioethics: Essays Commissioned by the President's Council on Bioethics,* Washington, DC, pp. 129–153, www.bioethics.gov (last accessed August 31, 2009).

Schrotenboer, B. (2006, May 24) College athletes caught in tangled web. *San Diego Union-Tribune,* www.thefire.org/article/7068.html (accessed June 21, 2010).

Seate, M. (2009) Sexting arrests provide warning, February 3, www.pittsburghlive.com/x/pittsburghtrib/opinion/columnists/seate/s_609935.html?source=rss&feed=7 (accessed June 21, 2010).

Slane, A. (2009) Sexting, teens and a proposed offence of invasion of privacy, March 16, www.iposgoode.ca/2009/03/sexting-teens-and-a-proposed-offence-of-invasion-of-privacy/ (accessed June 21, 2010).

Smit, R. (2001) The impact of labor migration on African Families in South Africa: Yesterday and today, *Journal of Comparative Family Studies,* 32, available on subscription at: www.questia.com.

Stanley, M. (1978) *The Technological Conscience: Survival and Dignity in an Age of Expertise,* The Free Press, New York.

Taylor, C. (1991) *The Ethics of Authenticity,* Harvard University Press, Cambridge, MA.

Vorster, J. M. (2003) HIV/AIDS and Human Rights. *The Ecumenical Review,* 55, available on subscription at: www.questia.com.

Warren, S., and Brandeis, L.A. (1890) The right to privacy, *Harvard Law Review,* 4 (5), 193.

Winch, S.R. (1996) Moral justifications for privacy and intimacy. *Journal of Mass Media Ethics,* 11, 197–209.

Wright, G. (2009) Twitter with care: Web 2.0 usage offers few second chances, July 30, www.shrm.org/hrdisciplines/technology/Articles/Pages/TwitterCarefully.aspx (accessed June 21, 2010).

6

Social Responsibility Theory and Media Monopolies

P. Mark Fackler

Social responsibility of the media is the ethical claim that the technologies of information, advertising, and entertainment which now constitute a nearly worldwide global matrix do not operate as ends in themselves, but as tools in the development of civil society whereby people find identity, knowledge, and enrichment. The social responsibility theory of media creates a moral trajectory toward human prosperity and communal transformation, challenging "free market" notions of maximum profit or "controlled culture" notions of state hegemony.

The virtues associated with social responsibility of media may seem an entirely idealistic and impractical overlay to work normally done by writers, producers, and other specialists who comprise the media professions. Finding a credible source or winning page placement are far more measurable objectives for busy professionals than those which capture the ideals of social responsibility. Media professionals who harbor ideals at all may find a term such as "social responsibility" too obscure to guide the daily discipline of the craft. For some, particularly academics, the notion of responsible media may be regarded as a mask for neoliberal profit-making with a courtesy bow to moral rhetoric, much like other public agencies whose real work mocks the terms and slogans generated to inject moralistic judgment into craft and business. Nevertheless, social responsibility of the media is an active, poignant term used to create alternative moral appeals to press-public theories founded on Enlightenment individualism and authoritarian systems of all kinds.

Media professionals today confront social responsibility in a wide range of workers' associations, each with its code of conduct. Some media companies articulate a credible social mission, a public service calling, as it were. Indeed, numerous academic training programs are sustained by a vision for social healing and peaceful change. Understandably, "social responsibility" takes many forms as its core concepts filter through complex processes of symbol-making for mass audiences. The effort to clarify the meaning of

The Handbook of Global Communication and Media Ethics, First Edition. Edited by Robert S. Fortner and P. Mark Fackler.
© 2011 Blackwell Publishing Ltd. Published 2011 by Blackwell Publishing Ltd.

Social Responsibility Theory and Media Monopolies 99

social responsibility and articulate professional practices which achieve its mandates is frustrated by global monopolization in media industries and by legal systems world-wide which have failed to achieve necessary protections for dissent against political power and for protection of creative process. Media can hardly be expected to operate in a manner typified by concern for human prosperity if owners and employers remain ensconced in the profit mandate or beholden to a regime which holds every key to business success, including the keys to prison when public messages offend.

Despite these formidable obstacles, "social responsibility" remains a viable, gen-erative concept with which to examine and improve the service provided by all mass media, publically operated or privately held. "Social responsibility," against considerable pressure, asserts a fundamental commitment to the prosperity of the communal whole and a fundamental *telos* to achieve the good in its sphere of sym-bolic activity and influence.

The notion that media intended for public use or sale carry a social responsibil-ity has never been doubted. Just as agriculture carries inherent obligations to food security and education to emerging ideas, so media once established engage moral obligation. Language itself carries inherent mandates for verisimilitude and human care. "Freedom of speech" is never a license to falsify and mislead, or cre-ate unnecessary harm. Language and its public projection has always engaged moral responsibility, but to whom, and for what? In this respect, media responsi-bility has been a subset of political morality. Aristotle set the terms: *dunamis* or *arete*, take your choice. The former leads to empire, the latter to eudaemonia.[1] In media, the classical terms constitute a moral choice between service to public or exploitation of audiences for the aggrandizement of those who control symbol-making processes.

Three Stories, Three Mandates

"Tell the power story" is the mandate most frequently met in the long history of mass media. Use all means – architecture, costume, language, written records, art – to cre-ate a culture in which power is compounded for the powerful, limited to the under-class. Examples of this version (or inversion) of responsibility abound. The artisans who drafted stories of "the Greats" – Alexander, Peter, for example, – were not impartial historians sifting objective evidence. The media which kept masses in Russia subservient to the Czars, and then the Stalinist czar-alikes, were carefully planned to produce results which fortified the control of leaders and secured a future for their designates. Edward Bernays famously called this peculiar invention, public relations, the "engineering of consent."[2] Critics of the modern American press claim that the same version of responsibility is evident in "democratic" media. American czars are business leaders; America's core value is profit. Everything else is window dressing.

The "power story" version of responsible media will employ every appeal to moral sentiment in its effort to justify its prescriptive agenda. Religious life must comply (for the king is God's vice regent). Entertainment must serve power's purposes (our songs celebrate royal victories). The power story is self-referential.

Life gathers around the word of the king, a word amplified by media. The king and his agents keep the books. Using media signals submission and puts users (and media producers) in "good books" with power hierarchies organizing every detail of consciousness. Where consciousness itself has a well-managed center, people fill roles without demanding moral review. Gramsci, Hall, and many others have devoted much ink to exploring these lost voices.[3] Siebert made the case explicit in legal history.[4]

The Enlightenment challenged this model of media responsibility. At its theoretical apogee, the Enlightenment effected a transvaluation of values, resetting individual choice and conscience as the power center, while leadership hierarchies became servant to the electorate. Thereafter universal suffrage is the benchmark of democratic process, with freedom to articulate the convictions of conscience a universal corollary. Where a vote freely chosen can be cast by every member, leaders are stewards and media become the people's tool for monitoring political process.

This theoretical high-ground is easier to maintain in books about media than in the reality of a people's history; democracies can present precious few examples of media which genuinely and consistently served this "watchdog" function. Yet in the heroic investigations of Ida Tarbell and the summons-to-justice of William Lloyd Garrison, democrats in America can cite instances in which vigorous dissent led to turning-point social change: economic fairness, racial reconciliation. In these cases, media as servants of *dunamis* were challenged by media as channels of *arete*, and evoked the second story of media, indeed its second *telos*.

"Tell the justice story" as a model for media responsibility met "tell the power story" and, at least in the West, demolished the former's foundational beliefs. Vast stretches of the world still regard this revolution as heresy. Elements of the justice story and its fit as a media archetype will constitute much of this essay's consideration of social responsibility theory. Global expressions of the "justice story" (as opposed to media serving power elites) will be noted, yet these notations are still inadequate to the moral challenge. Much more needs to be written concerning the role of media in achieving social fairness, equity in law, human rights, and open information exchange. If justice is indeed a foundation for human prospering, there exist many untold stories of the courage to speak and duty, the telling of which would serve to inspire reform in many places today where, as Graham Greene described in *The Power and the Glory*, people have "passed into a region of abandonment."[5]

A final story, "the profit story," is the nadir of the Enlightenment's call to courageous media. Indeed, Western media critics have built academic disciplines on the premise that the justice story is a ruse for economic power, a variant of the authoritarian model described earlier. "Tell the profit story" shifts responsibility from king or electorate to markets, and as Jacques Ellul taught us, from human ballads and conflicts to the subtle, disabling force of efficiency in every sphere, wherein a surfeit of data deprives the individual of any ability to act on it.[6] News happens when tomato farmers develop an edible product two days earlier than last year's crop. Less care is good, less cost is best. Profit in some measurable form drives every interaction, from having babies to selecting circuit judges. The profit story documents a culture's responsibility to maximize benefits with consistency sufficient to provide a trajectory that predicts the future which a majority of stakeholders affirm. The profit story seeks compliance from market sectors and steers from widespread change that may upset prediction models. Its entertainment celebrates everyman's desire to find something better, whatever commodity "better" represents. Better advertising is, of course, the point of the symbolic exercise.

Because profit *per se* sounds crass or possibly inhumane, the rhetoric of the profit story must be dressed in language which speaks to emotive or other dimensions of life. These dressings skillfully done do not fool intelligent insiders (nor intend to) but provide a palliative to those not informed or not within the benefit stream. This was the plan of social/psychological engineers such as Edward Bernays, who fashioned a new information profession along lines of perceived and disguised need developed by his uncle Sigmund Freud. This skillful overlay permits powerful business interests to continue building their empires while a naive public comes to perceive the corporation as an ally in public progress. Joel Bakan has called this the new moralism, and advises that the "best business minds" recognize it as immoral.[7] Milton Friedmann cites one and only one social responsibility for all businesses: make as much money as possible for shareholders.[8] Peter Drucker warns: "If you find an executive who wants to take on social responsibilities, fire him. Fast."[9] Many mediated messages produce profit. One cannot bemoan the entire economic sphere. Some media seek profit as an end in itself, subordinating other consideration. Paul Starr's important history of the parallel development of telegraphy in the United States and the United Kingdom illustrates the point.

> Nationalization in Britain in 1870 brought to the telegraph a public-service ethos. The mandate of the Post Office was to improve service and reduce rates, and...it immediately embarked on an expansion plan to make telegraph office and hours more convenient to the public.[10]

By contract, telegraph development in the United States tended to promote private investment and monopoly. The service was available to those who most needed it to sustain business.[11]

The Hutchins Commission

Social responsibility of media emerged as a sensitized concept in the 1940s as part of a small, now obscure effort to monitor prospects of state control under the New Deal, in the 1930s until World War II. The story of the Commission's origin and irritating results (to the press and its prime sponsor Henry Luce) has been told often and in depth. The most popular telling, and the reason "social responsibility theory" has entered the parlance of academic reflection on media, is the 1956 book, an after-thought to a study now forgotten, authored by three pillars of media scholarship at the University of Illinois, and titled simply *Four Theories of the Press*. Even today, reference to the "four theories" evokes immediate recognition throughout the world, as this book has enjoyed more than a half-century of global influence. The Social Responsibility Theory, named therein, was clearly the preferred model of the authors, and still is the anchor of efforts to elaborate the mission and moral responsibility of democratic media. Reflection on the book's shortcomings and modern versions of the theory have tended to underscore, not dismiss, the commission's fundamental contributions to media-state-public accountability.[12]

The twelve commissioners who produced *A Free and Responsible Press* in 1947 were a mixed lot of thinkers and leaders, headed by the archdeacon of liberal learning, the president of the University of Chicago and codesigner of the classical curriculum espousing "the Great Conversation," Robert Maynard Hutchins. Known foremost for university leadership, Hutchins described his two great passions as "the search for standards and the search for community."[13] For the former, Hutchins focused his vision on propositions which were self-evident, necessary, immutable, and axiomatic,[14] the rhetoric of the Vienna Circle naturalists but guided by the Greeks and Romans, where indeed Hutchins would begin his search for community. Hutchins' primary group were those gathered at the table of the Great Conversation, the notables of Western Civilization and the many, Hutchins among them, who made contemporary use of their ideals. One important ideal, raised to the level of immutable truth, was the consistency of human nature throughout history and around the world. Hutchins acknowledged cultural variety, but held nonetheless to an abiding and common human nature, "the same in any time or place."[15] The needs of that common nature were described by Aristotle and applied by Hutchins: to understand reality as it is, lived by people and manifest in the natural sciences.[16] Media had no rational purpose if not to aid and promote people toward their *telos* – whole, fit to live well, conscious of the past and adaptive to a prosperous future. Hutchins' humanism fit nicely with other forms of liberal progressivism soon to be overwhelmed in the era of pointless war (Vietnam), civil rights protest, and postmodern revisionism. Hutchins and Haight-Ashbury could not long coexist.

Hutchins was chair but by no means the only voice on the Commission on Freedom of the Press. The writings of William Ernest Hocking were foundational to commission recommendations; those writings too inspired a vigorous negative reaction among media leaders when Commission recommendations were publicized in 1947. Hocking's *A Framework of Principle* shows his "wider empiricism," a critique of the scientific naturalism that reduced legitimate metaphysical claims to data-driven measurables. Democracy, he claimed, was not a product of scientific inquiry, but springs from the "ethical nature" of humankind.[17]

As antidote to the narrow empiricism which reduces ideals to chemistry and thus to claims without authority,[18] Hocking advocated a recovery of classical political theory as a wisdom-seeking discipline – a realism above positivism, as he put it, a "super-natural realism... a Realism of the Absolute."[19] Hocking wrote:

Social Responsibility Theory and Media Monopolies   103

> Democracy cannot rest its case on either the biological or the psychological human creature. Democracy is not based on what is but on what ought to be.... The bond of equality and fraternity is to be found, not in scientific measurement, but in common devotion to a goal which is beyond them all. Let me lose... their direct awareness of a divine thread in history, and the bonds of liberal union are cut at the knot.[20]

Hocking is best known for his appeal to a duty to communicate. As this duty is foremost in the human armoire, the state must give way. No law or exertion of power justifies quietude when conscience rises to add insight to the conversation. Hocking again:

> Whatever one's final philosophy, it can never be held as a purely private result: as a supposed body of truth about the living world, there is inseparable from it the impulse to knead it into the self-consciousness of the world.... All life has this self-propagating impulse.[21]

Hutchins' classical humanism and Hocking's idealism, matched with the neo-Augustinianism of Reinhold Niebuhr, gave social responsibility theory a triangulated depth that its first critics failed to observe and its advocates have largely failed to develop. Niebuhr's transition from progressive liberalism to "Christian realism" is a journey well told.[22] Suffice it here that the events of two world wars shattered for Niebuhr the myth of enlightened humanism, broke the glass ceiling of naturalism, and in Niebuhr's telling, demanded first an accounting for evil, then of restoration and redemption.[23] Media play their important role while other institutions give framework and bear witness to both the tragic brutality of history and its hopefulness. Niebuhr's vision for media arose from his subtle accounting of humankind as a finite creature of thought and matter, moral impulse and pride. Humans are creatures and creators in an open-possibility universe accountable to the beneficent divine. For Niebuhr, self-giving love and order-keeping justice were two complementary poles of the moral order, yet neither leads to the eschaton envisioned by earlier liberals. "No society, not even a democratic one, is great enough or good enough to make itself the final end of human existence,"[24] he wrote pessimistically. Love and justice are the universal moral standards, prone to twists and bends, duplicity and shallow posturing. Without these guideposts we falter for lack of moral direction. Stuck with them we realize habitual failure. It is enough to press forward, and here media play important leadership roles, while stumbling often in the moral darkness before finding the dawn once again.[25]

Other Hutchins' Commission notables warrant mention to provide historic context for this turning-point in media-state relations. Archibald MacLeish, the last surviving member (d. 1982), was Librarian of Congress during Commission proceedings, and already a poet of distinction. He emerged from service in World War I, a writing sojourn in France and Harvard law school with a strong sense that American democracy was the middle ground between mercantilism and the "monstrous oversimplification" of Marxism.[26] MacLeish's commitment to the intellectual tradition of the West and its politics of dissent and debate in America led him to see the press as an extension of that tradition, akin to his library, in which he vested the survival of culture.

> If the cultural tradition, the ancient and ever-present structure of the mind, can still be saved, it can be saved by restructuring its authority. And the authority of art and learning rests on knowledge of the arts and learning. Only by affirmation, only by exhibiting to the people the nobility and beauty of their intellectual inheritance, can that inheritance be made secure.[27]

The press would help secure this beloved democratic ideal.

Zechariah Chafee Jr. is known to every student of First Amendment law, a champion of free speech in the classical liberal tradition, and certainly also in the American democratic tradition. He was planted and rooted in New England progressivism. Chafee lived within 50 miles of the Rhode Island land cleared by Thomas Chafee in 1635. As a professor at Harvard law school, Chafee criticized the Palmer raids of 1920, and survived his "trial" at the Harvard Club in 1921 by noting that his opposition was not to the ideas of the cabal spreading Marxist notions, but to the fairness of their treatment at law. Cleared of charges of "radical sympathies" by a vote of only 6–5, Chafee's commitment to free speech intensified. Thus, at Commission proceedings, Chafee opposed the Commission's nemesis – government repression – as certainly as he did civic, nongovernment efforts to curtail speech, such as the Legion of Decency, the Hays office in Hollywood, and others. Chafee's classicism led him to hope that journalism would show its greatness not by compulsion or Freudian trickery but by leadership and intellect, by a vision of culture in which humans can thrive, learning and discerning the parameters of the common life as media spurred the open conversation.

> Compulsion… will do more harm than good as a remedy for the uncertainty that truth will prevail over error. The only direct cure for these evils [press failures] lies in the internal ideals of the enterprises.[28]

The others were a roster of mid-century academics and civil servants whose accomplishments make their Commission legacy a mere footnote to the active life. John Dickinson was a law professor whose forebear signed the Declaration of Independence. He joined the New Deal administration as assistant secretary of commerce and then assistant attorney general. A medieval scholar and professor at the University of Pennsylvania, Dickinson came to believe that mechanistic legal codes such as devised (at least attempted) by Montesquieu was an impossible dream.[29] In his era, European Fascism posed an immense threat to human rights worldwide, and Dickinson reacted, carrying his concerns into the counsel of the Hutchins Commission:

> Our American tradition is a different one than a planned society. It is a tradition which invests initiative and decision in all individuals everywhere and calls the result democracy. It puts a man's fate at the mercy of his intelligence and skill and therefore holds him entitled to an education. It expects him to develop enterprise and there throws him on his own resources to find and hold a job if he can.[30]

Social Responsibility Theory and Media Monopolies 105

Dickinson would not permit a central government to presume the role of editor/censor over democratic media.

Robert Redfield forged new ground in anthropology at the University of Chicago. He became dean of the University of Chicago's social science division (1934–1946) and joined Hutchins on several other boards. His commitment to values freely expressed in open media derived from presuppositions concerning human nature as reasonable and intuitively wise. Public media was to sharpen that wisdom with conversation and to advance reason with proliferation of usable knowledge. Democracy has no other resources, but these were sufficient.[31] Redfield urged the press to contribute to humanity's purpose, that is, to establish itself as humane.

> The end of man's existence is not cooperation. It is not even safety. It is to live up to the fullest possibilities of humanity. And man is human only as he knows the good and shares that knowing with those to whom he is, in humanity, bound.[32]

Beardsley Ruml, chairman of the Federal Reserve Bank of New York, worked in FDR's New Deal and invented, among other things, a foolproof tax collection scheme: withhold it from wages. It was the "most discussed plan ever laid before the American public."[33] That discussion, no doubt, along with his lifetime of "sitting and thinking,"[34] then speaking, contributed to his commitment to a media system as free of government intervention as possible, and as vibrant with creativity as a society could make it. He shared the optimism of the postwar generation:

> We are moving slowly toward the emancipation of the human spirit, the attainment of personal responsibility through freedom, and the recognition of the dignity and worth of each human person.[35]

George Shuster, president of Hunter College in New York, lent his influential voice to Catholic piety. He taught at Notre Dame, wrote for and edited *Commonweal*, then left when the magazine supported Franco in Spain. At Hunter, he supported the rights of students to speak against official positions of the Catholic church, and endured constituents' criticism of "radical" influence at a time when donors and churchmen were divided and suspicious of foreign influence from several fronts.[36] Shuster's mind is best understood against the mood of Catholic renewal during the 1920s and 1930s. American optimism and cultural self-confidence were declining. The denial of natural law, inalienable rights, free will, and human equality by American academicians had undercut the vision of those who had founded American democratic institutions. Catholics were more certain about progress because, in that community, progress depended on Aquinas' own optimism concerning the human search for perfection through reason, which for Aquinas survived the Edenic "fall" and is still a dependable human trait, if culture and education give it an environment

> harmonious with man's aspirations and passive to his desire for mastery... a moral culture where man was assured that as he followed the laws of nature and of nature's God, individual and social success would be his reward.[37]

Shuster appreciated the cultural contributions of antiquity, but insisted that Christianity had "stamped Greek civilization with the imprint of a new ideal,"[38] which gave value, dignity, and purpose to all, rather than the aristocratic few. Shuster's world included a sense of Kierkegaardian mystery[39] clothed in the garments of Catholic symbolism and liturgy. Truth, gradually and organically disclosed, was the responsibility of each individual to pursue, together with supportive social institutions. If ever an academic leader gave the press a high mission, it was George Shuster.

> It remains the most difficult task in the world to persuade man that he has a dignity within nature which is yet not that of nature. If all of him springs from the same matrix… why should his assumption of a greater meaningfulness be… anything more than a vain illusion?[40]

Let media be the channel which informs this most difficult task, Shuster urged his fellow commissioners, and thus helped shape, however idealistically, the social responsibility theory of the press.

Harold Lasswell, John Clark, and Charles Merriam left their marks on political science, communications theory, law, and economics. That such varied talents spoke as one voice must be credited to the wit and finesse of Hutchins himself, who lost his campaign to revolutionize undergraduate education at Chicago but won a legacy in press-state theory far beyond what he likely imagined. His biography, for instance, gives the Commission only a passing reference.[41]

Difficulties of International Application

Critics of social responsibility theory and the Four Theories tradition have noted the obvious Western perspectives that lurk everywhere in the recommendations and analysis of press-society relations. These same perspectives are the backdrop to understanding American political history. The so-called Founding Fathers were united in their distrust of monarchical power, yet how to reorganize under democratic principles following independence was by no means universally clear. One camp wanted strong central banks and legislatures, with a president empowered to lead; opponents believed that the best defense against tyranny was state power distributed locally where landowners and local elites could lead and be accountable to communities. In each camp were persistent beliefs that no one holds a moral right over another by virtue of birth (though race certainly factored in), and that voters held responsibility for choosing leaders apart from fear or favor imposed on free political choices (although gender exclusion and land ownership requirements took years to overcome). The libertarian theory of the press would lead to a public marketplace where voters' consciences could find expression. In American democracy, no one may suppress thought. The Star Chamber was out of business on this side of the ocean, the old authoritarian press model a relic of elite British stubbornness and misguided notions of inherited rights.[42]

What then of cultures which have no such antipathy to monarchial rule, where central authority is perceived neither in the mood of bureaucratic oppression (old line Communism) nor privilege (British peerage)? Yin has noted that press systems in Asia do not fit easily in Four Theories' "pigeon holes" due largely to different perceptions of state supervision and partnership in national economic growth.[43] This same partnership yielded, in Latin and African contexts, the Developmental model of the press as a fifth alternative, or as a variant, Hachten claims, of the authoritarian model. This model, however ill defined, takes as a springboard the ominous task of nation-building and the absolute requirement that all means available are to be summoned to the task. Impoverished young democracies can little afford an adversarial press. As the libertarians of the West have shown, mass communication is effective in consensus building. Little wonder that fragile independent governments would appropriate it to stabilize the base. However, the cost is high: information becomes the property of the state; media are positioned to support the state, not to challenge it, to build political consensus, not to raise alternative voices. This "guided press" may work to increase literacy, but not free access, as each sovereign state presumes its right to control international news flow and, invariably, to privilege certain ethnicities from whom trusted leadership is drawn and to whom the fruits of development (international investment, roads, schools) are directed.[44] Critics of the Four Theories found its key blindspot to be media monopolies, ownership patterns curtailing the watchdog function of the press over government (the libertarian theory's keynote) and the many-voices imperative of social responsibility theory. When social responsibility theory meets free market capitalism, or Asian leadership traditions, or African neodemocratic experimentalism, does it still offer a compelling vision for public media, a vision in which Niebuhr's call for love and justice survive alongside Hocking's appeal to the duty to speak?

The Political Economy Critique

In his brilliant history of the 1893 Columbian Exposition (World Fair) in Chicago, historian Erik Larson captures the drama of architectural pride and planning. The Fair *must*, its advocates claimed, show superior beauty to Paris's admittedly gorgeous Exposition Universelle in 1889 where, among other wonders, the Eiffel Tower was opened. In a conversation in New York, esteemed architects Richard Hunt, Charles McKim, and George Post were considering joining the planning committee whose building designs and landscapes would, they thought, be definitive for national pride and worldwide acclaim. McKim, an idealist, began the meeting "with a wandering talk," according to Larson, when his older and less idealist colleague Hunt blurted: "McKim, damn your preambles. Get down to facts."[45] This faceoff between architectural (a communicative medium itself) realist and idealist plays out in communication ethics as political economists slice through abstract theories of virtue and values, including social responsibility theory's high-minded call to public service. Dallas Smythe, Thomas Guback, Robert McChesney, Stuart Hall, and others have insisted that economic data drive theoretical progress, and those data bode ill for many of the pronouncements adorning social responsibility theory. A thorough examination of this line of research is beyond the scope of this chapter, but here we note that the capitalist press (profit-based media) invariably prioritizes its "love and justice," social service, and "watchdog function" as second to survival and profitability. Indeed, the basic mandate of the liberal-democratic press is investigation – bring to light the duplicity, chicanery, and corruption inevitable in public life, particularly in politics, where immense budgets are controlled by modest-salaried "public servants" elected by the people (whose allegiance and admiration has been bought through media "spin" and classic truth-twisting). It is cheaper for news media to do "official source stenography" than independent investigation, McChesney asserts; that cheaper choice is compelling for profit-based media.[46] Decisions are easy when priorities are clear.

Those priorities rule the "neoliberal" press; profit rules much of social life; there is no "society," only individuals "in fierce competition"; markets are infallible as the "superior way to regulate human existence."[47] Early political economists of media cited the transvaluation of values and the Marxian notion of consciousness emerging as a product of market forces. Current researchers are content to note the inexorable efficiencies of market-based media. Examples to substantiate their claims are plentiful, from local to national political coverage, to "puff" essays appearing on almost every "business" page in America. In American life, time is money. Public office seekers pay for press coverage indirectly through campaign management which engineers press coverage and fine tunes the message – always "on point." Direct costs include heavy investments in television advertisings and a large staff to handle phones and the Internet. Where such investment is made, the articulation of policies and programs in inevitably affected. Pure coverage of the type called for in social responsibility theory is heavily colored by the immense sums political power invests.

Professional journalists resist this analysis, of course, with noteworthy restatements of journalism's mission in democratic polity. Kovach and Rosensteil, who know the profession well, still maintain that

> a commitment to citizens... is the implied covenant with the people.... the notion that those who report the news are not obstructed from digging up and telling the truth – even at the expense of this owners' other financial interests – is a prerequisite [of news reporting].[48]

This freedom to speak, even if one's own economic interests hang in the balance, demonstrates how precarious is the truth-value of mass-mediated messages. The detachment from value required at every level of message production staggers the will of practical persons. The unlikelihood that integrity would ever trump hunger creates a first response of suspicion that only long-term commitment by media professionals overcomes – long-term and painful. Nelson Mandela makes the point that suffering solidifies a movement. Leaders must take the opposition's blows, if change is to be effected.[49]

Such statements are rarely taken at face value by power players in democratic cultures, critics contend.

The Communitarian Turn

The third "turn" in press theory since the era of the Four Theories is the application of communitarianism to the role and vocation of media as mediator of citizen and state. Elsewhere this author has described communitarianism as

> the social strategy which distinguishes peace-loving virtues from greed-hoarding impulses and argues for the former because human experience has shown that people prosper when tribalism and egoism give way to generosity and fair-play as first order responses.[50]

As a political philosophy, communitarianism may well have been the dominant ethos in early American life. Survival in the "New World" required cooperation, even the creation of new, amalgamated communities, for example cooperative effort of early settler and native American.

Applied to media, communitarianism became a "narrative construct that enables cultural beings to fulfill their civic tasks."[51] Media came to be seen as the center of symbolic convergence and civic dialogue, just as the human person was re-interpreted (at least in the West) as communal, that is, fundamentally identified by the relation between selves, rather than the self as ontological bedrock, and by mutuality, not as isolated persons. Christians, Ferré, and Fackler delivered in 1993 a philosophy of communication and an ethic of media based on this idea.

> To the extent that we know the communal, we understand persons.... We work from a philosophy of culture in which mutuality is the meaning center.... Universal solidarity is the normative core of the social and moral order.[52]

One of the striking features of this third initiative is its vibrant appeal to moral purpose. This is no mere descriptive picture of democratic life at the turn of the millennium. Rather, proponents of communitarianism insist its *telos*, civic transformation

> aims to liberate the citizenry, inspire acts of conscience, pierce the political fog, and enable the consciousness raising that is essential for constructing a social order through dialogue, mutually, in concert with our universal humanity.[53]

Such a lofty, nearly poetic explanation seems unlikely to attract much serious attention from media leaders, unless returned to the din and dash of story, deadline, newshole, ad sales, and market. Christians, Ferré, and Fackler make their attempt in chapter four of *Good News* where exemplars good and nefarious create poses that reflect the Niebuhrian moral couplet, love (in this chapter framed as "making covenant," inclusiveness, significance,) and justice, the grant of reasoned fairness that secures peaceful relations. The authors of *Good News*, however, are not keen to reward media which simply plays fair with readers. Rather, taking note of Hocking's call to positive duty, communitarian media, they claim, requires the "courage of moral resolve" to expose to public view "the stories that justice requires."[54] A new vision of storytelling ought to, as Hannah Arendt capably noted, transform "private experience into a shared and therefore public reality."[55]

Can these initiatives turn media from profit to service, the truth in isolated facts to the whole truth with insight, from stories of power to narratives of people-in-relation? One such effort has been public journalism, so-called for its sense that in democratic cultures, "the public" is a vital if currently forgotten concept. Trading on work by John Dewey and James Carey,[56] advocates of public journalism urged media to recapture its purpose: "to see the public into fuller existence."[57] *The Wichita Eagle* under Davis "Buzz" Merritt Jr's leadership became a national experiment in public journalism, turning a 1990 gubernatorial campaign into a "new style of election coverage aimed at strengthening that sense of connection to community" that engages citizens in a dynamic process of choosing a future together.[58] Others sound these themes without adopting the public journalism label. "A commitment to citizens… is the implied covenant with the people," noted Kovach and Rosensteil in their small classic.[59]

These initiatives, responding in large part to the failed promises of Enlightenment liberalism and especially the promise that a free press works best in unregulated markets, are not absent their critics. Any strategic partnership between government and media will necessarily compromise the neutrality of media, its capacity to produce reports on the day's events without fear or favor, critics claim. With the world spotlight so frequently on China during the summer Olympics, 2008, there was plenty to scrutinize. Western critics do not applaud forceful intimidation of journalists or, in European venues, the *fatwa* applied to producers of religious satire. Take your choice, critics say. Better to put matters of truthtelling, privacy infringement, and media offensiveness in the hands of a competent individual with full legal support for free speech, than to permit government bureaucracies – always suspicious of innovation, always cloaked in self-preserving layers of protectionism and patronage – from joining the debate on what stories air or what interpretations create our "maps of the world."[60]

Social Responsibility in the Southern Hemisphere

In the South where socialist or Marxist politics dominate, media tend toward strong state control not unlike the authoritarian or central control models described in *Four Theories*. In Zimbabwe, for example, under the regime of Robert Mugabe, state-controlled media are extensions of the ZANU-PF party's marketing bureau, which takes a rough approach to persuasion. In July 2008 a government "death list" surfaced, naming several unlicensed journalists. The final paragraph offered this chilling new threat to those operating outside the bounds of Zimbabwe's Access to Information and Protection of Privacy Act (AIPPA):

> The majority of those named on the list, although they are living in the bliss and security of the Diaspora and the anonymity of cyberspace, their family members will not be so lucky.[61]

The country's main opposition newspaper, *The Zimbabwean*, is printed in South Africa and trucked into the country. In late May 2008, following a government official blaming the paper for Mugabe's losses in March, the truck carrying a Sunday edition was hijacked and burned by eight gunmen with new AK-47 assault rifles. New and sharply higher VAT taxes and import duties – all payable in foreign currencies – have effectively cut circulation by 70%. Independent journalists are cautioned never to meet new sources in isolated locations, and to always make certain someone else knows exactly where they are. Mobile phones and emails are presumed bugged.[62] A "free press" will not emerge in places such as this until legal safeguards are approved and tested. However, ruling elites in Zimbabwe (and many other venues) claim that a controlled press best enables efficient government and is thus, ipso facto, the most socially responsible arrangement. Those who need news to advance the public interest can receive it; otherwise, what's the point. In Mugabe's case, an official adoption of Marxist ideology – to the degree that "comrade" is a common appellation has created a "narrowly defined public news sphere patronized by a small group" of party loyalists.[63]

The situation in emerging democracies is more complex. Kenya, for instance, achieved independence in 1963 but required a "second movement" in the late 1980s before multiparty elections enabled dissent from ruling elites and a press environment more robust than before.[64] During those early decades, newspapers too critical of ruling elites would be visited by police dressed as thugs, their presses ruined, offices and personnel ruffled. Some brave journalists went to prison after covering corruption. Reporting certain data common to Western news (such as the age of the president) was strictly forbidden. During that era, however, minority party newspapers were published, media reviews began to appear, and specialized magazines had their runs at covering the immense wealth that flowed into government ministries. These media knew their limits, but in selected offices, a worthy effort was made despite intimidation, bluster, and official lies.

Is a Press Monopoly Inevitable?

The scenario developed in this essay establishes the Western press as a business where profit is relentlessly pursued within a context of law and regard for social norm. "Regard" is meant to suggest that business is neither conducted in a moral vacuum nor determined by tradition when social custom interferes with profit. Pickard draws attention to the high 25% profit margin in America's leading media companies and its effect on the type of broad-based reporting urged in social responsibility theory.[65]

Profit drives business efficiency. It is thus impossible to foresee a reversal of monopolization in Western "free market" media. The system of ownership in which shareholders require management to maximize investment potential is not open to disruption of its principle aim and purpose.

Neither is the monopolization of state-controlled media likely to shift from its control of content and opinion. A long war in the Middle East, Russian incursions into Georgia, and a growing divide between radical and liberal Islamic movements have drawn boundaries that the Hutchins Commissions could not have foreseen. The democratic press is stalled as institutions devolve, constitutions change, leadership seizes power, and accountants (or petty bureaucrats) presume to give vision to media whose purpose is dialogue first.

New Directions

Media monopolies (apart from those mandated by states) are rational responses of shareholders to good-risk ventures which portend profit. Buy-outs and mergers do not occur due to sensitized evaluations that a merger enhances public service, though that feature is nearly always stipulated. When Dow Jones sold the Wall Street Journal to News Corporation in 2007, many were the claims by past and present owners that journalism independence (meaning the integrity of news coverage over profit calculations) would not diminish; history will decide, though skeptics surmise. Clearly, media monopolies result from buyout and mergers negotiated for cost-benefit advantage. What role can public service hope to maintain?

Parastatal Cooperation

Jaifei Yin, noted earlier, describes this relationship between media organization and state as characteristically Asian, where strength of country, symbolized by the royal family, is more important than "individual rights and freedom."[66] Middle range institutions join states as lesser powers in cooperative planning for national survival, if not prosperity. The development model of the press is a close kin to this modern arrangement in which the libertarian watchdog function is surrendered in a bow to state leadership, and self-censorship is a high barrier to innovative reporting. Tradition is honored above progressive initiatives. A factual approach is preferred to narrative form. Government is shown deference; corruption is rarely exposed, unless the state authorizes.

In Parastatal cooperative systems, concentration of media ownership is not considered a threat to editorial independence, since owners are rarely in full control and often carry multiple social roles. Yin cites Japanese media as successes in achieving immense audience reach, an expert corps of writers, and little incentive to provide citizens with alternative accounts of the day's events.[67]

New Challenges

At the turn of the millennium, an important set of analyses and working points were brought together by former UNESCO leader Federico Mayor with the assurance that an altogether uncertain and open future was nonetheless "in our hands… it will be exactly what we make of it."[68]

Mayor prefaced the core of his plan with a stunning series of assertions claiming that a "soul-sickness" has beset the West, a "curious void, indifference, passivity," and "ethical desert, passions and emotions are blunted."[69] Months after publication, passivity, such as it was, gave way to terror and rage. Blunted emotions quaked at the destruction at Ground Zero, New York. Where Mayor had noted a "loss of references, erosion of principles, and twilight of values,"[70] a watching and horrified world saw the fullest fiery expression of values, the antithesis of passivity, and an aggressively deadly assertion of values. Mayor claimed that "people's eyes are empty and solidarity evaporates."[71] After 9/11, eyes were wide-open, if not tearful, and solidarity had shown its best as well as its worst. Which sort of solidarity did the world want?

Despite his writing just before the defining event of the millennium, Mayor capably set the global development agenda, focused around four contracts: a social contract to eliminate poverty and stabilize urban growth; a natural contract to reverse environmental degradation; an ethical contract to promote peace; and a cultural contract to enhance communication. He noted that half the human race has never used a telephone, and over a half-million human settlements have yet to see electricity, not to mention the Internet.[72] Yet his plea for civility and solidarity did not seek a panacea through technological development. Rather, Mayor issued a call to a new level of global human care. The strains and stresses of global inequities would not heal through massive aid or international refinancing schemes, important as those devices are to southern development. Mayor urged that leaders look where leaders fear to tread: values, cultures, and properties for the sake of humankind. Cyberspace, now a dated code word for Internet development, was both a reason for hope and cause for concern. Race hatred grows on that medium, he noted, along with pedophilia and child prostitution.[73]

Mayor then refused the easy appeal to law or broadly ambiguous international pragmatism. Rather, he said simply, "Cyberculture must go hand in hand with the invention of a system of cyberethics."[74] This moral scheme would require courage and a deepened appreciation of core human values. Democracies were Mayor's home-base. What other political system is equal to the task? Yet the sword is double-edged. While democracy is the right (perhaps the only) polity in which to negotiate a new cyberethics, democracy positively requires the nourishment of cybermedia and every other kind of inform, to inspire and challenge, democratic bodies charged with creating this bold new ethic. In effect, Mayor was urging precisely the same social renewal as did advocates of social responsibility of newspapers and magazines, film and television – communications. Media whose influence grows exponentially with market success, but whose focus on human care as a guiding ethic has so regularly followed the inverse path.

Mayor's heart-rending call for responsible global action may be dismissed as uncommon (for UN professionals) sentimentality, or downright preposterous. Who today dares to advance a universal ethic?

In America media history, the name Elijah Parish Lovejoy is all but forgotten. In a generation of texts now gone, he was often cited as the first martyr for free speech since American independence.[75] In fact, he was shot by members of a mob in Alton, Illinois, in 1837, while defending a warehouse in which his press had been secretly stored, or perhaps not so secretly. Lovejoy's message was one all people now celebrate as ethically irreproachable, the abolition of persons of African origin from involuntary servitude in American industries and agriculture. At the time of Lovejoy's death, slavery was unsettled and so deeply woven into culture and economy that no workable national plan existed to end it. Lovejoy's plan was not workable either. Like Garrison and other Radicals, Lovejoy's message was freedom, immediate, and irreversible. His journey to that moral stand was a long, slow, and arduous series of dangerous, intellectually challenging decisions framed in editorials and news coverage which threatened Mississippi River business interests and, as the mob demonstrated, he had to go, an expendable spirit in the struggle between *dunamis* and *arete*. Finally, however, Lovejoy is vindicated. His struggle, now hardly noted in media history, was against media monopolies on the scale of the frontier press, no less formidable for their relative obscurity and chauvinism. Media corporations rarely challenge monopolies; people inspired with a message set up against media goliaths and eventually prevail, or so we democrats like to hope.

The new millennium began with hope for peaceful growth, as all "new days" tend to do. Not even a decade into it, however, the globe is increasingly threatened by a polluted atmosphere, sectionalism over oil reserves, seaways made unsafe by lawless piracy, superpowers all too ready to test new weaponry and strategies in limited wars, poverty born of both capitalist greed and inefficient central planning, and media systems trusted only by fanatics or the naive.

Mayor once more: "The moment of truth has arrived – in one or two decades, the fate of the human race itself may be at stake, so weighty will be the combination of dangers jeopardizing the future."[76]

Surely a socially responsible press would be an energetic boost toward honest definitions and plausible solutions. Such a "press" (though of course the reference is synecdoche for media systems digital and light-speed) must entertain diversity yet coalesce to cooperative action. It must respect contradictory hermeneutical traditions yet pull to the foreground a common cause based on shared moral ground. Such a press must be free to seek truth under all its varied disguises in a climate deeply suspicious of any claims to have found it.

This task is not unlike the one confronting the Hutchins Commission, or the American abolitionists, or Kenya's "Beyond" in the late 1980s, or the samizdat of Cold-War Russia, or perhaps also of the first erstwhile symbol makers who responded to the urge to make thought public and thus to risk the wrath of adversity for the sake of an idea given greater permanence than speech and greater distribution than voice. In each era, ours no less than our forebears, an ethic of free and responsible conversation has separated human culture from all the alternatives. The ethic underlying public communication has rarely preceded its application, but at our best, that ethic comes along.

Socially responsible media in the decades Mayor cites as most dangerous will do well to hover near a communitarian framework. The future of communications media does not need a revival of Enlightenment individualism, but a more inclusive and convincing embrace of social and moral theory promoting the linkage between us and the varied languages among us, inscrutable in sound and grammar, common in core values – justice, fairness, freedom, love.

Notes

1 Aristotle (1985, pp. 1099b2, 1118a23).
2 Bernays (1952, p.157).
3 Fiske (1996, pp. 212–222).
4 Siebert (1965, passim).
5 Greene (1971, p. 147).
6 Ellul (1965, p. 87).
7 Bakan (2004, pp. 34–35).
8 Friedman (1970).
9 Bakan (2004, p. 35).
10 Starr (2004, p. 178).
11 Starr (2004, p. 184).
12 Nerone (1995, p. 1).
13 Hutchins (1965, p. 33).
14 White (1972, p. 291).
15 Hutchins (1954, p. 66).
16 Hutchins (1954, p. 116).
17 Hocking (1940, p. 432).
18 Hocking (1912, p. 290).
19 Hocking (1942, p. 290).
20 Hocking (1942, pp. 61–62).
21 Hocking (1926, p. 317).
22 See Meyer (1960); Merkley (1975); Harries (1986).
23 Niebuhr (1953, 1944) introduces readers to this journey.
24 Niebuhr (1960, pp. 132–133).
25 Niebuhr (1957, p. xv).
26 Sickles (1943, p. 226).
27 MacLeish (1940, p. 34).
28 Chafee Jr., (1947, p. 43).
29 Dickinson (1931, p. 834).
30 Dickinson (1943, p. 32).
31 Firth (1962, p. x).
32 Redfield (1955, p. 58).
33 *Newsweek* (1943, p. 30).
34 *Newsweek* (1943, p. 30).
35 Ruml (1945, p. 4).
36 *Time* (1940, p. 60).
37 Shuster (1974, p. 72).
38 Shuster (1943, p. 513).
39 Shuster (1960, p. 10).

40 Shuster (1944, p. 26).
41 Ashmore (1989).
42 The definitive history is Fred S. Siebert, one of the Four Theories authors, (1965).
43 Yin (2008, p.8).
44 Hachten (1999, pp. 31–35).
45 Larson (2003, p. 79).
46 McChesney (2008, p. 42).
47 McChesney (2008, p. 15).
48 Kovach and Rosenstiel (2001, p. 51).
49 Mandela, (1994, passim).
50 Fackler, (2009, p. 302).
51 Christians, Ferré, and Fackler (1993, p. 14).
52 Christians, Ferré, and Fackler (1993, p. 14).
53 Christians, Ferré, and Fackler (1993, p. 14).
54 Christians, Ferré, and Fackler (1993, pp. 93, 95).
55 Arendt cited in Christians, Ferré and Fackler (1993, p. 115).
56 Carey's (1989) is a classic in contemporary communication studies.
57 Rosen (1999, p. 21).
58 See Christians, Rotzoll, and Fackler (2005, p. 49).
59 Kovach and Rosenstiel (2001, p. 51).
60 Lippmann (1922, p. 16).
61 Mbanga (2008, p. 53).
62   Mbanga (2008, pp. 51–53).
63 Mano (2008, p. 510).
64 Kenya's press history is told by Obonyo (2005); and Fackler and Baker (2010).
65 Pickard (nd).
66 Yin (2008, p. 9).
67 Yin (2008, p. 8).
68 Mayor (2001, p. 1).
69 Mayor (2001, p. 5).
70 Mayor (2001, p. 5).
71 Mayor (2001, p. 5).
72 Mayor (2001, p. 285).
73 Mayor (2001, p. 284).
74 Mayor (2001, p. 284).
75 Lovejoy (nd).
76 Mayor (2001, p. 14).

References

Aristotle (1985) *Nicomachean Ethics*, (trans. T. Irwin, Hackett, 1985), Indianapolis, IN.
Ashmore, H.S. (1989) *Unseasonable Truths*, Little, Brown, Boston, MA.
Bakan, J. (2004) *The Corporation*, Free Press, New York.
Bernays, E. (1952) *Public Relations*, University of Oklahoma Press, Norman.
Carey, J. (1989) *Communication as Culture*, Unwin Hyman, Boston.
Chafee Jr., Z. (1947) *Government and Mass Communications*, University of Chicago Press, Chicago.

Christians, C., Ferré, J.P., and Fackler, M. (1993) *Good News: Social Ethics and the Press*, Oxford, New York.

Christians, C., Rotzoll, K.B., and Fackler, M. (2005) *Media Ethics: Cases and Moral Reasoning*, 7th edn, Pearson, Allyn and Bacon, Boston.

Dickinson, J. (1931) Legal rules: Their function in the process of decision, *University of Pennsylvania Law Review and American Law Register*, 79 (May), p. 834.

Dickinson, J. (1943) Planned society, in *Bulletin of the College of William and Mary in Virginia*, June, 32.

Ellul, J. (1965) *Propaganda* (trans. K. Kellen and J. Lerner), Knopf, New York: Knopf.

Fackler, M. (2009) Communitarianism, in *The Handbook of Mass Media Ethics*, (eds L. Wilkins and C. Christians), Routledge, New York, p. 302.

Fackler, M., and Baker, E. (2010) Kind of Selfless, in *Ethics and Evil in the Public Sphere*, (eds R.S. Fortner and M. Fackler), Hampton, New York, pp. 63–78.

Firth, R. (1962) *The Papers of Robert Redfield, Vol. 1: Human Nature and the Study of Society*, University of Chicago Press, Chicago.

Fiske, J. (1996) Opening the Hallway, in *Stuart Hall: Critical Dialogues in Cultural Studies* (ed. D. Morley and K-H. Chen), Routledge, New York, pp. 212–222.

Friedman, M. (1970) The social responsibility of business is to increase its profits, *The New York Times Magazine*, September 13.

Greene, G. (1971) *The Power and the Glory*, Penguin, London, p. 147.

Hachten, W. (1999) *The World News Prism: Changing Media of International Communication*, Iowa State University Press, Ames, pp. 31–35.

Harries, R. (ed.) (1986) *Reinhold Niebuhr and the Issues of Our Time*, Mowbray, London.

Hocking, W.E. (1912) *The Meaning of God in Human Experience*, Yale University Press, New Haven, CT.

Hocking, W.E. (1926) *Man and the State*, Yale University Press, New Haven, CT.

Hocking, W.E. (1940) Democracy and the scientific spirit, *American Journal of Orthopsychiatry*, 10 (July), p. 432.

Hocking, W.E. (1942) *What Man Can Make of Man*, Harper and Brothers, New York.

Hocking, W.E. (1944) *The Crisis of our Time*, University of Chicago Round Table, 353, December 24.

Hutchins, R.M. (1954) *Great Books: The Foundations of a Liberal Education*, Simon & Shuster, New York.

Hutchins, R.M. (1965) First Glimpse of a New World, *Saturday Review*, December 4.

Kovach, B. and Rosenstiel, T. (2001) *The Elements of Journalism*, Crown, New York.

Larson, E. (2003) *The Devil in the White City*, Vintage, New York.

Lippmann, W. (1922) *Public Opinion*, Macmillan, New York.

Lovejoy, E.P. (nd) www.altonweb.com/history/lovejoy/index.html (accessed June 21, 2010).

MacLeish, A. (1940) *A Time to Speak*, Houghton Mifflin, Boston.

Mandela, N. (1994) *Long Walk to Freedom*, Little, Brown, New York.

Mano, W. (2008) The media and politics in Zimbabwe: Turning left while indicating right, *The International Journal of Press and Politics*, 13 (4), 510.

Mayor, F. (2001) *The World Ahead*, Zed, New York.

Mbanga, W. (2008) Zimbabwe: Telling the Story, Reporting the News, *Nieman Reports*, Fall, 53.

McChesney, R. (2008) *The Political Economy of Media*, Monthly Review Press, New York.

Merkley, P. (1975) *Reinhold Niebuhr: A Political Account*, McGill-Queen's University Press, Montreal.

Meyer, D. (1960) *The Protestant Search for Political Realism, 1919–1941*, University of California Press, Berkeley.

Nerone, J.C. (ed.) (1995) *Last Rights*, University of Illinois Press, Urbana.

Newsweek (1943) Ruml's Turn-Up of Tax Clock Finally Comes to a Showdown, May 24, 30.

Niebuhr, R. (1944) *The Children of Light and the Children of Darkness*, Charles Scribner's Sons, New York.

Niebuhr, R. (1953) *Christian Realism and Political Problems*, facsimiled by Charles Scribner's Sons, New York.

Niebuhr, R. (1957) Introduction to *Responsibility in Mass Communication* by Wilbur Schramm, Harper Row, New York.

Niebuhr, R. (1960) *The Children of Light and the Children of Darkness*, reprinted edn, Charles Scribner's Sons, New York.

Obonyo, L. (2005) Growing in the cradle, dissertation, Temple University.

Pickard, V. (nd) Whether giants should be slain or persuaded to be good, unpublished paper.

Redfield, R. (1955) *The Redfield Lectures: The Educational Experience*, The Fund for Adult Education, Pasadena.

Rosen, J. (1999) *What Are Journalists For?*, Yale University Press, New Haven.

Ruml, B. (1945) *Tomorrow's Business*, Farrar and Rinehart, New York.

Shuster, G.N. (1943) The Greek tradition, in *Commonweal*, September 10.

Shuster, G.N. (1944) Education and religion, *Saturday Review of Literature*, September 16.

Shuster, G.N. (1960) *Education and Moral Wisdom*, Harper and Brothers, New York.

Shuster, G.N. (1974) *On the Side of Truth*, University of Notre Dame Press, Notre Dame.

Sickles, E. (1943) Archibald MacLeish and American Democracy, *American Literature* 15 (November), 226.

Siebert, F.S. (1965) *Freedom of the Press in England, 1476–1776*, University of Illinois Press, Urbana.

Starr, P. (2004) *The Creation of the Media*, Basic, New York.

Time (1940) "Shuster to hunter," September 16.

White, M. (1972) *Science and Sentiment in America*, Oxford, New York.

Yin, J. (2008) Beyond the four theories of the press: A new model for the Asian and the world press, *Journalism and Communication Monographs*, 10 (1), 8.

7

Ethics and Ideology
Moving from Labels to Analysis

Lee Wilkins

Back to the Beginning

The word ideology has its original home in political philosophy dating at least as far back as the ancient Greeks. As its origin is within this intellectual domain, it is important to review the core theoretical approach of what both Plato and Aristotle called politics.

All political philosophy responds to three questions:

1 What is the nature of the human?
2 What is the nature of the state?
3 What is the relationship between the two?

A thoroughgoing discussion of ideology in political philosophy answers these three questions and connects them to policy implications – everything from the structure of government to the sorts of laws government should pass. For example, Thomas Hobbes responded to these questions as follows:

1 What is the nature of the human: outside community, solitary, nasty, brutish and short; within community, capable of contractual agreements, and of being governed.
2 What is the nature of the state: the goal of the state (the Leviathan) is to bring order out of the human chaos that precedes agreement to a social contract which establishes community; the monarch, as the embodiment of the state, has the goal of maintaining order by almost any means necessary.
3 What is the relationship between the two? The monarch strives to maintain order; those entering the social contract benefit from this order and are

---

The Handbook of Global Communication and Media Ethics, First Edition. Edited by Robert S. Fortner and P. Mark Fackler.
© 2011 Blackwell Publishing Ltd. Published 2011 by Blackwell Publishing Ltd.

responsible for obeying the monarch in all circumstances *until* the monarch orders the death of the citizen. At this rare juncture, and to preserve life, it is permissible to dissolve the social contract and begin anew.

From these relatively straightforward answers to these three crucial questions it is possible to deduce the "ideology" of the divine right of kings as well as its theoretical and ideological demise. Hobbes believed that flourishing human life could not exist outside a community, but when the state tried to take life (what many have suggested is a moral assertion) then the community could dissolve and reform around a different promulgation of civil order.

All Western political theory focused on these three questions until Karl Marx. With Marx, the second of these three questions is rephrased to "what is the nature of power" which allows Marx to respond that power is lodged in economic institutions and that those institutions, in turn, drive political institutions in important ways. Lenin, Mao, and others adopted Marx's question and responded to it in slightly different ways. At other places in Europe and in the US, political theorists such as John Dewey and later John Rawls began the work of lodging power within community. However, it would be a misunderstanding of the field to fail to note that Marx's rephrasing of this second, central question has influenced every major thinker who has written since Marx.

The term "ideology" when used by political scientists is intended to be both neutral and analytic. There are many subcategories of ideology – for example fascism or democracy. However, the concept itself it meant to allow comparison between and among distinct answers to these three formative questions. As in ethics, in politics, ideology is not something you have, ideology is something you do. For ideology to be something other than a purely academic exercise, it must take hold in the real world. It is impossible to live the life of a citizen in an organized political society without incorporating some level of political ideology into experience.

Beginning with Hobbes, and with particular emphasis on the social contract theorists Locke (the framework for the US Constitution) and Rousseau (the father of the French Revolution), the link between political ideology and policy began to strengthen (Barker, 1962). As Marx's work was adopted as a political blueprint in various nation-states (with significant alterations in the case of Mao and China), the connection between theoretical responses to the central questions of political philosophy and the actual workings of government solidified. When differing responses to the theoretical questions moved into lived experience, a focus on ideology emerged.

Contemporary definitions for this term include:

- A belief system that explains and justifies a preferred political order for society, either existing or proposed, and offers a strategy (processes, institutional arrangements, programs) for its attainment (Christenson *et al.*, 1975, p. 1).
- Sets of ideas by which men posit, explain and justify ends and means of organized social action, and specifically political action, irrespective of whether such action aims to preserve, amend, uproot or rebuild a given social order (Seliger, 1976, p. 14).

Moving from Labels to Analysis

- Ideology is first of all concerned with values: that is, how we ought to treat each other and live together is society. Ideologies offer rival visions of the "good society, the morally best kind of society for human beings to live in. ..." Ideologies, then are guides to political action, (Adams, 2001, pp. 3-4).

However, it is important to note that many political theorists believe ideology itself provides one of the weaker motivations for political action.

> It makes little sense to abstract from personal context the ideology and public actions of either political leaders or ordinary citizens, even though the direct interpersonal, proximal experiences of people are not the sole basis for the formation of political outlook and actions. But it is doubtful that ordinary and extraordinary people would even enter "the stream of history," as it is so loosely called, if they were not pushed into it partly by direct, proximal experience.... A hungry person is likely to believe some person or group is depriving him of food ... Ideology may with more or less accuracy rationalize and explain such actions, but it has little to do with causing them or the related attitudes.... Political reaction is far more personal, far less abstract and ideological, than either students of citizenry or citizens themselves are wont to recognize.... This is not to say that people are at a loss for words to express reasons for action but that the effect of words is far less than the individual experience (Davies, 1964, 188–189).

In one of the more enduring works by a political scientist about the subject, Daniel Bell (1960) suggests that ideology should be abandoned as a useful analytic concept. In *The End of Ideology*, Bell suggested that ideology was the purview more of the intellectual than the scholar and that the debates of the nineteenth century were exhausted. Bell grounded his assertion in history, noting "For radical intelligentsia, the old ideologies have lost their 'truth' and their power to persuade. No serious minds believe any longer than one can set down 'blueprints' and through 'social engineering' bring about a new utopia of social harmony," (Bell, p. 373). In an analysis that included the creation of culture, what Bell labeled the stultifying effect of television, he argued that if ideological debates were once again to emerge, they would arise not from the humanism of the nineteenth century but from the political and social problems of the second half of the twentieth century. "The ideologies of the 19th century were universalistic, humanistic and fashioned by intellectuals. The mass ideologies of Asia and Africa are parochial, instrumental and created by political leaders. The driving forces of the old ideologies were social equality and, in the largest sense, freedom. The impulsions of the new ideologies are economic development and national power" (Bell, 1960, p. 373).

Thus, for most political theorists, ideology is an analytic concept that operates at a level of abstraction at least one level (individual to institutional) removed from concrete political behavior. There is a soft and somewhat post hoc connection between the two – but ideology itself is seldom considered a strong motivating force for political activity. For many, ideology has minimal power to transform political thought and action. However, its basis in political philosophy remains.

Placing Communication at the Ideological Nexus

As both ideology and political philosophy live in the real world, it was inevitable that the vocabulary of ideology would be adopted by other fields without the thorough conceptual grounding provided by political philosophy. This is not all bad, as new approaches can often provide analytic power that enlivens longstanding intellectual traditions (Brock *et al.*, 2005).

The field of communication tended to focus on, initially, what are called "speech acts" and later, more broadly, political communication, and to equate those with ideology. From this view, ideology is tied to language and political action through symbols, speeches, popular culture, and most certainly news. Often, in this construction of the term, ideology, rather than serving as an analytic tool, is viewed negatively, what Marx called a false consciousness and which certain political factions, for example "liberals" and "conservatives" have tended to use as one method for designating an undesirable or less-than-moral "other". In much scholarship in mass communication, ideology and social construction of reality (Berger and Luckmann, 1967) are first cousins. This way of thinking about ideology has had significant help from the world of politics, particularly American political rhetoric in the latter half of the twentieth century. In the real world of American talk during this era, ideological labels became shorthand for how individuals believed power should be distributed in society. In the general usage of the word in the communication literature, "ideology" is equated with a particular line of reasoning or speaking without a thorough examination of all the central questions that a political scientist would insist the concept answers for citizens.

Take this contemporary example as illustration. In the wonderfully popular book (and subsequent film) *The Da Vinci Code* (Brown, 2003), Harvard Professor Thomas Langdon (whose academic specialty is religious symbolism, by inference a subset of semiotics) opens his lecture by asking students what various symbols – a pitchfork or a swastika – have meant through human history. Langdon's point is that culture imbues symbols with meaning. What Langdon does not ask the students – but which both the book and film explore in detail – is the political meaning of the symbols Langdon, first as scholar and then as real-life protector of the "divine feminine", is asked to explore and ultimately chose between. Langdon is confronted with one of the central questions of all political theory – what is the nature of the human – and two distinct ideological responses that emerge from the answer to that question. The ideological responses, of course, are highly symbolic and hence can be decoded in multiple ways. Which decoding (and the resulting ideology) is persuasive all emerges from how Langdon and his adversaries answer that initial question.

Mass communication scholarship, and the foregoing popularized element of it, tends to have a "thin" definition of ideology by focusing less on the analysis of the structure and interrelationships among political actors and more on decoding communication about those relationships. In a lose sense, communication about

Moving from Labels to Analysis

the relationships among political actors is viewed as the equivalent of the actual relationship as it exists in political society. In fact, most recent work on the concept has focused extensively on how institutional structures are portrayed. Here, ideology tends to be tied to the production of culture. Jorge Larrain explains the process of cultural production as a cycle wherein institutions create "public versions of identity which select only some features that are considered to be representative" and then "influence the way in which people see themselves and the way that they act through a process of reading or reception which is not necessarily passive and uncritical," (Larrain, 1994, p. 163). In this rendering, institutions dominate individuals.

This view of institutional power dominating individuals is particularly marked in members of the Frankfurt School who, taking their cue from Marx, focus scholarship on how power is manifest outside the traditional political realm. This body of work, which includes scholars such as Foucault and Marcuse, emphasizes the production of culture. Marcuse, particularly in *One Dimensional Man* (1991), argues that a dominant way of speaking, for example, accepting the tenants of capitalism by the creation of business pages or channels without matching labor pages or channels, reinforces cultural belief that capitalism is the only appropriate economic system, that labor is and should be subservient to ownership, and that the lack of authentic and differing points of view in media makes "man" one dimensional – unable to think critically outside the box. Marcuse does not spend much time on the nature of human beings – but surely lazy and dim-witted would be among their psychological attributes. Hobbes, when compared to Marcuse, has both a more optimistic and a better developed concept of the human than many members of the Frankfurt School.

The underlying assumption of almost all of this work is that reality itself is changed by ideology, particularly an ideology that disconnects human beings from authentic experience, specifically the authentic experience connected to work and to the creation of culture. "Because the commodity exchange valorizes things rather than the procurers of those things, human activity is reduced to a subordinant position, as 'abstraction of the human labour incorporated into commodities' (Lukács 1971, p. 87). Reification thus functions as a natural byproduct of the division of labor. As work becomes increasingly compartmentalized, workers lose touch with the consumer of that work and become subject to a psychological fragmentation that mirrors the fragmentation of the commodity's production," (Decker, 2004, p. 57).

This project of teasing out the ideology in speech is worthwhile on a descriptive level, but to have analytic power, it must focus some energy on responses to underlying questions and how different responses might produce different content. Mass communication scholarship seldom explores the nature of the human political animal as a central actor in the creation and promulgation of ideology. Equally, it fails to analyze the notion of "the state" or "power" except as manifest in various speech acts that most often originate with economic institutions or within communication as it occurs throughout a particular culture at a particular time in history.

In mass communication, language becomes the "flashpoint for ideology," (Decker, 2004, p. 22). Scholars make visible the hidden hand of ideology in language (speech acts) and this visibility promotes analysis. Discovering the source (or bias) of discourse could become the first step in changing it – as well as the first step in making sure it remains unchanged and perhaps unexamined. In some scholarship, ideology has also been connected to the role of particular groups in society, for example, the military or journalists. Thus, there has been some significant work on the "ideology" of objectivity (Schudson, 1981) as it is applied to journalism. Ideology, here, becomes another label for pervasive professional values and norms.

In contrast to its use in political science, ideology in mass communication is connected with powerful impacts, particularly at the institutional level. Mass communication scholars suggest that ideology frames how institutions are built and how they maintain their status in society. In this approach, scholars often suggest that hegemony – of ownership and of message – results in institutional structures that tend of favor the economically powerful at the expense of workers, the poor, or institutions rooted in community. This domination of message content – and the structures that create that content – is assailed as profoundly undemocratic. At the individual level, message hegemony literally makes it impossible to behave or to think in "nonhegemonic" ways. That very abstract generalization having been made, mass communication scholars are far less clear about the relationship between speech acts (construed broadly) and specific political action at the individual level. From the point of view of a discipline in which words and symbols matter a great deal, it makes some common sense to imbue words and symbols with power, including the power of causality. How that power interacts with humans and with the other influences on humans remains largely unexplored.

Historians, too, deal with ideology (James, 1963). In some work, ideology is equated with intellectual history – what ideas and people have motivated a society throughout its history or in a specific era. William Raymond Williams' (1995) work particularly blends the insights of mass communication and intellectual history. For other historians, an examination of ideology includes an examination of culture, particularly the dominant myths of particular cultures. Myths, of course, have symbolic value – which means this element of historical analysis overlaps substantially with the definition of ideology that appears to dominate mass communications. For others, ideology can represent the grand sweep of history, as it did for Hegel (Edelman, 1964).

What historians bring to the table is a deep understanding of the connections between the past and the present. As historian G.L. Waite notes in his biography of Hitler, "It may well be protested that the kind of selective historical writing found in this chapter exploits the past for purposes of illuminating present problems. And in a sense it does. But the present is always involved with the past: the past shapes the present and the present may determine, if not the past, at least our understanding of it" (Waite, 1972, p. 244–245).

Thus, political philosophy and mass communication approach the concept of ideology quite differently. The disciplines share a concern with institutions.

Moving from Labels to Analysis 125

However, political philosophy is far more concerned with the nature of the human than is the field of mass communication. While mass communication focuses much scholarship and theorizing on the maintenance of power and by inference its distribution, political philosophy is equally concerned with the shifting power dynamics among institutions and how those shifts do and do not involve individual response. Tucked deeply into the theorizing in both fields are ethical questions. Isolating them and then articulating them make ideology a useful analytic tool.

The problem of power

In beginning that ethical exploration, it is important to discuss power. Outside of the field of political science, power is often viewed as an end in itself. In other words, the goal of a particular party, institution, or message is to gain power. For political scientists, power is instrumental – it makes other things possible. For political psychologists, power is an instrumental human need. In other words, it is difficult to imagine human beings accomplishing much of anything – making friends, attending a PTA meeting, voting, passing laws, forming community, without some measure of individual power. That individual power has a history in culture. Individual power is magnified, and sometimes emerges from, community. Thinking of power instrumentally, rather than as an end in itself, allows one to examine both distribution and ends. By incorporating power into flourishing human functioning (remember, for Aristotle, politics was the highest, ethical human achievement) power itself no longer becomes ethically reprehensible. Individuals who seek it (as all do), are no longer morally culpable. Instead, power itself can be evaluated based on ends (a somewhat utilitarian approach) and on what it allows to emerge, what Martha Nussbaum (2006) calls the capabilities approach. Thus, by making the instrumental human, scholars can better analyze both present actions and employ the moral imagination.

Ideology and Ethics: Core Questions

Given this wealth of definitions and levels of analysis, it makes sense, when discussing communication ethics and ideology, to provide a definition of the term that promotes ethical analysis and reflection. For purposes of this chapter, it makes sense to develop a definition that implicates journalists and the institution of journalism. A melding of the foregoing insights suggests the following:

Ideology, in the field of mass communication, is the symbolic response – in the form of news and entertainment broadly construed – to questions of the distribution of power in society. In an ethical sense, this definition implicates concepts of justice, fairness, and care. As power is lodged at the individual as well as the institutional level, thinking about ethics and ideology also requires thinking about the nature of the human being within community. Ideological analysis of the media, because it (they) is (are) an institution of some power in modern political cultures and states, may also be the focus of ideological analysis. In other words, it is important for scholars to articulate how power is distributed at the institutional level and the relative power and dominance of the media when compared to government structures, religion and the church, and so on. Thinking about ideology – consistent communication content and response over decades and centuries – can be one way to describe and analyze long-standing political structures and movements.

Ideological analysis, when coupled with ethics, must respond to the following questions:

What, if anything, does a particular ideology assert is the nature of humanity, particularly humanity as the creator of symbols, a political actor, and a participant in the political life well lived? Within this question, a subsidiary question logically occurs: How do particular ideologies frame the professional obligation of those who convey information about political power to the larger society?

How, and through what mechanisms of culture, speech, and structure, is power lodged, retained and expressed within a particular ideology? A subsidiary question occurs here, as well: What, if any, are the mechanisms of communication broadly and journalism specifically that connect the individual human to the power structures of any given society in particular historical moments?

What are the historic antecedents of culture and symbols that sustain one potential ideological interpretation of historic events and political actors and actions over others? Can analysis of political communication aid understanding of how power is shifted and retained? What sort of political community does a particular ideology ask humanity to imagine?

Finally, it is important to note that the responses to these three questions need to be connected to one another. Ideology is an integrated belief system – not merely opinion and far more than a disconnected collection of behaviors or messages. In this sense, ideology needs to become an analytic framework – not a label applied to various belief systems and those who adhere to them. (Such application of labels, particularly in the popular culture, is almost without exception derogatory.) For the concept to have analytic power, it must be capable of being compared across categories.

Having framed the discussion in this way, it is important to test whether such a framework can aid analysis.

The "ideology" of the *Control Room*: The difficult question of nations and professional obligations

It is not an understatement to say that the US-led invasion of Iraq raised ideological questions in public political debate worldwide. Former US President George W. Bush couched the rationale for the invasion in ideological language. The United States was invading Iraq to promote freedom and democracy – to overthrow a tyrant who had so bullied and neutered his citizenry that outside force was the only possible mechanism for change. Thus, at a crude but nonetheless high level of abstraction, the Unites States invasion of Iraq was a battle of

Moving from Labels to Analysis

conflicting ideologies: democracy versus fascism with a healthy dose of religious fundamentalism thrown in on both sides.

As a result of the war happening in the twenty-first century, contemporary media were expected to cover (report and analyze) the war. However, because the news organizations live within a culture and a history, and because there is ample scholarly and anecdotal evidence to suggest that journalists, too, take sides in war, getting the "whole" picture of this conflict was going to be extraordinarily problematic, particularly for professionals working under deadline. While there is an emerging body of literature about how journalists, particularly US journalists, did their jobs, relatively few studies of any sort attempted to focus on the work of journalism at the time it was being produced. One of the exceptions was the documentary *The Control Room*, an in-depth look at how Al-Jazeera covered the war – as it was happening.

A brief summary of the film is in order. *The Control Room* (2003) documents how journalists working for Al-Jazeera conceptualized and then practiced their journalism during the early days of the invasion and occupation. It shows journalists from this news organization interacting with sources, particularly with US military sources during the daily briefing process. Through interviews of both the sources and the journalists themselves, viewers begin to see the struggle to frame the early days of the invasion from a non-US (the film suggests an Arab) point of view. Clips of then-President George W. Bush, Secretary of Defense Donald Rumsfeld, as well as the military commanders on site, are included in the film. The narrative structure of the piece is the narrative structure of the invasion itself – from the days before the invasion through the "fall" of Bagdad. Viewers see the resulting journalism that aired on Al Jazeera. Through interviews with these journalists and their editors, viewers are also able to understand – from their point of view – why certain news reports were broadcast and to understand some elements of specific content. Those who see the film must remember that *The Control Room*, like all journalism and documentary film, is edited to tell a story.

This documentary film takes on the concept of "ideology" on at least three levels. First, it accepts the scholarly connection between ideology and social construction of reality. Through its examination of the production of news by a non-Western news organization, it is possible to see how individual journalistic choice influences news coverage and to connect those choices to political ideology informed by recent Middle Eastern history. Audience members can watch the film and how one news organization on the "other" side of the conflict constructed the reality of this invasion, can compare it to some memories of news coverage by other, most likely US-based, news organizations. Through this interior monologue, which I believe the film's producers wanted to evoke, it is possible to see how the workings out of two apparently competing ideologies result in distinctive news accounts. Second, the film also focuses on professional ideology – the values and ethics of these particular journalists as they do their jobs. It takes great care to include interviews with Al Jazeera staff – many of whom began their professional careers at the BBC, about their sense of professional obligation and the values that inform their choices. It also evaluates the institution of journalism – in this case Al-Jazeera – against other, powerful institutions, for example the US military and various Arab states. Third, and by implication, is asks whether it is possible to have a robust journalistic system within a certain sort of centralized political system where control over information is a key element in retaining power. The answer to this question – at least from the point of view of the film – is that what matters is the centralization of power, whether it is in the form of the US military and its control of information or the Arab governments which, depending on nation state, range from monarchial to dictatorial.

So, what does *The Control Room* conclude? From the point of view of those in the film, it is clear that the ideology that dominates is the one that coalesces around shared professional values that many – regardless of country of origin – would recognize: a drive to tell the truth, a relationship with a viewing audience, and sympathy for fellow professionals. Compared to this, political ideology rooted in the nationstate has some power and it certainly circumscribes options. However, it is the shared values of the profession rather than political vision that motives human action of the journalists in the film. Individual experience matters. These journalists know that their role is important, but that they share power with other, important institutions. They function as much on the notion of capabilities as they do on utilitarian considerations. It is possible, indeed it is one of the goals of the filmmakers, to imagine journalists such as these working in much the same way in a different ideological system because they function not within a single ideological framework but within layers of ideology.

The sort of professional community the film asks its audiences to imagine is a professional world that functions much along the lines of the sort of journalistic cosmopolitanism outlined by Ward (2008): "The cosmopolitan attitude is concerned with the priorities and limits of our attachments … Cosmopolitanism does not deny that people can have legitimate feelings of concern toward their country or compatriots. But it also insists that moderate patriotism be evaluated form a cosmopolitan perspective," (p. 54). In Ward's vision, which is to a modest extent reflected in the journalists featured in *Control Room*, cosmopolitan professional values would promote journalists who act as global agents and have some loyalty to the citizens of the world. The film itself illustrates the professional results of such allegiances: an attempt to promote nonparochial understandings.

If there is a lesson here, it is that hegemony is much more difficult to create and sustain than the somewhat abstract discussion of Marcuse, for example, would suggest.

My Fellow Citizens: The Inaugural Speech of Barack Obama

Surely if the understandings of political philosophers and mass communications scholars can find common ground in understanding ideology, it would in an analysis of significant political transitions. One such instance would be the peaceful passing of power in American democracy on January 20, 2009, when Barack Obama was inaugurated as the 44th President of the United States (Associated Press, 2009).

Moving from Labels to Analysis 129

In terms of political philosophy, Obama's inaugural address included responses to the three central questions political philosophy asks.

1 What is the nature of humanity?
2 What, then, becomes the nature of the state. And, in political communication, how is the power of the state portrayed?
3 What is the relationship between the state and the citizens? What are the historic and cultural symbols that fund specific interpretations of events?

What is the nature of humanity?

From President Obama's perspective, as articulated in his inaugural address, it is one of shared responsibility, noted from the very first words of the address: "my fellow citizens." Obama's speech focused on human capabilities – the capacities for hope, hard work, sacrifice, and creativity. Furthermore, all of these human qualities are lodged within political community.

This focus on human capabilities in some real sense is a challenge to any particular ideology. Obama began his speech by noting his belief that he was elected to help proclaim an end "to the petty grievances and false promises, the recriminations and worn out dogmas, that for far too long have strangled our politics." Yet, while Obama's statement challenges the thin articulations of liberalism and conservatism that have dominated American political discourse since the early 1980s, it is also infused with a small "d" democratic ideology – that of equal opportunity and a positive vision of human capability within political community. Obama himself is a powerful symbol of this democratic value: he is a person of color who came from what many would have characterized as a "broken home." Thus, news reporting of these events, in the context of Obama's life narrative and of American history, does carry a powerful ideological message – a message that focuses on the potential of democracy for the possibility of individual achievement. Thus, Obama's speech and journalistic reporting of it allows some insight into the thinking about the nature of the human being within political community. Journalistic coverage that frames answers to this question as debatable in the highest sense of the word also becomes a worthy professional goal.

What, then, becomes the nature of the state. And, in political communication, how is the power of the state portrayed?

In his inaugural address, President Obama outlined both a foreign and domestic agenda for a powerful federal government – from building roads and bridges, wiring the country for Internet communication, and transforming schools and colleges. On the international levels, his priorities included curtailing nuclear threats and meeting the challenges of global warming, all while maintaining national security from a US-centric perspective. The state here has a role, but Obama also circumscribed that role with pragmatism – government will do what works and, when something does not work, government will abandon that effort. DeToqueville (1835/2000) was among the first to note the American pragmatic streak, but entire political movements, for example Progressivism, have been built on the notion that good government is smart government that works. What is less clear from Obama's speech is the loci of countervailing power for this ambitious agenda. The President gave the market its circumscribed due, but other than that, there does not appear to be a single domestic institution that Obama believes, at this particular time in history, has a power equal to the democratic state.

This portion of Obama's speech handed both traditional journalists and the less traditional political satirists such as Jon Stewart and the blogosphere its marching orders: figure out what's working and not working and report and comment on it. Such an approach allows for a diversity of views, must be based on analysis (Obama himself used the words data and statistics), but must also consider the human potential that democratic theorists and Obama himself alluded to it in the same speech. Obama's invitation here is explicit: he invites citizens and their representatives, among them journalists and their various news organizations, to hold him and the government he heads to account. This is far easier said than done. Journalists, particularly, would do well to remember the history of the George W. Bush administration where dissent was morphed into sedition and a powerful executive branch made fact-based reporting on central issues of power extraordinarily difficult. Thus, while Obama sought to illustrate a contrast between his administration and the Bush years, journalists may not find such a profound difference. To some extent, the differences journalists do find will depend on the government's willingness to be transparent – a concept that does not find itself well represented in any political ideology. Here, it is professional values – much like those showcased in the *Control Room* – that may dominates individual action. There is a great deal of work here for journalists to do – in the service of both the citizenry and the state – in that order.

What is the relationship between the state and the citizens? What are the historic and cultural symbols that fund specific interpretations of events?

The symbolism of the nation's first African-American President echoes through the past and into the future. The President himself noted it. "We are shaped by every language and culture, drawn from every end of this earth, and because we have tasted the bitter swill of civil war and segregation, and emerged from that dark chapter stronger and more united, we cannot help but believe that old hatred shall someday pass." Obama in this sentence provided not only history, but a context in which it interpret it. For both journalists and scholars, the question thus becomes whether this context is the appropriate one, whether others provide additional explanatory power, and whether a specific context fuels a specific response where human potential is, in some systematic and organized way, denied. Obama seemed to suggest that the

Moving from Labels to Analysis

citizens were the final, and most powerful, check on the state. "For as much as government can do and must do, it is ultimately the faith and determination of the American people upon which this nation relies.... But those values upon which our success depends – hard work and honesty, courage and fair play, tolerance and curiosity, loyalty and patriotism – these things are old. These things are true" (Associated Press, 2009). Omitted from this list are the intervening institutions – schools, the church, corporations and other inhabitants of the market, and the institutionalization of freedom of speech in the media broadly construed, that have traditionally checked broad government power. In President Obama's address, it is not clear what institutions and through what mechanisms the power of the democratic leviathan can be restrained and redistributed. Surely this is a pertinent question for journalists to explore.

Thus, President Barack Obama's 2009 inaugural address would seem to be the appropriate focus of ideological analysis from a perspective that includes the questions most likely to be raised by both political philosophers and mass communication scholars. It also provides a set of follow up questions and stories for journalists. Such analysis provides food for philosophic thought as well as professional goals.

The role of ethics in ideological analysis

As the foregoing suggests, when ethical analysis is paired with ideology, a consistent set of questions emerges. Answering these questions, with particular emphasis on the ethical underpinnings of those answers, has the capacity to move the concept of ideology away from that of label and toward that of analytic tool. The questions that an ethical approach suggests are:

1   How does a particular ideology define what it means to be human – and who is allowed in that category. How are human capabilities defined and imagined? How does news and entertainment programming provide answers to these questions, not only in individual messages but also in a consistent span of messages over time?
2   How does a particular ideology frame power, and how is that power distributed not just among individuals but also among social institutions, including the media. Does media content, as well as institutional structure, reflect this distribution of power? How is power linked to the concept of human capabilities, as individuals, as individuals in community, and as individuals who inhabit professional roles? How is political power differentiated from other power centers in political society?
3   How easily, and under what circumstances, can the distribution of power be shifted? Is power regarded as something capable of being shared, or is it the province of only a particular set of institutions and individuals? Are there specific loci of power – for example the nationstate – which present special problems in light of ethical insight? How does political communication and professional obligation, both construed broadly, respond to these difficult questions?

A focus on ethics, thus, enables scholars to pull apart the concept of ideology and to use it as a tool in multiple levels of analysis. As Aristotle originally noted, and which the field of political philosophy has long accepted, ideology is best understood through an analysis of actions as well as statements about those actions. To move the project of ethics and ideology forward, it is necessary to analyze the relationship between ideology speech acts and human and institutional response to those acts, always remembering that people and institutions are complicated and that, when the topic is politics, parsimony is not always the most accurate explanation.

References

Adams, I. 2001. *Political Ideology Today*, 2nd edn, Manchester University Press, Manchester, UK.

Associated Press (2009) Text of President Barack Obama's inaugural address. http://yahoo.com /s/ap/20090120/ap_on_go_pr_wh/inauguration (last accessed January 20, 2009).

Barker, E., (ed) (1962) *Social Contract: Locke, Hume, Rousseau*, Oxford University Press, New York.

Bell, D. (1960) *The End of Ideology*, Macmillan, New York.

Berger, P., and Luckmann, T. (1967) *The Social Construction of Reality: A Treatise in the Sociology of Knowledge*, Doubleday, New York.

Brock, B.L., Huglen, M.E., Klumpp, J.F., and Howell, S. (2005) *Making Sense of Political Ideology: The Power of Language in Democracy*, Rowman & Littleifled Publishers, Inc., Lanham, MD.

Brown, D. (2003) *The Da Vinci Code*, Random House, New York.

Christenson, R.M., Engel, A.S. Jacobs, D.N. *et al.* (1975) *Ideologies and Modern Politics*, Dodd, Mead, New York.

Control Room (2003) (Director, Jehane Noujaim), Lionsgate Studios, Santa Monica, CA.

Davies, J.C. (1964) *Human Nature in Politics*, John Wiley & Sons, Inc., New York.

Decker, J. (2004) *Ideology*. Palgrave Macmillan, New York.

DeToqueville, A. (1835/2000) *Democracy in America*, Bantham Classic Books, New York.

Edelman, M. (1964) *The Symbolic Uses of Politics*, University of Illinois Press, Champagne.

James, C.L.R. 1963. *The Black Jacobins*, Vintage Press, New York.

Larrain, J. (1994) *Ideology and Cultural Identity: Modernity and the Third World Pressure*, Polity Press, Boston, MA.

Lukács, G. (1971) *History and Class Consciousness*, MIT Press, Cambridge, MA.

Marcuse, H. (1991) *One Dimensional Man: Studies in the Ideology of Advanced Industrial Societies*, Beacon Press, Boston, MA.

Nussbaum, M.C. (2006) *Frontiers of Justice*, Harvard University Press, Cambridge, MA.

Schudson, M. (1981) *Discovering the News: A Social History of American Newspapers*, Basic Books, New York.

Seliger, M. (1976) *Ideology and Politics*, The Free Press, New York.

Waite, R.G.L. (1972) *The Psychopathic God*, Da Capo Press, Cambridge, MA.

Ward, S.J.A. (2008) A theory of patriotism for journalism, in *Media Ethics beyond Borders*, (eds S.J.A. Ward and H. Wassermann), Heinemann, Johannesburg, South Africa.

Williams, R.W. (1995) *The Sociology of Culture*, University of Chicago Press, Chicago.

8

Fragments of Truth
The Right to Communication as a Universal Value

Philip Lee

At the conclusion of his book *The Descent of Man*, Charles Darwin asserts that:

> Man with all his noble qualities, with sympathy which feels for the most debased, with benevolence which extends not only to other men but to the humblest living creature, with his god-like intellect which has penetrated into the movements and constitution of the solar system – with all these exalted powers – Man still bears in his bodily frame the indelible stamp of his lowly origin (Darwin, 1871, p. 405).

It was a bold statement, since nothing in the known fossil record of the time supported that view. Today, it is absolutely certain that Darwin was right. Incontrovertible evidence has been produced from the study of mitochondrial DNA, pioneered in the United States in the late 1970s. Scientists discovered that mitochondrial DNA (a collection of genes outside the cell nucleus), as an exception to all other genes, is inherited only through the mother, and that the Y chromosome (the sex-determining chromosome in most mammals) is inherited only by men:

> These two sets of gender-linked genes are passed on unchanged from generation to generation... and can therefore be traced right back to our ancestors, to the first mammals, and even beyond to worms and worse (Oppenheimer, 2004, p. xviii).

Based on worldwide studies of mitochondrial DNA, an intricate mosaic of human gene trees has been pieced together that indicates where our ancestors and their gene lines traveled – where they came from and where they went to. The world is not a genetic melting pot that has produced a homogenous alloy that can no longer be separated into its constituent parts – although the complete story is extremely complicated as Richard Dawkins (2005) has shown. Most people have remained in

The Handbook of Global Communication and Media Ethics, First Edition. Edited by Robert S. Fortner and P. Mark Fackler.
© 2011 Blackwell Publishing Ltd. Published 2011 by Blackwell Publishing Ltd.

the same localities since well before the last ice age (20 000 years ago) and retain genetic material that links them to particular places and epochs. In order to grasp the import of these findings more fully, we need to summarize them, which can only be done using modern geographical terms as reference points.

According to the Bradshaw Foundation (2008) the genetic map shows that, between 160 000 and 135 000 years ago, different groups of people began journeying out of East Africa southward to the Cape of Good Hope, and southwest to the Congo Basin and the Ivory Coast. Between 135 000 and 110 000 years ago, another group traveled up the Nile across a green and fertile Sahara to the Levant. That branch died out 90 000 years ago when global freezing turned that region and North Africa into extreme desert.

Between 90 000 and 85 000 years ago a group crossed the mouth of the Red Sea and began a long trek as beachcombers along the southern coast of the Arabian Peninsula toward India. All non-African people are descended from this group. Between 85 000 and 75 000 years ago they continued along the Indian Ocean coast toward Indonesia, then a landmass still attached to Asia. Still following the coast they moved on to Borneo and South China.

Around 74 000 years ago a catastrophic volcanic eruption of Mt Toba in Sumatra caused a six-year nuclear winter and an instant 1000-year ice age with a dramatic population crash down to less than 10 000 adults. Between 73 000 and 65 000 years ago repopulation of India took place and groups crossed by boat from Timor into Australia and from Borneo into New Guinea. There was intense cold in the global North, which made it uninhabitable.

Between 65 000 and 52 000 years ago dramatic warming of the climate meant that groups were finally able to move north up the Fertile Crescent returning to the Levant. From there, some 50 000 years ago, they moved into Europe via the Bosporus. Between 52 000 and 45 000 years ago there was a mini-ice-age, but after that period it was possible to travel north and northeast to the steppes of Central Asia and Indo-China. By 25 000 years ago people had reached the Arctic Circle and North-East Asia, crossing the Bering land bridge into North America some 22 000 years ago.

However, during the most recent ice age, 22 000 to 19 000 years ago, Northern Europe, Asia and North America were depopulated, with isolated surviving groups locked in refuges. In North America the ice corridor closed and the coastal route froze. Later, as the climate got warmer between 19 000 and 15 000 years ago, survivors of the ice age began moving south through North and Central America to South America

Finally, between 15 000 and 12 500 years ago, with the global climate improving all the time, people moved down the west coast of the Americas and the east coast of South America. Between 12 000 and 10 000 years ago reoccupation of North America took place. People followed the retreating ice northward to become Inuit, Aleuts and Na-Dene speakers and Britain and Scandinavia were recolonized. The end of this ice age heralded the dawn of agriculture.

What is the Relevance of this to Universal Values?

The profound implications of these discoveries are still being assessed and debated, but one is inescapable. It is incontrovertible that all human beings are genetically related and, therefore, "universal" in a primordial sense:

> In the end, humans are the products of the same evolutionary forces as all other animals and will continue to be so. Hopefully, we will come to appreciate this before it is too late (Oppenheimer, 2004, p. 363).

The inescapable logic of this finding is that all people share intrinsic equality and worth as human beings. They share a foundational genetic constitution that runs deeper than race, gender, and physical attributes. This is as profound a revelation as we could hope for in the search for evidence that might undergird a universal ethics for all humankind.

While the possibility of genetic dissimilarity or outright difference existed, all kinds of insidious claims could be made as justification for discrimination: state-sponsored violence, forced sterilization of persons deemed genetically defective, the killing of institutionalized populations, and so on. In the 1930s the Nazis used it in Germany to justify their racial policies and, ultimately, the Holocaust, and in 1994 the Hutu authorities in Rwanda used it to promote genocide. Apart from the inherent immorality of such acts, if no distinction or discrimination can be made on the grounds of genetic heritage, if, in short, every human being carries the same genetic passport, we are all equal in the eyes of God and of each other. A universal ethics becomes ipso facto possible.

This discovery also calls into question whether it is ever possible to argue that "cultural specificities" permit exceptions to the universal rule. Is it ethically tenable that a caste system, for example Dalits in India, or sociocultural designations such as "indigenous" or "first peoples" should be used to establish alternative standards whereby people are looked down upon or discriminated against? While a cultural context may inflect the application of a moral principle, it should not alter that principle's claim to validity. It is vital to recognize a universal principle of human existence that unequivocally affirms the equality of all people. Some believe that this is enshrined in the Universal Declaration of Human Rights (UDHR), which recognizes "the inherent dignity and the equal and inalienable rights of all members of the human family [a]s the foundation of freedom, justice and peace in the world." The UDHR states categorically that, "All human beings are born free and equal in dignity and rights."

Even so, there have been many arguments for a hierarchical approach to such rights on the grounds of cultural specificities such as traditional social structures or religious beliefs. In recent years, widespread and recurrent challenges have led some to question the vitality, relevance, and applicability of the UDHR's principles.

However, such challenges tend to overlook the soundness of the Declaration's vision and ignore the ways governments fail to implement its norms and play political games with competing aspirations and scarce resources. Legitimate, independent, and effective institutions of governance are necessary to meet the UDHR's requirements of justice, effective participation, and genuine accountability. Viable public institutions – including the crucial role to be played by independent and nonpartisan mass media – are also needed to ensure that social justice, including equal access to food, education, health, proper housing, and other basic needs, is delivered in an effort to free people from structural violence and discrimination of all kinds.

Criticism has also targeted the very concept of universality on which the Declaration rests. This criticism has been expressed in the mistaken belief that universal principles obstruct pluralistic diversity or cultural specificity or free enterprise. Some skeptics argue that civil and political rights – as articulated in the Declaration – belong solely to Western traditions and to their political and economic agendas, and are not somehow applicable elsewhere. For their part, critics coming from liberal economic perspectives are wary of the Declaration's economic and social rights, which they regard as either hampering free market practices, or imposing cumbersome obligations on States or both. Finally, some have espoused rejectionist positions and recast them into self-serving doctrines simply to preserve privileges and power for themselves and a select few, while covertly denying the rights of everyone else.

Others argue cogently that universal human rights law cannot exclude anyone and must be all-inclusive:

> Within limits dictated by the autonomy principle, international human rights law accommodates the greatest diversity of alternative cultural conceptions of human dignity;... it is the most tolerant of cultural pluralism. Second, [it] is the uniquely appropriate mechanism to counterbalance the threats to human dignity posed by the nation-state, its offshoots, and its instrumentalities. To acknowledge the universality of human rights, then, is not to deny cultural pluralism or the relativity of value. It is to recognize the normative force of the system of international human rights in the face of cultural relativist challenges (More, 2005).

A universal approach to human rights law finds a place in the *Foundations of the Metaphysics of Morals* put forward by Immanuel Kant (1785/1997), where he asks, "Is it not of the utmost necessity to construct a pure moral philosophy which is completely freed from everything which may be only empirical and thus belong to anthropology?" (p. 5) Kant carefully distinguishes moral philosophy from any practical inflection that might limit its scope, arguing:

> Thus not only are moral laws together with their principles essentially different from all practical knowledge in which there is anything empirical, but all moral philosophy rest solely on its pure part. Applied to man, it borrows nothing from knowledge of him (anthropology) but gives man, as a rational being, a priori laws. No doubt those laws require a power of judgment sharpened by experience partly in order to decide in which cases they apply and partly to procure for them access to man's will and to

provide an impetus to their practice. For man is affected by so many inclinations that, though he is capable of the Idea of a practical pure reason, he is not so easily able to make it correctly effective in the conduct of his life (Kant, 1785/1997, p. 5).

In the same book, Kant formulates a general principle of humanity that is entirely relevant to a discussion of universal ethical principles: "Act so that you treat humanity, whether in your own person or in that of another, always as an end and never as a means only" (Kant, 1785/1997, p. 46). It is echoed in the Declaration Towards a Global Ethic endorsed by the Parliament of the World's Religions (1993) where it is stated that:

> By a global ethic we do not mean a global ideology or a single unified religion beyond all existing religions, and certainly not the domination of one religion over all others. By a global ethic we mean a fundamental consensus on binding values, irrevocable standards, and personal attitudes.

Leonard Swidler has pointed out that the Global Ethic was drawn up in a spirit of ecumenism and was specifically aimed at uniting religious and nonreligious positions (Swidler, 1994). As such it was fundamentally a humanist endeavor – and none the worse for that. Swidler proposed combining the principles of the Universal Declaration of Human Rights with those of the Global Ethic to create a *Universal Declaration of a Global Ethic* based on several fundamental assumptions:

1 Every human possesses an inalienable and inviolable dignity.
2 No person or social institution exists beyond the scope of moral order.
3 Humans as beings endowed with reason and conscience should act rationally.
4 Humans are an inextricable part of the universe and as such should act in harmony with nature.

Swidler (1994) claims that the principles of universality, of humanity, and of the autonomy of the human will are found and empirically formulated in all cultures, religious and secular ethical traditions as a practical precept of the ethic of reciprocity. These basic principles are subsumed in his Section IV "Basic Principle" of his *Universal Declaration of a Global Ethic*:

1 Every person is free to experience and develop every capacity as long as it does not infringe on the rights of others or does not disrupt the harmony with the rest of the universe (IV:1).
2 All humans should treat each other as ends, never as means, respecting their intrinsic dignity. This respect should be extended to the community, nation, world and cosmos – to all living creatures and nonliving parts of the universe according to their intrinsic values (IV: 2 & 3).
3 All humans should be granted a right to hold their own beliefs and strive to achieve explanations for meaningful life. A rational dialogue is the only method of arriving at a consensus whereby people can live together (IV, 7).

These principles reinforce Kant's formulation of the categorical imperative that human beings are to be treated as ends, and never as means only: in other words, their freedom and rights are to be respected and their agreement to be sought in the resolution of conflict. We shall return to this notion in a later discussion of communication rights.

Meanwhile, the struggle to construct universal principles with respect to genetics has proved, if anything, even more problematic. Although mitochondrial DNA provides a direct link between all human beings, and people everywhere might be supposed to have a vested interest in protecting their human heritage, there is no sign of a consensus on the ethics of genetic experimentation. If anything, governments, scientists, humanists and people of all faiths and none are in total disarray.

The Declaration of Helsinki (1964) set a standard for human biomedical research to be based on prior laboratory and animal research, introduced ethical reviews by independent panels, and promulgated clinical standards of qualification for researchers. Often revised, it has served as the primary international standard for regulatory ethics in the biomedical field and has evolved from a set of general principles to a more prescriptive set of guidelines. However, since ethical values are, to a large degree, shaped by culture and religion, global consensus is difficult to achieve and as the Declaration has become more prescriptive its relevance and utility has been called into question. Thus, at the international level consensus appears to be more and more elusive.

Approval on March 8, 2005 of a UN nonbinding declaration banning all human cloning did not appreciably change this picture. In addition, international conversations are ongoing with regard to implementing a consensus on protections for the human genome and restrictions on germ line modification. One potentially significant effort is the Universal Declaration on the Human Genome and Human Rights, approved unanimously by the General Conference of UNESCO on November 11, 1997. Article 1 reads, "The human genome underlies the fundamental unity of all members of the human family, as well as the recognition of their inherent dignity and diversity. In a symbolic sense, it is the heritage of humanity."

The Declaration has been cited in many academic and popular journals, and has been referred to in much national and regional legislation on medicine, privacy, and genetic research. UNESCO is currently evaluating the impact of the Declaration worldwide, in accordance with its Guidelines for the Implementation of the Declaration (UNESCO, 1999). These Guidelines outline the action that different groups must take if they are to be fully implemented.

Lack of a consensus regarding application of some biotechnologies to humans, including lack of agreement about the moral status of early-development-stage human embryos, has helped forestall the formulation of rules for human gene research and therapy, and kept researchers away from pursuing certain areas of inquiry. Without clear guidance, scientists working in certain areas of biotechnology find themselves caught in a cultural and moral vacuum, postponing research while awaiting the emergence of a consensus about the acceptability of utilizing human embryos in research and therapy.

The ETC Group is one NGO that advocates socially responsible development of technologies and addresses international governance issues and corporate power. The ETC Group works in partnership with civil society organizations to provide information and analysis of socioeconomic and technological trends and alternatives. It is clearly alarmed by the lack of regulation of human genetic research and the lack of public debate about such developments and their consequences. A recent publication commented:

> Genetic engineering is passé. Today, scientists aren't just mapping genomes and manipulating genes, they're building life from scratch – and they're doing it in the absence of societal debate and regulatory oversight (ETC Group, 2007, p. 7).

Genetics is one human trait that is foundational and the mitochondrial DNA of human beings marks us as intrinsically equal. Human beings share other similarities that point to universal principles. One such is water.

The Importance of Water to Human Life

> Every scenario you have ever read concerning the conditions necessary for life involves water – from the "warm little pond" where Darwin supposed life began to the bubbling sea vents that are now the most popular candidates for life's beginnings (Bryson, 2003, p. 257).

Next to air (in the shape of oxygen, which we will come to next), water is the most essential factor in human life. Water is vital to the functioning of every single cell and organ in the human body, which cannot survive longer than seven days without it. Water makes up more than two-thirds of the weight of the human body: the brain is 75% water; blood is 83% water; bones are 22% water; muscles are 75% water; and lungs are 90% water.

Water regulates body temperature (through perspiration), serves as a lubricant to form the fluids surrounding joints and bones and provide cushioning. Water helps the body to absorb nutrients in the intestines, plays a role in regulating metabolism, and constitutes saliva (necessary for consuming and digesting food). Water carries nutrients and oxygen to all the body's cells and facilitates all the chemical processes that occur in the body. Water is essential for the efficient elimination of waste products through the kidneys. Water also plays a role in the prevention of disease.

Access to potable water underlies the existence and survival of all civilizations and communities worldwide. The very earliest began in river valleys: Mesopotamia around the Tigris and Euphrates, Egypt on the Nile, the dynasties of Xia and Shang along the Yellow River. The Indus Valley Civilization (2600–1900 BC) was one of the first to build towns and open up trade routes. Without functional water management techniques, this would have been impossible. No wonder that throughout the ages, monarchs and despots tamed rivers, dammed lakes, and exercised control over water resources. No wonder that water etiquette is immediately apparent wherever it is scarce. In the Namib desert (Africa's second largest) the first act of greeting and hospitality among travelers is to offer water.

More striking still is the time it took for the international community to begin to think about a regime of water rights to safeguard this precious commodity. It was only during the 1980s that the defense of human rights began to assume a prominent place in development discourse. With some consternation, it was discovered that no human right to water had ever been articulated. It was not until 1989, and then only in the context of the International Convention on the Rights of the Child, that a right to drinking water and sanitation was asserted. In 1996 the new South African Constitution endorsed the claim that it was necessary to recognize the human right to water. In 2002 the UN Committee on Economic, Social and Cultural Rights (CESCR) stated that, "the right to water clearly falls within the category of guarantees essential for securing an adequate standard of living, particularly since it is one of the most fundamental conditions for survival" (CESCR, p. 2, para. 15). It called on governments progressively "to extend access to sufficient, affordable, accessible and safe water supplies and to safe sanitation services."

Under pressure from the Millennium Development Goals (2000), in which heads of state and government pledged to "reduce by half the proportion of people without sustainable access to safe drinking water", the World Health Organization proposed taking a rights-based approach to water. It produced *The Right to Water* (WHO, 2003), backing CESCR's position that, "The human right to water entitles everyone to sufficient, safe, acceptable, physically accessible and affordable for personal and domestic use."

A rights-based approach to water means that water is a legal entitlement, rather than a commodity or service provided on a charitable basis. It means that achieving basic and improved levels of access should be a priority; that the "least served" should be better targeted and therefore inequalities decreased; that communities and vulnerable groups will be empowered to take part in decision-making processes; and that the means and mechanisms available in the UN human rights system will be used to monitor progress in realizing the right to water and in holding governments accountable.

It was not long before the churches began to take an interest. The Protestant and Roman Catholic Churches of Brazil and Switzerland (2005) issued an "Ecumenical declaration on water as a human right and a public good." The Declaration called for:

- The human right to water to be recognized at the local and international level in the same way as the right to adequate food. This right must be respected by all sectors of society but States have a particular responsibility in this area.
- Water to be treated as a public good. The State must take over the commitment to guarantee access to drinking water to all of the population. This guarantee

The Right to Communication as a Universal Value

includes fixing an affordable price for water, making the necessary technical and financial means available, as well as involving local councils and communities in decisions relevant to them on the use of available water resources. Treating water as a public good also implies the commitment of States to regulate the use of water resources by peaceful means, in such a way that the right to water for all of the inhabitants of neighboring States also be respected.

- The right to water to be regulated through an international convention on water to be adopted by the UN.
- In terms of water consumption, legal priorities must be laid down. The first is quenching the thirst of human beings and animals and ensuring the supply of water to food crops. This presupposes a preventative approach to environmental policy, in a spirit of solidarity between local government, countries and peoples.

What does the right to water or the lack of it mean in practice? The following example comes from the work of independent investigative journalist John Ross, a foreign correspondent in Mexico, 2006.

A quarter of all Mexico's water has its source on Indian lands, yet many indigenous communities have no access to water. The Mazahua women of San José Villa de Allende, Mexico State, were so incensed by this inequity that they formed the Zapatista Army of Mazahua Women in Defense of Water (unrelated to the Zapatista Army of National Liberation.) Mazahua land extends on both sides of the banks of the Cutzamala river system, the main outside water source for Mexico City 100 miles to the east, 16 000 l³/s rush by their lands and yet eight of their villages have no water supply, a problem that the Mazahuas have been trying to resolve since the 1980s when the Cutzamala system was inaugurated. Repeatedly rebuffed by the water authorities, the Mazahuas have threatened to shut off the valves that allow water to be piped to Mexico City. In response, the National Water Commission (CONAGUA) sent the state police to occupy their villages.

In March 2006, the Zapatista Army of Mazahua Women in Defense of Water marched on Mexico City to present their case to the World Water Forum taking place there. Mexico City was an appropriate place to hold the fourth World Water Forum (WWF), a once every-three-years conclave organized by the World Water Council, the NGO created by industrialists, big agriculture, and water profiteers who preach privatization and the free market of water. Today's Mexico City – the watery paradise that was Tenochtitlan in the days of the Aztecs – has all but dried up. What little water remains in its aquifers is being pumped out at twice the rate that it can be replenished and the metropolitan area's 23 million residents (2008) are suffering severe water shortages. In some impoverished *colonias*, the only available water source is the cistern truck sent by political parties encouraging people to sell their votes for a gulp of clean water.

Pulling the strings behind the scenes at the 2006 World Water Forum was AquaFed, the lobbying front for world water privateers. Another powerful lobbyist running the show at the WWF was the Washington-based public relations group Burson-Marsteller (which has had ethically dubious relationships with several countries including Nigeria, Romania, and Argentina, as well as the tobacco and oil industries) responsible for organizing the exhibition space and charging water conservation groups $600 a day.

According to Ross's coverage:

> The Zapatista Army of Mazahua Women in Defense of Water did not bother to pay admission. Availing themselves of sympathetic souls in the NGO community, they stormed past the ticket takers and went looking for the head of CONAGUA. Repelled by security guards, the women formed a picket line and began to shout "We want water." With their wooden rifles, sheathed machetes, long skirts, farmers' sombreros, and a look so stern that it could stop traffic, the women terrified the organizers (Ross, 2006).

Latin America is the world's most important water source, but has the smallest per capita consumption on the planet, according to World Bank data presented at the World Water Forum (WWF). The struggle to include the right to water in the WWF's final statement was carried to the forum floor by Bolivia's Minister of Water Abel Mamani, a popular leader from the Aymara city of El Alto, which has been locked in a titanic battle with the French conglomerate Suez, for years doing business in Bolivia as Aguas Ilumani. Mamani insisted that he would not sign the final declaration if water were not declared a universal human right. He was joined by Venezuela, Cuba, and Uruguay (and to a lesser extent by Honduras, France, and Spain) but the revolt was quickly crushed. "The right to water is not relevant to this forum," said Jamal Shagir, the World Bank's director of water and energy. Laic Fouchon, president of the World Water Council, called Mamani's remarks "discourteous and disagreeable" because the Bolivian had pointed out that 2 000, 000 babies die every year from a lack of clean water.

The irony is that, despite general recognition for the right to water, it is only in societies with sustainable democracies and economies that there is much prospect of effective mobilization against the kind neoliberal globalization that restricts access to water:

> The arbiters of land use, industry, agriculture, energy, transport and tourism, pursue their water demand and water conservation policies with the blessing of the world's international financial and trading institutions... they are not over-committed to environmental integrity or to sustaining the livelihoods of around 1 billion rural people at the edge (Black, 2004, p. 124).

The Importance of Oxygen to Human Life

Oxygen is a primary nutrient without which human life could not exist. People can live without food for weeks and without water for between three to seven days. But without oxygen, a person can only survive for 5 minutes. Oxygen is also one of the most significant antiaging components. The more the body's cells are saturated with stabilized oxygen (called oxygenation) the lower the rate of wear and tear.

The Right to Communication as a Universal Value

Oxygen plays a policing role in the body – its natural ability to oxidize bacteria, fungi, and viruses helps prevent degenerative diseases and sustains the natural immortality factor of the cell. Oxygen is also necessary to burn up toxins in the body, those generated internally and those that come from outside in food, water, and the environment. The purpose of the immune system is to fight invaders and prevent degenerative disease. However, the fulfillment of this purpose really hinges on the amount of oxygen saturation in the body. The lower the oxygen content, the less energy to fight disease, burn toxins and heal. The average concentration of oxygen in the blood stream is between 60% and 70%. At this level people generally feel all right, with average energy and alertness. The minimum concentration of oxygen needed to sustain life is about 52%, but at this level the body is not very alive.

With millions of square miles of oxygen-regenerating rainforest already destroyed (and disease growing in the remaining forests), and huge amounts of oxygen-producing sea algae compromised by pollution, the planet's great sources of oxygen are being severely damaged. Scientific studies reveal that while 200 years ago the concentration of oxygen in the air was somewhere between 36% and 38%, recent measurements show a mere 19%. That is a 50% reduction in what was available to our most recent ancestors. In some heavily industrialized areas with high pollution levels, the oxygen content can be as low as 9%.

Basically, the body starves without oxygen. Each one of the body's estimated 100 trillion cells requires oxygen for all of its metabolic processes. Oxygen is needed in order to combust foods to provide energy for the heart, brain, and cells. Without oxygen, the cells starve for energy. They become impaired and dysfunctional, they become vulnerable to invasion from pathogenic organisms or they themselves mutate and begin to attack their healthy counterparts. With a reduced supply of oxygen, the immune system suffers because it requires oxygen to kill off foreign invaders like viruses, fungi, and pathogenic bacteria. People also need oxygen to burn waste products in the body, including waste from their metabolic functions.

Given the importance of oxygen (and, therefore, unpolluted air) to human beings, is there a sense in which there is a right to oxygen or clean air? Canadians think so. In January 2006 the Office of the Auditor General of Canada and the Commissioner of the Environment and Sustainable Development received a "Petition Regarding the Right of Canadians to Clean Air, Clean Water, and a Healthy Environment." It was presented by David R. Boyd, Trudeau Scholar, University of British Columbia, Adjunct Professor, Resource and Environmental Management, Simon Fraser University, and Research Associate, POLIS Project on Ecological Governance, University of Victoria. The petition stated that:

Canadians are gravely concerned about the impact of environmental pollution on their health. Ninety percent of Canadians believe that environmental pollution has a negative effect on their health or the health of their children. Pollution ranks second after stress when Canadians are asked about the major factors having a negative impact on their health. The concerns of Canadians are warranted. There is extensive evidence that environmental degradation is harming the health and well being of Canadians (Boyd, 2006).

The scientist presented evidence from a recent study of ordinary Canadians proving the presence of dozens of toxic chemicals in their blood and urine, including pesticides, polychlorinated biphenyls (PCBs), flame retardants, and plastic softeners; that air pollution causes thousands of premature deaths, tens of thousands of hospitalizations, and hundreds of thousands of days absent from work and school annually; that the dramatic 448% increase in the prevalence of childhood asthma between 1978 and 1995 is linked to environmental factors; that drinking water contaminated by air pollution causes roughly 90 000 cases of gastrointestinal illness annually; that acute pesticide poisoning harms thousands of Canadians annually, mainly children and farm workers; that a number of cancers that have known environmental connections are increasing, including skin cancer (50 000 cases annually) and lung cancer linked to radon exposures (2500 deaths per year); and that lead poisoning causes a range of chronic impacts, primarily affecting children, menopausal women, and the elderly.

Boyd argued that the evidence showed that the right of Canadians to enjoy clean air, clean water, and a healthy environment is being regularly, routinely, and systematically violated. He pointed out that the right to a healthy environment has been explicitly recognized in the constitutions of at least 70 nations in recent years, France being at that time most recent nation to amend its constitution, in early 2005, to explicitly acknowledge the right to a healthy environment. In a number of countries whose constitutions do not explicitly recognize environmental rights, courts have interpreted other constitutionally protected human rights, such as the right to life, liberty, and security of the person, as including the right to a healthy environment (e.g., Italy, the Netherlands, Nigeria, and India).

Canada's *Charter of Rights and Freedoms* (1982) does not explicitly recognize the right to a healthy environment. However, Article 7 of the *Charter* does state that: "Everyone has the right to life, liberty and security of the person and the right not to be deprived thereof except in accordance with the principles of fundamental justice." Section 7 of the Charter, by virtue of its references to the right to life and the right to security of the person, incorporates an implicit right to a healthy environment. In addition, Canada signed the *Hague Declaration on the Environment* in 1989, along with 23 other nations. The *Hague Declaration* recognizes that all individuals have: "The right to live in dignity in a viable global environment, and the consequent duty of the community of nations vis-à-vis present and future generations to do all that can be done to preserve the quality of the environment" (*Hague Declaration*, 1989).

Boyd posed several questions to the Government of Canada including:

1 Does the Government of Canada recognize that Canadians have a right to clean water, clean air, and a healthy environment?
2 Does the Government of Canada recognize that the right of Canadians to clean water, clean air, and a healthy environment enjoys constitutional protection because this right is implicit in Article 7 of the *Charter of Rights and Freedoms*?

3 Would the Government of Canada support an amendment to the *Charter of Rights and Freedoms* to explicitly recognize the right to clean water, clean air, and a healthy, ecologically balanced environment?

In June 2006 the Minister of the Environment issued a joint response on behalf of the Departments of the Environment, Justice, Health, and Foreign Affairs. Addressing the three questions, and citing Canada-wide and provincial legislation aimed at tackling key issues of environmental protection and health risks, it stated that:

> The Government of Canada is of the view that existing legislation and management institutions provide the basis for ensuring that Canadians have access to clean air, safe drinking water, and a healthy, ecologically balanced environment. There is no plan to amend the Canadian Charter of Rights and Freedoms in this regard. Given the role of the Federal Government and that of the provincial and territorial governments in ensuring that Canadians enjoy safe drinking water, clean air, and a healthy environment, the Government of Canada will continue to support an effective regulatory system involving all levels of government that embodies the concept of sustainable development as it seeks to protect the health of Canadians and the environment (Minister of the Environment, 2006).

The response nowhere conceded that there might be a right to oxygen or clean air. Yet just two years later, in July 2008, the European Court of Justice (ECJ) ruled that citizens have a legally enforceable right to clean air. Individuals affected by high concentrations of particulate matter can now call on the courts throughout the European Union (EU) to ensure that effective measures are taken to improve the quality of the air. The authority involved must then draw up an action plan listing the measures to be taken in the short term. The measures must be capable of reducing to a minimum the risk that limit values might be exceeded and of ensuring a gradual return to a level below the ceilings in the long term. The ECJ issued its ruling in response to a complaint lodged by a German citizen against the Munich municipal authority for neglecting to take effective measures to reduce air pollution. Having failed to achieve his goal in the German courts, he was finally successful in Luxemburg. The ECJ quoted an EU directive that provides for comprehensive action plans to be drawn up to tackle the complex problem of air-borne particulate matter.

The matter is unlikely to rest there. While the World Health Organization (WHO) recognizes that air pollution is a major environmental risk to health and is estimated to cause approximately 2 million premature deaths worldwide per year and that exposure to air pollutants is largely beyond the control of individuals and requires action by public authorities at the national, regional, and even international levels, the WHO does not indulge in rights-talk. It is supremely ironic that human beings who depend on oxygen and clean air to survive do not have a right to either.

The Right to Communication

There are obvious parallels between the right to water, the right to oxygen, and the right to communication, which is the symbolic equivalent of both. Human beings are social communicators, making them dependent upon speech and communication in its many modes and guises to enable them to be the enduring living beings they are. For this reason Michael Traber emphasized that:

> Communication, both public and private, is a fundamental human right and, as such, the precondition for other human rights, because communication is intimately bound up with what it means to be human. The freedom to speak and to publicize, and to create works of communication (cultural goods) is not only an essential component of human dignity and cultural identity, but it is also necessary for any progress in other rights (Traber, 1992/2008, p. 202).

Human beings have intentions, plans and schemes; they have individual and communal relationships; they believe themselves capable of making rational decisions in accord with short- and long-term interests; they are self-created in communion with their physical and sociocultural environments. Human beings live in communities on which they depend for their survival, their ambitions, and the language that describes and identifies them. These factors create the ever-present possibility of minor or major conflict – the tensions that arise from dependence, interdependence, and, paradoxically, the freedom to make choices and to live differently.

Consequently, people and communities live in and through communication, by negotiation and treaty, creating dialogue and conversation based on assumptions, for example, that different sides in a discussion or dispute should be able to give and accept reasons for their actions and to recognize good and bad, valid and invalid. In the form of democracy that passes for the best attainable, everyone should be free to make choices, to act intentionally and lawfully and to take responsibility for the outcome of their actions. Therefore everyone needs to strive for consensus and be prepared to make concessions to obtain it. Everyone must accept the sanctity and inviolability of life, since to threaten either is to threaten themselves and everyone must understand, accept and honor their obligations.

As discussed earlier, Kant sees these elements as constituting a moral law that has an absolute character and whose rights cannot be arbitrarily denied or weighed against alternative outcomes. As Roger Scruton points out:

> I must respect your right, regardless of conflicting interests, since you alone can renounce or cancel it. That is the point of the concept – to provide an absolute barrier against invasion. A right is an interest that is given special protection, and which cannot be overridden or cancelled without the consent of the person who possesses it (Scruton, 1996, p. 112).

Communication is recognized as just such a right – which cannot be trampled on or denied and without which individuals or communities cannot exist or prosper.

Communication enables meanings to be exchanged, makes people who and what they are, and motivates them to act. Communication strengthens human dignity and validates human equality. How, then, can communication be reasonably denied? Furthermore, recognition, implementation and protection of communication rights enable the recognition, implementation, and protection of all other human rights (Girard and Ó Siochrú, 2003) and the different capacities of people and communities to use communication and the media of communication to pursue their goals in the economic, political, social, and cultural spheres are also enhanced (Lee, 2004). Communication rights, therefore, encompass issues of inclusion and exclusion, equality and inequality, accessibility and denial, all of which are questions of human dignity.

In addition to numerous articles in scholarly journals, the critical literature endorsing the notion of communication rights is extensive (see, inter alia, CRIS Campaign, 2005; Dakroury, Eid, and Kamlipour, 2009; Fisher, 1982; Fisher and Harms, 1983; Galtung and Vincent, 1992; Girard and Ó Siochrú, 2003; Golding, Harris and Jayaweera, 1992; Hamelink, 1994; Hamelink, 2004; Harms, Richstad and Kie, 1977; Lee, 2004, 2008; Somavía, 1979; Traber, 1990). There are, of course, many voices opposed to the notion of communication rights, which perhaps makes it less remarkable that they have not yet been assigned the status of a universal entitlement. Governments are afraid that communication rights properly implemented and guaranteed might lead to genuine democracy and political accountability. Media corporations are afraid that communication rights might limit monopolies and decrease their global profits. The rich are afraid that communication rights will enfranchise the poor and the world's hierarchies of despots – global, regional, national and local – are afraid that communication rights will lead to giving up their status, privileges, and power.

As with water, a rights-based approach to communication means that communication becomes a legal entitlement, rather than a commodity or service provided on a charitable basis. It means that achieving basic and improved levels of access should be a priority; that the "least served" should be better targeted and therefore inequalities decreased; that communities and vulnerable groups will be empowered to take part in decision-making processes; and that the means and mechanisms available in the UN human rights system will be used to monitor progress in realizing the right to communication and in holding governments accountable.

Many examples of infringements of communication rights can be found. The following story comes from Chile and illustrates the violation of human rights and how implementing communication rights can augment the potential for social justice.

In October 1973, in the Mapuche community of Maiquillahue, near San José de la Mariquina, government soldiers murdered José Matías Ñanco, aged 60, fisherman, Protestant pastor, and leftist-sympathizer. The National Truth and Reconciliation Commission Report, made public in June 1991, recorded the circumstances. It seems that military troops carried out an operation in the area, detaining some 13 people and lining them up for questioning. José refused to obey, speaking harshly to the soldiers, pushing away one of their rifles, so they shot and killed him. A uniformed soldier ordered that the body be removed but refused to allow the other detainees to do so. The soldiers themselves took it to an unknown place. During the investigation, it was established that among the soldiers was a member of the Maiquillahue community – a recruit – who must have given the authorities the names of members of the community, including that of José Matías. This was not an unusual situation in the first months of the Pinochet dictatorship, when old quarrels, or the urgency of avoiding possible reprisals, turned into hasty denunciations whose consequences were unforeseen.

In January 2007 the Chilean Supreme Court condemned to five years and one day's imprisonment retired army officer Héctor Rivera Bozzo, who directed the operation, handing down lesser sentences to five others complicit in the deed. The Court judgment records that "the victim's body was thrown from a helicopter into the waters of the Pacific Ocean in the evening of the same day" (*El Mercurio*, 2007). As the body of José Matías has never been returned to them, his family, while knowing he is dead, considers him as having "disappeared."

In 1990, 17 years after these events, reaching Maiquillahue still meant a 2-hour walk from the nearest point accessible to a vehicle from the city of Valdivia in southern Chile. Apart from the geographical difficulty of access, the community bore two other identification marks that made it even more "invisible": its people were Mapuche (indigenous inhabitants of central and southern Chile) and Protestant (in a predominantly Catholic and conservative country). The histories of this and other indigenous communities in the country were generally unknown at the national level. At the end of the winter of 1990, Patricia Farías, at that time editor of the magazine *Evangelio y Sociedad* published by SEPADE, travelled to Valdivia with the intention of preparing a report on another massacre at Chihuio, a case in which 14 of the 18 victims belonged to Protestant churches in the region. On the train, Patricia happened to meet Sandra Rojas, a colleague and friend, and to her surprise learnt that her journey had the same purpose. Quickly they decided to share contacts and undertake the painful trip together.

From the very first interviews with local human rights activists, they began hearing of a case about which little was known, where the victim was a Protestant Mapuche pastor. Once they had gathered all the information they needed about the Chihuio incident, they decided to face the difficulties of the road and press on to Maiquillahue. However, since they arrived unannounced, it proved difficult to overcome the community's inherent distrust and fear. Only Cornelio Tito, another of the sons of José Matías, was prepared to talk with the journalists. *Evangelio y Sociedad* (October–December 1990) published the report on the Chihuio victims, including a section on the death of Pastor José Matías Ñanco of Maiquillahue. This was a publication with a circulation restricted to Protestant and ecumenical groups. For the family, however, to have a written version of the story became a form of evidence that gave credibility to their testimony and an incentive to seek clarification of the truth for justice to be done.

There the story might have ended, except that in 2007 the two journalists got together to recall their experience in the interior of Valdivia Province. Although the degree of violence and the number of victims at Chihuio made it a more journalistically interesting case, it was their visit to Maiquillahue that remained in their memory. There was something metaphorical in that small community, so geographically isolated yet, at the same time, so profoundly riven by the realities and tensions that characterized twentieth century Chile, including the marginalization of the Mapuche people following the so-called pacification of the Araucania Region; the presence of the Protestant churches and their encounters and misunderstandings with Mapuche identity; finally, dictatorship, repression, human rights violations and the subsequent search for truth and justice. It did not escape the journalists' observation that a more recent conflict, but also one with national import, had once again marred the lives of the Maiquillahue fisher-folk: a project to construct a pipeline in Caleta Mehuín to dump industrial waste.

The journalists wondered how the Matías of Maiquillahue might be living the present and looking to the future? Convinced that this was an important question not just for them but also for a country that was getting ready to commemorate its bicentenary, the journalists proposed going back to Maiquillahue. In conversation it rapidly emerged that two other events made the question particularly relevant to Protestants in Chile: Chilean Pentecostalism – the Matías family church was also Pentecostal – was getting ready to celebrate its own centenary and October 31, the day José Matías was murdered, had been declared the "National Day of Evangelical and Protestant Churches." There was no doubt, therefore, that Chile needed to hear the story of the Matías.

A video documentary seemed to be the appropriate medium and, once the project had been approved and funded, contact was made with Valdivia Films to carry it out. Fernando Lataste, its director, knew the story and showed immediate interest, but at the same time he warned that it would not be easy to win the trust of the community in order for it to take part in the project. These doubts were dispelled when, on a joint visit to Maiquillahue, the family of the deceased pastor, recognizing the journalists, received them with open arms and much gratitude for the help rendered them by the *Evangelio y Sociedad* article, which had helped advance the judicial process. For the family, sharing their story in a documentary that would be screened publicly offered a new opportunity to come to terms with their grief and to continue with their lives in peace.

In March 2008 a gathering of the now dispersed Matías family was organized in the paternal home – the occasion on which filming took place. In the midst of the testimonies and family dialogue, José Matías's granddaughter emerged as the natural narrator of the film, interpreting the accounts of the elders and communicating them to a wider audience. The varied nuances with which each witness told his or her version of the events – which were not removed during editing – illustrated different of ways of viewing Chilean national history: Mapuche/non-Mapuche; Mapuche/ Protestant; victims/killers; civilians/armed forces; and other subtle differences. The right to communicate the individual (subjective) story of José Matías reinforced the communication rights of the Maiquillahue collectivity and moved them one step closer to justice and the possibility of reconciling themselves to the future.

The Right to Communication as a Universal Value

Are the rights to water, to oxygen, and to communication individual or collective rights? In the case of communication rights and communication ethics, the conundrum of individual/collective, of objective/subjective, seems to bedevil both. However, Clifford G. Christians believes that critical resolution can be found in philosophical anthropology (pace Kant) as long as normativity is adequately understood in terms of human wholeness (Christians, 1997, p. 6). It is human wholeness both at the level of the individual and the community that the above examples illustrate. Christians elucidates, pointing out that: "A commitment to universals does not eliminate all differences in what we think and believe. Normative ethics grounded ontologically is pluralistic. The only question is whether our values affirm the human good or not" (Christians, 1997, p. 18).

Edmund Arens implicitly supports this contention, quoting Jürgen Habermas's procedural rules of discourse ethics to argue that:

> Discourse ethics does not tie universalization to the reflection and imagination of isolated individual subjects who in each particular case seek to hypothetically assume for themselves the universal perspective. Instead, discourse ethics ties universalization to the real argumentation and the actual discourse of potentially all affected parties... universalization is supposed to guarantee that the interests of all are taken into account (Arens, 1997, pp. 54–55).

In the framework of emerging "information societies" and powerful reassertions of local sociocultural identities, communication ethicists realized the need to respond to the globalization of communications in an attempt to address the tensions created, on the one hand, by cultural homogenization and, on the other, by cultural resistance. These two trends had long been identified in Latin America where, after more than 50 years of theory and praxis, the continent had emerged at the forefront of the theoretical construction of models of democratic communication.

One leading proponent was Jesús Martín-Barbero, whose theorizing of mass communication as a locus of contending discourses includes the proposal that communication processes be addressed from the point of view of social movements rather than beginning with assumptions about media power. He argued that:

> Communication has become a strategic arena for the analysis of the obstacles and contradictions that move these societies, now at the crossroads between accelerated under-development and compulsive modernization. Because communication is the meeting point of so many new conflicting and integrating forces, the centre of the debate has shifted from media to mediations. Here, mediations refer especially to the articulations between communication practices and social movements and the articulation of different tempos of development within the plurality of cultural matrices (Martín-Barbero, 1987, p. 187).

Martín-Barbero problematized the ethics of globalization in terms of mediations and explored the sociocultural specificities that need to be taken into account when models of communication are imposed from the outside.

In a similar fashion, and in the context of addressing questions raised by genetics and genetic engineering, Suzuki and Knudtson initiated a search for ethical principles beyond the realm of Western science and philosophical thinking. They called for a new breed of cultural anthropologists who can sift through crosscultural knowledge for "fragments of truth" that might contribute to a crosscultural synthesis of moral values:

> It would be forged from elements drawn from the rich diversity of myths, rituals and other expressions of human values concerning such timeless topics as heredity, life and death, and the natural world. Out of a mingling of a moral vision of many cultures and the latest insights of molecular genetics might gradually emerge what could be called a new and scientifically relevant mythology for our times – one steeped not only in the myth-shattering truths of science but also in the values that might help us use that scientific knowledge wisely and humanely (Suzuki and Knudtson, 1990, p. 338).

If we put these propositions together – pluralistic normative ethics grounded in the nature of being (Christians), the universalization of the discourse of all interested parties (Arens), a plurality of cultural matrices (Martín-Barbero), and the potential offered by a crosscultural synthesis of moral values (Suzuki and Knudtson) – and if we accept the universality of mitochondrial DNA, water, oxygen, and communication as indicators of humanity, we can conclude that communication rights have universal moral validity. If human beings cannot meaningfully exist without communication, as they cannot exist without water and oxygen, it becomes self-evident that the individual right to communicate must be a protonorm of communication ethics.

From this we can state that communication rights frame a plurality of normative ethics interpreted via a plurality of cultural matrices. The two notions meet to satisfy Kant's requirement of an *a priori* moral law (the right to communication) that can be inflected by "a power of judgment sharpened by experience" (accommodation to cultural specificities) provided that individuals and communities "Act so that you treat humanity, whether in your own person or in that of another, always as an end and never as a means only."

We might prefer to concur with the somewhat cynical view of one of Edith Wharton's protagonists:

> What was the staunchest code of ethics but a trunk with a series of false bottoms? Now and then one had the illusion of getting down to absolute right or wrong, but it was only a false bottom – a removable hypothesis – with another false bottom underneath. There was no getting beyond the relative (Wharton, 1899/2007, p. 69).

However, we can only move forward if we countenance the affirmation that the right to water, the right to oxygen, and the right to communication occupy common ontological ground as universal values. The right to water, oxygen, and communication can be considered, therefore, imperatives held in common by all human beings and communities. They are universal human rights.

References

Arens, E. (1997) Discourse ethics and its relevance for communication and media ethics, in *Communication Ethics and Universal Values*, (eds C. Christians and M. Traber), Sage, Thousand Oaks/London/New Delhi, pp. 46–67.

Black, M. (2004) *The No-Nonsense Guide to Water*. Oxford: New Internationalist/Verso, Oxford/ London.

Boyd, D. (2006) www.oag-bvg.gc.ca/internet/English/pet_163A_e_28897.html (accessed June 23, 2010) and www.oag-bvg.gc.ca/internet/English/pet_163B_e_28898.html (accessed June 23, 2010).

Bradshaw Foundation (2008) *Journey of Mankind*, www.bradshawfoundation.com/journey/ (accessed June 23, 2010).

Bryson, B. (2003) *A Short History of Nearly Everything*, Transworld Publishers, London.

CESCR (2002) The right to water, General comment number 15.

Charter of Rights and Freedom (Canada) (1982) http://laws.justice.gc.ca/en/charter/ (accessed June 10, 2010).

Christians, C.G. (1997) The ethics of being in a communication context, in *Communication Ethics and Universal Values*, (eds C. Christians and M. Traber), Sage, Thousand Oaks/London/New Delhi, pp. 3–23.

CRIS Campaign (2005) *Assessing Communication Rights: A Handbook*, CRIS, London, www.centreforcommunicationrights.org/tools-and-training/40-tools/125–cris-campaign-assessing-communication-rights-a-handbook-.html?layout=citation(accessed June 23, 2010).

Dakroury, A., Eid, M., and Kamlipour, Y. (eds.) (2009) *The Right to Communicate: Historical Hopes, Global Debates, and Future Premises*, Kendall Hunt Publishers, Dubuque.

Darwin, C. (1871) *The Descent of Man*, Chapter XXI, general summary and conclusion.

Dawkins, R. (2005) *The Ancestor's Tale: A Pilgrimage to the Dawn of Life*, Weidenfeld & Nicolson, London.

Declaration of Helsinki (1964) www.wma.net/en/30publications/10policies/b3/index.html (accessed June 11, 2010)

El Mercurio (2007) January 20, http://diario.elmercurio.cl/detalle/index.asp?id=%7B19 c3df1e-69f0-4fbb-9ab6-47a404771b74%7D (accessed July 13, 1010).

ETC Group (2007) *Extreme Genetic Engineering: An Introduction to Synthetic Biology*, www.etcgroup.org/en/materials/publications.html?pub_id=602 (accessed June 23, 2010).

Fisher, D. (1982) *The Right to Communicate: A Status Report*, UNESCO, Paris.

Fisher, D., and Harms, L.S. (eds) (1983) *The Right to Communicate: A New Human Right*, Boole Press, Dublin.

Galtung, J., and Vincent, R.C. (1992) *Global Glasnost: Towards a New World Information and Communication Order*, Ablex, Norwood.

Golding, P., Harris P., and Jayaweera, N. (eds) (1992) *Beyond Cultural Imperialism: New Perspectives on the New World Information Order*, Sage, London.

Girard, B., and Ó Siochrú, S. (eds) (2003) *Communicating in the Information Society*, UNRISD, Geneva.

Hague Declaration (1989) www.nls.ac.in/CEERA/ceerafeb04/html/documents/lib_ int_ c1s2_hag_230300.htm (last accessed June 24, 2010).

Hamelink, C. (1994) *The Politics of World Communication: A Human Rights Perspective*, Sage, London.

Hamelink, C.J. (2004) *Human Rights for Communicators*, Hampton Press, Creskill, NJ.

Harms, L.S., Richstad, J., and Kie, K.A. (1977) *The Right to Communicate: Collected Papers*, University of Hawaii, Manoa.

Kant, I. (1785/1977) *Foundations of the Metaphysics of Morals and What is Enlightenment*, rev. 2nd edn, (trans. L.W. Beck), Prentice Hall, Englewood Cliffs, NJ.

Lee, P. (ed.) (2004) *Many Voices, One Vision: The Right to Communicate in Practice*, Southbound, Penang.

Lee, P. (ed.) (2008) *Communicating Peace: Entertaining Angels Unawares*, Southbound, Penang.

Martín-Barbero, J. (1987) *Communication, Culture and Hegemony: From the Media to Mediations*, (trans. E. Fox and R.A. White), Sage, London.

Minister of the Environment (2006) Response to Question 3, June, www.oag-bvg.gc.ca/internet/English/pet_163A_e_28897.html (accessed July 13, 2010).

More, E. (2005) The Universal Declaration of Human Rights in today's world. *International Communications Journal*, 11 (2), www.internationalcommunicationsjournal.com/issues/volume-11-no-2/the-universal-declaration-of-human-rights-in-today%92s-world-.asp (accessed June 23, 2010).

Oppenheimer, S. (2004) *Out of Africa's Eden. The Peopling of the World*, Jonathan Ball Publishers, Cape Town.

Parliament of the World's Religions (1993) Declaration toward a global ethic: No new global order without a global ethic, www.weltethos.org/dat-english/03-declaration.htm (accessed July 13, 2010).

Ross, J. (2006) When even water is not a human right. *Counterpunch*, March 26, www.counterpunch.org/ross03292006.html (accessed June 23, 2010).

Scruton, R. (1996) *An Intelligent Person's Guide to Philosophy*, Duckworth, London.

Somavía, J. (1979) *Democratización de las comunicaciones: Una perspectiva latinoamericana*, ILET, Mexico City.

Suzuki, D., and Knudtson, P. (1990) *Genethics. The Clash Between the New Genetics and Human Values*, Harvard University Press, Cambridge, MA.

Swidler, L. (1994) Toward a Universal Declaration of a Global Ethic. *Dialogue and Humanism, The Universalist Journal*, IV (4), 51–64. www.jsri.ro/old/html%20version/index/no_7/leonardswidler-articol.htm (accessed June 23, 2010).

The Protestant and Roman Catholic Churches of Brazil and Switzerland (2005) Ecumenical declaration on water as a human right and a public good, April 22, www.oikoumene.org/resources/documents/wcc-programmes/justice-diakonia-and-responsibility-for-creation/climate-change-water/water-as-a-human-right-and-a-public-good.html (accessed June 23, 2010).

Traber, M. (1990) *The Myth of the Information Revolution*, Sage, London.

Traber, M. (1992/2008) Communication as a human need and human right, in *Communicating Peace: Entertaining Angels Unawares*, (ed. P. Lee), Southbound, Penang, pp. 243–257.

UNESCO (1999) Guidelines for the Implementation of the Declaration, http://portal.unesco.org/shs/en/files/2409/10560185351guidelines_en.pdf/guidelines_en.pdf (accessed June 10, 2010).

Wharton, E. (1899/2007) A cup of cold water. *The New York Stories of Edith Wharton*, New York Review of Books, New York.

WHO (World Health Organization) (2003) The right to water, www.who.int/water_sanitation_health/rightowater/en (accessed July 13, 2010).

9

Glocal Media Ethics

Shakuntala Rao

The word globalization has become the currency among journalists and academics in the past 20 years. From terrorism to the environment, free trade to protectionism, population growth to poverty and social justice, globalization seems deeply implicated in nearly all of the major issues of the new millennium. Every discipline is seeking to find its own epistemological location in the globalization debate. Some equate globalization merely with free markets; others use the term interchangeably with concepts such as transnationalism or postnationalism. "Called upon to account for developments as diverse as the value of the euro," observe Held and McGrew (2003, p. 22), "the worldwide popularity of *Star Wars*, the rise of Third Way politics and religious fundamentalism, the discourse of globalization seem to offer an analysis of the contemporary human predicament." While human lives continue to be lived in local realities, these realities are increasingly being challenged and integrated into larger global networks of relationships. People's experiences are linked to economic realities, social processes, technological and media innovations, and cultural flows that traverse national boundaries with greater momentum. In the past two decades, liberalization and privatization of the media systems, first in Europe and North America and then in the countries of South has created a new media world order. The existing centers of power for the past few centuries – be it the European nations of Britain, France, Spain, and Italy and the post-World War II US – are currently renegotiating their place in world history and in increasingly transnational media flows. The old categories which had defined international communication are passé. The rise of 'Chindia' (the joint economic and political powerhouses of China and India); the postapartheid rise of South Africa; Middle East nations', such as United Arab Emirates, Qatar, Bahrain, and Saudi Arabia, vast repositories of natural resources; and the post-Soviet Russia's resurgent military and cultural dominance over Eastern Europe and Asian Republics challenge and render obsolete previous

The Handbook of Global Communication and Media Ethics, First Edition. Edited by Robert S. Fortner and P. Mark Fackler.
© 2011 Blackwell Publishing Ltd. Published 2011 by Blackwell Publishing Ltd.

Glocal Media Ethics

155

descriptions of the global mediascape. The rise of satellite television, the Internet, and geolinguistic media markets have created new structures of media production and consumption, undercutting the preexisting dominance of state-controlled media. The focus of academic work in communication has shifted from a paradigm of international communication to one of media globalization where cultural, economic, political, social, and technical analysis of communication patterns and effects between nations has given way to studies of exchanges between transnational corporations, local and regional media companies, consumers, and media workers (Thussu, 2006). Given the increasing global flow of information, culture, and capital, scholars are wrestling to lay the epistemic foundation for global journalism. Berglez's (2008, p. 845) question, "What is global journalism?" is a significant one if we are to theoretically proceed in our attempts to understand the ethical issues surrounding global media. Berglez asks, "Is a domestic news story in which a domestic event is connected to climate change still solely domestic news? And does it not seem too limiting to apply traditional foreign news theory, with its restrictions to "events in distant countries", to transnational processes such as world terrorism or the SARS epidemic?" (2008, p. 845). There is, Berglez argues, a lack of theoretical rigor in journalism studies where too much emphasis is placed on the traditional conceptual framework of domestic/foreign news. Berglez argues for a theoretical and empirical model of global journalism that transcends and transgresses the domestic/foreign news dichotomy and, instead, focus on a kind of journalism (in practice and in developing content) which is boundary-less, mobile, interconnected, and embedded with a progressive "global outlook" (p. 855). In the multilayered world of television, Internet, and quick connectivity, it seems imperative that scholars develop new models and theoretical approaches to analyzing journalism practices and news content. Discussions of media ethics also need careful and rigorous epistemic reorientation. In this chapter, I argue, that discussions of global media ethics needs to acknowledge the "local" as an integral and necessary component of defining or constructing ethics for journalists globally. Extending the approach advocated by Christians *et al.* (2008, p. 136) that scholarship in global media ethics must recognize that "the universal and the particular are intimately linked," I suggest that the discussion of global media ethics can anchor itself in theories of "glocalization" as advocated by Ronald Robertson (1997, p. 25), and that journalistic practices and ethics in India can be described as, and informed by, Robertson's notion of the reciprocity between the global and the local, or the "glocal." By studying journalism ethics codes and practices in India, I conclude that media ethics in different parts of the world, when studied carefully in writing and practice, is glocal.

Globalization as Glocalization

Most scholars agree that globalization has been responsible for major transformations in the structures of media production and reception. The process of globalization is changing people's "perceptions of time and space" (Lie and Servaes, 2000, p. 317);

the influences of globalization broaden boundaries, yet also strengthen existing boundaries of self, identity, and culture. Some globalists believe, in a deterministic sense of the word, that the mere presence of global forces is prima facie evidence that local culture can have no power of resistance, and that globalization requires "the local to surrender, now incapable of radical resistance" (Thornton, 2000, p. 80). "Few terms have been stretched as far or proved to be as infinitely extendable as the word globalization," writes Mattelart (2002, p. 591). As media worlds get rearranged, it becomes more necessary for scholars to reject globalization as a "technolglobal new-speak" (Mattelart, p. 592) which operates like a lingua franca and makes its pronounce-ments "as if they are self evident truths requiring no discussion." Everyday practice, however, has shown a simultaneous solidification of global flows and the consolidation of local identities. Wilson and Dissanayake (1996, p. 1) term this paradoxical condition "a new world-space of cultural production and national representation which is simul-taneously becoming more globalized (unified around dynamics of capitalogic moving across borders) and more localized (fragmented into contestory enclaves of difference, coalition, and resistance) in everyday texture and composition."

Glocalization as an epistemological and intellectual inquiry has been around for some time, although its use among journalism and media scholars has been limited. Glocalization as a theoretical formation has been floated by authors such as Giddens (1990), Sparks (2000), Sreberny-Mohammadi (1987), and Straubhaar (2007) but it is in the work of Robertson that glocalization is best articulated for the purposes of understanding the professional practice of journalism and media. Globalization, for Robertson, falls short of rendering the complexity of international dynamics and glocalization is offered as a more appropriate term and idea to theoretically ground the sometimes contestory and sometimes cooperative forces of the global and the local. Rejecting the false dialectical opposition of the global/local, center/periphery, universality/particularism models as inadequate, Robertson (1997, p. 29) writes that glocalization "captures the dynamics of the local in the global and the global in the local." Citing the definition from the *Oxford Dictionary of New Words*, Robertson notes that glocalization has been modeled on Japanese *dochakuka* (deriving from *dochaku* or living on one's own land), originally the agricultural principle of adapting one's farming techniques to local conditions, but also adopted in Japanese business for "global localization, a global outlook adapted to local conditions" (1997, p. 28). He proposes the theory of glocalization as a way of accounting for both global and local, not as opposites but rather as "mutually formative, complementary competi-tors, feeding off each other as they struggle for influence" (Kraidy, 2003, p. 38). His idea of glocalization allows media scholars to escape "the pull of the global/local polarity" and the fear that the local is dead (Robertson, 1997, p. 29). Rather than pitching global *against* the local, glocalization hopes to break down the "ontologi-cally secure homes" of each and present them as interconnected forces (Robertson, 1997, p. 30). While some social theorists have attacked the concept of glocalization as being particularly apolitical, "without any teeth or resistance to the sinister forces of globalization" (Thornton, 2000, p. 79), Robertson calls for both understanding of the global–local nexus and of seeing glocalization as a tool of resistance and accommodation. The central project of glocalization is to understand the reconfiguration of locality and local subjects, to account for new cultural forms emerging at the intersections of the global and local, and to counter the frequently expressed thesis that global flows of labor, culture, and capitals necessarily result in homogenization. Robertson's idea of glocalization recognizes that when ideas, objects, institutions, images, practices, performances, are transplanted to other places, they both bear the marks of history as well as undergo a process of translation. The appeal of glocalization is in its conceptual elasticity and its ability to understand that locales (global, regional, national, provincial, local) overlap and mutually influence practices, contexts, and identities. As symbolic materials circulate on an ever-greater scale, locales become sites where, to an ever-increasing extent, globalized media products are received, interpreted, and incorporated into the daily lives of individuals. While the term glocalization has become transdisciplinary in use, very little scholarly work in media studies has focused on glocalization of news, journalism, and media practices; globalization theorists have focused on studying cultural diffusion and cultural diversity rather than news content and journalism practice (Wasserman and Rao, 2008). Concepts such as hybridity, creolization, mestizaje, syncretism, bricolage, and flows have inundated the literature in media and reception studies, and even studies of the cultural, political, and economic aspects of journalism, but have remained curiously absent from scholarship about journalism and media ethics.

Global Media Ethics

The past few years has seen various efforts in the fields of media studies, journalism, and communication to develop a philosophically rigorous and epistemologically sound ethics for the global media (Babbili, 1997; Brislin, 2004; Christians and Traber, 1997; Couldry, 2006; Merrill, 2002; Rao and Lee, 2005). In one attempt to formulate global media ethics, *Journal of Mass Media Ethics* published a special issue titled "Search for a global media ethics" (2003). One of the authors in this issue writes that the profession's global scope and transnational media forces the question of whether there can be "universal ethical standards for journalism to meet the challenges of globalization" (Callahan, 2003, p. 3). Similarly, Ward (2005, p. 4) states that a global media ethics would imply that responsibility "would be owed to an audience scattered across the world," a development resulting from the increasingly global reach of media corporations facilitated through new technologies. Christians and Nordenstreng (2004) have proposed a theoretical formulation which reexamines the search for global media ethics, and proposes the social responsibility theory as a possibility for the press to adopt internationally. They offer the possibility of establishing several universal principles which they ground in "a morality rooted in animate nature" (p. 20). Stating that "global social responsibility needs an ethical basis commensurate in scope, that is, universal ethical principles rather than the parochial moral guidelines represented by codes", Christians and Nordenstreng list respect for human dignity (based on sacredness of human life), truth, and nonviolence as three universal principles (2004, p. 20). Ward and Wasserman (2008), in the introduction of their book *Media Ethics Beyond Borders: A Global Perspective*, one of the first comprehensive anthologies on global media ethics, write, "A global-minded media is of value because biased and parochial media can wreak havoc in a tightly linked global world. By the same token, media that claim to be 'global' yet fail to acknowledge the ways in which their ethical perspective are influenced by their own cultural, historical or political positioning, will be unable to help us make sense of the world in which we live" (p. 1). There is a clear sense among ethicists, journalists, and scholars alike that *any* invention, evolution, or construction of global media ethics must be highly nuanced both in its epistemological approach and practical applications. The multidisciplinary theoretical perspective laid out by Christians *et al.* (2008) in their essay on global media ethics has further opened up new avenues of discussions. While not specifically invoking glocalization, the essay lays the "theoretical foundation upon which further discussion about the application of a global media ethics to particular contexts could take place" (p. 138). It does not presume to provide conclusive answers to theoretical questions about the relationship between the local and the global, the universal and the particular, but puts forward an argument about ways in which current disagreements about the nature, possibility, and desirability of a global media ethics can be resolved. "Progress in developing a global media ethics is stymied by a number of widespread beliefs and presumptions," write Christians *et al.* (2008), "One issue is whether there *are* universal values in media ethics." Their answer is as follows:

> It appears there are universals. Even a cursory survey of many codes of journalism ethics would find agreement, at least on a denotative level, on such values as reporting the truth, freedom and independence, minimizing harm, and accountability. Yet, a survey would also find differences. Some media cultures emphasize more strongly that other such values as the promotion of social solidarity, not offending religious beliefs and not weakening public support for the military. Even where media systems agree on a value, such as "freedom of press" or "social responsibility," they may interpret and apply such principles in different ways (p. 138).

In opening up these tensions, the authors describe several theoretical positions which might coalesce to form our current understanding of global media ethics. In their attempts to avoid errors of the past, Christians *et al.* (2008) propose an outline of a theory of ethics consisting of levels that interact dynamically in experience, "the levels of presuppositions, principles, and precepts" (p. 140). Rooted in a holistic conception of theory where basic values and ideas emerge from a "common humanness in concrete contexts", such values can be seen as "context-influenced articulations of deep aspects of being human" (p. 139). The authors critique the failure of past ethicists to often understand their own theoretical location as imperialist or historically, culturally, and politically positioned. They hope that the global and local, Western and non-Western, colonizer and colonized, can be brought together in a reflexive, relational, and critical dialectic that could contribute to the development of global media ethics. Scholarship of media ethics, it appears, has

Glocal Media Ethics   159

been perpetually caught *between* the global and local, in an irresolvable quandary or open conflict. The question posed by Wasserman (2008, p. 92), "Is it possible to agree on ethical conduct for journalists around the globe?" has become an urgent one. The task for us, Christians *et al.* (2008), argue is to understand the intimate connections between the global and the local, not as opposites, antagonists, working against each other's interests, in order to displace one with the other; rather, global media ethics must recognize the particular or local as the basic unit of analysis in all attempts to globalize and universalize. If we are to accept globalization as the spatio-temporal compression of the world, we must acknowledge that it has led to the "creating and incorporation of new forms of locality" (Robertson, 1997, p. 25) which defy simplistic and unidirectional theoretical assertions of homogenization, Americanization, or "McDonaldization" (Ritzer, 2006, p. 32). Journalism, in particular, has stayed anchored in the local while adapting, appropriating, and localizing global practices and technologies. This chapter focuses on the journalism ethics in India to show that the local is not being destroyed by "waves of Western globalization" (Hafez, 2007, p. 23) but rather the local is adapting to and integrating the arrival of transnational media ethical practices in a multiple of ways. I argue that while journalism ethics and practices have indeed been influenced by globalization, such practices and ethical decisions continue to be highly localized.

Changing Indian Media Landscape

Like the rest of the economy, Indian media has been transformed given the rapid liberalization and deregulation beginning in the early 1990s. Following the breakdown of the Soviet Union in the late-1980s, the government of then Prime Minister, P.V. Narasimha Rao, faced a fiscal crisis and was forced to make policy changes which relaxed restrictions on multinationals, which then expanded and invested in the Indian market. It was the "onslaught from the skies" that radically changed Indian media with the arrival of international satellite-distributed television (Pelton, Oslund, and Marshall, 2004, p. 44). International television came with CNN's coverage of the 1991 Gulf War. Between 1991 and 1995, several Indian satellite-based television services, prominently among them Zee TV and Sony TV, were launched. Consequently, the Indian media economy changed considerably. Foreign channels like CNNI and BBC World, and domestic channels like Zee TV, NDTV, and Sun TV, suddenly and explosively increased the demand for cable. Before 1991, Indian viewers had received only two channels but, by 2007, they were receiving more than 90 channels. Before reforms, Indian audiences had depended solely on state-owned public broadcasting entity *Doordarshan*, to provide news; after reforms Indian audiences could choose between several 24-hour news channels. India is currently the third largest cable TV viewing nation in the world, after China and the US, with more than 100 million cable and TV households by the end of 2006 (Mehta, 2007). Unlike in the West where there has been a drop in newspaper circulation, India has witnessed a growth in the print industry (Ninan, 2007, p. 66).

The competition between newspapers has drastically changed; major newspaper publishers and media companies are trying to expand into geographic regions (to competing cities and smaller markets), initiating price wars and strategically marketing campaigns to specific readerships. With the economic reforms, the vernacular press and regional language TV channels have grown exponentially. Regional and vernacular publications continue to garner the largest circulations (Rao, 2008). Almost every district has at least one or more newspaper. Multiple editions are becoming common given the availability of the Internet and fax. Newspapers, such as *Eenadu* in the South, have editions coming out from every district of Andhra Pradesh; Rajasthan's *Patrika* publishes four editions and *Malayala Manorama* issues three editions. Eenadu even brings out half a dozen editions for different localities in Hyderabad city. Similarly, *Aaj, Nai Duniya*, and *Amar Ujjala* publish several editions (Ravindranathan, 2005, p. 55). Every cable package in India currently contains several language-based channels. In metropolitan cities such as Delhi and Mumbai, cable packages can include up to 20 regional language channels catering to a linguistically vast and diverse audience. With such profound changes in media landscape, professional media ethics too are undergoing sea changes.

Glocal Media Ethics

Glocal codes

Given the breadth and size of the Indian media, it is surprising to see how few ethics codes have been available for journalists. Such reality has not dimmed the fact that ethics of media practices remains a concern for journalists and public alike. The few talks and symposium that are organized often attract large number of people – both journalists and regular folks – who vigorously and thoughtfully contribute to discussions. The daily discourse of journalism ethics might take place in newsrooms but there are underlying set of values which are given expression in journalism codes of ethics. If you ask individual journalists they will quickly retort that hardly anyone ever reads the codes, but it would be mistake to underestimate their importance. Not many people read the Indian Constitution and yet the document continues to exercise a profound impact on the nation and its culture. Christians, Ferré, and Fackler (1993, p. 38) note that codes fulfill the function of moral sanction among peers, and that enforced codes characterized by such specific guidelines can serve journalism professionals on the minimum level of "rule obedience." Skeptics have asked: are codes relevant? Black, Barney, and Steele (1998, p. 26) answer pointedly:

> Carefully written codes highlight and anticipate ethical dilemmas so we don't all have to reinvent a decision-making process each time we face a new dilemma; they inspire us about our unique roles and responsibilities; they make each of us custodians of our profession's values and behaviors, and inspire us to emulate the best of our profession; they promote front end, proactive decision-making, before our decisions "go public."

Glocal Media Ethics

According to Ayish (2002, p. 140), there are four types of codes that one finds around the world: (1) Codes designed as guidelines for a specific publication; (2) National official codes ratified by governments, government-controlled or supported media councils; (3) National independent codes formulated by independent bodies of journalists within a country; and (4) Multinational codes designed by different international autonomous bodies. In India, journalists are most familiar with Press Council of India's (PCI) "Norms of Journalistic Conduct." While there are other codes such as one initiated by All India Newspapers Editors' Conference (AINEC) and the newly-formed News Broadcasters Association (NBA), PCI codes are considered most comprehensive and significant. PCI is a quasi-judicial, State supported organization which was set up in 1966 with the recommendation from the government of India appointed Press Commission. Among its many functions, one was to adjudicate any complaints against the press from the public and/or other constituents and interested parties. The other important function has been "to build up a code of conduct for newspapers and journalists in accordance with high professional standards," (PCI, 2005, p. 4) and "to ensure on the part of newspapers and journalists the maintenance of high standards of public taste and foster a due sense of both the rights and responsibilities of citizenship" (p. 4). PCI has existed somewhat independently from the government since its inception though it is clearly recognized by journalists as an arm of the State. The government has enormous discretionary power to approve who is to be one of the 28 members who comprise the Council; 13 of those 28 members are working journalists or editors. Time and again, the government has debated whether to give PCI the penal powers to punish delinquent newspapers/journalists but every time the Parliament has wisely decided that such powers could be misused and could infringe the freedom of press. PCI's ethics code titled, "Norms of journalistic conduct" have been periodically updated, most recently in 2005. There is recognition, among journalists and nonjournalists alike, that the sudden proliferation of multiple commercial media outlets (print, electronic, and internet) requires a more systemic presentation of the profession's ethical principles and normative guidelines.

Even a cursory look at PCI's code (2005) – which is a 46 page document – attests to the fact that the code has been localized in its content and in topics it addresses. There is a sense among the authors that Indian journalists face challenges that are unique and that the profession of journalism must also develop unique solutions to those challenges. There are two dominant themes in the code: *accuracy* and *restraint*. The code explicitly states the importance of accuracy in the writing and production of news. Using different languages the code weighs upon the reader the centrality of factual accuracy in the kind of work the journalists do. "The journalists should endeavor to ensure that information disseminated is factually accurate" (PCI, 2005, p. 7); "No fact shall be distorted or deliberately omitted" (p. 11) and "The Press shall eschew publications of inaccurate, baseless, graceless, misleading or distorted materials" (p. 12). Unlike Western ethics codes such as those of Society of Professional Journalists (SPJ) where truth is constantly emphasized, PCI code makes no or little reference to truth. The emphasis is more on "getting it right" rather than telling the truth. While fairness is mentioned, it is not a well-defined value. It is mentioned in sections titled, "Parameters of the right of the press to comment on the acts and conduct of public officials" (PCI, 2005, p. 23), "Privacy of public figures" (p. 31), "Caution in criticizing judicial acts" (p. 33), and "Covering communal disputes and clashes" (p. 34). While the notion of fairness has been understood in Western codes of ethics as "pursuing the truth, with both vigor and compassion and reporting information without favoritism, self-interest in prejudice" (p. 28), PCI codes give us no explicit definition of fairness. Instead, one has to infer that fairness could mean portraying individuals and issues with a sense of open-mindedness, avoiding biases and stereotypical portrayal of specific groups and communities, and unsubstantiated allegations. The emphasis on restraint pervades the code and given primacy over press freedom. It asks for restraint in reporting about government officials, judiciary, the parliament, violence, obscenity, election reporting, exit polls, suggestive guilt, social evils, caste, religion, and community references, AIDS, national unity, among many others. Hafez (2002, p. 228), in his analyses of ethics codes from 17 nations, found that codes can integrate the concept of freedom in three ways: one set of codes incorporates freedom as a central value that can only be limited when it interferes with other fundamental rights (e.g., most American and Western European codes); codes incorporating freedom as a central value that is, however, limited due to political, national, religious, or cultural considerations (e.g., codes from Algeria, Egypt, Malaysia, and Pakistan); codes that do not mention freedom rights at all (e.g., Saudi Arabia). PCI's code fall into the second group where freedom is mentioned but press restraint overshadows any explicit commitment to freedom. It addresses freedom, not as a separate right, but as part of "Right to reply" (PCI, 2005, p. 10). It states, "Freedom of the Press involves the readers' right to know all sides of an issue of public interest" (p. 10). Unlike Western codes of ethics, freedom is not assumed to be the motivation of all moral action; there is nothing in the Indian Constitution akin to the First Amendment. Some scholars have argued that it would be wrong to assume that the Western concept of press freedom would be made applicable to the newly emerged countries where circumstances are different (Bertrand, 2000; Deuze, 2007). The PCI code suggests that while freedom is key to ethical journalism, freedom *alone* cannot be a guarantor of responsible journalism and that a free press must function with *restraint*. On one hand, journalists should always seek freedom for themselves and others and, on the other hand, they need to dedicate themselves to causes of public good. Keeping in tradition with the rich history of developmental journalism in India, social justice is outlined in the code as a fundamental obligation of a free press. It is a way to empower the most marginalized and unrepresented members of the society. The code explicitly recognizes the significance of media globalization. It states: "Globalization and liberalization does not give license to the media to misuse freedom of the press and to lower the values of the society. The media performs a distinct role and public purpose. So far as the role is concerned, one of the duties of the media is to preserve and promote our cultural heritage and social values"

Glocal Media Ethics   163

(PCI, 20005, p. 29). While one could debate what "cultural heritage" and "social values" need special protection, the code gives us specific examples: "Columns in newspapers replying to personal queries of the readers must not become grossly offensive" (p. 14); "Information which constitutes an unwholesome exploitation of women and children for commercial gain" (p. 20); and "Columns which have a tendency to encourage or glorify social evils like *Sati Pratha* or burning of widows" (p. 20). Journalists are constantly reminded that even with the operational logic of globalization in place, they are required to remain grounded in and be cognizant of the day-to-day local and cultural practices of the audience. Several sections such as "Right to privacy" and "Recording interviews and phone conversations" (p. 38) also recognize that the precipitous technological changes have impacted the way journalists cover news-stories. PCI code, in all such instances, reminds journalists the value of restraint, thus prioritizing local values over so-called "universal" values.

Many Indian newsrooms have a well-oiled process for decision-making when it comes to ethics but the solution to ethical dilemmas increasingly lies more in deference to the logic of promarket forces and less in critical thinking and engaged discussions with peers and colleagues in the profession. Ethics of journalists are often influenced and formed by various forces of which journalism ethics is just one part. Hafez (2002, p. 225) is right to point out that "formal journalism ethics, laid down in the codes, is merely a part (sometimes not even the most significant part) of views concerning journalism ethics in a certain country." Ethics codes are just one element in a sometimes very long chain of social, economic, political, and cultural mechanisms working together to create ethics of journalism. The study of ethics codes in India show the deep influence of local sensibilities and cultural practices on writing of such codes. Global media ethics cannot be developed without a clear recognition of the local conditions in which journalists work and practice ethics.

Glocal media practices

After independence, Indian print journalists functioned with relative independence from government intervention with private ownership of media where most newspapers were owned by business families (for example, the Sahu Jain group has owned *Times of India* since 1948 and the Gupta family owned *Dainik Jagran* since 1942). Broadcast journalism, on the other hand, is a new profession and all round-the-clock news channels began their broadcasting operations post liberalization (the oldest privately owned 24-hours news channel is Zee News which began its first news broadcast in 1999). Indian journalism, both print and broadcast, has indeed been affected by globalization, especially in terms of news-gathering technologies, news practices, and strategies. Journalists have begun to take advantage of advances in technology and sharing of practices. *Star News* (with its parent company of News Corporation), for instance, is based in India and predominantly under Indian management, but adopts journalistic styles akin to its American sister network, Fox. The cheap and easy availability of cell phones, modems, and computers has led to radical changes in the way news is gathered and disseminated, kinds of news that gets covered, and audience feedback. Cheaply available software has allowed for quick editing and composing. It has made desktop publishing a reality for most newspapers. It is now common to see many newspapers in India filled with strong graphic treatment of a news story including graphs, pie charts, photographs, and illustrations. The 24-hours news channels similarly exploit new technologies that permit fast-cut editing, dramatic music, and graphics to accompany footage. Journalists are using technologies such as compact DV cameras, cell-phone cameras, miniaturized cameras with recording capabilities, and miniaturized microphones with taping mechanisms to capture off-the-cuff footage or, even more frequently, hide them from potential subjects. Such technology helped, for example, a reporter who woke up in her hotel room to an earthquake in the state of Gujarat; the footage she recorded on her mini-DV camera was broadcast within a few hours (such footage, made using hand-held and miniaturized technology, provided the first broadcast images and sounds from the 2004 Asian Tsunami). One effect of the advent of new technologies in the newsroom is the phenomenal use of hidden cameras to develop news-stories. While new technologies have empowered journalists to report news quickly and accurately, and have made them accountable to the public while holding the powerful accountable, the ethics of using such technologies are being increasingly debated (Mehta, 2007; Sanghvi, 2004; Shrivastava, 2005; Rao and Johal, 2006). Journalists have uncovered much of the political corruption rampant in Indian politics by deploying hidden cameras and mini-microphones. *Tehelka.com* (an online magazine) started the trend; *Tehelka* sent two journalists posing as agents from a fictitious arms company called West End, and tried hawking a nonexistent product – hand held thermal cameras – to politicians and bureaucrats. The journalists made the rounds of defense officials, military personnel, and politicians; they used bribes, and prostitutes, to push the deal through. They had captured all transactions on a spycam, and subsequently exhibited the footage at a press conference. While Indian audiences have been aware of political corruption, images and recordings of high-level ministers and defense officials accepting bribes shocked them as no print story had. Since the success of *Tehelka.com*, hidden camera operations have become common in covering stories ranging from corruption of Members of Parliament, local shopkeepers' selling onions at "black market" prices, greedy grooms demanding dowry from prospective brides, to trafficking of children into prostitution. While the use of hidden cameras has unalterably changed the course of Indian news-making, its use is often based on local ethical practices. Thus, the ethical questions posed about hidden cameras by Western journalists cannot be unequivocally transplanted to the use of the practice in India. Neither should hidden cameras be banned – as some government officials have suggested – as being foreign and "anti-Indian" (Neuman, 2002, p. A18). One can analyze a three part news-story broadcast on SUN TV's 24-hour news channel, *SUN News*, in December 2006 regarding the illegal use of sex determination tests in the Southern city of Hyderabad. Over a period of

Glocal Media Ethics

10 weeks, the station sent in several decoy couples requesting sex-determination tests or ultrasounds at a well-known city clinic. Each pregnant couple was asked to carry a hidden camera and to request the doctor or the nurse practitioner to disclose the sex of the child and, subsequently, request an abortion if the fetus appeared to be female. The couples were paid by the news stations to appear on the show; none of the couples had any journalistic background and only one had been an employee of Sun TV. While the level of deception would concern almost all Western newsmakers, especially the use of paid informants (and nonjournalists) as decoy couples, one could argue that the scourge of sex-determination practices in India outweighs possible concerns regarding the use of hidden cameras. Hyderabad, for instance, has had an alarmingly low sex-ratio between girls and boys even after the passing of the Regulation and Prevention of Pre-Conception and Pre-Natal Diagnostic Act (PNDA) which banned ultrasounds for sex-determination purposes. Sun TV's broadcast led to the closing of several of these diagnostic clinics and to the prosecution of several high-profile city doctors. While Indian journalism adopts global formats and practices, the local inflection of such practices and content is equally relevant. While "old" standards of journalism ethics are not always viable in this new news environment, the "new" journalism ethics is not bereft of older historically determined (and locally based) issues and norms. One does not find the deep-seated bias against female children elsewhere as one finds it in almost all regions of India. No country in the world has witnessed female infanticide in such large numbers as in India. Given such historical and sociocultural dynamics, the use of hidden cameras (as was the use of the technology of ultrasound among physicians), in this case, must be determined keeping in mind the ethical issue of social good and justice for the girl child which outweighs the ethical issue of privacy (for the clinics and doctors) and deception. This is not to say that Indian journalists must, therefore, ignore all ethical issues as they relate to the use of hidden camera technology. The distinction between the "viewer and the voyeur" must be maintained as a journalistic standard (Perry, 2005, p. 29). The increasing use of globalized format and technologies has simultaneously increased local news content. The content of local news is determined by "what people are talking about, what they care about, and what they deal on a daily basis" (Albizu, 2007, p. 257) and such localization has deep religious and cultural connotations in India. For example, astrology is considered as important news. Astrology would not be considered "news" by Western journalists but news channels and newspapers in India treat astrology as news worthy of column space and programming time slots. The Western standards of truth and accuracy in journalism cannot be applied in understanding the significance of astrology to Indian life and its categorization as news. Astrology or *Vaatsu Shahstra* plays a central role in Hindu social life where astrologers are consulted at every major life events including for planning marriages, during sickness, births, and career changes. Astrologers frequently appear as news consultants on shows. On *Jagran TV*, former Chief Justice of India's Supreme Court, Ranganath Misra, has his own show on astrology with the logo: "Astrology is an excellent science, unparalleled in the universe." In this program, Mishra

solicits calls from viewers, discusses the changes in the planetary systems, and gives suggestions for *griha dosh nivaran* (solutions for the bad influence of stars). After two Indian film stars, Abhishekh Bachchan and Aishwarya Rai, announced their marriage, anchors on *Aaj Tak* News interviewed astrologers to help predict the success of the marriage. A number of television news channels begin their early morning news shows with astrologers discussing the planetary movements and answering calls from viewers predicting how the day will go for specific sun signs. Such practices cannot simply be deemed unethical. Understanding the ethics of a profession includes understanding the multilayered ethics of the culture in which professionals practice. The role of a journalist – and the ethics of the profession – cannot be separated from the key role journalists play in strengthening (or, as some skeptics believe, weakening) the democratic system. Recent scholarship about journalism ethics in India has begun to focus on the connections between the consolidation and success of democracy and democratic institutions *and* a flourishing, independent, and ethical press. Some scholars have argued that globalization of news has created a façade of media plurality when in fact it was "contributing to a democratic deficit in the world's largest democracy" (Thussu, 2005, p. 65). What has not been accounted for, in such critiques, is that format changes borrowed from a globalized news media has increased journalism's emphasis on *janmat* (will of the people). "Will of the people" or the power of the *janata* (people) seems to underlie every news decision as reflected in titles of news segments and programs on various news channels: *Khabar hamari, faisla aapka* (Our news, your decision), *Aap ki adalat* (You are the judge), *Aap ka haq* (Your rights), and *Muskil safar, janmat ka asar* (People power). The content of these shows focus on issues of social justice, accountability of those in power, and issues that affect people's daily lives. For instance, *Aaj Tak* TV covered a story about a group of *adivasis* (tribals), in the southeastern state of Orissa, who were attacked by the police for protesting against a local politician's visit. One *adivasi* was shown shot and wounded. *Aaj Tak* continued covering the story until the State government decided to provide medical attention and monetary compensation to the wounded man. *Adivasis* comprise of one of the poorest segments of Indian societies, are often landless, and work predominantly as indentured laborers, and rarely generate interest in the news media. In another story, NDTV (New Delhi Television) followed young child-beggars trying to earn a living on the trains of Mumbai and presented a chronicle of their daily journey on the trains. The news story was titled, *Bacche bik gaye* (children for sale). Many of these children had been sold to "vendors" for less than Rs.100 ($2) by their parents. The reporter talked to the children, showed the viewers the streets where they live, and the traffickers who bought and sold them. The reporter described the difficulties of locating the traffickers who buy these children and put them to work, and the reluctance of all parties to giving on-camera interviews, thus humanizing and making emotionally compelling the endemic problem of child-trafficking in India. Just about every news story includes "regular folks" being interviewed on the streets, over the phone, or in the studios. In stories about topics ranging from flight and train delays to land grab, reporters are seen asking

Glocal Media Ethics

people for opinions. Indian journalists' appropriations of new technologies and journalism practices from the globalized media has allowed for a new sense of public and political awareness among audiences, especially about democratic institutions and how they are governed. One institution, the judiciary, has been under particular scrutiny as exemplified in the coverage of the murder of Jessica Lall. Lall was working as a bartender at a pub in Delhi when she was shot dead on April 29, 1999. Dozens of witnesses at the restaurant pointed to Manu Sharma, son of a wealthy and powerful politician, as the murderer. The trial lasted 7 years during which time Sharma remained free and many of the witnesses turned hostile towards the prosecution. Some of those witnesses feared for their lives and later claimed to have received death threats from Sharma's family. Due to the prosecution's inability to gather any evidence against him, Sharma was acquitted in February 2006. *Indian Express*, a Delhi based English newspaper, took up Lall's case and provided intense coverage including daily updates on the case and interviews with Lall's family. Reporters also followed the witnesses. *Tehelka.com* did a month long undercover investigation, in which the reporters surreptitiously taped interviews with several of the witnesses and published a series titled, *Killers of Justice*. With increased national media attention, the Delhi High Court retried the case on a "fast track" in December 2006. It reversed the lower court's decision, found Sharma guilty, and sentenced him to life in prison. While critics have pointed to the "class bias" in the coverage of Lall's case, there was widespread celebration of Sharma's conviction. All such examples suggest that the increase in media plurality has increased both accountability (of the democratic institutions and the state) and an increased emphasis on the "we" – *janata*, the people, and the audience. I advocate awareness of the return of the local (however transformed by global processes) as one of the effects of globalization for journalism ethics. One, thus, must reject all blanket assertions that imported journalism practices and technologies debase indigenous and local news culture and ethics and that the new logic of global media order, therefore, annihilates the local.

Conclusion

To understand the changes in Indian journalism practices and ethics, glocalization is a potentially inclusive theoretical framework. It helps scholars understand that the local and the global significantly overlap, often global issues sustain their energy through links to the local, and localization of all that is global is necessary to sustain viewer and reader interests. Critics have labeled the changes in global journalism practices, including those in India, as "the globalization of the US approach" and "the global influence of Western news networks" with increased focus on infotainment and less public interest and development news (Thussu, 2002, p. 205). If one looks exclusively at the US model, changes are identifiable from the 1970s when broadcast news became increasingly governed by commercial logic and the budgets at news divisions were cut. The pace of the news broadcast increased and its agenda changed to deemphasize politics and international news and focus more on stories that would provide moments of emotional involvement on the part of ordinary viewers. Since liberalization and privatization began in the early 1990s, Indian media has adopted global news formats, as critics charge, but one cannot unproblematically equate changes in Indian journalism to the transplantation, or imposition, of a "US approach" to journalism. Appropriations of new technologies, format, and skills have enabled public participation in the process of news-making and allowed for increased stories advocating social justice. Globalization has also sustained local content though the presentation of such content has radically changed as has the focus of news. The new media landscape, despite having been made possible by globalization and configured by market logic, has created the opportunity for a propeople journalism to evolve. In journalism practices and writing of ethics codes, we have witnessed unprecedented level of *localization*.

Christians *et al.* (2008) suggest that journalists must engage with the notion of universal or global media ethics from "within their own set of socio-cultural conditions, experiences and values" (2008, p. 170). They write that rather than simply posit universal propositions as standards that all public communicators should adhere to, we can "advance the idea that a global approach must take contingency, history, dialog, and local voices seriously and integral to the process of theorizing" (p. 170). As it has become increasingly important for journalists and journalism scholars to reflect on the epistemological and methodological foundations of understanding media ethics, I have offered the conceptual framework of glocalization. Glocalization is a way to move away from the global-to-local matrix as a subsystem that neatly fits on to a national, regional, provincial, or local system. In the framework of glocalization, local ethics *is* transformed but not to the extent that it ceases to be recognizable *as* local. Rather, global and local are contexts that mutually affect each other without being absorbed within each other according to any hierarchical order. The theory of glocalization helps us recognize the complexity of the multivalent connections that signify the contemporary global media order.

References

Albizu, J.A. (2007) Geolinguistic regions and diasporas in the age of satellite television. *The International Communication Gazette*, 69 (3), 239–261.

Ayish, M. (2002) Political communication on Arab world television: Evolving patterns, *Political Communication*, 19, 137–154.

Babbili, A. (1997) Ethics and the discourse on ethics in post-colonial India, in *Communication Ethics and Universal Values* (eds C. Christians and M. Traber), Sage, Thousand Oaks, CA, pp. 128–158.

Berglez, P. (2008) What is global Journalism? Theoretical and empirical conceptualizations. *Journalism Studies*, 9 (6), 845–858.

Bertrand, J. (2000) *Media Ethics and Accountability System*, Transaction Publishers, New Brunswick, NJ.

Black, J., Barney, R., and Steele, B. (1998) *Doing Ethics in Journalism: A Handbook with Case Studies*, 3rd edn, Allyn and Bacon, New York.

Brislin, T. (2004) Empowerment as a universal ethic in global journalism. *Journal of Mass Media Ethics*, 19 (2), 130–137.

Callahan, S. (2003) New challenges of globalization for journalism. *Journal of Mass Media Ethics*, 18 (1), 3–15.

Christians, C., and Nordenstreng, K. (2004) Social Responsibility Worldwide. *Journal of Mass Media Ethics*, 19 (1), 3–28.

Christians, C., and Traber, M. (Eds.) (1997) *Communication Ethics and Universal Values*, Sage, Thousand Oaks, CA.

Christians, C., Ferré, J.P., and Fackler, M. (1993) *Good News: Social Ethics and the Press*. Oxford University Press, New York.

Christians, C., Rao, S., Ward, S. J.A. *et al.* (2008) Toward a global media ethics: Theoretical perspectives, *Ecquid Novi: African Journalism Studies*, 29 (2), 135–172.

Couldry, N. (2006) *Listening Beyond the Echoes: Media, Ethics and Agency in an Uncertain World*, Paradigm Publishers, Boulder, CO.

Deuze, M. (2007) *Media Work*. John Wiley and Sons, Inc., Hoboken, NJ.

Giddens, A. (1990) *The Consequences of Modernity*, Polity Press, Cambridge, MA.

Hafez, K. (2002) Journalism Ethics Revisited: A Comparison of Ethics Codes in Europe, North Africa, the Middle East, and Muslim Asia, *Political Communication*, 19, 225–250.

Hafez, K. (2007) *The Myth of Media Globalization*, (trans. A. Skinner), Polity Press, New York.

Held, D., and McGrew, A. (2003) The great globalization debate: An introduction, in (eds. D. Held and A. McGrew), *The Global Transformations Reader: An Introduction to the Globalization Debate*, Polity Press, London, pp. 1–46.

Kraidy, M. (2003) Glocalization: An International Communication Framework? *Journal of International Communication*, 9 (2), 29–49.

Lie, R., and Servaes, J. (2000) Globalization: Consumption and identity, towards researching nodal points, in *The New Communications Landscape: Demystifying Media Globalization*, (eds G. Wang, J. Servaes and A. Goonasekera), Routledge, (pp. 307–332) New York, pp. 307–332.

Mattelart, A. (2002) An archeology of the global era: Constructing a belief. *Media, Culture and Society*, 24, 591–612.

Mehta, N. (2007) *India on Television: How Satellite News Channels have Changed the Way we Think and Act*, Harper Collins, New Delhi.

Merrill, J.C. (2002) Chaos and order: Sacrificing the individual for the sake of social harmony, in (ed. J.B. Atkins), *The Mission: Journalism, Ethics and the World*, Iowa State University Press, Ames, IA, pp. 17–36.

Neuman, S. (2002)) India cracks down on Tehelka months after bribery exposure. *Wall Street Journal*, August 23, A 18.

Ninan, S. (2007) *Headlines from the Heartland: Reinventing the Hindi Public Sphere*, Sage, New Delhi.

Pelton, J.N., Oslund, R.J., and Marshall, P. (2004) *Communications Satellites: Global Change Agents*, Lawrence Erlbaum, London.

Perry, A. (2005,) India goes Undercover. *Time*, March 21, 29–30.

PCI/Press Council of India (2005) *Norms of Journalistic Conduct*, www.presscouncil.nic.ic/norms.htm (last accessed October 11, 2005).

Rao, S. (2008) Accountability, democracy and globalization: A study of broadcast journalism in India, *Asian Journal of Communication*, 18 (3), 193–206.

Rao, S., and Johal, N. (2006) Ethics and news making in the changing Indian mediascape. *Journal of Mass Media Ethics*, 21, 286–303.

Rao, S., and Lee, S. (2005) Globalizing media ethics? An assessment of universal ethics among political journalists. *Journal of Mass Media Ethics*, 20 (2 & 3), 99–120.

Ravindranathan, R. (2005) *Regional Journalism in India*, Authors Press, New Delhi.

Ritzer, G. (2006) Island of the living dead: Socialization of McDonaldization, in *McDonaldization: A Reader*, 2nd edn, (ed. G. Ritzer), Pine Forge Press, Thousand Oaks, CA, pp. 32–40.

Robertson, R. (1997) Glocalization: Time-space and homogeneity-heterogeneity, in *Global Modernities*, (eds M. Featherstone, S. Lash., and R. Robertson), Sage, London, pp. 25–43.

Sanghvi, V. (2004) The paradoxes of Tehelka. *Seminar: The Monthly Symposium*, www.india-seminar.com/2004/533/533%20vir%20sanghvi.htm/ (last accessed September 12, 2004).

Shrivastava, K.M. (2005) *Media Ethics: Veda to Gandhi and Beyond*, Government of India Publications Division, New Dehli.

Sparks, C. (2000) The global, the local and the public sphere, in *The New Communications Landscape: Demystifying Media Globalization*, (eds G. Wang, J. Servaes and A. Goonasekera), Routledge, London, pp. 74–95.

Sreberny-Mohammadi, A. (1987) The local and the global in international communication, in *Mass Media and Society*, (eds J. Curran and M. Gurevitch), Edward Arnold, London, pp. 136–152.

Straubhaar, J. (2007) *World Television: From Global to Local*, Sage, Thousand Oaks, CA.

Thornton, W.H. (2000) Mapping the 'glocal' village: The political limits of glocalization. *Continuum: Journal of Media and Cultural Studies*, 14 (1), 79–89.

Thussu, D. (2002) Managing the media in an era of round-the-clock news: Notes from India's first tele-war. *Journalism Studies*, 3 (2), 203–212.

Thussu, D. (2005) Media plurality or democratic deficit? Private TV and the public sphere in India, in *Journalism and Democracy in Asia*, (eds A. Romano and M. Bromley), Taylor and Francis, London, pp. 54–65.

Thussu, D. (2006) *Media on the Move: Global Flow and Contra-Flow*, Taylor and Francis, London.

Ward, S. J.A. (2005) Philosophical foundations for global journalism ethics. *Journal of Mass Media Ethics*, 20 (1), 3–21.

Ward S. J.A., and Wasserman, H. (eds) (2008) *Media Ethics beyond Borders*, Heinemann/Pearson, London.

Wasserman, H. (2008) Global journalism ethics, in *Global Journalism: Topical Issues and Media Systems*, 5th edn, (eds A. DeBeer and J.C. Merrill), Allyn and Bacon, New York, pp. 85–95.

Wasserman, H., and Rao, S. (2008) Glocalization of journalism ethics, *Journalism: Theory, Practice, and Criticism*, 9 (2), 163–181.

Wilson, R., and Dissanayake, W. (1996) Introduction: Tracking the global/local, in *Global/Local: Cultural Production and the Transnational Imaginary*, (eds R. Wilson and W. Dissanayake), Duke University Press, Durham, NC, pp. 1–20.

10

Feminist Ethics and Global Media

Linda Steiner

In both its activist and theoretical dimensions, feminism is normative, promoting ways of thinking and acting that are concerned with human good. Feminism's transformative and interventionist traditions predict its investment in media processes, practices, and content. An incipient feminist approach to ethics already emerged in feminists' own journalistic practices as well as their critiques of mainstream media practices and products. Even if these did not add up to a full-fledged feminist ethics, they imply normative standards for journalism and nonnews content. For example, in 1966, its founding year, the National Organization for Women (NOW) established a task force on images of women. One clause of NOW's Statement of Purpose asserted: "IN THE INTERESTS OF THE HUMAN DIGNITY OF WOMEN, we will protest, and endeavor to change, the false image of women now prevalent in the mass media.... Such images perpetuate contempt for women by society and by women for themselves" (NOW, 1966). The statement went on to oppose all policies and practices – whether in church, state, college, or workplace – that foster in women "self-denigration, dependence, and evasion of responsibility, undermine their confidence in their own abilities and foster contempt for women."

Feminist theorizing is somewhat undeveloped as a resource for media dilemmas, in part because ethicists in the still-emerging feminist literature rarely address media per se. Such applications are appropriate, however, especially now that philosophers are thinking quite practically about how to promote civic society and civic virtues, democratic institutions, and community. Meanwhile, until quite recently, journalism and media ethicists rarely referenced feminist ethics. One of the exceptions is Wilkins (2010), who defines feminist ethics in terms of care, although she insists, as do I, that feminist ethics be informed by duty, in order to provide a "strong handshake between the profession's goals, institutional demands, and the individual circumstance that characterizes ethical choice for journalists and their news organizations" (p. 31).

The Handbook of Global Communication and Media Ethics, First Edition. Edited by Robert S. Fortner and P. Mark Fackler.
© 2011 Blackwell Publishing Ltd. Published 2011 by Blackwell Publishing Ltd.

This chapter outlines a feminist ethics broadly and then in ways relevant to contemporary media, as well as media research and media education. To set the context, I return to my beginning point, the importance of media and media ethics to the women's liberation movement. Then, I clarify my assumptions by proposing conditions for a properly feminist ethical theory. After summarizing ongoing debates in feminist ethics, I show how substantially revising the notion of care to underscore its political dimension helps resolve troubling dilemmas in media practice and research and promotes moral reasoning among practitioners. Feminist ethics accommodates other important philosophical and epistemological principles, yet potentially results in somewhat different forms of analysis and action than do other moral theories. The conclusion suggests how feminist ethics might be extended globally, despite profound and enduring obstacles to this.

Setting the Context

As were suffragists and other nineteenth century social-political reformers, many of the mid-twentieth century feminists were untrained and inexperienced in journalism; so journalism ethics per se were not prominent in their agenda. However, their appreciation of the importance of media was dramatized not only in their own newspapers and magazines but also by the radical feminists' invasions of mainstream organizations, most famously of the *Ladies Home Journal*. This interest and appreciation for media also emerged in the National Organization for Women (NOW), which, under the leadership of its president Betty Friedan, cultivated relationships with journalists, monitored newsroom hiring patterns, and critiqued media content. In 1966, NOW petitioned the US Equal Employment Opportunity Commission (EEOC) to amend regulations on sex-segregated "Help Wanted" advertisements, and vigorously protested the EEOC's failure to act quickly. In 1971 NOW asked the Federal Communications Commission to require broadcasters to include women in affirmative action programs. Meanwhile, women journalists filed sex discrimination suits against NBC, *Reader's Digest*, *Newsweek*, and the *New York Times*. On the affirmative side, NOW campaigned for the reinstatement of the TV series Cagney and Lacey, whose eponymous female police officers were regarded as strong role models.

To this day, feminist scholars regularly expose misrepresentations and seemingly unvarying sexist stereotypes in news, advertising, pornography, and popular culture, although recently, they more often celebrate women-friendly forms. Feminist activists arguably have never been well-organized to publicize feminist perspectives and perhaps are now experiencing decreasing success in eliminating sexism. For example, in 2007, journalists invited few feminists to present specifically feminist analyses of the intersecting sexism and racism embedded in Don Imus's description of women's basketball players as "nappy-headed hos" ("Imus' Non-Defense" 2010). In contrast, many African-American civil rights leaders were heard decrying Imus's racism. Feminists still find sexist hiring and promotion policies in newsrooms as well as male-oriented (i.e. antifemale) assumptions about news and power. Whether this merely demonstrates the law of diminishing returns, given feminists' earlier success in challenging the status of women in media (or perhaps feminists' inability or unwillingness to argue vociferously) is not clear.

Regardless of how much progress has been made or is still necessary, feminist standards have a permanent place in the discourse about representations of gender/sex and sexual orientation – as well as race and ethnicity, physical ability, class – whether carried on television, cable, film, or the Internet. More to the point, feminist theorizing carved space for discussion of how ethics and ethical decision-making reflect mutually-interacting structures of status and power. In this context we can discuss how to nurture people's collective ethical reasoning, both interpersonally and professionally, and build social institutions that allow for and encourage ethical thinking, rather than thwarting it. Feminist theories of knowledge have prompted spirited critiques of key concepts in journalism – ones that undergird journalism ethics – derived from liberalism. For example, it asks whose liberties and what kinds of democratic rights are specifically protected by conventional free press theory, whether in its classic laissez-faire version or the somewhat less individualized social responsibility version. It considers which audiences are served with what kinds of materials, and how audiences are constrained, perhaps in ways hidden by conventional notions of the public sphere. Feminist theorizing offers a means for analyzing other theories in pure and applied ethics – uncovering gender-biased assumptions, omissions, and blind spots in conventional ethical approaches.

From the outset, the term "feminist ethics" is controversial. After substantially revising her original proposal (this is elaborated below), Carol Gilligan (1995) distinguished between a "feminine" ethic of care, emphasizing special obligations and interpersonal relationships, and a "feminist" ethic of care, emphasizing connection. It was the latter, she said, that exposes disconnections in a feminine selflessness premised on a faulty, patriarchal opposition between relationships and autonomy. Arguing that feminine and feminist ethics are similarly problematic and are not distinct categories, Koehn (1998) called for "female ethics," which, in encouraging care-receivers to contest caregivers' expectations, incorporates the principles of male ethics into the consultative ethos of female ethics. African-American theorists draw from Christian theology, Black history, and feminism to suggest "womanist" ethics. I treat "feminist ethics" as acknowledging women's historical experiences and grounded in feminist theory, without suggesting that women and men live by different ethical standards or assuming that gender always trumps other dimensions of power and identity. Media scholars often conflate feminist ethics with the ethics of care. I see care as relevant, only if caring is understood politically as an acquired and motivated disposition to be cultivated broadly but whose actual application is not always equal. This understanding of care is different enough, then, to distinguish feminist ethics from the ethics of care.

In my view, a robust feminist ethics that is relevant to media:

1 Regards women as moral agents, capable of ethical action and decision-making no less than men, without assuming that women are either instinctually predisposed to be less or more moral than men, or that women are conditioned to be so; it assumes neither that women are ethically superior nor that they are all equally and inevitably vulnerable to men.
2 Starts with the lives of marginalized peoples, taking sex discrimination seriously, along with racism, homophobia, and other systems of inequalities, and thereby acknowledging the inter-structuring of various dimensions of identity and power.
3 Understands the human self as always embodied and interdependent, living in relationships and communities (potentially including professional communities) with particular histories and loyalties, even as we seek autonomy and self-determination.
4 Uses feminist understandings of a transformative politics to generate normative standards, rather than beginning with or remaining satisfied with descriptions of frequent behaviors.
5 Integrates theory, practice, and method in non-obvious ways; it applies to social practices as well as to research and other forms of knowledge-seeking.
6 Responds to changing dilemmas of specific times, places, and cultures, since, just as knowledge is socially situated, so historical and cultural contexts are meaningful.

Consistent with its general repudiation of dichotomous thinking and codification, feminist ethics is simultaneously utopian and aspirational. It suggests principles that help people aim, in practice, for ever-more virtuous ways of being, without condemning them for failures or breaches of rules; and understands that moral purity is impossible in a world where virtues, duties, and moral goods compete. It acknowledges that people may legitimately make meanings and take pleasures in highly diverse ways and have different visions of the good life. Just as people cannot be divided as either cultural dupes or wholly independent agents, and people cannot be categorized in terms of gender or race, so workplaces, practitioners, or content cannot be classified as either moral or sinful. However, aspirational ethics is not moral freedom – the notion that individuals determine for themselves how to lead a virtuous life and need judgmental mandates (Wolfe, 2001). Rather, the goal is to push for ideals, including cultural materials and work structures that are more ethical; institutional supports for ever more ethical practices; and more debate and discussion regarding the importance of removing barriers to moral action.

The Ethics of Care

Alison Jaggar (1992) accused Western ethics of failing women in several ways: It marginalized women's interests as opposed to men's rights; ignored private world problems as morally uninteresting; assumed women are less morally developed than

Feminist Ethics and Global Media

men; overvalued culturally masculine traits like independence, autonomy; undervalued culturally feminine traits like interdependence, community, connection; favored culturally masculine ways of moral reasoning – emphasizing rules, universality, and impartiality; and dismissed culturally feminine ways of moral reasoning that emphasize relationships, particularity, and partiality. Jaggar defined feminist ethics as prescribing morally justifiable ways of resisting oppressive practices, and envisioning morally desirable alternatives that promote women's emancipation, based on respectful, though not uncritical, reflection of women's and men's moral experience.

Much of feminist ethics at least began by trying to correct male bias, overturning the devaluation of women and whatever is culturally associated with the feminine – the "thin" version of Western feminist ethics (Jaggar, 2000). Carol Gilligan's (1982) ground-breaking work fundamentally distinguished women's ethics of care from a male-oriented ethics of rights, whose moral agents independently choose which moral principles to obey. Gilligan's interviews with women convinced her that women's maturation process was marked by an expanding circle of care and compassion, as opposed to boys, who are encouraged to detach themselves from family and are pushed into work/public domains. Trained as a developmental psychologist, Gilligan saw a "conventional" stage based in relationships and sense of responsibility, after girls have been socialized to care for family and friends. Finally came universal care, when women extend concern to humanity as a whole. The "caring" moral agent in a morality of responsibility, then, is enmeshed in a network of relations, and tries to maintain these relations.

Gilligan's theory of women's distinctive ways of analyzing moral dilemmas precipitated many elaborations. Nell Noddings (1984), for example, identified an intimate ethic of care that specifically privileged maternal caring as a model for and of ethical decision-making. Noddings reasoned that human interaction and dyadic caring relationships are ontologically fundamental; therefore, a mother's caring for her children is morally basic. Noddings claimed that genuine caring – directed at people in definite relationships – involves "engrossment" (thoroughly attending to the cared-for, ignoring one's own concerns) and "motivational displacement" (setting aside one's goals to focus on the cared-for) without judging or evaluating. Noddings posed a tough standard: Causing pain, as well as failing to relieve the pain of someone with whom one had a relationship, were moral evils. Granting that most real life relationships involve people who are unequal in knowledge or power, Ruddick (1989) similarly grounded ethics in maternal practices. A mother socializes her children, in great part by cultivating certain ethical virtues, and eschewing values and traits that she deems unethical, even if they seem necessary for social success. Ruddick never assumed that mothering is easy or a "natural" way of thinking; men who spend a lot of time caring for children also think like mothers.

Gilligan was accused of ignoring the historically-situated impact of sex stereotyping and falsely universalizing women (Steiner, 1989). In any case, Gilligan and Noddings soon moved from closely associating care with women, to denying that care and justice are opposites (much less that one is a higher form than the other) even if the two conceptions cannot be readily integrated, much less simultaneously deployed.

Eventually Gilligan suggested that men and women use both: Moral maturity requires using two different moral languages – of rights and of responsibilities. Moreover, all relationships, public and private, can be characterized both in terms of equality and attachment (Gilligan, 1987). Inequality and detachment are each grounds for moral concern, since everyone is vulnerable both to oppression and abandonment. Noddings added that direct personal caring of "caring-for" (or being cared-for) teaches "caring-about" and this is the grounds of justice. To care about strangers, "we draw upon an ethical ideal – a set of memories of caring and being cared for that we regard as manifestations of our best selves and relations" (2002, p. 13). So, lessons learned "starting at home" are the grounds for a sense of social justice.

Many scholars agree that the care ethics' emphasis on face-to-face, personal relationships (and other virtues and ways of thinking devalued or left invisible by masculinist thinking) mitigate the impersonality, universalizing, and disembodied abstractions of a justice ethic. But Noddings' caregiver cannot care for large numbers of people and the intimacy of the caring relationship cannot apply to those outside the community (so is untenable for journalists). Responding to Noddings' notion that caregivers are transformed by caring and adopt goals of the cared-for, Bartky (2002) warns that the unreciprocated caregiving that benefits men may easily become epistemically and ethically disempowering: If the female caretaker adopts (it is not inevitable) the morally questionable attitudes of the male cared-for, it leads to moral complicity; if she keeps her doubts to herself, she becomes inauthentic. Mendus (2000) concludes that the concept of care is too narrow, since political problems are usually large-scale. Moreover, she insisted, "[D]omestic virtues are deformed when they are translated to a public world" (p. 114). Bell (1993) criticizes Noddings' conceptualization as apolitical, impracticable, and overly personal. Concerned that even politicized ethics of care is unavoidably associated with maternalism, Macgregor (2004) criticizes ecofeminist notions as reinforcing patriarchal dualisms and ignoring women's political and intellectual agency. Koehn (1998) suggests that prevalent approaches to care offer little guidance in particular cases; they are politically naive and inadequately self-critical, over-privilege the earth mother, and too easily dismiss autonomy. Koehn's dialogic female ethics stresses human interdependence; requires empathy for the vulnerable; treats the domestic realm as having public significance; respects difference and individuality, taking this as intrinsic to ethical maturity (rather than consistency); emphasizes imaginative discourse and listening; and is transformative. Her correctives are literally interpersonal conversations. If dialogical ethics works between individuals (I am not convinced) it has little practical application to professionals.

So, rather than jettisoning care, feminists need to give it social and political heft, and to extend the world of moral considerability well beyond local and family relationships. Caring must accommodate much more than the relatively few and private relationships of nurses, teachers, social workers and others in "caring" professions, which, it may be added, tend to be low-paid. (A 1974 survey found that the female editors of women's pages earned much less than the few male editors of women's pages, Beasley and Gibbons, 2003, p. 25. Also, both entertainment forms associated with women such as soap operas, and women's "beats" in journalism are also underpaid and undervalued.) Caring for (some) strangers and distant communities must be included in order to be useful to media professionals – who interact not only with known and "seen" sources and subjects, but also audiences not known to media professionals personally. (Care of self is legitimate and people who ignore their own needs may become unable to provide good care to others.) It must address structural and institutional problems and abuses. Feminist theorizing emphasizes context but also the connection of the personal and political, so an adequate ethic must serve media professionals at work and at home.

Finally, the fact that people inevitably resort to both care and duty in both private/personal domains and in public/professional settings raises questions about how care and justice might be integrated. Many feminist scholars see care and justice as both necessary, although they are not always compatible. The debate is whether the two concepts are equal, or whether one or the other is more prominent. Alternatively, some propose different ways to incorporate caring (as well as justice) into a virtue ethic. Halwani (2003), for example, makes care part of a virtue ethics, because, unlike those who treat care as the most basic moral value, she does not see care as ontologically sufficient. Sander-Staudt (2006) concedes the similarities between these two theories but argues against such "assimilation." She advocates a freestanding feminist caring ethic: Feminism enables the incorporation of justice into care, making for more comprehensive moral theory.

Who Deserves Care?

Ironically, besides Gilligan's celebration of intimate relations, her notion of universalized care is also troublesome, since it problematically requires that all subjects be universalized, generalized, and treated equally. Tong and Williams (2008) say *fully* feminist ethicists seek the elimination of subordination of oppressed persons in all its manifestations: "A feminist approach to ethics asks questions about *power* – that is, about domination and subordination – even before it asks questions about *good* and *evil, care* and *justice*." Held (2006), however, makes social connectedness normatively prior to rights: We ought to respect the human rights of all persons everywhere, but we begin by developing our capacity for care. First, she says, we respect and meet the needs of particular others we take responsibility for, before developing solidarity at community and global levels. In either case, rather than seeing morality as the struggle between self-interest and impartial universal principles, Held sees caring ethics as addressing the region between the individual and universal. Indeed, without equating care ethics to feminist ethics and without claiming that care is sufficient to deal with all political questions, she defends the ethic of care as able to evaluate wrongful as well as morally admirable relations – including families or communities.

Sommers (1987) builds on Nozick's (1981) definition of ethical pull – when a person exerts moral claims on others because that person can expect to be well-treated by moral agents – to propose the notion of differential pull. Unlike Kantians and utilitarians, who assume all moral patients exert equal pull, the notion of differential pull allows for greater consideration of special cases. Here, the community of agents and patients is analogous to a gravitational field: Distance counts and forces vary with local conditions. Psychologically, people may be more responsive to those who are closer, geographically and emotionally. The moral call from a "real," close, and liked human voice is inevitably loud, but psychological responsiveness is not necessarily moral. So news professionals should minimize the pull of less deserving, albeit closer, subjects even if this means contravening the conventional newsworthiness of proximity.

With their more formal and even universalized notion of community, communitarians ignore feminists' concern with the profound impact of social context and their fear of the repression of certain communities. The "new communitarians" ignore the effects of patriarchy and sex discrimination, as well as race, sexuality, or class (nor do they address professional or practical dilemmas), leaving in place a "traditional" family deeply entrenched in sexual difference. While feminists and communitarians have not been allies (Weiss, 1995), feminists may develop a distinctive version of communitarian ethic. Denzin (1997) and Christians (2002, 2003) call for "feminist communitarian ethics," aimed at ennobling human experience, facilitating civic transformation, and promoting universal solidarity. Feminist communitarians presume "a sociocultural universe where values, moral commitments and existential meanings are negotiated dialogically" (Christians, 2002, p. 169). This view contends that "the community is ontologically and morally prior to persons" (Denzin, 1997, p. 274), even as it connects personal dignity and communal well-being.

Tronto (1995) helpfully distinguishes four phrases of care, each of which has a concomitant value: caring about, attentiveness; taking care of, responsibility; caregiving, competence; and care-receiving, responsiveness. Determining who needs or deserves which kinds of care requires knowledge and thus public deliberation, she says. Integrating justice with care, here treated as a political concept, raises broad questions about social and political institutions: "care is not solely private or parochial; it can concern institutions, societies, even global levels of thinking" (p. 145). Kittay (1999) and Engster (2005) derive our moral duty to care for others (including strangers) from our dependency upon others. Like Tronto, they advocate the ethic of care as a framework for moral and political judgment. Engster defines caring functionally, in terms of everything we do "to help individuals to meet their basic needs, develop or maintain their basic capabilities, and live as much as possible free from suffering, so that they can survive and function at least at a minimally decent level" (2005, p. 54). Moreover, this is accomplished with caring virtues – attentiveness, empathy, and responsiveness. The paradigmatic case involves personally caring for another individual in an attentive, responsive, and respectful manner. Alternatively, one may make sure that others are cared for by ensuring that their caregivers have the resources and support necessary to provide good care, or by supporting programs that directly help people. Collective caring is diffuse, but still "counts."

Arguing for "care informed by duty," Wilkins would substitute parenting of teenagers for the highly gendered mother–infant metaphor now haunting the care ethic. Not only do fathers parent teens, but parenting a teenager centers around helping to develop an autonomous adult. Simultaneously, teenagers' psychological development hinges on peer relationships and testing who they are in relation to a community. As she puts it, parenting teenagers is therefore "a negotiation between empathic care and the promotion of autonomy in community." This "empathic care informed by and implemented with duty" is a response that, I might add, means parents and teens need community support as well as control over their own emotions, both frustration and/or adoration. To use Fischman *et al.*'s (2004) terms, ethical development relies on vertical (mentors or role models, for example) and horizontal (peers) workplace supports – and at any moment, may be in tensions with these sets of relations. (Since institutional milieu and periodic inoculations are also important, the GoodWork Project offers workshops to strengthen ethical resolve and encourage good, meaningful, socially responsible work see www.goodworkproject.org/).

In my view, the most helpful formulation is Fraser's (1986) dialogical ethic of solidarity. This permits "critique of interpretations of needs, of definitions of situations and of the social conditions of dialogue, instead of establishing a privileged model of moral deliberation which effectively shields such matters from scrutiny" (p. 426). Fraser notes that dominant social groups (by gender, class, race) control interpretation and communication, including by controlling official vocabularies, rhetorical devices, and paradigms of argumentation accepted as authoritative in adjudicating conflicting claims. Rejecting both "universalist-" or "monological" ethics and Gilligan's relational-interactive model, Fraser emphasizes a contextual, collective dimension in order to advocate the standpoint of the collective concrete other. That area standing between unique individuality and universal humanity – the intermediate zone of group identity – leads to an ethic of solidarity:

> The norms governing these interactions would be neither norms of intimacy such as love and care, nor those of formal institutions such as rights and entitlements. Rather, they would be norms of collective solidarities as expressed in shared but non-universal social practices…. [T]o be autonomous here would mean to be a member of a group or groups which have achieved a degree of collective control over the means of interpretation and communication sufficient to enable one to participate on a par with members of other groups in moral and political deliberation; that is, to speak and be heard, to tell one's own life-story, to press one's claims and point of view in one's own voice (Fraser, 1986, p. 428).

Applying Moral Epistemology to Media

Given the connection between the power dimensions of empirical and moral discourse, feminist moral epistemology has multiple implications for journalism/media research –choice of topic, method and design, and how research is used – as well as for journalists' "ways of knowing." Rouse (2004) specifically denies that feminist science studies are an epistemological analogue to an ethics of care, although it was offered as a way of knowing *and* a moral perspective. Nevertheless, his discussion of how feminist researchers care about the effects of their investigations emphasizes holding knowers accountable for what they do. These attempts take place with the recognition that knowledge, inquiry, and representation are inevitably socially situated, partial and perspectival (not detached). Feminist researchers are self-conscious regarding who gets to speak, who is heard as authoritative and how knowledge claims become authoritative, who has access to research materials, and how the resulting authorization of knowledge changes people's lives. Unlike utilitarian or contractual rights-based theories, which represent morality as a set of law-like propositions, feminist epistemology uses an "expressive-collaborative" model of morality, making moral knowledge a continuing negotiation among people (Walker, 1998). This involves "socially situated and socially sustained practices of responsibility" (p. 201), modified over time through reflection and interaction. Similarly, feminist communitarians assume humans can articulate situated moral rules grounded in local community and group understanding; research guided by such principles will enhance moral reasoning, reflect multiple voices, serve the community, and enable participants to act to transform their social world (Christians, 2002; Denzin, 1997).

In particular, feminist standpoint theory emphasizes the importance of historical and cultural contexts. Standpoint feminists (such as Sandra Harding, Dorothy Smith, Nancy Hartsock, and Patricia Hill Collins) grant that all knowledge attempts are socially situated. Since some of these are better than others for generating knowledge, critical evaluation is necessary to determine which particular social locations tend to promote better knowledge claims. Crucially, such a standpoint is an achievement of groups coming to understand the social relations and social forces in which they are involved; it is decidedly not a "social given" or self-evident form of knowledge generated by individuals reporting their experience. Specifically, standpoint theorists assume groups who are marginalized must understand those who dominate them; conversely, people who are dominant do not need to understand those they dominate – and therefore do not. By beginning with the standpoint of women as a subordinated class, then, they foreground and incorporate bias into the method of knowledge-seeking and thus generate less distorted accounts.

The sociological and historical relativism involved in starting with the perspectives of those most subordinated, however, is not epistemological relativism. Harding (1993) insisted that "strong objectivity" requires not only self-critique but also strong reflexivity, such that the subject is on the same critical/causal plane as researcher and can "gaze back." Harding's assertion that people can achieve a "traitorous" identity, betraying their privileged positions so as to understand others, is controversial. In particular, critics charge that people cannot disregard their particular needs and concerns to take up another's standpoint.

The feminist case for knowledge-seeking grounded in and inspired by concrete, caring relationships and care as an epistemological virtue emerges in the questions posed for researchers who want to "work the [Self-Other] hyphen" (Fine *et al.*, 2003).

Feminist Ethics and Global Media

Among other questions, qualitative researchers would ask themselves: "Have I connected the 'voices' and 'stories' of individuals back to the set of historic, structural, and economic relations in which they are situated?" "Have I described the mundane?" (rather than surfing through transcripts to find what is exotic or sensational), "Have I considered how these data could be used for progressive, conservative, repressive social politics?" and "Where have I backed into the passive voice and decoupled my responsibility for my interpretations?" (Fine *et al.*, 2003). Such questions have no single right answer. Similarly, Denzin (1997) sees feminist communitarian ethics as building collaborative, reciprocal, friendly, trusting relations with ethnographic subjects, including by giving them a voice in research design. Rejecting positivism's principles (beneficience, anonymity and justice) and norms (validity and random selection), feminist communitarian ethics is instead is grounded in community. Properly linking research and practice, Denzin calls on ethnographers to function as public journalists and advocates a "communitarian journalism that treats communication and newsmaking as value-laden activities and as forms of social narrative rooted in the community" (p. 157).

Thus, caring is appropriate for journalists under two conditions. First, care must embrace (some) strangers and/or communities (territorial and affective, local and distant – and indeed, global). Failing to do so invites a sentimental notion that infantilizes its already highly gendered subjects. Indeed, until the 1960s, most women journalists faced the trap of the "sob sisters" or "agony aunts," literally and explicitly gendered as female. Women understood that such caring forms represented professional ghettoes, not socialization, much less natural instincts. Yet, journalists are ethically obligated to be sensitive to the voice of care and, more importantly, to evaluate and help readers evaluate claims to caring and suffering and to evaluate policies and proposals to ameliorate suffering. Just as feminist ethics is increasingly attentive to the global, journalists' caring would extend to global agendas. This notably includes problems in caregiving relationships and institutions. Care work is a public issue, so requires the kind of public deliberation that might follow from public and journalistic attention. Importantly for media work, this notion of care requires thought, evaluation, deliberation, informed debate. Not all intimate caring relationships and contexts are moral; not all political "causes" are inherently moral and progressive.

Second, as a matter of epistemology and ethics, feminist researchers are highly self-reflective and self-conscious about ethical and scientific responsibilities. We acknowledge our positioning and partiality, rather than maintaining distance. Feminist epistemologists insist on exposing power relations between researcher and participants, who are regarded as subjects, not objects; duping or deceiving subjects is prohibited. Researcher and researched both contribute knowledge to the relation, albeit not equally. Feminist researchers share conclusions and drafts with research participants, and attend to their feedback, despite the enormous investment of energy, emotion, time, and labor this requires.

Moral dialogue among a community of interlocutors helps people recognize and correct the biases in each other's views that, again, they cannot detect in themselves

(Friedman, 1993). Media professionals – like other people– would state their positions openly and offer mutual critiques, not as a matter of competition, but for transparency and correcting the overall value of their work. Durham (1998) shows how standpoint epistemology requires journalists "to rethink themselves and their craft from the position of marginalized Others, thus uncovering unconscious ethnocentric, sexist, racist, and heterosexist biases that distort news production" (p. 132). Becoming engaged in the consequences of stories for the disenfranchised would "subvert from within the hegemonies in current news practice" (p. 135). Although conventional ethics prohibits journalists from considering the implications or potential consequences of stories, the kind of self-reflexivity described above would presumably make journalism practice quite different. Feminist moral epistemology asks journalists to acknowledge their own positionality and even their privilege, to bracket their assumptions, and to be modest regarding truth claims. Even as we choose important topics with potential for transformative impact, we concede that a particular piece of reportage may be incomplete, situated as it is in a historically particular social/political moment. Since feminism encourages criticism and evaluation, caring requires reporters not to believe all subjects equally, much less to treat them as coequals in the processes of gathering or interpreting news, but to hear them out in their particularity.

Allowing caring voices to emerge may require asking more questions, new questions. At least journalists would listen more attentively to people, especially subordinated or powerless people, whose voices are typically silenced or marginalized, often merely because they speak in the vocabulary of care and connection; they would acknowledge to sources and to the people they cover "how" they care. Finally, they would avoid stereotypes that might otherwise lead them to hear women only when they speak in caring voices but remain deaf to men speaking in this vocabulary.

Empirical Data

In the late 1990s, developmental psychologists at Harvard (where Gilligan and Kohlberg did their pioneering work) interviewed journalists, actors, and scientists to see how professionals manage to do "good work" despite powerful market constraints and other ethical conflicts (Fischman *et al.*, 2004). Not surprisingly, journalists were largely frustrated, stressed, and "demoralized"; two-thirds of them considered leaving journalism. They navigated the ethical minefields by being devious, or, rarely, by defying problematic orders. Sometimes they cut corners or compromised their integrity outright, lest they lose their jobs or their credibility (e.g., by being scooped). Although they valued good work and hard work, these journalists expressed something like Wolfe's (2001) moral freedom. (These journalists were also unusually unreliable research citizens, whether because of the chaotic nature of the work, or declining standards in journalism or the lack of mentoring.)

If studying the moral epistemology of media professionals may indicate the conditions and contexts that allow for or constrain ethical practices among advertisers,

Feminist Ethics and Global Media

film producers, television programmers, and photojournalists, however, empirical data do not generate an ethical framework. Nor are data on how men and women resolve actual dilemmas dispositive. Do differences indicate women have been socialized into a separate normative track? Does sameness indicate that women have internalized the male-identified concerns of a male profession? In any case, whether women journalists "do" ethics differently than men is unclear. According to informal surveys by the International Women's Media Foundation (www.iwmf.org), some women say female journalists offer a more human perspective, although others said that "the news is the news," so identical ethical standards apply equally to all journalists. Nor do larger surveys or paper-and-pencil tests find that gender reliably predicts journalists' values or approaches to ethical decision-making (Weaver, 1997; Weaver and Wilhoit, 1996). Moreover, there are inconsistencies across media professions. For example, liberal political ideology generally correlates with higher level moral thinking, and it does for public relations professionals, but not for journalists (Wilkins, 2010). Professional expertise appeared to support higher-level moral thinking in journalism and public relations, but not advertising.

Consistent with such findings (but in opposition to efforts by women activists and scholars to show that gender matters), many women journalists adamantly deny that their moral reasoning is gender-specific; they deny that they report "like" or "as" women, beyond a tendency to report more about the problems of women and to use more female sources and more human context (Chambers, Steiner, and Fleming, 2004). The case for difference is most often made in the context of war reporting; but even here, most women reporters argue that good war reporting looks at both military and human costs, tactics, and context. Perhaps ironically, although caring has enjoyed little explicit resonance among journalists, it is a male former BBC-correspondent who ventures (briefly) a "journalism of attachment" – "a journalism that cares as well as knows; that is aware of its responsibilities; that will not stand neutrally between good and evil, right and wrong, the victim and the oppressor" (Bell, 1998, p. 19).

As suggested above, emotion is particularly difficult to subject for ethical analysis, overlaid as it is by the historic dichotomy between masculine/public/reason and feminine/private/emotion. Precisely because women are assumed to be emotional and instinctual (so needing the control of superior reason) women have been seen as incapable of full moral personhood. Feminists have also tried to rehabilitate various emotions – altruism and passion, for example – as not irrational, even if they are not rational, and as legitimate aspects of moral reasoning and public processes such as deliberation (Hall, 2007). Professional journalists rarely acknowledge their own emotions in their conventional front-page news, much less their status as persons. Willis (2003) barely mentions emotions in *The Human Journalists: Reporters, Perspectives, and Emotions* until the end, when he celebrates the cathartic value of self-analysis and says writers need "an understanding heart" (p. 115). Willis defended acknowledging journalists' "real" emotions in situations such as Oklahoma City in 1995 and September 11, 2001, when, he suggests that only robots could have suppressed their emotions.

The real problem may be compassion burn-out. Journalists apparently do not regularly suffer post-traumatic stress disorder. However, war correspondents and other reporters dealing with intense trauma – complicated by interviewing victims and witnessing the aftermath of horrific events, without much time to process their emotions – suffer PTSD-like symptoms, also called "vicarious traumatization," or "compassion fatigue" (Palm, Polusny, and Follette, 2004; Simpson and Boggs, 1999). Indeed, the fact that some war correspondents have been shot at and wounded, have seen colleagues killed or commit suicide, have had bounties placed on them suggests war reporting is both morally and physically hazardous. War journalists working for six major news organizations reported significantly more depression; their life-time PTSD prevalence rates were 28.6%, similar to those of combat veterans (Feinstein, Owen, and Blair, 2002). Male journalists drank twice as much and female journalists three times more alcohol than nonwar journalists (Feinstein, Owen, and Blair, 2002).

Wilkins also notes that specific traumas and negative environments can thwart individual moral development, as indicated by evidence that abused women and rape victims have stunted moral development. The impact of environment on the organism is reciprocal, symbiotic, and not at all neutral. Some environments make caring far more difficult than others – and, of course, the current crises in journalism and in news organizations pose their own set of challenges to journalists trying to act ethically. The question is whether membership in a profession (as a kind of environment) and the resulting professional expertise can make moral action easier or more likely. Since journalists are not trained to understand the hazards they face, they need information about PTSD, effective coping, and interventions (Palm *et al.*, 2004). Wilkins rightly calls for additional empirical research on ethical reasoning to clarify the impact of what is specifically cultural, as opposed to innate, or what changes at specific times of life or within specific roles.

Regarding leadership, "feminine" management style is said to be more interpersonal, democratic, constructive, collaborative; while masculine management is more autocratic, competitive, defensive (Arnold and Nesbitt, 2006). These gendered dichotomies are asserted without much data. Men run nearly all papers in both categories. The single large paper that engaged women in all its top management positions (between 1999 and 2003) was perceived as encouraging openness and family-friendly policies (Everbach, 2006), but did not espouse distinctly feminist ethics or, for that matter, content.

This raises the question of whether workplaces of feminist organizations, operated by feminists and/or designed along feminist principles sustain moral reasoning along feminist dimensions. Granted, the ethical principles of nineteenth and twentieth century feminist media organizations are not dispositive, since, as intended, these almost never made money. An ethics that bans or condemns fame and commercial success is silly and impractical. Nonetheless, these publications offer interesting models for making the personal political, despite considerable inconvenience. Nineteenth century suffrage editors and publishers, for example, created workplaces that took account of the domestic and personal lives of the volunteer staff. Second-wave feminists regularly refuse advertising inconsistent with feminism. *Ms.* Magazine eschewed all advertising in response to advertisers who demanded "complementary copy" or compromises to its reporting. This is not to say these organizations are ethically pure. In 1970 *off our backs* announced that its mission was to be "just" (i.e., not impartial), but the periodical nearly collapsed in 1980, when a member of the collective embezzled $5000. Although *oob* survived, many nonhierarchal collectives have dissolved in the face of internal arguments.

Sex and Sexual Harassment

Feminism as a way of thinking about social and political relationships offers ethical and epistemological principles that correct misogynist biases and incorporate values (such as community) and responsibilities (such as caring) that historically are associated with women, without assuming that all women around the globe are permanently or equally subordinated. Sex differences are inadequate grounds for feminist media ethics. Nonetheless, sexism causes problems differentially relevant to women, including, as noted before, sexual commodification. Hypermasculinity is increasingly insidious. However, hyperfeminity and sexualized images of women (here referring to women sexually objectified in news and entertainment) remain morally troubling. Indeed, the texts asserting that women should be unhappy about themselves, especially their bodies, and that imply that women are the sum of their body parts are unethical, even without the kind of behavioral effects that sometimes are asserted.

A second issue emerges in the relationship of women journalists to male colleagues or bosses (who remain the majority) and to male sources (usually people in power, also primarily men). In television journalism, few women protest when they are hired, treated, and evaluated in terms of physical beauty, although such discrimination is arguably unprofessional and unethical. Likewise most women say they do not mind the romantic attentions of coworkers or sources. They may believe – and it might be valid in the short run – in mildly exploiting their sexuality (Robertson, 1992). Nevertheless, even if they are not fired for such relationships with sources, among the ethical problems are that men resent female colleagues for enjoying a competitive edge; men apparently assume all women deploy their sexuality for professional gain, even those who refuse to engage in flirting. Second, women are thus less able to protest sexual harassment and to take it seriously as a continuing workplace issue for other women. A sexual harassment claim in 1991 against a US Supreme Court nominee provoked a spate of complaints, news stories about harassment, and research on newsrooms. Nearly 30% of women journalists surveyed in 1993–1995 reported verbal sexual harassment by coworkers (Walsh-Childers, Chance, and Herzog, 1996). The concern soon evaporated. Perhaps professionalism brought cultural change to newsrooms. More likely, women simply ignore it. In any case, women are morally obliged to confront their sexual harassers (Hay, 2005). Suggesting that being subjected to a moral harm imposes moral obligations on the victim sounds odd, but Hay derives this obligation from a woman's obligation to protect her own autonomy or moral agency.

Is a Feminist Ethics Distinctive?

Media ethicists increasingly cite deontological and consequentialist approaches, and now virtue ethics, as well. This mix may not please philosophers. Arguing against an inevitably unhappy marriage of virtue and care ethics, Sander-Staudt (2006) lists the propensity to dominate, overly criticize, overlook bad qualities, or seek to possess the other as among the many problems that plague both marital relations and relations among moral theories. Her warning that some combinations of moral theories may thwart theoretical alliances with yet other theories also speaks on behalf of collaborations. The feminist media ethics proposed here overlaps at least the broad outlines of other ethical approaches. Indeed, from a practical standpoint, for media applications, the differences may be irrelevant; in actuality feminist ethicists and rights-based ethicists are unlikely to resolve ethical dilemmas in polar opposite ways. Both the ethic of care and virtue theory, for example, emphasize the importance of habit and inclination: "Neither pretends to provide a calculus for moral decision making; rather they insist that the context coupled with the character of the actor and some general rules of thumb will provide all the cues" (Manning, 1992, p. 83). No media ethics condones sexist and exploitative images, discriminatory hiring practices, or patriarchal production cultures. All ethical theories address how journalism and other media practices can be just and fair. Sometimes the aim of this goodness is defined in terms of self-governance and autonomy, and sometimes, as in the case here, in terms of community and the collective good.

The difference feminism makes emerges more clearly with reference to specific "local" situations, when, in the face of competing duties and responsibilities, we must select which specific facts or events to deem morally relevant. Take, for example, Elliott's (1997) explicit repudiation of compassionate journalism, a case admirably made not on the basis of easy targets – the toddler down the well or the much-despised "if it bleeds it leads" mantra – but more difficult ones, like the person who desperately needs a kidney transplant. For Elliott compassion is appropriate only for individuals on their own time: "Acting in the interest of particular individuals in need is not morally acceptable for a social institution or for an agent working on behalf of a social institution" (1997, p. 218). News organizations that promote the cause of an individual in need harm needy others who do not get similar aid. Elliott says compassion prevents journalists from doing their jobs (telling people what they need in order to be self-governing). It produces unjustified harm – the same kind of institutional unfairness news organizations presumably seek to expose. Even if citizen-readers get the policy stories they need, she argues, journalists should not tell the stories of needy individuals – as a matter of justice.

However, a justice-based rule prohibiting compassion ignores how narratives may ethically attend to "distressed" individuals. On one hand, all individuals' sad stories are not equally in need of being told. On the other, stories of pitiful individuals may trigger community concern (compassion) and demand (passion) for larger institutional change. Powerful exposés of the plight of "hurting people" show how portraying the complexities of human need can be ethical (Craig, 2006). Compassion is not always relevant; and careless application of compassion can compromise journalists' independence. However, attending to vulnerable individuals does not always or necessarily prevent journalists from doing their work. The fact that it can – but need not – end in sentimental or paternal (or maternal) discourse blocking institutional change and reform should constitute a guideline and warning, not a prohibition.

For Robinson (1999), rights- and duty-based approaches to problems like poverty are too abstract and generalized to mitigate the actual suffering, so major national and international problems need care at the forefront of moral deliberation. Robinson claims that a critical ethic of care would help privileged people understand the connection between their affluence and others' poverty. Otherwise, rich people will use occasional charity to feel good rather than to solve problems. Notably, Silk (1998) points to "spectacular" television fund-raisers as evidence that mass media content can inspire responsive actions in distant contexts (third party beneficence) and that media audiences can care from afar. Furthermore, acting at a distance to produce mass media information that inspires self-help support groups is itself a form of beneficence. He concludes that the quasi-interaction facilitated by print and broadcast news content may relieve suffering, without the embarrassment of face-to-face interaction. In any case, media issues come to the fore.

The kind of figure-ground relationship Gilligan (1995) offered to soften the contrast between care and duty is useful here. Again, as a practical matter, both practitioners and audiences probably speak in, listen to, and heed voices of justice and connection. Pure justice is unlikely to be useful. The same is true of emotivism, which, in the context of photojournalism, Scott (1993) described as a "fairly simple and accurate method" for making ethical decisions. The notion that everyone is equal, or that all stories are equally important, has already been eclipsed. The feminist version of care proposed here means that journalists would privilege the problems, concerns, stories, and counter-stories of marginalized or subordinated people and others who need care. These issues are themselves interstructured. Stories that respect care-giving (at the society and global level) may encourage other people to speak – and be reported – in this register. Journalists and the people they report on and for are entitled to the same satisfaction from accomplishing caring and seeing caring accomplished that others enjoy.

Conclusion

Feminist media ethics allows for simultaneous deference to professional duty, responsibility and care, and allows compassion to come to the fore in testing and evaluating ethical solutions. At a minimum, it provides a coherent, enriched account of to whom and when media are important and why ethical media practices are important. Such politicization is important in news and entertainment content, in media workplaces, and in consideration of which audiences are to be served. Application of feminist ethics would emphasize designing ethical work routines, institutional structures, and professional practices. With its preference for contextualization and its resistance to universalizing, abstract, and disembodied conceptions, feminist ethics cannot be codified. Just as caregiving is highly labor- and time-intensive, so is the ethic of care. In contrast, the formalist insistence on neutrality, distance, and objectivity conveniently short-circuits external criticism by automatically forbidding the time-consuming process of considering context and particularity. Meanwhile, revising journalism mythology valuably gives ethical journalists permission and validation to do what they already want to do and try to do (Steiner and Okrusch, 2006). Journalists want to do good work: They want their work to have impact, including by changing readers' lives, to support democracy and to empower the disenfranchised.

The extent to which this (or any) feminist ethics works globally is debatable. A global media ethics is advantageous, for example, by mitigating against the tendency to romanticize cultural forms of femininity or masculinity as "traditional" even while these forms are condemned as antifeminist in the West. New technologies have dramatically changed the way that mediated content is produced, delivered, consumed, and understood. The Internet, mobile phones, and satellite television mean that media institutions and practitioners operate globally, circulating global content to global audiences and even facilitating border-crossing feminist moral discourse. All this presumably speaks on behalf of globalized ethics. Luo (2007) sees significant overlaps (centering on empathy) between early Confucian ethics and feminist ethics of care, as well as with agent-based virtue ethics. Luo uses the Confucian concept of *de* (moral virtue). In Confucian ethics caring is a relational moral virtue. Making the case for a global feminist ethics requires support from ethicists around the world similar to Luo. Perhaps if I could read other languages I might even find additional international defenses of the feminist ethics proposed above. Meanwhile, despite academic feminists' protests about universalizing and essentializing, activists across the globe argue for women's rights as universal human rights. It's difficult, but not impossible, especially at a time when we increasingly have hyphenated or even subaltern identities but also access to new media technologies that might allow us to speak for ourselves. The potential of new media is complicated and not at all guaranteed, so a feminist media ethics plays a role here, too.

On the other hand, not only is there no monolithic global feminist community, but women and men in some subordinated or colonized cultures resist the empirical and moral scrutiny of feminists whom they regard as privileged Westerners; they resent feminist interventions and deny that feminists' moral critiques apply to them, their experiences, or their often stigmatized cultural practices (Jaggar, 1998). Some African and Middle Eastern feminists argue that Western feminists' concerns about ethical treatment and representation of women "orientalize" women (to use Edward Said's famous concept) and excuse global sexism; to others, this "orientalism" misunderstands culturally different approaches to women's agency

Feminist Ethics and Global Media

and freedom; still others say specific "traditional" religious values can render Western concepts of rights and women's moral freedom irrelevant. The "epistemological indispensability of closed communities" to developing languages for each group to elaborate their heretical ideas produces a paradox, however: What liberates the thinking of these closed communities also restricts their moral reasoning. Silencing all dissent and insisting on conformity make for moral and epistemological hazards. For a globalized feminist ethics to enable legitimate scrutiny of alternatives to hegemonic moral systems, at a minimum, requires Western feminists to abandon their missionary stance, participate in inclusive dialogue, think very carefully about who is entitled to speak. In particular, the perspectives of non-Western women may literally "disturb" seemingly well-established feminist assumptions.

Twenty years after Jaggar (1989) disputed the notion of a unitary feminist morality, feminist theorizing and ethics still refuse to congeal as a homogenous or singular whole. Typologies used in the 1980s and 1990s to distinguish, for example, liberal, cultural, and radical feminism no longer seem important; but debates over feminist ethics remain fraught. Some feminists criticize attempts to rehabilitate canonical political philosophies (such as liberal egalitarianism or contractualism) or ideals (such as autonomy). Others decry inverting male values to privilege women's interests. Just as feminism does not prescribe one way to be a woman, Tong and Williams (2008) conclude that all women-centered approaches to ethics – "feminine," "maternal," and "lesbian" – aim for nonsexist moral principles, policies, and practices, but do not impose a single normative standard on women. They see this multiplicity as politically problematic and call on feminist ethicists to develop policies that serve the *most important* interests of the *widest* range of women, and to agree on a theory that achieves gender equality.

A "morally dangerous profession" in which situational pressures "are likely to overwhelm the resources of character" (Levy 2004, p. 113, 116) probably demands a sturdy multidimensional framework. Around the globe we are all innately moral beings, with moral impulses (which can be developed, or thwarted) to respect human dignity and minimize harm. Nonetheless, this does not solve the problem of sincere individuals or even institutions weighing competing values to resolve profound dilemmas. Feminist ethics may not result in absolutely consistent answers.

References

Arnold, M., and Nesbitt, M. (2006) *Women in Media 2006: Finding the Leader in You,* Media Management Centre at Northwestern, Evanston, IL.

Bartky, S.L. (2002) Emotional exploitation, in *Ethics in Practice: An Anthology,* 2nd edn, (ed. H. LaFollette), Blackwell, London, pp. 156–166.

Beasley, M., and Gibbons, S. (2003) *Taking Their Place: A Documentary History of Women in Journalism,* Strata Publishing, State College, PA.

Bell, L.A. (1993) *Rethinking Ethics in the Midst of Violence,* Rowman & Littlefield Lanham, MD.

Bell, M. (1998) The journalism of attachment, in *Media Ethics*, (ed. M. Kieran), Routledge, London.

Chambers, D., Steiner, L., and Fleming, C. (2004) *Women and Journalism*, Routledge, New York.

Christians, C.G. (2002) Norman Denzin's feminist communitarian ethics. *Studies in Symbolic Interaction*, 25,167–177.

Christians, C.G. (2003) Ethics and politics in qualitative research, in *The Landscape of Qualitative Research: Theories and Issues*, (eds N.K. Denzin and Y.S. Lincoln), Sage, London, pp. 208–244.

Craig, D. (2006) *The Ethics of the Story: Using Narrative Techniques Responsibly in Journalism*, Rowman & Littlefield Lanham, MD.

Denzin, N.K. (1997) *Interpretive Ethnography: Ethnographic Practices for the 21st Century*, Sage, Thousand Oaks, CA.

Durham, M.G. (1998) On the relevance of standpoint epistemology to the practice of journalism: The case for strong objectivity. *Communication Theory*, 8 (2), 117–140.

Elliott, D. (1997) The problem of compassionate journalism, in *Mixed News: The Public/ Civic Communitarian Journalism Debate*, (ed. Jay Black), Lawrence Erlbaum, Mahwah, NJ, pp. 218–226.

Engster, D. (2005) Rethinking care theory: The practice of caring and the obligation to care. *Hypatia*, 20 (3), 50–74.

Everbach, T. (2006) The culture of a women-led newspaper: An ethnographic study of the *Sarasota Herald-Tribune*. *Journalism and Mass Communication Quarterly*, 83 (3), 477–493.

Feinstein, A., Owen, J., Blair, N. (2002) A hazardous profession: War, journalists, and psychopathology. *American Journal of Psychiatry*, 159, 1570–1575.

Fine, M., Weis, L., Weseen S. *et al.* (2003) For whom? Qualitative research, representations, and social responsibilities, in *The Landscape of Qualitative Research: Theories and Issues*, (eds N.K. Denzin and Y.S. Lincoln), Sage, London, pp. 167–207

Fischman, W., Solomon, B., Greenspan, D. *et al.* (2004) *Making Good: How Young People Cope with Moral Dilemmas at Work*, Harvard University Press, Cambridge, MA.

Fraser, N. (1986) Toward a discourse ethic of solidarity. *Praxis International*, 5 (4), 425–429.

Friedman, M. (1993) *What Are Friends For?: Feminist Perspectives on Personal Relationships and Moral Theory*, Cornell University Press, Ithaca, NY.

Gilligan, C. (1982) *In a Different Voice: Psychological Theory and Women's Development*, Harvard University Press, Cambridge, MA.

Gilligan, C. (1987) Moral orientation and moral development, in *Women and Moral Theory*, (eds E.F. Kittay and D.T. Meyers), Rowman & Littlefield, Totowa, NJ, pp. 19–33.

Gilligan, C. (1995) Hearing the difference: Theorizing connection. *Hypatia*, 10 (2), 120–127.

Hall, C. (2007) Recognizing the passion in deliberation: Toward a more democratic theory of deliberative democracy. *Hypatia*, 22 (4), 81–95.

Halwani, R. (2003) Care ethics and virtue ethics. *Hypatia*, 18 (3), 161–192.

Hay, C. (2005) Whether to ignore them and spin: Moral obligations to resist sexual harassment. *Hypatia*, 20 (4), 94–108.

Harding, S. (1993) Rethinking standpoint epistemology: What is strong objectivity? in *Feminist Epistemologies*, (eds L. Alcoff and E. Potter), Routledge, New York, pp. 49–82.

Held, V. (2006) *The Ethics of Care: Personal, Political, and Global*, Oxford University Press, New York.

Jaggar, A. (1989) Feminist ethics: Some issues for the nineties. *Journal of Social Philosophy*, 20 (spring/fall), pp. 1–2.

Jaggar, A. (1992) Feminist ethics, in *Encyclopedia of Ethics*, (eds L. Becker and C. Becker), Garland Press, New York, pp. 361–369.

Jaggar, A. (1998) Globalizing Feminist Ethics. *Hypatia*, 13 (2), 7–31.

Jaggar, A (2000) Ethics naturalized: Feminism's contribution to moral epistemology, *Metaphilosophy*, 31 (5), 452–468.

Kittay, E.F. (1999) *Love's Labor: Essays on Women, Equality and Dependency*. New York.

Koehn, D. (1998) *Rethinking Feminist Ethics: Care, Trust, and Empathy*, Routledge, New York.

Levy, N. (2004) Good character: Too little, too late. *Journal of Mass Media Ethics*, 19 (2), 108–118.

Luo, S. (2007) Relation, virtue, and relational virtue: Three concepts of caring. *Hypatia*, 22 (3), 92–110.

Macgregor, S. (2004) From care to citizenship: Calling ecofeminism back to politics. *Ethics and the Environment*, 9 (1), 56–84.

Manning, R.C. (1992) *Speaking from the Heart: A Feminist Perspective on Ethics*. Rowman & Littlefield, Lanham, MD.

Mendus, S. (2000) *Feminism and Emotion: Readings in Moral and Political Philosophy*, St. Martin's Press, New York.

Noddings, N. (1984) *Caring: A Feminine Approach to Ethics and Moral Education*, University of California Press, Berkeley, MA.

Noddings, N. (2002) *Starting at Home: Caring and Social Policy*, University of California Press, Berkeley, MA.

NOW (National Organization for Women) (1966) www.now.org/history/purpos66.html (accessed June 22, 2010).

Nozick, R. (1981) *Philosophical Explanations*, Harvard University Press, Cambridge, MA.

Palm, K.M., Polusny, M.A., and Follette, V.M. (2004) Vicarious traumatization: Potential hazards and interventions for disaster and trauma workers. *Prehospital and Disaster Medicine*,19 (1), 73–78, http://pdm.medicine.wisc.edu (accessed June 22, 2010).

Robertson, N. (1992) *Girls in the Balcony*, Random House, New York.

Robinson, F. (1999) G*lobalizing Care: Ethics, Feminist Theory, and International Relations*, Westview Press, Boulder, CO.

Rouse, J. (2004) Feminism and the social construction of scientific knowledge, in *The Feminist Standpoint Theory Reader: Intellectual and Political Controversies*, (ed. S. Harding), Routledge, New York, pp. 353–374.

Ruddick, S. (1989) *Maternal Thinking: Toward a Politics of Peace*, Beacon, New York.

Sander-Staudt, M. (2006) The unhappy marriage of care ethics and virtue ethics. *Hypatia*, 21 (4), 21–39.

Scott, S.D. (1993) Beyond reason: A feminist theory of ethics for journalists. *Gender Issues*, 13 (1), 23–40.

Silk, J. (1998) Caring at a distance. *Ethics, Place and Environment*, 1 (2), 165–182.

Simpson, R., and Boggs, J. (1999) An exploratory study of traumatic stress among newspaper journalists. *Journalism and Communication Monographs*, 9, 1 (1), 1–26.

Sommers, C.H. (1987) Filial morality, in *Women and Moral Theory*, (eds E.F. Kittay and D.T. Meyers), Rowman & Littlefield, Totowa, NJ, pp. 69–84.

Steiner, L. (1989) Feminist theorizing and communication ethics. *Communication*, 12 (3), 157–173.

Steiner, L. and Okrusch, C.M. (2006) Care as a virtue for journalists. *Journal of Mass Media Ethics*, 21 (2&3), 102–122.

Tong, R., and Williams, N. (2008) Feminist ethics, *The Stanford Encyclopedia of Philosophy (Winter 2008 Edition)*, (ed. E.N. Zalta), http://plato.stanford.edu/archives/win2008/entries/feminism-ethics/ (accessed June 22, 2010).

Tronto, J.C. (1995) Care as a basis for radical political judgments. *Hypatia*, 10 (2), 141–149.

Walker, M. U. (1998) *Moral Understandings: A Feminist Study in Ethics*, Routledge, New York.

Walsh-Childers, K., Chance, J., and Herzog, K. (1996) Sexual harassment of women journalists. *Journalism and Mass Communication Quarterly*, 73 (3), 559–581.

Weaver, D. (1997) Women as journalists, in *Women, Media, and Politics*, (ed. P. Norris), Oxford University Press, New York, pp. 21–40.

Weaver, D.H., and Wilhoit, G.C. (1996) *The American Journalist in the 1990s: U.S. News People at the End of an Era*, Lawrence Erlbaum, Mahwah, NJ.

Weiss, P.A. (1995) Feminism and communitarianism: Comparing critiques of liberalism, *Feminism and Community*, (eds P.A. Weiss and M. Friedman), Temple University Press, Philadelphia, pp. 161–186.

Wilkins, L. (2010) Connecting care and duty: How neuroscience and feminist ethics can contribute to understanding professional moral development, in *Media Ethics beyond Borders: A Global Perspective*, (eds S.J.A. Ward and H. Wasserman), Heinemann, Johannesburg, South Africa, pp. 24–41.

Willis, J. (2003) *The Human Journalists: Reporters, Perspectives, and Emotions*, Praeger, Westport, CT.

Wolfe, A. (2001) *Moral Freedom: The Impossible Idea That Defines the Way We Live Now*, Norton, New York.

11

Words as Weapons
A History of War Reporting – 1945 to the Present

Richard Lance Keeble

The Media in Wartime: From Militarism to New Militarism

The traditional militarism of World Wars I and II, in which the mass of the population participated in the war efforts either as soldiers or civilians, is constantly the subject of nostalgic, patriotic celebration in the mainstream media in the United Kingdom. Yet both wars threw up serious problems for Western elites. Throughout the West, the old elites were discredited by appeasement and collaboration with the Nazis. Trade union militancy flourished in Britain and 2194 strikes were recorded in 1944 – up to then the highest ever (Harris, 1984, p. 66). Mass employment encouraged the further emancipation of women while on the continent a "transnational revolutionary mood" emerged between 1943 and 1947 (Gunn, 1989, pp. 7–8).

Since 1945, the democratic problems posed by mass conscription have been resolved in a number of ways. National service has ended while military strategy has emphasized low intensity operations away from the media glare or spectacular adventures against manufactured enemies (Curtis, 1998, 2003; Newsinger, 2002; Pilger, 2002). Following the secret launch of the United Kingdom's nuclear weapons program in the late-1940s, the emphasis has shifted to nuclear "deterrence."

Democratic advances were also witnessed in the United States during the world wars. Unions gained in strength and workers struggled for higher wages. Significantly mass conscription during the Vietnam War (though not a total war for the United States) was also accompanied by substantial social dislocation with the emergence of student, black, and feminist radicalism – and urban riots. Since then, until 2003, the emphasis had been on avoiding Vietnam-type confrontations. With a shift to an all-volunteer army in the 1970s, technical development became the army's top priority. So men (and the occasional woman) have given way on the "battle front" to the computerized machine.

The Handbook of Global Communication and Media Ethics, First Edition. Edited by Robert S. Fortner and P. Mark Fackler.
© 2011 Blackwell Publishing Ltd. Published 2011 by Blackwell Publishing Ltd.

While the two world wars provided the United Kingdom with enduring myths of patriotic glory, Vietnam threatened to destroy the beliefs in victory and triumph which are so central to America's national identity. As Tom Engelhardt comments (1995, p. 15): "It is hardly surprising that, after 1975, the basic impulse of America's political and military leaders (as well as of many other Americans) was not to forge a new relationship to the world but to reconstruct a lost identity of triumph." New militarism, in effect, provided the solution, manufacturing conflicts in which the United States could gain its necessary "victories" and so "kick the Vietnam syndrome." However, after the disastrous invasions of Afghanistan (2001) and Iraq (2003), the lies and myths on which New Militarism was built were exposed. US and UK troops became bogged down in unwinnable conflicts in Iraq, Afghanistan and Somalia. So New Militarism began its slow death.

Secret State, Secret Warfare, Silent Press

In addition, the enormous political and economic power exerted by the military/industrial complexes in the United States and United Kingdom has meant that militarism has become a core, defining reality for these societies. Warfare has become a technological imperative as the United States aims to assert its capitalistic, worldwide hegemony (Boyd-Barrett, 2004, pp. 36–38). At the same time, it has provided the crucial testing ground for professional soldiers (desperate for "a piece of the action") and new weapons systems (Keeble, 2003).

Yet most of US/UK imperialism has advanced essentially in secret. Both countries have deployed forces virtually every year since 1945 – most of them away from the glare of the media (Peak, 1982). At various moments they have chosen to fight overt, manufactured "wars." We, the viewers and readers, have to see the spectacle. It has to appear "real." In this process the permanent war economy is both legitimized and celebrated.

MacKenzie (1984) has described the "spectacular theatre" of nineteenth century British militarism when press representations of heroic imperialist adventures in distant colonies had a considerable entertainment element. Moreover, the Victorian "small" wars of imperial expansion in Africa and India were glorified for a doting public by correspondents such as William Howard Russell, G.A. Henty, Archibald Forbes and H.M. Stanley (Featherstone, 1993a, 1993b). However, Victorian newspapers and magazines did not have the social penetration of today's mass media and Victorian militarism was reinforced through a wide range of social activities and institutions such as the Salvation Army, Church Army, uniformed youth organizations, rifle clubs and drill units in factories.

By the 1980s, this institutional and social militarism had given way to a new mediacentric, consumerist, entertainment militarism in which the mass media, ideologically tied to a strong and increasingly secretive state, had assumed a dominant ideological role. Thus, instead of active participation in wars, people were being mobilized for New Militarism through their consumption of heavily censored media (much of the censorship self-imposed by the journalists) whose job was to manufacture the spectacle of war as entertainment.

New Militarism in the United States

The origins of the New Militarist consensus in the United States can be traced to America's involvement in World War II. Some revisionist historians now suggest that Japanese plans for the attack on Pearl Harbor were well known to US intelligence and administration (Rusbridger and Nove, 1991). Certainly the attack provided the opportunity for the United State's fledgling permanent war economy state to join the fight against the Nazis (now that the more serious enemy, the Soviet communists, had managed to survive the German onslaught).

The "vulnerable state" (as represented by the elite) was responding as the innocent victim of an unprovoked attack. War was waged. Journalists faced a regime of "total censorship." As Gary C. Woodward comments (1993, p. 6): "Everything written, photographed or broadcast was scrutinised by censors. Anything that did not meet the High Command's considerations of security was deleted. In the Pacific theatre, for example, Americans were not told initially of the heavy damage to the US navy inflicted by the Japanese at Pearl Harbour." The legendary journalist, Walter Cronkite, United Press war correspondent from 1941 through to the end of the war and the Nuremburg trials, commented: "All written copy was passed by censors. And I think this is the way it should be. We had total freedom at the front with no restrictions where we went" (Sylvester and Huffman, 2005, p. 13). With the nuclear bombings of Hiroshima and Nagasaki in August 1945, the first warning to the Soviet Union in the new Cold War was delivered.

Growth of Secret US State and Covert Presidency

Alongside the development of the Cold War ideological hegemony and the permanent war state was the growth of the power of the executive office of the president based around the National Security Council and the CIA (together with the many other covert organizations comprising the secret state within the state) (Moyers, 1987). Secrecy and the development of a centralized, nuclear state were to become the dominant features of the domestic political scene, so covert Low Intensity Conflict (LIC) strategies, away from the glare of newspaper headlines, were favored abroad.

Secret Warfare: Away from the Probing Press

Thus, since 1945 America's main war-fighting activity was in the shady covert area – and here (through a series of managed media leaks) a number of "successes" were claimed. The CIA's clandestine support for military coups against revolutionary or reforming regimes ranked up a number of significant "victories': Syria 1949, Iran 1953, Guatemala 1954, Congo 1960, Iraq 1963 and 1968, Brazil 1964, Indonesia 1965, and Chile 1973 (Ranelagh 1992). As Halliday points out, these successes were dependent on the relative vulnerability of the armed forces in the target country. He adds: "When the CIA went into action against the revolutions of the 1970s this option was not available precisely because the revolutionaries had destroyed the old state machine, including its army, and replaced it with their own revolutionary armed forces. As in the case of Cuba during the period 1959–1961, the CIA was thrown back on a surrogate form of covert action – aid to right-wing guerrillas" (Halliday, 1989, pp. 74–75).

The global economic recession precipitated by the oil price increases of 1973 and 1979 completely overturned the global balance of power (Baker, 1991, pp. 3–8). Initially, the Third World made extraordinary gains and 14 revolutions shook the imperial powers.[1] In response, the imperial powers, led by the United States, completely altered their economic orientation to the Third/Developing World. From being suppliers of US$50 billion a year of capital to the Third World in the two decades leading up to the mid-1970s, the imperial powers moved to drawing US$100 billion a year from the Third World by the 1990s. This US$150 billion shift was equivalent to the entire balance of payments of the United States, 15 times the annual investment of Iraq or Egypt. The result was a massive rise of global poverty and Third World instability.

With the advent of the Reagan administration, the US elite was determined to roll back the revolutionary successes of the previous decade. The offensive was typically multipronged. Under the direction of William C. Casey (1981–1986), the CIA ran a massive LIC offensive strategy – totally contradicting the media myth of defense. Counter-revolutionary movements in Cambodia, Afghanistan, Angola, Suriname and Nicaragua were backed from 1981 to 1988 – at enormous expense. In 1986 alone, the Afghanistan operation received an estimated US$470 million and more than US$2 billion over the whole period.

Bob Woodward's (1987, pp. 310–311) history of the CIA's covert wars of the 1980s details a complex web of clandestine activity. He also reports (1987, p. 456) Ben Bradlee, *Washington Post* editor, as saying of the CIA in the 1980s: "It's really out of control, isn't it?" At least 12 operations of security and intelligence support included those to President Hissène Habré of Chad, to Pakistan President Zia, to Liberia's Samuel Doe, to Philippine President Marcos, to Sudanese President Numeiri, to Lebanese President Amir Gemayel and to President Duarte of El Salvador (all of these dictators with appalling human rights record). Both Prades (1986, p. 383) and Treverton (1987, p. 14) suggest that by the mid-1980s the CIA was engaged in at least 40 major covert operations – but they were largely ignored by the media.

The Great Vietnam Media Myth

At the heart of LIC strategy and the Reaganite response to the Third World revolutions were American perceptions of the "Vietnam syndrome." For the American elite the defeat in Vietnam (in what the Vietnamese dub the "American War")

Words as Weapons

against a far less technologically sophisticated enemy – accompanied by assassinations, race and student upheavals at home – was a trauma of unprecedented proportions. Its legacy was, indeed, horrifying. Some 4 million were killed in Indochina and many millions more orphaned, maimed and made into refugees; three countries were devastated – Vietnam, Cambodia and Laos. It cost more than US$150 billion for the US alone. More than 58 000 US troops were killed and 304 000 wounded while an estimated 3 million Vietnamese and 1 million in Laos and Cambodia died (Goldenberg, 2006). By the time Saigon fell to the North Vietnamese Army in 1975, more than 70 foreign and local journalists had been killed. As Richard Pyle and Horst Fass report (2003, pp. xiv–xv): "An unknown number of Cambodians, who had worked for the Western press and would vanish in the Killing Fields, were eventually added to an uncertain final toll.'

A scapegoat was needed and the most obvious one was the messenger of the bad tidings – the media. Vietnam has been described as the "first living-room war." Long after the end of the war, it is argued, television images still dominate our perceptions of it – a US Marine Zippo lighting a Vietnamese village, the execution of a Vietcong suspect in a Saigon street, a Vietnamese girl running naked and terrified down a street after a napalm attack. Images such as these along with press criticism of the conduct of the war are said to have eroded public support.

Studies have shown this conventional wisdom to be a myth. Even the US army's own official history, *The Military and the Media 1962–1968*, concluded that the American mainstream media was "remarkably professional in its coverage of Vietnam" (Badsey, 1995, p. 58). Surveys showed that media consumption, in fact, promoted support for the war (Williams, 1993, pp. 305–338). The American military, after considerable deliberations on the issue since the Korean War, opted for an entirely voluntary censorship scheme for journalists – in the main because they did not have total control over access to the frontline (unlike, for instance, during the Gulf crisis of 1991 and Iraq invasion of 2003 when the military enjoyed total control). War censorship, it was felt at the time, could not be introduced since no war had been declared.

Journalists were allowed remarkable access to the frontline. Sandy Gall comments in his autobiography (1994, pp. 230–231): "You could go anywhere at any time to cover almost any story. If there was a battle being fought in any part of Vietnam involving American troops or South Vietnamese or both the Press could go there simply by climbing aboard a helicopter or fixed-wing aircraft." This meant that censorship operated – but subtly. For instance, Bob Schieffer, a young reporter for *Forth Worth Star-Telegram* (later CBS news correspondent in Washington DC) commented: "The military commanders would exert control by limiting transportation into areas where the news might be bad. If I wanted to travel to Danang, they would call flight operation and find a transport plane going there that afternoon and make a place for me. But when there was a battle where the news was not the way they wanted, it was very difficult to get transportation" (Sylvester and Huffman, 2005, p. 20). Nor did the relative freedom enjoyed by journalists result in them flagrantly ignoring the guidelines which outlined 15 categories of information reportable only with authorization. Between August 1964 and the end of 1968, for example, around 2000 news media representatives reported from Vietnam – yet only six committed violations so severe to warrant the military revoking their credentials (Gannett, 1991, pp. 14–15).

The easy access to the frontlines also, intriguingly, offered new opportunities to women reporters – even though they still suffered from acute discrimination. As Chambers, Steiner and Fleming comment (2004, p. 205) "It was this feature of easy access, rather than significant changes in attitudes about women, that allowed so many women to report from Vietnam." In all, the US military provided credentials to 467 women reporters in Vietnam.

Backing Our Boys in Vietnam

Virtually every Vietnam reporter backed the war effort. As the Gannett Foundation report comments: "Throughout the war, in fact, journalists who criticised the military's performance did so out of a sense of frustration that military strategy and tactics were failing to accomplish the goal of decisively defeating the North Vietnamese forces" (Gannett Foundation, 1991, p. 15). Veteran war correspondent Peter Arnett (1993, p. 88) commented: "The consensus of the American high command was that their efforts were paying off in Vietnam, but that winning would take longer than anticipated. The reporters generally concurred in that view and I heard no one voice doubts that the war was worth fighting." In 1966, he said, he was entirely caught up in the war's momentum. "I never asked myself whether it was right or wrong and the question did not come up in conversation, not with soldiers or my colleagues because we were all of us too close to the action. Too many of our friends had died; we were unwilling to write off that sacrifice" (1994, p. 193).

The coverage of the My Lai massacre of March 1968, when hundreds of Vietnamese were slaughtered by rampaging American soldiers, highlights graphically the failures of the mainstream media in Vietnam. Evidence of the massacre was presented to top national news media by Vietnam veteran Ron Ridenhour and others, but none dared to touch the story (Neale, 2001, pp. 102–104). It was not until November 1969, more than a year and a half after the massacre, that the small, alternative Dispatch News Service and dogged investigative reporter Seymour Hersh, who never set foot in Vietnam, published the story. The report was immediately followed up by 30 newspapers nationwide. However, according to Noam Chomsky (2000, pp. 167–168) in the context of the mass slaughter of civilians in Vietnam, My Lai was a tiny footnote to one of these operations. "It gained a lot of prominence later after a lot of suppression and I think the reason is clear: it could be blamed on half-crazed uneducated GIs in the field who didn't know who was going to shoot at them next, and it deflected attention away from the commanders who were directing atrocities far from the scene – for example, the ones plotting the B52 raids on villages."

Most commentators have seen a shift to more critical "advocacy" reporting following the Vietcong Tet offensive of 1968 by which time some 20 000 American had been killed. Such a shift occurred among the American elite with significant sections beginning to question the cost, effectiveness, and overall moral/political justification for the war. In 1968, the *Boston Globe* ran a survey of 39 major newspapers and found that none had editorialized against the war (Solomon, 2007, p. 223). The media followed the shift in the elite consensus rather than created it (Hallin, 1986, p. 21; Williams, 1987, pp. 250–254). Additionally mass public protests against the war impacted on mainstream coverage. As Jeff Cohen commented (2006): "It wasn't the mainstream media that turned the public against the war. Quite the contrary: it was the public – especially the ever-growing antiwar movement fortified by Vietnam veterans who spoke out against the war – that prodded mainstream media toward more skeptical coverage." Many in the US military after 1968 were concerned to show the difficulties and daily frustrations of the war to the American public and welcomed the press as potential allies in conveying the message (Woodward, 1993, p. 8).

Hidden from the Media: The Secret War against Cambodia

With the massive costs and casualties, the American military learned the dangers of overt warfare (Williams and Reece, 1987, pp. 7–8). The secret war waged in Cambodia for 14 months completely hidden from the international media through a combination of lies and misinformation, showed the US government shifting back to LIC strategy. Nixon's policy of Vietnamization, of "peace with honor," essentially confirmed this move. Yet documents released by the Clinton administration revealed that the tonnage of bombing was almost five times as high as the highest level previously known. Noam Chomsky commented (2007, p. 103): "This meant that Cambodia was the most heavily bombed country in history." Bill Kiernan, head of Yale University Cambodian Genocide Project, wrote about it in a small Canadian journal, *Walrus*, and it was also published on the alternative website, ZNET. The mainstream news media ignored the report entirely.

By turning over the burden of the ground campaign to the Vietnamese, the US army cut casualties from more than 14 000 in 1968 to just 300 in 1972. By 1974 there were only 35 permanent correspondents left in Saigon. LIC fighting strategy predictably attracted LIC media coverage. Arnett comments (1993, p. 284): "Saigon bureaus were closed or reduced. The Vietnam story moved from the top of the network nightly news into the back pages of the papers alongside Dear Abby columns." In fact, the secret air war intensified. One year after the Paris peace conference of 1973, the US Senate Refugee Committee reported that 818 700 refugees had been created in Vietnam and on average 141 people were being killed every day. As John Pilger (2002, p. 259) comments: "But this did not qualify as a big story."

Thatcherism and the Journalism of Deference

In the face of the post-1973 global recession and extraordinary spate of 14 Third World revolutions over the decade, Western capitalist states began an equally extraordinary counter-attack. In this context, Thatcherism, building on the inherent weaknesses of Labourism, in the United Kingdom can be seen as part of a much wider, global shift to the right.

New Militarism – glorified as media spectacle – lay at the root of the Thatcher offensive. In 1980, the Special Air Service Regiment (SAS), the archetypal covert paramilitary group (with the full connivance of dominant sections of the British media), set up the "no compromise" strong state tone of the decade with their assault on the Iranian embassy to rescue hostages seized by six terrorists demanding autonomy for the southern region of Khuzestan and the release of 91 comrades from Ayatollah Khomeini's jails (Geraghty, 1980, pp. 237–243; Kemp, 1995, pp. 149–154; Harclerode, 2000, pp. 386–408). According to Harclerode (2000, pp. 408): "Operation Nimrod sent a clear signal throughout the world that the authorities would deal firmly with any terrorist threat within Britain's own borders." It was, in fact, the first time the SAS was officially deployed on the British mainland – and they became instant media heroes. As *The Sunday Times* investigative "Insight" team commented: "Having shunned publicity for the force for the better part of thirty years, the Government seems now to have decided that the best way of making their deployment within Britain acceptable is to turn them into real-life James Bonds – objects of hero-worship. And it has to be said that the strategy has proved singularly successful" (Insight, 1980, p. 109).

The Birth of New Militarism in the United Kingdom: The Falkland/Malvinas "Bizarre Little War"

The Falklands/Malvinas conflict of 1982 was to set a hugely significant precedent repeated in Grenada (1983), Libya (1986) and Panama (1989). Here was a First World country with a considerable military tradition behind it taking on a Third World country almost entirely dependent on First World countries for supplying its armies. (Indeed, Argentine's most deadly weapons had been supplied either by Britain or its allies). Crucially Argentine was a militarist state, run by a corrupt military dictatorship and relying on a conscript army where morale and discipline were known by British intelligence to be low (Bramley, 1991; Witherow, 1989). Britain, on the other hand, relied on a small, nuclearized professional army strongly committed to fighting to win (Rogers, 1994, pp. 4–6).

Britain's national security was hardly at stake in this little adventure for control of an unknown group of islands populated largely by penguins (Belgrano Action Group, 1988). Reginald and Elliot (1985, p. 5) describe it as a "bizarre little war." The conflict solved nothing. Neither side admitted they were at war. Nuclear weapons

Words as Weapons

were secretly carried by British ships (and one was actually lost in the South Atlantic) (Rogers, 1994, pp. 4–5). The conflict was tightly limited by both sides. Though the Argentinean army withdrew from the islands, no formal ceasefire was signed (war never having been declared) and the conflict over the rights to the sovereignty over the Falklands remains to this day.

However, the logic of a permanent war economy is to fight wars and this the British military were all set to do. Involvement in the escapade for the British public could be realized only through their consumption of heavily censored, patriotic media. As Shaw (1987, p. 154) comments: "While Britain in the Second World War can be seen as the archetype 'citizen war' of total war through democratic mobilisation, the Falklands are the vindication of small professional armed forces, acting on behalf of the nation but needing no real mass participation to carry out their tasks. For the vast majority involvement was limited to the utterly passive, vicarious consumption of exceptionally closely filtered news and expressions of support in opinion polls."

In 1977, a secret Ministry of Defence paper on "Public relations planning in emergency operations" stated that "for planning purposes it is anticipated that 12 places should be available to the media, divided equally between ITN, BBC and the press ... The press should be asked to give an undertaking that copy and photographs should be pooled" (Harris, 1983, p. 149). Following the intervention of Mrs Thatcher's press secretary, Bernard Ingham, the Falklands reporting pool was increased from 12 to just 29 (all male) British journalists. In the end they came to identify closely with the military (Morrison and Tumber, 1988; Hooper, 1982). The patriotic imperative so deeply rooted in the dominant political and media culture, together with journalistic self-censorship and hyperjingoism and crude "enemy" baiting of the pops, all served to transform new militarism into a spectator sport with the war consumed as a form of entertainment (Luckham, 1983, p. 18).

Contrived delays in the transmission of television images meant that this was a largely bloodless war (Greenberg and Smith, 1982; McNair, 1995, p. 176). Harris reported (1983, p. 59): "In an age of supposedly instant communication, what were perhaps the most eagerly awaited television pictures in the world travelled homewards at a steady 25 knots." As satellite facilities were denied the media, Taylor (1992, p. 14) records how the Task Force sailed in April 1982 without any facilities for transmitting black and white photographs. Six weeks later, two press photographers had returned just two batches of pictures to London. In all, just 202 photographs were transmitted.

The consensus support for the "war" in the three major parties meant that any opposition, however faint, could be condemned as traitorous. The BBC, following a *Panorama* program which dared to feature some war doubters and skeptics, was publicly attacked by Ministers and Conservative MPs. The Glasgow University Media Group (1985, pp. 127–129), in their study of television coverage, show that the controversial program, "Can we avoid war" of May 10, 1982, in fact, contained more statements in support of Government policy than against. A study by McNair found that coverage, in general, was deferential to and supportive of dubious official claims of military success. The war was sanitized for the media and the nonmilitary possibilities of a resolution to the conflict were marginalized.

New Post-Falklands Media Mythologies

A significant new myth emerged following the Falklands adventure. This might be labeled the "myth of the technological threat." According to Mercer (1987), the Falklands conflict was a unique event (the same was to be said about the 1991 massacres in the Gulf); control of journalists was possible because of the peculiar, out-of-the way situation of the theater of war. Such control was seen as unlikely in the future – particularly given the possibilities for instant, uncensored reporting by the new satellite technology. Yet the Mercer scenario completely ignores the ideological constraints of the political consensus and the patriotic imperative of the professional culture that weights so heavily on journalists in time of war and promotes the journalism of deference and conformism. Moreover, it ignores the extent to which new militarist societies demonstrated their ability to create "enemies" and media-blitzed conflicts against relatively weak Third World adversaries.

The Creation of Enemies in Libya, Panama and the Gulf

Indeed, the conflicts in the Falklands, Libya (1986), Panama (1989) and the Gulf (1991) were all essentially "chosen" by the major powers. As Donald A. Wells (1967, p. 14) comments pointedly in his seminal analysis of militarism: "Military men choose their wars and governments choose the conflicts in which they propose to be involved." In addition these conflicts were all archetypally New Militarist:

- They were all quickie attacks. The Libya bombings lasted just 11 minutes. All the others were over within days.
- They were all largely risk-free and fought from the air. All resulted in appalling civilian casualties. Yet the propaganda – in Orwellian style – claimed the raids were for essentially peaceful purposes. Casualty figures were covered up and the military hardware was constantly represented as "precise." "surgical," "modern," and "clean." Diseases and deaths among "enemy" civilians and "allied" troops resulting from the use of depleted uranium in artillery shells and Tomohawk missiles were largely covered up (Boyd-Barrett, 2004, pp. 35–36).
- Media and military strategies were closely integrated. With journalists denied access to planes, the massacres were hidden behind the military's media manipulation and misinformation. Moreover, mainstream journalists' links with the secret state (the massively over-resourced MI5, MI6, and GCHQ, the Cheltenham-based signals spying centre, secret armies and undercover police units) grew closer during the 1980s and 1990s (see Dorril, 2000). By 1991, a military, intelligence, media system was in place which meant a conflict under the glare of 24-hour media gaze could be fought in secret.
- Following the end of the Cold War and the collapse of the Soviet Union, the military/industrial complex needed the manufacture of "big" enemies to legitimize the massive expenditure on the weapons of war. Thus, the threats posed

to US/Western interests, in all these military adventures, were either grossly exaggerated or nonexistent.

- Central to the new strategies was the demonization of the leaders of the "enemy" states. In the case of Grenada, they were "communists." Colonel Gadaffi, of Libya, was demonized in the United States and the United Kingdom mainstream media throughout the early 1980s as a "terrorist warlord" and his supposed links with the Soviet Union were constantly stressed (Chomsky, 1986). Immediately before the raids President Reagan dubbed him a "mad dog." Over the Panama invasion, the propaganda constantly focused on the demonized personality of "drug-trafficker" Noriega (Dickson, 1994, p. 813).
- All the invasions were celebrated in ecstatic language throughout the mainstream media. The editorial consensus remained firmly behind the military attacks. Administration lies were rarely challenged just as the global protests against the actions were largely ignored. Significantly James Combs commented on the United Kingdom's Falklands campaign and the United States invasion of Grenada the following year in this way (1993, p. 277):

It is a new kind of war: war as performance. It is war in which the attention of the *auteurs* is not the conduct of the war but also the communication of the war. With their political and military power to command, coerce and co-opt the mass, the national security elite can make the military event go according to script, omit bad scenes and discouraging words and bring about a military performance that is both spectacular and satisfying.

The Manufactured Gulf War of the 1991

In 1991 the Iraqi army was constantly represented in the media as 1 million-strong, the fourth-largest in the world, full of battle-hardened fanatics led by global monster Saddam Hussein. As thousands of Iraqi conscripts deserted in January and February 1991, Fleet Street still predicted the "largest ground battles since the Second World War." In the end there was nothing but a rapid rout: a barbaric slaughter buried under the fiction of heroic, necessary warfare.

As Noam Chomsky commented (1992, p. 54): "from August 1990 through July 1991 there was little that could qualify as 'war'. Rather there was a brutal Iraqi takeover of Kuwait followed by various forms of slaughter and state terrorism, the scale corresponding roughly to the means of violence in the hands of the perpetrators and to their impunity." Despite the appearance of 24-hour saturation coverage of the Gulf war of 1991, it was, in fact, a conflict entirely shrouded in secrecy. Journalists were the real prisoners of war, trapped behind the barbed wire of reporting curbs, according to William Boot (1991, p. 24). Very few journalists were allowed to travel with the troops; little actual combat was observed since reporters were denied access to planes; most were confined to hotels in Saudi Arabia.

Colin Powell, in his account of the conflict (1995) estimated that 250 000 Iraqi soldiers had been eliminated. Yet the media celebrated the allied strikes as "clean," "surgical," "precise," and "humanitarian." Shots from video cameras on missiles heading towards their targets (shown on television and reproduced in the press) meant that spectators actually "became" the weapons.

As Robins and Levidow argued (1991, p. 324): "The remote technology served to portray as heroic 'combat' what was mainly a series of massacres." According to Cummings (1992, p. 121) the 1991 conflict appeared not as "blood and guts spilled in living colour on the living room rug" but through a "radically distanced, technically controlled eminently 'cool' postmodern optic." Kellner (1992, p. 386) described it ironically as "the perfect war." Indeed, out of the 353 "allied" deaths only 46 were killed in combat. Of those, 24 (52%) were caused by so-called "friendly fire" (military jargon that has slipped so effortlessly into the lexicon of contemporary conflict).

We now know that 1600 people, mostly women and children, perished when the Ameriyya shelter in Baghdad was bombed by an American Stealth jet during the Gulf massacres of 1991 (Petley, 2003). Yet at the time most of Fleet Street blamed "Saddam," described it as a propaganda coup for the Iraqi leader or claimed it was inevitable (Keeble, 1997, pp. 166–172). All of this was part of a strategy to deflect blame for the atrocity away from its perpetrators. Phillip Knightley commented (2000, pp. 494–495): "One reason for this almost hysterical reaction was that the reporting of the Ameriyya bombing threatened the most important element in the military's propaganda strategy – an attempt to change public perception of the nature of war itself, to convince everyone that new technology has removed a lot of war's horror ... The picture that was painted was of a war almost without death."

From a military standpoint many soldiers among the thousands sent to the Gulf were irrelevant. As part of an attempt to revive the heroic images of World War II and as a symbolic assertion of the heroic possibilities of major warfare, they were essential. Most crucially, the manufactured conflict provided a theater in which the United States could win a "big" war and "kick the Vietnam syndrome." The Iraqi army could never pose a threat to the mightiest army ever assembled. Inevitably then, the emphasis by the media, military and politicians on the demonized Saddam Hussein as a "global monster', the "new Hitler" and "evil madman" was the crucial ingredient in the manufacture of the "big" war (Keeble, 1998).

Argentina, Grenada, Libya and Panama were all puny under-developed countries while the United States and United Kingdom's low-intensity military adventures and assassinations of enemy leaders were deliberately conducted in secret beyond the gaze of the media throughout the 1980s and 1990s. In 1991 with the 24-hour media coverage (though reporters, kept well away from any action, ended up interviewing other journalists) the "big" war could crucially be seen.

All the editors, safe in their Fleet Street bunkers, backed the Desert Storm assaults on Iraq as did the vast majority of commentators. So the New Militarist consensus held firm. As early as August 3, 1990, immediately after the Iraqi invasion of Kuwait, virtually all of Fleet Street had gone on a war footing calling for strikes against the new-found monster "Saddam." Only the *Guardian* expressed a certain skepticism throughout.

The New Militarist Wars of the 1990s

During the 1990s, Iraq became the focus of regular manufactured crises (Carapico, 1998). In January and June 1993, September 1996 and December 1998 US jets attacked sites in Iraq during rapid, risk-free actions and only an 11th hour intervention by UN secretary general Kofi Annan prevented strikes after a media-hyped crisis exploded in January-February 1998. Throughout 1999 and 2000, regular attacks on Iraq by US and UK jets had become institutionalized gaining hardly any mention in the media.

Predictably, the United States and United Kingdom led attacks on Yugoslavia in 1999 "turned out to be the most secret campaign in living memory," according to historian Alistair Horne (cited in Knightley, 2000, p. 501). They were risk-free and conducted entirely from the air (as were NATO's earlier strikes against Bosnian Serbs in 1995). Celebrated as "humanitarian" and "precise," thousands, in fact, died during the Kosovo attacks; many more were traumatized and military sites, broadcast stations, hospitals, and homes were bombed (Ali, 2000; Chomsky, 1999). Hundreds of thousands were left jobless. Neil Clark reports (2004) on the 1999 bombing of Serbia: "NATO only destroyed 14 tanks but 372 industrial facilities were hit – including the Zastava car plant at Kragujevac, leaving hundreds of thousands jobless. Not one foreign or privately owned factory was bombed."

The attacks were part of a desperate attempt by a newly-enlarged NATO to celebrate its fiftieth anniversary with a symbolic victory in a manufactured, spectacular "war" (Keeble, 1999, p. 16; Johnstone, 2000, pp. 8–9). Significantly, the Kosovo theater of war was transformed largely into a no-go area for the international media. The state systems of Yugoslavia, the United States and the United Kingdom found it in their interests to deny media access to the frontline.

The New Militarist consensus fractured on Fleet Street during the 1990s with the *Express*, *Independent* and *Guardian* all expressing criticisms of the attacks on Iraq. Then, with the Kosovo crisis the consensus reemerged with virtually all the editorials backing air strikes and even calling immediately after hostilities began for a ground assault against the new monster "Milosevic." Not even the generals dared adopt this battle plan of Fleet Street's armchair strategists. There was just one exception to the prowar consensus, the *Independent on Sunday* – and its editor, Kim Fletcher, was sacked just days after the strikes were halted. Newspaper columns, however, were opened up to debate on an unprecedented scale. Out of 99 prominent columnists I surveyed, 33 spoke out against the United States led attacks (Keeble, 2000a, 2000b). For the 2001 attacks on Afghanistan and the toppling of the Taliban, the whole of Fleet Street backed the action – but again there was a wide-ranging debate among columnists and letter writers (Keeble, 2001).

The Manufacture of the "War on Terror'

Within this context, it can be seen that the United States and United Kingdom responses to the September 11 atrocities, with the launch of the endless "war on terrorism," the assaults on Afghanistan in 2001 and Iraq in 2003 and the threats to the "rogue" states, Syria, Iran and North Korea, are not distinctly new strategies but accelerating long-standing strategies of military imperial adventurism (Curtis, 2003; Boyd-Barrett, 2004, pp. 36–38).

Al Qaida, blamed for the September 11 atrocities and a series of later attacks on Western interests, is a shadowy grouping. As Burke comments (2003, p. 6): "even when at its most organised in late 2001, it is important to avoid seeing 'Al Qaida' as a coherent and structured terrorist organisation with cells everywhere, or to imagine it had subsumed all other groups within its network." Certainly against such an elusive threat, traditional, war fighting strategies (involving major battle confrontations) are inappropriate. The attack on Afghanistan in 2001 produced the necessary risk-free "victory" against a quickly manufactured "enemy" but they remained largely invisible with journalists kept well away from the "frontlines" as the US proxy forces, the Northern Alliance, advanced on Kabul. More than 800 Afghan civilians were killed in the US airstrikes, though many tens of thousands died through hunger, disease, and exposure (Burke, 2003, p. 324). In the end, al-Qaida leaders Osama bin Laden and Mullah Omar escaped into the void.

With image and entertainment the dominant concerns in New Militarist adventures against hopelessly overwhelmed "enemies," soldiers end up becoming actors. As Philip Hammond comments (2003, p. 27): "The US special forces who went into Kandahar in October 2001 were essentially actors, staging a stunt and videotaping their exploits for the world's media." The operation was of dubious military value, Hammond argues, since army pathfinders had already gone in beforehand to make sure the area was secure. So the United Kingdom and the United States are left having to manufacture once again in 2003 a necessary spectacle of traditional "warfare." As US novelist Don DeLillo commented on the Iraq invasion: "I'm almost prepared to believe that the secret drive behind out eagerness to enter this war is technology itself – that has a will to be realized. And that the administration is essentially a Cold War administration looking for a clearly defined enemy which was not the case after September 11. Now there is a territorial entity with borders and soldiers in uniform" (see Campbell, 2003).

Hammond (2003, p. 23) also sees the "war on terrorism" primarily as a war of images. "Just as the September 11 attacks were calculated not simply to wreak terrible destruction but to create a global media spectacle by targeting symbols of American prestige and power, so too the response of the US and UK governments has been highly image-conscious. Particularly in those aspects of the war on terrorism which have involved actual war fighting, producing the right image appears to be at least as important as any tangible results achieved on the ground."

The Manufacture of the Myth of the 2003 Iraq War

US/UK jets had been bombing Iraqi targets regularly since the end of the 1991 conflict so there was no clear start to the conflict. With the president of the defeated state melting away into thin air there was no clear end. Casualties on both sides mounted as hostilities continued after the end of the so-called war. Thus the bombing of Baghdad on March 19, 2003 became the manufactured "start" of the "war" narrative; and there were two contrived endings: the symbolic toppling of the Saddam statue before the world's media on April 9, 2003 and the statement by President Bush before a gathering of US troops on May 1, 2003 that the "major combat operations" were over.

Significantly, on the 2003 conflict, defense expert John Keegan reported in the *Daily Telegraph* of April 8: "In truth, there has been almost no check to the unimpeded onrush of the coalition, particularly the dramatic American advance to Baghdad: nor have there been any major battles. This has been a collapse, not a war." AFP photographer Cris Reeves, with the US marines, saw hardly any action at all. "It was like two weeks of camping for me with 20-year-old marines. I was 48 so I was exhausted" (Guillot, 2003).

The 2003 Invasion of Iraq and the Crucial "Big" Lies over Weapons of Mass Destruction

The invention of "Saddam's" weapons of mass destruction (WMD) by the US/UK elites to legitimize the invasion of Iraq in 2003 (and dutifully reported throughout the mainstream media) was the inevitable culmination of the demonization process begun in 1990 by the US/UK elites desperate to manufacture a credible enemy to fight a "big" war.

Predictably the disinformation about Iraq's WMD was spread by dodgy intelligence sources via gullible journalists (Keeble, 2004). Thus, to take just one example, Michael Evans, *The Times* defense correspondent, reported on November 29, 2002: "Saddam Hussein has ordered hundred of his officials to conceal weapons of mass destruction components in their homes to evade the prying eyes of the United Nations inspectors." The source of these "revelations" was said to be "intelligence picked up from within Iraq."

Early in 2004, as the battle for control of Iraq continued with mounting casualties on both sides, it was revealed that many of the lies about Saddam Hussein's supposed WMD had been fed to sympathetic journalists in the US, Britain and Australia by the exile group, the Iraqi National Congress (Landay and Wells, 2004). Among the 108 articles listed between October 2001 and May 2002 were those in the *Sunday Times, Observer, Daily Telegraph, Guardian, Economist, Birmingham Post, Daily Express,* and the *Western Mail.* The most sensational assertion – that Iraq could deploy WMD in 45 minutes – had come from Iraq's

Prime Minister-designate, A'yad Allawi (a man with close ties to the CIA and MI6: see Cockburn, 2004). Allawi, according to the leaks, was also the source of allegations that Saddam Hussein and the leader of the 9/11 hijackers, Mohamed Atta, were working together (Beaumont, Harding, Harris *et al.*, 2004)

Significantly, on May 26, 2004, the *New York Times* carried a 1200-word editorial admitting it had been duped in its coverage of WMD in the lead-up to the invasion by dubious Iraqi defectors, informants, and exiles (though it failed to lay any blame on the US President: see Greenslade 2004). Chief among *The Times'* dodgy informants was Ahmad Chalabi, leader of the Iraqi National Congress and Pentagon favorite before his Baghdad house was raided by US forces on May 20, 2004.

Then, in the *Observer* (May 30 2004), David Rose admitted he had been the victim of "calculated set-up" devised to foster the propaganda case for war. "In the 18 months before the invasion of March 2003, I dealt regularly with Chalabi and the INC and published stories based on interviews with men they said were defectors from Saddam's regime." He concluded: "The information fog is thicker than in any previous war, as I know now from bitter personal experience. To any journalist being offered apparently sensational disclosures, especially from an anonymous intelligence source, I offer two words of advice: *caveat emptor*." Since then, no other British journalist or newspaper has apologized for being so easily duped over the WMD.

Hiding the Horror of War

Central to the manufacture of New Militarist warfare has been the constant propaganda focus on precise, clean weapons. War is a civilized, humanitarian business – that's the essential message. People do not die in them, massacres never happen – unless through mistakes or through the fault of the "enemy." During the 1991 massacres descriptions applied to the weapons of the US-led forces were always positive: sophisticated, super, spectacular, awesome, stunning, brilliant, smart, precise, accurate, amazing, incredible.

For the enemy the descriptions were the opposite: dirty, crude, primitive (the Iraqi supergun was an exception – but that was being constructed by British firms). Allied onslaughts always provoked superlatives – such as the "greatest aerial bombardment in history" – behind which all the terrible human suffering was hidden, silenced. Throughout the Iraqi crisis from the invasion of Kuwait in August 1990 until the formal start of Desert Storm onslaught on January 17 the military monopolized the agenda and the language in which it was articulated – the glorification of military technology was the inevitable consequence (Keeble, 1997, pp. 139–159).

Up to 10 000 civilians died during the Iraq invasion of 2003 (Pilger, 2004, p.xxiii). As J.K Galbraith comments (2004): "We are accepting programmed death for the young and random slaughter for men and women of all ages. So it was in the first and second world wars and is still so in Iraq. Civilised life, as it is called, is a great white tower celebrating human achievement, but at the top there is permanently a large black cloud. Human progress dominated by unimaginable cruelty and death."

Thus, the essential function of the mainstream media in New Militarist wars has been no longer to naturalize and humanize the possibility of nuclear holocaust as during the Cold War but to acclimatize the public to the acceptability of mass slaughters of the nameless "enemy." *New York Times* reporter Chris Hedges wrote (2004): "War is made palatable. It is sanitized. We are allowed to taste war's perverse thrill but usually spared from seeing its consequences. The wounded and dead are swiftly carted offstage. The maimed are carefully hidden in the wings while the band plays the majestic march."

All the mainstream media highlighted the use of 2000 precision missiles in the US's "shock and awe" opening attacks on Baghdad on March 20, 2003. Notice how the *Guardian* highlighted the precision claims on March 19, under the headline: "US microwave bomb to make debut in most hi-tech battlefield campaign ever" the new bomb is celebrated as "new and devastatingly effective." Reporter Stuart Millar continues:

> The so-called high-powered microwave (HPW) weapon, or ebomb, will be the most sophisticated new weapon to get its operational debut in Iraq during a campaign that promises to be the most hi-tech ever fought. The last Gulf war may have marked the introduction of space age weapons – from laser guided bombs to cruise missiles "smart" enough to know which set of traffic lights to turn left at but as collateral damage figures later proved, the technologies were still in their infancy (*Guardian*, 2004).

Let us examine closely this text since it shows how the *Guardian*, one of the most outspoken in its criticisms of the United States/United Kingdom rush to conflict, still promotes various dominant discourses that ultimately serve to legitimize the attack on Iraq. Note the use of the phrase "most sophisticated" in relation to the weapon – with all its positive associations of intelligence and efficiency. The reference to turning left at the traffic lights is such an extraordinary phrase reducing the horror of mass slaughter to the level of the familiar, ordinary discourse of the urban everyday. "Collateral damage" is that heartless militaryspeak euphemism for civilian deaths while the reference to the "infant technologies" of mass slaughter again reduce the horror of military power to the innocence of a baby.

Or let us take this story in the prowar tabloid *Sun* of March 20, 2004, as US jets began their attacks on Baghdad. Under the headlines: "The first 'clean' war" and "Civilian deaths could be zero, MoD claims," it reported: "The war in Iraq could have almost no civilian casualties, defence chiefs claimed last night." It continued: "A senior defence source said last night: 'Great attention to precision-guided weapons means we could have a war with zero casualties. We are a lot closer towards that ideal. We may be entering an era where it is possible to prosecute a humanitarian war.'" How extraordinary. Just as US/UK imperialism is reaching new levels of unnecessary aggression so the language used to legitimize it is reaching new heights of exaggeration. In effect, could not the military's rhetoric about precision and smart weapons have betrayed its ultimate ambition – to destroy war itself?

The Breakdown of the New Militarist Consensus

In 2003, with significant opposition to the rush to war being expressed by politicians, lawyers, intelligence agents, celebrities, religious leaders, charities, and human rights campaigners – together with massive street protests – both nationally and internationally, the breakdown in Fleet Street's consensus was inevitable. Yet still for the invasion of Iraq, the vast bulk of Fleet Street backed the action (though columnists and letter writers were divided). The *Independent*'s, carrying prominently the dissident views of foreign correspondent Robert Fisk, were the most hostile. Following the massive global street protests on February 15, the *Independent on Sunday* editorialized: "Millions show this is a war that mustn't happen."

The *Guardian* did not criticize military action on principle but opposed the US/UK rush to war and promoted a wide range of critical opinions. The *Mirror*'s were also "anti" in the run up to the conflict (perhaps more for marketing reasons since the Murdoch press was always going to be firmly for the invasion) with the veteran dissident campaigning journalists John Pilger and Paul Foot given prominent coverage. However, after editor in chief Piers Morgan claimed his papers' stance attracted thousands of protesting letters from readers, their opposition softened. The *Mails* managed to stand on the fence mixing both criticism of the rush to military action with fervent patriotic support for the troops during the conflict.

The Breakdown of New Militarism:
The Decline of the American Empire

A few months before his death, Edward Said (2003) identified the way in which the dominant discourse in the United States/United Kingdom before the invasion of Iraq fabricated an "arid landscape ready for American power to construct there an ersatz model of free market 'democracy'." He concluded with typical optimism: "Critical thought does not submit to commands to join in the ranks marching against another approved enemy. Rather than the manufactured clash of civilisations we need to concentrate on the slow-working together of cultures that overlap, borrow from each other and live together."

Indeed, while US/UK militarism has appeared out of control it is clear from this analysis that it is built on lies, misinformation, and myth. In Iraq and Afghanistan today the struggle against the occupying US and UK forces continues and a global movement for peace gathers strength. From 1976 to January 2004 as few as 900 US service people died overseas due to hostile action, about 38% occurring in Iraq during the 10-month period March 19, 2003 to January 2004 (Conetta, 2004, p. 13). Since then United States and United Kingdom casualties have been mounting along with appalling Iraqi and Afghani death tolls.

New militarism was built essentially on the premise of risk-free, rapid interventions as a response to the Vietnam trauma and as a way of legitimizing the permanent

Words as Weapons   211

war economy. With US/UK forces now humiliated in Afghanistan and Iraq and the economies in both countries collapsing in a large part under the weight of the massive costs of fighting these wars, Fleet Street's New Militarism consensus has broken down and voices calling for international cooperation and understanding are increasing. There are reasons to be cheerful: the US/UK military juggernaut can be halted.

Note

1   Halliday (1986, p. 92) lists Ethiopia 1974, Cambodia 1975, Vietnam 1975, Laos 1975, Guinea Bissau 1974, Mozambique 1975, Cape Verde 1975, Sao Tome 1975, Angola 1975, Afghanistan 1978, Iran 1979, Grenada 1979, Nicaragua 1979, Zimbabwe 1979.

References

Ali, T. (ed) (2000) *Masters of the Universe? Nato's Balkan Crusade*, Verso, London.
Arnett, P. (1993) *Live from the Battlefield: From Vietnam to Baghdad – 35 Years in the World's War Zones*, Bloomsbury, London.
Badsey, S. (1995) Twenty things you thought you knew about the media, *Despatches* (Journal of the Territorial Army Pool of Public Information Officers), Spring, 55–61.
Baker, C. (1991) The new age of imperialism, *Socialist Action*, Spring, 3–8.
Beaumont, P., Harding, L., Harris, P. *et al.* (2004) UN sidelined in choice of Iraqi leader, *Observer*, May 30.
Belgrano Action Group (1988) *The Unnecessary War: Proceedings of the Belgrano Enquiry*, November 7/8, 1986, Spokesman, Nottingham.
Boot, W. (1991) The press stands alone, *Columbia Journalism Review*, March/April 23–24.
Boyd-Barrett, O. (2004) Understanding the second casualty, (eds S. Allan and B. Zelizer) *Reporting War: Journalism in Wartime*, Routledge, London, pp. 25–42.
Bramley, V (1991) *Excursion to Hell*, Bloomsbury, London.
Burke, J. (2003) *Al-Qaeda: The True Story of Radical Islam*, Penguin, London.
Campbell, D. (2003) Notes from New York, a profile of DeLillo, *Observer*, May 4.
Carapico, S. (1998) Legalism and realism in the Gulf, *Middle East Report*, 206, 3–6.
Chambers, D., Steiner, L., and Fleming, C. (eds) (2004) *Women and Journalism*, Routledge, London.
Chomsky, N. (1986) *Pirates and Emperors*, Black Rose Books, Montreal/New York.
Chomsky, N. (1992) The media and the war: What war?, in *Triumph of the Image* (eds H. Mowlana, G. Gerner, and H. I. Schiller), Westview Press, Boulder, CO, pp. 51–63.
Chomsky, N. (1999) *Lessons from Kosovo: The New Military Humanism*, Pluto, London.
Chomsky, N. (2000) *Rogue States: The Rule of Force in World Affairs*, Pluto, London.
Chomsky, N. (2007) *What We Says Goes: Conversations on US power in a Changing World: Interviews with David Barsamian*, Metropolitan Books/Henry Holt and Co, New York.
Clark, N. (2004) The spoils of another war, *Guardian*, September 21.

Cockburn, P. (2004) Exiled Allawi was responsible for 45-minute WMD claim, *Independent*, May 29.

Cohen, J. (2006) The myth of the media's role in Vietnam. www.fair.org/index.php?page=2526 (accessed June 22, 2010).

Combs, J. (1993) From the Great War to the Gulf War: Popular entertainment and the legitimation of warfare, in *The Media and the Persian Gulf War*, (ed. R. Denton), Praeger, Westport CT, pp. 257–284.

Conetta, C. (2004) Disappearing the Dead: Iraq, Afghanistan and the Idea of "New Warfare," *Project on Defense Alternative Research Monograph*, 9, February 18, www.comw.org/pda/0402rmp.html (last accessed February 19, 2004).

Cummings, B. (1992) *War and Television*, Verso, London.

Curtis, M. (1998) *The Great Deception: Anglo American Power and World Order*, Pluto Press, London.

Curtis, M. (2003) *Web of Deceit: Britain's Real Role in the World*, Vintage, London.

Dickson, S.H. (1994) Understanding media bias: The press and the US invasion of Panama, *Journalism Quarterly*, 71 (4), 809–819.

Dorril, S. (2000) *MI6: Fifty Years of Special Operations*, Fourth Estate, London.

Engelhardt, T. (1995) *The End of Victory Culture: Cold War America and the Disillusionment of a Generation*, University of Massachusetts Press, Amherst.

Featherstone, D. (1993a) *Victorian Colonial Warfare: Africa*, Blandford, London.

Featherstone, D. (1993b) *Victorian Colonial Warfare: India*, Blandford, London.

Galbraith, J.K. (2004) A cloud over civilisation, *Guardian*, July 15.

Gall, S. (1994) *News from the Front: The Life of a Television Reporter*, London, Heinemann.

Gannett Foundation (1991) *The Media at War: The Press and the Persian Gulf Conflict*, The Freedom Forum, Columbia University, New York City.

Geraghty, T. (1980) *Who Dares Wins: The Story of the SAS 1950–1980*, Fontana, London.

Glasgow University Media Group (1985) *War and Peace News*, Open University Press, Milton Keynes.

Goldenberg, S. (2006) Bush to face the ghosts of America's last failed war, *Guardian*, November 17.

Greenberg, S., and Smith, G. (1982) *Rejoice: Media Freedom and the Falklands*, Campaign for Press and Broadcasting Freedom, London.

Greenslade, R. (2004) Saying sorry isn't enough, *Guardian*, May 31.

Guardian (2004) March 19, www.guardian.co.uk/world/2003/mar/19/usa.iraq1 (accessed July 14, 2010).

Guillot, C. (2003) Nassiriya: le soldat Reeves face à la foule en colère, *Le Monde*, April 17.

Gunn, S. (1989) *Revolution of the Right*, Pluto with the Transnational Institute, London.

Halliday, F. (1986) *The Making of the Second Cold War*, Verso, London.

Halliday, F. (1989) *Cold War, Third World: An Essay on Soviet American Relations*, Radius, London.

Hallin, D. (1986) *The "Uncensored" War*, University of California Press, Berkeley, CA.

Hammond, P. (2003) The media war on terrorism, *Journal for Crime, Conflict and Media*, 1 (1), 23–36.

Harclerode, P. (2000) *Secret Soldiers: Special Forces in the War against Terrorism*, Cassell, London.

Harris, L. (1984) State and economy in the Second World War, in *State and Society in Contemporary Britain: A Critical Introduction*, (eds G. McLennan, D. Held, and S. Hall), Cambridge, Polity Press, pp. 50–76.

Harris, R. (1983) *Gotcha! The Media, Government and the Falklands Crisis*, Faber, London.

Hedges, C. (2004) Evidence of things not seen, *The Nation*, May, www.thenation.com/article/evidence-things-not-seen (accessed July 14, 2010).

Hooper, A. (1982) *The Military and the Media*, Gower, London.

Insight (1980) *Siege!*, Hamlyn, London.

Johnstone, D. (2000) Nato and the New World order: Ideals and self interest, in *Degraded Capability: The Media and the Kosovo Crisis*, (eds P. Hammond and E. Herman), Pluto Press, London, pp. 7–18.

Keeble, R. (1997) *Secret State, Silent Press: New Militarism, the Gulf and the Modern Image of Warfare*, John Libbey, Luton.

Keeble, R. (1998) The myth of Saddam Hussein: New militarism and the propaganda function of the human interest story, *Media Ethics*, (ed. K. Matthew), Routledge, London, pp. 66–81.

Keeble, R. (1999) A Balkan Birthday for NATO, *British Journalism Review*, 10, 2, pp. 16–20.

Keeble, R. (2000a) New Militarism and the manufacture of warfare, in, *Degraded Capability: The Media and the Kosovo Crisis*, (eds P. Hammond and E.S. Herman), Pluto Press, London, pp. 59–69.

Keeble, R. (2000b) Hiding the horror of 'humanitarian' warfare, *The Public*, 7 (2), 87–98.

Keeble, R. (2001) The media's battle cry, *Press Gazette*, October 5.

Keeble, R. (2003) Making the conflict seem unreal, *Lincolnshire Echo*, April 19.

Keeble, R. (2004) Agents of the press, *Press Gazette*, August 27.

Kellner, D. (1992) *The Persian Gulf TV War*, Westview Press, Boulder/San Francisco/Oxford.

Kemp, A. (1995) *The SAS: Savage Wars of Peace*, London, Signet.

Knightley, P. (2000) *The First Casualty: The War Correspondent as Hero and Myth-Maker From the Crimea to Kosovo*, Prion, London.

Landay, J.S., and Wells, T. (2004) Iraqi group fed false information to news media, 15 March, www.realcities.com/mld/krwashington/8194211.htm (last accessed March 16).

Luckham, R. (1983) Of arms and culture, *Current Research on Peace and Violence*, No. IV, Tampere, Finland, 1–63.

MacKenzie, J. (1984) *Propaganda and Empire: The Manipulation of British Public Opinion 1880–1960*, Manchester University Press, Manchester.

McNair, B. (1995) *An Introduction to Political Communication*, Routledge, London.

Mercer, D. (1987) *The Fog of War*, Heinemann, London.

Morrison, D.E., and Tumber, H. (1988) *Journalists at War: The Dynamics of News Reporting during the Falklands Conflict*, Sage, London.

Moyers, B. (1987) *The Secret Government: The Constitution in Crisis*, Seven Locks, Washington.

Neale, J. (2001) *The American War: Vietnam 1960–75*, Bookmarks, London.

Newsinger, J. (2002) *British Counter-Insurgency: From Palestine to Northern Ireland*, Palgrave, Basingstoke, UK.

Peak, S. (1982) Britain's military adventures, *Pacifist*, 20, 10.

Petley, J. (2003) War without death: Responses to distant suffering, *Journal for Crime, Conflict and Media*, 1 (1), 72–85, www.jc2m.co.uk (accessed June 22, 2010).

Pilger, J. (2002) *The New Rulers of the World*, Verso, London/New York.

Pilger, J. (2004) *Tell Me No Lies: Investigative Journalism and its Triumphs*, Jonathan Cape, London.

Powell, C. (1995) *Soldier's Way*, Hutchinson (with Joseph Persico), London.

Prades, J. (1986) *President's Secret Wars: CIA and Pentagon Covert Operations from World War II through Iranscan*, William Morrow, New York.

Pyle, R., and Fass, H. (2003) *Lost over Laos: A True Story of Tragedy, Mystery and Friendship*, Da Capo Press, Cambridge, MA.

Ranelagh, J. (1992) *CIA: A History*, BBC Books, London.

Reginald, R., and Elliot, J.M. (1985) *Tempest in a Teacup*, Borgo Press, San Bernardino, CA.

Robins, K., and Levidow, L. (1991) The eye of the storm, *Screen*, 32 (3), 324–328.

Rogers, P. (1994) A note on British deployment of nuclear weapons in crises – with particular reference to the Falklands and Gulf Wars and the purpose of Trident, *Lobster*, Hull, December, pp. 4–7.

Rusbridger, J., and Nove, E. (1991) *Betrayed at Pearl Harbour: How Churchill Lured Roosevelt into War*, Michael O'Mara, London.

Said, E. (2003) A Window on the World, *Guardian Review*, August 2.

Shaw, M. (1987) Rise and fall of the military-democratic state 1940–85, in *The Sociology of War and Peace*, (eds M. Shaw and C. Creighton), Pluto, London, pp. 143–158.

Solomon, N. (2007) *War Made Easy: Presidents and Pundits Keep Spinning us to Death*, John Wiley and Sons, Inc, Hoboken. NJ.

Sylvester, J., and Huffman, S. (2005) *Reporting from the Front: The Media and the Military*, Rowman & Littlefield, Oxford/New York.

Taylor, P. (1992) *War and the Media: Propaganda and Persuasion in the Gulf War*, Manchester University Press, Manchester, UK.

Treverton, G.F. (1987) *Covert Action: The CIA and the Limits of American Intervention in the Post-War World*, I.B. Tauris and Co Ltd, London.

Wells, D. (1967) *The War Myth*, Pegasus, New York.

Williams, K. (1987) Vietnam: The first living-room war, in *The Fog of War*, (ed. D. Mercer), Heinemann, London, pp. 213–260.

Williams, K. (1993) The light at the end of the tunnel: The mass media, public opinion and the Vietnam War, in *Getting the Message: News, Truth and Power*, (ed. J. Eldridge), Routledge, London, pp. 305–328.

Witherow, J. (1989) On HMS Invincible for *The Times*, (eds M. Bilton and P. Kosminsky) *Untold Stories from the Falklands War*, Andre Deutsch, London, pp. 266–273.

Woodward, B. (1987) *Veil: The Secret Wars of the CIA*, Simon Schuster, London.

Woodward, G.C. (1993) The rules of the game: The military and the press in the Gulf War, in *The Media and the Persian Gulf War*, (ed. R.E. Denton), Praeger, Westport, CT, pp. 1–26.

12

Multidimensional Objectivity for Global Journalism

Stephen J. A. Ward

We are in the middle of the fifth revolution in journalism ethics since modern journalism began in the seventeenth century.[1] The changes are prompted by a broader media revolution where new forms of communication transform societies and create a media-linked global world.

The new global media ecology is a chaotic landscape evolving at a furious pace. Professional journalists share the journalistic sphere with tweeters, bloggers, citizen journalists, and social media users around the world. The future of professional journalism in various forms, such as investigative journalism at newspapers, is cast in doubt as audiences migrate online and newsroom budgets shrink. Much has been written on how new media expands our idea of who is a journalist, while generating controversial practices (Friend and Singer, 2007). This "democratization" of journalism – the spread of publishing technology among citizens – occurs as journalism acquires global reach and impact.

Ultimately, these changes challenge the foundations of journalism ethics. The intersection of the amateur and the professional in journalism creates both communication possibilities and ethical debates. Time-honored principles such as objectivity are questioned. Journalists adopt new descriptions of themselves, as "sherpas" guiding readers through the information maze, as global "aggregators" of bloggers and web sites, as facilitators of online dialogue. All work to the relentless demands of a 24-hour news clock.

A multimedia, global journalism creates a tension among values on two levels. The first level is due to online journalism. The culture of traditional journalism, with its values of accuracy, prepublication verification, balance, impartiality, and professional gate-keeping, rubs up against the culture of online journalism which emphasizes immediacy, transparency, partiality, nonprofessional journalists and postpublication correction.

The Handbook of Global Communication and Media Ethics, First Edition. Edited by Robert S. Fortner and P. Mark Fackler.
© 2011 Blackwell Publishing Ltd. Published 2011 by Blackwell Publishing Ltd.

The second level is due to the emergence of a journalism that is global in reach. If journalism has global impact, what are its global responsibilities? The result is a tension between local and global values, patriotic journalism and a more global approach to reporting (Ward and Wasserman, 2008).

Journalism ethics must do more than point out these tensions and describe the trends. It must develop a new and coherent approach to this tangle of values and issues. It must develop guidelines for problem areas, such as the pressure to report rumors online. Nothing less than a philosophical rethinking of journalism ethics from the ground up will do. As I will argue, we need to construct a multimedia, global journalism ethics.

The aim of this chapter is to explain the idea of a multimedia, global journalism ethics and to propose what I call "multidimensional objectivity" as one of its principles. I begin by describing three features that should characterize this new ethics: ecumenicalism, cosmopolitanism, and a commitment to "public-guided" ethics.

I then argue that a global journalism should embrace multidimensional objectivity since it is better suited to a multimedia, global journalism than earlier notions of journalism objectivity. Multidimensional objectivity is my updated conception of pragmatic objectivity, which I introduced in *The Invention of Journalism Ethics* (Ward, 2005a).

In describing a new ethics, I am not describing an existing entity. A global journalism ethics has yet to be constructed. It is, at present, a project, an ideal, a movement. Therefore, my method is philosophical and normative. Looking at current trends, I say how journalism ethics *should* change if it is to guide responsible journalism in the twenty-first century.

Shape of a Future Ethics

Layered journalism

To argue for a future ethics, I need to say how I envisage journalism in the future. For brevity, I focus on a few structural features of the newsroom in the future – those features that will have the most impact on ethics.

The newsroom of the future will practice "layered journalism."[2] Layered journalism brings together different forms of journalism and different types of journalists to produce a multimedia offering of professional-styled news and analysis combined with citizen journalism and interactive chat.

The newsroom will be layered vertically and horizontally. Vertically, there will be many layers of editorial roles, positions, and supervisor personnel. There will be citizen journalists and bloggers in the newsroom, or closely associated with the newsroom. Many contributors will work from countries around the world. Some will write for free, some will be equivalent to paid freelancers, others will be regular commentators. In addition, there will be different types of editors. Some editors will work with these new journalists, while other editors will deal with unsolicited

Multidimensional Objectivity 217

images and text sent by citizens via email, websites, and Twitter. There will be editors or "community producers" charged with going out to neighborhoods to help citizens use media to produce their own stories.

Horizontally, the future newsroom will be layered in terms of the kinds of journalism it produces, from print and broadcast sections to online production centers.

Newsrooms in the past have also had vertical and horizontal layers. Newspaper newsrooms, for example, have ranged vertically from the editor in-chief at the top to the cub reporter on the bottom. Horizontally, large mainstream newsrooms have produced several types of journalism, both print and broadcast. Today, many newsrooms exhibit the characteristics of layered journalism. Newspapers have interactive websites and employ bloggers. Online news websites, such as OhMyNews.com in South Korea, combine professional and citizen journalists in complex ways.

However, the future production of journalism will develop this layering to an even greater degree of complexity. Future newsrooms will have additional and different layers. Of course, not all sites for the production of journalism will exhibit the features of layered journalism. Some sites will be operated by a few people dedicated only to one format, such as blogging. However, a substantial core of the "new mainstream media" will consist of these complex, layered journalism organizations.

Ethics of Layered Journalism

What sort of ethics is most appropriate for layered journalism? Four types of problems will dominate: vertical, horizontal, public, and global.

First, there will be "vertical" ethical questions about how the different layers of the newsroom, from professional editors to citizen freelancers, should interact to produce responsible journalism. By what standards will professional editors evaluate the contributions of citizen journalists?

Second, there will be "horizontal" questions about the norms for the various newsroom sections. One set of questions will be about the values that all sections should honor, regardless of their medium, or "media platform." Another set of questions will revolve around whether to allow certain sections to operate according to different guidelines because of the distinctive nature of their media platform. For instance, should the online section be allowed to publish stories before the print section because of the speed and immediacy of the Internet? How important will "being first" be to the organization, and what protocols will be used when online journalists come under pressure to report unverified claims because the story is already "out there" on the Internet? Questions of consistency will loom large. Can "local variations" in the ethics of sections within a news outlet be justified? For example, if a newspaper requires the authors of letters to the editor in its print version to be signed, how can it justify allowing commentary on its online chat forum to be anonymous?

Third, layered newsrooms, and the rise of the citizen as both producer and consumer of media, will raise serious questions about the role of the public in journalism ethics. Is ethics a discussion for professionals only? Can the public do more than complain about bad journalism to news councils?

Fourth, there will be questions about the relationship of the newsroom to the world at large. As journalists use technology that influences citizens around the world, they will become tangled up in questions about international standards for journalists and about the responsibilities of journalism to a global world.

Finding a reasoned and coherent way of answering these difficult questions is the goal of a reinvented journalism ethics. This sketch of the ethical questions of the future leads to my claim that an adequate ethics will have to display three general properties. It should be ecumenical, public-guided, and cosmopolitan in attitude. I now explain each property.

Ecumenical ethics

The multimedia nature of the layered newsroom calls for an ecumenical approach to ethics. I borrow the term "ecumenical" from its original Christian context, which is the desire to find unity among the sects of Christianity, despite their differences. Ecumenicalism does not seek to impose a unity that ignores (or is intolerant of) differences. It is an attempt to recognize differences within a common framework of values. By analogy, ecumenicalism in journalism is the search for a new framework for today's mixed media, a unifying set of values that are realized in different ways by different forms of journalism.

Ecumenicalism starts with the notion that a healthy public sphere in a democracy is as free as possible, and populated by many forms of communication and a diversity of communicators. Different forms of journalism fulfill different public functions.

Ecumenicalism also believes that this freedom and diversity should be used in an ethical manner, if the public sphere is to be a place for reliable public information and reasoned debate. A core group of public informers must be dedicated to responsible journalism in the public interest. They must be committed to norms and principles that support informed and deliberative discussion on essential public issues. Ecumenicalism does not assume that all communicators will use their chosen medium in an ethical manner, especially not in an age where the number of citizen journalists and media producers grows exponentially. It does believe however, that, if deliberative democracy is to be possible, ethics needs to be taken seriously and by a substantial group of practitioners across media platforms.

Journalism ethics is ecumenical if it provides a unifying conception of the main goals and values of all forms of responsible journalism. It seeks to articulate what should be the (changing) roles of journalism in a democratic sphere. Such aims are often articulated in short phrases such as "informing a self-governing citizenry," or "serving the public interest." Journalism ethics must expand and clarify the meaning of such phrases as journalism and society evolve. In addition, ecumenical journalism ethics should articulate a number of general principles and standards as means toward the aforementioned aims. The principles may include truth-seeking,

Multidimensional Objectivity

editorial independence, minimizing harm to the vulnerable, and being accountable and transparent to one's public.[3]

Journalism ethics is ecumenical if it also adopts another central idea: these aims and principles can be interpreted and practiced in many different ways in a diverse public sphere. "Respecting differences" ecumenically means rejecting the idea that there is one set of aims and one set of principles that all journalists must adopt uniformly. Instead, ecumenicalism asserts that ethics should work from the assumption that journalists will not adopt uniformly the same set of aims and principles, and even where they agree, journalists will interpret principles and aims in different ways. This diversity of ethical interpretation can occur on several levels. With regard to aims, journalists can understand "serving the public interest" as objectively reporting on event, or as interpreting events, or as bringing about needed social change. Similarly, journalists can disagree on principles. An objective reporter may argue that journalists need to be neutral in serving the public interest; the investigative journalist and the blogger reject neutrality and argue for informed inquiry and discussion from a perspective.

Journalists can also disagree on specific standards and rules of practice. For example, the print reporter for a quality newspaper may argue for prepublication tests for accuracy and verification through careful editorial gate-keeping. The online journalist may argue that she works in a medium where speed and the transparent sharing of information as it arrives, even if it is not fully verified, is more important than withholding information. The online journalist can argue that she still subscribes to the overall goal of journalism to inform the public and stimulate debate, but that norms of practice need to reflect the nature of the medium.

Ecumenicalism responds to this diversity of views and forms of journalism by asserting what I call the principle of communicative intention: The norms of practice for any specific form of communication, including forms of journalism, is influenced by the nature and intent of the communication, as well as by what the public expects of this form of communication. So we should seek to shape the ethics of journalism to fit the communication form.

This two-fold approach of ecumenicalism – unifying aims and principles, and more particular norms of practice adapted to different forms of journalism – is one way that ethics can address the four kinds of questions of layered journalism noted above. Of course, not every practice can be justified by simply stating that it follows from the nature of one's medium. It is difficult to see how posting a flimsy (and false) rumor that does serious harm to a person's reputation could be justified whatever the medium. It may be that an online writer's love of immediacy and speed can never be reconciled with ethics. However, we should not rush to that conclusion.

Online journalism, for example, may develop new and reasonable norms of practice for dealing with the pressures of speed and immediacy. Online journalism may take advantage of the connected nature of the Internet to develop a postpublication process for checking and testing stories. Online groups and communities have already developed ways to monitor false claims and identify unreliable writers. Also, online journalism can use the Internet's global linkages to let readers check for themselves the veracity of reports by inserting hyperlinks to original sources. True, much of this testing will come after the posting, but we should not thereby conclude that protocols cannot be developed that enhance the responsible use of the medium.

Even where it appears that an ethical approach is impossible, such as the use of unverified video and text from little-known sources, norms of practice can evolve. For example, mainstream news coverage of demonstrations in Iran after the June 2009 presidential election is a vivid example of how newsrooms can develop protocols that allow amateur and professional journalism to coexist. In Iran, professional foreign journalists were forbidden to cover "unauthorized" demonstrations. Meanwhile, Iranian citizens used the new media of Twitter, YouTube, cell phones, and text messaging to circulate pictures and commentary around the world.

Major news organizations, such as the BBC and CNN, used this information carefully. News anchors repeatedly explained to the public the limitations on their own journalists and why they were using citizen-generated information. They warned viewers that they could not verify the veracity of many of the images, or the identity of the sources. Although bogus and erroneous information was circulated by these means, vital information was also made public. The Iran coverage shows that the ecumenical search for combining responsibly the old and new forms of journalism is possible and indeed developing.[4]

The ecumenical approach seems almost inevitable, given the direction of journalism. It is unlikely that the new vertical and horizontal questions will be resolved by insisting that the blogger, the tweeter, or the citizen journalist adhere completely to the more restrictive norms of practice that guide other forms of journalism, such as "straight" professional news reporting. Conversely, more traditional modes of journalism, such as verified reporting in the quality papers, should not abandon the values that have long defined their medium. They should not simply opt for the more freewheeling practices of the Internet. The ethical challenge is to maintain common values for journalism while showing how ethical norms of practice can legitimately vary according to the medium.

Public-guided ethics

If my argument is correct, the new ethics should be ecumenical. Yet, as noted above, multimedia technology, now available to the public, makes questions about the role of the public inescapable. This situation suggests a second feature that should characterize all plausible forms of new ethics. It is a commitment to a public-guided ethics.

As the walls between professional and amateur journalism crumble, it becomes clear that any future ethics should involve the public in a manner that goes far beyond current mechanisms for discussion. The new ethics will be "public-guided" if it creates opportunities for the public to have a voice in the formulation, monitoring, and reforming of the ethics of journalism – to construct norms that apply

Multidimensional Objectivity   221

to professionals and amateurs (Ward, 2005b). The public, as themselves producers of media content, would be asked to construct an ethics for their blogs and websites. The public would be asked: What do they expect, ethically, of today's news media? What norms of practice do they want bloggers to honor? What forms of editing should be used online? Do they want traditional media to remain committed to the values of gate-keeping and prepublication verification?

A public-guided ethics is to be contrasted to both an elite professional approach to ethics and an excessively egalitarian approach, or "populism," that simply asks the public to vote on ethical issues. Majority vote decides all. A professional approach thinks ethical policy and decisions should be determined primarily (or only) by professionals inside newsrooms. Most existing mechanisms of public involvement take this approach. News councils and ombudsmen are usually industry-funded agencies designed to arbitrate complaints about stories *after* they have been published. The role of the public is that of a disappointed consumer. Citizens complain to an agency if the news "product," like a cheap pair of new shoes, does not live up to expectations.

The interactive nature of online communication raises many possibilities for public discussion of journalism ethics, from virtual public forums to "citizen assemblies."[5] Even traditional mechanisms such as news councils can revise their modes of operation. Take, for example, an attempt at public discussion of ethics by the Washington State News Council (WNC) in Seattle. The state news council received a complaint from Secretary of State Sam Reed against KIRO7 Eyewitness News, a CBS affiliate. Reed complained that two stories (aired October 15 and November 3, 2008) about voting irregularities were "incorrect" and "sensationalized." KIRO did not reply to the WNC's invitation to respond to the complaint. Eventually, Reed decided not to seek a public WNC hearing.

With the complaint process stalled, the council took an unprecedented step. It held a "virtual public hearing" on the complaint. The WNC invited citizens to view the stories, read the complaint, then vote and comment as a Citizens Online News Council. Of about 100 people who voted online, only a few defended KIRO while most supported Reed's position.[6]

Public-guided ethics cannot be a series of online votes. We need to structure public dialogue online and offline so that it is representative, reflective, and based on the core principles of good journalism. Otherwise, ethics can devolve into shifting opinion polls. Nevertheless, in the meantime, we can start exploring how the new communication tools can contribute to a public-guided ethics.

Cosmopolitanism

A third property of the new ethics should be a cosmopolitan approach to journalism and its global responsibilities. Cosmopolitanism can provide a unifying perspective from which to see the ultimate aims of today's journalism.

The proposal to transform journalism ethics by adopting a cosmopolitan, global perspective swims against journalism history. Across the 400 years of modern journalism, from broadsides to blogs, its ethics has been parochial. It has been assumed that journalists serve the readers of a local newspaper, the audience for a regional news broadcast, or the citizens of a country. Most of the 400 codes of journalism ethics in the world today are for local, regional or national media. Little is said about whether journalists have a responsibility to citizens beyond one's town or country. However, in a global world, why not define one's public as readers within *and* without my country? Why not talk about global journalism ethics?

Some of the elements of a global ethics exist. When we compare codes of journalism ethics internationally we see agreement on basic principles such as to report the truth, to avoid bias, to distinguish news and opinion, and to serve the public. When African journalists drew up the Windhoek Declaration on Promoting an Independent and Pluralistic African Press in 1991 (MISA, 1991), they invoked the Universal Declaration of Human Rights to promote press freedom on their continent. Already, there is a growing movement of scholars, journals, and books on global media ethics (Black and Barney, 2002; Cooper *et al.*, 1989; Ward, 2005b; Ward and Wasserman, 2008). There exist a number of international declarations of news media principles. Of special note is the development of an international approach to the study of media communication and journalism. The studies provide a portrait of the "news people" around the world and how their media systems and values compare (Demers, 2007; Weaver, 1998).

However, it is possible to question the project of global journalism ethics. Why should we consider taking this audacious step? Is ethics not complicated enough?

There are several reasons. First, media corporations are increasingly global enterprises. Technology gives news organizations the ability to gather information instantly from remote locations. The reach of the Al-Jazeera and CNN networks, for example, extends beyond the Arab world or the American public. Global issues and the power of global media organizations call for an ethics that is global in its principles and in its understanding of media.

Second, global impact entails global responsibilities (De Beer, 2004; McPhail, 2006; Seib, 2002). Reports, via satellite or the Internet, reach people around the world and influence the actions of governments, militaries, and humanitarian agencies. A parochial journalism can wreak havoc. Unless reported properly, North American readers may fail to understand violence in the Middle East. Jingoistic reports can portray other cultures as a threat. A global journalism is required in a world where media bring together a plurality of religions and ethnic groups with varying values and agendas. Our world is not a cozy McLuhan village. Publication of cartoons of Muslim's Prophet Mohammed in one paper in one country, Denmark, spread violence around the world. In such a climate, we need to emphasize journalism as a bridge for understanding across cultures.

Third, a global-minded journalism is needed to help citizens understand the daunting global problems of poverty, environmental degradation, technological inequalities, and political instability. Fourth and finally, a global ethics is needed to unify journalists in constructing a fair and informed media. Without global principles it is difficult to criticize media practices in other countries, including severe restrictions on the press.

Multidimensional Objectivity

In sum, the sufficiency of parochial ethics has been undermined by the globalization of news media. Journalism ethics will not be credible if it avoids engagement with these new complexities.

Elements of global ethics

To develop a global ethics, journalists would need to place much greater weight on their responsibilities to people beyond their borders. The attitude needed is ethical cosmopolitanism. The roots of cosmopolitanism go back to the stoics, Roman law, the Christian notion of a brotherhood of man, and Kant's imperative (Kant, 1997) to treat all humans as "ends in themselves." Cosmopolitan ethics asserts that our ethical behavior should be based on the equal value of all people, as members of a common humanity.

Cosmopolitanism (Brock and Brighouse, 2005) has received increasing attention because of the debate over the responsibilities of developed countries to the appalling poverty and illness on this planet. Nussbaum (2006), for instance, has put cosmopolitanism forward as an antidote to parochialism in ethics and especially in issues of justice.

Cosmopolitan journalists see themselves primarily as agents of a global public sphere, rather than as agents of a local public. Journalism's contract with society becomes a "multisociety" contract with citizens in many countries. As I have argued elsewhere, a global approach would require a redefinition of the ultimate aims of journalism. The aim would become not just the flourishing of a local or national public but the flourishing of humanity at large (Ward, 2005c, 2010). For global ethics, a report would not be counted as accurate and balanced unless it included international sources and crosscultural perspectives. Also, global journalism would reject extreme patriotism. Journalists would become global patriots attached to the expansion of human rights, democratic life, and social justice around the globe.

Let us summarize where we stand.

In the introduction, I argued that journalism ethics is in turmoil because of changes brought about by a media revolution, characterized by the twin forces of multimedia technology and the globalization of journalism. I argued that we needed to reinvent journalism ethics as a multimedia, global journalism ethics, and I explained how this new ethics should be ecumenical, public-guided, and cosmopolitan.

In the second-half of this chapter, I propose multidimensional objectivity, a reformulation of the idea of journalistic objectivity, as a principle for this new ethics.

Multidimensional Objectivity

The traditional notion of journalism objectivity was developed into an explicit doctrine by American print journalists in the early 1900s. Traditional objectivity says a report is objective if and only if it is an accurate recording of an event. It reports only the facts, and eliminates comment and interpretation by the reporter. The report is neutral between rival views.

Traditional objectivity was never just an abstract ideal. It was, from the start, a *practical* system of norms that restrained and governed practice. It disciplined journalism's empiricism by subjecting reporting to standards of verification, balance, and neutrality. These standards were operationalized in newsrooms by rules on newsgathering and story construction: all opinion must be clearly attributed to a source, accompanied by direct quotation and careful paraphrasing; reporters must verify facts by reference to studies and numerical analysis; and news reports must be written from the detached tone of the third-person. Phrases that indicate a bias are eliminated, or translated into neutral language.

Traditional objectivity was a strict, reductive, one-dimensional form of objectivity. Objective reporters were *completely* detached; eliminated *all* of their opinion; reported *just* the facts. Objectivity was a policing action against the agents of error and bias – the reporter's desire to interpret, theorize, campaign, and judge.

The heyday of traditional objectivity was from the 1920s to the 1960s in the broadsheet newspapers of North America. However, the second half of the century is a story of challenge and decline due to new forms of journalism, new technology, and new social conditions. Today, we arrive at a dead end. Traditional objectivity is a spent ethical force, doubted by journalist and academic. In practice, fewer journalists, especially online journalists, embrace the ideal; "objectivity" gradually disappears from codes of journalism ethics, while newsrooms adopt a reporting style that includes perspective and interpretation. Nevertheless, the best option is not to abandon objectivity *tout court* but to reform the conception.

Pragmatic objectivity

Traditional objectivity went wrong when journalists, seeking to discipline the rush for news, adopted a popular but flawed version of objectivity – a stringent positivism of "just the facts." In addition, writers used the misleading metaphor of the objective journalist as a recording instrument who passively observes and transmits facts. When positivism and the passive model of journalism collapsed, so did traditional objectivity.

The morale is that we need a notion of objectivity that is compatible with the idea of journalism as an active, interpretive, cultural activity. We start by acknowledging that all works of journalism are interpretations to some degree. This follows from a fact about human cognition. What we believe to be true is the result of much interpretation, hypothesis, and theory. The task of objectivity is not to eliminate active inquiry and interpretation. The task is to test our interpretations, selections, and judgments according to certain criteria.

In *The Invention of Journalism Ethics* (Ward, 2005a), I developed an alternate conception that I called "pragmatic objectivity." I called the conception "pragmatic" because objectivity is valued, pragmatically, as a means to the goals of truth, fair judgment, and ethical action. The claim of objectivity is not absolute but rather a fallible judgment about a belief or report, based on a holistic weighing of several standards. Pragmatic objectivity is multidimensional. It attempts to evaluate the many dimensions of a story with a plurality of evaluative criteria.

How would multidimensional, pragmatic objectivity work in a newsroom? Journalists would construct stories according to a certain attitude, and then test the story according to criteria appropriate to journalism.

The attitude is what I call the *objective stance*. It consists in a number of intellectual virtues such as a willingness to place a critical distance between oneself and the story, to be open to evidence and counter-arguments, to fairly represent other perspectives, and to be committed to the disinterested pursuit of truth for the public. One is "disinterested" in not allowing one's interests to prejudge a story. This is not neutrality. It is the attitude of a critical inquirer.

However, it is not enough to have an objective attitude. One has to apply this attitude by using criteria to test the story for objectivity. The criteria come in at least five kinds.

First, there are criteria that test for *empirical validity*. These criteria test the story for carefully obtained and collaborated evidence, and the accurate presentation of that data. Empirical validity is broader than reporting facts. It includes placing the facts in context.

Second, there are criteria that test for *completeness and implications*. Where appropriate, we check to see if the story reasonably reports the likely implications for society, avoids hype, and includes both negative and positive consequences.

Third, there are the criteria that test for *coherence*. These criteria test the story for coherence with existing knowledge and the views of credible experts. Journalists respect these criteria, for example, when they compare the clinical trial of a drug with existing studies.

Fourth, there are criteria of *self-consciousness*. An objective story is self-conscious about the frame it uses to present a study or event, and the sources chosen. Have powerful sources manipulated the media to present the story in a certain light? Is the story on crime in poor city areas not also a story about social inequalities? Is the media's depiction of a war as a march towards freedom a biased perspective, ignoring the war's economic motivations?

Fifth, there are criteria that test for *intersubjective objectivity*. Objectivity encourages inquirers to share ideas and facts with other people – other journalists, experts, and citizens. Through this interaction, mistakes are spotted, counter-evidence noted, other interpretations brought forward. The objective reporter is open to varying perspectives.

Journalists and their reports are objective to the degree that they satisfy these kinds of criteria. To evaluate a story as objective, we must weigh, holistically, a group of criteria. Satisfaction of these criteria enhances the credibility, balance and depth of the report, while adding to the likelihood of its truth.

Some people may be surprised that I include such things as context and self-consciousness as elements of objectivity. This is partly because of our cultural baggage. We assume, at least in journalism, that objectivity is *not* multidimensional. It

226   Stephen J.A. Ward

reduces to facts. However, the language and the frames that we use can be as responsible for subjective reports as much as a lack of facts. Objectivity is a complex method that reflects the many dimensions of rational inquiry and evaluation.

Objectivity and uncertainty

The complexity of multidimensional objectivity may suggest that it is useful only in certain domains, like natural science, where there is clear evidence, tough methods, and established knowledge. However, objectivity as a method of thinking and testing is equally important in situations of uncertainty, where the journalist struggles to determine what is true or false, biased or objective.

At home or in foreign fields, truth-seeking inquiry in journalism is an imperfect process that only gradually separates fact from fiction, allegations from verified claims, and credible sources from manipulative partisans. Journalism truth is a "protean thing which, like learning, grows as a stalagmite in cave, drop by drop over time" (Kovach and Rosenstiel, 2007, p. 44).

In war zones, the journalistic search for truth faces many obstacles: restricted access to conflict areas, threats to the personal safety of reporters and the confusing customs of foreign cultures. Unlike soldiers and aid providers, many foreign journalists work completely alone, with relative little resources or field support. In addition, war correspondents must try to discern what is taking place, despite the fog of war, the intense propaganda, the tug of patriotic feelings, and the speed of modern warfare. The war correspondent has little time to verify atrocity stories or tales of heroic action. Under such conditions, what is fact? What source is reliable? Who or what is objective? Consider an example from Canadian foreign reporting.

In January 2002, Claude Adams flew to Kathmandu to do a story on Nepal's Maoist insurgency for the Canadian Broadcasting Corporation (CBC). He was investigating allegations that the army was executing civilians. He decided to focus on the killing of Khet Lamichhane, described as a peasant farmer in the mountain village of Bageswari, west of Kathmandu. Here is his experience, as he told it to me:

> When we arrived there, townspeople gave us their version of the story: Soldiers and police had arrived early in a December morning, looking for a rebel unit that had spent the night in the village. There was some kind of altercation and they opened fire. Khet Lamichhane was shot in the mid-section and another man, a peddler, was chased into the woods and killed. Lamichhane, bleeding profusely, begged for help and water. The soldiers prevented anyone from helping him, and then told the townspeople to go inside and close their windows and doors. One witness said she heard a soldier asking an officer: "Should we give this man medical treatment?" The officer reportedly answered: "Give him another bullet." Then there was a shot. When the people came out of their homes, Lamichhane's body was gone. A day or two later, his family arrived at the nearby headquarters town of Trisuli and asked for his body so they could bury it. They were told Lamichhane had been cremated. A half-dozen townspeople told me this story.

Multidimensional Objectivity 227

A local politician insisted that Lamichhane was not a Marxist supporter, as did his family. A police official in Trisuli, however, said the soldiers fired because they were ambushed, and that Lamichhane was taken back to hospital where he died. Could I see the weapon he was carrying? No. Could I meet the doctor who declared him dead? Could I talk to an army officer who had been on the scene? No. Could I see any evidence that Lamichhane was a terrorist? No. I would have to go to the Interior Ministry. I repeatedly, phoned, faxed AND emailed both the interior ministry and the army headquarters in Kathmandu for more information on the killing, and got no response ... I went back to the Human Rights Commission, but they could give me nothing more, other than to say that there were many similar cases of civilian deaths and disappearances. Weeks later, I contacted Amnesty International in London, but their inquiries on my behalf also could not raise any more information on the case."[7]

Adams eventually included the story of Khet Lamichhane in a report on civilian killings in Nepal, despite the limitations imposed on his reporting in Nepal. What do Adam's experiences in Nepal say about objectivity? Do the inherent limitations on conflict reporting make the idea of pragmatic objectivity irrelevant or useless?

I do not think so. To the contrary, it is precisely during complex journalistic assignments, that objectivity as a method of thinking and testing is crucial. Objectivity will not guarantee truth. No method can make such a claim. Following the method is better than *not* following it. In uncertain situations, the methods of objectivity are about the only defense the journalist has against bias and error. Adherence to objectivity encourages the journalist to question claims and to take into account the motivations of her sources.

Adams was trying to put a "human face" on a story, a human face on human rights abuses by focusing on one village and the death of one man. We see an experienced reporter struggling to retain the objective stance. Adams had an initial story angle but he seeks to follow the facts and to verify claims. He is open to sources. Adam's gave the police official's version of events in his story, as unlikely as it sounded. Adams put things in context, and he bears in mind existing knowledge of the conflict. He tried to make the whole story cohere. He treats objectivity as multidimensional. He weighs and balances various criteria.

However, this selecting and sifting process, frustrated by obstacles at every turn, never reached anything approaching certainty. Adams accumulated facts, testimony, and perspectives until the balance of probabilities tipped in favor of reporting the story.

If we see objectivity as a sort of perfection – a perfect knowledge of reality, or a perfect correspondence with fact, or a "proof" of a hypothesis, then we will not see how objectivity operates in journalism. We will interpret Adams's struggles to produce a credible report as the absence of objectivity and a victory for subjectivity. However, this is clearly a false depiction. Adams struggles to improve his evidence through hard work. He does not just make up the story, or think of what he reports as merely subjective. Nor does he think of his reports as certain and absolute. He practices pragmatic objectivity – he seeks a degree of objectivity, as much as possible given the circumstances.

In practical enterprises we may have to accept a less rigorous and precise methodology of objectivity, yet all the while continuing to believe in the methodology's importance.

Relevancy of Multidimensional Objectivity

I conclude by explaining why I think multidimensional objectivity is a suitable reformulation of objectivity for multimedia, global journalism.

In previous works I have argued for the continuing relevancy of objectivity in journalism, if our goal is an informed public journalism for democracy (Ward, 2005a). Objectivity, correctly understood, encourages journalists to subject their work to critical reflection and prods them to do better-researched stories. Adopting the objective stance helps to counter-balance a public sphere redolent with instant analysis, instant rumor, and manipulative sources. In other writings, I have argued that pragmatic objectivity is important for peace journalism, and should be incorporated into the principles of non-Western journalism traditions, such as developmental journalism (Ward, 2004).

In this section, my aim is not to justify objectivity as an ethical principle. It is to show how my idea of multidimensional objectivity fits with the construction of a new ethics characterized by ecumenicalism, public-mindedness, and cosmopolitanism. My point is: If you want objectivity to be part of the new ethics, multidimensional objectivity is an attractive conception.

Multidimensional objectivity fits ecumenicalism because it can provide a unifying methodological principle for different forms of journalism, yet it respects differences. Multidimensional is a flexible method that can be applied in different degrees and in different ways, according to the communicative intention of the form of journalism in question.

Even if journalists seek different goals – report the world, interpret it, or change it – responsible journalists can make multidimensional objectivity a method for testing whatever stories are produced, for whatever reasons. The form of objectivity that I have described is not identifiable with any one form of journalism, one style of writing, or one aim of journalism.

Traditional journalism objectivity applied only to one form of journalism because it reduced objectivity to a strictly factual description of news events. Objectivity, as "just the facts," was not applicable to forms of journalism that were more obviously interpretive, such as the writing of editorials and columns.

By rethinking objectivity as a holistic method, we see the possibility of using the criteria of objectivity to evaluate many aspects of many kinds of journalism. For instance, the criteria of empirical validity, coherence, and openness to perspectives can be used to evaluate investigative journalism, despite the latter's rejection of neutrality. In fact, good investigative journalism is clear case of using objective methods to ferret out the objective truth about what happened behind closed doors.

Multidimensional Objectivity

In the same vein, objective criteria such as coherence and self-consciousness are important elements in the construction of good interpretive journalism in the form of background pieces, analysis, and column writing. To be sure, the emphasis in this writing will be on argumentation and theorizing. That does not mean that the objective stance, and its intellectual virtues and criteria, cannot be a part of the journalism process. Satirical journalism is probably the form of journalism where the objective method is weakest. Satirical journalism seeks to state a truth or expose hypocrisy beneath the rhetoric of modern life and its politics. Often it does so through exaggeration and unfair portrayals, for dramatic effect. Yet in an open public sphere, satirical journalism plays an important role. Other forms of journalism are closer to objectivity in spirit, such as investigative journalism, as noted above.

Multidimensional objectivity is compatible with many motivations for doing journalism. Whether journalists want to act as watchdogs or impartial observers, they should be able to accept the idea of testing their stories. On this score, multidimensional objectivity is more attractive than traditional objectivity to advocacy and activist forms of journalism. There is no in-principle reason why a reporter for the *Jewish Chronicle* in Toronto or a gay rights magazine in New York cannot be committed to the advancement of their group but also committed to stories that satisfy multidimensional objectivity. A commitment to achieving certain group goals can weaken one's commitment to telling the whole truth where facts may damage the group's public profile. Putting that danger aside, it is also possible for reporters in these forms of attached journalism to refuse to distort the facts to suit their goals, and to seek a degree of multidimensional objectivity in their reports.

How does multidimensional objectivity fit with new media and its many platforms? The key is multidimensional objectivity's flexibility. Different forms of journalism may employ only some of its criteria, or lay more stress on some criteria than others. Not all forms of journalism need to enforce all of the criteria of objectivity to the full extent. It depends on the communicative intent and nature of the medium. Multidimensional objectivity can be an attractive conception for responsible online journalism. Practitioners of blogging, writing for websites and citizen journalism could employ at least some of the criteria of multidimensional objectivity to test their stories, aligning objectivity with their medium.

The claim of compatibility between objectivity and online journalism may surprise those who assume that objectivity is a principle limited to traditional forms of news media. Part of the problem is the view that journalism objectivity must be as traditionally conceived – it must insist on strict neutrality and on the elimination of the "voice" and perspective of journalists. Such demands run counter to the more personal nature of communication on the Internet. However, if we redefine objectivity as multidimensional and pragmatic, we see that the objective stance and several of its major criteria express much of the spirit of online journalism. For example, take the objective stance as an attitude of approaching stories with a critical attitude, of being open to where the facts lead, and so on. Such attitudes support the online value of the Internet as a free "space" to question stories and events. Or take the criteria of coherence and self-consciousness. One of the dominant aspects of good online journalism is to use interactive dialogue and linkages to examine how claims or stories cohere with what other people around the world know about the topic. Also, online journalists often see themselves as being self-conscious and critical of the frames used by mainstream news media on major stories, and to offer alternative perspectives. These values are central to multidimensional objectivity.

The criteria that test for intersubjective objectivity are conceptually close to online journalism notions about how stories are to be tested by online communities. Multidimensional objectivity agrees with the idea, put forward by many who use the Internet, that the testing of ideas and stories is best achieved through interactive dialogue, not the inquiry of individuals. The Internet provides a tool for testing that includes many more people, and at much greatest ease, than was available to pre-Internet newsrooms.

It is true that the idea of intersubjective objectivity in journalism has been understood differently. Traditional journalists talk about prepublication testing and verification by teams of professional journalists within newsrooms. Online journalism raises the possibility of new forms of verification and correction – a postpublication testing by the many linked readers of a story. In this process, communities of online citizens collectively monitor postings for bias, manipulation of facts, bogus studies, and bogus experts. Responsible journalists, online and offline, agree on the importance of a methodology that tests stories, although their methods may vary.

What this shows, at the very least, is that there is no inherent opposition between multidimensional objectivity and new forms of journalism. In fact, there is an overlap of values that ethicists can use to develop an ecumenical ethics.

So much for objectivity and ecumenicalism. However, is multidimensional objectivity compatible with a public-guided ethics, and a cosmopolitan ethics? There is no incompatibility between objectivity and including the public in the formulation and monitoring of ethics. The opposite is true. Given its stress on intersubjective dialogue and testing, multidimensional objectivity by nature welcomes as many voices into the ethical discussion as possible. Also, multidimensional objectivity would provide useful standards to guide public discussions.

Finally, what I said about objectivity and foreign reporting in an earlier section of this chapter supports the idea that multidimensional objectivity is well-suited to foreign reporting in a global age. Traditional objectivity advised journalists not to let their own biases, or the biases of groups within their own country, distort the accuracy and fairness of their reports. With a cosmopolitan approach to journalism ethics, objectivity becomes a global objectivity that asks journalists to not allow their bias toward their country distort reports on international issues.

Multidimensional objectivity is a stance and a method that would lead to better coverage of global issues from poverty to social justice. The objective stance is *just* the sort of attitude you would want in global reporters since it asks journalists to put a distance between them and their beliefs and parochial attachments. Also, the criteria of coherence, self-consciousness, and intersubjective testing are key values for cosmopolitan journalism.

The conceptual distance between a concern for the inclusion of crossborder perspectives in stories and an ethical cosmopolitanism, with its concern for humanity, is not great. Armed with a cosmopolitan ethic and a method based on multidimensional objectivity, journalism would will be less prone to be swayed by narrow forms of ethnocentricism and xenophobia. Journalists would be less swayed by narrow patriotism wherever the national interests of their country comes into tension with other national interests.

It is not implausible, then, to claim that multidimensionality objectivity can "cross borders" and put itself forward as a unifying principle for the construction of a multimedia global journalism ethics.

Conclusion

This chapter has put forward a philosophical proposal. It proposes that we construct a multimedia global journalism that is ecumenical, public-guided, and cosmopolitan. The chapter also proposes multidimensional objectivity as a principle for this new ethics.

I have not provided the content of the new ethics itself – a detailed list of principles, standards, and norms. Nor have I "solved" the many ethical issues involving new media. I have provided only a philosophical outline of how to approach this construction. I offer a way of thinking about these complex issues, a conceptual scaffolding upon which others can build.

A new ethics is a work-in-progress. Therefore, attention to these general philosophical matters is crucial. If we do not approach these issues in the correct way, or if we start from an inadequate conceptual base, we will fail to complete the necessary construction. There will be many false starts and little progress.

Whether my proposal is useful can only be determined pragmatically in the course of time. It will be judged by its usefulness for developing a coherent ethical approach and for addressing the questions that confront journalism ethics today.

The role of the philosopher in times of confusion and disagreement is to step back and take in the big picture, to reexamine basic assumptions and explore the options. The philosopher points out pathways to the future, and plants a few seminal ideas in the hope that they may eventually take root in public discourse and reflection.

Notes

1 I describe the five revolutions in "Journalism ethics" (Ward, 2009). The five revolutions are the invention of ethics with the seventeenth century periodic press, the fourth estate "public" ethics of the newspapers of the eighteenth century Enlightenment public sphere, the liberal ethic of the early nineteenth century and the ethics of professional objectivity in the mass commercial press of late 1800s and early 1900s. Today, the media revolution calls for a mixed journalism ethics.

2 I borrow the phrase, "layered journalism," from a lecture given in my ethics class by Prof. Lewis Friedland of the School of Journalism and Mass Communication at the University of Wisconsin-Madison in Spring 2009.

3 I take these principles from the influential code of ethics of the Society of Professional Journalists in the United States (www.spj.org). I could have chosen, as examples, other principles in other codes, such as advancing social solidarity, being a catalyst for civic engagement, and so on.

4 Increasingly, there are attempts to systematically discuss and codify the practices of online media, through the creation of associations such as the Media Bloggers Association (www.mediabloggers.org/) and the Online News Association (http://journalists.org/Default.asp?) and the development of codes of ethics on sites such as www.cyberjournalist. net/news/000215.php. Some recent discussions argue that there can be an ethics for "tweeting" by applying to Twitter such existing journalism standards as fairness, balance and accuracy. See for example, David Brewer's discussion at www.mediahelpingmedia. org/content/view/401/1/ (accessed June 23, 2010). This view is too conservative. The construction will result in a mixed journalism ethics substantially different from existing journalism ethics. The construction will change (and perhaps eliminate) some basic principles, and call for new norms of practice.

5 The idea of citizen assemblies has been used in Canada, the Netherlands, and other countries to explore questions about politics, forms of government, and so forth. For example, the province of British Columbia created a citizen assembly to consider new election systems, such as systems based on proportional representation. On assemblies, see www.auburn.edu/academic/liberal_arts/poli_sci/journal_public_deliberation/citizensassembly/pandemic.htm (accessed June 23, 2010).

6 For more information on the case, go to the WNC's website, www.wanewscouncil.org (accessed June 23, 2010).

7 Claude Adams, pers. comm., February 2003.

References

Black, J., and Barney, R. (eds) (2002) *Journal of Mass Media Ethics: Search for a Global Media Ethic*, Special issue, 17 (4).

Brock, G., and Brighouse H. (eds) (2005) *The Political Philosophy of Cosmopolitanism*, Cambridge University Press, Cambridge.

Cooper, T., Christians, C., Plude, F. *et al.* (eds) (1989) *Communication Ethics and Global Change*, Longman, White Plains, NY.

De Beer, A. (ed.) (2004) *Global Journalism: Topical Issues and Media Systems*, Allyn and Bacon, Boston, MA.

Demers, D. (2007) *History and Future of Mass Media: An Integrated Perspective*, Hampton Press, Cresskill, NJ.

Friend, C., and Singer, J. (2007) *Online Journalism Ethics: Traditions and Transitions*, M.E. Sharpe, Armonk, NY.

Kant, I. (1997) *Groundwork of the Metaphysics of Morals*, (trans. M. Gregor), Cambridge University Press, Cambridge.

Kovach, B., and Rosenstiel, T. (2007) *The Elements of Journalism*, rev. edn., Three Rivers Press, New York.

McPhail, T.L. (2006) *Global Communication: Theories, Stakeholders, and Trends*, Blackwell, Malden, MA.

MISA (Media Institute of Southern Africa) (1991) The Windhoek Declaration, www.misanamibia.org.na/fileadmin/user_upload/docs/Windhoek_Declaration.pdf (last accessed July 22, 2008).

Nussbaum. M.C. (2006) *Frontiers of Justice*, Belknap Press, Cambridge, MA.

Seib, P. (2002) *The Global Journalist: News and Conscience in a World of Conflict*, Rowman & Littlefield, Lanham, MD.

Ward, S. J.A. (2004) Objective public journalism for global media, in *Agents of Peace: Public Communication and Conflict Resolution in an Asian Setting*, (eds T. Hanitzsch, M. Loffelholz, and R. Mustamu), Friedrich Ebert Stiftung, Jakarta, pp. 25–49.

Ward, S. J.A. (2005a) *The Invention of Journalism Ethics: The Long Path to Objectivity and Beyond*, McGill-Queen's University Press, Montreal.

Ward, S. J.A. (2005b) Journalism ethics from the public's point of view. *Journalism Studies*, 6, (3), 315–330.

Ward, S. J.A. (2005c) Philosophical foundations for global journalism ethics. *Journal of Mass Media Ethics*, 20, (1), 3–21.

Ward, S. J.A. (2009) Journalism ethics, in *The Handbook of Journalism Studies* (eds K. Wahl-Jorgensen and T. Hanitzsch), Routledge, New York, pp. 295–309.

Ward, S. J.A. (2010) *Global Journalism Ethics*, McGill-Queen's University Press, Montreal.

Ward, S. J.A., and Wasserman, H. (eds) (2008) *Media Ethics beyond Borders: A Global Perspective*, Routledge, New York.

Weaver, D H. (ed.) (1998) *The Global Journalist*, Hampton Press, Cresskill, NJ.

13

New Media and an Old Problem
Promoting Democracy

Deni Elliott and Amanda Decker

When anyone can be a publisher, it can be hard to tell who counts as a journalist. This confusion, peculiar to the beginning of the twenty-first century, ironically allows for communitarian journalism to emerge in a way that was not possible in the largely one-way mass communication of the twentieth century. The ease by which one can produce and consume messages challenges citizens to participate in self-governance in entirely new ways.

This essay argues that recent technological advances allow for participatory democracy at an unprecedented level by analyzing the mechanisms for doing so and the implications of those mechanisms. The challenge for the major social institutions of government, education, and journalism is how to help citizens realize their responsibility to actively and civically participate in self governance and to provide improved mechanisms for them to do so.

Communications scholar Clifford Christians writes, "As our philosophies of life and beliefs are lobbied within the public sphere, we have a responsibility to make public the course we favor and to demonstrate in what manner it advances our common citizenship. The issue is whether our values help to build a civic philosophy and thereby demonstrate a transformative intent. This is worldview pluralism, which allows us to hold our beliefs in good faith and debate them openly rather than be constrained by a superficial consensus. The standard of judgment is not economic or political success but whether our worldviews and community formations contribute in the long run to truth-telling, human dignity, and nonmaleficence. Ethical principles grounded in being do not obstruct cultures and inhibit their development. On the contrary, they liberate us for strategic action and provide a direction for social change" (Christians and Traber, 1997, p. 18).

The Handbook of Global Communication and Media Ethics, First Edition. Edited by Robert S. Fortner and P. Mark Fackler.
© 2011 Blackwell Publishing Ltd. Published 2011 by Blackwell Publishing Ltd.

The Role of Journalists and Citizens in Democracy

The liberation of American journalism from the elite silos of the twentieth century provides the opportunity to create public communication values that advance what Christians calls "common citizenship" and others would call democracy. However, simple expression of opinion is not enough to move the practice of journalism, essential for educating citizens, forward. According to journalist Leonard Downie Jr. and journalism historian Michael Schudson, "The expression of publicly disseminated opinion is perhaps Americans' most exercised First Amendment right, as anyone can see and hear every day on the Internet, cable television, or talk radio. What is under threat is independent reporting that provides information, investigation, analysis, and community knowledge, particularly in the coverage of local affairs. Reporting the news means telling citizens what they would not otherwise know" (Downie and Schudson, 2009).

Journalism and citizens are separate and essential elements for sustaining democracy. Historically, the role of journalism has shifted from providing a platform for views to providing reasoned, authoritative accounting of important issues and events. According to Downie and Schudson, "Most of what American newspapers did from the time that the First Amendment was ratified, in 1791, until well into the nineteenth century was to provide an outlet for opinion, often stridently partisan... By the late nineteenth century, urban newspapers grew more prosperous, ambitious and powerful, and some began to proclaim their political independence" (Downie Jr. and Schudson, 2009). What developed through that independence was a change from "a preoccupation with government, usually in response to specific events, to a much broader understanding of public life that included not just events, but also patterns and trends, and not just in politics, but also in science, medicine, business, sports, education, religion, culture, and entertainment" (Downie Jr. and Schudson, 2009).

The social role of journalism in democracy is continually evolving, as much dependent on technology and marketing values as ethics, but partisan or not, profit-driven or nonprofit, journalism exists to notice and report the important events and issues that citizens need to know so that they can effectively govern themselves (Kovach and Rosensteil, 2001) (Elliott, 1986). "Tim McGuire, a former editor of the Minneapolis Star Tribune," [said] "We've got to tell people stuff they don't know" (Downie Jr. and Schudson, 2009).

A worldwide web of information at one's fingertips gives the illusion that citizens can find out anything that they want to know with no journalistic intervention. Yet, information is only as good as its source and is only as complete as the process used to develop it. "Independent reporting not only reveals what government or private interests appear to be doing but also what lies behind their actions.... Reporting the news also undergirds democracy by explaining complicated events, issues, and processes in clear language... Something is gained when reporting, analysis, and investigation are pursued collaboratively by stable organizations that can facilitate regular reporting by experienced journalists, support them with money, logistics, and legal services, and present their work to a large public. Institutional authority or weight often guarantees that the work of newsrooms won't easily be ignored" (Downie Jr. and Schudson, 2009).

If journalism is essential to provide watchdogs over important social institutions and to provide credible collections of important material, so that citizens can make educated decisions, citizens themselves remain the missing link in US democratic process. "When moral controversies such as those over abortion, gay rights, affirmative action, and assisted suicide are routinely decided by the courts, critics charge that it is no wonder that the office of citizenship comes to seem of marginal importance," according to political theorist, Stephen Macedo. "Citizens deprived of the opportunity and the responsibility to grapple with the most significant moral questions lose a vital part of the training in responsibility and self-control that citizenship should bring (Macedo, 1999, p. 3).

Yet, citizens are more apathetic than ever before. "Where people once might have deluged their elected representatives with complaints, joined unions, resisted mass firings, confronted their employers with serious demands, marched for social justice and created brand new civic organizations to fight for the things they believed in," writes columnist Bob Herbert, "the tendency now is to assume that there is little or nothing ordinary individuals can do about the conditions that plague them" (Herbert, 2009).

It is not that citizens do not maintain the interest or desire to be an active part of participatory democracy, instead they are finding other means in which to practice their democratic rights and responsibilities. "Technology can amplify and aggregate voices that used to be faint and muffled. Voters used to write letters to newspaper editors and hope they would be published. Now they can blog" (*The Economist*, 2008). The Internet provides a whole new array of options for citizens seeking to address grievances and this shift in ways of expression opens new doors to great opportunities for participatory democracy.

The Internet opens the doors to many new, accessible, and affordable means of mass communication. These open doors allow for the embracing of the public as the new citizen-journalists, who seek to promote good by seeking out information and dispersing it. Communication and interaction between citizens, media, and government are key components to a successful democracy (Dahlgren, 2005, p. 149). The Internet acts as a means to connect those dots by granting the ability to connect groups and people who are geographically dispersed.

The World Wide Web has introduced the public to a new forum for political discussion and new kind of accessibility to the mechanisms that allow them to do so. What has traditionally been referred to as the public sphere, "a constellation of communicative spaces in society that permit the circulation of information, ideas, debates… and also the formation of political will… in which the mass media and now, more recently, the newer interactive media figure prominently, also serve to facilitate communicative links between citizens and the power holders of society" (Dahlgren, 2005, p.148), has advanced and become more prominent since the introduction of the Internet. While public discussion may only encompass a small percentage of all the Internet's offerings, those discussions and the countless sites that host them serve as a direct route to the future of participatory democracy. As political communications scholar, Peter Dalhgren, puts it, "today's democracy needs to be able to refer to a past without being locked in it" (Dahlgren, 2005, p.159). Interaction and discussion among citizens in the new virtual public sphere is a way to ensure that progression.

The "worldview pluralism" as described by Christians expands the notion of the marketplace of ideas credited to Justice Oliver Wendell Holmes in his dissenting opinion in Abrams versus United States. Holmes says "when men have realized that time has upset many fighting faiths, they may come to believe even more than they believe the very foundations of their own conduct that the ultimate good desired is better reached by free trade in ideas – that the best test of truth is the power of the thought to get itself accepted in the competition of the market, and that truth is the only ground upon which their wishes safely can be carried out" (Abrams versus United States 250 U.S. 616). His concept of a free market of ideas corresponds with the ideas of nineteenth century philosopher John Stuart Mill (1991a), to be discussed later in this essay. The Internet is working to further develop the public sphere into an expansive free marketplace of ideas where the public can gather with others in the comfort of their own home to discuss, debate, and participate in current events.

According to scholar David Thompson, the Internet has a great capacity to connect people with similar values (Thompson, 2008). The rise of these kinds of Internet communities has become a staple in promoting participatory democracy; serving to enhance our "social ties by reinforcing existing behavior patterns" (DiMaggio *et al.*, 2001). These online communities, as defined by DiMaggio and coauthors (2001) "come in very different shapes and sizes, ranging from virtual communities that connect geographically distant people with no prior acquaintance who share similar interests, to settings that facilitate interactions among friendship networks or family members, to community networks that focus on issues relevant to a geographically defined neighborhood. Scholars have found that political participation of individuals can be greatly dependent on those individual's participation in social networks (Jang, 2009). This holds true even for the kinds of virtual social networks DiMaggio discusses, ones that are facilitated by the advancing technology available online.

Grassroots efforts give individuals the opportunities to speak out and organize (virtually), yet in order to create deliberative democracy, more than just those opportunities need to be realized. Deliberative democracy is the result of individual citizen choices and group initiatives that are the products of gaining knowledge and weighing alternative actions. According to political scientist James Fishkin, "American politics exhibits a near-fatal attraction to a too simple notion of democracy. Anything more direct and more majoritarian is thought to be more democratic"(Fishkin, 1994, p. 101). Fishkin observed that the use of technology to collect instantaneous reactions to a President's state of the union address created the appearance, but not the reality, of citizen engagement. He said, "Despite the unrepresentative character of the self-selected sample, and despite the unreflective and volatile character of the instantaneous reactions, the results were presented as the voice of the people" (Fishkin, 1994, p. 101)

To echo Christians, deliberation has a goal of improving the community. According to theorist Jane Mansbridge, "If a deliberative system works well, it filters out and discards the worst ideas available on public matters while it picks up, adopts, and applies the best ideas. If the deliberative system works badly, it distorts facts, portrays ideas in forms that their originators would disown, and encourages citizens to adopt ways of thinking and acting that are good neither for them nor for the larger polity. A deliberative system, at its best, like all systems of democratic participation, helps its participants understand themselves and their environment better" (Mansbridge, 1999, p. 211).

Fishkin would agree. "Polls, primaries and referendums bring power to the people, but they bring it under conditions where people have difficulty thinking about the power they exercise. Efforts at democratic reform appear enmeshed in a dilemma. It appears that we must choose between politically equal but relatively incompetent masses and politically unequal but relatively more competent elites" (Fishkin, 1994, pp. 106–107).

Citizens do not act without recognizing their power to bring about change. Recognition of power leads to the development of moral responsibility to use that power and to use that power to advance what individuals perceive to be in their interest. This suggests that citizens need education that involves recognizing the new opportunities embedded in new technology, but also their responsibility to do something with that. Political strategist Joe Trippi says that rather than call the change from traditional one-way media to new interactive media the coming of "the information age," it should be called "the empowerment age." The Internet is the most democratizing innovation we have ever seen – more so than even the printing press.... If Madison was right, and the people can only govern when they can "arm themselves with the power which knowledge gives," then the Internet is the first technology that truly gives people full access to that knowledge – and empowers them with the ability to do something with it" (Trippi, 2008, pp. 235–236).

One of the key features that can attribute to online discussion participation is the anonymity that is associated with the free space of the Internet. According to behavioral scholars Deanna A Rohlinger and Jordan Brown (2009), the anonymity associated with contribution to online political discussions, "can buffer the risks associated with activism" because the Internet is not in the direct control of any one political group (Rohlinger and Brown, 2009, p. 134). By hiding behind the virtual wall of one's own computer in the comfort of home, an online contributor may feel more willing to voice her personal opinion or speak out against those of others. This "buffer" described by Rohlinger and Brown (2009) grants the privilege for contributors to "express their dissent anonymously and without retribution," (p.135) which then increases the willingness and discussion contributions of individuals unlikely to participate. They also argue that the anonymous online contributions are likely to evolve into real world activism once contributors get comfortable with the expression of their views in political environments.

New Media and an Old Problem

Perhaps the most essential element in representative democracy is the privilege of individual citizens to drive to the polls, pull the privacy curtain shut, and express their opinion by means of casting a vote. Voting is highly regarded as "the most fundamental way individuals may influence their government within any democracy" (Thompson, 2008). With the availably, accessibility, and power of the Internet to other forms of democratic process, it is not surprising that it is considered a possible way to make voting easier and more accessible to individual voters and provide them with the opportunity to have a greater say in policy making (Thompson, 2008). The more one can expose oneself to the factors in making an educated vote, the easier that decision becomes.

Thompson argues that the Internet serves as a means of exposing the general public to political conversation. He points out that these conversations can take place in any variety of online community such as a chatroom or an email network. The Internet is flooded with a wide variety of local and national, issue-advocacy, alternative journalism, and discussion forums (Dahlgren, 2005, p. 152). The availability of exposure to political conversation is all over the Internet. Citizens can access candidate websites, log on to political interest group blogs, or even subscribe to up-to-the-minute campaign updates, all of which can provide information unparalleled in accessibility.

Political scholar Seung-Jin Jang says that political disagreements, while they may be experienced differently by individuals and thus result in "different political consequences," (2009, p. 883) exposure to political disagreements in political networks can encourage participation for some individuals. He considers specifically the polarization of American politics that result in two strongly partisan opinions and much debate. Exposure to those partisan-fueled discussions can "spill over the participatory democracy by differently affecting each segment of citizens," resulting in "a critical balance between activism of strong partisans and recognition of the voice of reason," (Jang, 2009, p. 894). This balance is an ideal environment for the harboring of political debate, discussion, and participation, thus giving citizens the information they need to make an informed decision and vote.

The idea has even been considered by some to use the Internet as a way for voters to place their ballot in the comfort of their own home might encourage higher voter turnout (Thompson, 2008). This idea, among others opens the door to even further advancement of virtual possibilities to promote the intentions of direct democracy.

Another essential element of democracy that the Internet helps to ensure is transparency. Journalism scholar Micah Sifry writes about the 2008 financial bailout legislation and the explosive public response that subsequently resulted in the website crash of both the government-owned www.house.gov and the privately-owned GovTrack.us. According to Sifry, this response signals a new age of transparency, where "as the tools for analyzing data and connecting people become more powerful and easier to use, politics and governance alike are inexorably becoming more open" (Sifry, 2009). The September 2008 financial bailout legislation resulted in increased participation on public examination sites such as

PublicMarkup.org (Sifry, 2009). These sites enable public to detour around road-blocks set up by public officials who do not want certain information distributed, says Sifry. He specifically cites the website EveryBlock.com, which grants users access to crime reports, restaurant-inspections, and the like, putting information directly in the hands of the user that is otherwise accessible to the public but hard to acquire.

The Paradigm Shift in Journalism and Resulting Shifting Standards

Like the Guttenberg press, the telegraph, wire transmission of text, photos, sound, and video, technology is once again creating a paradigm shift in American journalism. A paradigm shift begins, according to Thomas Kuhn (1962), the scientist who invented the term, when a significant number of relevant parties realize that old assumptions for how the social institution works no longer hold. New ideas are forming, but no new standard has yet been accepted or recognized. Yet, the importance of the institution requires that it continue to operate within some recognizable frame. The beginnings of paradigm shift are marked with a lack of consensus, about how the organization should operate(Kuhn, 1962).

Journalism, in the early twenty-first Century, is a practice seeking definition. "[I]t appears that there are two contrasting theories of journalism… One consists of established standards and practices that emanate from print and broadcast journalism and the belief that journalism has a social responsibility to inform citizens and nurture democracy, while the other is informed by suspicion of centrally managed, traditional media conglomerates and a belief, inspired by the open architecture of the Internet and flexibility of Web publishing, that citizens can participate in democracy by creating their own journalism" (Berkman and Shumway, 2003, p. 67).

Trippi revolutionized political campaigns through his use of the Internet in Howard Dean's 2004 presidential bid. He sums up the paradigm shift as a shift in power from corporate news to the people. "In America, for two hundred years, we have relied on some version of the media to interpret the events of the world for us, and at the same time to explain our governments' role in them.… People are no longer waiting for the media or the government to give information. Now they are going online and getting it, and then disseminating it. And with that information, they are gaining power" (Trippi, p. 232).

An organization's "news hole" is no longer bound by constraints of time and space. The ability to transmit instantly across multiple platforms has created audience expectation for instant transmission. The time it took for traditional reporting to funnel through the series of gatekeepers allowed for editing and for review of information for accuracy and lack of bias by editors along the way. However, citizens are no longer dependent upon the local newspaper and three broadcast networks to tell them about their world. The increasing participation to the online public sphere further democratizes media in that it takes the power away from the

New Media and an Old Problem

three major media giants and disperses that power to the active citizens. As the broadcast and print media become more narrowly-owned by corporate media giants, the world of online information of the public sphere continues to increase and expand diversity due to its many contributors.

Bias or lack of complete information from a single source does not lead to misperceptions if citizens develop their understandings from an aggregate of information sources. The partisan or objective nature of news does not matter as much as truth in labeling and each presentation being an honest attempt to present reality. Reality is ripe with interpretation from many sides and many perspectives. Media plurality can exist when journalists strive to include many sides in a story – when they include two sides, creating polarity, they often lose the story. Or, media plurality can exist simply through a multitude of sources.

The concern is that citizens have not been educated on the importance of seeking opinion different from their own or for the need of reviewing opinion that is in opposition to their own views. Instead, they gravitate toward the sources who reflect their own biases, with the potential result of misconceptions. For example, after declaration of the first Gulf War in 1991, research showed that the level of misunderstandings that citizens held regarding the need, goal, and even outcomes of that war correlated with their primary news sources. Polls taken soon after the beginning of the 2003 Gulf War revealed three major misconceptions held by American citizens: the United States had found weapons of mass destruction in Iraq; Saddam Hussein was involved in the 9/11/01 attacks on the US; and that the US had the support of other countries for its invasion of Iraq. A poll conducted by the University of Maryland's Program on International Policy Attitudes (PIPA) found that, "80 percent of those who said they relied of Fox News and 71 percent who said they relied on CBS believed at least one of the three misperceptions. The comparable figures were 47 percent for those who said they relied most on newspapers and magazines and 23 percent for those who said they relied on PBS or National Public Radio. Twenty-three percent of the public believed that WMD have already been found in Iraq, according to the PIPA survey. [The pollster] said he thought such a notion seemed to be ideologically driven in part, because significantly higher percentages of Republicans believed this, particularly 'Republicans following Iraq news closely.' Eighty percent of respondents said that they depended more on television and electronic media for their news, and a particularly high proportion of Republican respondents cited Fox TV, which has been especially jingoistic in its war coverage, as their main source" (Lobe, 2003).

The easy ability to access a variety of credible (and incredible) beliefs, opinions, and arguments also eliminates the need of journalists to depend on the usual suspects' style of sourcing, sometimes referred to as the Golden Rolodex. Now, sources are no further from the reach of traditional journalists than the ability to click to a provocative blogger. An important change from past eras when speakers might struggle to reach audiences who would reinforce and amplify their perspectives and agenda, crowds are no longer essential to signify the credibility or importance of a speaker's idea. All that is necessary is that the speaker be 'clickable' and indexed by keywords for easy search engine access. Contemporary scholars suggest that traditional journalists embrace rather than eschew such involvement. "News organizations should... move quickly and creatively to involve their audiences and other citizens in the gathering and analysis of news and information" (Downie Jr. and Schudson, 2009).

However, aggregation of information has resulted in a new style of majoritarian rule called Wikiality – the mistaken belief that open sourcing and editing results in truth. According to one writer, "The millions of bloggers who are constantly watching, fact-checking and exposing mistakes are a powerful example of 'the wisdom of crowds' being assisted by a technology that is as open and omnipresent as we are" (Naim, 2006, p. 31).

The Moral Citizen

American democracy is steeped in talk of citizen rights – the right to know what government is doing in our name and to know what we wish about our candidates for public office; the right to speak freely and to hear diverse views; the right to vote and to develop ballot initiatives to engage other citizens in perceived reform. Yet, there is relatively little attention paid to citizen responsibilities. Legal responsibilities of citizenship include obligations to obey the law, serve on juries, and pay taxes. "Democracies need more than an occasional vote from their citizens to remain healthy. They need the steady attention, time, and commitment of large numbers of their citizens who, in turn, look to the government to protect their rights and freedoms"(State, 2008).

Nineteenth century British philosopher John Stuart Mill enumerated the duties of citizenship with an eye toward the aggregate good. In his essay, "Of the Liberty of Thought and Discussion," he tells us that the duty of every citizen is "To form the truest opinion they can" (Mill, 1991a, p. 23). The way that citizens form true opinions and continually test out the correctness of their opinions is through seeking divergent opinion and weighing their opinion against those of others.

Mill would agree with Christians and other political communication theorists in arguing that articulating one's opinion is but a piece of the vehicle on the road to democracy. Mill says that most people "have never thrown themselves into the mental position of those who think differently from them, and consider what such persons may have to say; and consequently they do not, in any proper sense of the word, know the doctrine which they themselves profess" (Mill, 1991a, pp. 42–43).

However, the seeking and expressing of one's opinion has instrumental worth for the active citizen. The true goal, as Mill explains in "Utilitarianism," is advancement of the overall good of the community, in which the citizen realizes that her happiness is dependent upon the happiness of others. "He comes, as though instinctively, to be conscious of himself as a being who of course pays

New Media and an Old Problem

regard to others. The good of others becomes to him a thing naturally and necessarily to be attended to, like any of the physical conditions of our existence.... If differences of opinion and of mental culture make it impossible for him to share many of their actual feelings... he still needs to be conscious that his real aim and theirs do not conflict, that he is not opposing himself to what they really wish for, namely, their own good, but is, on the contrary, promoting it" (Mill, 1991b, pp. 165, 167).

In his essay on the "Agentic Power of the Internet," Scott Waring (2006) discusses the concept of agency, or "having the power or authority to act." Waring emphasizes how maintaining personal agency is necessary to be an active part of any participatory democracy. He describes the youth of America as associating agency with historical figures that they learn about in school, and underestimate or do not even consider themselves capable of making change through their own actions. This disassociation with agency among children can be attributed to the way they are taught, brought up, and the experiences they encounter. It is essential that children understand their ability to contribute to political action and, as Warren states, the Internet can provide that missing link due to its "global and decentralized nature" (Waring, 2006 p. 63).

The Internet, because of its vastness, makes almost any information available to almost any user. "Small causes have large effects [online], thus enabling actors to have agency at a distance or from anywhere in the world," (Waring, 2006, p. 63) allowing for networks to organize and even quiet voices to be heard. Civic participation can be embraced and developed through the Internet, and helping young students acquire the skills to do both those things will help to advance the Internet's capabilities for democratic participation.

Warren also provides us with a list of online forums and agencies that help to promote civic participation. Among those is Congress.org (www.congress.org), a nonpartisan company designed to help users communicate with elected officials and learn more about this country's legislature. Another, e-advocates (http://e-advocates.com) assists individuals in advocacy and consults for advocacy strategy. Others, such as Action!Network (http://actionnetwork.org), an environmental activist group, and Amnesty International (www.amnesty.org), for human rights advocacy, provide opportunities for collective agency through the World Wide Web. Sites like these help the promotion of democracy by allowing for access and facilitation through taking steps toward agency and by offering networks and collective virtual meeting areas for initiatives (Waring, 2006, pp. 65–66).

By teaching our youth and partaking in the many democracy-promoting resources available on the Internet, citizens are working toward embracing their own agency while at the same time serving society. As Warren says, "through the power of the Internet, every individual has the ability to serve as an agentic force for change within a society. The Internet provides a way for individuals to fulfill promises of democracy and to become empowered agents for social change" (Waring, 2006, p. 70). Embracing the capacity of the Internet fulfills the role of a citizen to be an active member of society and democracy as a whole.

The Future of Democracy and Journalism's Role

A new understanding of journalism is essential to provide support for newly empowered citizens. Joe Trippi, a pioneer in the use of the Internet in political campaigns frames the future this way: "I am convinced that Internet politics and government will be defined by its opposite, broadcast politics, and by its potential to fix many of the problems broadcast politics creates: Civic disengagement,… the dumbing down of the American electorate,… the insidious corruption of our politics and our government due to the disproportionate influence of wealthy donors, special interests, and corporations. The Internet shines a light on these dark recesses and quickly organizes millions of Americans cheaply, without relying on billionaires who want something for their money" (Trippi, 2008, pp. 225–226).

Yet, the future of democracy is not the choice of citizen-journalist over traditional journalist or the choice of living in cyberspace over physical space. According to media scholar Alex Jones, "Online news consumers are going to want all of what the Web offers. And there is no reason to think that those who read print newspapers will not also go online for news and vice versa. Print newspapers and their brother publications online do different things and satisfy in different ways, and if that is recognized, they can both thrive"(Jones, 2009, p. 210).

The new era is one in which news media and active citizens recognize their mutual dependency. Trippi notes: "The little-known secret in newsrooms across the United States is that right now reporters are beginning every day by reading the blogs. They're looking for the pulse of the people, for political fallout, for stories they missed" (Trippi, p. 229).

According to Sifry, "we are heading toward a world in which one-click universal disclosure, real-time reporting by both professionals and amateurs, dazzling data visualizations that tell compelling new stories, and the people's ability to watch their government from below (what the French call sousveillance) are becoming commonplace" (Sifry, 2009). This world is one of increased exposure to the public sphere and acknowledgement of the agentic capabilities of everyday citizens.

Ultimately, whatever the source of information, citizens need to have some basis for trusting the accuracy of the information provided. Credibility is the ultimate value of mass communication whether the medium is a traditional newspaper (in print or online) or a blog. Just as advertising rates are determined in traditional media by the size of the audience, bloggers' income is determined by the number of clicks to their posts. "Honest debate requires at least some consensus on what the facts are, and honesty, not obfuscation, where there is genuine confusion over the nature of the facts… What we need, in other words, is to welcome the new partisan and participatory outlets while finding ways to nurture and improve independent journalism"(Dionne, 2006).

Freedom of expression, whether in speech or the press, is of instrumental, not intrinsic, worth. Journalistic freedom exists to support the dissemination of material necessary for active self-governance throughout the populace. As Jones points out, "America has been a place where difference in knowledge – like difference in wealth – was not a yawning chasm and where a 'reality-based' press was, for all its shortcomings, premised on the belief that reality is something all Americans should know about" (Jones, 2009, p. 222). The reason for active self-governance is so that citizens recognize their duty and power to transform their local and global community into the best of all possible worlds, that is, in the words of Clifford Christians, that citizens express "ethical principles grounded in being" (Christians and Traber, 1997, p. 18).

However, an ignored responsibility for new media is in motivating citizens as well as informing them. Citizens need to understand that the information they gain from any source is not to fulfill their personal interest but to provide opportunity for them to work in the public interest. Enlightened citizens understand themselves to be actively involved in creating the good community. Ideal news organizations promote the growth and maintenance of community by giving citizens' information and priorities for their consideration and by, at least, reminding citizens of how to turn information into community action. In his essay, "On Liberty," Mill provides unwavering support for free expression of a diversity of views. In "Utilitarianism," he tells us, ethically speaking, what we are supposed to do with all of that freedom. The simple answer is that we should do what we each can to support the good of all.

Just as aggregate good expresses a "sum greater than its parts" consideration of community good; the sum of individual expression produces democracy that is vibrant in tension and thought. How that plays out in the future is but anyone's guess. The trust is in the process, for Mill, as well as for Clifford Christians, instead of allegiance to some particular outcome. A century after the writings of John Stuart Mill, Clifford Christians has operationalized these thoughts in works that have inspired thinkers around the world. The technology of the twenty-first century has allowed true experimentation of the theories of political communication.

References

Berkman, R., and Shumway, C. (2003) *Digital Dilemmas, Ethical Issues for Online Media Professionals*, Iowa State University Press, Ames.

Christians, C. (1997) The ethics of being in a communications context, in *Communication Ethics and Universal Values*, (eds C. Christians and M. Traber), Sage, Thousand Oaks, CA, p. 18.

Christians, C., and Traber, M. (eds) (1977) *Communication Ethics and Universal Values*, Sage, Thousand Oaks, CA.

Dahlgren, P. (2005) Internet, public spheres and political communication: dispersion and deliberation. *Political Communication*, 22 (2), 147–162.

DiMaggio, P., Hargittas, E., Neuman, W.R. *et al.* (2001) Implications of the Internet. *Annual Review of Sociology*, 27, 307–336.

Dionne, E. (2006) The making of democracy: How the new media and the old media could live together happily and enhance public life. Theodore H. White Lecture,

Joan Shorenstein Center of Press, Politics and Public Policy, Kennedy School of Government, Harvard University, Cambridge, MA, November 16.

Downie, J.L., and Schudson, M. (2009) The reconstruction of American journalism. *Columbia Journalism Review*, October, www.cjr.org/reconstruction/the_reconstruction_of_american.php (accessed June 28, 2010).

Elliott, D. (1986) Foundations of press responsibility, in (ed. D. Elliott), *Responsible Journalism*, Sage, Thousand Oaks, CA, pp. 32–44.

Fishkin, J.S. (1994) Bringing deliberation to democracy, in *The Ethics of Liberal Democracy*, (ed. R.P. Churchill), Berg Publishers Ltd, Oxford, pp. 101–110.

Herbert, B. (2009) Changing the world. *New York Times*, October 27, p. A25.

Jang, S.-H. (2009) Are diverse political networks always bad for participatory democracy?: Indifference, alienation, and political disagreements. *American Politics Research*, 879– 898.

Jones, A. (2009) *Losing the News*, Oxford University Press, New York.

Kovach, B., and Rosensteil, T. (2001) *The Elements of Journalism*, Three Rivers Press, New York.

Kuhn, T. (1962) *The Structure of Scientific Revolutions*, University of Chicago Press, Chicago.

Lobe, J. (2003) Mistrust and misconceptions, July 3, www.atimes.com/atimes/Middle_East/EG03Ak01.html (accessed July 22, 2010).

Macedo, S. (1999) *Deliberative Politics, Essays on Democracy and Disagreement*, Oxford University Press, New York.

Mansbridge, J. (1999) Everyday talk in the deliberative system, in *Deliberative Politics, Essays on Democracy and Disagreement*, Oxford University Press, New York, p. 211.

Mill, J.S. (1991a) Of the liberty of thought and discussion, in *Utilitarianism and Other Essays*, (ed. J. Gray), Oxford University Press, New York.

Mill, J.S. (1991b) Utilitarianism, in *On Liberty and Other Essays*, (ed. J. Gray), Oxford University Press.

Naim, M. (2006) TheYouTube effect. *Los Angeles Times*, December 20, p. 31.

Rohlinger, D., and Brown, J. (2009) Democracy, action and the Internet after 9/11. *American Behavioral Scientist*, 133–150.

Sifry, M. (2009) A see-through society: How the Web is opening up our democracy. *Columbia Journalism Review*, 47 (5), 43–45.

The Economist (2008) *The Economist*, February, p. 18.

Thompson, D. (2008) Is the Internet a viable threat to representative democracy, *Duke Law Technology Review*, www.law.duke.edu/journals/dltr/articles/2008DLTR0001.html (accessed June 28, 2010).

Trippi, J. (2008) *The Revolution Will Not Be Televised*, Harper, New York.

Waring, S. (2006) The agentic power of the Internet, *International Journal of Social Education*, 21 (1), 59–72.

14

The Dilemma of Trust

Ian Richards

In her Pulitzer Prize-winning autobiography, former *Washington Post* publisher Kate Graham relates an incident which occurred during the industrial trouble that afflicted the newspaper in the mid-1970s (Graham, 1997). The late Ms Graham tells how, on one occasion, after the printers had been locked out because it was feared they would destroy the printing presses, their leader (Jim Dugan) convinced a management representative (John Prescott) to allow them back in to the building – whereupon they "slashed a lot of the blankets that surround the rollers on the presses and tore out all the webs, stopping the whole night's work" (Graham, 1997, p. 524).

John sadly said to Dugan, "You told me you were in here to operate these presses."
"Well, I lied," was Dugan's simple response (Graham, 1997, p. 524).

Apart from demonstrating the brutality of newspaper industrial relations during this period, the incident illustrates one of the most common understandings of how trust works in practice – one party gave a verbal undertaking which a second party trusted would be honored, but the first party proceeded to breach that trust by failing to adhere to the undertaking and, indeed, acting in a way which directly contravened that undertaking. In this way, as is frequently the case in everyday life, trust was given – and betrayed.

Such trust interactions appear to be easily understood by most people. From birth, children learn to trust, then learn not to trust. Broken promises of all kinds, broken relationships, and broken assumptions about the social world litter most lives, such that we (who have learned these lessons well) might think a person naïve and untested if "simple trust" were the first response to advertising or sales messages, or even to contract negotiations, job offers, or sadly but poignantly,

---

The Handbook of Global Communication and Media Ethics, First Edition. Edited by Robert S. Fortner and P. Mark Fackler.
© 2011 Blackwell Publishing Ltd. Published 2011 by Blackwell Publishing Ltd.

romantic overtures. Promises once considered sacrosanct are widely and wisely now taken as conditionals. Blind trust is reserved for movie figures, children, and monks.

As the incident above demonstrates, common understandings of trust are as relevant to the news media as to any other section of society. Thus, they are evident in the findings of those public opinion polls, conducted in many countries, in which an increasing number of people say they do not trust journalists. Indeed in some countries, journalists are often considered as corrupt as political leaders, but not as clever and hence, not as wealthy. Many explanations for this situation have been put forward. In the US, for example, Zelizer has described American journalists as a group "somewhat out of touch with itself, its critics and its public" (Zelizer, 2009, p. 32):

> Givens such as the needs of the audience, the changing circumstances of news-making or the stuff at the margins of the newsroom – like inspiration and creativity – have remained relatively unaddressed. It is no surprise, then, that in the US journalists rank at the bottom of nearly every opinion poll of those whom the public trusts (Zelizer, 2009, p. 33).

Declining levels of popular trust are only one aspect of the part played by trust in journalism. Almost two decades ago, Stuart Adam wrote that journalism is defined by reporting but also involves criticism, editorializing, and "the conferral of judgments on the shape of things" (Adam, 1993, p. 12). His observation fell at the intersection of intense debates of the time – such as whether journalism was a craft or a profession, an institution, a business or something else. These tensions continue today, along with many more. Financial crisis, the rise of the blogosphere, the expansion of corporate media, audience fragmentation, and the increasing tendency of audiences to get their news from alternative sources have all posed serious challenges to those practitioners who see their role in Adam's terms, and to those who employ them. There is little clarity about what comprises "journalism" and what constitutes a "journalist," and even less about the part played by trust. Yet while it is frequently acknowledged that trust in the news media is in decline, and that good reasons can be found to explain this, what is meant by "trust" is seldom, if ever, made clear. Although most people appear to have little difficulty responding when asked whether they trust journalists (or any other group in society, for that matter), they invariably fail to explain what they mean. This lack of clarity is a common characteristic of many trust discussions, and not only those relating to the news media. At a recent academic gathering attended by the author, for example, an invitation to 30 participants to write down the word they considered most accurately reflected the meaning of "trust" produced 28 different responses. Such definitional imprecision permeates the literature on trust, and points to the difficulty of acting on trust. Where the practice of trust is weak or discounted, the understanding of trust is fragile and ambiguous.

Defining Trust

Since Francis Fukuyama first raised its role in the formation of social capital (Fukuyama, 1995), it has become widely accepted that trust is at the heart of our social relations. Today, there is general agreement that trust is important to the quality of our lives and the quality of our relationships with the wider society in which we live. By virtue of expanding bureaucracies and the impossibility of knowing personally all, or even most, of the people on whom life depends, we are in a precarious situation which requires trust while at the same time our learned skepticism and suspicion work against depending on it. Nonetheless, we place trust in others every day in all sorts of ways, whether those others are individuals – friends, relatives, work colleagues, shop assistants, taxi drivers, dentists, doctors, teachers – or institutions – government departments, local services, the police, the courts, hospitals, the armed forces. The part played by such generalized trust in the strengthening of civil society has received considerable attention, and it seems clear that social trust provides vital bonds among an otherwise anonymous citizenry. It also assists in the development of democratic institutions, although some have argued that, while democracy requires trust from citizens, it also presumes distrust – for example, of those in authority (Uslaner, 2002, p. 222).

Fukuyama described trust as "the expectation that arises within a community of regular, honest and cooperative behavior, based on commonly shared norms" which could "be about deep 'value' questions like the nature of God or justice, but ... also encompass secular norms like professional standards and codes of behaviour" (Fukuyama, 1995, p. 26). Much attention has been devoted to the notion of trust since then, and there has been a multitude of attempts to pin it down. One definitional strand is exemplified by Kenneth Newton's "working definition" of trust as "the belief that others will not deliberately or knowingly do us harm, if they can avoid it, and will look after our interests, if this is possible" (Newton, 2007, p. 343). Another strand consists of those who propose far more comprehensive explanations. Thus, Daryl Koehn, for example, describes trust as "a dynamic expectation of goodwill that evolves in and through relations" which "assumes its most fully realised form in good friendships, but ... exists in relations of pleasure and utility as well" (Koehn, 1998, p. 24). Koehn has identified four forms of trust – goal-based, calculative, knowledge-based and respect-based (Koehn, 2003, pp. 4–7). Goal-based trust "arises between two people who think they share a common objective, while calculative trust develops when one party attempts to predict what the other will do by seeking evidence for the other's trustworthiness." One might think of business partners or marriage partners in the first instance, and perhaps a client-vendor or entertainer-audience in the latter instance. Such pairings become difficult to maintain with clarity, as types of trust bleed across academic boundaries. In many cases, trust is simply the calculated value of utility. "The would-be trustor calculates the perceived benefits and liabilities of trusting. If benefits outweigh the costs, then the individual chooses to trust the party in question" (Koehn, 2003, p. 5). With each party cautiously computing the value of add-on trust, social relations grow trustful as the common-sense meanings of words begin to determine behaviors.

Knowledge-based trust arises when people are familiar to each other and/or interact frequently; relations based on such trust "may evolve when the two parties delight in each other's company, fine wit and good temperament ... neither the trusting nor the trusted party may be especially concerned about reaping some particular benefit" (Koehn, 2003, p. 5). Then again, imagine high-level Cold War summits resulting in international peace, and you can picture the tonnage of shared knowledge necessary to bring suspicious players together. Respect-based trust develops when two parties have a similar love of virtue, excellence, and wisdom and are willing to engage in dialogue and ongoing conversation with a view to understanding each other better (for fuller discussion, see Koehn, 2003). These interactions are more difficult to plan and develop, but guilds and religious groups, for example, have often found this type of trust the glue binding them together. Conversely, the breach of trust is a repellent and bleeds into all other trust relationships.

While such interpretations offer many useful insights, no single definition of trust has been universally endorsed. The social sciences have yet to produce a commonly accepted definition and, indeed, many interpretations of trust are regarded as being problematic because they "inform us about the purpose of trust, and its social value, but they don't tell us what it is" (Dwyer, 2008, p. 1212). The topic is so fiercely contested that it has been argued that that there is a "remarkable diversity in conceptualizations of trust" (Bigley and Pearce, 1998, cited in Provis, 2001, p. 31) and even that it is "a mistake, in general, to try to capture contested philosophical terms in a 'definition'" (Flores and Solomon, 1997, p. 76). It seems that about all we can say with any certainty is that "the concept of trust is subtle, diffuse and elusive" (Nooteboom, 1996, p. 243).

Exploring Trust

It seems evident from the literature that trust is "redundant when action or outcomes are guaranteed" but necessary "precisely when and because we lack certainty about others' future action" (O'Neill, 2002a, p. 13). Beyond that, distinctions are often made between horizontal (social or interpersonal trust) and vertical (political) trust; between trust in people and trust in institutions; and between specific ("thick") trust and more abstract ("thin") trust (for fuller discussion see, for example, Giddens, 1990; Newton, 2007; Putnam, 2000) "The former is based on personal first-hand knowledge of individuals (trust in a friend), the latter on more general information about social groups and situations" (Newton, 2007, p. 344). It has been argued that trust is an attitude based on beliefs and values typically involving feelings and implying behavior (Govier, 1994, p. 238) while others make a distinction between simple trust (naïve trust or trust as yet unchallenged); blind trust (stubborn, obstinate, possibly self-deluding trust); basic trust (the basic sense of physical and emotional security most of us take for granted); articulate trust

(trust articulated as belief); and authentic trust (an attitude that has wholly taken into account the arguments for distrust "and has nevertheless thrown itself on the side of trust)" (Flores and Solomon, 1997, pp. 57–58). These categories doubtless change from culture to culture, based as they are on lived social experience.

Although there is a considerable range of theories as to how trust originates, most of these can be grouped into one of three categories (Newton, 2007, pp. 349–352): those which view the decision to trust as a rational choice, a product of rational calculation and an underlying recognition that we have to treat others in a trustworthy way if they are to trust us; those which are social-psychological and which postulate that trust is learned in early childhood and influenced by individual life experience; and societal theories which regard trust as a collective feature of societies based on the daily experience of social relations:

> we place trust in a system that trains people for their jobs, monitors their performance and health, regulates their working hours, checks the safety of brakes, engines, machinery, the public health provisions of public places, and the brick and metalwork of buildings, bridges and railways (Newton, 2007, p. 352).

Growing awareness of the social and personal costs of distrust, and the work of those operating from the perspective of feminist ethics such as Annette Baier and Trudy Govier, has led to an appreciation of trust as an ethically significant social practice. In the process, it has become apparent that many forms of trust are inextricably inter-twined with such inherently ethical notions as betrayal, honesty, and dishonesty, and that many of the ethical questions surrounding trust are derived from the state of vulnerability which lies at the heart of the act of trusting. In Onora O'Neill's words, "at some point we just have to trust" (O'Neill, 2002b); in other words, we are all inescapably vulnerable and have no choice but, at some point, to accept this vulner-ability. How to reconcile the conflict occasioned by this fact of life between the competing claims of accepted vulnerability and justified distrust is one of the central challenges posed by trust (Koehn, 2003). When we decide to trust rather than dis-trust, we cannot be certain that our decision will prove to be justified because there is no way of guaranteeing that someone will be deserving of our trust. We cannot rely on introduced mechanisms for accountability because, rather than reducing atti-tudes of mistrust, these tend to encourage "a culture of suspicion reinforced by obsessions with blame and compensation" (O'Neill, 2002c). Under the circum-stances, the only safeguard for trust might, ultimately, be human nature itself:

> The integrity of the individual human being is a bulwark against dishonesty and betrayal, and we have counted on it for centuries. These last decades have reminded us that in vulnerable human beings, integrity can be dissolved in a flash under the influence of a powerful and corrupt culture. Then the trustworthiness breaks down; the greedy doctor starts prescribing a multitude of pills from his own pharmacy; the greedy accountant starts signing off on dubious deals to enrich himself; trustworthiness disappears in a matter of a few years, and trust is wiped away in a minute. (Newton, Hodges, and Keith, 2004, p. 171)

252   *Ian Richards*

Many characteristics of trust have been identified (Richards, 2010, pp. 86–87). Trust is always relational, and one cannot be trustworthy by oneself. In trust relations, there are at least two parties – one who places trust and one who is trusted – and there must be a possibility for one party to betray the expectations or understandings of cooperation of the other. Although it can be destroyed in a moment, trust is not a short-term matter. If someone has won our trust, we do not necessarily interpret a minor failure on their part as a warning that we should no longer trust them. Trustworthiness also needs to be distinguished from confidence and reliance: "Confidence obtains when the truster has identifiable reasons to expect something, for example, a doctor's credentials give patients confidence that he is competent to treat them. Reliance consists of depending on another to successfully act in a certain way, for example, the way we rely on the train to be on time" (Brien, 1998, cited in Borden, 2007, p. 74). Sports officials are trusted to be outcome neutral, whereas lawyers are trusted to be client-outcome driven. A federal elected official must have local constituents primarily in view (reelection depends on their trust) but the common good as political guide. Keeping trust is complex.

Some scholars have argued that trust is a necessary condition for participation in social life as, by trusting, the agent subjectively reduces the overwhelming complexity of social reality (Luhmann, 1979). Others argue that the expectation of trustworthiness has an important role to play in the professions as it functions as an indirect control mechanism: if professionals want to sustain trust they must act ethically (Borden, 2007). It also seems that deception is the greatest enemy of trust. In Onora O'Neill's words, "Deceivers do not treat others as moral equals; they exempt themselves from obligations that they rely on others to live up to" and, because they mislead intentionally, there is " a deliberate intention to undermine, damage or distort others' plans and their capacities to act, that damages trust and future relationships" (O'Neill, 2002c). Historical accounts often gloss over failures of trust among heroes of the culture, in order to maintain a stereotypical "good person" against which to monitor current conditions. However, history even celebrates great deceivers, as in celebrity crooks or (someone else's) tyrant. Mobutu Sese Seko had his admirers, and Al Capone is still a cultural icon.

Social Capital and the News Media

Social capital has been described as the "features of social organization such as networks, norms, and social trust that facilitate coordination and cooperation for mutual benefit" (Putnam, 2000, p. 67). Although this interpretation has been contested, it is generally acknowledged that social capital involves "connections among individuals – social networks and the norms of reciprocity and trustworthiness that arise from them" (Putnam, 2000, p. 19). Trust is a fundamental component of these connections because it is fundamental to the principle of generalized reciprocity: "I'll do this for you now, without expecting anything immediately in return and perhaps without even knowing you, confident that down the road you or someone

The Dilemma of Trust   253

else will return the favour" (Putnam, 2000, p. 134). In this way "trustworthiness lubricates social life" (Putnam, 2000, p. 21).

The news media are often blamed for the decline of social capital in many countries in recent decades or, at least, accused of being an accomplice in the process. A common element in such accusations is the negativity of news:

> Our whole journalistic culture has been skewed this way, focusing on people's failures and weaknesses of character without the concomitant drive to understand why they have these faults, what the context is, and how they link up with their strengths and virtues (Midgley, 1998, p. 40).

However, it is not so much that the media create distrust but, rather, that "they circulate stories of mistrust, cynicism and disengagement in forms that maximize their selection and retention. It is in this sense that the media must bear part of the blame for the cynicism and mistrust found in society" (Cappella, 2002, p. 239). At the same time, however, the consistent decline in public confidence in the news media – as reflected in the public opinion polls referred to earlier – is consistent with the general decline of public confidence in advanced industrial societies. Falling public trust in the news media parallels the decline in public trust in everything from democratic government and the established churches to public education and the system of justice. The news media appear to have fallen victim to this process as much as any other element in society:

> Public confidence in the medical profession, in organised labor, in the military, religion, political parties, and the media and … our … educational system, has dropped and in some cases plummeted like a kite in a dead wind (Cappella, 2002, p. 231).

Trust and Journalism

Most journalists have their own understandings of what is meant by trust. Thus, in discussions of the role and responsibilities of the news media, practitioners frequently invoke the notion of journalism's "public trust," and statements of journalism's public trust are commonly included in professional codes of ethics and codes of practice. At the core of this interpretation of trust is the late James Carey's view that "the role of the press is simply to make sure that in the short run we don't get screwed" (Carey, 1978, p. 855). The concept of journalism's public trust reflects the social responsibility theory of the press (Siebert, Peterson, and Schramm, 1956), according to which the responsibilities of the press (and by extension the broadcast news media) are emphasized over its freedoms, and the press is considered subject to moral and ethical restrictions. Among its obligations are servicing the political system by providing information, discussion and debate on public affairs; enlightening the public so as to make it capable of self-government; and safeguarding the rights of the individual by serving as a watchdog on government.

To act as the public media which clarified the goals and values of a society is a high calling indeed, one that the social responsibility theory places on the press. Oddly, it is often noted, no one or no agency bestows that responsibility; rather, it accrues from readers/viewers who turn to the press for information about the world beyond personal sight and sound. Thus the press is responsible not to government or institution, but to all – to the public – a remarkable social role. The press gains trust by telling the stories of other power-centers, as mentioned above. Trust underlies each of these roles because "If we can't trust what the press report, how can we tell whether to trust those on whom they report?" (O'Neill, 2002d). Technological change has challenged some of these functions, in part because it can no longer be assumed that the journalist is a direct witness to events (Alia, 1996, p. 169) but it has also highlighted the importance of other roles because many look to journalists to provide guidance in an increasingly complex world:

> When awash in a sea of information, it becomes incredibly important that there be a trustworthy navigator who can be relied upon to care about setting a true course; a person who has the skill and disposition to assist by making an accurate interpretation of the mass of data that washes aboard (Longstaff, 1994).

Another understanding of trust commonly acknowledged in journalism is the type which arises between individual journalists and their sources (Richards, 2010, p. 84). Sources with access to information that others would prefer to hide or suppress must be able to trust those journalists to whom they reveal such information to respect their confidences and, in some circumstances, to protect their identities. This type of trust is emphasized in journalists' codes of ethics, which customarily contain clauses similar to clause two of the Australian Media Entertainment and Arts Alliance journalists' code of ethics, which states that "Where confidences are accepted, respect them in all circumstances" (MEAA, 1999). This means that sources should be able to trust that a journalist to whom they reveal confidential information will not reveal their identity under any circumstances, regardless of the consequences, and even if these include imprisonment. This view underlies moves to introduce shield laws in some countries, under which journalists would be legally entitled to decline to reveal their sources in courts of law, regardless of the wishes of the court. The operation of grand juries in US law has presented a particular crisis of trust for journalists. Grand juries are investigative juries, and their records and testimony are secrets. When a journalist enters the grand jury chamber, no one among the public can know what he/she will say, or not say. Closed door events are antithetical to the open public forums which democratic media celebrate and illuminate. The underlying point as far as this discussion is concerned is the central significance of trust – sources must be able to trust that journalists will respect their confidentiality and journalists must be able to trust that the source is acting in good faith. "Trust, the keeping of promises, and loyalty are the foundations of confidentiality, and it is against these cherished values that third parties who seek to breach the cloak of confidentiality must compete" (Day, 1997, p. 158). Confidentiality helps prevent harm to others, and serves the ends of social utility because:

without assurances of confidentiality, the trust surrounding certain professional relationships would be eroded. Clients would be less than candid with their attorneys, which could undermine the cause of justice. Patients might lose confidence in their doctors, which would diminish the quality of personal health care. And, of course, reporters argue that confidential sources are often essential to uncovering crime and bringing it to the public's attention (Day, 1997, p. 138).

A third aspect of journalism where issues of trust have undergone some examination is journalistic interviewing, most notably in regard to what Alia (2004) labels the "open interview" in which the interviewer behaves in a non-judgmental way "striving to create an atmosphere of trust, empathy and support" (Alia, 2004, p. 116)

> The ethical risks of "open" interviews include manipulation, in which the interviewer creates a false climate of trust and betrays that trust through the deceptive use of phoney empathy. Caught off guard, the interviewee may reveal information that they had intended to keep private (Alia, 2004, p. 117).

As Pulitzer Prize-winning American journalist Janet Malcolm has written, in many journalistic interviews the subject and the interviewer both end up saying more than they intended because "they are always being seduced and distracted by the encounter's outward resemblance to an ordinary friendly meeting" (Malcolm, 1994, p. 173). This may be compounded when the interview is written up because of the "moral ambiguity of journalism" which "lies not in its texts but in the relationships out of which they arise – relationships that are invariably and inescapably lop-sided" (Malcolm, 1990, 262). Malcolm's assessment built on the ethical concerns raised in the 1960s following publication of *In Cold Blood* (Capote, 1965), Truman Capote's famous account of the murder of the Clutter family in a lonely Kansas farmhouse and the author's subsequent relationship with those responsible. Malcolm's own difficulties in faithfully conveying interview information to the public are publically available for review in the court records of the perilously difficult case brought by Jeffrey Masson (Masson v. New Yorker Magazine, Inc. (89-1799), 501 U.S. 496 (1991)). Similar concerns have been expressed many times since, for example, in the United Kingdom in relation to Gitta Sereny's *Cries Unheard: The Story of Mary Bell* (Sereny, 1998), which relates the tale of Mary Bell, an 11-year-old girl who murdered two children in Newcastle-on-Tyne in 1968. In an Australian context, similar questions were raised after the publication of Helen Garner's *Joe Cinque's Consolation*, which told of the murder in 1997 of Joe Cinque by his lover, law student Anu Singh (Garner, 2004).

Despite these excursions into the way trust and distrust operate in journalism, we still do not fully understand what forms of trust lie at its heart. We do not fully appreciate the roles that trust relationships play, the contexts in which they thrive or fail to thrive, the levels at which trust operates, and where or how notions such as betrayal fit. We shudder to contemplate the threats to journalistic trust posed by owners bent on profit, businesses bent on covering their own trust-faults, and celebrities of all kinds bent on regulating their images. The Western press structure

256   *Ian Richards*

is itself a business, and all too common are the tales of so-called virtuous media which tried to defend trust against all odds, only to succumb to their own vanishing bottom line. What keeps this enterprise from simply writing scripts or producing sound or visual which simply entertains or sells?

Future Directions

Many of the interpretations of trust discussed earlier appear to have relevance to journalism (for full discussion, see, for example, Richards, 2010). If we return briefly to Daryl Koehn's definition, we can see that it highlights the dynamic nature of trust which appears to be especially relevant to journalism because journalists and journalism are being buffeted by so many strong and shifting forces. Another relevant aspect of Koehn's definition is that what she describes as an "expectation of goodwill that evolves in and through relations" seems to summarize the situation which exists in many relationships in journalism. Many of those interviewed by journalists have an expectation of goodwill, at least to the point of expecting their comments to be reported accurately and fairly, and journalists often have an expectation of goodwill in as much as they expect those they interview to provide accurate information, and to do so without malicious intent. Sources who provide confidential information have an expectation of goodwill insofar as they expect their identity not to be revealed to others, and many of those who comprise the audience for the work of journalists have an expectation that the content will contain information they require or provide entertainment and distraction. Nooteboom refers to "competence trust," meaning another party's ability to perform according to implicit or explicit agreements (Nooteboom, 1996) and this, too, appears to have relevance to journalism because news audiences implicitly trust their newspaper or news bulletin to provide the information they want in a form that is relevant to their needs. Interpretations of trust which incorporate emotion also have relevance to journalism because many trust decisions in journalism – such as the decision by a reader, listener or viewer to trust a particular reporter or presenter – appear to have aspects which are less than rational.

Trust is clearly relevant to media ethics, as even a cursory examination of the central currents flowing through the field over the past decade or so makes obvious. Three issues underlie much contemporary discussion in this field (Nordenstreng, 1995): the conflict between universal and particularist values, represented by the ongoing dispute between those who are concerned to respect local conditions and values and those who argue that there are basic journalistic values which can be applied universally; the conflict between freedom and control, as embodied in the debate as to whether journalists' ethical standards should be subject to external regulation and enforcement or left to self-regulation; and the conflict between individualism and communitarianism, which focuses on the extent to which journalists should be prepared to compromise their professional autonomy in favor of a commitment to considerations of community (Nordenstreng, 1995). Trust is central to each of these discussions. Neither those who consider that journalists should respect local conditions nor those who argue that journalists should embrace common universal values could mount a convincing case if, depending on the position being adopted, most journalists could not be trusted to defend or embrace those values. Self-regulation of ethical standards could not be defended for a moment if most journalists could not be trusted to apply common standards to themselves and their colleagues. Much of the heat in the conflict between individualism and communitarianism is a product of whether the protagonists consider that journalists can or cannot be trusted to behave in ways which strengthen rather than undermine a sense of community.

How to investigate trust in relation to journalism is a difficult question. Some idea of just how difficult can be gained by reminding ourselves that:

> trust can be simultaneously cast as (1) both an individual and collective property; (2) a private and a collective good; (3) something that individuals and society can produce and consume; (4) both a possible cause and consequence of a wide range of important social and political attitudes and behaviors; and (5) both a foundation and product of democratic institutions and politics (Newton, 2007, p. 356).

The situation is further complicated by the fact that "in the past 10 years the media has changed more rapidly than any large-scale global industry, and one of the areas that has changed most is news gathering and reporting" (Baume, 2009, p. 31). These pressures are compounded by external forces such as attempts to control the flow of information to the media. In Australia, for example, it has been claimed that the Federal Government's "media machine" is controlling the day-to-day discharge of information and that central control of media inquiries has become "the cornerstone of the government's strategy" (Callaghan and Warne-Smith, 2009, p. 21):

> The Rudd media bubble is inflating as the pool of journalists has shrunk, thanks to staff cutbacks on newspapers, TV networks and radio stations, reducing the number of reporters able to deliver substantive stories and investigative pieces (Callaghan and Warne-Smith, 2009, p. 21).

Similar observations have been made in many countries. As media become more and more part of multinational corporations, the trust of the public in the integrity of news reports can be seriously undermined. What editor can claim no consideration given to a story that negatively impacts a sister company in the growing chain of sisters to which most media houses belong? In many countries only the very wealthy can produce media, and the very wealthy are also the politically powerful – a social cauldron of mistrust from the start. Then there is the issue of trust in the newsroom and trust relationships between colleagues and management. This is no easier to investigate, because power relationships in organizations are "complex, multi-faceted and heterogeneous" as well as being gendered and "negotiated and re-negotiated daily" (Peters, 2008, p. 18).

A common way of investigating trust is to tackle the topic under the umbrella of professional ethics, but it seems unlikely that such an approach will be very productive in regard to journalism. Leaving aside the extended debate over whether journalism is a profession or not (see, for example, Richards, 2005, pp. 2–4), it seems clear that the primacy of trustworthiness in professional ethics rests on several conditions that do not apply in a straight forward way to journalism. As Borden has demonstrated, the conditions of trustworthiness raised in the professional ethics literature – "a pronounced power asymmetry between the trusted and the trustor; a significant personal investment by the trustor in the decision to trust; an attribution of goodwill; and a proximate relationship between the two parties" (Borden, 2007, p. 74) – do not work in the same way in journalism (for fuller discussion, see Borden, 2007), which today is a profession in which professional entry is precarious at best, and risk-behavior among the ranks of novices is an extremely ill-advised tenure strategy. The rare stories of professional courage among journalists – the Woodward and Bernstein investigation of Watergate, for instance – seem like anomalies of the trade, hard indeed to replicate and, in any case, too costly for all but the most stable media house to undertake.

Another common way of trying to understand trust is to separate trust in individuals from trust in institutions. Once again, this approach is problematic in journalism because what is meant by "journalist" and "journalism" is itself under serious challenge. The diversity and complexity of journalism today suggests that it is less an institution than may have once been the case, as "the news media" can include everything from mainstream commercial newsrooms to small community operations, from public broadcasters to corporate conglomerations, from slick operations in advanced economies to unsophisticated publishing outputs in developing nations. A "journalist" can be anyone from a highly educated, well-trained professional to an untrained amateur with no experience, from a news reporter to a blogger to a citizen journalist, from someone who never moves beyond their backyard to someone who operates transnationally. In this situation, the individual–institution division may not be especially useful.

Any attempt to investigate trust in journalism also needs to resist the temptation of reductionism, which afflicts a great deal of journalism research. The problem was ably summed up by James Carey when he observed that "most social science studies of journalism ... are seen through the lens of social studies, not through the lens of journalism" (McKnight, 2000, p. 17). Scholars in media studies who produce such studies are themselves a step or two removed from the newsroom, a giant step indeed in the eyes of most newsroom workers. The context of journalist as a lived experience is not that of slow, calibrated, meticulous reports for which a dozen readers is considered a significant audience. Carey himself would have made an excellent big-city editor, but could he have written with such craft and wisdom about big-city media if he had? As Carey told McKnight:

> In the act of studying it, they almost always reduce journalism as a practice to its least and lowest common denominator. If one were to study education the way you studied

journalism, then the only thing you would study would be the most elementary introductory course offered by a department, and to confuse that with the entire discipline (McKnight, 2000, p. 17).

This failure to distinguish between basic journalism and more sophisticated forms is serious because it means that they (social scientists) "have no critical language for talking about journalism in a way that distinguishes good from bad, as inevitably you must have if you are going to write about literature or the theatre or poetry" (Carey in McKnight, 2000, p. 18). As a result, when subjected to scholarly study, journalism, in effect, disappears because "when it's good, people starting calling it sociology or history or literature or something else" (Carey in McKnight, 2000, p. 18).

Yet, for all the difficulties it poses, the case for trying to understand trust in journalism is strong. At one level, it can be argued that trust is both an instrumental good and an intrinsic good – "something that is good in itself" and "part of being a good human being" (Provis, 2001, p. 33) – and thus a fundamental part of being a good journalist. At a broader level, understanding trust is important because journalism is a vital part of communication and, without trust, communication has no meaning:

> Imagine a society, no matter how ideal in other respects, where word and gesture could never be counted on. Questions asked, answers given, information exchanged – all would be worthless. Were all statements randomly truthful or deceptive, action and choice would be undermined from the outset. There must be a minimal degree of trust in communication for language and action to be more than stabs in the dark (Bok, 1979, pp. 19–20).

This is no less the case today than when Sissela Bok wrote these words three decades ago. It is perhaps a sign of the thirst we sense for recovery of trust that Bok's eloquence still speaks, and too few have tried to join her chorus.

While it is not unusual for journalists to acknowledge that trust is important to them, the picture we have of such trust is far from complete. This is the case with journalism at all levels, from the intensely local to the expansively global. Trust accommodates such variation because it can be both universal and rooted in particular contexts. Like honesty, integrity, sincerity, and loyalty, trust is a value which "expressed in different and distinctive ways" transcends particular cultures and national boundaries (Grace and Cohen, 2000, p. 182). Clifford Christians has made a strong case that "our international web is not primarily political power or economic interdependence or information technology but a commitment to conscience that preconditions the ethos of these external apparatuses" and that our "mutual humanity is energized by moral obligations that activate our conscience toward the bondedness we share inescapably with others" (Christians, 1997, p. 12). It is difficult to see how this bondedness can have genuine meaning unless those involved are able to trust one another. In short, without connectedness there can be no communication and without trust there can be no connectedness. Yet even words such as "bondedness" and "connectedness" suffer from ambiguities of

260   *Ian Richards*

their own, and a certain professional disdain among journalists worldwide. The concepts they explore, however, ride the same wave of social significance as the one this essay has underscored. Plainly, we need to know much more about how humans develop together and come to trust the words and actions of the other. Trust is, as Bok said, a "precious resource, easily squandered, hard to regain" (Bok, 1979, p. 249). We need to know much more about trust than we do.

References

Adam, G.S. (1993) *Notes Toward a Definition of Journalism*. Poynter Institute, St Petersburg, Florida.

Alia, V. (1996) *Deadlines & Diversity: Journalism Ethics in a Changing World*, Fernwood, Halifax, Nova Scotia.

Alia, V. (2004) *Media Ethics and Social Change*, Edinburgh, Edinburgh University Press.

Baume, P. (2009) How technology is changing journalism. *The Australian*, April 13, 31.

Bigley, G.A., and Pearce, J.L. (1998) Straining for shared meaning in organizational science: Problems of trust and distrust. *Academy of Management Review*, 23 (3), 405–421.

Bok, S. (1979) *Lying: Moral Choice in Public and Private Life*, Vintage Random House, New York.

Borden, S. (2007) *Journalism as Practice: MacIntyre, Virtue Ethics and the Press*, London, Ashgate.

Brien, A. (1998) Professional ethics and the culture of trust. *Journal of Business Ethics*, 17, 391–409.

Callaghan, G., and Warne-Smith, D. (2009) Rise of Rudd's sentinels of spin. *The Weekend Australian*, June 6–7, 21.

Capote, T. (1965) *In Cold Blood*, Random House, New York.

Cappella, J. (2002) Cynicism and social trust in the new media environment. *Journal of Communication*, March, 229–241.

Carey, J. (1978) A plea for the university tradition. *Journalism Quarterly*, 55 (4), 846–855.

Christians, C. (1997) The ethics of being in a communications context, in *Communication Ethics and Universal Values*, (eds C. Christians and M. Traber), Sage, Thousand Oaks, CA, pp. 3–23.

Day, L. (1997) *Ethics in Media Communications: Cases and Controversies*, Wadsworth, Belmont, CA.

Dwyer, R.J. (2008) Benchmarking as a process for demonstrating organizational trustworthiness. *Management Decision* 46 (8), 1210–1229.

Flores, F., and Solomon, R. (1997) Rethinking trust. *Business and Professional Ethics Journal*, 16 (1–3), 47–76.

Fukuyama, F. (1995) *Trust: The Social Virtues and the Creation of Prosperity*, Free Press, New York.

Garner, H. (2004) *Joe Cinque's Consolation*, Pan Macmillan, Melbourne

Giddens, A. (1990) *The Consequences of Modernity*, Stanford University Press, Stanford, CA.

Govier, T. (1994) Is it a jungle out there? Trust, distrust and the construction of social reality. *Dialogue*, 33 (2), 237–252.

Grace, D., and Cohen, S. (2000) *Business Ethics*, Oxford University Press, Melbourne.

Graham, K. (1997) *Personal History*, Phoenix, London

Koehn, D. (1998) *Rethinking Feminist Ethics: Care, Trust and Empathy*, Routledge, London.

Koehn, D. (2003) The nature of and conditions for online trust. *Journal of Business Ethics*, 43, 3–19.

Longstaff, S. (1994) Can we avoid trusting the media? St James Ethics Centre, www.ethics. org.au/about-ethics/ethics-centre-articles/ethics-subjects/journalism-and-media/ article-0027.html (last accessed May 22, 2009).

Luhmann, N. (1979) *Trust and Power*, Wiley and Sons, Ltd., Chichester.

Malcolm, J. (1990) *The Journalist and the Murderer*, Vintage, New York.

Malcolm, J. (1994) *The Silent Woman: Sylvia Plath and Ted Hughes*, Picador, London.

Masson v. New Yorker Magazine, Inc. (89–1799), 501 U.S. 496 (1991). http://supreme. justia.com/us/501/496/case.html (accessed October 14, 2010).

McKnight, D (2000) Interview with James Carey. *Australian Journalism Review*, 22 (2), 17–22.

MEAA Media Entertainment and Arts Alliance (1999) *Journalists' Code of Ethics*. Sydney, Australia.

Midgley, M. (1998) The problem of humbug, in (ed. M. Kieran) *Media Ethics*, Routledge, London, pp. 37–48.

Newton, K. (2007) Social and political trust, in (eds R. Dalton and H. Klingemann), *Oxford Handbook of Political Behavior* (seventh edition), Oxford University Press, Oxford, pp. 342–361.

Newton, L., Hodges, L., and Keith, S. (2004) Accountability in the Professions: Accountability in Journalism. *Journal of Mass Media Ethics*, 19(3&4): 166–190.

Nooteboom, B. (1996). Trust, opportunism and governance: A process and control model. *Organisation Studies*, 17 (6), 985–1010.

Nordenstreng, K. (1995) Introduction: A state of the art. *European Journal of Communication*, 10 (4), 435–439.

O'Neill, O. (2002a) *Autonomy and Trust in Bioethics*, Cambridge University Press, Cambridge.

O'Neill, O. (2002b) Called to account. *Reith Lectures*, BBC Radio. Retrieved May 10, 2009 from www.bbc.co.uk/radio4/reith2002/

O'Neill, O. (2002c) Trust and transparency. *Reith Lectures*, BBC Radio. Retrieved May 10, 2009 from www.bbc.co.uk/radio4/reith2002/

O'Neill, O. (2002d) Licence to deceive, *Reith Lectures*, BBC Radio, www.bbc.co.uk/ radio4/reith2002/ (accessed June 28, 2010).

Peters, M. (2008) The organized self: Managing time, space, work and life in the ever present. Paper presented at International Communication Association conference Communicating for Social Impact. Montreal, Canada, May 22–26.

Provis, C. (2001) Why is trust important? *Reason in Practice*, 1 (2), 31–41.

Putnam, R.D. (2000). *Bowling Alone: The Collapse and Revival of American Community*, Simon & Schuster, New York.

Richards, I. (2005) *Quagmires and Quandaries: exploring journalism ethics*. Sydney: University of NSW Press.

Richards, I. (2010) 'The strange case of trust in journalism' in (eds M. Fackler and R. Fortner), *Ethics and Evil in the Public Sphere: Media, Universal Values and Global Development* Hampton Press, Cresskill, NJ, pp. 79–92.

Sereny, G. (1998) *Cries Unheard: The Story of Mary Bell*, Macmillan, London.

Siebert, F., Peterson, T., and Schramm, W. (1956) *Four Theories of the Press*, University of Illinois Press, Urbana.

Uslaner, E. (2002) *The Moral Foundations of Trust*, Cambridge, Cambridge University Press.

Zelizer, B. (2009) Journalism and the academy, in (eds K. Wahl-Jorgensen and T. Hanitzsch), *The Handbook of Journalism Studies*, Routledge, New York and London, pp. 29–41.

15

The Ethical Case for a Blasphemy Law

Neville Cox

Introduction

The concept of a modern day blasphemy law seems intuitively anachronistic and oppressive to a typical Western liberal audience.[1] It carries undertones of an Old Testament style stoning of the kind parodied in Monty Python's *Life of Brian*, or of individuals being harshly punished by the law for doing something which a state fears may incur the wrath of God against it. This popular view that a blasphemy law is an inevitably and unacceptably illiberal one, best reserved for a theocracy and having no place in a modern democracy has been expressed a great deal recently and in the context of a number of different newsworthy events;

- In Sudan a British school teacher faced corporal punishment for her role in naming a class teddy bear "Mohammad."[2]
- In the United Kingdom, Christian groups attempted to bring a private prosecution for blasphemy against the producers of the stage show *Jerry Springer the Opera*.[3]
- In Ireland, legislation was enacted which *inter alia* included a statutory crime of blasphemy.[4]
- The United Nations Human Rights Council, in dealing with the issue of freedom of expression has been regarded by some as focusing excessively on how to ensure that religions generally (and Islam especially) are suitably protected against insult.[5]
- Most notably, in Denmark, in 2005, there was much condemnation of the reaction by Muslims to the publication in a well known Danish newspaper of caricatures of the Prophet Mohammad.[6]

The Handbook of Global Communication and Media Ethics, First Edition. Edited by Robert S. Fortner and P. Mark Fackler.
© 2011 Blackwell Publishing Ltd. Published 2011 by Blackwell Publishing Ltd.

In all these cases, the expressed view of many Western commentators was that both the existence and the application of a blasphemy law must be entirely and self-evidently inappropriate[7] and a blasphemy law is therefore nothing more than a tool for intolerant zealots to enable them to pursue an agenda against those who disagree with them.

What was especially stark about the reaction from many *European* commentators to these stories is that, as we shall see, a modern day blasphemy law is essentially one which seeks to protect religious sensitivities from abuse and in most European states and under the European Convention on Human Rights,[8] there is no absolute legal objection (of the kind that exists, for example in America) to the notion of free speech being curtailed because of the offensiveness or moral unacceptability of its content. An obvious example (and one on which I shall focus) is a law prohibiting holocaust denial.[9] Another example is arguably a law which prohibits so called "hate speech." Yet the same commentators who condemn blasphemy laws are not as vehemently opposed to these other kinds of law. This indicates that the *principled* objection to such laws (if any) shared by these commentators cannot be at the level of classic liberalism whereby one should be prepared to die for the speech one hates and whereby, consequently, speech should never be restricted simply because it is offensive.[10] Rather the objection appears to be more specifically to the *concept* of a blasphemy law itself, or, possibly, to the notion of the law protecting *religious* sensibilities from grave offence (even though it might validly protect other forms of sensibilities). Moreover, this line of principle gets such commentators a very long way, in that it allows them to conclude that any such blasphemy law must self evidently be an affront to democracy.[11]

In this chapter the question of whether it is possible to make an ethical case for a twenty-first century blasphemy law is considered. Emphatically, however, it is not the author's intention to argue that a blasphemy law *should* be enacted in any jurisdiction or jurisdictions nor to consider the proper content of any such law. Rather the hypothesis of this chapter is simply that the desire on the part of certain individuals for the law to step in to prevent blasphemy (and punish the blasphemer) is no different in principle to the desire (for example) of other persons for the law to be used to prohibit holocaust denial and thus that any principled view that one such desire is inherently unacceptable within a democracy must necessarily cover the other and *vice versa*.

Three central points will be made in this chapter as to why such a link between support for holocaust denial laws on the one hand and blasphemy laws on the other can be drawn.

- First, in both cases what is significant is not merely the fact that an individual is personally offended by the material in question, but more importantly, that the material is profoundly[12] offensive to the nation (or in the case of a religion, "quasi-nation") as a whole, such that if the material is permitted to go unchecked by law, this represents an affront to the moral core of the nation.[13]
- Second, it will be further argued that the reason *why* an affront to the core of a nation is seen by many people as something which may legitimately be restricted

by law is arguably because of the huge significance of a nation, not as a geographical territory but as a unifying source of self-identification for its citizens. In other words, many citizens rightly feel that they owe a respect bordering on reverence to their nation, because it is the source of much of the collective consciousness which binds that society together. The importance of such a collective consciousness is therefore the reason why it may be acceptable for a nation not to permit the gravest insults to what may loosely be termed its "soul" to go unchecked – but rather to check them in a highly public and dramatic way. This is, for example, the logic behind Chief Justice Rehnquist's powerful Supreme Court dissent in *Texas v. Johnson* when he felt prepared to uphold the constitutionality of law prohibiting the burning of the national flag despite the fact that this would necessarily entail a restriction on the putative flag burner's rights to freedom of speech.[14] For Rehnquist, (expressing the view of many Americans) the American flag was not merely a piece of fabric with a particular design, in the same way as "America" was not simply a geographical region in which they live. Rather both were fundamental sources of identification for Americans and of the collective conscience of the nation as a whole, and hence were sufficiently precious (at an almost primal level) that it was legitimate to protect them by law from mockery or desecration.[15]

- Finally, it will be argued that the kind of deeply profound offence which, for example Germans as members of the German nation appear to suffer through holocaust denial may also be felt by persons in respect of their religious sensibilities, precisely because many people in the world (and this chapter, perhaps inevitably will focus on Muslims and on the approach of Islam to this issue) define themselves according to their religion. In other words, the sense of self identity which "Germany" gives to Germans and German society is the same as the sense of self identity which, for example, Islam gives to Muslims (and Muslim society globally), and hence if a deeply offensive comment on the "soul" of Germany can *as a matter of principle* be prohibited by law for this reason, so also can an attack on the soul of Islam.

This is the proposition that is considered in this chapter; in order to consider it carefully though, we assess first the nature of the crime of blasphemy (or what the crime has come to mean), second, the nature of what might be termed an *inappropriate* blasphemy law – namely one which exists to protect the religious sensibilities of devotees against insults to religion yet in circumstances where there is no need to do so because the level of offence suffered at a corporate level is insufficient and, finally, the circumstances in which such a law might be appropriate.

Before doing so, however, one final introductory point should be made; this chapter is entitled "The Ethical Case for a Blasphemy Law" and it is important to address the question of the identity of the audience to whom the "case" is being made. After all, as will become clear, my argument assumes that individual rights and freedom of expression and so on, are important values (and self-evidently so), to the extent that it is necessary to justify restrictions on them. However, in a number of countries (including, for example, certain Sharia law led theocracies) such a proposition simply is not accepted, such that blasphemy or apostasy can be criminalized with no further debate, in that the interests of God, religion or religious feelings are at the upper end of the scale of national priorities, and there are either no such things as individual rights or freedom of expression, or else they rank very low on any such scale. Hence this chapter seeks to make the ethical case for blasphemy law to persons who are familiar with and supportive of what may simplistically and broadly be termed "Western human rights values," and who, in consequence see rights as important social possessions which, however, are not absolute and which may be limited where this can be justified.

What is Blasphemy?

In 1660 the common law courts took jurisdiction over the crime of blasphemous libel (in place of the Star Chamber and ecclesiastical courts).[16] At first, the law existed to protect *religion* and later it operated as a vehicle by which the offended sensibilities of religious devotees could be assuaged. These two stages in the life of the crime of blasphemy will be considered shortly, but it is worth mentioning briefly, that in fact, certainly on one analysis, "blasphemy" is properly an offence against neither religion nor a religious person but exclusively against God. So the Old Testament terms for blasphemy all stem from the words *Naats* and *Naqab* meaning to "pierce" or "sting" and the word *Gadaph* meaning to revile.[17] This is a not unimportant point, in that it suggests that most modern so-called blasphemy laws, whereas they undoubtedly prohibit the utterance of blasphemy, are in fact not actually blasphemy laws at all, but rather laws which restrict speech in the interest of preventing offence to persons affected thereby. Indeed it is also arguable that the very *name* of the crime of blasphemy is one of the reasons why it attracts so much criticism, as people perceive it to be anachronistic and "medieval" in nature.[18]

Blasphemy as Treason

Originally, the common law offence of blasphemy, existed for a specific reason, namely to protect the established church as a part of the law of the land[19] – and indeed to protect society from the wrath of a Divine force angered by insults.[20] As Feinberg put it:[21]

> The original blasphemies in an earlier time when religion was austere, did more than merely offend, as any vulgar insult might offend … the punished words were thought to be not merely offensive but dangerous to the collective interest or positively harmful in themselves. A solemn interdiction had been laid upon sacred words when used

for the purpose (or with the effect) of blasphemy, and disobedience threatened the whole community with divine vengeance. For that reason, blasphemy was not merely offensive, but dreadful, that is, likely to be accompanied in the speaker's mind and to arouse in all listeners a great dread of awful consequences.

This justification for the law meant both that even simple denial of the authority of the Anglican religion or any of its precepts constituted blasphemy (for it was a quasi treasonable denial of the authority of the law)[22] and also that it was only possible to commit blasphemy against the established religion.[23]

Blasphemy and Offence to Religious Sensitivities

This was certainly the law in England until 1842.[24] Later, however, owing to the efforts of reform bodies,[25] and politicians,[26] and public frustration with certain long running prosecutions,[27] the position changed, such that by 1883, the law had an entirely different focus[28] and existed to protect the religious devotee from comments that would offend his or her sensibilities. Hence in 1883 Coleridge LCJ commented that[29]

> the mere denial of the truth of Christianity is not enough to constitute the offence of blasphemy ... the law visits not the honest errors but the malice of mankind. A wilful intention to pervert, insult and mislead others by means of licentious and contumelious abuse applied to sacred subjects...is the criterion and test of guilt.

This change (which was copper-fastened by the decision of the House of Lords in *Bowman v. Secular Society*,[30]) naturally meant that the law would no longer be concerned with seditious or heretical blasphemy (including that most seditious kind, namely expression of unbelief) but only with what might be termed *offensive* blasphemy – in practice, publications involving the must scurrilous treatment of sacred things.[31]

What was not clarified in either *Bowman v. Secular Society* nor in *R v. Lemon*,[32] – the famous 1970s case in which redoubtable social campaigner Mary Whitehouse took a private blasphemy prosecution against the publishers of the magazine *Gay News* – was whether this new blasphemy law continued only to apply to publications involving aspects of the established religion.[33] Logically, in as much as this historic limitation was utterly based on the old rationale for the blasphemy law (the sedition justification) this should no longer have been the case, but in *R v. Bow Street Magistrates, ex parte Choudhury*,[34] (in the context of the extreme political tension surrounding the publication of Salman Rushdie's book *The Satanic Verses* which is considered later[35]) the English High Court held that the law still only covered the Anglican faith and that any change in this position would have to be made by parliament.[36]

Blasphemy Law and the Balancing of Rights and Interests

Accordingly then, the contemporary common law offence of blasphemy is one which appears to involve a balancing of rights and interests, namely the right to freedom of expression being balanced against the interests of various persons not to be offended in respect of their religious sensitivities. Different commentators and indeed law reform bodies naturally take different views as to whether as a matter of principle it is legitimate at all for speech or expression to be restricted because it is offensive,[37] or, more specifically, whether religious sensitivities should be protected from offence in the same way as might be the case for (for example) racial or ethnic sensitivities.[38] Nonetheless, what is notable is that the "new" blasphemy law (in as much as it involves a balancing between the right to freedom of expression and the interest of people in not being gravely offended by such expression) operates at a level of principle that is immediately cognizable within normal Western constitutional language. There is, after all, a large number of instances in which the law of various jurisdictions will restrict speech or expressive conduct on the basis that it is offensive, with obvious examples being laws against public nudity, racist or other hate speech, obscenity or holocaust denial. The modern version of the common law offence of blasphemy, simply takes the view that offence to *religious* sensibilities fits within that class of offenses which may justify restricting the right to freedom of expression, and proceeds accordingly by an assessment of whether the offence in question is grave enough to warrant suppression of the material.

In other words, a blasphemy law of this kind is *prima facie* consistent with normal Western rights theory (in the way in which a law which existed to prevent God from being offended would not be). To put it another way, if one is to submit that as a matter of principle this kind of a blasphemy law can *never* be acceptable, then it is necessary to argue either:

- that speech/expressive conduct should *never* be restricted simply by reference to its offensiveness – the principle which essentially emerges from the decision of the United States Supreme Court in *Texas v. Johnson*;[39] or
- that there is something about religion and religious sensibilities which renders them unworthy of legal protection even though other kinds of sensibilities *may* warrant protection.

We will now consider these two issues in turn.

The Significance of Offense and the Objectification of an Offense Principle

To take the first issue first, the broad question of whether the offensiveness of speech or conduct should ever be a ground for its legal restriction is so vast, that it is simply beyond the scope of this chapter. Nor indeed is it necessary to address the question, in that the purpose of this chapter is to make an ethical case for a blasphemy law premised on the notion that such a law is indistinguishable in principle from a holocaust denial law. On the other hand what *is* necessary is for us to assess the question of why holocaust denial is so offensive in Germany, and more particularly why the law steps in to prohibit the cause of this offense, in order to assess whether the offense caused by blasphemy could ever rise to this level.

In doing so, we immediately encounter what many commentators regard as the most significant objection to any kind of "offense principle" namely that the subjectivity of taste and tolerance is such that *anything* can be offensive to somebody,[40] hence an offense principle could lead to a situation where virtually all speech, especially speech which was dynamic and thought provoking could be prohibited. At the very least, it is strongly arguable that unless some "objectifying limitations" are placed on such an "offense principle" it could have very serious consequences as far as the right to freedom of expression is concerned.[41] Where religion is involved, moreover, this is a particularly problematic issue in that religious like atheistic beliefs (even deeply and sincerely held beliefs) lack objective basis because of the unprovability of the existence or nonexistence of God, let alone the content of his or her mind. In other words, it is possible to believe in anything or to subscribe to any kind of doctrine and hence to be offended by any kind of remark or comment, however objectively innocuous.

Hence if any kind of "offense principle" is to be employed within a legal system, it is presumably wise to impose some constraints on such a principle. It is suggested in this chapter that one way of objectifying an offense principle (although by no means the only appropriate way) is for a nation only to restrict offensive speech which offends not only an individual but also the collective ethos or "soul" of the state itself at some deep and profound level. It will later be suggested that this is precisely what is at issue when, for example, Germany prohibits holocaust denial and that it may also explain why Islam (as a quasi nationstate) is so outraged by blasphemy. Before doing so, however, it is apposite and salutary to consider the problems that may arise where there is a "misfit" in principles; that is, where a state restricts speech because of its alleged offensiveness to individuals, yet where the state itself has no interest in restricting the material in question. By way of example, let us consider recent developments in the blasphemy law of the Republic of Ireland.

A Disconnect in Principles – Blasphemy Law in Ireland

One of the most extraordinary features of the Irish Constitution is that whereas it guarantees a limited right to freedom of expression[42] it also specifically takes the unusual step of providing that the publication or utterance of blasphemous, seditious, or indecent matter; is an offence which shall be punishable by law. The only clue as to the ambit of the constitutional crime of blasphemy given at the time of the document's enactment came from the then Taoiseach (Prime Minister) Mr. Eamonn de Valera, who suggested that the constitution did not create a new offence of blasphemy but simply supported the existing common law offence.[43] This was not a remarkable conclusion given that it was in England that this common law offence was formed and developed and furthermore, during the bulk of the time when this offence was being developed, Ireland was under English legal control. The constitution came into being in 1937, and hence, if Mr. De Valera was correct, the constitutional offence of blasphemy existed in the scurrilous treatment of sacred things which has the capacity grossly to offend the religious sensitivities of devotees.

Despite (or possibly as a result of) its overtly religious ethos, there have been remarkably few prosecutions for blasphemy in Ireland either before, or after independence. The first such prosecution occurred in 1703,[44] when one Thomas Emlyn, a Unitarian minister was arrested because of a book he had written entitled *A Humble Enquiry into the Scriptive Account of Jesus Christ*. The Chief Justice, Richard Pyne, conducting the prosecution with great zeal told the jury that if *it* acquitted Emlyn, the Bishops sitting in Ecclesiastical Courts would not. Almost as a matter of course, Emlyn was convicted, sentenced to one year in prison, fined £100 and ordered to produce sureties for good behavior for life. The next major Irish blasphemy case took place in 1852,[45] and concerned Brother John Syngean Bridgeman, a Franciscan Friar living in County Mayo who was charged with *unlawfully, wickedly and blasphemously* setting fire to a bible which had the unfortunate status of being both English and Protestant. Ultimately Brother John was found to be not guilty but the court did indicate that blasphemy existed to protect the established religion (the Anglican Church). Finally in 1855, a Redemptorist priest named Padre Petcherine[46] had organized a bonfire aimed at facilitating the destruction of some of the works of the devil, particularly *vile English novels, whose very names are an abomination*. In his zeal to destroy such literature, he had neglected to notice that, encased in a bundle of disreputable books was a bible, which was thrown unto the fire and burned. This act of bible-burning generated a charge of blasphemy for which he was acquitted, with Baron Green again endorsing the view of blasphemy law as a protector of the legal establishment.[47] Equally this view of the law was unsustainable in 1937 both because of the developments in England which we have considered, and more pertinently because in 1869, the Church of Ireland was disestablished and since then no religion has been established, such that a denial of its precepts would be a denial of the law.

The first time in which an independent Irish Supreme Court dealt with the application of the "new" constitutional clause pertaining to blasphemy was some 140 years later in *Corway v. Independent Newspapers*.[48] The *Corway* case arose out of the publication in the biggest selling Irish Sunday newspaper, of an article which questioned whether the recent acceptance of divorce by the Irish people signaled a move away from the historic impact that Catholic doctrine had on Irish constitutional and social policy. The article was accompanied by a cartoon depicting a stout priest in priestly vestments holding aloft the Eucharistic host and offering it to three prominent political leaders who are seen to be walking away from this offer. The applicant in the case felt sufficiently aggrieved and offended by what he saw as

The Ethical Case for a Blasphemy Law

the contemptuous treatment of something so sacred as the Eucharist for the purpose of making a crude and rather obvious political point, that he sought leave, under the terms of s.8 of the Defamation Act of 1961, to bring a private prosecution against the newspaper.

The case proceeded to the Supreme Court which took the unusual step of deeming the constitutional clause in question, and specifically the notion of blasphemy, to be too obscure for it to interpret. Thus, having considered a dictionary definition of the term *blasphemy*,[49] the Supreme Court encountered what it regarded as an insuperable obstacle. Since 1869, Ireland has had no established church and hence there has been no possibility of any particular religion forming part of the law of the land.[50] Yet, (according to the Supreme Court) the crime of blasphemy exists to protect religion *as* an aspect of the law of the land. A combination of these two factors meant that it was impossible to say with any degree of certainty what the constitutional reference to blasphemy actually entailed. Indeed the problems in this regard were exacerbated by the fact that, even if such an established or (as in the case of the Roman Catholic Church) a quasi-established religion could be found, a constitutional guarantee would sit uneasily with the constitutional guarantee of religious equality. In the circumstances, the Supreme Court felt that the constitutional reference to blasphemy simply transcended judicial definition, and that its meaning should be determined by the legislature. Thus, the court concluded that[51]

> In this state of the law, and in the absence of any legislative definition of the constitutional offence of blasphemy, it is impossible to say of what the offence of blasphemy consists ... The task of defining the crime is one for the legislature and not the courts. In the absence of legislation and in the present uncertain state of the law, the court could not see its way to authorising the institution of a criminal prosecution for blasphemy.

There are many criticisms that can be made of the Supreme Court judgment in *Corway v. Independent Newspapers*.[52] First, it may be suggested that the Supreme Court misjudged its role in the case. After all, this was merely a case in which leave was being sought to bring a prosecution and hence all that had to be made out was a prima facie case. Second, it is surprising that the Supreme Court did not consider that the change in focus brought about by the nineteenth century blasphemy cases, and brought to full fruition in *Bowman v. Secular Society* obviated the need for any connection between a blasphemy law and an established church. Most pressingly, however, it is extraordinary that any Supreme Court – whose job after all is *inter alia* to interpret the constitution, should refuse to do so, on the basis that it felt unable to define a particular legal term.[53] Indeed the weakness of the Supreme Court argument that blasphemy is indefinable is highlighted by the fact that at the beginning of its judgment it had actually referred to a perfectly workable legal dictionary definition of blasphemy. For what it is worth, it is submitted that the cartoon was probably not blasphemous in the legal sense – in that however tasteless and tacky it was, it was not a genuinely scurrilous treatment of something sacred.

This conclusion, however, albeit one for a jury, is very different to a statement from the highest court in the land that it could not interpret one of the legal words used in the constitutional text.

The Defamation Act 2009 and the Statutory Crime of Blasphemy

It should be remembered that the Supreme Court, having accepted that blasphemy *is* a crime in Irish Law (because the constitution says that it is) called for legislative clarification of the nature of the offence.[54] In 2009 the Irish legislature enacted a new Defamation Act to repeal and replace the Defamation Act 1961.[55] This step posed a constitutional problem, however, in that the 1961 Act contained the procedural basis for taking a blasphemy action; hence simply to abolish such procedure without replacement would, at least on one level, emasculate the crime of blasphemy – a step with obvious constitutional implications. It would have been possible for the government to seek to amend the constitution and abolish the reference to blasphemy but politically that would have been an expensive and potentially complex step.[56] Accordingly the decision was taken simply to clarify what was meant by blasphemy (thereby doing what the Supreme Court in *Corway* had suggested) and to encapsulate the offence in statutory terms. Hence s.36 of the Act provides as follows

1   A person who publishes or utters blasphemous matter shall be guilty of an offence and shall be liable upon conviction on indictment to a fine not exceeding €25,000.
2   For the purposes of this section, a person publishes or utters blasphemous matter if –
    a)   he or she publishes or utters matter that is grossly abusive or insulting in relation to matters held sacred by any religion, thereby causing outrage among a substantial number of the adherents of that religion, and
    b)   he or she intends, by the publication or utterance of the matter concerned, to cause such outrage.
3   It shall be a defence to proceedings for an offence under this section for the defendant to prove that a reasonable person would find genuine literary, artistic, political, scientific, or academic value in the matter to which the offence relates.
4   In this section "religion" does not include an organisation or cult –
    a)   the principal object of which is the making of profit, or
    b)   that employs oppressive psychological manipulation –
       i   of its followers, or
      ii   for the purpose of gaining new followers.

A point to note about this law is that it is virtually nonenforceable. Indeed given that one must *intend* to cause outrage, one must succeed in causing outrage and the material must objectively have no literary (and so forth) merit, it is difficult to see *what* could be covered that is not already covered by Irish law relating to

The Ethical Case for a Blasphemy Law   273

incitement to hatred.[57] In other words, if the legislature was aiming at adhering to the words of the constitution while actually killing off the crime of blasphemy, the law is arguably a success. Despite this, the reaction to the new law has been almost entirely negative from both commentators in Ireland and abroad who regard it as unnecessary, retrograde, and sinister.[58] Even if we ignore the fact that most such comments are rather unrealistic in that they do not pick up on both (a) the constitutional obligations which faced the legislature and (b) the fact that the legislature was simply doing what the Supreme Court had asked it to do (and was doing so in a way that rendered the law unenforceable), what is notable about such comments is the fact that they almost uniformly (and irrespective of the source of such comments) regard a blasphemy law as an anachronistic blot on the Irish legal landscape. In other words, the law is perceived to violate rather than underpin any grounding ethic of the state. For many, therefore, the only appropriate step is for the constitution to be amended and the reference to blasphemy to be deleted.

That this is the case may be surprising to many external observers who would associate Ireland with deep religious piety and indeed who would observe that the text of the Irish constitution is imbued with overtly religious terminology. The point should be made, however, that despite certain racial stereotypes, certainly the Republic of Ireland (if not Northern Ireland) in 2011, is a place of considerable religious tolerance if not apathy. In fact, it is a radically different nation ideologically to that which existed when the Constitution came into being in 1937. At that time, the state was clearly extremely religious (though arguably more nationalistic than genuinely religious) and there was so little religious diversity beyond Roman Catholicism that the state could legitimately be seen as a monoreligious quasi theocracy.[59] It is unsurprising that a state of this kind would seek to be underpinned by a constitution which quite overtly found its ultimate authority in the Christian[60] (and arguably the Roman Catholic[61]) God. In 1937, moreover, at least in theory, the publication of blasphemy could have been massively offensive to vast numbers of people and, more importantly, it could have been seen as offensive to the values and beliefs that lay at the heart of the nation itself.[62] This may explain and possibly legitimate the constitutionalization of the crime of blasphemy in 1937 at the time; it was a case of a newly independent and rather vulnerable state determining that certain publications or utterances were so anathema to its core values that they simply transcended acceptability. The only analogous publication which could have generated such offence in an Ireland of the time might be one lampooning the events of the great famine of 1847, or mocking those people who had lost their lives in the fight for Irish independence.

Significantly, though, for a number of reasons, the core grounding ideology for Ireland is now completely changed – and has been so changed for at least 15 years[63] – and this ideological change has been reflected in legal developments. Thus since 1992, Irish law has been amended in a number of ways that involved the legalization of matters which had formerly been illegal because they violated the Catholic centered public morality of the state. Homosexual behavior was decriminalized as a new era of equality laws was ushered in;[64] contraceptives were legalized and

274   Neville Cox

contraceptive use encouraged;[65] the constitutional ban on divorce was removed by referendum in spite of strong opposition from the Roman Catholic hierarchy;[66] most dramatically, following a traumatic constitutional case in which the state attempted to injunct a 14 year old alleged rape victim from travelling to England for an abortion,[67] the absolute ban on abortion in Ireland was undercut. In all of these things, it is possible to see the law reflecting the fact that the grounding ethic of the state was changing, to the point that now the essential aspects of Irish public morality owe a great deal more to contemporary visions of human rights and equality, and considerably less to the teaching of the Catholic Church. Put another (and more accurate way), Christian teaching will, no doubt, influence the moral vision of the nation and will be reflected in law, but this will be because people approve of the essence of the teaching (with its focus on love, mutual respect, and the inalienable dignity of all people) and not because it *is* Christian teaching.

The point is that Ireland, while still by European standards a "religious" nation, is now in what many would regard as a "post-Catholic" era. Recent reports[68] into the systemic level of child abuse by priests and other religious leaders and the complicity of the whole Catholic hierarchy and leadership both in Ireland and in the Vatican at the time, have led to public revulsion at the extent to which such practices were allowed to go unchecked by the law and also to a significant mood of anticlericalism in the Ireland of 2011. In consequence, the Church is facing criticism and vitriol such as was unthinkable only 20 years ago, and there are increasing calls for a complete separation of church and state. In such an era, and whereas no doubt individuals will continue to be offended by blasphemies, blasphemy will not "offend the nation" to the point where it transcends legal acceptability.

For present purposes, therefore, what is relevant is that not only does a blasphemy law not "fit" in twenty-first century Ireland (not because it is inconceivable that a blasphemy law could ever be acceptable as a matter of principle, but rather because it is simply not warranted at the moment), but indeed the *existence* of a blasphemy law may be offensive to contemporary values. This is arguably why the proposed change in 2009 met with such criticism, albeit that some of that criticism suggested an objection to blasphemy laws that was positioned at an inappropriately general level of principle.

Offense to the Nation – The Example of Holocaust Denial

The Irish experience is, it is submitted a salutary one. Whether or not a blasphemy law can ever be justified (in principle), it clearly does represent an intrusion into the realm of free speech, and thus if an ethical case is to be made for a blasphemy law a key element of the argument, (certainly as it is made to those versed in and supportive of the Western view of rights) must be that such a law is actually sufficiently necessary that the interests of those offended by blasphemy can trump the rights to freedom of expression of the would be publisher of blasphemy. It will now be suggested that, in order for this appropriately to happen, it is necessary not only that individuals be

The Ethical Case for a Blasphemy Law 275

offended by the relevant material, but also that it offends the collective conscience of the nation as a whole and for this reason, transcends legal acceptability.

In order to consider this proposition, let us analyze another context in which speech has famously been restricted because of its inherent offensiveness, namely the approach of German constitutional law to the controversial issue of holocaust denial. In 1994, when the German constitutional court held that the "revisionist historian" David Irving's right to free speech under Article 5 of the German Basic Law (the constitution or *Grundgestz*) could be limited to prevent him from speaking his holocaust denial theory, its conclusion was based, in large measure, on the fact that such speech struck at the very essence of the nation by insulting the dignity of both holocaust survivors and those who has perished in that context.[69] Put another way, and whereas no doubt individual Germans would have been offended by the speech, the reason why it could validly be restricted was because it was grossly offensive (or in the terminology of Joel Feinberg *profoundly offensive*) at an objective and nationwide level, in that it struck at something fundamental to the collective consciousness of the nation. In dramatic terms it pierced the *soul* of the nation. Indeed as has been discussed earlier, it was for similar reasons that Chief Justice Rehnquist of the American Supreme Court was prepared to restrict free speech where flag burning was at issue in *Texas v. Johnson*.[70]

These two factual examples are important. Put simply, it is common knowledge that the US flag is of enormous emotional, cultural, and social significance within America, and hence that the wanton destruction of such a symbol (an act which involves a deliberate affront to something which, for whatever reason is a basic aspect of the American psyche) would be genuinely and offensive both to individuals and to the collective conscience of the nation. Similarly, it is common knowledge that, again, holocaust denial in Germany is something which (perhaps, and for obvious reasons, peculiarly to countries like Germany and Austria[71]) transcends normal levels of offensiveness and strikes at a particularly sensitive chord within the national psyche. Hence it may be argued that the prohibition of such activities within a nation is acceptable for that nation (and even, possibly, for a country like America which does not normally permit the prohibition of speech or expressive conduct on the grounds of its offensiveness) precisely because, on this basis, the level of offence which it causes is *objectively* sufficient and impacts on the people *collectively* and not merely *individually*.

This view of the matter may also explain why the decision in *Holocaust Denial* is arguably justifiable in spite of one superficially sizable gap in the case made for its restriction, namely that it would be remarkably easy for sensitive persons to avoid any offense arising out of Irving's speech. The point is that in order for someone to be offended by the words *themselves* as uttered by David Irving at the meeting for which he was denied a license to speak, it would be necessary for that person actually to attend at the meeting and actually to hear the words being spoken (or possibly to read the words in print), yet there was no suggestion that this was likely to happen. After all, it is simply inconceivable that anyone going to the meeting (organized by the far-right NDP) would not know in advance exactly what was to be discussed. Attendees at the meeting would presumably fit either into the category of persons who would support Irving's ideology, or else into the category of persons who opposed it – in other words, there would be no random strangers who would be *surprised* by what they heard. Yet for people in the first category, no offence would be suffered and for people in the second it is strongly arguable that they had actually knowingly sought out any offence which was suffered and must therefore, be taken to have consented to it.[72] Put simply, they would be in the position of someone who voluntarily attends at a movie or reads a book that [s]he knows will offend him or her and then seeks to take legal action against the producer of the movie or publisher of the book because of the offence which [s]he suffered. Hence (and again at a superficial level) anyone likely to be offended by Irving's words would either not hear them (because they would not go to the meeting) or would have sought out the offence suffered and hence their injured feelings should not receive redress. At a superficial level, this would suggest that the speech should therefore not be restricted because of its offensiveness.

Yet what this analysis fails to take into account is the fact that in as much as the speech offends the nation, what is repugnant is not the words in and of themselves, but rather the mere fact that they exist; or more accurately, that the law (and hence the state) *permits* them to exist unchecked.[73] As Ellis points out[74] "As a matter of psychological fact, what people find offensive is not the contents of erotic books, but the books themselves." Where something as serious as holocaust denial is at stake, the bare and unchecked existence of such speech becomes a national abomination.

In this light, moreover, the utilitarian argument that such kinds of speech should be permitted in order to avoid giving the speaker publicity which will enhance his cause also breaks down. In fact, publicity becomes very important in that what is being trumpeted by a decision such as that in *Holocaust Denial* is nothing less than the content of a national ideal with a concomitant "outing" of the forces and factors which strike at this ideal. No doubt if David Irving had been allowed to speak his theory and a debate was to ensue, the obvious academic limitations of his argument might have shone through and he might have faded into relative obscurity. If his speech had just been offensive to individuals this might have been the sensible thing to do. But from much of the jurisprudence of the German constitutional court an inference can be drawn that the court views itself as having a responsibility to uphold and herald the ideals of the new Germany.[75] Thus, the restriction on speech in this case was (on this view) both legitimate (in restricting speech the concept of which offended the nation) and productive (in that it was a vehement statement of the ideal of the nation and a rallying cry to those who supported such an ideal).

Thus, in conclusion it may be suggested that the logic behind a holocaust denial law in Germany is that it may be valid for a nation to restrict free speech by law where the speech, by its very existence, is offensive both to members of the nation *and* also to the "soul" of the nation itself. This logic is important in that it both objectifies the offense principle, and also allows for offensive speech to be permitted save in the most extreme circumstances – namely where the speech is profoundly offensive to the collective conscience of the nation rather than simply to individuals within it.

Offense to the Nation and the Case of Blasphemy against Islam

As has been mentioned at the outset, however, many people (and in particular we will focus on the position of many if not most devout Muslims) define themselves by reference to their religion and not their nationality. The question therefore arises as to whether a similar logic as was applied in the case of holocaust denial may be applied in the context of certain blasphemies. In other words, does the fact that both Muslims and Islam are outraged by certain blasphemies mean that such speech, like holocaust denial in Germany, *may* be legitimately prohibited by law and as a matter of principle?

In order for this to be remotely possible (or to be understandable), two initial hurdles must, however, be overcome.

Jurisdictional Concerns

The first such hurdle is a jurisdictional one. When Germany (for example) restricts holocaust denial, it does so in circumstances where the boundaries of its jurisdiction are obvious and recognizable within the law of nations. Hence, whether or not we approve of such restrictions, we can easily (or relatively easily) accept the legitimacy of a sovereign nation sorting out questions of the appropriate balance to be drawn *for itself* as between rights, interests, and ideals (and indeed we can say that the approach of the law is, perhaps, only understandable in Germany). Yet where Islam is concerned (and unless we are talking about a state which is governed by Islamic Law) we are talking about a quasi-nation that knows no recognizable boundaries because it works on the assumption that its legal order is predicated on universal truth. In other words, the ultimate source of this "nation's" authority is God, whose jurisdiction is the entire universe. Thus if a case can be made that Islam is as offended by blasphemy as Germany is by holocaust denial, we still run up against the argument that this should be dealt with through religious teaching *by Islam* and private religious observance and not by use of law in a democratic state.

The hypothesis of this chapter, however, is not that Muslims can legitimately require all temporal governments in the world to enact blasphemy laws because Islam is affronted by insults to God, or worse, that they can assume the mantle of the state and take retributive action against publishers of such blasphemy. It is not even that individual states *should* restrict blasphemy as a recognition of the validity of the Islamic reaction. The purpose of this chapter rather is simply to suggest that the desire of Muslims individually and Islam generally to prohibit certain allegedly blasphemous publications and the view that the interests of justice require such prohibition are, in principle, no different from the equivalent views of Germans and the German state where holocaust denial is at issue or those of Chief Justice Rehnquist in the context of flag burning in America. Rather in all these cases there is a view that the very notion that the speech in question should be allowed to proceed unfettered represents an insult to the national ideal and an abomination which must be targeted *in the name of that national ideal.*

In other words, whereas this initial objection raises strong concerns in respect of practicalities (and also in respect of the question of the extent to which democratic states with strong Muslim populations should, in the interests of democracy, regard the interests of such Muslims as being a component part of the national interest) it does not really relate to the *ethical* case which may or may not be made for a blasphemy law.

The "Violent" Islamic Reaction to Blasphemy

The second initial hurdle to be crossed in order for this theory to be comprehensible relates to the popular perception that the attitude of Islam towards blasphemy is fundamentalist, disproportionate, and violent and hence should be opposed rather than supported. The first two of these three perceptions can be dealt with easily; the Muslim attitude to matters concerning God is indeed fundamentalist, but there is nothing necessarily wrong with being fundamentalist about one's beliefs. After all, those who argue for an untrammelled right to freedom of expression are also fundamentalist in their views. It is one of the remarkably subtle forms of racism in twenty-first century Western culture that the term "Islamic fundamentalist" has been ascribed sinister undertones. Second, the contention that the reaction is disproportionate is merely a subjective value judgment. No one in Western society would say that, for example, imposing criminal sanction on a convicted rapist is a disproportionate reaction. This is, of course, because of the view which Western society takes of the value of bodily integrity and (arguably) because of its perceptions of the importance of equality. Similarly in Islamic societies, the importance of reverence for God and for the divine law is such that punishment for irreverence or for violation of the precepts of God will never appear disproportionate.

The third perception – that the Islamic reaction to blasphemy is also a violent or crazed and certainly illegal one – is more troubling. When an average Western audience looks at controversies such as, for example those which arose when Salman Rushdie published *The Satanic Verses* in 1988, or in the context of the so called Danish cartoons controversy in 2005 it is inevitably drawn to images of riots by Muslims both in the country in which publication initially occurred and worldwide. Indeed in the case of Rushdie, the defining memory of the controversy for many is surely the act of a senior Muslim leader (the Ayatollah Khomeini in Iran) in pronouncing a death sentence on the author and calling for a general effort on the part of all people and especially Muslims, to execute him. Thus the public reaction is that the response of Muslims to so called blasphemies is unacceptable in nature, and hence that even if they do genuinely suffer offence in such situations, it would be inappropriate and bad policy for the laws of any civilized nation to grant any concessions to such people.

The Ethical Case for a Blasphemy Law

It is, however, my submission, that in fact the view that "Muslims inherently react violently to Blasphemy" is simply incorrect. It is, at best, a gross oversimplification of what is actually happening and at worst an insidious form of stereotyping by persons with an interest in ensuring that the claims of Muslims generally are not given due consideration. In fact, to take both the Rushdie case and the case of the Danish cartoons, it is strongly arguable that in both cases, what occurred was a multifaceted response to the publication in question, of which the violent or illegal aspect was simply one (albeit a highly publicized) component and, in the case of the Danish cartoons, it was also very much the last element in a chain of reactions. That this is the case is made out by a brief evaluation of actually happened in both cases.

Take first of all the case of Rushdie's *The Satanic Verses*. At the outset, it is necessary to make the point that despite a myth that radical Muslims targeted the book because it criticized Islam, in fact the book was genuinely offensive to Muslims.[76] So, to take just a few examples the author uses the word *Mahound* to describe the Prophet-like figure who is one of the central characters in the book.[77] The term means *devil* and is inherently insulting to Muslims. The Prophet (who of course is the most sacred figure within Islam other than Allah himself) is portrayed as being unscrupulous, lecherous, and manipulative, and as a magician, a conjurer, and a false Prophet who fabricated the Koran. His companions, Salman-al-Farsi and Bilal, who are sacred figures in the Islamic faith, are referred to as *some sort of bums from Persia* and as *clowns*, and *profligates*. In addition, God is referred to as the *destroyer of men*, and Abraham, the father of Ishmael who was the founder of Islam, who is revered by Islam as a Prophet, is vilified.[78] The Archangel Gabriel, another sacred figure, is reduced to being a "pet" obeying its master. Further insult is generated by, for example, a sequence set in a brothel, where the whores are named after the Prophet's twelve wives, who, within the Islamic faith are reverently called the *mothers of Muslims*. Finally by the very title of the book, Rushdie suggests that the Koran, which, according to Islamic belief has been preserved in its original form to this day, was subject to regular man made alterations.[79] The book was therefore deeply insulting for individual Muslims and, as with holocaust denial in Germany, it can be regarded as insulting to Islam itself as well and by reason of its existence.

This is something which perhaps requires one further comment. No doubt the Rushdie case involved many pressing political realities. So for example it seems clear that one reason why the Ayatollah announced his fatwah against Rushdie was to shore up his own domestic authority. More pertinently, however, a political reality which explains why the book offended Islam as a religion, is the fact that both politically and sociologically, Muslims, especially those living outside of Islamic nations see themselves as being in a vulnerable position within the world.[80] Since the time of the crusades, after all, Christianity and Islam have, however covertly, been at war. This tension has increased since the latter half of the twentieth century (and especially since the events of September 11, 2001).[81] There is, in other words a perception that the West proclaims its own morality as constituting universal truth and undermines the Islamic view of truth, holding it up as something to be mocked and reviled. Thus Webster says,[82]

What Muslims see in Rushdie's fictional adaptation of ancient stereotypes is not simply hatred, but the long, terrible, triumphalist hatred which the West has had for Islam almost since its beginning.

Certain protests both national and international greeted the publication of the book.[83] Most notably, for present purposes, the British Muslim Action Front attempted to use the British blasphemy laws to have the book banned.[84] As we have seen, the High Court, however, *per* Watkins, J. found against the Muslim petitioners, and said that existing case-law required that the offence of blasphemy continue to be confined to the protection of the established church. The court accepted that this was a gross anomaly,[85] but saw it as one that arose from the chains of history, which could be unlocked only by parliament. Moreover, because of the difficulty inherent in defining the term religion and the fact that an extended blasphemy law could amount to a significant dilution of the value of free expression, the Court suggested that even if it had the power to extend the blasphemy laws it would refrain from doing so. Indeed, there was an implication that the total abolition of all blasphemy laws would be its preferred solution.[86]

From the Muslim perspective, this represented a clear statement that the establishment in England simply did not have respect for them or for their interests. Protests followed as Muslim groups, first in Bradford,[87] and then in other British cities, burned copies of the book.[88] Muslim activists petitioned the government for an extension of the blasphemy laws to cover faiths other than Christianity. But again, in response, the Secretary of State for the Home Department said that existing legal mechanisms were inappropriate for dealing with matters of individual faith and Western journalists bemoaned the lack of tolerance of Muslims who denounced the book. British Muslims were particularly galled by these reactions which their opposition to the publication of the book aroused both because it indicated a disrespect for them on the part of the establishment and also because the Western liberals who criticized the Muslim reaction, appeared to be championing Rushdie's right to freedom of expression in writing the book, but denying their right to protest against its publication.[89] Finally the view that their interests were not being taken seriously was solidified both when the second issue of the newly created *Independent on Sunday* newspaper was almost entirely devoted to Salman Rushdie (and contained an article by Rushdie entitled *In Good Faith* in which he set out his intentions in writing *The Satanic Verses*[90] and suggested that the hostile reactions to his book were based on Muslim *misreading and misunderstanding* of what was in actuality, merely a dissent from orthodoxies) and later when the book was republished in paperback.

Despite the obvious increase in tension, Rushdie himself appeared oblivious to the risks involved[91] until February 14, 1989, when the Ayatollah Khomeini, the religious leader of Iran issued his now famous *fatwah*, an order for the execution of Rushdie and anyone else connected with the book.[92] Ettore Capriolo, translator of the Italian edition of the book, was beaten and stabbed. Hitoshi Igarashi, the Japanese translator was murdered as was Abdullah-al Ahdal, director of the Belgian

The Ethical Case for a Blasphemy Law

Islamic centre, who denounced the *fatwah* and said that the book should not be banned in a democratic country.[93]

So there were violent and illegal elements within the overall reaction to the book. Significantly, though, what should be clear is that it is unfair to characterize all Muslim reaction to *the Satanic Verses* as being inherently violent or illegal. In fact the vast bulk of such reaction was peaceful if passionate and was utterly genuine and indeed it is certainly arguable that the violent reaction followed the unfair characterization of the peaceful reaction as being nothing more than the shouts of intemperate zealots. In addition, what is key is that the *peaceful* reaction of shock and horror (while undoubtedly and no more than holocaust denial something that has been fuelled by its own controversy) indicates that what was at stake was material which both in and of itself and also by reason of the political and social context in which it was published, was something which was grossly offensive both to Muslims and to Islam itself

A similar analysis can be applied to the Danish cartoons controversy. The facts briefly are as follows. In September 2005, Flemming Rose, editor of the Danish newspaper *Jyllands Posten* commissioned 12 cartoonists to draw cartoons depicting the Prophet Mohammad. This was in itself a reaction to the fact that children's author Kåre Bluitgen had sought to publish a children's book about the life of the Prophet but had been unable to find an illustrator to work with him. The general perception was that such illustrators were scared to do so because of possible violence from Islamic extremists. Moreover, there was a significant basis for such fears in that there is, within Islam a cultural prohibition on any visual depiction of the prophet. On September 30, 2005, the 12 cartoons were published. Naturally they were all different, but the one link between them was that, in one form or another, they all represented the Prophet as having involvement with terrorism (and thus carried the implication that Islam was itself, connected with terrorism).

It will be obvious that these cartoons were grossly offensive to individual Muslims and to Islam as a religion. This is for two reasons; first (and far less significantly despite popular misunderstanding of the issue), there was the fact that *any* visual depiction of the Prophet is unacceptable to Muslims. Second, and more significantly however, the particular depictions at stake in this case were grossly offensive. We have already seen the extent to which the figure of the Prophet is revered within Islam. To treat the Prophet irreverently is thus unacceptable. Worse still, to lampoon him in any way by grotesque caricature, let alone to depict him as a terrorist is obviously incredibly offensive. At another level, however, there is an even more dramatic offensiveness at issue. The point is that most Islamic devotees would contend that, properly understood, Islam is a religion of peace, yet the cartoons carry the implication that it is a quasi-terrorist organization. Such a depiction is most grievously offensive for Muslims, in that it perverts the basic essence of their religion – and in doing so feeds off and refuels the Western stereotypes that, as has been discussed, have left Muslims in what they perceive to be a situation of vulnerability. Indeed the impact of these stereotypes were particularly marked in Denmark at the time, where there was a significant and vocal body of antiimmigration opinion and where Prime

Minister Rasmussen had himself come to power on a strong antiimmigration platform and with the support of the antiimmigration Danish People's Party. Moreover, on this analysis, the link between these cartoons and the situation of holocaust denial in Germany is thus readily understandable in that both offend what I have termed the "soul of the nation" rather than simply offending an individual reader.

Finally, in so far as the Islamic cartoons were concerned, there is, again, the additional Islamic perception that Western liberals (including Western governments) were using issues like the Danish cartoons controversy, deliberately to perpetuate a stereotype of Islam as an inherently and entirely evil organization where the most extreme views of radicals came to be regarded as an expression of mainstream doctrine which all Muslims shared, in order for western liberalism to gain and retain the moral high ground in its ongoing war with Islam (particularly in the post-9/11 era). The success of this perceived effort at racial stereotyping is evidenced, for example in the view held by many Americans at the time of the invasion of Iraq in 2003 that there must be a connection between Sadaam Hussein and Osama Bin Laden, despite the fact that the two were poles apart in ideological terms.[94]

As with the Rushdie affair, (indeed arguably more than the Rushdie affair), the initial reaction from Muslims was both muted and peaceful. In October 2005 11 ambassadors from Muslim majority countries who had been petitioned by Danish Imams asked for a meeting with Prime Minister Rasmussen to discuss a range of issues which they felt amounted to a general smear campaign against Islam, of which the cartoons controversy was but one example, and they asked the Prime Minister to "take all those responsible to task under the law of the land in the interest of inter-faith harmony, better integration and Denmark's overall relations with the Muslim world."[95] The Prime Minister wrote a letter in reply, noting that because of the nature of the right to freedom of expression, any governmental intrusion in what the press was doing would be impossible in Denmark and, despite further clarification from the Egyptian government that what was being sought was simply an official statement that there was an obligation to respect religions and to avoid offending members of a religion, the Prime Minister refused to meet the ambassadors – a decision which met with considerable criticism both at home and abroad.

Denmark does, in fact have a law which prohibits blasphemy, hence in October 2005 various Muslim groups made a complaint under this law.[96] Both the Regional Public Prosecutor in Viborg and later the Director of Public Prosecutions, however, determined that there should not be a prosecution as there was no evidence to support the argument that what had occurred constituted a criminal offence in that, according to both prosecutors, what was at issue was a matter of public interest and in such circumstances, the blasphemy law could not be enforced having regard to the need to protect the right to freedom of expression of the media.

Significantly then, the initial "Muslim response" to the cartoons, at both a political and public level was peaceful and in accordance with normal legal principles. Yet in both instances these responses were effectively ignored or rejected. The groups petitioning for a prosecution were told that the insult to their faith which

The Ethical Case for a Blasphemy Law   283

they perceived was a matter of public interest. Worse, the senior Islamic diplomats who had written to the Prime Minister were effectively told that their concerns were so insignificant that he could not even be bothered meeting with them to discuss such concerns. Moreover, much of the Western world (inevitably) took the side of the Danish publishers. Thus for example, Italian reform minister Roberto Calderoli (who again endorses a strongly antiimmigration stance) had t-shirts made depicting the cartoons and offered to hand them out to anyone who wanted them.[97] Moreover, the photos were republished in over 50 newspapers throughout Europe and the world. On the other hand, representatives of the Governments of the United States, Canada, the United Kingdom (and, indeed, Ireland) as well as the United Nations and the European Union all made statements essentially endorsing the right to free speech but stating also that it must be accompanied by responsibilities, one of which involved being sensitive to the beliefs of others.

In any event, dissatisfied with the lack of reaction of the Danish government to the issue, two Danish Imams prepared a dossier in respect of the issue and formed an umbrella group comprising various other Islamic organizations.[98] Representatives of this group then travelled to various middle eastern and Islamic countries distributing the dossier and making their case for support for their position. It was as a result of this that the issue became well known and sensationalized (and indeed hyped) and what followed was a succession of riots and violent acts with a widespread boycott of Danish goods, with embassies being burnt, and with over 100 deaths and various further high profile death threats being made.[99] In other words, at a certain point and in certain locations the vehemence of the reaction led to violence but, as with the Rushdie issue, it is simply wrong to suggest that there was an *inherently* violent reaction against the cartoons on the part of Muslims. Moreover, and making suitable allowances for the agendas pursued by political forces on both sides, the events indicate that where blasphemies of this kind occur, the offense in question is not merely suffered by Muslims but by the whole Islamic religion.

That being the case, we can overcome the opposition that sees Islamic reaction to blasphemy as inherently violent (we would not, for example, say that a holocaust denial law was inherently unacceptable because of sporadic illegal acts by those offended by holocaust denial) and move to the more substantive question of whether an ethical case can, on this basis, be made for a blasphemy law.

The Nature of Religious Belief

What the above analysis demonstrates is not that a blasphemy law is a good or a desirable thing, but merely that in so far as Islam as an ideology (and an individual Muslim or Muslims as a devotee) is concerned, the simple unchecked existence of certain blasphemies is profoundly offensive, in that they strike at something which, within the collective consciousness of Islamic ideology, should be off limits. Moreover, it is unnecessary in the case of blasphemy, that the words actually be heard or read by someone liable to be offended by them. Rather it is the concept that such blasphemies should be permitted to go unchecked and unpunished which is relevant, for it amounts to the legalized degradation or perversion of the essence of its value system. In other words, these blasphemies are offensive in exactly the same way as Holocaust denial is offensive in Germany or flag burning is offensive in America. Thus, if we are prepared to accept the principled nature of the opposition to holocaust denial, then we should logically accept the principled nature of a blasphemy law as being cut from the same cloth.

We now turn, however, to the second of the principled objections to a blasphemy law which was considered earlier, namely the view that there is something different about religion, such that whereas we may protect certain sensitivities from offence (including sensitivities in respect of holocaust denial), religious sensitivities do not come within this class.

As an initial point, it is worth noting that such a restriction on an offense principle is simply not one which is universally recognized at the level of International Human Rights evaluation, in that the notion that the right to free speech may be restricted in order to protect religious sensitivities is a well known and indeed often accepted one. Thus in its dealings with free speech, the United Nations Human Rights Council has controversially been concerned with the concept of defamation of religions, and has sought to take measures aimed at preventing the same.[100] Similarly, as far as the European Court of Human Rights is concerned, it would appear that a blasphemy law which restricts offensive speech in order to protect religious sensitivities is consistent with the requirements of Article 10 of the European Convention on Human Rights – albeit that this is perhaps in large measure a concession to the "margin of appreciation" afforded by the European Court to individual states where a proposed restriction on liberty is justified by reference to an element of the public morality of that state.[101] Hence in *Otto Preminger Institute v. Austria*,[102] the court upheld an Austrian blasphemy law and in doing so spoke of a right not to be offended in one's religious sensitivities.

Opponents of the notion of a blasphemy law (those who oppose such law genuinely on principle) will, however, point to what they may regard as two fundamental differences between a blasphemy law and a law prohibiting holocaust denial which, they will contend, explains why the former if not the latter is inherently unacceptable. First, they will say that religion is simply incapable of replacing nationality as a source of self-identification. Second, they will argue that a holocaust denial law protects the sensitivities of a citizen in respect of a vital aspect of his or her national identity, and that this is appropriate because one's national identity (like one's gender, color, or sexual orientation) is something self-defining and over which one has no control. Yet religion on the other hand (so the argument runs) is a matter of voluntary choice and if one chooses to be religious, one must deal with the consequences of such a choice, including the consequence that one may be routinely misunderstood by the society in which one lives and one cannot rely on the law for protection in this regard.

The Ethical Case for a Blasphemy Law

Let us first deal with the argument that religion is not a genuine source of self-identification. It is submitted, that such an argument ignores most starkly the reality of the nature of religion. The point is again worth making, that for a huge number of people in the world, their principle source of self-identification is *not* the name of the country in which they were born or happen to be resident (and of course one can quite easily choose and change one's nationality) but is instead their religion. Indeed it is further submitted that much of the intolerance displayed by allegedly liberal commentators in the face of Islamic reaction to "blasphemy" is arguably reflective of a failure to accept or process this point (and presumably it is, in fact, a virtually incomprehensible logic for people who do not come from such a position).

To understand this notion of religion replacing nationality as a primary source of self-identification it is of course necessary to understand what belief in God entails – namely a view that at some eternal and infinite level, there is a divine being in overall control of the planet, whose "jurisdiction" (to put it crudely) is the universe, and whose subjects are every life form within that jurisdiction. If one genuinely tries to understand the nature of a belief of this kind (without of course, having to subscribe to such a belief), and bears in mind the gigantic and eternal nature of the dominion of any such entity (should he or she exist) then it must surely be accepted that it is possible that the sense of identification and belonging which it provides to the believer is an incredibly profound and strong one. Logically such a sense of identification and belonging must also (arguably) be a somewhat vulnerable one (as compared to the sense of identification which one receives from one's nationality) in that, unlike one's nationhood, the identity which one receives from one's religious beliefs is constantly under threat from the possibility that God does not exist, and hence that one's beliefs are based on a falsehood. Nonetheless, the argument remains that if a nation may be protected from an attack on its fundamental values because of its inherent preciousness; there is no reason why religion may not similarly be protected.

What of the argument that the analogy between nationality and religion is invalid in that one chooses one's religion but is born into one's nationality (and even more emphatically into one's ethnicity or gender)? Again it is submitted that the argument that religion is a voluntary matter is a flawed one.[103] Quite apart from the fact that a person's religion may be more fundamental to him or her than race or gender, it is simply incorrect to suggest that religion is in any but the most literal sense a voluntary matter. After all, each of the major monotheistic religions requires an allegiance which transcends rationalization.[104] This does not mean that it is impossible to present rational arguments either for or against the truth of a particular religion. Furthermore, it does not preclude the possibility that some people will seek to approach religion from an intellectual or questioning standpoint. It does, however, mean that for many, perhaps even most seriously genuine followers, the decision to commit to a particular religion, while possibly the result of an accident of birth, is nonetheless one that is made on faith and without any methodical consideration of the truth or otherwise of alternative religions, nor is deviation from this religion possible in psychological terms for that person. In other words the likelihood of renouncing the religion into which one is born and to which one has clung devoutly, in favor of another religion, while by no means impossible, is slim – and arguably slimmer than the decision to change nationality. Fundamental in nature, religious faith for those who are genuinely committed is, thus, essentially involuntary, self-defining, and inexorable.

If this is true, then, that one's religion can become the essence of one's self-identification and is not genuinely a voluntary matter for many if not most people, it is presumably also true that something which demeans that religion at a fundamental level can be as powerfully and profoundly offensive an attack as is, for example, a statement which strikes at the very core of a nation's value system – in the manner that, for example, holocaust denial appears to do in Germany. Again this is not to say that either holocaust denial or blasphemy *should* be legally prohibited, but simply that it is difficult to explain why an Islamic leader or an individual Muslim who wishes the publication of blasphemy to be a crime must inevitably be classifiable as an intolerant religious fundamentalist, whereas a German who supports a law prohibiting holocaust denial (whether or not we agree with him or her) may be regarded as having a fair point, or why certain commentators might argue that the latter restriction on speech *is* potentially acceptable as a matter of principle but the former is inevitably not, being archaic and reactionary. Indeed there may be a hint in the reaction of many in the West to the notion of a blasphemy law, that their condemnation of perceived intolerance may carry deeply if unintentionally ironic undertones. On this basis, it is difficult to see why, in the right circumstances, blasphemy laws cannot simply be justified on normal principles applying to the restriction on free speech

Conclusion

All of the above of course does not amount to any sort of argument for the proposition that any particular nation should enact a law which limits free speech in order to protect the religious sensitivities of devotees. Indeed more particularly, it does not even attempt to deal with:

- The particular jurisdictional complications connected with the notion of a nation within a nation, and the question of whether a recognized sovereign country like Britain or Denmark (or indeed Ireland) should ever consider enacting a law which is aimed at preventing offence which, whereas it does not constitute a grave insult to the nation as a whole, nonetheless does constitute such a grave insult to members of a religion within that nation, whose status as members of that religion may be more important to them than their status as citizens of the state; and
- The *content* of a blasphemy law, including such vexed questions as how to define religion or how to assess whether there is genuine offence suffered or whether, instead, the reaction of the person allegedly offended is simply unreasonably vitriolic.

Rather, as has been explained, the hypothesis of this chapter is more modest than this, namely to propose that in as much as membership of a religion may be a form of virtually involuntary citizenship to certain people – and especially those who regard their religion as a form of global nation – the links between the kind of attack on the dignity of the nation which we see with holocaust denial in Germany and the kind of attack on Islam which is felt by many in the context of certain blasphemies may give us pause for thought. In particular an appreciation of such links may go some way to dispelling the notion that the only people who could support a blasphemy law (or a law protecting religious sensibilities) *in appropriate circumstances* are intemperate, illiberal reactionary zealots. Rather they, like those who objected to Nazi marches in Skokie Illinois, or flag burning in Texas, or to David Irving's posturing in Germany, may simply be people who see the entity from which they derive their sense of belonging as being grotesquely undermined by a particular statement or other communication, and who wish to use the law to prevent this from happening. At the very least, such an understanding of the issue commits those who support free speech to argue against a blasphemy law at a more advanced level of principle, rather than permitting them to assume that it is their opponents and not they whose views are rooted in intolerance.

Notes

1 See for example the comments of the Reporters without Borders group at www.rsf.org/spip.php?page=article&id_article=35672 (accessed June 28, 2010).
2 See "Sudan charges British teacher in Muhammad teddy bear case," *New York Times* November 28, 2007, "Sudan jails teacher for teddy bear name," *Herald Sun* December 1, 2007
3 See "Jerry Springer the Opera puts Blasphemy in the Dock," *Daily Telegraph*, November 20, 2007. In *R (on the application of Green) v City of Westminster Magistrates' Court & Ors* [2007] EWHC 2785 it was held by the English High Court that a prosecution would not be permitted to proceed against the producers of the show in question.
4 See on this issue (which is dealt with in more detail later) O'Dell (2009).
5 Thus in March 2009, the Human Rights Council passed a resolution condemning "defamation against religion." See generally www.reuters.com/article/idUSTRE52P6 0220090326 (accessed June 28, 2010). See also http://daccess-dds-ny.un.org/doc/UNDOC/GEN/G06/139/90/PDF/G0613990.pdf?OpenElement (accessed June 28, 2010).
6 Again this issue is dealt with in detail later. See generally Cowell (2006).
7 See for example Greenslade "Ireland's new Blasphemy Law is a Disgraceful Inhibition of Free Speech" at www.guardian.co.uk/media/greenslade/2010/jan/06/freedom-of-speech-press-freedom (accessed June 28, 2010) and Healy (2009).
8 In fact Article 10(2) of the European Convention on Human Rights permits the right to freedom of expression to be restricted in the interests of "Public morality." To some extent the jurisprudence of the European Court of Human Rights is uncertain on this point. The court has regularly spoken of the freedom to "shock, offend and disturb" (*Handyside v. UK* (1976) 1 EHRR 737, (1979) 1 EHRR 737, [1976] ECHR 5, [1976]

ECHR 5493/72) but, as we shall see, it has always upheld the legitimacy of a state having a blasphemy law on its statute books. See for example *Otto Preminger Institute v. Austria* (1995) 19 EHRR 35. See also *Wingrove v. UK*, (1997) 24 EHRR.

9 For a bibliography of materials on the subject see www.york.cuny.edu/~drobnick/holbib.html (accessed June 28, 2010).

10 Generally on this issue see the decision of the US Supreme Court in *Texas v. Johnson* 491 US 397. See also Tucker (1986) and Barendt (2005).

11 On a related point see Dershowitz (2007).

12 Joel Feinberg famously used the term "profound offense" to denote those kinds of offense which are not specific to individuals by targeting their senses (and which constitute offensive nuisances) but rather which are impersonal and cause offense by reason of the fact that they affect the victim's sense of reverence or view of what is appropriate. See Feinberg (1985).

13 An example of this in practice may well be a law against public nudity. After all, nudity is an inherently natural state nor is there anything empirically *wrong* with being naked, but to many people the concept of public nudity (or worse, public fornication) is unacceptable because it is offensive and it is offensive because it strikes at a settled public consensus of what is and what is not acceptable upon which consensus the society is, at least in part, built. This analysis is, of course, not far removed from Lord Devlin's famous "social disintegration" theory which held that public morality could *in principle* be enforced because society was at least in part dependent on such public morals. See Devlin (1965).

14 Generally see Ely (1975).

15 The notion of the preciousness of nationality as a source of self-identification for both individuals and society is well illustrated by the nature of the reaction to the attacks on the Twin Towers on September 11, 2001. Naturally there was horror at the scale of atrocity, the loss of human life, and the possibility that future attacks might follow. Yet similar attacks in other countries (even when American targets were involved) did not and could not have provoked the level of reaction *by Americans* that followed on 9/11 – and this is obvious. The point is that what happened for many Americans on that day was an outrageous attack on something utterly precious – namely American values and beliefs and the very concept of America itself. Would people on September 12, 2001 have been prepared for the law to permit a jihadist group in New York to stage a celebratory parade or to lampoon the American situation in a crude newspaper cartoon (and apart from the obvious risk of counter violence this would entail)? The answer, surely, is no. The citizens of the nation are bound in reverence to the land which gives them a sense of identity and therefore that which undermines America hurts Americans at the most profound level possible.

16 Generally see Webster (1990), Blom-Cooper (1981), Walter (1977), Simpson (1993), Cox (2000a).

17 Simpson (1993, p. 7).

18 See Lee (1990), and Cox (2000a). See also Travis (2004).

19 See Cox (2000a, pp. 5ff).

20 *Taylor's Case*, (1676) 1 Vent 293, 3 Keble 607 (1676). See generally, Levy (1981).

21 Feinberg (1985) p. 194. See also Smith (1990, pp. 15–16).

22 *Woolston's Case*, Fitzg 64, 2 Str 834, 1 Barn KB 162 (1729).

23 As Baron Alderman put it in *R v. Gathercole* "If this is only a libel on the whole Roman Catholic Church generally, the defendant is entitled to be acquitted. A person without

being liable to prosecution for it, may attack Judaism or Mohammedanism or even any sect of the Christian religion save the established religion of the country, and the only reason why the latter is in a different situation from the others, is because it is the form established by law and is therefore a part of the constitution of the country" *R v. Gathercole* (1838) 2 Lew 237 at 284 ER 1140 at 1145.

24 The case seen as beginning a move to a "new" blasphemy law is *R v. Hetherington*, (1841) 4 St Tr 563, where the court found that mere denial of Christian doctrine did not constitute blasphemy. See Robertson (1993).

25 Generally see Calder-Marshall (1972).

26 In 1833 in a parliamentary address Lord Macauly said that "It is monstrous to see any judge try a man for blasphemy under the present law. Every man ought to be at liberty to discuss the evidences of religion. But no man ought to be at liberty to force upon unwilling ears and eyes, words and sights which must cause irritation." See Kenny (1923, p. 135).

27 Notable among these were the prosecutions arising out of Thomas Paine's seminal work *Age of Reason*. See for example, *Thomas Carlile*'s case, (1819) 1 St. Tr. (ns) 1387, *Mary Carlile*'s case, (1821) 1 St Tr. (ns) 1033. Generally see Clifford (1993).

28 *R v. Bradlaugh*, (1833) 15 Cox CC 217, *R v. Ramsay & Foote*, (1883) Cox CC 23. Generally see Calder-Marshall (1972, pp. 169ff).

29 *R v. Bradlaugh*, p. 236.

30 [1917] AC 406.

31 *R v. Gott*, (1922) 16 Criminal App Reps. 87. Finally, it is also clear that the modern (that is, twentieth century) blasphemy law was also a crime of strict liability, to the extent that the fact that the publisher may not have considered that the impugned material *was* blasphemous is irrelevant.

32 [1979] AC 617. Generally see Cox (2000a) pp. 23ff, Robertson (1993, p. 249), Buxton (1978). The most significant clarification of blasphemy law afforded by the House of Lords judgment in this case is that the crime may be committed unintentionally – that is one can be convicted of blasphemy without intending to blaspheme.

33 Lord Sumner (at pp. 457ff in *Bowman v. Secular Society*) did suggest that the new blasphemy law continued to apply only to the established church, but this proposition was not endorsed (nor indeed rejected) by the rest of the court. For criticism of this suggestion by Lord Sumner see Cox (2000a, p.17).

34 [1991] 1 All ER 306.

35 See *inter alia* Cox (2000a) pp. 38ff, Ahsan and Kidwai (1993), Eralp (1989), Easterman (1992).

36 For analysis of the social problems which this statement created see Lee (1990, p. 88). Generally see Robertson and Nicol (1993 p. 163) for the view that "To punish Rushdie ... would have been offensive to justice, but no more so than the punishment of the editor of *Gay News*." See also Cox (1997).

37 See for example Conway (1974), Ellis (1984). See also the Law Commission (UK) (1985), Law Reform Commission (Ireland) (1991).

38 See Blom-Cooper (1981, p. 12) and, for a different view Simpson (1993, p. 21). See generally Feinberg (1985, p. 193) for the view that "It is because most people hold some things to be sacred ... that blasphemous epithets ... can be so powerfully offensive and so effective as insults, exclamations, oaths and the like."

39 See also Blom-Cooper (1981, p. 12) for the view that "Public outrage at the contents of an idea expressed should never be sufficient to warrant the suppression of that idea.

If this were not so, toleration of the views of minorities would be jeopardized whenever they were sufficiently unpopular with majorities."

40   See for example Cox (2000a, p. 173).

41   Moreover, this does not even take into account the additional fact that some people are simply more sensitive than others.

42   Article 40.6.1.

43   O'Higgins (1960, p. 153), Cox (2000a, chapter 3). See also the Law Reform Commission (Ireland) (1991) p. 81 and *Corway v. Independent Newspapers*, [2000] 1 ILRM 426 at 436. It is not clear how the Irish statutory prohibition on blasphemy fits into this equation. Under section 13(1) of the 1961 Defamation Act the punishment for publishing or printing a blasphemous or offensive libel consisted of a fine of £500 or two years in prison. Section 13(2) of the same act provided for extensive provisions for search and seizure on suspicion of the existence of blasphemous materials. This Act has been repealed by the Defamation Act 2009 which, as we shall see, provides for a statutory offense of blasphemy. The other statutory provision concerned with blasphemy is s.7 of the 1923 Censorship of Films Act which permits a certificate for a film to be refused on the grounds *inter alia* of its blasphemous content.

44   See Law Reform Commission (Ireland) (1991) para 1:14 also O'Higgins (1960) p. 159. See also Levy (1981, p. 334) and Matthews (1839).

45   See Law Reform Commission (Ireland) (1991) para 1:15 and Kenny (1923, p. 140.

46   *Padre Petcherine Case* (1855) 7 Cox 79. See Kenny (1923, p. 140), the Law Reform Commission (Ireland) (1991) para 1:16 and O'Higgins (1960, p. 160).

47   *Padre Petcherine Case* (1855) 7 Cox 79, p. 84.

48   [2000] 1 ILRM 426.

49   [2000] 1 ILRM 426 at p. 430. The definition from Murdoch (1988) said that "The crime … consists of indecent and offensive attacks on Christianity or the scriptures or sacred persons or objects, calculated to outrage the feelings of the community …the mere denial of Christian doctrine is not sufficient to constitute the offence."

50   [2000] 1 ILRM at 435.

51   [2000] 1 ILRM 426 at 436–437.

52   See Cox (2000a, pp. 56ff), Cox (2000b), Ranalow (2000, p. 95,) Purcell (1999), Synon (1999), O'Hanlon (1999, p. 19).

53   Cox (2000a, p. 57). See O'Hanlon (1999, p. 19).

54   Indeed the call is resonant of that made by the Supreme Court in respect of Article 40.3.3 of the constitution (the clause protecting the right to life of the unborn) in *AG v. X* [1992] IR 1, where legislative *inactivity* was popularly blamed for something of a constitutional crisis faced by Ireland in respect of a 14 year old rape victim who wished to travel to the United Kingdom for an abortion but who faced an application by the state for a court order preventing her from doing so. What is, perhaps, surprising, therefore, is the reaction of many who would have supported the Supreme Court's view as to the culpability of the legislature in failing to legislate for abortion, yet who characterized the recent legislative step in doing precisely what the Supreme Court called for it to do in *Corway* as being unnecessary. The point is, perhaps worth making, that genuine principles must be consistently held; the alternative is simply to admit that one wants what one wants and not on the basis of principle.

55   The Act came into force on January 1, 2010.

The Ethical Case for a Blasphemy Law   291

56   The reason *why* the step of holding a constitutional referendum on the issue in 2009 was
     so problematic was because clearly this would have led to significant expense being
     incurred (which would be unacceptable in a recessionary era) unless it was held on the
     same day as some other national plebescite (and this was what the Law Reform Commission
     had essentially recommended in 1991). But the only plebescite to be held that year was
     one in respect of the European Union focused Lisbon Treaty, which, in the view of the
     government vitally needed support. One major strand of opposition to this treaty came
     from people who argued that it would involve a devaluing of national values, especially
     religious values. Hence to hold a referendum asking the people to remove the constitu-
     tional reference to blasphemy on the same day as that relating to the Lisbon treaty would
     have imperiled the passage of the latter in that it would have created a link in the voters'
     minds between it and the removal of legal protection for national religious values.
57   Prohibition of Incitement to Hatred Act 1989.
58   See among the many such comments Reidy (2009), O'Neil (2009). A notable response
     came from the group Atheist Ireland which published 25 quotes on its webpage which,
     it claimed, might generate prosecution for itself. With respect, it is the view of this
     author that this was something of a feeble stunt. See generally www.blasphemy.ie
     (accessed June 28, 2010). For reporting see Adam (2010).
59   Generally see Farrell (1988).
60   So for example (and quite apart from the constitutional reference to blasphemy) the
     preamble to the constitution states that the document is "In the name of the most holy
     Trinity" and acknowledges "all our obligations to our Divine Lord, Jesus Christ."
     Article 6 provides that "All powers of government, legislative, executive and judicial,
     derive, under God, from the people" and Article 44 provides that "The State acknowl-
     edges that the homage of public worship is due to Almighty God. It shall hold His
     Name in reverence, and shall respect and honor religion." Finally, the *interpretation* of
     the constitution, was, for many years informed by a Thomistic view of natural law. So
     in *Ryan v. AG* [1965] IR 294 Kenny J, held that the type of rights protected by the
     Irish constitution, albeit not enumerated therein were those which flowed from the
     "Christian and Democratic nature of the state." See also Walsh J's judgement in *McGee
     v. A.G.* [1974] IR 274.
61   Up until 1973 the Constitution had provided (Article 44.1.3) that "The State recog-
     nises the special position of the Holy Catholic Apostolic and Roman Church as the
     guardian of the Faith professed by the great majority of the citizens." Following the 5th
     amendment to the constitution, however, this clause was removed.
62   This perhaps explains why there was so little reporting of sexual abuse by priests at the
     time (and why any such reporting tended not to be acted on). In other words, an alle-
     gation that a priest was abusing a child was seen as a blasphemy, being an attack on the
     whole *modus operandi* of the state.
63   For a somewhat partisan account of such changes see Bacik (2004).
64   The decriminalization of homosexual behavior was effected by the Criminal Law
     (Sexual Offences) Act 1993, albeit foreshadowed in large measure by the decision of
     the European Court of Human Rights in *Norris v. Ireland* (1991) 13 EHRR 186,
     (1988) 13 EHRR 186, [1988] ECHR 22, [1988] 13 EHRR 186, 13 EHRR 186.
65   The statutes which genuinely liberalized the law on contraceptive use in Ireland were
     the The Health (Family Planning) (Amendment) Act, 1992 and the Health (Family
     Planning) (Amendment) Act, 1993.

292   *Neville Cox*

66   The original constitutional ban on divorce was lifted by the 15th Amendment to the Constitution in 1995. See Burley and Regan (2002).

67   *AG v. X* [1992] IR 1

68   See the Ryan Report (2009) and the Murphy Report (2009). Both reports disclosed widespread and systemic abuse of children by representatives of the Roman Catholic church, and a massive failure of the institutional church to deal with something which it knew was occurring.

69   From the huge amount of literature on this topic, see for example Teachout (2006), Fish (2001), Kahn (2006), Knechtle (2008), Rosenfeld (2003).

70   A similar logic is found in the opinion of Judge O'Connor in the US Supreme Court's decision in *Virginia v. Black* 123 S. Ct. 1536; 155 L. Ed. 2d 535 from which an inference can be drawn that one of the reasons why cross burning could, in her view, legitimately be restricted was because of its long and pernicious history within American culture.

71   In February 2006, David Irving was, in fact, sentenced to three years in prison in Austria for holocaust denial. See http://news.bbc.co.uk/2/hi/4733820.stm (accessed June 28, 2010). In December 2006 he was released when an appeal judge suspended the final two thirds of his sentence.

72   On the significance of reasonable avoidability of offence see Feinberg (1985, pp. 60 et seq).

73   To this extent, it may in fact be the immoral nature of any publication rather than its offensiveness which is the real reason why people would like to see it prohibited.

74   Ellis (1984, p. 21).

75   See for example the *Luth* case 7 BverfGE 198 (1958).

76   Mahmood Ahmed Mirpuri, secretary of the Islamic Sharia Council in Britain said that the book was *a blatant insult to Islam*, see *New Statesman*, October 15, 1988. For further analysis of the reasons why the book was offensive, see Webster (1990, pp. 34–44, 96–97), see also Lee (1990, p. 307). In addition see Umar Azam (1990), Akhtar (1989), Ahsan and Kidwai, (1993) and Eralp (1989).

77   The term *Mahound* is used predominantly in chapter 2 of *The Satanic Verses.*

78   This vilification, apart from the references to Abraham as a *bastard*, concerns Abraham's treatment of his Egyptian slave girl Hagar. See Genesis, chapter 16, and also, Chapter 21: 8–21.

79   One of the most controversial topics in the whole Rushdie affair is the question of the *Satanic Verses* themselves. The title of the book refers to an historical incident the veracity of which is uncertain and a matter of controversy for Islamic scholars. The verses in question are in Arabic, *tilk al-gharaniq al-ula wa inna shafaata-hunna la-turtaja*, which translated, means *these are exalted females whose intercession is to be desired* (See Rushdie, 1988, p. 340). The verses comprising this sentence are said to have been added to the 53rd Sura of the Koran entitled *Surat-annajm*, in order to acknowledge the validity of the goddesses Lat, Manat and Al'Uzza. The tradition goes on to say that the verses were later withdrawn and denounced as of Satanic origin. Some commentators, and Islamic historians accept the validity of this tradition, but the prevailing Muslim view is that it is a fabrication created and developed by Western orientalist unbelievers to imply that the Prophets were not infallible. See Muir (1986). See also Dashti (1985), especially pp. 32ff, Haykal M.H. (1976) especially pp. 105ff, and Bashier (1991) especially pp. 173ff. Most notable, in this context, because of its similarities with Rushdie's book is Watt (1956).

The Ethical Case for a Blasphemy Law 293

80 Webster (1990). Also Armstrong (1988).

81 See Webster (1990, p. 38) for a description of anti-Arab racist cartoons in the United States at the time of the OPEC oil crisis in 1973, which depicted Muslims as being anti-Semitic and greedy.

82 Webster (1990, p. 40). As Samuel (1992, p. 3) points out "The Muslim world is deeply sensitive to the plot of international racism mounted against it ... and to anything that attacks it, from American and Israeli F-1 8s to the various other Arab regimes themselves. The kind of attack sustained by a trendy cultured Indian/British writer will be taken as an attack not only on the hermeneutic intricacies of Islam, but also on the code of living which has historically always been manipulated by the west for the latter's benefit." For an interesting analysis of Western bias against Islam as it is shaped in our print and electronic media see Edward Said (1981).

83 The book was published in September 1988. In October 1988, the book was banned in both India and South Africa. On November 8, 1988, it won the annual Whitbread award for best novel. Also in November 1988, it was banned in Sudan and in Bangladesh. In December 1988 it was banned in Sri Lanka. Since then it has been banned in Pakistan (February 1989), Iran, Tanzania, Singapore and Indonesia, (March 1989), and Venezuela (June 1989).

84 *R v Bow Street Magistrates Court ex parte Choudhury* [1991] 1 All ER 306.

85 *R v Bow Street Magistrates Court ex parte Choudhury* [1991] 1 All ER 306, p. 317. Watkins J. is in fact quoting the comments of the 1914 Attorney General Sir John Simon.

86 *R v Bow Street Magistrates Court ex parte Choudhury* [1991] 1 All ER 306, pp. 318–320. The court also rejected an argument based on the European Convention of Human Rights, on the basis that an extension of the blasphemy law to encompass Salman Rushdie, would offend against Article 7's prohibition on retrospective criminal offences.

87 Bowen (1992).

88 These book burnings occurred predominantly in January 1989, significantly, one month before the *fatwah* was announced.

89 This inconsistency prompted Rana Kabbani to ask *Is the Western conscience not selective?* Kabbani (1989). In addition as Samuel (1992, p. 3) points out, the International Media's response to the Rushdie situation *was stereotypically and informationally dead-ended*. Most notable, in his view, was the fact that in covering the Rushdie incident, few Western journalists saw the need to interview third world intellectuals.

90 This is reprinted in Rushdie's 1992 collection of essays *Imaginary Homelands*. See Lee (1990, chapter 15) and Webster (1990, chapters 3 and 4).

91 He had after all said that *It would be absurd to think that a book can cause riots*. See *The Indian Press*, September 18, 1988. In fact, in February 1989, 12 people died in anti-Rushdie riots in Bombay. In August 1995, the Indian distributor of Rushdie's (1995) new book *The Moors Last Sigh*, delayed release of the book in Bombay due to Hindu protests.

92 On Teheran Radio, July 14, 1989 just prior to the 2.00 pm news the following announcement was made on behalf of the Ayatollah Khomeini; "In the name of God Almighty ... I would like to inform all the intrepid Muslims in the world, that the author of the book entitled The Satanic Verses ... as well as those publishers who were aware of its contents have been sentenced to death."

93 Webster (1990, p. 4) and Smith (1990, p. 20).

94 According to a March 2006 Zogby International Poll, 90% of Americans fighting in Iraq believed they were doing so in order to avenge Saddam Hussein's role in the 9/11

attacks. In similar vein in a speech given on September 25, 2002, President George W Bush said "You can't distinguish between Al Qaeda and Saddam when you talk about the war on terror."

95   For a copy of this letter see www.rogerbuch.dk/jpabrev.pdf (accessed June 28, 2010).

96   S. 149 and 266b of the Danish Criminal Code.

97   He subsequently resigned. See "Italy cartoon minister quits" at http://news.bbc.co.uk/2/hi/europe/4727606.stm (accessed June 28, 2010).

98   This was the European Committee for Prophet Honouring.

99   See "Muslim Cartoon Fury Claims Lives" at http://news.bbc.co.uk/2/hi/4684652.stm (accessed June 28, 2010).

100   The UN Human Rights Council has regularly passed resolutions calling for increased restrictions on speech which involves "defamation of religions'" most recently (at the time of writing) in March 2009. For analysis see www.reuters.com/article/idUSTRE52P60220090326 (accessed June 28, 2010). Since then (December 2009) the 3rd Committee of the General Assembly of the United Nations passed a similar resolution and recommended it to the General Assembly, see www.un.org/News/Press/docs/2009/gashc3966.doc.htm (accessed June 28, 2010). For analysis see International Humanist and Ethical Union (2009).

101   See for example the decision of the European Court of Human Rights to uphold the legitimacy of Ireland's statutory ban on religious advertising in *Murphy v. Ireland* (2004) 38 EHRR 13, [2003] ECHR 352.

102   (1995) 19 EHRR 35. See also *Wingrove v. UK*, (1997) 24 EHRR 1.

103   In the *Otto Preminger Institute case*, the European Court of Human Rights said that "[Religion is] one of the most vital elements that go to make up the identity of believers and their conception of life."

104   Thus in the context of Islam, JND Anderson (1971) writes that "It has often been remarked that, in the past at least, the life of an orthodox Muslim was dominated by the twin sciences of theology and the sacred law. It was the law moreover that could claim pride of place, for Islam has always been much more explicit and unequivocal about the way of life God has ordained for his creatures than about any self-revelation of his own character or nature."

References

Adam, K. (2010) Atheists challenge Irelands new Blasphemy Law with Online Posting, *Washington Post*, January 3, www.washingtonpost.com/wp-dyn/content/article/2010/01/02/AR2010010201846.html (accessed July 19, 2010).

Ahsan, M.M., and Kidwai, A.R. (1993) *Sacrilege versus Civility; Muslim Perspectives in the Salman Rushdie Controversy*, Markfield Islamic Foundation, Leicester.

Akhtar, S. (1989) *Be Careful with Muhammad*, Bedlew, London.

Anderson, J.N.D. (1971) Modern trends in Islam: Legal reform and Modernization in the Middle East, *International and Comparative Law Quarterly*, 20, 1.

Armstrong, K. (1988) *Holy War; the Crusades and their Impact on Today's World*, Macmillan, New York.

Azam, U. (1990) *Rushdie's "Satanic Verses"; An Islamic Response*, www.dr-umar-azam.com/islamic_response/islamic_response_intro.htm (accessed July 19, 2010).

Bacik, I. (2004) *Kicking and Screaming: Dragging Ireland into the Twenty First Century*, O'Brien Press, Dublin.

Barendt, E. (2005) *Freedom of Speech*, 2nd edn, Oxford University Press, Oxford.

Bashier, Z. (1991) *The Makkan Crucible*, Islamic Foundation, Leicester.

Blom-Cooper, L.J. (1981) *Blasphemy; An Ancient Wrong or a Modern Right?*, Essex Hall Lectures, London.

Bowen, D.G. (ed.) (1992) *The Satanic Verses; Bradford Responds*, Bradford & Ilkley Community College, Bradford, UK.

Burley, J., and Regan, F. (2002) Divorce in Ireland; The fear, the floodgates and the reality, *International Journal of Law, Policy and the Family*, 16 (2), 202–222.

Buxton, R. (1978) The Case of Blasphemous Libel, *Criminal Law Review*, 673–682.

Calder-Marshall, A. (1972) *Lewd, Blasphemous and Obscene*, Hutchinson & Co, London.

Clifford, B. (1993) *Blasphemous Reason*, Bevin Books, London.

Conway, D.A. (1974) Law, Liberty and Indecency, *Philosophy*, 49, 135–148.

Cowell, A. (2006) Dane defends press freedom as Muslims protest cartoons, *New York Times*, February 1, www.nytimes.com/2006/02/01/international/europe/01danish.html (accessed July 19, 2010).

Cox, N. (1997) Sacrilege and sensibility the value of Irish blasphemy, Dublin University Law Journal, 19, 87–112.

Cox, N. (2000a) *Irish Blasphemy Law*, Edwin Mellen Press, Lampeter, UK.

Cox, N. (2000b) Passive judicial activism, *Dublin University Law Journal*, 22, 201–207.

Dashti, A. (1985), *Twenty Three Years: A Study of the Prophetic Career of Mohammed* (trans. F.R.C. Bagley), Allen & Unwin, London.

Dershowitz, A. (2007) *Blasphemy, How the Religious Right is Hijacking our Declaration of Independence*, John Wiley & Sons, Inc., Hoboken, NJ.

Devlin, P. (1965) *The Enforcement of Morals*, Oxford University Press, London.

Easterman, D. (1992) *New Jerusalems, Reflections on Islam, Fundamentalism and the Rushdie Affair*, Grafton, London.

Ellis, A. (1984) Offence and the liberal conception of the law, *Philosophy and Public Affairs*, 13, 3.

Ely, J.H. (1975) Flag desecration: A case study in the roles of categorization and balancing in First Amendment analysis, *Harvard Law Review*, 88, 1482.

Eralp, I.H. (1989) *Salman's End: Exposing the Absurdity of* The Satanic Verses, Minerva, London.

Farrell, B. (ed) (1988) *De Valera's Constitution and Ours*, Gill and Macmillan, Dublin.

Feinberg, J. (1985) *Offence to Others*, Oxford University Press, New York.

Fish, S. (2001) Holocaust denial and academic freedom, *Valparaiso University Law Review*, 35, 499.

Haykal, M.H. (1976) *The Life of Muhammad*, 8th edn, (trans. Isma'il Ragi and al Faruqi), North American Trust Publications, Plainfield, IN.

Healy, A. (2009) Blasphemy law a return to middle ages – Dawkins, *Irish Times*, July 13, www.irishtimes.com/newspaper/ireland/2009/0713/1224250543694.html. (accessed July 19, 2010).

International Humanist and Ethical Union (2009), *Speaking Freely about Religion: Religious Freedom, Defamation and Blasphemy*, www.iheu.org/files/Speaking%20Freely%20 about%20Religion.pdf (accessed June 16, 2010).

Kabbani, R. (1989) *Letter to Christendom*, Virago, London.

Kahn, R.A. (2006) Cross burning, holocaust denial and the development of hate speech law in the United States and Germany, *University of Detroit Mercy Law Review*, 83, 163, www.law.udmercy.edu/lawreview/recentissues/v83/issue3/83_udm_law_review_rev163.pdf (accessed July 19, 2010).

Kenny, C.S. (1923) The evolution of the law of blasphemy, *Cambridge Law Journal*, 127, 135ff.

Knechtle, J.C. (2008) Holocaust denial and the concept of dignity in the European Union, *Florida State University Law Review*, 36, 41.

Law Commission (UK) (1985), *Report on Offences against Religion and Public Worship*, Report no. 45.

Law Reform Commission (Ireland) (1991) *Consultation Paper on the Crime of Libel*, Law Reform Commission.

Lee, S. (1990) *The Cost of Free Speech*, Faber & Faber, London.

Levy, L. (1981) *Treason Against God*, Shocken Books, New York.

Matthews (1839), *An Account of the Trial on 14th June, 1703 by the Court of the Queens Bench, Dublin, of the Revd. Thomas Emlyn*, Dublin.

Muir, W. (1986) *Mahomet and Islam: A Sketch of the Prophet's Life from Original Sources*, Derf, London.

Murdoch, H.S.P. (1998) *Dictionary of Irish Law*, Topaz Publications, Dublin.

Murphy Report (2009) Report of the Commission of Investigation into the Catholic Archdiocese of Dublin, November 2009, www.dacoi.ie (accessed June 16, 2010).

O'Dell, E. (2009) Blasphemy provisions clash with the Constitution, *Irish Times*, July 22, www.irishtimes.com/newspaper/opinion/2009/0722/1224251063583.html (accessed July 19, 2010).

O'Hanlon (1999) Why it's open season for blasphemy, *Sunday Business Post*, November 21.

O'Higgins (1960) 'Blasphemy in Irish Law, *Modern Law Review*, 23, 151, 153.

O'Neil, P. (2009) Ireland's new Blasphemy Law labeled return to Middle Ages, *Calgary Herald*, August 23, www.calgaryherald.com/life/Ireland+blasphemy+labeled+return+Middle+Ages/1922182/story.html (accessed July 19, 2010).

Purcell (1999) Court withdraws Another Protection from Religion, *Irish Catholic*, August 5.

Ranalow, S. (2000) Bearing a Constitutional Cross, *Trinity College Law Review*, 3, 95.

Reidy, P. (2009) Who asked for Ireland's Blasphemy Law, *Guardian* July 9, www.guardianco.uk/commentisfree/libertycentral/2009/jul/09/ireland-blasphemy-laws (accessed July 19, 2010).

Roberts, S. (2010) Atheist Ireland protests Blasphemy Law by publishing book of religious quotations by famous people, *New York Daily News*, January 2, www.nydailynews.com/news/world/2010/01/02/2010-01-02_atheist_ireland_protests_blasphemy_law_by_publishing_book_of_religious_quotation.html (accessed July 19, 2010).

Robertson, G. (1993) *Freedom, the Individual and the Law*, 7th edn, Harmondsworth, Penguin.

Robertson, G., and Nicol, A. (1993) *Media Law*, 3rd edn, Harmondsworth, Penguin.

Rosenfeld, M. (2003) Hate speech in constitutional jurisprudence; A comparative analysis, *Cardozo Law Review*, 24, 1523.

Rushdie, S. (1988) *The Satanic Verses*, Picador USA, New York.

Rushdie, S. (1992) *Imaginary Homelands: Essays and Criticism 1981–1991*, London, Granta Books.

Rushdie, S. (1995) *The Moors Last Sigh*, Jonathan Cape, London.

Ryan Report (2009) Report of the Commission to Inquire into Child Abuse, May, www.childabusecommission.com/rpt/pdfs/ (accessed June 16, 2010).

Said, E. (1981) *Covering Islam*, Routledge and Kegan Paul, London.

Samuel, J. (1992) Salman Rushdie's *Satanic Verses*, in *US/THEM, transition, Transcription and Identity in Post-Colonial Literary Cultures*, (ed. Gordon Collier), Atlanta GA, Amsterdam.

Simpson, R. (1993) *Blasphemy and the Law in a Plural Society*, Haslemere, UK, Grove Books.

Smith, F. LaGard. (1990) *Blasphemy and the Battle for Faith*, Hodder and Stoughton, London.

Synon, M.E. (1999) The New Secular Orthodoxy and its "liberal" catechism, *Sunday Independent*, August 8.

Teachout, P.R. (2006) Making "holocaust denial" a crime: Reflections on European anti-negationist laws from the perspective of US constitutional experience, *Vermont Law Review*, 30, 655–693.

Travis, A. (2004) Medieval law has had its day, *Guardian*, October 18.

Tucker, D.F.B. (1986) *Law, Liberalism and Free Speech*, Rowman & Littlefield, Totowa, NJ.

Walter, N. (1977) *Blasphemy in Britain*, Rationalist Press Association, London.

Watt, W.M. (1956) *Muhammad in Mecca/Medina*, Clarendon, Oxford.

Webster, R. (1990) *A Brief History of Blasphemy*, Orwell Press, Southwold, UK.

16

The Medium is the Moral

Michael Bugeja

The Medium *Was* the Message

Technology and its nature are often misunderstood by new media proponents, and as a result this chapter calls into question certain fundamental premises regarded as basic to communication theory and/or media ethics. The title of this work alludes to "The medium is the message," which happens to be the title of the first chapter of Marshall McLuhan's *Understanding Media: The Extensions of Man*, which posits that new technologies alter culture in specific place and time, a thesis he tests by this measure:

> Today when we want to get our bearings in our own culture, and have need to stand aside from the bias and pressure exerted by any technical form of human expression, we have only to visit a society where that particular form has not been felt, or a history period in which it was unknown (McLuhan, 1964, p. 19).

In other words, if you want to measure cultural change caused by any new technology, you should visit a place that lacks it. This was the concept behind a 1973 study by Tannis MacBeth Williams of the University of British Columbia who analyzed the cultures of three Canadian communities: "Notel," which had no TV reception but would soon acquire a transmitter; "Unitel," which only received the Canadian Broadcasting Company; and "Multitel," which had US network channels. Williams studied viewer behavior in all three towns before Notel had television and then returned to each place two years later to assess any differences in culture. She discovered that there was no significant difference in physical and verbal aggression among Unitel and Multitel children; Notel children, however, showed nearly twice as much aggression toward each other after TV as before (Ledingham *et al.*, 2003). The full

---

The Handbook of Global Communication and Media Ethics, First Edition. Edited by Robert S. Fortner and P. Mark Fackler.
© 2011 Blackwell Publishing Ltd. Published 2011 by Blackwell Publishing Ltd.

The Medium is the Moral

experiment is explained in Williams' (1986) book, *The Impact of Television: A Natural Experiment in Three Communities*. Jane Ledingham, director of the Child Study Centre at the University of Ottawa, summarized the cultural effect of television's impact on community in her paper "The Effects of Media Violence on Children":

> [Williams' study] found that people spent less time talking, socializing outside the home, doing household tasks, engaging in leisure activities such as reading, knitting and writing, and being involved in community activities and sports after television became available. They even slept less. ... It is clear that television's impact on children arises not only from the kinds of behaviour it promotes, but also from the other activities it replaces.

In addition to utilizing McLuhan's "medium is the message," the premise of this chapter also rests on two other widely held concepts in media ethics: *Values are inherently relativistic and subjective* "because cultures vary over place and time" (Bond, 2001, p. 1746). *Principles are inherently universal and impersonal* and "concern behavior that is possible for any rational person in any society at any period of history" (Gert, 2001, p. 1169).

Consider this: If we glance at pedestrians in the digital street tweeting, texting, and chatting into palms – rather than observing their neighbors and environs as they did a decade ago – we have witnessed "the medium is the message" altering culture in a specific time and place. If we believe that values are subjective – as in a criminal swearing a *loyalty* oath in gangland Chicago during Prohibition – then we also acknowledge the relativistic nature of that italicized concept above, grounded in place, time, and culture. Finally, if we believe some precepts are so inherently ethical that few philosophers anywhere question them, throughout history – such as "it is right to tell the truth" or "it is wrong to hurt a child" (Sommers, 1993) – then we are identifying principles that *transcend* place, time and culture.

This chapter questions all three widely held beliefs. It does so because of technology's nature to transform everything that it touches without itself being changed much at all. Then the medium no longer is the message; it becomes the means, ends, and essence that subjugates media ethics as we have known and theorized about the discipline for decades – an argument that first appears in my 2005 book, *Interpersonal Divide: The Search for Community in a Technological Age*, and which was developed subsequently in other book chapters, articles and presentations, whose concepts are assembled here with new data in a summary work.

The Medium Splits the Senses

I have hypothesized here and elsewhere that the message of the digital media is inherently amoral because technology does not enhance and extend the human senses but diminishes and splits human consciousness, eroding ethical awareness. In documenting that effect, we look to the work of the French-Maltese philosopher

Jacques Ellul (1912–1994) who stated that the nature of technology neither endures "any moral judgment" nor tolerates "any insertion of morality" in the technician's work (Ellul, 2003, p. 394). Ellul believed that technology is a self-determining organism ("an end in itself") whose autonomy transformed centuries' old systems "while being scarcely modified in its own features" (2003, p. 386).

How transformative is technology? What forces can adjust for its effects? Why do we lack sufficient theory to deal with technological saturation in an industry whose watchdog character is illustrated by the concept of The Fourth Estate, or fourth branch of government, holding federal systems and officials accountable for the public good?

The role of journalism in US history has been defined by the notion of the Fourth Estate. In sum, we opposed the value system of England whose royalty believed that bloodline and authority supersede truth – a view successfully challenged in the 1735 seditious libel trial of John Peter Zenger who criticized royal Gov. William Cosby in the *New York Weekly Journal*. Zenger was acquitted on the arguments of his attorney, Andrew Hamilton, who stated, "It is pretty clear that in New York a man may make very free with his God, but he must take special care what he says of his Governor" (Hamilton, 2003).

For purposes of this chapter, the Zenger case is an example of a value versus a principle. Should bloodline determine who rules, as it does even today in Great Britain in the House of Lords? Should the false or disenfranchising proclamations of authority go unchallenged so that the social order is maintained? In some cultures, including eighteenth-century England, the answer was "yes" – an antiquated idea even by Colonial standards. The principle of truth superseding authority, which came to define US society, transcends time and place. We identify as a culture according to that precept.

In discussing universal principles, Deni Elliott states that the argument for their existence, "like moral development theories, builds on the notion of similarities among human behavior that stretch across space, culture, and time" (1997, p. 68). However, the Internet and other communication technologies operate in an environment that is asynchronous, acultural, and virtual. In illustrating those web characteristics, I often cite Nicholas Negroponte whose 1995 book, *being digital* (1995), influenced the state of technical affairs in which we operate today. Here are excerpts:

- *Place without Space*: "[T]he post-information age will remove the limitations of geography. Digital living will include less and less dependence upon being in a specific place at a specific time, and the transmission of place itself will start to become possible" (Negroponte, 1995, p. 165).
- *Being Asynchronous*: "A face-to-face or telephone conversation is real time and synchronous" while email is not. ... The advantage is less about voice and more about off-line processing and time shifting" (Negroponte, 1995, p. 167).
- *Mediumlessness*: "Thinking about multimedia needs to include ideas about the fluid movement from one medium to the next. ... [M]ultimedia involves translating one dimension (time) into another dimension (space)" (Negroponte, 1995, pp. 72, 73).

In the last definition, Negroponte alludes to McLuhan's *Understanding Media: The Extensions of Man*, in which the word "culture" is the third word of his opening paragraph:

> In a culture like ours, long accustomed to splitting and dividing all things as a means of control, it is sometimes a bit of a shock to be reminded that, in operational and practical fact, the medium is the message. That is merely to say that the personal and social consequences of any medium – that is, of any extension of ourselves – result from the new scale that is introduced into our affairs by each extension of ourselves, or by any new technology (McLuhan, 1964, p. 7).

The phrase "extension of ourselves" represents McLuhan's mixed metaphor about media and conveys an optimistic belief in progress and the transformative power of technology. According to his theory, "media hot and cold," each communication platform enhanced or extended the human senses. The more defined (as in the technical term "high definition") the less the audience had to work to receive the message. For example, he writes, a movie is a "hot medium" that "extends one single sense in 'high definition'" whereas the television is a cool medium because its images are formed by dots and bands of lines (McLuhan, 1964, p. 22). Reading McLuhan today, one struggles to fathom why *Understanding Media* has been so influential in subsequent research in light of logic like this:

> High definition is the state of being well-filled with data. A photograph is, visually, "high definition." A cartoon is "low definition," simply because very little visual information is provided. Telephone is a cool medium, or one of low definition, because the ear is given a meager amount of information. And speech is a cool medium of low definition because so little is given and so much has to be filled in by the listener. On the other hand, hot media do not leave so much to be filled in or completed by the audience. Hot media are, therefore, low in participation, and cool media are high in participation or completion by the audience. Naturally, therefore, a hot medium like radio has different effects on the user from a cool medium like telephone (McLuhan, 1964, pp. 22–23).

Rhetoric cannot predict the future, an activity in which technology advocates from McLuhan to Negroponte often have engaged. Neither can it sway or guide the empirical. The phrase, "the medium is the message," is merely a poetic sound-bite of the times in discerning how single-platform technology reorganizes society, from the telegraph by which the US Civil War was fought to the television around which families once gathered as if by phosphorus campfire in the 1950s. When McLuhan spoke of "the global village," he was referring not to the Internet but to television which, he posited, would unite society and various cultures and countries so they became citizens of the planet, rather than of place. So excited was he by the specter of television that he failed to see it as a commercial tool, over-estimating its educational possibilities in the same manner that we witness today with the technorati. Television would engage and enlighten learners far more than books would,

McLuhan prophesied, chiefly because its "cool" low definition features stimulated rather than dulled the senses.

McLuhan's mistake was to use a biological metaphor to represent the nature of technology. A telephone, he stated, extends the human ability to hear over the vast expanse of oceans. By emphasizing "hearing," McLuhan bases his premise on biology rather than on physics (i.e., the distance sound travels transoceanically). Omitting physics, McLuhan ends up viewing people as information systems rather than as people *in information space*. This is why he fails to foresee cyberspace.

In *Interpersonal Divide*, I document how high-tech communication defies physical laws, relying on the saying, "If a tree falls in the forest and no one is around to hear it, does it actually make a sound?" The answer is *no*. Falling timber creates a sound *wave* that enters the ear when a person is there and that does not when the person is 100 miles away. Technology overcomes the distance by redirecting the wave from one place to another so that a person, technically, is in two places simultaneously: the real and the virtual. If one places a microphone near that falling tree and transmits the sound to the person 100 miles away so that he or she hears it on a receiver, then one can say with certainty that a tree *does* makes a sound when it falls, even if no one is at the actual site to experience the event. From a biological perspective, it is easy to see why McLuhan believed the microphone extended the range of the ear. In actuality, it does not. Technology creates *two sets of senses* – one in real place (where the person with the cell phone actually is) and one in virtual place (where the video phone recorded the event). Essentially, that person hearing the transmission of falling timber violates physics by being in two places at the same time. There is a downside. When consciousness is split, so is perception. The senses are not extended and enhanced; they are divided and diminished. When the senses are diminished, common sense (as well as ethical awareness) also is diminished, along with our notion of community.

This simple thesis from *Interpersonal Divide* predicted what McLuhan, for all his rhetoric, could not. Split consciousness due to technology is responsible for a variety of likely phenomena, from increased traffic fatalities caused by driver inattentiveness to widespread distractions in the digital classroom. Far from enhancing the senses so that people become information systems, people are lost in information space, unaware of their surroundings, texting while driving, checking social networks at work, and answering cell phones at wakes and weddings. The real and virtual worlds vie for their split attention.

The Medium Realizes Itself

This is technology's nature, best depicted by Ellul who saw technology as a viral essence. Introduced into any system, however previously independent or inherently powerful – from the news media to ethical theory – technology would reconfigure the principles of that system to adhere to its own protocol. Unlike McLuhan, social scientists and media ethicists have been able to use Ellul's theory to predict

The Medium is the Moral

outcomes long before they occur. Ellul died in 1994 before the technology boom that would ensue in the late 1990s. However, his view of technology proved correct even during the hype of the dot.com days. Technology's nature is akin to that of the scorpion; it is what it is. McLuhanesque rhetoric cannot change that. Ellul was particularly prescient when observing technology's influence on the economy. "Like political authority, an economic system that challenges the technological imperative is doomed," he wrote, adding that technology's nature is to obey its own determination; "it realizes itself" (Ellul, 2003, p. 392).

The medium has always been the message; but throughout history, it has not always been the moral. Ethicists debate schools of thought, rights, wrongs, theories, and applications seemingly unaware of technology's overpowering effects often occurring before their eyes.

The Internet obfuscates reality by providing an alternative virtual one. In the process it also obliterates linear time and homogenizes local, regional, and national culture – a chief reason why applications, websites, and search engines are banned in certain countries. However, the Internet also comes with other features that McLuhan could scarcely envision. His was a world of single platform media, primarily newspapers, radio and television. Each one of those platforms changed culture in the spirit of the medium is the message. In the current day, multimedia adds to that concept a type of cultural white noise emanating from convergence and resulting in a multitasking virtual community programmed by corporations that promised a global mall and delivered a global village. As I have argued in books, articles, and presentations for the past decade, the village may seem global because content is accessed or created from a variety of locations and countries. However, those introduced to the Internet tend to cluster at 30 top sites dominated by US providers such as Microsoft, Yahoo and Google (as of November 1, 2006).

Ellul believed that technology does not free us; it forces us to conform. It subsumes other systems; else, it fails to operate. Ultimatums abound: Lectures must conform to distance education digital parameters. Exams must be multiple choice for computer grading. Instructors using audience response systems ask questions answerable only by keypad. Automated answering systems also offer keypad customer service. At a typical presentation, the guest speaker and audience members wait while technicians hover over a laptop and projector, trying to extract from a Wal-Mart memory stick an IBM PowerPoint and then make it compatible with Apple hardware. We have become so accustomed to these aftereffects that we experience culture shock when student exams require written essays, college instructors ask complex questions, customer service representatives answer phones, and new media presentations operate without glitches.

Heidegger believed that technology may seem complex or complicate whatever it touches, but its essence is easily revealed (2003, p. 255). Using that premise, we can ask, "What is the moral of the medium?" Of course, the effects of the Internet and mobile technologies have changed all manner of social mores as well as personal and professional values. In *Interpersonal Divide*, I document the amorality of technology as it affects community, instilling in users the belief that someone somewhere else is more important than the place you are or the person you are with, an effect evident daily on interstate highways as drivers access the Internet Highway via any number of gadgets, endangering others not because their consciousness is extended as McLuhan might have believed but because it has been split, frequently with devastating results.

Several states are creating laws to ban texting in moving vehicles. Ramifications of that activity were widely reported in 2007 in the deaths of high school cheerleaders in Canandaigua, NY. The 17-year-old driver with four other recent high school graduates had sent and received text messages before a head-on collision with a truck, killing all five girls (Associated Press, 2007). A year later one of the worst train accidents in recent US history occurred when the operator of a Southern California commuter train was texting, missed a red light and collided with a freight train, killing 25 people and injuring more than 130 others (Washington Post, 2008). Even as I write a trolley operator in Boston was texting his girlfriend when he crashed into another trolley, sending nearly 50 people to the hospital (Bierman and Ryan, 2009).

Journalists use those same mobile devices with services such as Twitter, texting what they are doing at the moment to an audience that follows their momentary activities. Reporters tweet. Perhaps no other device in recent memory documents Ellul's thesis that technology changes everything it touches without itself changing much at all. Technology realizes itself; however, people rarely realize technology's effects on principles of their disciplines or professions. Journalists on the scene of spot news should be focusing on the place they are at and people they are with, especially when covering accidents as described in the previous paragraph. However, their concentration is split as they observe and text 140 character bursts of Morse Code-like dispatches to others who also are ignoring the place they are at and the people they are with. True, every now and then a tweet from a person involved in spot news has merit. For every one of those, reporters must endure hundreds of marketing pitches and mindless messages with each tweet racking up revenue in the process of affirming rather than informing users.

Those users are so affirmed in marketing themselves like catalog products in Facebook, blogging to an audience of none on Typepad, realizing what they can never become as avatars in Second Life, or coveting someone else's life via Twitter, that they have forgotten why they need factual information that serves democracy but assails their psychographics. Hence, they want news only about themselves or their affinity groups. The greater the ego, the larger the target market. A few social critics foresaw the likely outcome decades ago. McLuhan contemporary Henry Fairlie analyzed the commercial effects of mass media on Americans in this 1976 exegesis from *The Spoiled Child of the Western World*, which was prophetic:

> He has never encountered the world, or anything or anybody who is other than himself. If he feels anger, he has never seen anyone else angry; if he is afraid, he has never seen anyone else who was willing to exhibit fear lest it disturb him; if he wishes

to be selfish, he imagines that he alone, embraced by such givingness, bears such a guilt (Fairlie, 1976, p. 169).

The Medium is the Money

Everyday mobile gadgets and brands – iPhones, iPods, BlackBerry, Bluetooth, Twitter – are programmed for revenue generation, primarily because they are tools of convergence with each hitherto single platform combining with others typically for a hidden fee or datamining cookie. Use the cell phone to text like a telegraph, and the digital cash register *ca-chings*. Use it like a radio to download a ring tone, and it *ca-chings* again. Want video? Internet access? *Ca-ching, ca-ching!* The cultural effects of such widespread use are as multifold as the multimedia that the devices use or access, including the Internet developed by military and enhanced by business whose primary functions are to surveil and sell (and sometimes both simultaneously). Perhaps no one has crafted a better case for that assertion than the inventor of the web, Sir Tim Berners-Lee, who in 1999 already was criticizing how search engines drove commerce under the guise of delivering information. To illustrate that effect, he used a shoe store analogy. When someone wants to buy shoes, the search engine does not return addresses and listings of every available store, but only ones that have deals with its parent company. Berners-Lee writes, "It's like having a car with a Go Shopping for Shoes button on the dashboard; when pushed, it will drive only to the shoe store that has a deal with the carmaker. This doesn't help me get the best paid shoes for the lowest price, it doesn't help the free market, and it doesn't help democracy" (Berners-Lee, 1999, p. 133).

As communication companies have invested heavily in technology, and thus deliver much of the digital content, consumers are not only influenced by the medium's message; they are saturated with messages. As Avery Cardinal Dulles professed in 2004, on the occasion of the fifth anniversary of the Center for Ethics and Culture at Notre Dame, discussing ethical challenges in the modern era,

> The communications industry is driven by commercialism. It is almost totally in the hands of advertisers, who use it to market their wares and increase their profits. Their dominant concern is not to relieve poverty or promote justice, but rather to stimulate people's eagerness to buy (Dulles, 2004).

Journalism has a special role in democratic society: defending the Constitution and the rights of citizens by holding government accountable. Technology has changed that role, again as Ellul prophesied, by using devices and applications programmed for revenue generation at the expense of personnel – an effect we tested in a study of premier media companies as identified by *Advertising Age* (Media 100, n.d.). We analyzed financial data from the top 12 companies that also made their financial data public. Additionally, we gathered or verified data from corporate annual reports and the Google finance website. Those data and accompanying charts will

306   *Michael Bugeja*

become part of a larger study to document automation of employees over time as new media is introduced in 1990, 1995, 2000, 2005, and 2010. However, some of the highlights of our study are worth noting here to document how much emphasis media companies put on revenue generation, a concept to be explored later in this chapter with respect to media ethics.

In 2007, Time Warner, the top communication company, earned US$537 986 in revenue per employee. To arrive at that figure, we used a calculation as simple as Occam's Razor, that scientific standard of truth which suggests the simplest explanation is almost always the correct one: We divided its annual revenue by the number of its employees. After a decade that gave us Enron and the hieroglyphics of mark to marketing accounting – facilitated by the Internet and the broadband boom (Thomas, 2002), combining to create oxymoronic proprietary financial disclosures – we felt an Occam's Razor approach had merit. After all, Enron fell when *Forbes* senior writer Bethany McLean asked – "How, exactly, does Enron make its money?" – which no one could answer:

> Details are hard to come by because Enron keeps many of the specifics confidential for what it terms "competitive reasons." And the numbers that Enron does present are often extremely complicated. Even quantitatively minded Wall Streeters who scrutinize the company for a living think so. "If you figure it out, let me know," laughs credit analyst Todd Shipman at S&P. "Do you have a year?" asks Ralph Pellecchia, Fitch's credit analyst, in response to the same question (McLean, 2001).

In descending *AdAge* rankings, following Time Warner, were Comcast, as the second top company generating US$308 950 per employee; (3) Walt Disney, US$259 197; (4) NewsCorp, US$540 660; (5) General Electric, US$528 251; (6) CBS, US$587 105; (7) EchoStar, US$1 029 380; (8) Viacom, US$1 242 880; (9) Gannett, US$161 377; (10) AT&T, US$383 639; (11) Charter, US$363 758; and (12) Cablevision, US$448 102.

As is evident in Figure 16.1, *AdAge*'s top companies do not necessarily have to have the highest per-employee revenue. With the exception of a few companies, such as Gannett, vast amounts of revenue had to be generated per employee to maintain Wall Street performance expectations, with Viacom and EchoStar surpassing US$1 million per employee.

We used a similar, simple calculation to divine a different financial profile: We divided annual profits by the number of employees with Time Warner earning US$208 160 per person; (2) Comcast, US$197 200; (3) Walt Disney, US$49 496; (4) NewsCorp, US$188 868; (5) General Electric, US$222 651; (6) CBS, US$239.616; (7) EchoStar, US$60 053.33; (8) Viacom, US$554 852; (9) Gannett, US$61 057; (10) AT&T, US$197 816; (11) Charter, US$182 182; and (12) Cablevision, US$248 299.

Inconsistent with *AdAge*'s rankings are the amounts of per-employee profit (see Figure 16.2), which vary widely. For example, Viacom generates 2.5 times more than top company Time Warner and more than 10 times more than third-place

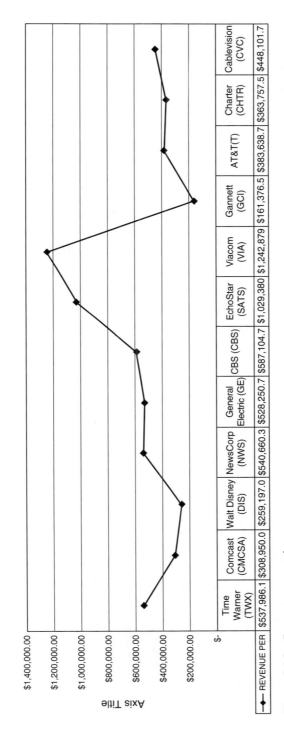

Figure 16.1 Revenue per employee.

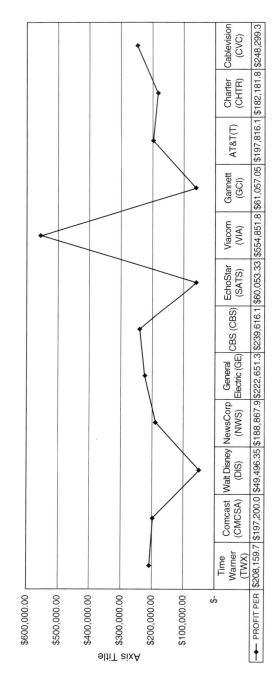

Figure 16.2 Profit per employee.

The Medium is the Moral

Disney, the lowest performing company on this metric. (However, there are other ways to view the data, such as Viacom recouping 45% of its revenue per employee and Disney 19%.) We created another simple graph to illustrate what we called the "the revenue-profit gap," or the difference between what companies generate compared to what they actually earn (see Figure 16.3).

The largest revenue-profit gap was EchoStar's with US$969 327 followed by Viacom, US$688 028; (3) NewsCorp, US$351 792; (4) CBS, 347 489; (5) Time Warner, US$329 826; (6) General Electric, US$305 599; (7) Walt Disney, US$209 701; (8) Cablevision, US$199 802; (9) AT&T US$185 823; (10) Charter, US$181 576; (11) Comcast, US$111 750; and (12) Gannett, US$100 320.

This gap seems fairly consistent for several companies, but others like Gannett's and Comcast's show a much smaller gap when compared to that of Viacom and EchoStar, indicating all manner of variables beyond the scope of this pilot study. For instance, Viacom and EchoStar may require vast amounts of revenue to earn relatively small amounts of profit because their operations require investment in costly production equipment or the manufacturing thereof. Or perhaps senior management is less effective. Nonetheless, the statistics here are revealing when one considers a traditional media company like Gannett with low revenue per employee and lower profit margins versus the size of its work force, indicating that even in 2007, with a stock price of $37.69 (compared to $4.31 in May 2009), the company was in trouble because too few of its employees were generating revenue required for the pricey tech-driven communication industry. In sum, too many Gannett managers were spending money reporting the news rather than feeding technology's insatiable appetite that requires technicians, support, maintenance, utilities, monitoring, security, applications, software, licenses, upgrades, accessories and, lest we forget, access.

Figure 16.4 shows the size of the revenue-profit gap in absolute terms without the per-employee revenue or profit lines for comparison. Considering the disparity in profit gaps, which may indicate the skill sets of senior management, we researched CEO compensation for the various companies and list them here from the largest to smallest: (1) CBS CEO, US$36 816 828; (2) Walt Disney CEO, US$27 699 200; (3) NewsCorp CEO, US$27 548 460; (4) Cablevision CEO, US$23 876 752; (5) AT&T CEO, US$21 981 984; (6) Comcast CEO, US$20 802 728; (7) Viacom CEO, US$20 597 090; (8) General Electric CEO, US$19 591 580; (9) Time Warner CEO, US$19 574 158; (10) Gannett, US$7 546 710; (11) Charter, US$6 227 866; and (12) EchoStar CEO, US$894 124.

As Figure 16.5 indicates, most CEOs tend to earn compensation in the US$20–30 million range, with the exceptions of Charter, Gannett, and EchoStar, whose CEO salaries are in the lower end. Here is another slice of Occam's Razor, depicting the importance of some personnel (CEOs) over others (employees) and their machines in the digital age. CEO salaries greatly dwarf what initially seemed to be enormous amounts of revenue and profit per employee – so much so, in fact, that it is difficult to see the employee revenue and profit bars on this graph (which proves the point).

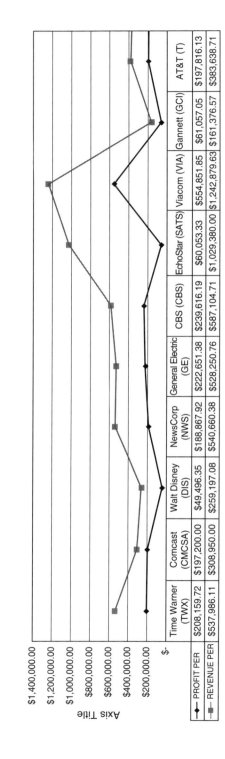

Figure 16.3 Per-employee revenue and profit.

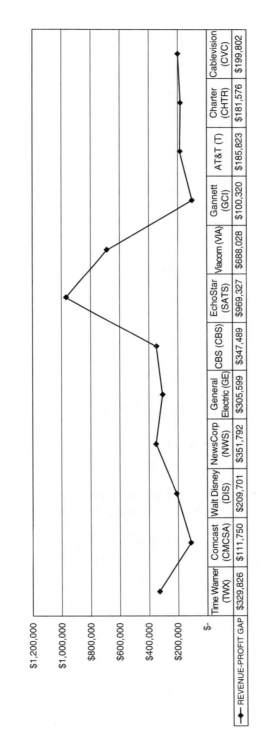

Figure 16.4 Per-employee revenue-profit gap.

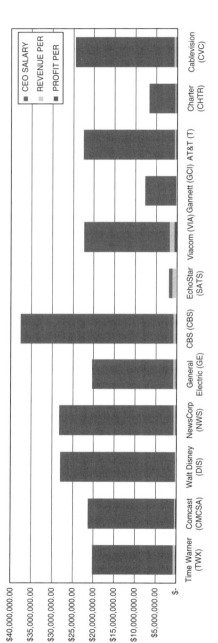

Figure 16.5 Per-employee ratios relative to CEO compensation.

The Medium Demoralizes the Message

What has happened to common sense? These are business models doomed for failure. Media ethics even as portrayed in this book were formulated around certain theses that many of our best theorists believed would be with us in perpetuity, grounded in or transcending time, culture, and place. We believed that no system, however autonomous, would render moral principles into mere propositions, especially concerning the Fourth Estate and society. In his essay "Why we need better ethics for emerging technologies," James H. Moor (2008) writes, "[B]ecause new technology allows us to perform activities in new ways, situations may arise in which we do not have adequate policies in place to guide us. We are confronted with *policy vacuums*" (p. 32). Moor correctly argues that absent ethical theory, decisions concerning technology often are made on a "cost-benefit" analysis, leaving ourselves "vulnerable to a tsunami of technological change" (p. 39). In light of that, ethical theory often overlooks phenomena that trigger such change – in our case, the reason for journalism itself – subsumed by technology's autonomous nature that subjugates other systems on its own terms or not at all.

To test that assertion, determine what theory of the press applies to media's current vacuous situation. Through much of the last century, before new media infiltrated journalism, practitioners operated within "social responsibility." Other countries relied on media values that fell under "libertarian," "authoritarian," and "communist" as described along with social responsibility in *Four Theories of the Press* by Fred S. Siebert, Theodore Peterson and Wilbur Schramm originally published in 1956 and until the technology boom of the 1990s, believed to be the definitive work on the topic. In recent years, these theories have been challenged by the emphasis on profit by media conglomerates and the advent of new media and worldwide communication technologies. Some ethicists are seeking a unifying theory of media that takes into account the "marketplace" – *both of commerce and ideas* – without realizing the rhetorical nature of that italicized phrase. The stock market is measured in figures; the creative consciousness, in figures of speech. Some creative ideas have monetary merit; most do not and ones that do are difficult to locate in the cacophony of the blogosphere. Other ethicists believe the blogosphere upholds the tenets of social responsibility by serving the political system through information and debate, by enlightening the public to make intelligent choices in the voting booth, by providing a forum for buyers and sellers to conduct commerce, by entertaining the populace, and by maintaining independence from special interests. However, the theory of social responsibility informs and is informed by such ethical systems as teleology with its focus on consequences, utilitarianism with its focus on happiness, and especially deontology with its focus on duty. None of these paradigms seriously consider cost-benefit analysis as the primary factor in consequences, happiness, and duty. In fact, social responsibility "reflects a dissatisfaction" with the interpretation of revenue generation by some media owners and operators; and while the theory "accepts the role of the press in servicing the economic system … it would not have this task take precedence over such other functions as promoting the democratic processes or enlightening the public" (Siebert and Schramm, 1974, p. 74).

For more than a decade I have tried to reconcile the reality of new media with the theories of press and journalism ethics. In every case, I have come to see that the medium is more than the message; it is the moral as in the moral of a story being written before our multitasking eyes with the end not yet scripted but hurdling toward an Ellulian conclusion. It is a moral that cannot even define the "mass" in "mass communication" upon which once again most of our ethical theories are based, at least in part, believing that journalists with socially responsible consciences disseminate news that informs rather than affirms. Successful online business models from Facebook to Google believe information, especially timely information, has no value so as to be given away for free via a platform that generates revenue by vending information *about* information that sells more than once in the spirit of marketing rather than Fourth Estate. Finally, the moral of the story is what has *not* occurred because of the Internet and integrated platforms that promised democracy and delivered "technopoly," the title of Neil Postman's prescient 1993 book about the surrender of culture to technology, in which he states that anyone who practices criticism of the kind presented here must endure being asked, "What is the solution to the problems you describe?" (Postman, 1993, p. 182).

Like me, Postman had no answers in 1993 as I have none 16 years later. He, however, provided the method to resist society's inevitable surrender to the autonomous nature of technology. Postman believed that an individual person can act "irrespective of what the culture is doing" and assess the culture "irrespective of what any individual is doing." At least for me, his methods helped me formulate the theory of the "interpersonal divide" – or the void that technology creates when it seduces people to the extent that they believe someone somewhere else is more important than the place they are or the person they are with. Countering this effect, Postman placed the future in the hands of individuals with certain character traits, whom he called "resistance fighters." They possessed attributes that can guide others in the digital age, helping us deal with a reality no longer grounded in place, time, and culture; that splits rather than extends the senses; and that will not reshape journalism as much as the reason for doing it.

Paraphrasing Postman (1993), we must refute the technological belief that efficiency is the primary goal of human relations and that precision is a synonym for truth and information, a synonym for understanding. We must be skeptical of technological progress or arguments based on that notion, especially using words that we associate with progress, such as "innovation," "engagement," and "interactivity." Innovation in one area might spell setback in another, and ethicists need to focus on the latter before embracing the former. Postman asked us to expect people in the room when consumers heard the 1979 AT&T slogan, "Reach out and touch someone." Likewise, I expect to travel to a real destination, reading, "Where would you like to go today?" These precepts remind us to admire technological ingenuity but not connote that with the highest form of human achievement (Postman, 1993, p. 184).

The Medium is the Moral   315

I incorporate those assessments in my criticism of technology's nature. I also am a student of history as well as philosophy, realizing it takes several generations before the overlooked or unanticipated effects of technology are addressed in theory or practice. As I write in *Interpersonal Divide*,

> Nobody can predict what will be invented or transformed to meet this challenge; but there will be distinct hallmarks: a shift from economic toward transcendent truth, from corporate toward collective empowerment, and from social disenfranchisement toward civic engagement. Until such a person uses media and technology to affirm that truth is greater than market or market share, we will suffer a diminished sense of community (Bugeja, 2005, p. 112).

In the end, all ethical theory, in one aspect or another, addresses community. According to Deni Elliott (1997), our social nature pivots on "the need for being-in-community" (p. 80) and "the socialization of the moral being takes place in the individual's relationships with others" (p. 80). Consequently, in our theories and hypothesizes, we need to acknowledge technology's indomitable nature, assessing how it undermines the hitherto unquestioned foundations of our arguments without our even realizing that, as we cite the works of other ethicists long since rendered irrelevant. Most of all, we must guard against a diminished sense of community grounded in place, time, and culture, without which journalism's role and reason for being will measured by the costs and benefits of economy rather than of morality.

Acknowledgment

The author wishes to acknowledge the work of research assistant Sam Berbano especially in the section titled "The Medium is the Money."

References

Associated Press (2007) Texting to blame for crash that killed 5 teens? July 14, www.msnbc.msn.com/id/19764563/ (accessed June 28, 2010).

Berners-Lee, T. (1999) *Weaving the Web*, Harper, San Francisco.

Bierman, N., and Ryan, A. (2009) *Boston Globe* online, 11 May, http://www.boston.com/news/local/breaking_news/2009/05/trolley_driver.html (accessed July 19, 2010).

Bond, E.J. (2001) Value, concept of, in *Encyclopedia of Ethics* (ed. L.C. Becker and C.B. Becker), Routledge, New York.

Bugeja, M. (2005) *Interpersonal Divide: The Search for Community in a Technological Age*, Oxford University Press, New York.

Dulles, A. (2004) Challenges to moral and cultural renewal, *Notre Dame Center for Ethics and Culture*, from http://ethicscenter.nd.edu/archives/dulles.shtml (accessed June 28, 2010).

Elliott, D. (1997) Universal values and moral development theories, in *Communication Ethics and Universal Values*, (eds C. Christians and M. Traber, Michael), Sage, Thousand Oaks, CA.

Ellul, J. (2003) The "autonomy" of the technological phenomenon, in *Philosophy of Technology: The Technological Condition*, (eds R.C. Scharff, and V. Dusek), Blackwell, Malden, MA, pp. 386–397.

Fairlie, H. (1976) *The Spoiled Child of the Western World: The Miscarriage of the American Idea in our Time*, Doubleday, Garden City, NY.

Gert, B. (2001) "Moral rules" in *Encyclopedia of Ethics*, (ed. L.C. Becker and C.B. Becker), Routledge, New York.

Hamilton, A. (2003) Andrew Hamilton, Statement at Trial of John Peter Zenger, 1735, in *A Patriot's Handbook: Songs, Poems, Stories, and Speeches Celebrating the Land We Love*, (ed. C. Kennedy), Hyperion, New York, pp. 229–325.

Heidegger, M. (2003) The question concerning technology, in *Philosophy of Technology: The Technological Condition* (R.C. Scharff and V. Dusek), Blackwell, Malden, MA., pp. 252–264.

Ledingham, J.C., Ledingham, A., and Richardson, J.E. (2003) The Effects of Media Violence on Children, www.hc-sc.gc.ca/hppb/familyviolence/html/nfntseffemediarech_e.html (accessed June 28, 2010).

McLean, Bethany (2001) Is Enron overpriced? March 5, *Forbes*, http://money.cnn.com/2006/01/13/news/companies/enronoriginal_fortune/index.htm (accessed June 28, 2010).

McLuhan, M. (1964) *Understanding Media: The Extensions of Man*, McGraw-Hill, New York.

Media 100 (n.d.) Index to the 2007 Media 100, *Advertising Age*, Data Center, http://adage.com/datacenter/article?article_id=131198 (accessed June 28, 2010).

Moor, J. (2008) Why we need better ethics for emerging technologies, in (eds J. Van Den Hoven and J. Weckert), *Information Technology and Moral Philosophy*, Cambridge University Press, New York, p. 432.

Negroponte, N. (1995) *Being Digital*, Knopf, New York.

Postman, N. (1993) *Technopoly: The Surrender of Culture to Technology*, Vintage Books, New York.

Siebert, T.P., and Schramm, W. (1974) *Four Theories of the Press* University of Illinois Press, Urbana.

Sommers, C.H. (1993) Teaching the virtues. *Chicago Tribune Magazine*, September 12, reprint.

Thomas, WC. (2002) The rise and fall of Enron, *Journal of Accountancy*, www.journalofaccountancy.com/Issues/2002/Apr/TheRiseAndFallOfEnron.htm (accessed June 28, 2010).

Washington Post (2008) Engineer in deadly LA train crash was texting. *The Washington Post*. September 18, http://voices.washingtonpost.com/washingtonpostinvestigations/2008/09/conductor_in_deadly_la_train_c.html (accessed June 8, 2010).

Williams, T.M. (1986), *The Impact of Television: A Natural Experiment in Three Communities*, Academic Press, Orlando, FL.

17

Development Ethics
The Audacious Agenda

Chloe Schwenke

*There it was again: the noble cause, the great saving illusion. I didn't say
anything. I thought of Somalia and Sudan, all of that vainglorious rhetoric
about pasting nations back together with a few bags of food. No aid worker who
stayed long in that part of the world imagined the kind of aid we gave could
do more than keep a few people going for another day and perhaps, as one of
Emma's Operation Lifeline colleagues wrote to me, open some "space for the
oddities of relief, tragedy, misery, sex, and personal extravagance" – which is
to say, some space for life itself. But it seemed impossible to transmit this small,
personal knowledge back to the West; in every case it became garbled, mutated
into visions of grandiosity or metastasized into furies of disappointment. It was
never enough to have helped one person, to have opened some tiny window of
compassion. There was no allowance for the years of warfare, no time to study the
messy politics. If Africa couldn't be saved in a very short time and at very little
cost, then to hell with it – anyone who went there must be a saint.*

(Scroggins, 2004, p. 344)

Introduction

Adventure, not sainthood, was my goal when I first ventured to Africa. Other than
being prepared for intense heat, I had few preconceptions of Africa. As the doorway of the Kenya Airways Boeing 707 opened and I stepped out onto the airport's
apron, I was enveloped by the surprisingly cool air of a July Nairobi night in 1979.
So much for the intense heat; it was the first of countless Africa's lessons during my
14 years of living and working on the continent. The one Africa lesson I most
wanted to master continues to elude me: making some sense of Africa's grinding

---

The Handbook of Global Communication and Media Ethics, First Edition. Edited by Robert S. Fortner
and P. Mark Fackler.
© 2011 Blackwell Publishing Ltd. Published 2011 by Blackwell Publishing Ltd.

poverty. I have observed how Africa's poor persevere: stripped of any vestige of dignity, devoid of all but the most meager hopes for a better future. I have sought to understand how they can endure each day of unrelenting harshness, especially while they witness the coddled comfort and security of elites and expatriates. How can anyone rationalize a global society that allows such enormous diversity in wealth and poverty, comfort and suffering, privilege and destitution?

Perhaps the most evocative description of poverty I know comes from the simple declaration of a poor Ethiopian man (Narayan *et al.*, 2000, p. 33): "Life has made us ill." These five words embody a sweeping, incisive condemnation of the global status quo, while begging the question of our relationship to his "illness." In an age where human prosperity for many people has reached levels unimaginable at any prior time in human history, vast numbers of people around the developing world, and some in the more developed countries as well, must still contend with the moral outrages of poverty, child malnutrition, the widespread incidence of preventable disease, and the deprivation of those qualities we normally associate with the "truly human" life. Who cares about these persons? Who is responsible for reconciling the morally impermissible coexistence of such wealth and such poverty? Are we in the developed world complacent – or complicit – in tolerating the moral distance between "us" and "them"? Ought there not to be a global moral order, perhaps a premise of universal human dignity, which would provide the rationale for a minimum threshold of well-being for all human beings?

A global moral order, or any similar concept of a moral law seems at best a fanciful notion compared to the reality of the poor throughout the less developed countries of the world – the "global South" as these countries are termed in the jargon of international development. As Jonathan Glover pondered: "The challenge to the moral law is intellectual: to find good reasons for thinking that it exists and that it has any claim on us" (Glover, 1999, p. 1). Yet there are many people who are convinced that such a framework of moral interconnectedness, perhaps moral interdependency, exists – perhaps not so definitively structured as a moral law, but with clear claims upon our awareness, compassion, resources, energies, and action. This conviction forms the foundation of a serious undertaking, and bears with it our modest but earnest hopes for a morally coherent future for this planet. This conviction underpins and defines development ethics.

An Overview of Development Ethics

> Morality is for human beings. It is possible because of certain facts of human nature, and it is necessary because of other facts of human nature (McKinnon, 1999, p. 5).

Development ethics is ethical reflection on the ends and means of socioeconomic change in poor countries and regions. Development ethicists agree that the moral dimension of development theory and practice is just as important as the scientific and policy components. What is often called "development" – economic growth, for instance – may be bad for people, communities and the environment. Hence, the process of development should be reconceived as beneficial change, usually specified as alleviating human misery and environmental degradation in poor countries (Crocker, 1999, 2001).

One of the best known leaders in the field of development ethics is the philosopher David Crocker, who asks the philosopher's question, "In what direction and by what means should a society 'develop'" (Crocker, 2001, p. 1)? His succinct description of development ethics encompasses a complex endeavor by philosophers, ethicists, development practitioners, and others to create and apply a rigorous intellectual discipline and philosophical grounding to the challenges of development, and to the many moral questions to which the concept of "development" gives rise. Development ethics provides a comprehensive set of moral approaches to facilitate reflection upon – and consideration of appropriate responses to – the many urgent moral concerns, motivations, obligations, and competing priorities associated with development particularly in the global South, but arguably also in the more developed countries – the global North. Development ethics reinforces and places in a general framework such norms as human dignity, social justice, human flourishing, the common good, safety and security, interdependence, care and compassion, participation and inclusion.

Development ethics is a relative newcomer in applied ethics, having only begun to take explicit and self-conscious form in the 1980s (Crocker, 2001). Since that time, however, there have been robust additions to the body of thought framed by development ethics, and the literature within the new discipline is now substantial. The best known contributions have come from philosophers and ethicists, both in the North and the South, including the recent release of David Crocker's *Ethics of Global Development: Agency, Capability, and Deliberative Democracy*. My own book, *Reclaiming Value in International Development: The Moral Dimensions of Development Policy and Practice in Poor Countries*, also was released recently. The literature of development ethics includes works by Sabina Alkire, Charles Beitz, Peter Berger, Luis Camacho, David Crocker, John D'Arcy May, Nigel Dower, Des Gasper, Denis Goulet, Godfrey Gunatilleke, Herman Kahn, Onora O'Neill, Martha Nussbaum, Thomas Pogge, Mozaffar Qizilbash, E. Roy Ramírez, Ramon Romero, Amartya Sen, Peter Singer, and Paul Streeten, among others. Development ethics, by intention, seeks to extend beyond academia and involve development practitioners such as this author, policy makers, and others. This expansion has taken form, for example, in the International Development Ethics Association (IDEA), a small organization active in fostering a widening dialogue on a variety of development issues by means of a newsletter, website, international conferences, and networking (Gasper, 1994).

The ethical focus on development extends beyond the domain of development ethics, whose boundaries in any event are loosely defined. Closely related to the concerns of development ethics, significant work is being advanced in research and dialogue on social and human capital, environmental ethics, business ethics, political theory of development, leadership studies, urban and regional planning theory, development economics, and geography. The many-faceted attention now placed on the moral dimensions of development does call into question whether there is a need to establish some "territorial" boundaries for development ethics – should development ethics extend into trade relations, military affairs, migration, international organized crime networks, stabilization and security studies, gender and diversity studies, and/or corruption? Should it address such concerns in both the South and the North? These issues remain unresolved and continue to elicit spirited debate.

In the context of international development, where resources are scarce and needs are urgent, many of the decisions made by individuals, institutions, groups, and governments affect others for good or for ill. Sometimes, such decisions mean either life or death for certain stakeholders. Engaging in ethical reflection on decisions that pertain to critical development issues therefore is not merely an intellectually stimulating academic pastime. The normative dimensions of the decisions as to what we or others *ought* to do (or ought to have done) in response to poverty, exclusion, marginalization, and urgent need warrant our careful thought and evaluation: factually, conceptually, and ethically. Political and cultural leaders, policy makers, development practitioners, civil society activists, and many others confront ethical issues on a daily basis, and the choices they must make may be harmful for some – or many – persons. When resources are scarce, human needs great, and existing economic distributive mechanisms ineffective or skewed, the moral weight of decisions can be particularly acute. As noted by Guido Calabresi and Philip Bobbitt, such decisions on allocations must be made in "ways that preserve the moral foundations of social collaboration" (Calabresi and Bobbitt, 1978, p.18). Failing this, violence and civil unrest may ensue or poverty may worsen, with the associated increase in human suffering. Such choices must also be made with the full knowledge that we are living in a world of human imperfections – greed, hunger for power, ignorance and short-sightedness, prejudice and ethnocentrism – and that social, cultural, political, and economic institutions often reflect these imperfections (Dower, 1998a).

The Moral Discourse on Development

Moral reflection as described above is part of a moral discourse. According to the late Denis Goulet, who together with Louis Joseph Lebret can be considered as the pioneers of development ethics, moral discourse concerning development occurs on four distinct levels:

1 Determination (including clarification and defense) of the most general and fundamental ends of development;
2 Establishing the criteria for specifying when these ends have been achieved or already exist;
3 Formulation of strategies (adoption of the most efficient and morally permissible package of means to achieve important ends); and
4 Separate consideration of individual means (Goulet, 1995, pp. 11–14).

The Audacious Agenda 321

A four-level reflective process of this character operates in several contexts. It applies as much to the resolution of moral dilemmas in the formulation and implementation of development policies as it does in the assessment of the moral dimensions of foundational development theories. This four-level reflective process also describes aspects of the deliberative participation of stakeholders in development decision-making.

Goulet properly begins at the beginning – by asking what development is. The determination of the ends or objectives of development has to do with the conception of development itself, which is at the heart of many of the debates within development ethics and related fields of inquiry. Development was originally conceived as being equivalent to economic growth, modernization, or industrialization, but development ethics has brought a values focus to refine the concept and definition of development. The economic growth model failed to focus on the well-being of individuals, and it became clear that the alleviation of poverty was not a necessary by-result of economic growth, unless some form of authority intervened or directed that growth (Dower, 1998a). Some also questioned whether the image of the good life – characterized by materialism, consumerism, and individualism, and associated with the economic growth model – is fundamentally Western in value (Schumacher, 1973). This Western concept of the good life may not be appropriate, they argue, to all cultures and societies (Dower, 1998a). Even subsequent evolutions of the economic growth model, such as the *growth with equity* model, in which the state directed some of the benefits of growth to the poor, or the *basic needs approach*, which created specific programs targeted at the basic needs of the poor, are considered by many to have failed adequately to address the dimension of individual human well-being or flourishing (Dower, 1998a). Despite these misgivings, the majority of development theorists consider that economic growth is either central or at least necessary (but not sufficient) to development, although more radical views reject this premise (Dower, 1998a).

The philosopher and Nobel Laureate economist Amartya Sen moved the debate about the goals of development more firmly into the moral sphere when he argued that economic growth is not the fundamental end of development but is at best (and not always) a good means. Development, Sen argues, should be conceived as a process of expanding the real freedoms that people enjoy so that their lives may become more truly "human" (Sen, 1999). Since its inception in 1990, the United Nations Development Programme, in which Sen was and continues to be a major influence, also frames its view of development in relation to the goal of increasing the freedoms, of which it lists seven (UNDP, 2000, p. 1):

1   Freedom from discrimination,
2   Freedom from want,
3   Freedom to develop and realize one's human potential,
4   Freedom from fear,
5   Freedom from injustice,
6   Freedom of thought and speech and participation, and
7   Freedom for decent work.

322   Chloe Schwenke

When and where has genuine development occurred? When is real progress being made? How should one assess the quality, effectiveness, and appropriateness of development strategies, policies, or interventions? Goulet's second step or level – establishing the criteria for specifying basic development goals – depends in part upon a process of discernment and ethical reflection. This, in turn, must be based upon the application of norms and moral values. How does one select and justify the choice of moral values, among many competing moral theories? This question raises several fundamental divisions of thought within development ethics, which Crocker summarizes in three meta-ethical views: *universalists,*[1] *particularists,*[2] or a position based on crosscultural consensus, embracing elements of both (Crocker, 2001, p. 9). This third position attempts to transcend the stand-off between universalists and particularists. As stated by Crocker:

> On this view, development ethics should forge a cross-cultural consensus in which a society's own freedom to make development choices is one among a plurality of fundamental norms and in which these norms are of sufficient generality so as not only to permit but also to require sensitivity to societal differences (Crocker, 1999, p. 42).

It can be argued that other moral approaches fit well within this third position, including the capability approach and the UNDP's human rights approach. Amartya Sen, who – along with Martha Nussbaum and David Crocker – pioneered the ethical theory and development perspective known as the capability approach, seeks to be sensitive to cultural differences while still insisting on a threshold of "moral minimums" (Crocker, 1991; Nussbaum, 2000; Sen, 1987).

In summary, development ethics has raised the profile of the moral dialogue within the context of development theory, policy, and practice. Development ethics directly addresses the most fundamental – and the most controversial – topics in development, generally considered: the dignity and worth of each human being, the moral dimensions that motivate development actions, who should make development decisions, and the meaning of development itself. Development ethics similarly provides a valuable and insightful perspective on the meaning and role of such important concepts as the extent and nature of our moral obligations towards – and claims on – others, the moral demands of social justice, the moral legitimacy of government and its leaders, the moral requirements of gender equality, and the moral justifications for broad-based stakeholder participation in analysis, deliberations, and decision-making on development and governance.

Returning to Goulet's four levels concept of moral reflection, level three pertains to the formulation of strategies or sets of means designed to achieve development ends. Strategies are the means by which to achieve and sustain development goals. This means-ends thinking is closely related to the theory-practice[3] relationship which Crocker clarifies, since not only do development ethics formulate and defend certain ethical principles and goals for development but they can also be viewed as an essential strategy for achieving the desirable objectives of development in the South.

Recall that Goulet identifies the fourth or most concrete level of moral reflection within development ethics as the consideration and choice of individual means (within sets of means). This disaggregation is somewhat problematic in the context of development, where most means of development are closely interrelated and interdependent. Nevertheless, there is certainly scope for targeted ethical reflection of specific critical "means," such as specific programs or tactics to achieve or protect decent standards of employment, opportunities for popular participation in decision-making, equitable access to development resources, local empowerment[4] for decision-making on local issues, and so forth.

If it is to be effective, reflection on the means and ends of development in the South can and should take many forms. Within the development context, development ethics can be effectively applied on Goulet's four levels and in many different ways: (a) participatory integrated development planning, (b) codes of ethics, (c) ethical oversight of the public sector by civil society, and (d) moral education, to mention but a few.

Thinking Morally

A moral agent is a rational, dignified human being who enjoys the freedom to "prioritize and coordinate their various inclinations, affiliations, and roles" (Crocker 2008, p. 245). Moral agents make informed choices, and accept the responsibility for the consequences that flow from their actions. Operating at this level of ethical consciousness, freedom, and accountability requires moral grounding. The impacts of development policy and practice directly affect the moral agency of all of the stakeholders involved, ideally expanding and strengthening such agency. In some cases, however, development policy and practice is a blunt and poorly directed instrument, devoid of clear purpose, or structured in such a way as primarily to serve interests other than the purported beneficiaries. The test of moral grounding is simple: when challenged with the "development for what?" and the "development benefiting who?" questions, the answers should be either apparent or readily to hand. If, however, development policy and practice is not rooted in the moral values experience and convictions of human beings – individually, within interdependent relationships, and in society – then those involved in designing, planning, or implementing development policies and practice will stumble in their attempts to answer these two basic questions, and be unable even to differentiate between development means (instrumentality) and development ends (objectives).

In the absence of a clear articulation of the priority moral values that shape our character, actions, relationships, and communities, our ability to achieve effective moral agency is very much in doubt. Sometimes these moral values are situated in our intuitive response to a situation in which specific people are in need, when we simply act out of our direct caring and concern. In other instances, our moral agency is best directed by recourse to trusted ethical ideals, principles, and freedoms, derived from or associated with priority moral values. While by no means a definitive list, these ideals, principles, and freedoms include the premise of human dignity; social justice; human well-being and flourishing; the common good; safety and security; and participation and inclusion. Each of these is described in further detail below.

The premise of human dignity

The concept of human dignity has its roots in the idea of social honor; *dignitas* in Latin means just this – honor. The Israeli philosopher, Avishai Margalit, in his work on portraying the attributes of the "decent society," claims that the achievement of such a society depends on universal acceptance throughout society that everyone deserves social honor in equal measure, which is best expressed in the concept of human dignity. Dignity, according to Margalit, also constitutes the external aspect of self-respect, and the tendency to behave in a dignified manner that attests to one's self-respect (Margalit, 1996).

Margalit, as well as Rousseau and Kant before him, offers many reasons for respecting human nature, a concept closely associated with human dignity and intrinsic worth. Kant, for instance, listed many attributes of humanity that give it value, including (but not limited to): (a) being a creature who gives things values, (b) having the capacity for self-legislation, (c) having the ability progressively to pursue perfection, (d) having the capacity to be a moral agent, (e) being rational, and (f) being the only creature able to transcend natural causality (Margalit, 1996).

At the other extreme, the simple fact that people believe that they are worthy of respect – but not due to any particular human attribute – is considered even by some skeptics as adequate grounds to justify treating human beings as creatures with dignity, deserving of respect (Margalit, 1996). Removing even this level of abstraction, the simple acknowledging that human relationships are frequently about offering care and receiving care provides its own motivation for alleviating poverty (Noddings, 1984).

Margalit however makes another sobering observation, of particular relevance to the life of the poor in the South, and directly tied to my own questions about the nature of poverty: "Survival takes priority over dignity" (Margalit, 1996, p. 136). For the poor in a society to achieve the most basic level of human dignity, they must also be able to meet their most basic needs. Without acceptance of the moral right to human survival, discussions of human dignity become merely theoretical, particularly when that sense of dignity is insufficient to motivate others with access to more substantial resources to secure that survival threshold for all persons.

Social justice

Social justice is associated with fair, even-handed treatment of all individuals and groups within a society. An alternative formulation, indebted to John Rawls, is that conceptions of distributive justice[5] clarify and defend how major social institutions should distribute burdens and benefits, however conceived (Rawls, 1971).

The important point at this juncture is to indicate that different conceptions of justice have different conceptions of burdens and benefits as well as different conceptions of the proper principles of distribution.

On social justice, philosopher Thomas Pogge remarks:

> Its current most prominent use is in the moral assessment of social institutions, understood not as organized collective agents (such as the United States government or the World Bank), but rather as a social system's practices or "rules of the game," which govern interactions among individual and collective agents as well as their access to material resources … Prominent within our political discourse, then, is the goal of formulating and justifying a criterion of justice, which assesses the degree to which the institutions of a social system are treating the persons and groups they affect in a morally appropriate and, in particular, evenhanded way (cited in Paul, Miller, and Paul, 1999, p. 337).

Both Thomas Pogge and Douglas Rasmussen make reference to the close relationship between social justice and human flourishing. According to Rasmussen, social justice is the prerequisite for the achievement of human flourishing (Paul, Miller, and Paul, 1999).

Manfred Max-Neef, an economist and noted development practitioner, considers that social justice has become, in some instances, conflated with economic growth. He criticized the prevalent thinking that simply by "growing" the economy there will be more to share, without having to tackle the more thorny issues of distributing or redistributing the proportions of the total. Max-Neef contends that it is ineffectual to focus on the maintenance of static distributive proportions while growth proceeds; the reality is that the poor usually get less and less: "even with growth, the poor's share of the cake diminishes" (Max-Neef, 1992, p. 51).

Some feminists offer a significantly differing view on the issue of social justice. Carol Gilligan notes that from a social justice perspective, the individual as a moral agent is challenged to judge the conflicting claims of self and others against some principle or standard of equality (e.g., the Golden Rule). As an alternative less based on abstract notions of equality, she proposes instead that the caring relationship becomes the determinate of self and others, under which the self as a moral agent perceives and responds to the perception of need within and around her. The moral question shifts from "what is just?" to "how to respond?" as caring, it is argued, only becomes meaningful when it is linked to a commitment to action (Kittay and Meyers, 1987, p. 23). Nel Noddings also speaks to this approach, now commonly known as the ethics of care, when she argues: "It is precisely because the tendency to treat each well is so fragile that we must strive so consistently to care" (Noddings, 1984, p. 99).

Human flourishing and well-being

The notion of human well-being, which is sometimes but not always identified with human flourishing, is intuitively understood by each of us, perhaps without consciously attempting to be precise in its definition. For the sake of development strategies, this intuitive understanding may suffice. Yet many philosophers have wrestled with this notion, formulating and justifying their varying conceptions, which in turn are challenged by other philosophers. I offer below an overview of the range of these conceptions, not to step into the philosophers' debates by arguing for any one position, but instead to impart something of the conceptual richness and diversity of this important objective of human development.

The concept of flourishing, if not well-being, is to some extent at least agent-relative. That is, no one concept of human flourishing is wholly relevant for all, and each person's sense of "the good life" may differ in many respects. To a considerable extent, the notion depends upon knowledge of the possibilities open, and the availability of freedoms and resources essential to pursue those opportunities. Despite agent-relative differences in conceptions of the good, there may still be a defensible crosscultural conception of *basic* well-being or at least of a human life not going badly.

Nuanced definitions of well-being and flourishing do exist. Philosophers such as Amartya Sen, David Crocker, and James Griffin distinguish between well-being, minimal well-being, and flourishing or "the good life" (Crocker, 1998, pp. 366–385; Griffin, 1996, pp. 85–86; Sen, 1999, pp. 70–76). Sen and Crocker identify well-being with enlightened self-interest (Crocker 1998, p. 373; Sen 1999, pp. 74–76). Other philosophers have attempted to characterize the ideal of human flourishing or the less robust notion of human well-being. Rasmussen, for example, proposes a neo-Aristotelian conception of human flourishing, in which he states that human flourishing is a way of living and acting, not something static. It is desirable because of what it is, and while not the only activity of inherent worth, it is the ultimate human goal (Paul, Miller, and Paul, 1999). This is not meant to imply that human flourishing is achieved as some end-state of well-being; instead flourishing is seen in a life that is worthwhile as a whole. Aristotle viewed human flourishing, among other things, as a self-directed activity. The neo-Aristotelian position, according to Rasmussen, dictates that human flourishing is not a direct result of luck or factors beyond one's own control and that it must be achieved through one's own efforts if it is to have value and meaning. Moral consideration also is required to determine what form of flourishing is best for each individual (Paul, Miller, and Paul, 1999). Charles Larmore has a more nuanced view; he argues flourishing is more than a self-directed accomplishment: how one responds to factors beyond one's control is also important to the achievement of human flourishing and well-being (Paul, Miller, and Paul, 1999).

Leading thinkers in the ethics of care tradition construe human well-being and flourishing in terms of our innate desire to "meet the other morally" (Noddings, 1984, p. 4), and the nurturing of conditions that will permit caring and healthy interdependencies to flourish as the basis for what constitutes a meaningful life. Within ethics of care, flourishing is viewed as both self-directed and individually defined, but also as a product of our interrelatedness with others. While rejecting some generalized notion of universal caring, the fundamental recognition

The Audacious Agenda

of this relatedness is described by Noddings in terms of specific relationships comprised of the "one-caring" and the "cared-for." To Noddings, what one might become and achieve is dependent, at least in part, on this caring relationship between specific people. As she states: "The very goodness I seek, the perfection of the ethical self is, thus, partly dependent on you, the other" (Noddings 1984, p. 6).

Sen and Crocker, by contrast, capture this relationship between self and others, self-direction, and well-being quite differently. They differentiate the agency dimension of human beings from a person's well-being dimension, and do not conceive of well-being necessarily as a product of interrelatedness with – or caring for – others. For Sen and Crocker, being self-directed also does not have to mean pursuing higher levels of well-being. Someone can be very self-directed and intentionally lower her/his well-being, through religious fasting, making sacrifices for others or for a cause, even through suicide (Sen, 1999, 190–195).

For John Rawls, human flourishing is best portrayed as the formulation and successful execution of a rational plan of life, by which the person determines the good for himself or herself (Rawls, 1971, p. 408). Pogge explains flourishing as a composite of experience, success, character, and achievement, and offers an encompassing definition of human flourishing:

> That human persons are flourishing means that their lives are good, or worthwhile, in the broadest sense. Thus, the concept of human flourishing, as I understand it, marks the most comprehensive, "all-in" assessment of the quality of human lives (cited in Paul, Miller, and Paul, 1999).

The common good

In its most general sense, the "common good" may be said to consist of the policies and actions that best serve to promote the essential components of human well-being or flourishing for all. Identifying the "common good," or its equivalent phrase, the "public interest," is a controversial issue because of different conceptions of human well-being or flourishing, as described above. In utilitarian thinking, the common good is the aggregated best net score of individual interests in the community – a concept that obviously sacrifices some people's interests to that of others. Others contend that the common good can be articulated only roughly, and is often subject to moral disagreements. On this view, it is through a deliberative democratic process of reasoning together that the common good can be agreed upon and mutually acceptable decisions can be made (Gutmann and Thompson, 1996). Amy Gutmann and Dennis Thompson describe a process in which people in conflict reason reciprocally, recognizing the moral worth of the opposing person, even when they consider his or her position to be morally wrong. Under this concept of deliberative democracy, there exists a mutual obligation of respect towards opponents. From this respect a common good, acceptable to (almost) all, often can be agreed to: "Deliberation is not only a means to an end, but also a means for deciding what means are morally required to pursue our common ends" (Gutmann and Thompson, 1996, p. 12).

In serving the public good, Richard Flathman has observed that a moral demand is placed upon members of a society to regard themselves as morally obligated (but not physically coerced) to obey particular commands and to conform to particular policies that they may regard as contrary to their personal interests. A moral justification must be provided to justify this sacrifice of perceived self-interest, and not simply the weight of majority interests. The fact that many individuals present such a demand does not alter the situation. Number – that is, force – is not a criterion of right. Flathman further observed that this "is the timeless message of Rousseau's distinction between the will of all and the general will" (Flathman, 1966).

Safety and security

Safety and security refer generally to conditions of stability, order, predictability, and freedom from bodily harm (Rosan, Ruble, and Tulchin, 2000, pp. 14, 76). Within the development context, these concepts can be interpreted in a wide variety of ways. They may be reflected in public health and environmental concerns, such as being able to live without becoming ill or being subject to environmental disasters. These concepts may extend to economic security, in which access to employment and/or other forms of welfare ensures access to adequate resources for human flourishing, or at least, human survival.

In human rights terms, security encompasses many negative rights and freedoms. Achieving a sustainable sense of security involves certain critical freedoms, such as the freedom *from* poverty and *from* violence. Positive rights and freedoms are also included – the ability *to* achieve a decent standard of living.

The United Nations Development Programme (UNDP) makes the point that no other aspect of human security is more vital as security from physical violence. It lists several sources of threats of violence, including (a) the state (torture, arbitrary arrest and detention),(b) other states (war, support for oppressive regimes), (c) other groups of people (ethnic conflicts, street violence, crime), (d) threats directed at women (rape, domestic violence, trafficking), and (e) threats directed at children (child abuse) (UNDP, 2000, p. 35).

Participation and inclusion

There are many kinds and intensities of participation, ranging from Gutmann and Thompson's deliberative democracy model to voting, from open and advisory public hearings to visioning workshops. Each has its benefits and limitations. I argue for a model of *deliberative participation*, claiming that the notion of a truly deliberative, participatory process is important to the achievement of sustainable development. In this respect, a deliberative participatory process either assumes or includes – through a partially structured or facilitated dialogue – the ideals of human dignity, social justice, human flourishing, and well-being, the common good, safety and security, caring and compassion, and similar ideals. Deliberative participation also offers a way to specify, weigh, trade-off, and sequence (the realization) of these ideals (Schwenke 2008, pp. 45–56).

When decisions are made in the public interest, the decision-maker's moral legitimacy, credibility, and motivation deserve scrutiny. This scrutiny should begin by, but not be limited to, assessing the extent to which opportunities for popular participation exist, the degree to which decision-makers view themselves as influenced by and accountable to that participatory process, and the fairness, representativeness, and effectiveness of the participatory process itself. Effective participation is an excellent means to morally based decision making, but in addressing issues of power relationships and human rights, it is not the only means.

If all rational human beings are regarded as equally dignified and valuable, all rational human beings within a society ought to be empowered to participate in the critical decisions that affect them – that limit or create opportunities and freedoms for each to flourish. Including all people in all aspects of all decision-making is not practical, so societies have developed various forms of political leadership and representative decision-making. Under this conception, political leaders and elected or appointed representatives act on the presumption of a vested public trust, to which they are accountable. The delegation of decision-making authority to political leaders is not by necessity absolute – where possible and appropriate, opportunities ought to exist to allow all citizens and residents of any given society to be well informed about the issues, and to participate in identifying priorities, strategies, and desirable actions.

In practice, political leadership in the South is generally top-down or even autocratic – neither accountable to, nor inclusive of, the citizenry. Some try to justify top-down leadership as a way to avoid the difficulties and expense in structuring and sustaining a deliberative participatory process sufficiently robust regularly to register, discuss, and reason through the various concerns, aspirations, claims, and demands of citizens and stakeholders. These "difficulties" may be only self-serving excuses, but equitable, inclusive, and – certainly – deliberative participation is hard to accomplish, and it can be expensive.

The problems begin with the stakeholder identification process, in which usually the elected and/or appointed decision makers in national or local government invite a range of participants to join in the formulation of specific development priorities, policies, and actions. It is seldom possible to select a representative body of stakeholders that reflects a reasonable approximation of the diverse interests, demographic, and social characteristics (age, gender, ethnicity, religion, LGBT diversity, etc.), and power structure of the area under review. If stakeholder selection can be accomplished to the general satisfaction of all, without the exclusion of any one group, further difficulties ensue. The participatory process must be time sensitive but ought not to be rushed – participants ought to have the opportunity to be informed on the issues, to be heard by all, to engage in a give and take of reason giving and assessing, and to have conflicts resolved in terms of outcomes to which all can give their consent. Ideally, the participatory agenda will be rich enough so that participants are not simply being polled, but instead have an opportunity to engage in a deliberative process in which all stakeholders are able to put forward their own arguments and ideas, to seek common ground, to demand reasons, and to record disagreement. In some cases, participants may need training to learn necessary public speaking skills, and/or to find assistance from trusted, articulate advocates.

Credibility demands a participatory process that has a procedural rationale, justified in language that the average stakeholder will easily understand. In some cases, such as in more radical models of participation, outsiders and experts are intentionally excluded. In other situations, particularly where participation addresses complex technical and/or procedural issues, the stakeholders as well as the experts shape the final process. This participation rationale – the rules and objectives of the participatory game – should persuade stakeholders that a framework is in place through which participants (stakeholders) will be respectfully encouraged to reflect upon, evaluate, and express their considered views – and their reasons for such views – on a wide list of development issues. Some of the values and principles that the larger society (the nation) already has formally agreed upon or accepted as universal – in treaty, law, or policy – may need to be restated. Those values and principles that are relative to that particular group of stakeholders may need to be articulated openly – perhaps for the first time in a public forum. In this sense, "careful structuring" of the participatory process should mean ensuring that principles of fairness and a commonly agreed upon agenda are adhered to, and not that the participation is manipulated towards predetermined outcomes. Participants should be exposed to and consider different views of means and ends within the larger context of a holistic view of human well-being, human development, and good governance, but those participating will first need to agree on process – how best to resolve disagreements and accommodate dissent.

Challenging a Moral Approach to Development

It might be argued that given the many procedural and logistical difficulties in participation, adding moral concerns such as concepts of social justice, the common good, human dignity, human rights and freedoms, caring and compassion, will only make the entire process more difficult and therefore less likely positively to influence public policy and planning. The same critique can be applied to development generally. First, many consider moral issues to be largely arbitrary and subjective in nature, changing in scope and intensity depending on which individuals are participating (or not) in any particular public deliberative forum. The forum may itself be problematic; the choice of agenda, chairperson, and/or social and cultural constraints may greatly constrain the quality, honesty, depth, and subject matter covered.

Second, seeking common ground on moral concerns risks upsetting the status quo. Those in power may never have had to justify the moral source of their authority, and may shrink from the moral obligations implicit – but seldom clearly articulated – in public service. Those who are most affluent may be morally challenged by those less affluent to justify why the gap between rich and poor should widen even further in pursuit of short-term "development" goals. Cities or towns may be morally emboldened to demand greater autonomy from the central government. Are some questions best left unasked? It is not surprising that there are few institutions within global, national, or local societies that demonstrate through their actions a commitment to ethically based decision-making, even if some make rhetorical gestures in this direction.

Third, the quality of a moral dialogue on substantive issues depends upon tolerance, reflection, mutual respect, and a deliberative ethos representative of the diversity of stakeholder interests and concerns. These attributes are moral ones that individual participants ought to bring to the process or acquire through it. Situations, however, may exist where such virtues are in scarce supply, and the quality of the moral dialogue or the developmental enterprise consequently deteriorates.

Fourth, many consider moral values and systems to be largely unreliable in policy making; many values are discounted because they are relevant only to a particular culture, time, and context, or are mistrusted as imposed by outsiders in the name, for example, of moral universalism,[6] skeptical realism,[7] or cosmopolitanism.[8] On the other hand, some values are questioned as being too focused on the interests, concerns, and perceptions of a particular community or society, rejecting claims of a broader moral obligation or accountability.

Fifth, moral values, along with many qualitative factors in development, are extremely difficult to measure, monitor and evaluate, so the impact of policies intended to respond to such concerns is hard to gauge. For this reason alone, many public policy makers avoid reliance on hard-to-measure moral justifications for allocation of scarce public resources.

Defending a Moral Approach to Development

The five objections described above apply to participatory processes specifically, but also generally to morally-based approaches to development. If left unanswered, they undercut my fundamental premise of the importance of moral appraisal in the definition, formulation, and implementation of development means and ends. I therefore offer the following brief responses.

The first objection is the claim that moral issues are largely arbitrary and subjective in nature, and that attending to moral issues in a participatory process is fraught with procedural difficulties. In practice, this objection has merit. Moral issues, if raised at all in participatory workshops or other development processes, are seldom addressed explicitly in a rigorous, unrushed manner through deliberations, reasoned justifications (and challenges to these justifications), and dialogue addressed at reducing disagreements and consensus-building. Common models of participatory practice and development decision-making largely ignore moral issues, or at best channel moral concerns into narrow outlets such as vision statements. Morality is not, however, arbitrary, as the systematic and critical study of moral beliefs, values and concerns – ethics – makes abundantly clear. In ethics, our values and beliefs are organized into various (and to some extent, competing) systems, each of which exhibits coherence more or less internally and more or less matches our considered judgments and deeply felt beliefs. In this way, individual moral concerns are given context, so that they can be argued from a systematic, well-reasoned set of relationships based on principles that in turn can be argued and justified. It is not practical or appropriate, however, to use the limited time and resources of a participatory workshop on development to justify a complete ethical theory (much less compare it to other contending theories, from first principles). Instead, various process tools can be derived from several well-established theories within the field of development ethics. These tool-based approaches could be applied in a time-constrained participatory process without preliminary philosophical justifications, using language accessible to the diverse range of stakeholders engaged.

The second objection is the claim that attending to moral concerns risks upsetting the status quo by challenging the existing economic and power relationships within any given society. This claim is accepted and may serve as a sufficient (but not publicly stated) reason for politically insecure leaders to avoid a participatory approach, or to seek to control the development process. Whether through participatory processes or by recourse to other means such as the courts, challenging the status quo is often important to the moral approach to development. The existence of widespread poverty, corruption, injustice, gender inequality, and the lack of universal respect for human dignity demand a challenge, and the moral approach offers some fresh insights into the means and ends of changing the status quo in ways which lead to more just, compassionate, and decent societies, and to the protection of the status quo when it is judged to be reasonably just. The changes need not be immediately radical or revolutionary. The fulfillment of such claims will, however, *ultimately* entail radical changes to the status quo.

The third objection is the concern that moral issues must be addressed and deliberated by participants, and decisions made by persons who exhibit moral virtues, and that such participants and decision-makers may be few in number. If this claim were accepted, it would be difficult to imagine a society's moral progress over time. The leadership of morally virtuous persons may well inspire and motivate others towards being receptive to the deliberation of moral issues, but that leadership is not a necessary condition. The commitment of social, political or religious institutions (and, by treaty provisions, even nations) to moral principles goes some distance in bringing the moral approach to participatory and development processes. If stakeholders are able to accept the credibility of an ethical framework, such as a human rights approach, and a way can be found to apply this (such as through a derived set of participatory process tools) to the development agenda under discussion, then the requirement for a wise and virtuous person to preside over the proceedings no longer pertains.

The fourth objection is that asserting values in public policy, whether within a participatory forum or through other operations of governance and development, is inappropriate because values vary in their moral justifications, from the universal to the relative. This dichotomy between the universal and the relative is a venerable old chestnut of philosophical debate, and a great deal is written and argued in the literature on this subject. I argue for an approach that accepts certain values as universal and fundamental to human nature, while also accepting that the local culture, tradition, and context ought significantly to influence and shape the implementation of development initiatives responsive to these universal values.

Finally, the fifth objection to morally based approaches to development is that the qualitative dimensions of moral values make them impractical in the public policy context. This, I contend, is a superficial argument. Measuring moral performance may be more difficult than monitoring nonmoral criteria through gathering empirical data and identifying trends. Empirical data, however, can say a great deal about the changes in achieving morally desirable goals, and the presentation of such data in participatory workshops can be informative. The birth weight of babies is a good proxy for measuring the shortcomings in the quality of life of people and the need for better nutrition and health care. An extensive amount of work is being carried out around the world to identify appropriate empirical indicators that measure quality of life. The degree to which national laws reflect internationally recognized human rights principles is also measurable. Qualitative factors in the experience of poverty, the enjoyment of basic freedoms and opportunities, and the prevalence of respect for human dignity are all subject to meaningful evaluation through a variety of techniques, from focus groups to surveys. The claim that I have confronted on a regular and frequent basis in three decades of development practitioner experience is that moral issues should not influence public policy or be raised in participatory workshops because they are troublesome to monitor and evaluate. Such an argument speaks more of a failure of political will or methodology than of a basic fault inherent in ethics or in evaluative technique.

Addressing Poverty

For most in the South, the prospect of large-scale external assistance from the North in the near future is unrealistic, and my own experience living and working in developing countries convinces me that no one in such countries seriously expects to receive such aid. Instead, there is a growing acceptance that initiatives to eradicate poverty and improve governance will continue to depend in large measure on the quality and effectiveness of local and national leadership in the South. Effective local leadership in turn is linked to progress in decentralization – bringing an appropriate level of institutional capacity, resources, and political control from the national to the local level, for urban and rural residents alike.

Moving power and resources closer to local residents by means of decentralization is but part of the solution; good governance at any level also requires political leadership that is ethically responsive to the broader context of sustainable human development and poverty alleviation. Development ultimately is a moral challenge; effective development policy and their implementing interventions therefore must come to terms with moral content, beginning by recognizing, respecting, and responding to the principal of human dignity, and the moral obligations that arise from this recognition. Similarly, development interventions and planning ought to recognize the human interdependence, and the many caring relationships that characterize development. This recognition and acceptance of our common caring and our human dignity – our moral equality – are the prerequisites for determining what it means for political leadership to be "ethically responsive," what ought to characterize the "good" of good governance, and who development ought to serve. The development challenge is not just to bring about economic growth, for growth is but a means to something else. Human dignity is fundamental, but human care and compassion, social justice, human flourishing, the common good, participation and inclusion, and safety and security variously suggest the objectives of development as a moral endeavor.

Institutionalizing Development Ethics

The recognition of development as a moral enterprise seems intuitively correct, and upon rational and rigorous examination this premise is only strengthened in its persuasiveness. Despite this, leading actors in international development continue with a deeply ambivalent view towards morality and ethics in development policy and its associated implementing programming. Throughout my own career, I have joined with leading ethicists and philosophers – along with concerned practitioners – in advocating for institutionalizing a more explicitly ethical perspective within the major development institutions: the World Bank (IBRD), the United Nations Development Programme (UNDP), the major regional development banks (IDB, AfDB, ADB), the US Agency for International Development (USAID), and the United Kingdom's Department for International Development (DFID). The goal was straightforward: to increase and deepen ethics awareness, and to ensure that ethically sensitive development planning and evaluation becomes a routine component of good development policy and practice.

Hopes were raised in 1998 when the Inter-American Development Bank (IDB) established within its walls the Inter-American Initiative on Social Capital, Ethics and Development (ISED) – the very first time that a functional unit of a multilateral or bilateral development organization was dedicated specifically to ethical concerns. It owed its existence in large measure to former IDB President Enrique Iglesias' initiative to rethink the values of development, its goals and means, and to put ethics and human rights – broadly defined – in more prominent focus. Iglesias made a series of statements that, if taken as more than mere rhetoric, had the potential to alter development practice in a significant way. He argued that ethics must become a central consideration in any reflection on development, and claimed that: "Ethics needs no justification. Values like … equity, respect for life, personal growth and self fulfillment, respect for culture, and affinity for cooperation, are ends in themselves." He ended the speech with a forceful assertion: "Today we must vigorously defend the human being's right to development."

The Audacious Agenda   335

The main focus of the Initiative on Social Capital, Ethics and Development (ISED) was not quite this ambitious, but it was bold in its way: to put ethics on the agenda throughout Latin America, not merely within the IDB. This was to be achieved through outreach, encouraging dialogue with different groups in Latin American and Caribbean societies, with a significant focus on universities and educational institutions, voluntary organizations and business. Among the methods used were: (a) to arrange large conferences and other events in different countries in the region with high-profile invited speakers and broad attendance; (b) to establish a university network; and (c) to improve access to written material on ethics and social capital through the initiative's website.

In its first years, the ISED received overwhelming response to its outreach activities, which clearly reflected a hunger for a dialogue on ethics and development within Latin America and the Caribbean. However, when compared to the ambitions set out by Iglesias, ISED still faced major challenges. No effort was made to monitor or measure ISED's impact, so it can be debated to what extent if any the ambition to encourage people to "put values first" had been achieved. One certainly still sees frequent conflicts between the goal of economic growth and other values. What was clearly discernable, however, was that the ISED had very limited impact on encouraging ethical reflection *within* the IDB – in fact most employees within the IDB did not even know of its existence. All of ISED's energies had gone into outreach, and none into changing the institutional ethos of the IDB itself.

Bringing ethics to the center stage of the daily considerations of a development bank official is not an easy task. The IDB was established with a specific financial purpose: to provide funding for development projects in the Latin American and Caribbean region by acting as a financial intermediary in capital markets and channeling concessional funds from donors. As such, it has to relate to many different stakeholders – including donors, investors and investment banks, rating agencies and borrowing governments – not all of whom are accustomed to placing moral values such as equity and the strengthening of human rights as priorities above economic considerations. Moreover, over the course of the years, the IDB added a number of other issues to its "economic" agenda: environmental protection, gender equity, and concern for traditionally excluded groups (such as indigenous peoples). In addition, major emphasis was placed on improving the overall development effectiveness of the Bank. Thus, IDB officials already had multiple demands – some of them perhaps contradictory.

Once President Iglesias had left, the IDB's experiment in institutionalizing ethics lacked any well-placed vocal champion within the upper reaches of its bureaucracy. The Initiative on Social Capital, Ethics and Development then lost its own director amid very credible charges that he had engaged in corruption; it was claimed that he used staff on the ISED payroll to carry out personal consulting assignments under contract to the UNDP, while retaining the fees for himself. It was an inglorious and sad end to a potentially groundbreaking effort to bring ethics into the IDB, but after eight years few within that institution were even aware that it had ever existed. Perhaps the ISED had adopted an unwise strategy, but without doubt this particular invitation to engage in a moral dialogue was not warmly embraced – or possibly simply was not understood – by those in senior leadership within the IDB in the post-Iglesias era.

Still in Washington, DC, the World Bank made its own tentative efforts to address ethics within its scope of operations and concerns (World Bank, 1997). Starting in 1998, the World Bank issued statements that supported the realization of human rights, and linked human rights to development directly – while being careful to retain its own focus on its strict mandate as contained in its Articles of Agreement (World Bank, 1998). Under the leadership of former President James D. Wolfensohn, the Bank did not eschew the use of moral language, as evident in his 2002 address to the Annual General Meeting. Wolfensohn forcefully argued that the developing world demanded a global system that was "based on equity, human rights, and social justice" and immediately added "It must be our demand too" (Wolfensohn, 2002). Programmatically, however, these lofty aspirations were not evident. Instead, the World Bank adopted a lateral (and some would argue peripheral or even superficial) approach towards ethics and development, getting at moral values issues by funding small, internal programs on culture or religion, neither of which was sustained. The World Bank did embrace ethical dimensions more directly in its continuing work on governance, gender, and environment, but seldom in an explicitly moral context. Perhaps best known of its ethical initiatives, the Bank made significant strides in targeting human rights, yet even this has been largely conceptualized at the level of human rights laws, treaties, and legal principles, and not the human rights moral framework that underpins such laws.

The well-attended April 2006 *Global Ethics Forum on Leadership, Ethics and Integrity in Public Life* at Keble College in Oxford, England was a particularly interesting exception to the World Bank's indirect approach to ethics. This three day conference was a very high profile explicitly ethics-based initiative led by the World Bank, and supported by USAID, DFID, the Australian Agency for International Development, the International Institute for Public Ethics, the United Nations University, Griffith University, and others. I delivered a paper at the conference on ethics and leadership, and I left the conference with buoyant expectations for a vigorous new receptivity of development ethics, at least within the participating sponsor institutions. Unfortunately the energy and momentum of the conference was not carried forward. Instead, the conference was followed by a faltering effort, tentatively facilitated by the World Bank, called the Global Integrity Alliance (GIA). Its goal was to bring together experts from nongovernmental organizations, multilateral agencies, businesses, and governments who shared a common purpose in strengthening good governance through capacity building, research, dialogue, partnerships, and anticorruption initiatives. None of the Bank's senior leadership took a public stand in advocating for the GIA, and the initiative foundered as the Bank sought in vain for some appropriate non-Bank entity to take on the leadership of the fledgling entity. The GIA also suffered its own inner lack of clarity about its ethics-based purpose; in its short life it never directly absorbed or made use of the many resources and perspectives offered by development ethics.

The GIA's last significant effort consisted of a research program led by political scientists and economists that explored leadership and governance while expressly and intentionally omitting ethics-based perspectives!

It is worth noting, however, the longstanding existence of the Friday Morning "Values for Development" Group at the World Bank, which until 2009 convened at the Bank from 8am to 9am on almost every Friday morning since 1981. This unique gathering provided Bank staff (active and retired), as well as others like me active in or concerned about international development, a physical, institutional, intellectual, and even emotional space to meet and discuss ethical challenges, resources, opportunities, and concerns. Often they invited a speaker, but other times they simply engaged in free ranging, often-provocative discussions and reflections that were rich in moral relevance, and seasoned by direct practitioner experience. Sadly, the Friday Morning Group's membership dwindled and it closed. With its passing the Bank and its staff lost a special ethical resource and a center of gravity for a community of ethics oriented persons to gather.

Just a few blocks away in downtown Washington, DC, there is more upbeat news. In 2006 some staff at the United States Agency for International Development (USAID), under the active leadership of Neil Levine, started their own informal equivalent of the World Bank's Friday Morning Group. This ethics focused gathering meets biweekly, and retains its vibrancy. It is also the only institutionalized presence of development ethics within USAID, albeit informally. USAID has not embraced any formal recourse to the insights and tools of development ethics, despite the deep and significant resources that development ethics is able to offer. This is not to say, however, that value issues are not being recognized by some within USAID as an important part of the development discourse, particularly so in the context of leadership, human rights, gender equity, conflict, and citizen "ownership" of development policies. Still, USAID consideration of the ethical dimensions of development remains at best a peripheral afterthought, not an integral part of its policy or programming. Occasionally there are glimmers of a change in receptivity, as in 2005 when the philosopher David Crocker and I were engaged by USAID to prepare a short publication titled *The Relevance of Development Ethics for USAID* (Crocker and Schwenke, 2005). This publication contained several modest recommendations for piloting elements of an ethics-based approach within one of USAID's most common activities, the democracy and governance country assessment methodology. Despite apparent signs of interest among the USAID staff who reviewed this document, and the large number of USAID staff who attended the presentation on it, none of its recommendations pertaining to the assessment methodology have ever been incorporated.

The resistance to ethics based development is puzzling. Approaching values issues in the structured, robust manner typical to development ethics can (a) clarify what development is; (b) defend normative positions by critical and rational thinking about ethical alternatives; and (c) identify the complexities involved in the rational and moral choice of means. More broadly, development ethics can provide a basic understanding of the human condition and of morally relevant facts. The committed development worker or policy maker at USAID engaged with concrete problems and in-country public discussion can gain much from the thinking and analytical frameworks offered by development ethics, and at the same time keep such reflection firmly rooted in and informed by development practice. The publication that Crocker and I wrote provided USAID with an up-to-date if brief overview of the field and the literature of development ethics, and of the best current thinking from that field in human rights moral theory in the context of international development.

Conclusion

Development ethics is well established within academia, with a thriving literature and sophisticated moral resources in normative analysis, and in the design, strategic planning, and monitoring of development interventions. Development ethics continues to inform deliberative democracy and meaningful participation, and to assist in balancing culturally sensitive development with important universal moral values. As international foreign assistance structures, institutions and policies evolve, experts conversant with development ethics do have some influence – although not nearly as much influence as if they were working on the inside of major multilateral and bilateral aid and development institutions. The effectiveness of development ethics to shape and improve development itself still remains highly constrained by the troubling resistance of the development establishment to embrace it as a valued resource.

Notes

1 The universalist position in development ethics seeks to formulate and justify – in the light of universally valid ethical principles – a set of development goals that ought to apply equally to all human beings and human societies.

2 Moral particularism, in its strongest version, is the claim that there are no defensible moral principles; that the morally perfect person should not be conceived as the person of principle; and that moral thought does not consist in the application of moral principles to cases. There are more cautious versions, however. The strongest defensible version, perhaps, holds that though there may be some moral principles, the rationality of moral thought and judgment does not depend on a suitable provision of such things – the perfectly moral judge would require more than a grasp on an appropriate range of principles and the ability to apply them. Under this view, moral principles are, at best, simply aids that a morally sensitive person would not require, and indeed the use of such aids might even lead us into moral error (Dancy, 2001). A variant of this, Aristotelian particularism, holds that moral judgment must be sensitive to the particularity of specific moral situations. Certain Aristotelian thinkers, such as Nancy Sherman, argue that Aristotle was advocating a third way between particularism and general ethical theories,

The Audacious Agenda 339

in which there is room for general moral rules or principles, even if these are not deemed to be universal (Sherman, 1997, p. 244).

3 A concept linking up both normative and empirical development theory with development policy, politics, and practice. Crocker argues: "Theory normally informs practice: it tells us what is and why, what is (likely) to be and why, and how to arrive at the better future from the actual present. Relatively pure theory is possible. But it is typically and, more importantly, often desirable to have a 'practice-theory' or a 'theory-practice' in which more or less abstract thought, site specific experience, and practical conduct are dialectically related" (Crocker, 1991, pp. 468–469).

4 Something can be both an end and a means. Local empowerment is both; but as a means it refers to a general level of capability and confidence to pursue what is potentially a very wide range of development goals. Also, before local empowerment can operate as a means, it must be generated; other means first will need to be identified and implemented to bring about local empowerment.

5 Distributive justice is a principle of social justice that requires the distribution – according to some pattern or process – of some good, for instance, resources, wealth, or opportunities (Dower, 1998a, p. 755). This contrasts with retributive and compensatory justice, which are concerned, respectively, with justified punishment for perpetrators of bad deeds and justified reparation to victims of bad deeds.

6 Universalism is the view that values or norms, and associated obligations apply equally to all people and all cultures. Utilitarians and Kantians, for example, argue that the correct or justified ethical principles apply to all societies and all individuals. A variant is "minimum universalism," which accepts some moral diversity but contends that there is a universally valid body of values which can be accepted by people from different moral and religious communities (agreed on, not discovered) that can be used to judge public policy (Dower, 1998b, pp. 43, 155).

7 Dower defines *skeptical realism* as the calculation of power and national interests, as often used in evaluating relations between states within a competitive framework. These norms of international relations are more maxims of prudence than moral norms – they are abandoned whenever prudence dictates, but are often used in moral rhetoric that Dower claims is generally hypocritical (Dower, 1998b, p. 18).

8 *Cosmopolitanism* is an ethical approach based upon the moral premise that the world is one moral domain, out of which arise certain universal or global moral obligations, values, and responsibilities (Dower, 1998b, p. 20).

References

Calabresi, G., and Bobbitt, P. 1978 *Tragic Choices*, W.W. Norton & Company, New York.

Crocker, D.A. (1991) Toward development ethics. *World Development*, 19 (5), 457–483.

Crocker, D.A. (1998) Consumption, well-being and capability, in *Ethics of Consumption: The Good Life, Justice, and Global Stewardship*, (eds D.A. Crocker and T. Linden), Rowman & Littlefield, Lanham, MD, pp. 366–390.

Crocker, D.A. (1999) Development ethics, in (1999) *Routledge Encyclopedia of Philosophy*, (ed. E. Craig), Routledge, London, p. 42.

Crocker, D.A. (2001) Globalization and human development ethical approaches, Institute for Philosophy and Public Policy, College Park, MD.

Crocker, D.A. (2008) *Ethics of Global Development: Agency, Capability, and Deliberative Democracy*, Cambridge University Press, Cambridge.

Crocker, D.A., and Schwenke, C. (2005) *The Relevance of Development Ethics for USAID*, US Agency for International Development, Washington, DC. www.developmentvalues.net/files/Publications/development%20ethics%20and%20usaid.pdf. 2005 (accessed July 18, 2010).

Dancy, J. (ed.) (2001) *Stanford Encyclopedia of Philosophy*, Stanford University Press, Stanford, see Moral particularism, http://plato.stanford.edu/entries/moral-particularism/#1 (accessed June 29, 2010).

Dower, N. (1998a) Development ethics, in *Encyclopedia of Applied Ethics*, (ed. R. Chadwick), Academic Press, San Diego, pp. 755–766.

Dower, N. (1998b) *World Ethics: The New Agenda*, Edinburgh Studies in World Ethics, Edinburgh University Press, Edinburgh.

Flathman, R.E. (1966) *The Public Interest: An Essay Concerning the Normative Discourse of Politics*, John Wiley & Sons, Inc., New York.

Gasper, D. (1994) Development ethics – An emergent field? in *Market Forces and World Development*, (eds R. Prendergast and F. Stewart), St. Martin's Press, New York, pp. 160–185.

Glover, J. (1999) *Humanity: A Moral History of the Twentieth Century*, Yale University Press, New Haven.

Goulet, D. (1995) *Development Ethics: A Guide to Theory and Practice*, The Apex Press, New York.

Griffin, J. (1996) *Value Judgement: Improving Our Ethical Beliefs*, Clarendon Press, Oxford.

Gutmann, A., and Thompson, D. (1996) *Democracy and Disagreement*, The Belknap Press of Harvard University Press, Cambridge, MA.

Kittay, E.F., and Meyers, D.T. (eds) (1987) *Women and Moral Theory*, Rowman & Littlefield, New York.

Margalit, A. (1996) *The Decent Society*, (trans. N. Goldblum), Harvard University Press, Cambridge.

Max-Neef, M.A. (1992) *From the Outside Looking In: Experiences in Barefoot Economics*, Zedd Books, London.

McKinnon, C. (1999) *Character, Virtue Theories and the Vices*, Broadview Press, Peterborough.

Narayan, D., Chambers, R., Shah, M.K., and Pepesch, P. (2000) *Voices of the Poor: Crying Out for Change*, Oxford University Press, Oxford.

Noddings, N. (1984) *Caring: A Feminine Approach to Ethics and Moral Education*, University of California Press, Berkeley.

Nussbaum, M.C. (2000) *Women and Human Development: The Capabilities Approach*, Cambridge University Press, Cambridge.

Paul, E.F. Jr, Miller, F.D., and Paul, J. (eds) (1999) *Human Flourishing*, Cambridge University Press, Cambridge.

Rawls, J. (1971) *A Theory of Justice*, The Belknap Press of Harvard University Press, Cambridge, MA.

Rosan, C., Ruble, B.A., and Tulchin, J.S. (eds) (2000) Urbanization, population, environment, and security. A Report of the Comparative Urban Studies Project, Woodrow Wilson International Center for Scholars, Washington, DC.

Schumacher, E.F. (1973) *Small is Beautiful: Economics as if People Mattered*, Harper and Row, New York.

Schwenke, C. (2008) *Reclaiming Value in International Development: The Moral Dimensions of Development Policy and Practice in Poor Countries*, Praeger, Westport, CN.

Scroggins, D. (2004) *Emma's War: A True Story*, Knopf Doubleday, New York.

Sen, A. (1987) *On Ethics and Economics*, (ed. J.M. Letiche), Blackwell, Malden, MA.

Sen, A. (1999) *Development as Freedom*, Alfred A. Knopf, New York.

Sherman, N. (1997) *Making a Necessity of Virtue: Aristotle and Kant on Virtue*, Cambridge University Press, Cambridge.

UNDP (United Nations Development Programme) (2000) *Human Development Report 2000*, Oxford University Press, New York.

Wolfensohn, J.D. (2002) A Time to Act. Address to the Board of Governors at the World Bank's Annual General Meeting of 2002. http://web.worldbank.org/WBSITE/EXTERNAL/NEWS/0,,contentMDK:20069713~menuPK:34472~pagePK:34370~piPK:34424~theSitePK:4607,00.html (accessed June 28, 2010).

World Bank (1997) Ethics and values: A global perspective. Associated Event of the Fifth Annual World Bank Conference on Environmentally and Socially Sustainable Development; Partnerships for Global Ecosystem Management: Science, Economics and Law, World Bank, Washington DC.

World Bank (1998) *Development and Human Rights: The Role of the World Bank*, Washington DC.

18

Indigenous Media Values
Cultural and Ethical Implications

Joe Grixti

This chapter examines some of the characteristics which distinguish indigenous media productions from more mainstream Western media. Mainstream Western media are here broadly taken to be usually characterized by commercial concerns – which among other things lead to a situation where the overriding objective in media production is to generate capital by attracting as many viewers as possible, as consumers or targets for advertising. Indigenous media, on the other hand, are approached here as an evolving cultural category which usually involves comparatively small-scale, low-budget and locally based productions, and often forms part of broader movements concerned with cultural autonomy and political self-determination (Ginsburg, 2002a, p. 211). Indigenous media obviously do not constitute a homogeneous category, and it is simplistic to lump them together indiscriminately – not least because indigenous peoples inhabit vastly different cultures, histories, and landscapes, and the details of their religious beliefs, myths, and cosmologies are also very different. However, as this chapter will show, indigenous media coming from different parts of the world can also be seen to share a number of common motivations and characteristics which can have challenging implications for more mainstream global media. As a broad category, "indigeneity" itself is also not easy to pin down, and definitions of what it can be taken to include can be quite flexible. Indeed, as was noted by the United Nations Working Group on Indigenous Populations in 1996, the guidelines that modern international organizations and international legal experts consider relevant to understanding the term "indigenous" are anything but definitive or comprehensive. As summarized by Stewart and Wilson (2008, p. 14), the UN's general guidelines in this area include: "(a) priority in time with respect to occupying and using the resources of a particular territory; (b) the voluntary perpetuation of cultural distinctiveness (which may include language, social organization, religious and spiritual values, modes of

---

The Handbook of Global Communication and Media Ethics, First Edition. Edited by Robert S. Fortner and P. Mark Fackler.
© 2011 Blackwell Publishing Ltd. Published 2011 by Blackwell Publishing Ltd.

Indigenous Media Values 343

production, laws, and institutions); (c) self-identification, as well as recognition by other groups or by state authorities as a distinct collectivity; and (d) an experience of subjugation, marginalization, dispossession, exclusion, or discrimination, whether or not those conditions persist."

Indigenous media are usually distinguished from "multicultural media" and the media produced by and for minority groups who came to various countries as immigrants, slaves, or "guest workers" (Ginsburg, 2002a). Discussions of indigenous media thus generally focus on indigenous groups who live as a minority within a historically colonial nationstate dominated by an originally European settler society, as is the case with Native American, Australian Aboriginal, Maori, and Inuit societies, who have had to struggle against the biases (not always unconscious) and institutionalized racisms inherent in national media systems that generally target the majority population (Glynn and Tyson, 2007, p. 207). This understanding of "indigenous media" draws attention to important cultural and ethical values underscoring global indigenous media productions, and it is to a consideration of some of these value systems that this chapter first directs itself. However, there are other examples of indigenous media which come from politically independent postcolonial communities whose experiences and practices reflect striking variations from those of minority indigenous communities living within broader nationstates. Examples of such groups include small island communities which have gone through a form of colonization which did not involve major settlement by the colonizing power and who thus continue to constitute the majority of their now independent nationstate. One interesting example of this phenomenon is the small Mediterranean island of Malta, where the complex intermingling of colonial and global influences with indigenous practices, belief systems, and traditions has given rise to a distinctive media landscape and media practices which provide an interesting illustration of some of the problems which can be created by indigenous media values when they become institutionalized in a postcolonial context. Some of those problems and their broader cultural and ethical implications are discussed in the later sections of this chapter.

Indigenous Media and the Disjunctive Flows of Globalization

Perhaps the most widespread understanding of indigenous media productions is that they are the work of activists who use Western media technologies in order to counter dominant media misrepresentations of indigenous people by documenting indigenous cultural traditions from an indigenous perspective, and in the process articulate indigenous cultural identities and futures. In this perspective, indigenous media are seen as powerful arenas of cultural production, in that they simultaneously work towards challenging and changing the assumptions informing the visual landscape of mainstream media, while also providing innovative contexts and practices through which new forms of indigenous solidarity, identity, and community are created (Dowell, 2006, p. 376).

Indigenous media productions are in this sense part of a larger global process in which global media culture is not so much replacing local cultures as getting inflected by being made to coexist with them. The local and the global have become deeply intertwined, paradoxically reinforcing as they symbiotically transform each other (Grixti, 2006). There have thus been some very dramatic developments in the ways indigenous people living in different parts of the world perceive themselves and their relation to their local and global environments. Anthony Giddens (1991, p. 5) has argued that as tradition loses its hold and daily life becomes reconstituted in terms of "the dialectical interplay of the local and the global," individuals are increasingly being forced to negotiate lifestyle choices among a diversity of options. Though this allows greater control over whether, when and how to assume a given social identity, it can also lead to confusion and lack of direction, especially among members of indigenous minority groups traditionally dependent on the once-powerful solidarities provided by land, locality, kinship, and ancestry. Several commentators have thus noted that the constant bombardment of tantalizing images of the good life in the glamorized "global mall" can often leave groups and individuals dispirited by the reality of their own life and economic prospects. As Meyrowitz and Maguire (1993, p. 43) put it, "television and other media have enhanced our awareness of all the people we cannot be, the places we cannot go, the things we cannot possess," so that for many segments of Western and other societies, television and other media have raised expectations but provided few new opportunities. According to Appadurai (2000, p. 5–6), in a world dominated by these type of "disjunctive flows" – as in the case of "Media flows across national boundaries that produce images of well-being that cannot be satisfied by national standards of living and consumer capabilities" – globalization "produces problems that manifest themselves in intensely local forms but have contexts that are anything but local."

Indigenous groups from different parts of the world appear to have developed strategies of responding to these "disjunctive flows" and the mainstreaming thrust of the international commercial media marketplace by taking active control of new media technologies and applying their indigenous value systems, world views and protocols to the ways they represent themselves to themselves and to others. One underlying concern among many indigenous media makers is the need to give the youth of their communities a strong sense of their heritage and cultural identity, especially in view of the fact that young people coming from minority groups often appear to be overawed by more mainstream ("Western") perspectives and lifestyles, with consequent confusions of identity. In a sense, the concern derives from a realization of the responsibilities of what Jerome Bruner memorably called "the mythologically instructed community" in providing its members "with a library of scripts upon which the individual may judge the play of his [or her] multiple identities" (Bruner, 1979, p. 36). As in most postcolonial communities, the "libraries of scripts" available to the youth of minority indigenous communities have inevitably become strongly inflected (or hybridized) by the commercial imperatives of global media. The challenge for indigenous media makers has been that of taking more active and culturally informed control of that process of hybridization so as to ensure that it does not entail a loss of roots and the hope which comes from self-understanding.

The rest of this chapter explores some of the ways in which indigenous media makers from different parts of the world have gone about addressing the "relations of disjuncture" (Appadurai, 1990) created by global media by applying their traditional value systems to their own creative use of new media technologies. One recurring motif in accounts of indigenous appropriations of new media technologies is the idea that past and future can be seen as mutually reinforcing rather than mutually exclusive. In Maori thinking, for instance, one moves into the future with one's eyes firmly focused on the past. In Mason Durie's striking phrase, "Maori values are not simply about celebrating the past but have always had a rationale that is premised on the future – survival" (New Zealand Law Commission, 2001, p. 30). What the more idiosyncratically creative forms of indigenous media seem to be doing is highlighting recognition of the fact that survival involves adaptation and change – not least in the ways cultural identity is defined and understood. What is involved here is a creative process of cultural regeneration which recognizes that in increasingly globalized and technologically mediated contexts, a community's cultural resources do not lie exclusively in the past – though continued contact with that past remains paramount. Cultural identity is never static and all societies and cultures are constantly changing and evolving, not just indigenous ones. Everywhere, as Hall (1992, p. 310) argues, "cultural identities are emerging which are not fixed, but poised, *in transition*, between different positions; which draw on different cultural traditions at the same time; and which are the product of those complicated cross-overs and cultural mixes which are increasingly common in a globalized world" (Hall's italics). In his discussion of how Jamaican Rastafarians borrowed from and radically transformed a text that did not belong to them (the Bible) in their creation of Rasta, Hall (in Grossberg, 1996, p. 143) thus insists that cultural and political survival are often inseparable from hybridization and "transformation through a reorganization of the elements of a cultural practice." In appropriating and "turning the text upside down" in order to "get a meaning which fit their experience," Hall argues, the Rastafarians actually "remade themselves; they positioned themselves differently as new political subjects; they reconstructed themselves as blacks in a new world: they *became* what they are."

Appropriating Media Technology to Preserve Indigenous Cultures

One of the most striking characteristics of global indigenous media productions is the self-awareness of many indigenous media practitioners. This is particularly noticeable in their understandings of how media can be used to reexamine and revitalize cultural identities and traditional practice. Of their very nature indigenous media are hybrid formations, in the sense that they are produced by intercultural dynamics which are inherently complex and often highly charged. They often involve intricate processes of negotiation or resistance necessitated by their need to define themselves against the idealized or stereotypical images that dominate the popular culture and discourses of mainstream societies. Whatever their location, motivation and orientations, indigenous media are also inevitably produced and consumed within a broader process of globalization that has been dominated by a combination of dramatic developments in technology, worldwide processes of deregulation in broadcasting, and the growth of massive multinational media conglomerates which command interests that span a range of key media sectors and operate across the major world markets. Faye Ginsburg (1991) famously described this situation as a "Faustian dilemma," in that, by using new technologies for cultural self-assertion, indigenous film, video-makers and broadcasters are also spreading a technology that might ultimately foster their own disintegration. The challenges of working within this broader global context are well reflected, for instance, in the ways indigenous media producers often describe their work as having to compete against the popular appeal of mainstream media products (music, film, television, Internet games), as well as needing to learn from and adapt some of the techniques which make these products popular. As one Australian Aboriginal radio broadcaster put it during a National Media Forum in 1996:

> Today hunting is mostly done on Nintendo video games and they're talking like New York rappers. Can our culture or our language or our morals and ethics survive? Are our leaders aware of this very loud invasion that is staring us in the face? Are we in a position, if not to stem the tide, at least to come to a compromise and still maintain our culture and identity in this very multiracial community which is Australia? Those are some of the questions which we as media, Indigenous media, are faced with today. (Hartley and McKee, 2000, p. 177)

The type of compromise mentioned here appears to have been the target of the indigenous filmmakers and actors responsible for the movie version of the Aboriginal stage hit musical "Bran Nue Dae" (released in 2010), for whom the film project is an expression and endorsement of indigenous cultural identity. The film's funding through the Melbourne International Film Festival and the star appeal of non-Aboriginal Oscar winners (actor Geoffrey Rush and cinematographer Andrew Lesnie) draw attention to the broader global context. Yet for Rachel Perkins (the film's director) "the musical was like the soundtrack of our lives" and "a life affirming story for black Australia," while for Stephen Page (the film's choreographer), the film "really is an Aboriginal film" because "its stories are embedded around a language, the music and the land here that really shapes the people, and the people tell the stories" (Nicholson, 2008).

The emphasis on using film and other media to tell stories which affirm cultural identity is a recurring motif in accounts of indigenous media productions from several countries. The importance of storytelling for many indigenous communities derives from the fact that, before the arrival of written language, it was primarily

Indigenous Media Values   347

through stories that cultures and traditional knowledge were kept alive and renewed from generation to generation. Maori television producer Tainui Stephens, for instance, describes himself and his colleagues as "the inheritors of a magnificent story-telling tradition", following in the lines of tribal orators who "interpreted the world they knew and observed, for the benefit of other people" (Stephens, 2004, p. 107). The same is true of the way Aboriginal Australian communities responded to the arrival of satellite television in the 1980s by appropriating the new technology as a means of facilitating the preservation and renewal of cultural traditions (Michaels, 1994; Parks, 2005), and "putting them to work for remembering, imagining, connecting, and becoming-in-relation to the Ancestral" (Deger, 2006, p. xx). Similarly, the Igloolik-based Inuit film- and video-making collectives of Northern Canada describe their work as educating and engaging their audiences in Inuit histories, providing "a storage method that allows aesthetic, artistic, and interpretative practices to be reaccessed as mnemonic records of place deeply rooted in community" (Cache Collective, 2008, p. 77). According to Ginsburg (2002b, p. 41), the satellite television transmission to Inuit communities of their own small-scale video productions played a dynamic and revitalizing role "as a self-conscious means of cultural preservation and production and a form of political mobilization." This is how the award-winning Inuit filmmaker and broadcaster Zacharias Kunuk describes his community's reaction to the arrival of television in Igloolik in 1983:

> We finally got one channel of TV in 1983 and, since then, things developed fast. We had to understand TV and how films are made. When I was growing up, I went to the movies, and when you watch a good movie, time flies. It was like they just dropped from the sky, and you didn't even think about what goes on behind the camera.
>   We had to understand all these things and we wanted to do it. We wanted to do it for real. The elders were very scared because TV was coming. We had to make it work for us, to preserve the culture (Chun, 2002, p. 22).

The Canadian Aboriginal Peoples Television Network (APTN) officially went to air in 1999 as the world's first national cable TV system to be fully operated by Indigenous peoples. It was the culmination of two decades of Inuit agitation for expanded media access, inspired by a determination to preserve and revitalize cultural traditions under threat.

These media makers emphasize the fact that their works speak primarily to and for their indigenous community, often in ways which may remain opaque to outsiders, especially when they employ "an experimental strategy that leaves the audience looking for what is unexposed" (Cache Collective, 2008, p. 85), and in the process "challenge conventional Western assumptions about the ontological nature of media and the kinds of cultural worlds that they engender" (Deger, 2006, p. xx). As a result, many indigenous media productions are "possessed of an aesthetic that does not conform to the formal patterns or technical standards of mainstream fiction or documentary" and as such they have often been dismissed as amateurish or somehow naïve (White, 2005, p. 56). Such dismissal misses the crucial function performed by these productions as cultural mediators and as reactions to the misrepresentations of indigenous cultures which have traditionally characterized the technical and aesthetic proclivities of mainstream media. They are thus not simple reflections of reality but "the mediated presentation of someone with a vested interest in the proceedings documented" (White, 2005, p. 56). In this sense, indigenous media making is one aspect of a larger project concerned with cultural maintenance, revival and regeneration in an increasingly globalised world.

Indigenous Media and Cultural Empowerment

Zacharias Kunuk, prominent among those producing work for new indigenous television networks and director of the award winning 2001 feature film *Atanarjuat: The Fast Runner*, describes his work as providing Inuit audiences with culturally authentic images of themselves and of their ancestry "because our culture has never *really* been exposed from the inside" (Chun, 2002, p. 23). He therefore sees the Inuit themselves as his first audience:

> It's very challenging when we do feature-length because there are [elders] that are viewing it on the screen and one slight mistake we make, they all notice it. So we have to do everything right (Svenson, 2002).

Kunuk and his community-based Inuit production company Igloolik Isuma see themselves as using media technologies to get back in contact with "four thousand years of oral history silenced by fifty years of priests, schools, and cable TV" (Kunuk, 2002, p. 13). The film *Atanarjuat* stresses community values and responsibilities. It is set in the ancient past and retells an Inuit legend that has been told and transmitted through centuries of oral tradition. The story deals with the problems created by rivalry and how the lust for power leads to discord, suffering and the breakdown of community. At the start of the film, an evil shaman commits murder and places a curse which plagues the lives of two generations. The characters themselves compound the problem by breaking taboos – the main character, for instance, breaks the taboo of claiming and then marrying a beautiful girl who had been promised to someone else. The curse is finally lifted when great human courage and the invocation of benevolent spiritual forces allow the community to confront the evil and begin the process of healing and growth. According to Kunuk,

> It's an old story that's been passed down from generation to generation, and when we first heard it, we were kids living off the land. *Atanarjuat* is just one of the stories that parents were telling to their children as a bedtime story. It's a lesson about what happens to people when they act, and it has *everything* because when we were growing up, there was no school system, and the Inuktitut way of teaching was telling these stories. Then you start to choose how you want to lead your life (Chun, 2002, p. 21).

Kunuk and his team insist that Inuit community values were at the centre not just of the story but also of their technique of filmmaking. Determined to let their unique story shape the filmmaking process in an Inuit way, they wrote their script "by a unique process of cultural authenticity" (Igloolik Isuma Productions, 2007). They first recorded eight elders telling versions of the legend as it had been passed down to them orally by their ancestors. These versions were then combined into a single detailed treatment in Inuktitut and English by a team of five writers, who developed the various drafts of the script following a bicultural and bilingual process involving regular consultation with the elders for cultural accuracy as well as with a Toronto-based story consultant. Norman Cohn, Kunuk's coproducer and cinematographer, describes the film as "coming from a different set of cultural and aesthetic values, different from what you're used to" because it is concerned with "empowering people in their own voices, putting tools in the hands of people, letting them present themselves, in a non-didactic form, watching and listening rather than telling and being told" (Fuchs, 2002). Kunuk's style of direction reflected these community values:

> Well, we don't work like [they do] in film, like how they do down here [in the US], where you have a director, an assistant to the director, and then another assistant to that director. We don't work like that. All the heads come together, we talk about what it's going to be like and understand each other at length; if we're going to do a scene where tents are – we ask each other "Are they right?" It's everybody's job to get it right, and so we all talk about it: "Should that be there?" "No – I think it should be there. Oh, let's get Anele to tell us where it is." … We just work like that (Svenson, 2002).

The emphasis on empowering people in their own voices is especially reflected in the way many indigenous media producers see themselves as playing a crucial role in nurturing young people's pride in their ancestry and cultural identity. Kunuk's application for funding to make the film *Atanarjuat* made this point forcefully:

> *Atanarjuat* will reach Inuit youth and give them hope. Young Inuit have the highest suicide rate in Canada, seven times the national average. At our rate, in Montreal or Toronto, they would wake up to 15 youth suicides every day. It seems that when our elders stopped talking, our children began killing themselves. *Atanarjuat* will pioneer the use of video and TV to give new life to our past and to show youth that a living past means a living future (Cited in Ginsburg, 2003, p. 828).

Global commercial media's tendency to compound the problems which young people encounter as they forge their personal and cultural identities have been well documented. In contexts where the entertainment media focus on selling dreams of successful lifestyles linked to images of attractive ("Western") young men and women disporting themselves in healthy abandon, those who do not fit these "norms" often come to be seen, and also come to see themselves, as the other (Grixti, 2008). Elizabeth Bird's (2003, p. 168) description of the cultural impact of the introduction of television and "the arrival of images of blonde, thin, imported beauties" into a Fijian culture is instructive in this regard:

> In a society that traditionally valued generous female proportions, young girls quickly learned disgust for their bodies, discovered the binge/purge syndrome, and told interviewers: "I want their body, I want their size. I want to be in the same position as they are ... We have to have those thin, slim bodies."

My own research (Grixti, 2004, 2006) into how indigenous youth in Malta forge their personal and cultural identities in an increasingly globalized media landscape, similarly drew attention to the fact that young people living in minority cultures frequently associate being young, forward-looking, modern, technologically advanced and enlightened with being in tune with what comes from more main-stream Western societies – or more specifically in the case of Maltese youth, with what comes from Western Europe, Britain and the United States, particularly through the media. Being "old fashioned" and backward tends to be linked with an inability to move beyond the more obviously indigenous and traditional. It is precisely these perceptions and the problems which they give rise to that indige-nous media makers like Kunuk have tried to counteract.

Indigenous Media as Revelatory Ritual

Concern about the importance of giving the younger generations hope and cultural pride through a stronger connection with their community, ancestry and heritage is also reflected in Jennifer Deger's (2006, p. 75) account of how members of the Aboriginal Yolngu community of northern Australia saw young people's enthusias-tic endorsement of mainstream Western videos and music as making them "forget who they are" and blind and deaf to their own culture and traditions. Like other indigenous media makers working in other parts of the world, the Yolngu realized that advances in media technologies and global communications have created a situation where the only way tradition can be revitalized is through an informed use of those very technologies. Deger describes the passionate interest of one Yolngu man (Bangana Wunungmurra) in using modern media to reach indigenous youth "in a Yolngu way" – by exploiting the potential of television technologies to "repro-duce the potent, socially constitutive effects of highly restricted revelatory ritual" (Deger, 2007, p. 103). "Just as media can produce perceptual blockages leading to blindness or forgetting," Bangana insisted, "so too it can be used to open eyes, ears, hearts and minds" (Deger, 2006, p. 76). The blending of media technology with ritual forms was thus seen as potentially offering Yolngu youth "an encompassing sense of meaningfulness and belonging in the face of the often enormously debili-tating pressures of contemporary life" (Deger, 2007, p. 117). To achieve these ethical demands and political aspirations, the challenge was to use mainstream Western technology in terms that were not dictated by Western imaginations.

Working with Deger and an indigenous television production company from central Australia, Bangana conceived, produced and codirected an innovative 90-minute "cultural video" entitled *Gularri: That Brings Unity* for broadcasting on local community and regional television. Made in local languages and in accordance with Yolngu cultural protocols and priorities, the video tells the story of Gularri, the sacred fresh waters that flow through the waterholes, rivers, and seas of Yirritja clan countries across northeast Arnhem Land. It focuses on the waters as they flow through the various clan lands, with the visuals often showing nothing but the shimmering surface of the water itself. For Yolngu, these waters are a foundational source of Yolngu identity (Deger, 2006, p. 138). Bangana's concern was that, though the younger generation knew this and could also "sing and dance their identity in relation to these waters", they did not fully understand and had never fully experienced the "big picture" of how Gularri "connects everyone up" (Deger, 2007, p. 106). Such understanding had traditionally been imparted to the young through the restricted initiatory ceremonies known as *ngarra*. His video therefore set out to impart that ancestral knowledge of community connectedness by drawing inspiration and authority from *ngarra* revelatory ceremonies.

When the film was broadcast for the first time on the local channel, "an almost eerie stillness descended on the community" (Deger, 2006, p. 182), creating a total contrast to the noisy, semi-distracted way in which Yolngu normally watched television. Their normal hubbub came to a near complete halt so that "as the conjunction of camera and microphone, screen and speaker mimetically amplified Ancestral presence, Yolngu settled down to watch: respectful, attentive, and engaged" (p. 183). This is how Deger describes the community's reaction to the first broadcast:

> For many if not most of the viewers, this was the first time they had seen certain locations. Bungirrinydji, as the site of the starting point for Gularri, holds enormous significance for all Yirritja clans. Yet so many people, even those with close clan ties, have never visited it, given the difficult terrain and its inaccessibility by road or air... Nevertheless, people visit Gularri *ringgitj* [sacred places] in other ways. Depending on their age, their ritual experience, and their relationship to the countries and clans featured, they would have built up a picture of these places in their mind's eye. They would be able to envisage these *ringgitj* with imagery assembled from the poetic details of song, enhanced by layers of associated imagery from the *rangga* [sacred objects] and *wangarr* [Ancestral past] connected to these places. Indeed, many would have expressed their connections to this and other locations in funerals and other ritual performances, generating an embodied, effective constellation of memories and knowledges of places that, until this moment, they had never directly laid eyes on (Deger, 2006, p. 183).

The video technology of Western culture had thus, at least temporarily, been transformed from a medium of distractions leading to forgetting into a communal means of producing "a collective and politicized identity among the clans of the region, enabling the audience to make a new sense of what it might mean to be Yolngu in ways that are derived from locality as a lived experience of the underlying truths of the Ancestral" (Deger, 2006, p. 146).

Indigenous Media and the Production of Social Consciousness

This type of use of new media technologies extends and revitalizes the ritual traditions and constructions of cultural identities which it recreates and reinscribes. However, it also inevitably modifies them. Indigenous media producers are thus often very much aware of the fact that their works play a key role in constructing reality and cultural identity, rather than simply reflecting them. According to Terence Turner (1992, p. 14), the Kayapo of the central Amazonian community of Gorotire are interested in the representational possibilities of new media "because they are keenly aware that the social circumstances affecting their presentation of themselves to one another are changing." Their idiosyncratic use of video is therefore both responding to and actively molding the ongoing transformation of their culture and their conception of themselves. On the one hand, their camerawork and editing techniques are guided by Kayapo cultural and aesthetic values – as when a video of a men's naming ceremony "replicates, in its own structure, the replicative structure of the ceremony itself, and thus creates 'beauty' in the Kayapo sense" (Turner, 1992, p. 9). At the same time, however, the act of filming itself is also understood to have a performative function because it helps to establish the facts it records. The Kayapo thus see representation as "an act that contributes to the material social reality of the thing represented rather than merely reflecting a pre-existing objective reality separate from the act of representation" (Turner, 2002, p. 247). This is why, when they were approached by a documentary crew from Granada Television in 1987, they actively embraced the new possibilities which became available to them by demanding video cameras, VCR, monitor, and videotapes for their own use in return for allowing themselves to be filmed. With this equipment they subsequently documented their traditional knowledge of the forest environment and recorded their own traditional ceremonies, demonstrations, and encounters with whites (Shohat and Stam, 1996, pp. 150–151). They used video as part of their struggles to defend their land, rights, and environment. In Turner's (1992, p. 13) striking phrase, the Kayapo threw themselves "into inter-cultural adultery on a grand scale": "The Kayapo were not simply passively succumbing to 'objectification' and absorption by an irresistible Western force of representation, but pursuing what they perceived as their own interests as they both conflicted and converged with those of the enveloping national society. They were, in other words, acting very much as the 'subjects' of their own history as Kayapo."

The Kayapo's embrace and appropriation of new video technology thus also played a key role in transforming their social consciousness, partly because it allowed them to develop a clearer understanding of how social reality can be objectified, and also because it heightened their sense of their own agency by providing them with a means of active control over the process of objectification itself.

Language and Cultural Identity

One important and potentially contentious area where the transformation of social consciousness through indigenous control of media shows itself powerfully is in the use of indigenous media as a means of preserving and reviving the languages of minority indigenous communities. The Welsh-language television broadcaster Sianel Pedwar Cymru (S4C) is often cited as an instructive illustration of the media's important role in the construction and maintenance of a national community. Like a number of other indigenous broadcasters, S4C was born out of political protest, "a testament to the capacity of individuals to work in cultural groups both to contest their own cultural erosion and, more positively, to develop a media institution that may speak to that community in its own tongue" (McElroy, 2008, p. 233). The preservation and enhancement of the Welsh language (a Celtic language distinct from the Gaelic spoken in Scotland and Ireland) was thus seen as having a dynamic relation to Welsh cultural identity. The struggle for the establishment of an indigenous Welsh television channel was a response to the key role played by the mass media in establishing English as the dominant language of both the home and the public sphere – with the consequent erosion of Welsh-language culture and the drastic drop in the number of Welsh speakers from just under half the population of Wales in 1911 to a state of terminal decline by the 1950s. There is evidence to suggest that since the launch of S4C in 1982, and in conjunction with the introduction of Welsh as a compulsory school subject, the decline has been reversed. The success of S4C is often cited as "an example of how the mass media can help maintain linguistic and cultural heterogeneity and foster a modern sense of community" (McElroy, 2008, p. 235).

The links between language, cultural identity, and political activism are perhaps most clearly illustrated in the way Maori radio and television were successfully introduced as New Zealand's national indigenous broadcasters with the clear intention of playing a major role in promoting, normalizing, and revitalizing Maori language, culture, and custom. Here too, control over media technology and broadcasting was recognized as playing a crucial role in helping to preserve and regenerate indigenous culture and values by remolding social consciousness. As was the case in Wales, the demand for Maori radio and television was largely driven by a desire to counteract the erosion of the Maori language, which had been "brought to the very brink of extinction, more than anything else by the influence of monolingual broadcasting" (Fox, 1993, p. 132). The situation of Maori as the original inhabitants of the land becoming a minority over time is significantly different from the experience of comparable groups in Australia, Canada or the Americas because the entry of an external culture into Aotearoa/New Zealand was formalized through a legal agreement between equal parties. The Treaty of Waitangi, signed in 1840 between the British Crown and more than 500 Maori Chiefs, guarantees the First People of Aotearoa/New Zealand "*tino rangatiratanga*" or "absolute authority over all their resources." In this sense, the Treaty is far more all-encompassing than any comparable document between Native American tribes and the United States, British, or Canadian government, and there is no comparable document stipulating Aboriginal and British or Australian relationships (Browne, 1996, pp. 131–132). The Treaty became the focus of Maori resource claims after the Waitangi Tribunal was established in 1975 to deliberate and rule on alleged breaches of the Treaty, mostly in relation to land claims but also other cultural "treasures" such as language (King, 2003, p. 487). It was within this context that Maori activists and lobby groups eventually won their long legal battle for public funding of Maori broadcasting on the grounds that "the public broadcasting system is a vital present-day resource, and as such Maori are legally entitled to an equal share of it" (Fox, 1993, p. 126).

The introduction of Maori radio was the result of many years of sustained activism, protest, and legal challenges against a national radio network (first set up in 1926) and individual private stations which for many years "operated as if Maori culture, including the language, either did not exist or were irrelevant to New Zealand society" (Browne, 1996, p. 155). Despite staunch and persistent conservative opposition, Maori programs appropriately informed by Maori values and perspectives were gradually introduced on the national radio network, and separate Maori radio stations were established over the period 1989 to 1994. There are now 21 Maori radio stations in the country funded by the Maori broadcasting funding agency, Te Mangai Paho – a Crown Entity established in 1993 "giving life to the acknowledgement of successive governments that *te reo Maori* [the Maori language] is a *taonga* (treasure) warranting its active protection and support" (www.tmp.govt.nz/about/about.html). The establishment of a dedicated Maori television network in 2004 was also the result of a lengthy and often bitter struggle. The official Maori Television website (www.maoritelevision.com) describes the channel's aim as that of playing "a major role in revitalising language and culture that is the birthright of every Maori and the heritage of every New Zealander." The channel was successfully launched after the Maori Television Service Act of 2003 provided a sufficient, sustained public funding package, as well as a lengthy establishment phase for this new public service network (Dunleavy, 2008, p. 807). The occasion was described by Maori scholar Ranginui Walker (2004, p. 402) as "a cultural celebration of triumph over adversity, a dawning of a new age of Maori modernity" because it finally gave Maori the means of televising their own stories and images of themselves. Like Maori radio, Maori Television gives paramount importance to the Maori language as "the cornerstone of Maori culture":

> It provides a platform for Maori cultural development and supports a unique New Zealand identity within a global society. It is a taonga (treasure), at the very heart of Maori culture and identity, and for that reason alone it must be preserved and fostered (Corporate Maori Television Website, n.d.).

The network plays a significant role in the construction of positive notions of being Maori (Poihipi, 2007), and it has also endeared itself to New Zealanders more generally by maintaining an emphasis on local material and reconciling its

Indigenous Media Values 355

funding limitations with the imperative to build its audience via a unique range of programs (Dunleavy, 2008, p. 807). In this sense, the introduction of Maori Television has been seen as forming part of a strategy of decolonization which seeks to critique and interrupt the hegemony of New Zealand settler society by affirming an indigenous form of social agency from within the mediated public sphere – "a practice of incorporation that poses a counter discourse to prevailing national orthodoxies" (Smith, 2006, p. 28).

One way in which that counter discourse reveals itself is in the style of broadcasting adopted by both Maori television and radio. Commenting on his visits to several Maori radio stations between 1991 and 1996, the Minnesota-based communications researcher Donald R. Browne (1996, p. 162) argues that many of the varied broadcasting practices he noted were considerably different from what would be the case on public or commercial radio in New Zealand or elsewhere. Informational programming and news reports tended to be more detailed and delivered in a considerably more relaxed pace and style than their counterparts on mainstream media. Browne was particularly struck by the way indigenous radio talk shows "displayed a more truly discursive approach than did their counterparts in the United States and Canada, and their hosts were far more interested in showing compassion, respect, and kindness toward their guests and callers than U.S. and Canadian talk shows are prone to display." Group discussion and community consultative programs also feature prominently on Maori Television. The reason for this lies very much at the heart of the Maori values which the establishment of Maori broadcasting was meant to preserve and revitalize. As summarized in a 2001 New Zealand Law Commission Study Paper, Maori values give central prominence to relationships, mutuality and reciprocity of responsibilities:

> Of all of the values of tikanga Maori [the Maori way of doing things], whanaunga-tanga is the most pervasive. It denotes the fact that in traditional Maori thinking relationships are everything – between people; between people and the physical world; and between people and the atua (spiritual entities). The glue that holds the Maori world together is whakapapa or genealogy identifying the nature of relationships between all things. That remains the position today. In traditional Maori society, the individual was important as a member of a collective. The individual identity was defined through that individual's relationships with others. It follows that tikanga Maori emphasised the responsibility owed by the individual to the collective. No rights enured if the mutuality and reciprocity of responsibilities were not understood and fulfilled (New Zealand Law Commission, 2001, pp. 30–31).

Group identity and wellbeing are also crucially linked to the land, not least because "the signs or marks of the ancestors are embedded below the roots of the grass and the herbs" (New Zealand Law Commission, 2001, p. 47). The Maori word for "land" (*whenua*) also means "placenta," and in Maori idiom, the people's identity is deeply rooted in the land, which nourishes them like a mother. The connections with land and reciprocal care of the natural world are thus reflected in all the values underlying the Maori way of doing things (Christ and Rountree, 2006, pp. 187–189).

Communal Identity and Its Discontents

There is of course a danger of over-romanticizing the benefits of traditional and community-based values as the underlying driving forces in indigenous media productions. In order to place this in a more balanced perspective, this concluding section examines how the traditional community-based values and practices which usually inform the establishment and structure of indigenous media can also give rise to more complex problems.

On one end of the spectrum are the risks of what Ginsburg calls the "Faustian bargain" into which indigenous media makers are forced to enter. Thus, because the predominance of global consumer culture has turned the international commercial media marketplace into a "global mall" where an "ethnic-food-court approach creates a One-World placelessness" (Klein, 2000, p. 117), there is also a danger that the cultural differences informing indigenous media-making can become neutralized through incorporation into the global marketplace as aestheticized attributes to be traded. This risk is of course endemic to the fact that all contemporary cultures are to some extent hybrid, and hybridity, as Kraidy (1999, p. 460) points out, is "a zone of symbolic ferment where power relations are surreptitiously re-inscribed." On the other end are the types of risks identified by Ruth McElroy (2008, p. 235) in her discussion of indigenous media projects which are "deeply imbricated in broader political projects": that indigenous media can become agents for maintaining cultural essentialism and for propagating cultural exclusions and national exclusivity.

All identity construction, as Kennedy and Danks (2001, p. 3) have noted, "requires the summoning of difference, the relativization of the self as against the 'other' imagined as separate, outside – and perhaps also as marginal, inferior and dangerous." The preservation of shared commonality within an indigenous community or nation is thus usually paralleled by a strong sense of cultural and linguistic discontinuity with respect to outsider-groups or nations, so that the construction of a collective identity "generally involves active strategies of inclusion and exclusion whereby the boundaries of a given collectivity are policed" (Schlesinger, 1994, p. 27). As an inevitable characteristic of community groupings and protocols, the policing of boundaries can often lead to complex social and moral dilemmas when indigenous broadcasting becomes institutionalized. Some of the lessons and risks involved here are well captured in the ways patterns of indigenous media production and news reporting have been influenced by long-established community and village life orientations in the traditional and highly politicized context of the small Mediterranean island of Malta.

The media landscape in Malta forcefully draws attention to the hybrid complexity of indigeneity and communication in an increasingly globalized context. Traditional dependences on kinship and community networks have here created a situation where patronage and rivalry dominate the social and political landscapes. Politics and political debates in Malta are conducted in a uniquely passionate and colorful fashion – one which the Dutch anthropologist Jeremy Boissevain (1965) influentially compared to the patterns of patronage and rivalry which traditionally characterized village allegiances to patrons and saints. This is also reflected in the way the local media situation has evolved. In a country which has traditionally been staunchly Roman Catholic in its beliefs and customs, the establishment of indigenous broadcasting and media production have taken a distinctly local emphasis – one whose discourse is dominated by politics and religion. Nonprofit advocacy broadcasting and journalism are deeply ingrained in indigenous Maltese media practice (as is indeed the case in a number of other Mediterranean societies) and they coexist with public and commercial set-ups.

Malta, an island nation and former British colony with a population of just over 400 000, is located in the central Mediterranean Sea some 93 km south of Sicily and is one of the oldest and most densely populated countries in the world. As a result of its distinctive features as a small island community with its own language, a long history of foreign domination, small-scale economic conditions and limited audience reach, the media system which has evolved in Malta is quite unique. Hybridity and cultural adaptation have been the main hallmarks of the island's long history and, as in other aspects of Maltese life, the Maltese communications landscape has evolved into a complex mixture of staunch insularity and global village orientations. The Maltese are keen users of all forms of communications technologies, through which they have access to an increasingly broad range of both local and foreign transmissions. Indigenous media products (in Maltese and English) to a large extent dominate the Maltese media landscape with a lively and flourishing range of newspapers, radio and television stations. Though these outlets are becoming increasingly influenced by commercialization, their historical origins and distinctly local cultural biases also mean that they are markedly different in a number of significant ways from the mainstream European or Anglo-American models with which they rub shoulders and also frequently emulate.

When local broadcasting became available to private companies with deregulation in 1991, the country's major political parties and the Catholic Church were the first to be granted licenses. As a result, Malta is now the only European democracy in which large segments of the broadcasting and print media are owned and controlled by the two main political parties and by the Catholic Church. State-sponsored public service radio and television stations as well as commercial broadcasters are carefully monitored by the local Broadcasting Authority, which has considerable supervisory and regulatory powers. There is, however, precious little control on how the officially partisan radio and television stations use their privately owned media outlets to propagate biased party political viewpoints with the aim of preserving and revitalizing partisan identities and communities. In her detailed analysis of the complex sociocultural contexts of Maltese journalistic practices, Carmen Sammut (2007) argues that one of the good qualities of partisan Maltese broadcasting is that it still tends to address its audiences as citizens and voters rather than consumers. Unlike situations where profit-driven media organizations make money by selling audiences to advertisers, in the Maltese context, most journalists do not normally feel constrained by polls. In most cases, news items tend to be selected for reporting either because they are believed to be of "news value" or because of institutional interests. This means that though Maltese media are anything but impartial, they are not likely to be primarily dominated by commercial constraints and perceptions of financial profitability. There is also a clear understanding by reporters and audiences alike that because all reports are filtered through institutional biases, they always need to be read and interpreted in the light of those biases. Some of the journalists interviewed by Sammut thus insisted, for instance, that they consciously declare their political and other biases openly because they consider this to be democratically healthy and appropriate – precisely because they know that they are presenting an institutionally or politically biased perspective. Similarly, the comments made by audience groups can often come across as having been made by "active receivers," precisely because these audiences are very conscious of the fact that they are constantly trying to make sense of news reports and local media content which are obviously contradictory and blatantly partisan.

All this suggests that the contrasting models of advocacy, commercial, and public service broadcasting need not be mutually exclusive, especially in a situation like the one which prevails in Malta, where community-based or partisan broadcasting is counterbalanced by the parallel availability of a public service model, local commercial broadcasting, and a plethora of imported overseas networks. This does not mean, however, that the Maltese media landscape is anywhere near meeting the requirements of a rational public sphere as advocated by Habermas. The institutional constraints that have made the Maltese media system the idiosyncratic mixture that it is today have also led to many journalistic excesses, and news reports and broadcasting more generally often focus on the preservation and revitalization of exclusively partisan communities. Through news and current affairs programs which interpret social reality on behalf of their listeners, partisan radio and TV have become what Sammut (2007, p. 213) calls "the main shrines where party pilgrims gather to discuss missions and revere relics." In this sense, partisan broadcasting plays a major role in extending cohesion and a sense of belonging at party level. The essentializing exclusivity of such forms of belonging, however, has also been highly divisive and detrimental at broader national and inter-community levels.

Postmodern Fluidity and Intersubjective Ripples

The intricate, complex and often convoluted ways in which indigenous belief systems, habits, and cultural practices intermingle with global media trends raise challenging questions about mainstream approaches to global media ethics and to the study of media more generally. In global Western media, consumerism draws on and nourishes rampant individualism, which is a prized value of Western societies. In contrast, many indigenous societies place value instead on the collectivity (family, community, the village, the tribe) rather than the individual. Their media

Indigenous Media Values

productions are motivated by a desire to enhance this collectivity rather than nurturing, rewarding, or deliberately frustrating individuals who want to be richer, more beautiful, more successful, more cool, or more admired than other members of the same society. The underlying value systems and political and ethical motivations are quite different.

Zygmunt Bauman describes the criteria which drive and underscore postmodern consumer cultures as motivated by the imperatives of transience, or what he memorably calls the *fluidity* or *liquidity* which characterizes the consumer market's propagation of "rapid circulation, a shorter distance from use to waste and waste disposal, and the immediate replacement of goods that are no longer profitable" (2005, p. 59). As Bauman points out, a consumer market catering for long-term needs, not to mention eternity, would be a contradiction in terms. As a result, the thrust of the international commercial media marketplace is to subordinate cultural creativity and cultural difference to the demand for instant consumption, instant gratification, and instant profit. This means that difference becomes an attribute to be traded, while cultural creations are required to "accept the prerequisite of all erstwhile *bona fide* consumer products: that they legitimize themselves in terms of market value (and their *current* market value, to be sure) or perish" (Bauman, 2005, p. 59).

This is in very marked contrast to the motivations informing the work of indigenous media makers concerned with fostering and preserving language, tradition and ancestral custom, with using "visual, poetic and oral imagery … to transfer intergenerational memories from elder to community" (Cache Collective, 2008, p. 85). Bauman's metaphor of "liquidity" and the (Western) associations of flowing impermanence and superficiality which he brings to it are also starkly different from the ways in which the shimmering and flowing surfaces of sacred waters are viewed as a conduit to spiritual experience and deeper understanding in Australian Aboriginal art. From Bauman's European (materialist) perspective, liquids are anything but timeless or durable because they "do not keep to any shape for long and are constantly ready (and prone) to change it" (Bauman, 2000, p. 2). From a Yolngu Aboriginal perspective, however, the shimmering and dappled luminescence of flowing water can create abstract and aesthetically engaging effects that provide the possibility of an experience of the Ancestral. Viewed from this different cultural perspective, solidity is not a prerequisite of durability or enduring value. As Deger (2006, p. 215) puts it, "in Yolngu hands, photographs, audio recordings, video, and radio generate mimetic ripples that reach beyond the 'everyday' time and space, amplifying an invisible yet sensuously encompassing intersubjective field of unity."

The preservation and revitalization of personal and communal identities among indigenous as well as other cultures are inextricably entwined with the realities of globalization and the complex transnational constructions of what Appadurai (1990) calls "imaginary landscapes." One belief shared by several indigenous communities from different parts of the world is the conviction that human life and communal identity are crucially bound to the land, not just pragmatically, but also ethically, in the sense that all are considered part of the same moral universe. For indigenous Australians, for instance, because all life is part of one vast unchanging network of relationships which can be traced to the Great Spirit Ancestors, all that is sacred is in the land. It both sustains and is sustained by the people and cultures which have evolved with it, changing it and changing with it. With globalization, the land and the landscape have evolved in ways which, though unprecedented in their details and challenges, can still be encompassed by the ethics informing this world view. As one of Bruce Chatwin's characters in *The Songlines* puts it: "Aboriginals believed that all the 'living things' had been made in secret beneath the earth's crust, as well as all the white man's gear – his aeroplanes, his guns, his Toyota Land Cruisers – and every invention that will ever be invented; slumbering below the surface, waiting their turn to be called" (Chatwin, 1987, pp. 14–15).

By embracing, adapting and indigenizing new communications technologies, the best examples of global indigenous media are not simply preserving the lessons and wisdom of ancestors, they are also actively choosing to forge imaginary landscapes which have the potential to inspire communally informed and empowered cultural identities. As Norman Cohn (2002, p. 27) puts it, in the course of his description of community-based Inuit filmmaking:

> As artists bridging the past and future we practice a third way, different from either the Inuit way or the White way, both solitudes separated by centuries of fear and mistrust since Columbus and Frobisher "discovered" the New World. Inuit skills of working together join with southern ideas of community videomaking in a new model of professional production that can expand film and television in Canada and around the world.

All this suggests that there are a number of important lessons which more mainstream Western media could learn from a dispassionate consideration of the values (and potential pitfalls) underscoring the production of global indigenous media and from an open-minded study of their content and of how they appeal to, communicate with, instruct, and often empower their target audiences. One key area is the emphasis on community values and the preservation and revitalization of a shared heritage and identity. In this context, the spiritual and emotional wellbeing of the group as a whole are often seen as paramount, and media practitioners approach each other and their audiences as mutually supporting, equal and (in the case of the young) developing community members, rather than agents or targets of marketing. This does not, however, equate with a simple-minded or myopic entrenchment in traditional values, or with an unrealistic romanticization of those values. At their creative best, the types of indigenous media products discussed in this chapter are the results of a conscious acceptance of the fact that survival and the revitalization of ancestral wisdom inevitably depend on the ability to adapt as a prerequisite to moving into the future. Among other things, such adaptation calls for a culturally-informed understanding of, engagement with, and control over new media technology. In this perspective, the old and the new, the local and the global, are approached as always crucially needing to be balanced and enlightened by each other.

References

Appadurai, A. (1990) Disjuncture and difference in the global cultural economy. *Public Culture*, 2 (2), 1–24.

Appadurai, A. (2000) Grassroots globalization and the research imagination. *Public Culture*, 12 (1), 1–19.

Bauman, Z. (2000) *Liquid modernity*, Polity, Cambridge.

Bauman, Z. (2005) *Liquid life*, Polity, Cambridge.

Bird, S.E. (2003) *The Audience in Everyday Life: Living in a Media World*, Routledge, New York.

Boissevain, J. (1965) *Saints and Fireworks: Religion and Politics in Rural Malta*, The Athlone Press, London.

Browne, D.R. (1996) *Electronic Media and Indigenous Peoples: A Voice of our Own?* Iowa State University Press, Ames.

Bruner, J. (1979) *On Knowing: Essays for the Left Hand*, Harvard University Press, Cambridge, MA.

Cache Collective (2008) *Cache*: Provisions and productions in contemporary Igloolik video, in *Global Indigenous Media: Cultures, Poetics, and Politics*, (eds P. Wilson and M. Stewart), Duke University Press, Durham, pp. 74–88.

Chatwin, B. (1987) *The Songlines*, Viking Penguin, New York.

Christ, C.P., and Rountree, K. (2006) Humanity in the web of life. *Environmental Ethics*, 28 (2), 185–200.

Chun, K. (2002) Storytelling in the Arctic Circle: An interview with Zacharias Kunuk. *Cineaste*, 28 (1), 21–23.

Cohn, N. (2002) The art of community-based filmmaking, in *Atanarjuat: The Fast Runner*, (eds P.A. Angilirq, N. Cohn and S. d'Anglure), Coach House Books & Isuma Publishing, Toronto, pp. 24–27.

Corporate Maori Television Website (n.d.) About Maori Television, http://corporate.maoritelevision.com/Default.aspx?tabid=178 (accessed June 29, 2010).

Deger, J. (2006) *Shimmering screens: Making media in an Aboriginal community*, University of Minnesota Press, Minneapolis.

Deger, J. (2007) Seeing the invisible: Yolngu video as revelatory ritual. *Visual Anthropology*, 20 (2), 103–121.

Dowell, K. (2006) Indigenous media gone global: Strengthening indigenous identity on- and off-screen at the First NationsFirst Features Film Showcase. *American Anthropologist*, 108 (2), 376–384.

Dunleavy, T. (2008) New Zealand television and the struggle for "public service." *Media, Culture & Society*, 30 (6), 795–811.

Fox, D.T. (1993) Honouring the treaty: Indigenous television in Aotearoa, in *Channels of Resistance: Global Television and Local Empowerment*, (ed. T. Dowmunt), British Film Institute, London, pp. 126–137.

Fuchs, C. (2002) Interview with Zacharias Kunuk and Norman Cohn, director and producer of "Atanarjuat, The Fast Runner." *PopMatters*, 20 June, www.popmatters.com/film/interviews/kunuk-zacharias.shtml (accessed June 29, 2010).

Giddens, A. (1991) *Modernity and Self-Identity: Self and Society in the Late Modern Age*, Polity Press, Cambridge.

Ginsburg, F. (1991) Indigenous media: Faustian contract or global village? *Cultural Anthropology*, 6 (1), 92–112.

Ginsburg, F. (2002a) Mediating culture: Indigenous media, ethnographic film, and the production of identity, in *The Anthropology of Media: A Reader*, (eds K. Askew and R.R. Wilk), Blackwell, Oxford, pp. 210–235.

Ginsburg, F. (2002b) Screen memories: Resignifying the traditional in indigenous media, in *Media Worlds: Anthropology on New Terrain*, (eds F. Ginsburg, L. Abu-Lughod and B. Larkin), University of California Press, Berkeley, pp. 39– 57.

Ginsburg, F. (2003) *Atanarjuat* off-screen: From media reservations to the world stage. *American Anthropologist*, 105 (4), 827–830.

Glynn, K., and Tyson, A.F. (2007) Indigeneity, media and cultural globalization: The case of *Mataku*, or the Maori *X-Files*, *International Journal of Cultural Studies*, 10 (2), 205–224.

Grixti, J. (2004) *Broadcasting and the Young Adult Consumer: Local and Global Media Influences on Maltese Youth Culture*, Broadcasting Authority, Malta.

Grixti, J. (2006) Symbiotic transformations: Youth, global media and indigenous culture in Malta. *Media, Culture & Society*, 28 (1), 105–122.

Grixti, J. (2008) Desirability and its discontents: Young people's responses to media images of health, beauty and physical perfection, in *Social Studies of Health, Illness and Disease: Perspectives from the Social Sciences and Humanities*, (eds P. Twohig and V. Kalitzkus), Rodopi, Amsterdam and New York, pp. 49–74.

Grossberg, L. (1996) On postmodernism and articulation: An interview with Stuart Hall in *Stuart Hall: Critical Dialogues in Cultural Studies*, (eds D. Morley and K. H. Chen), Routledge, London, pp. 131–150.

Hall, S. (1992) The question of cultural identity in *Modernity and its Futures*, (eds S. Hall, D. Held and T. McGrew), Polity Press, Cambridge, pp. 274–316.

Hartley, J., and McKee, A. (2000) *The Indigenous Public Sphere: The Reporting and Reception of Aboriginal Issues in the Australian Media*, Oxford University Press, Oxford.

Igloolik Isuma Productions (2007) www.isuma.tv/hi/en/atanarjuat/filmmaking-inuit-style (accessed July 14, 2010).

Kennedy, P., and Danks, C. J. (2001) *Globalisation and National Identities: Crisis or Opportunity?* Palgrave, Basingstoke.

King, M. (2003) *The Penguin History of New Zealand*, Penguin, Auckland.

Klein, N. (2000) *No logo*, Flamingo, London.

Kraidy, M.M. (1999) The global, the local, and the hybrid: A native ethnography of glocalization. *Critical Studies in Mass Communication*, 16 (4), 456–476.

Kunuk, Z. (2002) I first heard the story of Atanarjuat from my mother, in *Atanarjuat: The Fast Runner*, (eds P.A. Angilirq, N. Cohn, and S. d'Anglure), Coach House Books & Isuma Publishing, Toronto, pp. 12–15.

McElroy, R. (2008) Indigenous minority-language media: S4C, cultural identity, and the Welsh-language televisual community, in *Global Indigenous Media: Cultures, Poetics, and Politics*, (eds P. Wilson and M. Stewart), Duke University Press, Durham, NC, pp. 232–249.

Meyrowitz, J., and Maguire J. (1993) Media, place, and multiculturalism. *Society*, 30 (5), 41–48.

Michaels, E. (1994) *Bad Aboriginal Art: Tradition, Media, and Technological Horizons*, University of Minnesota Press, Minneapolis.

New Zealand Law Commission (2001) Maori custom and values in New Zealand law: Study paper (NZLC SP9) for the Maori customary law project. New Zealand Law Commission, Wellington, www.lawcom.govt.nz/ProjectStudyPapers.aspx?ProjectID=112 (accessed June 29, 2010).

Nicholson, A. M. (2008) Bran Nue Day dawns in Broome. *ABC News (Australia)*, 9 December, www.abc.net.au/news/stories/2008/12/09/2441518.htm (accessed June 29, 2010).

Parks, L. (2005) *Cultures in Orbit: Satellites and the Televisual*, Duke University Press, Durham, NC.

Poihipi, V. (2007) The impact of Maori Television on being Maori: A geographical approach. *MAI Review*, Issue 1, Intern Report 6, http://ojs.review.mai.ac.nz/index.php/MR/issue/view/2 (accessed June 29, 2010).

Sammut, C. (2007) *Media and Maltese Society*, Lexington, Lanham, MD.

Schlesinger, P.R. (1994) Europe's contradictory communicative space. *Daedalus*, 123 (2), 25–53.

Shohat, E., and Stam, R. (1996) From the imperial family to the transnational imaginary: Media spectatorship in the age of globalization, in *Global/Local: Cultural Production and the Transnational Imaginary*, (eds R. Wilson and W. Dissanayake), Duke University Press, Durham, NC, pp. 145–171.

Smith, J.T. (2006) Parallel quotidian flows: Maori Television on air. *New Zealand Journal of Media Studies*, 9 (2), 27–35.

Stephens, T. (2004) Maori television, in *Television in New Zealand: Programming the Nation*, (eds R. Horrocks and N. Perry), Oxford University Press, Melbourne, pp. 107–115.

Stewart, P., and Wilson, M. (2008) Introduction: Indigeneity and indigenous media on the global stage, in *Global Indigenous Media: Cultures, Poetics, and Politics*, (eds P. Wilson and M. Stewart), Duke University Press, Durham, NC, pp. 1–35.

Svenson, M. (2002) Zacharias Kunuk Interview. *Native Networks*, www.nativenetworks.si.edu/eng/rose/kunuk_z_interview.htm (accessed June 29, 2010).

Turner, T. (1992) Defiant images: The Kayapo appropriation of video. *Anthropology Today*, 8 (6), 5–16.

Turner, T. (2002) Representation, polyphony, and the construction of power in a Kayapo video, in *Indigenous Movements, Self-Representation, and the State in Latin America*, (eds K.. Warren and J. Jackson), University of Texas Press, Austin, pp. 229–250.

Walker, R. (2004) *Ka whawhai tonu mātou: Struggle without end*, Penguin, Auckland.

White, J. (2005) Frozen but always in motion: Arctic film, video, and broadcast. *Velvet Light Trap*, 55, 52–64.

19

Media Ethics as Panoptic Discourse
A Foucauldian View

Ed McLuskie

Morals reformed ... by a simple idea in Architecture! ... A new mode of obtaining power of mind over mind.

(Bentham, 1995, from the 1787 title page of Panopticon; or The Inspection-House)

Humanity ... installs each of its violences in a system of rules and thus proceeds from domination to domination.

(Foucault, 1977b, p. 151)

Visibility is a trap.

(Foucault, 1977c, p. 200)

The literature of media ethics recognizes that any medium, globalized, or regionalized, is more than a technology. Ever since the alphabet met papyrus and the scribe, shifts in media relations have meant shifts in social relations and our actions in the midst of both. Even the nature of sociality and our understandings of it accompany media. Newspaper reading on the 1920s streetcar (Hardt, Brennen, and Killmeier, 2000) fixed displays of the private into public view. Microbroadcasts of class, literacy, contemporality, and content interests thus extended cues of surveillance while providing conventionalized invitations to possible conversation. Today's brand names announce e-readers shrouding potentially shareable interests, as flesh-and-blood screen readers seem increasingly immune from conversational bids or personal judgments about who they are and with whom they associate. A shifting media world shrinks the social environment during material transport – the subway, perhaps, or even the greener version, walking – while faster, one-way windows ensure that people are no longer judged by the covers they hold or the

---

The Handbook of Global Communication and Media Ethics, First Edition. Edited by Robert S. Fortner and P. Mark Fackler.
© 2011 Blackwell Publishing Ltd. Published 2011 by Blackwell Publishing Ltd.

Media Ethics as Panoptic Discourse

virtual pages they turn. Surveillance and suppositions about others has gone digital. Meanwhile, "monopolies of knowledge" (Innis, 2008) associated with "changes in the technology of preserved communication" (Havelock, 1963, p. xi) acquire a Foucauldian read: scribes become metaphors for human subjects working within and through regimes of power-knowledge (Foucault, 1980), as concrete human beings inscribing themselves through the power of the panopticon (Foucault, 1977c).

To Michel Foucault, media developments tell the modernist story of discourse, broadly understood as new ways of seeing the world through alterations in work, life, and languages. Not only do they open new vistas; they extend surveillance and create professions for knowledge-life relations. Among them are a few Foucault identified: practices tied to studies of medicine, the psyche, literature, and the social. Once Foucault moved Weberian analyses of bureaucracy into connections with, instead of separations between, power and knowledge – "power-knowledge" (1977a), "the reconfiguration of professionalism and profession" (Boon, Flood, and Webb, 2005, p. 47) implicated knowledge and bureaucratic surveillance in the midst of contests over the status and power of professionalism and its dictates for professional practices.

Since Foucault, the list of professions grew and further intertwined knowledge with life, expanding into a secondary literature of professionalism. Foucauldians in that literature offer critical assessments in a range from the therapeutic professions (Mackey, 2007) to accounting (McPhail, 1999). There, we read of professional discourses as sets of narrow incubators that grow self-subjugating practitioners. "Ethical professionals" appear as a "threat" even to professional practitioners (McPhail, 1999, p. 833), occasioning resistance to normalization from within, as well as transgressions and counter-technologies capable of cultivating a counter-ethics. Such a critique surfaces occasionally in the study of media professions, as when Dodson ties professional discourse in journalism to forms of "ideological fantasy" in the 2003 Iraq invasion, one version of professional ethics that "militarises journalism" (Dodson, 2010, p. 99).

The professionalization of knowledge and its intersections with "the professions" await a specialty-canvassing review of ethics in fields of communication and media, though the prospect has been proposed (Fortner and Hoag, 1980, p. 41). "Few treatments of media ethics," however, "are historical," tending instead to the "anecdotal," reaching no "further back than a generation" (Ferré, 2009, p. 15). Thus media ethics as a literature generally produces case studies to unpack media professions, providing recommendations grounded elsewhere for moral-professional dilemmas. The sources of this grounding in turn have become the subject-matter of an academic-professional specialty approaching canonic status. As "media ethics," differences converge in shared appeals to universal, normative principles intended to (re)frame media practices for their errant ways or compliance. A recent text reached its eighth edition reiterating classic distinctions for media ethics, distinctions that attempt to bring case-based (a)morality into alignment with ethical principles. The text rejects professional-media intersections and self-interpreting actors as sources of a media ethics, wary of "relativism" and "normlessness," and associating both with Foucault as well as others (Preface to Christians *et al.*, 2008). We read there of a postmodern falling from grace. Indeed, Foucault's analyses "cannot be captured in a history of moral codes or social rules" (Laidlaw, 2002, p. 321). In a more modest articulation, Christians insists that "there are protonorms that precede their reification into ethical principles"; one such protonorm is "dialogic communication understood as intersubjective universalism," an ethics for "the whole of humanity" (Christians, 1997, p. 8) that explains "our duty to preserve life" as "timeless and nonnegotiable" (p. 7). Foucault might respond, "That may be, unless I'm the one incarcerated in the unanticipated ways of duty." Yet Foucault might agree with such an interlocutor, per a later interview: "In the serious play of questions and answers, in the work of reciprocal elucidation, the rights of each person are in some sense immanent in the discussion. They depend only on the dialogue situation" (Foucault, 1980, p. 108). Literature revealing Foucault's modernism (for example, Bruns, 2005) problematizes the broad brush of the postmodern worries. The matter of truth in ethics – a concern for hard-to-soft normativists as well as for journalists – occupies much in Foucault's last lectures on truth-telling (Foucault, 2001). There, truth-telling is invoked for the constitution of a moral subjectivity.

However, getting there is neither natural nor expected. Indeed, Foucault seems a deliberately moving target, refusing to settle into imagined, universalized universes, demanding the situatedness of the details for any universals moving beyond specific situations to track surveillance practices. A tolerance for what some may read as Foucault's inconsistency here is required, as his "ethic of an intellectual" means to "break loose from himself" (Flynn, 1985, p. 532) as an ethics of transformation, a point among others that accords Foucault equal status as a conversation partner for analyses of ethics. Where media ethics carves out norms of reciprocity as a criterion, complementarity instead of vast distances suggests itself when Foucault moves through technologies of the self-forming process, the dynamics whereby normative appeals "stick." They are of similar, if not truly mutual, interest (cf. Ingram, 2005).

The occasional power analyst, reading power and domination in forms of mutuality, however differentiated, finds appeals to "communication" and "dialogue" actually describing the "maintenance of interests" rather than "freedom from domination and consensus seeking" (Flyvbjerg, 2000, p. 5). Meanwhile, appropriators and detractors of Foucault's work find silence about media-work and its relations to ethics and morality in the Foucauldian oeuvre.

It turns out that Foucault stands within "a series of French-led shifts" producing a "critique of [both] subject-centered reason [and] general truth claims," a post-structuralist "critique of 'foundationalism'" extending the critique of metaphysics "into an attack on all claims to an external standpoint" (Calhoun, 1993, pp. 77–78). For any variation of applied ethics, recourse to overarching principles is foreclosed on condition that Foucault is properly positioned there. But he inherits Durkheim as well, certainly no poststructuralist or postmodernist, who wrote that every society possesses and requires a morality: "Chaque société a en gros la morale qu'il lui

Media Ethics as Panoptic Discourse

faut" (Durkheim, 1967, p. 81). Foucault deciphered that morality needed its minders, keepers of the keys to moral conduct who, once conduct of all types come into view, expanded the pool of willing subject themselves. This is the power of the panopticon.

Innovative in its day, Bentham's panoptic prison was teeming with participants. The original brick-and-mortar panopticon hid the prison guards from view to intensify any prisoner's feeling of being watched. A 24-hour, seven-day-a-week surveillance mechanism, it cultivated chronic mental uncertainty about being watched. The "major effect of the panopticon" was the assurance that power would function automatically. Once "surveillance is permanent in its effects," if not in its enactments, "the perfection of power should tend to render its actual exercise [of observation by the guards] unnecessary." The guiding panoptic principle was that "power should be visible and unverifiable": today's analog of the "inmate will constantly have before his eyes the tall outline of the central tower from which he is spied upon," but can never ascertain "whether he is being looked at at any one moment" (Foucault, 1977c, p. 201) – an achievement rivaling in practice any principle invoked for any media ethics. The panopticon "is polyvalent in its applications," able to instruct, distribute, and locate "bodies in space," effectively GPSed and arrayed as individuals regulating one another, by defining their places in and for "channels of power" and "the instruments and modes of intervention of power." The panopticon is "a generalizable model of functioning" that defines "power relations in terms of the everyday life" (Foucault, 1977c, p. 205). The panoptic vision in the eighteenth century led to "the swarming of disciplinary mechanisms" (Foucault, 1977c, p. 211), now faster-tracked in twenty-first century celebrations of "the hive," that global, Internet-infused source of alleged wisdom certainly connected, visible, but questionably communicative except, perhaps, as the surveillance function of media. Foucault saw the panopticon in "the Christian School" training "docile children," institutions producing mentors, soon-to-be adults in the ways of control who reproduce a morality to "exercise regular supervision" from family to neighbors, all checking to see whether all "know their catechism and their prayers" (Foucault, 1977c, p. 211).

Foucault also saw the morphing of the panopticon through institutions of modernity, into full-blown governmentality enacted upon, in, by, and through microactions of collective and self-surveillance. They are virtually indistinguishable practices. A Foucauldian ethics responds with "fearless speech" (Foucault, 2001), problematizing the practice of "surveillance" as though it were a duty. In the name of "ethics" and other articulations aimed at right, just, or otherwise appropriate conduct, regimes of power assert their requirements as recurring occasions for the systematically silenced and compliant, in order to capture and imprison autonomy itself.

Against this background, Davidson (1994, pp. 115–116) regards Foucault's ethics as "potentially transformative for the writing of the history of ethics" and the conceptualization of ethics. One of its key features is to keep the actor in the fray of the panoptic world. Foucault's ethics would have to include, and did, themes and practices of transgression predicated on self-care, on looking out for oneself, but without falling into narcissism while avoiding utopian appeals. "Transgressions," after all, "do not form their own orders" (Cresswell, 1994, p. 57) because "the order of things" (Foucault, 1970) persists. Nor do they articulate an animating dimension of human agency, free choice. As an inevitable actor caught up in normed and regulated lives, the panoptic actor already is a power actor. The question is whether this actor can pit power against power. How could this actor be considered the bearer of an ethical position, much less a producer of one? To address the issue, language and cultures of reception intervene.

Davidson calls the move to Anglo-American readings of Foucault's works on ethics "markedly disjointed" (1994, p. 116). English translations add layers of problematic interpretations as Foucault looks back to antiquity. For example, when Foucault quotes Plato's *Laws* (Plato, 2006, p. 783e), the English reading privileges the ideas "fine or noble" over the idea of "the beautiful" (O'Leary, 2006, p. 55). However, according to the French reading, parents must give to the city "les enfants les plus beaux et les meilleurs possibles" (Foucault, 1976, p. 140) – "the most beautiful and the best children possible" (as translated by Annas, 1993). A standard English translation (Foucault, 1988d, p. 123) ignores the aesthetic reading, preferring "the beautiful" even while noting the aesthetic dimension of a Foucauldian ethics. We may already be misled simply by linguistic and cultural sensibilities alone, for Foucault could be doing "no more than exploiting possibilities" in Greek thought as mediated by "French-speaking philosophers and historians": rather than interrogate the perhaps mistaken but frequent conclusion that Foucault wishes to "aestheticize" Greek morality, O'Leary suggests that we consider the possibility that "English speaking philosophers [are] blind (or hostile)" (p. 55) to an aesthetics of self-care articulated in French philosophical traditions.

Aesthetic relations of subjectivity describe the art of relating to the self. They are forms of power-knowledge enacted as a power relation to oneself. Aesthetic self-governance echoes the classical Greek concept, *enkrateia*: "the dynamics of a domination of oneself by oneself and the effort that this demands" (Foucault, 1988d, p. 65). Nothing is eradicated or banished here. Like the medium of the artist's clay, the self is controlled and molded by the artist. Thus, Foucault's ethics of this self is a contest for control of the self. Greek society counseled training for this contest, *askesis*. To know oneself through training to control the self meant the prospect of success in power relations with others. The point, however, was not to value control as an end, but as a strategy of freedom for the always-integrated. Indeed, Foucault's ethics displays "impatience for ... a freedom" that promotes "self-creation" (Bernauer and Mahon, 1994, p. 155).

Since Foucault's archaeology of knowledge (1972), the pervasiveness of power would seem to trump human agency at any level, whenever, and wherever a human subject might, if she could, enact that movement of the celebrated human subject, "agency." While sounding much like the Nietzschean *Zeitgeist* suspicious of civilization, Foucault's interest in self-(re)creation is no mere subjective rage against the machine. His genealogies (Foucault, 1997) are "a kind of historical writing that integrates into a single investigation the tasks of the history of institutions and conceptual history" (Honneth, 1994, pp. 158–159). They are concerned to determine the "nature of the present" (Foucault, 1988b, p. 36) as more than an exposé, but also as a search for connections between human subjectivity, truth, and, especially, "the constitution of experience" (Foucault, 1988a, p. 48). Thus Foucault reads Heideggerian subjectivism not to be caught in its ontology, but for its transformative potential (Rayner, 2007), and he finds in ancient Greek orientations to the body an unending, not a transcending, perfectibility project.

Foucault's attention to the ethics of other times is not an exercise in valorization of the search for timeless lessons. We can appeal neither to modernity nor to the classics. He was once asked, "Do you find [the Greeks] admirable?" "No," Foucault replied, because the "operation of self-governance in antiquity applied only to free men [in] a society based on slavery and the subordination of women" (Foucault, 1988e, p. 253). Instead, Foucault looks for subjectivity in its moments of transition, including, so to speak, from the contested terrain of the inside. It is an ethics that, as a self-politics, promotes if anything technologies that focus on shifting moments in subjectivity. While no promised lands lurk beyond such hermeneutic horizons and daily life practices, much can be done in the face of false promises.

In his last interview, "The Return of Morality" (1988f), Foucault elevates moral action as an escape from entrenched, rearticulated modes of subjectivity. Moral practice becomes at its core a form of critique necessary as a means of survival of the self. Critique may be as close as one gets to a "principle" for a Foucauldian ethics predicated on care of the self. Critique *is* a technology of the self to Foucault, and this technology "is virtue" (quoted in Sharpe, 2005, p. 97).

Critique-as-ethics is aimed at desubjugation but also desubjectivation, reaching beyond "technologies of the self" (Foucault, 1988g) to the author of the categorical imperative, whose maxim demands ethical action according to a principle "we" would reason to be the universal law. Foucault's essay echoing Kant's "What Is Enlightenment?" (Foucault, 1984b), however, avoids the counterfactual universal while approaching self-care almost teleologically. Foucault stresses *Mündigkeit* inflected as mature action, to "exit from the immaturity of subjection to authority" (Milchman, 2009, p. 81).

In a move approaching media ethics debates over what qualifies as ethics, Foucault asks, "which is the aspect or part of myself or my behavior which is concerned with moral conduct?" He continues:

> For instance, you can say, in general, that in our society the main field of morality, the part of ourselves which is most relevant for morality, is our feelings. [But] it's quite clear from the Kantian point of view, [that] intention is much more important than feelings. And from the Christian point of view, it is desire [though] in the Middle Ages it was not the same as the 17th century (1984a, p. 352).

Foucault's ethics considers all when his ethics concentrates on the ancients' perfection of the self. There we face, not duty, but choices to care for the body as a liberatory practice that, for our time, negotiates power relations, too. Foucault's ethics, while critical of tradition, more often urges simply their description as inscription into the self. While he eschewed theory beyond practice, his influence for media ethics is its grounding in the media practices of a carceral society. There, the lesson of the Greeks also prompts an objection:

> I am not looking for an alternative; you can't find the solution of a problem in the solution of another problem raised at another moment by other people. You see, what I want to do is not the history of solutions – and that's the reason why I don't accept the word *alternative*. I ... do the genealogy of problems, of *problematiques*. My point is not that everything is bad, but that everything is dangerous, which is not exactly the same thing as bad. If everything is dangerous, then we always have something to do. So my position leads not to apathy but to a hyper- and pessimistic activism. I think that the ethico-political choice we have to make every day is to determine which is the main danger (1997, p. 104).

This requires experimentation as an ethical practice, an ongoing critical self-revisionism of practices to explore techniques of the self by analyzing those "practices by which individuals" came to "decipher, recognize and acknowledge themselves as subjects." There, they "discover, in desire, the truth of their being be it natural or fallen" (1988d, p. 5). Foucault's ethics operationalizes truth itself – as "intentional and voluntary actions" that people "not only set [for] themselves [as] rules of conduct, but [as rules that] seek to transform themselves ... to make their life into an oeuvre that carries certain aesthetic values and meets certain stylistic criteria" (Foucault, 1988d, p. 10).

Beyond the individual subject, one can imagine in idealized Foucauldian universes populations prone to resistance, impulses considered ethical, vital to the survival of the human subject as well as its institutions. This, then, is the image one must imagine for any version of media ethics. Media would be enlisted to encourage resistance, even transgression, because in Foucault's interrogations of history, history has yet to reveal practices free of systematic, identity-defining, action-orienting domination. Above all, a media ethics would aim for virtue as critique.

It is for others to say whether a power analytics contributes to democratic social change. Astride divides, Foucault and one of his more prominent critics agree on one thing, at least, and one important qualifier, in particular: ethics and morality "shield the peculiar vulnerability of socialized individuals" *if* they can find a way to object (Habermas, 2004, p. 5). In this, media ethics has friends across universal-particular, subjective-intersubjective divides. Still, appeals to codification invoked for or from the applied-inclined professions occur within the panoptic iterations of the times. The human subject, who gets her name from pervasive practices of subjugation, can only address these violences against the self through an alternative "self-fashioning" understood as an empowered freedom against power. Ethics in this light focuses on "techniques of the self." Put differently, a Foucauldian ethics is always and everywhere a response and an enactment of bio-power.

As history produces power regimes that overpower choice, a Foucauldian media ethics would encourage reading history with a horizontal eye, focusing on the surveillance practices of the subjugated. While other versions of media ethics proceed into spheres of the professions with corrective intent, Foucault's corrective is critique. Could that be a standard in a panoptic age, one that invites a hermeneutics of doubt as an ethical technology resisting the contents of universals and a plunge into cynicism? *Discipline and Punish* (1977a) described (re)interpretation practices of panoptic control superglued to behavior while creating interlocked categories of individuals, the feared versus the fearful. Where professions and their knowledge industries bend to demands for legitimacy and harmony, Foucault would highlight instead the relation of knowledge-regimes to concrete practices. Perhaps he would take up the university for his analyses, a twenty-first century panoptic institution where the academic professions have grown "risk-averse," threatening "to impoverish ... intellectual vitality" (Fritschler and Smith, 2009, p. A80). Foucault would feature the word, "vitality."

Were Foucault to consider declining/reconfigured ranks of reporters, he might redirect the media ethics discourse of justice to Craig's observation that moral commitment is "squeezed out ... under the pressure of competition and profit" (2009, p. 203), but with the twist that reporters themselves already are part of corporatized panoptic pressures. Where media ethics speaks the language of institutions, Foucault enters to analyze the panoptic and the critical. When *The Handbook of Mass Media Ethics* references Foucault, the "technology of the self" looks for "the bones of truth" after announcing, "truth is an ideology," and the "truth in pictures" in photojournalism as "about truth in self," a "search for moments of empathy as gateways to moments of revelation about the story of the self" (Newton, 2009, p. 91). Elliott (1988) grounds her applied ethics in "essential shared values," an appeal that echoes Trapp's (1978) argument for social responsibility of the press, if not in subject matter, then in the communitarian appeal described by Fackler as the "orientation of conscience toward mutuality" (Fackler, 2009, p. 314). Foucault would redirect such discussions to avoid any hint of an out-of-body appeal, whether to subjectivist or collectivist ontology, or to an actual Other considered, as a matter of human nature, panopticon-free and, therefore, capable of or ready for mutual recognition. Lest such Foucauldian foci signal for media ethics unbridgeable differences, Foucault sees occasions of power-knowledge and power relations where all involved exemplify to some degree – and it's always to *some* degree – the virtue of critique.

Thus a recursive inevitability attaches to Foucault's ethics. The predicament and enactment of power persists while *Müdigkeit* beckons from within. For a media ethics of communication, the call to maturity enacts "the *free speaker*" who becomes "the *fearless speaker*" who actually speaks regardless of "fear of ridicule, torture, or death, where the chance for silence is present" (Zapata, 2005, p. 153), as is the chance of professional excommunication. Foucault regards knowledge-regimes as contestable sites of power relations that can encourage diversity and critique, assume reorganized forms in the course of contestation, as part of panoptic maintenance, but also as shaper and reshaper of traditions.

When a media ethics appeals to traditions, it appeals to power that is always embedded in relationships practiced by media professionals, not only power from above (Foucault, 1988c). Its ubiquity makes ethics itself always a likely agent of the panopticon. As power relations take the form of micropractices of power to enact and resist (Foucault, 1977a), they depend and actually extend societal regimes of power (Foucault, 1988c). A media ethics that is a Foucauldian ethics cannot take itself out of the regime. "So what kind of ethics can be built now, when we know that between ethics and other structures there are only historical collisions?" Foucault answers:

> What strikes me is the fact that in our society, art has become something which is related only to objects and not to individuals, or to life. That art is something which is specialized or which is done by experts who are artists. But couldn't everyone's life become a work of art? Why should the lamp or the house be an art object, but not our life? (Foucault, 1988c, p. 350).

The journalist, the blogger, the wordsmith may become be an artist pursuing a critical fashioning as an ethics of the self in a panoptic world. She might write counter visions to the panoptic vision of a globalizing media. Failure in this can only be described from loftier standpoints we cannot know. Instead, we can suffer but also appropriate the consequences of subjugation. On that petard, a media ethics finds itself.

Foucault's histories of the present leave a legacy of looking for "unsuspected dimensions of reality" where "phenomena of power" do not mean incremental progress or revolution "from combat to combat" toward "universal reciprocity" (Honneth, 1994, pp. 157–158). Humanity, instead, "proceeds from domination to domination," (Foucault, 1977b, p. 151), informing our knowledge of ethics. That knowledge, like all knowledge, can never be severed from systems of power, due to the "indissoluble connection between power and knowledge" (Honneth, 1994, p. 158), a connection that produces historically specific ways "of rendering" docility and utility (Foucault, 1977a, p. 305). The connection is a policy of governmentality, requiring specific relations of power-knowledge that inevitably reindividualize all subjects.

Specialties in ethics have proliferated. Some address achieving results designated "moral." Others interrogate how to arrive at moral values through a normative ethics. Some describe moralities already underway, and leave it at that. Others "go meta" or "subterranean." Some say we cannot decide, inviting charges of relativism. Then White (1997) describes the "Teflon subject," a seemingly unaffected soul living subjugation harmoniously and recommending it. This Teflon subject is perhaps Foucault's equivalent to the unbridled sedentary habits among us. Do the habits suggest a self in need of exercise?

The current masthead of the *Journal of Mass Media Ethics* locates its knowledge-regime at an intersection of "academic and professional groups" where considerations are "subdisciplines of communication and ethics." The hope is for "mutually beneficial dialogues," where "academicians and professionals" take their focal cues from "philosophical bases of decisions" already accomplished or underway. Post hoc analyses of mass-mediated content and conduct describe the "behavior of practitioners" who work in "journalism, broadcasting, public relations, advertising, and other mass communication disciplines" (*Journal of Mass Media Ethics*, 2009). To Foucault, the masthead presses upon the existence of agency to technologies of the self in reactive and proactive self-reflection.

References

Annas, J. (1993) *The Morality of Happiness*, Oxford University Press, New York.

Bentham, J. (1995) *The Panopticon Writings*, (ed. M. Bozovic), Verso, London.

Bernauer, J.W., and Mahon, M. (1994) The ethics of Michel Foucault, in (ed. G. Gutting), *The Cambridge Companion to Foucault*, 2nd edn, Cambridge University Press, Cambridge, pp. 141–158.

Boon, A., Flood, J., and Webb, J. (2005) Postmodern professions? The fragmentation of legal education and the legal profession. *Journal of Law and Society*, 32 (3), 473–492.

Bruns, G.L. (2005) Foucault's modernism,, in (ed. G. Gutting), *The Cambridge Companion to Foucault*, 2nd edn, Cambridge University Press, Cambridge, pp. 348–378.

Calhoun, C. (1993) Postmodernism as pseudohistory. *Theory, Culture and Society*, 10 (1), 75–96.

Christians, C.G. (1997) The ethics of being, in *Communication Ethics and Universal Values*, (eds C.G. Christians and M. Traber), Sage, Thousand Oaks, CA, pp. 3–23.

Christians, C.G., Fackler, M., McKee, K.B. *et al.* (2008) *Media Ethics: Cases and Moral Reasoning*, 8th edn, Allyn and Bacon, Boston.

Craig, D.A. (2009) Justice as a journalistic value and goal, in *The Handbook of Mass Media Ethics*, (eds L. Wilkins and C.G. Christians), Routledge, New York, pp. 203–216.

Cresswell, T. (1994) Putting women in their place: The carnival at Greenham Common. *Antipode*, 26 (1), 35–58.

Davidson, A.I. (1994) Ethics as ascetics: Foucault, history of ethics, and ancient thought, in (ed. G. Gutting), *The Cambridge Companion to Foucault*, 2nd edn, Cambridge University Press, Cambridge, pp. 115–140.

Dodson, G. (2010) Australian journalism and war – professional discourse and the legitimation of the 2003 Iraq invasion. *Journalism Studies*, 11 (1), 99–114.

Durkheim, E. (1967) *Sociologie et philosophie*, Presses Universitaires de France, Paris.

Elliott, D. (1988) All is not relative: Essential shared values and the press, *Journal of Mass Media Ethics*, 3 (1), 28–32.

Fackler, M. (2009) Communitarianism in *The Handbook of Mass Media Ethics*, (eds L. Wilkins and C.G. Christians), Routledge, New York, pp. 305–316.

Ferré, J.P. (2009) A short history of media ethics in the United States in *The Handbook of Mass Media Ethics*, (eds L. Wilkins and C.G. Christians), Routledge, New York, pp. 15–27.

Flynn, T.R. (1985) Truth and subjectivation in the later Foucault. *The Journal of Philosophy*, 82 (10), 531–540.

Flyvbjerg, B. (2000) Ideal theory, real rationality: Habermas versus Foucault and Nietzsche. Political Studies Association, London, April 10–13.

Fortner, R.S., and Hoag, R.L. (1980) The professional communicator and the interplay of history and ethics: nuclear power plant development in Grundy County, Illinois. *Journal of Communication Inquiry*, 6 (1), 41–53.

Foucault, M. (1970) *The Order of Things: An Archaeology of the Human Sciences*. Random House, New York.

Foucault, M. (1972) *The Archaeology of Knowledge*, (trans, A.M.S. Smith), Pantheon, New York.

Foucault, M. (1976) *Histoire de la sexualité: l'usage des plaisirs. Bibliothèque des histoires*, Gallimard, Paris.

Foucault, M. (1977a) *Discipline and Punish: The Birth of the Prison*, (trans. A. Sheridan), Pantheon, New York.

Foucault, M. (1977b) *Language, Counter-Memory, Practice: Selected Essays and Interviews*, (trans. D.F. Bouchard and S. Simon, ed. D.F. Bouchard), Cornell University Press, Ithaca.

Foucault, M. (1977c) Panopticism, in *Discipline and Punish: The Birth of the Prison*, (trans. A. Sheridan), Pantheon, New York, pp. 195–228.

Foucault, M. (1980) *Power/knowledge: Selected Interviews and Other Writings, 1972–1977*, (ed. C. Gordon), Pantheon, New York.

Foucault, M. (1984a) *The Foucault Reader*, (ed. P. Rabinow), Pantheon Books, New York.

Foucault, M. (1984b) What is enlightenment? in *The Foucault Reader*, (ed. P. Rabinow), Pantheon Books, New York, pp. 32–50.

Foucault, M. (1988a) An aesthetics of existence, in *Politics, Philosophy, Culture: Interviews and Other Writings, 1977–1984*, (ed. L.D. Kritzman), Routledge, New York, pp. 47–56.

Foucault, M. (1988b) Critical theory/intellectual history, in *Politics, Philosophy, Culture: Interviews and Other Writings, 1977–1984*, (ed. L.D. Kritzman), Routledge New York, pp. 17–46.

Foucault, M. (1988c) *The History of Sexuality. Vol. 1, Introduction*, (trans, R. Hurley), Vintage Books, New York.

Foucault, M. (1988d) *The History of Sexuality. Vol. 2, The Use of Pleasure*, (trans, R. Hurley), Vintage Books, New York.

Foucault, M. (1988e) *Politics, Philosophy, Culture: Interviews and Other Writings, 1977–1984*, (ed. L.D. Kritzman), Routledge New York.

Foucault, M. (1988f) The return of morality, in *Politics, Philosophy, Culture: Interviews and Other Writings, 1977–1984*, (ed. L.D. Kritzman), Routledge, New York, pp. 242–254.

Foucault, M. (1988g) *Technologies of the Self: A Seminar with Michel Foucault*, (ed. L.H. Martin, H. Gutman and P.H. Hutton), University of Massachusetts Press, Amherst.

Foucault, M. (1997) On the genealogy of ethics, in (ed. P. Rabinow), *Ethics: Subjectivity and Truth: Essential Works of Michel Foucault 1954–1984, Vol 1*, The New Press, New York.

Foucault, M. (2001) *Fearless Speech*, (ed. J. Pearson), Semiotext(e), Los Angeles.

Fritschler, A.L., and Smith, B.L.R. (2009) The new climate of timidity on campuses, *The Chronicle of Higher Education*, February 15, p. A80.

Habermas, J. (2004) Public space and political public sphere – the biographical roots of two motifs in my thought, Commemorative Lecture, Kyoto, November 11.

Hardt, H., Brennen, B., and Killmeier, M. (2000) *In the Company of Media: Cultural Constructions of Communication, 1920s–1930s*, Westview Press, Boulder, CO.

Havelock, E. (1963) *Preface to Plato*, Harvard University Press/Belknap Press, Cambridge, MA.

Honneth, A. (1994) Foucault's theory of society: a systems-theoretic dissolution of the *Dialectic of Enlightenment*, in *Critique and Power: Recasting the Foucault/Habermas Debate*, (ed. M. Kelly), MIT Press, Cambridge, MA, pp. 157–183.

Ingram, D. (2005) Foucault and Habermas, in *The Cambridge Companion to Foucault*, 2nd edn, (ed. G. Gutting), Cambridge University Press, Cambridge, pp. 240–283.

Innis, H. A. (2008) *The Bias of Communication*, 2nd edn, University of Toronto Press, Toronto.

Journal of Mass Media Ethics (2009) masthead, 1 (24).

Laidlaw, J. (2002) For an anthropology of ethics and freedom. *The Journal of the Royal Anthropological Institute*, 8 (2), 311–332.

Mackey, H. (2007) "Do not ask me to remain the same": Foucault and the professional identities of occupational therapists, *Australian Occupational Therapy Journal*, 54 (2), 95–102.

McPhail, K. (1999) The threat of ethical accountants: an application of Foucault's concept of ethics to accounting education and some thoughts on ethically educating for the other. *Critical Perspectives on Accounting*, 10 (6), 833–866.

Milchman, A. (2009) Review of *Foucault's Heidegger*, by Timothy Rayner, *Foucault Studies*, (6), 79–82.

Newton, J. H. (2009) Photojournalism ethics: A 21st-century primal dance of behavior, technology, and ideology, in *The Handbook of Mass Media Ethics*, (eds L. Wilkins and C.G. Christians), Routledge, New York, pp. 84–100.

O'Leary, T. (2006) *Foucault and the Art of Ethics. Continuum Studies in Ethics*, Continuum, New York.

Plato (2006) *Laws*, (trans. B. Jowett), Dover Publications, Mineola, NY.

Rayner, T. (2007) *Foucault's Heidegger: Philosophy and Transformative Experience. Continuum studies in Continental Philosophy*, Continuum, London.

Sharpe, M. (2005) "Critique" as technology of the self. *Foucault Studies*, 2, 97–116.

Trapp, M.E. (1978) Consequences of an individualist theme in American views of journalistic responsibility. *Journal of Communication Inquiry*, 3 (2), 13–26.

White, S.K. (1997) Weak ontology and liberal political reflection. *Political Theory*, 25 (4), 502–523.

Zapata, F.R. (2005) Review of *Fearless Speech*, by Michel Foucault. *Foucault Studies*, (2), 150–153.

20

Ethical Anxieties in the Global Public Sphere

Robert S. Fortner

Introduction

In Arne Gron's (2008) study of Søren Kierkegaard's work on anxiety, he makes several telling remarks: "Anxiety is part of being human, but the question is how" (p. 3); "To Kierkegaard anxiety is not just extraordinary. It is fundamental in any human life" (p. 4); "Anxiety points toward the future" (p. 5); and finally (although not exhaustively) "anxiety is an ambiguous power. What is it that both attracts us and frightens us? ... The situation is urgent by being indeterminate. That is to say we can take a stand in different ways vis-à-vis the situation. ... What evokes anxiety is that we not only can but must take a stand towards our situation, a situation that opens before us as indeterminate or settled" (p. 15). Gron's explanation of this concept of anxiety includes two important points. First, that anxiety must be linked to modernity and its concomitant experiences of "emptiness and loss of meaning" (p. 3), and second, that anxiety is akin to dizziness: "you are gazing into a deep hole or an abyss that threatens to swallow you" (p. 6).

In Kierkegaard's original Danish, the word anxiety (angest) was used in the sense of "dread." Another word associated with it was "angst" or even "despair." It is a difficult book. Gordon D. Marino calls it "maddeningly difficult" (1998, p. 308). But what does anxiety have to do with communication or the global public sphere?

The modernity that an increasing proportion of the global population is experiencing is in many ways defined by its ability to connect and interact with others. Most of the "others" reached using new technologies such as voice and texting on mobile telephones, via email and or social network sites on the Internet are known others, but not necessarily. Twitter provides a means for strangers to follow the other, people may request that anyone "friend" them on Facebook or similar sites,

---

The Handbook of Global Communication and Media Ethics, First Edition. Edited by Robert S. Fortner and P. Mark Fackler.
© 2011 Blackwell Publishing Ltd. Published 2011 by Blackwell Publishing Ltd.

Ethical Anxieties in the Global Public Sphere

YouTube videos are available for anyone to view, and individuals can forward texts, photos or videos received from one other to many others. So connections may occur between complete strangers, either near-by or on different continents. People can also appropriate others' intellectual work for their own purposes: they can "Photoshop," remix audio or recut video to share on public sites. The phenomena of file sharing or pirating films and music (or CDs and DVDs) to sell on the street are well-known problems in the digital age. People "trash" one another, or comment to, or argue with, one another, on blogs or "walls." They compete against one another via game consoles or cooperate with one another in different roles (avatars) on "World of Warcraft" or in other virtual realities such as "Second Life." They "meet" on dating sites (chemistry.com) or create profiles on "compatibility" via e-Harmony.com. Interactions can be both planned and spontaneous, with both known and unknown others, synchronous or asynchronous in nature. Although none of this was part of the modernity of Kierkegaard's day, this modernity is certainly rapidly spreading from one part of the globe to another.

According to Gron's explanation, anxiety is linked to this modernity as to any modernity. The future is unknown – will anyone respond to my overtures – friend me, follow me, like my postings or mixes, appreciate my videos? The interactive capability of this modernity encourages people to "put themselves out there," take (at least) virtual risks, take on new identities, represent themselves (presumably accurately) in new ways. There are, however, no guarantees, no requirements. A pedophile may represent himself as a trusted friend, or even a prospective mate. People can even "fall in love" with someone they have never actually met face-to-face – and may be surprised by when they do. Is it any wonder that anxiety would result from all this representation and virtuality?

Of course "emptiness and loss of meaning" are always a danger. Relationships can end with a much larger mess in the virtual world than in the physical one (and perhaps with more callowness). People make and remake meaning from the streams of digital consciousness they encounter. The six degrees of separation famously linking the people of the planet may reasonably be said to apply to the layers of hyperreality that can quickly emerge from a single posting on mobile or hardwired networks and which compound the original polysemy of the initial post (see Fortner, 2007).

Also, as Gron (2008) explains, this anxiety is similar to that experienced by anyone looking into the proverbial "bottomless pit," the abyss, where one wrong step may take you deep into the frightening unknown. People can experience the potential abyss every day – every time they drive a car or get on an airplane, every time they turn on the television to watch the news or a press conference, every time they log on to the Internet to surf or check their email. Life is full of uncertainty. This is Kierkegaard's point – modernity brings with it the dangerous abyss of uncertainty. As the public spheres of communities, or nations, have merged into the developing global public sphere through engagement with international organizations, financial institutions, NGOs and the various technologies and sites of connection, anxiety can do little but become more pronounced.

There appears to be a consensus that a global public sphere exists, as well as a global civil society. However, scholars do not agree as to the implications of the existence of these phenomena (Stevenson, 2005, pp. 67–68). The difficulty of assessment is the result of a variety of factors. These include: (1) the overtly political context within which Jürgen Habermas' concept of the public sphere first developed, (2) the locus of political legitimacy and loyalty at the level of the nation state, (3) the concomitant notion of civil society which cannot always be cleanly hived off from that of the public sphere, thus confusing the two concepts, and (4) the reluctance of Western scholars, building on the Habermasian idea – itself was constructed atop Enlightenment democratic ideals of individualism and rationality – to impose these analytic concepts on non-Western societies that may approach the problem of civic engagement, citizenship, politics, and society from entirely different directions.

For the purpose of this essay I intend to take the following positions on these four points: (1) the global public sphere is not concerned merely with politics, but with a variety of other issues including humanitarian and relief efforts in areas of the world suffering from violence or natural disasters, economic and community development, education, and technological and media development; (2) neither political legitimacy nor loyalties are a major concern, and although the nationstate is relevant in some cases, in others more relevant are localized or regional collectives within national boundaries, or ethnic groups, tribes, or other groups that cross national boundaries; (3) the global public sphere and global civil society may develop in sync or out of sync – they are not synonymous or identical but often support each other; and (4) although individualism and rationality may be present or developing in some cases, in others the connections of history, culture, tradition, language, religion, or ethnicity may be far more important in the creation and maintenance of a public sphere. Societies are organized differently and all do not follow the Western model, nor is it required that they do so, for a public sphere to exist.

Some of these positions may be controversial within public sphere scholarship, but I wish to avoid the problems of definition or characteristics here in order to concentrate on the anxieties posed by existing or developing public spheres regardless of their specifics. By broadening the scope of this phenomenon, I hope to show that there is much to learn about the dynamics of anxiety within in the global public sphere, and the role that ethics plays both in exacerbating and in alleviating such anxiety.

Ethical Anxiety and the Global Public Sphere

If modernity creates angst, despair, and anxiety akin to the dizziness created by looking into the unknown abyss of the future, then ethics is potentially a point of reference to stop the light-headedness, a handhold that can stabilize one's world. Since globalization is not a homogenous phenomenon, however, but one whose characteristics vary from context to context, the question of what ethics is one source of potential anxiety. Like it or not, the globalization of business and

Ethical Anxieties in the Global Public Sphere 379

commerce (along with the norms of such transactions), of trade and manufacturing, of currency exchanges and stock market connections, of the work of NGOs and the spread of various competing religious traditions, of tourism and air transportation, of media expansion and the distribution of popular culture on a worldwide basis, all of these throw ethical systems committed to varying foundational precepts into close proximity, and potential conflict, with one another.

Such a confusion of intertwined ethical systems and the social space that contains them could result in paralysis altogether. Or it might result in the struggle to hang on to "oases of meaning and relevance amidst a featureless desert," as Zygmunt Bauman (1993) has called it, the effort to maintain one's own mobility – based on his or her own inculcated values – and to limit the mobility of others (p. 158). This is due to the fact that, as Bauman argues, globalization's perspective is one in which "the vision of a global spread of information, technology and economic interdependency. ... conspicuously does not include the ecumenization of political, cultural and moral authorities" (p. 43).

This is one of the causes of anxiety – the conflicting demands of moral systems in a global environment that have not been ecumenized. The United Nations has made some efforts to accomplish this ecumenization, but its efforts are based in law rather than ethics. The Universal Declaration of Human Rights, the UN Global Compact's Ten Principles on human rights, labor, the environment and anticorruption, and the UN Principles on Responsible Investment all address different aspects of corporate behavior across national boundaries, but such documents are dependent on governments and individual transnational companies' endorsements, contain no enforceable consequences for entities that violate them, and have a merely quasi-legal basis rather than an ethical one, even when addressing issues that are both legal and ethical in nature. So, while they are laudable efforts to articulate expectations for corporate social responsibility, they lack the gravitas and the universalism needed for ecumenization.

Of course such conventions, principles, or commitments also address only a fraction of the issues that might pull people back from contemplating the abyss. The ones they do address (other than human rights) are largely concerned with the materialist issues of economics. So, while useful, they are insufficient when considered from an ethical perspective. Even those that deal with human rights can be at variance with cultural traditions. The notion of individual human rights is a Western Enlightenment ideal, not one that resonates in cultures where identities are more corporately construed. What may matter far more than an individual's rights in some contexts are family, tribal, or community rights. So, while all members of such groups are included individually within the guarantees, there is relatively little said in such documents about the rights of various aggregations of individuals. The Universal Declaration of Human Rights does mention the family (Article 25) and the community (Articles 27 and 29), but the word most used in the Declaration is "one" or "everyone," indicating its individual rights focus.

Another source of ethical anxiety in the global public sphere is what has been called the "digital divide." CNet Networks International Media claims (but with no date) that 600 of every 1000 people in the developed world have access to a computer, compared to fewer than one in every 1000 in the developing world (www.bridgethedigitaldivide.com). Pippa Norris (2001) calls this the "global divide" – "the divergence of Internet access between industrialized and developing countries" (p. 4). She explains that "UNESCO emphasizes that most of the world's population lack basic access to a telephone, let alone a computer, producing societies increasingly marginalized at the periphery of communication networks. ... Initiatives have been launched to address this problem but disparities in the distribution of information and communication technologies are deep seated, suggesting that they will not easily be eradicated or ameliorated" (2001, p. 6).

Of course this was 2001. Research undertaken in the years since then have confirmed the deep seated nature of this divide. The International Center for Media Studies, which has conducted surveys in both East and West Africa, and in parts of Asia, reports the continuing low access to computers, and in the poorer and less-infrastructure-developed parts of Asia, even mobile telephones. In one study undertaken in Uganda, southern Sudan, the eastern Congo, and in the refugee camps of northern Kenya, no Acholis (an ethnic group living in internally-displaced persons camps) had ever used a computer, just above 5% of Bari speakers (southern Sudan) had done so, and even among the Luganda speakers (the largest language group in Uganda) less than 14% had ever used a computer. The two language groups with the greatest access to computers were the Dinka and Nuer Sudanese in internationally-funded refugee camps (Fortner, 2008a). In 2009 8.8% of Ivorians had a computer in their home (Fortner, 2009a). Similar results were found in Togo and Niger (Fortner, 2008b, 2009b). Among the Bugese people on the island of Sulawesi in Indonesia only 2.1% of those interviewed, or any member of their family, owned a computer (Fortner, 2008c). Less than 1.5% of the Makassarese who lived on Sulawesi and Selayar islands in Indonesia owned a computer (Fortner, 2008c). Qualitative research undertaken in Banda Aceh and West Timor in Indonesia, northern Luzon island (Philippines), and eastern Nepal by ICMS suggest that only in Banda Aceh, where extensive redevelopment work has been undertaken by the international NGO community after the 2004 tsunami, has significant Internet access. Lack of computers – and thus the Internet – in all of these places is the result, not only of lack of landline telephone lines that could be used to provide at least rudimentary dial-up access, but also the lack of available electricity to run computers. This also means low access to televisions or even radios in areas where batteries are scarce and expensive and incomes are low to nearly nonexistent (see also Chinn and Fairlie, 2004).

The ethical anxiety introduced by the global divide is of several types. First is the anxiety among those in highly developed countries that are committed to egalitarian access. The evidence of their anxiety is reflected in the academic literature that emerges from them, the various reports of the existence of this divide and its ramifications from international organizations such as UNESCO, the International Telecommunication Union and the World Bank (Millennium Development Goals). The second anxiety occurs among those nations that fear what increased access to information and communications capacity might mean for their own stability or

Ethical Anxieties in the Global Public Sphere

legitimacy and that, therefore, take various steps to restrict access, such as banning satellite dishes, controlling bandwidth or routing Internet traffic through controlled servers, blocking websites, shutting down mobile telephone towers in time of crisis, limiting infrastructure development to prevent high speed access to the Internet, or making access too expensive for most people to use. These two anxieties are often at odds in international discussions as egalitarians emphasize the need for freedom of speech and press and their human rights dimensions, and controllers respond with the need to protect cultures, language, or "innocents," to stop insurrections, or object to interventions into internal affairs.

A third, but related, ethical anxiety occurs within individual countries as individuals with access attempt to use existing systems to press their own agendas that are in opposition to those of the ruling authorities. A cat and mouse game of circumvention and response not only creates anxieties in those attempting to bypass controls, and those in control who attempt to maintain it, but also among those on the outside with whom circumventers attempt to communicate. The most recent example of this occurred during the postelection protests in Iran as Iranians attempted to bypass government controls to provide news of the street protests and the crackdown of authorities to outside news organizations via social networking sites. Many Chinese bloggers and dissidents have also experienced the negative response of the government to their activities, with some ending up in prison, or refused reentry into China once they have visited the West. In many respects these activities are merely a continuation of the efforts to avoid the jamming of radio signals from the West during the Cold War by those behind the "Iron Curtain," but in the more recent cases, it is not merely the reception of outside information that is at issue, but also the provision of information to the outside. All of this makes technologically-based information sharing systems a battleground between groups that define sovereignty, legitimate protest, political exigency, legitimate restrictions, or human rights in diverse ways.

Last is the ethical anxiety that develops in recognition of the sometimes severe disparities of access to information or knowledge that comes as a function of distance, poverty, language facility (including literacy), topography, and lack of transportation, electricity or telecommunications infrastructure. This digital-divide-induced anxiety leads to isolation and places people on the fringe of economic, political, social, health, education, and cultural development (for instance, see Foulger, 2002). Whatever inequalities might have been ameliorated by expansion of access to technologies of connection (from mobile telephones to satellite TV to the various varieties of Internet access) are frustrated by structural deficiencies in these basic elements of existence. The result: "improved global communication [has] led to an increased awareness among the poor of income inequalities and heightened the pressure to emigrate to richer countries. In response, the industrialized nations have erected higher barriers against immigration, making the world economy seem more like a gated community than a global village" (Scott, 2001, p. 1).

Still another type of anxiety is created by the intersection of two facts. First is the fact, long understood by development economists, that economic growth could be improved and cyclical poverty reduced by empowering women, especially through education (Coleman, 2010, p. 1). Second is the fact that in many societies women continue to be underappreciated, dominated by men, ill-educated, in some cases sold in sexual slavery, raped or otherwise exploited by tradition, religiously-based gender inequalities, or simple devaluing (Coleman, 2010; see also Darwish, 2008, Kristof and WuDunn, 2009, and Mam, 2008). This plays itself out in the realm of information and communication when men control access to technology. In most developing societies, better-educated men decide what will be heard on the radio in their household; they control the "remote" to access football matches, they are more likely to use mobile telephones and computers. Women are relegated to receiving knowledge that their husbands, fathers, brothers, or even male children are willing to share with them. All of this frustrates the ability of women to provide the economic boost to their family's welfare that might otherwise be possible.

This anxiety resulting from the clash of these two facts raises ethical concerns because it pits the welfare of families against the traditions of family in many parts of the world. To improve health, sanitation, nutrition, and the other manifestations of poverty and unequal treatment requires changes in behavior that are sanctioned by history, culture, and religion. The dozens of families interviewed by ICMS during October and November 2009 raised my own consciousness about how difficult, or even devastating, such changes might be. Most of those interviewed, regardless of caste, adhered to the inequalities of the caste system, as well as that of the male-dominated family structure, with little reflection. Educational opportunities were few and even those who were the best educated had apparently not had their strongest cultural, social, or religious beliefs challenged by the school or university. Children were routinely pulled from school when they were needed in the fields. Women continued to give birth in their homes with little assistance because the distance to the hospital was too far. People denied that respiratory problems were a major issue even while coughing and wheezing when answering questions – the result of indoor, unventilated wood fire cooking. Men dominated every household and women bore large numbers of children to help harvest crops that would only feed the family for half of each year, never considering the better nutrition that would result from having smaller families. They were cut off not only from the world outside Nepal (except for when a relative managed to work abroad in Malaysia or the Gulf, or joined the British or Indian armies) but from their own government as well. For most of them, Kathmandu was a three-day bus ride away and there was little visible evidence of central authority, police protection, or government services in the region. Where would change begin in such circumstances? Who would champion it? Who would assure that change, once begun, would continue? Who would negotiate the relationship between history and tradition, on the one side, and economic sufficiency and knowledge on the other? There was simply no organization or individual in the region with the ability to do it.

Another source of anxiety in the globalized public sphere is caused by the struggle over control of the system itself. The development of connectivity worldwide that is required for the existence of the global sphere itself necessitates massive

Ethical Anxieties in the Global Public Sphere

capital investment. Satellites must be put into orbit and controlled from the ground to assure they do not stray from their orbits. Undersea fiber optic cables must be laid on ocean floors and maintained. Cell towers and Wi-Fi connections have to be installed, maintained, and interconnected. Satellite dishes (LNAs), telephones, receivers, computers, modems, and all the other technical paraphernalia needed to be a part of this global technical system must be made available in every country at prices that locals can afford. Systems of subscription, including payment systems, have to be put into place, often in places where banks do not exist, postal service is irregular, and climatic conditions are not always kind. Somehow the relationship between corporate or government investment in the system, and participant investment in it, must be rationalized. Subsidies must come from somewhere. The production costs of content must be borne by someone. Expansion of services – increasing bandwidth – must be anticipated.

Yet there is an ethical conundrum created by this reality. The whole point of creating a global public sphere is for dialog to happen – for people to participate in the ongoing discussion of events, activities, people, ideologies, and so on, that inform the decisions that affect their everyday lives. This is where the global public sphere and the notion of a civil society intersect.

The notion of a civil society requires that ethical dimensions function within the operation of the public sphere. Civility itself requires a "willingness to be considerate of other people as we pursue our own individual ends" (O'Brien, 1999, p. 2) Such consideration implies that others will be taken seriously, regardless of the distinctions made within any society (caste, tribe, class, race, education, age, gender, and so on). Everyone's opinion, prima facie, is equal. Distinctions may result from the quality of argument, the use of evidence, the appearance of bias, and so forth, but at least at the outset of discourse, the divisions that may cleave society or culture generally are not to be determinative. Tutsis and Hutus must be heard. Brahmins and Dalit, men and women, young and old, PhD professors and illiterate peasants – all must have the opportunity to participate without a priori discounts made on the basis of basic human, or socially constructed distinctions.

This is, of course, part of the justification for the "right to communicate." It is also the source of much ethical anxiety in the global public sphere. Humans have a propensity to dismiss others whose characteristics do not mirror their own. We see the manifestations of this is racism, ageism, discrimination against the disabled, condescension to the poor, ill-educated or younger people, male domination, dismissal of rural dwellers as "rubes." People want to believe there is a meritocracy operating in society (including global society) and that they are at or near the top of it. However true civility is based on the equality of humans and "to be fully human we must be able to imagine others' hurt and to relate it to the hurt we would experience if we were in their place. Consideration is imagination on a moral track" (Forni, 2002, p. 7). It is application of the "Golden Rule." Michael Edwards (2009), showing the moral foundation of the public sphere that makes the development of civil society possible, explains that "what takes place in the public sphere is, or is assumed to be, marked out by the normative values of the good society – for example, tolerance for dissent, a willingness to argue without quitting the debate when other, more persuasive, voices take the stage, and a commitment to 'truth telling'" (pp. 67–68). Stephen L. Carter (1998) agrees, writing that "civility ... is the sum of the many sacrifices we are called to make for the sake of living together. ... Yielding to [the] very human instinct for self-seeking ... is often immoral, and certainly should not be done without forethought. We should make sacrifices for others not simply because doing so makes social life easier (although it does), but as a signal of respect for our fellow citizens, marking them as full equals, both before the law and before God. Rules of civility are thus also rules of morality; it is morally proper to treat our fellow citizens with respect, and morally improper not to. ... And because morality is what distinguishes humans from other animals, the crisis is ultimately one of humanity " (p. 11–12). Carter's implied definition of civility – and thus of the requirements for civil society – is what Daniel Bell (1976) called "civitas," that spontaneous willingness to obey the law, to respect the rights of others, to forego the temptations of private enrichment at the expense of the public weal" (p. 245).

The control of the means of connection among those who would participate in the global civil society within the global public sphere by large corporate entities was identified by Habermas (1989) in his initial proposal of the existence of the public sphere itself as a serious problem (see also Boyd-Barrett, 2006, and Kellner, n.d.). In the original conception, too, there was emphasis on both the rationality of the discourse within the public sphere and on the fact that this sphere was outside the realm of monopolized political discourse controlled by the state. The take-up of Habermas' original notion by a variety of other scholars has expanded the vocabulary of the public sphere to encompass nonrational representations such as visual arts, poetry, and popular media (soap operas, TV sitcoms and the like) and to reengage politics in discussions of "global governance" that are informed by discourse within the public sphere and its constituent civil society (see Picciotto, 2001).

Ingrid Volkmer (n.d.) argues that the new global public sphere no longer requires citizens – as Habermas argued – but anyone who participates in "a multi-discursive political space, a sphere of mediation (not imperialism)" that includes both "subnational 'network' modes. ... and 'authentic' worldwide available newsgroups and individual homepage viewpoints" (Volkmer, 2003, p. 4; see also Couldry and Dreher, 2007). She calls these various components "dialectical spaces," and suggests that they "increasingly impact public participation, notions of political identity and 'citizenship,' and the agendas and formats of political journalism within the global public sphere" (Volkmer, 2003, p. 4). Based on focus group research conducted in four countries (Austria, Germany, India and Mexico) she concludes that various media – examined for their impact within age cohort groups – were understood within the complex life-worlds that differed from one age cohort group to another (Volkmer, 2003). The meaning provided by news media to these groups was closely tied to its specific symbolic life-world universe (p. 17).

The various anxieties occasioned by the intrusions of corporately-controlled media into what had been indigenous life-worlds is not a new phenomenon, to be sure. International radio and television broadcasts have been endeavoring to do this for decades. What is new is the ability of some people within such indigenous life-worlds to participate more actively in the discourse occasioned by news that is delivered to them within an international (or globalized) system. Although many people are still left out of this discourse (for reasons already mentioned), the single most prevalent reason mentioned by people who do use the noninteractive media of radio or television in the developing world for participation is to hear the news. In ICMS interviews their reasons for doing so are largely unarticulated beyond keeping up with events. However, these events have, by and large, little impact on their day to day situation because most of them are far removed from the events discussed and their ability to respond to them outside merely attending is largely absent. Perhaps they use the connection for orientation to the world and, in that respect, they may be on the fringe of the global sphere as delivered by the media. More likely to provoke some action on their part are reports from knowledgeable and trusted members of their own communities who travel outside the immediate environs and report back what they have experienced. This is what they are anxious – at least in some cases – to see for themselves.

There are differences of opinion on the level of engagement provided by the global public sphere (see, for instance, Braman, 1996, Selverston-Scher, 2000, and Youngs and Allison, 2008). Nkosi Ndela argues that despite the lack of Internet connections in Africa outside major cities, it "is increasingly becoming a major mass medium" in these cities. Thus, he says, "even though African voices and viewpoints are limited in the international public sphere, the internet makes Africa's participation in the global public sphere possible. For example, civil society websites facilitate transnational African debates on diverse issues such as gender, religion, politics, development and human rights. The internet [sic] also enables diaspora communities to constitute diasporic public spheres" (2007, p. 328). But what is the result? A World Bank study reported in 1999, based on consultations with the poor in 23 countries, that people thought "they were worse off now, have fewer economic opportunities, and live with greater insecurity than in the past" (Narayan *et al.*, 1999, p. 2) The sense of being worse off was a function of feelings of powerlessness, bad social relations, insecurity, lack of material benefits and physical weakness (p. 5). Although some of this might have been ameliorated 10 years later, ICMS's experience in interviewing the poor confirms that, at least for the countries it has covered, this conclusion would still apply. Similarly, Shelton A. Gunaratne (2009, p. 60) claims that even those who we might expect to have input into the global public sphere from non-Western regions have been marginalized because their perspectives do not fit within the framework of Western cosmologies.

Ethical Responses to the Anxieties within the Global Public Sphere

Several ethical responses to the dynamics introduced by the global public sphere have already been suggested. In order for civil society (whether national or transnational) to function properly, everyone within the sphere must be seen as equals. There can be no discrimination, or devaluing, of people because of some identifiable (or imagined) characteristic. The affirmation of human dignity is thus an ethical necessity.

Also, there must be an ethical equivalence for moral systems and differing "street level cosmology" (Douglas, 2001, p. 152). This begins by adhering to universals across traditions (with the affirmation of human dignity being one of these), and by committing to basic requirements for truth-telling in communication. Deception would make civil society impossible for when it is discovered, it will raise defenses, and perhaps cause retribution, among those duped by prevarication. Beyond this is the fact that different peoples define the world cosmologically using different categories. As Mary Douglas (2001) explains, the down to earth (or "street level") cosmologies "can be coherent only if the population is stable enough to have a shared history. [They] also need a high degree of interdependence in the people's lives. They must have enough involvement with each other to be anxious not to hurt the feelings of their fellows, to wish not to annoy by seeming indifference to grief or frivolity about serious matters. Most significantly, the members of such ... communities recognize clearly their dependence on each other. Their patent need for solidarity makes it possible for them to overlook the weakness of the great cosmic analogies which anchor their certainties. A community that is tight enough, and closed enough, can regard outsiders as a threat, ridicule and exploit them. Xenophobia is one of the knowledge-protecting devices" (p. 152). The use of taboos would be another. The global public sphere can never be more than a loose community. It shares none of the solidarity that Douglas describes here, and is ever unlikely to develop it given the clear distinctions of wealth, education, gender, age, geography, and so on, that will define the human condition regardless of technological change or commitments to moral equivalence. Nevertheless, if such cosmologies (and their accompanying moral distinctions) are not accepted within the global sphere – or find themselves disadvantaged by others with more general acceptance – the expectations of full inclusion will be a chimera. It will never occur. So, although committing to moral equivalence does not solve the problem entirely, as definitions of truth may vary, it is nonetheless a necessary starting point for engaging in civil discourse.

Also required is a commitment to extend the infrastructure and connectivity required for full participation in the global public sphere into the remotest parts of the planet, develop systems for translation, extend literacy education and other educational opportunities, and provide the technologies needed to participate (along with the requisite power). Clearly, this commitment would be a long-term one, but if it is not part of the ethical response the failure to extend would essentially eliminate the possibility of claiming the equality of all persons. The inequalities in access and ability to participate are so egregious that failing to address them systematically and with adequate resources would make a mockery of any commitment to a truly global public sphere – ethically speaking.

Even more difficult is the requirement that the global public sphere not be developed primarily as a profit-based corporately-controlled system. Some corporate

Ethical Anxieties in the Global Public Sphere

involvement will be required if the system is to develop on a reasonable time schedule, but it will be necessary – to avoid having such interests define the public sphere on their own terms – to have clear requirements for universal service and for subsidies to be provided so that the poor can truly participate. Otherwise we will continue to celebrate the existence of a "global" public sphere that is merely "urban, middle-class," "metropolitan," rather than truly inclusive of all. Imagining a global village is one thing – actually creating and maintaining it is something else altogether. Nalaka Gunawardene (2007), a Sri Lankan citizen journalist, looking at the situation in Asia, says that the policies of governments there have "edged out" the public. "Most of those who occupy the public spectrum don't support the public interest. ... The duopoly long enjoyed by governments and the military was slightly eased to let in big money corporations – while keeping out practically everybody else." Other than Nepal and, more recently, India, "all other South Asian countries licensed commercial FM channels but stubbornly excluded communities and civil society from broadcasting." This is also true in many parts of Africa.

Next would be the requirement of interoperability of discrete systems. What this means is that individuals must have the ability to interconnect via various technologies that have developed independently. Some of this is already occurring as smartphones develop the ability to browse the Internet via Wi-Fi, WIMAX, and 3G/4G systems, but most of the current roll-out of such advanced connection capability is occurring in already highly-advanced countries. People need to be able to connect to audio and video streams, even from local stations, via their mobile telephones, to browse the Internet, use email, connect and contribute to blogs, post photos (and perhaps videos), talk via VOIP, and so on, with as much transparency between different systems as possible. Most domestic broadcasting stations around the world are currently analog, so this creates some problems for interconnection with digital systems, but chips can be installed even in simple mobile telephones to allow for radio listening at least (as many such phones are already capable of doing in Africa). More sophisticated phones will have to be more widely distributed to allow television on such devices. The significance of such developments would be to reduce the need for the poor to invest in more than one electronic technology to participate in the global public sphere. Currently they must choose, usually not more than a single technology (radio, mobile telephone, or television), each of which provides connection to a particular type of information and/or capacity for interaction. Forcing such choices effectively excludes those in remote areas, the poor, and the uneducated from participation.

All of these improvements in the global public sphere would be required to reduce the anxieties occasioned by the current unfavorable situation, at least for those on the fringe of the global public sphere. "One of the great ethical challenges of this extraordinary age of scientific discovery is to ensure that we deploy our new knowledge so that it will strengthen our communities and yield the greatest benefits to our entire society. New knowledge by itself has little moral or ethical content. It is, by itself, neither a good nor a bad thing. New knowledge achieves its moral and/or cultural relevance only when we decide how we will use it" (Shapiro,

2000, p. 3). Since all new discoveries or inventions are based on the development of knowledge and its application, they all raise such ethical issues. "The question constantly before us is: Will our new knowledge be focused on uses that give greater meaning to our lives and the lives of others or will it be used for trivial or even frightening and, therefore, immoral purposes?" (Shapiro, 2000, p. 3).

The notion of the "other" has a long and not particularly stellar history. As one Brooklyn College (CUNY) website puts it, "The Other is an individual who is perceived by the group as not belonging, as being different in some fundamental way. Any stranger becomes the Other. ... The Other is almost always seen as a lesser or inferior being and is treated accordingly" ("The Other", n.d.) The impact of such definitions can clearly be seen in the genocides and ethnic cleansings of the 1990s (see Fortner, 2006, 2008d, 2010). In order that the global public sphere, and global civil society, are allowed to continue development and to thrive under the regime outlined above, and thus be fully inclusive of all "others," it is necessary that we define one another in more basic, human, and positive terms. As Kelle Lynch-Baldwin (n.d.) put it, "We can learn about the stranger, but they remain 'other' to us; our shared feelings and experiences do not dissolve the distinctions that maintain our individuality. Through the realization of a global community, we encounter more and more diverse peoples in our day-to-day activities. In these interactions with those of different religions, ethnicities, races, economic classes, etc., we must resist the urge to strip away the humanity of the person in pursuit of a common denominator." Although this may sound antithetical to the argument of seeking basic, human and positive inclusion, what are actually talking about are the "misused rallying calls" that take on "fetish-like status," rather than a stance of "solidarity, a posture that does not usurp the individuality of the persons involved" and that can serve as the foundation for true social justice (Lynch-Baldwin, n.d.)

It is, in the end, the requirements of social justice that must define ethics within the global public sphere. Under the UN Charter, social justice is justice among people, and if a global public sphere is to operate as it should, this should be the focus rather than the nationstate (see Department of Economic and Social Affairs, 2006, Chapter 1). Justice itself, "in its most general sense, ... implies order and morality. That is, justice means predictability in the daily life of a community and its individual members and the observance of basic rules governing right and wrong behavior" (Montville, 2001, p. 129). Such commitments to justice (and social justice) must be such that they transcend the public sphere envisioned and defended in the West. This sphere is one based merely on rationality, but the global public sphere must also encompass cosmology and its accompanying moral claims, traditions, histories, differing argumentative styles and presentation, even the differences in intellectual abilities and educational opportunity. Otherwise, it would simply replicate the post-Enlightenment imperialism of Western philosophy, and not truly open the public sphere to equality among "others" (see MacIntyre, 1988, p. 6).

This will take vigilance. For people are prone to prostrate themselves before the idols of ideology, bureaucracy, patriotism, tribalism, and a host of other abstractions that obscure the common humanity of all. As Václav Havel (1991) puts it, "all of us, East and West, face one fundamental task from which all else should follow. The task is one of resisting vigilantly, thoughtfully, and attentively, but at the same time with total dedication, at every step and everywhere, the irrational momentum of ideologies, systems, apparat, bureaucracy, artificial languages, and political slogans. We must resist its complex and wholly alienating pressure, whether it takes the form of consumption, advertising, repression, technology, or cliché – all of which are the blood brothers of fanaticism and the well-spring of totalitarian thought" (p. 267).

Michael Ignatieff (1984), who puts similar thoughts into a more existential context (perhaps the difference between living under a totalitarian state and not doing so), says that "there is no such thing as love of the human race, only the love of this person for that, in this time and not in any other. These abstract subjects created by our century of tyranny and terror cannot be protected by abstract doctrines of universal human needs and universal human rights. ... The problem is not to defend universality, but to give these abstract individuals the chance to become real, historical individuals again, with the social relations and the power to protect themselves" (pp. 52–53). Although Ignatieff sees that "beneath the duties that tie us to individuals, there ought to be a duty that ties us to all men and women whatever their relation to us" (p. 52), he takes the position that everything is historically and socially grounded. There is no genuine, altruistic care.

This is precisely what ethics applied within the public sphere must do if a true global civil society is to be the result. People must be protected from the linguistic, intellectual, ideological, nationalistic, chauvinistic, judgmental bullies that are the part of every community, physical or virtual. Any expression – provided it does not foster such bullies (as, for instance, hate speech, pornography, or allowing self-promoting (or self-righteous) demagogues does). Allowing this type of speech is to quash civility, and with it, the possibilities for a robust civil society to grow up within the global public sphere. In this respect we should adopt the idea of the "imagined community," in which each of us has an equal stake, and an equal voice, and which is constructed as a safe haven for addressing humankind's most egregious and primordial issues (see Anderson, 1991, Chapter 2). It is these issues that are the source of humankind's most pressing anxieties. Living in a modern world, as Thomas Mann put it, "cultivates 'a sympathy for the abyss'" (Bell, 1976, p. 51).

Let me end this essay by sharing two quotations, the first from Daniel Bell, and the second by David Nicholson. It will be clear, I think, why their perspectives are the final word.

First, Daniel Bell (1976, p. 12): "The modalities of culture are few, and they derive from the existential situations which confront all human beings, through all times, in the nature of consciousness: how one meets death, the nature of tragedy and the character of heroism, the definition of loyalty and obligation, the redemption of the soul, the meaning of love and sacrifice, the understanding of compassion, the tension between an animal and a human nature, the claims of instinct and restraint."

And last, David Nicholson (1995, n.p.): "The more technology invades our lives, the more it obscures the real issue – the fact that our lives are really about love and work and death, about creating and sustaining and maintaining relationships that sustain us, about finding meaningful vocations, and about living with the knowledge that, alone among all creatures, we know one day we're going to die. Technology may affect the material conditions of our lives, but it hasn't done much yet for our souls."

References

Anderson, B. (1991) *Imagined Communities*, rev. edn, Verso, New York.

Bauman, Z. (1993) *Postmodern Ethics*, Blackwell, Cambridge, MA.

Bell, D. (1976) *The Cultural Contradictions of Capitalism*, Basic Book, New York.

Boyd-Barrett, O. (2006) "Cyberspace, Globalization and Empire." *Global Media and Communication*, 2, 21–41.

Braman, S. (1996) Interpenetrated globalization: Scaling, power, and the public sphere, in *Globalization, Communication, and Transnational Civil Society*, (eds S. Braman and A. Sreberny-Mohammadi), Hampton Press, Cresskill, NJ, pp. 21–37.

Carter, S.L. (1998) *Civility: Manners, Morals and the Etiquette of Democracy*, Basic Books, New York.

Chinn, M.D. and Fairlie, R.W. (2004) The determinants of the global digital divide: A cross-country analysis of computer and internet penetration. Center Discussion Paper No. 881.

Coleman, I. (2010) *Paradise beneath Her Feet: How Women are Transforming the Middle East*, Random House, New York.

Couldry, N. and Dreher, T. (2007) Globalisation and the public sphere: Exploring the space of community media in Sydney. *Global Media and Communication*, 3, 79–100.

Darwish, N. (2008) *Cruel and Usual Punishment: The Terrifying Global Implications of Islamic Law*, Thomas Nelson, Nashville, TN.

Department of Economic and Social Affairs, UN Secretariat (2006) *Social Justice in an Open World: The Role of the United Nations*, United Nations, New York.

Douglas, M. (2001) Dealing with uncertainty. Multatuli Lecture, Leuven, Belgium. *Ethical Perspectives*, 8, 145–155.

Edwards, Michael. (2009) *Civil Society*, 2nd edn, Polity Press, Malden, MA.

Forni, P.M. (2002) *Choosing Civility: The Twenty-Five Rules of Considerate Conduct*, St. Martin's Press, New York.

Fortner, R.S. (2006) Markers of evil: The identification and prevention of genocide and ethnic cleansing. *International Journal of Interdisciplinary Social Sciences*, 1, (2), 149–157.

Fortner, R.S. (2007) *Communication, Media and Identity: A Christian Theory of Communication*, Rowman & Littlefield Publishers, Inc, New York.

Fortner, R.S. (2008a) *Africa: Audience, Message and Media*, International Center for Media Studies, La Mirada, CA.

Fortner, R.S. (2008b) *Niger: A Report on Audience Research*, La Mirada, CA: International Center for Media Studies.

Fortner, R.S. (2008c) *Indonesia: Audience, Message and Media*, International Center for Media Studies, La Mirada, CA.

Fortner, R.S. (2008d) The media in evil circumstance, in *The Handbook of Mass Media Ethics*, (eds L. Wilkins and C.G. Christians), Lawrence Erlbaum, Mahwah, NJ, pp. 340–352.

Fortner, R.S. (2009a) *Ivory Coast: Media and Audience*, International Center for Media Studies, La Mirada, CA.

Fortner, R.S. (2009b) *Togo: A Report on Audience Research*, International Center for Media Studies, La Mirada, CA.

Fortner, R.S. (2010) Genocide as civic engagement: When the public sphere turns evil, in *Ethics and Evil in the Public Sphere*, (eds R.S. Fortner and M. Fackler), Hampton Press, Cresskill, NJ, pp. 185–207.

Foulger, D. (2002) Seven bridges over the digital divide. IAMCR and ICA Symposium on the Digital Divide, November 2001. January 12, http://evolutionarymedia.com/papers/digitalDivide.htm (accessed June 28, 2010).

Gron, A. (2008) *The Concept of Anxiety in Søren Kierkegaard*, (trans. J.B. Knox), Mercer University Press, Birmingham, AL.

Gunaratne, S.A. (2009) Globalization: A non-Western perspective: The bias of social science/communication oligopoly. *Communication, Culture & Critique*, 2, 60–82.

Gunawardene, N. (2007) Protecting the spectrum for media freedom. Panel remarks made during the OUR Media 6, International Conference, Sydney, Australia, April 9–13.

Habermas, J. (1989) *The Structural Transformation of the Public Sphere*, MIT Press, Cambridge, MA.

Havel, V. (1991) *Open Letters: Selected Prose 1965-1990*, (ed. P. Wilson), Faber and Faber, Boston, MA.

Ignatieff, M. (1984) *The Needs of Strangers*, Picador USA, New York.

Kellner, D. (n.d.) Habermas, the public sphere, and democracy: A critical intervention. www.gseis.ucla.edu/faculty/kellner/kellner.html (accessed June 28, 2010).

Kristof, N.D. and WuDunn, Sl. (2009) *Half the Sky: Turning Oppression into Opportunity for Women Worldwide*, Alfred A. Knopf, New York.

Lynch-Baldwin, K. (n.d.) To walk a mile in the shoes of a stranger: An integrative approach to social justice education. Boston College, www.religiouseducation.net/member/06_rea_papers/Lynch-Baldwin_Kelle.pdf (accessed June 28, 2010).

MacIntyre, A. (1988) *Whose Justice? Which Rationality?* University of Notre Dame Press, Notre Dame, IN.

Mam, S. (2008) *The Road of Lost Innocence: The True Story of a Cambodian Heroine*, Spiegel & Grau, New York.

Marino, G.D. (1998) Anxiety in the concept of anxiety, in *The Cambridge Companion to Kierkegaard*, (eds A. Hannay and G.D. Marino), Cambridge University Press, Cambridge, pp. 308–328.

Montville, J.V. (2001) Justice and the burdens of history, in *Reconciliation, Justice, and Coexistence: Theory and Practice*, (ed. Mohammed Abu-Nimer), Lexington Books, New York, pp. 129–143.

Narayan, D., Chambers, R., Shah, M., and Petesch, P. (1999) Global synthesis: Consultations with the poor. Draft for discussion, September 20, Poverty Group, World Bank, Washington, DC.

Ndela, N. (2007) Reflections on the global public sphere: Challenges to internationalizing media studies. *Global Media and Communication*, 3, 324–329.

Nicholson, D. (1995) The pitfalls of a brave new cyberworld. *The Washington Post National Weekly Edition*, October 9–15.

Norris, P. (2001) *Digital Divide: Civic Engagement, Information Poverty, and the Internet Worldwide*, Cambridge University Press, Cambridge.

O'Brien, R. (1999) Civil Society, the Public Sphere and the Internet. www.web.net/~robrien/papers/civsoc.html (accessed June 29, 2010).

Picciotto, S. (2001) Democratizing globalism, in *The Market or the Public Domain: Global Governance and the Asymmetry of Power*, (ed. D. Drache), Routledge, New York, pp. 335–359.

Scott, B.R. (2001) The great divide in the global village. *Foreign Affairs*, 1–8, January/February www.foreignaffairs.com/articles/56664/bruce-r-scott/the-great-divide-in-the-global-village (accessed June 28, 2010).

Selverston-Scher, M. (2000) Building international civil society: Lessons from the Amazon coalition. Draft paper prepared for UCSC Conference.

Shapiro, H.T. (2000) Moral anxiety: The interface between biomedicine, public policy and ethics. Martin Memorial Lecture, American College of Surgeons, October 26, Chicago, IL, www.princeton.edu/~hts/PDFs/Moral_Anxiety.pdf (accessed June 29, 2010).

Stevenson, N. (2005) Media, Cultural Citizenship and the Global Public Sphere, in *The Idea of Global Civil Society: Politics and Ethics in a Globalizing Era*, (eds R.D. Germain and M. Kenny), Routledge Ripe Studies in Global Political Economy, New York, pp. 67–83.

The Other (n.d.) www.academic.brooklyn.cuny.edu/english/melani/cs6/other.html (last accessed July 1, 2010).

Volkmer, I. (n.d.) International communication theory in transition: Parameters of the new global public sphere. *MIT Communications Forum*, Web.mit.edu/comm.-forum/papers/volkmer.html (last accessed January 6, 2010).

Volkmer, I. (2003) Dialectical spaces in the global public sphere: Media Memories across generations. Working Paper Series. The Joan Shorenstein Center on the Press, Politics and Public Policy, Harvard University, Cambridge, MA.

Youngs, G., and Allison, J.E. (2008) Globalisation, communications and political action: Special issue introduction. *International Journal of Media and Cultural Politics*, 4, 3–8.

21

Universalism versus Communitarianism in Media Ethics

Clifford G. Christians

The question is whether we must choose between communitarianism and universalism when establishing a theoretical framework for media ethics. Both are alternatives to the individualistic rationalism that has served as the primary basis for mainstream communication ethics. However, in their offering a new perspective, they appear to be at odds with each other. Communitarianism contends that the community is axiologically (in terms of values) and ontologically (in terms of being) prior to persons; therefore ethical principles reflect community values and arise from dialogue among persons-in-relation.[1] Universal human solidarity, on the other hand, is considered the most far-reaching alternative to both individual autonomy and communalism. Transnational and crosscultural principles are seen as necessary for guiding the global mass media, with individual decision-making and community-based ethics out of sync with today's worldwide technology. Zygmunt Bauman puts the debate this way: "To the defenders of the situated self ('communitarians' as they came to be known), universalistic ambitions and universalizing practices are, of course, an outrage – vehicles of oppression, an act of violence perpetrated upon human freedom" (1993, p. 41).

The answer to the question revolves around the definitions of universalism and communitarianism. In the Enlightenment version of universals, and a functional understanding of community, these two concepts are in opposition. This chapter presents a counter-Enlightenment perspective on universals and a dialogic communalism that enables both ideas to feed off one another rather than contradict each other.

The intellectual strategy for a media ethics that is international, crosscultural, gender inclusive, and ethnically diverse goes like this: Individual autonomy is the problem and its analysis is the first step. Instead of addressing this problem by appealing to the community, the second step is developing universal protonorms. Third, since we live in community and practice our professions within them, the

---

The Handbook of Global Communication and Media Ethics, First Edition. Edited by Robert S. Fortner and P. Mark Fackler.
© 2011 Blackwell Publishing Ltd. Published 2011 by Blackwell Publishing Ltd.

final step is establishing principles for the media that are consistent with universals. Obviously not all communities are morally upright; therefore standards from outside them are needed to establish a common good. Rather than stopping with universalist generalizations, universal principles become a crucial step toward a media ethics that is actionable and pluralistic.

Universal Theories

A foremost challenge is the structure of theory itself. Rigor in and agreement regarding the formation of universal theories will enable us to work fruitfully on the universal–communitarian problem. A universal theory is not just a system of conduct binding on all rational creatures, the content of which is ascertainable by human reason. Theories of ethics that are credible transnationally are ontological instead, constitutive of our humanness. This latter kind of theory can be the centerpiece of a new generation of communication ethics.

Enlightenment universals

Ethical rationalism has been the prevailing paradigm in Western communication ethics. Consistent with mainstream philosophical ethics generally, media ethics has presumed that rationality marks all legitimate claims about moral obligations, so that the truth of those claims can be settled by formal examination of their logical structure. "Since Parmenides, Greek philosophy assumed the identity of being and reason…. In the thought of Aristotle only the active *nous*, precisely the mind which is not involved in the soul, is immortal; and for Plato the immutability of ideas is regarded as proof of the immortality of the *nous*"(Niebuhr, 1964, pp. 6–7). Through confidence in reason, we dare to disobey divine and cultural regulations. Philosophical ethics in this tradition is "based on the common principle" that we ought to "do the good which stands the test of reason" (Landmann, 1974, p. 110).

This is the unilateral model carried forward by René Descartes (1596–1690), the architect of the Enlightenment mind. Descartes insisted on the noncontingency of starting points, with their context considered irrelevant. His *Meditations II* presumed clear and distinct ideas, objective and neutral. His *Discourse on Method* (1637) elaborated this objectivist notion in more detail. Genuine knowledge is built up in linear fashion, with pure mathematics the least touched by circumstances. The equation two plus two equals four is lucid and testable, and all valid knowledge in Descartes' view should be as cognitively clean as arithmetic.

Descartes contended, in effect, that one could demonstrate the truth only of what can be measured. The realm of the spirit was beyond such measurement, a matter of faith and intuition, not truth. The physical became the only legitimate domain of knowledge. Descartes' spiritual world was left to speculation by the divines, many of whom shared the Cartesian bias that theirs was an ephemeral pursuit. A split between facts and values was bequeathed to the Western mind as science gained a stranglehold on truth. In terms of philosophical mapmaking, entire regions of human interest which had engaged the intense efforts of earlier cultures and non-Western peoples, simply ceased to appear.

The eighteenth century carried over Cartesian mathematics in conceiving of human nature as defined by rational choice. Instead of using the primitive tools of theology and the arts, morality could be ordered with sophisticated procedures of induction and logic. Kant (1724–1804) represented this linear rationality, schooled as he was in Descartes, mathematics, and Newtonian physics. In 1755, his first major book, *Universal History of the Nature and Theory of the Heavens*, explained the structure of the universe exclusively in terms of Newtonian cosmology (Kant, 1981). What is called the Kant-Laplace theory of the origin of the universe is based on it.

Then, in the *Critique of Practical Reason* (1788) and *Groundwork of the Metaphysic of Morals* (1785), Kant assimilated ethics into logic. Society was presumed to have a fundamental moral structure embedded in human nature as basic as atoms in physics, with the moral law the analog of the unchanging law of gravity. The rational individual derives universal laws mentally, by identifying those imperatives that one calculates ought to be true for everyone. Through the mental calculus of willing an individual's action to be universalized, imperatives are understood to emerge unconditioned by circumstances – treat others as ends in themselves, do not kill, no harm to the innocent, do not deceive, obey the law, for example. By the formal test of calculating rules without exception one concludes, for example, that everybody ought to keep their promises.

Reason made the human species distinctive and only through rationality were moral canons legitimate. Humans act contrary to moral duties only by enduring the illogic of self-contradiction. In the Cartesian version, reason was considered "the same for all thinking subjects, all nations, all epochs and all cultures" (Cassirer, 1951, p. 6). By making cognitive processes explicit and combining them with the ancient Western emphasis on reason's universality, basic rules were constructed that autonomous moral agents considered obligatory and against which all counter claims about moral obligation could be measured.

> Just as Western science has held that there are universal truths about the world, discoverable through reason and accessible in principle to people of all times and places, so Western philosophers such as Plato, Aristotle, and Kant have held that there are timeless moral truths, arising out of human nature and independent of the conventions of particular societies (Paul, Miller, and Paul, 1994, p. vii).

In a context-free rationality, moral principles are derived from the essential structure of a disembodied reason. This is a correspondence view of truth with an extremely narrow definition of what counts as morality. Instead of prizing care and reciprocity, for example, our moral understanding becomes prescriptivist, arid, and absolutist. This scientific version of universals is what communitarians object to. They are linear abstractions laid out like the arcs of longitude and latitude over the globe. Instead of transcendent metaphysical universals, we need norms that are historically

396   *Clifford G. Christians*

embedded across space rather than absolutist over time. For communication ethics to be meaningful over the long term, a new kind of universal is necessary.

Alternative theories of universals

I introduce here the latest scholarship on this new kind of universal in ethical theory. These are credible attempts to shift the field unequivocally from individual autonomy to universal humanity. These universals are compatible with communitarianism. In recovering the idea of moral universals, they recognize this must be done without presuming first foundations, without the luxury of an objective reality from which to begin.

1   Seyla Benhabib (1992, cf, 2002) has developed the principle of interactive universalism, not subject to Lyotard's (1988) objection that grand narratives are no longer possible. She defends universalist ideals in moral and political life by addressing the contemporary assault on universals. In the process, she gives serious attention to the respective contributions of feminism, communitarianism, and postmodernism. She argues that a universalist communication ethics must respond adequately to these perspectives (1992, pp. 1–21, chapters 1, 2, 6, 7). For example, the concept of participation in communitarianism (that community emerges from common action) must be carried into a universal theory for it to be legitimate. In her reformulation of discourse ethics, she depicts humans as dialogic selves whose moral agency follows norms implicit in Habermas' ideal speech situation: universal moral respect and egalitarian reciprocity (Bracci, 2002, 128–130). Her idea of interactive dialogic rationality keeps ethics close to people's everyday experience, so that diversity in cultures is recognized and differences do not disappear into an abstract metaphysics.

2   Kwasi Wiredu (1996) writes from an African philosophical perspective: the human species lives by language.[2] It is through the intrinsic self-reflexivity of natural language that we arbitrate our values and establish our differences and similarities. The shared lingual character of our existence makes intercultural communication possible. Through the commonness of our biological-cultural identity as *homines sapientes*, we can believe that there are universals, notwithstanding that concomitantly we live in our local communities. In his words, "human beings cannot live by particulars or universals alone, but by some combination of both." Their incompatibility in philosophy and anthropology is illusory. "Without universals intercultural communication must be impossible," while our natural formations are in the vernacular (Wiredu, 1996, pp. 1, 9). Wiredu's argument can be summarized this way: All 6500 known languages are equally complex in phonetic and phonemic structure. All humans learn languages at the same age. All languages enable their speakers to deduce and generalize, to make inferences and identify abstractions. Languages are the *sine qua non* of cultural formation. All languages can be learned and translated by native speakers of other languages; in fact, every language includes speakers who are bilingual.

Universalism versus Communitarianism 397

In Wiredu's terms, as cultural beings we are sympathetically impartial to other cultures. "Human beings do have a basic natural sympathy for their kind," the difficulty being that this "sympathy is often quite sparse and ... easily extinguishable" (1996, p. 41).

> The survival of human society is possible in the face of quite a lot of defaults and defections from the observance of the ethical principle, but unless it held a certain minimum of sway in the thought and action of some individuals at least, there would be a collapse of human society. This necessary connection of the principle with the survival of the group and, by and large, of the species, invests it, as in the case of non-contradiction, with the status of an evolutionary force (1996, p. 41).

Universals are not driven by cognition, but a mosaic of cultural habitats in which we engage sympathetically and impartially at the same time. We embrace an Other with deep personal sympathy, and simultaneously universalize impartiality – wishing conceptually that the whole human race were like the Other, and defining the Other as the universal ideal.

3 In a study of ethical principles in 13 countries across four continents, the sacredness of human life[3] was consistently identified as a universal value (Christians and Traber, 1997; cf. Christians, 2008). The rationale for human action was affirmed to be reverence for life on earth – respect for the organic realm in which human civilization is situated. Veneration of human life represents a universalism from the ground up. Various societies articulate this protonorm in different terms which they illustrate locally, although every culture can bring to the table this fundamental norm for ordering political relationships and social institutions such as the media. There is at least one generality of universal scope underlying systematic ethics. Rather than generating an abstract conception of the good, the primal sacredness of life is a catalyst for binding humans universally into an organic whole. Its universal scope enables us to avoid the divisiveness of appeals to individual interests, cultural practices, and national prerogatives. The sacredness of life, evident in nature itself, grounds a responsibility that is global in scope and self-evident regardless of cultures and competing ideologies. Its dynamic and primordial character contradicts essentialist and static views of human nature. The veneration of human life is a protonorm similar in kind to the proto-Germanic language – *proto* in Greek meaning underneath – a lingual predecessor underlying the Germanic languages as we know them in history. Out of this primordial generality basic principles emerge such as truth, human dignity, and nonviolence. The notion of protonorms is a way of rooting our universals in ontology, rather than in the rationalist epistemology of the Western tradition.

4 Cees Hamelink (2000) finds in international human rights the foundation for freedom, justice and peace in the world, and thus for the moral standards of the media as well. He estimates human rights to provide the only universally available principles for the dignity and integrity of all human beings. The world political

community has recognized the existence of human rights since the adoption of the United Nations Charter in 1945 and has accepted the attending international legal machinery for their enforcement. Member states of the United Nations have pledged to promote universal respect for, and observance of, human rights. They have also committed themselves to upholding the dignity and worth of the human person, to foster social progress, and to safeguard the right of recognition before the law without any discrimination. Core human rights include the right to life, to food, to health care, to due process, and – not least – to free expression and to open public deliberation. To ensure democratic participation, in principle and practice, therefore, all peoples must have the right of access to communication channels in a manner independent of governmental or commercial control.

5   Martha Nussbaum (2000, cf. 2006) uses extensive research into the daily lives of women in the nonindustrial regions of India to argue for capabilities that are true of humans universally as they work out their existence in the world. The idea of capabilities respects "each person's struggle for flourishing; it treats each person as an end, and as a source of energy and worth in her own right" (2000, p. 69). There are common values that are evident from people's daily toil to meet their basic needs. Various social goods emerge which people aspire to reach and are capable of achieving. Bodily health is one example: "Being able to have good health, including reproductive health, to be adequately nourished; to have adequate shelter" (2000, p. 78). Affiliation is another social good: "Being able to engage in various forms of social action; to have the capability of justice and friendship; freedom of assembly and political speech" (2000, p. 79). All human beings are fully capable in principle of achieving these standards of a quality life. The countless ways of doing them overlap and establish the possibilities of universals. Social arrangements are just when people have the opportunity to develop the full range of their abilities. That, in turn, means that it should be possible to work out a conception of what all people must have to flourish. For Nussbaum, "theory is valuable for practice; … universal norms of human capability can provide the underpinning for a set of constitutional guarantees in all nations" (2000, pp. 35–36).

Universalist positions have discredited themselves over history by breeding totalitarianism. Those who claim knowledge of universal truth typically use it to control or convert dissenters. In the face of this objection, it must be reiterated that the universalist appeals from Benhabib to Nussbaum are not foundational *a prioris*. Interactive universalism, sympathetic impartiality, the sacredness of life, international human rights, and overlapping capabilities in the theoretical models are not objectivist absolutes. They are presuppositions that intellectual work needs as a starting point. Infinite regression is conceptually impossible. These five theories are interpretive schemes that arise from and explicate our fundamental beliefs about the world. They yield meaningful portraits, and not rationally precise formulations derived from artificially fixed conditions as in Enlightenment science. Theorizing is redefined not as an examination of external events, but the power of the imagination to give us an inside perspective on reality. As an intellectual strategy, it shifts transcendental criteria from a metaphysical and vertical plane to horizons of community and being, but universal norms they remain nonetheless.

The Communitarian Paradigm

The idea of universals needs to be revolutionized for universalism and communitarianism to live together in harmony rather than in opposition. It also requires a specific form of communitarian thinking. Communitarians cut their teeth on liberal democracy. This social philosophy has matured into a dialogic version that is more ecumenical in character and broader in scope intellectually. Dialogic communitarianism works in concert with ontological universalism, with the latter feeding into the former rather than standing isolated in its own domain.

Political philosophy

Communitarian's basic formulation is in political theory and it is this version that cannot account for universals. It developed in the 1980s as a challenge to individualistic liberalism. In the sociopolitical theory of Michael Sandel, Carole Pateman, and Charles Taylor, an atomistic democracy of individual rights should be replaced by social, deliberative democracy instead. These scholars (plus Michael Walzer and Alasdair MacIntyre) are not promoting a political movement as is Amitai Etzioni, who aims at restoring traditional community values. The philosophical communitarians understand the issues in fundamental terms as revolving around the relationship between persons and community, the nature of the common good, and the impact of the excesses of individualism on morality (Sandel, 1984).

The communitarian argument can be summarized in three steps: First, in a politics of individual rights, the process of fairness has priority over a conception of the common good. Second, we can accept such a priority only by presuming that our individual identities can be established in isolation from history and culture. Third, since our human identities are actually constituted within a social conception of the good, we cannot make individual rights the cornerstone of the political order.[4]

In the communitarian worldview, what is worth preserving can only be ascertained within specific social situations where human identity and interests are framed. The communal – our commonness, *communitas* – is the context in which ethics can be understood. Individualist democracy since John Locke confuses an aggregate of individual goods with the common good. Our selves are understood to be constituted antecedently, that is, in advance of our engagement with others. A sense of community describes a possible aim of individuated selves but is "not an ingredient of their identity" (Mulhall and Swift, 1996, pp. 49–52; cf. Sandel, 1995, pp. 59–65) Liberal political theory presumes that people are distinct from their ends; the domain of the good is extrinsic. Intrinsic valuing is defined out of existence. Individual liberty has priority over the moral order, and therefore ethics is exterior.

For Sandel, however, the utilitarian picture of persons as separate from their conceptions of the good is unacceptable. "Who, the communitarian asks, is the shadowy 'person' that exists independently of, and able freely to choose, the ends that give her life meaning and value" (Mulhall and Swift, 1996, p. 10)? A voluntaristic relation between a self and its ends, in Sandel's view, leads to an impoverished understanding of political community. Communal goods are then only one contender among many. Community is a possible aim but not an ingredient of our human identity. In this perspective, citizens think of themselves as "participants in a scheme of mutual cooperation, deriving advantages they could not have gained by their own efforts, but not tied to their fellow citizens by a bond whose severance or alteration would change their identity as persons" (Mullhall and Swift, 1996, p. 54, cf. Sandel, 1995, pp. 15–23). In communitarianism as a political philosophy, unless our freedom is used to help others prosper, our own wellbeing is negated. Citizenship is not achieved through a voluntary contract with other citizens, but arises from and depends on the reciprocal bonds which constitute human existence.

Dialogic communitarianism

Communitarianism that works itself in and through dialogic theory is the most mature version of communal normative theory at present. It embodies the commitments of the political version and the insights of feminist social ethics (cf. V. Held, 2006), while benefiting from the breadth and range of dialogic communications theory. A normative dialogic paradigm is a decisive alternative to relativism and a fruitful framework for communications in an age of globalization and multiculturalism.

In terms of the dialogic perspective, when we talk with each other about our mutual responsibilities, we seek to discover a good reason for acting. We are not simply being open to the other party's perspective. We are actively listening and contributing with a view to uncovering nonidiosyncratic truths capable of withstanding the test of critical dialogue. A reason to act is a nonarbitrary thought-satisfying determination supporting one course of action over others. The thinking person finds the reason convincing and is compelled to act upon it precisely because the determination it makes is nonarbitrary. In the contribution of feminist ethics, dialogic theory does not think of morality as an impersonal action-guiding code for an individual, but rather as a caring process in which individuals continually adjust their positions in light of what others have said and done (Koehn, 1998, pp. 156–161). Emmanel Levinas (1905–1995) shifts the starting point in dialogic ethics to the Other, thus displacing motivations from oneself to engrossment in the needs of the Other (1985). Charles Taylor summarizes the fundamental character of the dialogic this way:

> We become full human agents, capable of understanding ourselves, and hence of
> defining our identity, through ... rich modes of expression we learn through exchange
> with others. Discovering my own identity doesn't mean that I work it out in isolation,

but crucially depends on my dialogical relations with others. ... In the culture of authenticity, relationships are seen as the key loci of self discovery and self affirmation (Taylor *et al.*, 1994, pp. 32, 34, 36).

Whereas political communitarianism centers on the North Atlantic liberal tradition since Locke and Mill, the dialogic version is articulated in various areas of the world not conditioned by Enlightenment thinking. Their lineage cannot be traced to a single source. Good ideas are seldom unique; often they surface in several places at the same time triggered by similar conditions and needs.

Martin Buber is typically used as the supreme example of dialogic ethics. For Buber, restoring the dialogic ought to be our primary aim as humankind (1965, pp. 209–224). He makes the dialogic fundamental in his famous lines, "in the beginning is the relation" (1970, p. 69) and the relation is "the cradle of actual life" (1970, p. 60). He thinks of the interhuman relation ontologically as a category of being. Human relationships, not individuals per se, have primacy. "Persons appear by entering into relation with other persons" (1970, p. 112). For face to face encounters and community life, "the one basic word is the word-pair I-Thou" (1970, p. 3). This irreducible phenomenon cannot be decomposed into simpler elements without destroying it. There are not three components, sender-message-receiver, to be dismembered for scientific analysis. Buber (1970) speaks prophetically that only as I-Thouness prospers will the monologic I-It modality recede.

Mark Fackler's description of communitarianism focuses on relationships in virtually the same terms as describe Buber: "The identity of the individual in communitarian theory emerges as an ontological recognition of the primacy of relationships.... Communitarianism insists that mutuality defines and constitutes the person. Without relationships and therefore communicative sharing, the idea of personhood vanishes" (2009, pp. 305–306). Verlinden, in his work on media ethics and globalization, also integrates Buber and the communitarian worldview. Buber's Judaic dialogism he considers the best alternative to "abstract universalist imperialism" (2008, p. 199). Buber's antifoundationalism can be summarized this way: "'True norms,' Buber says, never become a maxim: they do not command our obedience to authority but they command our-*selves*; they address us *directly* in the situation where we are and leave us to respond with our whole being" (Verlinden, 2008, p. 202; cf. Buber, 1965). For Buber, the I becomes We when people come together affirming Thouness to one another. "True community is not just a collection of individuals pursuing common interests, needs or appetites, but is instead the 'vital interaction' between complete and thoroughly responsive persons" (Verlinden, 2008, p. 206).

In Paulo Freire's (1970) language, only through dialogue do we fulfill our ontological and historical vocation of becoming fully human. Following the work of the Spanish philosopher Eduardo Nicol (1965), Freire makes dialogue the distinctive element in his emancipatory strategy. Without dialogue, Freire argues, there is conquest, cultural invasion, manipulation, and imprisonment in antagonistic relationships. Society is macroanthropos rather than microcosmos, and dialogue is therefore the only morally acceptable tool for liberation. In analyzing dialogue as a human phenomenon, Freire understands the word to be the essence of the dialogic itself. However, the word is more than just an instrument which makes dialogue possible. It has two constituent elements – reflection and action – in continual tension. "There is no true word that is not at the same time a praxis. Thus to speak a true word is to transform the world" (Freire, 1970, p. 75). Liberation is a process of self-reflection achieved in dialogue. Freire argues that the fundamental right of dependent or oppressed societies is exactly that of gaining its own voice, the right to pronounce its own word.

Thus a revolution in our language is an integral component in the process of human liberation. Freire confronts the evils of starvation, poor housing, environmental abuse, unemployment, health hazards, and a lack of essential commodities. These problems, however, cannot be solved in the absence of a true word about the human condition, a word which enables us to decenter the reality in which we live, no transformation is possible. In the face of a culture of silence, Freire insists on a theory of our universal humanness, not as romanticism but as a barrier against nihilism. While tearing down our idols and rejecting evil structures, Freire refuses to condemn all our cultural creations. His program of resistance ruptures our situated experience, while retaining a redemptive ambience through a language of possibility.

In his work on human rights and Asian values, China scholar William deBary (1998) uses a historical approach to develop the relationship between Confucianism and communitarianism. He defines values as "the core or axial elements of a culture, the traditional ground on which rest the culture's most characteristic and enduring institutions" (p. 1). While endorsing the standard conclusion that the civil cultures of Japan, Singapore, Taiwan, South Korea, and the People's Republic have been deeply influenced by Confucianism, he elaborates on the nuances and applications through the major dynasties in China, and accounts for different kinds of allegiance to Confucianism in different periods, and for today's "tough environment and limiting conditions" (p. 13). In his effort to illuminate human rights in the Orient, he resists the "individualistic West" versus "communitarian Asia" formulation. Rather than argue that Confucianism has produced the premiere version of communitarian thought because the two understand reality in similar terms, deBary outlines a more general task, that is, "to consider what communitarianism has meant in the Confucian context, in the longer development of Confucianism and especially of neo-Confucianism" (p. 12).

Two cases are of special interest to him as evidence of "Confucian communitarian thought": community schools and community organizations known as community compacts. Community schools in villages, outside the bureaucratic system – for farmers in some periods – were rooted in both the moral uplift of the *Great Learning* and communitarian values (chapter 4, pp. 41–57). The ritual of compacts (*xiangyue*) survived into the twentieth century, where members of communities entered into a contract of voluntarism, mutual aid in distress, rotating leadership, engagement in rites and customs in order to limit the intervention of the state in

Universalism versus Communitarianism

local affairs (chapter 5, pp. 58–89). These examples of communitarianism are "authentically Confucian" in that they illustrate "the wider range of efforts by Confucians to strengthen community life and build consensual fiduciary institutions" (p. 13). These communitarian efforts under authoritarian regimes did not survive, but if they had flourished "they might have contributed to a Confucian version of a civil society" (p. 14).

Ubuntu is a traditional African concept in the Zulu and Xhosa languages that is typically translated as "humanity toward others." The term is derived from the Zulu maxim *umuntu ngumuntu ngabantu*, meaning "a person is a person through other persons" or "I am because of others" (Louw, 2004, p. 2). *Ubuntu* defines humans as social beings, with human dignity central to and integrated into both rationality and morality. Prinsloo (2003) explains that "according to *ubuntu* thinkers, there is no dualism in this position because both rationality and morality are acquired from community life and do not follow from so-called universal categories or fixed ideologies. In this sense one can speak of communitarian morality and rationality" (p. 43).

For Khoza (Prinsloo, 1998, p. 41), *ubuntu* represents "the collective consciousness of the people of Africa," and in Louw's (2004, p. 2) perspective, *ubuntu* is an indigenous aphorism that "serves as the spiritual foundation of African societies." "Despite Africa's cultural diversity, threads of underlying affinity do run through the beliefs, customs, value systems, and socio-political institutions and practices of the various African societies" and one of the value systems "found in most of these societies is the *ubuntu* system" (Kamwangamalu, 1999, p. 26). In this sense, *ubuntu* is the basis for sustainable African values and the African renaissance. Simultaneously *ubuntu* is understood as a universal value, with humans everywhere able to understand human life according to its terms.

Since *ubuntu* is not merely African, but embodies a fundamental truth about humanity, it serves in this essay to illustrate dialogic communitarianism as a normative system for understanding the press (cf. Christians, 2004b, pp. 241–251). Schutte (1993, p. xii) observes that although *ubuntu* is "opposed to the dominant forces of contemporary European thinking…. it finds sympathetic echoes in many non-African ideas" such as Schumacher's "small is beautiful," Ivan Illich's "conviviality", and Simone Weil's "need for roots." Dialogic communitarianism likewise contradicts Western liberalism, thereby making its intersection with *ubuntu* conceptually congenial (see Masolo, 1994).

Humans as cultural beings

In the philosophical framework opposed to Descartes' rational being, the definition of humans as cultural beings is the best pathway to dialogic communitarianism. The philosophy of language provides the basis for a shift to the lingual definition of humans. Communities as linguistic entities, by reason of this fact, are moral in character, and this phenomenon is central to the dialogic version of communitarianism.

Ernst Cassirer's *Philosophy of Symbolic Forms* (1923–1929/1953–1957, 1996) brought this intellectual domain to fulfillment.[5] In Cassirer's view, "we are language-using and culture-incorporating creatures whose forms of experience, conduct and interaction take shape in linguistically and culturally-structured environments, and are conditioned by the meanings they bear" (Schacht, 1990). His four-volume work in the 1920s brought to completion the symbolic tradition established by Ferdinand de Saussure's *Course on General Linguistics* (1916). For Cassirer, symbolization is not merely the hallmark of human cognition, but our representational capacity that defines us anthropologically. Cassirer (1944) titled his summary monograph, *An Essay on Man*. He identified our unique capacity to generate symbolic structures as a radical alternative both to the *animale rationale* of classical Greece and of Descartes' modernity, and to the biological being of evolutionary naturalism. Cassirer's creative being is carved out against a reductionism to intellectus and disciplined thinking on one hand, and a naturalistic neurophysiology and biochemistry on the other.

In his definition of *homo sapiens* as *animale symbolicum*, Cassirer sees the symbolic realm as intrinsic to this form of living being.[6] Humans alone of animate creatures possess the creative mind, the irrevocable ability to reconstruct, to interpret. From this perspective, communication is the symbolic process expressing human creativity and grounding cultural formation. Culture is the womb in which symbols are born and communication is the connective tissue in culture building. Realities called cultures are inherited and built from symbols that shape our action, identity, thoughts, and sentiment. Communication, therefore, is the process of building and reaffirming through symbols, and culture signifies the constructions that result.[7]

James Carey (1989) described communication-as-symbolic-process the ritual view. Rituals are ceremonies or sacraments through which we define meaning and purpose; they are events of celebration such as weddings and birthdays where values are affirmed, and not merely exchanges of information. Humans have enveloped themselves in linguistic forms, artistic images, and religious rites and therefore their reality is known through their own symbolic matrix. When defining humans as cultural beings, culture is understood as a created reality that establishes a meaningful cosmos. Communication is the catalytic agent, the driving force in cultural formation, and if cultures are sets of symbols that orient life and provide it significance, then cultural patterns are inherently normative. Assuming that culture is the container of our symbolic capacity, the constituent parts of such containers are a society's values. As ordering relations, values direct the ends of societal practice and provide implicit standards for selecting courses of action.

In this shift from rational being understood through mathematics to cultural being understood through language, symbol systems are not a vehicle of private meaning but belong to a community where they are nurtured in reflection as well as action. Communities are knit together linguistically; however, the lingual is not neutral but value laden, so our social bonds are moral claims. Defining humans as cultural beings moves discourse from its Enlightenment home in cognition to an interpretive axis in values, beliefs, norms, the human spirit, that is, in culture. If the interpretive domain is lingual, then human bonds are not through reason or action, but through the moral imagination. Our communal relations are not inscribed, first of all, in politics or economics, or in the transportation or data. Our mutual humanness is actually an ethical commitment rooted in the moral domain all humans share. Communities are woven together by narratives that invigorate their common understanding of good and evil, happiness and reward, the meaning of life and death. Recovering and refashioning moral discourse help to amplify our deepest humanness and provide the soil in which democracy can flourish.

Community-Universals Convergence[8]

Universals that are ontological reach toward diversity, and dialogic communitarianism has a worldwide and crosscultural orientation. These definitions of universalism and communalism eschew dichotomies and open pathways to convergence. Three such trajectories are suggestive of a media ethics that is oriented first of all by the universal rather than by individual autonomy: (1) universals anchor community values and professional ethics;[9] (2) moral literacy becomes the press' primary mission; and (3) global journalism and cosmopolitan democracy take center stage.

Universals as framework

Not every community ought to be celebrated. Some are sexist and others have racism in their language and institutions. Matt Hale's Worldwide Church of the Creator is blatantly anti-Semitic and thrives on hate rhetoric. Through universal norms we raise questions about communal values that are exclusionary and oppressive. Cultures need norms beyond their own values in order to be self-critical. "Only an 'outside' lets us know that we are limited, and defined by those limitations; only an 'outside' shapes us" and enables us to evaluate and move forward constructively (Fleischacker, 1992, p. 223).

For media values and practices, universals serve as the ethical framework also. As an illustration, note how the sacredness of life as one universal protonorm applies. As we begin systematizing the idea that the lives of all humans are sacred, it entails ethical principles such as truthtelling, human dignity and nonviolence. Given the three step strategy that the convergence model suggests, after moving from the problem – step one, to its alternative – step two, universals need to shape community structures and professional practices in step three. What follows is a summary of how these principles grounded in the sacredness of life work communally.

Of the three principles, we have concentrated the most in communications with the first and second – truth and human dignity. Truth is central to media practice and appears everywhere in our codes of ethics, mission statements, classes, and textbooks on communication ethics. We disagree on the details, not always sure what truth means and how it applies. There is still in news a heavy emphasis on facts and unbiased information that is no longer defensible epistemologically. The general concept of truth is an unwavering imperative.

However, if we broaden our understanding of truth from the Occidental tradition to a definition rooted in the sacredness of life, the view of truth as accurate data is too narrow. With a framework oriented to the universal, the concept is more sophisticated as authentic disclosure. Truthful statements entail a comprehensive account of the context which gives them meaning. The fact-value dichotomy of Eurocentric science no longer is credible. "The facts never 'speak for themselves'. They must be selected, marshaled, linked together, and given a voice" (Barzun and Graff, 1992, p. xii). News defined as disclosure of the inside meaning rings true, that is, it is authentic as both fact and interpretation to those being covered. This kind of news brings to light the underlying issues that enable communities to work constructively on social problems themselves.[10]

Increasingly, human dignity has taken a central position in media ethics. For two decades now, media professionals have worked on ethnic diversity in hiring, racist language in news, and sexism in advertising. Human dignity that arrives on the media's agenda from the universal, takes seriously lives that are loaded with cultural complexity. Gender, race, class, and religion are understood as decisive contexts for fashioning human identity. The imperative of human dignity grounded in the sacredness of life moves the field beyond an individualistic morality of rights to a social ethics of the common good. It enables media organizations and practitioners to recognize that the flourishing of all the voices of self-discovery, and self-affirmation among a society's cultural groups, are urgent for the civic agenda.

However, the third ethical principle, nonviolence, is still underdeveloped. Flickers of peace are emerging on our media ethics repertoire, but only glimmers compared to truth, and of late, human dignity. Johan Galtung has developed the principle most thoroughly as peace journalism, concerned not only with the standards of war reporting, but nonviolent resolution of all types of human conflicts (e.g. 2004). Peace journalism recognizes that military coverage as a media event promotes the very violence it reports, and therefore is developing strategies that make peace paramount (Lynch and McGoldrick, 2005; Lynch, 2008). However, the broad task remains of bringing this third principle to maturity (cf. Christians, 2007). We need a rich venue at present for doing so – international magazines and newspapers, town hall discussions, the world wide web, educational multimedia presentations, documentaries, online journalism, theater, and music – together bringing nonviolence into its own across cultures and from the bottom up.

Moral literacy

The argument of this chapter is that the ontological version of universals obligates us to choose the dialogic version of communitarianism. If in the dialogic model, communities are moral orders and not merely functional structures, moral literacy ought to be privileged in the media's mission. Rather than merely providing readers and audiences with information, the aim of the press is morally literate citizens.

Dialogic communitarianism challenges reporters to participate in a community's ongoing process of moral formation. The possibility exists in principle. Moral judgments may appear to be instinctual, but "agents manifesting them are often capable of explaining just what it is about human beings that merits" reactions or involvement; in other words, "we articulate our intuitions by developing a particular ontology of the human" (Mulhall and Swift, 1996, p. 103). Our moral intuitions are often "purely instinctual, like reactions of nausea to certain tastes." However, humans are capable of explaining what merits their obligations and they typically do so in terms of their beliefs about the nature of humanness. Agreements and disputes about the good life can be articulated and sifted. Discussions among people typically specify the character and identity of our moral intuitions. Therefore, as journalism deals with the moral dimension in news, editorials, features, investigative reporting and so forth, it is meeting a crucial human need. In communitarian perspective, media practitioners open windows on the moral landscape in interactive terms – with reporters, those in persuasion, script writers, and producers resonating critically with the same debates over authentic social existence as the public themselves. Citizens are helped to distinguish beneficent communities from bad ones, and to articulate a common good within the fallible and irresolute voices of everyday discourse.

In other words, given the character of dialogic communitarianism, the various technologies of public communication ought to stimulate the moral imagination. This language often appears in a sanitized sense: "Do these programs have any redeeming social value?" In this regard, investigative reporting has been deficient and it ought to be rectified:

> The hard-hitting stories, the investigative stories, lack a morally sensitive vocabulary. They don't talk about moral issues in moral terms. They go to great lengths to do what, in a morally technical language, might be called "objectifying morality" by taking moral claims and making them appear to be empirical claims (Glasser, 1992, p. 44).

Recovering and refashioning moral discourse helps to amplify our deepest humanness and provide the soil in which democracy can flourish. Whenever one observes reenactments of purposeful history and justice, one sees the results of moral literacy.[11]

Despite unrelenting pressure from media commercialism, public broadcasting often resonates with a redemptive accent and stirs the human conscience.[12] We all know stations and reporters who have refused infotainment and sought to awaken the civic conscience. Major league awards are still won by professionals in journalism who distinguish themselves for public service. In the Tsunami disaster, December 2004, the news included the overwhelming acts of kindness around the world, and our moral imagination was invigorated. Historical documentaries on the horrifics of the Holocaust sometimes include the benefactors of Anne Frank in the Netherlands, and the resistance of Dietrich Bonhoeffer. Out of the turmoil in the Middle East are the inspiring stories of Jews and Muslims working on water projects in Palestine, and teaching their children each other's religion. Editorials have raised consciousness of anti-Semitism and heightened our moral awareness of racism and gender discrimination. In the debates over war and worldwide trade in military arms, the moral issues in terms of just-war theory and pacifism have emerged at various times in news and commentary. Affirmative action, environmental protection, health care reform, gun control, unemployment, and immigration policy raise moral conflicts that journalists can help the public negotiate. Building on the unique capacities of news as a genre, and with ontological universals and dialogic communitarianism as the ethical framework, reporters can empower us toward moral literacy by appealing to our conscience.

Global Journalism

Current thinking on democracy is moving beyond deliberation to cosmopolitanism. Political theorists are seeking to make democracy more responsive to, and more viable in, a world where global trade and communication have fundamentally altered the demands of nation state democracy. Political participation now extends beyond national boundaries and requires forms of democracy sensitive to regimes of power not defined by geography. David Held (2006) thus calls for implementing a model of "cosmopolitan democracy," one that extends and deepens the mechanisms of democratic accountability across the globe. He envisions an assembly of democracies rather than an inclusive United Nations with governments of all kinds (1995, pp. 228–229). The model is not that of a world government, but "the development of democratic decision-making in emerging cross-border and transnational communities and associations" (Gould, 2008, p.21). These include, for example, international agencies working on economic issues, Internet forums, and larger regional associations like the European Union.

Held's cosmopolitanism focuses on what he understands to be a new and pressing need for a global democratic order, to deal with those international issues confronting democratic life at present – global warming, food supply and distribution, risks of nuclear and chemical warfare, health and disease. This structure recognizes local, national, and regional authority but also coordinates it in ways that build an even larger democratic community: "an international community of democratic states and societies committed to upholding democratic public law both within and across their own boundaries" (2006, pp. 229–235).

Along with David Held, Nigel Dower uses cosmopolitanism as his framework in his *World Ethics: The New Agenda* (2007). He speaks of a number of cosmopolitan theories that have two common aspects: "First, a set of values as values to be accepted everywhere. Second, some notion of active responsibility to further those values" (chapter 5). Kwame Anthony Appiah (2006) settles for the term as well, while rejecting the superiority complex of the so-called cosmopolitan frequent-flyer who does not engage the world deeply in its diversity. Kathleen Roberts and her colleague Ronald Arnett have drawn the same conclusion, calling their recent book *Communication Ethics: Between Cosmopolitanism and Provinciality*.

Actually *polites* – citizen-of-the-cosmos – has had resonance since the expression was first introduced by the cynics of the fourth century BC. In its complexity it designates two interwoven strands: (1) the idea that we have obligations to others, beyond our kin and communities, and (2) the idea that we value not just human life in general, but human lives specifically (Appiah, 2006). Instead of the fragmented "act locally and think globally," we think and act locally and globally simultaneously. Local allegiances and human solidarity have rarely functioned well in philosophy – even among those with cosmopolitan instincts. However, for the twenty-first century we have no other option but to get it right. Cosmopolitanism sets the highest and most accurate standard for our theoretical work at present as the sociopolitical context for understanding the ethics of news.

Stephen Ward (2005) has developed a global journalism ethics that rethinks journalism's principles and standards by adopting a cosmopolitan perspective. Cosmopolitanism regards people as citizens of the world. It emphasizes such international principles as human rights, freedom, and justice. The cosmopolitan values "humanity's common aspirations, vulnerabilities, and capacities, as well as its potential for suffering…. The cosmopolitan attitude does not deny that particular cultures and traditions are valuable for life and may be psychologically necessary for the development of ethical character. The claim of humanity acknowledges that we live simultaneously in two communities: the local community of our birth and a community of common human aspirations. It insists only that … we should not allow local attachments to override fundamental human rights and duties" (Ward, 2005, p. 15). For journalists to serve cosmopolitan's claim of humanity, they must follow three imperatives (p. 16): act as global agents for a well-informed and tolerant public; serve the world's citizens and not only local and national readers and audiences (cf. Comers, 2008, pp. 86–93); and enhance nonparochial understandings with a diversity of perspectives. The media-connected world brings together a daunting array of ethnic groups, traditions, religions, political agendas, technological inequalities, and cultural conflicts; Global journalism ethics makes sure "we do not withdraw into an insular ethnocentrism" and insists on "reporting from an informed and nuanced international perspective" (p. 5). The convergence of universals and communitarian thinking encourages this enlargement of the boundaries of media ethics.

Conclusion

The different trajectories in this article converge on the view that media ethics in an age of global technology requires a more sophisticated theoretical framework than hitherto available. Communication ethics rooted in Enlightenment rationalism, and therefore emphasizing personal decision-making, cannot serve journalism with its global reach and technological complexity. Kantian-style categorical imperatives are absolutes across time and space that require a Newtonian cosmology and have no credibility post-Einstein and Heisenberg. Appeals to face-to-face communities or political communitarianism are not sufficiently crosscultural.

However, theories in which ontological-linguistic universals and dialogic communitarianism converge are not reductionistic and open the pathways to media ethics of the future. Such theories do expect diversity of opinion and epistemological differences in the pursuit of a new generation of media ethics, but in good faith anticipate salient agreements beyond the status quo.

Our communal identity is defined by what we consider good or worth opposing. As a result for journalism, its moral framework cannot be reduced to professional ethics. The focus ought to be not on professional practice, but on the moral life as a whole. How the moral order works itself out in community formation is the issue, not first of all what practitioners consider virtuous in their own codes of ethics. To resonate intelligently with a community's values means that professional communicators need to know ethical principles that they share with the public at large, such as truthtelling, justice, human dignity, keeping one's promises, and no harm to the innocent. Theories of universals and community, properly understood, converge on that demanding but inspiring task.

Notes

1   Referring to African communitarianism, Fackler (2003) concludes that for the Nigerian A. Okechukwu Obgonnaya and the Ghanian Kwasi Wiredu, the world is constituted communally. They regard "community as nothing less than 'the way things are', a presupposition, a *prima facie* truth. To speak meaningfully is to address social reality in communitarian terms" (2003, p. 320).

2   Wiredu was head of the Philosophy Department at the University of Ghana until his retirement in 1999. His first major book, *Philosophy and an African Culture* (1980), deals with African philosophy in terms of the folk thought preserved in oral traditions and critical reflection. He contends that philosophical work is culture-relative but can be universal too. African philosophy uses historical resources and engages them in indigenous languages but then actually does philosophical work relevant outside these boundaries. As editor-in-chief of the Blackwell *Companion to African Philosophy* (2004) he provides comprehensive coverage of African philosophy across the ages – including Ancient Egypt, North African thinkers, precolonial philosophy, and African political thought in the nineteenth and twentieth centuries.

3   The term "sacredness" is standard in religious vocabulary, referring to deity. It is also an anthropological term with its etymology from the Latin *sanctum*, meaning "set apart." The protonorm is presuppositional, pretheoretical, deep, primordial. On that level, sacredness as a term grants extraordinariness to human life, but is not invoking the higher level of organized religion, its doctrines, and institutions.

4   These three propositions are adapted from Amy Gutmann (1985).

5   Cassirer (1960) developed the most systematic treatment to date of the nature of the cultural sciences. See especially his "Naturalistic and Humanistic Philosophies of Culture" (1960, pp. 3–28) and "Nature-Concepts and Culture-Concepts" (1960, pp. 117–158). Cassirer is particularly valuable for the counter-Enlightenment orientation of this chapter, since he refers to Vico's humanism throughout his career, using Vico's philological emphasis as the most compelling alternative to Enlightenment rationality.

Universalism versus Communitarianism

6 Symbolism as a special endowment of the human species, to the exclusion of other organic beings and their sign language, is a fundamental question that is not resolved in Cassirer. His basic task in the *Philosophy of Symbolic Forms* is to trace the evolution of cultural symbols from early history to modern times, where he of necessity focuses on the origin and role of language in *homo sapiens*. What is needed to contradict Cassirer's exclusivism is proof that any animal has made the decisive step to propositional language, that is, advancing from direct or indirect sign-responses to symbols of meaning.

7 This is a semiotic definition, which stands in contrast to anthropology where culture refers to entire civilizations as complex wholes, and in contrast to common parlance where culture is identified as refined manners. Most definitions of culture are expansive, encompassing under the term virtually all human activity. Culture is thus said to involve technologies, customs, arts, sciences, products, habits, political and social organizations that characterize a people. Others such as Jacob Burckhardt (1943) find the broad definition inchoate and distinguish culture from political and social structures, from direct efforts to understand nature (such as chemistry, physics, astronomy), and from religious institutions. Culture thus becomes essentially people's communicative activities and refers primarily to the products of the arts and languages. The term is used here in Burckhardt's sense.

8 This section serves as a propaedeutic, the concept in the humanities for introductory principles that serve to guide future thinking and research.

9 Having community life judged by universal norms follows the intellectual strategy of Jürgen Habermas (1984). For an ethics of discourse to operate effectively in the public sphere, he presumed an ideal speech situation as its context. His communicative rationality opposes objective reason as does the concept of ontological-linguistic communities proposed in this chapter. Presuming an inherent desire in speech acts for mutual understanding, Habermas argues for an ideal speech formulation of full participation, mutuality and reciprocity as a goal for citizens and a critical standard by which to judge consensus. In *Moral Consciousness and Communicative Action* (1990), Habermas argues that the principle of universalization acts as a rule of argumentation and is implicitly presupposed by discourse (pp. 86–94). In moral consciousness, universals are the bridging principle which makes agreement possible (pp. 57–68).

10 For an elaboration of news as authentic disclosure in theory and practice, see Christians (2004a).

11 For a historical review of the way communitarianism applies to the mass media and sociopolitical life, see Fackler (2008, pp. 306–312). Fackler (2003) applies communitarian theory to the media in Africa, including the oncoming internet technologies (pp. 318–126).

12 Fackler challenges communitarianism to "provide an account of the conscience" for the sake of its long-term vitality (2008, p. 313).

References

Appiah, K.A. (2006) *Cosmopolitanism: Ethics in a World of Strangers*, W.W. Norton, New York.

Barzun, J., and Graff, H.F. (1992) *The Modern Researcher*, 5th edn, Harcourt Brace, Orlando, FL.

Bauman, Z. (1993) *Postmodern Ethics*, Blackwell, Oxford.

Benhabib, S. (1992) *Situating the Self: Gender, Community, and Postmodernism in Contemporary Ethics*, Routledge, New York.

Benhabib, S. (2002) *The Claims of Culture: Equality and Diversity in the Global Era*, Princeton University Press, Princeton, NJ.

Bracci, S.L. (2002) The fragile hope of Seyla Benhabib's interactive universalism, in *Moral Engagement in Public Life: Theorists for Contemporary Ethics*, (eds S.L. Bracci and C.G. Christians), Peter Lang, New York, pp. 123–149.

Buber, M. (1965) *Between Man and Man*, (trans. R.G. Smith), Macmillan, New York.

Buber, M. (1970) *I and Thou [Ich und Du]*, (trans. W. Kaufmann), Scribner, New York.

Burckhardt, J. (1943) *Force and Freedom: Reflections on History*, Pantheon, New York.

Carey, J.W. (1989) *Communication as Culture: Essays on Media and Society*, Unwin Hyman, Boston.

Cassirer, E. (1923–1929/1953–1957, 1996) *The philosophy of symbolic forms*, (trans. R. Manheim and J.M. Krois), 4 vols., Yale University Press, New Haven, CT, [original publication 1923–1929].

Cassirer, E. (1944) *An Essay on Man: An Introduction to the Philosophy of Human Culture*, Yale University Press, New Haven, CT.

Cassirer, E. (1951) *The Philosophy of the Enlightenment*, Princeton University Press, Princeton, NJ.

Cassirer, E. (1960) *The Logic of the Humanities*, (trans. C. Howe), Yale University Press, New Haven, CT.

Christians, C.G. (2004a) The changing news paradigm: From objectivity to interpretive sufficiency, in *Qualitative Research in Journalism: Taking It To the Streets*, (ed. S.H. Orio), Erlbaum, Mahwah, NJ, pp. 41–56.

Christians, C.G. (2004b) *Ubuntu* and communitarianism in media ethics. *Ecquid Novi: South African Journal for Journalism Research*, 25 (2), 235–256.

Christians, C.G. (2007) Non-violence in philosophical and religious ethics, *Javnost: The Public*, 14 (4), 5–18.

Christians, C.G. (2008) The ethics of universal being, in *Media Ethics Beyond Borders: A Global Perspective*, (eds S.J.A. Ward and H. Wasserman), Heinemann, Johannesburg, pp. 6–23. Christians, C.G., and Traber, M. (1997) *Communication Ethics and Universal Values*, Sage, Thousand Oaks, CA.

Comers, M.S.R. (2008) Gobal ethics and world citizenship, in *Ethics in an Era of Globalization*, (eds M.S.R. Comers, W. Vandekerckhove and A. Verlinden), Ashgate Publishing Limited, Aldershot, UK, pp. 75–94.

deBary, W.T. (1998) *Asian Values and Human Rights: A Confucian Communitarian Perspective*, Harvard University Press, Cambridge, MA.

deSaussure, F. (1959) *Course in General Linguistics*, (trans. W. Baskin), Harper and Row, New York [original publication 1916].

Descartes, R. (1998) *Discourse on Method*, (trans. D.A. Cress), Hackett Publishing Co., Indianapolis, IN [original publication 1637].

Dower, N. (2007) *World Ethics – The New Agenda*, Edinburgh University Press, Edinburgh.

Fackler, M. (2003) Communitarian theory with an African flexion, in *Mediating Religion: Conversations in Media, Religion and Culture*, (eds J. Mitchell and S. Marriage), T & T. Clark, London, pp. 317–327.

Fackler, M. (2009) Communitarianism, in *The Handbook of Mass Media Ethics*, (eds L. Wilkins and C. Christians), Routledge, New York, pp. 305–316.

Fleischacker, S. (1992) *Integrity and Moral Relativism*, E. J. Brill, Leiden, Netherlands.

Freire, P. (1970) *Pedagogy of the Oppressed*, Seabury Press, New York.

Galtung, J. (2004) *Transcend and Transform: An Introduction to Conflict Work (Peace by Peaceful Means)*, Pluto Press, London.

Glasser, T.L. (1992) Squaring with the Reader: A Seminar on Journalism, *Kettering Review*, Winter, p. 44

Gould, C. C. (2008) The New Global Ethics in Three Faces in *Ethics in an Era of Globalization*, (eds M.S.R. Comers, W. Vandekerckhove and A. Verlinden), Ashgate Publishing Limited, Aldershot, UK, pp. 13–26.

Gutmann, A. (1985) Communitarian Critics of Liberalism, *Philosophy and Public Affairs*, 14 (3, Summer), 311.

Habermas, J. (1984) *The Theory of Communicative Action, Vol. 1: Reason and the Rationalization of Society*, (trans. T. McCarthy), Beacon Press, Boston, MA.

Habermas, J. (1990) *Moral Consciousness and Communicative Action*, (rans.C. Lenhardt and S. W. Nicholsen), MIT Press, Cambridge, MA.

Hamelink, C. (2000) *The Ethics of Cyberspace*, Sage, Thousand Oaks, CA [original publication 1999].

Held, D. (1995) *Democracy and the Global Order: From the Modern State to Cosmopolitan Governance*, Polity, Padstow, UK.

Held, D. (2006) *Models of Democracy*, 3rd edn, Polity, Cambridge, UK.

Held, V. (2006) *The Ethics of Care: Personal, Political and Global*, Oxford University Press, Oxford, UK.

Kamwangamalu, N.M. (1999) *Ubuntu* in South Africa: A sociolinguistic perspective to a pan-African concept. *Critical Arts*, 13 (2), 24–41.

Kant, I. (1964) *Groundwork of the Metaphysic of Morals*, (trans. M. Gregor), Cambridge University Press, Cambridge, UK [original publication 1785].

Kant, I. (1981) *Universal Natural History and Theory of the Heavens*, (trans. S.L.), Scottish Academic Press, Edinburgh [original publication 1755].

Kant, I. (1997) *Critique of Practical Reason*, (trans. M. Gregor), Cambridge University Press, Cambridge, UK [original publication 1788].

Koehn, D. (1998) *Rethinking Feminist Ethics: Care, Trust and Empathy*, Routledge, New York.

Landmann, M. (1974) *Philosophical Anthropology*, (trans. D.J. Parent), Westminster Press, Philadelphia.

Levinas, E. (1985) *Ethics and Infinity: Conversations with Philippe Nemo*, Duquesne University Press, Pittsburgh, PA.

Louw, D.J. (2004) *Ubuntu:* An African assessment of the religious other. www.by.edu/wcp/Papers/Afri/AfriLouw.htm (last accessed July 1, 2010).

Lynch, J. (2008) *Debates in Peace Journalism*, University of Sydney Press, Sydney.

Lynch, J., and McGoldrick, A. (2005) *Peace Journalism*, Hawthorn Press, Stroud.

Lyotard, J.F. (1988) *The Post-Modern Condition: A Report of Knowledge*, (trans. G. Bennington and B. Massumi), University of Minnesota Press, Minneapolis.

Masolo, D.A. (1994) Western and African communitarianism: A comparison, in *A Companion to African Philosophy*, (ed. K. Wiredu), Blackwell, Oxford, pp. 483–498.

Mulhall, S., and Swift, A. (1996) *Liberals and Communitarians*, 2nd edn, Blackwell, Oxford.

Nicol, E. (1965) *Los Principios de la ciencia [The principle of knowing]*, Fundo de Cultura, Mexico City.

Niebuhr, R. (1944) *The Nature and Destiny of Man, Vol 1: Human Nature*, Scribner, New York [original publication 1941].

Nussbaum, M. (2000) *Women and Human Development: The Capabilities Approach*, Cambridge University Press Cambridge.

Nussbaum, M. (2006) *Frontiers of Justice: Disability, Nationality, Species Membership*, Harvard University Press, Cambridge, MA.

Paul, E.F., Miller, F.D., and Paul, J. (eds) (1994) *Cultural Pluralism and Moral Knowledge*, Cambridge University Press Cambridge.

Prinsloo, E.D. (2003) *Ubuntu* culture and participatory management, in *The African Philosophy Reader*, (eds P.H. Coetzee and A.P.J. Roux), Routledge, London, pp. 41–51.

Roberts, K.G., and Arnett, R. (2008) *Communication Ethics: Between Cosmopolitanism and Provinciality*, Peter Lang, New York.

Sandel, M. (1984) Morality and the liberal ideal. *The New Republic*, May 7, 17.

Sandel, M. (1995) *Liberalism and the Limits of Justice*, 2nd edn, Cambridge University Press, Cambridge.

Schacht, R. (1990) Philosophical anthropology: What, why, and how. *Philosophy and Phenomenological Research*, 50, Fall, 155–176.

Schutte, A. (1993) *Philosophy for Africa*, University of Cape Town Press, Cape Town.

Taylor, C. K. et al. (1994) *Multiculturalism: Examining the Politics of Recognition*, Princeton University Press, Princeton, NJ.

Verlinden, A. (2008) Global ethics as dialogism, in *Ethics in an Era of Globalization*, (eds M.S.R. Comers, W. Vandekerckhove and A. Verlinden), Ashgate Publishing Limited, Aldershot, UK, pp. 187–215.

Ward, S. J. A. (2005) Philosophical foundations for global journalism ethics, *Journal of Mass Media Ethics*, 24 (1), 3–21.

Wiredu, K. (1980) *Philosophy and an African Culture*, Cambridge University Press, Cambridge, UK.

Wiredu, K. (1996) *Cultural Universals and Particulars: An African Perspective*, Indiana University Press, Bloomington.

Wiredu, K. (2004) *A Companion to African Philosophy*, Blackwell, Oxford.

22

Responsibility of Net Users

Raphael Cohen-Almagor

Introduction

The Internet burst into our lives in the early-1990s without much preparation or planning, and changed them forever. It has affected virtually every aspect of society. It is a macrosystem of interconnected private and public spheres: household, literary, academic, business, and government networks. The Internet has produced major leaps forward in human productivity and has changed the way people work, study, and interact with each other. The mix of open standards, diverse networks, and the growing ubiquity of digital devices makes the Internet a revolutionary force that undermines traditional media and challenges existing regulatory institutions based on national boundaries. The Internet has created new markets and is profoundly changing the way people interact, find leisure, explore the world, and think about human phenomena. In the Internet age, people often have cyber life in addition to their offline life. The two are not necessarily one and the same.

Information is organized and exchange is enabled on the Internet by the World Wide Web. Websites have addresses, based on their unique Universal Resource Locator (URL), which allows users to locate and exchange information using a web browser (White, 2006, pp. 14–15). The Internet has no central management or coordination, and the routing computers do not retain copies of the packets they handle. The Internet's design and *raison d'être* are complete freedom, but soon enough people began to exploit the Net's massive potential to enhance partisan interests, some of which are harmful and antisocial. As can be expected, given that the Internet has been a part of our lives for a relatively short time, the discussions concentrate on the social production, technological, architectural, geographical aspects of the Net (Benkler, 2006; Kellerman, 2002; Lessig, 1999, 2002, 2004;

The Handbook of Global Communication and Media Ethics, First Edition. Edited by Robert S. Fortner and P. Mark Fackler.
© 2011 Blackwell Publishing Ltd. Published 2011 by Blackwell Publishing Ltd.

Schneider and Evans, 2007; Slevin, 2000; Zittrain, 2008 to name a few). The discussions about the costs and harms of the Internet, and how to address them, are – on the other hand – in their infancy. The transnational nature of the Internet makes it very difficult, some say virtually impossible, for national authorities to unilaterally implement laws and regulations that reflect national, rather than global, moral standards (Thornburgh and Lin, 2002; National Research Council 2001).

Generally speaking, the Internet is perceived as a free highway, and the way to combat problematic speech is said to be by more speech. In the United States, still the home of the majority of Internet sites in the world and the land of the First Amendment, emphasis is put on education (Atkinson, n.d; Boucher, n.d; Corn-Revere, 2003a, 2003b; Harris, n.d.; Head, 2005; Moreno-Riano, 2006; Nakaya, 2005; Nelson, 1998; Rutkowski, n.d.; Thierer and Crews (2003) and Shiffrin and Silberschatz, 2005, among others). Organizations and associations were set up to protect and promote freedom of expression, freedom of information, and privacy on the Internet.[1] The dangers of the Internet are recognized but it is commonly argued that the Free Speech Principle shields all but the most immediately threatening expression. In the United States, among the limited boundaries to free expression on the Net are direct and specific calls for murder ("true threats"),[2] child pornography, direct calls for terrorism and spreading of viruses and material protected by copyright legislation. On the other hand, threats of general nature, hatred, bigotry, racism, instructions how to kill and maim, how to seduce children, are protected forms of speech under the First Amendment. Speech is afforded protection except when a life-threatening message is directed against identified individuals.[3] Blanket statements expressing hatred toward certain groups are given free sway, even if individual members of such groups are put at risk.[4] For free speech advocates, the substantive danger is that of censorship. Freedom of expression is perceived as a fundamental human right and censorship should not be allowed to inhibit the Net's free flow of information. Salimipour (2001/2002) argued that government actions "limiting the spread of harmful content should be carefully designed to ensure that measures taken do not restrict hate or offensive speech on the Internet" (Salimipour, 2001/2002, p. 395). This statement may sound strange to European ears but American courts have followed this doctrine in cyberspace, affording this form of speech broad protection. Thus, most hate speech on the Internet will not be considered threats, harassment, fighting words, or libel, since it is generally directed broadly and not at a particular person (Delgado and Stefancic, 2004, p. 127).

Most Netusers act within the law. The argument is that we cannot punish the majority of users because of the small numbers who exploit the Internet. Therefore, in the United States there are far more protections on free expression than restrictions on speech. We should not allow the abusers to dictate the rules of the game. We should of course fight against those who abuse this freedom.

In this essay I wish to address the ethical problems rooted in technology in response to potential risks on the Internet. The Internet is not the problem. The problem arises when it is utilized to undermine our wellbeing as autonomous beings living in free societies. This study focuses on articulating possible solutions to specific problems and on providing a framework within which these problems can be identified and resolved by accentuating the concepts of moral and social responsibility. It strives to suggest an approach informed by the experiences of democratic societies with different norms and legal cultures; one that harnesses the strengths and capabilities of Internet users in offering practical solutions to pressing problems. The second section introduces the underpinning concepts of this essay, moral and social responsibility. The following section discusses the responsibility of people who are using the Internet, Net agents. The final section focuses on readers' responsibilities. Do readers of websites have any moral and social responsibility to warn against potentially harmful uses of the Net which might be translated into real, practical harms?

Moral and Social Responsibility

We need to distinguish between legal, moral, and social responsibility. Legal responsibility refers to addressing the issue by agencies of state power. In moral responsibility, the personal responsibility of the agent to conscience is at issue, with appeals to moral consideration. Social responsibility relates to the societal implications of a given conduct.

Aristotle was the first to construct a theory of moral responsibility. In discussing human virtues and their corresponding vices, Aristotle in *Nicomachean Ethics* III.1–5 explores their underpinnings (Aristotle, 1962). He states that it is sometimes appropriate to respond to an agent with praise or blame on the basis of her actions and/or dispositional traits of character. Of course, if one is acting out of coercion one cannot be held responsible for one's deeds. One is responsible when one is informed, aware of what one does (1110b15–25). Only a certain kind of agent qualifies as a moral agent and is thus properly subject to ascriptions of responsibility, namely, one who possess a capacity for decision. For Aristotle, a decision is a particular kind of desire resulting from free deliberation, one that expresses the agent's conception of what is good. Choice is important, to have desirable ends and relevant means to pursue the end (1111b15–1113b22). Aristotle spells out the conditions under which it is appropriate to hold a moral agent blameworthy or praiseworthy for some particular action or trait. He proposes that one is an apt candidate for praise or blame if and only if the action and/or disposition are voluntary. A voluntary action or trait has two distinctive features: the action or trait must have its origin in the agent. That is, it must be up to the agent whether to perform that action or possess the trait – it cannot be compelled externally. The agent must be aware of what it is she is doing or bringing about (1110a–1111b4) (Aristotle, 1962).[5]

Thus, by moral responsibility it is meant that autonomous agents have the understanding of the options before them, have access to evidence required for making judgments about the benefits and hazards of each option, and able to weigh the relative value of the consequences of their choice.

In a recent article, William J. FitzPatrick further explains that all cases of moral responsibility for bad actions must involve a strong form of akrasia, that is acting against one's better judgment (FitzPatrick, 2008, p. 590). If an agent does something bad, either she does so in full knowledge that she should not be doing it, which is clear-eyed akrasia, or the agent is acting from ignorance. In the former cases the agent will be held responsible. In the latter case whether the agent is responsible or not will depend on whether or not the agent's ignorance is culpable. The agent's ignorance will be culpable only if the agent is responsible for some earlier failure that gave rise to that ignorance. And the agent will be responsible for that earlier failure again only if that was a case of clear-eyed akrasia. We do not establish culpability until we arrive at a relevant episode of clear-eyed akrasia (FitzPatrick, 2008, p. 593). Ignorance, whether circumstantial or normative, is culpable if the agent could reasonably have been expected to take measures that would have corrected or avoided it, given the agent's capabilities and the opportunities provided by the social context, but failed to do so either due to akrasia or due to vices such as overconfidence, arrogance, dismissiveness, laziness, dogmatism, incuriosity, self-indulgence and contempt (FitzPatrick, 2008, p. 609).

The accompanying concept of social responsibility refers to the responsibility of individuals, groups, corporations, and governments to society. People are not islands to themselves. We live within a community and have some responsibilities to it. The responsibilities are positive and negative. That is, we have a responsibility to better the society in which we live, and a responsibility to refrain from acting in a way that knowingly might harm our community. The responsibility is ethical in nature. The assumption is that we are rewarded by the social framework in which we live, we care about society, would like to maintain it and to contribute to it. The contribution is proactive. We take active steps to do good and to avoid harm.[6] We care for one another, communicate with respect and do not stand idly by while seeing that others might be in danger.

In the Internet age, an interesting phenomenon emerged that confuses the concept of moral and social responsibility. In the offline, real world, people know that they are responsible for the consequences of their conduct, speech as well as action. In the online, cyberworld, we witness responsibility shake-off. You can assume your dream identity and then anything goes. The Internet has a dis-inhibition effect. The freedom allows language one would dread to use in real life, words one need not abide by, imagination that trumps conventional norms and standards. It is about time to bring to the fore discussion about morality.

Agent's Responsibility

An agent is morally responsible insofar as the agent has the capacity to choose ends freely and act in accordance with such choices (Fischer, 1999, p. 96). An agent would be held accountable for speech that directly led to harm. The issue is more complicated when it is impossible to prove a direct link between the Net posting and the real harm. However, please bear in mind that the subject at hand is moral, not legal responsibility. To be legally culpable it is incumbent on the prosecution to show that the speech under scrutiny directly led to the harmful action. Preaching is all right. Incitement is illegal. This is in accordance with John Stuart Mill's theory, in which he was the first to distinguish between advocacy and incitement (Mill, 1982). However, no such temporal association is insisted upon when we speak of moral culpability. There are many cases in which it will be difficult to prove legal responsibility but the speech still might seem morally wrong and we will hold the Net speaker as accountable. An agent will be held responsible for bad conduct when the agent clearly intends to "do bad" or when the agent can be held culpable for ignorance in making bad choices. As Aristotle said, an autonomous agent is aware of her action.

Words can wound. Words can hurt. Words can move people to action. The anonymity of the Internet is most convenient for spreading unfounded allegations, for backstabbing, for malicious rumors. JuicyCampus.com (Juicy Campus, n.d.a) became a focus of attention in recent years as it had been used to ruin the name of young people. The site described itself as "the world's most authentic college website, with content generated by college students for college students. Just remember, keep it Juicy!" The site contained a variety of information, data, messages, and other materials that users of the site created and posted, including detailing sexual activities of named individuals, their physical attributes (D.P., on the site the full name was explicit, "has the hairiest asshole in the world. You try to go down on her and you get lost in the dirty tangled bush. Seriously that shit makes me want to vom. Like wtf go get your asshole waxed and get those old stinky dingle berries out of there. Like wtf and get a tan holy shit i could use you as a fucking night light. skank.") (Juicy Campus, n.d.b), that your named dorm mate was spreading sexual diseases, attacks on people's integrity, accusing students of using others for social climbing, and so on. The site's managers were well aware of what was done in their forum. They did not care.

The site's terms and conditions unsurprisingly said the following:

> Please use caution and common sense when viewing the Site. You understand and agree that any Content is the exclusive responsibility of the person who posted it, and that you will be solely responsible for any Content that you post via the Site. You acknowledge that JuicyCampus is not responsible for, does not control, does not endorse and does not verify the Content posted to the Site or available through the Site, and that it makes no guarantee regarding the reliability, accuracy, legitimacy or quality of any such Content. You agree that you will bear any and all risk of reliance on the accuracy, validity or legitimacy of such Content. You agree that JuicyCampus has no obligation to monitor the reliability, accuracy, legitimacy or quality of such Content, nor to enforce any standards … in connection with such Content. Under no circumstances will JuicyCampus be liable in any way to you for any Content, including, but not limited to, any errors or omissions in any Content or any loss or damage of any kind incurred as a result of the use or existence of or exposure to any Content posted or otherwise transmitted via the Site (Juicy Campus, n.d.c).

Most if not all the comments posted on the site were anonymous and JuicyCampus did not remove posts based on students' objections. "The second someone's name appears on the site, it's a death sentence," said one student (Holahan, 2008). This, of course, was an exaggeration, but it showed the extent people were troubled by this influential website. Behind the shield of anonymity, agents dust away all responsibility. JuicyCampus closed down on January 5, 2009[7] but on other forums people can say whatever they wish, notwithstanding how damaging, defamatory, or degrading their words might be, without expecting to be accountable for the consequences.

To counter JuicyCampus, Connor Diemand-Yauman, 20-year-old president of the Princeton 2010 class, created a new website, OwnWhatYouThink.com, that asks students to pledge not to visit anonymous gossip sites and to stand behind their online statements. Own What You Think seeks to unite people and bring personal accountability back into the ways in which people communicate and interact with each other. It is about encouraging individuals to voice their opinions respectfully and constructively while refusing to participate in anonymous and malicious character assassination. This refreshing initiative is also about taking a personal stand for something and encouraging others to do the same. Ultimately, "Own What You Think is about collaborating, dissenting, learning, and disagreeing in a constructive manner that allows us to grow as individuals and a society as a whole."[8] "This is about changing the way our generation and our culture look at the way we communicate with one another," Diemand-Yauman explained. "Anonymity = Cowardice" (Holahan, 2008).

On the Web we find extensive discussions on suicide pills[9] and "exit bags" (do-it-yourself suicide kit).[10] In 2005, in Japan alone there were more than 17 000 Japanese websites that offered information on suicide and its methods (Hagihara, Tarumi, and Abe, 2007). One site calls on people to "save the planet, kill yourself."[11] It advises people to "do a good job" when they commit suicide, saying: "Suicide is hard work. It's easy to do it badly, or make rookie mistakes. As with many things, the best results are achieved by thorough research and careful preparation."[12] The site goes on to discuss the pros and cons of death by shooting, hanging, crashing a car, jumping, slitting your wrists, drowning, freezing, overdosing or gassing yourself with nitrous oxide, exhaust fumes and oven gas. Another site describes using guns, overdosing, slashing one's wrists, and hanging as the "best methods to commit suicide." Other site titles suggested various suicide methods (Malamuth, Linz, and Yao, 2005). Yet another site illustrated various methods including lethal doses of poison, their availability, estimated time of death, and degrees of certainty methods (Malamuth, Linz, and Yao, 2005). Notwithstanding the extent of the agents' liberalism, they should consider the prudence of such postings given the vulnerability of the people that such sites might attract. Indeed, some people report being encouraged to use suicide as a problem solving strategy by suicide web forums. Cases of cybersuicide, attempted or successful suicides influenced by the Internet, were documented (Biddle *et al.*, 2007; Beatson, Hosty, and Smith, 2000; Cubby, 2007, Thompson 1999). The Internet facilitates group suicides, providing a forum for like-minded people to meet in order to arrange their collective death.[13] Thus, such a behavior that encourages suicide constitutes a clear-eyed akrasia, behavior that is stripped of any moral and social responsibility that cannot be justified nor legitimized.

In November 2008 a federal statute designed to combat computer crimes was used for the first time to prosecute what were essentially abuses of a user agreement on a social networking site. Previously this statute was used to address hacking. Let me discuss this tragic story in some detail.

The Meier tragedy

Lori Drew, 49, her daughter Sarah, who was then 13, and Ashley Grills, 19, a family friend and employee, created on the computer mediated community, MySpace,[14] a fictitious teenage boy "Josh Evans" to communicate with Sarah's nemesis, Megan Meier, who was 13 and had a history of depression and suicidal impulses. Meier received treatment for attention deficit disorder and depression and had been in counseling since third grade (Deutsch, 2008b; Jones, 2008). "Josh's" profile and communications were geared to the needs of an insecure and volatile teenage girl, carefully designed to exploit Megan's vulnerabilities and to play on her emotions. After six weeks of online courtship with "Josh" who told Megan he loved her "so much," (Deutsch, 2008a) in October 2006 "Josh" suddenly wrote to Megan "I don't want to be friends with you anymore because you're not nice to your friends" (McFadden and Fulginiti, 2008). The distraught Megan tried to understand why "Josh" no longer wanted to be her friend, involving her MySpace friends in a discussion. The query escalated into a barrage of insults and fierce exchanges. Megan received other emails from "Josh" in which he called her "fat" and "slut," (Jones, 2007) and that "You're a shitty person, and the world would be a better place without you in it" (Collins, 2008). Shortly after that last message was sent, Megan wrote back, "You're the kind of boy a girl would kill herself over" (Steinhauer, 2008). Megan hanged herself that same afternoon in her bedroom. Drew, who masterminded the cyber affair, was convicted of computer fraud in creating a phony account to trick Megan and obtaining information in order to inflict emotional distress on the girl. The indictment charged Drew and her coconspirators for using "the information obtained over the MySpace computer system to torment, harass, humiliate, and embarrass the juvenile MySpace member" (Deutsch, 2008b).

Undoubtedly, Lori Drew and her coconspirators are blameworthy and morally culpable for her involvement in this tragedy, for playing on Megan's emotions in a crude and cynical way without thinking which way this game might lead. They were fully aware of what they were doing. No one coerced them to take this crude path. They chose it freely, exhibiting a strong form of clear-eyed akrasia, acting against their adult better judgment. Megan's parents discovered the Drews' involvement six weeks after the suicide. Then the Drews sent the grieving parents a letter in the mail, "basically saying that they might feel a little bit of a responsibility but they don't feel no guilt or remorse or anything for what they did"

(Lauer and Lewis, 2007). One month after Megan's death, Drew told sheriff's deputies that the neighborhood had grown hostile because people had "found out her involvement in Megan's suicide." The report recounts Drew's admission that she "instigated and monitored" the fake MySpace profile (Jones, 2008). Later on, when Drew realized that she might be held responsible for the vicious prank she orchestrated, she tried to shrink the magnitude of her involvement. Ashley Grills said after the tragedy that Drew suggested talking to Megan via the Internet to find out what Megan was saying about her daughter. Soon "Josh" began to flirt with Megan. Grills admitted she wrote the message to Megan about the world being a better place without her. The message was supposed to end the online relationship with "Josh" because Grills felt the joke had gone too far. Indeed it did. "I was trying to get her angry so she would leave him alone and I could get rid of the whole MySpace," Grills explained (Sawyer and Roberts, 2008; Deutsch, 2008b). The result was the Megan left the world. The messages distressed Megan and caused her so much pain that she decided to take her life.

Megan's weaknesses were well known to the Drews. She had accompanied the Drews on several vacations, and they knew that she was taking medication (Collins, 2008). Still they carried out the deception for weeks. They must have been aware of the rollercoaster state they had entrusted upon Megan. The initial idea of knowing what Megan thought about their daughter escalated very quickly into an online affair. After the suicide, Lori Drew denied her involvement, pointing the finger at Grills as the mastermind of the hoax. Grills insisted that Lori was deeply involved in the deception. Lori never took responsibility, saying that she did not create or direct anyone to create the fake MySpace account. Grills, on the other hand, said that was not true and was willing to take responsibility for her part. Grills said that Kurt Drew, Lori's husband who also became involved in this tragedy, insisted after the suicide that she quickly close the MySpace account, and that Lori instructed her to keep quiet. Grills maintained that she and the Drews are blameworthy: "I'm partially to blame. They are partially to blame ... I do know what I did, and I take responsibility for it every day" (Sawyer and Roberts, 2008).

What about parental responsibility? Knowing Meagan's delicate personality, her parents were proactive in trying to protect her. They authorized Megan's MySpace account, with some restrictions: "1. Your dad and I are the only ones who know the password. 2. It has to be set to 'private.' 3. We have to approve the content. 4. We have to be in the room at all times when you're on MySpace" (Collins, 2008). Only the parents had the password to the account. Megan could not sign on without them. One of the parents was in the room watching (Lauer and Lewis, 2007). Megan had a timed amount online, usually in the presence of her mother (Lauer and Larson, 2007). The vigilant parents could log into the account at anytime. They monitored her Internet use. They were aware of Megan's MySpace friends. They were reluctant to authorize the contact with "Josh," as Meagan did not know him. Only after she begged and insisted to have contact with that "hot" guy did they agree to add him to Megan's list of friends (Stossel, Vargas, and Roberts, 2007). Still, Tina Meier warned Megan of this guy, as he could be for all they knew a

Responsibility of Net Users

"40-year-old pervert" (Stossel, Vargas, and Roberts, 2007). She even called the police to see whether there was a way to confirm who owned the "Josh" account (Collins, 2008). She was told there was nothing to do unless a crime had been committed (Jones, 2008). Megan's parents did not wish to force their daughter to delete "Josh" as they knew this would upset Megan and would cause a bitter rivalry. At least, so they thought, this way they could monitor the chats and Megan does not go behind their backs. Megan called her mother when "Josh" suddenly turned against her. Tina returned home and saw her daughter distraught. She turned the computer off (Jones, 2008), thinking that Megan needed some time to calm down. Yet despite this direct and observant involvement, more vigilant than the involvement of most parents, Megan's parents did not prevent the tragedy.

The story of Megan Meier is tragic but unfortunately it is not unique. Cyberbullying (typically teenagers targeting, humiliating and/or intimidating other minors, typically among teens who know each other from school, neighborhood or after-school activities) charged more victims who could not cope with the malicious attacks and the vile language.[15] Research shows that almost one in four children between the ages of 11 and 19 have been the victim of cyberbullying. The same research shows that approximately 65% of kids know of someone who has been cyberbullied.[16] According to a national phone survey of 935 teenagers conducted by Pew Internet and American Life in November 2006, one in three online teens have experienced online harassment. Teens who share their identities and thoughts on social networking sites, such as MySpace and Facebook, are more likely to be targets than are those who do not use social networking sites. Nearly 4 in 10 social network users (39%) have been cyberbullied in some way, compared with 22% of online teens who do not use social networks (Reich, 2008). Internet agents should be made aware of the consequences of their free expression.[17] Stories like that of Megan Meier should be brought to classes and discussed openly and fervently. People, especially young people, should be made aware of the power of the word and settle the confusion between online and offline responsibility. Sites like www.netsmartz.org and http://kids.getnetwise.org/tools/ are instrumental in providing information and promoting awareness regarding the possible harms of social networking forums on the Internet. We need to teach our children that silence, when others are being hurt, is not acceptable. Safety should be maintained online and offline and studies should be carried out about the connections between the two. As stopcyberbullying.org holds, the task is to create a generation of good cybercitizens, controlling the technology instead of being controlled by it.[18] Agents are morally and socially responsible for all their conduct, whether in the cyber or physical environment.

Internet users, when acting collectively, have power – they are able to change companies' policies and conduct. Yahoo!, a US-based Internet service provider, had adult items on its shopping pages since 1999. Then, in 2001 it quietly expanded its offering of hard-core videos and DVDs in search of new revenue. When the *Los Angeles Times* reported this, the company was swamped with angry calls and emails. Under pressure, Yahoo! announced that it would stop selling X-rated videos and other pornographic material on its webpages. It would also stop entering into new contracts for banner advertisements for adult merchandise. Yahoo! has also come under fire for serving as a host to online chats by hate groups (Bergstein, 2001). It began donating ad space in the chat rooms to Tolerance.org, set up by the Southern Poverty Law Center. The ads also appear when users enter words such as "Nazi" or "hate" on Yahoo! search engine (Bergstein, 2001). Agents' collective action, driven by moral and social responsibility considerations, may affect business to better their Internet conduct in fear of revenue losses.

Readers' Responsibility

John is walking on the beach listening to his IPod. He sees a little child drowning in the water nearby. John is a good swimmer and could easily save the child, but he decides to keep on walking, enjoying the music he loves so much. John leaves the little child to his own fate, and the child drowns. Following Aristotle, we would hold John morally culpable for his decision to walk away and for the tragic consequences of his failure to act. He voluntarily chose to enjoy his music over saving the little child's life. It is a case of clear-eyed akrasia. There was no ignorance, only self-indulgence and contempt for human life.

Now consider a person who posts on the Internet a desire to blow up the world and to exit the world stage in a hail of fire, leaving corpses behind him. Suppose James reads this posting on the Net. Is he morally culpable to try and stop that person? If he does not, can we hold him morally responsible for failure to act?

As the Internet continues to grow, the responsibility of the reader is especially important in the identification of new websites that serve as a vehicle for the expression of murderous thought that potentially leads to murderous action.

Kimveer Gill was a 25 year-old man from Montreal who decided to depart the world, leaving corpses behind him. He voiced his aim explicitly on an Internet site called VampireFreaks.com. Gill was not reprimanded for his postings on vampire-Freaks.com. Quite the contrary; he received moral support from his website friends. On Tuesday, September 12, 2006, just a day before he went on rampage shooting at Dowson College in Montreal, "Caranya," a 19-year-old member from Indiana, wrote to Kimveer, "Can I go play with you?? I wanna go hunt down the preppies with you!" (Hanes, Silcoff, and Hamilton, 2006). Subsequent postings from visitors to Caranya's webpage were not kind: "Congratulations on inspiring a psycho to go on a murderous rampage killing innocent kids," wrote one. Another posted: "One has to wonder where he was able to get his moral support from" (Lithwick, 2006) Gill's blog was immediately removed after the killing, but not before a stream of online comments were posted, most of them denouncing Gill. However, one read: "I've been to Dawson College. The people there are so superficial I actually thought about shooting the school up myself. Thank you, unknown guy with a Mohawk. I salute you" (Robertson, 2006). A 16-year-old VampireFreaks member named Melissa from Sherbrooke, Quebec expressed her surprise that Gill was responsible for the Montreal tragedy. "I found him super cool," she said, "There was nothing strange about his blog" (Agrell, 2006). There was nothing strange in the fact that his screen name was Fatality666. Apparently there was nothing strange that his favorite video game was Super Columbine Massacre. Nothing strange in the way Gill described himself: "His name is Trench. You will come to know him as the Angel of Death ... He is not a people person. He has met a handful of people in his life who are decent. But he finds the vast majority to be worthless, no good, conniving, betraying, lying, deceptive" (Couvrette, 2006b). Indeed, apparently there was nothing strange in the pictures that Gill chose to upload, more than 50 pictures depicting him dressed like his heroes from Columbine, long black trench coat and boots to match while carrying various weapons. In one of the pictures, titled "You're next," he was seen pointing a handgun at the camera (Pona, 2006). In another picture he held a sign in order to deliver a message – "My Gothic Princess Leaves a Trail of Tears. God Has Forsaken Her. God Will Pay" (*Toronto Sun*, 2006) In his last photo on the VampireFreaks blog, he was wearing his signature trench coat and holding up an automatic weapon with a text message "ready for action" (*National Post*, 2006). The readers found nothing strange in the fact that Gill decided to post a virtual tombstone on which he wrote "Kimveer – Lived fast. Died young. Left a mangled corpse" (Couvrette, 2006a). Apparently there was also nothing strange in the list of a vast array of people, places, and things that he hated, among them were comedies, governments, sunlight, and country music.[19] The readers of VampireFreaks.com who saw all this information and said nothing should have had better judgment.

In spite of the very violent messages included in Kimveer Gill's profile and postings, nobody reported him to the police. The readers' failure to report this disturbed state of mind involves a strong form of akrasia. Readers of websites should be alert of problematic postings, and speak out when they read warnings of troubled individuals who seem to be on verge of explosion. Teachers, administrators, parents and peers, often are the first-hand recipients of the expressions of rage. They can help prevent violence by seeking treatment for people showing the type of behavior that might erupt into violence (Swanson and Nguyen, 2007). Web readers should contact police if they see information that looks like a threat to public safety.

Jed Kahane, who covered the Gill murder story from the very beginning for CTV, reported that one of the questions everyone raised in Montreal after the rampage was "how could Kimveer Gill post such violent pictures on his own website and talk about it for so long and no one bothered to report him or raise an alarm bell" (Oliver and Taber, 2006).

In the aftermath of the Megan Meier's suicide new websites popped up to commemorate Megan, but also another startling site named Meganhaditcoming.com. The anonymous blogger claimed to be a former classmate of Megan's. She described Megan in vicious terms as an aggressive, vulgar and unpopular girl who victimized the Drew girl. More than 5000 comments were posted within three days – many of them denouncing the blog as "sick" and suggesting it was the work of the Drews (Jones, 2008).

Internet hotlines

An important initiative is the voluntary establishment of Internet hotlines, by Internet Services Providers from different countries. The term "hotline" characterizes organizations ensuring communication from users about Internet content they find of significant concern. Such communication can take place by phone, fax or email. The connection is usually qualified by easy accessibility, high availability, and an assured response. Some hotlines in the private sector where enterprises offer direct access to "help desks" or related services dealing with consumer and client requests (Waltermann and Mahill, 2000, p. 46).

Hotlines have to be transparent. Users should be aware – at the point of entry – of the persons/organizations responsible for running the hotline system and those persons and organizations on whose behalf hotlines are operated. Transparency also means that the rules and procedures according to which concerns are being processed and explained at the point of entry: for example, which concerns will not be processed; which concerns will be handled over, when, under what criteria and to which public authorities. The system should be explained in sufficient detail and additional help should be available (Waltermann and Machill, 2000, p. 48).

Users should have the ability to track their concern throughout the process and they should be informed of the final outcome of the process. To this end, hotline operators should be informed accordingly by public authorities so that they can provide this information. Organizations running hotline systems should, at regular intervals, make publicly available reports on the basic statistics and experiences with their systems (Waltermann and Machill, 2000, p. 49). Parents and teachers can become involved in children's Internet activities and establish healthy Internet-use guidelines and principles (Weimann, 2006, p. 235).

In Britain, the IWF Hotline provides internet users with a means of reporting potentially illegal content that are located on websites, newsgroups and online groups.[20] Police officials have set up an online network that young people can use to report crimes anonymously without having to tell their parents. The tactic has worked well in catching pedophiles.[21] Through hotlines, anyone can make a report of something they suspect to be illegal on the Internet. The hotline investigates these reports to determine if they are illegal, and if so, trace the origin of the content. If the content is illegal, the hotline refers this onwards to local law enforcement agencies as well as the Internet Service Provider for removal.

In the United States, since 1998 the Department of Justice is funding the CyberTipline®, at www.cybertipline.com. The cyber tip line is operated by the National Center for Missing and Exploited Children to act as a national clearing-house for reports of Internet-related child pornography and other Internet-related sex crimes committed against children.[22] The majority of concerns are with child pornography, child prostitution, and child sex tourism (Wolak, Finkelhor, and Mitchell, 2005).[23] A 24-hour, toll-free telephone line, 1-800-THE-LOST® (1-800-843-5678), is available in Canada, Mexico, and the United States for those who have information regarding missing and exploited children. Similar hotlines are suggested for alerts about violent messages that threat committing of murders. Readers who might not wish to alert the police directly should be able to contact a similar cyber tip line and evoke attention to violent threats and signals.

Some of the existing hotlines are associated in a global organization named INHOPE (The International Association of Internet Hotlines),[24] which enjoys the support of law enforcement agencies, local governments, and child welfare organizations. As sites can be accessed by anyone anywhere, illegal content may be reported by a person in one country, while the site can be hosted somewhere else. Once the source is traced, hotlines pass reports over to the relevant country. INHOPE has set processes for exchanging reports, to ensure a rapid response is taken. These hotlines deal mainly with three sorts of illegal contents: child pornography, illegal activity in chat rooms, and hate speech[25] as well as with online grooming (mostly pedophiles preying on children).[26] The 2007 Global Internet Trend Report[27] reveals that most reports refer to child pornography (50%), adult pornography (28%) and other child related-content (19%). Only 0.7% of the reports (an average of 130 reports per month) refer to other illegal contents, a category which is comprised of promoting violence against an individual, terrorism and drugs.[28]

The use of hotlines can establish new routes of communication between users, in particular, parents, media-industry initiatives, and law enforcement authorities. A hotline enables users to respond to illegal Internet content by drawing attention to where it is to be found. The hotline receives the report and, if necessary, sets in motion a process of response. The response includes processing the report, providing the user with feedback and a decision about whether to forward the report to law enforcement or a self-regulatory authority (Waltermann and Machill, 2000).

Conclusion

The Internet is a vast ocean of knowledge, data, ideologies, and propaganda. It is ubiquitous, interactive, fast, and decentralized. The ease of access to the Internet, its low cost and speed, its chaotic structure (or lack of structure), the anonymity which individuals and groups may enjoy, and the international character of the world wide web furnish all kinds of individuals and organizations an easy and effective arena for their partisan interests. It contains some of the best products of humanity, and some of the worst ones. It serves the positive and negative elements in society.

The Internet does not have any borders but it does have limits. Its short history provides us with a crash course in understanding why order is preferable to anarchy, and why a balanced approach is needed to address and resolve conflicting freedoms. People have the freedom to express themselves, within reason. Two underpinning principles, in the heart of liberal democracy, are respect for others, and not harming others. We should strive to uphold them also on the Internet.

In this essay I stressed the concepts of moral responsibility and of social responsibility. We can reasonably expect people to know and to take certain steps to know the difference between good and bad, between that which is of benefit and that which is evil, and then to act accordingly. Given the agents' social context, basic capabilities and the level of knowledge people are expected to cooperate in the struggle against antisocial activities on the Internet. Readers may encounter problematic material during their surf of the Internet. They should contact the authorities via a tip line and alert about the problematic content.

Acknowledgments

I thank Janet Spikes for her excellent research assistance, and to Sam Lehman-Wilzig for his constructive comments.

Notes

All websites, unless otherwise stated, were last accessed between February 5 and February 8, 2009.

1 Among them are The Center for Democracy and Technology (CDT), http://cdt.org/ ; The Electronic Frontier Foundation (EFF), www.eff.org/; The Electronic Privacy Information Center (EPIC), http://epic.org/ ; The Global Internet Liberty Campaign (GILC), http://gilc.org/; The Internet Society, www.isoc.org/; The Association for Progressive Communication, www.apc.org; Save the Internet, http://savetheinternet.com/

2 A statement is a "true threat" when a reasonable person making the statement would foresee that the statement would be interpreted by those to whom it is communicated as a serious expression of an intent to bodily harm or assault. See *Planned Parenthood of Columbia/Willamette, Inc. v. Am. Coalition of Life Activists*, 290 F.3d 1058, 1080 (9th Cir. 2002). See also *Watts v. United States*, 394 U.S. 705 (1969); *United States v. Kelner*, 534 F.2d 1020 (2d Cir. 1976); Rothman (2001); Andrews (1999); Karst (2006).

3 In *Planned Parenthood of the Columbia/Willamette, Inc. v. American Coalition of Life Activists*, 23 F. Supp. 2d 1182 (D. OR 1999), an Internet site listed the names and home addresses of doctors who performed abortions. The site called for the doctors to be brought to justice for crimes against humanity. The names of doctors who had been wounded were listed in gray. Doctors who had been killed by antiabortionists had been crossed out. The court found this speech to be threatening and not protected under the First Amendment. See Delgado and Stefancic, (2004): 127. Another pertinent case is *The Secretary, United States Department of Housing and Urban Development, on behalf of Bonnie Jouhari and Pilar Horton v. Ryan Wilson and ALPHA HQ*, before Alan W. Heifetz, Chief Administrative Law Judge (decided July 19, 2000), available at www.hud.gov/utilities/intercept.cfm?/offices/oalj/cases/fha/pdf/wilson.pdf

4 See Anti-Defamation League (2000); Delgado and Stefancic (2004, p. 127).

5 For further discussion, see Meyer (1993); "Moral Responsibility," *Stanford Encyclopedia of Philosophy* (2004).

6 See Kaliski (2001); Marshall (1994); Christians and Nordenstreng (2004); Bunton (1998); Rivers, Schramm, and Christians (1980).

Responsibility of Net Users   429

7   Juicy Campus published the following: "Unfortunately, even with great traffic and
    strong user loyalty, a business can't survive and grow without a steady stream of reve-
    nue to support it. In these historically difficult economic times, online ad revenue has
    plummeted and venture capital funding has dissolved. JuicyCampus' exponential
    growth outpaced our ability to muster the resources needed to survive this economic
    downturn, and as a result, we are closing down the site as of Feb. 5, 2009." http://
    juicycampus.blogspot.com/ (last accessed February 4, 2009).

8   http://ownwhatyouthink.com/

9   www.saves.asn.au/resources/newsletter/jul1998/item4.php; http://kittyradio.com/
    soapbox/mental-health/25048-suicide-sleeping-pills.html

10 www.beliefnet.com/News/2002/07/Exit-Bags-Stir-Up-Death-Debate.aspx; www.ncbi.
    nlm.nih.gov/pubmed/12043438;www.finalexitnetwork.org/newsletter/newsletter1204.
    htm

11 www.churchofeuthanasia.org/index.html

12 www.churchofeuthanasia.org/index.html

13 http://news.walla.co.il/?w=/402/639665 (Hebrew).

14 MySpace is a social networking service that allows members to create unique personal
    profiles online in order to find and communicate with old and new friends. The services
    offered by MySpace include any MySpace branded URL (the "MySpace Website"), the
    MySpace instant messaging service, the MySpace application developer service and
    other features (for example, music and video embedded players), MySpace mobile serv-
    ices, and any other features, content, or applications offered from time to time by
    MySpace in connection with MySpace's business (collectively, the "MySpace Services").
    The MySpace Services are hosted in the United States. See www.myspace.com/
    index. cfm?fuseaction=misc.terms. It is estimated that every month over 10 million
    American teens log on to MySpace.

15 Several suicides in the United States were recorded as the result of cyberbullying. Ryan
    Halligan was bullied relentlessly. He received emails and instant messages from class-
    mates ridiculing him and calling him a loser. When a pretty girl at school pretended to
    like him online but later revealed she was only joking, the taunting emails and instant
    messages increased, only with even more venom. A few weeks later, in October 2003,
    Ryan hanged himself in his family's bathroom. Like Megan, he was 13 years old. See
    Long (2008); Fink (2008). In the UK, Sam Leeson, a 13 year-old student from
    Tredworth, Gloucestershire, hanged himself in his bedroom apparently after suffering
    months of bullying online. See http://mashable.com/2008/06/14/bebo-suicide/

16 www.cyberbullying.info/whatis/whatis.php

17 For discussion on suicide and ethics, see Cohen-Almagor (2005).

18 www.stopcyberbullying.org/take_action/take_a_stand_against_cyberbullying.html

19 Killer likened life to a video game, *Globe and Mail* (September 15 2006): A9. For fur-
    ther discussion, see Cohen-Almagor and Haleva-Amir (2008).

20 www.iwf.org.uk/public/page.31.htm

21 Police virtually powerless to find killers online: experts (2006) *Cornwall Standard
    Freeholder* (Ontario), September 15, 8.

22 Also see www.missingkids.com/en_US/publications/NC144.pdf (accessed June 17,
    2010).

23 See www.missingkids.com/cybertip/ (accessed June 17, 2010). See also www.
    stopitnow.org/ (accessed June 17, 2010).

430   *Raphael Cohen-Almagor*

24 www.inhope.org/ (accessed June 17, 2010).
25 See "Anti-Semitism on the Internet, an overview," (April 28–29, 2004), www.inach.
    net/content/INACH%20-%20Antisemitism%20on%20the%20Internet.pdf (accessed
    June 17, 2010).
26 www.inhope.org/en/problem/overview.html
27 www.inhope.org/en/system/files/inhope_global_internet_trend_report_v1.0.pdf
28 www.inhope.org/en/system/files/inhope_global_internet_trend_report_v1.0.pdf,
    pp. 49, 61.

References

Agrell, S. (2006) Troubled kids gravitating to vampire site, *National Post*, September 15, A6.
Andrews, A.S. (1999) When is a threat "truly" a threat lacking First Amendment protec-
    tion? A proposed true threats test to safeguard free speech rights in the age of the
    Internet, *UCLA Online Institute for Cyberspace Law and Policy*, May.
Anti-Defamation League (2000) *Combating Extremism in Cyberspace: The Legal Issues
    Affecting Internet Hate Speech*, ADL, New York.
Aristotle (1962) *Nicomachean Ethics*, (ed. M. Ostwald), Bobbs-Merrill, Indianapolis, IN.
Atkinson, R.D. (n.d.) www.innovationpolicy.org (last accessed February 7, 2009).
Beatson, S., Hosty, G., and Smith, S. (2000) Suicide and the Internet, *Psychiatric Bulletin*,
    24, 434.
Benkler, Y. (2006) *The Wealth of Networks: How Social Production Transforms Markets and
    Freedom*, Yale University Press, New Haven, CT.
Bergstein, B. (2001) Yahoo takes the xxx out of its www, *The Philadelphia Inquirer*,
    April 14, A1.
Biddle, L., Donovan, J., Hawton, K. *et al.*, (2008) Suicide and the Internet, *British Medical
    Journal*, 336, 800–802.
Boucher, R. (n.d.) www.boucher.house.gov/
Bunton, K. (1998) Social responsibility in covering community: A narrative case study,
    Journal of Mass Media Ethics, 13 (4), 232–246.
Christians, C., and Nordenstreng, K. (2004) Social responsibility worldwide, *Journal of
    Mass Media Ethics*, 19 (1), 3–28.
Cohen-Almagor, R. (2005) *Speech, Media, and Ethics: The Limits of Free Expression* Palgrave-
    Macmillan, Houndmills and New York.
Cohen-Almagor, R., and Haleva-Amir, S. (2008) Bloody Wednesday in Dawson College –
    The story of Kimveer Gill, or why should we monitor certain websites to prevent mur-
    der, *Studies in Ethics, Law and Technology*, 2 (3), article 1.
Collins, L. (2008) Friend Game, *New Yorker*, 83 (44), January 21, 34–41.
Corn-Revere, R. (2003a) Caught in the seamless Web: Does the Internet's global reach
    justify *less* freedom of speech?, paper based on amicus brief in *Yahoo!, Inc. v. La Ligue
    Contre Le Racisme Et L'Antisemitisme*, Case No. 01-17424 (9th Cir.).
Corn-Revere, R. (2003b) *United States v. American Library Association*: A missed opportu-
    nity for the Supreme Court to clarify application of First Amendment Law to publicly-
    funded expressive institutions, in (eds A. Thierer and C.W. Crews), *Who Rules the Net?*,
    Cato Institute, Washington, WA.

Cornwall Standard Freeholder (Ontario) (2006) Police virtually powerless to find killers online: experts, September 15, 8.

Couvrette, P. (2006a) College gunman liked Columbine role-play, *Sun-Sentinel*, Fort Lauderdale, FL, September 15, 20A.

Couvrette, P. (2006b) Rampage shooter an angry loner, *Pittsburgh Post-Gazette*, September 15, A4.

Cubby, B. (2007) Lost in a tragic web: Internet death pacts increasing worldwide, *Sydney Morning Herald*, April 24, 2.

Delgado, R., and Stefancic, J. (2004) *Understanding Words That Wound*, Westview, Boulder, CO.

Deutsch, L. (2008a) Neighbor indicted in Missouri MySpace suicide case, *Associated Press Online*, May 16.

Deutsch, L. (2008b) Woman indicted in Missouri MySpace suicide case, *Associated Press Online*, May 16.

Fink, P. (2008) The case of a teenager who committed suicide after being bullied online shows that the Internet can be a weapon against the psychiatrically vulnerable. What can we do to help these patients?" *Clinical Psychiatry News* February 1.

Fischer, J.M. (1999) Recent work on moral responsibility, *Ethics*, 110, 93–139.

FitzPatrick, W.J. (2008) Moral responsibility and normative ignorance: Answering a new skeptical challenge, *Ethics*, 118, 590.

Globe and Mail (2006) Killer likened life to a video game, September 15, A9.

Hagihara, A., Tarumi, K., and Abe, T. (2007) Media suicide-reports, Internet use and the occurrence of suicides between 1987 and 2005 in Japan, *BMC Public Health*, vol. 7., 321, www.biomedcentral.com/1471-2458/7/321 (accessed June 17, 2010).

Hanes, A., Silcoff, S., and Hamilton, G. (2006) Gunman fantasized about rampage, *National Post*, September 15, A1.

Harris, L. (n.d.) www.cdt.org/staff/lharris.php (accessed June 30, 2010).

Head, T. (ed.) (2005) *The Future of the Internet*, Greenhaven Press, Farmington Hills, MI.

Holahan, C. (2008) The dark side of anonymity, *Business Week*, May 12.

Jones, T. (2007) Cyber-bullying by classmate's parents ends with teen's life, *Chicago Tribune* November 16.

Jones, T. (2008) A deadly web of deceit, *The Washington Post*, January 10.

Juicy Campus (n.d.a) www.juicycampus.com/posts/ (last accessed January 1, 2009).

Juicy Campus (n.d.b) www.juicycampus.com/posts/gossips/all-campuses/ (last accessed January 1, 2009).

Juicy Campus (n.d.c) www.juicycampus.com/posts/terms-condition (last accessed January 1, 2009).

Kaliski, B.S. (ed.) (2001) *Encyclopedia of Business and Finance*, Macmillan, New York.

Karst, K.L. (2006) Threats and meanings: How the facts govern first amendment doctrine, *Stanford Law Review*, 58 (March), 1337.

Kellerman, A. (2002) *The Internet on Earth: A Geography of Information*, Blackwell, Oxford.

Lauer, M., and Lewis, G. (2007) Teenager, Megan Meier, takes her own life after falling victim to a cruel Internet hoax; Megan's parents discuss importance of monitoring children's online activities, *NBC News Transcripts*, November 19.

Lauer, M., and Larson, J. (2007) Tina Meier talks about her daughter, Megan, who committed suicide over MySpace relationship that turned out to be hoax by adult neighbor, *NBC News Transcripts*, November 29.

Lessig, L. (1999) *Code and Other Laws of Cyberspace*, Basic Books, New York.

Lessig, L. (2002) *The Future of Ideas: The Fate of the Commons in a Connected World*, Vintage, New York.

Lessig, L. (2004) *Free Culture: How Big Media Uses Technology and the Law to Lock Down Culture and Control Creativity*, Penguin, New York.

Lithwick, D. (2006) Networking born killers, *Slate Magazine*, September 23.

Long, C. (2008) Silencing cyberbullies: Digital sticks & stones can't break bones–but they can hurt even more. What educators can do to curb bullying in cyberspace, *NEA Today*, May 1.

Malamuth, N.M., Linz, D., and Yao, M.Z. (2005) The Internet and aggression: Motivation, disinhibitory and opportunity aspects, in *The Social Net: Understanding Human Behavior in Cyberspace*, (ed. Y. Amichai-Hamburger), Oxford University Press, Oxford, pp. 163–190.

Marshall, M.L. (1994) Ensuring social responsibility, *Thrust for Educational Leadership*, 23 (4), 42–43.

McFadden, C., and Fulginiti, M. (2008) Searching for justice; online harassment, *ABC News Transcript*, March 24.

Meyer, S.S. (1993) *Aristotle on Moral Responsibility: Character and Cause*, Blackwell, Oxford.

Mill, J.S. (1982) *On Liberty*, London.

Moral Responsibility (2004) *Stanford Encyclopedia of Philosophy*, http://plato.stanford.edu/ (accessed June 17, 2010).

Moreno-Riano, G. (ed.) (2006) *Tolerance in the Twenty-first Century: Prospects and Challenges*, Lexington Books, Lanham, MD.

Nakaya, A.C. (ed.) (2005) *Censorship: Opposing Viewpoints*, Greenhaven, Farmington Hill, MI.

National Post (2006) Montreal shooting – The Blog: Excerpts "I hate this world … I hate so much." September 15, A4.

National Research Council (2001) *Global Networks and Local Values: A Comparative Look at Germany and the United States*, National Academy Press, Washington, DC.

Nelson, M.R. (1998) Sovereignty in the networked world, *Emerging Internet*, Aspen Institute, Queenstown, MD.

Oliver, C. and Taber, J. (2006) Jed Kahane on Montreal shooting, *CTV Television*, September 17.

Planned Parenthood of the Columbia/Willamette, Inc. v. American Coalition of Life Activists, 23 F. Supp. 2d 1182 (D. OR 1999).

Planned Parenthood of Columbia/Willamette, Inc. v. Am. Coalition of Life Activists, 290 F.3d 1058, 1080 (9th Cir. 2002).

Pona, N. (2006) Net violence unchecked, *Toronto Sun*, September 15, 4.

Reich, P.C. (2008) The Internet, suicide and legal responses, in *Cybercrime and Security* (ed. P.C. Reich), Oxford University Press, New York,.

Rivers, W.L., Schramm, W., and Christians, C.G. (1980) *Responsibility in Mass Communication*, Harper and Row, New York.

Robertson, L. (2006) Web links to shooting, *CTV Television*, September 14.

Rothman, J.E. (2001) Freedom of speech and true threats, *Harvard Journal of Law & Public Policy*, 25 (1), 283–367.

Rutkowski, T. (n.d.) www.itu.int/TELECOM/wt95/pressdocs/profiles/rutbio.html

Salimipour, N. (2001/2002) The challenge of regulating hate and offensive speech on the Internet," *Southwestern Journal of Law and Trade in the Americas*, 8, 395.

Sawyer, D., and Roberts, R. (2008) The MySpace suicide: Ashley Grills tells her story, *ABC News Transcript*, April 1 (online).

Schneider, G.P., and Evans, J. (2007) *New Perspectives on the Internet: Comprehensive*, Thomson, Boston.

Shiffrin, M.A., and Silberschatz, A. (2005) Web of the free, *The New York Times*, October 23.

Slevin, J. (2000) *The Internet and Society*, Polity Press, Oxford.

Stanford Encyclopedia of Philosophy (2004), http://plato.stanford.edu/ (accessed June 17, 2010).

Steinhauer, J. (2008) Verdict in MySpace suicide case, *New York Times*, November 27.

Stossel, J., Vargas, E., and Roberts, D. (2007) The hoax; MySpace suicide, *ABC News Transcript*, December 7.

Swanson, S., and Nguyen, K. (2007) Web rants raise red flags for violence: But police can do little to prevent attacks, *The Gazette*, Colorado Springs, CO, December 16.

The Secretary, United States Department of Housing and Urban Development, on behalf of Bonnie Jouhari and Pilar Horton v. Ryan Wilson and ALPHA HQ, before Alan W. Heifetz, Chief Administrative Law Judge (decided July 19, 2000).

Thierer, A., and Crews, C.W. (2003) *Who Rules the Net?* Cato Institute, Washington DC.

Thompson, S. (1999) The Internet and its potential influence on suicide, *Psychiatric Bulletin*, 23, 449–451.

Thornburgh, D., and Lin, H.S. (2002) *Youth, Pornography, and the Internet*, National Academy Press, Washington, DC.

Toronto Sun (2006) September 15, 4.

United States v. Kelner, 534 F.2d 1020 (2d Cir. 1976).

Waltermann, J., and Machill, M. (eds) (2000) *Protecting Our Children on the Internet: Towards a New Culture of Responsibility*, Bertelsmann Foundation, Gütersloh.

Watts v. United States, 394 U.S. 705 (1969).

Weimann, G. (2006) *Terror on the Internet: The New Arena, the New Challenges*, US Institute of Peace Press, Washington, DC.

White, A.E. (2006) *Virtually Obscene: The Case for an Uncensored Internet*, McFarland & Company, Inc., Jefferson, NC.

Wolak, J., Finkelhor, D., and Mitchell, K.J. (2005) *Child-Pornography Possessors Arrested in Internet-Related Crimes: Findings from the National Juvenile Online Victimization Study*, National Center for Missing & Exploited Children.

Zittrain, J.L. (2008) *The Future of the Internet – And How to Stop It*, Yale University Press, New Haven, CT.

23

Media Ethics and International Organizations

Cees J. Hamelink

The leading question for this chapter is: have international organizations contributed to the codification and implementation of media ethics?

In other words, have international organizations played a role in the (moral) standard-setting for media performance and were they actors in the development of best moral practices for media performance? Answering this question demands first a clarification of the notion "media ethics."

Ethics is often used interchangeably with morality but there are good arguments to distinguish between ethics and morality.

Morality refers to the set of moral standards (basic values and behavioral norms derived from these values) that are important to individuals and groups. Morality (often codified in laws and professional rules, but also to be found in unwritten codes of conduct) tells people how to behave. It helps them to distinguish between "good" and "bad" and it provides guidance in the moral choices that people make (almost permanently) in both their personal lives and in social settings.

Ethics refers to the philosophical discipline that reflects on morality. Ethics or "moral philosophy" addresses such basic, existential questions as "why be moral?" Ethics also explores different approaches (such as deontological, consequentialist, or discursive methods) to making moral choices and investigates methods for the justification of such choices.

I find the distinction between morality and ethics useful because it helps us to see that whereas "morality" tends to be strongly bound to historical times and places, "ethics" can evolve into a more global process of reflection on the significance of local moralities and possibly eventually lead us to a shared morality.

Therefore, in addition to the question about codification and implementation, there is the critical issue of whether international organizations act as open, public platforms for the reflection on moral standards for media performance and their related practices.

The Handbook of Global Communication and Media Ethics, First Edition. Edited by Robert S. Fortner and P. Mark Fackler.
© 2011 Blackwell Publishing Ltd. Published 2011 by Blackwell Publishing Ltd.

International Organizations

International organizations are those social institutions that states and nonstate parties have developed for the management of their crossborder affairs.

Although throughout human history people traded and fought and travelled great distances, most people stayed home.

For the longest period of world history the capacity to interact between remote places was very limited. Ideas and people have moved between ancient Rome and China of the Han-dynasty. Yet, contacts were so superficial that such interaction could remain unregulated. Even when in the seventeenth century an international system began to develop, the state of the world remained anarchic. Since the Peace of Westphalia (1648) which (together with the Treaty of Utrecht in 1713) laid the basis for a Eurocentric international economy, contacts between European governments increased. Apart from the more than 60 wars fought between 1648 and 1800, most contacts were of a rather shallow and formal diplomatic nature. The bulk of contacts were in fact conducted through international traders and merchants. No institutional arrangement evolved to address issues stemming from the states' international relations and indeed little need was felt to regulate these relations.

The Westphalian system of sovereign units had no common conventions or norms and rules. Equally the world outside Europe did not establish forms of multilateral politics for its international relations.[1]

The creation of international organizations that function as fora for multilateral policy making by states is typically a nineteenth century phenomenon. Throughout the seventeenth and eighteenth century the conduct of states remained largely defined by the narrow interests of nationalism and individualism. Although these interests continue to be forceful in the early twenty-first century, socioeconomic developments of the nineteenth century made states more aware of the need to regulate their relations. The "interaction capacity" (Buzan, 1993, p. 331) between states increased and the prevailing anarchy began to cause too much inconvenience. With more contact and more conflict between states a desire for minimal rules in such areas as the control of armed force emerged. A first clear point in time was the Vienna Congress of 1814/1815. This Congress established the rules for international diplomacy and agreed to meet at regular intervals in peacetime in order to prevent war.

The industrial revolution was an important factor in the increase of interaction capacity. With the development of mass production, improved communication and transport means, the growth of markets expanded within Europe and between Europe and other parts of the world. At the same time another revolution hit Europe. The French revolution fostered nationalism in Europe and reinforced the sovereignty of the nationstates. The two movements created a peculiar tension between rapidly increasing crossborder movements of goods, capital and people and the firm national control over these movements. The first multilateral institutions accommodated this tension by providing international interaction under norms and rules controlled by independent nation-states. These institutions were the Congress of Vienna, 1815, the Hague Conferences of 1899 and 1907, and the administrative bodies that dealt with issue areas such as post, telegraph and intellectual property.

The nineteenth century also saw the rise of a considerable number of public and private multilateral associations.

All this international activity could not prevent World War I. At the end of this war the victorious states gathered in the Versailles Peace Conference of 1919 in order to create an international system that would employ peaceful means in the resolution of inter-state conflicts. An important task of the 1919 Peace conference was the establishment of multilateral institutional arrangements that could promote international cooperation and contribute to the achievement of peace and security. Basic was the desire to shape the kind of postwar international relations that could prevent a collapse of the international system into another devastating war. The most important multilateral institution was the League of Nations.[2]

Concerns About the Growth of the Mass Media

With the proliferation of printed and especially broadcast media (in the late-nineteenth and early-twentieth century) serious concerns about the social impact of the mass media emerged.

There was considerable excitement about the positive and constructive contribution of the media to peaceful international relations. Such positive expectations were expressed in the 1933 Convention for Facilitating the International Circulation of Films of an Educational Character. This Convention was signed at Geneva on October 11, 1933. The contracting parties to the Convention, which was registered with the secretariat of the League of Nations,[3] considered the international circulation of educational films which contribute "towards the mutual understanding of peoples, in conformity with the aims of the League of Nations and consequently encourage moral disarmament" highly desirable. In order to facilitate the circulation of such films the signatories agreed to exempt their importation, transit, and exportation from all Customs duties and accessory charges of any kind.

There was however also a serious concern about the negative social impact of the mass media. A moral, educational concern was expressed regarding the spread across borders of obscene publications. This concern resulted in the adoption of the 1910 and 1924 treaties on traffic in obscene publications. The 1924 International Convention for the Suppression of the Circulation of and Traffic in Obscene Publications declared it a punishable offence "to make or produce or have in possession (for trade or public exhibition) obscene writings, drawings, prints, paintings, printed matter, pictures, posters, emblems, photographs, cinematograph films or any other obscene objects." It was also punishable to import or export said obscene matters for trade or public exhibition and persons committing the offence "shall be amenable to the Courts of the Contracting Party in whose territories the offence … was committed."

Media Ethics and International Organizations

Concern about the negative impact of the mass media also arose from the increasing use of the mass media (in the course of the nineteenth century) as instruments of foreign diplomacy. Although this was particularly the case with the newspapers, the development of wireless radio did significantly increase the potential for this new form of diplomacy. Increasingly diplomats shifted from traditional forms of silent diplomacy to a public diplomacy in which the constituencies of other states were directly addressed. In most cases this in fact amounted to the propagandistic abuse of the radio. During World War I an extensive use was made of the means of propaganda. This psychological warfare continued after the war had ended and international short wave radio began its proliferation.

In the immediate postwar period the League of Nations initiated discussions about the contribution of the international press to peace. The underlying concern with the role of the press in international relations found expression in a resolution that was adopted on September 25, 1925 by the Assembly of the League of Nations. This resolution called for a committee of experts representing the press of the different continents "with a view to determining methods of contributing towards the organization of peace, especially: (a) by ensuring the more rapid and less costly transmission of press news with a view to reducing risks of international misunderstanding; and (b) by discussing all technical problems the settlement of which would be conducive to the tranquillisation of public opinion" (Kubka and Nordenstreng, 1986, p. 71). The resolution referred to the press as "the most effective means of guiding public opinion towards that moral disarmament which is a concomitant condition of material disarmament."

In August 1927 the League convened a first conference of press experts in Geneva to deal with such problems as the provision of information that would "calm down public opinion in different countries" (Kubka and Nordenstreng, 1986, p. 54). The conference made the appeal to the press "to contribute by every means at its disposal to the consolidation of peace, to combat hatred between nationalities and between classes which are the greatest dangers to peace, and to prepare the way for moral disarmament." In September 1931 the Assembly of the League of Nations adopted a resolution that requested the Council of the League, to consider the possibility of studying with the help of the Press, "the difficult problem of the spread of information which may threaten to disturb the peace or the good understanding between nations." The increasing concern of the League for moral disarmament evidently reflected the actual historical developments of the period, such as the emergence of Nazism in Germany.

When the World Disarmament Conference opened in February 1932 the press was given great importance in moving public opinion towards moral disarmament.

A second conference with press experts was convened in Copenhagen (1932) and one of its resolutions addressed among other issues the problem of inaccurate news. Following the Copenhagen conference a conference of governmental press bureaux and representatives of the press was held in Madrid in November, 1933. This conference adopted a resolution on the right to correct false information.

In 1931 the League of Nations decided to ask the Institute for Intellectual Cooperation (the predecessor of UNESCO) to conduct a study on all questions raised by the use of radio for good international relations. In 1933 the study was published "Broadcasting and Peace") and it recommended the drafting of a binding multilateral treaty. Under the war threat emanating from Germany after 1933 the treaty was indeed drafted and concluded in 1936 on September 23, with the signatures from 28 states. The fascist states did not participate. The International Convention concerning the Use of Broadcasting in the Cause of Peace entered into force on April 2, 1938 after ratification or accession by nine countries, Brazil, the United Kingdom, Denmark, France, India, Luxembourg, New Zealand, the Union of South Africa, and Australia. Basic to the provisions of the Convention was the recognition of the need to prevent, through rules established by common agreement, broadcasting from being used in a manner prejudicial to good international understanding. These agreed upon rules included the prohibition of transmissions which could incite the population of any territory "to acts incompatible with the internal order or security of contracting parties" or which were likely to harm good international understanding by incorrect statements. The contracting parties also agree to ensure "that any transmission likely to harm good international understanding by incorrect statements shall be rectified at the earliest possible moment." In 1994 the Convention was still in force and had been ratified by 26 member states of the United Nations.

The development of industrialization and urbanization in late-nineteenth-century Europe brought about important social changes. A modern society was constructed with "a new sense of self, of subjectivity and individuality" (Eyerman, 1992, p. 38). This modern society gave rise to the emergence of a multitude of voluntary, nonstate associations, such as the trade unions.

In the negotiations leading towards the first multilateral agreements on media and telecommunication these non state actors played an important role.

Nongovernmental Organizations

Towards the end of the nineteenth century the increasingly international character of journalism stimulated the organization of journalists across national borders. In a number of European capitals associations of foreign correspondents were founded and in 1893 the first international press congress took place in Chicago. Among the topics addressed by the congress participants was the international role of the press. The following year an international congress at Antwerp (1894) established the first international organization, the International Union of Press Associations (IUPA). The congress, taking place from July 7 to 12, 1894 was attended by journalists, press owners and associations, and publishers from 17 countries (almost all from Europe). The IUPA was to address many different issues, such as property rights, work on Sundays, women's emancipation, wages, working conditions, professional training, professional ethics, and the problems of international dissemination of false news and war propaganda.

In the early 1920s many new international organizations were set up, the IUPA became marginalized and held its last assembly in 1936.

Meanwhile the International Federation of Newspaper Publishers Associations (FIADEJ) had been established in 1933 (which was after World War II was replaced by the International Federation of Editors of Journals and Publications (FIEJ)). Other organizations that appeared in this period were the International Association of Journalists accredited to the League of Nations in 1921, the International Sporting Press Association (ISPA) in 1924, the International Federation of the Periodic Press (IFPP) in 1925, and the International Catholic Union of the Press (UCIP) in 1927.

In 1926 the French Journalists' Syndicate took the initiative for the establishment of an international organization of journalists. At a conference in Paris (June 1926) it was decided that this organization would be formally constituted as the International Federation of Journalists (IFJ) by a congress in Geneva at the International Labor Office (ILO) headquarters. This congress took place in September 1926 and was attended by journalist organizations from several European countries and representatives of the ILO, the League of Nations, and the International Institute of Intellectual Cooperation.

In 1926 the League of Nations had commissioned the ILO to study the working conditions of journalists. When this study was published in 1928 ("Conditions of Work and Life of Journalists") it pointed among others to "an evil from which journalism has suffered since its beginnings, but which was becoming more and more threatening as the profession developed – incoherence, arbitrariness, the absence of a code which would define rights and duties, and which would introduce a little order, and at the same time a little justice, in the conditions in which this great modern profession is unfolding. The absence of a code, which is beginning to be remedied in certain countries, is a veritable anachronism" (Kubka and Nordenstreng, 1986, p. 95). The second congress of the IFJ in November 1928 at Dijon discussed the establishment of an international tribunal of honor for journalists and decided to mandate the permanent commission to elaborate a professional code and to set up a tribunal of honor (Kubka and Nordenstreng. 1986, p. 60). The next year the IFJ executive committee discussed at length the principles to guide the tribunal (October 1929, Antwerp) and at the third IFJ congress the establishment of the tribunal was a key item on the agenda. The Berlin congress of 1930 adopted a fundamental declaration with the principles for the judgments by the tribunal. The preamble referred to the wish to create an institution which contributes to establish and maintain a good understanding among peoples, to uplift the professional dignity by prescribing for journalists special duties, and to secure the legitimate rights of the members of the professional organizations. Next to the declaration a procedural code was adopted formulating the rules of dispute settlement by the tribunal. "The International Journalists' Tribunal of Honour" was solemnly inaugurated at the Hague (in the Palace of Peace) on October 12, 1931. In his inaugural address the president of the Tribunal, the Dutch jurist B.C.J. Loder mentioned that the "great danger for the people, even in our modern times, the source of many of their conflicts is that they do not know each other, do not understand each other, that they see only that what divides them instead of being aware of that what could unite them" (Kubka and Nordenstreng, 1986, p. 68).

The tribunal consisted of a president, a vice president, two permanent judges, four alternate judges, a public prosecutor, and two alternates. The tribunal was to deal with disputes relating to honor which might arise between journalists of different nationalities, or between a journalist and a nonjournalist of different nationalities.

In 1937 the issue of a deontological code was on the agenda and the seventh and last FIJ congress in 1939 at Bordeaux adopted a "Professional Code of Honour for Journalists."

Also the organization of publishers was concerned about the issue of professional responsibility and especially about the spreading of false information. It drafted a convention in 1933 that included the immediate correction of false news. By 1938 the convention was adhered to by member associations from eight countries.

The origins of concern with the social responsibility of the mass media are found in the late-nineteenth century. They were related to the emergence of journalism as an independent profession in this period. The emergence of the culture of professionalism in Europe stemmed from the rise of the middle class in the eighteenth and nineteenth centuries. This class resisted the aristocracy and needed, in this struggle, emancipatory symbols. Such a symbol was the existence of a class of independent professionals. The idea of the independent profession proliferated rapidly in the late-nineteenth and early-twentieth century in such fields as medicine, law, and the clergy. Journalism also developed as a profession. For many professions the formulation of an ethical code meant the recognition of autonomy and public status. Out of the development of professionalism grew the ethics of journalism. The first formal ethical code was probably formulated by newspaper publishers in Kansas in 1910. The oldest international code of conduct for journalists was probably the "Code of Journalistic Ethics" adopted by the first Pan-American Press Conference at Washington in 1926. This Code was confirmed in October 1950, at New York, by the Inter-American Press Conference as the guideline for the IAPA (Inter-American Press Association). The International Federation of Journalists made serious attempts at professional self-regulation through the adoption of a professional code of honor in 1939. Other professional organizations also adopted principles of conduct, such as the International Union of Press Associations in 1936. In the mid-1920s the International Federation of Journalists asked the League of Nations and the International Labour Office (with the International Association of Journalists accredited to the League) to study the position of journalists throughout the world in regard of their material conditions of work and in terms of professional status and social responsibilities.

All these developments ended temporarily when World War II began.

Developments since 1945

After World War II the international community established the system of the United Nations and its specialized organizations. Among them the United Nations Educational, Scientific and Cultural Organization (UNESCO) became particularly relevant for standard-setting in the media field.

An important contribution to international standard-setting was also offered by a rapidly growing group of international nongovernmental organizations (INGOs). These INGOs were partly really international in terms of membership and activities, partly they were nationally-based but with activities that had an international impact. Obviously, they did not have the legal power to issue binding decisions, but they could influence the policy making processes of the intergovernmental organizations as expert groups or as lobbying agents. They also defined standards for their own conduct with political significance beyond the members of the group they represented. Illustrations are the efforts of the international professional bodies in journalism to arrive at a self-regulatory code of conduct, or the self-regulatory codes that are adopted by the International Public Relations Association and the International Advertising Association.

Focus on Freedom and Responsibility of the Media

The international debates on freedom of information have always had an association with reflections and viewpoints on the social responsibility of the media of mass communication. The key normative provisions on freedom of information permit freedom of expression "without fetters," but also bind this to other human rights standards. The clear recognition of the right to freedom of information as a basic human right in the Universal Declaration of Human Rights was positioned in a standard-setting instrument that also asked for the existence of an international order in which the rights of the individual can be fully realized (Article 28). This implies that the right to freedom of information is linked with the concern for a responsible use of international media. This linkage laid the basis for a controversy in which one position emphasized the free flow principle, whereas another position stressed the social duty principle.

Already the UNESCO Constitution, adopted in 1945, contained the tension between the two approaches. It accepted the principle of a free exchange of ideas and knowledge, but it also stressed the need to develop and use the means of communication toward a mutual understanding among nations and to create an improved factual knowledge of each other. The two approaches can also be seen in the postwar development of the professional field. On March 26, 1946 the IFJAFC convened a World Congress of Journalists that was held at Copenhagen, June 3–9, 1946. This congress was attended by some 165 delegates from 21 countries. In the invitation letter the Executive Committee of the IFJAFC indicated among the purposes of the congress, "to discuss methods of assuring the freedom of the press" (Kubka and Nordenstreng, 1986, p. 10). The discussions largely focused on the establishment of a new international professional organization, a provisional constitution was unanimously adopted and the International Organization of Journalists was created. Special attention was given to the debate on the liberty of the press and at the end of the Congress a Statement of Principle on the freedom of the press was adopted. "The International Congress of Journalists affirms that freedom of the press is a fundamental principle of democracy and can function only if channels of information and the means of dissemination of news are made available to all" (Kubka and Nordenstreng, 1986, p. 115). The Statement stressed "the responsibility of every working journalist to assist by every means in his power the development of international friendship and understanding and instructed the Executive Committee to examine the various codes of professional ethics adopted by national bodies, particularly in respect of any journalist deliberately and knowingly spreading – whether by press or radio or news agencies – false information designed to poison the good relations between countries and peoples."

The social duty dimension was even stronger present in the resolution on press and peace that stated that "this congress considers the cementing of lasting international peace and security the paramount aim of humanity, and calls upon all the 130,000 members of the IOJ to do their utmost in support of the work of international understanding and co-operation entrusted to the United Nations." The provisional constitution, read under aims and objectives:

> Article 2. (a) Protection by all means of all liberty of the press and of journalism. The defence of the people's right to be informed honestly and accurately. (b) Promotion of international friendship and understanding through free interchange of information.

As the Cold War was already warming up by 1948 the social duty principle and the free flow principle collided in the early UN debates largely as East/West ideological confrontations. For instance in the General Assembly of 1947 the Yugoslav delegation proposed legislation to "restrict false and tendentious reports calculated to aggravate relations between nations, provoke conflicts and incite to war." This was unacceptable to the Western delegations and eventually a compromise text (proposed by France) was adopted that recommended the study of measures, "to combat, within the limits of constitutional procedures, the publication of false or distorted reports likely to injure friendly relations between states" (UNGA, Resolution. 127(II)).

After 1948 the principles of freedom of information and social responsibility largely followed separate paths and could be found as separate provisions in standard-setting instruments that were adopted since 1948. Some instruments also linked the two principles, such as the International Covenant on Civil and Political Rights (1966) and the UNESCO Mass Media Declaration (1978). Article 19 of the Covenant, for example, acknowledges the freedom of information, whereas article 20 states important restrictions, "Any war propaganda shall be prohibited by law … Any advocacy of national, racial or religious hatred that constitutes incitement to discrimination, hostility or violence shall be prohibited by law."

After World War II the 1948 UN Conference on Freedom of Information at Geneva articulated normative prescriptions for the conduct of the mass media. After the Conference the United Nations Sub-Commission on Freedom of Information and of the Press became involved in a very extensive attempt at the formulation and adoption of a professional code of conduct.

Media Ethics and International Organizations   443

In 1950 a group of experts serving on the Sub-Commission drafted an international code of ethics that was sent by the UN Secretary General to some 500 professional organizations in the mass media field. Based on the replies which in majority indicated that respondents thought a code would be useful, the Sub-Commission produced a second draft which it submitted (in 1952) to the Economic and Social Council of the United Nations (ECOSOC). In the same year the Council adopted the draft international code of ethics as resolution 442B (IV). The Code proposed that media should strive towards factual accuracy, should desist from willful slander, plagiarism, calumny, and libel, be responsible and devote themselves to the public interest. The Draft International Code of Ethics was sent to professional associations and mass media enterprises. Commercial organizations such as the Motion Pictures Association of America and the US National Conference of Business Paper Editors had no objections to the code. Also in 1952 the UN General Assembly called upon media professionals to arrange for a conference to elaborate the draft and to discuss its implementation (UNGA Res. 635 (VII) and 736 (VII)). No further action was taken and the proposed Code never developed beyond its draft status.

Also in the 1970s UNESCO entered the debates on journalistic ethics. The organization convened a consultation on ethical principles in 1973 and a consultative meeting with working journalists in 1978.

Discrimination

An important provision in international law that affects the social performance of the mass media concerns discrimination. Article 20 of the International Covenant on Civil and Political Rights contains next to the propaganda provisions, a paragraph that states, "Any advocacy of national, racial or religious hatred that constitutes incitement to discrimination, hostility or violence shall be prohibited by law." This was even stronger formulated in Article 4 of the International Convention on the elimination of all forms of racial discrimination (adopted as UNGA Resolution 2106 A(XX), December 21, 1965). Here "all dissemination of ideas based upon racial superiority or hatred, incitement to racial discrimination, as well as acts of violence or incitement to such acts against any race or group of persons of another colour or ethnic origin" was declared a criminal offence. Essential to this provision is that states are also required (in Article 4b.) to declare organizations which promote and incite racial discrimination illegal. The UNESCO 1978 Declaration on Race and Racial Prejudice mentioned in this context the mass media specifically in Article 5. The Declaration provides a strong prescription for media conduct as it urges the "mass media and those who control or serve them" to "promote understanding, tolerance and friendship among individuals and groups and to contribute to the eradication of racism, racial stereotyped, partial, unilateral or tendentious picture of individuals and of various human groups." The mass media are also told to be "freely receptive to ideas of individuals and groups which facilitate communication between racial and ethnic groups."

The UNESCO Mass Media Declaration

The issue of racial discrimination was also addressed in the most extensive regulatory instrument to address the concern for social responsibility in the mass media, the UNESCO Mass Media Declaration. This Declaration originated from the 19th General Conference of UNESCO (in 1979 in Nairobi) when a first multilateral discussion about a draft declaration on fundamental principles governing the use of the mass media in strengthening peace and international understanding and in combating war propaganda, racialism and apartheid, took place. The heart of the controversy at that meeting was a proposed Article XII of the draft declaration which stated "States are responsible for the activities in the international sphere of all mass media under their jurisdiction." For many member states this reference to state responsibility suggested the possibility of state control over the mass media. Also the phrasing on "the use of the mass media" in the title of the draft declaration was deemed unacceptable. In particular for Western member states this meant that standards would be set for the mass media by users and among those users states could play a prominent and potentially dangerous role. The draft declaration that was proposed at the 19th General Conference had been adopted in 1975 during an experts' conference. The Group of Nine EC countries (the Federal Republic of Germany, Denmark, Ireland, Britain, France, Italy, Belgium, Luxembourg and the Netherlands) had walked away in protest from this meeting. For them the text was unacceptable because of its reference to the United Nations General Assembly Resolution 3379 on Zionism as a form of racism and because of the fact that the state was accorded an important role with regard to the mass media. During the General Conference of 1976 there were three positions.

For the Western countries, Japan and some Latin American countries the draft declaration was totally unacceptable. Several delegations from the East-European countries pushed for the adoption of the draft declaration. A group of African and Asian countries supported the draft declaration but did plead for postponement in order to design a new text with better chances for consensus.

The decision taken in Nairobi referred the draft to the Director General and the General Conference invited him "to hold further broad consultations with experts with a view to preparing a final draft declaration which could meet the largest possible measure of agreement ... and to submit such a draft declaration to member states at the end of 1977 or early in 1978." It was also decided to establish a commission for "a comprehensive study on the problems of communication in the modern world." This became the International Commission for the Study of Communication Problems, usually called after its chairman Sean MacBride, the MacBride Commission. During the 20th General Conference of UNESCO in 1978 in Paris the amended draft declaration was unanimously adopted as "Declaration on fundamental principles concerning the contribution of the mass media to strengthening peace and international understanding, the promotion of human rights and to countering racialism, apartheid and incitement to war."

Media Ethics and International Organizations 445

The Conference also adopted a resolution aiming at practical recommendations concerning the Mass Media Declaration. The resolution proposed the holding of a congress to discuss the application of the declaration and was accepted with 61 votes in favor (the socialist and developing countries), one vote against (Switzerland) and 26 abstainers (all of them Western countries). During the 1980s there was no follow-up to the Declaration.

An attempt was made cojointly by the leading journalists' bodies, the IFJ and the IOJ, to arrange an international congress to discuss the declaration. Largely due to the unwillingness to cooperate expressed by the International Federation of Editors of Journals (FIEJ) and the International Press Institute (IPI) the meeting never took place.

Nongovernmental Actors

In the nongovernmental community the two main professional bodies in journalism did address issues of social responsibility.

The IFJ (founded in 1952) adopted in 1954 at its Second Congress in Bordeaux, an International Code of Ethics, The Declaration of Principles on the Conduct of Journalists. This "Bordeaux declaration" stated among its principles, "The journalist only accepts, professionally, while recognizing the acknowledged right of every country, the jurisdiction of his equals, to the exclusion of any other interference, governmental or other."

The IOJ adopted at its various international conferences resolutions that articulated the organization's concern about journalistic ethics.

In 1956, a meeting organized by the IOJ at Helsinki (June 10–15) was attended by 200 journalists from 62 countries who adopted among other resolutions a statement on professional ethics. This read in part "The journalist profession imposes a great moral responsibility on those that exercise it. It demands that he acts in accordance with the aspirations of peoples for peace, mutual understanding and cooperation. Reporting must be truthful and impartial in order to help people understand events taking place in the world and in their countries. A journalists' professional ethics requires him to work for a better future for mankind, for peace and for social progress and to oppose war propaganda.… We believe the ethics of journalism requires every journalist to fight against the distortion of the truth and to oppose all attempts at falsification, misinformation and slander.… He should support freedom of the press in those countries where it is restricted, should oppose mass communication media monopolies that hamper the discharge of his duty, should protect against the persecution of journalists, their imprisonment, the banning of newspapers and discriminatory press legislation."

The second meeting of journalists organized by the IOJ in Baden-Baden, October 1960 stated "We are convinced that professional ethics imply, at the present time, the duty of every journalist not to tolerate the distortion of the truth and to take a stand against all attempts at falsification of information and slander.

Each journalist should be aware of the responsibility which rests with him. All journalists should safeguard professional ethics and morality."

From the UNESCO consultative meeting with working journalists in April, 1978, in Paris emerged the so called Consultative Club. This was a network of professional organizations that regularly convened to discuss matters of professional importance, such as ethics.

Meetings took place in Mexico City (1980), Baghdad (1982), Prague and Paris (1983), Geneva (1985), Brussels and Sofia (1986), Cairo and Tampere (1987), and Prague (1988).

The Club met under UNESCO auspices, but without direct involvement of the organization. It also liaised with the International Labour Office (ILO) and the International Committee of the Red Cross. At the first meeting it was agreed "to examine possible common grounds for a definition of basic ethical principles of the journalistic profession." At the second meeting in Mexico this examination produced a draft document that was adopted by the representatives of the attending organizations as the "Mexico Declaration."[4] The meeting also appointed a working group with the brief to produce a draft international code of ethics. In its preparatory work the working group changed the notion of an international code to a set of ethical principles. It seemed to the group that the concept of code was more adequate for national or regional efforts than for an international type agreement. The group retained the basic structure of the Mexico Declaration and presented a draft at the Prague meeting of 1983. As a result of some reservations expressed by the IFJ it was decided to postpone a final decision on the document till the consultative meeting to be held late 1983 in Paris. The Paris meeting, after more amendments, decided to adopt the text even in the absence of the IFJ.

Self-regulation

The professional organizations have by and large preferred self-regulatory measures over public regulation. Voluntary professional regulation has found expression in codes of conduct, but also in the establishment of national press councils (for example in Australia, Austria, the Netherlands, Norway, Sweden, and the United Kingdom) which hear complaints from individuals about the performance of the press. Some countries developed in addition to the press council the institute of a Press Ombudsman (Sweden) who may arbitrate in conflicts between the public and the press, in other countries the newspapers themselves have their own ombudsman (for example in Canada). Guidance for decisions about complaints is often provided by the standards articulated in professional codes of conduct. It is common that the outcome of the council's proceedings is the obligation for papers to publish its decisions.

The effectiveness of self-regulation is dependent upon the compliance by the offenders. It remains a voluntary arrangement with no formal obligations towards the complainants.

Other Media Products

The concern with social responsibility has to a large extent addressed the issue of international news provision. This should however not obscure the fact that also other media products have given rise to a similar concern. This can be illustrated in the fields of advertising, consumer information, and public relations.

When in the late-nineteenth century advertising emerged as an industry, it confronted suspicion and opposition. There were accusations of distortion, waste of resources, and the creation of false needs. The establishment of active consumer groups in many countries led to self-regulation of the industry. In many countries national advertising industries developed their own self-regulatory structures and mechanisms. In spite of the fact that advertising was becoming a global business, very little effort developed to align self-regulatory policies across national borders. Probably, the first international attempt was made in 1911 at the Convention of the Associated Advertising Clubs of the World at New York City. This was the Truth in Advertising Resolution. The first comprehensive self-regulatory code was formulated in 1937 by the International Chamber of Commerce (revised in 1973). Among the standards the Code sets are "All advertising should be legal, decent, honest, and truthful ... Every advertisement should be prepared with a due sense of social responsibility.... No advertisement should be such as to impair public confidence in advertising." The ICC has played a very active role in the past decades to coordinate efforts "to establish a common ground upon which national systems of marketing self-regulation may be based. It has sought to outline the principles and to encourage business communities in many countries to set up the machinery for their observance" (Neelankavil and Stridsberg, 1980, p. 7). Efforts at self-regulation have generally been seen by the industry as an attractive way "to protect both the consuming public against deceptive advertising and themselves against unfair competition on the one hand and overzealous government regulatory bodies on the other" (Neelankavil and Stridsberg, 1980, p. 2).

Also in the field of consumer information the need for guidelines arose. Increasing pressure was mounted by consumer organizations to provide information in a responsible manner. Important steps were the unanimous adoption by the United Nations General Assembly of the Guidelines for Consumer Protection in 1981 and the listing a year later (1982) of products harmful to health and the environment. The increasing concern with consumer information was strongly motivated by accidents due to deficient product information, including instructions for use. The British Medical Journal has claimed (2001) that a lack of data on underlying causes, incidence, prevalence, long-term consequences and costs of injury results in "patchy and often ineffectual efforts to prevent injury."

Like in the advertising field the world's Public Relations professionals also felt the need of self regulation. On May 12, 1965 the General Assembly of the International PR Association (IPRA) adopted an International Code of Ethics at Athens. This so called Code of Athens (which was modified on April 17, 1968 at Teheran) provided that all IPRA members would observe in the course of professional duties the moral principles and rules of the Universal Declaration of Human Rights. Members would also refrain from "taking part in any venture or undertaking which is unethical or dishonest or capable of impairing human dignity and integrity." The preamble of the Code refers to the issue of social responsibility by stating that Public Relations practitioners can substantially help to meet social needs.

European Convention on Human Rights

In the European Convention on Human Rights and Fundamental Freedoms (1950) an essential standard for media behavior is codified in Article 10 on the freedom of information. Part of this article reads "Everyone has the right to freedom of expression. This right shall include freedom to hold opinions and to receive and impart information and ideas without interference by public authority and regardless of frontiers."

In the opinion of the European Court of Human Rights this article constructs a right to receive information and ideas, not just broadcast signals and it imposes upon broadcasters the duty to accommodate this receivers' right. According to the jurisprudence of the European Court the European citizen has the right to be properly informed. In several opinions the Court has stated that not only do the mass media have a right to impart information, they have the task "to impart information and ideas on matters of public interest," and the public has a right to receive such information and ideas. The European Court has ruled that the media are purveyors of information and public watchdog. This matches the classical opinion of the US Supreme Court in the *Red Lion Broadcasting v. the FCC* in 1969: "the right of the viewers and listeners, not the right of broadcasters is paramount."

Another example is the variety of rules on a right of reply in different legislations. These rules vary from the entitlement to respond to critical opinions to a right of reply to factual allegations. In countries that recognize this provision the reply is usually published in the offending newspaper. If newspapers refuse this, the persons who feel wronged may in some countries (for example in France and Spain) seek redress through the assistance of a court of law

World Summit on the Information Society

In 2003 (Geneva) and 2005 (Tunis) the United Nations convened a world summit on the information society (WSIS). The two gatherings of the Summit focused primarily on technology issues and offered little, if anything, in terms of guidance for or reflection upon media performance. During the preparatory meetings there were some (sometimes heated) exchanges about the media, but the summit never became a platform to discuss the key moral issues confronting the media in the twenty-first century.

Conclusion

The international community (both governmental and nongovernmental organizations) has produced a fairly large volume of moral standards for media practices and has codified them in both binding law and voluntary self-imposed codes.

There are standards for media performance that address among others the freedom of information, the protection of privacy, discrimination, incitement to violence, presumption of innocence, propaganda, and exposure of prisoners of war. However impressive all this rule-setting may be most of it remains largely ineffective. In relation to media practices the international community faces a problem similar to most other social domains: the absence or weakness of tools of implementation.

With regard to the performance of media it is ironic that robust mechanisms of rule implementation would have caused great risks to the professional autonomy of media practitioners. The final adjudication of the (non)enforcement of rules almost inevitably implies a degree of arbitrariness and thus a space for the abuse of rules, certainly in case governmental organizations are involved.

Serious problems also occur in the case of professional voluntarily accepted rules of conduct. Codes of conduct fulfill important purposes, such as the identification of an autonomous professional community. They provide a common set of moral rules for the members of a profession which contribute to the credibility of their professional performance. A code of conduct tells clients what quality to expect from the professional conduct.

Codes can be a starting point for ethical inquiry, but – given the variety of choice-situations and the almost inevitable general nature of their rules – they are not likely to produce concrete moral guidance. Prescriptions in a Code suggest an almost universal applicability which is of course not realistic since actors, situations, and interests differ greatly over time and place.

Codes tend to reflect the "common sense morality" that most people will share anyway and – as a result – they are rather superfluous for most day-to-day moral choices. A professional code of conduct may tell the professional what the collective consensus of colleagues is but it does not help in knowing what to do in a concrete case. The Code may proscribe the receiving of bribes, but it does not tell whether accepting a special gift in a special situation is alright.

It is rather pointless to present prescriptions as general principles for professional conduct without explaining how these principles have to be applied in concrete choice situations.

In the daily practice of moral decision making a growing scepsis emerged about the usefulness of the conventional theories in the resolution of moral choices in real-life situations. Concrete experiences in such fields as medical and business ethics have led "to a serious if not widespread erosion of confidence in the power of normative theory to decisively guide the resolution of real practical problems" (Winkler and Coombs, 1993, p. 3). In the quest for a more adequate approach it has been proposed to conceive of morality as "an evolving social instrument" that is part of a specific cultural context (Winkler and Coombs, 1993, p. 3). This suggests a contextual approach to moral decision-making which "adopts the general idea that moral problems must be resolved within the interpretive complexities of concrete circumstances" (Winkler and Coombs, 1993, p. 4).

In the contextualist approach the moral argument begins casuistically with the concrete choice-situation and moves towards a selection of applicable moral principles. From this perspective, a primary task in the situation of choice is the precise interpretation of the moral issue at stake. The first step is the attempt to understand in detail what the basic choice is in a concrete case.

In the course of this inductive moral reasoning, questions are asked about the institutional setting and the cultural context in which choice-situations are located. In this connection questions are also asked about the consequences of different choices (what benefits versus which damages, who are winners versus losers) and about the interests that are at stake.

Contextualism offers the possibility of a more eclectic model in which the ethical dialogue moves back and forth between general moral principles and specific details of choice-situations. This dialogical type of ethics views the resolution of moral choice-situations as a mutual learning experience. It is a process in which people learn from each other, listen to the outsider and try to understand the rationale of the outsider. In the ethical dialogue people also discover that the moral practices of "us" are not always morally defensible and that those by "them" are not always morally despicable. The attempt to understand different moral premises and conclusions may lead to feelings of mutual respect in spite of fundamental disagreement.

Over the years there have been inspiring and fascinating debates about best (and worst) media practices in a variety of public fora such as the UN institutions and the professional associations. However, there never was the concrete effort to develop an international platform for ethical reflection: a place where the global ethical dialogue among those involved (policymakers, regulators, practitioners, and audiences) could be conducted.

If such a place had been established, the dialogue would not depart from a consensus on fundamental moral values, but would work on the basis of an agreement on common procedure to seek those solutions to moral dispute that optimally accommodate the parties' interests and principles. In the dialogue moral choice is conceived as a reiterative and dynamic process since situations and moral standards change over time and space. There are no single good answers to the questions media ethics raises. However, in the process, growing consensus on what constitutes best practices could emerge.

More important than the development of institutional tools for the implementation of standard-setting in the field of the media is indeed the issue of ethical reflection on professional media morality.

The emergence of a global communication ethics needs an independent global forum for permanent dialogue among professionals and users to identify common ground and common sense for "best media practices."

Notes

1 An exception may be found in the ancient Greek councils that established multilateral cooperative arrangements in order to prevent warfare between the participating parties.
2 Copies of League of Nations/ United Nations Treaties are available at http://untreaty. un.org/English/CTC/CTC_04.asp (accessed June 30, 2010)
3 Signatories of the treaty establishing the League of Nations were the United States, Belgium, Bolivia, Brazil, the British Empire, China, Cuba, Czechoslovakia, Ecuador, France, Greece, Guatemala, Haiti, Hejaz, Honduras, Italy, Japan, Liberia, Nicaragua, Panama, Peru, Poland, Portugal, Romania, the Serb-Croat-Slovene State, Siam, and Uruguay.
4 Participating international organizations in the Mexico Declaration were the International Organization of Journalists, the Latin American Federation of Journalists, the International Catholic Union of the Press, the Latin American Federation of Press Workers, the Federation of Arab Journalists, the Union of African Journalists and the Confederation of ASEAN Journalists.

References

British Medical Journal (2001) Editorial: The continuing global challenge of injury, June 30, 322. 1557–1588, www.bmj.com/cgi/content/full/322/7302/1557 (accessed July 20, 2010).

Buzan, B. (1993) From international system to international society: structural realism and regime theory meet the English school. *International Organization*, 47 (3), 327–351.

Eyerman, R. (1992) Modernity and social movement, in *Social Change and Modernity*, (eds H.Haferkamp and N.J.Smelser), University of California, Berkeley, pp. 37–54.

Kubka, J., and Nordenstreng, K. (1986) *Useful Recollections, Part I*, International Organization of Journalists, Prague.

Neelankavil, J.P., and Stridsberg, A.B. (1980) *Advertising Self-Regulation: A Global Perspective*, Hastings House, New York.

Winkler, E.R., and Coombs, J.R. (eds) (1993) *Applied Ethic*, Blackwell, Oxford.

24

Making the Case for What Can and Should Be Published

Bruce C. Swaffield

Journalists have an absolute responsibility to be fair, honest, and ethical. The media cannot always publish everything it is legally allowed to report. There are ethical boundaries to the news. From time to time, editors and reporters must draw the line when a story or photograph goes over the edge. They have to decide when something is objectionable or offensive even to a small number of viewers and readers.

Making decisions that involve moral and ethical values are not easy. Many factors on various levels need to be considered, including the overall effect on the audience, the news value and timeliness of an item, the rationale for running a particular piece or picture and, most of all, the impact on the public. Each issue must be weighed carefully and completely, especially when dealing with death and destruction. These are extremely sensitive subjects that must be treated with compassion. Too often, reporters go too far and offer too many details – descriptions that make for a great story but, in the end, do more harm than good.

When deciding what to report, journalists have to make the right decision the first time. They do not have a second chance. In "What is News? The Answer is Not Blowing on a Whim," Deni Elliott and Paul Martin Lester (n.d.) analyzed a photograph that caused tremendous controversy many years ago. The picture involved the body of a young boy who had drowned in a lake in Bakersfield, CA. At issue was the graphic nature of the picture – showing the dead boy, face and all, in a body bag.

A classic controversy over a tragic situation occurred in Bakersfield, California in 1986. With a caption head titled, "A family's anguish," there is no doubt that the image by John Harte of the Bakersfield Californian of 5-year-old drowning victim, Edward Romero, halfway zippered in a dark, plastic body bag with family members crying and a bystander awkwardly reaching for one of the survivors, is a powerful and disturbing image.

The Handbook of Global Communication and Media Ethics, First Edition. Edited by Robert S. Fortner and P. Mark Fackler.
© 2011 Blackwell Publishing Ltd. Published 2011 by Blackwell Publishing Ltd.

What Can and Should Be Published 453

But was that scene worthy of the newspaper's front page? Many readers didn't think so. The paper received 500 letters, 400 phone calls, 80 subscription cancellations, and one bomb threat. (Elliott and Lester, n.d.)

Immediately after the incident, Managing Editor Robert Bentley said the paper was justified in publishing the picture. He explained it was a dramatic photograph that might serve as a warning to prevent further drownings in the area. A short time later, however, Bentley recanted. "The reaction was too intense and widespread to just shrug it off and say we're just doing our job," he said (quoted in Hodges, 2003). Harte, on the other hand, maintained all along that the picture was newsworthy and the paper did the right thing by publishing it.

> Managing editor Robert Bentley was called into the offices of the Bakersfield Californian that Sunday evening to decide whether one of Harte's gripping photos should run. He was persuaded that the photo would serve as a potential warning and help stem the high number of drownings in the county.
>
> A week later, Bentley explained his decision in an editorial column. "Some claimed the Californian showed callous disrespect of the victim. Others felt the photograph had forced their visual intrusion on what should have been a family's private time of shock and grief. Most combined the dual protests."
>
> Bentley eventually decided that the photo should never have been published. He has said that by publishing the photo, he learned that journalists are seriously out of touch with their readers' sensibilities (Hodges, 2003).

At first glance, most journalists would have agreed about the impact of the photograph. It contained all of the ingredients of news: drama, impact, tragedy, and power. Yet, there was more to consider. How did the family feel, for example, when they saw the incident replayed over again on the front page of the newspaper the next day? This picture was the last one ever taken of their five-year-old son and brother; it was a lasting reminder of how he died. In addition, how did the young boy's friends and schoolmates react to seeing Edward in a body bag?

The real question in this case is whether a great photo should be published simply because it is dramatic. There is no doubt that people would take notice of such a picture, but would they be thinking at that moment about the underlying tragedy? Some justification could be made for saying the photo would make the community more aware of the number of recent drownings in the area. However, would the picture actually prevent future accidents? What the newspaper failed to do, most of all, was to consider the family more than the many reasons it had to publish the picture. The paper was well within its rights, legally – but what about ethically? Did they have the moral right to show a dead five-year-old in a body bag to the entire community? One has to wonder whether the image would have appeared in the paper if it involved a member of *The Bakersfield Californian*. Would the managing editor have made the same decision if he was a relative of the young boy or even a friend of the family? That should be the real question to ask when determining what should and should not run.

Tragedies almost always produce interesting and engaging stories. For journalists, there is the risk of stepping over the line by offering graphic descriptions that might offend or hurt others, especially relatives. The story of the blaze at the Happy Land Social Club in New York City on March 25, 1990, is a perfect example. *Newsday* writers Kevin Flynn, Chapin Wright, Joseph Queen and Michael Powell (Flynn *et al.* 1990) reported on the aftermath of a fire that killed 87 persons. The story appeared on page five the next day, Monday, March 26, under the headline "87 Die: Bronx Social Club Tragedy" with the subhead "Sights and Sounds of Death: For firefighters, a journey into blackness and horror."

> Firefighter Saturnino Reyes clung to the side of the first hook and ladder truck as it lurched onto Southern Boulevard early yesterday morning. He saw flames licking at the darkness outside the Happy Land Social Club, heard wood crackling and popping.
>
> There were no screams, no sobs, no one in sight. It snapped like a bonfire and Reyes felt sick. ...
>
> Reyes paused in the retelling yesterday morning, his face ashen beneath a mask of soot. ...
>
> "Then I realized that entire floor was human beings, I was crawling across dozens of bodies," the firefighter whispered.

The details and descriptions are excellent. The reader experiences what Reyes encountered as he climbed through the debris. The tragedy becomes all the more real as we realize the dead bodies "felt like wet, smoldering cardboard." What is the overall effect, not only on family members who might read the story, but on the public in general? The active verbs create so much intensity and realism that readers would associate – whether consciously or subconsciously – the lives of the 87 individuals with how they died: "There were no screams, no sobs. It snapped like a bonfire and Reyes felt sick. 'It was the sound of death,' he said.... 'Then I realized that entire floor was human beings, I was crawling across dozens of bodies,' the firefighter whispered." Little imagination is needed to recreate the entire scene, beginning to end, in our mind. From the "flames licking at the darkness outside the Happy Land Social Club" to the "wood crackling and popping," the details offer a graphic account of exactly what was going on inside the club as dozens tried to flee the inferno.

The story goes on to provide even more accounts of the scene. The grim details tell the entire story, especially how it all began and then more descriptions of those who died:

> On the second floor, they felt the soft floor, covered with bodies.
>
> "They looked like mannequins," Reyes recalled. "Bodies were fused together, men and women, lying next to each other, holding each other, lying on top of each other, arm in arm."
>
> Farther from the door there were men in neat afros, women with their hair coiffed, high heels and miniskirts. They lay beneath tables, legs tangled, hands wrapped around beer bottles.
>
> "If you didn't know better, it was like they were sleeping," said Assistant Fire Chief Anthony De Vita with the citywide fire command. "That's how peaceful they were."

What Can and Should Be Published   455

For the typical reader, the information offers all the excitement of an exciting story. There is action, suspense, tragedy, and reality. What about the families, friends and relatives of the 87 persons who perished in the fire? How would they feel as they learned about the death of their loved ones? The narrative here is almost too real and poignant. "The club lit up like a funeral pyre" and "Bars covered the windows." There was no escape; they were trapped inside a cage. "Within seconds, the heat was like that of a cauldron" while " 'Lungs are seared by the hot gases, and it becomes impossible to take a second breath.' " Next came the "cyanide gas" and "death for those in the club came instantly." Ironically, "a sprinkler system was in place but ... by the time it started spraying water, everyone was dead." "The bodies layered four deep by the upstairs door, however, suggest panic and pain."

On the one hand, this article bears the marks of good, solid reporting because it puts the reader on the scene, directly in front of the fire as an eyewitness. On the other hand, for those who knew someone who died in the fire, the story perhaps provides too much information. Coping with loss is extremely difficult. Harder still is accepting how a person died. Journalists need to be fair both to the public as well as those involved in a story. Again, the primary question to answer, before a story is published, is whether a piece would harm and offend certain groups or individuals. It is critical to weigh the overall impact and effect of a story on everyone, not only the general reader. Greater numbers of journalists today are taking a more personal approach to the news. They are asking the hard question: How would I feel if this story was about me or my family in some way?

The story about the Happy Land Social Club certainly raises the question of how far the media should go in re-presenting an incident. How much detail is needed and how much should be omitted? Consider the following details that *Newsday* included in their coverage. "People were screaming; they were all burned." "Two charred bodies lay in the downstairs doorway. Seventeen more were scattered across the first floor." "On the second floor, they felt the soft floor, covered with bodies. 'They looked like mannequins.... Bodies were fused together, men and women, lying next to each, holding each other, lying on top of each other, arm in arm.' Farther from the door there were men in neat afros, women with their hair coiffed, high heels and miniskirts. They lay beneath tables, legs tangles, hands wrapped around beer bottles." In the end, one firefighter said he had not seen anything like this since his days of fighting in Vietnam.

The paper did an outstanding job of covering this breaking story. However, the question of ethics arises again. Is the story fair to all those family members who would read it the next day? How would the facts and information make them feel? To be sure, there is no absolutely right or wrong answer. What the media do in each special situation depends on editorial perspective and viewpoint. One point of view that must be considered in all cases is, once again, the personal effect of the news.

In 1996, *Newsday* published another series of articles that involved the deaths of 229 persons on a plane bound for Paris from New York. The stories were awarded the Pulitzer Prize for Spot News Reporting. The day after the crash, July 18, writer

Philip Dioniato wrote about what happened when Trans World Airlines flight 800 exploded over the Atlantic near Long Island.

> I looked at the bay and saw a reflection on the water, then I looked up and I saw a big orange fire ball falling into the ocean, said Robert Siriani, who was outside his parents' home in Mastic Beach. I'd say it was one hundred feet wide and a couple of hundred feet long, the whole thing was flames, the flames were so bright I didn't see anything else. ...
>
> Professional and volunteer rescuers found mostly body parts strewn among the torn seat cushions and mangled metal.

The story continues with the grim task of recovering the bodies:

> At the Coast Guard base in East Moriches, rescue workers – armed with latex gloves and body bags – began bringing in the bodies of the dead. A police official said that a boat with about 20 bodies sat outside the inlet, which was too narrow for it to enter. Workers transferred the bodies – many of which were burned and not whole – into smaller boats, which brought the dead to the shore. ...
>
> In East Moriches, the hundreds of tense rescuers began turning their attention to finding enough refrigerated trucks to hold the mounting number of corpses.

The story provides comprehensive information on both the crash and the aftermath. Readers are able to find answers to most any question they might be pondering. Yet, what about those family members who are waiting for news about someone on the flight? How did they react to certain details?

Phrases such as "body parts strewn among the torn seat cushions and mangled metal" and "a boat with about 20 bodies sat outside the inlet" would make relatives and friends more distraught.

Two days after the explosion, *Newsday* published an even more explicit story on the recovery operation. Under the headline "Probers focus on possibility of bomb or missile; toll at 230," staff writers included the following (*Newsday* Staff, 1996):

> By last night, remains of 140 of the 230 people TWA officials said were on the flight had been fished from the water. The bodies were placed on Coast Guard cutters whose decks were stained with blood, then brought by smaller boats to a makeshift morgue at the command center in East Moriches.
>
> The remains were often badly burned and mangled beyond recognition. One was just a charred torso with no arms, legs or head, another's clothes and hair were burned off, and a third was a woman still wearing a black dress and a gold necklace.

Another story, "In the Morgue, Somber Tasks," dealt the continuing problem of identifying the remains (Schaer and Yan, 1996):

> "We have a large amount of what appears to be virtually heavy blunt force, some drownings and also postmortem burns," Dr. Charles Wetli, Suffolk's medical examiner, said between autopsies. ... Victims' fingers will be shriveled after hours in ocean

water, making it harder to get good fingerprints. Their teeth, the most durable part of the body, may be blackened by fire, requiring dental experts to clean them before comparing them to records.

There were more depictions of the dead. On the same day, in "Shards of a Disaster on a Sunny Beach Day," Phil Mintz and Lauren Terrazzano (1996) covered another angle of the story. They quoted a helicopter pilot who was picking up bodies. "The first body that I saw was intact, a male wearing blue jeans, face down," Baur said last night from the Air National Guard station at Westhampton Beach. The helicopter hovered 20 feet above the crash scene. "Then, all of sudden, at least 20 to 30 bodies in different states of configuration. A lot of people without heads. We marked them in the area. I picked up two." Still another story, "Just the Shell of their Souls," explained the adverse effect on rescue workers (Evans, Baker, and Slackman, 1996):

> Shortly after a State Police boat unloaded its grim cargo of 17 body bags, a medical examiner turned to one of the black plastic pods and zippered it open.
> Inside, the body of a girl lay wet and still.
> The sight left a rescue worker who watched from nearby shaking with emotion, and another worker tried to console him.
> "Remember, it's just the shells of their souls," he said softly. As hopes that a single survivor might be found faded in the dawn light...

Scattered throughout were more references to those who died:

> "A lot of them were burned, and some were pretty badly mutilated," Kelly said. "It was very sobering."
> As bodies were brought aboard, decks and equipment became smeared with blood, which crew members washed away with bleach.
> By morning, more than 100 bodies had been placed in black plastic body bags and carried by emergency workers in white jumpsuits and surgical gloves to a temporary morgue in a Coast Guard boat warehouse near the water's edge.

There is plenty of information in this story. Perhaps too much, though. One could argue *Newsday* was just covering the story, but others might contend that all of these details, each more gruesome than the next, were not needed. A few descriptions of the scene and the bodies being covered would have been sufficient to capture the somber mood.

Fortunately, a great many details were never seen by or reported to the public. In "Footage Too Sad to Televise," reporter Rita Ciolli (1996) wrote about a broadcast news crew that was on the scene. They witnessed more than they reported.

> WNBC News Director Paula Walker told the pilots of Chopper4, whose state-of-the-art cameras provided the most gripping images of the fiery wreckage on Wednesday, not to zoom in on any of the human remains floating in the ocean.

"I told them, 'Don't go too close,'" said Walker, who described the images as "very sad and disturbing." She also put out an electronic message to all her producers instructing them not to broadcast any pictures of bodies. "We don't need to show everything we've got to tell the story," said Walker.

When working on such a story, journalists need to guard against getting caught up in the moment and, as a result, going too far. Excitement can easily replace good judgment. Although journalists face constant deadlines to report the news as quickly as possible, it is well worth taking time to consider the ethical responsibility of being both fair and fair-minded.

The world will never forget the horrid images of people plunging to their deaths from the upper floors of the World Trade Center Towers on September 11, 2001. One by one, dozens of people jumped to escape the fire that was about to engulf them that morning. Writing one year after the incident, Dennis Cauchon and Martha Moore (2002) of *USA Today* wrote about the roughly 200 individuals who leaped from the two buildings:

> At first, it seemed like debris. Large objects were falling from the top of the World Trade Center's north tower, just a few minutes after American Airlines Flight 11 hit.
> "It took three or four to realize: They were people," says James Logozzo, who had gathered with co-workers in a Morgan Stanley boardroom on the 72nd floor of the south tower, just 120 feet away from the north tower. "Then this one woman fell."
> "The look on her face was shock. She wasn't screaming. It was slow motion. When she hit, there was nothing left," Logozzo says.

How much detail does a reader need to see or vicariously experience the event? As journalists, we must ask ourselves when and if we have crossed the line from simply being descriptive to becoming morbidly graphic, as seen in other parts of the article:

> For those who jumped, the fall lasted 10 seconds. They struck the ground at just less than 150 miles per hour – not fast enough to cause unconsciousness while falling, but fast enough to ensure instant death on impact. People jumped from all four sides of the north tower. They jumped alone, in pairs and in groups....
> Intense smoke and heat, rather than flames, pushed people into this horrific choice. That drove people to the windows 1,100 to 1,300 feet above ground.

In spite of the magnitude of the tragedy, *USA Today* made the decision to analyze precisely how many victims were involved:

> To make its estimate of the number of people who plunged from the Trade Center, USA TODAY reviewed videos and photographs, interviewed witnesses and analyzed the time and location of the jumping. The newspaper discussed its conclusion with officials in the fire department and medical examiner's office who, while not making calculations of their own, deemed an estimate of 200 jumpers as accurate.
> On the east side, people plummeted into the plaza, best known for its globe sculpture. Blood covered the glass walls and revolving doors that led to the plaza from the second-floor mezzanine in the north tower.

Eric Thompson, who worked on the 77th floor of the south tower, went to a conference room window after the first jet hit. He was shocked when a man came to a north tower window and leapt from a few floors above the fire. Thompson looked the man in the face. He saw his tie flapping in the wind. He watched the man's body strike the pavement below. "There was no human resemblance whatsoever," Thompson says.

On the first anniversary, the events of 9-11 were as vivid as the day they happened. Sharp and clear, the images have not faded at all, especially for those who knew one or more of the 2752 persons who died when the two jets crashed into the twin skyscrapers. The *USA Today* story allows reflection on what happened – specifically why these people jumped – and why, but it does a great deal more. The close details take the reader beyond the news and into an area of the curious and inquisitive. Many of the items in the story seem excessive a year later, such as the following: The falling people "seemed like debris." The entire description of a woman with olive skin who was wearing a white blouse and black skirt. How *USA Today* went to great lengths to verify the number of people who jumped. People "jumped alone, in pairs and in groups." "People plummeted into the plaza" and "Blood covered the glass walls and revolving doors." "The windows were red … and bits of bodies were outside." After one person hit the ground, "there was no human resemblance whatsoever." The story has tremendous impact and drama, but does it help the audience understand the events of that day any better? Or do we simply come away feeling nauseous and sick.

An article in *Esquire Magazine*, published on the second anniversary of 9-11, discussed the now-famous photograph known as the Falling Man. It is the picture of a man falling head-long next to one of the towers; he is perfectly vertical and his left leg is bent at almost a right angle. Tom Junod (2003) wrote that the man "appears relaxed, hurtling through the air. He appears comfortable in the grip of the unimaginable motion." Throughout the story, Junod probes the possible identity of the Falling Man.

> Of course, the only way to find out the identity of the Falling Man is to call the families of anyone who might be the Falling Man and ask what they know about their son's or husband's or father's last day on earth. Ask if he went to work wearing an orange shirt.
>
> Should those calls be made? Should those questions be asked? Would they only heap pain upon the already anguished? Would they be regarded as an insult to the memory of the dead, the way the Hernandez family regarded the imputation that Norberto Hernandez was the Falling Man?

Does the identity of the Falling Man truly matter – to the public, the family, his friends or co-workers? Or do we just want to know so we can put a name to the face? As a journalist, Junod wonders if such questions should even be asked or investigated. After all, the answer will not change the outcome.

Not every situation is the same and not every story is identical. Each one requires a different approach, a special perspective, with its own unique set of questions and answers. The most critical step in publishing the right kind of story, one that is fair and informative for everyone, is for those in the media to keep questioning themselves. They need to evaluate what they report through the lens of their own personal lives (i.e., how they would feel if the story they are telling involved them in some way). Certainly, journalists must remain impartial and objective, but they need not become detached from the details or the effect.

One of the primary ethics is to "Show compassion for those who may be affected adversely by news coverage" (SPJ Code of Ethics, n.d.). Considering the effect of any story is as important as gathering all of the correct information. Both are necessary to make certain a story is fair and appropriate for everyone. The media in today's society cannot afford to remain apart from the stories they report. Rather, they need to become a part of them to make sure they are making the right decisions about what can and should be published.

References

Cauchon, D., and Moore, M. (2002) Desperation forced a horrific decision. *USA Today*. September 11, www.usatoday.com/news/sept11/2002-09-02-jumper_x.htm (accessed July 1, 2010).

Ciolli, R. (1996) Footage too sad to televise. *Newsday*, July 19, www.pulitzer.org (accessed July 1, 2010).

Dioniato, P. (1996) 229 Perish in jet crash: Coast Guard says no survivors are found. *Newsday*. July 18, www.pulitzer.org (accessed July 1, 2010).

Elliott, D., and Lester, P.M. (n.d.) What is news? The answer is not blowing on a whim. *News Photographer*, http://commfaculty.fullerton.edu/lester/writings/what_is_news.html (accessed July 1, 2010).

Evans, M.C., Baker, A. and Slackman, M. (1996) Just the shell of their souls. *Newsday*, July 19, www.pulitzer.org (accessed July 1, 2010).

Flynn, K., Wright, C., Queen, J. *et al.* (1990) 87 Die: Bronx social club tragedy, *Newsday*, March 26, http://docs.newsbank.com/s/InfoWeb/aggdocs/AWNB/109E86084D5180F4/102B43015865E5CC (accessed July 14, 2010).

Hodges, L. (2003) Taste in photojournalism: A question of ethics or aesthetics? *McGraw Hill*, http://highered.mcgraw-hill.com/sites/dl/free/007288259x/151121/Tastein Photojournalism.pdf (accessed July 1, 2010).

Junod, T. (2003) The falling man. *Esquire Magazine*, September 11, www.esquire.com/features/ESQ0903-SEP_FALLINGMAN (accessed July 1, 2010).

Mintz, P., and Terrazzano, L. (1996) Shards of a disaster on a sunny beach day. *Newsday*. July 19, www.pulitzer.org (accessed July 1, 2010).

Newsday Staff (1996) Searching for answers: Probers focus on possibility of bomb or missile; toll at 230. *Newsday*, July 19, www.pulitzer.org (accessed July 1, 2010).

Schaer, S. C. and Yan, E. (1996) In the morgue, somber tasks. *Newsday*, July 19, www.pulitzer.org (accessed July 1, 2010).

SPJ Code of Ethics (n.d.) The Society of Professional Journalists Code of Ethics. www.spj.org/ethicscode.asp (accessed July 1, 2010).

25

Ungrievable Lives
Global Terror and the Media

Giovanna Borradori

I lived firsthand the attacks of September 11, 2001, from the 11th floor of my apartment on the Upper East Side, in Manhattan. However, I learned what was happening only a few miles away through a phone call from Rome, while wondering why I was hearing so many sirens howling on the street. As I was agonizing about the safety of my two children, stranded in their schools at the opposite ends of town, I was watching the Twin Towers collapse on TV and speaking to a terrified friend in Brussels who had called me on my mobile. On that day, original and copy, event and representation were literally indistinguishable. Since that day, the global media – the complex communicative network without either center or periphery, unregulated by laws and unmarked by boundaries – shrunk the planet, by transforming "the local event simultaneously into a global one and the whole world population into a benumbed witness" (Borradori, 2003, p. 28) These words, spoken by philosopher Jürgen Habermas a few weeks after the attacks, announce that September 11, 2001 inaugurated not only a set of brand new questions at the geopolitical level, but also important and permanent modifications in the structure of perception and experience of the world population at large.

Luckily, it took only a day for the major television channels to realize that repeating over and over again the scenes of the two planes penetrating the Twin Towers had a traumatizing effect on both viewers worldwide and the relatives of the victims. The endless reiteration of the same horrific images intensified anxiety in viewers from Chile to Norway, and made the very real tragedy of families from New Jersey to the Bronx into an obscene spectacle. By contrast, as it was predictable, it took years for journalists, political scientists, media theorists, and philosophers like me to come to grips with the kind of untamable beast terrorism is, due to its slippery meaning and the immense and unique ethical challenge it poses to whoever studies it, writes on it, reports on it or films it: for the internal logic of a terrorist

The Handbook of Global Communication and Media Ethics, First Edition. Edited by Robert S. Fortner and P. Mark Fackler.
© 2011 Blackwell Publishing Ltd. Published 2011 by Blackwell Publishing Ltd.

attack in the age of the global media is such that informing the world audience of the events on the ground cannot be done without divulging and aggrandizing them, thereby contributing to the fulfillment of the attack's psychological, political, financial, and military objectives.

In this essay, I will start by examining the difficulties concerning the very definition of terrorism and then turn to its encounter with the pervasive network of the global media. In particular, I will analyze the impact of terrorism on the global media in terms of the biopolitical figure of autoimmunity, first used by French philosopher Jacques Derrida to describe the fine line that separates information on from support of terrorist attacks. Biologically, the immune system is a network of organs, cells, and molecules that work together to defend the body against aggression by foreign invaders such as bacteria and viruses. I propose to read the global media as part of the immune system of the democratic body politic, whose survival depends on free and informed participation in the public sphere. Since the collapse of the Twin Towers, terrorism has occupied a prominent position on the world stage at the level of geopolitics but also at the level of the media's operation and self-conception. The impact of terrorism on the global media looks like an autoimmune response because the media cannot but disseminate, and consequently augment, terrorism's terrifying effect. Once terror as an emotion migrates into the political sphere it opens the way to rigid polarizations and the undercutting of civic freedoms. Such autoimmune response destroys the pluralism of the democratic body politic and does so by colonizing the public arena with images and narratives of destruction and dehumanization. These images and narratives by themselves invite us to apprehend the other according to the complementary schemes of victimization and demonization. Such an extreme degree of polarization produces a numbing of perception and affect that allows viewing of the other as not fully real, or human, precisely because it is either demonized or victimized. Following Judith Butler's (2009) idea that others appear to us as truly living only if their lives are framed as vulnerable, or at the risk of being lost, and thus grieved, I will claim that the only way the media can control its own replication of terror is by embracing a hyperbolic ethics that privileges responsiveness to the vulnerability of the other over normative principles, rights, and duties. Embracing such an ethics means to accept as a fundamental obligation the dismantling of any proclaimed "we" or "them." Anyone reporting, writing, filming, posting world events, whether officially for a news organization or by taking photos from their own cell phone, should elect as their founding obligation to question the unity and cohesion of any collective actor. Reporting seems to have forgotten, and let its public forget, that a group, a nation, or a culture is not only delimited by other groups, but also internally differentiated in factions and subgroups, and even more deeply, in interdependent, unique individuals. If what Butler (2009) calls the "precariousness" of individual lives is brought into focus, along with the range of material and discursive conditions that are needed to sustain even the simplest human existence, a commitment to a more egalitarian distribution of those conditions is likely to emerge, over and beyond any ideological divide.

Boundless Terror

The difficulty in dealing with the concept of terrorism starts from a simple and disconcerting realization: in spite of the fact that it has been and still is used as a self-evident term, "terrorism" does not designate a specific type of action or event. This makes it an elusive, confusing, and dangerous term.

A symptom of the fogginess that surrounds the concept of terrorism is the anarchy with which names are attributed to the various events associated with it: September 11, 2001, or 9/11; and March 11, 2004 (the train bombings in Madrid, Spain), go by date. However, the marking of dates varies according to national or regional conventions. As a consequence, some terrorist attacks have several names: For example March 11, 2004 is also known as 11/3, 3/11, M-11, and 11-M. Some other terrorist attacks go instead by the name of their targets as in the attack against the USS Cole that occurred on October 17, 2000 in the harbor of Aden, Yemen. Other attacks go by their location, like the Oklahoma City Bombing and there are some that do not have a "proper" name at all, as in the case of the suicide missions carried out by Islamic extremist groups and factions against ordinary Muslims in countries like Iraq and Pakistan.

The confusion that reigns at the level of individual events is puzzling but is only a symptom of a much more serious definitional issue that arises whenever the general categorization is invoked, either as a noun, "terrorism," or as a predicate, "terrorist." Formal documents offer hundreds of definitions of terrorism. The Department of State has one, the Department of Defense has another, the Federal Bureau of Investigation has yet another. However, none is wholly satisfactory, a complaint voiced by many terrorism experts, including Walter Laqueur, an authority on the topic since the 1970s, who concluded that the only features common to all available definitions is that terrorism involves violence and the threat of violence. Laqueur's laconic conclusion is still unfortunately the current situation even though, since 2001, the United States Code has expanded its section dedicated to terrorism considerably. The Code's priority, however, is clearly to spell out the kinds of offenses a crime of terrorism entails as well as various jurisdictional issues. As a consequence, there is nothing in it that clarifies any of the political and conceptual ambiguities haunting the term.

The first ambiguity concerns the alleged political nature of terrorism, which is usually left to the public declarations in which a given group "claims responsibility" for a given attack usually providing a sketch of its ideological justifications. The media and the political establishment validate the legitimacy of the practice by restricting their attention to the authenticity or inauthenticity of these declarations. It is not at all clear to me that the political content of terrorism should in fact be determined through this sort of pronouncement. Given the elusive meaning of the term, violent actions for which vague claims of responsibility are issued could conceivably be classified and prosecuted as criminal activity. To gather the degree of confusion surrounding the use of the term "terrorism" let us look at the following case. In August 2002, *The New York Times* reported a study conducted by the World Markets Research, a centre of economic intelligence based in London, which worked out a world ranking of countries at risk of terrorist attacks. It gave Colombia the first place and the United States the fifth. In this case just like innumerable other ones, the label "terrorism" covered over abysmal differences in context. Colombia's tumultuous political front, copiously fraught with assassinations, is complex and fragmented: drug-lord mercenary armies fight alongside paramilitary private groups, hired by land-owners, against the historical so called terrorists (the members of the Revolutionary Armed Forces of Colombia, or FARC), the police force, and the official army. How can this splintered play of forces, deeply entrenched in contradictions specific to Latin American modern history, be so easily assimilated to the attacks of 9/11, or the suicide bombers on the Tube in London? Similarly, where is the common ground between international terrorist networks such as Al Qaeda and domestic terrorist groups or individuals in the United States? Interestingly, this parallel is seldom drawn, if at all.

Habermas' solution to this problem is to reconstruct the political content of terrorism as a function of the realism of its goals. In this perspective, terrorism becomes nothing more than a historical category. Habermas' solution applies very efficiently to the case of national liberation movements that succeed in their scope: these are situations where those who are considered terrorists, and possibly even convicted as terrorists, become, in a sudden turn of events, the new political leaders. Here is a classic example: At the head of the military Zionist faction known as *Irgun*, Menachem Begin, one of the founding fathers of Israel, was the mastermind of the Jewish uprising against the British authorities controlling Palestine, which began in 1944, increased in pace and scope immediately after World War II, and continued until late 1947. Begin ordered many of *Irgun*'s operations, including the famous Acre prison breakout that allowed the liberation of many members of the underground organization, and the bombing of the central British administrative offices in the King David Hotel, which caused the death of 91 people, among which were 15 Jews. Following the establishment of the State of Israel, in 1948, Begin disbanded *Irgun* and became the leader of the parliamentary opposition until 1977.

It would be a mistake to think that a case like Begin's does not have a chance to happen anymore. As recently as November 2009, the world learned that the man who was elected president of Uruguay, José Mujica, was a cofounder of the Tupamaros guerrillas, an armed and very active "terrorist" organization that during the 1960s and 1970s regularly conducted kidnappings, bombings, and armed robberies. While the country was suffering under an oppressive military dictatorship that lasted two decades, Mujica was in prison, enduring torture and solitary confinement; an experience, he declared, that cured him of the belief that armed revolution can achieve lasting social change.

The second level at which the concept of terrorism remains dangerously ambiguous concerns its conceptual coherence. Take one of the official definitions of "terrorist activity," which has been widely adopted by the FBI and the CIA as well as the Departments of State and Defense. The document states that terrorists are to be considered those "violent acts intended to intimidate or coerce a 'civilian' population or intended to influence the policy of a government by intimidation or coercion" (*United States Code Congressional and Administrative News*, 1984). None of the primitive terms is given any substantive clarification. For example, what counts as "intimidation" of both civilians and governments? If it is true that intimidation is the chief characteristic of an act of terrorism, it is also a major component of military strategy in war. What separates terrorism from war? Has there ever been a war completely free of terrorism, namely, the killing or abuse of civilians for the sake of the intimidation or swaying of their government? Were the carpet bombings of London, at the hand of the Nazis, or of Dresden, Germany, Hiroshima and Nagasaki, Japan, at the hands of the allies, acts of war or acts of terrorism? The definition provided by the United States Code does not help to dispel the confusion either. In title 22, Section 2656, terrorism is presented as a "premeditated, politically motivated violence perpetrated against noncombatant targets by subnational groups or clandestine agents, usually intended to influence an audience." What it is that separates civilian and military targets – one of the historical obstacles to the peace process between Israeli and Palestinians? The Code speaks of "subnational groups or clandestine agents" as the sole possible agents of terrorism. On what grounds do we discount the possibility that a legitimate government may commit acts of terrorism? Virtually any authoritarian regime, not to speak of dictatorships, has used terrorism as a means to subdue the opposition. So, if we draw a line between state and nonstate terrorism, are we also to discuss their respective legitimacies according to different parameters? Is there a difference in kind between state and nonstate terrorism? What is one to make of the other distinction between national and international terrorism, upheld after 9/11 as a truism? Once terrorism erupts on the geopolitical scene, it becomes hard to distinguish clearly between institutions such as the army and the police, or even between war and peace, with the result that it is not absurd to wonder whether we are ever really at peace in the presence of the potential occurrence, or recurrence, of a terrorist attack.

For political discourse as a whole the encounter with terrorism equals stepping on a landmine and experiencing the devastating blast – the effects produced by terrorism in the material sphere, where people and objects are physically torn apart by explosive devices, and replicated in the theoretical sphere, where laws and definitions are imploded by the collapse of age old conceptual architectures. What is certain is that terrorism exposes the global system of communication to a new set of responsibilities *vis à vis* both realms.

A Spectral Fight, Not a War

As disturbing as it is to face it, the global media has an unwilling but constitutive role in the production and dissemination of terror. One of the suggestions of this essay is that the figure of autoimmunity may help clarify it; and in so doing, pave the way for a strategy of containment of its destructive effects. In order to throw light on this crucial point, I will first explain the broad semantic umbrella of the term immunity, which I will recover from its long and singular history. I will then show how Derrida first used autoimmunity to describe the relation between the attacks of September 11, 2001 and the history of the American participation in the Cold War.

The Latin term *immunitas* originates from the legal concept of exemption. In ancient Rome the exemption was meant for individuals who were excused from military service or paying taxes, whereas in the in the Middle Ages it applied to the exemption that the Church's property and personnel enjoyed from civil control. Although the first medical use of the term dates to the fourteenth century, when it indicated being miraculously saved from contagion in the plague epidemic, medical historian Arthur M. Silverstein noticed that its first biological application occurred in the poetry of the Roman Marcus Annaeus Lucanus "to describe the famous resistance to snakebite of the Psylli Tribe of North Africa" (Silverstein, 1989, p. 1). This history of the term makes clear the ambiguity haunting the meaning of immunity, which, very much like the Greek word *pharmakon*, means *both* "cure" and "poison." In fact, this oscillation between cure and poison well describes the role that the global media plays *vis à vis* the democratic body politic. On the one hand, the media is the guarantor for the circulation of information, opinion formation, and its free expression. On the other hand, if it falls prey to the colonization of its space by a hegemonic political agenda, the media becomes the democratic body politic's most destructive poison.

Historically, the term immunity did not earn formal medical currency "until the nineteenth century following the rapid spread of Edward Jenner's smallpox vaccination." (Silverstein, 1989, p. 1) Yet, even after its definitive medical adoption as the heading for a new branch of studies called "immunology," the concept of immunity retained that same semantic fluctuation between the realms of biology and law. On the one hand, the legal meaning survived in expressions such as "diplomatic immunity," "charitable immunity," and "parliamentary immunity;" on the other, as literary scholar W. T. Mitchell writes, "the whole theory of the immune system, and the discipline of immunology, is riddled with images drawn from the socio-political sphere – of invaders and defenders, hosts and parasites, natives and aliens, and of borders and identities that must be maintained" (Mitchell, 2005, p. 917). Before looking carefully at how the cross over between biology and politics evolved to the point of intersecting the phenomenon of terrorism in the post-9/11 phase, I wish to examine more closely the biology of immunity.

Biologically, the first identification of the immune system in its current understanding was carried out by a Persian physician and alchemist in the ninth century AD, Al-Razi, who distinguished between smallpox and measles, and indicated that exposure to these agents conferred a lasting protection against them. However, it was only with the French scientist, Louis Pasteur, in the second half of the nineteenth century that immunology was born as the study of how various pathogens, including bacteria and viruses, cause disease, and how after an infectious episode the human body or other organisms gain the ability to resist future attacks. From Pasteur on, the immune system has been likened to a sixth sense. Its workings can be compared to a sophisticated set of learning tools, able to distinguish between invading pathogens and the organism's own healthy cells. Since the receptors coordinating this selection are the antibodies, we can say that the immune system's main function is to produce antibodies, which are its most intelligent components. The way antibodies learn is by "mirroring" the invading antigens, binding themselves to them, and killing them.

"Clonal selection" is the theory that explains immunological memory as a two-prong cloning of lymphocytes (the blood cells that are the basic components of the immune system). While one clone actively combats infection, the other remains in the immune system for a longer time, which results in protection, or immunity, to that antigen. The challenge of the immune system is that pathogens can mutate rapidly and produce adaptations able to bypass it. If the antibodies do not keep up either with the aggressiveness of the pathogens or with their mutations, the organism falls prey to an infection. What happens if the whole system of recognition of the host's own cells fails? The immune system turns against itself: it is these misdirected immune responses that are referred to as autoimmunity. Autoimmunity is thus the phenomenon by which an organism attacks its own defenses against foreign invaders.

The figure of autoimmunity renders ambiguous a set of opposites traditionally at the center of political and military discourse: friend and enemy, native and foreign, defense and attack. It is precisely because of this ambiguity that Derrida used it to elucidate the nature of the violence responsible for the collapse of the Twin Towers and a section of the Pentagon. Derrida's argument concerning autoimmunity starts from a double consideration: the aggression came from within the United States and the commando that carried it out was an aberrant product of recent American history. The attacks against the Twin Towers and the Pentagon were conducted by a small group of men who, with a ruse, got hold of an American plane, on the grounds of an American airport, and used it to destroy an American building complex, internationally recognized as a symbol of American global financial power and leadership. The notion of the pure foreignness of the attacks that was being promoted by the media and fueled by the Bush Administration literally as they occurred, and that remained uncontested for a long time thereafter, is compromised already at this minimum level. Moreover the commando, insofar as it was part of Al Qaeda, was a late outgrowth of a large group of intelligence and military operatives that had been armed, financed, and trained by the United States in the context of the Cold War. At that time, Washington backed the religiously inspired resistance against the Soviets in Afghanistan, the *mujiahidin*, which included Bin Laden in its ranks. The *mujiadhin* movement, which would evolve into the Taliban regime, was thus part of the United States' own system of defense against the USSR.

Derrida appealed to the figure of autoimmunity to describe what he called a case of double suicide: the commando's "own (and one will remain forever defenseless in the face of a suicidal, autoimmunitary aggression – and that is what terrorizes most) but also the suicide of those who welcomed, armed, and trained them" (Borradori, 2003, p. 96). The phenomenon of autoimmunity captures the self-destruction of the terrorist commando as well as their destruction of those to whom they owed their political life: the United States of America. In either case, it legitimately describes an immune response misdirected at the organism's own cells.

The kind of violence that exploded on September 11, 2001 can be illustrated by the phenomenon of autoimmunity in yet another sense: its self-propagating quality. The internal logic of autoimmunity is such that the organism undergoing the phenomenon becomes structurally and indefinitely defenseless because it has lost the protection of its own immune system. Medically, weakening the immune system is often the only option, since in this way its aggressive misfiring is also going to be weakened. Similarly, the threat of an attack aimed at spreading terror, particularly against a mass of ordinary citizens as it was the case in downtown Manhattan and Washington may be over physically but is never really over discursively, symbolically, and psychologically.

A terrorist attack is never over because it is future-oriented: it always promises more than it is able to deliver. As Derrida suggested, "a weapon wounds and leaves forever open an unconscious scar; but this weapon is terrifying because it comes from the to-come, from the future … traumatism is produced by the *future*, by the *to come*, by the threat of the worst *to come*, rather than by an aggression that is "over and done with" (Borradori, 2003, p. 97). As horrific as the events of September 11, 2001 were, if they had been conclusive, there would have been the possibility, after mourning the dead and grieving the losses, to turn the page. However, in Derrida's view, one of the structural features of an act of terrorism is precisely not offering this chance. Any wound, he claims, leaves a scar, and with the scar comes the fear to be wounded again. What is specific to terrorism, however, is that it projects its threat into the future so powerfully that the worst is always and systematically expected as yet to come. "What is put at risk by this *terrifying* immunitary logic is nothing less than the existence of the world," (Borradori, 2003, p. 98) he ominously concluded. In the same way that the organism's life is threatened by a misdirected immune response, the existence of the world itself is threatened by an act aimed at spreading terror, especially in an age in which images of chemical, bacteriological, and nuclear attacks are part and parcel of what terror is about. In fact, the aftermath of the attacks of September 11, 2001, proves Derrida's point. Their consequences have been incalculable both at the domestic and international levels. Apart from the problematic response of the Bush Administration to the attacks, any reaction on the part of a state or a continental alliance is fraught with a very high margin of error: there are the risks of overreaction and underreaction, on top of the game of guessing the reliability of data provided mostly by intelligence. The fight against terror is thus a spectral fight, not a war.

Autoimmunity and Weaponization

Derrida's argument insists on the autoimmunitary character of the violence unleashed by the Cold War as the historical context for the emergence of the Afghan religious resistance against the Soviets, which eventually produced clandestine organizations, such as Al-Qaeda, who then turned back against their original lifeline, the United States. In Derrida's footsteps, I propose to turn the figure of autoimmunity to examine the relation between the phenomenon of terrorism and the global media, which any attack aimed at the dissemination of terror seeks to weaponize. Indeed, the turning of a physical object such as a commercial airliner into a weapon is only the most tangible aspect of a broader mechanism of weaponization, which extends to the media and religion among other things.

Suppose that the sprawling network of communication, information, and representation that constitute the global media performs the same function that the immune system plays in a biological organism. Like the immune system the global media would thus be a sixth sense able to learn from the encounter with external stimuli how to distinguish between invading pathogens and the organism's own healthy cells. In my parallel, this selection corresponds to the expansive as well as defensive role of the global media: on the one hand, the recognition of healthy cells creates the conditions of possibility for participation in the democratic life of the body politic, nourishing and protecting the public sphere's pluralism of opinions and their free expression; on the other, the selection between the organism's own cells and the pathogens should defend that same body politic from any colonizing attempts by private interests or the interest of given political associations as well as the instrumental use of information, communication, and representation.

Biologically, the selection between one's "own" healthy cell and "invading" pathogen occurs via a mirroring in which antibodies, the agents of the immune system, "photograph" or "film" the invaders, bind themselves to them, and kill them. In the same way, the global media mirrors whatever it encounters, by photographing, filming, and generally reporting on it. This is what I call its analytical function. Like the biological immune system, the global media expresses a critical function too, which consists in denouncing hegemonic attempts at centrally controlling, and thus impoverishing, what it is set to protect: the democratic body politic. The mirroring of the world, which per deontological mandate the media has to conduct as freely, deeply, and objectively as possible, is thus, and at the same time, the enabling condition for the media's detection of any infringements of its own freedom of movement and operation.

In the global arena, the media's analytical and critical roles have become less distinguishable, a fact that has brought new challenges. A reason for it is the blurring of the boundaries between news and entertainment, known as infotainment, which has complicated the distinction between analysis and critique by exploding the genre of the political commentary. Infotainment has reinvented and spectacularized political commentary allowing it to become more ideological, more dependent on populist rhetoric, and in general more commercially oriented by ratings than by any reflective attempt at a critical appraisal of the issues.

Another reason for the merging between the media's analytical and critical functions rests with the exponential acceleration of the circulation of information, which includes instances of radical disenfranchisement from professional journalism. The ever more carefully staged studios producing mostly polarized, and polarizing, political commentary seem to be working in a stale format, remote from the vividness of what lands directly on the blogosphere, which bypasses both the cable networks and the printed press. This structural modification at the level of how information circulates represents both a challenge and a promise in terms of the global media's commitment to enact communicative democracy.

The phenomenon of this mostly informal reporting that tends to land on blogs and social networking sites is epitomized, I believe, by private cell phones, which allow the dissemination of vocal and visual messages around the world in real time, even in areas or situations that do not offer the immediate availability of a computer. Their role emerged clearly during the harrowing minutes between the impact of the planes against the Twin Towers and their collapse. Every second of that tragic segment of time was reported, denounced, and commented on by employees trapped in their offices in the upper floors of the North and the South towers. The callers were desperately trying to inform their families and the world of what was happening. The same has been true during the upheaval following the presidential elections in Iran, in June 2009. The pictures of the violence against demonstrators protesting the allegedly manipulated reelection of the conservative hawk, Mahmoud Ahmadinejad, went around the world before the political establishment could even try to control what left the streets of Teheran.

An article that appeared in *The Guardian* (Tate and Weaver, 2009) exemplifies how Neda Soltani became the face of the Iranian upheaval. "Shortly after 5pm on Saturday afternoon, Hamed, an Iranian asylum seeker in the Netherlands, took a frantic call from a friend in Tehran. 'A girl has just been killed right next to me,' the friend said. It had all happened quickly. A young woman, chatting on her mobile phone, had been shot in the chest. She faded before a doctor, who was on the scene, could do anything to help. There was more. Hamed's friend, who does not want to be named, filmed the incident on his phone. Within moments the footage had landed in Hamed's inbox. Five minutes later it was on YouTube and Facebook. Within hours it had become one of the most potent threats faced by the Iranian regime in 30 years."

The dissemination and radical decentering of news production and circulation that has made Neda Soltani the face of a major political process is at the same time terrifying and promising, in proving and disproving what media theorist Murray Edelman has been claiming for years. "The spectacle constituted by news reporting continuously constructs and reconstructs social problems, crises, enemy, and leaders and so creates a succession of threats and reassurances" (Edelman, 1988, p. 1). Problems and personalities, according to Edelman, thus play a pivotal role in the dynamics of approval and disapproval of political causes, and it is especially this constitutive role with respect to public opinion that is "masked by the assumption that citizens, journalists, and scholars are observers of 'facts' whose meaning can be accurately ascertained by those who are properly trained and motivated" (Edelman, 1988, p. 1). Neda's brief and poignant agony has rallied behind it public opinion from the four corners of the planet. As teenagers and some of their younger parents were browsing Facebook or checking the most popular videos on YouTube, Neda's face irrupted in their lives silently pleading for their attention. Congruently with Edelman's view, it is that irruption that has constructed the public opinion's uprising against the Ahmadinejiad authoritarian regime. I am not sure that ideological interests were at play there. This changes the conditions under which the media can exercise its critical role, which thus needs to be reexamined.

Edelman is right in stating that the spectacle of news reporting constructs and reconstructs social and political issues. I also agree with him that, "because a social problem is not a verifiable entity but a construction that furthers ideological interests, its explanation is bound to be part of the process of construction rather than a set of falsifiable propositions." (Edelman, 1988, p. 18) Reducing a complex construction to a set of verifiable propositions runs the risk of forfeiting the deconstruction of the "ideological interests" the construction serves, which is, I believe, an essential aspect of the liberal-democratic mission of the media as a public watchdog. This deconstruction is certainly not encouraged by the positivist default assumption about the solidity of the distinction between fact and value, which makes facts and not values, or evaluations, the objects of reporting. This positivist assumption, based on the reduction of ambiguity to certainty, is indeed a dangerous and simplistic idealization that imports into the uneven and open-ended sphere of discourse the orderly methodological abstraction of quantitative reasoning. Unfortunately such idealization serves the interests of most mainstream news organizations: embedded in large corporations, these organizations are "more concerned about representing shareholders interests than embracing public-interest standards that might better serve democracy." The subservience of the press to the corporate world parallels what political scientists Lance Bennett, Regina Lawrence, and Steven Livingston (2007) call the "tendency of the press to record rather than critically examine the official pronouncements of government." The massive failure of the American media in expressing their critical function with regard to the Iraq War and its alleged preemptive legitimacy is the product of that tendency.

The deconstruction of particular political, corporate, and ideological interests is an essential aspect of the liberal-democratic mission of the media: as media theorist Simon Cottle put it, it consists in "a combination of normative expectations deeply embedded in civil societies, regulatory requirements, and the professional raison d'être of journalism itself, all mandate a central responsibility in the communicative enactment of democracy" (Cottle, 2006, p. 22). However, what Neda's story shows is that, in its process of globalization, which is not only a question of geographical expansion but also a modification in the modes of production of our everyday existence, a considerable segment of information circulates independently from institutional or corporate-minded settings as well as structures of political dominance and control. This fact renders the media's position as hopeful but also more fragile: on the one hand, information is being produced and exchanged over and beyond corporate and political constraints, thus representing a token of enacted communicative democracy. On the other, the spontaneous proliferation of data renders discriminating between reality and fiction, legitimate and counterfeit narratives, even more demanding. What are the new filters going to be? Will the cascade of informal production of news, circulated in the blogosphere, make the disoriented traditional media outlets even more dependent on the political and financial structures of dominance and control?

In the same way that biological autoimmunity disables the immune system from distinguishing between an organism's "own" healthy cells and the invading pathogens, an attack aimed at the spreading of terror eats at the media's ability to pursue its critical commitment to the communicative enactment of democracy. Minimally, this enactment consists in denouncing any attempts to colonize the space in which information circulates and communication occurs. Weakened in its ability to appropriately select between healthy reporting and the pathological colonization of its space by both corporate pressure and the informal news production landing directly on the blogosphere, the media may easily become an agent of diffusion of terror, a panic that takes hold of the public stage by incrementally silencing all other voices, images, and figures. It is as if an act of terror was able, in the context of the global media network, to disrupt the mechanism of clonal selection, whereby lymphocytes are replicated according to a dual division of labor. After mirroring the attackers, one clone combats the infection, while the other protects the organism from future invasions by transforming the pathogen's imprint into immunological memory. In the presence of the terrorist threat the clone fighting the infection is muted, so that the pathogen is free to colonize the host and its immunological memory.

In the case of the violence against the Twin Towers and the Pentagon, the colonization of the media, and as a consequence of the public sphere, was easily achieved at the visual level: the image of the gutted Towers and of their eerily elegant implosion smothered the global flow of information effortlessly in the short-term. Long-term, however, the violence produced equally destructive consequences at the level of political and social discourse, which seemed to succumb under the weight of a constricting rhetoric of demonization and victimization. Undoubtedly, the political responsibility for that rhetoric falls squarely onto the Bush administration that imposed it as the only respectable mode of response to the attacks. However, in addition to it, I am also suggesting the presence of a systemic malfunctioning of the media that, for lack of a better description, may be compared to an autoimmune response. Terrorism, and this is my argument, is like a virus that gets hold of the media's software and disarms it to the point of making it self-destruct. This is what I have called weaponization, an effect that terrorism, now projected on the global stage, seems to be able to produce on the entire discursive field.

In the face of this challenge, different media ought to respond in ways tailored to the specific structure. Also, given the different formats in which information is being circulated, each medium has to apply distinct criteria in judging those formats in relation to the concurrent risks of colonization and weaponization. In other words it is necessary to examine, as Cottle put it, "how established media forms mediatize, that is shape, facilitate, and condition the communication of conflicts, sometimes in the most decisive of ways" (Cottle, 2006, p. 21). For example, studies focusing on television as a specific medium, such as David Altheide's (1987), have sought to understand how "'event-type' reports associated with regular evening news broadcasts tends to focus on the visuals of the aftermath and tactics of terrorism, while 'topic-type' format associated with interviews and documentary presentation are more likely to include materials about purposes, goals, and rationals" (Cottle, 2006, p. 21) Altheide's argument is that event-type reports, focused on images of destruction and dehumanization, feed into media colonization and weaponization more than topic-type formats. The polarization between victims and perpetrators, which became the language of information in the aftermath of the collapse of the Twin Towers, is an instrinsic feature of those kinds of images which, in the absence of adequate topic-type reporting, obstruct the communicative enactment of democracy.

The global media is thus at constant risk of falling prey to a "take over" that, as an autoimmune response, may spin out of control. I think that since September 11, 2001 such a take-over did spin out of control as evidenced by the new hegemony of the most alarmist format of all: "breaking news." Cottle put figures on my intuition that, in the post-9/11 phase, this kind of format seemed to have permanently taken over television news programs. According to his research, a total of 74.3% of all news deliver either "thin" updates on the events on the war on terror, or news stories dominated by a single external news source, usually the institutional and political elites, which during the Bush administration years replicated and deepened the polarizing language of Al Qaeda's own press releases. Another cumulative 19% is taken by what Cottle calls the "contest" and "contention" frames. The contest frame is one in which "conflictual news stories are framed in terms of binary opposition, with opposing views and arguments generally given approximately equal weight or representation and structured in adversarial terms." (Cottle, 2006, p. 27) The contention frame is a variation of the contest frame because, in it, "an increased array of voices or perspectives may be represented, in contrast to only two opposed views" (Cottle, 2006, p. 27). Finally, a meager 0.3% of all news is covered using the "exposé/investigative" frame, "based on intensive research and exploratory fact-finding as well as exposé journalism of public and private affairs," (Cottle, 2006, p. 28) which is the frame best suited to disrupt colonization attempts and more apt at securing public engagement. These are stunning statistics and they apply to perhaps still the most politically influential global media today: television. Any segment of the media establishment should review its operations in light of these numbers, if it does not want to mindlessly reproduce the same violence that terror encourages. A violence that is "visualized, incessant, universal, ahistorical, without a political context or motivation" (Cottle, 2006, p. 37)

There Shall Be No Mourning

Instead of protecting the pluralism of the democratic body politic the autoimmune response tends to destroy it and does so by flooding the public arena with images and narratives that do not only represent and voice terror but repeat its violence incessantly, intimating its indefinite multiplication. Repetition is thus at the center of my proposal to rethink the critical role of the media on the global stage. Biological immunity is, again, a useful analogy to illustrate it.

If immunity is a kind of cellular memory that allows the body to learn by experience how to fight a given pathogen, and then to never forget it, amnesia leaves the body without defense – but is amnesia not the endless repetition of the same? In articulating a similar point, Mitchell notes "the convergence of cloning and terrorism as cultural icons of the principal techno-scientific anxieties of our time" (Mitchell, 2005, p. 914). From Hollywood to Bollywood cloning is associated with images of horror and dehumanization, eugenic experiments and cyborgs. "The figure of the clone itself, as a mindless, even headless repository of 'spare parts' ... all turn out to be handy images of the terrorist himself. Terrorist and clone," Mitchell continues, "unite in the stereotype of the mindless automaton, an organism whose individuality has been eliminated, fit only for a suicide mission" (Mitchell, 2005, p. 914). The exact replica of a lifeform, namely, the clone, is also used to describe terrorist networks as organic tissues whose "cells" tend to clone themselves. Repetition, thus, picks out in many converging ways how narratives of terrorist identity as well as images of the terrorist's inhumanity and destructiveness are aired and circulated.

The effect of repetition is that all kinds of differences fade. Whether it is the difference between places, contexts, or faces, repetition empties out whatever is distinctive and irreducible, singular, and unique. Any difference in kind, if repeated long enough, becomes a difference in degree, a quantitative matter and as quantity sets in as the fundamental evaluative parameter, attention is turned away from what it is that is being counted, statistically analyzed, and numerically interpreted. Consequently, the identity of the units belonging to a given set is simplified because the focus now shifts onto pitting set against one another, or grouping them together in order to taxonomically organize them. As it happens to stories and characters strictly adhering to a literary or cinematic genre, from detective novels to Western films, storylines as well as faces crystallize into easily recognizable molds that eventually essentialize all identity, whether it is the identity of a group or an individual, rendering it substitutable and irrelevant.

The popularity of Pavlovian experiments with conditioned reflexes, whereby a given response can be made to occur to almost any stimulus simply by exposing the subject to the same chain of events over and over again, is behind the default positivist assumption that repetition produces recognition. My argument stems, instead, from the opposite standpoint: that repetition does not produce recognition, because recognition involves a cognitive operation of selection of its own.

Nineteenth century philosopher, Georg W.F. Hegel, gave an account of recognition that seems eerily close to the basic grammar of immunity, which, as we saw, is based on the cellular memory's ability to select between what is the organism's "own" and what is "foreign" to it, what is friendly to it and what is inimical. Said very roughly, to recognize means, for both Hegel and biological immunity, to be able to differentiate between what is the same and can be seamlessly repeated, and what is different, assumed as what stands in the way of the repetition of the same. In a parallel manner, the human subject in the Hegelian tradition and the individual organism in immunological science both face what is different by engaging in a struggle aimed at subduing it. Hegel defines this struggle as dialectical in nature because, whether it ends in the elimination of what is different, the other, or in its subjugation, it involves a contact with it that leaves its trace in the self. For Hegelian philosophy, the dialectical relation characterizes the social bond, the relation of interdependence between the individual and the community. In the case of the immune system, a similar dialectics defines the relation between host and invader: the assimilation of the invader by the host is obtained via the formation of antibodies that mirror the structure of the invading pathogen and remain permanently stored in the organism's immunological memory. Biology and politics, and more specifically, immunology and Hegelian political theory converge in a description of recognition as a dialectical relation, and thus a relation of interdependence, between self and others, host and invaders.

As Hegel himself claimed in a famous chapter of his *Phenomenology of Spirit*, entitled "Absolute Freedom and Terror," the experience of terror annihilates all sense of interdependence. With its spectacularization of violence and all-consuming focus on the enemy, any act associated with spreading terror demands an extreme polarization that reduces the world to irreconcilable opposites: perpetrators and victims, oppressors and oppressed, evil and good. As a last argument of this essay I wish to suggest an interpretation of acts of terror as those acts that deny all human interdependence.

The global media that under ordinary conditions has the function of the immunitary system, faced with acts of terror responds by deploying an autoimmunitary response whose distinctive feature is, as we have seen, the inability to recognize its own healthy cells from the invading pathogen. While in a biological organism that confusion brings the immune system to destroy its own tissue, in the social and political realm the confusion makes the global media lose its critical force and replicate terror, by disseminating it in all corners of the planet and projecting it onto an indefinite future. Alongside theorist Judith Butler, I want to claim that what connects two partners in a relation of mutual dependence is the recognition of "precariousness," understood as their shared exposure to vulnerability and the risk of loss. Butler's (2009) suggestion is that we recognize each other to be different but also interdependent if and only if we are able to recognize under what conditions the life of the other, like mine, can be sustained. This recognition is predicated on the awareness that we are both facing vulnerability and the risk of loss. In other words, I recognize the other for its difference from me only in the context of our common exposure to the possibility of grief. Grievability, therefore, is a necessary condition for the recognition of the other. My argument is that, in order to enact some control over the autoimmunitary response caused by terrorism, the global media's ethical mandate is to reinstate precariousness both on deontological grounds and because of its present uneven distribution. Reinstating precariousness in public discourse would reduce the political manipulation of grievability and mourning, which is part and parcel of the social and political use of terror.

The notion of precariousness, in Butler's theory, is founded on her assumption that to be a body, human or otherwise, is to be exposed to "social crafting." Butler writes, "the body is exposed to socially and politically articulated forces ... that make possible the body's persisting and flourishing" (Butler, 2009, p. 3). Butler's point here is that the body is neither a purely biological entity nor a socially self-sufficient one. Rather, like the human subject, the body is constituted through "norms, which, in their reiteration, produce and shift the terms through which subjects are recognized" (Butler, 2009, pp. 3–4). The set of norms, or normative conditions, that produce subjects and bodies by making them recognizable have "historically contingent ontologies." Since they are historically contingent, these ontologies can be analyzed as politically saturated frames.

Butler (2009) observes that existing norms allocate recognition differentially, as a function of a given population, nation, or community's political weight, social relevance, and visibility by and access to the global media. As a consequence, since recognition means apprehending the precariousness of the life of the other, there are others whose precariousness is not recognized. These are expendable lives, lives without needs, lives represented as not facing mortality. These are lives that are reductively perceived as simply "living" and thus as not belonging to an individuated agent. If precariousness means that life is subject to social and economic conditions that put my existence in the hands of others, a life perceived as nonprecarious is a life whose vulnerability is obscured, and thus a life that cannot be grieved or mourned. Concurrently, a lack of recognition of a life's precariousness entails to be relieved of all responsibility for it.

My claim is that acts seeking to spread terror work precisely by obscuring life's vulnerability. The question is how that concealment occurs. The more explicit way is by dehumanizing the lives of the victims' who, in spite of being mostly innocent civilians, are taken to be siding with the supposed enemy just by virtue of working in a given office building, praying at a mosque or a temple, or staying at a hotel. However, vulnerability is obscured in other ways too, which are generally harder to spot. In discussing nationalism, Butler claims that it "works in part by producing and sustaining a certain version of the subject ... produced and sustained through powerful forms of media." We cannot forget, Butler admonishes, "that what gives power to their version of the subject is precisely the way in which they are able to render the subject's own destructiveness righteous and its own destructibility *unthinkable*" (Butler, 2009, p. 47). What Butler says about nationalism, one of the historical motivations for terrorist activity, can be easily applied to the workings of the kind of terrorism from the post-9/11 era. For the occlusion of vulnerability does not only concern the victim's life but also the perpetrator's life and goes hand in hand with her sense of untainted righteousness, whether the agent is an individual, a group, or a state. There is yet another way in which precariousness is concealed: through the high symbolic power of the target of the attack. Anything entailing the context evaporates under the symbolic force of the attack. This vaporization clouds the precariousness that would make the devastation and the maiming of the urban environment unbearable to watch. So, not only the precariousness of the victims, but also the precariousness of the perpetrators as well as of the context in which the violence takes place are all buried under the rubble.

In the face of the immense ethical challenge of reporting violence aimed at spreading terror and in order to control its own role in disseminating more violence, the global media has to keep precariousness in sight because it is the media, even much more powerfully than the ideological justifications embraced by the agents of destruction, that can operate on what we have indicated as the norms that regulate the recognizability of life. Terrorism sustains its practices by acting on the global audience's sensibility, its "structure of feeling and reference" to use an expression by theorist Edward Said. Such structure gets crafted so that the public exposed to the spectacle of violence will apprehend the world selectively. For example, the practice of "embedded journalism," which was implemented by the Bush Administration since the invasion of Iraq and was accepted by the media organizations to get closer to action on the battlefield, crucially contributed to crafting the public's structure of feeling and reference toward the Iraq War for years on end. It did so by seeking to control not only "what" the public was being exposed to and shielded from seeing or hearing, but also by determining "how," namely, from what perspective the public was apprehending others, their vulnerability and invulnerability, humanity and inhumanity. That perspective, as Butler notes, "is a way of interpreting in advance what will and will not be included in the field of perception." Scenes of war "are meant to be established by the perspective that the Department of Defense orchestrates and permits, thereby illustrating the orchestrative power of the state to ratify what will be called reality: the extent of what is perceived to exist" (Butler, 2009, p. 66). The perspective does not address "what" the public was being exposed to during the Bush years but "how" whatever was being presented to it had been selected. By calling attention to the fact that perspective is an a priori interpretation of what can be included *and* excluded by the framing of the media, Butler makes a subtle point, dense with theoretical and practical consequences. Contrasting acts of terror with acts of war clarifies why. Acts of war have a state behind them that regulates the perspective of their frames intentionally at least at some degree. Thanks to its "orchestrative power," to keep with Butler's terms, the state ratifies "what will be called reality." By contrast, acts of terror in the post-9/11 phase, express an iconic violence whose intention is hard to spell out in terms of immediate strategic goals. In this sense, the frame engendered by an act of terror structures as much by excluding that which should not be recognizable from the perceptual field, as they do by including in it that which is deemed appropriate or necessary to be recognized. Unlike acts of war, and as a consequence of the autoimmune response of the global media, the violence expressed in the act of terror becomes itself the agent behind the regulation of perspective. In replicating and circulating the bare images and narratives of a violent attack, the media excludes the very issue of precariousness from the perceptual field.

Although there is plenty of space for self-criticism by the media establishment we should resist the temptation of picturing the dissemination of terror as an intentional strategy because terror is not fully and exclusively in the media's hands. Responsibility for obscuring precariousness cannot be attributed to any Chief Puppeteer or to the overarching will of any individuated agent. Rather, as Butler cogently affirms, that obscuring "takes place by virtue of the structuring constraints of genre and form on the communicability of affect – and so sometimes takes place against one's will or, indeed, in spite of oneself" (Butler, 2009, p. 67). As life unfolds, actions and events are figures emerging from a background that cannot be represented comprehensively, but only pointed at in terms of its delimiting role. The media's necessary framing of those events and actions, besides the deliberations of its editors, carries within it additional influences that include the structuring effects of norms, which perhaps can be captured by what the German tradition of Critical Theory referred to as "mentalities," a term close in meaning to what today we call culture but with a much sharper critical edge than culture. A mentality is a structure of feeling and reference. It is also the invisible pattern of those convictions, dispositions, attitudes, and preferences of an individual or an organization, only apparently disconnected from one another. If bound together into a "mentality," the pattern looks like the expression of deep "personality" trends that reveal the internalization of the norms of recognizability of life, which govern the uneven distribution between the lives united in precariousness, and thus grievable, and the lives beyond vulnerability, and thus ungrievable.

In this context, the media's primary commitment should be to instigate the recognition of shared precariousness by articulating how that recognition readily translates into a call to securing the conditions for sustainable lives on egalitarian grounds. Concurrently, the media should take very seriously the interminable task of self-scrutiny. Due to the simultaneous production and circulation of discourse, this means attempting to reconstruct the hidden presence of a structure of feeling and reference, attitude and mentality within its own process of framing. The kind of self-scrutiny I have in mind could then be driven by the following questions: Do our framings include enough strong normative commitments to equality and the universalizing of rights for basic human needs? Are we taking into account only material needs, or are we trying to identify symbolic, communicative, or representational needs? Does the framing we use most frequently give voice to the uneven distribution of precariousness that went undetected thus far?

The fault with the way in which the global media responds to violence aimed at spreading terror is much deeper, and graver, than a strategic penchant for market-friendly sensationalism that many impute to the coverage of terrorist attacks. The fault sinks very powerful roots in the functioning of a media grown global very rapidly and facing the constant evolution of the modes in which we produce our ordinary existence. The story of how the agonizing face of Neda Soltani became the face of the Iranian resistance in June 2009 illustrated some of these changes. This is why the media's regulating ideal cannot anymore be balanced and analytical reporting. If examined through the figure of autoimmunity, the fault in media reporting is a pathological flattening and shrinking of the parameters of recognition. Flooded by images and narratives of destruction and dehumanization, it is as if the global media faced the panic of being forced to recognize as real what had been safely presented and experienced as unreal, in films, video-games, and other mass cultural products. Under that pressure, the immune system of the democratic body politic but also of our individual and collective sensibility, as embodied by the global media network, begins to misfire. As more disturbing images and narratives invade the communicative arena, a numbing of perception and affect sets in and allows the public to form a view of the other as not fully real, or human, because it is either demonized or victimized to the extreme. In either case, the lives of distant others are not framed as vulnerable, mortal, and thus grievable. While those "others" are oftentimes grouped and objectified into a "them," they would need to recover the multifaceted reality that constitutes our shared humanity, vulnerability to suffering, and constant exposure to the risk of loss. The same reification, however, haunts the "we," whether it refers to we, the viewers, we, the citizens of a mature constitutional democracy, or we, the members of a criminal organization aiming at spreading terror.

The founding obligation of the global media is thus to disrupt any proclamation of both "we" and "them" by any collective actor, since a group, a nation, or a culture is not only delimited by other groups but also internally differentiated. Any group contains a sub-group, which is oftentimes related to other groups and their own subgroups in a complicated, sometimes conflictual, manner. Moreover, every group has a history that shapes its self-understanding and its mission and by looking at a group through the lens of time one automatically separates its apparent cohesion of membership and purpose, namely, its unity. Finally, any "we" as any "them" is also internally differentiated into singular unique individuals whose identity is crafted and recrafted constantly by their relations to others and themselves, by the forces shaping the context in which they live or which they left behind, by all the discursive framings and their distinct effects on each self.

The work of self-scrutiny, deconstruction of frames and reconstruction of mentalities, does not offer the guarantees of a classical normative ethics, founded on governing principles and individual rights and duties. The ethics that I envision is hyperbolic because it is ultimately an interminable but not impossible endeavor. It requires steady commitment to the enactment of communicative democracy, high tolerance for confusion and ambiguity, and the willingness to take risks. It also entails putting a positive value on the most difficult kind of recognition: the recognition of the spectrality of freedom in an interconnected world and, even more importantly, among interdependent human subjects.

References

Altheide, D.L. (1987) Format and symbols in TV coverage of terrorism in the United States and Great Britain. *International Studies Quarterly*, 31, 161–176.

Bennett, L.W., Lawrence, R.G., and Livingston, S. (2007) *When The Press Fails. Political Power and the News Media from Iraq to Katrina*, The University of Chicago Press, Chicago.

Borradori, G. (2003) *Philosophy in a Time of Terror. Dialogues with Jürgen Habermas and Jacques Derrida*, The University of Chicago Press, Chicago.

Butler, J. (2009) *Frames of War. When Is Life Grievable?*, Verso, New York.

Cottle, S. (2006) Mediatizing the global war on terror: Television's public eye, in *MEDIA, Terrorism, and Theory. A Reader*, (eds A. Kavoori and T. Fraley), Rowman & Littlefield, Oxford, pp. 19–48.

Edelman, M. (1988) *Constructing the Political Spectacle*, University of Chicago Press, Chigao.

Mitchell, W.T.J. (2005) Picturing terror. Derrida's autoimmunity, *Cardozo Law Review*, 27 (2), 913–925.

Silverstein, A.M. (1989) *A History of Immunology*, Academic Press, San Diego.

Tate, R. and Weaver, M. (2009) How Neda Soltani Became the Face of Iran's Struggle, *The Guardian*, June 22.

The United States Code Congressional and Administrative News (1984.) 98th Cong., 2nd session, Oct. 19, 1984, vol. 2, par. 3077, 98 STAT. 2707.

26

Journalism Ethics in the Moral Infrastructure of a Global Civil Society

Robert S. Fortner

Ethics is disturbing.

(Simon Blackburn, 2000, p. 7)

Nothing can be accomplished by denying that man is an essentially troubled being, except to make more trouble.

(William Barrett, 1990, p. 279)

The presence of the public in us depends on our willingness to recognize and to take responsibility for the other, that other person who appears to us, in our space, in our world, and whose presence cannot be ignored. It also depends on honesty and integrity, however pious this sounds, of the communications we construct for each other.

(Roger Silverstone, 2007, p. 39)

In the past decade or more the world of reporting events has expanded from the old categories of reporter, commentator, columnist (both serious and gossip), paparazzi, stringer, and journalist to include citizen journalist, blogger, news aggregator, tweeter, facebooker, youtuber, and mash-upper. Arguably, people referred to as "spinners" and "flacks" could also be added to these lists. These are not precise names, of course, and there is a fair amount of overlap in the activities of one sort of reporter and another. People who report events on Facebook, or via email, are likely also to be tweeters, YouTube users and possibly constructors of mash-ups. Some bloggers are also news aggregators or gossip columnists (Matt Drudge) or perhaps even journalists (HuffingtonPost). Some large media corporations (CNN, Fox) now invite citizen journalists to submit stories to their websites. Some print newspapers (e.g., *The Washington Post*) also employ bloggers. Some websites thrive on reports from their own constituents as citizen reporters (e.g., OhmyNews

---

The Handbook of Global Communication and Media Ethics, First Edition. Edited by Robert S. Fortner and P. Mark Fackler.
© 2011 Blackwell Publishing Ltd. Published 2011 by Blackwell Publishing Ltd.

International from South Korea). How can any global ethical system be applied in such a complex and confusing context?

We must admit, first, the essential truth of Blackburn's observation that ethics is disturbing, perhaps more so in an age of unedited reportage and the propensity to conflate journalism with reporting. None of us would be likely to challenge Barrett's observation – at least on a rational basis – the foundation, rationale, or first justification for observation and reporting since newspapers gave up their singular attention to commerce and began to carry stories on politics, crime, and sensationalistic accounts of human depravity in the mid-nineteenth century. Of course, human nature being what it is (and I will leave that to each of you to define), it is always the "other" who is of interest. People object when the "other" is themselves – their privacy has been violated, their peccadilloes trotted out for the entertainment of the masses. Roger Silverstone's (2007) suggestion that for people to embrace the public aspects of character requires that they take responsibility for the other means that they must, first, know of the other – as someone dependent, or owed, care. To do that, as he continues, requires honesty and integrity in what we say and hear about the other.

We might think of this as the first obligation, then, in this complex environment, for practicing life ethically. Seeing it in all reports of the other, regardless of source, is, of course, a chimera. Jean Baudrillard goes so far as to argue that it cannot be done. In our digitalized world, he says (2005), everything has become an image – even what we consider text on a screen (2005, p. 76). These images are no longer representational; they are merely information to be manipulated, processed, distributed, combined, and recombined. They tell no stories; they have no meaning. "It is this failure of representation which, together with a failure of action, underlies the impossibility of developing an ethics of information, an ethics of images, an ethics of the Virtual and the networks. All attempts in that direction inevitably fail" (2005, p. 78). So the question is, what must ethicists and journalists do – or what can they do, if anything – to assure that this obligation for honesty is met, given the complexity we now face, the essentially troubled character of humankind, and this new environment within which any global civil society must be constructed?

Baudrillard's pessimism about the digital world is a good starting point for exploring the question of journalism ethics. This may seem odd, given his denunciation of the world as ethics-less, but his contention that our present context is one of information alone does provide a foothold. His characterization of our predicament is correct, of course, insofar as it applies to the challenge, even if we can (and should, or must) challenge his conclusion. It is not merely his pessimism that should give us pause, but also his implicit denial of the possibility for a robust ethical response to this environment. The human concern for ethics has too long a history to be dismissed so easily. So this essay will attempt to make a case for ethics in an unstable information-laden digital world.

First, let us hear Baudrillard's argument. As everything has become undifferentiated information, Baudrillard doubts that the world itself can be "reflected or represented; it can only be refracted or diffracted now by operations that are, without distinction, operations of brain and screen – the mental operations of a brain that

Journalism Ethics in a Global Civil Society

has itself become a screen" (2005, p. 78). In other words, everything suffers distortion – perhaps entropy – in its display and human beings who use information systems (e.g., computer screens) do so on the terms of the screen. "Image-feedback dominates, the insistent presence of the monitors – this convolution of things that operate in a loop" (2005, p. 79). Everything, then, is duplicity – because nothing is true, or authentic, as represented in such systems we all lose our sensibility about what matters, what represents. The countryside becomes a landscape, merely a representation of itself – not merely on the screen, but in the physical world as well, as people become incapable of seeing the countryside for what it is. They merely see it within the context of the artificial construct we call "landscape," based on the way that we have become accustomed to seeing it on the screen (2005, p. 79).

What we see on the computer screen, Baudrillard argues, is only a "machine product" – the products of a machine itself (2005, p. 80). "they are artificially padded-out, face-lifted by the machine, the films are stuffed with special effects, the texts full of *longueurs* [overlong passages] and repetitions due to the machine's malicious will to function at all costs (that is *its* passion), and to the operator's fascination with this limitless possibility of functioning" (2005, p. 80).

Baudrillard also denies that the Internet provides the "freedom" that is often claimed for it. He calls what the Internet provides merely simulation (2005, p. 81). Although people may have the illusion that they are interacting, he says, they are merely doing so "with known elements, pre-existent sites, established codes. Nothing exists beyond its search parameters. Every question has an anticipated response assigned to it. You are the questioner and, at the same time, the automatic answering device of the machine. Both coder and decoder – you are, in fact, your own terminal" (2005, p. 81). This, he says, "is the ecstasy of communication" (2005, p. 81). The computer is a "prosthesis" (2005, p. 82).

As to news/journalism/reporting, Baudrillard says we are hostages, "but we also treat it as spectacle, consume it as spectacle, without regard for its credibility. A latent incredulity and derision prevent us from being totally in the grip of the information media. It isn't critical consciousness that causes us to distance ourselves from it in this way, but the reflex of no longer wanting to play the game" (2005, p. 84). At first blush, this argument appears to have a positive streak. People are not "totally in the grip." However, what he really means by that is that, because we maintain a bit of distance from the portrayals we view, we are mere spectators of spectacle. We see what we see as mere observers, detached as a result of our own cynicism, not as a result of critical consciousness. So what appeared potentially optimistic quickly fades.

Finally, Baudrillard provides some perspective on morality – but again with a condemnatory spin. Since everything becomes an image represented on the computer monitor, Baudrillard is concerned with the nature of that image. He says (2005) that violence is done to images as we see them. They are exploited "for documentary purposes, as testimony or message," they are exploited "for moral, political or promotional ends, or simply for the purposes of information ..." (2005, p. 92, ellipsis in original). All images are thus illusions, destroyed "by overloading them with signification; we kill images with meaning" (2005, p. 92).

There are at least three points to be made about Baudrillard's concerns. First, some of what he says has been argued by others, so his objections are not necessarily unique. The problem of news as spectacle, particularly, is a point of view that many critics of news – and particularly television news – have raised before.

Second, there is truth and reality here. It is true, I think, that many people have gone down the route that Baudrillard illuminates: they fail to maintain an arm's length relationship with the data flow that emerges from their computer screens. They seek it out; immerse themselves in it, as some recent examples of Internet addiction or videogaming have demonstrated. According to research conducted in Sweden, immersion in violent video games can lead to loss of bladder control from stress activation of the vagas nerve or to symptoms similar to premenstrual syndrome (Hurtado, 2008). Internet addiction treatment centers have also begun operation in some countries, including the United States and the Netherlands (Clark, 2006). A Council of the American Medical Association recommended to that body's annual policy meeting that video game addiction be added to the diagnostic manual used to classify mental illness (Tanner, 2007). In South Korea a 28-year-old man collapsed and died after playing a video game for fifty straight hours with few breaks, little food or sleep ("S. Korean dies after video games session," 2005).

Third, although Baudrillard argues that the mutation of experience into data streams makes concerns for ethics meaningless, what he is describing actually calls for an ethical response from societies where unbridled freedom has provided the philosophical justification for death by cyber-immersion. It seems to me that one task for journalism is to respond to social changes that do fundamentally shift the terrain for the expression of humanity and engagement with technology, which – if we take Baudrillard seriously – is exactly what he is arguing about society.

So on what basis, or using what criteria, might we develop such an expression and engagement? Second, is it reasonable to expect journalism to take the lead in developing appropriate expression, or showing the way forward in engagement with technology? This is an especially pressing and difficult question to address given the collapse of journalism itself in the United States as a result of falling circulations and revenues and the rise of the blogosphere as an alternative to the professional press. It is doubly a problem because journalists are as likely to mislead or misinform the public about technology as a result of their own needs (or those of their sponsoring organizations) as they are to illumine. These are global claims, and they require some elaboration here.

The decline of the print media – especially newspapers – in the United States is perhaps so well known that it goes without saying (see Ahrens, 2009; "Charting US newspapers' decline," 2009; Henry, 2007; "Who killed the newspaper?" 2006). The Project for Excellence in Journalism's annual report on the news media began its 2009 report by stating that "newspaper ad revenues have fallen 23% in the last two years.... By our calculations, nearly one out of every five journalists working for newspapers in 2001 is now gone." It was not just newspapers. Local television news staffs "are being cut at unprecedented rates.... In network news, even the rare programs increasing their ratings are seeing revenues fall." The ethnic press is likewise "troubled." "Only cable news really flourished in 2008, thanks to an Ahablike focus on the election, although some of the ratings gains were erased after the election." Matt Cover (2009) reported, too, that an internal report within the Federal Communications Commission written by commissioner Michael Copps, examined "the decline of broadcast journalism over the past several years and [tried] to explain why traditional forms of journalism have declined while other, newer forms have been on the rise" (see also Merritt, 2005; Meyer, 2009; and Tunstall, 2008).

It is not just in the United States that journalism is thought to be declining. Graeme Turner (2005) has written about the decline, at least of current affairs journalism, in the Australian Broadcasting Company's programming. Steven Barnett and Ivor Gaber (2001) also argue that political journalism in Britain is on the decline, not because of financial woes or the Internet, but because of "the culmination of a number of interacting structural factors over which journalists have little control (p. 2)." If such concerns are correct, then the conclusion reached by Daniel C. Hallin and Paolo Mancini (2004) is particularly worrisome: "A powerful trend is clearly underway in the direction of greater similarity in the way the public sphere is structured across the world. In their products, in their professional practices and cultures, in their systems of relationships with other political and social institutions, media systems across the word are becoming increasingly alike" (p. 2).

On to the second claim: journalists are as likely to mislead or misinform as to enlighten when it comes to technology. The advent of what I call "pre-news" as a form of reporting has become so ubiquitous that perhaps many people do not notice it. By "pre-news" I mean the reporting of what someone is going to do, or is expected to do, later in the day or the week at a press conference, or through a press release or some other form on a matter of public interest. This makes the actual event almost anticlimactic. The only thing to wonder about is whether the event will affirm what has already been reported. In the area of technology this type of reporting has figured greatly in the phenomenon of "vaporware," promised software advances that either never appear or appear at later dates as originally promised or in forms other than those that were originally reported. J. D. Kleinke (2000) has argued that even the "health care Internet" is an example of vaporware. Robert Prentice (1996), reviewing the antitrust case *United States v. Microsoft Corp.*, quoted Judge Stanley Sporkin, who noted "that 'vaporware,' the high-technology industry's marketing ploy of preannouncing products that do not exist at the time of the announcement and may never come into existence in anything like their described form, 'is a practice that is deceitful on its face and everybody in the business community knows it'" (p. 1; see also Haan 2003).

It is not just the hyping of software that results in journalistically reported misleading information. The advent of so-called "neuromarketing," based in brain studies has resulted in a variety of claims about known functional brain centers that could be appealed to by marketing campaigns. Max Sutherland (2007) calls this "toutware." Its impact is exacerbated by media "overclaiming."

"The media love sensationalist stories that can carry a headline like 'Buy centre of the brain found." As a result, journalistic reporting is prone to outstrip the scientific substance." Peter Lunenfeld argued as early as 1996 that many technology theorists were prone to similar excursions, leading to "science-fictionalized discourse."

The frames used by journalists to report about technology can also be misleading. Journalists often look for an on-going narrative within which to place a story. This provides a means to discuss a new development efficiently by placing it within a context with which the audience is already familiar. The "gee-whiz" nature of much technological development (or at least announcements of developments) provide one convenient hook upon which to hang a story. Another such device is placing a story within a narrative structure with mythical qualities. Peppino Ortoleva explains some dimensions of this activity in this way:

> Technology has been able, in the age of the great faith in progress, to create a world wonderful and realistic in the same time, the world of the great Expos, in which things that were becoming part of everyday life were at the same time projected into the myth of unlimited expectations, in which each single achievement got its meaning (both intellectual and esthetic) from the great endeavor of creating a whole new world of shared welfare.... More recently, another myth has succeeded in creating a symbolic (and illusionistic) remedy to a real condition of meaninglessness: that of interactivity .... The idea of a "prosumer", of the consumer of computing who is made an hero by the technology itself he/she uses, is a very interesting case in which a concrete phenomenon .... overlaps with a plurality of aggressive marketing campaigns (2009, pp. 5–6).[1]

Myths attached to the development of technology in the United States are not new (Dery, 1997, especially pp. 10–11). Leo Marx (1997/2001, p. 26) writes about the "ideology of progress," an ideology that often leads to "the archetypal sentence: 'Technology is changing the way we live.'" He refers to this archetype as hazardous. This is because when the word technology is used in that way, it becomes "*hazardous* to the moral and political cogency of our thought." In the United States reports about the spread of technology are often sprinkled with phrases such as "the global village," a reference to the ubiquity of connection to the world that has overstated the reality since it was coined by Marshall McLuhan nearly a half-century ago. Reports of how health problems are diagnosed using the Internet or mobile telephones are used to stop price gouging in Africa are not uncommon (see, for instance, Grady, 2006). However, research undertaken by the International Center for Media Studies (www.center4media.org) in several developing countries over the past two years suggests that for the poor of the world even the arrival of a new technology does relatively little to change their situation beyond enabling them to stay connected on an infrequent basis with relatives working in other countries. Although the reports of instances where new technologies have assisted the poor may be true, they mislead by suggesting that they are merely one or two instances among many that could be reported – and thus poverty or isolation is reduced on a global scale. To repeat and paraphrase Marx's point: when such reports are made within a context of mythologies and are taken as archetypes of reality on a global scale, they are hazardous. They distort the moral and political convictions of our thought.

Journalists thus contribute to the data streams of everyday life, but how they report the facts, and the context within which they place them can both distort these streams. Narrative structures make certain demands on the nature of their reporting. Commonly held mythologies can provide easy interpretive structures that result in facile interpretations. The use of isolated examples or anecdotes as a way to humanize stories or to provide instances of impact can distort interpretations made by audiences and diminish very real problems affecting the planet. All of these activities, whether intentionally used or not, mislead audiences – or can do. They also diminish the reality – and thus, I will argue, the humanity of those outside the usual understandings of audiences.

What, then, should publics expect from journalists, and – more importantly for this essay – what makes these expectations legitimate, or defensible, in a globalized, yet fragmented, world? As Christians and Traber put it (1997) in their introduction to a book on ethics and universal values, "Communication ethics ... has to respond to both the rapid globalization of communications and the reassertion of local sociocultural identities. It is caught in the apparently contradictory trends of cultural homogenization and cultural resistance" (p. viii). Christians himself offers the prospect that what he calls "proto-norms" as basic commitments (p. 6). Such norms would be to Kant (1998) a "categorical imperative," or to others nonnegotiable principles or axioms (see Elliott, 1997, p. 81). The difference is that in Christians' formulation (1997), these protonorms emerge from a kind of consensus among those who practice different religions, feminists, and the international community at large as evidenced in declarations on human rights (pp. 8–13). Universals are possible because, as Gomes (1997) puts it, "human beings are imbued with a moral conscience that determines their daily actions.... [They] are moral by their very nature" (p. 211).

This sentiment itself is not universally endorsed. Zygmunt Bauman (1993) does not disagree with the point that human beings are moral by nature, but he does object to the idea that any sort of universal values can be imposed or even articulated within vastly different societies. "No universal standards, then. No looking over one's shoulders, to take a glimpse of what other people 'like me' do" (p. 53). His claim, instead, is that "Only rules can be universal. One may legislate universal rule-dictated *duties*, but moral *responsibility* exists solely in interpellating the individual and being carried individually. Duties tend to make humans alike; responsibility is what makes them into individuals" (p. 54). He continues, "one may say that the moral is what *resists* codification, formalization, socialization, universalization" (Bauman, 1993, p. 54). Morality, in the end, Bauman argues (1993), is "irredeemably *non-rational*" (p. 60) (All emphases in original).

This is because, as he puts it (p. 69), "reason is, by definition, rule-guided; acting reasonably means following certain rules."

Figure 26.1 A continuum of approaches.

Between these two positions are a multitude of other approaches. We might put them on a continuum as shown in Figure 26.1.

This is by no means a perfect representation of ethical perspectives. Kohlberg and Colby (1987) and Noddings (2003) both would argue that ethics develops within people who are a society and would thus likely fit between Bok and Rawls. Bok (1999) argues that society cannot afford to accept untruths for their own sakes. Mill (1978) takes the position that it is the greatest good for the greatest number that must be the clincher when choices must be made. Rawls (1971) suggests that only when social, political and economic positions are put aside can anyone decide what the right course of action is. Kant demands that the categorical imperative be paramount in choice. So from the left to the right of this chart is a movement from innate, or emotional, morality (postmodernistic ethics) toward greater and greater application of rationality, a movement toward negotiated rules, then inviolable principles, determined by rationality or essential qualities (often based in religious traditions).

Is being human the same thing, then, as being moral? We all know enough about the atrocities visited upon both individuals and groups of people (think of Rwanda, Congo, Cambodia, Kosovo, Ukraine, Nazi Germany, etc.) to answer this question in the negative. There is nothing intrinsically moral about human beings. They may have a predilection (or merely a desire) to somehow make the "right" choice, but this begs the question – what is the source of that predilection? Perhaps it evolved as people discovered that working together made hunting easier or community life safer. Perhaps truth-telling became a norm because people found the consequences of lying potentially too horrible to contemplate. This would be the default position of those who will not accept the idea of a created order in which the expectations of the creator are hardwired into humanity. In either case, though, the exceptions to moral (or right) behavior are legion.

Given that reality, and the fact that none of us can be sure whether morality is hardwired, evolved, or developed within society, it is problematic to assume that any particular individual will act rightly, or even more to the point, altruistically, or as Daniel Bell (1976) puts it, with *civitas*. In many respects, however, this is the expectation that society has of journalists. The very notion of objectivity is premised on the fact that journalists will report news by putting their own personal biases (including moral biases) to the side. They will not be influenced by personal commitments, but examine and report facts independently of pressure, without subjective interpretation, and in a manner that is fair to all parties. In a real sense, without certainty as to moral standards or extant moral behaviors shared broadly across a society, the expectations of such reporting are ludicrous. Ethical codes written for professional societies of journalists, editors, publishers, and so on, all assume a rational perspective – they should be followed because they will result in trust, or profit, or professional status, provide for social acceptance of the product on offer. However, if universal principles cannot be trusted, or are negotiable, or if morality itself is not a rationality-based activity, then the basis for ethical expectations is fatally flawed. As Harry G. Frankfurt (2008) put it, "if we have no respect for the distinction between true and false, we may as well kiss our much-vaunted 'rationality' good-bye" (p. 66).

Yet the journalistic function in any society is too important to allow it to sink into a morass of subjectivity, relativism, or shifting allegiances. Hence the struggle among philosophers, moralists, theologians, and sociobiologists to determine some basis for right behavior. If the Commission on Freedom of the Press was right (1947), then there must be some basis for determining the truth of events, campaigns, contexts and movements, for the press to accomplish its first task: "providing a truthful, comprehensive and intelligent account of the day's events in a context which gives them meaning" (p. 20).

It seems equally far-fetched to tell journalists to do as they will and the public will sort it out. The expectation that in a contest between truth and falsity, truth will always win out (at least eventually) is as fatally flawed as that journalists will act ethically in a morally-perverse world. People tend toward reading, listening, watching, or searching for facts that affirm their prior beliefs (see Carey, 1989). They don't go looking for demonstrations of their own mistaken intellectual or emotional commitments. What is more likely is that the middle ground of commitments wherein reasonable conversations can occur among those with different beliefs will shrink and information that is more outrageous or fanatical will flourish, drawing people to ever more extreme positions – and thus destroying any possibility of genuine dialog.

The argument that is made here is that the role of journalism must be to open up prospects for genuine dialog. This simple statement rests on a foundation outlined by James W. Carey (see Carey's chapters on journalism in Munson and Warren, 1997) and others concerning the necessity for journalism to function in such a fashion in order that democracy might flourish. (After all, dialog is not required in a dictatorship.) Beyond that, however, is the assumption that if journalism does not pursue this role, the chances that civil society can develop or be maintained in places where it may be lacking are slim at best and likely to slide into barbarity at worst.

The implications of this are two-fold (at least). First, it is necessary that some institution act to protect the language of discourse. If those who seek power are allowed to define terms or concepts as they choose without being called to account for distortions, unflattering (to brutal) portrayals of others, or prevarications, legitimate genuine dialog is impossible. Journalists are in the best position to assure that this occurs. They have more day-to-day connection with publics than do other wordsmiths such as storywriters, novelists, screenwriters, magazine writers, or educators, so their influence is more crucial. Also, they are both obviously engaged in dealing with matters of public import (legislation, campaigns, movements, protests, meetings, stump speeches, debates, spin, advertising, public relations, etc.) than are others, and they do so not from a position of power-seeking, but from one of dispassionate observer, fact-checker, and analyst (at their best).

It is, of course, the power of the unembellished truth that is most useful to genuine, or authentic, dialog in the public sphere. It is what protects the language of discourse itself, and what provides journalists with their power as watchdogs over the contests between ideologies or partisan positions that are part of the public sphere. This unembellished truth can only be guaranteed by adherence to one overarching requirement: the practice of ethics.

The second implication concerns the practice of journalism under a regime of ethics. Ethics in this sense is not about what journalists should be doing to adhere to some set of professional standards nor is it fundamentally about journalists functioning in a particular way because doing so would enhance their credibility. It is more fundamental than either of these rationales. The reason underlying such an expectation of protecting the language of discourse and thus accepting the limitations of an ethical regime (whatever it is), is that it makes the public sphere possible. Other forms of information or opinion contribute to the public sphere, but it is journalism that assures that honest discourse occurs. It calls people to account for their claims and vocabulary. It explicates the institutional or historical memory that is assumed without defense or even accuracy. It compares and contrasts the implications of differing approaches to public policy. It holds participants in the public sphere accountable.

Being able to accomplish such tasks, however, depends on the perceived credibility of journalists and this, in turn, depends on the way that journalism is practiced and defended. If journalism is merely another input into the public sphere, perceived to be little different than that provided by bloggers, aggregators, public relations workers, advertising, political bombast, crackpots, conspiracy theorists, or the uninformed but opinionated masses who believe what they hear from such sources, then there is little reason to be concerned about journalism itself. Journalism is only valuable to the degree that it does adhere to ethical standards of one sort or another, enforces them within its fraternity, and defends them within the public sphere.

At a minimum the requirements for journalists (as opposed, here, to mere reporters) is that they would, as the Hippocratic oath puts it for physicians, "do no harm." Of course the "harm" that journalists might do differs from that for physicians, who are to assure that whatever treatment they accord to a patient does not make things worse. In the symbolic world of journalism it would always be problematic as to how this same expectation might work. A person could ask, "worse for whom?" Or "define worse." The practice of journalism, if practiced rightly, would often result in a worse outcome for someone. A politician whose sexual peccadilloes are exposed is probably worse off for the publicity. A corporation whose polluting practices are outed, likewise, would consider itself worse off than when it controlled knowledge of its activities. Liars and criminals often do not appreciate having their true motives or behaviors held up to the light.

So what would it mean to do no harm? Our most minimal expectations, I will argue, are that journalists adhere to what Clifford Christians (Christians and Traber, 1997) has called "protonorms," those universal values that societies and religious traditions agree are basic and non-negotiable "in terms of our human wholeness" (p. 6). The most basic of these is acknowledging the sacredness of life (p. 12). Based on that protonorm, Christians argues, are the ethical principles of "human dignity, truth, and nonviolence" (p. 13). Every issue opened for public debate should then have particular questions answered: "Do they sustain life, enhance it long term, contribute to human well-being as a whole? The challenge for the mass media is not just political insight on the news and aesthetic power in entertainment but moral discernment. This is the discourse that irrigates public debate, refusing simply to focus on politics or entertainment per se but connecting the issues to universal norms, speaking not only to our minds but vivifying the spirit, grafting the deeper questions underneath the story onto our human oneness" (p. 15).

This is a good first step – but our expectations for journalism must go deeper. One might argue that these basics adhere to all public discourse, whether by journalists or not. The demand for truth-telling, for instance, is for Sissela Bok (1999) the most basic requirement for interpersonal relations. Living in a society where people cannot trust others to be telling the truth in conversation is unthinkable. Felipe Fernández-Armesto goes one step further: "It is, I think, impossible to be human without having a concept of truth and a technique for matching the signs you use to the facts you want to represent as true" (1997, p. 4). Not only that, but human beings, according to Fernández-Armesto, have an innate characteristic of seeking coherence (p. 31). "No people known to modern anthropology is without it." Desiring either equilibrium or coherence (or both) within a society is what leads them to seek truth – the most important "contribution to equilibrium or particip[ant] in cohesion" (p. 32).

Even "sacredness of life" could use more precision. It is not merely a requirement that people's lives be spared, or that journalists report on activities that result in the taking of life (criminal activities, terrorism, genocide, war, etc.), but also that torture be banned (Tesón, 2001, p. 381). Beyond that are so-called "second-generation" human rights, rights that adhere to humankind by international agreement, that are part and parcel of definitions of a fully human life, although the lack of them may not, in itself, threaten the basics of human physiology. These include the "right to physical integrity, the right to participate in the election of one's government, the right to a fair trial, freedom of expression, freedom of association, freedom of movement, or the prohibition of discrimination" (Tesón, 2001, p. 381) All such rights must be part of moral discourse, according to Fernández-Armesto because such discourse must be universalizable (p. 385) to have any meaning in the international arena (or sphere) of human rights.

Although there may be differences of opinion concerning the basis of such rights (with Asians, for instance, objecting to the Western individualist notion of rights rather than rights located within the collective), beginning from a different foundation can sometimes lead to the same conclusion: "the Buddhist conception provides an alternative way of linking together the agenda of human rights and that of democratic development. Whereas in the Western framework these go together because they are both seen as requirements of human dignity, and indeed, as two facets of liberty, a connection of a somewhat different kind is visible among Thai Buddhists of the reform persuasion. Their commitment to people-centered and ecologically sensitive development makes them strong allies of those communities of villagers who are resisting encroachment by the state and big business and fighting to defend their lands and forests" (Taylor, 2001, pp. 418–419). This different conception is based in the "fundamental value of nonviolence" (p. 418).

So we much go deeper – beyond merely a Western conception of individual rights to be protected (whether that is the "civil liberties" under the US Constitution or various human rights accords signed in the international arena). Journalists must not only do their tasks with these basics in mind ("do no harm"), but also carry out their tasks in defense of community. This is at once both obvious and controversial. It is obvious within the Western journalistic tradition where journalists have a type of fiduciary relationship with the public: they are watchdogs of government, they expose corruption in high places, they represent the public's interests when the public does not have the access to the information or individuals who can provide the truth on particular issues. However, it is also controversial, because a question can legitimately be posed as to what communities are to be protected. There are minority communities of Muslims, people of African descent (Africans themselves, Caribbean-Africans, African-Americans), Arabs, and indigenous peoples, and others in many Western countries. Outside the West there are tribal and clan groups, castes, people of European descent and indigenous peoples, refugees, internally-displaced persons, expatriate communities, and so on. So, what community?

The answer is complicated, as there are two distinct ways to approach it. One way is to say the answer is all communities and no single community. In other words, journalists should not see their task as representing merely the most oppressed, or poorest, or least engaged community that may exist within a given society. The people in such communities should be represented, of course, but not to the exclusion of other communities that may be wealthier, more engaged, or powerful. This would mean that all communities should be represented, but none preferred. However, there is a caveat to this approach. That is that the universals cannot be violated.

Journalists can only avoid violating universals if they are committed to traditional values within the journalistic profession – especially fairness, balance, accuracy, and avoidance of conflicts of interest. Journalists who fail to commit to these traditional values cannot be trusted in the public sphere. A corollary to these values is a commitment to social justice – a step beyond simple fairness. As Joseph V. Montville explains (2001), "in its most general sense, justice implies order and morality. That is, justice means predictability in the daily life of a community and its individual members and the observance of basic rules governing right and wrong behavior. Justice serves the interests of life and the advancement of the human species, because it is perhaps the most fundamental element of peace. [Peace and justice must be defined] as progress toward the optimum environment for the fulfillment of human developmental potential" (p. 129).

This wider commitment to social justice is an important obstacle (if a true commitment) to preventing domination of the public sphere by the privileged in society. This is – according to Rawls (2001) the "first virtue" of social institutions (p. 4). Privilege may come from the exercise of political power, wealth, notoriety, celebrity or status (based, for instance, on race or gender). None of these can be allowed by true journalists acting ethically to influence the types of stories reported, the approach to them, or the perspectives and facts included. If these factors do influence reports, then what the public sees is the same as what defines current political discourse: an overvaluation of "individualism, confrontation, hyperbole, winning, and entertainment, while [undervaluing] community, understanding, compassion, and information" (Allen, 2002, p. 98).

This responsibility implies that those who have achieved some prominence in society, whatever the reason, should have no more access to journalists than do ordinary people. It also implies that, although no quantifiable favoritism should be shown to those from nonprominent elements of society, that attention must be given to engaging them in the wider conversation within the public sphere that comprises society. This could be done, as Jürgen Habermas suggests (Allen, 2002, p. 112) by controlling the press to prevent it from forging relationships with society's most powerful elements, but such an approach would elevate legal requirements above ethical responsibility. Seyla Benhabib suggests an approach that retains the focus on ethics – a "radically democratized, conversational" discourse ethics "rooted in the Kantian tradition of ethical universalism [that] posits an idealized form of practical reason that transcends cultural boundaries" (Bracci, 2002, p. 126).

These boundaries may be those from one society to another, but they may also be seen within a single society, as many cultures may exist within a single social corpus. These cultures may be defined by ethnicity, gender, age cohort groups, class, caste, and so on. If journalists can succeed in identifying and using the collective knowledge that exists within such cultures as part of the due diligence we should expect as they exercise their fiduciary obligation to the public, this would devalue notoriety and thus radically democratize the nature of the reporting they do to open up the social conversation on matters that affect the lives of everyone.

The second answer begins with the question: what is the role of the press – is it to represent the public's interests or is it to invite them into a conversation? It can be argued either way, of course. The traditional arguments for the First Amendment – for instance, that the public has a right to know and thus the press's access to information must trump other considerations (short of national security), or that the independence of the press is sacrosanct because it is a watchdog on behalf of the public, are both essentially claims that journalists represent the public's interests. In such cases journalists act on behalf of the other, and remain apart from it (for instance, see Gurevitch and Blumler, 1977, pp. 280–281). As Martin Linsky put it (1988), "at least as presently organized and under its current conventions, the press is a substantial barrier to overcome in attempting to move toward a richer, more participatory, broader, more explicative dialogue on public affairs" (p. 211). Why? "Journalists and news organizations like to see themselves as observers of public affairs, not as participants in them." So they must stay "independent" and potentially "irresponsible" (Linsky, 1988, p. 211). Similarly, McQuail's (1977) characterization of mass media as an institution that "can help bring certain kinds of public into being and maintain them" also suggests the separation between journalists and citizens (pp. 90–91).

Contrast this with the expectations of journalists put forth by John Dewey and James W. Carey. Dewey (1954) in typically abstruse fashion argues that the American polity developed in a period characterized by intimate community life, but that much was lost in the expansion of the country to a continent-wide nation that led people to organize themselves into interest-based groups disconnected from one another. To create what he called the "great community" (itself defined by democracy) two things were necessary. One was interconnection among these groups via the transmission and circulation technologies of the modern age. The second was the intelligence generated by the social sciences applied in daily news reports by journalists who were free of the distortions created by interests of elites that controlled the press (Chapter 5). If journalists were choosing news voluntarily (for instance, in the interests of their audiences) rather than at the instruction of their money-driven producers, they would be acting morally (Dewey, 1960, p. 8).

Carey (1997), although building on the foundation of Dewey's ideas, is more direct and expectant about the relationship of citizens and the press. He argues that the press that is independent of the conversation of culture would be "a menace to public life and an effective politics" (p. 218). He continues with the observation that the press and the public must be connected, that the press without connection to its public is a vacuous notion. "The notion of a public, a conversational public, has been pretty much evacuated in our time" (Carey, 1997, p. 218). "From this view of the First Amendment, the task of the press is to encourage the conversation of the culture – not to preempt it or substitute for it or supply it with information as a seer from afar. Rather, the press maintains and enhances the conversation of the culture, becomes one voice in that conversation, amplifies the conversation outward, and helps it along by bringing forward the information that the conversation itself demands" (p. 219).

In this perspective journalists are participants in the culture, representing, encouraging, including, questioning, agreeing or disagreeing, with the variety of opinions voiced by members of the public as concerns. They are not apart. They are integral, intimate with the public, using their positions as journalists to assist the public in its deliberations. It does not pander to their baser instincts, but elevates the conversation by adding intelligence that emerges in their examination of issues. These examinations are to uncover the various opinions, facts, allegiances, biases, and connections emerging in public consideration of issues relevant to their own wellbeing.

So, both the universal and the particular must inform the practice of journalists. Commitment to the universal establishes journalists as humane practitioners. Such a commitment would mirror the ethic of *primum non nocere* – "first, do no harm." It sets journalists apart from those who are committed to an ideology, or political platform, or who pursue self-aggrandizement, in their communication practices. When these motivations are fundamental to communication, they allow rationalizations that justify lying, distortions, and – as Harry Frankfurt (2005) claims – the most dangerous of all, "bullshit."

The particular includes commitments grounded in community-defined norms. In the United States, for instance, such norms would include the guarantees of the First Amendment, not merely for a free press, but for freedom of speech and association. It also includes expectations for social responsibility, the protection of minority opinion and whistle-blowers, and willingness to spend the time and finances necessary to get to the bottom of controversies, and economic, political, and social practices. It demands that journalists eschew the "partisanship [that] is unabashed on the Web, and increasingly on cable" and the "rise of niche journalism ... taking place as old-line organizations more frequently chase tabloid melodramas" (Kurtz, 2009).

In other words, it is through the practice of ethics itself that journalists actually become journalists. Journalistic style has been compromised by the sheer number of news sites on the web (which has supplanted much of what people used to think of as news sources) and the different approaches taken to reporting on them. Different perspectives, uses of language (both descriptive and vitriolic), and attention to different types of minutia have all contributed to a confusion of reportage. How are journalists to be known – to be identified in such a chaotic environment? It is by their ethics that we will know them. Although there are ethical dimensions to such activities as blogging, they are not the same ethics as those that should define truly journalistic activity.

This does not mean that journalists will always get it right or that aspects of news will always be reported first or more completely by them. Sometimes other sources – in some cases, perhaps, hugely biased ones – may accomplish this. However, by putting ethics first, before economics, style, publisher demands, or personal predilections, journalists can reestablish themselves as worthy of public trust. Their activities will reflect public questions, concerns, and fears, their reporting will include the representation of all segments of the society, helping people to understand the "other side," because journalists are representing the "other," whoever that may be. News will not be dominated by sensationalism, elite pronouncements, angry retorts, vindictive comments, because journalists will see their ilk as anomalous, self-serving, or designed to throw true debate to one side in favor of peculiar biases or idiocies. What will matter is what those with whom journalists are participating within the culture are worried about or do not understand. This does not mean that the public's own silliness or uninformed perspectives are the focus of journalism, because journalists should be elevating the level of public understanding and debate by providing the intelligence necessary to accomplish this. However, they do not have to assume that the President, for instance, or the Senate majority leader, or celebrities, are always the most knowledgeable, articulate, or understandable in the public sphere that matters. Their job is still interpretation and contextualization of facts, explanation, provision of multiple perspectives, but within a public arena of accountability to the common man. People should be able to see that journalists are on their side, are their champions, are concerned about the same things that they are. It is only through new vigilance in following the universals of ethics, and knowing intimately the community nuances that influence application of these universals within a particular context, that journalists can distinguish themselves from other reporters or writers and reimagine their function within a democratic society. It is only through such work that journalists will be able to see the value of their activities to the public that they should wish to serve.

Note

1 The allure of reporting "scoops" in technology for journalists can be seen in Valvovic (2000, pp. 4–5).

References

Ahrens, F. (2009) The accelerating decline of newspapers. *The Washington Post*, October 27. www.washingtonpost.com/wp-dyn/article/2009/10/26/2009 (last accessed November 9, 2009).

Allen, D.S. (2002) Jürgen Habermas and the search for democratic principles, in *Moral Engagement in Public Life: Theorists for Contemporary Ethics*, (eds S.L. Bracci and C.G. Christians), Peter Lang, New York, pp. 97–122.

Barnett, S., and Gaber, I. (2001) *Westminster Tales: The Twenty-First-Century Crisis in Political Journalism*, Continuum, New York.

Barrett, W. (1990) *Irrational Man: A Study in Existentialist Philosophy*, Anchor Books, New York.

Baudrillard, J. (2005) *The Intelligence of Evil or the Lucidity Pact*, (trans. Chris Turner), Berg, New York.

Bauman, Z. (1993) *Postmodern Ethics*, Blackwell, Cambridge, MA.

Bell, D. (1976) *The Coming of Post-Industrial Society: A Venture in Social Forecasting*, Basic Books, New York.

Blackburn, S. (2000) *Being Good: A Short Introduction to Ethics*, Oxford University Press, New York.

Bok, S. (1999) *Lying: Moral Choice in Public and Private Life*, Knopf Publishing Group, New York.

Bracci, S.L. (2002) The fragile hope of Seyla Behnabib's interactive universalism in *Moral Engagement in Public Life: Theorists for Contemporary Ethics*, (eds S.L. Bracci and C.G. Christians), Peter Lang, New York, pp. 123–149.

Carey, J.W. (1989) *Communication As Culture: Essays on Media and Society*, Unwin Hyman, Boston.

Carey, J.W. (1997) "A republic, if you can keep it": liberty and public life in the age of glasnost, in *James Carey: A Critical Reader*, (eds E.S. Munson and C.A. Warren), University of Minnesota Press, Minneapolis, pp. 207–227.

Charting US newspapers' decline (2009) www.guardian.co.ukmedia/organgrinder/2009/oct/28/us- newspapers, (last accessed November 9, 2009).

Christians, C.G. (1997) The ethics of being in a communications context, in *Communication Ethics and Universal Values*, (eds C.G. Christians and M. Traber), Sage, Thousand Oaks, CA, pp. 3–23.

Christians, C., and Traber, M. (1997) Introduction, in *Communication Ethics and Universal Values*, (eds C.G. Christians and M. Traber), Sage, Thousand Oaks, CA, pp. vii–xvi.

Clark, A. (2006) Detox for video game addiction? July 3, www.cbsnews.com/stories/2006/07/03/health/webmd/main1773956.shtml (last accessed September 24, 2009).

Commission on Freedom of the Press (1947) *A Free and Responsible Press*, University of Chicago Press, Chicago.

Cover, M. (2009) FCC Commissioner circulates document on "The State of Media Journalism." July 9, www.cnsnews.com/public/content/article.aspx?RsrcID=50761 (accessed July 14, 2010).

Dery, M. (1997) *Escape Velocity: Cyberculture at the End of the Century*, Grove/Atlantic, Inc, New York.

Dewey, J. (1954) *The Public and Its Problems*, The Swallow Press, Chicago.

Dewey, J. (1960) *Theory of the Moral Life*, Holt, Rinehart and Winston, New York.

Elliott, D. (1997) Universal values and moral development theories, in *Communication Ethics and Universal Values*, (eds C.G. Christians and M. Traber), Sage, Thousand Oaks, CA, pp. 68–83.

Fernández-Armesto, F. (1997) *Truth: A History and a Guide for the Perplexed*, St. Martin's Press, New York.

Frankfurt, H.G. (2005) *On Bullshit*, Princeton University Press, Princeton, NJ

Frankfurt, H.G. (2008) *On Truth*, Alfred A. Knopf, New York.

Gomes, P.G. (1997) Communications, hope, and ethics, in *Communication Ethics and Universal Values*, (eds C.G. Christians and M. Traber), Sage, Thousand Oaks, CA, pp. 211–224.

Grady, B. (2006,) Wireless technologies help less developed countries grow. *Oakland Tribune*, March 12, findarticles.com/p/articles/mi_qn4176/is_20060312/ai_n16155359/ (last accessed November 20, 2009).

Gurevitch, M., and Blumler, J.G. (1977) Linkages between the mass media and politics: A model for the analysis of political communications systems, in *Mass Communication and Society*, (eds J. Curran, M. Gurevitch and J. Woolacott), Edward Arnold, London, pp. 270–290.

Haan, M.A. (2003) Vaporware as a means of entry deterrence. *The Journal of Industrial Economics*, 51 (3), 345–358.

Hallin, D.C., and Mancini, P. (2004) Americanization, globalization and secularization: Understanding the convergence of media systems and political communication in the U S and Western Europe, in *Comparing Political Communication: Theories, Cases, and Challenges*, (eds F. Esser and B. Pfetsch), Cambridge University Press, Cambridge, www.mediacritica.net/courses/491m/hallin.pdf (last accessed November 19, 2009).

Henry, N. (2007) The decline of news. *San Francisco Chronicle*, May 29, www.sfgate.com/cgi-bin/article.cgi?f=c/a/2007/05/29 (last accessed November 9, 2009).

Hurtado, C. (2008) The real danger of violent video games, November 26, www.popsci.com/entertainment-amp-gaming/article/2008-11/real-danger-violent-video-games (accessed July 2, 2010).

Kant, E. (1998) *Groundwork of the Metaphysics of Morals*, (eds D.M. Clarke and M. Gregor), Cambridge University Press, Cambridge.

Kleinke, J.D. (2000) Vaporware.com: The failed promise of the health care Internet. *Health Affairs*, 19 (6), 57–71.

Kohlberg, L., and Colby, A. (1987) *The Measurement of Moral Judgment, Volume 1: Theoretical Foundations and Research Validation*, Harvard University Press, Cambridge, MA.

Kurtz, H. (2009) Media notes: Howard Kurtz on the evolution of media in the awful aughts, December 28, *The Washington Post*, C01.

Linsky, M. (1988) The media and public deliberation, in *The Power of Public Ideas*, (ed. R.B. Reich), Harvard University Press, Cambridge, MA, pp. 205–228.

Lunenfeld, P. (1996) Theorizing in real time: Hyperaesthetics for the technoculture, *Afterimage*, 23 (4), p. 16ff.

Marx, L. (1997/2001) *Technology*: The emergence of a hazardous concept, in Technology and the Rest of Culture, (eds A. Mack), The Ohio State University Press, Columbus, OH, pp. 23–46.

McQuail, D. (1977) The influence and effects of mass media, in *Mass Communication and Society*, (eds J. Curran, M. Gurevitch and J. Woolacott), Edward Arnold, London, pp. 70–94.

Merritt, D. (2005) *Knight Ridder and How the Erosion of Newspaper Journalism is Putting Democracy at Risk*, AMACOM, New York.

Meyer, P. (2009) *The Vanishing Newspaper: Saving Journalism in the Information Age*, University of Missouri Press, Columbia, MO.

Mill, J.S. (1978) *On Liberty*, (ed. E. Rapaport), Hackett Publishing Company, Inc., Indianapolis, IN.

Montville, J.V. (2001) Justice and the burden of history, in *Reconciliation, Justice, and Coexistence*, (ed. M. Abu-Nimer), Lexington Books, New York, pp. 129–143.

Munson, E.S., and Warren, C.A. (1997) *James Carey: A Critical Reader*, University of Minnesota Press, Minneapolis, MN.

Noddings, N. (2003) *Caring: A Feminine Approach to Ethics and Moral Education*, 2nd edn, University of California Press, Berkeley, CA.

Ortoleva, P. (2009) Modern mythologies, the media and the social presence of technology. *Observatorio (OBS*) Journal*, 8, 1–12.

Prentice, R. (1996) Vaporware: Imaginary high-tech products and real antitrust liability in a post-Chicago World, *Ohio State Law Journal*, 57, Heinonline.org (last accessed November 19, 2009).

Project for Excellence in Journalism (2009) *The State of the News Media 2009: An Annual Report on American Journalism*, www.stateofthemedia.org/2009 (accessed July 2, 2010).

Rawls, J. (1971) *A Theory of Justice*, The Belknap Press of Harvard University Press, Cambridge, MA.

Rawls, J. (2001) *Justice as Fairness: A Restatement*, (ed. E. Kelly), Harvard University Press, Cambridge, MA.

Silverstone, R. (2007) *Media and Morality: On the Rise of the Mediapolis*, Polity Press, Malden, MA.

S. Korean dies after video games session (2005) August 10, news.bbc.co.uk/2/hi/technology/4137782.stm (accessed July 2, 2010).

Sutherland, M. (2007) Neuromarketing: What's it all about. The Inaugural Australian Neuromarketing Symposium at Swinburne University, Melbourne, February, www.sutherlandsurvey.com/Columns_Papers/Neuromarketing-What's it all about- March 2007.pdf, (last accessed November 19, 2009).

Tanner, L. (2007) Is video-game addiction a mental disorder? June 22, www.msnbc.msn.com/id/19354827/ (accessed July 2, 2010).

Taylor, C. (2001) A World Consensus on Human Rights? in *The Philosophy of Human Rights, Paragon Issues in Philosophy*, (ed. P. Hayden), Paragon House, St. Paul, MN, pp. 409–423.

Tesón, F.R. (2001) International human rights and cultural relativism, in *The Philosophy of Human Rights, Paragon Issues in Philosophy*, (ed. P. Hayden), Paragon House, St. Paul, MN, pp. 379-396.

Tunstall, J. (2008) *The Media Were American: US Mass Media in Decline*, Oxford University Press, New York.

Turner, G. (2005) *Ending the Affair: The Decline of Television's Current Affairs in Australia*, University of New South Wales Press, Brisbane.

Valvovic, T. (2000) *Digital Mythologies: The Hidden Complexities of the Internet*, Rutgers University Press, New Brunswick, NJ.

Who killed the newspaper? (2006) August 24, www.economist.com/opinion (last accessed November 9, 2009).

The Handbook of Global Communication and Media Ethics

Volume II

Handbooks in Communication and Media

This series aims to provide theoretically ambitious but accessible volumes devoted to the major fields and subfields within communication and media studies. Each volume sets out to ground and orientate the student through a broad range of specially commissioned chapters, while also providing the more experienced scholar and teacher with a convenient and comprehensive overview of the latest trends and critical directions.

The Handbook of Children, Media, and Development, *edited by Sandra L. Calvert and Barbara J. Wilson*
The Handbook of Crisis Communication, *edited by W. Timothy Coombs and Sherry J. Holladay*
The Handbook of Internet Studies, *edited by Mia Consalvo and Charles Ess*
The Handbook of Rhetoric and Public Address, *edited by Shawn J. Parry-Giles and J. Michael Hogan*
The Handbook of Critical Intercultural Communication, *edited by Thomas K. Nakayama and Rona Tamiko Halualani*
The Handbook of Global Communication and Media Ethics, *Robert S. Fortner and P. Mark Fackler*

Forthcoming
The Handbook of Global Research Methods, *edited by Ingrid Volkmer*
The Handbook of International Advertising Research, *edited by Hong Cheng*
The Handbook of Communication and Corporate Social Responsibility, *edited by Oyvind Ihlen, Jennifer Bartlett and Steve May*
The Handbook of Gender and Sexualities in the Media, *edited by Karen Ross*
The Handbook of Global Health Communication and Development, *edited by Rafael Obregon and Silvio Waisbord*
The Handbook of Global Online Journalism, *edited by Eugenia Siapera and Andreas Veglis*

The Handbook of Global Communication and Media Ethics

Volume II

Edited by

Robert S. Fortner and P. Mark Fackler

A John Wiley & Sons, Ltd., Publication

This edition first published 2011
© 2011 Blackwell Publishing Ltd

Blackwell Publishing was acquired by John Wiley & Sons in February 2007. Blackwell's publishing program has been merged with Wiley's global Scientific, Technical, and Medical business to form Wiley-Blackwell.

Registered Office
John Wiley & Sons Ltd, The Atrium, Southern Gate, Chichester, West Sussex, PO19 8SQ, United Kingdom

Editorial Offices
350 Main Street, Malden, MA 02148-5020, USA
9600 Garsington Road, Oxford, OX4 2DQ, UK
The Atrium, Southern Gate, Chichester, West Sussex, PO19 8SQ, UK

For details of our global editorial offices, for customer services, and for information about how to apply for permission to reuse the copyright material in this book please see our website at www.wiley.com/wiley-blackwell.

The right of Robert S. Fortner and P. Mark Fackler to be identified as the authors of the editorial material in this work has been asserted in accordance with the UK Copyright, Designs and Patents Act 1988.

All rights reserved. No part of this publication may be reproduced, stored in a retrieval system, or transmitted, in any form or by any means, electronic, mechanical, photocopying, recording or otherwise, except as permitted by the UK Copyright, Designs and Patents Act 1988, without the prior permission of the publisher.

Wiley also publishes its books in a variety of electronic formats. Some content that appears in print may not be available in electronic books.

Designations used by companies to distinguish their products are often claimed as trademarks. All brand names and product names used in this book are trade names, service marks, trademarks or registered trademarks of their respective owners. The publisher is not associated with any product or vendor mentioned in this book. This publication is designed to provide accurate and authoritative information in regard to the subject matter covered. It is sold on the understanding that the publisher is not engaged in rendering professional services. If professional advice or other expert assistance is required, the services of a competent professional should be sought.

Library of Congress Cataloging-in-Publication Data
The handbook of global communication and media ethics / edited by Robert S. Fortner and P. Mark Fackler.
      p.   cm. – (Handbooks in communication and media; 7)
   Includes bibliographical references and index.
   ISBN 978-1-4051-8812-8 (hardback)
      1. Communication–Moral and ethical aspects.   2. Mass media–Moral and ethical aspects.
I. Fortner, Robert S.   II. Fackler, Mark P.
   P94.H354 2011
   175–dc22

                                                          2010043496
A catalogue record for this book is available from the British Library.

This book is published in the following electronic formats: ePDFs 9781444390605; Wiley Online Library 9781444390629; ePub 9781444390612

Set in 10/13pt Galliard, SPi Publisher Services, Pondicherry, India
Printed and bound in Singapore by Markono Print Media Pte Ltd

1   2011

Contents

Volume I

Notes on Contributors	ix
Preface	xix

1 Primordial Issues in Communication Ethics   1
  Clifford G. Christians

2 Communication Ethics: The Wonder of Metanarratives
  in a Postmodern Age   20
  Ronald C. Arnett

3 Information, Communication, and Planetary Citizenship   41
  Luiz Martins da Silva

4 Global Communication and Cultural Particularisms: The Place
  of Values in the Simultaneity of Structural Globalization
  and Cultural Fragmentation – The Case of Islamic Civilization   54
  Bassam Tibi

5 The Ethics of Privacy in High versus Low Technology Societies   79
  Robert S. Fortner

6 Social Responsibility Theory and Media Monopolies   98
  P. Mark Fackler

7 Ethics and Ideology: Moving from Labels to Analysis   119
  Lee Wilkins

8 Fragments of Truth: The Right to Communication
  as a Universal Value   133
  Philip Lee

9 Glocal Media Ethics   154
  Shakuntala Rao

10	Feminist Ethics and Global Media *Linda Steiner*	171
11	Words as Weapons: A History of War Reporting – 1945 to the Present *Richard Lance Keeble*	193
12	Multidimensional Objectivity for Global Journalism *Stephen J.A. Ward*	215
13	New Media and an Old Problem: Promoting Democracy *Deni Elliott and Amanda Decker*	234
14	The Dilemma of Trust *Ian Richards*	247
15	The Ethical Case for a Blasphemy Law *Neville Cox*	263
16	The Medium is the Moral *Michael Bugeja*	298
17	Development Ethics: The Audacious Agenda *Chloe Schwenke*	317
18	Indigenous Media Values: Cultural and Ethical Implications *Joe Grixti*	342
19	Media Ethics as Panoptic Discourse: A Foucauldian View *Ed McLuskie*	364
20	Ethical Anxieties in the Global Public Sphere *Robert S. Fortner*	376
21	Universalism versus Communitarianism in Media Ethics *Clifford G. Christians*	393
22	Responsibility of Net Users *Raphael Cohen-Almagor*	415
23	Media Ethics and International Organizations *Cees J. Hamelink*	434
24	Making the Case for What Can and Should Be Published *Bruce C. Swaffield*	452
25	Ungrievable Lives: Global Terror and the Media *Giovanna Borradori*	461
26	Journalism Ethics in the Moral Infrastructure of a Global Civil Society *Robert S. Fortner*	481

Contents vii

Volume II

27 Problems of Application   501
    P. Mark Fackler

28 Disenfranchised and Disempowered: How the Globalized
    Media Treat Their Audiences – A Case from India   516
    Anita Dighe

29 Questioning Journalism Ethics in the Global Age:
    How Japanese News Media Report and Support
    Immigrant Law Revision   534
    Kaori Hayashi

30 Ancient Roots and Contemporary Challenges:
    Asian Journalists Try to Find the Balance   554
    Jiafei Yin

31 Understanding Bollywood   577
    Vijay Mishra

32 Peace Communication in Sudan: Toward Infusing
    a New Islamic Perspective   602
    Haydar Badawi Sadig and Hala Asmina Guta

33 Media and Post-Election Violence in Kenya   626
    *P. Mark Fackler, Levi Obonyo, Mitchell Terpstra,
    and Emmanuel Okaalet*

34 Ethics of Survival: Media, Palestinians,
    and Israelis in Conflict   655
    Oliver Witte

35 Voiceless Glasnost: Responding to Government Pressures
    and Lack of a Free Press Tradition in Russia   677
    Victor Akhterov

36 Media Use and Abuse in Ethiopia   700
    Zenebe Beyene

37 Collective Guilt as a Response to Evil: The Case of Arabs
    and Muslims in the Western Media   735
    Rasha A. Abdulla and Mervat Abou Oaf

38 Journalists as Witnesses to Violence and Suffering   752
    Amy Richards and Jolyon Mitchell

39 Reporting on Religious Authority Complicit
    with Atrocity   774
    Paul A. Soukup, S.J.

40 The Ethics of Representation and the Internet   785
    Boniface Omachonu Omatta

41	Authors, Authority, Ownership, and Ethics in Digital Media and News *Jarice Hanson*	803
42	Ethical Implications of Blogging *Bernhard Debatin*	823
43	Journalism Ethics in a Digital Network *Jane B. Singer*	845
44	Now Look What You Made Me Do: Violence and Media Accountability *Peter Hulm*	864
45	Protecting Children from Harmful Influences of Media through Formal and Nonformal Media Education *Asbjørn Simonnes and Gudmund Gjelsten*	891
46	Ethics and International Propaganda *Philip M. Taylor*	912
47	Modernization and Its Discontents: Ethics, Development, and the Diffusion of Innovations *Robert S. Fortner*	933
48	Communication Technologies in the Arsenal of Al Qaeda and Taliban: Why the West Is Not Winning the War on Terror *Haydar Badawi Sadig, Roshan Noorzai, and Hala Asmina Guta*	953
49	The Ethics of a Very Public Sphere: Differential Soundscapes and the Discourse of the Streets *Robert S. Fortner*	973

| Index | 992 |

27

Problems of Application

P. Mark Fackler

One of the easiest declarations a writer on global communication ethics can make is that the world is diverse and the moral life of the world reflects that diversity. Let each follow his/her path; let each culture carve its own totem. Diversity is standard operating procedure for human culture. It could not be otherwise, given the challenges of survival in different geographies, given the "up for grabs" nature of moral choice. Accepting such a situation as morally true, a chapter on the difficulty of applications would reduce to cultural anthropology: various symbol systems and traditions carry different moral values, and therein lies the tale. The best observers may do is to learn the rules characteristic of a region, its moral syntax. In the 2007 film *Mongol*, the story of Ghengis Khan, a Buddhist monk is told by the imprisoned Temudgin (Ghengis' given name, played by Asano Tadanobu) to "kill the guard and steal his keys," thus enabling Temudgin's escape. The monk responds, "It is against my faith to kill." Without hesitation or flicker of doubt, the weary Temudgin replies, "It is not against mine." Thus it is: one may kill in faith while the other would choose to die before violating a sacred rule prohibiting violence against another. The world, even among near neighbors, is remarkably diverse.

One of the most contentious declarations a writer can make about ethics is that some communicative actions, done anywhere or place, are morally wrong and ought to be condemned, while other communicative actions are right and good, no matter when or where. Who dares express such cultural myopia today? Surely one who is naïve by nature, boxed by custom, and xenophobic by orientation. Yet without some declaration approaching this far-out claim, a chapter on the difficulty of applying ethics to global problems washes out. Our only reason to proceed is the belief that some actions are good, others not, and that we may justifiably talk across cultures about both. Temudgin is right to admit his propensity toward violence, but wrong to act on it, which he did with brutal regularity. Dismiss that claim and

The Handbook of Global Communication and Media Ethics, First Edition. Edited by Robert S. Fortner and P. Mark Fackler.
© 2011 Blackwell Publishing Ltd. Published 2011 by Blackwell Publishing Ltd.

the movie and a million like it lose all point and purpose. In each human life, the moral dilemma leads to searching, justifying, testing, advocating, and then a vision of the good. Ghengis conquered the eastern world, but if his life had been without moral quest, we need pay no attention.

This chapter seeks to elaborate on why global communications present a serious claim on our collective moral awareness, and concludes with a proposal to guide us toward clarity, cooperation, and possibly peace. The mention of peace reminds us that cultures on the world's stage at the start of the second decade of the twenty-first century are radically different in mood, tradition, and ambition. Can we find sufficient common ground to abide the other's company, fueled as they are by entrenched ideologies and passionate rhetoric? Peace in many places seems a long way off; in some places, more distant yet by the disdain in which peace is held to be a failure of nerve, a softness and erosion of discipline. It was failure of discipline, was it not, which taught young Mohamed Omar Ismail to morally excuse his theft of 10 shirts and 10 trousers in Kismayo, Somalia, and "hard peace" which led the Sharia courts, backed by al-Shabab, to declare the ancient penalty as prescribed in the Quran (BBC Africa, 2010). It was education in "hard peace" that required the people of Kismayo to assemble in Freedom Park to witness the severing of Mohamed's right hand. Then "soft peace" spoke from a big-city office of Amnesty International, calling on the Titan of Soft Peace, the United Nations, to investigate this gross abuse of human rights, an investigation and report which will get a hearing in no place close to Kismayo.

Do such narratives lead to improved communication and understanding between East and West? No, in fact, they lead to a maimed youth, a more fearful city of people trying to hold life together, and distant grandstanders on both sides growing more certain than before that the ways of living they oppose are even more fearsome and intractable than they previously imagined. On top of that, all we (who live beyond the dust and din of Kismayo) know about Ismail's crime and punishment is learned via a report from a news agency steeped in its own ideology, and thus not to be trusted as a reliable source of anything beyond propagandists' lies. In a world such as this, discussion concerning the problems of applying ethics to communications issues would occur only to those who have grown soft by a surplus of goods safely stored for tomorrow, little to dread, rather in control of their fortunes, a luxury of the so-called developed world. Soft minds, soft wills, soft bodies – peace such as Ghengis so enjoyed demasking. In Kismayo, this conversation might seem quite irrelevant to the more urgent demand of putting thieves in their places.

Cataloging the Challenges

Even a brief review of the development of mediated communication reveals constant threats to veracity, covalent concerns for truth tempered by commercial considerations, and obvious intrusions of political power in the production of messages. Christians cites the major problems of communications ethics to be

Problems of Application 503

justice, diversity, violence, and privacy (2005, vol. 1, pp. 367–9). Statements presented as authentic are everywhere tempered by considerations of self-interest, sometimes of survival. Money speaks loudly in the public square. Those who hold and exercise power did not achieve it through passivity; control of social messages is perhaps the most important device available for political tenure. Everywhere messages are filtered, refined, and often trashed because the cost of speaking/writing is believed to outweigh benefits. Yet public speech (in any format) is still a treasured resource among democrats who need an informed public to achieve responsible consent. Cornell West (2004, p. 39) urges:

> Democracy depends, in large part, on a free and frank press willing to speak painful truths to the public about our society, including the fact of their own complicity in superficiality and simplistic reportage. There can be no democratic *paideia* – the critical cultivation of an active citizenry – without democratic *parrhesia* – a bold and courageous press willing to speak against the misinformation and mendacities of elites.

That "bold and courageous press" is the product of a long learning curve that has taught democratic free-speech advocates to prize dissent as the signal that pursuit of truth and responsible public action is renewable and vital. A proper measure of communicative justice is not what is forbidden, but what is allowed (Carter, 1995, p. 6).

Dissent is not everywhere treasured, obviously. In Guinea, on African's west cost, independence came on October 2, 1958. Ahmed Sekou Toure, a trade union organizer and first national chief executive, so offended the French (dissented from French designs on continued colonial influence) that Charles de Gaulle terminated all aid, withdrew French civil servants and army units, including doctors who provided care to the civilian population, and all French property, even furniture and fixtures in the former governor's house, to make Toure's move-in less exquisite. The new executive cared nothing about de Gaulle's pull-back. The cost of freedom might be dictated by French sensitivities but never again curtailed by them. Toure spoke with the boldness of his Ghanaian mentor, Kwame Nkrumah, "We prefer poverty in freedom to riches in slavery" (Meredith, 2005, p. 67). Once in power, that strong rhetoric metamorphized into leadership by paranoia. Convinced he was vulnerable, Toure found plots and conspiracies at every turn. In 1961 when teachers demanded equal pay for equal work (dissenting from Toure's corrupted ministry), prominent intellectuals were detained and imprisoned, and the Soviet ambassador was expelled, apparently under the notion that the Soviets were plotting. A cholera epidemic in 1973 was called a counter-revolutionary plot. The 1976 defeat of Guinea's soccer team in African championships was further evidence of a scheme against him, Toure believed (Meredith, p. 217–74). Such was the fear he inspired that years after his death in 1984 in an American hospital, older Guineans would refuse to answer questions about his regime because they feared that news of his death was planted by Toure to uncover silent disloyalty.[1]

News of Africa is "almost exclusively about poverty, wars and death," wrote one Western observer (Dowden, 2009, p. 4). Even in the great surge of independence in the 1950s and 1960s, international media struggled to find stories about anything other than poverty, wars, and death. Democracy was there, alive and growing on the continent, but obscured by blood, money, and traditional channels of power.

> The essence of democracy is not at all alien to Africa. Although few African societies were pure democracies, some ... were almost egalitarian, at least among men. They did not have kings or chiefs and decisions were taken after debate at meetings of the male elders. Discussions tended toward consensus rather than adversarial debate (Dowden, p. 71).

In one state, however, monarchical control was deeply entrenched. Haile Sellassie (1892–1975, Emperor 1930–1974) based his power on alleged blood connections to Solomon of ancient Israel. When rains failed in the early 1970s, he forbade Ethiopian media to discuss or admit to a famine. Dissenting university professors traveled to the ravaged provinces, returning with photographic proof. Government response to the evidence was weak and corrupt; officials were unable to deliver grains to the people without calloused profiteering. When international media began reporting, Ethiopia officially denied any problem and claimed, despite all, its internal affairs were being unfairly exaggerated by the international press.

Nevertheless the story was out, and worldwide response began to rush supplies to save those who could be helped. However, it was too late to help the leadership. By February, 1974, a student uprising and military coup led to a Coordinating Committee of the Armed Forces (called the *derg*, "committee"). Its leader, Major Mengistu Haile Mariam, nationalized land and industries, tolerated no dissent, and purged and executed at will (Marcus, 1994, p. 181). Accounts of this era tell of fear, arbitrary control, a failed economy, and then the inevitable counter-revolution. In all this, the Ethiopian press was totally incapable of informing its own people, or the world, of realities of poverty, war, and death hidden behind utopian rhetoric and a drought of both rainfall and political transparency. Only in 2004 was the first-ever graduate program in journalism offered at the University of Addis Ababa, and then, some of its most vocal sponsors were still facing jail terms for dissent against the "democratic" regime which replaced the *derg*.[2]

Examples from the developing world inform advanced democracies on the extent to which ideals of freedom are vulnerable to realities of political control and conservation of power and resources. Dissent in the "free world" is hard won and rarely without struggle. Dissent in the developing world is still, in many places, an occasion of extreme personal courage and sacrifice. In no case is the application of a vision of the good, or communication ethics, an easy roll-out.

Our examples also serve to point out the dialectical relationship between democracy and a responsible and free press. One does not build the other; one is not the cause or origin of the other. Rather, each plays a reciprocal role in the development of the other. In the west, the press is corrupted by the economic might of large corporate players, whose role in public life is often subtle but

Problems of Application 505

powerful, as king-making and deal-breaker. McChesney writes (2008, p. 308): "Today the regulatory and policymaking process is arguably more corrupt than ever, as tens of millions of dollars have made members of congress and regulators beholden to powerful corporate lobbies."

In the developing world, the press is equally vulnerable to the influence of money coupled with state power. Even where democracy has taken hold, ownership and office frequently overlap, presenting reporters and editors with a phalanx of opposition which makes even the importing of newsprint and ink, or the power to arbitrarily tax, a considerable pressure-point to reporting the news. The history of the *Economist* magazine in Kenya is a case in point. Its staff regularly uncovered flaws in government offices, bribery and kick-backs, schemes and trickery. Its editor, Peter Warutere, was one of the most admired journalists in the country, for integrity and clarity, and for avoiding detention, which he claimed was due to his careful, redundant research and his airtight agreement never to reveal a source.[3] During a European trip by Warutere in 1999, taxes evasion charges were brought against the magazine. It could not pay, and the premises were closed. Clever bureaucrats have many ways of dealing with sophisticated journalists.

Educated citizens ready to work for their rights, and a press ready to articulate a way to achieve those rights, must work hand in hand. Tabloids and television have proven that citizens in most democracies are codependent on media for entertainment and escape. A much smaller population in East or West – small in ambition and will – is ready to engage in participatory democracy: the heart of the enterprise for a free press.

Unless there is a citizenry that depends upon journalism, that takes it seriously, that is politically engaged, journalism can lose its bearings and have far less incentive to do the hard work that generates the best possible work (McChesney, 2008, p. 34).

Culture as Moral Arbiter

The first edition of a popular text in media ethics proposed to do ethical analysis using the Potter Box, a four-part sequenced process helpful in isolating key issues in moral dilemmas (Christians *et al.*, 1983, p. 6). Now 30 years later, the ninth edition (due in 2011) still uses that methodological frame. The famed and porous "third quad" in the box is Cultural Values. The reason culture plays such a significant role in the Box is the authors' belief that we humans, in all times and places, are shaped, defined, and nurtured by culture. Our values derive from relationships of all kinds, all culture-based. Our education is determined by culture, our choices constrained by culture, even our very names emerge from culture. How indeed could values *not* be shaped by culture? Understanding culture is the key to moral insight. Bernard Adeney notes that many people claim to follow a timeless morality, but all such claims are understood relative to the culture in which they are articulated. Virtues "are formed out of the habitual actions of real people" (Adeney, 1995, pp. 20, 27).

"Relative to the culture" reads as if values are indeed *relative*, and that is not the conclusions to which this essay points. Relativism – the belief that "because moral judgments vary across cultures and historical periods, all moral systems are equally good" (Christians *et al.*, 1993, p. 59) – is to let culture dictate, an unacceptable strategy. Christians points to the incongruity of seeking an ethic while granting permission to all options, so long as a social group lays claim to it.

> Without a normative basis for moral decision making, relativists frequently accept a utilitarianism that seeks at least noxious resolution for the distribution of limited goods and resources. However, relativism is the most conservative of moral strategies, because it seeks stability with established mores and has no reason to consider counter-claims from outside the group.... To believe that ethics is the code of the majority would allow the majority to tyrannize the minority (Christians *et al.*, 1993, p. 59).

Edward Purcell's (1973) weighty dissection of American thought in the twentieth century projects relativism as the antidote to *der Feuhrer* and *el Duce*. Dismissing absolutes as the regime of tyrants followed in the wake of social Darwinists and critical scholars such as William Graham Sumner, Ruth Benedict, Rudolph Carnap, and others, Purcell claims. The language of moral norms is now a foreign syntax. People do not use such terms anymore (1973, p. 202).

The critics of absolutism and relativism observe that tyranny draws its energy from both polarities. This essay promotes neither. Instead, we advise a normative ethics based on life and its liberties, responsibilities, and discoveries held in common and in trust across human societies. We need not "start from scratch" in devising moral norms, but neither do we recite ancient verities as final answers. The human community is not like that – monochromatic, inscribed norms, timeless judgments on application or substance. The human community grows, tests, tilts, and repositions its notions of the good, always with continuity to the past, always with the hope that futures will open to less struggle, more fertility, less bombast, more wisdom. However, we still need a moral center to the orbiting values and readjustments that human communities devise. We need a discourse that leads to responsible change. As Appiah observed, peoples do not alter their ethical norms as a result of long discussions over theory or principle, but gradually acquire "a new way of seeing things" (2006, p. 73). Is there an environment where we can see things anew, together, with good results for all?

Addressing the Problem

Communicative problems associated with greed, power, and suspicion (failure of trust) begin to coalesce around the meta-problem, a vacuous ethical center. Relativism plagues the trust–recovery process. No standpoint under heaven seems capable of sustaining the weight of widespread public belief and consequent action. No right-minded soul will "take the leap" into moral certitude while waters are churning, no break in the cloud-cover.

Problems of Application

These problems are not new. Sissela Bok (1978, p. 9) has noted the skeptic Cratylus, who adopted a language of gesture only to signal he had heard a sound, but that audible reply was meaningless given the variance of words and meanings; or Pyrrho, who 23 centuries ago gave up knowing anything, then surrendered speaking. Today, we have come to widespread dismissal of the correspondence theory of truth, or as Taylor (2007) has written at considerable length, we have arrived at the secular age – no more assurances, no cosmic platforms on which to weigh the veracity of claims to know.

Courting this epistemic abyss (to use Peters' artful phrase of 2005), a surge in communications scholarship has isolated and articulated postmodern universals grounded on fundamental human identity, that is, the web of relationships that sustain identity and culture, without which humanity cannot exist. Clifford Christians (2005, p. 238) has turned the soil on much of this ground, arguing the case for feminist communitarianism as best suited to address contemporary pleas for caregiving and peace. Remarkably, scholars from quite diverse traditions are reflecting the themes which now appear regularly in Christians' voluminous writing. Haydar Sadig (2010, p. 240), as a hopeful case in point, takes a communitarian strategy in his presentation of "reformed Islam" based on the teachings of Ustadh Mahmoud Mohamed Taha, whose own work before his untimely death in Sudan sought above all to address the lost trust disabling social progress:

> Fear, whatever form it takes, is the legitimate father of all moral perversion and behavioral distortion. Man will never perfect his manhood, and woman will never perfect her womanhood, as long as they remain frightened to any degree or in any fashion. Perfection is obtained through the process of liberation from fear (Taha, 1987, p. 84).

Many contributors to these debates seek to revitalize what pragmatists call procedural virtues: tell the truth, keep promises, negotiate fairly, avoid name-calling, control hyperbole, respect diverse traditions. Often these virtues become like proverbs to the communications professional, sometimes collected in small booklets and bound for easy transport.[4] Some follow the lead of Piaget, aiming to track the varied rates (based on age, place, gender, education, genes) of moral development (Coleman and Wilkins, 2009). Would that such well-developed persons gifted with a sense for word and symbol found their way into corporate public relations offices, global advertising agencies, or press services. Some contributors link the moral life to inherent gendered intuition and practice (Steiner, 2009). Some scholars are exploring the teachings of the stress-less faiths. Buddhism comes down to basics such as "intend no harm" or "do some good" (Stocking, 2009). Across the world in academic conferences probing the possibilities that journalism might actually promote peace, Taoism has become the favored tradition (Christians, 2009).

Do commonalities emerge from this pulsating conversation? Clearly the effort here is to respond with practical guidance to the digital age, to a one-world communications network, in the face of heightened tensions between disparate cultural centers spinning antagonistically away from *Gemainschaft* and the I-Thou. In many world conflict areas, Buber's (1970) classic typology must appear as nonsense language, so divergent are the cultural orientations.

All this ethical work is important to the field, academy, and communication professions. Gradually we might expect to see positions coalesce around shared norms and practices, though some (Alleyne 2009) see trends in other directions – no common standards, little to no shared norms.

This essay contends that the problem of universal norms and applications must be resolved within communities and cultures set toward an ethic of sustainable human advancement. Such communities will explore both ethical practice and moral substance, fail often, but consistently reach for life-sustaining realities. That is the common thread in efforts to find the moral center.

Eschatological Communitarianism

The concept behind this 13-syllable, 30-letter term shows up around the world wherever people gather to contemplate the uncertainties of the future and the hope for peace. In my own tradition, the concept appears as people, gathering, church, and congregation. *Eschatology*, what the future looks like, derives from the Greek *eschatos*, furthest out. *Communitarianism* – an arcane term that looks a lot like community, commune, and communicate – gathers ideas explained throughout this essay, namely, that we humans are grounded in time and place, relationships, traditions, habits of thinking, and embodied values. We live and breathe in relation to others. As John Mbiti (1969, p. 109) said, "We are, therefore I am." (Longer explanations of communitarianism are readily available. See this author's essay in Wilkins and Christians, 2009). Together, the phrase "eschatological communitarianism" denotes a trajectory, a future, which must be hammered out in time and place, but regularly in the history of humankind points toward a social order which the Jewish scriptures typify as *shalom* (e.g., Isaiah 9:7) and the New Testament writings (e.g., Revelation 11:15) call the *kingdom of God*. Both traditions speak in terms of a future which is present and "not yet" – apparent and accessible in part, with fulfillment still ahead (Ladd, 1974, p. 114). Each contributes to a vision of social peace, justice, and transparency as essential qualities for human prosperity and fulfillment (the Greek *Makarios*, completion). Historical reflection has brought hopes and fears of many years past to bear on our present responsibility for setting moral trajectories, however novel our rhetoric may be. We rarely invent virtues today.

Clarifying the dynamic of the ancient Jewish or Christian communities lies well outside the range of this chapter. Indeed, a vast literature explores the many dimensions of the long evolution of a people associated around both traditions. Early in the Christian movement, there was recognition that its origins reached back to "the beginning" and forward to "the end," and that the journey between would be difficult. Paul's salutation in his Letter to the Philippians (and in most of

Paul's writing) expresses this reality with endearing attachments to the people with whom he will experience this "new life." In light of much contemporary criticism of the Christian movement, its founding texts and praxis reflect a vision of community centered on fellowship (Greek *koinonia*) and struggle. Richard Hays (1996, pp. 196–197) notes:

> The community … is called to embody an alternative order that stands as a sign of God's redemptive purposes in the world. Thus, "community" is not merely a concept … it points to the social manifestation of the people of God…. The community expresses and experiences the presence of the kingdom of God by participating in "the *koinonia* of his [Jesus'] sufferings" (Philippians 3:10). Jesus' death is consistently interpreted in the New Testament as an act of self-giving love, and the community is consistently called to take up the cross and follow in the way that his death defines.

That theme is famously rendered by Dietrich Bonhoeffer. Community appears in all his work, but his 1939 *Life Together* is devoted to it. Bonhoeffer wrote the book while teaching in an underground seminary (the Nazis had outlawed it). *Life* criticizes the "visionary dreams" of people who imagine that community is cheerful, pleasant, or ideal. Bonhoeffer scolds such expectations which remove community from oppositional struggle. Gratitude is the first sign of genuine community, and in Bonhoeffer's case, gratitude for the virtues enable perseverance (1954, p. 29). Community is neither position nor status, but bounded action. The boundaries, today fluid, were at the start rather clearer. As N.T. Wright explains, the early Christian community functioned much like a family, with care for the needy, particularly widows and orphans, quite in accord with social obligations widely practiced within family circles.

> This called for a new socio-political orientation. On the one hand, there was 'another King,' and this King required allegiance and worship of a sort that radically subverted the allegiance and worship demanded by Caesar, and other lesser lords. On the other hand, the subversion in question was not that of the ordinary political revolutionary, and in the normal run of things Christians must submit to legitimate authority … The early church was thus marked out from the first familial community, loyalty to which overrode all other considerations (Wright, 1992, p. 449).

Gratitude, care, and love lead to action, and are not contemplated as moral destination. The destination is communal shalom. Virtues themselves could not be acquired in the older, classical way, by dint of effort and rational contemplation. Rather, this community, being and becoming, was itself the work of divine though mystical intervention, yet all too evidently human (Stassen and Gushee, 2003, p. 25). Its *telos* was not moral perfection, *eudaemonia* in Aristotle's rendering, the product of sufficient will and training, but community itself, that is, being together with God. Augustine caught the heart of it in his elegant phrase, *ipse praemium*, "he himself is our reward" (O'Donovan, 1994, p. 249). Yet action and passion, to borrow Oliver Wendell Holmes Jr's timely phrase,[5] was still the means and motive of this community's common life, and all action requires coordinated purpose. What, then, is the purpose of this community's social engagement? Nicholas Wolterstorff (1983, p. 19) writes:

> They are to struggle to establish a holy commonwealth here on earth. Of course it is the mandate of all humanity to struggle toward such a community; what makes Christians different in their action is that they have in fact committed themselves to struggling toward this goal, that they recognize it as God's mandate, and that they struggle toward it not just in obedience to God the creator but in imitation of Christ. It is because Christians are committed in obedient gratitude to work for the renewal of the earthly community that they will render their obedience in such ordinary earthly occupations as tailor, merchant, and farmer.

The time-place-political-economic community never reaches its high goals of justice and peace, yet presses on. Commenting on the "Christian realism" of Reinhold Niebuhr, Keith Ward (1986, p. 61) writes:

> The Christian faith enshrines as a central part of its teaching a positive hope for the material world and a positive purpose for the historical process. The world of history … is somehow to be transfigured, renewed, redeemed, to express fully the purpose of a loving God…. Insofar as [Christianity's] hope is for a society of justice and peace … its hope is political – it is about the founding and sustenance of a *polis*, a city or society of persons, bound together in the love of God.

Niebuhr himself, quoted later in Ward's essay, wisely observed that "the Kingdom of God is an impossibility in history;" Christian hope must be "in the fulfillment of life beyond the limitations of temporal existence" (Ward, p. 69).

Thus, a community with direct linkage to ancient Hebrew traditions received from its founders a new mission, energy, and familial mutuality, with assurance that never getting to Zion, so to speak, would not be reason for hopelessness. Heaven would come to them, all in good time (Wright, 2008).

Must the Jewish and Christian scriptures or their commentators be invoked to sustain a discussion of eschatological communitarianism? Kant thought not. His third formulation of the Categorical Imperative pointed toward a "universal kingdom of ends" which echoes his Lutheran catechism yet without the encumbrance of divine revelation. All the insight needed to enact this kingdom (*Reich*, realm) was inherent in each person, the reasonable self, whose first obligation was to be loyal to universal law, not for what rewards it might offer, including the long-sought reward of a just and happy society, but for itself, for the moral life itself, because that is indeed the human life. Yet this responsibility, borne by all people, is not able to be fulfilled by solo agents acting independently of each other. The moral obligation must be realized in the village and among the people. Sullivan (1994, p. 86) writes:

> This duty … cannot be satisfied just by the efforts of individuals concerned only with their own moral lives, for the goal is a collective, social good, not merely an aggregate

of the moral achievements of individuals. Therefore, our obligation to promote the kingdom of ends is a special duty, unlike any other. It involves the human species as a whole, requiring each of us to recognize that our moral destiny is inextricably tied to our relations with one another in a communal endeavor.

Kant was skeptical of the human tendency to do good for the rewards of doing good, much like a child will obey for a candy or an adult will "do good" in view of a pending promotion, more money, or prestige. Social hope was crucial to sustained moral action, Kant insisted, but the just society was to be a by-product of morality, as it were, not a critical motivation for it, lest passion override reason and ends become falsely justified means. Clearly, however, people seek answers to the moral quest which are "comprehensive as well as final" (Sullivan, 1994, p. 84):

> Kant concluded that the complete final good for the human species, our ultimate "necessary end," consists in both our obligatory end – good moral character – and our natural end – happiness or well-being (Sullivan, 1994, p. 89, paraphrasing Kant, 1785/1990, p. 396).

Postmodern critics would dismiss grand theory such as this, but never its local expressions. Always and at all times people of "good character" will advocate and sacrifice for a broader reach of human rights and ready supply of basic needs for all people. No moral argument forbids the hope of a better day tomorrow, and much moral effort is expended in finding it. People of all ideological traditions and faith-groups hope for the elusive "kingdom [realm] of ends" and will test and try any new path to get there, minimizing moral fall-out and maximizing human prosperity. The eschatological community is a people with hope and vision, anywhere, everywhere.

Moral diversity and respect for the varied traditions find here a point of meeting: human relationships matter. Aristotle's courage may be superseded by more nuanced thinking on behalf of slaves and women; revenge as primal value no longer works (Posner, 1996); but mutuality in human community seems to stick. Richard Rorty, writing as a modern Crytalus, presents a triad of values to herald the secular age: contingency, irony, and solidarity. The latter derives not from reflection on the essence of human nature, but from stories of pain and humiliation that spark within us a realization that we are more like each other, despite cultural differences, than we are unlike. Indeed, writes Rorty (1989, p. 192), "there is such a thing as moral progress, and this progress is indeed in the direction of greater human solidarity ... thought of as the ability to see more and more traditional differences (of tribe, religion, race, customs, and the like) as unimportant when compared with similarities."

Such claims are found everywhere, from citadels of academia to the conference halls where business and leadership literature chieftains create the next surge of entrepreneurship. There sounds the call to a communal consciousness. Peter Block (2008, p. 1), writing for the marketplace, advises:

The essential challenge is to transform the isolation and self-interest within our communities into connectedness and caring for the whole. The key is to identify how this transformation occurs.... A key insight in this pursuit is to accept the importance of social capital in the life of the community. This begins the effort to create a future distinct from the past.

Communal consciousness is the modern reflection of traditional moral proverbs such as the Golden Rule. Such sayings are heard around every human hearth and boma. Settling differences to coordinate action requires constant attention to skillful communication. Marcus Buckingham (2005, p. 59) urges leaders to focus on what lies ahead, the eschaton, as it were: "Great leaders rally people to a better future.... What defines a leader is ... preoccupation with the future. In his head he carries a vivid image of what the future could be, and this image drives him on."

The rhetoric of many leaders respected throughout centuries would attest to this futuristic bent, alive with hope and challenge. The Rev. Jesse Jackson, well known as a champion of civil rights, captures the core message:

Wherever you are tonight, I challenge you to hope and to dream. Don't submerge your dreams. Dream above all else. Even on drugs, dream of the day you'll be drug free. Even in the gutter, dream of the day that you'll be up on your feet again. You must never stop dreaming. Face reality, yes. But don't stop with the way things are. Dream of things as they ought to be. Dream. Face pain, but love, hope, faith, and dreams will help you rise above the pain. Use hope and imagination as weapons of survival and progress (July 17, 1984, in Torricelli, 1999, p. 374).

That is what this chapter means to say. Communities with moral vision respect the past but fix on the future, respect the individual but work toward the common good, know the reality of their times but conceive conditions and relationships that offer hope to all. Leaders in such communities say the words that make the quest vital and perhaps even possible. They open the future with vision and symbolic power, guiding communities toward survival and progress.

The reader may ask: why communitarianism, or this version of it? What criteria of social or ontological significance permits confidence that this approach salts in any sense the stew of ethical conundra which seems able to adapt like a virus to every moral pharmacology? In our era, latching on to virtues or programs or even moral traditions is like serial marriage – one moves around searching but rarely satisfied.

Polanyi (1962) directs the "secular age" away from its bipolar epistemology of evidence/subjectivity to a unified process of inquiry that builds on informed belief. Acknowledging his debt to Augustine, Polanyi (1962, p. 266) advises:

We must now recognize belief once more as the source of all knowledge. Tacit assent and intellectual passions, the sharing of an idiom and of a cultural heritage, affiliation to a like-minded community: such are the impulses which shape our vision of the nature of things ... No intelligence, however critical or original, can operate outside such a fiduciary framework.

Problems of Application

History offers plenty of examples of knowledge and commitment generated apart from community, or in deliberate resistance to community. The result is usually power unbridled by norms that this essay and communication professionals worldwide seek and adopt. Jung Chang's (2005) brilliant study of Chairman Mao describes a life of tactical judgments morally disconnected from even the people's movement he is popularly celebrated for, as if "chairman" was the wrong prescript altogether: Mao was chairman-in-chief of his own grasp for place and power. The rest is façade, by Chang's account. Greene's (1998) acclaimed *48 Laws of Power* is a rogues' gallery of morally vacuous advice, all the while using alleged moral "softies" as pawns.

Belief for Augustine was in a good God who speaks and acts (Webber, 1980, p. 74), for Polanyi in "personal acceptance which falls short of empirical and rational demonstrability."

> This then is our liberation from objectivism: to realize that we can voice our ultimate convictions only from within our convictions – from within the whole system of acceptances that are logically prior to ... the holding of my particular piece of knowledge ... I must aim at discovering what I truly believe in (1962, pp. 266–267).

This essay advises that the process of articulating identity, focusing moral commitment, achieving social gain, and overcoming the considerable resilience of greed and oppressive power, is best done in the context of eschatological communitarianism. This framework forbids the orphanage of any human being from the whole while respecting the integrity and freedom of individuals. It knows the past but works toward open futures conceivably more abundant of human happiness than the present. It mediates between the "perfectionist" tradition, in which state and civil society help people achieve a substantive vision of the good life, and the "procedural" tradition, which remains open to substance from the people while the state enables wide liberties of thought and action (Madsen and Strong, 2003, p. 2). It is the stratosphere of the responsible press, however much its atmosphere is smoky with crass residue of the hour. It requires visionary leadership grounded in presuppositions pregnant with human yearning, grounded in values that celebrate life. Problems of applying moral norms to communications practice may pick and choose codal proverbs as the fix of the day, but new technologies and audience configurations will require regular revision. A peaceful destination must be fixed, a trajectory of human prosperity established. Meaning must invade sterile process. Love will generate sustained action. Eschatological communities toil in the now, aim at the future, and take measure of human life in artful reflection of its own errors and efforts.

We tend to get what we hope for.

Notes

1 pers. comm. with Robert Bolt, 17 January 2010.
2 This author had the privilege of delivering the first lectures at that program, and interviewing the academics and students in the first class.

3 pers. comm., October 1998.
4 The "Code of Conduct & Practice of Journalism in Kenya" is such a booklet. On its effectiveness, see Fackler (2010).
5 "I think that, as life is action and passion, it is required of a man that he should share the passion and action of his time at peril of being judged not to have lived." Holmes delivered this line in a speech at Keene, New Hampshire, on Memorial Day, May 30, 1884. Quoted in Sheldon, 1989, p. 176.

References

Adeney, B. (1995) *Strange Virtues: Ethics in a Multicultural World*, IVP Press, Downers Grove, IL.
Alleyne, M. (2009) Global media ecology: Why there is no global media ethics standard, in *Handbook of Mass Media Ethics*, (eds L. Wilkins and C. Christians), Routledge, New York, pp. 382–394.
Appiah, K.A. (2006) *Cosmopolitanism*, W.W. Norton, New York.
BBC Africa (2010) Somali justice Islamist-style. 7 January, http://news.bbc.co.uk/2/hi/africa/8057179.stm (accessed July 19, 2010).
Block, P. (2008) *Community: The Structure of Belonging*, Berrett-Koehler, San Francisco.
Bok, S. (1978) *Lying*, Pantheon, New York.
Bonhoeffer, D. (1954) *Life Together*, (trans. J. Doberstein), Harper & Row, New York.
Buber, M. (1970) *I and Thou*, Scribners, New York.
Buckingham, M. (2005) *The One Thing You Need to* Know, Free Press, New York.
Carter, S. (1995) *The Dissent of the Governed*, Harvard University Press, Cambridge, MA.
Chang, J. (2005) *Mao*, Knopf, New York.
Christians, C. (2005) Communication ethics, in *Encyclopedia of Science, Technology, and Ethics*, (ed. C. Mitcham) Macmillan, New York, pp. 364–371.
Christians, C. (2009) The Tao and Peace. Presented at the National Communication Association, Chicago, November 13.
Christians, C., Ferré, J.P., and Fackler, M. (1993) *Good News*, Oxford University Press, New York.
Christians, C., Rotzoll, K.B., and Fackler, M. (1983) *Media Ethics, Cases and Moral Reasoning*, Longman, New York.
Coleman, R., and Wilkins, L. (2009) Moral development: A psychological approach to understanding ethical judgment, in *Handbook of Mass Media Ethics*, (ed. L. Wilkins and C. Christians), Routledge, New York.
Dowden, R. (2009) *Africa*, Public Affairs, New York.
Fackler, M. (2010) Journalism makes you kind of selfless, in *Ethics and Evil in the Public Sphere*, Hampton, Cresskill, NJ.
Greene, R. (1998) *The 48 Laws of Power*, Viking, New York.
Hays, R. (1996) *The Moral Vision of the New Testament*, Harper, San Francisco, New York.
Kant, I. (1785/1990) *Foundations of the Metaphysics of Morals*, (trans. L.W. Beck), 2nd edn, Macmillan, New York.
Ladd, G. (1974) *The Presence of the Future*, Eerdmans, Grand Rapids, MI.
Madsen, R., and Strong, T. (2003) *The Many and the One*, Princeton University Press, Princeton, NJ.

Marcus, H. (1994) *A History of Ethiopia*, University of California Press, Berkeley.

Mbiti, J. (1969) *African Religion and Philosophy*, Praeger, Westport, CT.

McChesney, R. (2008) *The Political Economy of Media*, Monthly Review Press, New York.

Meredith, M. (2005) *The Fate of Africa*, Public Affairs, New York.

O'Donovan, O. (1994) *Resurrection and Moral Order*, Eerdmans, Grand Rapids, MI.

Peters, J.D. (2005) *Courting the Abyss*, University of Chicago Press, Chicago.

Polanyi, M. (1962) *Personal Knowledge*, University of Chicago Press, Chicago.

Posner, R. (1996) *Overcoming Law*, Harvard University Press, Cambridge, MA.

Purcell, E. (1973) *The Crisis of Democratic Theory*, University of Kentucky Press, Lexington.

Rorty, R. (1989) *Contingency, Irony, and Solidarity*, Cambridge University Press, New York.

Sadig, H. (2010) Ustadh Mahmoud Mohamed Taha and Islamic reform, in *Ethics and Evil in the Public Sphere*, (eds R. Fortner and M. Fackler), Hampton, Cresskill, NJ.

Stassen, G., and Gushee, D. (2003) *Kingdom Ethics*, InterVarsity Press, Downers Grove, IL.

Steiner, L. (2009) Feminist media ethics, in *Handbook of Mass Media Ethics*, (eds L.Wilkins and C. Christians), Routledge, New York, pp. 366–381.

Stocking, S.H. (2009) Buddhist moral ethics, in *Handbook of Mass Media Ethics*, (eds L. Wilkins and C.G. Christians), Routledge, New York, 291–304.

Sullivan, R. (1994) *An Introduction to Kant's Ethics*, Cambridge University Press, New York.

Taha, M.M. (1987) *The Second Message of Islam*, (trans. A.A. An-Na'im), Syracuse University Press, Syracuse.

Taylor, C. (2007) *The Secular Age*, Harvard, Cambridge, MA.

Torricelli, R. (1999) *In Our Own Words*, Free Press, New York.

Ward, K. (1986) Reinhold Niebuhr and the Christian Hope, in *Reinhold Niebuhr and the Issues of Our Time*, (ed. R. Harries), Eerdmans, Grand Rapids, MI, pp. 61–87.

Webber, R. (1980) *God Still Speaks*, Thomas Nelson, Nashville.

West, C. (2004) *Democracy Matters*, Penguin, New York.

Wilkins, L., and Christians, C. (2009) *Handbook of Mass Media Ethics*, Routledge, New York.

Wolterstorff, N. (1983) *Until Justice and Peace Embrace*, Eerdmans, Grand Rapids, MI.

Wright, N.T. (1992) *The New Testament and the People of God*, Fortress, Minneapolis.

Wright, N.T. (2008) *Surprised by Hope*, Harper, New York.

28

Disenfranchised and Disempowered
How the Globalized Media Treat Their Audiences – A Case from India

Anita Dighe

Introduction

Since 1991, India has witnessed an explosion in the print and electronic media. The new economic policies of liberalization have permitted an unregulated entry of private players and opened up the Indian media to foreign investment. Privatization and deregulation have enabled cross-border flow of capital and technology. These changes have opened new ways for media businesses to expand into international markets through joint ventures, joint production arrangements and sales, thereby ensuring that media are commercialized and profit-driven.

The extent of the massive change in the Indian media scene can be gauged if one realizes that before 1991, Indian viewers had access to only two television channels. By 1999, they had access to more than 50 channels (Crawley and Page, 2001). Television broadcasting has grown at such a phenomenal rate that by 2008, there were more than 250 diverse television channels reaching 112 million Indian homes (Joseph, 2008a). This process of transformation, however, has been relentless and is so complex that it would be difficult to capture all the nuances of the changes that are taking place in India today. An attempt, however, is made to describe broad contours of the media scene in the present times. This essay will focus attention on three media – print, radio, and electronic, with a small section on the growth of the new media, and will highlight issues of media ethics that have arisen due to the fast-paced changes taking place in the Indian media.

The Handbook of Global Communication and Media Ethics, First Edition. Edited by Robert S. Fortner and P. Mark Fackler.
© 2011 Blackwell Publishing Ltd. Published 2011 by Blackwell Publishing Ltd.

An Overview of the Globalized Media Scene in India

India has experienced, post media-deregulation, an explosion in the Indian language newspapers. While it is difficult in India to get accurate figures of the circulation of daily newspapers, even figures from the official Registrar of Newspapers indicate that the circulation of daily newspapers doubled between 1993 and 1998. The circulation of Indian dailies has continued to grow – at least 10 newspapers now count their daily copy sales in millions. Of these three are in English, another three in Hindi, and the rest in various regional languages. According to Joseph (2008b), with 62 483 newspapers and periodicals in 101 languages and combined daily circulation of 99 million copies, India is the second biggest newspaper market in the world despite its poor literacy rates.

Further, Joseph (2008b) quotes the National Readership Survey (NRS) 06 data, according to which vernacular dailies grew from 191 million readers in 2005 to 203.6 million in 2006, while the English dailies stagnated at 21 million during the same period. In her book, *Headlines from the Heartland: Reinventing the Hindi Public Sphere*, published in 2007, media critic Sevanti Ninan describes the on-going newspaper revolution in the country's Hindi-speaking states, where the circulation of Hindi newspapers has grown rapidly, especially in small towns and rural areas. While their content targets a local readership, multiple editions have now become common, given the availability of the Internet and fax. Eanadu in the South has editions coming out in every district of Andhra Pradesh. Rajasthan's Patrika publishes four editions and Malayala Manorama issues three editions. Aaj, Nai Duniya, and Amar Ujala similarly publish several editions. As a result of this trend, Indian language publications have come into their own – with growth in circulation and share of advertising leading to a parallel growth in self-confidence (Joseph, 2008b).

One of the hallmarks of the Indian press is that it has remained relatively robust and unfettered over the six decades since independence. It has been successful in warding off State attempts to curb its freedom of expression and has been characterized by relative autonomy and its commitment to serving the public interest. This has happened despite the fact that it has traditionally been recognized that Indian newspapers are controlled by "monopoly capitalists." The situation, however, is fast changing, with a new trend of "corporatization" that has now set in the Indian newspaper industry. A related development is that of the increasing dependence on advertising for a newspaper's revenue. India's advertising industry grew by an average of 30% a year through the 1990s, is currently worth Rs.196.4 billion and is expected to shoot up in the coming years (Joseph, 2008b). While the English language newspapers previously took the lion's share of the industry's advertising revenues, the situation is gradually changing, with the regional press showing a growth in advertising volumes.

Radio, on the other hand, has always been used as an extended arm of the State. While the government has focused on extending the network of radio stations and transmitters, the fact remains that post-independence, the medium has been used as a tool of public policy. The practice of appointing a civil servant as the Director General of All India Radio (AIR) began in 1947. Due to its bureaucratization, the credibility and effectiveness of AIR's news operations have thus been naturally compromised. The advent of cheap transistor radio sets by the late 1960s popularized the medium in India and brought about a major expansion in its reach.

Television came to India as recently as 1959. A pilot project was set up confined initially to Delhi and its surrounding areas and was restricted to educational and other "developmental" content and was limited to three days a week (Joseph, 2008a). In the initial years, television was handled by AIR and it was only in 1976 that Doordarshan, a separate organization, was formed with its own Director General. Both radio and television were blatantly used to project the personality of the then prime minister and during the emergency, were tightly controlled by government censorship. Indian television, however, remained an urban phenomenon until the 1980s, as it was confined to affluent sections of the society.

A rapid expansion and development took place during the 1980s so that by the mid-1980s, indigenous satellite technology enabled Doordarshan to broadcast nationally for the first time. The national reach paved the way for the emergence of an all-India market for television advertising, which not only brought new commercial influences to bear on programming but made television a powerful vehicle for the promotion of consumerism (Joseph, 2008a). The global coverage of the Gulf War by the US-based Cable News Network (CNN) International in 1991 heralded the era of private satellite television in India. Thereafter, the entry of Hong-Kong based Satellite Television Asia Region (STAR), which brought some news and a great deal of entertainment to Indian audiences, began what came to be known as the "invasion of the skies" challenging the hegemony of Doordarshan's supremacy over television airwaves.

Between 1990 and 1999, access to television grew from 10% to 75% of the urban population. Cable television and foreign movies became widely available for the first time in India. Satellite programming from foreign sources such as CNN and BBC World, and the development of domestic channels like Zee TV, Sun TV, suddenly and explosively increased the demand for cable television. Viewers now had access not only to the major international cable stations such as CNN and BBC World but also to MSNBC, Star News, and Headlines Today, as well as to privately owned channels such as NDTV, India TV, Aaj Tak, and Zee News.

With satellite broadcasting, India's large and expanding middle class has enthusiastically welcomed the greater diversity that the new satellite television channels have to offer. Having depended entirely on the State-owned Doordarshan to provide news, Indian audiences have not lamented the breaking down of the state's stranglehold on broadcasting. With the opening up of the economy after 1991, they can now choose between several 24-hour news channels. While Doordarshan, has remained under centralized bureaucratic control, it has since 1992, been forced to seek 80% of its operating costs from advertising. As a result, it is in direct competition with the proliferating satellite and cable stations. It is now widely recognized that there is a new dynamism on the Indian media scene, with increased viewer choice, better entertainment, broader international coverage, and more credible news reporting (Crawley and Page, 2001).

Radio has also shown considerable resurgence. The National Readership Survey (NRS, 2006) reported that radio had increased its reach from 23% to 27% of the population, meaning that more than a quarter of the population now listens to a radio station in an average week, bringing the number of listeners almost equal to the number of readers. AIR presently has a network of 208 broadcasting centres, including 74 local radio stations, technically covering the entire Indian population (almost 99%) across much of the country (Joseph, 2008a). The establishment of FM stations has been a significant step that has been taken to break the government's monopoly over radio airwaves. According to indiantelvision.com, by 2007, a total of 281 FM channels, including 161 of AIR and 120 privately owned channels, were operational, and it expected this number to rise. However, with no news or current affairs programs thus far permitted on FM radio in India, it is at present primarily a medium of entertainment, reaching out to a predominantly young audience with a menu of Indian and Western pop music and chat shows (Joseph, 2008a).

Community radio, to serve the information, communication, and entertainment needs of small, local communities, was until recently a distant goal that was pursued only by a few nongovernment organizations (NGOs) on an experimental and pilot basis. Despite the landmark Supreme Court judgment in 1995, declaring the airwaves to be public property, it was not until 2002 that the Ministry of Information and Broadcasting issued guidelines to enable at least educational institutions to launch what it defined as community radio. Exercising extreme caution, such stations at present are not permitted to broadcast news. According to the current guidelines, programs are to be of immediate relevance to the local community, focusing primarily on issues concerning development, agriculture, health, education, the environment, social welfare, community development, and culture. Furthermore, the broadcast range of such stations is restricted.

There has also been a tremendous growth of the new media in recent years. According to Saxena (2008), the Internet, mobile telephony, and other new technologies have changed the way media organizations collect, present, and disseminate news. They have also changed the definition of news and who controls it, and created new revenue models for media companies. Tracing the growth of the new media in India, Saxena (2008) describes how the first Internet hubs were created in the early 1990s. They had limited range and limited access. Then came the Software Technology Parks of India (STPI) Internet service. It used dial-up connections and leased lines to connect technology parks located in Bangalore, Hyderabad, and Noida.

It was in August 1995 that the first public Internet service was launched in India. It was, however, made available only in the four metros of Delhi, Mumbai, Kolkata, and Chennai. Gradually, the services were extended to other Indian cities but the connections were slow and the technology was not very effective. However, the Internet sparked people's enthusiasm so that by 1998, the number of internet subscribers had increased to 1.4 million.

Between 1996 and 1998, some major websites were set up. The traditional media, too, moved to the Internet and three major English dailies – the *Hindu*, *Times of India*, and the *Indian Express* – launched their websites in 1996. The language newspapers soon followed. Initially, however, the media websites were low-tech websites that made downloading of pages and reading very slow and cumbersome.

The year 1998 marked a turning point in the evolution of the Internet in India as the government in power, ended the monopoly of the public Internet service provider and allowed the private sector to set up Internet facilities. This made possible the Net-savvy media groups to diversify and to offer a host of services.

The popularity of mobile phones opened a new revenue source for media companies. Several newspapers and television channels in English as well as in regional languages tied up with VAS (value-added services) companies to provide non-news content like ringtones, jokes, Bollywood gossip, forecasts, contests. This was because they found that readers were more willing to pay for value added services than news (Saxena, 2008).

In the new millennium, several newspaper companies launched the e-paper as it offered major benefits to them. While initially, they were offered as paid products, soon it became apparent that Internet users were not willing to pay any access fee. As a result, the e-papers today are largely free.

An important development was the launch of broadband in 2004, first in the metros and then in smaller towns. This made downloads easier and faster. The post-2004 period also witnessed a great interest in user-generated content. Users thus started posting text, images, and video. As a result, India witnessed a rush for social networking sites. Another important development has been the evolution of blogs in Indian languages.

The rapid changes that are being brought about by the new media become evident if one considers that while there were 1.4 million Internet users in 1998, that number went up to 42 million in 2007.

What are the manifestations of this process of globalization on the Indian media? An attempt will be made to highlight what are some of the significant changes that are being brought about in the Indian media – electronic and print – that are raising ethical questions about the role and the responsibilities of the media in the Indian context.

Impact of Globalization on the Indian Media

The discourse surrounding the impact of globalization from a communications point of view is one of the most vigorously debated. The complexity of global media systems in the contemporary world has made it clear that the older paradigms under which the processes of media globalization had been understood, for example, communication and development, dependency, and cultural imperialism, have to be reexamined. Broadly, there are two media theories of globalization. One strand relates to the cultural imperialism/homogenization perspective, which emphasizes domination and hegemony while the cultural heterogenization perspective stresses the proliferation of cultural fusion and hybridity (Gordon, 2008). The cultural imperialism perspective on globalization was particularly dominant during the 1960s and the 1970s when countries from the developing world began voicing their concerns over what was perceived as a one way flow of information and cultural goods from the North to the South. Such countries felt that their cultural sovereignty was being undermined due to the dominance from the more industrialized countries. There was therefore a demand to set up a New World Information and Communication Order.

Proponents of media imperialism suggest that media play a central role in shaping cultural processes and practices that are dominated by Western ownership. As a result, the cultural products and media outputs from the lesser developed countries are forced to occupy a position of subordination not only on the international scene but at the local level as well. This results in global imbalances, for conditions are created for information dependency by lesser developed countries on the West. According to these theorists, media imperialism becomes hegemonic because imported programs cultivate a taste for things North American or European while undermining those values that are espoused locally. The critics who challenge this perspective suggest that instead of creating homogenization, globalization succeeds in producing a heterogenization of cultures. They make an important observation that since local programming is more culturally proximate or relevant than imported programming originating from culturally disparate places, they are therefore preferred by local viewers. As a result, even though the Western media have been imported in developing countries, they have only made a limited impact on the local culture. For in order to gain local acceptance, many transnational corporations (TNCs) such as Sony Entertainment Televisions, Star TV, have had to localize their products and advertising. This is based on the argument that local audiences still prefer local programming to imported content and will support local productions as long as they are of good quality. In other words, a question can be raised about the homogenizing influence of the global media industry on local identities and cultures.

In India, while there were fears of cultural invasion in the early 1990s that accompanied the advent of Star TV and CNN, it was Indian satellite to cable channels that captured the allegiance of the local audience based on their offerings of local program content produced in Hindi (Gordon, 2008). India has experienced, post media-deregulation, an explosion in the vernacular press and Indian language television channels. In the North, Hindi dailies are claiming three to four times more sales than English dailies. Every cable package currently contains several language-based channels. In Delhi and Mumbai, cable packages can include up to 16 regional language channels catering to a linguistically vast and diverse audience, and these channels often have the highest television ratings. Such a scenario allows media scholars to hope that globalization does not necessarily and uniformly lead to cultural homogenization, but rather, to reinvigorate cultural diversity in new ways (Wasserman and Rao, 2006). Building on the notion of "glocalization," that has come to give cultures a vocabulary for their experiences, Wasserman and Rao (2006) aver that in order to understand the complexity of media ethics in a rapidly changing world, it is necessary to understand how local resistance is taking place against homogenization. The theoretical framework of glocalization helps us to understand that the "threat of imported media" does not necessarily eliminate local resistance to imported cultural or political ethos. The earlier understanding that media globalization as a one-way traffic from the centre to the periphery has now made way for a more nuanced understanding of the multidirectionality of the process (Wasserman and Rao, 2006).

The rise of local television channels and newspapers has resulted in a phenomenal rise in the use of hidden cameras in recent years. This has precipitated public debate among media professionals and academics about the ethics of such news gathering techniques. While in the West, hidden cameras have been judiciously and rarely used, in the past few years, Indian magazines and channels like Tehelka, Star News, Zee News and India TV, in the name of investigative journalism, have been aggressively using hidden cameras as a tool of news-gathering, calling these news stories "sting operations." Tehelka.com (an online magazine) started the trend when it aired video footage that revealed professional cricketers were involved in match-fixing and in taking bribes.

There are divergent views about the rampant use of the hidden cameras. Thus, there are those who argue that due to market pressures, newspapers and television channels are more image driven and less public service oriented. It has been said that tabloidization of news is resulting in an increase in deceptive practices that are bordering on entrapment (Wasserman and Rao, 2006). On the other hand, there are those who argue that the hidden camera tactics have allowed for more accountability in a system that is thoroughly and completely corrupt. There are several instances to show how the hidden cameras have helped to uncover some of the social ills and practices that plague Indian society. Thus, Cobrapost.com, another Internet news portal, and Aaj Tak TV channel, broadcast hidden camera footage of 11 members of Parliament (from various political parties) accepting bribes for asking questions in Parliament. Then there was the case of the hidden camera exposing on a news channel broadcast, footage of doctors disclosing the sex of the fetus after an ultrasound and offering abortions to those couples with a female fetus; both practices being illegal under the Indian law. What shook the nation, however, was when in 2001 Tehelka exposed the level of corruption in the defense establishment; the hidden cameras showing how politicians, army officers and some arms deals organizers, were involved in the deal. The visuals of party leaders and senior army officers eager to take bribes from a fictitious company, created a storm in the Indian Parliament (Vasudevan, 2001). That the audiences are responding positively to these "sting operations" is evident from the very high ratings the television channels that show such programs are getting. While on the one hand, globalization has led to commodification and tabloidization of news, on the other, globalization has also increased the availability and use of new technologies that seem to be benefiting local audiences.

Sensationalization of news is another phenomenon that is now characterizing the Indian media. In a bid to catch eyeballs and get sound-bytes, the various television channels and the press now vie with one another and thereby violate their own norms of media ethics. Rather than reporting facts, the media have now started expressing opinions and sitting in judgment. This has happened in a number of cases and is a cause for alarm. The media have been sitting in judgment over matters of life and death for those facing trial. Thus, in the case of the attack on the Indian Parliament that took place in 2003, the television channels ran an SMS poll on whether Afzal Guru should be given the death penalty. According to Indira Jaisingh, a noted Supreme Court lawyer, this was a first in Indian legal history, when an SMS poll could decide the penalty by influencing public opinion That public opinion did influence the outcome of the case was to some extent evident from the fact that the judges who decided the case said that the "collective conscience of society" was outraged by the attack on Parliament (Jaisingh, 2008). A virtual trial by the media was carried out in the Scarlett Keeling murder case. All sorts of theories were floated; that it was a conspiracy to malign the tourist destination of Goa, that it was a plot to sully the fair name of the Goan people and from all this, it was finally surmised that it was the girl's mother, Fiona, who was responsible for the tragedy because she was an irresponsible mother. The manner in which every rule of journalistic restraint was thrown to the winds was highlighted in the media handling of the Aarushi Talwar murder case recently. On most television channels, there was the same high-pitched coverage, the wild theories, the showing of gory details, as well as character assassination of the worst kind. Throughout, there was a certain smugness and self-righteousness that was the sub-text of the media reporting. Were they not acting in the public interest?, acting as a watchdog and exposing the ineffectiveness or venality of the enforcement agencies?, they asked (Sivadas, 2008). While it is true that the media was responsible for having brought issues like failure of justice in the Jessica Lal murder case or Priyadarshini Mattoo case to public notice and thereby created a public outrage that eventually led to the reversal of the sentence that had been passed earlier, there is no denying the fact that no matter how significant a role the media can play in exposing the failure of justice, it cannot replace the justice delivery system (Jaisingh, 2008).

Yet another phenomenon which characterizes the current Indian media scene is that due to "corporate hijack" of the media agendas, as described by the famous Ramon Magsaysay award winner, P. Sainath, who is also the Rural Affairs Editor of the Hindu, there has been a "structural shut-out of the poor in media coverage." As reported in the Hindu, according to Sainath (2008, p. 14), there has been a dangerous shift of the Indian media towards corporate agendas that have led to the failure of the media in adequately reporting events like the current crises in food, agriculture and labour. Some newspapers had even begun to have what they call private client treaties with a company. 'They acquire a stake into a company … and the marketing of (their) products is sold as news. These treaties privilege the right of giant corporations' surrogate selling above the rights of reader to be informed.' Citing a report by the Centre for Media Studies, P. Sainath averred that the share of entertainment in news channels was nine times that of agriculture, education, health, and environment combined. It was therefore common for newspapers to have dozens of reporters covering business beats and entertainment and completely neglecting problems of labor or the agricultural sector.

That the discrimination shown by the media against the poor and the dispossessed can be blatant and disgraceful was highlighted in an incident that took place in a village called Khairlanji in Maharashtra in September 2006. On September 29, 2006, the inhabitants of Khairlanji lynched four members of a dalit (the lowest social group in the caste hierarchy) family residing in their own village – a mother, her daughter and two sons – in one of the most gruesome ways possible. Those who committed the crime were backward castes and tribals. The immediate provocation for the massacre was that the mother and daughter had given evidence against some of the villagers who had assaulted a dalit from a neighbouring village. The government and the civil society were at first indifferent to the incident. The dalits themselves took over a month to react. When they ultimately reacted, the response of the government was swift and ferocious. The government unleashed terror on them and gunned down some of them. Later, when the dalits took to the streets in their thousands, the media gave some attention to the development but were unsympathetic to those who had died. In reviewing the book by Teltumbde, Sebastian (2009) recounts how the media had carried out a sustained, vociferous and aggressive campaign in the cases of Jessica Lall and Priyadarshini Mattoo (upper caste, rich women), but the same campaign was missing for the deaths of Surekha and Priyanka, the mother and daughter in the Khairlanji case. Also, while four dalits had died and more than 100 injured, the media bemoaned the damage to public property, inconveniences suffered by the "citizens," the loss to the exchequer and the savagery of the agitators – not mentioning a word about Khairlanji or the misdoings of the government of Maharashtra. What the Khairlanji case had served to highlight was that the ruling classes of India had still not accepted that 25% of India belonged to the dalits and the tribals and that the media which is monopolistically controlled by the rich and the upper castes, carries out media campaigns to protect its class interests, while the rest are excluded from its campaigns.

The caste bias of the media was made evident following the media's antireservation campaign in 2006. A survey conducted by the Centre for the Study of Developing Societies showed that of the 315 key decision makers from 37 Delhi-based (Hindi and English) publications and television channels, almost 90% of decision makers were found to be "upper caste"; Brahmins alone constituted 49% of this segment, and 71% of the total were "upper caste" men. Not one of the 315 key decision makers was a dalit or an adivasi (tribal); only 4% were OBCs (Other Backward Classes) and 3% were Muslims (who constitute 13.4% of the population). This caste composition indicates who wields power and authority on the Indian media scene.

The latest example was the terrorist attack on some places in Mumbai on November 26, 2008. More people died in Chattrapati Shivaji Railway Terminus than at the Oberoi and the Taj – the elite hotels of Mumbai. However, the focus of the media attention initially was on the Oberoi and Taj Mahal hotels. The media described the Taj Mahal hotel as the second home of the citizens of Mumbai, without realizing the number of citizens of Mumbai who could ill-afford to spend tens of thousands of rupees a day to stay at the Taj. The people who stayed at the Taj were described as "citizens"; while the rest were excluded from the category of citizenship. In the television program, "We, the People," on November 30, 2008 on NDTV, one of the noted television channels, an impression was created that the rich and the famous who participated in the panel discussion, were representative of the people. Commenting on the power of the media that gives the illusion that we are all participating in it, Mannathukkaren (2008) avers that that is why the suffering and tragedies of the few elites who lost their lives in the terror attack at the Taj and Oberoi hotels became more important than that of the other victims. That is why the media spectacle of terror has the habit of ignoring the systematic horrors and tragedies undergone by millions of Indians on a day-to-day basis. That also explains why the moral angst of the media was not aroused all these years even when 150 000 farmers committed suicide in a period of mere eight years from 1997 to 2005 due to neglect of the farmers by the government. Or, hardly any channel aired exclusive "breaking news" stories when India, the second fastest growing economy in the world, secured the 94th position, behind even Nepal, in the Global Hunger Index Report.

While it was noted at the Beijing meeting in 2006 on gender policies in broadcasting organizations that all the staples of media coverage such as conflicts, natural disasters, politics and economics, crime and punishment, involve and impact women as do most other issues that media need to cover such as poverty, environment, culture and health, women's experiences and perspectives are largely missing from media coverage of such events and issues. In India, policies that address women and communication are practically nonexistent. Women were largely perceived as objects of welfare until 1980s. The concept of women's empowerment began to be considered as a development strategy only in the 7th Five Year Plan (1985–1990). The National Policy for Empowerment of Women (2001) focuses on gender sensitization measures through training personnel, also removing degrading, demeaning images of women in the media. However, the policy has had limited success. Women's empowerment faces an uphill battle from mainstream media – satellite television in particular. Mass media actively promote images of modern "new women" who are ambitious and actively pursue a career of their own. They also depict women through the prism of firmly entrenched traditional perceptions and expectations of women's roles in society and in family who are caught in an "image trap." Working class women, on the other hand, are invisibilized and their concerns and problems are rarely reflected in the various television channels. If they do make the news, there is a tendency to sensationalize news as it happened recently in the case of a school teacher who was blatantly accused of promoting sex trade, without even ascertaining and verifying facts. Another case related to a woman who had remarried, thinking that her first husband who had disappeared, was no longer alive and had even conceived from the second husband. The various television channels conducted a virtual media trial and even arrived at a judgment that since her first husband had made an appearance, she should now go back to him.

While women have now entered the media industry in large numbers, the fact remains that women still have very little real decision-making power within the media. This is in conformity with the international experience that shows women's lack of power within media industries. As state-run media cede control to commercial interests, struggle for change has become even more complicated. In her study of the Indian Press, Ammu Joseph (2000) concludes that with the trend towards market-driven, consumer-oriented media, journalists who take strong positions on issues of justice risk derision, if not marginalization. They are often referred to as "crusading, campaigning or committed journalists or even – Mother Teresas of the Press" (Joseph, 2000, p. 285).

In order to deal with the deep-seated sexism which is evident in the contemporary media content, efforts at dialogue and interaction between researchers, activists, advertisers, journalists, and radio and television producers such as by those convened by the Centre of Advocacy and Research are more likely to succeed in a media environment of public responsibility. The global trend toward rabidly commercial, market-driven media places a question mark over the future viability of such strategies.

The coverage on television channels of the incidents in Mumbai on 26/11 has raised larger issues relating to the role and responsibility of the media. Due to the intense competition among the news channels there was "unrestrained coverage" of what was happening on that day and for 60 hours thereafter. The attack was unprecedented but the reporting failed to put the ongoing and dramatic battle in any perspective. For example, few outside Mumbai would have realized that the battle was confined to the southern tip of a very big city, and that the rest of the city was unaffected. Even the immediate past was erased as television crews forgot that 58 people had already been killed at the Chhatrapati Shivaji Terminus even before the attackers laid siege on the two elite hotels. The present was endlessly telecast, with reporters expected to talk ceaselessly with very little new information (Sharma, 2009). Conflicting information kept flashing on different channels. The numbers of attackers varied, estimates of the dead and the injured kept changing, the number of people held hostage in each hotel remained uncertain. No one appeared to be in charge, and the media attempted to get information from multiple sources, often telecasting it live without double-checking. As aptly described in the *Economic and Political Weekly* (Rammanohar, 2009, p. 5) two themes contended for attention in the political reaction to the media coverage of Mumbai's horror: "First was the concern that relentless live coverage may well have limited the scope and effectiveness of the security operations. Second was the worry that media coverage had deeply dented public confidence, fuelled anxieties and created an environment in which the appearance of drastic action, rather than prudence, became the priority."

Once the crisis ended after an unprecedented continuous live coverage by the media over three nights and two days, the media's role became the focus of considerable criticism and discussion. Was there too much live coverage? Did the media obstruct the work of the security forces? Were the cameras and the journalists too intrusive and insensitive in the face of such a human tragedy? Was there too much unsubstantiated and incorrect information conveyed on live television, causing panic? Was the tone of the reporters such that it added to the tension and the panic?

According to Sharma (2009), behind these questions lies a demand that the media, as a principal source of information in disaster and conflict situations, must remain accurate, professional, sensitive, and responsible. While these questions should apply to the media at all times, they become particularly relevant during times of crisis as November 26 demonstrated.

What is evident from the above discussion is that while the media have proliferated enormously since 1991, the economic factors, rather than other considerations, exercise an even greater pressure on them. Thus the "TRP (television rating points) wars" have increasingly come to impact television content. TRPs are critical because they influence the flow of advertising revenue. TRPs are often cited as the determining factor in much of what is currently seen on television today. Sometimes, a trivial event is shown to be "breaking news." It is the TRP that determine the sensational manner in which crime programs, entertainment programs that stick to populist genres such as the "saas-bahu" (mother-in-law and daughter-in-law) serials, mythological serials, reality shows that seem to have a mass following despite their often dubious values, are aired. There is, however, no denying the fact that with the proliferating satellite and cable stations, there is a relentless pursuit of the middle-class audience, the main target of the advertisers. This has led to transmitting a diet of programs that are largely adapted from Western entertainment formats – soap operas, quizzes, pop video and variety shows – as well as 24 hour news. Star Plus became the country's top cable channel, largely to the success of its version of the game show "Who wants to be a millionaire?" The media audience is increasingly subjected to a fare of entertainment-driven programs. While, on the one hand, there has been an increased choice in programming, on the other, due to ratings and circulation battles, there is a narrowing of program range and an increasing intrusiveness of advertising.

The consequences of liberalization in India have brought about a change in the communication priorities. Wasserman and Rao (2006) quote Thomas (2005) who has referred to a shift from "predevelopment to a pro-market focus." This promarket globalization of the Indian media has been characterized by over-commercialization and profit-driven journalism. Wasserman and Rao (2006) also quote Sonwalkar (2002), according to whom a new phenomenon called "Murdochization of the byline" has set in This is a move towards a corporate culture in the newsroom that gives overriding primacy to marketing rather than editorial, and thus distances the press from its social obligations. Likewise, the drive for higher ratings influences, if it does not actually govern, editorial decisions in television newsrooms (Joseph, 2008a).

With the proliferation of satellite television channels, broadcasting has moved from the public to the private sphere, where the private is privileged at the expense of the public media. This is reflected in the way the audience is perceived in the broadcasting industry. People are seen increasingly as consumers rather than as citizens, as spectators rather than as participants.

Due to intense competition for advertising revenue among the country's proliferating broadcast channels and print media, questions are now being raised about the role and the responsibility of the media and of their accountability to the public at large. Significant ethical dilemmas have surfaced for the Indian media. Some

528   *Anita Dighe*

ethical violations have caused great public concern and resentment. The IFJ Press Freedom Report for South Asia (2007–2008) comments that such ethical violations have led to a debate on media regulation to be overtaken by the advocacy of extreme measures. The Government and the judiciary in India remain prepared to expand their supervisory jurisdiction over the media because public trust has been eroded by the increasing evidence that media follows no norm other than that of profit maximization.

That all norms of media ethics were violated became evident in the recent Aarushi Talwar murder case. Acting on a public interest litigation petition, the Supreme Court of India expressed serious concern over the media coverage of the case and issued notice to the Government to lay down norms and guidelines for the print and electronic media in covering criminal cases in which investigation was still pending. While the need for a suitable regulatory framework is clearly felt, there is no consensus as to how this would become feasible.

The Existing Regulatory Mechanisms for the Media

Following the recommendations of the First Press Commission (established in 1952), the first Press Council of India was established in 1965 through an Act of Parliament. It was swiftly dissolved during the Emergency in 1975 by an ordinance, but was revived by the Press Council Act of 1978 giving it its present charter. The Council consists of a Chairperson (usually a retired judge) and 28 other members (including representatives of the press and Members of Parliament). The mandate of the Press Council of India is to safeguard the freedom of the press and to promote professional ethics and standards.

The philosophy behind the establishment of the Press Council has been aptly captured by a previous Chairman of the Council. Thus, the Council was set up to be a self-regulating body, consisting ordinarily of peers in the profession, with the representatives of the public, with the readers also having a say in the matter, since freedom of the press is essentially the freedom of the people to be informed adequately and accurately on matters having a bearing on public interest. Needless to say, the effectiveness of such a body depends on its independence, integrity, competence, representative character, and acceptability by the media.

The problem with the Press Council of India is that it has remained a toothless body. According to A.G. Noorani, a well-known lawyer, scholar, and political commentator, the Press Council suffers from two inherent defects. First, while the composition of its membership might be distinguished, it is not representative. Second, with a retired judge as the chairman of the Council, a question can be raised about the intellectual equipment of such a person to do justice to such a position, in matters outside the law. As a result, the press does not own it as its own and even the chairpersons do not behave as if they belong to it (Noorani, 2009).

Presently, there are proposals to amend the Press Council Act of 1978 and to give more powers, including the power to withhold advertisements for the erring newspapers. According to Noorani (2009), these are dangerous proposals. While recommending a "speedy burial" of the Press Council by a statute, he is also of the opinion that that would impose on the media a burden it must bear if it is to deserve freedom. The print media would then have to set up a credible, representative body to oversee a code of conduct drawn up by the media itself.

With regard to the electronic media, the problem is even more complicated. Since the electronic media was restricted to the State sector until the 1990s, the government did not perceive the need for more laws to regulate and control radio and television since the existing laws, albeit antiquated, seemed to serve the purpose. The onslaught of satellite television, however, seemed to have caught the government unawares. The subsequent efforts were slow, hesitant, and somewhat confused. The government's first attempt to regulate satellite media focused on cable operation and resulted in the Cable Television Networks (Regulation) Act, 1995. The Act was an attempt to set up a regulatory mechanism for the burgeoning cable market that was beginning to thrive. The next major attempt was to draft the Broadcasting Services Regulation Bill, 2006. This draft Bill which was later withdrawn, was widely criticized for the draconian powers that it gave to the government and its representatives to cripple the media through pre-censorship and a particularly severe and potent form of inspector Raj. No process of public consultation and discussion had preceded the drafting of the legislation (Joseph, 2008a).

In July 2007, the Ministry of Information and Broadcasting unveiled yet another draft Broadcast Bill, this time accompanied by a Content Code. Echoing the Supreme Court landmark judgment in 1995 that airwaves were public property and the purpose of regulating them was to ensure that they serve the public interest, the document, however, conveyed the impression that the legislation would have essentially enabled the government to regain control of the broadcast media. While there was agreement among the critics that there was need for greater attention to ethics and social responsibility in media practice, they were also of the view that the draft Content Code was not the best way to achieve this, especially since there was apparent contradiction in the government issuing guidelines for self-regulation by the media. The tussle between the government and the industry over the draft legislation resulted in a stalemate, with the government keeping the Broadcast Bill in abeyance, pending the establishment of a system of self-regulation by the latter (Joseph, 2008a)

Even the courts have been active in advocating more responsible behaviour by the broadcasters. Due to cases involving sting operations and insensitive, sensational coverage of some criminal cases, courts have also proposed judicial intervention against irresponsible broadcasters. As mentioned earlier, in a public interest litigation pertaining to the media coverage of the Aarushi Talwar murder case, the Supreme Court announced its intention to lay down norms for media coverage of ongoing criminal investigations. With the pressures mounting on the private channels, the News Broadcasters Association (NBA) produced its own Code of Ethics and Broadcasting Standards and in August 2008, announced the setting up of the News Broadcasting Standards Disputes Redressal Authority. The Authority, headed by a former Chief Justice of India, began functioning on October 2, 2008. The Authority will keep a watch on news broadcasts to ensure that they do not violate the NBA code of ethics and broadcasting standards. It will also act on the complaints received from the viewing public.

While it is still too premature to comment on the effectiveness of the regulatory body that has been set up by the private broadcasters, there is no denying the fact that with the broadcast sector changing and expanding at a rapid pace, there is need for it to be regulated in some way, preferably through responsible, effective self-regulation. If such a regulatory body is not effective, there is every possibility that the government would feel free to introduce a system of official regulation. Many sections of the public may even support such a step given the considerable, widespread disenchantment with the way some television channels, particularly news channels, have been functioning in recent times (Joseph, 2008a).

Information and communication technologies (ICTs) are transforming the global economy and creating new networks that cross continents and transcend cultures. However, there are disparities with regard to access and skills needed. As a result, the benefits of knowledge and technology are not available to a large majority of the world's population. Developing countries and particularly the rural areas in these countries are severely disadvantaged since they are not able to respond to the transformation that the development of ICTs has produced. In order to use ICTs, several conditions have to be met. Thus in order to access the Internet, it is necessary to:

- Be able to read and write, primarily in English, since the Internet continues to be English dominated.
- Be able to use software that is largely Microsoft dominated.
- Be able to have access first to electricity, second to a telephone line with decent bandwidth and third, to a computer with a reasonably fast modem.

For a large number of rural populace, the Internet is frustrating and inaccessible often due to the costs of access, technical problems, lack of training and knowledge. In most cases, women find themselves excluded in terms of the benefits offered by ICTs. They are faced with problems of access to ICTs, and ability to participate and to exercise control of ICTs. Experience is now showing that women can take advantage of ICTs only if there are conducive policies, an enabling environment in their countries to extend communications infrastructure to where they live, and increased educational levels.

In order to ensure that access to information for all remains a fundamental right, UNESCO has been promoting the establishment of Community Learning Centres in rural areas so that communities can have access to ICTs. Since the opportunity to use one's language on global information networks such as the Internet will determine the extent to which one can participate in emerging knowledge societies, UNESCO has been supporting the development of multilingual cyberspace to ensure wider and more equitable access to information networks as well as to offer possibilities through ICTs for the preservation of endangered languages. Recently, UNESCO convened the first Regional Conference for the Asia Pacific to raise questions on the ethical dimensions of the Information Society. Among the set of priorities for the region were included the need for all countries to continue working on closing the digital divide, the importance of promoting media and information literacy, the need for promoting multi-lingualism, among others.

The Way Forward – The Need for Promoting Community Broadcasting

It is evident from the above discussion that the private commercial broadcasters with predominantly economic interests, do not serve the interests of people and groups who face social and economic marginalization, especially those who live in rural areas, and women among them. The economic interests of the private broadcasters are so pervasive, that they tend to openly flout all norms of media ethics. While there have been attempts to set up regulatory mechanisms to ensure that the media become accountable to the people at large, the attempts so far have not inspired much confidence in the ability of the media to set up an effective self-regulatory mechanism. Even the new media, particularly the Internet, which was once regarded as the panacea for all ills, has shown that it tends to exacerbate the gap that presently exists between the haves and the have-nots.

Development experts have noted that people faced with social and economic exclusion also face systemic obstacles to Freedom of Expression that are associated with the conditions of poverty – low levels of education and literacy, poor infrastructure, lack of access to electricity and general communications services, discrimination and so on. Community broadcasting, in the broader context, is now seen by many development experts as a vital tool to empower the poorest people and communities. Local media invite participation from marginalized and vulnerable populations that are often overlooked by the larger media. Although it is not guaranteed that marginalized groups such as women for example, will be included in the dialogue, community media has the potential to provide an inclusive and interactive platform for expressing views and opinions and for decision-making.

In order to encourage international debate and reflection on the impact of globalization on media products, UNESCO has been focusing on improving the endogenous production and distribution of quality audio-visual programs in developing countries. It has also been promoting and fostering community broadcasting. According to a UNESCO document (UNESCO, 2009); the various studies on community broadcasting have outlined some characteristics of good practice which can be summarized in the following key points:

- Community broadcasting should be recognized in policy and law as having distinct characteristics and guaranteed for and equitable access to the radio frequency spectrum and other broadcast distribution platforms, including digital platforms.

- Procedures for the award and regulation of broadcast licensing and frequencies for community broadcasting should be fair, open and transparent, and under the administrative responsibility of an independent regulatory body.
- Community broadcasters should have access to a diversity of funding sources without unreasonable restrictions. This may include public funds administered in such a way that this does not compromise their independence.

Based on the experiences of countries that can be mentioned as good examples, the characteristics of community broadcasting can be generally referred to as broadcast media which are independent, civil society based and which operate for social benefit and not for profit.

India has been encouraging the development of community radio stations. However, the approach has been hesitant and overly cautious. The UNESCO document notes that India has put in place regulatory arrangements for community broadcasting but has been less effective in actually implementing them (UNESCO, 2009).

What is apparent from the Indian experience is that there is a lack of political will that is required to implement legal and regulatory provisions in a manner designed to encourage and not restrict the growth and development of community broadcasting.

This essay has attempted to present how globalization has affected the Indian media scene. Media ethics is an issue that has not received concerted attention of the media professionals so far. According to a study (Rao and Johal, 2006) although journalists encounter serious ethical issues, media ethics is not a topic being widely discussed in Indian newsrooms and television stations. Marketing pressures, the tabloidization of news, and management and economic pressures are affecting media ethics and issues such as accountability, independence, and conflict of interests. A lack of professional training, especially ethics training, is affecting journalists' understanding of concepts such as privacy and accuracy. Considering that the private broadcasters are rendering the poor and the disadvantaged groups in India invisible, the need for promoting community broadcasting is mooted. However, the track record of the Government of India does not inspire much confidence in ensuring that community broadcasting would indeed become a tool for giving voice to the marginalized groups.

References

Crawley, W., and Page, D. (2001) Enlightened regulation: The future Indian way? Democracy News Analysis, www.opendemocracy.net (accessed February 9, 2009).

Gordon, N.S. (2008) *Media and the Politics of Culture; The Case of Television Privatization and Media Globalization in Jamaica (1990–2007)*, Universal Publishers, Sydney.

Disenfranchised and Disempowered

IFJ Press Freedom Report for South Asia (2007–2008) *In the Balance: Press Freedom in South Asia*, 6th annual report.

Jaisingh, I. (2008) Media on trial: Driven by sensationalism, *Hindu Magazine*, August 3 Weekly Edition-2, 1.

Joseph, A. (2000) *Women in Journalism: Making News*, Konark Publishers, New Delhi.

Joseph, A. (2008a) The 24x7 broadcasting revolution, *Infochange News & Features*, September, http://infochangeindia.org/Media/Backgrounder/The-24x7-broadcasting-revolution.html#2 (accessed February 19, 2009).

Joseph, A. (2008b) The world's 'last great newspaper market', *Infochange News & Features*, September, http://infochangeindia.org/Media/Backgrounder/The- world's-last- great-newspaper-market.html (accessed February 19, 2009).

Mannathukkaren, N. (2008) 'Whose media? Which people?' *Hindu Magazine*, December 21, Weekly Edition-2, 1.

Noorani, A.G. (2009) The Press Council: An expensive irrelevance, *Economic & Political Weekly*, January 3, 13–15.

Rammanohar, R.C. (2009) When the media becomes the story, *Economic and Political Weekly*, 44 (4), 5–6.

Rao, S., and Johal, N.S. (2006) Ethics and news making in the changing India mediascape, *Journal of Mass Media Ethics*, 21 (4), 286–303.

Sainath, P. (2008) Sainath decries "corporate hijack" of media agendas, *Hindu*, May 5, p. 14.

Saxena, S. (2008) The march of new media, from ERNet to IPTV, *Infochange News and Features*, November, http://infochangeindia.org/Media/Backgrounder/The-march-of-New-Media-from-ERNet-to-IPTV.html (accessed February 19, 2009).

Sebastian P.A. (2009), Dalits in Indian society, *Economic & Political Weekly*, January 24, 33–34.

Sharma, K. (2009) Sensitivity and professionalism: The twin mantras for conflict reporting, *Infochange India News & Features* http://infochangeindia.org/Agenda/Reporting-conflict/Sensitivity-and-professionalism-The-twin-mantras-for-conflict-reporting.html (accessed February 19, 2009).

Sivadas, A. (2008) Need for restraint, *Hindu Magazine*, August 3, 08, Weekly edition-2, 1.

Sonwalkar, P. (2002) Murdochization of the Indian press: From by-line to bottom-line, *Media, Culture, and Society*, 24 (6), 821–834

Thomas, P. (2005) Contested futures: Indian media at the crossroads, in *Democratizing Global Media* (eds R.A. Hackett and Y. Zhao), Rowman and Littlefield, New York, 81–99.

UNESCO (2009) *Freedom of Expression, Access to Information and Empowerment of People*, UNESCO, Paris.

Vasudevan, R. (2001) Tehelka and media ethics, *India News Online*, http://news.indiamart.com/news-analysis/tehelka-and-media-et-5247.html (accessed February 7, 2009)

Wasserman, H., and Rao, S. (2006) Media globalization and journalism ethics: A view from the South, International Communication Association Conference, Dresden, Germany, June, http://www.allacademic.com/meta/p90202_index.html (accessed June 10, 2008)

29

Questioning Journalism Ethics in the Global Age
How Japanese News Media Report and Support Immigrant Law Revision

Kaori Hayashi

Immanent Nationalistic Views inside Modern Journalism

This essay discusses how "fact-oriented" conventional journalism ethics works to support the ideology and politics of "nationstate" by taking up a case study of reports on Japan's policy on immigration. Timothy E. Cook described in his book *Governing with the News: The News Media as a Political Institution* "how the development of the current news media has always been closely fostered by practices and public policy, how the news media perform governmental tasks, how reporters themselves (like it or not) are political actors" (Cook, 1998, p. 164). He regarded practices, rules and conventions of news media as an "institution" and worked to strengthen the government policies, from the theory of so-called "new institutionalism." Extending Cook's argument, I argue here that the news media in Japan has been serving not only as a political institution, but also as a major factor in the politics of nation building in its modern history and thus experiencing difficulties adjusting to the globalization and change to a multicultural environment that Japanese society is undergoing.

My aim here is not so much to criticize the content of the reports themselves, but to examine the process by which nation-centered discourse overwhelms more liberal, pluralistic discourse which is indispensable at the time of globalization. The problem I identify here is that it is not, as is often believed in general, powerful conservative actors who silently manipulate public opinion from the shadows towards the formation of more nationalistic opinion; rather, it is those professional rules and ethics such as disinterested detachment, the separation of fact from opinion, and the balancing of claim and counterclaim that cause the media to turn their back on examining social changes and acknowledging the emerging needs of new members of society.

The Handbook of Global Communication and Media Ethics, First Edition. Edited by Robert S. Fortner and P. Mark Fackler.
© 2011 Blackwell Publishing Ltd. Published 2011 by Blackwell Publishing Ltd.

The Professional Ethics of Japanese Journalism

For the purpose of analysis, I identify two characteristics of Japanese journalism and its views on rules and ethics. These rules may also be observed in other liberal industrialized countries, but the nature and degree to which Japanese journalists comply with them institutionally and systematically are symbolic due to the history and structure of Japanese journalism.

First, the media coverage in Japan can be characterized by its impressively heavy inclusion of "official facts." This is attributed to its exclusive Press Club System for newspaper and broadcasting journalists. A press club is a group of major news organizations, including national daily newspapers, key TV stations and wire services that belong to the Japan Newspapers Publishers and Editors Association. There are hundreds of press clubs nationwide, and in most cases, members are given space in government and industry buildings including those of the prime minister, the Diet, ministries, local governments, and police.

Press club journalists feel they are compelled to be loyal to their duties and report facts obtained from respective official sources. They are trained to stick to "objective reporting," and not to express their "private" opinions – "not being aware that their objectivity is a politician's subjectivity" (Uemae, 1982, p. 42). Furthermore, according to their ethical professional rules, all the official announcements, and all the statements by "accredited" and prominent sources connected to press clubs, should be covered immediately and "correctly," and all of them should receive a timely follow up for impacts and reactions so that no single paper falls behind in coverage of any story. Criticisms that Japanese newspapers all look alike may be attributed to this rigid professional ethic. Additionally, because each newspaper publishes a morning edition as well as an evening edition and most readers subscribe to them both as a "set", and as each morning/evening edition is printed in several versions to include corrections and additions, journalists are required to update their information constantly until their final version is finished.[1] This means at the same time that a majority of Japanese reporters work uninterruptedly throughout the day to keep up with their "latests" so that they can use the most up to date information. The "professional ethics" and working environment of Japanese journalists are designed for total devotion to following up "just facts."

Unfortunately, however hard-working they are, Japanese journalists more often than not skip or neglect reporting some of the important issues. It is said that their news standards have become too mechanical to recognize new phenomena that utilises journalists' own definition and interpretation. More often than not they become parochial in judging what is important to society at large due to limited capacity for reflection after long working hours. Consequently, the dose of nation-centric, if not always nationalistic, discourse receives high news priority while other issues get buried in oblivion.

Second, due to market forces, Japanese media have been increasingly required to reflect "public tastes" in selecting their topics and how they describe those topics.

Down-to-earth, grass-root angles are theoretically justifiable if one considers that journalism has its mission to serve people's right to know, but such a call would leave room for nation-centric, populisitc discourse. This is especially the case with Japanese media because Japan's media audience consists mainly of those who can speak Japanese and identify themselves as Japanese.

It is no doubt that such a "user-oriented" tendency for the contents of mass media arose in tandem with the decline of the corporate media. Like other industrialized countries, with the Internet becoming an everyday tool to obtain information (often free of charge), many people, especially the young generation, turn to digital news source.[2] In the face of a shrinking business, journalists are urged to be friendly and accountable to the public to win back their customers. Inside the industry, this call has often been translated into a normative form of being "reader-friendly" or "needs-sensitive" on the ground that journalists ought to serve society.

Keeping in mind these journalistic practices, rules, and ideology in Japan, I demonstrate how the revision of the Immigration Control Law, one of the most sensitive and new issues[3] in Japan, was reported. In the following, I will first briefly explain the background of the immigration policy in Japan. After that I will touch upon the framing methodology I employed for the analyses. Next, I will present three discursive frames identified in the coverage of the revision of the Immigration Control Law. I will then examine how these frames compete with each other in the process of reporting and analyze the mechanism by which one becomes dominant. Last, I will reflect on the meaning of journalism ethics, rules, and practices in the rapidly changing globalized world.

Research Background and Method

On May 17, 2006, the Japanese Parliament approved the revision of the Immigration Control Law. This law was originally enacted in 1952 and provides the basic framework of immigration policy in Japan (Tanaka, 1995: 35ff). Although modeled on the system in the United States, this law from its inception was not designed to encourage migrants to settle in the country, to say nothing of including them as members of society. It can be said that Japan has kept its door shut to most migrants throughout its postwar history.

Some key statistical figures by the Immigration Bureau provide a broad picture of the movement and migration situation in Japan.[4] The percentage of foreign residents against the total population remains around 1.7% at the end of 2007. As the international comparison figures in Figure 29.1 show, it is fair to state that Japan remains exceptionally cautious towards accepting migrants.

Figure 29.1 shows that Japan, together with South Korea, have a relatively small foreign population. Tanaka Hiroshi, urging a radical review of immigration policy as well as consciousness change on the part of the Japanese people, maintains that according to Japan's way of thinking, its principle has been "no

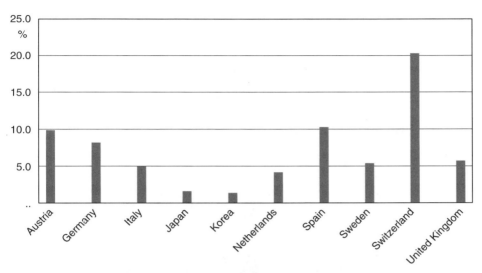

Figure 29.1 Foreign nationals in selected OECD countries, 2008.

foreigners", and those few foreigners who are accepted are treated "as exceptions" (Tanaka, 1995, p. 243).

However, Tanaka saw a slight change in attitudes on the part of some Japanese when he wrote his book *Zainich Gaikokujin. Hō no Kabe, Kokoro no Mizo* (Foreign Residents in Japan: Legal Barriers and Mind Gap) in 1995. Indeed, slight signs of change towards liberalization had been identified in some of the policy revisions made in the 1990s including banning fingerprinting of foreigners altogether and opening the door to foreign-born Japanese as an unskilled labor force.

With the enforcement of the most recent revision, however, all non-Japanese adults entering Japan are again obliged to be fingerprinted and photographed on entry. It is expected that the country will accumulate biometric data on more than 7 million people a year with this new enforcement. With this revision, Japan became the second country in the world after the United States to introduce the system of requiring visitors to give biometric information on entry.

Many activists and scholars see this new revision as anachronistic against the tendency toward liberalization since the late 1990s, however modest that tendency may have been in its scale. It is estimated, for example, as of the end of 2008 that some 2 266 000 people from overseas live in Japan. Of them 2 152 973 are registered and 113 072 (as of January 1, 2009) are undocumented foreign residents. Some 430 000 foreign residents have a status of residence called "special permanent resident." These residents are people, and their offspring, who were forced to migrate to Japan from Korea and China which were colonized by Japan before 1945. Altogether, the number of foreign residents has steadily increased, especially since the late 1980s as Figure 29.2 shows. The number of registered foreign residents has hit a record high.

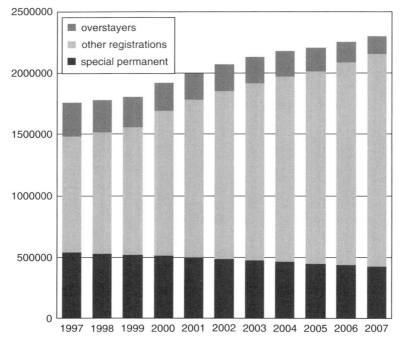

Figure 29.2 The number of foreign residents in Japan 1997–2007.

Therefore, ever since the government first proposed revising the law, experts and NGO leaders have been very critical about this change. Even some conservative politicians and bureaucrats were skeptical about whether such tightened border control should be implemented in Japan since it totally goes against the borderless age we are in.

On the other hand, the government explained the necessity of this revision citing two reasons. One is to reduce visa overstayers who are believed to contribute to the rising crime rate and general deterioration of public security in Japan. The government, therefore, sought support for revision of the law on the grounds of maintaining "the people's life and security." This argument was in line with the action plan adopted by an initiative under Prime Minister Jun'ichro Koizumi in December, 2003 to reestablish Japan as "the safest country in the world." This action plan aimed to halve the number of those entering the country illegally or overstaying their visas in the five-year period between 2004 and 2008.

Another reason cited by the government was "the war on terror." In this respect, the government had already issued antiterrorism action plan in December 2001 at the Emergency Anti-Terrorism Headquarters established within the Cabinet Office under the top-down leadership of Prime Minister Koizumi. This plan included the blueprint of the revision in that it explicitly discusses the policy that requires all foreign visitors to submit biometric information when entering Japan. The stated purpose was to "forcefully advance comprehensive and effective emergency measures against terrorism." This action plan also clearly states that an increase in

Table 29.1 The number of articles for analysis

		Year	<Revision of the Immigration Control Act>* 「入管法改正」	<New Immigration Control> 「新入国審査」	<Immigration Control> 「入国審査」	<foreigners>+ <fingerprinting> 「外国人」+「指紋」
Asahi		2004	3			
		2005	5			
		2006	15			
		2007	–	19	71	37**
Mainichi		2004	1			
		2005	0			
		2006	10	1		
		2007	–		62	28**
Yomiuri		2004	1			
		2005	3			
		2006	2			
		2007	–	7	79	30**

The numbers include articles published in local pages of each national daily.
*The key phrase <Revision of the Immigration Control Act> sometimes refers to the 1989 revision. I read all the articles and omitted irrelevant ones.
**Only in November 2007 when the Act was enforced.

the number of foreign aliens entering Japan is one reason why Japan had been transformed from a "peaceful country" into an insecure one. Thereby justifying the importance of the surveillance of foreigners entering Japan.

While investigating how the issue of the revision of the Immigration Control Law was reported I examine the development of discussions of the legal revision in Japan's three major national newspapers: the *Asahi Shimbun* (daily circulation of 8 million), *Mainichi Shimbun* (6 million), and *Yomiuri Shimbun* (10 million). These dailies are considered to represent the liberal (Asahi and Mainichi) and conservative (Yomiuri) views of the nation and, as their circulation figures indicate, are well-read. Consequently, they set the direction of national public opinion on important political issues.[5]

For a broad overview, data was collected from the data bank on the Japanese press maintained by "Nikkei-Telecon." I began with explorative investigations using several keywords and picked up at last three key phrases: "revised immigration law (改正入管法)" "new immigration law (新入管法)" and "fingerprinting (指紋押捺)." These key phrases covered almost all the articles published during the period between January 1, 2004 and December 31, 2007. All the articles were also confirmed either from the newspapers themselves or from each paper's reprinted compact paperback editions (called "shukusatsu-ban"). Data were also collected from local and regional newspapers, although there are few systematic search engines in this area. For a breakdown of these sources see Table 29.1.

The research employed media frame analysis. Media frame analysis has its theoretical origin in the concept of "frame" by Goffmann (1975). Goffmann's frame analyses were conceived to identify and abstract rules as to how people organize subjectively their daily experience. He argues that frames bridge between social dynamics and individual actions and behaviors. Although he remained hesitant about claiming any connection between frames and social institutions or organizations, media frame analysts try to bridge the gap between individual understandings of events or texts and the organizational mechanisms of broader cultural, social meanings of discourse. According to Gamson, a frame is considered to be "culturally available" if there is any organization or advocacy network within the society that sponsored it (Gamson, 1992, p. 215). Robert Entman also emphasizes the power of culture in the production of frames: "Those frames that employ more culturally resonant terms have the greatest potential for influence" (Entman, 2004, p. 6). It is this cultural and social hegemonic power that I wish to problematize in the construction of media coverage.

News Framing of the Coverage on Revision of the Immigration Control Law

After having examined government documents, related literature and articles in the period from 2004 to 2007, I was able to identify the following three main discursive frames in newspaper reporting:

1 Critical interpretations focusing on the violation of foreigners' human rights
2 Commentary on the government's policies for "combating terrorism" and "counteracting the rising incidence of crimes committed by foreigners"
3 "Objective reporting" on implementation and execution

Critical interpretations focusing on the violation of foreigners' human rights

In this frame, the revision of the Immigration Control Law was reported from the standpoint that the human rights of foreigners in Japan were being violated since fingerprinting remains a key symbolic issue in the critique of discrimination and human-rights violations against foreigners in postwar Japan.

Japan used to take fingerprints as part of the registration process for all foreign residents, a policy which has been the subject of much controversy, especially among Zainichi Koreans. Historically, these Zainichis are one of the legacies of Imperial Japan. Tanaka discovered that the debate about whether or not to make fingerprinting obligatory for "foreigners" goes back to the late 1940s after Japan lost the war and its colonies. At that time, Koreans and Chinese abruptly became "foreigners" and continued to be deprived of their civil rights. Even their descendents, already in the second or third generations who have never been in their "homeland" and are not familiar with their "native" culture and language, were treated as foreign residents with the obligation of fingerprinting (Tanaka, 1995, 81ff).

In the 1980s and 1990s, the campaign against this obligatory fingerprinting of foreigners was led mainly by these ethnic Korean residents in Japan. After many years of campaigning, this ethnic group succeeded in abolishing the requirement on the grounds of human rights infringement. In 1999 the Alien Registration Law was further amended to eliminate fingerprinting of foreign residents in general. Following this change of law, Japan banned fingerprinting altogether in the year 2000.

In fact, in light of this historical background, the most recent revision exempted the so-called permanent residents including Zainichi Koreans, which makes up, 20% of all the registered foreign population in Japan. This has led to a consequence that the countermovement against this revision floundered.

Commentary on the government's policies for "combating terrorism" and "counteracting the rising incidence of crimes committed by foreigners"

As previously mentioned in 2004, the Japanese government adopted an "Action Plan for the Forestallment of Terrorism," which included revision of immigration legislation as one of its concrete goals for the prevention of terrorism. In reference to concerns that Japan had shifted from being a "society at peace" to an "unstable society," this action plan also cited increased crossborder movement (in other words, the entry of larger numbers of foreigners into Japan) and especially the entry of illegal aliens and criminals as a cause of social instability. Both "combating terrorism" and "counteracting the rising incidence of crimes committed by foreigners" were thus included within the same framework in the revision of the Immigration Law.

This approach by the government was in close conformity with the public mood at the time. Even while the events of 9/11 were still fresh in people's minds, there were reports in the media about terrorist acts by Islamic extremists in such places as Moscow and Madrid, and mention of the possibility that terrorists had entered Japan. These reports were combined with popular perception about the increased incidence of (nonterrorist) crimes by foreigners in Japan. As a result, this was the most easily accepted frame of discourse among the public in the years 2004 to 2006.

"Objective reporting" on implementation and execution

Much of the newspaper reporting on this topic gave much space on how efficiently the new immigration procedures were being implemented. Indeed, such reporting accounted for a larger volume of news than coverage of the debate on legislative revision. On the first day of the new law's implementation, large numbers of journalists were mobilized to report intensively on whether or not the law was being successfully implemented. Much attention was paid to such "factual matters" as the new machinery installed at the passport control gates, the response of the immigration staff, and the length of time foreign tourists had to wait in line at the airports, typically with a photo of a foreign visitor putting his/her finger on the newly-installed equipment at the passport control. Such coverage surrounding a social event or the introduction of new administrative systems has been typically regarded as "news worth printing" in Japanese journalism. On the one hand, it could be understood as a fulfillment of journalism's public duty in that it monitors achievements by the government and authority. On the other hand, however, it serves to divert attention away from the background and significance of the event by giving prominence to the minutia of administrative procedures (Hayashi, 2008). This narrowness of focus is all too typical of Japanese political reporting that adheres to the press club system (Krauss, 2000: 25ff, 53ff).

Altogether, in the course of the various phases of the revision process (planning, legislative debate, implementation), these three discursive frames appeared and disappeared – competing and interacting with each other. At any particular time, one of them may have come to the fore while the others retreated into the background. In the next section, I look in detail at this process of competition and interaction among the frames.

The Tradeoff between Foreigners' "Human Rights" and "Combating Terrorism"

As already mentioned, the proposed revision to the Immigration Law was first incorporated as part of the "Action Plan for the Forestallment of Terrorism" finalized on December 10, 2004 by the government's "Headquarters for the Promotion of Countermeasures against International Organized Crime and Terrorism." At the time of the initial announcement of this plan, discussion focused mostly on the issue of human rights contravention. On December 11, 2004, for instance, *Yomiuri Shimbun* carried a 1200-character article explaining the plan under the following headline: "Terrorism Prevention Plan Countermeasures: Respect for Human Rights by International Standards and Adequate Explanation Required." In its discussion of the plan's significance, while making mention of the establishment of an underground Al Qaeda cell in the city of Niigata in May earlier the same year, it points out that human-rights problems would remain if the legal revision was adopted. The conclusion of the article reads as follows:

> There is the possibility that parts of the currently adopted plan stipulating fingerprinting of foreigners and restrictions on the daily life of nationals will give rise to debate from the viewpoint of human rights. However, the reality of the approaching danger of terrorism cannot be ignored. Besides respecting human rights, the government also has a duty to explain and obtain the understanding of the people.

By portraying a state of tension between "human-rights" and "terrorism countermeasures," the article presents revision of the Immigration Control Law as an issue of finding a balance between the two options. The inclusion of the words "respect for human rights" in its headline also casts doubt on whether terrorism countermeasures were a sufficient justification for the gathering of biometric information from all foreigners entering the country.

Asahi Shimbun's article, published on December 8, 2004, almost at the same time as the prior Yomiuri article, was 600 characters long and bore the following headline: "Human Right Problems Remain: Government Issues Terrorism Prevention Action Plan." "Human Rights" thus appears as the top headline. The lead immediately below the headline reads as follows: "Some measures are sure to lead to human-rights problems, and questions are likely to arise concerning the balance between counteracting terrorism and respecting human rights when it comes to concrete issues such as implementation and operation."

Like *Yomiuri*, *Asahi* also presented "human rights" and "terrorism countermeasures" as being in a trade-off relation. This closely reflects repeated statements made by responsible government high-rank officials when appealing for support of the revision: "There is no time to lose before Al Qaeda makes Japan one of its targets" (Taro Kono, Deputy Minister of Justice); and "Terrorism is a major threat. It's a question of balancing the weight of different values, so all we can do is to have some people endure" (Kunio Hatoyama, Minister of Justice).

When the revised law passed the Lower House of the Diet on March 31, 2006, *Asahi Shimbun* once again took up the issue of "balance" in its editorial, mentioning "human rights" and "the war on terror" as opposing values. The lead "Revised Immigration Law: the Merits and Demerits of Fingerprinting reads as follows:

> The House of Representatives has passed the revised Immigration Control Law which stipulates the fingerprinting and facial photographing of foreign visitors to Japan. The stated purpose of the revision is to forestall acts of terrorism [as well as] [...] counteracting illegal immigration.[...]
>
> However, there is also deep-seated caution. The obligatory fingerprinting of foreign nationals residing in Japan was criticized as a violation of human rights and was abolished in 2000. [...].
>
> Security is of the utmost importance, but there remains a danger that Japan's image may be seriously damaged. We urge the Upper House to consider the merits and demerits of this system from a wider perspective. (*Asahi Shimbun* Editorial March 31, 2006)

Thus, *Asahi Shimbun* pointed out the existence of both "merits" and "demerits" to the revised law. It maintained its noncommittal stance in this editorial, which is one of the few spaces where the newspaper has an opportunity to express its own opinions directly. "Forestalling terror," "counteracting illegal immigration," and the "affront to the dignity of foreign nationals" are each given equal prominence and the editorial concludes by simply observing that "revision of the law will have major effects."

Meanwhile, *Mainichi Shimbun* refrained from taking its own position on the issue at all and strove instead to represent the opinions of numerous experts and people concerned. The frame of "human-rights violations" was particularly prominent in this debate, as the following extracts illustrate:

> Fingerprinting in Japan is restricted to circumstances in which a person is remanded in custody as part of a criminal investigation or when a warrant has been issued. However, requiring almost all foreign nationals to give their fingerprints is going too far. There are even greater problems related to the maintenance and use of fingerprint information. There is the visible intention to go beyond the original purpose of counteracting terrorism and use this information in order to combat crime and control immigration. Since it treats all foreigners (including those free of suspicion) as potential criminals or illegal immigrants, the law lends itself to discriminatory practices (Nanba Mitsuru, Lawyer, *Mainichi Shimbun*, March 23, 2006).

> Fingerprints are one of the most sensitive forms of personal information. Fingerprinting should be considered cautiously lest there be a danger of belittling privacy. We must avoid a situation in which the majority is forced to provide their fingerprints in order not to be severely disadvantaged by their inability to use automated gates (Hisashi Sonoda, Professor of Information and Criminal Law, Konan Law School, *Mainichi Shimbun*, March 28, 2006).

These comments were both published prior to the passing of the law in the Lower House on March 31, 2006. Just before the law passed the Upper House on May 1, 2006, *Mainichi* published a "debate" between the former chief of the Tokyo

Immigration Bureau, Sakanaka Hidenori, and the deputy chairman of the Japan Federation of Bar Associations, Seiichi Ito.

In all these discourses in *Mainichi,* the word "fingerprinting" was laden with symbolism in the context of the "human rights" frame. This symbolism derived from memories of the highly significant human-rights campaign in the 1980s to abolish obligatory fingerprinting of resident foreign nationals.

In the final instance, however, both *Asahi* and *Mainichi* failed to adopt a clear position on the controversial revision of the Immigration Law and instead adopted the role of an "opinion forum." This forum was structured according to the binary opposition between the "war on terror" and "human rights."

Despite their slightly different distribution of opinions on the debate, all three national newspapers, *Yomiuri, Mainichi,* and *Asahi* demanded that their readers adopt the same basic approach of balancing the two frames of "national security" versus the "infringement of foreigners' human rights through the compulsory provision of fingerprint data" at this early stage of discussion.

The positing of these two frames as mutually exclusive alternatives was even more pronounced in the regional newspapers. *Shimotsuke Shimbun* (a local newspaper based in Tochigi Prefecture) and *Yamanashi Nichinichi Shimbun* (a local newspaper based in Yamanashi Prefecture) both carried the same wire-service report about the revision of the Immigration Law, but the headlines they each added to the article suggest entirely "opposite" readings:

> May 17, 2006
> House of Councilors Justice Committee to Approve Revised Immigration Law Today: Aiming at Preventing Entry of Terrorists (*Shimotsuke Shimbun*, p. 5).
>
> Fingerprinting Made Obligatory at Immigration Inspection: Revised Immigration Law to Pass the House of Councilors Justice Committee Today (*Yamanashi Nichinichi Shimbun*, p. 2).

These contrasting headlines indicate opposing editorial positions on the same report, one emphasizing the issue of "fingerprinting" and the other stressing "preventing entry of terrorists." We need, however, to question the underlying assumption behind this binary opposition: Is the protection of foreigner's human rights necessarily opposed to the protection of Japan from terrorist attacks? Lurking beneath the surface of the debate is an unspoken equation of "foreigners" with "terrorists." This in the end is what provides the link binding together the various issues of "combating terrorism," "criminal acts by foreigners," "illegal entry," and "illegal residency." I will consider this further in the next section.

The Origins of the "Terrorists = Foreigners" Discourse

In the period between the publication of the 2004 government action plan and the passing of the revised law in May 2006, *Yomiuri Shimbun* only carried three articles on the issue. This is rather small in number compared to *Asahi*'s nine articles and *Mainichi*'s six. However, the *Yomiuri* editorial published on April 18, 2006 (while the bill was being debated in the Diet) contained the following very clear statement of opinion as the government started to articulate the significance and purpose of the revision:

> The Revised Immigration Control and Refugee Recognition Law has been passed by the House of Representatives and has been sent to the House of Councilors.... According to the Government, the revised law is "an avoidable measure designed to protect the lives and property of the nation. Besides forestalling acts of terror, it will also serve as a means to deal with crime by foreigners, illegal entry and illegal prolongation of stays." The revised law is highly necessary and should be enacted in the current session of the Diet. (April 18, 2006 *Yomirui Shimbun* Editorial "Proposed immigration law revision: Move toward fingerprinting seen worldwide")

In this editorial, there is no longer any mention of "human rights." Starting with this article, Yomiuri abandoned the "human-rights" frame completely. The news angle has shifted instead to "combating terrorism" which the government exactly argued for in its proposal.

It is notable that the *Yomiuri* uncritically adopts the government line by listing "forestalling terrorism" and "crime by foreigners, illegal entry and illegal staying" as if they were self-evidently related. At the time of the revised law's implementation in November, 2007, *Yomiuri* once again listed terrorism countermeasures and crime by foreigners in the same context and emphasized the concrete benefits of the law to persons with Japanese nationality residing in Japan. The headline and lead published by *Yomiuri* on this occasion was as follows:

> Fingerprint data and facial photographs will be taken. The revised Immigration Law will be implemented on the 20th and the new immigration inspection system will swing into action. Its main objective is the prevention of terrorism and the entry of foreign criminals. If it succeeds, Japan's reputation as a safe country will surely be enhanced. (November, 19, 2007 *Yomiuri* Editorial "Revised Immigration Law: Use fingerprints and facial photographs to improve public order")

Yomiuri took over this unreflective identification of terrorism with foreign nationals from the government discourse contained in the 2003 "Action Plan for the Realization of a Society Resistant to Crime" and the 2004 "Action Plan for the Forestalling of Terrorism." In contrast to *Yomiuri*'s lumping together of the issues of combating terrorism, crime by foreigners, and illegal immigration, *Mainichi* pointed out the separate nature of each of these objectives. While recognizing that the revised law would have some effect in combating these separate problems, *Mainichi* drew attention to difficulties with its implementation.

> [...] However, it will certainly demonstrate its effectiveness against illegal entry on false passports. Of the 56,000 people deported last year, approximately 7300 had been deported previously. These are people who should never have been allowed into the country in the first place, and the system of immigration control was under

Questioning Journalism Ethics in the Global Age   547

constant criticism for being ineffective. (November 24, 2007 *Mainichi Shimbun* Editorial "New immigration law: Secure system desired")

While it gives recognition to the effectiveness of the new law as a way of dealing with "illegal immigration," the principal point of this editorial is to point out the need for urgent measures to improve more practical side of the issues such as data management.

Asahi raised doubts about the inclusion of immigration control issues together with "combating terrorism" despite the fact that initial discussion cited the latter as the purpose of revising the Immigration Control Law. It also contested the effectiveness of the new law in dealing with terrorist threats.

> [...] However, some experts question their effectiveness in countering terrorism. A former chief of the Tokyo Immigration Bureau points out the following: "How can we check fingerprints when there is hardly any data of terrorist fingerprints in Japan? The first thing we need to do is establish our own data collection capacity." (November 19, 2007 *Asahi Shimbun* Column "New immigration procedures starts tomorrow: Fingerprints and facial photographs collected")

The above extracts, however liberal and critical they may initially appear, demonstrate that there has hardly been any debate on the definition of the word "terrorism." There is an unspoken assumption that "terrorism" is an external problem created by organizations outside Japan such as Al Qaeda. This assumption is not, however, as self-evident as it may initially appear in Japan. Only the English-language *Japan Times*, whose readership consists mostly of foreign nationals resident in Japan questions the identification of "terrorism" with "foreigners." This paper carried extensive discussion of the revised Immigration Control Law around the time of its passage through the Diet in, 2006, including the following:

> Does anyone really believe that all terrorists are foreigners? The Tokyo subway sarin attack comes to mind (6000 injured, 12 dead), so does the bombings of Mitsubishi Heavy Industries in Tokyo in, 1974 (20 injured, 8 dead) and the Hokkaido Prefectural Government office in Sapporo in, 1976 (80 injured, 2 dead). The obvious prejudice here is palpable (Dioguardi, 2006).

> The new law does not cover "special" permanent residents, i.e. Koreans and Chinese, which for some throws into question the whole basis of the fingerprinting requirement – preventing terrorist attacks – since Japan's nearest threat is neighboring North Korea.
> Exempting the very large North Korean community in Japan is an area of the law that some legal experts see as problematic" (Joseph, 2006).

The same August 22, 2006 article pointed out the vagueness of the law's provisions even after deliberation in the Diet:

> And despite plans to implement the changes to law from November 2007 some Japanese officials spoken to by The Japan Times suggest awareness of the law in

government circles is limited. One Foreign Ministry official admitted: "We have not heard of that law yet. Are you sure it applies to permanent and long-term residents?"(Joseph, 2006)

To those who are to have their fingerprints taken, the "war on terror" and "foreigners' human rights" are not in a situation of trade-off. There is no direct relation between terrorism and "crime by foreigners" and "illegal immigration."

The desire to treat terrorism as something belonging to foreigners – that is, the culturally different "Other" – has already been pointed out by scholars such as Edward Said (1997). In the revision of the Immigration Control Law, the history of terrorist acts committed by Japanese citizens has been entirely forgotten. With the emergence of the frame treating the Immigration Control Law as a means of "combating terrorism," "terrorists" came to be seen more and more like invaders threatening the internal peace of Japan from the outside. As a result, the focus of debate shifted almost automatically to the questions of how to prevent the entry of "illegal foreigners" and how to combat the growing problem of "crime by foreigners."

Avid Coverage of Implementation

Another frame that was particularly important in coverage of the revision of the Immigration Control Law concerned issues of implementation and administrative management.

The "implementation and execution" frame functioned at first as a counterweight to the frame of "controlling terrorism and foreigners." For example, at the earlier stage of the Action Plan, *Mainichi* published the following commentary on December 11, 2004, in which "terrorism countermeasures" and "implementation issues" are discussed together:

> Since Japan has been named by Al Qaeda as a possible future target of attacks, the danger of terrorism for Japan has increased. However, systems have to be invented that would place restrictions on individual rights and impose extra burdens on individuals and businesses in order to strengthen the control against terrorism. As the government considers fingerprinting and photographing foreign nationals at entry and the creation of a data base, there is apprehension about possible information leaks and worry for the state becoming the collector of the "ultimate form of personal data." (*Mainichi Shimbun* December 11, 2004 Commentary: "Terrorism prevention outline plan: Government adopts 'Action Plan' – Law to be revised in 2005 or 2006")

In this article, the issue of personal data management is cited as a potential threat to individual rights. Rather than relying on memory of the struggle against the fingerprinting of foreign residents in the 1980s as *Yomiuri* and *Asahi* did at the

Questioning Journalism Ethics in the Global Age   549

early stage, *Mainichi* criticizes the revised law from the standpoint of personal data protection. The two frames of "terrorism/foreigner countermeasures" and "implementation and execution" are thus placed in opposition to each other. When, however, the law went into implementation in 2007 the debate shifted in the direction that "flawless implementation" would serve the purpose of terrorism countermeasures.

As I have already suggested, the prominence of this frame derives largely from the general understanding of the professional ethics of "monitoring power" and "objectivity" in Japanese journalism. As a fulfillment of this professional duty, journalists put their greatest efforts into observing the implementation of the law at airports around the country and interviewing entering foreigners to obtain their reactions. This becomes evident simply by examining the number of the headlines indicated in the Table 29.1 as well as the sheer quantity of column inches.

Unlike the case of the other two frames, all three national newspapers followed roughly the same line in their reporting on this third frame. This is true to the extent that they all carried very similar photographs of foreign nationals being fingerprinted and photographed at the immigration gates. Indeed, many journalists may have seen this frame as the one that matched the classical ethic of their profession most closely. For example, the previously cited *Yomiuri* editorial (2007, p. 3) that strongly supported the revised Immigration Law nevertheless contained the following demand to the government: "Operation will continue to require thorough consideration so that chaos does not occur as a result of system failures or excessive time taken to complete the procedures."

By thus urging the government to be efficient and cautious in its implementation of the law, journalism is considered to formally fulfill its function in the narrowest sense of monitoring and criticizing those in power.

It might appear at first glance that the newspapers were fulfilling their role of scrutinizing the government by focusing debate on the condition of legal enforcement. However, this debate was premised on acceptance of the law's existence, and little consideration was given to the background issues of "combating terrorism" and "dealing with illegal immigration" that lay behind the adoption of the law in the first place. By focusing almost exclusively on the efficiency of implementation after the law went into effect, Japanese journalism no longer questioned the justification and basis of the revision. This reflects the fact that the "implementation" frame was subsumed and assimilated into the justification for "terrorism countermeasures."

On the day after the new law went into effect, *Asahi* carried a commentary article, "Start of the New Immigration Law: Caught between human rights and security – Increased staff at Narita Airport", the lead portion of which is quoted below:

> Amid concern about the invasion of privacy, the new immigration inspection system proclaimed as a measure in the "war on terror" went into operation on the 20th.

At Japan's number one gateway, Narita Airport, entering foreigners were compulsorily fingerprinted and photographed one after another. Asked to choose human rights or security, foreigners leaving the gates expressed various opinions about the new law, some in favor and some against. Some intellectuals issued warnings about the advance of social surveillance.

In this article, *Asahi* maintained its restrained position of favoring neither side in the balance between "combating terror" and "human rights." The "implementation" frame also makes its appearance with the mention of the lack of trouble at the gates and reference to the opinions of various foreigners passing through. There was similar coverage in local editions of newspapers.

following introduction of the new immigration procedures involving fingerprinting and photographing, there has been a succession of mishaps in the taking of fingerprints [...]. According to the Immigration Bureau, fingerprints could not be taken from a total of 21 people, due to reasons such as wearing away of fingerprints.

At Hakata Airport [...] errors occurred in the cases of several tens of people when reading fingerprints magnetically. The procedure was repeated, but in the case of four people [...] fingerprinting was abandoned and they were admitted at the discretion of the Immigration Bureau. Similar problems occurred at Narita, Chubu, Tokachi-Obihiro and Fukuoka. (November, 20th *Mainichi Shimbun*, "Immigration inspection: Fingerprinting of arriving foreigners, 21 people could not give fingerprints2)

On the 20th, the revised Immigration Control and Refugee Recognition Law was implemented, requiring all foreign nationals over the age of 16 to be fingerprinted and photographed, in order to preempt the entry of terrorists. At Narita Airport, 70 extra staff of the Tokyo Immigration Bureau were mobilized, forming a total force of 210, to guide arriving passengers and explain the procedures.

Some users had to repeat the procedures because reading of their fingerprints or photographs did not go smoothly. This caused arriving passengers to have to wait in line. (November 21, 2007 *Yomiuri Shimbun*, "Immigration fingerprinting and facial photographing made obligatory: 210 staff mobilized to guide and explain")

As these articles illustrate, on this first day of the law's implementation, all the major newspapers mobilized large numbers of their staff from branches all over the country to cover the story. The amount of labor expended in this one effort far exceeded what was used to cover deliberations on the law during its passage through the Diet.

Paucity of the Coverage

So far we have discussed three frames and the competition among them. However, there is another, perhaps most dominant, frame for the coverage: i.e. its paucity.

On June 6 2006, in the aftermath of the law's approval in the Diet, *Asahi* reflected – somewhat apologetically – on the rather half-hearted tone of the debate, as follows:

Table 29.2 Coverage of the law revisions: Immigration Law vs. Education Basic Law searched on each paper's data base for the period January 1, 2004 to December 31, 2007

	Revision of basic education law	Revision of immigration law
Asahi	1057	52
Yomiuri	604	58

[...]

The paucity of debate can be attributed to the understanding that "the problem has little to do with Japanese people." Besides Japanese citizens, the revised law omits 470,000 special permanent residents as targets for fingerprinting.

A top official in the Ministry of Justice called this omission a "policy judgment." Special permanent residents are citizens of North and South Korea who resided in Japan before the end of the Second World War or are descended from such persons. (June 6, 2006 *Asahi Shimbun*, "Immigration control: Differences in the deliberations between Japan and the UK on the provision of biometric information such as fingerprints and facial photographs")

Asahi cites the exceptional treatment of special permanent residents and the perception that "it is someone else's problem" as causes of the relative lack of debate compared to the case of Great Britain. Robert Entman (2004) claims that magnitude measures and helps determine a news event's political importance: "the sine qua non of successful framing is magnitude" (Entman, 2004, p. 31). Such paucity may be a proof that the immigration issue is not a matter with cultural resonance in Japanese society. For example, there was far less coverage on revision of the Immigration Law compared with revision of the Basic Education Law, which was on the political agenda almost at the same time in the year 2006.

Figures show that the number of articles on revision of the Immigration Control Law remains as few as about 5% in *Asahi* and 10% in *Yomiuri* of the total headlines on revision of the Basic Education Law (see Table 29.2). It is understandable that domestic issues such as education reform have a higher news value in national media coverage. Nevertheless, the issue of the Immigration Law had to do with long standing political controversies regarding how open Japan can and should be to migration in the face of the increased border-crossing forces of globalization. Special permanent residents, of whom the majority are Zainichi Koreans, have long fought for their rights to stay in Japan without fingerprinting, and to them, the "revision" of this law appears nothing but anachronistic. However, because on this occasion, they do not belong to the concerned social group their voices were not raised against this change in the Law. Ultimately only around 60 articles were written in the full four years, which indicates that this issue never became a national concern, with the greatest weight being put on description of operational enforcement at ports and airports.

Conclusion

Through its "objective reporting" on the balance of debate between the demands of national security and the human rights of foreign nationals, the Japanese media failed to commit itself to the rights of foreign migrants. After all, any kind of advocacy is considered to be strictly inhibited in the world of journalism. As a result, the debate concerning the revision of the Immigration Control Law followed closely the discourse put out by "officially recognized" sources, such as government officials or intellectuals. In summary, among the "human rights frame," the "combating terror frame," and the "administrative implementation frame" within which the revision was reported, the last two were foregrounded.

Japanese journalists, who are mostly Japanese-speaking, monocultural people working lifelong for corporate media and living in the arena of nation-centric discourse, are not particularly sensitive to the need to listen to culturally and ethnically diverse voices. I conclude that the revised Immigration Control Law, which is targeted at foreigners who generally do not patronize the Japanese media and represent "total otherness" in their cultural and ethnic backgrounds, was practically irrelevant to the Japanese media due to cultural and linguistic barriers. My investigation confirmed that the newspapers all effectively gave support to the government policy line directly and indirectly through their journalistic practices and norms, whether they wanted to or not. So far, it would be fair to say that the direction of migration politics in Japan has been mostly determined by politicians and government officials with insufficient public scrutiny.

At least for issues that are not yet widely recognized as a social agenda within the national public sphere, it can be assumed that journalists select frames that are easy to understand to a wider audience such as war on terror or public safety so that their stories will be printed. The real challenge in the global age will therefore be to find out at which point and by which means new perspectives and values will grow to be an agenda for national debates and receive popular recognition in the world of domestic journalism.

Acknowledgments

I appreciate David Buist for his careful and competent translation and proofreading. I also thank Daimon Sayuri, news editor of the *Japan Times* for her numerous suggestions. This chapter owes much to the joint symposium by the University of Tokyo and the Japan Times Ltd. held in 2008.

Notes

1 Major newspapers belonging to the Japan Newspaper's Publishers and Editors Association agree to set its final deadline at 1.25 a.m. for its morning edition and 10.00 a.m. for its evening edition. Newspapers cling to these deadlines strictly (and sometimes blindly) to

keep the peace among them. A majority of reporters work until the last minute of these deadlines.

2 The total newspaper circulation declined from 53 669 866 in 1998 to 51 491 409 in 2008, a fall of about 4% in 10 years, according to Japan Newspapers Editors and Publishers Association. In addition, according to figures by Dentsu, Japan's largest PR company, the share of newspapers in the advertising market has been falling continuously, from some 25% in the mid-1980s to 12.4 % in 2008, whereas that of the Internet has been rising steeply in the past five years. Its market share stands at 10.4% and it is expected to exceed that of newspapers in the very near future.

3 So far Japan's immigration policy remains ambivalent. Some social and economic factors such as foreseeable labor shortages due to demographic changes are pushing some in the political and business sector towards a more open immigration policy. However, factors such as concerned popular sentiment about public security and growing apprehensions about international terrorism are prompting Japanese politics to adopt stricter immigration controls.

4 All the figures were cited from www.immi-moj.go.jp/toukei/index.html (accessed July 21, 2010)

5 Besides the large number of circulations, each newspaper company is operationally and formally associated with a large commercial TV broadcasting station.

References

Cook, T.E. (1998) *Governing with the News. The News Media as a Political Institution*, The University of Chicago Press, Chicago.

Dioguardi, M. (2006) *Japan Times*, June 6, 16.

Entman, R.M. (2004) *Projections of Power: Framing News, Public Opinion, and U.S. Foreign Policy*, The University of Chicago Press, Chicago.

Gamson, W.A. (1992) *Talking Politics*, Cambridge University Press, Cambridge.

Goffman, E. (1975) *Frame Analysis. An Essay on the Organization of Experience*, Penguin, Harmondsworth.

Hayashi, K. (2008) Mass Media wo Shihaisuru "Saidai Tasū no Saidai Fukou": Shokugyōrinri no Kentō to sono Sasshin no Kanousei [Innovations of Professional Ethics for Mass Media Journalism]. *Ronza*, July, 26–31.

Joseph, K. Jr. (2006) *Japan Times*, August 22, 16.

Krauss, E. (2000) *Broadcasting Politics in Japan: NHK and Television News*, Cornell University Press, Ithaca, NY.

Said, E.W. (1997) *Covering Islam: How the Media and the Experts Determine How We See the Rest of the World*, rev edn, Vintage Books, New York.

Tanaka, H. (1995) *Zainichi Gaikokujin – Hō no Kabe, Kokoro no Mizo*, Iwanami Shoten, Tokyo.

Uemae, J. (1982) *Shitenchô Wa Naze Shindaka*, Bunshun Bunko, Tokyo.

30

Ancient Roots and Contemporary Challenges
Asian Journalists Try to Find the Balance

Jiafei Yin

In the age of the global media, sometimes it is difficult to distinguish what are Asian media and what are Western media. However, that does not mean that there exist global journalists in Asia who follow a global code of ethics in executing their journalistic duties. East or West is still a useful shortcut in describing today's world in many contexts. However, in the post Cold-War era, the distinction between the East and the West is much less geopolitical than cultural.

Generally speaking, the West is often associated with advanced science and technology, individual freedom and rights, democracy, and higher living standards. In contrast, the East, for the most part, is often seen as less developed, more traditional, more group-oriented, and more focused on duties and responsibilities (Yin, 2008). The Western media, another name for the global media, are free, rich, powerful, and defiant of authorities, while the media in the East are often controlled, tame and depend on the authorities for resources or guidance. In summary, the East today does not compare favorably with the West.

The East, or Asia in particular, has not always been in that humble position. Asia has a magnificent past with civilizations dating back thousands of years, a past that the people in Asia can still be proud of. It is common knowledge that India and the Middle East were the birthplace of world's major religions, including Hinduism, Buddhism, Judaism, Christianity, and Islam. Besides being the birthplace of Taoism and Confucianism, China also invented paper and movable-type printing, two indispensables in the age of modern print media.

Even today the Asian media are attracting the attention of the world – the Asian press dominates the world's press industry today with well-established press giants like Japan and South Korea and newcomers with phenomenal growth in the industry such as China and India. In the world today there are only two newspapers that have circulations greater than 10 million – the *Yomiuri Shimbun* and *The Asahi Shimbun*,

The Handbook of Global Communication and Media Ethics, First Edition. Edited by Robert S. Fortner and P. Mark Fackler.
© 2011 Blackwell Publishing Ltd. Published 2011 by Blackwell Publishing Ltd.

both published in Japan, which also claimed the top five spots of the largest newspapers in the world. Of the 100 largest newspapers in the world, 75 of them are published in Asia, according to statistics of the World Association of Newspapers. Of the 75 Asian newspapers, 21 are published in Japan; 22 in China, and 17 in India.

The fast growth of the Asian media led by China and India is unprecedented in history even though the development of the Asian media as a whole is rather uneven. As Asian societies open up and develop, their media are being globalized. Foreign-owned media firms, joint ventures, and joint media productions are increasing in Asia, including China. Global media products – news, entertainment, and commercials – are readily available in the Asian media. Almost every Asian country has English-language newspapers, where journalists who are native English speakers are hired as news and copy editors. CNN, BBC, and Western wire services set news agenda for the world, including Asia.

The impact of global media is tangible in Asian societies much to the dismay of the older generations. Teens around the world are becoming more alike. They wear jeans, eat fast food, listen to rap music, and worship pop stars. Teens in Asia are no exceptions. They are less bound by traditional cultural values, defiant of the wisdom of their elders and much more accepting of fads from the West. Generation gaps sometimes lead to serious cultural clashes. The influence of the global media, which have spread Western cultural values, beliefs, and lifestyles and weakened local cultures, poses strong challenges to Asian societies as well as Asian media and journalists. Traditionally Asian media were regarded more as public utilities than businesses because of its influence and power in society. They were expected to inform, educate, and advocate for just social cause, and they were also expected not only to report but also to be responsible for the social impact of their report, which often led to self-censorship of "inappropriate" materials, be it political or moral in nature. In contrast, the global media are run as businesses, the ultimate goal of which is profit and market share. To achieve their goal the global media often resort to sensationalism. To provide news, journalists are supposed to be detached observers and support full disclosure upholding the principles of press freedom and democracy. In a global media environment today, what is the role of the Asian media? How can Asian media successfully compete against the powerful global media? Can Asian media remain commercially viable and culturally relevant? How should Asian journalists adapt to the challenges? Should they follow the examples of the global media in their relentless pursuit of market share and profit margins or should they chart a new course, which will allow the Asian media to successfully compete with the global media while still maintaining deep-rooted cultural values?

Dual Currents

These questions are raised in relation to bigger concerns over where Asian societies are heading. As a continent, Asia is undergoing major transformations and is at a historical crossroad. In the debate in search of a path most conducive to the development of Asian societies, dual currents emerge with one school ready to abandon traditional culture and instead, follow the footsteps of the West on the road to modernization while the other school insisting on relying primarily on traditional cultural values, not to exclude the best part of Western culture, in order to move forward. Nowhere is this debate taken more seriously than by Asian philosophers. Writing about contemporary Indian thinking, Bina Gupta (1997, p. 531) cited Narayana J.S.R.L. Moorty as saying that the contemporary Indian philosopher could embrace the analytical and verificationist approach of the West or choose to rejuvenate the tradition of Indian philosophy. In Japan, the study of European thinkers dominated the Japanese philosophical scene before the 1970s (Nagatomo, 1997). Since then, however, a new trend appeared in which Japanese philosophers began to recognize the flaws of the Eurocentric philosophy and its resultant science and technology, which yielded "mindless" or "heartless" societies, pollution, and global ecological crises impacting all parts of the Japanese archipelago (Nagatomo, 1997, p. 523).

The strongest reactions to traditional culture are perhaps from the Islamic world. Initial responses to Western influence led to sharp criticism and even rejection of national cultural and philosophical traditions, which were seen as responsible for the "backwardness" of the Islamic world (Stepaniants, 1997, p. 573). This negative attitude among Muslim intellectuals contributed to their unreserved pursuit of Western values and institutions as the only solutions to problems in Islamic societies (Stepaniants, 1997). However, according to Stepaniants, such negative attitudes toward national philosophical traditions lasted mostly during the first half of the twentieth century before they were criticized by those who believed progress should be built on the foundations of national culture with the assimilation of the valuable elements of other cultures. Iran might provide the best example of Westernization of an Islamic society turning sour. The impact of the Islamic Revolution after the failure of imposing the Western model is still being felt in the Iranian society today. According to Stepaniants, "the emergence of Islamic fundamentalism has been caused by the failure of all the efforts to rehabilitate the system by borrowing from the West, by the realization that 'there is no solution from without'" (Stepaniants, 1997, p. 578).

Across Asia, amid signs of McDonald's, KFC, and Pizza Hut, national cultures are stubbornly reasserting themselves. *Newsweek* reported that young Chinese returned from studying overseas promoted national pride more than Westernization (Liu and Hewitt, 2008). The article said, "In the West there's long been an assumption that this cohort would import Western values along with their iPods" (Liu and Hewitt, 2008, p. 31). However, it turns out that despite their Westernized lifestyles, the last thing they want is to build their homeland in the West's image. Instead, they want "a China that lives up to their sense of national greatness." According to Liu and Hewitt, the pacesetters of these returnees do not aspire to be "modern," a synonym for Western. Instead, these prosperous young returnees tend to see themselves emphatically as modern Chinese. Such attitudes and self-perceptions are in line with the philosophical thinking of Tu Weiming, a prominent Confucian scholar, who contends that the Western assumption that

Ancient Roots and Contemporary Challenges   557

human beings are rational animals endowed with inalienable rights and motivated by self-interest to maximize their profit in the marketplace is hardly an inspiring ideology (Tu, 1997). Instead, Tu believes that "The Chinese, especially the Confucian, idea of the intellectual – politically concerned, socially engaged, and culturally sensitive – seems to have special relevance for contemporary professionals in the academy, government, mass media, business, and civic organizations" (Tu, 1997, p. 23). Tu is convinced that given the need for a global ethic in combating global challenges such as the environment, social disintegration, and the lack of distributive justice, "Confucian inclusive humanism" seems more compatible with the spirit of our time.

In such a context of overwhelming social changes and debate, Asian journalists are seeking an ethical guide that respects traditional cultural values as well as globally accepted practices and standards in order to compete in a global media environment. In this chapter a brief overview of major philosophical, religious, and moral influences was provided to lay the foundation for the discussions of their applications in media practices in the Asian context and their compatibility or incompatibility with the global culture. As Asia is a culturally, economically, and politically diverse continent, discussions in this chapter reflect diverse moral influences as well as unique challenges Asian journalists face in their societies.

Dominant Asian Moral Influences

Some of the ethical challenges faced by Asian journalists are common to journalists around the world, such as stretching the truth in order to expand market share, pocket-book journalism for exclusives, or bribing journalists; other ethical challenges are unique to Asian media as they are inevitably heavily influenced by the traditional Asian cultures. In their development over thousands of years, Asian cultures interacted with each other, and dominant influences emerged and reached different parts of the continent as well as different parts of the world. According to Yong Choon Kim (1973), the sixth century BCE was one of the most significant periods in our entire human history since the great thinkers of the East were born during that time – Sakyamuni, founder of Buddhism in India; Confucius, founder of Confucianism, and Lao-Tzu, the legendary founder of Taoism in China. Hinduism, Buddhism, Confucianism, Taoism, and Islam have been the dominant spiritual influences across Asia for thousands of years and up to the present day. With the exception of Hinduism whose influences are largely confined to India and ethnic Indians overseas, all the other religions and philosophies crossed borders and took root in neighboring countries.

Hinduism is one of the oldest if not the oldest religion that originated on the Asian continent. Reincarnation, karma, and the individual effort to achieve a mental state free from desire and "selfish motive for the fruit of action" (Kim, 1973) are the key beliefs in Hinduism. The cause and effect logic in karma is not unique to Hinduism. Heaven and Hell in Christianity embody similar ideas. The other moral exhortation, to try to be free from desires and selfish motives in order to achieve inner peace, seems to be in direct opposition to the American ideal of the pursuit of happiness and private property. The commercialism in today's society seems to be pulling the world in another direction. One negative impact of Hinduism is the caste system, which was banned by the Indian government but still has influence in people's thinking in the Indian society today.

Buddhism, which also originated in India, claims followers in as many as one hundred and thirty countries and was born within the social and religious context of Hinduism (Kim 1973). It adopted key beliefs and moral principles of Hinduism, including reincarnation, karma, self-effort and self-strength in trying to liberate oneself from lust and illusion of self. It emphasizes the impermanence, suffering, and non-ego state of human existence. The one major difference between the two is that Buddhism rejected the caste system and teaches equality and salvation of all. In Buddhism, everyone can become a Buddha and enter Nirvana through self-effort at surrendering ego, pride, and desire. Buddhism also encourages compassion for all perhaps because it has witnessed the human tragedy and suffering under the caste system.

The idea in Buddhism that everyone can enter Nirvana through meditation, morality, and wisdom is very close to the foundational belief of Western democracy that all men are created equal and that their dream can come true if they try hard enough. However, the destinations of the two are very different. Nirvana was "Nothingness or Emptiness" (Kim, 1973), or peace without desires, which is the complete opposite of Western consumer culture emphasizing material possessions.

Originating in China, Taoism shares with Hinduism and Buddhism the rejection of materialism by strongly discouraging desires, and even pride and knowledge, which are considered objects of desire themselves. According to Lao Tzu, "There is no disaster greater than not knowing contentment with what one has; no greater sin than having desire for acquisition" (Fung, 1948, p. 101). Taoism also encourages the cultivation of "a spiritual sanctuary outside the lived world here and now" (Tu, 1997, p. 12) in order to get to the truth of the world, which is perhaps comparable to the concept of a detached observer in journalism. Taoism also shares one thing in common with Western thought – the celebration of individualism. Zhuang Tzu, a student of Lao Tzu, exalted individual freedom of the mind: "Alone he associates with Heaven and Earth and spirit" (Tu, 1997, p. 14). Zhuang Tzu was also influenced by Yang Chu, perhaps the only Chinese philosopher who promoted self interest without reservation – each one for himself. The part of Taoism that promoted individualism, minimum government, and self interest seems to reflect the values of the Republican Party in the United States.

The only similarity between Confucianism and Taoism is perhaps the emphasis on harmony with nature as the idea of harmony is central to Confucian thinking – harmony with nature and harmony in society. In every other aspect, Confucianism, which formed the moral foundation in East Asia and parts of Southeast Asia, is a complete opposite of Taoism. The primary concern of Confucianism is the collective

Ancient Roots and Contemporary Challenges   559

or the group – order and stability of the society and the welfare of the people rather than freedom and rights of the individual. To Confucius, a person is not viewed as an isolated individual but a center of relationships as human beings can only survive in groups (Tu, 1997). So his moral teachings address proper behaviors in different kinds of social relationships and emphasize duties and responsibilities in those relationships. In order to achieve those goals, Confucius encouraged "right thinking" – "have no depraved thoughts" according to the *Analects* (Fung, 1948), a collection of Confucius' teachings – and "right behavior." To ensure "right thinking" and "right behavior" and overcome the natural human tendency to be self-centered, Confucius strongly promoted education, especially the molding of noble and moral character, the essential qualities to be a just and wise leader. In fact, Confucius despised people who seek only personal gains – "little men" as he called them versus "gentlemen," people of noble character. "Joe the plumber," promoted by the McCain campaign in the 2008 US presidential election as an embodiment of the American ideal of self-interest, would be a typical "little man" by Confucian standards.

There are clear differences between Western philosophies and Confucian thinking – individual versus the group, freedom versus discipline, rights versus duties and responsibilities, right to think freely versus right thinking, competition versus harmony, and democracy versus meritocracy. The one thing in common across cultures and religions is the emphasis on individual efforts for self-improvement and success, which, nevertheless, have very different definitions based on different cultures. The influence of Confucianism on the media in Asia is long and widespread.

One other major moral influence in Asia is Islam, which is one of the dominant influences in South and Southeast Asia. In Islam there is a classification of moral acts: (1) those that should be practiced, (2) those that are recommended, (3) those that are permitted, (4) those that are disapproved, and (5) those that are forbidden (Albertini, 1997). These classifications seem to match the Confucian line of thinking – what is right versus what is wrong, rather than freedom of choice. Some Islamic philosophers believe the majority of people are disposed towards evil (Wahba, 1997), which is very similar to the beliefs of the Legalists in China around the third century BCE. They believe a social hierarchy is needed because some people have no virtues, others have some, and still others – the philosophers – have them all. Thus, philosophers must rule, while those without virtues or with only some virtues must be ruled and guided, which is clearly advocating a system of meritocracy and even authoritarianism similar to Confucian beliefs. One major influence of Islam on the media is that criticism of Islam and sex in the media are not tolerated.

Asian Values in Asian Media

Given traditional cultures that emphasize harmony, public good, order, stability, duties, responsibilities, and morals that discourage desires and self-interest, the ethical dilemmas Asian journalists face often vary from those their Western counterparts have to deal with, and those ethical challenges are often collective in nature, that is, personal ethical choices by individual journalists are often influenced or pressured by the social and political environment in which the media operate. Nonetheless, those ethical choices are still individual decisions – some Asian journalists are true believers in nation building; others remain tame for the good of the company or advances in their personal careers; and still others choose to become independent journalists and are pushing the boundaries everyday in trying to reveal the truth to the public.

To Be a Partner or a Watchdog?

Asian cultures emphasize harmony, consensus, cooperation, social order, and stability. An adversarial relationship in whatever social context is hardly a goal any institution would pursue. So to be a partner with the government or to be a watchdog of the government is perhaps the most difficult ethical question with which Asian news media must contend. Many Asian media organizations have to weigh on a daily basis whether to release certain information or not. Part of the reason, of course, is whether the government will tolerate such publication, but another part is that Asian journalists are culturally conditioned to be more aware of the possible impact of full disclosure even though truth, full disclosure, and freedom of the press are increasingly becoming the universally accepted goals of journalism. Such concern with media self-preservation and the potential social impact of media coverage results in widespread practice of self-censorship among Asian journalists and conservative mainstream media in Asia, regardless of their political environments – democratic, authoritarian, or Communist – or even their press freedom rankings assigned by Freedom House. The mainstream media in Asia tend to keep cooperative rather than adversarial relations with the government. They are mostly proestablishment as they are part of the establishment. Most of them are not known for aggressive, independent, and investigative reporting but known for much-researched and well-documented practices of self-censorship, such as in Hong Kong, Japan, South Korea, Thailand, India, Afghanistan, Pakistan, Sri Lanka, Malaysia, Singapore, and China. The only exceptions are perhaps Taiwan and the Philippines, where media exposés can topple governments. There are opposition papers or liberal media in various Asian societies, but their influence cannot compete with the mainstream media.

There are many reasons why there are not more watchdogs among Asian media as each Asian society faces its own unique challenges. One common thread is the emphasis on national security and social stability given the turbulent history of this part of the world, the unstable situations many societies still face today, and the widespread poverty in many of the Asian societies. Asia is a continent full of conflicts and a continent desperate for economic development in order to feed its large population, approximately 60% of the world's total. The concern with stability and the need for development plus authoritarian governments in many Asian societies often motivates Asian journalists to choose to be partners with, rather than watchdogs of, their governments.

Singapore is one of the richest and most technologically advanced countries in the world today, but it had to overcome much under a strong leader, Former Prime Minister Lee Kuan Yew, to be where it is today. In the nation's determined drive for fast economic development and against social chaos and unrest, the media played the role of a partner in that national endeavor. Lee knew the challenges his country faced firsthand and perhaps summarized the paramount goal of Asian societies the best. Challenged by a Western journalist over the control of his country and its media, Lee said emphatically, "Without order and stability, nothing can be achieved" (Singapore, 1997). Many Asian journalists would concur, and the mainstream media in Singapore certainly seem to agree with that despite repeated criticism from the West and from the opposition in the country.

Lee Kuan Yew might be the Confucian student that the sage would be most proud of. Confucius was born and raised during a time of great turmoil in China. Throughout his lifetime, he witnessed the endless suffering of the people and the destruction of the country due to constant wars. Therefore, Confucius' primary concern with the society was order and stability rather than freedom and rights of individuals. In the case of Singapore, when Lee became the leader of Singapore after World War II in 1959, the country was flattened by the war and brewing for mayhem as crime and strikes swept through the country. With a firm hand and 31 years in office as prime minister, Lee was able to turn Singapore from a fishing village into one of the busiest trading ports in the world. Traditional societies tend to be deferential to authoritative figures, and Asian societies have long traditions. Given what Lee had accomplished for his country, it is easy to understand the respect that his people and the media have for him. Some well-educated Singaporean professionals believed that people were willing to accept his policies and a high degree of social discipline because people realized that they had to make those sacrifices in order to achieve development goals (Singapore, 1997), which include a strong economy, higher living standards, quality education, a low crime rate, and a government mostly free of corruption, a rare feat among many corrupt Asian governments. Singapore was ranked the fifth least corrupt country in the world by the Berlin-based organization Transparency International and the fourth least corrupt by the World Democracy Audit.

Against such a background, the mainstream media in Singapore are conservative, focusing their coverage on world news, positive stories about the country and less sensitive topics such as science and technology, health issues, accidents, petty crimes, euthanasia, and comparative wages instead of muckraking the government. Most journalists in the country censor themselves on topics concerning ethnicity, religion, or relations with neighboring countries in order to prevent potential conflicts given the history of disastrous social turmoil in that part of the world. However, times are changing. Younger generations of Singaporeans, who have grown up in affluence, are looking for more rights and freedom, including the right to criticize their government. Dissenting journalists founded opposition media, such as the *New Democrat*, which often tries to break away from the tradition of self-censorship and provides an alternative voice to the public. However, these journalists often face charges of criminal defamation or violation of national security, which can result in a prison sentence. For Singaporean journalists, they have to choose between covering "what is right for society" and the right to cover, and between trusting the government and trusting the people.

Journalists in neighboring Malaysia face very similar challenges. Like Singapore, Malaysia is one of the more-developed and less-corrupt countries in Asia. However, it is perhaps more influenced by Islamic morals than by Confucian teachings with the majority of the population being Muslims. News coverage and editorials by both print and broadcast media generally support government policies. Journalists censor themselves to avoid public discussion of divisive and potentially explosive issues such as ethnicity and religion in order to avoid disrupting harmony or social stability. They also censor themselves for profanity, nudity, and violence to uphold Islamic values. The top concerns of the government with the media seem to be national security and respect for Islam. The media generally pose little challenge to the government's ban on the coverage of race and religious issues to prevent the "Islamization" of the country. However, in 2006 journalists from some bold pro-opposition media outlets, such as the *Guang Ming Daily*, defied the ban by reproducing the controversial Danish cartoons of the prophet Muhammad. The paper was suspended temporarily. In recent years, however, there has been greater criticism of government policies in the mainstream press, according to the 2007 report by Freedom House.

The concern with national security, ethnicity, and religious issues weigh more heavily on the minds of journalists in South Asia, which is the most explosive part of Asia due to the ongoing war on terror, disputes over territories, guerrilla warfare, and historical religious and ethnic conflicts. Random bombings, assassinations, military skirmishes and guerrilla warfare force journalists to think hard about what should be printed in the papers and what should not be. Editorial decisions depend not only on "news values," but also on the immediate impact of publication. Editors must weigh the balance between the freedom of the press and accountability for using that freedom.

The media in India are among the freest in Asia. However, the mainstream media in the country are rather conservative despite their diverse and vigorous news coverage, including criticism of the government. Terrorist attacks, such as the one in Mumbai, India's financial center, random bombings on public transportation, and skirmishes in Kashmir put the nation on high alert and prompt journalists to exercise self-censorship regarding the publication of security-related information. National security concerns tend to bring governments and the media together as partners in security building rather than as adversaries. The media in India also cooperate with the government in trying to transform Indian society and culture. Like many nations in Asia, India, despite its fast economic growth, is still a traditional society, which often inherited some unjust systems and practices from the past. The media and the government become partners in trying to

Ancient Roots and Contemporary Challenges

eliminate the unjust caste system and discourage the predatory practice of extorting dowry from the bride's family.

Journalists in Pakistan face even tougher challenges with more serious threats to national security on the border with Afghanistan, potential conflicts with India over the Kashmir region and over religious differences as nearly all of the population are adherents of Islam. The media are partners with the government in trying to protect national security and respecting the ban on negative coverage of the military, the courts and most of all, Islam, by exercising self-censorship as they believe coverage on these sensitive issues could trigger violence. However, some media outlets in Pakistan still provide diverse views including criticism of the government. In Sri Lanka, the people experience the highs and lows of guerrilla warfare waged by the separatist rebel group, the Tamil Tigers. Often journalists have to put the concern over national security and social stability before their concern over people's right to know by exercising self-censorship. The burden of press responsibility weighs as much as press freedom on the minds of journalists in South Asia if not more.

In the case of China, readers might ask: do journalists in China actually have a choice between whether they want to be a partner or a watchdog? Do watchdogs exist in China? Is investigative reporting even allowed in the country? The New York-based Committee to Protect Journalists (CPJ) reported that in the past two decades, "China's media have undergone profound changes, resulting in more dynamic, aggressive, and prolific reporting on a wider variety of topics than ever before" (Beech, 2002). The report said: "Chinese journalists have transformed themselves from state propaganda workers and government mouthpieces into professional reporters" who cover topics prohibited twenty years ago, despite the fact that political reporting is still tightly controlled. As a result of the changes, investigative reporting in China, particularly on crime, official corruption, police abuses, and illegal financial dealings, is becoming increasingly popular as such reporting attracts public attention and sells papers. Aggressive reporting and exposés sometimes lead to removal of editors, and in more serious cases, result in threats, harassment, arrests and even deaths to journalists in China. However, more often than not, such investigative reporting is done by nonmainstream tabloids or weekend papers in the country, such as the *Southern Weekend*, which was regarded as "the conscience of Chinese journalism" (Chan *et al.*, 2004).

Caijing, an independently-owned hard-hitting financial magazine, is another vanguard in pioneering investigative reporting in China. It made a name for itself in 2001 when it exposed a Shenzhen-listed Guangxia Industry Co. for inflating its profits by $50 million. Also in 2001, journalists in Guangxi Province were beaten and threatened with death for exposing cover-up efforts by local officials after a mining disaster, and even reporters from the China Central Television were beaten while investigating industrial environmental pollution in Shanxi Province (Beach, 2004). At the Beijing Foreign Studies University one American author and journalist invited to teach First Amendment, free press, and American-style journalism was able to set up an English-language, university-approved, student-written web log, where he posted student opinion pieces on the arrest of Zhao Yan, a Chinese journalist working in Beijing for the *New York Times* (Bosco, 2005). Students' opinions varied from nationalistic sentiment to "Zhao is a victim of (a) political power struggle!" and "When can we be free to tell?"

No doubt it is very risky for a media outlet or a journalist to be a watchdog. That explains why the mainstream media, for the most part, lags behind in investigative reporting despite better resources and better-trained staff. Exposés are often turned down by the mainstream media before they surface on the Internet or in tabloids, and then they are often picked up by the mainstream media due to public outcry. Many journalists are content with the status quo. A study by Chan *et al.* (2004) revealed that journalists in Shanghai, the second largest city in China, derived job satisfaction from autonomy; however, those who preferred government-sponsored media as ideal news outlets actually reported higher levels of job satisfaction. The study demonstrates that even under a Communist government like the one in China, there is still plenty of room for journalists to choose what kind of journalism they want to practice – to play it safe and avoid controversies or to investigate and publish the truth. This is one major dilemma and challenge that Chinese journalists face today given the ongoing transformation of the media in the country. That dilemma juxtaposes with the fact that exposés sell papers while safe coverage tends to be bland, and the fact that Chinese media are being transformed into commercial entities.

These overwhelming changes in the Chinese media send Chinese journalists struggling to try to find their balance. One editor in Guangzhou expressed the frustration of many when he told an American journalist that journalists in China today are never really sure where they stand (Kunkel, 2007, p. 2). The frustration is understandable given the fact that the government itself is trying to strike a delicate balance between openness and control when it comes to ruling the country. As a result, the central government often gives vague orders. The situation leaves Chinese journalists perplexed, torn between two masters: the Party and the people (Chan *et al.*, 2004).

One American journalist teaching journalism in China was optimistic about the future of the Chinese media. He said, "When a free press becomes a reality in China – and it surely will – it will come after countless small victories and even more tragic sacrifices by brave, persistent souls" (Bosco, 2005). He predicted that the process would be slow but "unstoppable." The pace of that process depends on the choices of the media in the country – to be a partner or to be a watchdog, to serve the party or to serve the people.

The same choice challenges journalists all across Asia – how close they can be to the government and still be able to cover the government objectively. In countries like India and Pakistan, it is very difficult to maintain media independence as many media organizations depend on the government for advertising dollars and for newsprint. Some may argue that in some Asian countries, journalists do not really have a choice as laws and regulations and government pressure make it impossible for the journalists to make a choice with free will. In each one of these countries discussed above including China, there are those brave and independent journalists who are at the forefront of pushing the boundaries set by the government, who

Ancient Roots and Contemporary Challenges   565

carry out serious investigative reporting, and who risk their career and even lives in pursuing authentic journalism. Press freedom is never a Christmas present. The call for the "Fight for freedom" rings loud in Asia today in the age of global media.

At the other end of the spectrum, there are Asian media that are considered too free by the public when they muckrake government officials without the support of facts. In Taiwan, if some media organizations suspected wrongdoing by a government official, they would publish a story alleging an affair by the official, and then they would wait for phone calls tipping the reporters about the real misconduct by that official, such as embezzlement or money laundering, but not an affair (Neal, 2008). Once they obtained the real story, they did not publish corrections of their earlier stories. Such "investigative reporting" without the support of facts or balance, sometimes encouraged and financed by political opponents, can also be found in Cambodia, the Philippines, and Indonesia, prompting an outraged public in Cambodia to label the media as a "mad dog" instead of a watchdog (Loo, 2006).

To Make Nice or to Make News

Not all the Asian media choose to be partners or censor themselves in news coverage because of concerns over national security, social stability, or the need for economic development. The mainstream media in Japan, South Korea, and Hong Kong, societies that are economically developed and heavily influenced with Confucian thinking, choose to "make nice" with the government and big businesses to minimize conflict and maintain a harmonious relationship, which also serves the self-interest of the media.

With a few exceptions, Asian governments are corrupt. The most notorious example might be the 3000 pairs of shoes in the palace of Mrs. Imelda Marcos, former first lady of the Philippines. In contrast, the national media in many Asian countries are not known for being diligent watchdogs of the government with hard-hitting investigative reports – they are often referred to as lapdogs.

In their reports Freedom House consistently ranks Japan highly in its assessment of press freedom in Asia, but the Japanese media has long been criticized for its self-imposed press club system, which discourages independent and investigative reporting of the government and competition by enforcing self-censorship in exchange for exclusive access to the government. In order to prevent controversies and conflicts, newspapers in Japan avoid dealing with uncomfortable truths (Gamble and Watanabe, 2004, p. 37). Instead, the media in Japan keep cozy relationships with the government and big businesses. Often they value good relations with sources over critical reporting (Kambayashi, 2006). On television talk shows, hosts nod their heads all the time instead of asking hard questions. With such softened news programming, the mainstream media can hardly uncover hidden truths.

It is little wonder that freelance journalists and racy tabloid weekly magazines in Japan, which are kept outside the press club system, are spearheading investigative reporting, and they are often the first in exposing government scandals and official corruption. There are about 3000 freelance journalists in Japan, who are a select group of resourceful and determined investigative journalists. They often cover issues that the national media "cannot" or will not touch, topics including political corruption, fiscal waste, police accidents, the insurance industry, suspicious suicides, and accidents where no autopsy was performed (McNicol, 2006). However, these independent journalists, who have a low status in Japan's company-centered society, often face continued battles against obstructive government officials, who intimidate freelance journalists and weekly magazines with charges of defamation and even imprisonment (McNicol, 2005).

Japan is a democracy. The government did not force the press club system on the national media; it is the highly profitable national media that willingly impose the system on themselves as the system benefits the media at the expense of the public. The national media organizations have made their choice, and individual journalists have their own choice to make as well. In this case, the answer seems to be obvious given the clear differences in social status and compensation between the national media and the alternative media. However, that may not mean that journalists working for the national media are happy with their "make nice" role as some studies show that some of scandal magazines' scoops came from journalists in the mainstream media (McNicol, 2005). Ironically the loudest protest against the Japanese press clubs comes from the global media – Western journalists, who are denied access to those exclusive government press conferences.

In South Korea, even though the press clubs have been phased-out, traditional deference to authority and close ties with the establishment remain. In Hong Kong, some newspapers soften their criticism of the central government in Beijing in order to protect the business interests of their owners.

To Be An Advocate or a Detached Observer

The Western ideal of a professional journalist is to remain an observer rather than a participant in order to avoid conflicts of interest and remain neutral. It is the perceived violation of this principle that makes civic journalism controversial in America. In contrast, Asian media, by and large, are unapologetically activist in nature. It is no coincidence that development journalism, which emphasizes the role of the media in nation-building, originated in Asia and has become popular even though it may not be mainstream in every Asian society. Development journalism as a theoretical concept was criticized by some Western media scholars as a disguise for government control as it may focus news coverage on government economic plans, policies, and perhaps propaganda. Defenders of development journalism, which is particularly well received in South Asia and the Philippines, argue that it can be community-based and identified examples of community media in South Asia.

India is proudly the largest democracy in the world, but sadly it also has one of the highest poverty rates in the region. Community media in the country, especially

Ancient Roots and Contemporary Challenges 567

in its rural areas, play a huge role in disseminating information about technology, health, small business management, and new ways of farming in hopes of improving the life of millions. One example of development journalism at work was the one-man enterprise run by Shree Padre, who was a farmer and a journalist (Rain man, 2007). He was the founder-editor of *Adike Patrike*, a magazine "by, of and for" farmers, and headed a movement called "Pen to Farmers" that trained hundreds of farmers to write about their experiences. His major project was to collect and document information about rainwater harvesting in fighting drought. He studied unique traditional water harvesting systems such as man-made caves for collecting water and traditional percolation ponds of coastal areas. He published 10 books documenting success stories of rainwater harvesting and drought-proofing from around the world. He made sure that only successful methods, which were: low cost, completed without government subsidy, and replicable were selected. He disseminated such information through his columns and slide shows. The practical methods of water conservation he promoted contrasted with government's empty talks about building big dams. Here is one convincing example that development journalism does not necessarily entail government control; it can be practiced at different levels depending on the inspirations, aspirations, and passions of a journalist. Community media are particularly strong in South Asia. The primary target of development journalism in Asia is its vast rural populations, many of whom live in poverty.

The drive for national development also calls for a progressive society while many Asian societies still observe good and bad traditions. Development media play active roles in advocating social justice, gender equality, and civic virtues. In the early days of China's economic reforms and opening to the outside world, the media launched a nationwide campaign promoting good behaviors and manners, including civilized behavior, courtesy, sanitation, order and morals, beautiful heart, beautiful language, beautiful manners, and beautiful environment, which could be the first steps toward Confucian values of humanity, righteousness, decorum, wisdom, and trust (*ren, yi, li, zhi,* and *xin*).

The reason for the emergence of development journalism in Asia is that the continent as a whole is desperate for development in order to reduce poverty, which skyrocketed to more than 40% in Pakistan in 2008 (Poverty, 2008). It is an activist and interventionist type of journalism, the goal of which is to bring desired social changes rather than just to inform people. Development journalism is in perfect step with Confucian teachings of being politically involved, socially engaged, and committed to humanity.

To Educate or To Entertain – To Give the Public What It Should Know or What It Wants To Know

Asian cultures are known for their emphasis on education and their strong sense of right and wrong. Confucius, a civic-minded philosopher, placed high hopes on the role of education, which he believed would lay a solid foundation for building a strong society. In his teachings, Confucius emphasized the sense of duty and responsibility, the sense of right and wrong, and the importance of character. He was convinced that education would teach people right from wrong and would help build noble and moral characters. Confucius was acutely aware of human weaknesses, and he strongly advocated life-long efforts at "self-cultivation" (*xiushen*) through transcending and overcoming oneself. His best known maxim on education was, "Never bored with learning and never tired of teaching." Until the commercialization of the media in China, there was very little entertainment in the Chinese media. News was intended to inform and educate, not to entertain. There were no pop stars in China, and celebrities were model workers who devoted themselves to their jobs. Science, technology, and culture were given plenty of space to keep the public up to date and nurture the "right interest" among young people. There was no "inappropriate material" – sex and violence – in the media. Today the commercial media in China are not that "clean," but the educational role of the press still remains. The *21st Century*, a tabloid targeting high school students and published by the English-language *China Daily* Group, regularly carries English teaching materials and sponsors English writing and speech contests. There are also specialized math newspapers for high school students.

Press in the Islamic world can be very serious about its educational role as well. *Dawn*, the leading English-language newspaper in Pakistan, publishes a special education section. One article on the Alzheimer's disease explained the importance of education well: "Education is one of the most important ways to transform Pakistan from a developing to a developed country. Education is not only an engine of economic and intellectual development but is also critical for maintaining a population in good health and protecting it from disease" (Xhaferri and Iqbal, 2008). Another article in the section discussed how to raise a child with the right values (Patel, 2008). Further headlines in the section included excellence in higher education, work ethic, and tips for preparing exams. In a country with a literacy rate of only 50%, the press has a special role to play in promoting education.

While serious-minded Asian journalists try to inform, to enlighten, and to inspire the public, the global trend toward entertainment media makes those goals increasingly difficult to accomplish. One Indian journalist criticized the commercialization of the media in his country by saying, "The pivotal role of the media is its ability to mobilize the thinking process of millions. But in today's highly commercialized market, the press is losing its main focus. Journalism had deviated from the path of responsible journalism to more saleable journalism" (Commercialization, 2008). That description can be applied to many media outlets across Asia. In China, a popular local television station, Hunan TV, turned an old rape case into a love story and was later sued by the rape victim for invasion of privacy (Li, 2005). In Cambodia, graphic journalism dominates the front pages of the Khmer papers in the pursuit of shock value (Loo, 2006). In India where the country is facing mounting challenges in reducing mass poverty, the media resort to sensationalized journalism through "sting operations" in the pursuit of ratings (Commercialization, 2008).

Ancient Roots and Contemporary Challenges 569

Media are businesses, but many Asian journalists still believe they have a higher purpose than to make money. After all, Confucius made a distinction between the profit-seeking "little man" and the noble "gentleman." He said, "A gentleman is always carefree; only a little man constantly worries about petty gains and losses." Confucius despised those who would give up morals for the sake of personal gains. In the age of the global media, the market seems to be taking over throughout the world. Can media professionals resist being "little men"?

To Be The Voice of The People or The Voice of The Elite

Since the beginning of the human society, there have always been distinctions between the powerful and the powerless, and between the rich and the poor. Even in the United States, which was once proud to be a classless society, the gap between the rich and the poor is widening. Of the two groups, which one will the media represent? In a commercial society, there can be only one answer. The commercial media, particularly the broadcast media, are snobbish by nature. Media's target audiences are the elites, those with money, good education, influence, and power. In China, the elites are party and government officials and the emerging middle class; in India, the elites are the new millionaires and the expanding middle class, which still accounts for a very small portion of its 1.1 billion population.

Facing the vast challenges of the country, Palagummi Sainath, an award-winning rural affairs editor of *The Hindu*, lamented that "the moral universe of the Indian media has shifted; outrage and compassion among journalists has died" (Commercialization, 2008). He pointed out that the structural shutout of the poor was evident in the way beats were organized in the newsrooms. He gave the poignant example that very few national media reporters covered the agrarian crisis in Vidarbha, but 512 journalists attended the Lakme Fashion Week in Bombay, and when the media did organize a panel discussing issues facing farmers, there were no farmers or people familiar with farming on the panel. The media were out of touch with reality as the media's accountability and professionalism were declining, according to Sainath (Commercialization, 2008). An article in the *Hindustan Times* sharply criticized the press' excessive coverage of lavish weddings of the rich and famous while ignoring stories of rape (Not fine print, 2007). The writer of the article warned that another story on those weddings could be the funeral of the press.

In the Chinese media, the spotlight is often on pop stars rather than on the concerns of ordinary citizens. When it comes to controversial issues, the party's voice dominates. China's economic reforms have undoubtedly lifted millions out of poverty and improved the living standards of the general population, but they have also caused many new problems, such as the dissolution of China's social safety net and the deteriorations of labor protection due to the privatization of state enterprises. However, in most cases, grievances of the people are missing in the Chinese media even though Chinese editors today have greater leeway in making editorial decisions. Theoretically, the Chinese media are the voice of both the party and the people as the party is supposed to represent the interests of the people. When the party and the people disagree with each other, the party's voice prevails. In the Chinese news media today, there is plenty of criticism of party policies so long as the targets of criticisms are the policies and not the party. Some media outlets reflect people's concerns in those criticisms more than others. In today's China, that is a choice made possible through the opening-up policies.

More enterprising journalists in Asia take to the Internet to publish what is turned down by the mainstream media. The Internet provides a much-needed alternative avenue for reflecting the voice of the people in Asia through citizen journalism.

To Inform or To Provoke and Polarize

Asian societies are diverse, which contributes to the richness of Asian culture but also tends to spawn conflicts. In journalism, conflict is one prominent news value. It is one thing to cover the conflict, but it is quite another to fan the flames and intensify the conflict, thus producing more drama for the media. Indonesia is a country still contending with its ethnic and religious differences, some of which have led to massive unrest and violence against minorities. During the height of one such communal conflict in the Maluku Province, the Jawa Pos media group promoted the conflict by starting a new paper, *Ambon Express*, which supported one side of the conflict while the group's established paper, *Suara Maluku*, advocated the other side. The media group split the community along ethnic and religious lines by publishing two rival papers, one called a "Muslim" daily and the other a "Christian" paper (Nurbaiti, 2005). Almost all of the media outlets at the time were accused of providing biased rather than balanced reporting.

On the international level that kind of "provocative reporting" can be more dangerous. When tension broke out between Indonesia and Malaysia over the disputed Ambalat offshore oil block in the Sulawesi Sea, the national media in Indonesia focused on the possibility of war instead of advocating a peaceful settlement, and the local media preferred to cover the deployment of troops and the recruitment of volunteers to attack Malaysia (McNicol, 2005).

In domestic politics, polarized reporting prompted the public in Cambodia to call the media a "mad dog." Many partisan Khmer publications were unrestrained in slandering their opponents. All were fair targets except for the king (Loo, 2006). Impartial reporting was rare while partisan press was commonplace in the forms of taking sides in the news and ideological positioning. The same kind of reporting occurred in the Philippines and Indonesia after their dictators were overthrown. In Sri Lanka, many private media outlets are becoming increasingly polarized even though there are some privately owned newspapers and broadcasters that still scrutinize government policies and provide diverse views.

Ancient Roots and Contemporary Challenges 571

Polarized reporting helps sell papers, but during international conflicts journalists, and not just Asian ones, have to decide if they want to be journalists or patriots.

To Be An Anchor or A Salesman

With the accelerated pace of commercialization of the media, the line between news and commercials seems to be disappearing, thus the term "infomercial." In America it would be unimaginable if a news anchor of a major television network was spotted endorsing a product in a commercial. In Japan, however, well-known television news anchors promote commercial products in the media without repercussions to their reputations or careers or even much discussion about conflict of interest among journalists and media critics (Kambayashi, 2005). Shuntaro Torigoe, one of the best-known television and print journalist in Japan, appeared in a television drama and print advertisements selling insurance even though he had discussed ethical issues in journalism in his books. Torigoe's employers claimed that his endorsements of products did not impact his journalistic work. Torigoe was not alone. Seiichi Kanise, an anchor for TV Asahi and Tokyo Broadcasting System, also appeared in advertisements promoting Japan Telecom. ALICO Japan, a subsidiary of the American Life Insurance Company, flooded Japanese television with commercials that imitate actual news reporting, with former television anchors explaining the benefits of products. These commercials looked so much like real news programs that a little note had to appear at the top of the screen reminding the audience that they were not watching a real news program. Even though a few journalism professors criticized such practice, most of the media critics remained silent because of their close ties to the industry. Employers of these "amphibious anchors" hid behind the excuse that these journalists were freelancers, so the companies did not have exclusive contracts with them. While many freelance journalists in Japan have upstaged the mainstream media in investigative reporting, others have chosen to profit from their fame. When there are commercial media, are there also "commercial journalists"?

To Push the Envelope Or to Accept the Envelope – of Cash

While some Asian journalists are pushing the envelope in the topics they can cover, others are accepting envelopes filled with cash from news sources for favorable coverage. Journalists have power, and power corrupts even though journalists are supposed to be watchdogs against corruption. In South Korea, China, Indonesia, the Philippines, Cambodia, and many other Asian countries, it is standard practice that journalists are handed an envelope containing cash at press conferences. In Cambodia it is called "gas money" or "coffee money." In Indonesia the envelopes became so enticing that they attracted hundreds of "bogus journalists" to press conferences in Jakarta alone (Paid, bogus press, 2005). In Cambodia they are called "fake journalists." In many newsrooms in China, there are rules against "red envelopes" of cash or gifts from sources, but the rules are sometimes not rigorously enforced, leaving individual journalists to their own discretion.

Such envelopes of cash are not limited to press conferences; they are ubiquitous around news events and between news sources and reporters. In Cambodia, such direct cash payments for covering news events could be really small, amounting to 5,000–20,000 riels (about US$1.25–$5). Still there were many "fake journalists" who used their media pass to gain favors or seek bribes from their sources (Loo, 2006). In Indonesia, the influence of "envelope journalism" was pervasive among both private and state media organizations. Many news sources willingly bribed the media for favorable coverage or to prevent exposés. Everyday about 2000 journalists make their fortune by asking lawmakers for money, resulting in "bogus journalism" (Luwarso, 2002) In the case of Cambodia and Indonesia, sometimes salaries for journalists were so low that cash payments from news sources became almost an accepted form of subsidies for the profession. Even in higher-income societies such as South Korea, corruption among journalists also occurs. Gifts include stocks, free trips, and free meals. In Vietnam, one journalist was exposed to have received a bribe of up to US$200,000 (News often wounds, 2001). In the Philippines, envelope journalism became such an accepted practice that one reporter was stunned by the matter-of-fact manner in which an envelope stuffed with a thick stack of cash was handed to her when she was investigating corruption charges against a government official and his wife (Magsino-Lubis, 2005).

In China a well-known young reporter, Li Min, who covered the legal affairs beat for China Central Television (CCTV), was accused of taking bribes from a news source and was arrested in 2008. Ironically, the reporter's defense was that the gifts were not bribes but presents from a suitor as the news source was courting Li (Procurators, 2008). One more twist in the case was that the procurators who arrested Li were targets of Li's investigation for inappropriately interfering in a civil business dispute. The case shows that if the media are corrupted, it is then very difficult for the media to be an effective watchdog for the public.

Even worse than bribery, blackmailing targets of investigation for money is reported from time to time in the Chinese press. One reporter from the *Southern Metropolis Daily* was fired for blackmailing the owner of a health clinic for alleged wrongdoing. While the usual amount of hush money was several hundred yuan, this particular reporter demanded 15 000 yuan, nearly US$2000 (Cody, 2007). The outraged supervising editor said the case was a disgrace to himself and to the paper, which was a paper respected in the country for daring to cover topics that other papers would not. Such cases can also be found in other countries where bribing journalists is a way of practicing journalism. In some instances, people impersonate reporters to try to extort money from local businesses or officials.

The economic reforms in China have turned media from political tools into money-making businesses in order to compete with the global media. The adoption of capitalistic practices seems to have opened up the eyes of millions of Chinese to the value of money. Communist doctrines of "serving the people" or Confucian distinctions between "little men" and "gentlemen" have all been tossed aside in the pursuit of profits. Some journalists in that pursuit have lost their way even though there are still many journalists with a conscience in China and in other parts of Asia, who are trying to keep the profession credible. The path to authentic journalism is going to be a long one given the economic realities of many Asian societies and the highly infectious human addiction to greed.

To Tell The Truth Or To Run

For those conscionable Asian journalists, the ultimate challenge is whether to tell the truth or to run as telling the truth may cost them their lives. Being harassed, attacked, detained, or even murdered for trying to tell the truth is not a possibility but a reality for journalists in Pakistan, Sri Lanka, Indonesia, the Philippines, India, and China. South Asia and the Philippines are among the most dangerous places for journalists to work in the world. Murder and harassment of journalists were documented in almost all countries in South Asia (Seneviratne, 2007). A culture of impunity emboldens those who commit violence against journalists. Often attackers can be criminal gangs, police officers, or hired hit men of political parties or local officials.

In South Asia, terrorism, insurgency and guerrilla warfare make reporting news a very dangerous occupation. Journalists in Pakistan had to work in a worsening security environment following the assassination of former leader Benazir Bhutto and with the ongoing unrest in the tribal areas bordering Afghanistan. "Police, security forces, and military intelligence officials subjected journalists to physical assaults, intimidation, torture, and arbitrary arrest and detention" in order to silence critical voice in the media, according to the 2007 Freedom House report. Islamic fundamentalists and hit men hired by feudal landlords or local politicians harassed journalists and attacked newspaper offices for reports they did not like. In 2006, more than 100 such instances were reported. In Sri Lanka, there was also a rise in attacks against journalists, particularly ethnic Tamils. More than two dozen Tamil journalists were abducted, assaulted, or killed in 2006, according to a report by the Colombo-based Centre for Policy Alternatives. Journalists covering human rights issues or official misconduct faced intimidation and threats from security forces and government officials. In India journalists were particularly vulnerable in rural areas and insurgency-infested states. Two journalists were killed for exposing official misconduct and corruption in 2006, Freedom House reported in 2007.

In Southeast Asia, the Philippines rivals Indonesia as the most dangerous country in the region for journalists. In the past 15 years, 32 journalists have been killed in the Philippines for exposing corruption. The perpetrators often enjoyed impunity. Violence against journalists was also a serious problem in Indonesia, where journalists were threatened, attacked, or killed for covering official corruption or for offending Islam.

In China, not only journalists but news sources for exposés were detained, jailed, or sent to labor camps. To stop such police abuses, a "Witness Protection Law" was proposed as investigative reporting invites reprisals (Pan, 2006). For journalists, the results can be deadly. In one case, an editor was beaten to death by local police for an embarrassing exposé (Newspaper editor dies, 2006). Attacks against journalists have increased in China in recent years as news reporting has become more aggressive (TV reporters attacked, 2006). At least 100 journalists were physically attacked in 2003 (TV reporters attacked, 2006). In Nepal, leading newspapers are fighting back by leaving editorial spaces blank, some with black borders, after Maoist activists attacked the country's biggest publishing houses (Pasricha, 2008).

Compared with their Western counterparts, journalists in Asia face tougher challenges in their jobs. Knowing that their stories may cost them their lives, many journalists, especially those in the local press, are still pushing to uncover official corruption, police abuses, and crimes by gangs or insurgents. They are taking full advantage of the freedom granted them by their constitution. They are the hope of Asian journalism.

Ethical standards of journalism in Asia are rather uneven given the large differences in traditions, resources, the training of journalists, the level of development of the media, and influences of the global media. Caught between traditions and influences of the global media, Asian journalists are seeking the right balance. As if to provide some moral guidance, Tu Weiming, the prominent Confucian scholar, believes that motivators such as self-interest are hardly inspiring (Tu, 1997, p. 22). Tu is convinced that the Confucian intellectual – politically concerned, socially engaged, and culturally sensitive – and "Confucian inclusive humanism" are more compatible with the spirit of our time and more conducive to solutions to world's problems. Self-interest or inclusive humanism – that may be the key question for journalists, not just for journalists in Asia but journalists throughout the world.

References

Albertini, T. (1997) Islamic philosophy: An overview, in *A Companion to World Philosophies*, (eds E. Deutsch and R. Bontekoe), Blackwell Publishing, Malden, MA, pp. 99–139.

Beach, S. (2004) In China, new journalism and new threats. *Committee to Project Journalists*, August 24, http://cpj.org/reports/2004/08/china-8-04.php (accessed July 19, 2010).

Beech, H. (2002) Let one hundred cultures bloom. *TIMaisia*, November 11, www.time.com/time/asia/features/china_cul_rev/opener.html (accessed July 19, 2010).

Bosco, J. (2005) A moment in Beijing. *The Quill (Chicago, Ill)*, 93 (May, 4), 45.

Chan, J.M., Pan Z., and Lee, F.L.F. (2004) Professional aspirations and job satisfaction: Chinese journalists at a time of change in the media. *Journalism and Mass Communication Quarterly*, 81 (2, Summer), 254–273.

Cody, E. (2007) Blackmailing by journalists in China seen as "frequent." *The Washington Post*, January 25, section A, A01.

Commercialization (2008) Commercialization of journalism in India, September 17, *ANKWD*, www.ankwd.com/commercialization-of-journalism-in-india/ (accessed July 19, 2010).

Fung, Y. (1948) *A Short History of Chinese Philosophy*, Macmillan, New York.

Gamble, A., and Watanabe, T. (2004). *A Public Betrayed – An Inside Look at Japanese Media Atrocities and their Warnings to the West*, Regnery Publishing, Washington, DC.

Gupta, B. (1997). The contemporary Indian situation, in *A Companion to World Philosophies*, (eds E. Deutsch and R. Bontekoe), Blackwell, Malden, MA, pp. 531–541.

Kambayashi, T. (2005) Prominent Japanese journalists defy ethical standards. *Japan Media Review*, www.japanmediareview.com/japan/stories/050411kambayashi/print.htm (last accessed July 16, 2007).

Kambayashi, T. (2006) Making nice instead of making news. *Japan Media Review*, www.japanmediareview.com/japan/stories/060628kambayashi/print.htm (last accessed July 16, 2007).

Kim, Y.C. (1973). *Oriental Thought: An Introduction to the Philosophical and Religious Thought of Asia*, Charles C Thomas, Springfield, IL.

Kunkel, T. (2007) East Greets West. *American Journalism Review*, 29 (1), 2.

Li, J. (2005) TV station sued over invasion of privacy in outing a rape victim. *Beijing Morning News*, December 5, http://media.news.hexun.com/detail.aspx?lm=1979&id=1434171 (last accessed July 29, 2006).

Liu, M., and Hewitt, D. (2008) Rise of the sea turtles. *Newsweek*, August 25, www.newsweek.com/2008/08/08/rise-of-the-sea-turtles.html (accessed July 28, 2010).

Loo, E. (2006) Cambodian journalism "flying blind." *WACC*, www.waccglobal.org/lang-en/publications/media-development/50-2006-3/594-Cambodian-journalism-flying-blind.html (last accessed July 26, 2007).

Luwarso, L. (2002) "Freakdom" of the press: Keeping Indonesia free for all. *Taipei Times*, April 5, p. 13.

Magsino-Lubis, M. (2005) Passing the envelope. *PJR Reports*, online edition, November, p. 12.

McNicol, T. (2005) Media criticized for stoking hatred over Ambalat 2005. *The Jakarta Post*, April 1, www.asiamedia.ucla.edu/article.asp?parentid=22564 (accessed July 28, 2010).

McNicol, T. (2006) Walls in front of freelance journalists. *Japan Media Review*. www.japanmediareview.com/japan/stories/060928mcnicol/print.htm

Nagatomo, S. (1997) Contemporary Japanese philosophy, in *A Companion to World Philosophies*, (eds E. Deutsch and R. Bontekoe), Blackwell Publishing, Malden, MA, pp. 523–530.

Neal, R. (2008) A free press comes with responsibility. *The Quill (Chicago, Ill)*, 96 (5), 70.

News often wounds (2001) News often wounds, but more often it heals. *Saigon Times*, October 5.

Newspaper editor dies (2006) China: Newspaper editor dies after police beating. *Committee to Protect Journalists*, February 6, Retrieved July 25, www.cpj.org/news/2006/asia/china06feb06na_2.html (last accessed July 25, 2006).

Not fine print (2007) The *Hindustan Times*, www.hindustantimes.com/News-Feed/offtrack/Not-fine-print/Article1-209724.aspx (accessed July 28, 2010).

Nurbaiti, A. (2005) A balance between profit, readers' needs and idealism. *The Jakarta Post*, December 30, www.asiademocracy.org/content_view.php?section_id=11&content_id=619 (accessed July 28, 2010).

Paid, bogus press (2005) Paid, bogus press mars free press, integrity *The Jakarta Post*, March 20.

Pan, H. (2006) Protecting whistle blowers means protecting the social conscience. *Beijing Youth Daily*, June 20, from http://china.ynet.com/view.jsp?oid=10059620 (last accessed July 29).

Pasricha, A. (2008) Nepal media protests attack by Maoist activists. *Voice of America News*, December 23, www.cnielts.com/voa/40487.html (accessed July 28, 2010).

Patel, Z. (2008) A controversial subject. *Dawn*, December 14, www.dawn.com/weekly/education/education1.htm (last accessed December 19, 2008).

Poverty (2008) Poverty rate has crossed 40 percent. *Dawn*, December 19, www.dawn.com/2008/12/19/top20.htm (last accessed December 19, 2008).

Procurators (2008) Procurators from Shanxi arrested CCTV reporter in Beijing. December 8, http://news.sina.com.cn/c/2008-12-08/104516804604.shtml (last accessed December 23, 2008).

Rain man (2007) "Rain man" of Indian journalism makes sure well stays full. *Indo-Asian News Service*, July 5, 2007, www.dmanewsdesk.com/professional_journalist_rain_water_hravesting_information_flow-2-398-298.html (accessed July 28, 2010).

Seneviratne, K. (2007) Media experts criticize report on press freedom. *IPS (Latin America)*, May 8, www.highbeam.com/doc/1G1-163076923.html (accessed July 28, 2010).

Singapore (1997) Singapore: The price of prosperity. A BBC Production (video recording), Films for the Humanities & Sciences, Princeton, NJ.

Stepaniants, M. (1997) Contemporary Islamic thought, in *A Companion to World Philosophies*, (eds E. Deutsch and R. Bontekoe), Blackwell Publishing, Malden, MA, pp. 573–580.

Tu, W. (1997) Chinese philosophy: A synoptic view, in *A Companion to World Philosophies*, (eds E. Deutsch and R. Bontekoe), Blackwell Publishing, Malden, MA, pp. 3–23.

TV reporters attacked (2006) TV reporters attacked in Shenzhen. *Southern Metropolis Daily*, February 7, http://cmp.hku.hk/look/article.tpl?IdLanguage=1&IdPublication=1&NrIssue=1&NrSection=100&NrArticle=514 (last accessed July 25, 2006).

Xhaferri, R., and Iqbal, K. (2008) Learning and Alzheimer's disease. *Dawn*, December 14, www.dawn.com/weekly/education/education3.htm (last accessed December 19, 2008)

Wahba, M. (1997) The concept of the good in Islamic philosophy, in *A Companion to World Philosophies*, (eds E. Deutsch and R. Bontekoe), Blackwell Publishing, Malden, MA, pp. 484–492.

Yin, J. (2008) Beyond the four theories of the press: A new model for the Asian & the world press. *Journalism & Communication Monographs*, 10 (1), 3–62.

31

Understanding Bollywood

Vijay Mishra

When that great art of mechanical reproduction – cinema – came to India with the release of Dhundhiraj Govind (Dadasaheb) Phalke's *Raja Harishchandra* in 1913, it drew its soul from India's ancient epics (which continued to be orally transmitted), its theatricality from a vibrant Parsi theatre of colonial India, its representational format from the paintings of Raja Ravi Varma (1848–1906) and its gestures (dramatic *mudrās*) from both classical dance forms and folk theatre, notably Nautanki. When sound came to Indian cinema in 1931 (with the first talkie *Alam Ara*) these features were given greater prominence through the use of music and dialogue (largely derived from the Persian mathnavi-inspired performances and nondiegetic music of Parsi theatre) and poetic language: Hindi-Urdu for the cinema primarily based in Bombay, regional languages for cinemas based in other parts of India.

There is now an extensive bibliography on Indian cinema, especially on Bollywood cinema, which examines this cinema from perspectives derived from the discipline of film theory and criticism generally. Although the word "Bollywood" is now a respectable term which refers to a quite specific form of cinema and is not a derisory term for a second rate imitative cinema (based on the deference to Hollywood in the descriptor) and has indeed made its way into the *Oxford English Dictionary* (OED), a few general comments about the cinema must be made as a prelude to the chapter proper. Bollywood, the cinema based largely in Mumbai (Bombay), has produced some 9000 films since the coming of talkies to India in 1931. (This must not be confused with the output of Indian cinema generally, which would be four times greater.) The triumph of Bollywood (over other regional cinemas) is nothing less than spectacular and indicates, furthermore, the growing global sweep of this cinema not just as cinema qua cinema but as cinema qua social effects, national cultural coding, and entrepreneurial nous. The Hyderabad-based Ramoji Film City

The Handbook of Global Communication and Media Ethics, First Edition. Edited by Robert S. Fortner and P. Mark Fackler.
© 2011 Blackwell Publishing Ltd. Published 2011 by Blackwell Publishing Ltd.

constructs stage-sets for any locality in the world, and in doing so gives another definition of the global nature of Bollywood. Indeed it was Bollywood which provided the metaphor for the shift from Melbourne to Delhi for the Commonwealth Games in 2010. The Melbourne closing ceremony was marked by Bollywood pop stars Aishwarya Rai and Saif Ali Khan doing a veritable Bollywood romp. International games (the Olympics, World Cup Soccer, Asian Games, Commonwealth Games, and so on) are often expressions of a nation's own emerging modernity. For India that modernity, in the realm of culture, is increasingly being interpolated by Bollywood.

This essay brings together four key elements of Bollywood cinema:

1 the lure of the mythological;
2 the allure of the Muslim courtesan, and Urdu, Bollywood's language of love;
3 the hegemony of melodrama; and
4 the persistence of song and dance.

The essay concludes with an examination of a classic 1963 film which may be used as the touchstone for the items discussed under the subheadings.

The Lure of the Mythological

The *Mahābhārata* claims, "what is not here is nowhere else to be found" (I. 56.34). Given this claim, it may be suggested that the epics (both the *Mahābhārata* and its lesser sister epic the *Rāmāyana*) laid the foundations of Indian cultural forms, foundations so old and influential, yet their impact remained pervasive. It may therefore be argued that modern Indian cultural forms, and notably cinema, connected directly with the epics, which were also repositories of religious belief, albeit sometimes in heavily mediated ways.

It must be said at the outset that Indian modernity has not parted company with religion; nor has modernity transformed religion into coded narratives and characters through whom an alternative version of the sacred may be imparted. There are no figures (be they Superman, Gandalf, Saruman, or the Principal of the Hogwarts School of Witchcraft and Wizardry) whose bodies and language mark out an alternative, postmodern sacred. In Bollywood (the variety of Indian cinema which is our archive here) gods and goddesses or divine personages generally come down to earth themselves, which is a time-hallowed mode of travel in the Hindu scriptures. Indeed Indian cinema began with mythologicals, a genre which continues to shadow Indian cinema generally by providing it with some of its basic narrative structures as well as ethical norms.

The mythological is primarily an episode from the epics or the later Puranic texts. It is marked by a story which has a distinctly human dimension, in which gods may figure, and humans in the end must bow down to their will. What is important, however, is that it is never God-centered, nor is it devotional in the strict sense of the word. Although piety and submission to the will of God (here as pre-written *karma*) are crucial, the narrative is not defined by the discourses of devotion. The latter is characterized by prayers, *bhajans* (hymns), sacrifice, worship, transvaluation of sacred spaces, the '*act of manifestation* of the sacred (*hierophany*)'[1] and by the overriding discourses of *bhakti* or devotion. Encounters with gods and goddesses are not with the absolutely other (*ganz andere*) within the framework of sublime awe, the *mysterium tremendum*,[2] but as part of an interconnected system.

Narratives formed through the mythologicals, beginning with *Raja Harishchandra*, made as we have noted by the legendary Dhundiraj Govind (Dadasaheb) Phalke (1870–1944) in 1913 introduced the hero as renouncer.[3] The renouncer-ideal permeates Indian cinema, and the grand text of this ideal, after Phalke's seminal film, was *Raja Harishchandra*. Since 1913 no fewer than eight versions of this story have been made, 3 silent films and 5 talkies: *Raja Harishchandra* (dir. D.G. Phalke, 1917), *Raja Harishchandra* (Kohinoor Productions, 1924), *Harishchandra* (dir. N.D. Sarpotdar, 1928), *Harishchandra* (dir. K. Rathod, 1931), *Satyawadi Raja Harishchandra* (dir. J.J. Madan, 1931), *Harishchandra* (dir. Dhirubhai Desai, 1958), *Harishchandra Taramati* (dir. B.K. Adarsh, 1963), *Harishchandra Taramati* (dir. B.K. Adarsh, 1970). What is important to underline is that the mythological established the narrative and thematic norms of Indian cinema: what is not there is nowhere else to be found. These norms fall under the following general categories/groups/themes: unqualified adherence to the principles of *dharma* or the eternal law; the hero as the follower of the complete Christian 10 commandments with the proviso that Hindu polytheistic monism replaces the Judeo-Christian God and images of gods are a necessity; the woman as the sacrificial/devoted wife/mother/female companion; the hero bereft of the seven deadly sins; the narrative constructed around a theory of a secular, impartial nation based on the idea of the common good for all; the triumph of good over evil. Around these, many more themes may be added but all within the over-riding principles of acts which are not linked to fruits of action.

Of the nine versions already mentioned, the 1963 *Harishchandra Taramati* (remade in color by the same director seven years later) is representative of the form. The tale of Hariścandra is itself something of an anomaly since, as fleshed out by Bollywood, it does not exist in this extant form in the literature. Although it is recorded in the great epic, in one of the *Brahmanas* and in the *Markhandeya Purāna*, the tale is present there only in skeletal form. In Book Two of the *Mahābhārata* (the *Sabhāparvan*) when Yudhisthira asks Nārada, "What feats did Hariścandra accomplish?" the latter replies: "He was a mighty monarch (rājā balavān), an emperor who ruled over all the kings (samrāt sarva mahīksitām)." The epic tells no more than this. It may stand to reason then that stories simply grew around this king. The tale itself was gradually embellished by other cognate stories of piety and self-sacrifice.

The film begins with a variation on the Judgment of Solomon scene. It is Queen Tārāmatī (Jaymala) and not King Hariścandra (played by Prithviraj Kapoor fresh from his success as Emperor Akbar in *Mughal-e-Azam*, 1960) who dispenses the correct judgment by declaring that the child claimed by two women should be cut in half and given to both. At this the first woman declares that she would rather see the child given away to the other woman than so inhumanely divided. The other woman remained silent. The Queen, in a repeat of Solomon's judgment, orders that the child should be given to the first woman as only a real mother would rather lose her child than see him slaughtered. In these establishing shots we are also told about the King's promise to save one Candramani from her evil paramour, Ānandkāl. We are informed that the King has a son, and that the King belongs to the lineage of the Sun kings of the Kingdom of Ayodhya of which, later, Lord Rāma is also a prince. Further, we are informed that such is the King's dedication to the path of truth that even the heavens are afraid of him since fidelity to absolute truth – he is called *satyavādī* – threatens the primacy of gods. To challenge the King's fidelity to truth, he is tempted.

What follows is a series of trials and tribulations in which the King and his family are tested by the powerful guru-saint Viśvamitra. The King works as a laborer, as a cobbler, as a man-servant, as a potter; the Queen as a maid; and the child Rohit (Babloo) earns money through kick boxing to pay their guru *daksina* (or guru gratuity) to Viśvamitra. Whenever a *daksina* is collected, Viśvamitra cheats them and in the end they are sold into slavery to pay their guru debt. More intense difficulties follow, often framed within well-known narratives.

The worst is yet to come as the pious king, the follower of the eternal *dharma*, the upholder of truth – all ancient Hindu verities – takes on the job of a *candāla* responsible for burning the dead. This act, an unclean act, is however followed through with the same sense of dharmik propriety since following one's *svadharma* (the *dharma* of one's caste) is more important than following another *dharma* (the *Bhagavadgītā* 18.47). In this role the King not only asks his wife, who has brought their dead son to the cremation grounds, to pay him before the son can be cremated (which she does by stripping her own sari and thereby compromising her modesty), but he condemns his own Queen and accuses her of murdering their child. She is charged forthwith and condemned to be executed. In all this, to the world the King never declares his identity; he suffers, and this is ennobling suffering, the kind of intense sacrifice of the self which again threatens the order of the universe, just as his dedication to truth had done before. The cosmos is threatened with *pralaya* (apocalypse); the gods are afraid, for such *tapas*, such austerity, such an act of renunciation, if unstopped, would make the King a god himself. So Vishnu, the Preserver, intervenes, and the King's son is brought back to life, his Kingdom is returned and the moral order reestablished. In all its severity, this is the definitive allegory on which the genre of the religious film is based. Beyond that, Bollywood cinema, as a single interconnected text, will find much of its idiom as well as its narrative model in this story.

It is not the aim of this chapter to declare the extent to which *Raja Harishchandra*, like Gogol's overcoat (of which Dostoevsky declared all writers were children), has spawned all other Bollywood films. It is sufficient to argue that the genre of the mythological film (which Salman Rushdie has termed "theologicals"[4]) has provided cinema with some of its key structural and thematic forms. There are four ways in which mythologicals have functioned in Bollywood: as a reenactment of the life of Rāma as God incarnate (*Sampoorna Ramayan*, Homi Wadia/Babubhai Mistry 1961); as an exemplary text of *bhakti* (devotion) and saintliness, as in the demi-god Hanumān's unqualified love for Rāma (*Bajrangbali*, dir. Chandrakant, 1976); as the absolute instance of brotherly love and duty, as in the relationship between Rāma and his brother Bharat (Manibhai Vyas's *Ram Bharat Milan*, 1965); and as God's transhistorical or synchronic presence in our midst (*Jai Santoshi Maa* 1975, dir. Vijay Sharma; 2006, dir. Ahmed Siddiqui). It is the latter form which continues to energize Bollywood, although with less obvious divine intercessions.

Rewriting Mythologicals I: *Jai Santoshi Maa*

Released in 1975, *Jai Santoshi Maa* is a cheaply produced religious film, yet one of the great hits of the year and, arguably, the most influential devotional film of all time. The film was remade with the same general theme but placed in a late modern Indian context in 2006. A number of issues of worship, faith, and devotion within the apparati of Hindu belief systems come together in these films. We shall consider these issues with reference to both versions of the film. The 1975 film brought together well-known stars of religious/devotional films: Trilok Kapoor, Manhar Desai, and Bharat Bhushan. Mahipal and Anita Guha are the last two best-known actors who played the roles of Rāma and Sītā respectively. *Jai Santoshi Maa* declares its eponymous goddess' connections with the establishment pantheon immediately as she is the daughter of Ganeśa himself. Santoṣī Mā, however, has no establishment genealogy like the other Hindu goddesses. The aim of the film is to construct one for her. How then does the text work its spell on the spectator and effectively start the worship of a little-known goddess, at least for a decade or two after the film's release? The remarkable effects of the film on the Hindu imagination may be explained in a number of ways. The first is the need for synchronous revelations in Hinduism, or the actual presence of divinity among us from time to time. The pervasiveness of cults such as that of Śirdi Sai Bābā (1836–1918), popular among filmmakers, and of the still-alive Satya Sai Bābā (1926–) are instances.[5] One may wish to add claims of many gurus, including Bhagwan Shree Rajneesh, to the list. In this respect a story in which Śantoṣī Mā comes into the lives of people here and now confirms the idea of the eternal recurrence of divinity among us. The second is the way in which the film is encoded in the discourses of popular religiosity, notably those derived from the Tulsīdās *Rāmāyana*.[6] Wrapped in a red cloth, Satyavati's father (Bharat Bhushan) chants from it and in doing so foregrounds yet again the film's lineage in the tradition of *bhakti*. Third, the film actually constructs a new *āratī*, a new prayer-hymn for this goddess. It takes the form of the song *mai to āratī uteri re santoṣī mātā kī/jai jai santoṣī mātā jai jai mā* written by Bollywood's preeminent devotional lyricist Pradeep and sung by Usha Mangeshkar, sister of the prima donna Bollywood high-pitched crooner Lata Mangeshkar.

Fourth, the film confirms, as indeed the extended final sequence of dance, homage, and *āratī* in the temple scene shows, the very Hindu idea that gods may enter into our lives at any time, in any form: *nā jāne kis bheś mem nārāyan mil jāye*. Finally, the sacrificial woman is seen as the embodiment of the quintessential Indian woman, a point made in a background song sung by one of Bollywood's rare classically-trained singers, Manna Dey: *mat ro mat ro āj rādhike jo dukh se ghabrā jāye vah nahīm hind kī nārī* ('Do not cry today, Rādhā, for whoever is flustered by suffering is no woman of Mother India').

A religious film which makes money has to be repeated and so we get another *Santoshi Maa*, 30 years later, in 2006. It is not my aim here to connect religious texts with shifts in capital – from an immediately postcolonial social democrat capitalism to a late modern free market capitalism, the first producing the 1975 text, the second its late modern avatar. Nor am I concerned, given the metaphysical rather than distinctively materialist tenor of this chapter, to explore how the *Santoshi Maa* films critique heteropatriarchal social formations or how internal to these texts is the presence of the Muslim as writer and/or director. It is sufficient to allude to these productive and critically self-aware modes of analysis but move on to the more formal dimensions of the religious film and its place in the construction of the Bollywood film syntagm.

Santoshi Maa (dir. Ahmed Siddiqui, 2006) pays direct homage to the 1975 original at the outset: dedication to Pradeep the lyricist, the chanting of the *āratī*, *mai to āratī utāri re santośī mātā kī*, the uncanny resemblance of the Santośī Mā statue with the Satyavati of the 1975 film, and ongoing allusions to the original film throughout. In this 2006 version, the tale of a latter-day Santośī Mā devotee is presented as a framed narration. A modern media girl, Preety (Garima Kapoor), interviews Mahima (Nushrat Bharucha) about the miraculous birth of her son when science could not cure her infertility. Mahima is observing the 16th Friday *vrat* (fast) of Santośī Mā and invites Preety, who is in the throes of a divorce, to her home. Mahima then recounts her life story which parallels the life of the earlier Satyavati. In Mahima's case, too, she is separated from her husband Anurag (Rakesh Bapat) and is abused by her extended family. Like the Satyavati prototype, Mahima is sorely tested and undergoes suffering only to triumph in the end. Although the other divinities in the Hindu pantheon do not figure in this version, Santośī Mā's presence is felt throughout the film as once again she participates in person in the final *pūjā* to tell her followers: "Arise my children, be content, be happy, this is my blessing."

In a foundational essay on the 1975 *Jai Santoshi Maa*, Veena Das pointed out a number of fascinating features of this film.[7] First, it seems Santośī Mā is very much a creation of Bollywood cinema along the lines of earlier creations, though not by Bollywood, of goddesses such as Śītal in Bengal to explain a smallpox epidemic there in the nineteenth century. However, unlike Śītal, Santośī Mā is not related to an epidemic and hence is not constructed as an embassy of death to be appeased. Nor is she a purely rural phenomenon as she has been appropriated, via cinema, by the Indian middle class. Second, Santośī Mā belongs to what may be called the tradition of tribal and not savior religions[8] in the sense that she does not bring any huge metaphysical baggage with her. There is no commentarial tradition behind her, no personal history such that attributed to Lakṣmī or Pārvati, goddesses whose reincarnations are interwoven into the textures of Hinduism. Instead what Santośī Mā symbolizes is the efficacy of renunciation as a constituent feature of devotion. In other words, both Satyavati and Mahima, as model devotees (hence figures to aspire to), are marked by intense sacrifice and suffering; their rewards coming only after their sufferings have been so acute and so painful that there is indeed no more that can be asked of them short of death itself. The renouncer ideal is therefore embedded into the figure of the person-of-the-world, the two no longer seen as irreconcilable items in a binary set of oppositions but as a sequential order in which to suffer or to renounce is a precondition for a divinely sanctioned, contented life in this world. Finally, the emergence of what is in effect a new deity (Santośī Mā's presence in the canon is completely marginal) shows how Hinduism constructs new gods out of old in response to the requirements and needs of a changing social order. In reaffirming sacrifice and moral uprighteousness even as modernity effectively precludes such absolutes, the new cult, and the cinema which has created this new cult, refines the received tradition and simplifies it through emphasis on personal worship. The *heimlich* (homeliness) of Santośī Mā (she has no major temples) makes her a presence in a home centered around the figure of the homely wife who imbibes the grace of this goddess. The centrality of the heteropatriarchal order is disturbed because the Friday *vrats* are undertaken by women who alone are granted a personal vision of the goddess. The Arjuna-Krishna classic bonding of the *Bhagavadgītā* gets rewritten as the Satyavati-Santośī Mā dialogue.

Rewriting Mythologicals II: *Ekalavya*

A principle of structuration: no Bollywood film is unaffected by the absolutist norms of Hindu culture, the norms of *dharma* and *karma*, of law and of individual action as constitutive of the higher moral order; our acts, in other words, condition not only our lives in this world but also in the next. Any number of Bollywood films may be cited to make this point but I want to turn to the case of *Eklavya* (2007) since this film comes at a time when the religious film is either truly dead or it cannot uncritically reaffirm the old moral absolutes. Located in the midst of a late Indian modernity, globalization, and the Indian diaspora as a key market for Bollywood, *Eklavya* indeed shows how much more difficult it is now to represent, even as allegory, the religious canon.

The story of Ekalavya is found in the *ādiparvan* (1. 123: 1–39) of the *Mahābhārata*.[9] The preeminence of Arjuna, the great archer and favorite pupil of Drona, is challenged by Ekalavya, a hunter's son who asks Drona to be his guru. Drona declines on grounds of caste. Ekalavya, however, retreats to the forest, makes an image of Drona, pays homage and reverence to the image as if it was Drona himself and, following the rules of a pupil, masters the craft of archery to an unparalleled degree. One day Arjuna and his brothers and cousins go hunting. Their dog smells a black hunter wrapped in uncouth clothing and keeps barking. Annoyed by the sound, Ekalavya shoots seven arrows into the mouth of the dog (without of course seeing the dog). The dog, its mouth filled with arrows, walks back to Arjuna and his brothers. Arjuna is taken aback by the hunter's prowess, locates him in the forest, and sees for himself his immense dexterity with bow and arrow. Worried that there is an archer superior to him, he returns to Drona demanding that he keep his promise that no "pupil of his should ever excel him." Drona locates the aboriginal Ekalavya ("his body caked in dirt, hair braided, dressed in tatters") shooting arrows with great precision. Ekalavya touches Drona's feet and acknowledges him as his guru.

> tato drono 'bravīd rājann ekalavyam idam vacah
> yadi śiśyo 'si me tūrnam vetanam sampradīyatām
> ekalavyas tu tac chrutvā prīyamāno 'bravīd idam
> kim prayacchāmi bhagavann ājñāpayatu mām guruh
> na hi kim cid adeyam me gurave brahmavittama
> tam abravīt tvayāngustho daksino dīyatām mama (1. 123: 33–35)

Then, O king [Yudhisthira, the narratee], Drona said to Ekalavya, "If you are my pupil, you must give me a fee." Having heard this, Ekalavya said happily, "What can I give you, sir? Let my guru give his command. Greatest of Brahman-scholars, there is nothing I would not give my guru." He replied, "You must give me your right thumb."

Such is the eternal law, the unchanging Law of *Dharma* that a guru's request must be honored. Without hesitating and delightfully, Ekalavya slices off his right thumb and gives it to Drona. Ekalavya enters Hindu everyday life as the symbol of honor and as the tragic hero who commands respect.

To understand *Eklavya* we need to know the eponymous hero's function in the epic narrative and we also need to know how "Ekalavya" circulates in culture and the symbolic role he plays in it. Of special importance is the place given to Ekalavya in current Dalit literature and everyday life. The Dalits (formerly "Untouchables") see in Ekalavya an earlier Dalit sacrificed for the greater glory of the higher castes. Their reasoning is that Nisāds (hunting caste) were in fact proto-Dalits and aboriginal peoples, people born out of interbreeding and consequently rejected. This view also resonates with the Damodar Kosambi thesis about autochthonous elements in the epic.[10] In some Dalit circles the author of the later epic, the *Rāmāyana*, Vālmīki, is also seen as a Nisād. Ekalavya for the Indian Dalits then symbolizes in a graphic, albeit poetic form, an alternative ennobling which the high caste epic must reduce to a cipher, to a moral anecdote, so as to advance its own perverse definition of *dharma* and demonstrate its fear of miscegenation. Although the connection between Nisād and Dalit is ingenuous (though not totally indefensible) in everyday Dalit life it has gained an epic grandeur in which Ekalavya is lifted

Understanding Bollywood

to the status of a mythic hero, a dying god figure, the unnameable signifier (the characters within the Ekalavya episode in the *Mahābhārata* do not name him) who must be sacrificed before fertility can return. In this respect the Dalit is the sacrificial victim whose blood renews the land. It is this reading of the Ekalavya-Nisād-Dalit which underpins *Eklavya*, the film.

At the outset a voice-over connects the film with its epic antecedent: "It is a story from the *Mahābhārata* ... an aboriginal child ... who followed the eternal *dharma* by honouring the request of his guru." The addressee is a child who repeats the manner in which the dog is shot: "without any sign of blood or pain." As the voice-over ends and the credit stills fade we enter into a tale of intrigue, murder, revenge, and honor. The tale combines capitalist modernity with feudal structures and values since the subject of the film is a postcolonial Indian principality which somehow functions both as part of a democratic polity and outside of it. Located in this ambivalent, if radically contradictory, position is the new Ekalavya (Amitabh Bachchan) who is at once biological father of the heir apparent and defender of the principality. In this reworking of the myth, one would have expected a bold statement connecting Ekalavya to his Dalit origins. Instead the Dalit role is given to a deputy superintendent of police, Pannalal Chohaar (Sanjay Dutt) in whom is located the new social order of India. For *Eklavya* the film can do no more than construct his moral dilemma in an instrumental modernity. The Sanskrit axiom *dharma madhyata rudhyate* ("*dharma* must be restrained by reason") is often repeated to underline this new morality. When it becomes clear to Ekalavya that the heir apparent Harsha (Saif Ali Khan) had in fact killed his putative father (Boman Irani) to save his biological father, who is himself, Ekalavya is faced with an epic dilemma. It is Harsha who reminds him of his duty, "Now you must follow your *dharma* and kill me, isn't that so?" In the epic Ekalavya must sacrifice what he loved most, his right thumb, for without it he could no longer be an archer. If the Law of *Dharma* were to be followed to the letter (and not with the rider "dharma madhyata rudhyate") Ekalavya must sacrifice his son (angūsthā, "thumb" also means soul), which is what he prepares to do. But he doesn't and with the strains of the Gāyatrī mantra, the Hindu Lord's Prayer (tamaso mā jyotir gamaye ...), interwoven into the dialogue, Ekalavya concludes, "This time I didn't cut off my thumb." The father and son embrace.

The eternal *dharma* of the mythologicals in late modern Bollywood now becomes a matter of postmodern contingency, not a transcendental absolute. As Georg Lukács wrote, in the age of capitalism, the epic can no longer be written because the unities that the epic stood for (the unity of work value and use value for instance, the primacy of the artisan, the certainty given to felt life through ethical absolutes, and the like) can no longer be replicated.[11] The epic gives rise to its degraded avatar, a genre such as the novel which, through irony, tries to come to terms with the world's fragility. In these terms *Eklavya*, the film, can no longer rewrite the epic tale of Ekalavya since *dharma* now is contingent, the epic absolutes are gone. Still what *Ekalavya* the film cannot do is declare Ekalavya himself a Dalit (in line with this new alternative, subaltern historiography) and thereby allegorically suggest that the Indian nation state (for the principality is a microcosm of the nation here) itself has a Dalit/Aboriginal origin.

The religious film is dead; long live the religious film. In a deeply religious culture, religious narratives are replicated as well as invoked; they have a dynamic narrative (that is plot) as well as structural (that is systemic or absolutist) function. From *Achhut Kanya* (dir. Himansu Rai, 1936) to *Om Shanti Om* (dir. Farah Khan, 2007) and *Rab Ne Bana Di Jodi* (dir. Aditya Chopra, 2008), "salvation" or indeed the "good life" lies in humility, in detachment, in equanimity, indeed, in the qualities of the renouncer. Where once the renouncer-ideal worked with twice told texts (which were orally transmitted from mother to child) and established the foundational genre of Indian cinema, it now functions as thematic, driving the machines of Bollywood. In spite of the lure of a capitalist modernity, the eternal verities of the religious film – verities of *dharma*, the law, and *karma*, correct action – continue, even if ambiguously and impossibly as in *Eklavya*, to define Indian cinema. In this respect the legacy of the religious film is deep and enduring: what is not in Bollywood cinema is to be found nowhere else.

The Allure of the Muslim Courtesan and Urdu, Bollywood's Language of Love

We have noted in passing Urdu plays performed in Parsi theatre, none perhaps more influential than *Laila Majnun*, a play derived from the Persian Sufi poet Nizami's poetic rewriting of an Arab tragic romance. The Arabic tale seems to have originated in the late-seventh century and was reputedly based on a *Romeo and Juliet*-style tragic love of one Qays ibn al Mulawwaht for his beloved Layla. In Nizami's version, the story gets overlaid with strong mystical symbology and the relationship of the lovers is also rendered as an allegory of human love for the divine. Parsi theatre used the story in its more secular "Shakespearian" form and Bollywood too emphasized its secularity. The story, though, has deeper significance in that its narrative was often presented as the quintessentially Muslim story around which the tale of the tragic Muslim courtesan unfolded. This figure of the "Muslim courtesan" remains pivotal to the Bollywood conception of the heroine but also suggestively points to the at-once central and marginalized Muslim in Bollywood. Without the power of Urdu and Muslim culture, the distinctiveness of Bollywood cannot be fully grasped. Yet this power, pervasive and aesthetically dominant as it is, is nevertheless captured in a figure of cultural exclusion and erasure. A quick look at four films – *Anarkali*, *Mughal-e-Azam*, *Pakeezah*, and *Umrao Jaan* – should make this ambivalence clear.

Where and how the Anarkali legend began, no one is too sure. We know that a silent film about her was made in 1928 by Imperial Film Company (directed by R.S. Choudhry) and it stands to reason that a play of sorts predated the film. We know that the Urdu dramatist Afga Hashar Kashmiri wrote a play on the subject early in the twentieth century and the fact that the names of the characters and the story line have remained unchanged tends to suggest that the origin of the legend may well have been literary. It seems clear that the original writer felt that the great Arab-Persian love story should be given an Indian context and what better way to do it than by locating it in the court of the great Mughal Emperor Akbar. The story line is then about Akbar's son, the Mughal Prince Salim (later Emperor Jehangir), falling in love with the court dancer Nadira, named Anarkali by none other than Akbar himself. This leads to political and dynastic tensions, open warfare between father and son, the sentence of death on both Salim and Anarkali, a final reprieve to the son but Anarkali's death by being entombed alive not revoked. The 1928 silent version as well as Imperial Company's talkie version (with the same director and lead actors) of 1935 adheres to this story line. The same fidelity to the narrative is shown in the 1953 film version (*Anarkali*, dir. Nandlal Jaswantlal) perhaps the best rendition of the story. It is interesting that in this version it is Emperor Akbar himself who enters into extensive dialogues with Anarkali on the question of love and the law, agreeing with her that perhaps love is higher than the law. The proof of the latter lay in the love of Anarkali herself (about which for a while he remains ignorant). Much of the performance is staged, but Marshall Braganza's cinematography is so good that the film captures the fragility of Anarkali remarkably well. Then there is also the haunting use of song, especially the song yah zindagī usī kī hai jo kisī kā ho gayā pyār hi me kho gayā ("life is for those who love, who get lost in it") with which the film more or less begins and ends, and a song, in both its original version and later avatar, as pyar kiyā to darnā kya, celebrated by both M.G. Vassanji (in *The Book of Secrets*, 1994) and Salman Rushdie (in *Shalimar the Clown*, 2005).

The establishing shots of *Anarkali* (1953) juxtapose a tomb and a song, one signifying death, the other transcendence over it. As a film of the Muslim courtesan, *Anarkali* lays claim to the soul of Bollywood cinema as a "Muslim" soul of love and longing, of poetry and self-denial. It also lays claims to a central tension between law, justice, cultural norms, and love. In this battle, love triumphs even if tragically. The Muslim theme and the film's historical location also lays claim to a syncretic Indo-Muslim heritage and argues that the Muslim is crucial to Indian cultural identity, especially for those people who speak Hindi/Urdu, the language of Bollywood. In a much grander version of the Anarkali theme, K Asif's *Mughal-e-Azam* (1960), the centrality of the Muslim is given a retrospective legitimacy through the recasting of Akbar, the great Indian emperor, in the codes of ancient Hindu dharma, so that justice is not simply a matter of jurisprudence, a philosophy of what is just and right, but relies on codes that predate the arrival of Muslims and into which the Muslim establishment also reinserts itself. So in this epic remake K Asif distorts the myth by letting Anarkali escape death because Emperor Akbar had given his word to Anarkali's mother, who had brought good tidings to the King on the birth of his son, that if and when she asked for a favor of the king, her wish would be granted.[12] What neither of the films erase is the centrality of the *mujra*, the dance of the courtesan in Bollywood whose definite form is the pyār kiya to darnā kya ("why be afraid when in love") dance of Anarkali in *Mughal-e-Azam*. At the same time, the endorsement isolates the form, confines it within a specific genre so that in effect there is no type of recognizable Muslim film other than a version of *Anarkali*.

"Anarkali," sign as well as theme, is the antecedent of two key courtesan filmic dramas: *Pakeezah* ("The Pure One," dir. Kamal Amrohi 1971) and *Umrao Jaan* (1981). The first of these takes the figure of the *tavayaf*/courtesan but presents it not so much as a sign of absolute exclusion (which in reality it is: a figure of illicit desire, but a threat to normative family values) as a symbol (precisely because of its otherness) through whom values of high aestheticism and love may be expressed. The courtesan thus becomes, in Bollywood's version of Muslim culture, emblematic of an elusive but aesthetically pure and culturally pivotal formation without which the culture itself is emaciated and forlorn. At the same time, though, the culture cannot endorse or celebrate the courtesan in social practice: no courtesan can become a mother or a wife; she can only be the desirable Other through whom love, often absent in arranged marriages, can be given felt expression. Indeed, the courtesan affirms a fact of Indo-Muslim culture generally (where cousin marriages are the norm): only in the courtesan outsider (who by definition cannot be part of a family) is desire fulfilled. So in the case of *Pakeezah* the excluded courtesan (whom the respectable man marries but cannot bring into his family) must live her life twice over, once as herself, and again as her daughter before she is incorporated back into respectability by the nephew of precisely the man who had rejected his courtesan wife (it is the nephew who marries Nargis, the courtesan's, daughter Sahibjaan).

In *Pakeezah* the courtesan enters the text fully formed; she is what she is and it is Shahabuddin's fate to fall in love with her. It is a love signified by both mother (and later by her daughter) through the symbology of a caged wingless bird (pinjre kī cidiyā) and the torn kite (katī patang) hanging from the branch of a tree – both established metaphors of loss in Indian art. In *Umrao Jaan* the courtesan is part of patriarchal violence towards women, as the young girl Amiran is forcibly taken from her village by men seeking revenge of wrongs done to them by her father. They take her to the city of Lucknow to be sold. Poet Muzaffar Ali, the director of this film, however, uses the tragic history of rape, abduction, and sexual slavery to extend the link between the aesthetic and the courtesan. It may be that Muslim poetic forms derive much of their strength from the figure of the courtesan whose *khotā* (brothel) provides a space where dance and song, desire and passion, sex and poetry can fuse into one, uninhibited by either religion or family. The *khotā* is a space of romantic transformation, where reality is changed into fantasy. In *Umrao Jaan* the poetic impulse itself is connected to the courtesan. It is she who writes poetry and who seduces as much through song as through body. The film then becomes a vehicle for the transmission of high Urdu dialogue and verse as the courtesan masters both music and literature, mastering the rules of both *khayāl* and *alfāz*, both poetic suggestiveness and sound combinations, as in the establishing song of the courtesan: dil cīz kyā hai āp merī jān lijiye. Yet in spite of lovers' trysts that fill the film with exquisite moments of romantic love, the exclusion of the

Understanding Bollywood 589

courtesan from society is not negotiable. When she finally returns home, she is rejected as the bazārū aurat (the available woman of bazaars). The final shot of the film is of Umrao Jaan looking at herself in a mirror: the courtesan is only an image, a reflection, a sign into which is poured romantic meaning but of itself is only a mirage, unreal, and like poetry in the end untranslatable.

Muslim courtesan films demonstrate both the centrality of Muslim culture in Bollywood and at the same time their exclusiveness. For that culture can only exist as a source for poetry and dance, for expressions of that elusive desire that cinema, as the art of the imaginary, always endorses. Without that cultural input Bollywood cannot be what it is; and yet the texts through which that culture is signified also exhausts that very culture, confining it in expressive terms, to just one form. When the form is reinterpreted through what Rajadhyaksha had called a "techno-realism," where the sites of the culture are "simulacrally" displaced,[13] as happens in the highly finessed 2006 remake of *Umrao Jaan*, then the legacy of the genre itself is strained, its centrality misplaced. Where Muzaffar Ali's *Umrao Jaan* made a statement about the necessity as well as the tragedy of the courtesan in Muslim high culture, the 2006 version (dir. J.P. Dutta) transforms her into a pious, uncontaminated figure of sentimental remorse, replacing in effect the character by the star Aishwarya Rai. We need to keep in mind the 1981 version so as to remember that to understand Bollywood the Muslim as expressed in the canonical genre is pivotal: it is the Muslim and her language and culture that has mediated what has come to be known as Bollywood.

The Hegemony of Melodrama

If Parsi theatre provided Bollywood with a narrative structure, a mode of representation, songs, dialogues, and a repertoire of cast, Hindu culture gave it a vast archive of myths about gods and man as well as key moral absolutes, Muslim culture provided poetry, a courtly language, and the figure of the dancer-courtesan, it was English/colonial melodrama, suitably indigenized with *rasas* (notably of love-longing and the tragic), which gave Bollywood its distinctive content. We can follow this through the singular achievement of *Devdas* (1935) and its later remakes. The person who was instrumental in creating the figure of the melodramatic hero was Pramathesh Chandra Barua (1903–1951), often referred to as Prince P.C. Barua, the son of a ruler of a tiny native state in Bengal-Assam.[14] However, given that his father was, in fact, nothing more than a large landowner, the title of prince was not a little misplaced. His life, though, was anything but simple, expressing a mixture of oedipal longings (he had his first solid food at the age of nine – one imagines he survived on nothing but milk up to this time!) and guilt. Aged 14 he married a girl of 11 (Madhurilata), had many unhappy affairs, married four times in all (the last remained secret to the end) and was struck by tuberculosis (seen then as very much the disease that affected artists, rich in a kind of Bloomsbury cultural excess). All these items added to his melodramatic persona and mystique. His visit to England in 1926 after his mother's death a year earlier was clearly a defining moment in sharpening his sense of exile, and released his nascent nationalism. A key motif in his films therefore became the idea of the journey, and here Saratchandra Chattopadhyay's (Chatterjee's) 1917 novel *Devdas*,[15] the film's source, was the perfect text as it provided Barua with key components of a distinctly Bollywood melodrama: the renouncer who cannot win his beloved; his tragic life; his escape from the world indicated through mis-en-scenes of drunkenness, the lonely train ride or the walk towards the horizon. *Devdas* and its remakes (Bimal Roy, 1955; Sanjay Leela Bhansali, 2003) established the melodramatic frames of reference within which Bollywood operates. Its tenacious grip on the form may be seen in Bhansali's *Saawariya* (2007).

Saawariya is based on Dostoevsky's sentimental romance "White Nights,"[16] a short story written in 1848, in which the hero, like Dostoevsky's criminal, takes upon himself the act of mourning, loss and melancholy which, in his absence, would have been borne by others. It follows, as Bakhtin suggests in another work, "that we might substitute for our own life an obsessive reading of novels, or dreams based on novelistic models (the hero of [Dostoevsky's] *White Nights*)."[17] The short story was made into a film by Luchino Visconti in 1957 (*Le Notti Bianche*) with Marcello Mastroianni and Maria Schell.[18] It is a film which provides Bhansali with a visual as well as an interpretative model with which both the narrative of the Dostoevsky original and the received Bollywood tradition of the sentimental romance are mediated.

Dostoevsky's "White Nights" tells the tale of a man aged 26 who falls in love with a woman over four nights and then loses her. It ends with the melodramatic hero's declaration of what can only be read as perverse gratitude:

> May your sky be always clear, may your dear smile be always bright and happy, and may you be forever blessed for that moment of bliss and happiness which you gave to another lonely and grateful heart!
> Good Lord, only a *moment* of bliss? Isn't such a moment sufficient for the whole of a man's life?[19]

The Bollywood spectator's memory takes him (the masculine gender is consciously used because of the paragraph's autobiographical subtext – visual pleasure here is masculine) back to what he may call the "Bollywood sentimental syntagm." He recalls his first moments of watching the Raj Kapoor films: *Aag* ("Fire," 1948), *Barsaat* ("Monsoon," 1949), *Awara* ("The Vagabond," 1951), *Aah* ("Sighs from the Heart," 1953), *Jagte Raho* ("Stay Awake!" 1956), even *Sangam* ("The Confluence," 1964). He thinks of *Devdas* (1935) and its remakes (1955, 2003); he thinks through what circulates in popular terminology as the *bicāra* complex (the hero who makes a virtue of self-pity[20]); he thinks of Dilip Kumar in *Andaz* ("Style," 1949) and *Deedar* ("Sight," 1951), Dev Anand in *Bambai Ka Babu* ("A Gentleman of Bombay," 1960), Guru Dutt in *Pyaasa* ("The Thirsty One," 1957) and *Kaagaz Ke Phool* ("Paper Flowers," 1959), Rajendra Kumar in *Dil Ek*

Mandir ("The Heart is a Temple," 1963) and *Sangam*, Rajesh Khanna in *Anand* (1970), and even Shah Rukh Khan in *Kal Ho Na Ho* ("Even if Tomorrow Never Comes," 2003). Like the unnamed hero of Dostoevsky, he sings songs from these films – zindā hūm is tarah ke game zindagī nahīm ("I live without living" (*Aag*)), chor gaye bālam ("My beloved has left me" ' (*Barsaat*)), ham tujh se muhabbat kar ke sanam ("Having fallen in love with you" (*Awara*)), huem ham jin ke liye barbād ("For whom I've sacrificed everything" (*Deedar*)), yād nā jāye bīte dinom kī ("It is hard to forget those once forgotten days" (*Dil Ek Mandir*)), dost dost nā rahā ("My friend you are no longer a friend" (*Sangam*)) – till his voice goes hoarse. He knows that this is what Bollywood romance is, and even when the ending is happy, which is true of most films, the path towards that moment of happiness is marked by a discourse of sentimentality, even if presented as tableaux. The auteur who looms large in this version of romance is Raj Kapoor (1924–1988). That filmic dominant, that history of romance and sentimentality, especially in the achievement of Raj Kapoor, find their most consummate and artistically most accomplished form in Bhansali's magnificent *Saawariya* (2007), a film which shows the artistic possibilities of the genre. Bhansali is no Dostoevsky (who can be?) but from him he learns how to construct an artistic monad out of the predictable genre of the sentimental romance. The form that he adopts though depends heavily on Visconti too as he creates a filmscape which is not grounded in any recognizable [Indian] geographical space. This space, like Visconti's, is "artificial and meant to be seen a such," evocative of the "*réalisme poétique* of Carné."[21] There is then a master text which carries the genius of Dostoevsky; but there is also Visconti's operatic melodramatic interpretation which is then fed into the major tradition of Bollywood itself as made exemplary in the early films of Raj Kapoor. The weight of the lineage is heavy and complex; it is to Sanjay Leela Bhansali's credit that he pulls it off.

Saawariya, released by Columbia Pictures (the first Bollywood film to be financed by Columbia Tristar Pictures), is memorially constructed but unlike "White Nights" not from the point of view of the unnamed hero. The narrator is in fact the courtesan Gulabji (Rani Mukherjee) whose first words make it clear that her tale is located in a city of dreams (khvābom ki ek śahar). The establishing shots reveal this city of dreams through a bluish-violet color palette, a digitally constructed city of canal, bridge, street and quadrangle. The bar in which this courtesan works has neon lights with the sign "RK." The homage to the great Bollywood auteur and actor Raj Kapoor is clear as is the presence of *Le Notti Bianche* where Visconti introduces the figure of the prostitute as a "permanent feature of the landscape"[22] and as a contrastive point of reference (although not as narrator) to the deeply confused and apparently hysterical Natalia (Natasha). Raj Kapoor, whose films changed the idea of the sentimental romance forever and whose title song (āvārā hūm) in the film *Awara* had a similar effect on film music, stands as the crucial reference point throughout the film. Like Visconti's studio set with its "Esso," "Farmacia," "Assic," "Sport Bar" signs, Bhansali's streets are lit up with neon signs with no other significance beyond an affirmation of the *réalisme poétique*: "Lilianjis," "Windermere," "Capitol," "Ace," "Old Town," "Clifton Hotel," "Sheskhomar,"

"Symphony," "Rockstar." There are pictures of the Mughal Queen Mumtaz in whose memory the Emperor Shah Jahan built the Taj Mahal; there is the muezzin's cry, "Allahu Akbar," and statues of gods replicating the trinity of gods captured in the dream sequence in the film *Awara* in which Nargis, Raj Kapoor's favorite actress, sings ghar āyā merā pardesī ("My long lost lover has come home"). The mise-en-scenes here are under strict directorial control so as to ensure that background and theme remain interwoven throughout.

Although there is a play with "double time," the film's internal time remains confined to a few days. It is in the RK Bar that Gulabji first meets the sentimental hero (Ranbir Kapoor) whose name (as he later tells his landlady Lilianji (Zohra Sehgal)) is Ranbir Raj, which, as any Bollywood spectator knows, are Raj Kapoor's first names.[23] He is also the wanderer of Visconti's *Le Notti Bianche*, and not the city-based hero of Dostoevsky. The homage therefore gets underway in the opening scenes: the name of the bar and the name of the person both are brought together. Like many of Raj Kapoor's own heroes, Ranbir Raj is a singer and a musician. Through Gulabji he gets a job in the bar where, as a trial run, he sings the first verse of the film's title song and then again, a little later, sings another song to the courtesans of this fantasy town. At Lilianji's he finds board after his characteristically excessive sentimental discourse persuades her that through him she could regain the spirit of her dead son Vincent and smile again. However, our hero is alone, and as Gulabji says, "he was ours but he had no one."

After the neon sign ("RK"), and the name ("Ranbir Raj"), comes the third crucial reference to the intertext: that evening, for so it seems, our hero sees a woman (Sonam Kapoor) with an umbrella. Behind the image stands another umbrella and a haunting song from Raj Kapoor's *Shree 420* (1955). In the latter scene Raj (Raj Kapoor) and Vidya (Nargis) share a cup of tea in the rain; they walk together alternately using an umbrella, and then, as common sense dawns on them, they share it. A musical note harkens towards Raj Kapoor's signature *rāg bhairavī* and the voices of Manna Dey (for once not Mukesh, Raj Kapoor's preferred background singer) and Lata Mangeshkar define the song pyār huā ikrār huā hai, pyār se phir kyūm dartā hai dil ("Love has blossomed, a confession made, then why is the heart so afraid of love?"). The rain continues to pour throughout the song sequence, a sequence which, alongside, Raj Kapoor's own āvārā hūm ("I am a vagabond") song (in *Awara*) and the hall of mirrors song pyār kiyā to darnā kyā ("Why be afraid when in love?") in *Mughal-e-Azam* ("The Great Mughal," 1960), has continued to define the Bollywood song and dance sequence.[24] We must pause to take in the first encounter between Raj and the woman. We may assume it is Dostoevsky's first white night. The woman with the umbrella is being hounded by hooligans; Raj offers to help but she says no. Her look, her momentary gaze, captivates Raj who breaks out into a song, māśā allāh ("My God, how extraordinary!"). During the song sequence (the third song in the film) we see the painting of the Mughal Queen, we see the girl running umbrella in hand, we see them both on a boat in the canal and we also see them against the backdrop of gods. As the song ends, he asks her if he could take her home. She hesitates, again says no, and

Understanding Bollywood 593

umbrella up, she walks on the bridge. The hooligans reappear, but so does our hero, and with each holding the folded umbrella at one end he takes her home. They jump over potholes. It continues to rain and they both come together under the one umbrella in a direct homage to the scene from Raj Kapoor's *Shree 420*. He writes down her name – Sakina, which means "tranquillity."[25] At Lilianji's, draped only in a towel, he sings his fourth song: "since our gaze met".

It is the second white night. Raj meets the girl again. He holds her hand and takes her to the top of a building from where they both see the simulacral city. A conversation ensues with snippets of dialogue from the scene in *Awara* between Rita (Nargis) and Raj (Raj Kapoor) before that memorable song: dam bhar jo udhar muh phere ("If only the moon could turn its face away for a moment"). The words of the dialogue in *Saawariya* (lafangā, āvārā bhī hūm, aur janglī bhī, aur buddhū bhī, " I am a braggart, a vagabond too," "And yes you are uncivilized, and stupid as well") replicate parts of the earlier dialogue, both in continued homage to the definitive auteur of romance and to the genre. He declares his love but she says she is waiting for someone else, a man called Imaan, whom she loves a lot. She tells her story in which a green color palette is also introduced. She lives with her blind grandmother (Begum Para) and their servant Jhumri. The blind grandmother ties the ends of her dress to her petticoat so that she is always there to talk and read to her. She ties Jhumri's skirt to her grandmother's and gets away at night. Financially stretched, the grandmother needs to keep a tenant and one rainy night a lodger arrives. He knocks, Sakina opens the door and sees a man in the rain who greets her with māśā allāh ("My God, how extraordinary!"). The lodger tells her grandmother that he drinks milk, not tea, in a direct echo of Raj's own first words to the barman at the RK Bar, "A glass of milk please?" She falls in love with the lodger and one night enters his room. Later the lodger takes the family to see a rerun of the classic *Mughal-e-Azam*, a film which like Visconti's grandmother character (who recalls snatches of the arias of Rossini's *Barber of Seville*), Sakina's grandmother too can memorially recall. Then, abruptly, he leaves promising to return. He gives her a coin as a token of remembrance. Her tale at an end, "The coin is fake; your tale untrue," says Raj. As Sakina and Raj stand together in the rain a drunken stranger comes along singing barsāt mem ham se mile tum sanam ("In monsoonal rain we meet my beloved") from Raj Kapoor's second film *Barsaat*. Raj feels as if she is falling in love with him and sings his fifth song, thorī badmāś ho tum, thorī nādān ho tum ("A little wicked are you, and a little innocent too"). The song complete he tells her that Imaan is not going to come. She then gives him a letter to deliver to Imaan and leaves him. Left alone on the bridge, letter in hand, Raj pauses to reflect. Then, abruptly, he burns the letter and drops it in the water. Later, in a scene dominated by the courtesans (which ends in a song, the sixth in the film, sung by them) Gulabji tells Raj to ask for Sakina's forgiveness for burning the letter.

The third white night – a boat, an umbrella, and a woman. Raj surveys the scene. Sakina walks on the bridge with her umbrella. The umbrella flies out, she calls, "Raj." Another scene intervenes: Raj dances and sings with the dervishes as Muslims await the new moon, marking the end of fasting. This, the seventh song, ends and by the bridge Sakina asks if Raj had received the reply to her letter. Instead of answering her, Raj again declares his love, saying he wants to marry her. These protestations Sakina treats as a joke.

The scene shifts to the RK Bar at which Sakina finally comes with him. This may be the fourth white night or the seamless merging of two nights into one. She stands up to leave and he sings the film's theme song, "sāvariyā," replicating Visconti's dramatic staging of a rock 'n' roll number in the café to which Mario brings a tense and hysterical Natalia. He thinks Sakina is his and he phones Lilianji (whom he calls Lillipop). However, as he phones, Sakina rushes out. "Forget him [Imaan]," cries Raj and adds, "I love you." She does not reply. Bereft of love, he seeks out Gulabji declaring to her that at least he can love her physically. At this Gulabji calls her pimps and he is beaten. Hurt, he makes his way to the bridge. There he tells Sakina that he had burnt the letter. She concedes that Imaan may not come and smiles when he asks if there is some room in her heart for him. Under the conspicuous RK neon sign they dance with the umbrella and reenact a classic Raj Kapoor-Nargis pose in the film *Barsaat* which, after that film, became the iconic emblem of the RK (Raj Kapoor) film. Snow begins to fall ("It's snowing, it's snowing," Mario and Natalia delightfully scream in Visconti's *Le Notti Bianche*); the color palette brings a dash of red to Sakina's clothes. The ninth song, jāne jā, is sung. The song ends, and they walk towards Lilianji's house. A bell tolls, she looks back and sees a man on the bridge. "He has come, I have to go," exclaims Sakina, "please forgive me, you understand?" He shakes his head. "A moment's love is enough," he says.[26] He holds the umbrella and gives the coin back to her. On the bridge Imaan gives a subtle hint about his life – quite possibly that of a Muslim terrorist – when he asks her, "Do you accept a painful life with me?" She nods and they walk away. A blue-grey color palette dominates as Raj watches and waves his bowler hat. He walks down an alleyway where the potholes are. He jumps over them, and picks up the anklet Sakina had dropped in one of them during their first meeting there. The umbrella opens up again.[27]

The Persistence of Song and Dance

Aishwarya Rai and Saif Ali Khan's Bollywood kitsch alluded to in the opening paragraph of this essay said something which is internal to the structure of Bollywood as a genre. For here, as in our exemplary melodramatic film *Saawariya*, song and dance constitute the indispensable ingredient of the film, and this structural universal of Bollywood is not to be confused with Hollywood-inspired musicals. Bollywood films are not musicals in the Western sense of the word. Bollywood is a multilayered, capacious genre which has grown out of prior similarly coded literary texts. The third-fourth century playwright Kalidasa's great dramatic fable *Śakuntalā* (primarily in Sanskrit) opens with its stage director (the sūtradhāra) uneasy about how the gathered audience would respond to the play that day.

He needs to distract them for a while and make them feel at ease. The lead actress asks, "what can we do to help?" to which the stage director replies:

kim anyat asyāh parisadah śruti pramodahetor imam nāticirapravrttam upabhoga ksamam grīsmakālam adhikrtya gīyatām tāvat[28]

What else, but sing about this recently arrived season of summer, the season of enjoyment. Yes, bring joy to the audience with a song.

The director goes on to suggest possible ways in which the song may be sung, and in particular ways which would bring metaphor and feeling together. Taking up the challenge (given in the latter part of the director's speech in poetic metre) the lead actress sings, not in Sanskrit but in Prakrit, that is, in the vernacular:

Sensitive women adorn their bodies
With mimosa flowers
Delicate filaments of which
Are kissed fleetingly by bees.

The director is ecstatic – "susthu gītam," "beautifully sung," he declares – and is so carried away that he forgets the name of the play which is to be staged.

Although I have referred to a text which predates Bollywood cinema by close to two millennia, the snatches of dialogue from *Śakuntalā* recalled above have a direct bearing on the role of song and dance in Bollywood cinema. It is clear that Kalidasa's song has a function in drama-as-performance and that its language, Prakrit, decouples the play from its patrician patrons who, one suspects, are the spectators referred to by the director and who speak Sanskrit. Love (both in separation and in union), seasons, desire within a predominantly pastoral/romantic discourse, are also the themes of the Bollywood song. Beyond its thematic specificity the Bollywood song in its poetic variety is grounded in Indian *ragas*, musical forms, or are variations on the dominant notes in any given *rāga*. Thus, while the song āvārā hūm is intrinsic to the film *Awara* it is also rendered in *raga bhairavī*, Raj Kapoor's signature *rāga* which marks key songs in all his major films. So zindā hūm is tarah ke game zindagī nahīm (*Barsaat*, 1949), āvārā hūm (*Awara*), rājā ki āyegī bārāt (*Aah*, 1953), merā jūtā hai jāpānī (*Shree 420*), merā nām rāju, (*Jis Desh Mem Ganga Behti Hai*, 1960) and dost dost nā rahā (*Sangam*, 1964) are all *rāga bhairavī*s, most of which are written by Shailendra, the perfect sentimental Bollywood lyricist. *Rāgas* constitute a parallel narrative (a narrative which may be constructed through moods rather than through actual narrative events) in all great Bollywood films including films such as *Baiju Bawra* (1952), *Mother India* and *Mughal-e-Azam*. More recently the use of *rāga bhairavī* by A.R. Rahman whenever he wants to return to an indigenous form (in songs such as rādhā kaise na jale in *Lagaan*, 2001 or jiyā jale jām jale naino tale in *Dil Se*, 1998) are important indices of the persistence of classical musical forms. So, the "dolā re dolā" song in Bhansali's *Devdas* is in fact a variation of *rāga hindola* (hence the play on the word dolā).

In their introduction to their book on Hindi song and dance in Bollywood, Gopal and Moorti note, "To talk of Bollywood is inevitably to talk of the song and dance sequence" which, they continue, is "the single most enduring feature of popular Hindi cinema."[29] This feature of Hindi cinema now occupies different contexts and has created hybrid musical forms such as the Trinidadian "chutney," the Greek "indoprepi," the Javanese "dangdut," ("a hybrid pop music extremely popular among the lower classes"[30]), the Nigerian "bandiri," among many other hybrid forms yet to find a distinct name. Yet, and very appropriately, Gopal and Moorti make it clear that the presence of song and dance as a structural universal (a deep structure) in Bollywood does not mean that Bollywood films are variations on the Western musical. Indeed the point of the volume is to demonstrate that Bollywood is a distinct genre which has its sub-generic forms such as the social, the mythological, the stunt, the romance and so on. Further, the circulation of song and dance and the capacity of spectators (and not necessarily just Indian spectators) to memorially reconstruct films through songs is a special feature of Bollywood. Song and dance in fact function as parallel texts of cinema for purposes of recall. Some of the classic films – *Awara, Mother India, Pyaasa, Kaagaz ke Phool* for instance – are in fact remembered through their songs. A song writer such as Shailendra becomes crucial for the success of Raj Kapoor's films, his lyrics becoming part of Bollywood romance.

Beyond the idea of a parallel text, the circulation of film songs through technological advances in the medium of transmission (from radio to iPod and the Internet), their varied reception in significant "circuits of globalization: metropolitan, diasporic and subaltern,"[31] and, within India, their role as a form that dilutes "ethnocentrism," are other important features of this cinema.

The commercial success of film songs by and large depended on the success of the parent film although it must be conceded as well that films without great songs were, as a general rule, never successful. Hence among the great auteurs – Mehboob Khan, Raj Kapoor and Guru Dutt – songs were part of the success of their films, be they *Andaz* (1949) and *Mother India* (1957) (Mehboob Khan), *Awaara* (1951) and *Shree 420* (1955) (Raj Kapoor) or *Mr and Mrs 55* (1955) and *Pyaasa* (1957) (Guru Dutt). Since India does not have a separate equally vibrant independent popular song industry, film songs have traditionally occupied that role and became a form which changed styles in line with western popular taste in songs. This being so, for a while Radio Ceylon's Binaca Geetmala program which played Hindi film songs when the latter were banned from the All India National Radio Program was the rage in the 1950s. (Dr Balkrishna Vishwanath Keskar, Minister of Information and Broadcasting in the first Nehru Government, called filmgit or film song fit for no one but "raw and immature people like children and adolescents"[32]). These were precassette and CD days; in recent years the picture is very different and the circulation and reception of film songs are not linked to radio or indeed television. They have a different value as a commodity which can be packaged, easily disseminated, copied, and endlessly replayed. Technology creates new forms of social relations outside of the dominant ideologies of the nation state.

The success did not come early as film song struggled against tremendous odds to establish its legitimacy as a key cultural artefact. In spite of colonial denigration

Understanding Bollywood 597

and postcolonial cringe, the form nevertheless grew in strength and was embraced by some of India's finest Urdu-Hindi poets (Sahir Ludhianvi, Shailendra), musicians (Timir Boran, O.P. Nayyar, A.R. Rahman) and singers (K.L. Saigal, Mohammad Rafi, Lata Mangeshkar, Kishore Kumar, Mukesh).

"At what point do the musical insertions stop being complimentary spectacles and assume a life of their own, and begin to destroy a basic integrity of storytelling," is the question asked by Anustup Basu.[33] Would it not follow that such an assertion privileges realistic narrative over the pageant, the carnival and the like? Basu reads film song as a free market commodity, free-floating, eccentric, and eminently consumable. He calls it the logic of "geotelevisual" production which "dis-locates" performance and places it in a transnational idiom. This disjunctive, nonnarratological relation of event to dominant text often without any anchoring (the song and dance can be located in variable global centers) thus points to an alternative worlding, one which is not located in an identifiable archival memory but works through modern technology towards an alternative, global aesthetic which in turn functions as both texts within discrete filmic narratives and as autonomous moments with their own logic.

In the Indian diaspora, film song and dance sequence function as a form of cultural memory, bringing India's heterogeneous communities together. Song and dance function as transferable cultural capital which the diaspora can then declare as its own. Filmgit or film songs make their way into American hip-hop and other popular genres. There is, however, another side to this consumption which E.K. Chan has referred to as the "dirty pleasures" of the film song and of Bollywood generally.[34] Thinking through the reception of the film song not by the diaspora but by NBCs ("nontraditional Bollywood consumers"), Chan argues that the songs "promote a kitchy 'otherworldliness.'" They are outlandish, excessive, and an example of "exotic kitschification" (recall Shah Rukh Khan's rendition of Roy Orbison's "Oh, Pretty Woman" in *Kal Ho Naa Ho*, 2003), because in the absence of an "abstract" (in effect essential or metaphysical) negotiation of the film song, an NBC's consumption of it will always be "dirty." The liberal imagination wants us to enter into the song's "abstraction"; the reality is that Bollywood songs as consumed by the NBCs are marked by an excess – a lurid, extravagant delight in its form, indeed a different mode of consumption which is akin to Chan's appropriation of Vivan Sobchack's cinesthetic film theory in which he spoke about "bodies not merely objectively beheld but subjectively lived."[35] An NBC's subjective living of the film-song body creates an excess, a stain in the diaspora's own response to it.[36]

Conclusion: *Gumrah* (1963)

The first frame of *Gumrah*, B.R. Chopra, the producer's logo, carries a voice over which repeats the great Hindu religious text's one-verse manifesto (*Bhagavadgītā* 2.47): karmanyevādhikāraste mā phaleṣu kadācana ("Your entitlement or duty is to the act itself, never to its fruits"). The directive is clear – your life is meaningful in terms of the purity of action, not its consequences – and the film, although modern and secular in its theme, must be read as an allegory of the failure to uphold this directive. Should the sonority of the Sanskrit verse (which is not translated either through subsequent voice-over or subtitle) be missed by the spectator, the film's next frames are scenes from the *Rāmāyana* which deal in quick succession and in the style of Mughal miniatures, with Sītā's request to Rāma for the skin of the golden deer, Rāma's seeming death-cry for help, and Laksman's departure from their hut upon Sītā's insistence that he does so to help Rāma. Before he leaves he draws a line in front of the hermitage with an arrow and tells Sītā not to cross it under any circumstance. The line is known as *laksman rekhā* ("Laksman's line") which, as we know, Sītā does cross when Rāvana arrives in the guise of an itinerant *sādhu* to abduct her. The scenes at an end, the voice-over now declares the moral: aurat kā suhāg isī ke andar hai ("A woman's state of wifehood, her married bliss, is contained within this line"). The film, as the voice-over makes even clearer, will allegorize the moral: isī tarah kī lakīr kī kahānī yah hai ("This is a tale of a similar *laksman rekhā*"). For a woman there is always a *laksman rekhā* which she must never cross. Invoked through a graphic citation from a religious text, the obvious patriarchal underpinning of the *laksman rekhā* (the act of female containment) is seemingly erased as what emerges is a larger principle of *dharma* rather than patriarchal control mechanism. The film *Gumrah*, which confronts head-on both premarital sex and postmarital affair, and is in this respect quite radical, must address these transgressions in the context of the eternal *dharma* which, momentarily, even divine Sītā transgresses. In the end, in spite of Sītā's innocence, she pays a mighty price for her error as upon her return to Ayodhya, the vox populi is so rigidly moralistic that she has to be banished yet again. In *Gumrah* the husband, Ashok (Ashok Kumar), does not follow the path of Lord Rāma although Meena (Mala Sinha) continues her affair with her lover Rajendra (Sunil Dutt) even after her marriage. The scenes themselves produce one of the finest songs of forlorn love in Bollywood cinema: calo ik bār phir se ajnabī ban jāye ham dono ("once again let us, you and I, become strangers to one another"). Modernity now recodes Sītā's transgression through a post-Enlightenment narrative of lost love and forgiveness.

I conclude this chapter with a reference to a film from Bollywood's realist period to establish a more general principle about the nature of this cinema and our understanding of it. What the film does is bring together the various strands of Bollywood. The reference to *dharma*, the eternal law that governs Hindu society, takes us back to the beginnings of Indian cinema since the principle governed all the mythologicals, beginning with Phale's *Raja Harishchandra*. The use of high Urdu poetry for the songs – āp āye to khayāle dile nāsād āyā ("beautiful thoughts arise when you come") and calo ik bār phir se ajnabī ban jāye ham dono – affirms the tenacity of Muslim influences on this form, as well as shows the link between film and song in Bollywood, reinforcing the point made earlier that for a long time great Bollywood films were also the ones with immensely catchy and highly poetic songs. Finally even duty or *dharma* cannot exist outside of melodrama. So Meena must sacrifice her love for Rajendra and marry her brother-in-law Ashok because she finds it hard to let go of her nephew and niece upon the death of her sister Shanti. The seeds of the sacrifice are fed to her by her own father who points out the evils of a

Understanding Bollywood

step-mother and the subsequent loss of his grandchildren should Ashok remarry someone other than a family member. In this respect, like much else in Bollywood, the mythological included, the genre of melodrama underpins the form and the form cannot be any other. Audience reception, the corner stone of rasa aesthetics, is built around intense moments of melodramatic dialogue. *Gumrah* too is not free from the power of genre.

However, in as much as *Gumrah* enters into a difficult arena of sexual politics and explores it even when its answers do not question the eternal norms of *dharma*, the film points to the role of Bollywood as the site where ethical issues are debated. Slavoj Žižek referred to the Eastern sublime as offering "a useless solution to a real problem" whereas the Western sublime offered a "practical solution to a problem that does not arise."[37] The ethical questions raised by *Gumrah* are a "real problem" in Indian culture; the solution offered is a useless solution in that it simply reinforces the sanctity of eternal *dharma* and not the power of desire. Although Bollywood cinema now circulates as more than just culture-specific texts consumed by people who know it as one single interconnected text, one can therefore conclude by saying, with Žižek, that in the end Bollywood too offers no practical solutions to real problems. The verities of the mythological, suggestively encased in melodrama and poetically suffused with Urdu lyrics, it seems, remain intact. Bollywood triumphs over social reality.

Notes

The names of Bollywood films and proper names generally in this essay are given in the film industry's own romanized forms. In places this chapter draws on essays published in *The Sage Book of Film Studies*, 2008; *Textual Practice*, 2009; *Postcolonial Studies*, 2009; and *Brill's Encyclopædia of Hinduism, II*, 2010.

1   Eliade (1987, p. 11).
2   Otto (1977).
3   The classic study of the renouncer and the man-in-the world in Hindu culture is Louis Dumont (1960).
4   Rushdie (1988, p. 16).
5   Dwyer (2006, pp. 94–95).
6   Tulsīdās (1947).
7   Das (1981, pp. 43–56).
8   Munz (1970, pp. 188–199).
9   Sukhantar (1942, pp. 549–553); Brodbeck, (2006, pp. 1–34).
10 Kosambi (2005, pp. 248–275).
11 Georg Lukács (1971).
12 The granting of a boon, even at the expense of great personal loss, has its textual antecedent in the *Rāmāyana* where King Dasaratha gives his kingdom to Prince Bharata and banishes his eldest son and heir to the throne Rama because Keikeyi, mother of Prince Bharata and the king's youngest wife, demanded that boons given her by the King must be honored.
13 Rajadhyaksha (2003, pp. 25–39).

14 Nandy (2001).
15 Saratchandra Chattopadhyay (1876–1938) was alive when P.C. Barua made both the Bengali and Hindi versions in 1935. The moment of *Devdas* also signals Bollywood's debt to the realist-sentimental novel. Indeed what Barua did was bring Sarachandra Chattopadhyay's novel, a colonial literary form, self-evidently bourgeois, and different from the texts of Parsi theatre, into cinema.
16 Dostoevsky (1968).
17 Bakhtin (1987, p. 32).
18 Visconti (1970).
19 Dostoevsky (1968, p. 201).
20 Mishra (2002, pp. 6–7).
21 Nowell-Smith (1973, p.122).
22 Nowell-Smith (1973, p.128)
23 In real life Ranbir Kapoor is the auteur Raj Kapoor's grandson. His father Rishi Kapoor is Raj Kapoor's second son.
24 Recall the jānam dekh lo mit gayī dūriydā m ("Beloved, see our separation has gone") song in the film *Veer Zaara* (dir. Yash Chopra, 2004). This song, which constructs a fantasy around an impossible love, also ends in the rain.
25 See Dawood (1999, p. 248): "Therein shall be tranquillity from your Lord." Dawood footnotes "tranquillity" as follows (p. 36): "This is the meaning of the Arabic word *sakīnah*, which, however, may well be related to [the Hebrew word] *shekhīnah* (the Holy Presence) in the Old Testament."
26 The dialogue echoes Visconti: "Try to forgive me" (Natalia) … "Go to him, God bless you for the moment of happiness you've given me" (Mario).
27 In Visconti Mario gathers his disheveled coat, shakes it, puts it on his shoulder and walks slowly. A stray dog (seen earlier in the film) comes to him. Mario continues walking, followed by the dog.
28 Kālidāsa (2006, p. 52).
29 Gopal and Moorti (2008, p. 1).
30 Gopal and Moorti (2008, p. 179).
31 Gopal and Moorti (2008, p. 7).
32 Gopal and Moorti (2008, p. 90).
33 Gopal and Moorti (2008, p. 153).
34 Gopal and Moorti (2008, p. 279).
35 Gopal and Moorti (2008, p. 284).
36 The excess, the kitsch that Chan writes about finds a place in queer readings of film song, especially among the queer Indian ("desi") diaspora. This is the point made by Rajinder Dudrah's essay on gender and sexuality in Bollywood films ("Queer as Desis") in the Gopal and Moorti (2008, pp. 288–307). Dudrah examines, very smartly, the ways in which the Bollywood aesthetic is appropriated by queer desis, and indeed how seemingly heteronormative representation gets reinflected towards queer aesthetics. The point is also made that in India itself, cinema halls patronized primarily by men, constitute a darkened space for homoerotic desires. The "new libidinal possibilities" of Bollywood, often implicit in the common Bollywood buddy semantics of *yaar* and *dosti* (friendship) and parodied in *Kal Ho Na Ho*, relocate desire and redefine the erstwhile heterosexual reception of the form.
37 Žižek (2002, p. cvii, n. 124).

References

Bakhtin, M.M. (1987) *The Dialogic Imagination*, (ed. M. Holquist, trans. C. Emerson and M. Holquist), University of Texas Press, Austin.

Brodbeck, S. (2006) Ekalavya and *Mahābhārata* 1.121–28, *Hindu Studies*, 10, 1–34.

Das, V. (1981) The mythological film and its framework of meaning: An analysis of *Jai Santoshi Ma*. *India International Centre Quarterly*, 8 (1), 43–56.

Dawood, N.J. (trans.) (1999) *The Koran*, Penguin, Harmondsworth.

Dostoevsky, F. (1968) White nights, in *Great Stories of Fyodor Dostoevsky*, (trans. D. Magarshack), Harper & Row, New York, pp. 145–201.

Dumont, L. (1960) World renunciation in Indian religions. *Contributions to Indian Sociology*, 4, 33–62.

Dwyer, R. (2006) *Filming the Gods: Religion and Indian Cinema*, Routledge, London and New York.

Eliade, M. (1987) *The Sacred and the Profane: The Nature of Religion*, (trans. W.R. Trask), Harcourt Inc, New York.

Gopal S., and Moorti, S. (eds) (2008) *Global Bollywood: Travels of Hindi Song and Dance*, University of Minnesota Press, Minneapolis.

Kālidāsa (2006) *The Recognition of Shakúntala*, (ed. and trans. S. Vasudeva), New York University Press, New York.

Kosambi, D.D. (2005) *Combined Methods in Indology and Other Writings*, (ed. B. Chattopadhyaya), Oxford University Press, Delhi.

Lukács, G. (1971) *The Theory of the Novel*, (trans. A. Bostock), Merlin, London.

Mishra, V. (2002) *Bollywood Cinema: Temples of Desire*, Routledge, New York and London.

Munz, P. (1970) India: Homo hierarchicus or generalised exchange of souls, *Pacific Viewpoint*, 11 (2), 188–199.

Nandy, A. (2001) Invitation to an antique death: The journey of Pramathesh Barua as the origin of the terribly effeminate, maudlin, and self-destructive heroes of Indian cinema, in *Pleasure and the Nation: The History, Politics and Consumption of Public Culture in India*, (eds. R. Dwyer and C. Pinney), Oxford University Press, Delhi, pp. 139–160.

Nowell-Smith, G. (1973) *Visconti*, Viking Press, New York.

Otto, R. (1977) *The Idea of the Holy*, (trans. J.W. Harvey), Oxford University Press, New York.

Rajadhyaksha, A. (2003) The "Bollywoodization" of the Indian Cinema: Cultural Nationalism in the Global Arena. *Inter-Asia Cultural Studies*, 4, 25–39.

Rushdie, S. (1988) *The Satanic Verses*, Viking, London.

Sukhantar, V.S. (ed.) (1942) *The Mahābhārata*, vol. 1, *ādiparvan*. Bhandarkar Oriental Research Institute Poona, 1942, pp. 549–53 (1. 123: 1–39).

Tulsīdās (1947) *Rāmcaritamānas*, Gita Press, Gorakhpur.

Visconti, L. (1970) *Three Screenplays: White Nights, Rocco and His Brothers, The Job*, (trans. J. Green), Orion Press, New York.

Žižek, S. (2002) *For They Know not What They Do: Enjoyment as a Political Factor*, Verso, London.

32

Peace Communication in Sudan
Toward Infusing a New Islamic Perspective

Haydar Badawi Sadig and Hala Asmina Guta

Introduction

On March 31, 2009, addressing the Sudanese expatriates in Doha, Qatar, Omer Hassan Al-Bashir, the president of Sudan, enumerated his grievances with the West in general, and the United States in particular. He condemned the United States for the Native American "genocide." He also talked about US atrocities committed in Iraq, "based on a lie," he said. Then he went on to say that the Sudan government ordered the Ambassador of "Great Britain" out of the country.

The use of the word "genocide" is of special significance here because Al-Bashir stands accused of crimes of war and crimes against humanity by the International Criminal Court (ICC). (Neither the United Sates nor Sudan are signatories to the ICC.) In essence, Al-Bashir was saying that countries which have "concocted" allegations against him have their own crimes to contend with. Hence, they should mind their own business and leave Sudan alone.

The use of the empire name "Great Britain" also has great rhetorical significance because the British colonized Sudan from 1898 to 1956. Thus, kicking the ambassador of "Great Britain" out of Khartoum touches a special patriotic nerve, which conveys a special meaning to the ears of his Sudanese and Arab audiences in Doha – where Al-Bashir was visiting – and elsewhere in the Muslim world.

Al-Bashir read many verses of Qur'an to support his arguments, insisting that controlling Sudan's resources and wealth are the reasons why his country is targeted by hegemonic powers led by the United States. He claimed that Sudan is poised to become a "super power" with the help of its friends. This implies China's partnership in development projects, including its oil industry and dam construction. This, he insisted, is the reason why the country is being targeted, through its leadership.

The Handbook of Global Communication and Media Ethics, First Edition. Edited by Robert S. Fortner and P. Mark Fackler.
© 2011 Blackwell Publishing Ltd. Published 2011 by Blackwell Publishing Ltd.

Al-Bashir was speaking passionately, feverishly, and very loudly while the crowd cheered "Alahu Akbar" (God is Greatest) between statements. He himself used the cheer "Alahu Akbar," as he always does, to conclude his very emotionally charged address. Shortly before he spoke, Sami Al-Haj, one of the Guantanamo Bay prisoners (released in 2008) presented him with a symbolic shield plaque.

Mr. Al-Haj is a journalist with al-Jazeera, which is a globally far reaching TV channel, dubbed the "CNN of the Arab World." Based in Doha, Qatar, al-Jazeera is seen by many as the main conduit of Osama bin Laden's mediated terror to the world. Mr. Al-Haj was a terrorism suspect who spent more than 5 years in Guantanamo Bay before being released under special conditions irrelevant to this essay.

Variations of this scenario have been a staple of Sudan government rhetoric since June 30, 1989, the day general Omer Al-Bashir overthrew the democratically elected government of Sudan in a bloodless coup. The blood flowed in streams thereafter. Claiming to be mandated to rule in God's name, Al-Bashir, together with Hassan Al-Turabi, the ideologue of "Thawart Al-Ingaz" (Salvation Revolution), ruled with an iron fist. By many estimates, more than 2 million people perished. More than 6 million were displaced, and since then millions more continue to be oppressed, by various means. The latest manifestation of the continuing unspeakable suffering of Sudan conflicts is the Darfur crisis.

The Sudan is not alone in this regard. According to Stockholm International Peace Research Institute (SIPRI), as of 2008, 16 major armed conflicts were active in 15 locations around the world, 2 more than in 2007. Major breakthroughs have been made in the world's most intractable conflicts, like Sudan's, Comprehensive Peace Agreement (CPA), which was signed in 2005. Yet signing a peace agreement is but a first step in a long journey toward sustained peace.

An alarming fact is that 31% of the civil wars in the world resume within the 10 years of the end of the conflict. This makes the quest for sustainable peace – not just the absence of war – more pressing (Bigombe, Collier, and Sambanis, 2000, p. 323). While peace agreements bring violent conflicts to an end, sustainable peace needs more than ceasefire. Achieving sustainable peace requires changing hearts and minds. Peace communication lends itself well to such a noble mission. The Sudan is not alone in its urgent need for deliberate and well attuned peace communication, but it is unique in that the National Congress Party (NCP), the party that has the upper hand in power today, claims to have a mandate from Allah (i.e., from God) to rule the Sudanese!

The purpose of this essay is twofold: (1) to situate conflicts of the current Sudan within global peace communication literature and (2) to introduce a unique Sudanese Islamic reformist perspective, in hopes of enriching the literature concerning global ethics of peace communication.

We shall be looking at this reformist perspective within the confines of Sudan's current affairs. By the end, however, we hope, readers will realize that the situation in Sudan has huge implications for other parts of the world. This realization will help in advancing our understanding of terrorism as a product of festering fanaticism. This, in turn, may help us point in new directions for how to tackle terrorism the world over, intelligently, not impulsively, as we do today.

We shall start with basic concepts in peace studies, then media effects research. Finally we shall return to the Sudan case. We believe that the dynamism in the Sudan situation, despite all its complexities – perhaps because of them – offers the world a rare opportunity to rethink how to reengage the Islamic world anew in a shared global project of peace communication.

Hanged While Smiling

On January 18, 1985, the Sudanese government executed Al-Ustadh Mahmoud Mohammed Taha, founder of the reformist Islamic group, The Republican Brothers. All the Republicans, men and women alike, consequently, endured tremendous emotional torture, physical displacements, alienation, humiliation, and unspeakable pain. The single exhibit before the judge who convicted Al-Ustadh was a leaflet (see later). In announcing his decision to boycott the proceedings, Al-Ustadh Mahmoud provided a strong statement which was translated by An-Na'im (Taha, 1987, p. 14):

> I have repeatedly declared my view that the September 1983 so-called Islamic laws violate Islam itself. Moreover, these laws have distorted Islamic Shari'a and projected it in a repugnant way. Furthermore, these laws were enacted and utilized by the government to terrorize the Sudanese people and humiliate them into submission. These laws also threaten the national unity of the country by discriminating against the non-Muslim segment of our society.
>
> This is my objection to these laws at the theoretical level. At the practical level, the judges enforcing these laws lack the necessary professional qualifications. They have also failed morally when they placed themselves under the control of the executive authority, which used them to violate people's rights, to humiliate political opponents, and to insult intellect and intellectuals. For all these reasons, I am not prepared to cooperate with any court that had betrayed the independence of the judiciary and allowed itself to be a tool in the hand of the government to humiliate our people, insult thinkers and free thought, and persecute political opponents.

Shortly after the execution of Al-Ustadh, trade unions and some political organizations rallied the country into a huge rage against Islamic fundamentalism. The outrage resulted in a full-scale uprising that, in turn, resulted in the overthrow of the dictatorship on April 6, 1985. A transitional military government took over to arrange for elections. One year later, there was an elected civilian government ruling the country.

Republicans jubilantly started to regroup and collect their shattered lives. Most were professionals, doctors, university professors, lawyers, teachers, diplomats, and college students. Many had a sense that their days of misery were over, but it did not last long. In less than four years, fanaticism returned. The elected government was overthrown by a military coup, this time with a vengeance and an added dose of fanaticism and rage. The totalitarian junta, steered by civilian fanatic Islamic ideologues, ruled with an iron fist, and the result was cultural, structural, and direct violence (Galtung, 1990).

As mentioned earlier, it was under Al-Bashir's watchful eye and protection that the lord of terror, Osama bin Laden, found refuge and sanctuary in Sudan before leaving for Afghanistan. Since then, Islamic fundamentalists have wreaked havoc in Sudan, other areas in the Middle East and North Africa, and the world. Now, without a doubt, they have the initiative in shaping international politics. This is why tackling this issue from a peace communication perspective is urgent.

Why Peace Communication?

When a peace agreement is signed, the disputants declare the end of violent exchanges. Broom and Hatay (2006) stated that conflicts, even after resolution through political peace agreements, leave societies suffering from distrust, trauma, and grievances that last long after conflict resolution and can be transmitted through generations. Therefore, reversing these adverse consequences needs more than political agreements. It needs social change and interaction through sustained good-faith and goodwill communication.

When you add Al-Bashir's retrieval of historic and current grievances with the West to the present disputants' mistrust of each other, you get an even muddier scene. By confronting the West and by using religious discourse, Al-Bashir is blatantly saying that the Sudanese and all Muslims are victims because of who they are – Muslims – and because their old oppressors want to conquer their land and exploit it again!

Mass communication has long been used to bring about desirable changes in communities. However, it is equally effectively manipulated by the elites in power to augment their standing and continued control of the message and the political scene at large. Such is the situation in Sudan today, where the NCP has a firm grip on national broadcasting media, and which until recently heavily censored print media.

In conflict situations change agents need communication media to intervene as conduits of paradigmatic shifts and transformation. The field of peace communication promises to provide a platform through which strategic help could be offered to such agents of change. Due to its interdisciplinary nature, this field brings rich resources from peace and communication studies as well as from conflict management and resolution literature. New paradigms of peace communication to help forge sustainable peace are certainly overdue.

Peace and Conflict Studies

Although violence and violent conflicts have characterized human history, it is not until the late-1950s that peace studies emerged as a cohesive academic discipline. Even today, there is no universally accepted concept of what encompasses peace studies. Analysis of the literature on peace and conflict studies reveals that these two contradictory terms, peace and conflict, have always been linked together in research.

Moreover, peace has often been defined by studying its binary opposite: conflict. The field of peace and conflict studies is a product of the field of conflict resolution, which gained momentum at the height of the Cold War in the 1950s and 1960s (Miall, Ramsbotham, and Woodhouse, 1999; Okoth, 2008). Peace studies can be traced back to the work of Quincy Wright and Lewis Richardson in the early-1940s. During this early phase, peace was thought of as the absence of war. Thus, peace research focused on the struggle of power among nationstates and suggested that this power struggle is the main cause of wars. Wright and Richardson introduced a new perspective that conceptualizes peace as a balance of forces in the international system (Beer, 2001; Elias and Turpin, 1994; Groff and Smoker, 1996).

Later in the 1960s, Galtung (1969) introduced the concept of "positive peace." Galtung identifies two concepts of peace, "negative" and "positive" peace. Negative peace is defined as simply the absence of violence. Positive peace, on the other hand, aims at achieving the ideal of general and complete peace (GCP), a state of *pax omnium cum omnibus* (everyone loves everyone) will be the rule, explains Galtung (1964). These two concepts of peace greatly influenced theorizing about peace and what has encompassed peace studies.

This new perspective of peace broadened peace studies from just studying war to studying other causes of violence including all forms of injustice. This period witnessed the rise of civil rights as well as feminist movements which produced new perspectives about issues of peace and conflict. The new perspective extends the concept of negative peace and positive peace to include not only the macro and international levels but also the microlevel of individual relationships (Bratic, 2005; Elias and Turpin, 1994; Galtung, 1964, 1969, 1990; Groff and Smoker, 1996).

These shifts in the theorizing of peace and war are accompanied, as Alger (1994) notes, by three fundamental transformations in peace thinking: The first transformation is the broadness of the definition of peace, as reflected in the United Nations Declaration on the Preparation of Societies for Life in Peace, of 1978. Peace is no longer defined as the absence of violence, but rather includes addressing structural inequalities, as well as cultural and global threats to our social fabric and natural environment, among others. This transformation in the definition of peace was accompanied, as a consequence, by the recognition of the role of grassroots peace building.

Since peace has not hereby been limited to the absence of violent conflict or the binary opposite of war, peace is no longer perceived as a leaders-only business. The third transformation is the perception of "peace as unfolding from the pursuit of peace" (Alger, 1994, p. 283). Peace is no longer a means to an end; it is an end in itself. In other words, "there is no way to peace, peace is the way."

These transformations are demonstrated in the new directions of peace movements, both in the developed and developing world. As Alger (1994) notices, "in building coalitions … the peace movement has broadened itself to economic issues such as jobs for peace and military conversion" (p. 283). As a response to these perspectives, emphasis was put on peace education. As a result, peace research centers were formed in the United States, Japan, and Latin America as well as Europe (Elias and Turpin, 1994).

In the 1980s, with the nuclear power race, peace studies programs witnessed a surge in interest as concern grew for the fate of the planet. Peace and antinuclear and disarmament movements emerged. Conflict resolution and mediation gained popularity. Research on nonviolent approaches to conflict management was undertaken (Elias and Turpin, 1994). After the end of the Cold War, the focus on war and peace studies shifted from an international dimension to internal power structures, or what is known as the domestic regime effect, and the democratic peace hypothesis emerged.

According to the democratic peace hypothesis, democratic governments are less likely to go to war with each other, although they may continue to engage in conflicts with more authoritarian regimes. The hypothesis suggests that there is a strong link between democracy and peace (Beer, 2001). Accordingly, peace research embraces issues of democratization, social justice, economic development, and human rights, as well as the traditional political science and international relations fields.

Another transformation in the thinking about peace and conflict is what Galtung (1964, 1990, 1996) calls the triangle of violence. Galtung (1990) introduced three concepts of violence: direct violence, structural violence, and cultural violence. Direct violence can be thought of as the physical act of violence, while structural violence is the type of violence that results from social injustices. Cultural violence can be attributed to:

> Those aspects of culture, the symbolic sphere of our existence – exemplified by religion and ideology, language and art, empirical science and formal science (logic, mathematics) – that can be used to justify or legitimize direct or structural violence. Stars, crosses and crescents; flags, anthems and military parades; the ubiquitous portrait of the Leader; inflammatory speeches and posters (p. 1).

In general, the three levels of violence (direct, structural, and cultural) are connected. Violence, as Galtung (1990) explains, can start from any corner of this triangle: "The underlying assumption is simple 'violence breeds violence'" (p. 295). If society starts with cultural violence that preaches, teaches, and legitimizes structural violence, injustices would be seen as normal conditions in "every" society. This, in turn, results in direct violence either from the oppressed rejecting oppression or counter violence from the oppressor. Therefore, the violence from the oppressor and the counter violence from the oppressed intensify as a result of the dehumanization stemming from cultural and structural violence. On the other hand, direct violence leads to poverty and displacement, resulting in structural violence. Direct violence, according to Galtung (1990), "is an event, structural violence is a process and cultural violence is an invariant 'permanence'" (p. 294).

Galtung's concept of peace and violence goes beyond scholarly theorizations that conceptualize peace as "international peace" to encompass broader dimensions of peace. This trend started with the rise of civil rights and feminist movements in the West and with struggle for freedom in the global South. What also contributed to the broadening of the discipline is that this concept of peace allows us to understand peace on both macro and micro levels. It provides an opportunity for multiple levels of analysis, starting from interstate relations to the family level.

To change the vicious triangle of violence, we need to work with a virtuous triangle of peace. "This virtuous triangle," argues Galtung (1990), "would be obtained by working on all three corners at the same time, not assuming that basic change in one will automatically lead to change in the other two" (p. 302).

While political negotiation deals with direct violence and policies deal with structural injustices, addressing "cultural violence requires attitude change" (Bratic, 2005, p. 68). Broom and Hatay (2006) discuss how conflicts, even after resolution through political peace agreements and ending of direct violence, leave societies suffering from distrust, trauma, and grievance that last long after conflict resolutions and can be transmitted through generations.

Conflicts, especially those along ethnic and religious lines, can deeply affect cultural norms and profoundly divide societies, creating vicious cycles of cultural, structural, and direct violence. Cultural violence creates negative interdependence, whereby each party sees the elimination of the other as a prerequisite of its own survival. Conflicts create a state of polarization in the affected society that may lead to a physical separation. When considering the effects of conflict, it is essential to address that polarization and distrust among conflicting parties.

Peace and Media Effects Research

In conflict situations, media institutions can be manipulated to perpetuate cultural violence. On the other hand, they can also be used to promote cultural peace. The relationship between communication (especially mass media) and peace is well articulated in the UNESCO constitution, which reads, "since wars begin in the minds of men, it is in the minds of men that the defenses of peace must be constructed." Media represents one of the most important sources of information that help people understand the world around them. Media influence in the political sphere has been an enduring field of research (Downing, 1996; McQuail, 1994). As argued by McQuail (1994), "the entire study of mass communication is based on the premises that the media have significant effects" (p. 327).

The mass media role in inciting and escalating violence has been the subject of numerous studies in the field of mass communications (Allan and Seaton, 1999; Seib, 2005). The case of the hate radio station Radio-Television Libre de Mille Collines that fueled the genocide in Rwanda in 1994, is one illustration of the role of media as provocateur in conflict situations (Kellow and Steeves, 1998). Since many scholars have concluded that media can incite conflict, it is then logical to assume that media can influence peace building as well. Media can be a double-edged sword in the context of peace and conflict, argues Hattotuwa (2002):

> The media can emphasize the benefits that peace can bring, they can raise the legitimacy of groups or leaders working for peace, and they can help transform images

of the enemy. However, the media can also serve as destructive agents in a peace process and can choose to negatively report on the risks and dangers associated with compromise, raise the legitimacy of those opposed to concessions, and reinforce negative stereotypes of the enemy (p. 1).

However, the nature and the extent of mass media effects on audiences are still matters of debate among scholars. As a result of this debate, varieties of approaches and theoretical frameworks have been adopted in communication research to explore mass media influence on society and audiences.

Historically, media effects research has witnessed significant changes. These changes are basically due to developments in the field of mass communication research. As argued by Bryant and Miron (2004), these changes are tied to rapid transformations in media content, ownership patterns, as well as in media technologies. On the other hand, there are also major changes in the social, economic, and political spheres, globally. All these changes contribute to growing and significant changes in mass communication research.

McQuail (1994) argues that the history of mass communication research can be divided into four broad phases. The first phase started after the end of World War I. After the war, attention was drawn to the role of media in war propaganda. A book by Lasswell entitled *Propaganda Technique in the World War* was considered the beginning of systematic research on media effects (Mattelart and Mattelart, 1998). During that period, research was dominated by positivist approaches that sought to understand social phenomena through "objective," "value free," and "scientific" empirical inquiry. Primarily drawing on social psychology and psychology traditions, media effects models such as the magic bullet theory were developed. The magic bullet theory (also known as hypodermic needle theory) proposed that media are immensely powerful and have strong and direct effects in shaping public opinions. The strong effects paradigm assumed a direct correlation between exposure to media messages and the shaping of public opinion. Audiences were thought to be passive, susceptible, and vulnerable to media messages.

Following the positivist approach of empirical inquiry, systematic studies, using surveys, were conducted to determine the effects of media on audiences' attitudes and behavior, especially towards political campaigns. However, instead of confirming the strong effects paradigm, they produced a new assessment of media power. Scholars such as Lazarsfeld, Berelson, and Gaudet (1944), as a result of the study of media influence on voters in the 1940 presidential election, paved the way to a new paradigm known as the two-step flow communication paradigm. During this second phase, the strong and direct media effects paradigm was reconsidered. Exposure to media was no longer considered a sufficient cause of attitude changes. Rather, audiences were thought of as part of social networks and particular social and cultural contexts. Media were thought of as factors, not necessarily the primary factor, of attitude changes (Mattelart and Mattelart, 1998; McQuail, 1994).

A new phase of research started developing to understand long term, cognitive, rather than short term media effects. This phase of research, which dominated the 1970s, revisited the strong effect paradigm and cultural effects theories. Researchers sought to understand media effects in terms of broader contexts. Unlike the magic bullet theory and direct effects paradigm, which were characterized by experimental and psychological models, this phase of mass media research sought to understand the "intervening variables of context, disposition and motivation, and collective phenomena such as climates of opinion, structures of belief, ideologies, cultural patterns and institutional forms of media provision" (McQuail, 1994, p. 331).

The present stage, influenced by "social constructivism," started in the 1980s. This stage of media research combines elements from both the limited and strong effects theories of mass media in a new perspective that recognizes that "the human agency for communicative practices" (Hardt, 1999, p. 179). This approach sees media effects as products of interaction between media and audiences (Bryant and Miron, 2004; MacBride, 2004; Scheufele, 1999; Williams, 2003). Mass media, within this paradigm, have significant effects by "constructing meanings and offering these constructs in a systematic way to audiences" (McQuail, 1994, p. 331). However, unlike previous approaches, audiences negotiate with these constructs to come up with personal interpretations.

As argued by Hardt (1999), this paradigm shift was a result of introducing an alternative theoretical approach to the study of communication that "proposes that facts cannot be separated from the domain of values, that the relationship of meaning and language to culture is central to constituting reality" (p. 180). That is to say, this emerging theoretical approach considers communication a process "which entails studying media institutions, not in isolation, but in relation to other institutions in broad social, national and international context" (MacBride, 2004, p. 226). This new approach does not adopt the linear and simplistic traditional mass media research model that conceptualizes the communication process as a sender-message-receiver relationship, but rather considers communication a process that results from the interaction between the media and recipients.

Communication and the Global South: The Shift to Hearts and Minds

The development in theorizing about communication research was accompanied by development in what may seem to be an unrelated field, development studies. Great dissatisfaction has followed the failure of many development projects in the global South. New philosophical approaches started to emerge and modernization theory, as a philosophical approach, faced criticism. The universality of many concepts such as development and human rights was questioned.

Many global South scholars (especially from Africa and Latin America) started getting their voices heard in the scholarly debates about the role of communication in development. As a result, a new paradigm has emerged advocating communication for development. One of the major features of this alternative paradigm is that people are considered active agents of change, not passive recipients. This major shift led the field of communication for development into becoming an instrument for social change. Development is no longer about transmitting information but about exchanging meanings to effect change.

This shift in theorizing about communication for social change is particularly significant in peace and conflict transformation. Sustainable peace, more than any other human need, demands active engagement from the people affected by conflict. Building sustainable peace requires more than signing agreements; it demands change in hearts and minds.

In conflict situations, the way people perceive a conflict serves as the interpretive lens through which disputants see, conceptualize and interpret the conflict. It is important to understand that such a frame is not an objective device, but rather a subjective perception or "view that one person [or group] has of what is going on" (Goffman, 1974, p. 8). Gamson and Modigliani (1989) argued that media discourse is presented in a "set of interpretive packages" or frames that serve as the central organizing idea of any news story (p. 3). The literature suggests that the way issues of peace and war are framed can influence the way they are understood and eventually addressed (Avraham, Wolfsfeld, and Aburaiya, 2000; Benford and Snow, 2000; Reese, Oscar, and Grant, 2001; Watkins, 2001). Johan Galtung, in developing a framework of peace journalism, emphasizes these concepts and argues that the way conflict is framed differentiates peace journalism from war journalism. By highlighting peace initiatives, focusing on peace makers, toning down ethnic and religious differences, and by focusing on people's suffering and the adoption of interpretative approaches, the peace journalist works towards preventing further conflict. On the other hand, war journalism focuses on "our" suffering and frames the conflict as an us/them dichotomy (cited in Lynch and McGoldrick, 2005).

Conflict, Peace and Media in Sudan

When studying media in the context of peace and conflict, it is also important to understand, as Carragee and Roefs (2004) emphasizes:

> Journalistic framing of issues and events doesn't develop in a political vacuum; it is shaped by the frames sponsored by multiple social actors, including politicians, organizations, and social movements. News stories, then, become a forum of framing contest in which political actors compete by sponsoring their preferred definition of issues (p. 216).

In other words, media reflects the power relationships in a given society, as the dominant group's frames have more access in media. Sudan is an apparent example of how control over the means of communication reflects the struggle of control over knowledge.

Sudan stands out in twentieth century history as a country that was embroiled in one of history's longest civil wars. The war pitted Northern Sudanese,[1] who are culturally Arab and mainly Muslim, against other ethnic groups who are seen as African and who practice both traditional folk religions and Christianity. Many scholars hold that the conflict was rooted in the hegemony of Northern Sudanese over other ethnic groups, but the Sudanese conflict is more complicated and multidimensional. This conflict had an economic dimension that pitted a more-developed North against less-developed peripheries. At one level, it was an ethnic conflict, as the civil war was between Arabized Northerners and what might loosely be called the Black population. On another level, it was a religious conflict between Islam, Christianity, and traditional folk religions. Both the ethnic and religious conflicts combined to form a cultural conflict (Loisa, 2005).

Sudan's past is closely bound to its present challenges. The historical process of dichotomizing the country into the Arabized North and African South dates back to the seventh century. At the time, the Arab-Muslim Empire invaded the Sudan, and concluded peace accords with Northern people that established remote Arab control over the country and opened communication channels with the Arabs. Through conquest, intermarriage, trade, and settlement, Northern Sudan underwent Arab-Muslim assimilation. Arab migration and settlement toward the South was hindered by the tough geographical terrain and harsh tropical climate. Relationship between Arabs and Southerners were limited to those who were engaged in the slave trade (Daly and Sikainga, 1993; Deng, 1995; Khalid, 2003).

This division was further enforced during the 58 years of colonization under an Anglo-Egyptian administration (1898–1956). During colonization, both Northern and Southern Sudan were administered as separate colonies under a Governor General. This separation of administration, however, reinforced Arabism and Islam in the North, while Southern Sudan was ruled as an African colonial territory, where the practice of African culture and Christianity were encouraged.

In addition, the British introduced the concept of "Closed Districts" by which the British closed the South to all Northerners, including Northern government officials (Sarkesian, 1973). Closed Districts included Southern Sudan, the Nuba Mountains of Southern Kordofan, and the Funj areas of the Southern Blue Nile. Britain's declared justification for the "Closed District" policy defended the policy as a means of protecting Southerners from Northern slave traders. Along with this, British colonizers formalized a "language policy" that allowed vernacular languages to be taught in primary schools in Southern Sudan, where English was designated as the official language. Consequently, Arabic was not used in schools and government offices in Southern Sudan (Biong, 2003; Collins, 1983).

Northerners had undergone centuries of assimilation into Arab and Islamic cultures. Since independence, they dominated governments that continued the process of assimilation through deliberate policy. All regions of the country, including the South and the West (Darfur, Kordofan, and Blue Nile), were fair game for official policy of extending the influence of Arab-Islamicism. Not all policy involved direct violence, but cultural violence fostered the conditions for it. In fact none of the wars began with directed violence, which makes the country a good example of what Galtung (1990) said about the interconnectedness of cultural and direct violence.

Successive postindependence central governments in Sudan have adopted different policies aimed to construct a united Sudan with the Arabic-Islamic culture as the key determinant for national unity (Khalid, 1990; Sarkesian, 1973).

All these factors – the heritage of master-enslavement history, the British separation policy, in addition to preservation of the pattern of exclusion by successive postindependence government – prevented Sudanese from the North and South from interacting and identifying with each other and resulted in deep polarization among ethnic, religious, and regional lines (Khalid, 2003).

Though not as common as in the past, it is still possible to hear Northerners cry out "abid!" (slave) to Southerners as fights break out between people from different ethnic groups (Jok, 2001). It is essential that postconflict social institutions in Sudan, such as media, education, and religious organizations, critique the cultural aspects of Sudanese life which legitimize prejudices and foster violence.

Communication in this chapter is regarded in the broad sense that includes all forms of mass communication operating through social institutions. That definition of communication includes mass media, education, and religious institutions, among others. As argued by Bratic (2005) "inherently media [among other social institutions] are responsible for good or bad interpretations of the things outside our immediate perceptions; in wars, media frame our enemy for us" (p. 69). In this context, mass media, among other social institutions, play an essential role in defining Us and Them. The representation of We and Others through mass media is influential in shaping collective minds, or public opinions of different groups. Keen (1991) states: "We first kill people with our minds, before we kill them with weapons" (p. 18).

Sudan Government and Othering: Minds Killing People

Mass communication is always a dynamic process, rooted in a sociocultural and political context. Mass communication, as a terrain of struggle over control of knowledge, has always been manipulated by elites and dominant groups to advance their ideas. The media in Sudan is no exception. In fact, it is a rich source of all kinds of study of communication in general, and mass communication in particular, not least because of its historical, cultural, and religious dimensions.

Sudanese mass media, as well as its educational system, has always been a victim of political control. Radio and television in Sudan are governed by the state-owned media corporation Sudan's Radio and Television Corporation (SRTC), which is the only broadcaster with transmission facilities inside Sudan. Private broadcasting can use its facilities after obtaining a license, which, obviously, subjects private broadcasters to the whims and flows of power elites. SRTC broadcasts throughout Sudan, including the South, through four repeater transmitters and regional stations. Different regimes have used mass media to advance their political agenda. Thus, it is of great importance to understand the ideological principles that guide the current ruling elite. This will lead us to appreciate how those ideologies inform communication practices in Sudan.

When the current ruling party, the National Congress Party (NCP – known previously as National Islamic Front, NIF) came to power in 1989, it sought to revive the "Islamic Umma," or "Islamic Global-Community" with Sudan at the forefront (El Turabi, 1994; Al Mubarak, 2001). El Turabi, the ideologue of the Al-Bashir regime – before they parted ways in 1999 – sought to make Sudan the uniting power of all Muslims throughout the globe.

Many Muslim fanatic leaders flocked to Sudan, where the high ranking among them were given Sudanese diplomatic passports. Osama bin Laden was one such leader. Not only was he accommodated as one of the pioneers of the Umma, but he was transformed into the global menace that he has become. It is a well established fact that till then his ambitions were regional in scope and nature. Control over knowledge, therefore, has been of great concern for the current regime.

Islamic zealots within the ruling party have always viewed mass media as a suitable platform to impose their dream of reviving the Islamic Empire. One of these government officials explained how the control over knowledge is an important tool for domination: "A vision for life, which is based on the Islamization of knowledge, is a vision for the Sudanese and Muslim excelling in and dominating the world" (Abdul Rahman Ahmed, quoted in Al Mubarak, 2001, p. 10). Hence, Islamization of knowledge is declared as a means and weapon in the struggle to dominate the world. To achieve this goal, the mass media system has been manipulated to shape young minds to be soldiers with a "holy mission" as defined by the NCP. Radio and TV became frontline weapons in the project of Islamization. This project is manifested in many areas, but the major manifestation was in identity, representation, and national history.

The current regime introduced an official version of Sudanese identity that is associated with Islam. To understand how this new version of Sudanese identity works, it is useful to link it with the citizenship and passport law of 1994. In 1994, a new law was issued that gave The President the right to grant citizenship to any foreigner. It was declared by the head of legal affairs in the Transitional National Council that "the citizenship and passports which are recognized in our Shari'a state are the words 'la ilaha illa Allah' there is no God except Allah and thus Sudan is open for all Muslims" (quoted in Al Mubarak, 2001, p. 100). Although there are no definite figures for how many non-Sudanese Muslims had been granted citizenship according to this law, the overflow of Arab Afghans to Sudan in the 1990s was a clear result of these stipulations. This new definition of Sudanese identity, as much as it coincides with the ruling class ideology, is in opposition to the constitutional stipulation, which states: "Sudan is an independent, sovereign State. It is a democratic, decentralized, multi-cultural, multi-lingual, multi-racial, multi-ethnic, and multi-religious country where such diversities co-exist" (Sudan Constitution, 2005). However, the version of Sudanese identity that is defined according to the Islamic symbols excludes non-Muslims from being Sudanese. This is reflected throughout radio and TV programming.

This exclusionary version of "Sudanese identity" has far-reaching implications for the possibility of obtaining social cohesion and harmony among different groups. Deng (1995) makes a significant statement on the relationship between the official policies and conflict in Sudan. He states that a crucial factor in determining the critical turning point in Sudan's conflict has always been "the extent to which policies or actions of the central government have promoted or diminished a sense of belonging or identification with the country on more or less equitable footing with the North." He further explains that official policies, including those that deal with mass communication, have "delineated the margin, the dividing line between peace and war, cooperation and conflict, unity and polarization" (p.177).

In their study of the role Radio Rwanda played in inciting violence during Rwanda's genocide, Kellow and Steeves (1998) state that one of the frames that the radio perpetuated is the "risk and danger frame." The "risk and danger frame" puts citizens in a defensive situation and provokes horror against a real or perceived enemy. That is what the Sudanese mass media, perpetuate. The ruling elite, through different social institutions – schools (including curriculum), media, and religious organizations – aims at reinforcing the theme of a "nation at war."

One program, on the air before the CPA, clearly illustrates the role mass media played in building the perception of a "nation at war." The program entitled "Sahaat Elfedaa," ["In the Battlefields of Sacrifice"] was an example of extreme cultural violence, which projects real violence even against civilians in the form of Jihad. In this program, images and the poetry of war were constant themes. Heroism was associated with war, and history episodes were borrowed from Islamic history and summarized as a history of wars against "Kufar," or infidels, a term that included all non-Muslims. Inflammatory statements, such as "enemies' armies," "enemies' conspiracy," and "enemies' abhorrence," were diffused through the scripted shows. "Enemies" take many forms; sometimes they are Kufar, other times they are Jews, and many times they are not specified, allowing the audience the option to identify whoever they consider as their enemy. The relentless message is that there are always enemies, and they were always there to be engaged. These "enemies" included indigenous Sudanese.

In this strategy, community identity is presented solely as Islamic collective identity. Thus, the concepts of brotherhood/sisterhood are limited to Muslims, and fall short of embracing the whole. This exclusive collective identity denies any calls for national unity in a multireligious country like Sudan. The message is that whoever does not share our faith does not belong to us. With this univocal construction of collective identity, it is more likely that audiences will identify "others," who are not Muslims, as their enemies. War has always been fueled by the myth of an evil enemy: "We first kill people with our minds, before we kill them with weapons. Whatever the conflict, the enemy is always the destroyer. We're on God's side; they're barbaric. We're good; they're evil" (Keen, 1991, p. 18). Thus, religious rhetoric became an effective weapon in the arsenal of the Sudan government against those who were deemed "Others" by the National Islamic Front, which morphed into today's National Congress Party.

What is "Othering"?

As articulated by Keen (1991), "We first kill people with our minds, before we kill them with weapons" (p. 18). Historically, direct violence has always been fueled by the myth of an evil enemy. Mass media always have been at the forefront of creating and fueling the enemy image, fomenting the irrational hatred that bred the Holocaust, the Rwanda genocide, Darfur, and countless other catastrophies. However, enemy images do not grow in a vacuum; they are "culturally influenced, grossly negative and stereotyped evaluation of the 'other'." Others, explained Hase and Lehmkuhl (1997), "are classified as 'enemies' if their appearance is coupled with some kind of extreme threat perception" (pp. 2–3). As there is always a threat perception associated with the "Other," exclusion is the most logical response to such a threat. Spyrou (2002) points out how "in ethnically divided societies … nationalism … plays a key role in defining a political sense of 'self' in relation to 'others'" (p. 56). Harold (1997) explains that for self-identity to develop in opposition, or in relation, to the "Other," a person "must generate *discourses* of both *differences and similarities* and must reject and embrace specific identities" (p. 4 [italics in the original]). The process of labeling and identifying those who are different from oneself has been defined by many scholars as a process of Othering.

A growing body of literature has dealt with the Othering concept. Johnson (2004) defines Othering as "a process that identifies those that are thought to be different from oneself or mainstream" (p. 253). According to Holliday, Hyde and Kullman (2004), "the foreign Other … refers not only to different nationalities, but also to any group of people perceived as different – perhaps in terms of so-called ethnicity, religion, political alignment, class or caste, or gender" (p. 23). Yet, according to Charon (1992): "it is through others that we come to see and define self, and it is our ability to role-take that allows us to see ourselves through others" (p. 107). Todorvo (1982, cited in Harold, 1997, p. 5) identifies three dimensions of relationship between Self and Other: (a) value judgment (Other may be perceived good or bad, equal or inferior); (b) social distance; and (c) knowledge (to what extent Self knows about the Other's history, culture and values system) (cited in Harold, 1997, p. 5).

Othering, thus, is based on perceived differences. People tend to identify Others as those who are racially, religiously, or culturally different. Othering, as Canales (2000) states, could take two forms: exclusionary and inclusionary. However, she asserts, "in the multicultural, feminist, and critical literature, the prevailing discourse presents Othering as a negative, exclusionary process with dire consequences. It was this exclusionary perspective that strongly influenced my perceptions of the Other and the Othering process" (p. 19).

The Otherness can be articulated by minorities and majorities, that is to say, the politics of otherness is not related only to politics of power. However, "the discourses of identity articulated by majority populations are likely to be univocal and monologic because it is easy for dominant groups to express and confirm their shared identity publicly" (Harold, 1997, p. 6). Schools and mass media can play an effective role in such articulation, because they are "essential transmitters of stereotypes and stereotyped perceptions of the external and internal enemy" (Hase and Lehmkuhl, 1997, p. 13).

The literature provides many strategies that majority groups use to deal with minorities that are defined as "Others." Beck (1997) explains how enemy images are characterized by "existential exclusion": enemy's images are never neutral, only with us or against us. Accordingly, the society is dichotomized into "We" and "They." "The binary opposition of we/they becomes important here," states Apple (1996), because always " 'we' are law abiding, hard working, decent, virtuous, and homogenous. The 'theys' are very different. They are lazy, immoral, permissive, and heterogeneous ... The 'theys' are undeserving" (Apple, 1996, p.7).

In this context, mass media, among other social institutions, plays an essential role in defining *Us* and *Them*. The representation of *We* and *Others* through mass media and daily interaction is very influential in shaping collective public opinion. The Other is defined according to difference: race (White/Black); country of origin (native/immigrant, citizen/foreigner), gender (male/female), or religion and sect (Muslim/Christian, Catholic/Protestant, believer/non-believer) (Apple, 1996; Groiss, 2004; Sefa Dei, 1997; Spyrou, 2002).

Back to the Sudanese Republican (Islamic Reform) Ideas

The Republicans fostered the idea that all Muslims should rethink their relationship with their religion. They advocated a deep socioeconomic transformation, not possible without an enlightened vision of Islam. That new vision, according to the Republicans, must be based on major intellectual, theological, and legal reforms. The consistent exposition of this perspective gave the Republicans a prominent place in the intellectual map of Islamic reformism, especially in Sudan.

The reformist ideas of Al-Ustadh Mahmoud Mohamed Taha are the antitheses of those of the reactionary strands of Muslim thought. Such reactionary strands include the Wahabiya and Muslim Brothers (the confluence of which produced al-Qaeda) and the Shiite ayatollahs in Iran. To the Republicans, these strands do not represent the essence of Islam, for the word "Islam" is from the root "salam," which in Arabic means "peace." Peace, by definition, demands understanding and accommodating the "Other" as long as he/she is not a threat to security and peace itself.

According to the Republicans, the leaders of the fanatic groups do nothing less than distort Islam, the religion of peace. By manipulating religious sentiments, the Republicans contend, these leaders deliberately misappropriate and abuse popular aspirations for socioeconomic change in Muslim countries (Sadig, 1988). As the Republicans see it, exploitation of religious rhetoric and feelings is the underlying current which explains the motives and actions of the fanatic leaders of reactionary Islam.

The only place in modern history before Afghanistan where this fanatical perspective of Islam found full opportunity for application was Sudan. In fact, Sudan in many respects was a launch pad of the current surge in terrorism. This is where

Osama bin Laden found refuge before he left for Afghanistan to apply the ideas he learned and nurtured there.

The shift in power toward Muslim fanatics in Sudan started in1983. In September of that year, Sudan's dictator, Jaffar Mohamed Numeiri, swayed by Hassan Al-Turabi, the charismatic head of what later came to be known as the National Islamic Front (NIF), enacted the so-called Shari'a Law.

The Republicans called those laws the September laws to clearly dissociate them from Islam and the Shari'a. Not only did the Republicans reframe the key terms of political and theological debates of the day, they also powerfully waged a campaign to educate the public about the real purpose of the use by fanatics of religious sentiment as a political tool (Sadig, 1988).

Two indicators show that the Republicans made their point. First, today in Sudanese political rhetoric, Numeiri's Shari'a are called the "September Laws." Second, many leaders today, even among the ranks of the so-called Islamic Movement in Sudan, acknowledge the ideological use of Islam as a tool of "Othering." Today, many former Islamic fanatics admit that Al-Ustadh Mahmoud's trial and execution were in fact a result of a political ploy in which theology was used as a tool of Othering and oppressing the Other.

Although different factors escalate conflict, Coleman and Raider (2006) note that most conflicts are identity-based conflicts (in the broader sense of identity). Therefore, the infusion of peaceful perspectives is very important in both conflict management and advancing an organic peace culture on the ground. Indeed, the Islamic reformist perspective of the Sudanese Republicans enlivened the debate on reforming Islam, working at universal values of equality, justice, freedom, and human dignity.

The leaflet "Either This or the Flood," the only exhibit presented as evidence in the trial of Al-Ustadh Mahmoud Mohamed Taha, was issued in protest against the enactment of September Laws. It was the only exhibit presented by the prosecution as evidence of a crime in the trial of Al-Ustadh and four of his associates. Al-Ustadh was executed less than a month from the day the leaflet was issued, Christmas Day in 1984.

Issuing the leaflet on that day had its own symbolic significance because the timing was deliberate. The Republicans meant to extend a hand from within the ranks of Islam to persecuted Christians. The leaflet aptly represents what the Republicans stand for. Here is a translated version of it:

"In the name of God, the Beneficent, the Merciful"
Either This or the Flood

"And guard against a turmoil that will not befall the unfair ones alone, and know that God is severe in punishment" (Qur'an, chapter 8, verse 25).

We, the Republicans, have dedicated our lives to the promotion of two honorable objectives namely, Islam and the Sudan. To this end, we have propagated Islam at the scientific level as capable of resolving the problems of modern life. We have also sought to safeguard the superior moral values and original ethics conferred by God upon this people (the Sudanese), thereby making them the appropriate transmitter of Islam to the whole of modern humanity, which has neither salvation nor dignity except through this religion (Islam).

The September 1983 laws (that is, the series of enactments purporting to impose Shari'a law in the Sudan) have distorted Islam in the eyes of intelligent members of our people and in the eyes of the world, and degraded the reputation of our country. These laws violate Shari'a and violate religion itself. They permit, for example, the amputation of the hand of one who steals public property, although according to Shari'a the appropriate penalty is the discretionary punishment (ta'zir) and not the specific (hadd) penalty for theft, because of the doubt (shubha) inherent in the participation of the accused in the ownership of such (public) property. These unfair laws have added imprisonment and fine to the specified (hadd) penalties in contravention of the provisions of Shari'a and their rationale. They have also humiliated and insulted the people (of this country) who have seen nothing of these laws except the sword and the whip, although they are a people worthy of all due respect and reverence. Moreover, the enforcement of the specified penalties (hudud and qassas) presupposes a degree of individual education and social justice which are lacking today.

These laws have jeopardized the unity of the country and divided the people in the North and South (of the country) by provoking religious sensitivity, which is one of the fundamental factors that have aggravated the Southern problem (that is, conflict and civil war in the non-Muslim Southern part of the country). It is futile for anyone to claim that a Christian person is not adversely affected by the implementation of Shari'a. A Muslim under Shari'a is the guardian of a non-Muslim in accordance with the "verse of the sword" and the "verse of Jiziah" (respectively calling the people to use arms to spread Islam, and for the imposition of a humiliating poll tax on the subjugated Christians and Jews –.(verses 5 and 29 of chapter 9 of the Qur'an). They do not have equal rights. It is not enough for a citizen today merely to enjoy freedom of worship. He is entitled to the full rights of a citizen in total equality with other citizens. The rights of the Southern citizens in their country are not provided for in Shari'a but rather in Islam at the level of fundamental Quranic revelation that is the level of Sunnah [The Second Message of Islam]. We therefore, call for the following:

1   The repeal of the September 1983 Laws because they distort Islam, humiliate the people, and jeopardize national unity

2   The halting of bloodshed in the South and the implementation of a peaceful political solution instead of a military solution (to the civil war in the Southern part of the country). This is the national duty of the government as well as the armed southerners. There must be the brave admission that the South has a genuine problem and the serious attempt to resolve it.

3   We call for the provision of full opportunities for the enlightenment and education of this (Sudanese) people so as to revive Islam at the level of Sunnah (the fundamental Qur'an). Our time calls for (The Second Message) not Shari'a (The First Message). The prophet, peace upon him, said "Islam started as a stranger, and it shall return as a stranger in the same way it started ... Blessed are the strangers... They (his companions) said "who are the strangers, O Messenger of God?" He replied, "Those who revive my Sunnah after it has been abandoned."

This level of Islamic revival shall achieve pride and dignity for the people. In this level, too lies the systematic solution for the Southern problem as well as the Northern problem (that is, socio-economic and political problems of the Northern part of the country). Religious fanaticism and backward religious ideology can achieve nothing for this (Sudanese) people except upheaval and civil war.

Here is our genuine and honest advice. We offer it on the occasion of Christmas and Independence Day (December 25 and January 1), and may God expedite its acceptance and save the country from upheaval and preserve its independence, unity, and security (The Republican Brothers, 1984).

The Second Message of Islam versus the First Message

According to the (Sudanese) Republicans, Qur'anic texts are comprised of two distinct, though not mutually exclusive, messages: Meccan texts, which were mostly revealed in Mecca, and the Medinese texts which were revealed at Medina. The classification of Qur'anic texts into Meccan and Medinese is very significant, not as signifiers of places of revelation, but as signifiers of a huge paradigm shift in the meaning and content of the message itself (Taha, 1987).

A little digression into the history of the revelation of the Quran may clarify the point. For 13 years, Quran continued to be revealed to the Prophet Muhammad in Mecca. It enjoined him to spread the word of Allah (God) graced with wisdom, good admonition, and to argue in good faith. It clearly stated, in many verses, that there was no compulsion in religion. It also enjoined him to preach the equality of men and women, in all walks of life. Soon, the new religion began to draw adherents from all sections of the community, particularly from among the ranks of slaves and other oppressed classes of Mecca. This appeal alarmed the Meccan religious and ruling circles who feared that their economic and political interests were being jeopardized (The Republican Brothers, 1980).

Statements like "Muhammad is corrupting our pages against us" became rhetorical tools among the elite for fighting and oppressing the new religion, which threatened their status and interests. This fear of the power circles in popular rhetoric, however, masqueraded as defense of the religion (idolatry) then dominant in Mecca. Waged in the name of defending the religion of the fathers, a fierce campaign of terror against the followers of Islam ensued. In that campaign the ruling elite resorted to every available means of torture to force the Muslims – who were mostly from the underclass and slaves – back into idolatry and the old exploitative ways. The campaign reached its peak in the plot against the life of the Prophet himself who was forced to emigrate to Medina (The Republican Brothers, 1980).

The treatment received by the Muslims at the hands of the Meccan elites, according to the Republicans, amply demonstrated the inability of most men at that time to respond intelligently to the peaceful call to progressive values. Consequently, when the Prophet settled in Medina, the grand Meccan texts which established fundamental human rights, including equality between men and women and absolute individual freedom, were repealed, and the Medinese texts began to be revealed.

The Medinese texts appointed the Prophet as a "guardian" over men who failed to embrace values that would liberate them. Furthermore, the Prophet and the Muslims in Medina were commanded to fight back in "self-defense," which was not allowed in the Meccan phase. The Meccans, however, did not sit idle as the Islamic faith began to take hold in Medina. They continued to plan to fight the Prophet Mohammed, who was received by the Medina tribes – which had historic disputes with Meccans – with open arms. The Medinese embraced the new faith in hordes.

The enmity between Meccan "infidels," as the Qur'an labeled them, and Muslims intensified as the Muslims gained more power and status. Hence, the command to fight in self-defense was extended to preemptive fighting, and later in fighting to spread the faith. That, in Republican terms, was a direct consequence of the failure of most men at the time to rise by persuasion and illumination to accept faith in one God. Faith in one God meant the demolition of the multiple idols that were erected in the site of the present day Kabba and were then worshiped in Mecca. By extension, the worship of a single deity has embedded within it equality between people as a derivative of worshiping a just and merciful God. This meant liberating slaves from bondage and ending other forms of exploitation, including using religious rhetoric to bolster economic interests and social status.

In Medina, not only was the Prophet commanded to preempt aggression by aggressive measures, including making war against enemies of Islam, he was further commanded to spread Islam by the sword. This effectively meant that people were no longer treated as equals in the Medinese texts. According to the Medinese texts, you can be overpowered by the faithful if you resist the call to Islam, contrary to the value of absolute individual freedom, abundantly expressed in Meccan texts.

On the social plane, men and women were no longer equals, and men became guardians of women (Sadig, 1985). While the Medinese texts were a great leap forward toward monotheism and equality by the standards prevailing at the time, they were utterly inferior to the Meccan texts by today's standards.

Thus, to Al-Ustadh Mahmoud Mohamed Taha, the division of Qur'an into Meccan and Medinese texts is a fundamental one. To him, the Meccan texts are the fundamental, original texts, because they contain universal values that ascertain fundamental human rights. The Medinese texts are the transitional, aberrational texts, revealed as tools of conflict management and tools of spreading an oppressed faith. In other words, they were revealed to pave the way for the return to the Meccan texts by organizing society in a period of transition (Taha, 1987).

Thus, the purpose of the "guardianship" of the Prophet, clearly stated in Medinese revelation, was to build an "Umma," or community of believers. The concept of "guardianship" in the Medinese texts replaced the concept of absolute individual freedom, which is the backbone of Meccan texts. The Republicans, however, do not see the concept of "guardianship" as a means of rhetorical assault on freedoms and equality, but as a transitional measure to organize

Muslims as a community of believers. This community, after solidly establishing itself, would then help prepare the human race into a global community capable of producing individuals who understand the responsibilities that come with practicing absolute individual freedom. On this division of Qur'anic texts (into Meccan and Medinese) is based the most radical statement in the history of Islamic thought. This radical paradigmatic shift sees Islam, as revealed in the Qur'an, not as one but two messages, addressing two different levels of audiences. The First Message of Islam, which was the one embedded in Medinese texts, addressed the needs of the seventh century (at the level of the audience of the time). It was revealed then, in the seventh century, only to provide evidence that people were called to embrace freedoms, but they could not, because they were not mature enough to do so. The Second Message, embedded in the Meccan texts, addresses our needs today.

Concluding Remark

The Second Message of Islam, as stipulated by the Republicans, is an inclusive understanding of religion that sees Christianity, Judaism, Eastern religions, and traditional African and other religions as part of a merciful God's scheme to unite all of humanity. By framing Islam as an encompassing element of global values, and as part of the human heritage, the Republicans have changed the course and nature of the debate of religious discourse and peace communication in the Sudan.

This will, indeed, have far reaching consequences beyond the Sudan, not only because of Sudan's strategic location as a Middle Eastern and African country but also because the West is now deeply interested in reaching out to Muslim reformists. The fact that there is still conflict in this troubled African country does not detract from the immense contribution of the Republicans to the ongoing reformative debates. On the contrary, it provides for a dynamic setting where new Islamic reformist ideas face their ultimate test as ingredients of lasting peace. If nothing else, the Republicans have intensely engaged the majority of the Sudanese educated elite, including the devoutly religious among them, by positing new, unsettling questions about the applicability of orthodox Islamic ideas. This, in no small measure, paves the way toward a new approach to peace communication in the Muslim World.

Note

1 For the purpose of this research the term "Northern Sudan" is defined according to Mukhtar (2004), who defines the North not as a geographical North, but rather the ideological and political North, whose geographical confinements are limited to the Muslim, Arabic speaking, central Northern Sudan. For more information on this please consult Mukhtar (2004).

References

Al Mubarak, K. (2001) *Turabi's "Islamist" Venture: Failure and Implications*, El Dar El Thaqafiai, Cairo.

Alger, C.F. (1994) A grassroots approach to life in peace, in *Rethinking Peace*, (eds R. Elias and J. Turpin), Lynne Rienner Publishers, Boulder, CO, pp. 282–289.

Allan, T., and Seaton, J. (1999) *The Media of Conflict: War Reporting and Representations of Ethnic Violence*, Zed Books, London.

Apple, M. W. (1996) *Cultural Politics and Education*, Routledge, New York.

Avraham, E., Wolfsfeld, G., and Aburaiya, I. (2000) Dynamics in the news coverage of minorities: The case of the Arab citizens of Israel. *Journal of Communication Inquiry*, 24 (2), 117–133.

Beck, U. (1997) The sociological anatomy of enemy images: the military and democracy after the end of the Cold War, in *Enemy Images in American History*, (eds R.F.-von Hase and U. Lehmkuhl, Ursula), Berghahn Books, Providence, RI.

Beer, F. (2001) *Meanings of War and Peace*, Texas A&M University Press, College Station.

Benford, R., and Snow, D. (2000) Framing processes and social movements: An overview and assessment. *Annual Review of Sociology*, 26, 611–639.

Bigombe, B., Collier, P., and Sambanis, N. (2000) Policies for building post-conflict peace. *Journal of African Economies*, 9 (3), 323–348.

Biong, L.D. (2003) Education in Southern Sudan: War, status and challenges of achieving education for all goals. UNESCO EFA Monitoring Report, UNESCO, Paris.

Bratic, V. (2005) In search of peace media: Examining the role of media in peace developments of the post-cold war, doctoral dissertation, Ohio University.

Broom, J., and Hatay, A. (2006) Building peace in divided societies: The role of intergroup dialogue, in *The Sage Handbook of Conflict Communication: Integrating Theory, Research and Practice*, (eds G. Oetzel and S. Ting-Toomey), Sage, Thousand Oaks, CA, pp. 627–662.

Bryant, J., and Miron, D. (2004) Theory and research in mass communication. *Journal of Communication*, 54 (4), 662–704.

Canales, M.K. (2000) Othering: Toward an understanding of difference. *Advances in Nursing Science*, 22 (4), 16–31.

Carragee, K.M., and Roefs, W. (2004) The neglect of power in recent framing research. *Journal of Communication*, 54 (2), 214–233.

Charon J. (1992) *Symbolic Interactionism: An Introduction, An Interpretation, Integration*, Prentice Hall, Englewood Cliffs, NJ.

Coleman, S.W., and Raider, E. (2006) International/intercultural conflict resolution training, in *The Sage Handbook of Conflict Communication: Integrating Theory, Research and Practice*, (eds G. Oetzel and S. Ting-Toomey), Sage, Thousand Oaks, CA, pp. 663–690.

Collins, R. (1983) *Shadows in the Grass: Britain in the Southern Sudan, 1918–1956*, Yale University Press, New Haven, CT.

Daly, M.W., and Sikainga, A. (1993) *Civil War in the Sudan*, British Academic Press, London.

Deng, F. (1995) *War of Visions: Conflict of Identities in the Sudan*, The Brooking Institution, Washington, DC.

Downing, J. (1996) *Internationalizing Media Theory: Transition, Power, Culture: Reflections on Media in Russia, Poland and Hungary, 1980–95*, Sage, London and Thousand Oaks, CA.

El Turabi, H. (1994) The Islamic state. Epicflow production of Channel Four [Video], Films for the Humanities & Sciences, Princeton, NJ.

Elias, R., and Turpin, J. (1994) *Rethinking Peace*, Lynne Rienner Publishers, Boulder, CO.

Galtung, J. (1964) An editorial. *Journal of Peace Research*, 1, 1–4.

Galtung, J. (1969) Violence, peace, and peace research. *Journal of Peace Research*, 6 (3), 167–191

Galtung, J. (1990) Cultural violence. *Journal of Peace Research*, 27 (3), 291–305.

Galtung, J. (1996) Cultural peace: Some characteristics, in *From a Culture of Violence to a Culture of Peace*, UNESCO, Paris, pp. 75–92.

Gamson, W.A., and Modigliani, A. (1989) Media discourse and public opinion: A constructionist approach. *American Journal of Sociology*, 95, 1–37.

Goffman, E. (1974) *Frame Analysis: An Essay on the Organization of Experience*, Harper and Row, New York.

Groff, L., and Smoker, P. (1996) Creating global/local cultures of peace, in *From a Culture of Violence to a Culture of Peace*, UNESCO, Paris, pp. 103–128.

Groiss, A. (2004) *Jews, Christian, War, and Peace in Egyptian School Textbooks*, Center of Monitoring Impact of Peace, Jerusalem.

Hardt, H. (1999) Shifting paradigms: Decentering the discourse of mass communication research. *Mass Communication and Society*, 2 (3–4), 175–183.

Harold, S. (1997) *The Language and Politics of Exclusion: Others in Discourse*, Sage, Thousand Oaks, CA.

Hase, R., and Lehmkuhl, U. (eds) (1997) *Enemy Images in American History*, Berghahn Books Providence, RI.

Hattotuwa, S. (2002) The role of the media in peace processes. 14th World Congress of Environmental Journalists, www.Cpalanka.Org/Research_Papers/Role_Of_Media_ In_Peace_Processes.Pdf (last accessed November 15, 2007).

Holliday, A., Hyde, M., and Kullman, J. (2004) *Intercultural Communication: An Advanced Resource Book*, Routledge, London/ New York.

Johnson, J. (2004) Othering and being othered in the context of health care services. *Health Communication*, 16 (2), 253.

Jok, M. J. (2001) *War and Slavery in Sudan*, University of Pennsylvania Press, Philadelphia

Keen, S. (1991) Why peace isn't covered. *Media and Values*, 56, 18.

Kellow, L.C. and Steeves, L. (1998) The role of radio in the Rwandan genocide. *Journal of Communication*, 48 (3), 107–128.

Khalid, M. (1990) *The Government they Deserve: The Role of the Elite in Sudan's Political Evolution*, Routledge, New York.

Khalid, M. (2003) *War and Peace in Sudan: A Tale of Two Countries*, Kegan Paul, London.

Lazarsfeld, P.F., Berelson, B., and Gaudet, H. (1944) *The People's Choice: How the Voter Makes up His Mind in a Presidential Campaign*, Columbia University Press, New York.

Loisa, K. (2005) Conflict, profit, and power: The case of Sudan. Sudanese Studies Association Conference, York University, Toronto, Canada.

Lynch, J. and McGoldrick, A. (2005) *Peace Journalism*, Hawthorn, Stroud, UK.

MacBride, S. (2004) *Many Voices, One World: Communication and Society Today and Tomorrow: Towards a New More Just and More Efficient World Information and Communication Order*, Rowman & Littlefield, Lanham, MD.

Mattelart, M., and Mattelart, A. (1998) *Theories of Communication: A Short Introduction*, Sage, London and Thousand Oaks, CA.

McQuail, D. (1994) *Mass Communication Theory: An Introduction*, Sage, London and Thousand Oaks, CA.

Miall, H., Ramsbotham, O., and Woodhouse, T. (1999) Contemporary Conflict Resolution: The Prevention, Management and Transformation of Deadly Conflicts, Blackwell, Malden, MA.

Mukhtar, Al-Baqir (2004) The crisis of identity in Northern Sudan: A dilemma of a black people with a white culture, in *Race and Identity in the Nile Valley: Ancient and Contemporary Perspectives*, (eds C. Lobban, and K. Rhode), Red Sea Press, Trenton, NJ.

Okoth, P.G. (2008) Peace and conflict studies in a global context, in *Peace and Conflict Studies in a Global Context*, (ed. P.G. Okoth), Masinde Muliro University of Science and Technology Press Kakamega, Kenya.

Reese, S.G., Oscar, H., and Grant, E.A. (eds) (2001) *Framing Public Life: Perspectives on Media and our Understanding of the Social World*, Lawrence Erlbaum Associates, Mahwah, NJ.

Sadig, H.B. (1985) Aspects of female participation in religious organization in Sudan: The case of the Republican Sisters. Thesis, University of Khartoum, Sudan.

Sadig, H.B. (1988) The Republican Brothers: A religio-political movement In Sudan. Master's thesis, University of Khartoum, Sudan.

Sarkesian, S.C. (1973) The Southern Sudan: A Reassessment, *African Studies Review*, 16 (1), 1–22.

Scheufele, D.A. (1999) Framing as a theory of media effects. *Journal of Communication*, 49 (1), 103–122.

Sefa Dei, G.J. (1997) Afrocentricty and inclusive curriculum: Is there a connection or a contradiction? in *The Language and Politics of Exclusion: Others in Discourse*, (ed. S. Harold), Sage, Thousand Oaks, CA.

Seib, P. (2005) *Media and Conflict in the Twenty-first Century*, Palgrave Macmillan, New York.

Spyrou, S. (2002) Images of 'the Other': 'The Turk' in Greek Cypriot children's imaginations. *Race Ethnicity and Education*, 5 (3), 255–273.

Taha, M.M. (1987) *The Second Message of Islam* (trans. A.A. An-Na'im), Syracuse University Press, Syracuse, NY.

The Republican Brothers (1980) *An Introduction to the Second Message of Islam*, Publications of the Republican Brothers, Omdurman.

The Republican Brothers (1984) *Either This or the Flood*, Publications of the Republican Brothers, Omdurman.

Watkins, S.C. (2001) Framing protest: News media frames of the million man march. *Critical Studies in Media Communication*, 18, 83–101.

Williams, K. (2003) *Understanding Media Theory*, Oxford University Press, New York.

33

Media and Post-Election Violence in Kenya

P. Mark Fackler, Levi Obonyo, Mitchell Terpstra, and Emmanuel Okaalet

"Peace journalism" is reportage that promises to reduce violence, especially when tensions flare between ethnicities, to moderate the politically stifling impasse, and to promote dialogue between antagonists where embedded suspicion threatens to disrupt already fragile communities. Advocates of "peace journalism" (hereafter PJ) have been particularly enthusiastic about this movement's potential in developing democracies where the franchise is sullied by widespread perceptions of corruption, vote rigging, and distrust between traditional cultural and language groups. This study is set in a social context in which everyone claims to want peace, media leaders want to participate in peace-keeping work, and few believe the cultural and political trajectory leads toward peace at all. It is the coming conflict that most foresee and fear.

In East Africa, Nilotes, Cushites, Bantus, and Westerners (noted by the all-purpose *wazungu*) were tucked within common national boundaries by European powers in 1886. The region, a geographically rich swath of earth, has bloodied its soil with periodic violence, destruction, and brutality: South Africa with apartheid, Rwanda in 1994, Burundi thereafter, Sudan since the 1980s, Eastern Congo since the regime of Sese Seko, Uganda from 1971 and onward in the north, Ethiopia in the 1980s and 1990s, Zanzibar in its quest to secede from Tanzania, and Somalia seemingly forever. Kenya "burned" in late 2007 and early 2008.[1]

This study considers the influence of media on pre- and postelection violence (hereafter PEV) in Kenya in the fall of 2007 and spring of 2008. The study seeks to understand what role media played in promoting peace or inflaming violence that left more than 1100 persons dead and 350 000 internally displaced (Waki Report, 2008, pp. 345, 351). After a brief review of the development of the press in Kenya, we lay out the tensions that led to this unprecedented civil disruption, then review media performance during December and January through a content analysis of

---

The Handbook of Global Communication and Media Ethics, First Edition. Edited by Robert S. Fortner and P. Mark Fackler.
© 2011 Blackwell Publishing Ltd. Published 2011 by Blackwell Publishing Ltd.

three newspapers, *Daily Nation*, *Standard*, and *People*. We follow with a summary of 25 long interviews with media and civic leaders conducted in Nairobi in July 2009.[2] Finally, we attempt to lay theoretical groundwork for a theory of the press based on *ubuntu*, an indigenous philosophy of the human person and community. Parallels between *ubuntu* as a basis for media performance and PJ will conclude this study.

We state at the outset that this research was conducted in an atmosphere of tension in July 2009, midway in the five-year cycle of national elections. An agreement between the contending parties (Peoples National Union, hereafter PNU and Orange Democratic Movement, hereafter ODM) in April, 2009, ended the burning, looting, and killing but did little to settle the underlying causes of PEV. Nor has Kenya's national leadership made progress toward an enduring democratic process. Nearly every interview was clear on this point: the next scheduled election in 2012 will be worse if substantial progress is not made to restore social trust. History will tell the story. A decade from now we will know whether war between Kenya and Somalia, stoked by unemployed youth enticed into rag-tag militias by the offer of the one prize their own economies cannot provide – bags of money, will redraw northern borders (as some suggest); whether the Lord's Resistance Army will migrate from eastern Congo to Kenya (as some predict), its corps of brutalized fighters strengthened by Kenyan "street boys" exported to the Democratic Republic of the Congo in the 1990s; or whether the Luo, Kalinjen, Kikuyu and Kamba leadership will send a once growing GNP into freefall (as many anticipate). Time will also tell, on the contrary, whether a determined and culturally renovated free press will help citizens achieve such a fair and open process that the nation's fractious constituencies and its wealthy and feckless leadership will emerge from the next national transition with confidence and hope.

Media Backdrop

Kenya's media divide loosely into three categories: the national press, the vernacular press and what euphemistically is referred to as alternative press. In 2000 the roster of Kenya's lively media was impressive: one major regional newspaper, several smaller regional newspapers, five national newspapers, and the alternative press reporting most scandals and sex escapades; four national television stations and several regional telecasters; two radio stations broadcasting internationally, one broadcasting within the region, at least two broadcasting nationally and nearly 50 others reaching sections of the country; at least two community based radio broadcasts broadcasting from Nairobi (see Maina, 2006, pp. 29–30, 38, 41). These media are staffed by some of the finest trained journalists in Africa, and from a design and presentation point of view, the Kenyan media is fairly competitive. However, a discussion on the competitive nature of these media has to take into account the diversity within them – that the more national ones have greater access to resources including advertising revenue with greater effect on their cultural impact.

The journey of Kenya's media to this stage started over a century ago with a little known newspaper, *Taveta Chronicle*, then edited by a Protestant Church minister. It soon withered, as did a host of other commercial publications, leaving the claim of longevity to the *Standard*, founded in 1902 by an Indian immigrant A.M. Jeevanjee (Scotton, 1972). Between the founding of the *Standard* and national independence in 1963, Kenya witnessed many media in many forms. Some were owned by the church. Those launched by the pioneers of African freedom, who also happened to be nascent politicians, folded as these amateur journalists took positions in the new government. The media that dominate Kenya's media scene today have a more recent history dating back to independence. Their history is the history of the nation.

The development of media in Kenya started with the European settlement and the arrival of Indian migrant workers (Ole Ronkei, 1995, p. 8). Colonial administration and missionaries initiated literacy programs; their capitals hosted printing presses and promoted the setting up of what Hachten (1971, p. 199) called the "settler" press. This press carried news from Great Britain, seldom African events (Faringer, 1991, pp. 9–10). Nearly half a century after its founding, Ainslie (1966, p. 100) wrote about the *Standard*:

> The *Standard* was, and remained consistently for nearly sixty years, the voice of settler demands for more independence from Whitehall, for funds and soldiers to deal with "the natives," for aid in developing the land ... anyone who saw the *East African Standard* during the years of Mau Mau rebellion might have been forgiven for seeing it as an extremist settler mouthpiece. It expressed all the White hysteria, all the angry settler demands for more and more repressive action by the Colonial Office, that made this period the ugliest in Kenya's history.

Besides the papers that were openly prostate, such as the *Standard*, the colonial administration often ran papers by proxy. From the turn of the century to the declaration of the state of emergency in 1952, the settler government founded and funded nearly 10 newspapers or newssheets: *Habari*, *Tazama*, and *Baraza*, and even cooperated with the *East African Standard* among others (Abuoga and Mutere, 1988; Kitchen, 1956; Scotton 1972). In some cases the government funded newssheets in vernacular languages. Altschull (1995, p. 239) noted that newspapers everywhere were agents of the central forces that drove the nation's agenda. These papers were helpful in entrenching the philosophy of the colonial government: *Pamoja*, *Mucemanio*, *Ramogi*, *Kamha*, *Embu Gazette*, and *Ramogi*.

The colonialist's control of the media prompted nationalists to set up their own media, starting with Harry Thuku's *Tangazo* and leading to nearly 50 others at the height of anticolonial agitation (Scotton, 1972). Understandably, the colonial administration banned most of them at the time of emergency in 1952. Schramm and Ruggels (1967, p. 65) suggested that media growth is dependent on literacy, urbanization, increased energy consumption, and high GNP. None of that would have been possible in a traditional African context, nor considered very important. As economies grew and diversified, media became significant (De Beer et al, 1995,

p. 213; Hachten, 1993, p. 14; Scotton, 1972). Victorian culture, as Scotton has observed, may have contributed to the atmosphere under which Kenyan media grew. It is the British "belief that an educated man (sic) should express opinions on the social and political questions of the day." Thus media developed (Scotton, 1972, pp. 87–88).

In Bourgault's (1995, p. 4; cf Abuoga and Mutere, 1988; Kitchen, 1956; Passin, 1963) survey of *Mass Media in Sub-Sahara Africa*, she observed that electronic media in countries with a British colonial legacy followed the BBC model, and not only in broadcasting. Kenya newspaper design and editorial content mirrors the best in Britain, and if American influence is evident in recent TV programming, the dominant accent on-air remains British.

Kenyan media have tended to be more robust, contentious, and progressive than counterparts in the region. Competition for advertising may explain some of this liveliness, as Kenya's economy grew and riches awaited media owners who knew how to find an audience. On the other hand, Kenya has always had an active civil society, even at the height of political oppression. The rambunctious press and active civil society have ensured the presence of competing voices in the media even if at times those voices paid a price for challenging the national ruling party. In the period following independence, newspapers, supported by the National Council of Churches of Kenya, often took positions contrary to the ruling elites'. Equally, Kenyan clergy have always expressed their opinions on social issues, many using the media as skillfully as the pulpit.

At independence Kenya had two main newspapers, *Daily Nation* and *Standard* (the vernacular language papers were banned in 1952). Church press writers and editors (Catholic and Protestant) were often either forced from their jobs or chose to go into exile to escape the regime (Ochieng, 1992; Scotton, 1972). Broadcasting was, for a long time, limited to one broadcasting house that would eventually change its name to the Kenya Broadcasting Corporation.

Since independence in 1963, the media, particularly print, has been dynamic, given periods of repression. The dynamism has been evident in staffing, media–government relationships, or the predisposition of media to national issues. Many publications were also established and disappeared off the stands in quick abandon. While the *Nation* in 1960 started out primarily as a paper targeting the African community, the *Standard*, which developed as a White settler paper, held that policy. Within two years after independence the *Nation* already had a native Kenyan at the top of its leadership. It took the *Standard* 10 years after independence to have an African hold the position of a senior reporter (Ochieng, 1992). In postindependence Kenya, media staffing has taken ethnic tones, a fact that informs the media dynamics in 2008 PEV (Rambaud, 2008).

Practicing journalism in Kenya has not been without its dangers. Kenya has had a long history of intimidating journalists through phone calls from the nation's high offices, jailing or detaining without trial those unwilling to "play ball," and censoring journalism through newsroom spies. When a journalist felt overly cornered by the government, he (almost always) has sometimes opted for life in exile.

Threats to media freedom have not always come from the government. Often Kenyan journalists have been accused of corruption, compromising standards either for commercial gain or due to ethnic loyalty. The near 40 million population comprises 43 tribes, but only a few of these communities are represented in newsrooms. Their representation almost mirrors the mosaic of national leadership often reflecting a journalism that has been more ethnically biased than influenced by professional and ethical standards (Opiyo, 1994). In spite of everything, Kenyan media have produced some of Africa's finest journalists, such as Hillary Ngweno and Philip Ochieng.

Nairobi's location has influenced how Kenya has been covered globally. This also has an impact on local media. Situated on the eastern seacoast of the continent, the city provides access to most of the troubled regions of eastern Africa, some which are constant flash points for news: the DRC, Rwanda, Uganda, Southern Sudan, and Somalia among others. Nairobi is well served by international flights that make it easy for journalists to access the region. As a result, nearly every major news company has an office in Nairobi. The high standards of these international journalists have invariably influenced local practice. This influence and presence has also meant that the Kenya government comes under closer scrutiny than other governments in the region. Too often this has irked the government, particularly during the administration of former President Daniel arap Moi. He frequently threatened to revoke the visas of journalists and occasionally carried out the threat. Events in Kenya also draw closer attention in the international media, and the tone this coverage takes is reflected in Kenyan media leading to a competitive journalism environment. Broadcast stations that are easily accessible in Nairobi include the BBC, VOA, Radio France International, Radio Germany, CNN, Al Jazeera, and the South African Broadcasting Corporation.

Several factors have influenced the growth of Kenyan media, primarily the national political structure. Mazrui (2007) provides a taxonomy of African leadership: mobilizer, reconciler, housekeeper, patriarch, disciplinarian, technocrat, warrior, and sage, among others. To use Mazrui's taxonomy, Kenyans have tended to venerate the state's chief executive, which on the downside has created opportunity for dictatorial tendencies and legal impunity. Colonialism has been replaced increasingly by leadership that looks like patriarchy. In this environment, media has tended to suffer suppression. State House aside, the legislative environment has not been helpful either. Throughout Africa, electronic media have been little more than the microphone of the leader, an extension of the president's pulpit. It was not until the late-1980s, in the heat of civic discontent, that the government relented and started freeing the airwaves, permitting frequencies and broadcast licenses to the system's private and corporate entrepreneurs.

In 1990, the first independent TV station in Kenya, KTN (Kenya Television Network) was launched. This followed relentless civic discontent that often included confrontations between bullish police and protesters. In Kenya, the slogan is, *Fanya fujo uone* (Do it and see what happens! Indeed, the government's police will come out swinging clubs.) Even though the government released its stranglehold on TV, the state monopoly in radio broadcasting still remained in place. With liberalizing underway, however, the KBC would not be the exclusive voice on radio for long. That began to happen in 1998 when the first radio frequencies for independent broadcasters were assigned. What started cautiously soon became a floodgate as the inside network began to hawk frequencies to the highest bidder resulting in nearly 200 countrywide frequencies issued by the time of Kenya's 2007 elections. However, not all frequencies were operational. However, there were now at least 13 religious broadcasting stations across the nation, nearly 20 stations broadcasting in some of the country's largest ethnic tongues, then about five stations broadcasting nationally and several broadcasting internationally including BBC, Radio China, and German radio.

With each phase of Kenya's national development, its state of press freedom has deteriorated according to the independent measurements by such institutions as Freedom House (Freedom House, 2008). The first republic under Jomo Kenyatta had a comparatively tension-free relationship with the media. Complaints against the media tended to emerge from the lackeys in State House rather than directly from Kenyatta. That was not the case with Kenya's second president, Daniel arap Moi, who was known to have a pesky relationship with the media that often degenerated into arrests and detention of journalists. The third president of Kenya, Mwai Kibaki, is a man who seldom makes his opinion known. However, during his tenure the media has suffered some of the worst, even if isolated, incidents of media violence since 1963. In one instance on May 3, 2005 the wife of the president marched at midnight into one of the media houses that had carried a story the first lady did not like. She held the newsrooms hostage, slapping journalists and demanding what no journalist could give (Karoney, 2005). In another incident, on March 2, 2005, armed goons suspected to be either state security or its agents, raided the second largest media house disabling the television station while burning copies of the print edition of the associated newspaper (Africa Confidential, 2006).

The vibrancy of the Kenyan media has been particularly evident when they have closed ranks under attack. While Kenya's constitution was inherited from British practice, legislation that London abandoned years ago is still in the Kenyan constitution. From time to time these articles are reviewed with the goal of harassing the press. For instance, the Books and Newspapers Act prescribes the conditions under which one can print and distribute a newspaper or a book. In 2002, parliament sought to amend this law to make it more punitive. Parliament sought to increase the bond any publisher would deposit with the government from Ksh. 10000 to Ksh. 1000000. Few media houses could afford this jump in fees, which obviously was intended to stifle the emergence of new publications. United media strongly opposed this, as they also stood in opposition to the raiding of *Nation* media, the raiding and banning of *KTN* and *Standard*, the legislation of Kenya Communications Amendment Act 2008, and the legislation requiring journalists to reveal sources.

If print media has witnessed turbulent relations with the state, the electronic media has had, on the other hand, a different type of relationship. The first broadcasting house in Kenya, the Kenya Broadcasting Corporation, was founded in 1927 under British administrative control and primarily to serve the settler community. Later on, to cater for the black population, colonial administrators founded several vernacular stations scattered across the country. Though established to serve the native population, these stations offered little more than British visions of life in Africa. At independence, the new government recognized the importance of broadcasting and assumed monopoly control over KBC. That monopoly remained in place until 1989.

Also in 1989 the beginning of the collapse of the authoritarian began. Many television and radio stations emerged. Two privately owned national channels NTV owned by the Nation group and KTN owned by the Standard group, began to compete for viewers with the KBC. These have been joined by Citizen TV and K24. NTV is owned by a publicly traded company but the controlling shareholder is the Paris based leader of the Ishmael religious community, the Agha Khan. Its broadcasts have adopted the same tradition as that of its parent company, the Nation group. KTN is the oldest private TV station in Kenya. Initially it was owned by the ruling party apparatchiks, but when KANU (Kenya African National Union) was dislodged from power, ownership changed hands and remains one of Nairobi's badly kept secrets. However, it is believed that the current owners closely identify with the current administration. Citizen TV is owned by a Nairobi based entrepreneur S.K. Macharia who also owns at least 13 other stations broadcasting in leading vernacular languages and Kiswahili. Macharia is believed also to be one of the confidants of the current president. K24 is Kenya's 24 hour news channel owned by Regional Media which also owns a vernacular station called Kameme FM, broadcasting in the central province and in the dominant Kikuyu language. The station is closely affiliated with the KBC. There are other TV stations such as STV and Family which broadcast nationally but have a limited following and are of little consequence in political debate.

The majority of Kenya's population is still rural. Given the terrain, the broadcasts reach only major urban centers. Given the cost of owning and running a TV receiver, it is still largely a medium for the urban middle class. Rural viewing tends to be community based. For the mass of the rural poor, the dominant media is still radio. According to Maina (2006) while only about 37% of Kenyans access TV, radio stations collectively reach 96% of the population.

Only two radio stations, KBC and Citizen, reach the entire country. Both broadcast in Kiswahili. However, nearly every major local community has a broadcast in the mother tongue. The biggest player in vernacular broadcasting is S.K. Macharia who owns Mlembe FM broadcasting in Luhya, Ramogi (Luo), Chamge (Kalenjin), Inooro (Kikuyu), and Musyi (Kikamba) which are the biggest communities in Kenya. Most stations broadcasting in English and Kiswahili are based in Nairobi. They have sliced the city population into smaller segments but spend more time playing music and engaging in "small talk" throughout the broadcast schedule. Community stations are few; their impact and influence is minimal.

Kenya's gutter or alternative press would best be described as "now-you-see-them-now-you-don't" after their nature of appearing only when there is a major scandal involving the nation's politicians or socialites. These papers range from a single A4 sheet to as many as 12 pages. It may be sold on newsstands, but more often on street corners for less than half the price of the daily newspapers. Most are technically and editorially mediocre with occasional but unpredictable flashes of brilliance. Generally, these publications have no fixed address, no known publisher, and tend to focus on rumor and sometimes make very spectacular claims. These papers often draw the ire of the Kenyan government. Three are worth mentioning: *The Weekly Citizen*, *Kenya Confidential*, and *Independent*. The later was recently shut down after the publisher-editor was arrested and jailed for criminal libel. He has since been released on presidential clemency.

Performance of Three Newspapers During PEV

This study analyzed the content of three leading Nairobi dailies during the month prior to national elections and the month after. The analysis intended to track how each daily newspaper reported PEV and whether any one of them showed credible interest in the principles of PJ. Those principles center on a "reinvigorated pursuit of objectivity" which honors all people as sources and citizens, situates events in context, and understands conflict as opportunity for public maturation.

The three dailies were *Nation*, *Standard*, and *People*. Started in 1958, the *Daily Nation* is now East Africa's most widely read newspaper with a daily circulation over 200 000 copies – three times that of the nearest competitor. The *Nation* is owned by Nation Media Group, which also owns and operates the weekly *The East African*, *The Business Daily*, Uganda's *Daily Monitor*, the Swahili *Taifa Leo*, the television station *NTV*, and the radio station *Easy FM*.

The *Standard*, founded in 1902, is Kenya's second most widely read newspaper with a circulation of 70 000. It is owned by The Standard Group, which also owns and operates the television station *KTN*.

Originally a weekly, the *People* has been a daily newspaper since 1998. Its circulation peaked around 2002 at 60 000. It is owned by veteran politician and businessman Kenneth Matiba, and runs a bold motto in each edition: Frank, Fair, and Fearless.

Leading up to the presidential election, the tenor of Kenyan political coverage was divisive. On 4 January 2008 a significant break occurred with the joint-headline "Save Our Beloved Country" appearing on the front page of the *Nation*, *Standard*, *People*, and three other Kenyan newspapers. Before this orchestrated call for unity, nearly all coverage was split into a two-party framework, pitting the PNU against ODM, instead of framing the coverage within the greater concern for national wellbeing. These headlines were typical: "The Giant Killers" (December 1, 2007); "Election Victory Talk" (December 12, 2007); "Battle of Dirty Tactics" (December 16, 2007); "It's attack mode in the eleventh hour" (December 23, 2007); "Standoff" (December 30, 2007). Such stories dichotomized the political race and later the ethnic conflict into an either/or reality: *either* you are for PNU and against ODM, *or* you are against PNU and for ODM. Coverage of this sort effectively erases middle ground. In addition, the diction favored in such headlines and stories is overtly militaristic, priming readers to accept an antagonistic relationship between supporters of their party and opponents. This conception of the political race and the ethnic conflict as a zero-sum game, in which every success for one side is inevitably a blow to the other, further diminishes the possibility of cooperation. One could, extending the militaristic diction, say that to be a mediator in such a context is to be in "no man's land," a vulnerable area between the two antagonistic poles. When compromise is framed as weakness or disloyalty, violent response becomes more attractive.

Newspapers' coverage approached the parties as war camps. The divide between them was clear, and it was ethnic. Leading up to the election, the negative themes of "accusations," "propaganda," "poll rigging," "bias," "devious plots," "intentional disenfranchisement," "hate messages," and "hate speech" were so recurrent that they aggravated the dividing line, creating a gulf of distrust and suspicion. Besides widening the social rift, the newspapers' emphasis on mudslinging between the parties resulted in a deemphasis on the real issues at stake. Instead of a focus on the core national issues, the focus was on the "meta-conflict" of the political elites arguing about so-and-so's hypocritical stance on an issue. Given such a preoccupation with political elites, the *wananchi* (common citizen) receded into the background. As told to us by Tom Maliti, AP correspondent, "The media failed to report politics beyond the frame of politics being a contest."

Another danger latent in the two-party framing of stories was the tendency to lapse into essentialism. Because each Kenyan journalist had to wrestle with political pressures and his/her own internalized biases from ethnic heritage and family ties, it was extremely difficult to keep a PNU-versus-ODM story from turning into an "us-versus-them" story. The further danger of the "us-versus-them" story is that the "them" inevitably becomes incriminated. "They" were portrayed as *de facto* the problem with no heed given to their circumstances. The *Standard* slipped into this often, with an antigovernment stance evident by word choice and imbalanced sources.

In the midst of divisive "objective" news coverage of conflict, the most lucid, levelheaded voices rang forth from the editorials, at times calling for crossethnic cooperation, tolerance, compromise, forgiveness, and a sense of national unity.

Most of the shortcomings in newspapers coverage of conflict are patterns of omission. One major omission was historical context. Reporters certainly knew their context. An article from *People* (December 2, 2007) approached a proper understanding of the nature of the postelection violence when it couched the early instances of the violence within a broader historical context:

> The clashes re-emerged last month invoking memories of past similar violence in Molo, Burnt Forest, and Kuresoi where hundreds of people lost their lives following upheavals largely attributed to political reasons owing to the fact that they occur every election year.

In every election year since 1992 – including even incumbent Mwai Kibaki's land-slide win in 2002 – Kenya had witnessed some degree of election-related violence. To fail to connect these recurring bouts of violence is to ignore the common denominator that is their root cause. Thus, the danger in reporting conflict as an event detached from historical context is the likelihood of leading readers to accept a superficial and short-term resolution to that conflict.

However, not all coverage reported as if the conflict was amputated from his-torical trajectory. One article in *Nation* highlights the "land factor" and how griev-ances over property dating back to colonialism are playing a part in "election violence" (January 5, 2008). Unfortunately again, though, the clearest voices of reason came through the editorials and not news reporting. During January, for example, a number of editorials appear in *Nation* that saw through the political surface of the conflict and suggested a number of more fundamental causes. *Nation*'s "Save Our Beloved Country" editorial hinted at Kenya's gaping eco-nomic disparity as in part prompting the chaos. One editorial suggested a sense of helplessness experienced in slums that drives slum-dwellers to riot (January 5, 2008); another suggested that the "genesis of this bloodletting goes back a long way," citing unresolved grievances from the colonialist-, Kenyatta-, and Moi-eras (January 6, 2008); still another, pulling ideas from the first two together, recog-nized that only a "comprehensive settlement that seeks to resolve many social, economic, and political issues, some going back to history," will end the conflict for good (January 8, 2008). In their diversity of opinion and willingness to recall the past, these editorials more accurately reflected the complex nature of conflict than the amnesiac "objective" news pages.

The very phrases most used by media to refer to the events of violence and vandal-ism surrounding the 2007 election – "postelection violence," "postelection chaos," and "postelection conflict" – are misleading in their implication of a complete cause-and-effect relationship between the botched election and the conflict. If anything, the botched election was only a spark to a heap of kindling of historical frustrations.

Themes from Interviews

What caused postelection violence?

The recurrent causal themes that emerged in the 25 long interviews gravitated around economic inequality, land disputes, the politicians, a culture of impunity, tribalism, and the media itself. However, because of their unique role in amplifying the other causes, the media will be dealt with separately, both in terms of inciting and pacifying the violence. Economic inequities had long historic roots and branched widely.

Quotations from interviews have been edited for verbal bridges and redundan-cies. All interviewees were promised anonymity. Their institutional affiliations are included in the notes at the conclusions of this essay.

Going all the way back to the history of the nation … people from certain areas of the country were marginalized … So when people talk about historical injustices, some of them stem from the colonial times.

The underlying causes of that bloodbath … The very deep seated animosities and the…economic equations…contributed to that fallout.

The top 5% own 70% of this country … The ones causing the chaos … had nothing to lose.

The average Kenyan would like to eat and drink and have a place to live … basic human rights … Those biting needs will lead people to irrationality … no alternatives but to fight … to survive.

It's actually about poverty, really … When there's nobody left to attack, people turned on each other.

Poverty inevitably led to land disputes that remained unresolved since independence.

Those who thought they were going to win … were declared non-winners. It contributed because it triggered, but that was the wound which caused blocking to land and other resource distribution … by the time they were declared winners people had already chased others out of their houses.

The land question … came in by default or design … But then over thirteen years of Kenyatta, twenty-four years of Moi and at least the five years of Kibaki … there was no effort really to reverse these things which had accumulated.

People have to own something. They didn't own anything, thus they are insecure … The politics began in 2002/2003 when people were hopeful for change but were let down … The land issue was not addressed.

As Kalenjins killed Kikuyus with the aim of regaining their land, Uhuru Kenyatta paid Mungiki to retaliate, to kill Kalenjins … He was helping his people.

As the clashes moved … young Kikuyu men armed themselves to defend their land. Greedy politicians pay gangsters to cause chaos, and … sponsor violence by claiming that they'll expel "the others" from the land and give it to the particular community.

Politicians had much at stake personally and tribally by retaining power at all costs. Political machinations were abundant, but so was uninformed acquiescence.

This referendum was about whether we want a new constitution to come into place … [T]here were contentious issues which they should have asked people to vote on, not … the whole constitution. But the whole thing was politicized.

It was politically instigated … when people started talking about the [new constitution's] draft … For instance, politicians from Rift Valley were saying that in it their land was going to be taken. The seeds were already planted. They just needed something to ignite it.

PNU created political chaos so they could steal the election. It's like they wanted it to happen ... Kibaki could have stopped it ... There was rigging everywhere, left, right, center.

We heard so much hate speech ... when the politicians were calling each other names.

The rest of society has left everything up to politicians ... and not to the experts, the professionals ... the Nobel Peace Prize Winner!

People still subscribe to the 'big chief' African mentality and don't take a look at the ideologies the politicians stand for; they simply follow.

So also that [historic injustices] politicians, with time, have been able to plan for using ... during the elections.

We ... lack a government which listens to what the public wants and responds accordingly. We ... come from a culture ... where people in power believe they are leaders and the people are the servants. They never understand that they govern on behalf of the people ... servants of the people.

The violence was planned ... and funded ... and logistically aided by politicians ... The botched election was just an excuse rather than the basis for the violence ... When the politicians said stop, the violence stopped ... [A] reckless political class ... use office to their own advantage at expense of public.

Almost three quarters of the reporters were communication workers for the political parties, so they were so blinded to even seeing if something was amiss and worth reporting.

There was a lot of bribing of the media by politicians.

Such misappropriation of power spawned a culture of impunity.

A culture of impunity has existed in this country since independence. Constitutional amendments ... have ... emasculated ... the role of citizens ... and their right in a democracy to determine their common agenda and destiny as a nation. [T]he powers of parliament were usurped by the executives ... and ... excesses of power led to certain deficiencies in our system.

Police brutality – the police were overstretched but they were also being paid off and even raping the people they were supposed to be protecting ... the guys who did are still out scot-free ... The judiciary is appointed by the President, the police commissioner is appointed by the President, so ... work for the President, not for the truth.

In Tanzania, when a leader is caught in an act of corruption, they quickly throw him out ... but here when a leader is caught in an act of corruption, we politicize it and he or she will survive.

The political class disconnects from the general public on the insistence for prosecution ... the general public wants the impunity cracked.

Tribalism was entrenched in every sector as an undercurrent ready to be manipulated and triggered.

A wrong start – we should have had the two biggest tribes come together and choose our first leader, but we didn't, and now they've been fighting ever since ... now it's been ingrained: "You're not a Kenyan; you're from this community or that community".

If I am Kikuyu I feel much stronger loyalty to being a Kikuyu than a Kenyan ... If I am required to defend my community in that context, I will defend them rather than my country.

During the campaign ... a lot of hate speech ... to divide Kenyans ... When violence broke out, it was tribal.

We Kenyans vote for our tribe, not for parliament ... When there is trouble, we revert to a tribe.

Missionary work allocated to themselves particular areas of influence ... so today denominations fit neatly with ethnic groups ... ethnicity has been maintained in the church to this day, making it hard for people to believe the church can address the issue of ethnicity because they are not bigger than it.

Church leaders gave into tribal divisions and supported candidates ... were partisan ... even though the NCCK warned them they could not later play a role of reconciler if they did.

At the root is the tribalization of the media ... leadership herding people into tribal cocoons.

How was media guilty of incitement?

People hired to operate local language stations, or to "string" for newspapers (called correspondents) are not properly trained. Moreover, they are paid only for what is published or broadcasted, thus creating incentive for the spectacular story.

Most media practitioners didn't know about the repercussions ... didn't know the history which enables journalists to cover particular issues and ask the right questions.

The people behind the microphones did not know how much power they had ... They don't understand how the community interprets [what they hear] ... We only

Media and Post-Election Violence in Kenya

know how to do the easy story. Glorify violence ... whip up emotions ... that is what we excelled in.

I can recognize hate speech when I see it but I know people who can't, who think it's a good story ... a good byte, who'll put it [out] ... some people are naïve ... not knowing ... what ... damage they could cause.

Expressive language, idioms – used by local/vernacular stations when broadcasting ... tarnished other.

They rallied people toward ethnocentrism over nationalism.

Editors and journalists had a preconceived angle to the story without even going out to cover the story.

Sloppy journalism – all it took was to get a byline, slap a name on it, and you have a story ... It's journalists who failed to do their jobs ... to have the bigger good of the country at heart. ... We all became supporters of political parties ... reporting conflict without proper grounding. ... We all agreed to be cowed ... to do consultancy work on the side for these politicians.

They give acres and acres of space to politicians who don't say anything important to benefit the country ... stories measured with a ruler and paid accordingly ... Journalists would make five or six dollars a story ... Poorly paid journalist would make more from politicians *not* to write a story ... Politicians can easily target journalists ... the brown envelope ... we don't have a free media ... Journalists are corrupt ... If you have a family, you'll be corrupt.

The media by ... portraying what was happening assisted people ... to ... respond in a certain ... either in terms of protest [or] ... revenge attacks, because the media would report attacks ... Those images ... then promoted revenge attacks.

Small community radio stations ... were informing where and when to meet for riots the next day.

The media never accurately had the results to go to the public with ... was terrified and was acting ... out of self-interest and ... fear of what this degeneration means ... We haven't been exposed to that kind of fall-out that is so bloody and violent and the country really turning on each other ... The media became paranoid ... did not know how to handle it ...became avenues or platforms for the people who were either preaching the peace or mobilizing security or what not ... abandoned the reporting.

I think eight billion was used in elections; three billion went to the media ... Media and the advertising companies were greatly benefiting from all this, from raising the temperatures ... But if you look at the media ownership ... some things are being reported in newspapers that are not being reported in others ... the media are irresponsible; they do not check their facts.

The Standard was so pro-ODM that the threat of chaos, if it brought government down, was okay with them ... The media should not have been announcing the votes, vote by vote ... Oh yes, good intentions – to stop rigging, but ... media contributed to violence by creating the impression that PNU could only win by cheating, and by constant reports that [PNU] intended to steal the election.

For the first time we had a pluralistic situation of media ... TV stations and radio stations ... going to specific groups ... Politicians used those medias and they were divided into two groups.

Some radio stations would call certain politicians [seeking their opinions] and incite listeners

Political priorities took the place of ethical/professional standards ... The media did not know it would escalate like it did ... They would fill in their [statistical] gaps by ECK's numbers or others' work ... It was so easy to doctor results – just add zeros to an SMS message sending in the results from a far out province ... [W]e were not coordinated. *Nation* would say, "We don't need to send someone there; *Standard* has someone there." Or they would rely on agents of the parties.

Text messages (SMS) – new media that is not being controlled did so much damage, more than any newspaper.

There was very little attempt by the media to go a bit deeper ... no one inquired about where the money for the campaigns was coming from, no one questioned the politicians' motivations ... The media failed in terms of checking out the ECK ... No one reported on the fact that the chairman was once Kibaki's lawyer! ... The media failed to cover the election beyond a straightforward contest.

How did media help restore peace?

Eventually the media also aided pacification, though from diverse motives. An initiative of Pamoja FM is a prominent example of broadcast media influence in calming the violence.

In Kibera in minutes ... planning to attack the Kikambas ... Pamoja FM radio ... decided to call some of the Kikuyu elders, the Luo elders, the Kikamba elders to the studio to discuss the implications of the rumor that was going around, and they allowed the callers to call in, ask questions.

And don't even ask them questions ... because you will ask stupid questions ... Just give them a frequency, a microphone to address their peoples' ... because journalists cannot command that kind of attention ... but elders can ... People listen to their elders

A joint radio broadcast and joint newspaper headline also had significant impact, among other media events.

The best that I've ever seen of the media was that joint broadcast ... given how powerful music is .. the patriotic songs were helpful. The decision to spend an entire day talking about peace was very powerful.

The media ... played its role ... to bring down the tensions when media owners ... resolved to give a common voice. Before, we were all doing it in our own, different, independent ways, bringing in music groups or whatever ... bringing in people to talk about peace and the need to deal with this issue. It was really when media owners ... resolved, 'Fine, let's find a common approach, common headlines, common DVDs being distributed to all media houses,' that each media house in a collective way was able to help bring down the passions.

There was a parliament reporter ... and somebody asked him ... "Why did you guys all have the same headline ... 'Save Our Country'?" And he said, "Let's be realistic.... It's not that we're really concerned about that, because conflict sells.... The reason we did that is we realized...we couldn't do business with the dead."

The media finally stopped airing politicians ... stopped inviting analysts, stopped talk shows for a while ... Things changed a lot when NGOs came in and set up media programs that promoted peace.

Moreover, they refused to carry some content, e.g., the *Nation* refused to carry certain ads.

The Swedish Embassy called me and asked me to rally around and get the senior women editors of the papers. And ... report the voices of women and the impact of this on ordinary people ... use their pen before even the editors choose the stories ... Get the message out that "Enough is enough!" and get ordinary women to speak on how they have suffered and how peace was paramount ... The impact was immense ... And it was called the White Ribbon Peace Campaign ... So this led the way for other women groups to rally ... The interventionist movement.

Will 2012 be better or worse for the people?

Opinion was divided and often nuanced. On the negative side, too many issues remain unresolved, so pressures keep building.

The country is going to burn ... the media needs to read the early signs ... White-collar Kenyans don't even know what happened – they're shocked ... when they see my photos ... When this country burns in 2012, it will be more than tribal, it will be a class war.

Immediately after parliament endorsed the constitutional amendments under the peace accord, the issues were forgotten again. It was like, "Phew! We have peace now!" – we are back to normal, back to bickering ... back to the usual corruption, back to failure to provide services and listen to the public.

> This country has not cured the underlying causes of that bloodbath ... call it a volcano ... The factors which contributed to that fallout are still in place, nothing has changed much ... The peace and coexistence are totally superficial ... The very deep-seated animosities and the political and economic equations ... are still unresolved, and ... could just erupt again.

> I can't see anything on the horizon that says it isn't a likelihood for 2012. Look at how they behave. 2007 didn't affect them at all – it didn't touch them ... Nothing would have changed come 2012.

> If anything we are preparing for more violence ... People say, "The last election caught us by surprise, the next one will not!" ... Poison arrows ... arms are being amassed ... in preparation, even before we ask what we need to fight for ... indicating that the violence could be worse than before.

> If nothing happens with Agenda 4, it will be full-scale [war]. Rwanda will be nothing ... Politicians think about themselves and are very shortsighted.

> People will migrate because of the dreaded 2012. The immediate temporary peace seems fragile.

Violence may be moderate, stemming more from economic disparities than from tribalism.

> I really doubt we will see this kind of chaos – ... no tribe of peasants [will rise] against a tribe of peasants ... We're not going to see the kind of chaos we saw, depending on how The Hague thing goes. Chaos will be created by the tension between the wealthy and the poor ... People have learned that there's nothing to be gained from violence, and the politicians have realized that they stand to lose a lot too.

> The citizens have learned who loses. It is them who lose ... They lost jobs, they lost homes, they lost businesses. They won't do that again. There will be very low voter turnout ... I foresee two major contesting parties ... Election may not be as tribalistic, but a class issue.

There is a more hopeful attitude in some, based on the media having learned their lessons.

> Very hopeful. We've [KBN] re-branded. We've added new people who can give much better balanced coverage ... Yes, there will still be sloppy journalism as we approach 2012, but no one wants to be known as the media house that pushed us into the conflict ... sexed up issues.

There is hope that results of the intervening by-elections in 2010, concerning the new constitutional referendum, along with the outcome of the Truth, Justice and Reconciliation Commission, will be oil on the waters.

2010 is when we are having the new referendum on the constitution ... [T]he previous referendum showed us that our politicians will politicize anything ... So that if we make it through the new referendum, I'm hopeful about 2012 ... At the same time, we have the TJRC two years from now ... If we make it through those processes, then yes, I'm hopeful about 2012 ... That was one of the reasons people were saying we went into violence, because the electoral body was incompetent.

The jury is still out on The Hague tribunal's examination of the violence perpetrators and whether they will hazard reconciliation by invoking impunity.

It could happen again. The tribunal [for prosecuting post-election violence perpetrators] could raise their [perpetrators'] profile. It will polarize Kenya ... And there's impunity.

Very much depends on ... the question of what to do with the perpetrators, because people are waiting to find out who they are ... So a lot depends on how this issue is handled ... There are many who're in jail, many in IDP [Internally Displaced People] camps, many who know the truth and many more who don't ... So it's still volatile ... even the peace, the calm that we see, is not that deep. There are still people who can't talk to each other to this very day ...I don't know whether enough's been done to help reconcile the communities.

Is *ubuntu* an ideal past its prime?

Ubuntu has suffered deterioration and marginalization. Regardless, it continues to retain viability in the opinion of many, and though languishing under the assault of capitalism, still holds the prospect of revival. Philosophical *ubuntu* is blunted by a practical problem, survival.

Ubuntu applies to our extended families but not beyond that, because of Western influence and Kenyan influence too.

I don't think it [*ubuntu*] does [figure into the future of the place], because a lot has changed. In our cultures, we have shed ... a lot of good things, and especially the people who have grown up in urban settings ... We're doing it [the same things as Americans – keeping your brother's problems as *his* problems, not yours] and we're going on with our lives – buying cars, houses, things. We're not helping ... anymore.

We've lost the core values, what it means to be human ... The problems are deeply rooted ... can only be sorted out by people having dialogue ... at the community level, because that is where the trouble is.

Communalism of Africa lost out to that capitalist materialism that took over ... acquire, accumulate ... There is none [room for ubuntuism] because journalism has appropriated those Western values ... compete, get the best story, sell your paper, and go home.

Ubuntu – not enough – not sufficient grounding for journalists covering conflict, because how many journalists coming in know about it? ... Capitalist thinking sneaking in ... eroded some cultural values ... We view each other through self-interest now ... We need to work hard at it [*ubuntu*], especially for the younger fellows.

It [*ubuntu*/traditional African communal values] is the only thing that can save Africa, if we can go back ... There is something within the individual ... which God has put in the individual – the contact to others.

Ubuntu is actually what kept us resilient in Africa after all these years and instances of war ... Can the United Nations claim to have taken care of all those IDP's? ... Relatives and neighbors [took] care of IDP's because of the *ubuntu* spirit. And as soon as the media picks up on that spirit and encourages it, then we will even reduce a lot of need for donor support you see around.

I think we are getting there ... And the reason I say we are getting there is, after we experienced the events of last year, we are asking ourselves, "Who are we?" And you see a lot of government programs, like Najuvunia kwa Kenya / I am proud to be a Kenyan ... a lot of campaigns ...and all saying it doesn't matter where I come from, I am a Kenyan, and that should be the uniting factor ... So it has started working, but among the younger generation. The older generation of our parents is still very tied to ... their tribes ... But the younger generation is actually adopting that.

The urban youth may not be able to explain *ubuntu*, but they practice it. They may not have a whole set philosophy, but as they're growing up, they keep wondering who's who. And the kind of socialization that we go through is that of relationships that are built from day one. And we're taught to care for the persons because they are members of the family (nuclear and extended). So *ubuntu* exists in the socialization, even though it might not be as deep among the youth, but it exists underneath the surface.

And now when you try to restructure the nation you have this concept of *ubuntu* ... But when it comes to the nation, it dissipates ... Now it is a new concept on which Africa has to rebuild itself ... It does not mean you cannot integrate it into ethics ... because that is how you build it up ... Rebuilding it now is bringing it into the mainstream of the nation ... Practical ways is people really starting to respect each other ... story of class discussion ... letting out all angers.

Could the media revive *ubuntu* values to bring healing? Absolutely! ... We have assumed from our education that the institution of elders has no place ... but ... Now for the media, we have picked up the model that news is a top-down affair ... that it's only the top that make news, names that make news; those down there are mere statistics ... Violence makes news ... However, give elders media platform to talk to their people ... Education system under the colonials were meant to serve the colonials ... and our syllabuses still reflect that and not community service ... The media were much more focused on helping the city ...We, however, hope as Kenya goes digital, rural areas could easily get signals to broadcast instead of expensive

Media and Post-Election Violence in Kenya

frequencies ... would like to see the media reporting from H-U-T to H-U-T, because that's where the heart of Africa is.

You see, our sense of community is stronger in terms of our ethnic community rather than our sense of nation ... There needs to be a deliberate working around to reinvent that belonging ... what should define us ... A sense of nationhood should come first ... We need to create that confidence in the government institutions that every-body is included ... Cross-ethnic marriages helping out ... the younger peoples are losing that strong sense of ethnicity ... When your parents come from different tribes you identify as Kenyan before a particular tribe.

As Kenyans this [*ubuntu,* the "brotherhood thing"] is where we should have a lot of optimism, because we're surrounded by all these conflict areas ...We should unite together because the forces outside are much worse than the forces inside ... Did that [ubuntuism] stop us from hacking each other? Have you been to Rift Valley today? If ubuntuism was alive today, they would say, "You can come back." But they have not come back...every town in the Rift Valley has a camp of IDP's ... The only way ubun-tuism can work with us is the leaders embracing it at the national level; then it will work at the ground level ... We need a voice like Mandela's that can unite us.

By virtue of how we are brought up, okay, *at least the way we were brought up* ... with this sense of community ... And *there used to be,* because it's going [away], that sense of, "So and so is in trouble!" – everybody comes to the rescue. And everything was a community thing ... And we are all part of the process. I think we are redefining who we are...we are losing that sense of community, and it is becoming more of what works for *me* ... [P]eople have failed to realize it's a new community – your new community is *those people you are with!* Fine, now you're in Nairobi. Your sense of community should be defined by '*Now* who are your neighbors?' – maybe not those who necessarily speak your language ... Our sense of nationhood is so fragmented ... So in that sense we are yet to grow, but it's happening everywhere in the world ... I think it was Martin Luther [King] who said, "Injustice anywhere is a threat to justice everywhere. "And our common prosperity is so intertwined – if they thrive it will help me thrive ... [It] will be about who can provide the services for the people.

What is the outlook for peace journalism in Kenya?

A proactive peace agenda for journalism holds promise of authentic cultural development and sustainable nation-building.

Peace Journalism needs to [be] taught in a larger context of development...Peace-building vs. peace-making ... peace journalism should encompass the reporting of every event.

Organize and increase exchange visits between people from different ethnic commu-nities. This initiative has been successful ... The media should highlight these and intensify training on development communication ... understand that what they say affects everyone ... shield certain information like other countries do instead of publishing it on the front page.

They [South African editors and journalists] understand their role in national development and their hold in democracy – only one hour of election news per night and no election numbers [vote tallying] and all parties get equal coverage. They made an assertion that other things were bigger, more important than who wins this election ... The coverage of news is to support the president in resolving an issue [positive coverage] not bringing down, sensationalizing an unresolved issue [negative coverage] ... South Africans took a proactive stance ... I think we still have a long way to go.

There are people who are going to the media to look for solutions....the whole idea of an intervention point: how do we bring in media that actually makes development an agenda of news reporting ... change their audiences to appreciate information that is more on development and peace than on conflict and drama?

The challenge for PJ: find a way to package it that has sufficient appeal to win financial support.

Peace sells for one day, the day of the handshake ... News is a business ... We need to find creative ways to report peace ... package peace so that it sells.

Friends ... are saying, "Peace journalism? That's advocacy work – you can't get funding for that!" ... Peace does not sell ... The challenge is to turn the idea into a product that sells and therefore media can promote it as a product.

Referring to [the joint headline] – Before the media came together...there was a lot of work that had already been done. The media and peace workers had met for two weeks, bringing in a lot of media personalities ... The media were very ... quick at grasping the whole idea of making peace in news and leading people to recognize each other as citizens ... [T]he way the media appeared, it looked like news that was also peaceful events, and it drove business.

"Does peace journalism veer away from business?" Not exactly. If ... [the media] can change their audiences, they will be ready to take a new package ... it's the media that drives the thinking, the mindset, the politics, the culture of a people. But if the media can deliver it without the strife ... I don't see them running out of business – still selling, but now with a different model.

It's a money thing ... Advertisers follow ... researchers like Steadman, who measure listenership and viewership, and then follow up why the audience prefers this station or that ... There is room for peace journalism, but it doesn't make front page ... it might earn a spot in the middle pages ... people appreciate it [peace journalism] – it makes great impact ... It has to gel with the newspaper's agenda.

Good stories, with appealing human-interest, could go far to win paying customers and loyal audiences.

The media has gone out documenting details of the violence as it is happening now and as it happened 20 years prior ... While the media is relaying those events, they should also be relaying the peace-making events in those same areas because there are a lot of good stories.

There's so many ... human-interest stories. So we have to look at who makes the news ... We need to focus on some of those ... human-interest stories, and move away from covering the politicians.

Where is most conflict experienced? Usually it's among those people who fear...the very poor in society. [H]ow are slums covered by the mainstream media? Whenever Kibera is on TV it's because they've done something bad...So we get the idea that nothing positive comes out of these areas. So already when you're feeling marginalized... like the underdog, you always try to exert yourself and make your presence known ... a way they get attention ... [T]hough it might not make much business sense to talk positively about the poor and the slum people ...there are a lot of positive things that happen in ... all these other places. From time to time can media focus on the positive aspects ... so that they don't have to struggle to make news?

Increasing income will prove decisive since full-fledged PJ will often require costly investigative reporting.

PJ was never part of our training ... The signs were there in terms of outburst ... conflict ...negative language about stereotyping ... the various ethnic types ... But we never summed up these things as some of the signs around conflict, simply because we never anchored them in the root cause of conflict.

It takes a seasoned journalist to be a peace journalist, not someone who's trying to get ahead. Most journalists make a name for themselves by the conflict they cover, so peace journalism needs ... someone who's willing to spend the time to investigate.

PJ is not just talk about the issues that *lead to* the conflict, because so often...the media just focuses on that, but let's go back to the issues that *caused* it. It's very expensive for media houses to support that ... We have to send reporters to some of these places, accommodate them, because issues-based journalism takes time. You need to do a lot of research, a lot of groundwork, to get to the root cause of the problem ... media houses may not be so willing to spend money on some of those things when I can discover conflict and it doesn't really cost much, but it still sells ... issues-based journalism takes a lot of investigative reporting, which is very costly...but then you're doing a service to the leaders, because they can address those issues. If you bring them to their attention ... then you're going to work towards some peace or at least resolving some of the causes of conflict.

[R]eport proactively ... The media should work closely with conflict analysts ... we are always able, based on past events and ... scenario-building ... to tell what issues are going to cause violence in the near future. If the media could begin to cover it at this stage .. journalists can deliberately do a conflict analysis and then identify a complex situation at its latent stage and ... be able to intervene by ... mediation ... we know... the root causes of conflict here ... some of the cultural problems that help trigger the violence ... the governance issues. Now the media is able to [do] an analysis of how these issues are playing in politics, in relationships between different communities.

In-depth reporting must overcome the reflex to sensationalize and replace it with vision-casting, community dialogue, and a variety of cultural features.

... morally bankrupt ... corruption ... impunity – that attitude, 'Who cares?' ... Bring in the media house to reflect ... focus on the issues, "What's eating us up?" News value for Kenya is ... if it's not sensational, it doesn't go ... Highly packed with rumors ... (they [Zambia and other African nations with solid journalism] seem to have better morals) ... The problems are deeply rooted ... can only be sorted out by people having dialogue ...at the community level, because that is where the trouble is.

"How do you persuade others to sacrifice their interests for the good of others?" We rarely engage that in our training directly, but that helps our trainers see the vision and what their role in the vision is ... [W]e help to see their current situation, and ... ask them what they want in the next five years. We give them plenty of time ... They describe their vision very ... beautifully for the next few years ... Then we talk to them about what they can do at the personal ... relational ... structural ... and cultural level ... in that way we don't prescribe but let them do it.

TV and radio have ... time that can be dedicated to ... other programs ... drama, entertainment ... So there is a lot of expression there that can be done ... But in the newspaper, not maybe the front pages, but elsewhere.

The whole package of PJ will demand strategic training, especially of the young.

The media were telling us, "We don't know how to do reconciliation – how do you do it? We were completely unprepared to deal with the conflict. We only know how to do the easy story ... We need more workshops."

That is now the challenge ... in peace journalism ... there are people out there who can write well; conflict analysts ... conflict journalists can be trained.

Make vernacular radio stations more professional and train the young ... A justice and truth commission by the UN is organizing training for people in order to prevent war.

We did not anticipate violence ... our training was much more focused on covering elections ... Looking back we should have included some training on peace journalism.

When the media brings in warring parties to the studio we are already playing mediator, and when the people see their leaders talking in the same studio they realize there is room to talk about things ... how to make Kenyans see beyond the otherness of the other to the common humanity ... We do not have time ... what [with]

Media and Post-Election Violence in Kenya   649

"unwitting bias" ... it even happens unconsciously ... We need more training to over-come the unwitting bias in Kenyan journalists ... that kept journalists from talking to each other in the newsroom.

in 2007 even the media houses were divided and wouldn't consult with one another ... Political priorities took the place of ethical/professional standards ... So what you call peace journalism was never there at all ... And we had a workshop looking at the context of peace journalism. And it was very interesting looking at how it could manifest itself here and the three C's of peace journalism ... conflict which they never defined, the contradictions that followed, and the way they were reporting ... It acted like a time bomb ... But have we learned anything? No, we have not – we have not developed any conflict-editorial guidelines – we don't have trained war correspond-ents like Europe ...We still cover conflict like any daily story item.

Ubuntu and "peace journalism" in Kenya

Press theory in the West was born in revolutionary England. Weary of royalty's claimed privilege to define reality, indeed to control the conscience, liberalism cited the rational individual as history's center and telos (Siebert *et al.*, 1956, p. 40). Able inherently to sort truth from error, as Milton claimed (1644, p. 719), the Enlightenment Self carried responsibility to establish its proper moral vision through logic, wisdom, and experimentation. Media filled a moral need, not to mention market needs. When markets dominate, or information is politicized, or the individual is not free, what then?

On the media side, the common response is a call to reform. The press in the United States came under reform of a reluctant sort in the mid-1940s with the Commission on Freedom of the Press led by Robert M. Hutchins of the University of Chicago. Commission sponsors clearly intended that the Commission's Final Report would underscore classical liberal values, saving the press from government interference and enabling the "watchdog function" and free-market competition among news providers. Instead, sponsors and public alike received a short book outlining the well-known Social Responsibility theory of media, a call for "full access to the day's intelligence" and a forum for clarifying the "goals and values of the society," among other recommendations (Leigh, 1947, pp. 27–28).

Kenyan media have their own loci of reform. The Media Council of Kenya pub-lished its Code of Professional Conduct in 2001 in shirt-pocket format for easy reference. Few journalists know the booklet, and fewer still carry it (Fackler and Baker, 2010). Nonetheless, Kenya presents a bright and profitable media climate. Several universities prepare graduates for work in the field. Freedoms impossible to exercise a decade ago are commonplace. Stories are told of the courageous few dis-senters who resisted government intimidation and won respect as advocates of democratic reform.

We conclude that Kenya and most of sub-Sahara Africa has the advantage of a framework of theory and social practice unlike anything imagined by the Hutchins Commission or any other Western media reform effort.

African life is communal. John Mbiti's famous revision of Descartes, "We are therefore I am," rings true from university seminars to village palaver (Mbiti, 1969, p. 109). The "philosophy" called *ubuntu* arises not from classical texts but "religion, proverbs, oral tradition, ethics and morals" (Mbiti, p. 2). The rational individual developed from Enlightenment categories required an information system capable of providing competitive advantage and early access to market news. That autonomous model of humanity and its communicational appetites are now under serious review in the West, which scrambles to locate alternative models.

In the communal South, *ubuntu* is part of the sinew of culture, often so close that to call it a "model" seems a superfluous abstraction. Clifford Christians (2004) has outlined the significance of *ubuntu* to professional journalism. He reconceptualized the task, mission, and social responsibility of media based on this social theory rising from African traditions without emulating European versions. *Ubuntu* permeates the "entire life of society" with "respect for the human in all humanity" (Magesa, 2002, p. 88). *Ubuntu* is summarized in the Xhosa proverb, *ngumuntu ngabantu umutu*, (a person is a person through other persons). DeGruchy calls *ubuntu* "essential for the recovery of democracy in Africa," suggesting that life in the village was once an inclusive palaver, a quest for consensus currently lost.

> This does not imply the denial of individuals or individual political rights. On the contrary, a respect for each person as an individual is essential....The emphasis is on human sociality, on inter-personal relations, on the need which each person has for others in order to be herself or himself. This is the root of African humanism (DeGruchy, 1995, p. 191).

Christians adds that *ubuntu* and communitarianism, its Western (rough) equivalent, revises for the West its Enlightenment priorities.

> Humans are dialogic agents within a language community. All moral matters involve the community. A self exists only within "webs of interlocution." ... We talk ... to discover a good reason for acting (Christians, 2004, p. 240).

If *ubuntu* is the basis for sustainable values, why is Africa "torn apart" by wars and conflict, putting eight million into refugee or displaced persons status? (Tarimo and Manwelo, 2007, p. 11). The "disintegration of value systems" cited by Tarimo and Manwelo is a denial that *ubuntu* is sustainable in the face of pervasive corruption, famine, or draught (p. 12). In our interviews, many worried that Kenya was doomed to repeat or increase pre- and postelection violence in the 2012 national elections.

> They [media owners and political party bosses] got absolutely nothing out of the experience. They live in a tribal cocoon. Media houses were divided by tribe. I know of one prominent Kikuyu media owner who actually participated in top-level PNU meetings at which vote-rigging was discussed (interviewee).

Media and Post-Election Violence in Kenya

PJ presents tensions between advocacy and objectivity (Lynch and McGoldrick, 2005, p. 203). Kenyan media leaders strongly disagree whether PJ holds promise for Kenya. The current head of the Kenya Union of Journalists, David Matende, told a Media Council of Kenya forum that media "have no business dabbling in advocacy and campaigning for dialogue and peace" (Namwaya, 2009, p. 24). Many disagree based on experience of media peace-building efforts in Sri Lanka and Sudan, and Kenya itself. Chaacha Mwita, former group managing editor of The Standard Group, urges media to take up the peace cause, even prior to anticipated violence and with strict impartiality on the divisive matter of tribal interests (p. 24).

Media professionals clearly prefer practices that support peace and dampen conflict, without sacrificing essential truth-telling. Toward that end, *ubuntu* becomes a sensitized concept and possible bridge to a more inclusive sense of the public sphere where the Other is neither feared nor oppressed, but considered a "gateway to new opportunity and unimagined beauty" (Kobia, 2003, p. 4). Kobia urges:

> The courage to hope means that we shall refuse to accept our current experience ... as permanent. We must negate the negation imposed by history ... Africans must be convinced that ... a better, brighter future is possible. ... We must defeat the Afropessimism that strangles nascent initiatives for transforming our present situation (p. 5).

International Media Support (IMS) urges that media coverage of tribal or ethnic violence purposely avoid blame and accusation, or unnamed sources without explanation of why attribution was deleted. IMS manuals advise newsroom diversity and a newsroom culture that can identify hate speech, gender discrimination, and xenophobia (Howard, 2008, pp. 13, 29).

Christians wants journalists animated by *ubuntu*-communitarianism to create interpretive accounts that reflect genuine features of a situation, rather than hurried conclusions of observer opinion.

> Given the moral dimension inscribed in the social order, interpreting its various configurations adequately means elaborating the moral component ... Eliminating the divisions among ourselves ... opens the pathway to crossing barriers and to reconciliation across cultures (Christians, 2004, p. 251).

Our review of PEV shows that cliché, redundancy, and conscious ambiguity distracted media from careful, thick, or propeace analysis as tensions heightened in Kenya. If moral literacy is the media's privileged mission in *ubuntu*-communitarianism, Kenyan media failed.

Perhaps Blankenberg's call for "liberatory journalism" (1999, p. 60) with its strategy of "discussion leading to solutions" and empowerment of the "interactive self" (Christians, 2004, p. 249) can be joined to Africa-based mediation strategies such as "Deep Democracy" (described in *Inside the No*) to reconfigure public journalism from information provider to agent of social change.

Our panel of interviews point to "a cracked foundation" in social trust in Kenya. A "culture of impunity" tells its people that the powerful eat their cake (Dowden,

2009, p. 415), while the peasant makes no claims on the state ("what we lacked was a government that listened") and seeks his/her pitiful portion from the dry earth. Where media reach, they frequently project a culture of violence and competition. For land, commerce, and patronage, the race goes to the swift and the connected.

In October, 2009, Kofi Annan returned to Kenya for consultations with all parties involved in the peace process. His report was telling:

> Progress is being made … But the pace of reform must be accelerated. Kenyans are concerned that the window of opportunity to deliver reform is rapidly closing … [A] recurrence of the crisis and violence … is a serious risk if tangible reform is not achieved … This cannot take place without the right protections of the democratic space. (Annan, 2009)

The foremost protection of the public sphere is a free and responsible press. The democratic world has recognized this for nearly four centuries. We still work at it, worldwide. In Kenya, that work faces obstacles, not the least of which is a culture of fear and a loss of trust between neighbors. This study adds then, for Kenya at this time, for democracy at all times, the need for a press inclined toward peace, motivated by the old *ubuntu* of the village, alert to the "opportunity for a new start" (Mayor, 2001, p. 464).

Acknowledgment

The authors wish to thank the McGregor Foundation, the Nagel Institute for the Study of World Christianity, and the Calvin College Alumni Association for their support of this work.

Notes

1 A photo essay titled *Kenya Burning* was published in Nairobi in April 2008, and thereafter withdrawn from bookshops due to is graphic yet forcefully truthful images. It may be secured privately from the photographer cited in References.
2 These media houses, agencies, and universities were represented in the interviews: Nation Media Group, Standard Publishing, Royal Media, Kenya Television Network, K24 (television), Kenya Broadcasting Network, Associated Press, Africa Women and Child Feature Service, Media Council of Kenya, National Council of Churches of Kenya, Catholic Peace and Justice Commission, Nairobi Peace Initiative-Africa, Daystar University, Tangaza College (Catholic University of East Africa), The Media Institute (Nairobi), and consultants in print, marketing, and visual communication.

References

Abuoga, J.B., and Mutere, A.A. (1988) *The History of the Press in Kenya*, ACCE, Nairobi.
Africa Confidential (2006) Biting the snake, March 17, p. 4.

Ainslie, R. (1966) *The Press in Africa: Communications Past and Present*, Gollancz, London.

Altschull, J.H. (1995) *Agents of Power: The Media and Public Policy*, 2nd edn, Allyn & Bacon, Boston, MA.

Annan, K. (2009) Remarks on conclusion to his visit to Kenya, 4–7 October 2009. www.marsgroupkenya.org/multimedia/?StoryID=269342 (accessed July 23, 2010).

Blankenberg, N. (1999) In search of real freedom. *Critical Arts*, 13 (2), 42–65.

Bourgault, L.M. (1995) *Mass Media in Sub-Saharan Africa*, Indiana University Press, Bloomington.

Christians, C. (2004) *Ubuntu* and communitarianism in media ethics. *Ecquid Novi*, 25 (2), 235–256.

de Beer, A.S., Kasoma, F.P., Megwa, E.R., and Steyn, E. (1995) Sub-Saharan Africa, in (ed. J. Merril), *Global Journalism: Survey of International Communication*, 3rd edn, Longman, New York, pp. 209–268.

DeGruchy, J. (1995) *Christian and Democracy*, Dave Phillip, Cape Town, SA.

Dowden, R. (2009) *Africa*, Public Affairs, New York.

Fackler, M., and Baker, E. (2010) *Journalism Makes You Kind of Selfless, Ethics and Evil in the Public Sphere*, Hampton, New York.

Faringer, G.L. (1991) *Press Freedom in Africa*, Praeger, New York.

Freedom House (2008) Freedom of the press – Kenya, www.freedomhouse.org/inc/content/pubs/pfs/inc_country_detail.cfm?country=7422&year=2008&pf (accessed July 21, 2010).

Hachten, W. (1971) *Muffled Drums: The News Media in Africa*, Iowa State University Press, Ames.

Hachten, W.A. (1993) *The Press in Africa*, Iowa State University Press, Ames.

Howard, R. (2008) *My Tribe is Journalism*, International Media Support, Copenhagen.

Karoney, F. (2005, May 3) YouTube, www.youtube.com/watch?v+QrxpPHQ17SU (last accessed December 29, 2009).

Kitchen, H. (ed) (1956) *The Press in Africa*, Ruth Sloan Associates, Washington, DC.

Kobia, S. (2003) *The Courage to Hope*, Action, Nairobi.

Leigh, R. (1947) *A Free and Responsible Press*, University of Chicago Press, Chicago.

Lynch, J., and McGoldrick, A. (2005) *Peace Journalism*, Hawthorne, Gloucestershire, UK.

Magesa, L. (2002) *Christian Ethics in Africa*, Acton, Nairobi.

Maina, L.W. (2006) *African Media Development Initiative*, BBC World Service Trust, London.

Mayor, F. (2001) *The World Ahead*, Zed, London.

Mazrui, A. (2007) Pan Africanism, democracy and leadership in Africa: The continuing legacy for the new millennium, http://igcs.binghamton.edu/igcs_site/dirton6.html (last accessed July 23, 2010).

Mbiti, J. (1969) *African Religion and Philosophy*, Praeger, Westport, CT.

Milton, J. (1644, n.d.) "Areopagitica" in *Complete Poetry and Selected Prose of John Milton*, The Modern Library, New York.

Namwaya, O. (2009) Peace-making versus professional independence. *The Media Observer*, June, pp. 24–26.

Ochieng, P. (1992) *I Accuse the Press: An Insider's View of the Media and Politics in Africa*, Initiatives Publishers, Nairobi.

Ole Ronkei, M. (1995) Emerging communication strategies in the press-Church alliance in Kenyan politics, doctoral dissertation, University of Oregon.

Opiyo, B.A. (1994) The press and Kenyan politics: A study of newsmaking in a newly democratic state, unpublished doctoral dissertation, University of Iowa.

Passin, H. (1963) Writer and journalist in the transitional society, in (ed. L. Pye), *Communication and Political Development*, Princeton University Press, Princeton, NJ.

Rambaud, B. (2008) Caught between information and condemnation: The Kenyan media and the electoral campaigns of December 2007, in *The General Elections in Kenya*, (ed. J. Lafargue), IFRA, Nairobi.

Schramm, W., and Ruggels, W.L. (1967) How mass media systems grow, in *Communication and Change in the Developing Countries*, (eds D. Lerner and W. Schramm), East-West Center, Honolulu, pp. 57–75.

Scotton, J.F. (1972) Growth of the vernacular press in colonial East Africa: Patterns of government control, doctoral dissertation, University of Wisconsin.

Siebert, F., Peterson, T., and Schramm, W. (1956) *Four Theories of the Press*, University of Illinois Press, Urbana.

Tarimo, A., and Manwelo, P. (2007) *African Peacemaking and Governance*, Acton, Nairobi.

Waki Report (2008) www.eastandard.net/downloads/Waki_Report.pdf (accessed July 23, 2010).

34

Ethics of Survival
Media, Palestinians, and Israelis in Conflict

Oliver Witte

The term "ethics" is woefully inadequate to describe a foundation for decision-making in the Arab-Israeli conflict. At its base, the conflict is a fight for survival – both national and individual – inflated by each side's conviction that it is doing the will of God.

On both sides there are people who are willing not only to kill for their side but also to die for it. Still more wrenching, they are willing to sacrifice themselves by killing people *on their own side* whom they see as insufficiently zealous or too cooperative with the other side. Examples cannot get more extreme than Yitzhak Rabin, prime minister of Israel, who was assassinated not by a Palestinian Arab but by an Israeli Jew, and Anwar Sadat, the president of Egypt, who was assassinated not by an Israeli Jew but by Egyptian Muslims. Their offense was the same: They wanted to make peace. Lesser-known individuals, including journalists (Committee to Protect Journalists, 2007) have also suffered the same fate for the same reason.

This chapter will distinguish between law, ethics, and morality. Law is defined as a rule of conduct established by a government with the power to enforce it. Offenses are punished by sanctions such as execution, imprisonment, and fines. Ethics is defined as the dictate of a social group such as a family, business, or profession. Offenses are punished by sanctions such as censure or banishment. Morality is defined as a personal value system. Offenses are punished by guilt.

Laws and ethics are externally created, published, imposed, and punished; guilt is imposed internally upon oneself by one's own conscience. Laws and ethics are subject to change; morality tends to stick.

Viewed as a pyramid, law would be the base. An ethical code typically would include obedience to laws and would add obedience to a set of social values. A moral code would incorporate obedience to laws and to a social code of ethics and would add obedience to one's own personal values.

The Handbook of Global Communication and Media Ethics, First Edition. Edited by Robert S. Fortner and P. Mark Fackler.
© 2011 Blackwell Publishing Ltd. Published 2011 by Blackwell Publishing Ltd.

A legal system is informed by a consensus of what is required for an orderly society, such as traffic laws and property rights, enforced by a judicial process. An ethical system is informed by a consensus of what is accepted by one's social, business, or professional group, such as what constitutes fair competition. A trade union or profession, for example, will control admission and membership. The right to call oneself a plumber or a doctor, for example, and to participate in group activities might be enforced by a legal process such as licensing or just by consensus of the group.

It is also important to be mindful of exceptions. Just because a government has enacted a law does not make it moral or even ethical. Consider, for example, the path from slavery to emancipation to separate-but-equal – all legal in their times but seen as immoral, then, by some, and as immoral, now, by consensus. For example: "I own slaves (immoral), but I treat them well (ethical) if they behave (lawful)." The example is relevant to the Arab-Israeli conflict, where Palestinians in the Occupied Territories see themselves as prisoners at best and slaves at worst – and badly treated slaves to boot. Israelis see themselves as fighting for their state's right to exist as a Jewish state and for their personal right to live freely as Jews. Neither is a given.

At one point in recent American history, professional groups such as lawyers and architects incorporated a fee schedule in their codes of ethics. The purpose was to promote competition on the basis of services, not price. However, the US Justice Department viewed it as price-fixing, which is against the law, and forced its elimination.

Under these definitions, international ethical systems might include the Fourth Geneva Convention on the Rules of War and various United Nations resolutions. The social group is the community of nations, its primary enforcement mechanism is censure, and Israel – the nation most often censured – is free to ignore the punishment. Even the Marquess of Queensberry rules might be considered an ethical system for boxers.

Some offenses, such as murder, would be contrary to the principles of all three: law, ethics, and morality.

Except …

On the evening of Jan. 15, 2005, Ella Abukasis, 17, and her younger brother Tamir were visiting friends in Sderot, Israel, a city of 19 000 about 1 kilometer from the Gaza Strip, when an air raid siren warned residents that a rocket would land somewhere in the city within 20 seconds. With no time to get to an air-raid shelter, she shielded her brother with her body. He survived; she did not (Israel Ministry of Foreign Affairs, 2005).

Their story is not unusual. Ella's death did not make the New York Times or the major news services. The rocket that killed her was one of thousands that have been fired at Israel. Most land harmlessly, but not all. Ella happened to be one of the last to die before Israel unilaterally began withdrawing its troops and settlements from Gaza.

Even Sderot is not particularly unusual. It used to be an Arab city called Najd until its residents were evicted during Israel's 1948–1949 war of independence and

Ethics of Survival 657

its buildings razed (Morris, 2004). Its former residents, now refugees, still consider the land theirs and the rocket attacks justified as self-defense.

One year after Ella died, a Palestinian election brought to power the Islamic Resistance Movement (better known by its Arabic acronym, Hamas), which is dedicated to the eradication of Israel, and the rocket attacks increased in number, range, and lethality (Reich, 2008, p. 276). In 2007, Hamas forced out its more moderate political rival, Fatah, and seized total control of Gaza.

Infuriated by the continuing rocket attacks on its civilians, Israel invaded the Gaza strip in 2008. By the time the shooting ended, 1 300 Palestinians and 13 Israelis had died. Both sides claimed victory – Israel for forcing Hamas to switch tactics from rocket attacks to what Hamas called a culture of resistance and Hamas for forcing Israel to withdraw unilaterally (Hamas, 2009).

What does this have to do with communication ethics? Plenty. By writing down its principles in a covenant, Hamas subjects them to scrutiny by the outside world. The outside world's opinion is relevant because both Palestine and Israel are kept afloat by foreign aid. Israel, for example, has been receiving about $3 billion a year in economic and military aid from the United States for decades. "The extra U.S. aid was crucial; it made it possible for Israel to take risks that otherwise might not have been adopted" (Reich, 2008, p. 149).

By and large, the donors disapprove of attacks on civilians, which worked to the disadvantage of Hamas. Israel's response to the provocation, deliberately disproportionate in Gaza, was viewed as unfair, which worked to the disadvantage of Israel.

Further, the Hamas covenant serves as a rallying point that defines correct opinions and conduct for its social group (Palestinians). In its own words, the covenant "clarifies its picture, reveals its identity, outlines its stand, explains its aims, speaks about its hopes, and calls for its support, adoption and joining its ranks" (Hamas covenant, retrieved from Avalon Project at Yale Law School, 1988). It says it aims to "obliterate" Israel. It quotes the Prophet (Mohammad): "The Day of Judgment will not come about until Moslems fight the Jews (killing the Jews), when the Jew will hide behind stones and trees. The stones and trees will say O Moslems, O Abdulla, there is a Jew behind me, come and kill him." Territorial compromise (land for peace) is clearly prohibited: "The Islamic Resistance Movement believes that the land of Palestine is an Islamic Waqf [sacred trust] consecrated for future Moslem generations until Judgment Day. It, or any part of it, should not be squandered: it, or any part of it, should not be given up." Thus, "Initiatives, and so-called peaceful solutions and international conferences, are in contradiction to the principles of the Islamic Resistance Movement." Hamas's political rival, the PLO, is accused of secularism, which the covenant rejects as contradicting Muslim ideology.

The covenant is keenly aware of the power of communication to tell its story and to promote unity. It advocates "issuing of explanatory bulletins, favourable articles and booklets, enlightening the masses regarding the Palestinian issue. ... Jihad is not confined to the carrying of arms and the confrontation of the enemy. The effective word, the good article, the useful book, support and solidarity – together with the presence of sincere purpose for the hoisting of Allah's banner higher and higher – all these are elements of the Jihad for Allah's sake."

Remedies for the injustice of occupation are limited: "There is no solution for the Palestinian question except through Jihad." And: "Jihad for the Liberation of Palestine is an Individual Duty. ... It is necessary to instill the spirit of Jihad in the heart of the nation so that they would confront the enemies and join the ranks of the fighters."

Jews are demonized by reference to the *Protocols of the elders of Zion* (1903), the infamous anti-Semitic hoax, to justify Hamas's accusations. The purpose of Jihad, says the covenant, is to "rid the land and the people of their uncleanliness, vileness and evils."

On the other hand, the covenant also presents a humanistic side. As it states, "[Hamas] takes care of human rights and is guided by Islamic tolerance when dealing with the followers of other religions. It does not antagonize anyone of them except if it is antagonized by it or stands in its way to hamper its moves and waste its efforts. Under the wing of Islam, it is possible for the followers of the three religions – Islam, Christianity and Judaism – to coexist in peace and quiet with each other. Peace and quiet would not be possible except under the wing of Islam."

The New York Times concluded: "In that tactical sense, the war (Israel's 2008–2009 invasion of Gaza) was a victory for Israel and a loss for Hamas. However, in the field of public opinion, Hamas took the upper hand. Its leaders have noted the international condemnation of Israel over allegations of disproportionate force, a perception they hope to continue to use to their advantage. Suspending the rocket fire could also serve that goal" (Bronner, 2009).

The Times noted that Khaled Meshal, who heads Hamas's political wing, Hamas's top position, was "eager" for a cease-fire and that his movement was seeking a state only in land seized by Israel in 1967. In June 2009, a total of two rockets were fired from Gaza, one of the lowest monthly totals since the attacks began in 2002, according to an Israeli military spokesman (Khodary and Bronner, 2009).

The discontinuity between covenant and comment became even stranger in February 2010, when the Associated Press moved a story quoting a Hamas spokesman expressing regret for the rocket attacks.

"We apologize for any harm that might have come to Israeli civilians," the Hamas government wrote. The statement quoted by the AP added that the rockets were not intended to hit civilians, but often strayed from their course. The purpose of the rockets, Hamas said, was to defend Gazans against Israeli military strikes, and the statement repeated its consistent assertion that Palestinians had the right to resist Israeli occupation. Before the week was out, Hamas had issued a clarification, again distributed by the Associated Press: "The report that was submitted regarding the Goldstone report does not include any apologies and what took place was an incorrect interpretation of some of its wording," according to the clarification (Jawad, 2010).

What's going on here?

Ethics of Survival

Hamas was responding to allegations by a team of United Nations' investigators, headed by Richard Goldstone, a South African jurist, that charged both Israel and Hamas with targeting civilians and that charged Israel with excessive force in its response.

By way of explanation, the AP quoted Gaza analyst Naji Sharrab, who said Hamas might have come under domestic pressure for apologizing. Hamas, he said, was addressing different audiences – the international community with the apology and local militants with the clarification.

Both Hamas and Israel, as expected, rejected the Goldstone report. The next step would be for the UN Security Council to refer the Goldstone report to the International Criminal Court, which was created in 2002 to prosecute individuals for genocide, crimes against humanity, war crimes, and the crime of aggression. It has the power to order reparations, individually, or collectively. Israel is not a member and Palestine, which is not a state, is ineligible to join. (Do not confuse the International Criminal Court with the International Court of Justice, which also sits in the Hague. The main function of the ICJ is to settle legal disputes referred to it by states or international agencies. Although both courts are limited in their punitive powers, they can exert a powerful influence in shaping world public opinion, which might become more important than force in future conflict resolution as laws and ethical codes – if not morals – are disseminated, studied and shared.)

Also in February 2010, Israel said it had reprimanded a brigadier general and a colonel for firing artillery shells at a built-up area. Some of the shells hit a United Nations compound in Gaza (Kershner, 2010).

The point is that Judge Goldstone has done a valuable service to the cause of peace not only by focusing the world's attention on rockets and retaliation but by focusing each side's attention on its own identity.

Meshal is faced with a decision: Should he say what he believes, which would be the ethical decision? Sticking with the apology could get him assassinated. What is more important – ethics or survival? Sticking with what the radical elements in his constituency want to hear could get him shunned by the world community. What's more important – his constituency or an amorphous world community? Waffling makes him an impossible negotiating partner, because agreements, at least initially, are based on trust, and it is not clear which Khaled Meshal to trust. The velocity of information today has made it increasingly difficult to straddle fences in an attempt to have it both ways.

Israel, on the other hand, must decide what it means to kill 1 400 Palestinians, many of them civilians. The Jewish Left, which sees Judaism as a religious doctrine based on social justice, worries that the refugees symbolize "such a fundamental transgression of Jewish ethics and morality that it threatens to render Judaism ... a theological impossibility" (Ellis, 2002). Ellis fears that the Torah scrolls will be replaced with the image of a helicopter gunship that "speaks of power and might without ethics or morality" (p. 1).

Certainly there is rage at the terror suffered by residents of border cities such as Sderot, but does random killing on such a scale square with Prime Minister Ariel

Sharon's speech to the United Nations in 2005? "The right of the Jewish people to the Land of Israel does not mean disregarding the rights of others in the land," Sharon said. "The Palestinians will always be our neighbors. We respect them, and have no aspirations to rule over them. They are also entitled to freedom and to a national, sovereign existence in a state of their own" (Sharon, 2005).

Except …

Lebanese Christian militiamen (Phalangists) met no significant resistance when they entered two Palestinian refugee camps in southern Lebanon about 6 p.m. on September 16, 1982. The Israel defense forces, having previously invaded Lebanon to attack the PLO, were firmly in control as far north as Beirut, but under orders not to enter the camps (Morris, 2001).

The Phalangists were under no such constraints, and they were in an ugly mood. Their leader had just been assassinated, shortly after being elected president of Lebanon. The time was ripe to settle some old scores, and the Israelis were in no mood to constrain them. In fact, there were indications that the Israeli Defense Forces, including Defense Minister Ariel Sharon, encouraged them and "coordinated" their entry into the camps. "I don't want a single one of them left," Sharon was quoted as telling Phalangist commanders (Morris, 2001, p. 546). Sharon later denied that they had spoken of the need for revenge or of the impending massacre.

For 18 hours, the Phalangists moved from house to house killing everyone they found. When the carnage was over, some 700 to 800 residents were dead and the names of the camps – Sabra and Shatilla – were seared into the memories of Arabs throughout the world.

As the news got around, public protests forced the Israeli cabinet to convene an independent court of inquiry. Its report described the operation with words such as massacre, murdered, butchered, barbarism, and despicable. The court, known as the Kahan Commission, found Israeli military leaders complicit in the slaughter. Sharon, along with the director of military intelligence and the division commander, was judged complicit and punished. He knew – or should have known – what was happening and prevented the crimes.

> "The massacre at Sabra and Shatilla was carried out by a Phalangist unit, acting on its own but its entry was known to Israel," the commission found. "No Israeli was directly responsible for the events which occurred in the camps. But … Israel had indirect responsibility for the massacre. … Mr. Sharon was found responsible for ignoring the danger of bloodshed and revenge when he approved the entry of the Phalangists into the camps as well as not taking appropriate measures to prevent bloodshed" (Reich, 2008, p. 143, summarizes the findings; the complete text is at Israel Ministry of Foreign Affairs, 1983).

Sharon and others at the top of chain of command were targeted by the commission, but the condemnation might be applied to everyone who knows about evil deeds and says nothing.

As the Kahan Commission put it: "The end never justifies the means, and basic ethical and human values must be maintained in the use of arms.… It therefore has importance from the perspective of Israel's moral fortitude and its functioning as a democratic state that scrupulously maintains the fundamental principles of the civilized world" (Israel Ministry of Foreign Affairs, 1983). And so Sharon was punished.

Except ...

Except he was not punished much. His demotion smacks of the revolving door punishments meted out by Israelis on Israelis and by Palestinians on Palestinians who commit crimes against the other side. Sharon lost his job as defense minister but remained as a member of the ruling cabinet and came back to be elected Prime Minister. He obviously had considerable support among the Israeli populace, especially among its zealots and super-patriots, who justified his crimes as being in their interest and viewed him as a war hero. It's a frame of mind that numbs the conscience to the principles embodied in the United Nations Declaration of Human Rights and leads cynics to conclude that ethics is only a code meant to apply to one's adversaries; one accepts one's own excuses and justifications. The issue becomes whether numbness is inevitable after decades of provocations by the other side and decades of rationalizations by one's own friends and leaders.

Except....

Yael Orbach, aged 29, had just put her wedding invitations in the mail when she and her fiancé went out to celebrate with friends in Tel Aviv. The nightclub they chose, the Stage Club, was a popular hang-out, and on this Friday, February 25, 2005, the eve of the Jewish Sabbath, it was crowded with revelers.

The club's popularity with Jewish young people had also caught the attention of a young Palestinian Arab, Abdallah Badran, 21, a student from the village of Deir al Ghusun. He was angry with the Palestinian Authority, which he accused of surrendering to the American military. Badran also was a member of an independent cell with ties to the Islamic Jihad, a terrorist organization.

On this Friday, Badran's anger boiled over. He left home at 6 a.m., telling his family that he would be sleeping over that night at a friend's home. Instead, he spent the day preparing to die, videotaping his last will and testament, and saying his last prayers. In the early evening, he strapped an explosive device to his body. Three friends drove him to Tel Aviv, where he got out and walked toward the Stage Club. A witness, Eran Jorno, quoted in the Jewish newspaper Haaretz, said he heard Badran's companions calling "Come back!" in Arabic. "Then he looked at me strangely," Jorno said, "and blew himself up" (Singer *et al.*, 2005, p. 1).

Himself, that is, along with Orbach and three of her companions. At least 50 others, including Orbach's fiancé and Jorno, were injured. The cycle of violence in the Middle East had claimed its latest victims.

Hatred gushed from survivors and relatives. Yael's father, Israel, delivered what Haaretz called a "fiery eulogy" at his daughter's funeral. "This girl is a descendant of King David," he told fellow mourners, urging them to seek vengeance, and pledging, "If they don't, I will" (Rotem, Azoulay, and Ashkenazi, 2005).

Palestinians took a different view. Their newspaper, *Al-Quds*, honored Badran as *shahid* – a holy martyr – in the cause of liberation from Israeli oppression (Cited in Witte, 2006).

This explosion might have been just another event in the seemingly endless routine of provocation and retaliation except for two remarkable – perhaps unique – responses: All the militant Palestinian groups, which usually compete with each other to claim credit for acts of violence against Israel, disclaimed responsibility. Even the Islamic Jihad distanced itself from Badran and his cell. The Israelis, for their part, declined to strike back. Both sides – for once – found it in their mutual interest to give peace a chance. The cease-fire in effect at the time was sustained.

The circumstances raise the question of why this particular cease-fire held – and continued to hold for several months afterward – when so many previous attempts had failed. The answer might be that the mood of the respective publics and their governments was pacific. The parties wanted the truce to hold. They refused to accept the custom of tit for tat. This one incident – although clearly horrific in its deaths and injuries – was viewed as an anomaly. For the moment, the desire for peace overcame the pride in revenge on the Palestinian side and the instinct for revenge on the Israeli side.

Palestinians wanted Sharon to keep his promise to withdraw from the Gaza Stip. Sharon wanted to withdraw, and if violence escalated, both sides knew his cabinet would balk. However, the cabinet approved his disengagement plan on February 20, and the withdrawal was completed later that year. Sharon's invitation to address the United Nations – quoted above – was his reward for pushing the withdrawal in the face of fierce resistance from a minority of Israelis.

Two words from the Tel Aviv bombing symbolize the role of ethical speech in the Arab-Israeli conflict: the Arabic word *shahid* and the Hebrew word *mkhabel*.

Shahid is the favored Arabic word for a suicide bomber. It usually is translated into English as martyr, but no English word is strong enough to convey the sense of holy, religious sacrifice. Since suicide is forbidden by the Quran, a more sanctified word is required to describe the bomber and to valorize his deed. Arabic media, including *Al Quds*, the only independent daily Palestinian newspaper, in its reporting of the Tel Aviv bombing, called Badran *shahid*, even though his sacrifice was not sanctioned by the leading terrorist groups.

Some Israelis prefer to describe the bomber as *mkhabel*, which means saboteur, rather than terrorist, and sabotage rather than terrorism to describe the bombers' work. The word for saboteur in Arabic is *mokharreb*. When used by the Israelis, it connotes cowardly, vicious, and random destruction. Mahmoud Abbas, the president of the Palestinian Authority, raised eyebrows on both sides of the conflict when he used *mokharreb* to describe the Tel Aviv bomber.

The two words – *shahid* and *mkhabel* – bear watching. As long as suicide bombers are sanctified as holy martyrs in the Palestinian media and saboteurs in the Israeli media, the prospects for rapprochement are likely to be dim. Further research will be needed to determine whether the cumulative repetition of such "fighting words" by the political and religious leadership and by the media trigger or reflect unthinking hate. The semantics are important. George Bernard Shaw (in his play Pygmalion) said the difference between a flower girl and a lady is not what they do but how they are treated. Similarly, the difference between terrorist and a freedom

Ethics of Survival 663

fighter is not what they do but how they are treated. It takes powerful inducements to persuade a mother to sacrifice her son for a political cause. As the eminently quotable former Prime Minister of Israel, Golda Meier, put it: "Peace will come when the Arabs will love their children more than they hate us" (Meier, 1957).

Other words are similarly loaded. The term *Zionists* originally described those who believed that the Jews had a right to a Jewish state. Some Jews always have and still do proclaim that they are not Zionists. However, in Palestinian invective, *Zionist* has come to mean all Israelis, all Jews worldwide, and their supporters. "Sharon often used the word 'terrorist' as a synonym for Palestinian" (Morris, 2001, p. 534).

The rhetorical distinctions go deep into how participants think of the conflict and of themselves. At Sabra and Shatila, "Israeli soldiers would claim they did not know what was happening in the camps. ... All of this is true. The Israeli soldiers did not see innocent civilians being massacred and they did not hear the screams of innocent children going to their graves. What they saw was a 'terrorist infestation' being 'mopped up.' ... There is no such thing as 'terrorists' being massacred" (Friedman, 1989, p. 163).

The role of local media in the Holy Land is circumscribed by a host of limitations not always evident to Western observers. Israeli media, although generally free to advocate extreme positions, are subject to government censorship (Limor, 2000). Dor (2001), who studied how Israel's two largest daily newspapers covered the first three weeks of the second Intifada, found that reports appearing in Maariv and Yediot Ahronot were "fragmented and highly censored" (p. 251).

Palestinian media are subject to censorship by both the Israeli government and a mixture of Palestinian political factions. The newspaper *Al-Quds*, which is published in Jerusalem, is generally recognized as relatively independent, in that it is not the organ of a specific party. However, as ever in the Middle East, it is risky for any person or medium to stray too far from accepted boundaries. On some touchy subjects such as refugees, Jerusalem and borders, more meaning might be conveyed between the lines than in the lines. The best that can be hoped for in an account that touches on the political or religious is accuracy. It might be unfair and incomplete, but still truthful in what it reports. *Al-Quds'* account of the Tel Aviv bombing, for example, agreed substantially in its facts with the account published in *Haaretz*, which historian Benny Morris described as Israel's leading daily (Morris, 2001, p. 308). Of all the journalistic virtues, accuracy comes the closest to being a pragmatically accessible goal. It is doubtful if any Palestinian medium can be accepted as representing the full range of opinion, considering the risks involved.

Except ...

Except for the clandestine pamphlets, especially those published during the first Intifada. They provided the leadership that is missing in the public media and some range of Palestinian opinion. Mishal and Aharoni assembled 53 leaflets, most of them issued between December 1987 and December 1988, and published them in their book, *Speaking Stones* (1994). Hamas is identified as the source of 25 of the leaflets. The others were issued by a short-lived organization called the United National Command (not to be confused with the United Nations), which was affiliated with the PLO. The 53 represent about a third of all the leaflets from the two groups during the formative years of the Intifada.

"An unmediated encounter with the leaflets will expose the reader to the ideological intensity, the political complexity, and the behavioral codes of the Palestinian uprising" (Mishal and Aharoni, p. xvi).

Their thesis is that behind the youngsters and the stones and the barricades are words. "They dictate the way of life and determine the borders of the permissible, they bring the people into the streets and instruct them what to do, when, and how. The population responds to the written directives and does not submit to the military pressures and economic sanctions. If one wants to know the why and wherefore of the Intifada's eruption, what the Palestinians think and what they are fighting for, how they operate and how they perceive Israel, the United States, and the Arab world, one should read the written words. The underground leaflets are the documents by which the Palestinians go forth and to which they return" (Mishal and Aharoni, p. xivi).

Although Hamas and the UNC had the same strategic goals – Israeli withdrawal and creation of a Palestinian state, their orientation and their tactics differed. Morris (2001) refers to the UNC as the United National Leadership of the Uprising, or UNLU (p. 575).

The leaflets exposed two conflicting influences among Palestinians: the national and the religious. The national camp included Fatah, the Democratic Front for the Liberation of Palestine, the Popular Front for the Liberation of Palestine, and the Palestinian Communist Party. The religious camp was represented by the Muslim Brothers and the Islamic Association.

The leaflets gave guidance on what was allowed and what was not. Hamas added instructions on prayer, charity, penitence, and general good behavior. With no formal leadership in the territories, the anonymous authors provided pamphlet leadership for the Intifada, according to Mishal and Aharoni. "If a leadership is measured by its ability to articulate values, define goals, and assure the public's obedience and compliance, the authors of the UNC and Hamas leaflets met those criteria," Mishal and Aharoni said (p. 29).

The Hamas leaflets left no room for diplomacy. A leaflet of March 13, 1988, said, "Let any hand be cut off that signs [away] a grain of sand in Palestine in favor of the enemies of God [i.e., the Zionists]." An undated leaflet, addressed to Israelis, said, "Our struggle with you is a contest of faith, existence, and life" (p. 31). Leaflets 6 and 13 (p. 213) ended with, "Allah is great, death to the occupiers."

"Death to the occupiers!" That's honest communication, in that it comes from the gut. It's ethical, in that it complies with a code of conduct (the Hamas covenant). It's even moral, in that its commission would not trouble the believer's conscience one bit. On the contrary, the perpetrators can expect praise and honor.

Is it, however, a guide to right action? Probably not, because – so far, after nearly a century of conflict – it is not working. The Israelis have not withdrawn completely, and the Palestinians do not have their freedom or their state. Furthermore, the occupiers have been having quite a bit to say about conduct based on a call for

Ethics of Survival

their extinction. An ethical or moral standard is useful only to the extent that it is practical and salable to the world community.

The same lesson might be considered by the Israelis. Subjugating and humiliating an entire people might be legal, ethic, and moral (to some Israelis), but such methods are not working, either. Killing off opposition leaders is not working; new leaders keep popping up. Bribery, torture, and various forms of state-sponsored terror are counter-productive, because the yearning for freedom and dignity lie at the heart of what it means to be human, and that can never be eradicated. The purpose of war, say the military historians, is to reduce the enemy's will to resist. After two Intifadas, it appears that the Palestinians' will to resist has, if anything, stiffened. Peace overtures seem to work better than terror in pursuit of the national objective of safety for the state of Israel and its citizens.

The UNC advocated violence because it seemed to produce favorable political results, but it also favored negotiations with Israel and supported a peaceful solution (Mishal and Aharoni, 1994, p. 43). Israel was not listening.

The demise of the UNC is told by Meijer (1998). The Israelis – tragically – did not distinguish between the pragmatic, approachable UNC and the religiously motivated Hamas. Israel attacked both with equal ferocity. With 35 000 to 100 000 copies of the UNC fliers being distributed throughout the Gaza Strip and West Bank, it was inevitable that the Shin Bet (Israel's intelligence service) would find out. On February 3, 1988, one of the distributors was caught with 35 000 copies of flier No. 6 in his van, and the entire Unified Command was arrested. New leadership promptly took over and was promptly arrested. After the third set of leaders was arrested and faced with continuous repression both externally and internally, the UNC ultimately was unable to continue.

Several conjectures are easily identifiable from the pamphlet affair:

1   When the Israelis supported Hamas as a rival to the hated PLO, they bet on the wrong horse, at least as of 2009. Hamas's leaflets gave early warning that its opposition to Israel was implacable, in part because it was imbued with religious fervor. The Hamas covenant, published in August 1988, confirmed its radical stance. The UNC, with a secular, pragmatic approach, was more likely to have been a productive negotiating partner.

2   The PLO leadership – even Arafat – was less of a problem than radical elements like Hamas and especially individual Palestinians. The leadership seems to have been more amenable to peace than the populace. It was not until much later that Israel switched its bets. Israel did not fully awaken to the Hamas threat until 2007, when it formally decreed that it was a terrorist organization (Reich, 2008, p. 343).

3   Violence – both internally (Morris, 2001, p. 584) and externally by Palestinian radicals – was a productive means of advancing their cause; violence by the Israelis was not, except perhaps in the short run.

4   Nor was Israeli censorship productive. A major benefit of a free press is the opportunity it affords for debate toward rational decisions. Throttled newspapers

and fliers appear – from the most radical elements. Rumors become taken for facts because responsible voices have been silenced, and minor incidents escalate into massacres, which then must be avenged.

5 It is a curious fact that the Arabs have failed to produce a leader strong enough, respected enough, and charismatic enough to lead Palestine into statehood. Arafat came the closest, but he was more follower than leader. Anyone with potential was arrested or assassinated by the Israelis or assassinated by Palestinian radicals. When Israel didn't get whom it wanted from local elections, they made appointments, who had no credibility with the Palestinian people. Mishal and Aharoni concluded that Israel was wrong when it believed that it could control the Arab populace in the absence of credible local leadership. Their study of the leaflets led them to conclude that the first Intifada erupted spontaneously and was led by youths and students. They found: "In the absence of an effective local leadership, nothing could contain the violent activity of the young generation. … The initiative passed into the hands of the youngsters, and no one, not Israel, not Jordan, and not the PLO, could control the unfolding events" (p. 22).

Rhetoric also over-ran reason in the run-up to the Arab decision to invade Israel in 1948. Politicians, the media, and the mob, inflamed by invective, drove the leaders and the military to go further than they intended. "Warnings went unheeded. Doubters were denounced as traitors," recalled the Arab Legion's British commander, Gen. John Bagot Glubb. The leaders found themselves enmeshed in a snare of pro-war rhetoric of their own making" (Morris, 2001, p. 220). Arab leaders were left with no other choice but war.

The situation reversed after the war. "The Israeli public 'drunk with victory' – in [David] Ben-Gurion's phrase in the cabinet meeting of December 19, 1948, – was unwilling to give up any of its hard-won territory or to allow back the refugees, the two consistent Arab demands" (Morris, 2001, p. 262). The Israelis expected to exchange peace for peace (Morris, 2001); the Palestinians wanted more, leading to former Prime Minister Abba Eban's famous remark that the Palestinians never passed up a chance to pass up a chance (Charney, 2002). The same might be said of Israel.

Various people, including US Senator Hiram Warren Johnson, have been credited with saying, "The first casualty of war is truth." Knightley (1975) took the title of his book *The First Casualty* from that quotation. They are wrong. The first casualty – even before truth – is reason. An early example in the Arab-Israeli conflict was the British attempt to establish self-governing institutions in its Palestinian mandate. The Jews, alarmed at the prospect that Arabs, who were in the majority, would control such institutions, refused to agree. Palestinian Arabs, alarmed that any Jews would be involved in their government, also refused to agree. The resulting stand-off led William Ormsby-Gore, British Undersecretary of State for the Colonies, to despair, saying famously: "Palestine is largely inhabited by unreasonable people" (cited in Isseroff, 2009). Endless examples followed.

Ethics of Survival

If truth and reason are casualties, memory is not. Every evil deed is remembered and magnified. William Faulkner was talking about the United States' South when he wrote that the past not only is not dead, but it is not even past (Faulkner, 1951), although he could have been talking about the Arab-Israeli conflict.

It is tempting to conclude that the story of the Arab-Israeli conflict is nothing but a never-ending parade of "horribles": assassinations, suicide bombings, torture, violence, crimes against humanity, evictions, expulsions, shootings, deportations, riots, beatings, strikes, kidnappings, vengeance, murders, blockades, checkpoints, searches, stoning, rockets, seizures, extermination, home invasions, demolitions, mass arrests, on-the-spot executions, looting, lynchings, expropriations, curfews, imprisonments, and terrors of all kinds.

Ethics? Ha! Morality? What is that in a war? As former Israeli Prime Minister Golda Meir put it: "To be or not to be is not a question of compromise. Either you be or you don't be. ... I prefer to stay alive and be criticized than be sympathized" (Shenker, 1974).

Except ...

Terrorism is not the whole story. It takes some digging, but stories of respect for human rights and dignity by Israelis and Palestinians who have a different kind of moral compass – at least on occasion – can be found.

The poster model for courageous leadership is none other than the reviled Ariel Sharon, for engineering the withdrawal of settlers and troops from the Gaza Strip in 2005. He promised US President Bush and Mahmoud Abbas that he would withdraw, and he kept his word, despite fierce protests from a militant minority of his own constituency: right-wing Israelis.

A comparable example is provided by Jordan's King Hussein, who angered much of the Arab world by signing a peace treaty with Israel in 1994. Even more remarkable than the treaty was the speed and trust with which it was concluded. Morris (2001, p. 631) comments repeatedly on the good feelings between negotiators for the two sides: "The evidence of real warmth between the two leaders, in smiles, body language, and handshakes, was unmistakable. ... The [treaty] document was far warmer in tone than the 1979 Israel-Egypt treaty." Agreements included borders and water – two of the so-called "final status" issues that have eluded other negotiators. Although Hussein is not a prototypical Palestinian, he comes close. Jordan was originally part of the Palestinian mandate awarded by the League of Nations to Great Britain. Moreover, Jordan annexed what is now called the West Bank and East Jerusalem in 1950 after capturing it in Israel's war of independence. Jordan then lost the territory during its Six-Day War with Israel and ceded its claims in 1988.

Neither Sharon nor Hussein rise to the level of Sadat, who led the first Arab country to sign a peace treaty with Israel, nor Rabin, who traded land in the Sinai for peace with Egypt. The leadership of all four men, taken together, suggests that peace might be possible when the parties act ethically and in good faith.

Palestinians have earned a reputation of being tough on their own people for cooperating with the Israelis. "A symptom of the PLO's frustration was the great increase in the killing of suspected collaborators; in 1991 the Israelis killed fewer

Palestinians – about 100 – than the Palestinians did themselves – about 150"
(Morris, 2001, pp. 611–612). Thus, criticism of Palestinians by Palestinians in the
Palestinian press is more difficult to find than criticism of Israelis by Israelis in the
Israeli press, but it does exist.

A content analysis of local newspapers' coverage of the 2005 suicide bombing in
Tel Avid was unusual for breaking out self-criticism (Arab on Arab, Israeli on
Israeli) as a separate category (Witte, 2006). Self-criticism was an interesting category because it reveals the range of potentially acceptable opinion and courses of
action. The two Israeli newspapers in the study – *Haaretz* and *Jerusalem Post* –
were significantly more likely to be self-critical in a way that Palestinians would find
offensive. On the other hand, self-criticism by the independent Palestinian newspaper *Al-Quds* and other regional Arabic media was more heavily weighted toward
conciliation. Caution was advised in interpreting the results because of the small
number of examples. Overall, *Al-Quds* also used significantly fewer inflammatory
words as a percentage of all coded words than the two Israeli newspapers.

Inflammatory was defined conceptually as likely to increase tensions to either
Israelis or Palestinians or both. *Conciliatory* was defined as likely to ease tensions.
Specific words were categorized operationally based on which vocabulary list they
were assigned.

What about the ordinary people? They were generally uninformed, especially in
the early stages of the conflict. "Throughout Israel's history, and especially in
1948–51 and again in the early 1970s, the government had successfully hidden
from the public the fact that there were Arab leaders who were willing to make
peace and to make concessions to achieve it" (Morris, 2001. p. 455).

Leaders of Arab countries were no different: "The Arab regimes – all of them
autocracies or dictatorships – subsequently hid from their constituencies the facts
about what had transpired. No Arab archive opened its papers to the scrutiny of
historians" (Morris, 2001, p. 268).

The literature does contain occasional examples of kindness by Israelis toward
Palestinians and by Palestinians toward Israelis. Tragically, the examples too often
are wrapped in violence.

Morris (2001) tells of 15 high school students who in 1988 went for a hike from
their settlement in the West Bank. A group of Arab youngsters pelted them with
stones. In the melee, four were killed and several were injured. It would have been
worse, but "a number of Arabs then protected the hikers until IDF (Israeli) troops
arrived" (p. 583).

During Israel's war of independence, hundreds of thousands of Arabs were
forced or frightened into fleeing by Israeli massacres or evictions. But not all.
Morris (2001) reports that the Jewish mayor of Haifa pleaded with its Palestinian
residents to stay. "All but three or four thousand of the Arabs left" (p. 211). Morris
notes that a contributing factor might have been the previous departure of prominent Arab military leaders, ostensibly to seek aid, which never came.

In Kfar Etzion, Arab villagers shouting "Deir Yassin, Deir Yassin" (a notorious
massacre of Arabs by Jews), rounded up 120 Jewish residents and "proceeded to

Ethics of Survival 669

mow them down ... Of the four survivors, three were saved by Arabs" (Morris, 2001, p. 214).

When Arab rioting broke out during the Mandate, Haganah officers proposed that a squad of militiamen be sent to defend the 600 Jews in Hebron. The community rejected the proposal, saying that it trusted the town's Arabic leaders to protect them. A mob attacked, killing 60 Jewish inhabitants, who had no weapons. Arab policemen fired into the air. Hundreds of Jews were saved by their Arab neighbors and, later, by Arab policemen (Morris, 2001, p. 114).

Analyzing early failures at bridge-building, Morris blamed both sides. Zionist leaders gave a higher priority to immigration, and the few Arabs who were willing to reach an agreement were silenced by the hard-liners.

Friedman posed the fundamental question for both Israel and Palestine: What kind of state do they want to have? The question goes deeper than boundaries and refugees. At it core, it requires introspection into the kind of values that legitimize a state and identify its citizens.

How the parties answer that question is relevant to the rest of the world. More than half the world's population – 3.6 billion of 6.8 billion[1] – count themselves Christian, Muslim, or Jew. All three consider holy one small part of one small city in one small country. For Jews, it is the Wailing Wall, for Muslims the Dome of the Rock, and for Christians the Church of the Holy Sepulcher – all with walking distance of each other in the Old City of Jerusalem. However, the significance of the sites goes beyond land they occupy, especially for the West.

When Syria killed thousands of its own people in Hama, it was not a crisis for the West because the West did not see any of its values based in Damascus (Friedman, 1989, p. 434). "The Jews historically were the ones to introduce the concept of a divine universal moral code of justice through the Ten Commandments. These divine laws, delivered at Mount Sinai, formed the very basis of what became known as Judeo-Christian morality and ethics. Modern Israel, therefore, is expected to reflect a certain level of justice and morality in its actions. But the Jews also played another role, which modern Israel is expected to live up to: as a symbol of optimism and hope. It was the Jews who proclaimed that history is not, as the Greeks taught, a cyclical process in which men get no better and no worse. No, said the Jews, history is a linear process of moral advancement, in which men can, if they follow the divine laws, steadily improve themselves in this world and one day bring about a messianic reign of absolute peace and harmony. ... Because Israel has inherited these two roles of the Jew in Western eyes – the yardstick of morality and the symbol of hope – the way Israel behaves has an impact on how men see themselves" (Friedman, 1989, p. 432).

The Arabs have a parallel connection, basing their values on Islamic Scriptures. The Hamas covenant, for example, is heavily documented with quotations from the Quran and the hadiths (sayings of the Prophet). The difference is both historical and cultural. The West does not have a tradition of reverence for the Qur'an. Thus it is difficult for a Westerner to understand that the Qur'an does not distinguish between law, ethics, and morality. Religion and politics are one. Attempts to separate mosque and state, as was proposed by the United National Command for Palestine, are likely to prove difficult.

Different Judeo-Christian and Arabic-Muslim histories blind Westerners to the inherent unfairness in how conflict in the Holy Land is communicated. "When the Palestinians are not victims of the Jews, but of other Arabs, or when they themselves are victimizers, the West in general is simply not interested in their fate. That becomes clear from even the most cursory reading of newspapers during the past few years. When Israelis were indirectly involved in the massacre of Palestinians at the Sabra and Shatila refugee camps in Beirut in 1982, the story was front-page news for weeks. When Lebanese Shiites were directly involved in killing Palestinians in the very same camps from 1985 to 1988, it was almost always back-page news – if it was reported at all. This despite the fact that some 3000 Palestinians were killed during the 3 years of fighting over the camps, including women who were shot by snipers while going out to buy bread and others who died of hunger after having run out of dogs to eat" (Friedman, 1989, p. 444).

Proposing a solution for the Arab-Israeli conflict is beyond the scope of this chapter. Nor is it intended to propose that communication professionals ignore risks to their life and safety by going behind the norms of their societies. The issue for communication professionals is how to present conflicting values and value systems in a fight for survival in the context of a quasi-war. Political and judicial systems have comparable decisions to make.

The best that can be hoped for in the absence of a comprehensive solution is for communication professionals to be aware of their role and to be aware of the power of the words they choose in shaping the attitudes of people toward conflict or conciliation. As Mishal and Aharoni (1994) emphasized, behind the stones are the words – words like *shahid* and *mkhabel* versus words like forgiveness and understanding.

The connection between words and deeds is enshrined in both scientific literature and common sense. George Gerbner *et al.* (1980) found a significant relationship between violence that viewers see on television and their attitudes toward violence in their daily lives. "Television demonstrably affects attitudes toward violence and mistrust among adolescents" (p. 24). Using violent acts depicted on television, Gerbner constructed a Violence Index, which suggests that time spent watching television correlates with the viewer's perception of social reality. In other words, heavy viewers of television are more likely to exaggerate the amount of violence they perceive in the real world. Whether watching violent television causes violent acts or whether violent tendencies cause people to watch violent television has not been established.

Public perceptions parallel Gerber's findings. When Joan Lefkow, a US district judge, gave the following testimony[2] before the US Senate Judiciary Committee on May 18, 2005, she was talking about violence against judges, but with a few ellipses, her comments could apply broadly: "In this age of mass communication, harsh rhetoric is truly dangerous. It seems to me that even though we cannot prove a cause-and-effect relationship between rhetorical attacks ... and violent acts of

Ethics of Survival

vengeance ..., the fostering of disrespect ... can only encourage those who are on the edge or on the fringe to exact revenge" (Coen, 2005, May 19). Judge Lefkow's husband and mother were ambushed and fatally shot by a man whose claims of medical malpractice the judge had dismissed.

Drawing on the notion of frames by psychologist Kenneth Burke, Mackin (1998) concluded: "Since frames result from symbolic interpretations of the world, rhetoric exploits the possibilities of identification and division inherent in these frames. Some rhetoric draws upon literary or religious catharsis, substituting the feeling of catharsis for actual change. Rhetoric in the frame of acceptance can, in this way, support an unjust regime. On the other hand, in the frame of rejection, rhetoric can lead to violent, bloody sacrifice in hopes of achieving a redeemed social order."

Reiner (1997) found two effects of media images: the amplification of crime and violent behavior and the creation of anxiety and fear of crime. In a study of media effects on panic, Young (1971) showed that some aspects of stereotypes and fantasies could become reality. As fearful people are more easily manipulated, they might be persuaded to accept repression (Signorielli, 1990).

Korn (2004) argued that the Middle Eastern media are complicit in the amplification of crime by focusing on the effects rather than the causes of violence, which would make some sense of the violence. Instead, terrorism usually is portrayed as senseless, irrational, or fanatic behavior.

Reporting on the effects of suicide bombing resurrects long-standing questions about whether newspapers lead public opinion, follow public opinion, reflect public opinion, or merely pick up what opinion leaders say. Mass society theories attribute an influential but often negative role to the media. Lazarsfeld *et al.* (1944) found limited effects. More recent research positions the media role as a two-way flow that mirrors what is going on in society (Katz and Lazarfeld, 1955, Walker and Whittaker, 1990, and other investigators).

Several commentators have put forward the notion of a symbiotic relationship between terrorists and the media. ABC news anchor Ted Koppel (1984) foregrounded the connection: "The media, particularly television, and terrorists need one another, that they have what is fundamentally a symbiotic relationship. Without television, terrorism becomes rather like the philosopher's hypothetical tree falling in the forest: no one hears it fall and therefore it has no reason for being. And television without terrorism, while not deprived of all interesting things in the world, is nonetheless deprived of one of the most interesting" (p. 497).

Weimann (1987) agreed: "The media are the terrorists' best friends" (p. 213). Tsesis (2002) suggests a parallel between the rhetoric of terrorism and hate speech, which can lead to the terrorism of genocide. Terrorism, like genocide, denies the right of its target to exist.

Weimann (1987) found rather few scholarly studies connecting rhetoric to terrorism – a lack he attributes to the complexity of the issues. His article, titled *Terrorism as Theater*, says, "Concepts such as climate of opinion, status conferral, cultivation and reconstruction of reality, knowledge gap, or agenda setting may serve as examples of these specific effects that caused, to some extent, a return to the concept of powerful mass media" (p. 104). Leets and Bowers (1999) also complained about the "dearth" of empirical work on the effects of verbally disturbing speech on terrorism (p. 325).

In contrast to the negative tone of most studies that relate media effects and violence, Doxtader (2003) took a positive approach in a study titled *Reconciliation – a Rhetorical Concept/ion.* Doxtader contended that reconciliation is a rhetorical concept that transcends violence and summons understanding. Reconciliation's promise, he says, demands significant faith in the work of words.

Labeling violent actors either as "terrorists" or as "freedom fighters" in the press encourages the cycle of violence. They become socially constructed – and legitimated – symbols, which become stimuli that encourage replication. Mead (1934) showed that the labels applied to people shape how they think and act. (Note previous discussion regarding the difference between a freedom fighter and a terrorist.) A similar point was developed by Korn (2004) who said language could densensitize as well as inflame. The wide use of the neutral phrase "killed in clashes" in Israeli newspapers to refer to Palestinian deaths, he said, "legitimated the high number of civilian casualties and contributed to the construction of the uprising as an armed conflict justifiably oppressed by military means" (p. 247).

Cable Network News (CNN), a frequent target for criticism from both sides, said, "There has been an intense internal debate over the use of words" (Fisk, 2002).

Dajani (2003), in a critical study of Palestinian coverage of the Israeli operation Defensive Shield into the Jenin refugee camp in 2002, urged newspapers to:

1 Banish highly emotional terms such as "massacres," "catastrophe," "hell," "disaster," and so forth, from headlines to avoid harmful ripple effects resulting in tragic consequences. Editors and reporters should anticipate that such terms have the power to intensify public fear, cause panic and could result in flight or incite violent revenge.
2 Filter and tone down stories of high drama and violence that may cause public anger and concern.

There is considerable evidence that the political climate in the Holy Land has changed to become more receptive to messages of reconciliation. Public opinion before and after the election of Mahmoud Abbas as President of the Palestinian Authority shows contrasting views about the prospects for peace.

In a poll taken in 2000 by the Palestinian Birzeit University, 60% of Palestinians did not believe that peaceful coexistence was possible and 80% supported military attacks against Israel (Said, 2000). The most recent poll was taken jointly in March 2005 by the Palestinian Center for Policy and Survey Research and Hebrew University. The same questions were asked to a representative sample of Israelis and Palestinians. One of the findings: General support for reconciliation among Israelis also increased and stood at 84% compared to 80% in June 2004; 81% of the Palestinians asked supported reconciliation compared to 67% previously. More

Ethics of Survival

important is the consistent, across-the-board increase in support for a list of specific reconciliation steps (Shamir and Shikaki, 2005).

The Arab-Israeli conflict will not be resolved until a consensus develops on both sides that peace is better than war. Facilitating consensus-building through dialogue and debate is what communication professionals do best. Reporting actions accurately causes both the actors and observers to examine the values that direct laws and ethics and, perhaps, to build a moral foundation for peace.

The nature of the Arab-Israeli conflict calls into question the principle of distinction in international humanitarian law. Article 48 of the protocol provides that "Parties shall at all times distinguish between the civilian population and combatants and between civilian objects and military objectives and accordingly shall direct their operations only against military objectives" (Protocol 1, Additiona to the Geneva Conventions, 1977).

Is this article still realistic? Is it reasonable to expect Palestinian militants to wear uniforms when they attack Israeli targets? If all Jews are identified as the enemy, who are the civilians? At the suicide bombing of the Tel Aviv night club, many of the injured were members of an army reserve unit. They were not combatants at that moment in time, but the Israeli military depends heavily on its reserves for combat missions. Even if the questions could be answered, who will enforce Article 48? It is easy to pass judgment when one's survival is not at stake.

The depth of the problem is illustrated by a story told by Friedman (1989, p. 388) who was interviewing a young man who had been arrested by the Israeli police.

> "So what exactly did you do that landed you here [in prison]" I asked.
> "I threw a stone at some Jews," said Mazen.
> "Why?"
> "Because I didn't have a grenade."

To which Golda Meir might have commented, as she so often said, "Peace will come when the Arabs will love their children more than they hate us."

Which raises one of the world's oldest moral questions: Can love of one's enemy, one's neighbor, one's self triumph over hate? All three religions with connections to the Holy Land say it should. Perhaps it will in Israel and Palestine.

Notes

1 World population estimated by US Census Bureau, www.census.gov/ipc/www/popclockworld.html (accessed August 2, 2010). Religious populations estimated at 2.1 billion Christians, 1.5 billion Muslims and 14 million Jews www.adherents.com/Religions_By_Adherents.html (accessed July 23, 2010).

2 The full quotation reads: "In this age of mass communication, harsh rhetoric is truly dangerous. It seems to me that even though we cannot prove a cause-and-effect

relationship between rhetorical attacks on judges in general and violent acts of vengeance by a particular litigant, the fostering of disrespect for judges can only encourage those who are on the edge or on the fringe to exact revenge on a judge who displeases them."

References

Avalon Project at Yale Law School (1988) Hamas covenant, August 18, 2010, from www. yale.edu/lawweb/avalon/mideast/hamas.htm (accessed July 23, 2010).

Bronner, E. (2009) Hamas shifts from rockets to culture war. *The New York Times*, July 23, p. A1.

Charney, M.D. (2002) Abba eban, eloquent defender and voice of Israel is dead at 87. *New York Times*, Nov. 18, p. A1.

Coen, J. (2005) Protect our judges, Lefkow implores. *Chicago Tribune*, May 19, p. 6.

Committee to Protect Journalists (2007) May 13, http://cpj.org/killed/2007/suleiman-abdul-rahim-al-ashi.php (accessed July 23, 2010).

Dajani, M. (2003) Press reporting during the Intifada – Palestinian coverage of Jenin. Palestine Israel Journal, 10 (2, June), www.frontpagemag.com/Articles/ReadArticle. asp?ID=9883 (accessed July 23, 2010).

Dor, D. (2001) *Newspapers under the Influence*, Babel, Tel Aviv, Israel.

Ellis, M.H. (2002) *Israel and Palestine out of the Ashes: The Search for Jewish Identity in the Twenty-First Century*, Pluto Press, London, p. 1.

Faulkner, W. (1951) *Requiem for a Nun*, Random House, New York.

Fisk, R. (2002) Quoted in Mid-East Realities. Posted September 2, www.middleeast.org/ premium/read.cgi?category=Magazine&standalone=&num=374&month=9&year=2 001&function=text (accessed July 23, 2010).

Friedman, T.L. (1989) *From Beirut to Jerusalem*, Doubleday, New York.

Gerbner, G., Gross, L., Morgan, M., and Signorielli, N. (1980) The "Mainstreaming" of America: Violence profile No. 11. *Journal of Communication*, 30 (3), 10–29.

Hamas (2009) *New York Times*, http://topics.nytimes.com/top/reference/timestopics/ organizations/h/hamas/index.html?inline=nyt-org (accessed July 23, 2010).

Israel Ministry of Foreign Affairs (1983) 104 Report of the Commission of Inquiry into the events at the refugee camps in Beirut- - 8 February 1983 Volume 8: 1982–1984. www. mfa.gov.il/MFA/Foreign%20Relations/Israels%20Foreign%20Relations%20since%20 1947/1982-1984/104%20Report%20of%20the%20Commission%20of%20Inquiry%20 into%20the%20e (accessed July 23, 2010).

Israel Ministry of Foreign Affairs (2005) Ayala-Haya (Ella) Abukasis, www.mfa.gov.il/MFA/ Terrorism-+Obstacle+to+Peace/Memorial/2005/Victims/Ayala-Haya+Abukasis.htm (accessed July 23, 2010).

Isseroff, A. (2009) Quoted in *Israel and Palestine: A brief history – Part I*, June 10, www. mideastweb.org/briefhistory.htm (accessed July 23, 2010).

Jawad, R.A. (2010) Hamas backtracks on missile apology. *Taiwan News*, February 6, www.etaiwannews.com/etn/news_content.php?id=1174859&lang=eng_news(accessed July 23, 2010).

Katz, E., and Lazarsfeld, P.F. (1955) *Personal Influence*, Free Press, New York.

Kershner, I. (2010) Israel rebukes 2 for U.N. Gaza compound shelling. *New York Times*, February 1, www.nytimes.com/2010/02/02/world/middleeast/02mideast.html (accessed July 23, 2010).

Khodary, T., and Bronner, E. (2009) Addressing U.S., Hamas says it grounded rockets. *New York Times*, May 5, p. A6.

Knightley, P. (1975) *The First Casualty*, Harcourt, New York.

Koppel, T. (1984) Harper's, quoted by Weimann, G., Terrorism as theater, in *Language and Communication in Israel: Studies of Israeli Society*, Vol. IX, (eds H. Herzog and E. Ben-Rafael) (2001), *Language and Communication in Israel: Studies of Israeli Society*, vol IX, Transaction Publishers, Piscataway, NJ, p. 467.

Korn, A. (2004) Reporting Palestinian casualties in the Israeli press: the case of Haaretz and the intifada. *Journalism Studies*, 5 (2), 247–262.

Lazarsfeld, P.F., Berelson, B., and Gaudet, H. (1944) *The People's Choice: How the Voter Makes up his Mind in a Presidential Campaign*, Duell, Sloan & Pearce, New York.

Leets, L., and Bowers, P.J. (1999) Loud and angry voices: The insidious influence. *Communication Monographs*, 66 (4), 325–342.

Limor, Y. (2000) The Printed Media: Israel's newspapers. *Israel Ministry of Foreign Affairs*. www.mfa.gov.il/mfa/facts%20about%20israel/culture/the%20printed%20media-%20 israel-s%20newspapers (accessed July 23, 2010).

Mackin, J.A. Jr. (1998) Sacrifice and moral hierarchy: The rhetoric of Irish republicans. *American Communication Journal*, 1 (3), 1.

Mead, G.H. (1934) *Mind, Self and Society*, University of Chicago Press, Chicago.

Meier, G. (1957) Statement to the National Press Club in Washington, DC, www. jewishvirtuallibrary.org/jsource/Quote/MeironPeace.html (accessed July 23, 2010).

Meijer, R. (1998) Inventory of the collection of the United National Command of the Intifada 1987–1990. International Institute of Social History, Amsterdam, www.iisg.nl/ publications/intifada.pdf (accessed July 23, 2010).

Mishal, S., and Aharoni, R. (1994) *Speaking Stones*, Syracuse University Press, Syracuse, NY.

Morris, B. (2001) *Righteous Victims*, Random House, New York.

Morris, B. (2004) *The Birth of the Palestinian Refugee Problem Revisited*, Cambridge University Press, New York.

Protocol 1, Additional to the Geneva Conventions (1977) Part IV: Civilian Population, Section 1: General Protection Against Effects of Hostilities, Chapter 1: Basic Rule and Field of Application, Article 48: Basic Rule, http://deoxy.org/wc/wc-proto.htm (accessed July 23, 2010).

Protocols of the Elders of Zion (1903) Referenced in the Hamas Covenant 1988, http:// avalon.law.yale.edu/20th_century/hamas.asp (accessed July 23, 2010).

Reich, B. (2008) *A Brief History of Israel*, 2nd edn, Facts on File, New York.

Reiner, R. (1997) Media made criminality: The representation of crime in the mass media, in *The Oxford Handbook of Criminology*, 2nd edn, (eds M. Maguire, R. Morgan and R. Reiner), Oxford University Press, Oxford, pp. 189–231.

Rotem, T., Azoulay, Y., and Ashkenazi, E. (2005) Tearful comrades-in-arms bid farewell to bombing victims. *Haaretz Daily*, February 2, www.haaretzdaily.com (accessed July 23, 2010).

Said, N. (2000) Development studies program, Birzeit University, http://home.birzeit.edu/ dsp/DSPNEW/polls/poll_2/ (last accessed March 20, 2005).

Shamir, Y., and Shikaki, K. (2005) Palestinians and Israelis disagree on how to proceed with the peace process. Survey Research Unit, Poll No. 15. Palestinian Center for Policy and Survey Research and Hebrew University of Jerusalem. Posted March 16, 2005, http:// pcpsr.org/survey/polls/2005/p15ejoint.html (accessed July 23, 2010).

Sharon, A. (2005) Text of Sharon's address before the UN General Assembly, September 15, www.zionism-israel.com/hdoc/Sharon_UN.htm (accessed July 23, 2010).

Shenker, I. (1974) Mrs. Meir, at Princeton, Offers Her Views In Talks Marked by Humor and Grimness. *New York Times*, December 12, p. 99 as renumbered by Microfilm Corp. of America from New Jersey edition (original page number obscured).

Signorielli, N. (1990) Television's mean and dangerous world, in *Cultivation Analysis*, (eds N. Signorielli and M. Morgan), Sage, Newbury Park, CA85–106.

Singer, R., Benn, A., Harel, A., and Regular, A. (2005) Four killed in Tel Aviv suicide bombing. February 27, *Haaretz*, 1.

Tsesis, A. (2002) *Destructive Messages: How Hate Speech Paves the Way for Harmful Social Movements*, New York University Press, New York.

Walker, M., and Whittaker, S. (1990) Mixed initiative in dialogue. 28th Annual Meeting, Association for Computational Linguistics, pp. 70–78.

Weimann, G. (1987) Conceptualizing the effects of mass-mediated terrorism. *Political Communication & Persuasion*, 4 (3), 213.

Weimann, G. (1976 quoted in *Language and Communication in Israel: Studies of Israeli Society*, Vol. IX, (eds H. Herzog and E. Ben-Rafael) (2001), *Language and Communication in Israel: Studies of Israeli Society*, vol IX, Transaction Publishers, Piscataway, N.

Witte, O.R. (2006) The Rhetoric of Terrorism and Conciliation in the Arab-Israeli Conflict. Meeting of the International Communication Association, June 19–23, Dresden, Germany.

Young, J. (1971) The role of the police as amplifiers of deviance, negotiators of reality and translators of fantasy, in *Images of Deviance*, (ed. S. Cohen), Penguin, Harmondsworth, pp. 27–61.

35

Voiceless Glasnost
Responding to Government Pressures and Lack of a Free Press Tradition in Russia

Victor Akhterov

A quarter century ago two Russian words, coined and popularized by charismatic Soviet leader Mikhail S. Gorbachev, became known throughout the world: Glasnost (openness; exact translation: voiceness) and Perestroika (rebuilding). In an effort to gather support for desperately needed reforms, Gorbachev chose to use the media to propagate a plan to rebuild the Soviet Union into a more democratic socialist country. Thus, Glasnost became a vital tool to energize the Soviet people to accept, support, and initiate change on a local level. Now, as Gorbachev, one of the least popular people in Russia, is paid to advertise luggage and Russian media is largely under government control, an examination of the history of Glasnost is in order.

The present political course of the country has been described as moving in reaction to the initial post-Soviet reforms; terms such as "quasidemocracy," "pseudo elections," and so forth, are prevalent in the works of many observers (e.g., Petrov, 2005; Shevtsova, 2006). As far as freedom of the press is concerned, Russian media exist in relative freedom (Greene, 2009) and some segments such as the Internet are almost completely unrestricted.[1] Despite these opportunities, Russian media have no meaningful or powerful enough independent voice to inform or transform society; the current situation in Russian media is actually a *Voiceless Glasnost*.

One of the deepest roots of this state of affairs is the lack of appreciation for a free press by ordinary Russians. The Academy of Sciences' Institute of Sociology demonstrates this in an authoritative report on bureaucracy and power in Russia (2005). When asked to identify the largest threats to democracy in Russia, only 9% mentioned the media's lack of independence. In contrast, nearly half of those interviewed identified the large gap between the rich and poor as a major threat, while selective applications of the laws (36.5%), or the unwillingness of people to fight for their rights (23.1%) was mentioned far more than the lack of a free press. People do not see media independence as a pillar of a democratic society. Instead,

The Handbook of Global Communication and Media Ethics, First Edition. Edited by Robert S. Fortner and P. Mark Fackler.
© 2011 Blackwell Publishing Ltd. Published 2011 by Blackwell Publishing Ltd.

they are ready to lose their freedom of speech to gain more social justice (Solodovnik, 2006, p. 46), however oxymoronic this may sound.

In addition, more than 70% of Russians at the onset of Putin's rule considered free media a sham and believed it had no influence on the decision-making process of the rich and powerful. Not only that, more than 30% of Russians believe the media should be controlled by the government, and more than 50% believe the government should coown and subtly control media (Solodovnik, 2006, p. 58). According to the Levada Center (2007), 26% think that even tighter government control would be beneficial for media, while 36% believe that stricter control would have no effect on it; 27% believe that control is already extremely strict and half of the population does not trust the media in reporting sensitive matters such as events in Chechnya (pp.160–162). While young people see media primarily as an entertainment tool, older Russians see it as a kind of paternalistic aid that allows them to bring their complaints to the government, as it used to be under the Soviet system (Solodovnik, 2006, p. 63). Interestingly, journalism is not a respectable career: it occupies 14th place in the ratings of the most popular professions. Still, almost a third of the Russian population sees media as the most powerful agent for forming opinions (Bureaucracy and power, p. 66).

Students of Russian national characteristics (Danilova, 2005) indicate several classifications of Russian mentality in an attempt to explain the media development in Russia:

- Looking for an authority figure, or national leader to lead them as opposed to government institutions.
- Subconscious mystical feelings that this leader is in one way or another sent by God, as opposed, for example, to the American view that rights are given to individuals by their Creator.
- Belief in the sacred nature of authority.
- And also internal, subconscious rebellion against authority, feelings of dependence and a desire to be free from it; spontaneous actions or verbal expressions against authority – as in a nonconsequential loud protest.

This lack of concern about media independence from government explains why Russian media lacks a consistent, powerful voice that can be seen by the public as a critical source of power for the people. Instead, Russia has a largely obedient media with some nonconsequential agenda-driven rebels who claim to embody "free press;" they are hardly popular or authoritative.

Brief Overview of Media Transformations in Russia

There are two early notable historical sketches by Grebelnikov and Andrunas that cover Russian (post-Soviet) media. First, Grebelnikov (1996) presents a large amount of information on the media, but the author demonstrates his failure to

Representing a more Western way of thinking in Russia, Elena Androunas (1993) presents a completely different framework for analyzing Russian media transformation. She regards the USSR as a totalitarian state and believes that the establishment of a new media system is not possible without a fundamental change of attitudes among journalists. Instead of fulfilling governmentally-assigned roles, journalists should be attentive to the informational needs of their readers, viewers, and listeners. She states: "It seems that journalists do not realize this problem. They mistake the absence of government control for freedom. But in most cases everything ends up by journalists serving another boss. Everyone is tired of the outgoing boss, while the new owner seems liberal and understanding" (p. 32). The recipe for healing the media is, according to Androunas, is in forming a true market for informational services. "Only economically independent structures, private property in exchange of informational services, selling of information for profit and not for ideological purposes as well as effective use of information as product will let us form a mass media market" (p. 114). This might be true in the Russian context, but the independence of ownership is not a guarantee of objective journalism.

The current media age can be labeled the Putin Age despite the election of the new president Dmitriy Medvedev in 2008; judging by the first two years in power, Medvedev has been continuing Putin's course and working with Putin as the prime minister. The Putin Age began at the dawn of the new millennium and brought with it a much stricter rule over media. However, the current system is hardly the Soviet system of total control. Becker (2004) calls Putin's era Russian media system *neo*-authoritarian. So, while the Russian media have been suffering under the presidency of Vladimir Putin, circumstances are in no way as dire as in the pre-Gorbachev period, nor even as bad as some journalists' rights organizations might suggest. By using comparative analysis and incorporating political science literature that offers typologies of nondemocratic systems of governance, Becker insists that contemporary Russian media find much in common with authoritarian regimes across the world. In many ways Becker is right. However, he seems to discount the power of self-censorship by journalists and fails to identify the deeper roots of Russia's current media problem.

Zassoursky (2005) identifies three periods in the transformational period of Russian media. The first period was Glasnost (1985–1990), when Gorbachev used the system of party regulations to bring more democracy to Soviet society. During the second period, (1990–1995), media was "largely independent" and was able to influence both society at large as well as the government. Then, from 1995 on, they label media as being "commercial" and "ruled by business structures." Yassen Zassoursky, the former dean of the school of journalism at Moscow State University, lamented the fact that *Echo Moskvy*, the station that MSU helped establish, came under the control of a business structure. "We are planning to create a university station, a new station," he stated (2005, p. 146). However, the dream of the famous late professor remains unfulfilled; his beloved station is now majority-owned by Gazprom, a government-controlled company (Greene, 2009, p. 60). As Soldner puts it, "it is no longer big business but state actors for who control of media outlets is of prior importance (2008, p. 172). Eventually, Yassen Zassoursky identified three periods of transformation: 1985–1995, 1996–1999 – the late Yeltsin period, and a third period that began with Vladimir Putin coming to power in 2000 (I. Zassoursky 2001).

McNair (1994) identified a short "Golden Age" of Russian media from 1990 to August 1991 (the period immediately following the passing of the new USSR Media Act), but how free was that age? By Soviet standards, the freedom was limitless; by democratic standards not so free. *Vzglyad* (The View), one of the most influential television programs of the early 1990s, was under constant scrutiny by government officials. According to *Vzglyad*'s director, Lysenko, every program produced 2 hours of hysterical response from his bosses, who were government bureaucrats (Mayoffice and Kukulin, 2007, pp. 47–49). In was during this "Golden Age" that Soviet media were transformed into Russian media.

One thing is undeniable: from 1985 to 2000 there was an unprecedented influx of freedom in different forms into the old Soviet system, and very soon this untrained freedom was tamed by the business interests and, later, stricter political control. However, it would be a mistake to equate this influx of freedom with journalistic excellence, which many Western and pro-Western Russian researchers do. Olessia Koltsova (2006) rightly states that we must take into account that while weaker Russia under Yeltsin's rule was more convenient for the West than a stronger Russia of the Putin Age, many feel the need to label Putin's Age as authoritarianism in the area of media. Koltsova states (2006, p. 228):

> In practice, I see little difference in, for example, the role of the Russian media in covering Yeltsin's and Putin's elections ... The difference in the degree of determinacy and institutional consolidation ... is, however, apparent. Routinization of new journalistic practices, professionalization of sources ... – all these stabilizing tendencies are easily observable.

These positive signs of stabilization and professionalization are commonly being ignored by pro-Western one-sided observers.

In any case, as both American and British experiences demonstrate, neither private nor governmental ownership of media by itself is the problem. The problem is in the absence of traditional articulation of media independence and the tradition that media's main goal is to inform their audiences, to see the audience as the main client. Koltsova rightly identifies the problem, saying that during the rapid changes of the 1990s, media top-managers made the fateful mistake in choosing their main clients. "Media's main clients were not audiences, and not even legal advertisers, but hidden promoters, propagandists, and external owners" (Koltsova 2006, p. 160).

Failure to Inform

For Gorbachev, Glasnost was never a value in itself; he simply used it as an instrument to bring a limited dose of democracy to the nation in order to accomplish radical, but limited, political reforms that would revive and strengthen socialistic society of the Soviet Union. Emancipated but still controllable, the media was the only reliable force he could use against the reactionary communist forces in the Soviet government.

Gorbachev was the first Soviet politician who understood the power of free media and used it as a political weapon and an image-making tool for his reforms. The enormous influence of media, particularly television, was demonstrated by the first live broadcast of the gatherings of the people's deputies. Ivan Zassoursky (2001, p. 62) calls it "an enormous soap opera;" streets were empty when these television broadcasts aired; everyone was at home watching. This, however, was not a nonconsequential entertainment show, but a raw, unexpected and direct influence on the masses. Along with dozens of documentaries and movies about the crimes of the Soviet government, these broadcasts have become a powerful tool that politicized the population of the Soviet Union.

However, as Gorbachev's openness became an integral part of Soviet society, economic conditions worsened, and Gorbachev felt the power of the media turn against his system. Government meetings where conflicts between leaders suddenly became open to the public affected the Soviet society in powerful and unexpected ways. During the next several years the nation experienced a complete turnaround in the way people viewed the government, the Communist party, and socialism as a political system. If not for the power of media, this revolution of minds would have taken years and, possibly, would have included a civil war.

It is important to remember that this revolution of minds was initiated by the general secretary of the Communist party, who was promoted to power by the head of the KGB; this was not a revolution generated by the media's response to some grassroots movements. In fact, at this time, when the media appeared vibrant, fresh, and free, it was still serving a government that was about to become bankrupt, at least at the beginning stages of Glasnost. Media was simply used as a tool in order to achieve specific results. During that time there was no effort or specific goal to establish the culture of media independence, objectivity, or a mere separation of reporting from rendering opinions. Solodovnik (2006, p. 70) plainly states: "In Russian media there is no separation of 'news' and 'views.'" Russian journalists see nothing wrong with inserting their opinions, attitudes, and feelings into their news broadcasts. In an extended conversation published by *Novoe Literaturnoe Obozrenie* (Mayoffice and Kukulin, 2007), many journalists who worked during the 1990s talked about those times as journalistic romanticism, ambiguous media transformations, social/political activism, and miscalculations.

It is of special note that all the hosts of the popular television show *Vzglyad* (The View) except one were elected congressmen; all of them said that politics was the continuation of their journalistic mission. They saw no contradictions in calling themselves journalists and pushing for specific political agendas. Later, there was a movement to establish some principles of objectivity for news reporting, but the dilemma of separating news from opinion still continues.

In some ways it was impossible to separate journalism from politics in the 1990s. Dmitry Zakharov produced several documentaries about communist leaders. In one of them he reports that the first action of the 1918 Bolshevik government in Moscow was to order 90 Rolls Royce cars; such reporting of facts was, of course, political by its very nature. Often, however, opposition to the communist government among new journalists was explicit. Reporter Politkovskiy was walking through the Kremlin with a nose clip he used whenever he came close to the "smelly communists." Vladimir Pozner,[2] perhaps the most respected journalist in Russia today, says that it is precisely during the Glasnost era that a new breed of reporters was born: those capable professionals such as Mitkova or Osokin who always expressed their opinions while reporting the news (Mayoffice and Kukulin 2007, p. 15).

It is important to note that most of these new wave journalists came from Soviet foreign media services and were familiar with BBC, CBS, AP, France Press, and so forth. French and American influence was especially strong. It is also remarkable that many of the most prominent broadcasters of the Glasnost era, such as Pozner, Zakharov, Lubimov, and Listyev were raised in capitalist countries. Malkin, who worked on the television show *Vzglyad*, described the team that came from the foreign services as "people of a different quality when it comes to … internal freedom" (Mayoffice and Kukulin, 2007, p. 224). However, they were also the propaganda workforce who for years simply carried out the government's program. This combination of powerful techniques of free media, strong personal conviction combined with the Soviet habit to indoctrinate under the pretence of informing proved deadly for Russian journalism – for years to come.

Mayoffice and Kukulin (2007, p. 234) conclude that all the media leaders they interviewed expressed the feeling that they did not fight for freedom but rather received it from the government. Most journalists interviewed admitted they failed to make sure that the public considers free media a necessary element for a free country.

Arutunyan (2009, p. 78) rightly states that "many of the problems that plague journalists today arise not from censorship or lack of security, but from failures of purpose, identification, and credibility." One of the mistakes that Russian journalists have made is that they aspired to still be the "pastors," "truth (Pravda)-tellers," and "engineers of human souls," often forgetting their mission to provide objective, clear, and impartial information. This failure to inform instead of indoctrinating (no matter in which way) has consistently undermined the journalists' credibility before the people. They failed miserably to become an independent voice that would be appreciated and respected by their audiences. Their habit of indoctrinating under the cover of informing made it easier for journalist to tolerate corruption in all its forms.

Corruption in Journalism

Ivan Zassoursky identified several serious problems with the new Russian journalism, from "black PR" to business promotional articles, such as "news" about new cell phone discounts to articles written to order. Zassoursky writes: "Nevertheless, articles written to order represent perhaps the least harmful type of bios in journalism …journalists rarely formed and defended their own positions, but preferred to solidarize with the position of the owner of the publication" (2001, p. 93).

Perhaps the biggest problem that such an environment gave birth to is that journalists themselves stopped believing in journalistic ethics in the 1990s. Andrew Jack, the *Financial Times* reporter, observed:

> Such was the cynical, mercantile atmosphere of the period that any critical article or broadcast was perceived as having been paid for. The reality was not always so simple. There was so much "dirt" in circulation that it was perfectly possible for a good journalist to unearth true but scandalous materials in all honesty and objectivity (Jack, 2005, p. 141).

The dirt was available on the journalists/media owners as well. The hostile takeover of Gusinsky's/Kiselyov's NTV channel is often portrayed as the end of real pluralism in the Russian media. However, Oleg Dobrodeyev, who cofounded NTV with Kiselyov, left in 2000, accusing Kiselyov and Gusinsky of twisting coverage over the years for their own political advantage. The mogul Gusinsky admitted "mistakes" of supporting Yeltsin during the 1996 elections, instead of giving the people objective information to help them make their own decision (Jack, 2005, p. 142). It was not a prodemocracy zeal that led oligarchs into troubled territory, however. When privatization of Svyazinvest, a telecommunications company, did not go according their interests (Gotova, 1997), they attempted to bring down the government. The former head of NTV news Vladimir Kulistikov recalls:

> NTV worked against the reformist government … Gusinsky and the journalists at NTV – who called themselves liberals and democrats – worked against it. We campaigned against the government until it was destroyed and re[laced by something much less liberal (Burrett 2009, p. 74).

Jack (2005, pp. 140–155) provides multiple examples of alleged corrupt deals by NTV, such as receiving tens of millions of dollars in exchange for positive press for various businesses – and in this case we are talking about the most prodemocratic channel in Russian TV. NTV received the license to continue broadcasting soon after the 1996 elections – by special presidential decree (Soldner, 2008, p. 165).

Corruption in Russian media brought forth the lack of trust from the general population. While the immediate goals of reelecting the anticommunist president and uncovering the evils of communism were achieved, the deeper issue of building media as a viable democratic tool necessary for a free society to function was left unattended. Failure to inform, coupled with blatant corruption is to be blamed for the following statistic, produced by the World Public Opinion organization in April 2009. Only 23% of responders felt "very strongly" that it is important for media to publish news and opinions without government control. This is the lowest number among the 22 countries surveyed.

Given such statistics, why would the government not exercise more control? Today this control is increasing. The Russian media professionals face more government control over media, as part of all-encompassing move towards a more "orderly" society. As the famous Russian writer Boris Strugatsky said in an interview given to *Novaya Gazeta*, " 'You wanted it, George Dandin …' We wanted this peace and order. We got it. Now it will stay with us for a long time" (Strugatsky, 2009).

Given the reality of the situation, what are the ethical ways to respond to it for Russian journalists? One, obviously, would be to do everything they can to keep their craft free of blatant corruption. However, the main challenge today is not to resist a temptation to publish something for money, but to withstand subtle government pressure to work in the regime of limited freedom, where some topics such as the situation in Chechnya or the direct criticism of the Putin-Medvedev tandem are off limits. Many, the vast majority of Russian journalists, decide to exercise some form of self-censorship.

Self-censorship

As sad as it is, perhaps the biggest breakthrough of the past couple of years on Russian television was the decision of Channel One executives to include in their festive New Year's program a cartoon of dancing and singing President and Premiere. Newspapers talked about "the event" for days: does it mean that the new times are coming? Yet, while TV is tightly controlled, there are still voices that criticize the government even there – in the right tone, of course. There are further opportunities to criticize the government via other media outlets, although not many decide to engage in such criticism.

Masha Gessen, the editor of an independent Moscow-based magazine, wrote a poignant essay about their editorial decision to publish or not publish newsworthy information that was critical of the government. Gessen concludes that "in an

Voiceless Glasnost

important sense we have returned to the late Soviet period, the Brezhnev era. At that point, Soviet terror was not total ... they just needed frequently to punish a few people at random" (Gessen, 2005b). In her article Gessen expresses the emotional torment of making this decision. She meditated on the lives of her two grandmothers, one of whom had chosen to compromise with the Soviet secret police, while the other withstood the pressure.

An objective observer could point out that Gessen openly wrote about her decision-making process in a Western newspaper, that she lives interchangeably between Russia and America, and at the worst case scenario she stands to lose her magazine, not her child, as in her grandmother's case. The torment, however, is of the same nature: do I conquer my fear and do what I think is right or do I succumb to the pressure, engage in self-censorship and survive? Alexei Simonov, the founder of the Glasnost Foundation, speaks eloquently about this moral dilemma, saying that the government is playing on the fears of journalists similar to the worst of the Stalin years. From time to time the government "touches that chord, which is now becoming increasingly real to people, and hears in response the tune it wants to hear" (Simonov, 2005).

In 2004 President Putin was asked about a free press in Russia. His ambiguous response still haunts him today. He said: "There is a phrase in a famous Italian film – 'a real man should always try, while a real woman should always resist.'" Since the only official source of the quote is the government's *Rossiyskaya Gazeta*, there is no clarity of how exactly Putin said it, and what he actually meant. What is interesting is the way the press reacted. The phrase was reprinted by numerous publications with clear understanding that the government, as a man, should try, while the press, as a woman, should resist (Arutunyan, 2009, p. 6). *Moskovsky Komsomolets*[3] columnist Alexandr Minkin openly accused the president of condoning rape (Minkin, 2006). The fact that Putin could have meant the press as a man and the government as a woman completely escaped the journalists. Indeed, Putin later clarified that this is what he meant, that the government will be always trying to cover its mistakes, and the press should be aggressive in uncovering them (Arutunyan, 2009, p. 6). The real issue is the reaction of the journalists who once again demonstrated how deeply they have internalized their subordinate role. Journalism was never truly free and independent in Russia, and this lack of tradition of freedom is the key problem.

All this occurs in the environment where Internet is free; there is no government control over it. Three largest Russian players, Yandex, Rambler, and Mail.ru are partially owned by foreign companies, which could be seen as an insurance policy against government control. However, the fact remains that an important sector of new media is free from government control for the most part, while there are some attempts to assert influence over it.[4]

This description of Russian journalism portrays journalists and their managers as spineless, unprincipled, and fearful amoebas afraid of government control shadows. Unfortunately, in many cases this is an all-too accurate depiction. Dmitri Bykov, a journalist, columnist, and TV personality states that he never experienced any pressure from the government. However, he said he has always experienced very strong pressure from his bosses, "who would always try to run in front of the government train. People are overly cautious without any basis in being so" (Arutunyan, 2009, p. 6).

If corruption in media obviously breaks the journalistic code, can self-censorship be perceived as a serious ethical problem? Gessen (2005a) reports an embarrassing alleged story of GQ German executives falsifying the "man of the year" poll results because Mikhail Khodorkovskiy, imprisoned by the Kremlin, came out as the winner. Bernd Runge, the publisher of the magazine, is a citizen of Germany and has little to be afraid of as far as personal retribution from the Russian government. Yet, compromises were made, with similar compromises are being made all the time; at what point do they clearly break ethical standards? Given van Dijk's assertion that the "unsaid" can sometimes be more important than what is "said," (van Dijk, 1991) is there a clear line between obvious lying and withholding information because of fear? Gessen concludes with an uncompromising statement that merely being mindful of the limitations of freedom makes one an enforcer of these limitations; the consequences of not being mindful, however, are too grave (Gessen, 2005a, p. 118). The choice today, however, is not necessarily between independent journalism and a prison camp; more likely it is between working for a more influential or less influential media outlet.

Real Control Exercised

Media watchdog groups have harshly criticized Russia's recent authoritative stance towards the media. In its 2001 annual report, the media rights organization Reporters sans Frontières described then President Putin's antimedia actions as "too grotesque to be true," and they named him one of the world's "predators of press freedom" (Reporters sans Frontières, 2002). The same organization's Worldwide Press Freedom Index ranks Russia 141st out of 173 countries reviewed in 2008 and 153rd out of 175 countries reviewed in 2009, trailing countries such as Sudan and Oman. Since Putin came to power in 2000, 65 journalists in Russia have been murdered, including seven who were murdered under President Medvedev's rule.

Although the Russian constitution provides for freedom of speech and the press, authorities are able to use the judicial system to harass and prosecute journalists for independent reporting. "Authorities also took advantage of legislation like the Law Against Extremist Activities, which prohibits the dissemination of information supporting 'extremist activities' and allows authorities to shut down media outlets after three warnings" (Karlekar, 2006, p. 202). Becker (2004) notes that this judicial pressure is meant to create a sense of uncertainty and, through that, cultivate self-censorship, "the most common and important limit on journalistic activity."

Evaluating the manner in which Russian media cover the foreign policy of the Russian Federation, Arman Djilavyan (2006) came to the conclusion that the

Russian media closely follow the official point of view. Furthermore, when the Kremlin's position is clearly defined, there are virtually no alternative positions for the Russian media. When the government position is more neutral, several positions may be presented. Djilavyan (2006) also points out that establishing an agenda for covering foreign policy is also a full prerogative of the Russian president and foreign minister and concludes that media has virtually no effect on the foreign policy of the Russian Federation. A comparison with America's coverage of the Iraq War, for example, is not possible.

Foreign policy is not an isolated area excluded from the influence of freedom in media, however. Analyzing the ways that media has changed in Russia's post-Soviet society, Danilova (2005) emphasizes that while media outlets changed their outer image, the manner in which they receive and transmit information is changing very slowly; for the most part, they still disseminate information provided to them by political elites.

While in most cases critical articles are not openly punished by the government, the government has been successful in creating an expectation of a crackdown, described by Gessen (2005a) above. One example is the case of Natalia Morar, who wrote for *The New Times* about corruption in parliamentary election campaign and presidential administration. There were no consequences for *The New Times*, but Morar, a citizen of Moldova, a former Soviet republic, was barred entry at the airport by the FSB (former KGB) in 2007. The reason given was that she "presented a threat to the Russian Federation" (Arutunyan, 2009, p. 77). While no one was imprisoned or murdered, Morar's career suffered greatly.

Comparing the censorship of the final years of the Soviet Union to today's pressures, journalist by the name of Alexandr Politkovskiy (his former wife Anna Politkovskaya, a famous journalist who wrote about Chechnya, was killed in 2006) states that in the past there were not as many limitations. At that time, the rules were harsh, but familiar and avoidable. Many of the journalists feel that the problem is not in open censorship, but in self-censorship of today's media personalities; it is almost impossible to define, but everyone knows it is there (Mayoffice and Kukulin, 2007, pp. 47–49). Many feel pressured to make a decision: use self-censorship and have some influence or lose an opportunity to practice journalism altogether one way or another.

In his state of the nation address in June 2000, Putin divided the media into *state* and *antistate* (or prosociety and antisociety – the distinction is obscured in Russian) categories and criticized private owners for turning media into "mass misinformation outlets" and "into a means of struggle against the state" (Albats, 2001; Coalson, 2000). Putin believes that the media should support his efforts to "bring order back" to Russia by strengthening the "vertical power structure." The media, for the most part, complied, serving the government once again.

The most coveted media the government would like to control is television. And they do. Vladimir Pozner, a respected TV journalist and President of Russian Television Academy, in an interview he gave to *Nezavisimaya Gazeta* in

2006 characterized the state of Russian television as dismal. Acknowledging that there is no censorship, he said:

> Now there is something different. In the first place control from above, consisting from meetings and telephone calls in which you are told what you can and cannot do. And in the second place an enormous amount of self-censorship, when those who work in television respond to the slightest hint that there may be danger ahead in the manner of Pavlov's dogs (Varshavchik, 2006).

As Dunn (2009, p. 44) notes, since Putin became president, there has been a significant depolitization of Russian television. Pozner's comments apply only to the slight programming segment where politics is discussed. This creates a feeling that there is a lot of freedom on Russian television, as channels present a variety of entertainment programs and shows about a wide variety of subjects, from cooking to international travel – it is nothing like tightly controlled Soviet media. Formerly influential journalists like Sorokina or Parfyonov are still allowed to make programs, but not about politics. Political satirists and humorists such as Shenderovich or Morzhov and Kapusta were replaced by apolitical Petrosyan and Galkin (Dunn, 2009, p. 45). Pozner himself hosts a program where he interviews newsmakers; he asks tough questions, but is noticeably muffled, does not push too far; his program airs at 1a.m. on Channel One. Another tactic used by the government is when high-rank nationalists like Zhirinovsky, Luzhkov, or Leontyev say aggressive and outrageous things on national television; compared to them, Putin and Medvedev seem like moderate, prodemocratic politicians.

Today, the main channels of Russian television – Channel One, Rossiya, NTV, Kil'tura, Sport are either directly or indirectly owned by the central government; only the first three provide news/commentary service. Channels such as CTC, Domashniy, DTV, and MTV provide only entertainment and educational types of programs and are registered as international companies. In 2006, television grossed almost half of the total Russian advertizing market. Nonpolitical CTC channel is rising to the third position after Channel One and Rossiya (Zassoursky, 2009, pp. 31–32).

In April 2001 the state gas monopoly Gazprom executed a hostile takeover of Russia's most prodemocratic national television channel NTV. When NTV reporters and commentators moved to TV6 to continue their independent reporting, the station was closed by court order in January 2002. When the journalists moved to yet another station, TVS, the Press Ministry pulled that station off the air in June 2003. Some see NTV's closure as a tragedy for media freedom, while others dismiss it as a failure of another oligarch's business. Those two views are not mutually exclusive. Koltsova rightly states, while it is true that NTV owners were "struggling for power, material resources, and other personal interests, a by-product of this activity was media diversity, since having a private national channel along with two state ones is definitely closer to the democratic ideals of press freedom" (2006, p. 204).

Alex Lupis (2005) notes that remaining national television channels, state-run Rossiya and Channel One along with new NTV, have revived the old Soviet approach to news reporting, focusing heavily on the president's daily meetings

Voiceless Glasnost

with national and international leaders as well as ordinary people, promoting him as a decisive and capable leader. Putin, of course, is a capable communicator who is often seen as direct, no-nonsense people's person, doing the work of the people – employing the qualities that Russian prodemocratic journalists often lack.

When Anna Politkovskaya, a famous crusader for the rights of the Chechen citizens suffering from the abuses of the Russian army, was killed October 7, 2006, on the 54th birthday of Putin, he, visiting Germany at the time, in an interview to the *Sueddeutsche Zeitung* newspaper said that the killing was despicable and those guilty of it must be punished. He also said that Politkovskaya's materials, in his opinion, were too radical, even though the press is supposed to be critical of the power structures. He also said, quite convincingly, that since she was better known in the West than in Russia,[5] her death is much more damaging to the image of the Russian government than her publications were, saying, in effect, that it would be stupid for the Russian government to order such a killing. In fact, he conveniently mentioned that he thinks that some anti-Kremlin oligarchs who moved from Russia have something to do with this murder, trying to raise a wave of antigovernment sentiments in the country.

Rated much higher than Great Communicator, Ronald Reagan, however, Putin became *Time* magazine's man of the year in 2007, with *Time*'s pronouncement that "the Tsar was born." Were they trying to draw parallels with the first Tsar of all Russia, John the Terrible, who reached such mountain peaks of manipulation, that he voluntarily left the throne on more than one occasion and made Muscovites ask him to come back as their ruler?

In any case, if government control is real and self-censorship only enables it, what are some practical and ethical ways of improving the situation? Some look for other sources of power that could in some way counterbalance the unmitigated power of the central government.

Polarized Pluralism

Hallin and Mancini (2004) describe the media situation in some southern democracies such as Italy or Greece as "polarized pluralism." In the environment of sharply polarized and conflicting politics, news content tends to be less dispassionate. Different worldviews are communicated to audiences through the news.

As mentioned previously, during the second part of the 1990s the "free media" was owned by commercial interests and clearly delivered nonobjective information (Zassoursky, 1998, p. 48). However, some measure of objectivity was achieved by the multiplicity of media outlets, before central government took control of the most powerful.

Analyzing Russian media of the early-1990s, John Downing (1996, p. 145) characterized the situation in the Russian media as a "competitive pluralism of power." Colin Sparks also noted that the struggle between different power centers may best explain the development of post-Socialist media in Russia (Sparks and Reading, 1998, p. 137). In part, Russia is still experiencing what can be called a "muffled polarized pluralism," where the central government monologism is broken not by independent journalists, but by journalists representing other views and interests, primarily of the local governments.

While national television channels are under firm control of the central government, regional television has developed a format of structured free speech, which permitted some criticism of the federal government. Despite tightening control of the federal government these local outlets enjoy some measure of freedom. Moscow's Third Channel, financed and controlled by the Moscow city government, from time to time expresses criticism of the national government, but is embarrassingly saccharine towards the Moscow mayor (Simonov, 2005, p. 81). Since the mid-1990s, regional media has been playing a larger role with 45% of Russians now using only regional media (Solodovnik, 2006, p. 63). Of regional media in Russia 85–90% is controlled by local governments (Gurevich, 2004). Before the mayor of Moscow was fired by the President on September 28, 2010, all federally-owned media TV channels placed negative programming about the mayor. The third channel spoke favorably about him. Some observers think that with the new appointed mayor of Moscow, local media outlets will be significantly weakened.

This timid, but nevertheless real, competition between powerful federal TV channels and local channels controlled by local governors is reminiscent of the polarized pluralism system identified by Hallin and Mancini (2004, p. 11). It differs from the liberal media model by emphasizing commentaries and analysis as well as a strong role for state entities. However, it brings some varied views to the overall environment of the Russian media.

Taking advantage of the paralyzed pluralism approach, however, will most likely lead to the same result: reaching short-term goals and losing more respect for the journalistic profession in the process. Unfortunately, many Russian journalists are following this prescription. The result will probably be the same, only more people will be asking not for more government control, but for more centralized government control.

Practicing Unbiased Journalism

The only real and long-term answer to the mistrust of the "independent" media is to practice professional, nonbiased, and informative journalism. There are several areas where, despite the growing government control, it can be done with considerable ease.

One area that exemplifies informative and free journalism is Russia's business press. Katja Koikalinen (2009) conducted an investigation of two Russian business dailies: *Kommersant* and *Vedomosti* and discovered that both newspapers work within well-established journalistic frameworks, very similar to one another. Since these publications do not directly comment on the politics, they operate with a greater amount of freedom. The readers of these dailies are businesspeople and those who are more interested in information than opinions. In fact, the older *Kommersant*[6] is proud of the fact that it rarely uses even expert opinions – echoing disconnect between Soviet-era experts and the new economy of the 1990s. *Vedomosti*, a newer publication, is incorporating expert opinion which, however, is clearly marked as analysis.

Voiceless Glasnost

This fact-hungry audience has helped the editorial offices of these publications craft policies that bring forth a consistent flow of reliable information. These practices include: taking into account business leaders' tendency to provide positive self-portrayal; choosing the real decision-makers for interviews and information, instead of the more eloquent ones; trading business information with their sources;[7] using variety of sources; double-checking facts; including an opposing opinion to the opinion expressed by an interviewee; careful use and clear identification of anonymous sources as anonymous; using the first voice of the person interviewed as much as possible, instead of retelling the story. These business publications, particularly *Kommersant*, are widening their coverage to include sports, culture, and entertainment, setting new journalistic standards in those areas; also, *Kommersant* has 14 regional editions, paying attention to the local issues.

Such fact-oriented and customer-oriented practices of business publications provide a great example to the rest of the journalistic community in Russia. Admittedly, media outlets that cover politics are operating in a more controlled environment, but there is a lot of room to grow, especially in making sure that the public is the main client of the publication.

What today's "free and loud" Russian journalism is associated with in minds of many Russians are oppositional publications such as *Novaya Gazeta*, the former home of Anna Politkovskaya, murdered in 2007, or the *Echo Moskvy* radio station. These, however, are hardly the models of pure informative media outlets.

As iniquitous and horrible the murder of Anna Politkovskaya was, as brave as this woman was in uncovering the horrors of Chechnya, she was more than an investigative journalist, she was a crusader. She had an agenda and expressed this agenda in her every article. She always gave specific recommendations. She always took sides. Vividly describing horrible abuses that one Chechen man experienced at the hands of other Chechens, loyal to the central Russian government, she only casually mentioned that he used to fight against the local authorities, but "only for a short time" (*Novaya Gazeta*, January 30, 2006). Then she gives admonitions and concrete recommendations. As noble and as brave the work of the advocate for the suffering is, such approach, again, is mixing opinions and arguments with news. The long-term result will be the same: people will reject opinion under the cover of news and reject "free journalism" as such.

Ideals of real free journalism could be nurtured not only in business publications, but also in media outlets that cover other areas that do not deal directly with politics, that is culture, entertainment, social life, basics of civil society, human interests, religious issues, and so on. If media outlets fully devote themselves to these particular areas and nurture journalistic idealism there, they can be both ethical and progressive in terms of building the tradition of objective journalism. In other words, the answer is not to leave journalism to protest censorship, but to leave political journalism. The market forces are pushing media into serving specialized audiences in any case.

Another successful model of journalistic excellence in Russia is the joint Russian-Western publications such as *Russian Newsweek*, *Russian Forbes*, *Russian Esquire*, and so on, – *GQ* obviously does not belong to this group. These publications are not merely translations of the Western version of these publications they are adapted to the traditions of Russians. When it comes to journalistic ethical standards and practices such as separating news from opinion, and the quality of writing, by many accounts Russian versions are superior to their parent publications. Often serving as standard-bearers, these publications influence the way Russian independent publishers practice journalism.

Such joint ventures, along with business publications, could serve as one of the ways to establish a liberal model of journalism in Russia – without corruption and with clear distinctions between news and opinion. There is an audience for such quality materials, and this audience is bound to grow.

A third option, less feasible, but one that could be extremely effective, is creating news organization directly funded by the people, similar to the National Public Radio or Public Broadcasting System in the United States. Such a noncommercial, public-supported media structure that sets independent and objective journalism as its highest value would create unprecedented support from the public. It might have been impossible to create something like this in the past, but today broad public financial support for various humanitarian projects is becoming a reality. If someone like Vladimir Pozner would start such radio network, it could become a new way to ignite people's interest in a free press. As long as it would be clear where the money is coming from and as long as the sizable portion of support comes from individual listeners, such a network could become a reality and it would be difficult for the government to control it.

Openly Opinionated Media

The fact that news should be separated from opinion does not mean that expressing opinion should always be avoided. Just the opposite: clearly defined opinionated pieces are exactly what the Russian media consumer needs. What is especially needed is a well-formulated, audience-based case for freedom of the press for a new generation of Russian people. There are several venues for achieving this, with various chances of success.

Internet

RuNet (so named for .ru domain), particularly the blogosphere, is the most free and diverse marketplace of opinions. Without going into a description of the RuNet, it will suffice to say here that, according to All Russian Center for Public Opinion Research, only 24% of Russians used the Internet in 2006, and of those less than 20% used it as a source of news. Even if these numbers doubled during the past 4 years, still less than 10 of the Russian population uses the Internet as a source of news and even fewer – as a source of commentary.

Thus, the influence of the Internet is not widespread – yet. In a strange way, the low numbers of users could be the greatest blessing for RuNet. Since in general the government continues its "hands off" policy towards the Internet, the culture of unrestricted freedom is being formed. When the Internet use explodes because of new technological achievements, it will be difficult to use censorship, especially given Internet's multiplicity of sources. Unlike Russian television of the 1990s with just a handful of channels, Internet will be a far more difficult animal to tame, especially if a considerable number of people will get used to receiving information and opinion free from the government control.

The habits of freedom are hard to break. Russia's most popular blogging site (Antropova and Grigoryev, 2007), *Livejournal.com* has become a virtual agora for Russian influential intellectuals, and when its Russian part was bought by SUP, a Russian Kremlin-friendly company, many became suspicious and voiced their opposition. However, no restrictions of any kind were introduced.

Only time will tell, of course, what role the Internet will play in the history of Russian journalism. Some think that the new Russian empire that controls the free press will melt in the Internet (Zassoursky 2009, p. 40) – again, setting political goals instead of striving to achieve the free press in Russia; in any case, the technology by itself will not bring the change. What is needed is an honorable tradition of free and independent press, and such tradition is still lacking in Russia. RuNet is a great platform for promoting the value of free press.

Newspaper/magazine opinion pages

While opinion sections in printed magazines and newspapers are functioning, there are two issues that plague them. First is declining audiences, especially for newspapers, reflecting the worldwide trend. Second, is the way opinion pages are written; for reasons of self-censorship and a desire to appeal to "cultured" audiences, many columnists use "Aesop's language"[8] to get the information across without getting into trouble. While such columnists might be successful in reaching elites, they are ineffective in affecting wide audiences. Arutunyan observes: "With a few notable exceptions, journalism is either too elite to make a profit, or too yellow to be considered quality journalism" (2009, p. 115).

Could it be, however, that "yellow journalism" is what's needed to propagate the value of the freedom of the press to the masses? *Moskovsky Komsomolets* (*MK*) is a vividly typical Russian tabloid, incorporating high and low, sophisticated and carnivalesque. It is one of three most widely read newspapers in Russia – the other two are *Komsomolskaya Pravda* and *Argumenty i Fakty*. *MK*'s circulation in Moscow is over 2 million. Resnyanskaya (2006, p. 228) characterizes *MK* as combining uncombinable: "Analysis sits next to epatage, intellectual writings about art are adjacent to intimate exposes from newsmakers; vivid commentary next to ideological tendentiousness."

It was *Moskovsky Komsomolets*, however, that was able to publish a front-page critical opinion piece two days before the 2008 Presidential elections. In part, it said:

> The problem is that election, by definition, is a show. And the only difference between ourselves and the Americans is that their show is "directed" by thousands and millions of people. In our spectacle everything to the last letter is choreographed in advance by a group of "producers" (Rostovsky, 2008, p. 1).

The title of the article was humorous, depicting Americans as not really needed as teachers of democracy in Russia. The style of the writing is also full of carnivalesque laughter. Yet the commentary is direct, harsh, and understandable. Because of their "not serious" style they are able to clearly and popularly express meaningful, consequential ideas. It could be that such an approach, connecting with the masses of common people could revive their interest in free media that will not be controlled by the government.

Television

Television that exists under the government control is yet to produce programs that could incorporate clear ideological views and discussions. There were several attempts to create battles of opinions on both more liberal NTV with Solovyov as the host and on more conservative Channel One with Shevchenko, but more liberal Solovyov's show was cancelled at the end of 2009, and more pro-Kremlin Shevchenko's show airs after midnight. Both hosts pretended to be journalists and not the ideologues that they are, as can be seen from their writings. Solovyov opened a similar show on the Rossiya Channel in the Fall of 2010, but the topics discussed seem less ideological. For now, there is no equivalent to openly ideologically partial hosts such as Sean Hannity of Fox or Rachel Maddow of MS NBC on Russian TV. The main problem is the audience's expectations or the lack of them. This chicken-and-egg problem will not be resolved soon because audiences' expectations, not because of Russian TV professionals' inability to produce opinionated programs. As *Russia Today*, the government-sponsored CNN-like English-language channel has demonstrated, even an openly pro-Kremlin channel can produce healthy discussion programs with opposing views (Arutunyan, 2009, p. 137), as long as audiences expect them.

Given the current political climate, the potential is there for television to propagate free media by exemplifying what it means to present interactive discussions that are not necessarily political, but personal and ideological in nature. The famous "television bridges" between Soviet and American audiences (Pozner-Donahue) were not political in nature. They were personal, people-to-people conversations, but they had world-view-shattering influence on the Russian psyche. They also shook the system. "Sunday Night with Vladimir Pozner" was another tremendously influential program. "This was a true talk show, where the audience played a key role," says Pozner (Mayoffice and Kukulin, 2007). Frank, passionate, people-to-people conversations were revolutionary for the Russian media and the Russian way of thinking. This could be repeated in the future, but a change in government would have to precede such a change.

Radio

Radio is a medium with great potential to present views that would help openly promote democratic ideals, among them the importance of free and independent media. Despite the lack of freedom for the press in Russia, radio remains the most emancipated medium, and many are listening: talk/news stations like *Mayak* and *Echo Moskvy* each get 10% of the audience (comccon-2.com). Yassen Zassoursky states clearly: "Freedom of mass media has been mostly realized in radio broadcasting"; he calls it the most independent and pluralistic (2005, p. 144). The popularity of radio in Russia is due to its ubiquity and availability (Keith *et al.*, 2004, p. 75).

Yudin, a well-known Russian researcher and journalist, gave a thorough overview of the development of Russian radio since the beginning of Glasnost (Yudin and Keith, 2003). She listed the number of privately-owned, independent radio stations, as the main and lasting achievement of Glasnost. Dozens of such stations are operating in Moscow and St. Petersburg alone, and thousands are in operation throughout Russia. Most of these stations have adopted a Western approach, emulating US programming models. Other researchers agree: "Programming is often an eclectic mix of Russian and Western rock and pop and can include weather and helicopter traffic reports and disc jockey patter that would be familiar to Western ears, although Russia has yet to develop an indigenous Howard Stern" (Terry and Richte, 2004).

While drawing close parallels between Russian and American radio environments, Yudin acknowledges that there is only one information-oriented commercial radio station in Moscow, *Echo Moskvy*, which receives little competition from state-owned *Radio Rossii* and *Mayak*, which clearly promote the state's point of view on current affairs. Yudin fails to mention that an American city comparable to Moscow has not only several independent public radio stations, but also commercial news stations and, most importantly, vibrant talk radio stations, where not only news, but ideological commenting on the news is present. Keith *et al.* (2004, p. 76) also arrives at a similar mistaken conclusion that despite "very different origins and traditions, modern Russian and American radio have grown to become exceptionally similar," also ignoring the weak positions of public and commercial talk radio in Russia.

Russian radio stations do promote particular values. The most discussed are: values of state, liberalism, patriotism, Western orientation, and high culture. There is no clash of these different values, however; government-owned stations subtly promote values of state and patriotism, while nongovernmental stations subtly promote liberal values (Ruvinskiy *et al.*, 2007). There is no dialogue; rather, most stations pretend they have no ideology and are simply in the business of informing the public. Again, this dishonesty is detrimental to both journalism and opinionated media.

As Chibita and Fourie (2007) conclude from their research of media influence, the very presence of different voices, different "public spheres" in broadcast media gives people a larger degree of participation in the way they live and are governed (2007, p. 23). With such an abundance of evidence for the *Voiceless Glasnost*, is radio going to become the last outlet open to people to express their political opinions and be heard by others? Or will it be further regulated, manipulated, and pressured to become as controlled as television?

Uncovering of the reasons for the absence of ideologically-driven dialogical talk radio in Russia are beyond the goals of this essay, but the opportunity to promote democratic ideals of free media on talk radio are both obvious and are obviously being ignored. What is needed is opinionated talk radio with the style similar to mischievous and often sharp Russian tabloids, similar to *Moskovsky Komsomolets*, with a powerful mix of entertainment and news analysis, humor and dissecting opinion pieces, among them open ideological propaganda of the benefits of free press. In fact, as music-oriented radio is being hit by new technologies such as MP3 players (Zassoursky, 2009, p. 36), radio could be saved by the news/talk radio format.

Conclusion

Thus, there are two obvious problems that led to the current state of apathy of the Russian population towards the free and independent media: (1) failure to objectively and impartially inform the population; and (2) the blatant corruption in Russian media during the transition period of the 1990s, as owners and business structures, and not the public was chosen as its main clients. In the environment where the ideals of media independence are brought from the outside, they were quickly forgotten, and the central government took control of most important media outlets under its soft control.

Russian media professionals responded in unproductive and unethical ways:

- continuation of ideological media under the disguise of objective journalism, only on a smaller scale,
- self-censorship, and
- becoming mouthpieces for local governments.

Such reactions will lead to the same results as the mistakes of the 1990s: people will see no need for independent media.

There are also two feasible solutions: (1) practice informative journalism in different media outlets and help people develop an appreciation for independent press – create Russian Public Radio and use nonpolitical media outlets to nurture a tradition of objective reporting; and (2) propagate the values and benefits of free media in openly opinionated media outlets, using opinionated talk radio and especially the Internet, as its availability spreads to wider circles of the population in the years to come.

Notes

1 While RuNet continues to enjoy almost complete freedom, some observers (for example, see Strukov, 2009, p. 219), notice that there is a growing list of legislations that attempt to classify Internet as the means of mass communication, which will bring it under the direct government control.

2 Born in France of Russian immigrant father and French mother, Pozner also lived in the United States, growing up in Brooklyn, before the family moved to Russia, escaping

accusations of espionage for Russia. Vladimir later became a Soviet "intellectual propagandist," broadcasting the Soviet virtues to Western audiences. When Perestroika came, he became one of the proponents and practitioners of the liberal model of journalism.

3 *Moskovsky Komsomolets* is a Russian tabloid that, while accused by many of being "yellow press," provides some sharp, thought-provoking commentary.

4 For example, in April 2007 a popular website gazeta.ru received an official warning for publishing an interview with Eduard Limonov, an anti-Kremlin activist, whose Nationalist Bolshevik Party was banned by court order several months earlier (Yashman, 2007).

5 This assessment of Putin is absolutely right not only concerning Politkovskaya, but concerning many radical antigovernment figures in Russia who, like the chess champion Kasparov, for example, are more popular in the West than in Russia.

6 In September 2006 the *Kommersant* publishing house was sold to a subsidiary of Gazprom, so it is now indirectly owned by the government (Soldner, 2008, p. 168).

7 While some may see it as a negative, such exchanges of reliable information build trust between journalists and their sources.

8 Highly allegoric language, referring to Aesop's fables, writings ascribed to a Greek slave storyteller.

References

Albats, Y. (2001) Press: As free as Putin says. *Moscow Times*, 16 January, www.themoscowtimes.com (accessed August 12, 2010).

Androunas, E. (1993) *Soviet Media in Transition: Structural and Economic Alternatives*, Praeger, Westport-London.

Antropova, T., and Grigoryev, A. (2007) DV-Reclama, www.dv-reclama.ru/?id=2676 (accessed August 12, 2010).

Arutunyan, A. (2009) *The Media in Russia*, Open University Press, Milton Keynes.

Becker, J. (2004) Lessons from Russia: A neo-authoritarian media system. *European Journal of Communication*, 19 (2), 139–163.

Burrett, T. (2009) Where did it all go wrong? Russian television in the Putin era, in *The Post-Soviet Russian Media: Conflicting Signals*, (eds B. Buemers, S. Hutchings, and N. Rulyova), Routledge, London and New York, pp. 71–86.

Coalson, R. (2000) Media morass, Committee to Protect Journalists Report, www.cpj.org/attacks99/frameset_att99/frameset_att99.html (accessed August 12, 2010).

Chibita, M., and Fourie, p. J. (2007) A socio-history of the media and participation in Uganda. *Communication*, 33 (1), 1–25.

Danilova, E.E. (2005) Media activities in open, closed, and transformational societies: methodological analysis. PhD thesis, Moscow State University.

Djilavyan, A.G. (2006) Russia and the world: Forming the foreign policy agenda setting in Russian media. PhD thesis, Moscow State University.

Downing, J. (1996) *Internationalizing Media Theory: Transition, Power, Culture: Reflections on Media in Russia, Poland and Hungary, 1980–95*, Sage, Thousand Oaks, CA.

Dunn, S. (2009) Where did it all go wrong? Russian television in the Putin era, in *The Post-Soviet Russian Media: Conflicting Signals*, (eds B. Buemers, S. Hutchings, and N. Rulyova), Routledge, London and New York, pp. 42–55.

Gessen, M. (2005a) Muzzled in Moscow fear and self-censorship in Putin's Russia. *The Boston Globe*, January 2, A2.

Gessen, M. (2005b) Nieman reports, www.nieman.harvard.edu/reportsitem.aspx?id=101154 (accessed August 12, 2010).

Gotova, N. (1997) Invest ili instest. *Moskovskii komsomolets*, July 30, p. 1.

Grebelnikov, A.A. (1996) *Media of Post-Soviet Russia*, Russia's University of People's Friendship Press, Moscow.

Greene, S. (2009) Shifting media and the failure of political communication in Russia, in *The Post-Soviet Russian Media: Conflicting Signals*, (eds B. Buemers, S. Hutchings, and N. Rulyova), Routledge, London and New York, pp. 56–70.

Gurevich, S.M. (2004) *Economics of Homeland Media*, Aspect Press, Moscow

Hallin, D.C., and Mancini, P. (2004) *Comparing Media Systems: Three Models of Media and Politics*, Cambridge University Press, Cambridge.

Institute of Sociology RAN (2005) Bureaucracy and power in Russia, www.isras.ru/analytical_report_bureaucracy.html (accessed August 12, 2010).

Jack, A. (2005) *Inside Putin's Russia*, Granta, London.

Karlekar, D.K. (2006) *Freedom of the Press 2006: A Global Survey of Media Independence*, Rowman & Littlefield Publishers, Lanham, MD.

Keith, M.C., Sterling, C.H., and Yudin, A. (2004) Privatizing Russian radio: A post-perestroika perspective. *The Radio Journal*, 2 (2), 67–76.

Koikalinen, K. (2008) Journalistic source practices in Russian business dailies, in *Media, Culture, and Society in Putin's Russia*, (ed. S. White), Palgrave Macmillan, New York, pp. 95–108.

Koltsova, O. (2006) *News Media and Power in Russia*, Routledge, London and New York.

Levada Center (2007) *Public Opinion 2007*, Levada Center, Moscow.

Lupis, A. (2005) Nieman reports, www.nieman.harvard.edu/reportsitem.aspx?id=101156 (accessed August 12, 2010).

Mayoffice, M., and Kukulin, I. (2007) Freedom as unconscious precedent: Notes on the transformation of media field in 1990. *Novoe literaturnoe obozrenie*, 83, 222–236.

McNair, B. (1994) Media in post-Soviet Russia: An overview. *European Journal of Communication*, 9 (2), 115–135.

Minkin, A. (2006) Who is Mr. Putin? *Moskovsky Komsomolets*, February 10, p. 1.

Petrov, N. (2005) Politicheskaya sistema Rossii posle Putinskih reform. http://polit.ru/research/2005/01/27/polit_system.html (accessed July 27, 2010).

Reporters sans Frontiéres (2002) Annual report 2002: Hard times for press freedom, www.rsf.org (accessed August 12, 2010).

Resnyanskaya, L.L. (2006) *Sredstava massovoi informacii*, Aspekt Press Moscow.

Rostovsky, M. (2008) Sami s USAmi. *Moskovsky komsomolets*, February 29, p. 1.

Ruvinskiy A.I., Semenov, Y.A., Thagushev, I.N. *et al.* (2007) *Radio Journalism and Politics*, Aspect Press, Moscow.

Shevtsova, L. (2006) Imitation Russia. *The American Interest*, November–December, 2, 46–49.

Simonov, A. (2005.) Media as mouthpiece. *Index on Censorship*, 34 (4), 78–82.

Soldner, M. (2008) Political capitalism and the Russian media, in *Media, Culture, and Society in Putin's Russia*, (ed. S. White), Palgrave Macmillan, New York, pp. 154–178.

Solodovnik, L.V. (2006) Russian media as a part of forming civil society: Institutional aspect. PhD thesis, Krasnodar State University.

Sparks, C., and Reading, A. (1998) *Communism, Capitalism and the Mass Media*, Sage, London; Thousand Oaks, CA; New Delhi.

Strugatsky, B. (2009) Return to sovok is the result of Putin's decade. *Novaya Gazeta*, February 9, p. 1.

Strukov, V. (2009) Russia's Internet media policies: Open space and ideological closure, in *The Post-Soviet Russian Media: Conflicting Signals*, (eds B. Buemers, S. Hutchings, and N. Rulyova), Routledge, London; New York, pp. 208–221.

Terry, H.A., and Richte, A. (2004) Russian radio, in *Encyclopedia of Radio* (ed. C.H. Sterling), Routledge, New York.

Van Dijk, T.A. (1991) The interdisciplinary study of news as discourse, in *A Handbook of Qualitative Methodologies for Mass Communication*, (eds K. Bruhn-Jensen and N.W. Jankowski), Routledge, London and New York, pp. 108–120.

Varshavchik, S. (2006) Vladimir Pozner: Pervyi, vtoroi i chetvertyi kanaly obolvanivaut naselenie. *Nezavisimaya gazeta*, April 4, p. 1.

Yashman, V. (2007) Pressure mounting on opposition, media, Radio Free Europe, www.rferl.org/content/article/1076073.html (accessed July 27, 2010).

Yudin, A., and Keith, M.C. (2003) Russian radio and the age of glasnost and perestroika. *Journal of Radio Studies*, 10 (2), 246–254.

Zassoursky, I.I. (1998) Russian media during global transformation. PhD thesis, Lomonosov Moscow State University.

Zassoursky, I. (2001) *Rekonstruktiya Rossii: Mass-media i politika v 90e*. Moscow University Press, Moscow.

Zassoursky, I. (2009) Free to get rich and fool around, in *The Post-Soviet Russian Media: Conflicting Signals*, (eds B. Buemers, S. Hutchings, and N. Rulyova), Routledge, London and New York, pp. 299–241.

Zassoursky, Y.N. (2005) *Teleradiobroadcasting: History and Contemporary Times*, Moscow University Press, Moscow.

36

Media Use and Abuse in Ethiopia

Zenebe Beyene

The fact that the press has the power to influence public opinion for better or worse has been well established. The press can make or break individuals or institutions.[1] Such a powerful institution needs freedom with responsibility. Journalists advocate for freedom, while governments advocate for responsibilities. Clearly, conflict of interest exists. As a result, a balance must be struck between freedom and responsibility. As a part of this effort for balance, this study seeks to investigate existing media practices and suggest viable legal protections for journalists in Ethiopia. Included in the legal protections are the corresponding responsibilities expected of journalists.

Freedom of expression is a pillar that supports democratic societies as shown in the First Amendment to the US constitution and also a basic human right as expressed in the 1948 Universal Declaration of Human Rights (UDHR). However, significant disparities exist in implementation of the universal principle behind freedom of expression. While exercising press freedom, journalists in many nations suffer frequent persecution and harassment. Rationalizations for restrictions on freedom include the media's poor performance, irresponsibility, and inaccurate reporting. Experiences in nations like Rwanda indicate that media outlets seem to incite violence and social disorder.[2]

Regardless, people expect journalists to play similar roles: protecting societies from government excesses and wrong doing. For those expectations to be met, journalists must have legal protections, in order to fulfill their professional and civic responsibilities. This study will provide a theoretical framework and present case studies to suggest a workable system of legal protections for journalists in Ethiopia.

Ethiopia has a total landmass of 1.13 million square kilometers of the Horn of Africa and a population of more than 77 127 000 in 2007.[3] It is the second most

---

The Handbook of Global Communication and Media Ethics, First Edition. Edited by Robert S. Fortner and P. Mark Fackler.
© 2011 Blackwell Publishing Ltd. Published 2011 by Blackwell Publishing Ltd.

populous nation in Africa, after Nigeria. Ethiopia's population is young: an estimated 40% of the population (28 500 000), are aged 14 years and under.[4] Of the total population, 64 438 000 live in rural areas, while the remaining 12 689 000 live in urban areas. About 43% of the adult population (aged 15 and older) is literate.[5]

Ethiopia, the oldest independent nation on the continent, is a nation with an ancient civilization, historic culture, and proud tradition. A landlocked nation in northeastern Africa, Ethiopia is separated from the Red Sea by Eritrea and Djibouti and from the Gulf of Aden by Somalia. It borders the Sudan to the west and Kenya to the south.

Ethiopia is the only African nation that has defeated a European army. The Italians were defeated in 1896 at the battle of Adwa. This decisive victory preserved Ethiopia as a nation never to be colonized by Europeans. Aalen's observation best summarizes the unique nature of Ethiopia.

> Ethiopia is considered to be an anomaly on the African continent with its early adoption of Christianity, imperial rule, written language and plough agriculture. The fact that it was the only country in Africa that remained independent during the colonial era adds to the image of Ethiopia as unique.[6]

With a population of more than 77 million, Ethiopia is the source of the Blue Nile, one of the largest rivers in Africa. Agro-climatic conditions enable this land to produce a broad range of grains, fruits, vegetables, cash crops, for example.

However, Ethiopia does not make use of its natural resources due to poor governance and poor economic policy.[7] The governments of King Haile Sellasie (1941–1974) and the Derg (1974–1991) led the nation into unstable political and economic conditions. Of course, the degree of insecurity that these governments caused varies significantly.[8]

The current government introduced press freedom in 1992. One could argue that until the May 15, 2005 election, an element of freedom of expression existed in Ethiopia. Ethiopians dreamed of the emergence of a new form of democracy in Africa – a democracy that could place Ethiopia at the forefront and create a progressive image of the nation.[9] They dreamed of a better form of democracy that would be as renowned as the monuments and historical sites of Axum, Lallibela, and Fasil. They dreamed of democracy that would elevate the stature of the nation and its people in the international community.[10] However, postelection events shattered those dreams.[11] The ruling party suffered unexpected losses in some parts of the nation, and the opposition parties' emotional responses led to political unrest.

Although Ethiopia is the oldest independent nation in Africa, it is still grappling with the formidable task of building democratic institutions. Freedom of expression, the lynchpin of democracy, was recognized by the current government, and a freedom-of-expression law was enacted in 1992.

Freedom of expression is protected by Article 19 of the Universal Declaration of Human Rights (UDHR). Ethiopia is a signatory to this declaration and other international conventions. In spite of such public declarations of commitments to freedom of expression, government practice limits media in their promotion of the democratization process.[12]

The main source of the laws in Ethiopia is Article 29 of the Constitution. Article 29 states "Everyone has the right to hold opinions without interference and to freedom of expression without any interference. This right shall include "freedom to seek, receive and impart information and ideas of all kinds, regardless of frontiers, either orally, in writing or print, in the form of art, or through any media of his choice."[13] This article and other laws related to the press seem to be drawn from Article 19 of the UDHR.

In his interpretation of the First Amendment to the US Constitution, Meiklejohn extends this notion of freedom of expression and asserts "no speech, however dangerous may, for that reason, be suppressed"[14] in a democratic society. Echoing how important free speech is in building and strengthening a democratic culture in a nation, Sunstein concludes: "The right to free speech is hardly in tension with democracy; it is a precondition for it."[15] Clearly, he assumes that democracy benefits from plural and diversified views and that free speech promotes diversified and plural views.

However, Meiklejohn argues that "no one can doubt that, in any well-governed society, the legislature has both the right and the duty to prohibit certain forms of speech. Libelous assertions may be, and must be, forbidden and punished. So too must slander. Words which incite men to crime are themselves criminal and must be dealt with as such."[16]

Smolla emphasizes the need for responsibility for one's action. He says, "The free communication of thoughts and opinions is one of the invaluable rights of man, and every citizen may freely speak, write, and print on any subject, being responsible for the abuse of that liberty."[17] According to Smolla, free speech assumes the responsibility of the speaker or writer rather than the government. Thus, freedom of speech does not mean freedom from control. It means self-regulation.

However, many developing nations have introduced repressive laws, and these undermine self-regulation.[18] USAID reported that repressive media laws hinder the democratic process in any nation. Such laws impede the free flow of information and do not allow freedom of expression, which is the natural right of any free human being and guaranteed by universal declaration. Repressive laws leave little or no room for dissenting opinions and pluralistic views. They do not offer forums for public debate. These are obstacles that significantly affect the role media play in promoting democracy.

On the other hand, granting maximum protection for the free flow of information and promoting freedom of expression is not intrinsically opposed to regulation in the public interest.[19] Indeed, law and order are as important as freedom of expression.[20] It can be argued that law and order are the precondition of peace and stability. Peace and stability, in turn, are fundamental to democracy. Promoting freedom of expression is at the heart of democratic principles, for democracy presupposes an informed citizen.[21] Democracy cannot function without an open, fair, and representative media system that promotes transparency and accountability.[22]

Fair and free elections also are at the heart of a democratic process, and media play a critical role in free election "The media treat elections as the lifeblood of the democratic process, and their coverage of them provides citizens with balanced information on which to base their vote."[23]

Democracy presupposes that citizens are informed and can make choices. Media facilitate this through monitoring and reporting activities of elected officials, identifying areas of weaknesses and strengths and reporting on them. This way media demonstrate their influential power in a democratic process. "The media have power: They determine the fate of politicians and political causes; they influence governments and their electorates."[24] Besides facilitating fair and free elections, media promote good governance through monitoring the activities of elected officials.[25] However, exposing corruption and wrong doing can make journalists targets and victims of government repression.

For example, Reporters without Borders (2006) reported five journalists were killed, 256 arrested and 213 physically attacked or threatened in Africa during 2005. That same year, 86 media outlets were reported to have been censored. According to CPJ and Reporters without Borders, the situation is not improving. In fact, the number of journalists being harassed, charged, jailed, and attacked is increasing.[26]

In Ethiopia, a total of 17 journalists were detained in 2005, more than any other African nation.[27] This affects the information flow and eventually the ability of people to express their opinions freely. It is difficult to think of good governance and transparency in the absence of such freedom. Lack of freedom encourages corruption and abuse.[28]

Although presently the government seems to have a cat-mouse relationship with media, it is under the current government that an independent press came into existence.[29] The end of the Cold War and the change of government in Ethiopia are two major factors in the introduction of press freedom.[30] Due to the important change of 1992, people have been optimistic about the future of journalism in the nation.[31] A large number of newspapers and magazines flourished during this period.[32] Regardless of the practical flaws, the independent press provided the public with an alternative source of information and began to contribute its share in promoting public debate.[33] However, journalists still face roadblocks to their work. Unlike journalists working for government media, journalists working for privately owned media lack access to government documents: "Reporters from private newspapers are not allowed to attend news briefings by government officials and are denied information through the appropriate government channels."[34]

The government has accused the private press of lacking ethics and professionalism. However, government media also have had difficulties in these areas.[35] Most of their reporting has been criticized for being biased and weak.[36] Critics think that government media are biased in favor of the government while the privately owned press is inclined towards opposition groups.[37] The problems in both government and private media highlight a major challenge that journalism faces in Ethiopia.[38]

704   *Zenebe Beyene*

How can these issues be addressed in a manner that will promote and consolidate the democratic process in Ethiopia and bring peace and stability to the nation? One way to address this problem is to develop a legal framework that would protect journalists from continuous prosecutions and promote critical and responsible reporting. It is hoped that the findings of this study will be useful to policy makers who would promote freedom of expression and/or the public right to know.

Press Freedom in Africa and the West

Various scholars define freedom of the press focusing on different aspects. Eribo, for example, says: "It is the availability of a free marketplace of ideas and information for all the citizenry without fear, favor, intimidation, or obstacles. The concept of press freedom abhors government control, censorship, interference, and undemocratic regulations aimed at abridging the freedom of opinion, expression, and transmission of information or ideas through the mass media and other channels of communications."[39]

Press freedom means more than the ability of journalists to report news and views as they see fit without any interference. It also means accessibility of the press so people can express their views without limitations. In addition, it means the availability of newspapers and other media when citizens need information.[40]

According to Kasoma, freedom of expression means more newspapers and greater access; hence, more venues to express ideas and more alternatives to choose from. By the same token, diminished freedom means fewer media outlets, making people dependent on fewer sources and limiting options.

Stein describes the danger of the latter: "When a newspaper shuts down, one fewer voice exists to inform us on what we should know; moreover, we have fewer editorial opinions to give us guidance."[41] When choices are limited, people are denied their basic rights of access to information. The basic principle of democracy is threatened. Information is vital for democracy; people have a right to get information from alternative and independent sources.

Do other rights mean anything in the absence of freedom of expression? Addressing this role of freedom of expression as a basis for all other rights, Sawant states: "Freedom of expression is the mother of all civil rights that forms the bedrock of a democratic system, and legal restrictions on free speech eventually operate as restrictions on other rights as well."[42]

UDHR emphasizes that any human being is born free to express opinions and to seek, receive, and impart information through any medium. In all its characteristics, a free press is there to enable people to express their ideas. By serving this purpose, "A free press stands as one of the great interpreters between government and the people. To allow it to be fettered is to fetter ourselves."[43]

Press freedom has become one of the indicators for the existence of freedom of expression. In fact, the importance of a free press might be described most clearly by Thomas Jefferson: "Where it is left to me to decide whether one should have a government without a newspaper or newspaper without a government, I wouldn't hesitate for a moment to prefer the latter. But I should mean that every person should receive these papers and be capable of reading them."

Press freedom promotes government efficiency through exposing corruption and wrong doing; enabling the public to monitor how well elected officials carry out their duties, eventually building public confidence in government. Press freedom also promotes economic and technological development through making information available to the public.

A free press also can benefit a nation by promoting public debate and democratic discussion. This fosters transparency and openness which "permits more public understanding of the government's action and also makes it more possible for the government to respond to criticisms and justify those actions."[44] Thus, freedom of the press plays another role in keeping the government honest, responsible and responsive to public demands. In other words, press freedom "allows citizens to monitor government activity and participate more effectively in the process of self government."[45] Everyone becomes part of the decision making process.

While serving this purpose, a free press also acts as a bridge between the public and those in power: "Elected officials need the press in order to reach the public upon whom they depend for electoral support, and to gain knowledge of the public's policy interests. Facilitating the connection between government and citizens is essential to good journalism.[46]

Hiding information or classifying documents for political purposes results in rumor. Rumors endanger the credibility of governments and government-owned media. Franz Kruger illustrated this using his experience in Ethiopia as a visiting professor:

> I arrived in June 2005 to teach a course at Addis Ababa University. It was very soon after some shootings; I think at the time the government was talking of 26 deaths – the unofficial figure at the time was around 43. I talked to the taxi driver who collected me about the incident, and he said the real figure was definitely ten times as high. You cannot believe what is in the papers, he said. Even now, I am not sure there is general consensus on the death toll. I think this shows how easily rumor spreads when factual reporting is not available. And rumor is always worse than the reality. It also shows how much damage is caused to a society if the media's credibility collapses.[47]

Rumors also endanger national security through creating prejudice and mistrust between the electorate and elected officials.[48] Conversely, granting access to information is a way of increasing political participation, one of the characteristics of democracy. Denying access marginalizes the public.[49]

However, this does not seem to be the orientation of many political leaders in the developing world. Asante indicates that political leaders in the developing world believe that people should not know what their governments do. Such leaders believe that the more access the public has, the greater the interference which endangers national security and public order. As a result, they see the free press as a danger to public safety and make every justification to deny access.[50]

Apparently, this perceived conflicting interest endangers the existence of press freedom in the developing world. If officials do not acknowledge the role of a free press in informing the public, promoting accountability, and transparency, if they do not want to prevent corruption and if they do not want to promote democracy, how can they empower journalism? No matter how strongly an international agency such as the United Nations tries to empower this sector through introducing laws, national leaders may have the last say. "Laws do not mean much if those who are supposed to adhere to them do not do so."[51]

Freedom of expression and of the press are among the most fundamental of human rights. In spite of the constitutional recognition of these rights in many nations, there seems to be significant disparities in implementing freedom.

Disparities occur partly because of media structure and policies, which vary depending on forms of government, the principles on which the nation is founded and its culture and social history. Various nations introduce different media regulations; in some the media are relatively free (e.g., the United States). In others, government regulates media, and in some press councils determine media roles (e.g., India).[52] The arguments and counter arguments for these media systems are presented as follows.

One argument for government control over the media asserts that "media are too important to be left in private hands."[53] Another argument claims the restraint of opinion may be morally wrong but politically right; therefore, government should have control over media outlets.[54] "Every society has a right to preserve public peace and order, and therefore has a good right to prohibit the propagation of opinions which have a dangerous tendency. It is not the magistrate that has such a right but society."[55]

Counter argument asserts that it is difficult to obtain fair, objective, and accurate information if governments monopolize media. Ochs (1986) asserts press freedom is almost nonexistent in areas where the press is owned by government. Djankov *et al.*'s findings further strengthen this claim. After surveying patterns of media ownership and their implications for press freedom in 97 nations worldwide, they report, "Countries with greater state ownership of the media have less free press, fewer political rights for citizens, inferior governance, less developed capital markets, and inferior health outcomes."[56]

Concerning government's control over the media and its implications for freedom of expression, Djankov *et al.* (2003) state two opposite theories: public-interest and public-choice. These two theories clash over who best serves the public interest. The public-interest theory favors government-owned media. Proponents of this theory argue that only under government ownership can media best serve the public interest.

Public-choice theory, rather, argues that the public's desire should be given priority over the government's agenda. According to this theory, government-owned media would distort information to serve the government's interest. Therefore, government-owned media outlets do not offer forums for free debate. Without free debate, informed decisions become difficult.[57] Unfortunately, the public interest model seems to dominate in many parts of Africa. Wilcox reported that in 85% of African countries, journalists can be fined or imprisoned for criticism of government officials or polices.[58]

In Malawi, "the parliament passed a law making the publication of a false report punishable by life imprisonment. (Malawi's president) Banda is the arbiter of whether a report is true or false."[59] Similarly, the former Nigerian President Sani Abacha declared that "all criticisms of his government be treated as treasonable offense."[60] In a situation where criticizing government is treated as treason, how can media expose corruption and/or wrong doing to promote good governance?

There seem to be more agreements than differences concerning a definition of press freedom. However, the following studies indicate battles over freedom of the press begin with questioning the extent of free press and who should correct potential problems.

The argument for certain limitations on press freedom emanates from the notion of ensuring public safety. Proponents of this notion seem to base their arguments on the social responsibility theory: "No rights are unconditional, because for every right there is a reason given for that right....Yet if that reason for its existence were no longer valid, there would be no need for the right. Thus, argue proponents of social responsibility, there can be no unconditional, inalienable rights."[61] The Commission on Freedom of the Press, for example, states: "The press can be inflammatory and sensational. If it is, its freedom will go down in the universal catastrophe."[62]

This implies that in order to avoid or minimize inflammatory, sensational and irresponsible reporting, government should be able to limit freedom of the press. The public should be protected from libel/defamation, pornography, or obscenity. Military secrets essential to public security should be protected.[63] These matters place limitations on press freedom. Although controversial, courts call for limitation on press freedom. In a court, anyone is innocent until proven guilty. A defendant has the right to a fair trial; the public has the right to know. These interests may conflict. As a result, where to draw a line can be contested.

Bollinger states "there is no guarantee that the press will not abuse the freedom it poses under the autonomy model, for the autonomous press is free to make omission or active misrepresentation."[64] This view speculates that some media outlets distort facts and mislead the public and therefore do not deserve protection. This may be one reason some scholars argue for regulation. The Commission on Freedom of the Press outlined a more serious concept of media freedom: "the media are free, in one sense, to publish a variety of opinion. But if they do not do so, if they do not uphold their moral responsibilities, they lose the moral right of freedom. Freedom of the media then is a conditional right."[65] This implies that press freedom is not absolute; how media behave determines their rights. Media should meet their obligations. If they do not, they jeopardize their freedom.[66]

Press freedom was granted so that media can serve the public and protect it from government wrong doing. If media abandon this responsibility and assume different roles, such as misleading the public or inciting violence, they invite government interference.

The argument for maximum protection for press freedom, on the other hand, is based on libertarian theory, which maintains that individuals are born with certain unconditional rights that can neither be taken away by government institutions nor forfeited by individuals.[67] Stevens argues that limiting press freedom prevents the press from performing its role in advancing democracy and exacting accountability for governmental wrongdoing.

To generalize that all media outlets discharge their responsibilities fairly and objectively is difficult. Some engage in sensational reporting; others preach supremacy of one ethnic or political group over another. Media engaged in such tasks may not deserve protection.

Groups that base their arguments on social responsibility theory argue that media were granted freedom so that they could provide citizens with fair and objective information that the public would use to make informed decisions. According to a proponent of this argument, "No rights are unconditional, and absolute; any one can lose them upon abuse."[68]

Protecting Press Freedom

Journalism is commonly referred to as the "fourth estate." It is perceived as an independent public institution that safeguards the public from wrong doing by powerful entities. Such a view assumes that journalists should "check the three official branches by exposing misdeeds and policies contrary to the public interest."[69] In order to assume this responsibility, the press should enjoy maximum protection. To this end, some scholars base their arguments on libertarian theory. Basing itself on the works of prominent thinkers such as John Milton, Thomas Jefferson, and John Stuart Mill, libertarian theory advocates for maximum protection for freedom of expression and individual rights and sees government involvement in the marketplace as a greater violation.[70]

However, for various political reasons, the press can be forced to neglect its responsibilities and fail to make information available for public consumption. During a crisis, for example, it is press freedom that may become the target. Citing previous studies, Mizuno reported that during World War I, it was "press freedom that became one of the early causalities of the war in the U.S."[71]

Similarly, press freedom became a victim during the controversial May 2005 election in Ethiopia. On the election evening, the prime minister appeared on television and declared a ban on mass demonstrations and public meetings. This was followed by a crackdown on the independent press.[72] In many such cases, the notion that describes journalists as "fearless seekers of truth and justice" tend to leave journalists to face injustice.

In an attempt to make an assessment of universal ethics among international political journalists, Rao and Ting Lee conducted a study in Asia and the Middle East. Many of the journalists interviewed for their study expressed concern over the ongoing attacks against them for doing their job. One of the journalists interviewed reported:

And what use would such a code be to me? The broadcasting code we have says that we cannot criticize even the seventh cousin of the sheikh, forget his brother or son. If the code includes "tell the truth" and if we tell the truth, we will be put to death for following such a code. They will find something in the Sharia laws (Islamic laws) to justify my hanging.[73]

Harsh measures against press freedom during crises seem to be more of a norm than an exception. After studying US government use of the Japanese-language press during World War II, Mizuno reported:

The Roosevelt administration took stricter approaches toward certain unpopular, minority press groups. ... The federal government placed close surveillance on publications of communists, fascists, anti-war black nationalists, and pro-Nazi extremists. Some were indicted. Washburn found that government officials seriously considered prosecuting dissident African American publications for sedition.[74]

In the United States, where press freedom and freedom of speech are assumed to be vital to democracy, experiences such as this may have a very chilling effect on the practice of freedom of expression in the United States and elsewhere.

On the other hand, Cross argues that press freedom should be maintained during both war and peacetime: "The right of the people to know should not be diminished. It should not be uncertain, precarious, or dependent on the grace of officials."[75]

However, this is not the case in many nations. In Ethiopia, for example, freedom of the press depends on the political ideology and the good will of the governments: "Successive governments in Ethiopia have muzzled the media despite claiming democratic governance and freedom of expression. In such an environment, the media must fight to articulate public concerns in the struggle for democracy."[76]

During the Emperor era, 1941–1974, the notion of freedom of the press was almost nonexistent. During the military dictatorship, there was no press freedom. Ethiopia's present government introduced freedom of the press. However, this freedom did not last long. After the May 2005 election, the government took measures against journalists and private publishers, eroding the rights of freedom of expression by accusing journalists of irresponsible reporting and putting them behind bars.[77] In order to protect journalists from such attacks and to make them more accountable, certain measures must be taken. Experiences and practices in other nations suggest the following possible measures:

Journalists need certain privileges. In the United States, for instance, most states have shield laws in place. These laws provide legal protections for journalists and their confidential sources. Although shield laws protect reporters from state (not federal) prosecutions, among other constitutional protections, this can be considered one step towards empowering journalists to discharge their professional and civic responsibilities with some level of confidence.[78] Journalists should protect the safety and confidentiality of their sources.

However, freedom of expression does not mean freedom from any control. Who should exercise this control? Many developing nations show that government's control over the media has been detrimental.[79] Does this mean that media should be left free so that media professionals can misuse freedom of expression? There seems to be more consensus than disagreement on regulating media outlets. Perhaps regulating media outlets has gained importance due to media roles in divided societies. For example, the situation in Rwanda during 1994 has conveyed a powerful message to responsible citizens. Radio Television Liber des Collines, "which stereotyped the Tutsi minority, and called for war to 'exterminate cockroaches'" is worthy of consideration.[80]

Media practices such as this endanger press freedom. Such irresponsibility invites government interference in the name of protecting public safety. Thus, regulating media outlets is part of empowering the profession and promoting freedom of expression, because freedom hardly exists without responsibility. In addition, "professional standards are not likely to be achieved as long as the mistakes and errors, the frauds and crimes, committed by units of the press are passed over in silence by other member of the profession."[81]

The importance of establishing self-regulatory mechanisms such as press councils has been reported by Bertrand. It "emphasizes the importance of self regulation by media owners and media professionals, who are asked not only to hold politics, business, and other systems of society accountable, but also to inquire if media professionals fulfill their primary responsibility, which is 'to provide a good public service'."[82]

Such justifications led India to become one of the nations that instituted a press council to govern the conduct of the media. Sewant argues that by establishing a press council, India makes its media vibrant, free and accountable – accountable to the press council, not to the government. The purpose of the council has been described as "preserving the freedom of the Press and of maintaining and improving the standards of newspapers and news agencies in India."[83]

Like India, Ghana, Nigeria, and South Africa have adopted mechanisms to regulate the media. Former President Dr. Limann expressed his readiness to protect press freedom in that nation when he came to power in 1980.[84] Established in 1978 Nigeria has a similar press council. According to Eribo, "The council, a self-regulatory body had powers to enforce a code of conduct and define duties of journalists."[85]

South Africa has set up the office of the Press Ombudsman and an Appeal Panel. This body is similar to press councils in other nations whose functions include to "mediate, settle and, if necessary, adjudicate complaints about what has been published in newspapers and magazines, in accordance with a Code and Rules of Procedure."[86] According to the South African National Editor's Forum (SANEF), the principle of press self-regulation was introduced in South Africa in 1962 and has been accepted for more than 40 years.

Press Freedom in Ethiopia

The sections below summarize the development of freedom of expression during three successive governments: the Emperor era, 1941–1974; the Derg era, 1974–1991, and that of the current government 1991 to the present.

The Emperor era: 1941–1974

This era is remembered as peaceful and stable, and the emperor's administration became a model for some developing nations. However, the status of press freedom during this period was not ideal. Those close to Emperor Haile Sellasie promoted a proverb in Amharic[87] whose English equivalent would read, "One cannot accuse the king because he is a descendent of the Lion of the tribe Judah – *a king cannot be accused as the sky cannot be cultivated*." As a result, The Emperor had absolute control over the press.

Despite this, freedom of expression was introduced in 1955 with the addition of an article to the Constitution of Ethiopia. Getahun wrote, "The idea of freedom of expression was first mentioned in the 1955 revised Constitution of Emperor Hailesellasie I. Article 41 declares: freedom of speech and of the press is guaranteed throughout the empire in accordance with the law."[88]

Nevertheless this right to exercise freedom of the press was restricted by the 1950 penal code that outlawed any writing or libelous accusation defaming the royal family and foreign heads of state.[89] Getachew summarized the Law:

> Other restrictions disallowed pronouncements against the imperial government and the constitution; a show of disrespect for government officials; any reference to unemployment, disputes between labor and management, student uprisings, religious and ethnic differences, the increase in prostitutions, and the number of beggars; any comment on the government budget; writing obscenities; ... land tenure; complaints by government employees; tax increases; inflation; comparing Ethiopia's living standards with other countries; propagating the social philosophy or ideology of other countries; and finally, reporting on parliamentary debates. In addition, the media had to be careful about criticizing the US government, as it was an ally of Ethiopia.[90]

In short, the press was free to say anything, so long as it was of no consequence at all. If one cannot comment on social and economic issues, cannot express frustration about corrupt practices, cannot comment on abuse of power, cannot hold public officials accountable, then what is the point of an article in the Constitution on press freedom?

The Derg regime 1974–1991

During the Derg regime, Ethiopia experienced both natural and manmade disasters. The era is remembered for its repressive laws. Freedom of expression was one of the casualties under this regime.

Like most democratic constitutions, the Derg constitution contained an article guaranteeing freedom of expression. For example, Article 47 (1) declared, "Ethiopians are guaranteed freedom of speech, press. ..." Furthermore, Article 47 (2) reads: "The state shall provide the necessary material and moral support for the exercise of these freedoms."[91] "Having officially declared socialism as the ideology of the state in 1975, the Derg demonstrated its intolerance to diversity of views by killing, torturing, or forcing into disappearance those who demanded rights. As views opposed to the regime had no political space, their views and opinions became unlawful for public consumption. In short, citizens did not have any right to express themselves nor to get access to governmental information."[92]

Press freedom 1991 to the present

The present government firmly departed from the previous regimes. This period witnessed the birth of many newspapers and the death of others.[93] Changes occurred in the restrictive policies that had existed in Ethiopia. However, the practice of journalism by privately owned media has remained problematic; getting information from government officials is difficult. Getachew observed: "Reporters from private newspapers are not allowed to attend news briefings by government officials and are denied information through the appropriate government channels.[94]

Lack of training is another major challenge for Ethiopian media. In his study, Tedbabe found that 35.7% of the journalists working for the privately owned press had experience in journalism while 23.8% had public relations experience. The rest, that is, 40.5%, did not have any journalism experience.[95] Only 9% of Ethiopian journalists surveyed were college graduates (Diploma).[96]

The above findings demonstrate a lack of professional credentials among media practitioners. Lack of professional skill greatly influences the quality of reporting. Upgrading the professional skills will increase the quality of reporting and improve journalism.

However, no study showed any effort to improve journalism in Ethiopia. Unfortunately, after the May 2005 election, the privately owned press became a victim of government action. "The government unleashed a sudden and far-reaching crackdown on the independent press."[97] Thus, in addition to lacking respect due to poor quality, practicing journalism in Ethiopia has become a risky business.

The preceding survey of the status of press freedom under the three successive governments in Ethiopia suggests that freedom of expression depends on government ideology.[98] Martin concludes, "the role of the press vis-à-vis the government varies from country to country, but in all cases the relationship is symbiotic and depends on the country's political ideology."[99] Noting this dependency of the media on the ideology and good will of the people in power, Getachew wrote: "Successive governments in Ethiopia have muzzled the media despite claiming democratic governance and press freedom. In such an environment, the media must fight to articulate public concerns in the struggle for democracy."[100]

In order to understand the context in which the media operate in Ethiopia, one should make reference to the Constitution. In Ethiopia, the main source of all the laws is Article 29 of the Constitution. Article 29 contains the following five provisions:

1 the right to hold opinions without interference;
2 the right to freedom of expression without any interference [including] freedom to seek, receive and impart information and ideas of all kinds, regardless of frontiers, either orally, in writing in or print, in the form of art, or through any media
3 freedom of the press and other mass media, and freedom of artistic creativity are guaranteed. Specifically include[ing] the following elements:
   a) prohibition of any form of censorship,
   b) access to information of public interest.
4 ideas and opinions that are essential to the functioning of a democratic order, the press shall. as an institution, enjoy legal protection to ensure its operational independence and its capacity to entertain diverse opinions;
5 All media financed by or under the control of the State shall be operated in a manner ensuring their capacity to entertain diversity in the expression of opinion.[101]

The current government has made progress towards guaranteeing a free press. However, some inconsistency exists within the government's commitment to this freedom. The introduction of the draft press law is considered highly constrictive of press freedom.[102] Amare argues: "It is totally unconstitutional and violates some of the international agreements the country had signed willingly to establish a free press."[103] Similarly, Alemayehu argues "the credibility of this press law is questionable because it was drafted without involving the main stakeholders – the journalists in the private press."[104] The law states that it would establish a press council whose directives and procedures will be determined by the government.[105]

After expressing its concern about the way some private newspapers report, the government accuses the private press of lacking responsibility and professionalism, and argues for a mechanism to overcome irresponsible reporting and sensationalism. The draft press law seems to be oriented toward development of such a mechanism. According to the government, the draft press law is designed to "encourage responsible journalism." However, the draft of the press law drew concerns from international press institutions and human rights groups. Fritz asserted:

> Under the proposed law, the independent media will have little chance to develop and the Ethiopian media scene will be further dominated by government-owned or government-supported media. There can be no coincidence in the fact that the most outspoken critic of this draft law, the independent Ethiopian Free Press Journalists Association (EFJA), has been suspended and its members prevented from associating.[106]

However, Minister of Information Berhan Hailu wrote: "Journalists were victims of partisan politics, and their reports were full of distortions and fabrications."[107] According to Hailu, the law is not the problem; it is "irresponsibility and lack of capable professionals in the sector that remain as stumbling blocks"[108] for press freedom in Ethiopia.

Hailu's remarks about the performance of the independent press and the probable impact of the press law are consistent with the social responsibility theory. "The media's social responsibility came to mean acting morally: keeping promises, not fabricating information, searching out the 'truth,' and so on."[109]

The arguments and counter arguments presented here reveal the controversial nature of the draft press law. Given the role of press freedom as "a means of advancing knowledge and searching for truth" and promoting democracy, maintaining this human right requires special care. Otherwise, in the attempt to avoid irresponsible reporting, we may end up preventing press freedom as a whole. "Any power capable of protecting freedom is also capable of endangering it."[110]

Censorship, Licensing, and Law

The following section presents conflicting values: freedom of expression versus concern for government's role in protection of children, traditional values, individual reputations, and national security. People constantly struggle to balance their love for and devotion to free expression with all those other legitimate and cherished values. It is difficult to illustrate ways to distinguish censorship that protects national security from censorship that protects a political administration or point of view. This section tries to address these conflicting values, and shows the difficulty in striking a reasonable balance.

The definition of censorship used in this article implies that it is a government's imposition against the will of the public. According to Daily: "The Latin term *censura praevia,* always claimed as a privilege of the Roman Catholic Church, is roughly translated as 'suppression'."[111] Tribe defined censorship as "restriction on ideas prior to, prosecution following, their publication." After 25 years of these definitions, censorship is defined as "much about displacing one version with another, and displacing texts from one channel to another, as it is about blocking access or destroying transgressive material."[112]

While freedom of the press means the right to gather, disseminate, and exchange information, opinions, and ideas, censorship is a practice against this. In Daily's words: "Intellectual freedom is the opposite of censorship, because whatever may be argued as the basis for the imposition of rules on the transmission of messages, the purpose is to govern the thoughts of others, to control curiosity."[113] Given these characteristics, censorship "is the hallmark of an authoritarian regime. A society can be strong only when it is truly free."[114]

However, this remark does not mean that censorship exists only in authoritarian nations. Although the degree varies, censorship exists in every nation.[115] "Nowhere in the real world could we have total freedom of expression."[116] The difference is that in a free society, regardless of government intent and action, "people see and read what they wish despite what the law says. Just as during prohibition, if you pass a law which everybody violates, it creates an attitude or climate of indifference toward the law and a disrespect which could generalize to other legitimate and valid laws."[117]

Media Use and Abuse in Ethiopia

People who argue for some forms of censorship say government has a responsibility to keep the people and their nation safe. To achieve this, they justify censorship. Citing the experience in the United States, Delgado and Stefancic argue that "the Supreme Court also has recognized that the government may restrict speech directed at a captive or unwilling audience."[118] The highest judicial power in the United States recognizes government's responsibility to prevent expressions that harm society.

The captive audience doctrine also arose in a case called *Lehman vs. Shaker Heights* and involved car cards on public transportation. Lehman, a candidate for state office, wanted to advertise his political messages on public transit vehicles. He brought the suit challenging the constitutionality of the municipal policy to disallow political messages in public vehicles. However, the state courts and the Ohio Supreme Court rejected his plea and concluded that the city's refusal did not violate the candidate's free speech, rather protected the captive audience.

Similarly, Delgado and Stefancic (1997) state that utterances that inflict injury or tend to incite violence are not protected by the First Amendment. They support their claims by presenting a case called *Chaplinsky vs. New Hampshire*. They maintain:

> In *Chaplinsky vs. New Hampshire*, the United States Supreme Court declared that words which by their very utterances inflict injury or tend to incite an immediate breach of the peace are not protected by the First Amendment. Racial insults, and even some of the words which might be used in a racial insult, inflict injury by their very utterance.[19]

The major argument for censorship focuses on maintaining national security; therefore, national security issues take priority over the public's right to know.[120] However, governments may not always be successful in winning cases involving military documents or "secrets." The Pentagon Papers is a classic example. When the *New York Times* published an article in 1971 on the US military involvement in Vietnam, Attorney General John Mitchell warned the *Times* against further publication. The *Times* refused, and the US government took the case to court. The Court granted a temporary restraint; the *Times* argued that this would violate First Amendment rights. The government failed to prove that the *Times* article endangered national security. As a result, the Supreme Court decided in favor of the newspaper.[121]

Another argument for censorship is the need to make sure that children are protected from some pornographic materials. MacKinnon argues that speech may not be restricted because of its type but because of its value or lack thereof. Based on this, pornography does not deserve protection because "protecting pornography means protecting sexual abuse as speech."[122] Sexual abuse should not be protected. Although the justifications might take different forms, Qualter argues for some level of censorship: "Some level of censorship is necessary and inevitable because without it, the cohesive fabric of society would be undermined, and its very existence endangered."[123] One can conclude that we could censor some expressions because of their "detrimental social impact."

Some of the opinions cited in this study favor some sort of censorship, but one favors censorship in general. However, some forms of censorship can be encouraged. The issue becomes who decides what and when to censor? Who draws the line between what should and should not be censored? How should a nation draw the lines so that, for example, censorship to protect national security does not become censorship to protect a politician? These questions must be considered before drawing any conclusions on such a sensitive topic.

Licensing is required in some nations, but not in others. Licensing is generally considered a way of collecting fees. However, Asante maintains licensing and certification of journalists is one form of control over information. He argues that: "Perhaps one of the pervasive ways of keeping citizens away from mass media channels is the licensing and certification of journalists in a country. By doing so, government authorities are able to control who gets access to the media."[124] In brief, licensing authorities, mostly government agencies, use licensing to silence critical voices. In other words, to be critical of government that decides the fate of media is practically impossible.

Journalists do not need a license to practice one of their democratic rights – freedom of expression. McQuail objects to any licensing procedure, saying it is a means to suppress freedom.[125] He further argues that whenever a government thinks that the press is critical of policies or officials, it tends to regulate the press. Along the same line, Wilcox argues that "any license to permit publication can be withdrawn if the periodical becomes too critical or skeptical of government policies and officials."[126] In a number of nations, critical newspapers were suspended for allegedly failing to comply with licensing procedures.[127] In reality, these newspapers became targets mainly for their critical reporting on government corruption, human rights abuses and restrictions on civil liberties.[128]

A number of nations worldwide demand licensing of journalists for "public safety." In the United States, for example, a Commodity Futures Trading Commission (CFTC) rule requires publishers and website operators who provide futures-trading information to register with the government.[129]

Although not major, there are arguments and counter arguments on the issue of registration and licensing. Clearly, governments may put a system in place to track down who does what. However, governments should make sure that licensing should not be abused for political purposes.

The discussions so far indicate that press freedom can be affected by a number of factors. One of these, defamation law, limits press freedom. Defamation can be defined as "The intentional communication of a falsehood about a person, to someone other than that person, that injures the person's reputation. ... Being required to pay damages for defamatory statement restricts one's freedom of speech. Intentional communication to damage reputation can be a serious crime and should be dealt with accordingly. Sometimes, differentiating between intentional and innocent communication might be difficult. Attempting to redress damages and silence critical voices make defamation a focus and it "has been the subject of more discussion and study during the last 20 years than most of us would care to admit."[130] One reason that researchers give so much attention to defamation law is that governments tend to use this law to silence critical voices. The high cost of litigation of such cases and their impact on press freedom also provide reasons for such great attention.[131] "A growing fear among the media is that large damage awards and expensive litigation costs will have a chilling effect on the media's willingness to report on controversial news stories."[132]

Contrary to their original purpose, defamation laws have been abused by governments. Article 19 states "Governments and government officials are abusing defamation and insult laws to suppress criticism of official wrongdoing, maladministration and corruption, and to avoid scrutiny. These laws often flout international principles and standards. They are also often unconstitutional."[133]

Defamation is the issuance of a false statement about another person or entity, which causes harm to his or her reputation. Therefore, although difficult to generalize, the main purpose of defamation law is to protect reputation, not to suppress critical voices. A longitudinal study conducted during a 10 year period (1974–1984) by Benzanson, Cranberg, and Soloski discovered: "Most plaintiffs reported that they sued in order to punish the media and to restore their reputations. Only about a quarter of the plaintiffs said that they sued to win money damages."[134] According to this finding, the central reason behind defamation cases is to redress damaged reputations, not to make money.

However, some studies indicate that governments and big corporations abuse defamation law.[135] For example: "A libel suit can be used as a weapon to silence a critic and warn other potential critics that they might suffer the same fate if they persist in attacking the plaintiff."[136] Indeed, Benzanson, Cranberg, and Soloski (1985) maintain that the more states use libel laws to silence criticism and punish journalists, the less effective the press becomes in investigative reporting.

Defamation laws can have both constructive and destructive roles in promoting press freedom. Defamation laws can have destructive roles if they are used for political reasons. Unfortunately, many criminal libel laws are used primarily to silence critical voices and discourage free public debate.[137] The studies conducted by Article 19 indicate that criminalizing defamatory statements is not necessary to redress damaged reputation. They should be replaced with appropriate civil laws."[138]

Defamation laws can be constructive by providing the basis for accountability. The fact that an "honest mistake" has been committed does not change the fact that a false statement has been made.[139] Such situations may lead to libel suits. To try to avoid such suits, journalists and editors check and double check for accuracy and credibility. As Nelson stated, "Libel can be overcome if journalists always check their facts."[140]

Ethiopian Applications

Amare Aregawi, editor and publisher of *Reporter*, a newspaper based in Addis Ababa, was charged for an article that appeared in the February 8, 2004, edition, which alleged widespread corruption at Ethiopian Telecommunication. While the case was pending, the Ethics and Anti-corruption Commission of Ethiopia accused many of the Ethiopian Telecommunication's high-level managers. After the story was published, the government fired 16 high-level managers and dismissed CEO in 2006.[141] The prosecutor argued that the article was defamatory while the other government body, that is, the Ethics and Anti-corruption Commission, accused the officials of corruption.

Similarly, Daniel Kifle, editor of *Fendisha*, an Amharic-language weekly newspaper, was charged with publishing an article alleged to be defamatory. The article ran in the January 14, 1998, issue of the newspaper and discussed corruption by Tamrat Layne, then Prime Minister. Layne was charged with corruption and sentenced to 18 years. However, the court found the editor guilty and sentenced him to a 18 months of imprisonment. Why was the journalist who exposed the corruption sentenced to 18 months in prison? The dilemma behind this case is: "Did that journalist deserve recognition or punishment?"

Artist Sileshi Demissie, commonly known as "Gash Abera Molla," has played a vital role in changing litter-filled public areas in Addis Ababa into garden and recreational areas (BBC, 2001). He managed to do this through mobilizing about 30 000 school children in Addis Ababa and obtaining strong financial support from some organizations. A journalist working for *Maebel*, a weekly newspaper, wanted to get 2000 birr (US$225) from him. He called and threatened to blackmail the artist unless he gave the stated amount of money. According to personal communication with Sileshi, the journalist published an article alleging the artist was taking the school children away from their studies. As a result, the article held the artist accountable for a possible growing trend of delinquency among the students. More seriously, the article alleged the artist embezzled millions of dollars from the Royal Netherlands Government for the project. The article concluded with the promise to publish stories of the artist's "corrupt" practices.[142] After the publication, the artist arranged a meeting to give the journalist the money. The meeting turned into a fight in which the journalist had a tooth knocked out. The conflict was settled through arbitration by professional associations.

Avoiding responsibilities is also a major threat to press freedom in Ethiopia.[143] Tedbabe's study found that people are employed to serve as "tapelas," or persons listed on the editorial staff who serve jail terms for those journalists who do the editorial work, but are not identified."[144] These "journalists" publish whatever they want and the "tapelas" "take the heat." Such practices will not lead to quality journalism or a responsible free press in Ethiopia.[145] Attacks by political and economic powers, unethical, and irresponsible reporting, coupled with abuse of press freedom by journalists endangers press freedom. How can a situation like this be handled?

The cases in this section show that something must be done to protect journalists from government attacks and society abuse by the journalists. Some argue that government control over the activities of the press is dangerous for press freedom. However, some of the above examples show that the abuse of this right by journalists is equally dangerous: "There is no guarantee that the press will not abuse the freedom it possesses."[146]

Summary of Cases

- In all the cases, the press defendants are charged by prosecutors.
- In most cases, the press defendants are accused of defamation and disseminating false and inaccurate information.
- In almost all cases, the decisions rule against the press defendants.
- Unlike the situation in the United States, the press defendants need to prove that they are innocent.
- Unlike experiences in the United States, the cases in this study show that criticizing (defaming) government officials was least tolerable.
- The US 5th Amendment guarantees that "no person ... shall be compelled in any criminal case to be a witness against himself." Contrary to this basic principle, the press defendants' answers while in police custody are used as evidence for prosecutors and against themselves.

Defamation

Case one

In May 2006, Abraham Reta, a journalist working for *Addis Admas*, the privately owned Amharic weekly newspaper, was sentenced to a year for libel.[147] The press defendant was first convicted of libel in 2006 over an article reporting that three government officials had embezzled funds in 2002, when he was editor of another Amharic weekly newspaper *Ruh*.[148] Abraham was arrested on April 24, 2006 and spent three months in prison before conditional release, pending the outcome of his appeal. The Federal Supreme Court rejected his appeal and decided to send Abraham back to prison to complete the one-year sentence he received in May 2006 for allegedly libeling the three government officials (information about the identity of the officials and the content of the article unavailable). According to Reporters without Borders, throughout the court hearings, the press defendant insisted on his innocence but was forced to identify his source.

Case two

Wossenseged Gebre Kidan, editor-in-chief of *Ethop*, the privately owned Amharic weekly newspaper, was charged with violating the Press law by disseminating false information in 2002 concerning explosions in the Tigray Hotel in Addis Ababa. According to the court document, Wossenseged was prosecuted for publishing a false report in the September 18, 2002, issue that alleged that Mr. Sekuture Getachew, editor-in-chief of *Abiyotawi Democracy*, an organ of the ruling party, was wounded during the attack in the hotel.

The prosecutor's witness, Mr. Sekuture Getachew, about whom the report was written, explained to the court how the report has damaged his reputation and affected his and his family's lives. He further explained that he went to the newspaper and asked Wossenseged to publish corrections or retractions which the defendant did. However, at the end of the correction, a footnote indicated that the report was true and the newspaper was ready to present evidence upon court request. As shown in the court document, the prosecutor used a witness and a copy of the newspaper to make his points. The court sentenced the editor-in-chief to 16 months imprisonment.

Case three

Tesahelene Mengesha, editor of *Mebruk*, an Amharic-language weekly, was charged for a defamatory article that appeared in the newspaper's August 28, 1998 issue that alleged Army Captain Risom served as an undercover agent for two governments.

The prosecutor used a witness and a copy of the newspaper to make his points. The witness was Army Captain Risom, the person who was allegedly defamed by the article. The court sentenced Tesahelene Mengesha to 18 months imprisonment.

What makes this case questionable is the fact that the court based its decisions on the published article and the testimony of the subject of the article: Army Captain Risom. The captain is the plaintiff, but his testimony was used to make the prosecutor's case.

Case four

According to Reporters without Borders, Tilahun Bekele, editor of *Fetash* (an Amharic-language weekly) was accused of publishing a report alleging that an Ethiopian mineral water company was financed by the US Central Intelligence Agency (CIA) and was taking water from polluted sources. The articles appeared in *Maebel*.

The writer of this paper interviewed the owner of Crown Mineral Water Company, Mr. Ermias Amelga by phone. In the interview, the owner indicated that a journalist threatened to cause damage to his company unless the owner paid money (5000 birr/ US$500).[149] The owner refused; the journalist published a fabricated story; the market reacted and the mineral water company went out of business. This outcome was confirmed with other informants.

The above cases show major problems in the Ethiopian media. The problems are explained in terms of the following: First, the principle of libel (defamation) laws. Libel laws protect private citizens against libel far more than they protect public officials. In the United States it is nearly impossible for a public official to win a libel suit. "Public officials and public figures have to prove a higher level of fault than do private individuals."[150]

Government or public officials must prove actual malice to win libel lawsuits. Cases such as *New York Times vs. Sullivan* are evidence of this. Public officials should be open to public scrutiny. How can journalists investigate and expose government wrong doing if government officials are protected by defamation laws?

What makes these particular decisions more questionable is that the courts found the press defendants guilty of libel without proof of actual damages. Under the principle of defamation, proof must exist that an official's reputation has been damaged as a result of intentional or reckless conduct. The prosecutors did not prove actual malice. Publications of false statements (by themselves) are not sufficient conditions for defamation. In *New York Times vs. Sullivan*, the US Supreme Court said: "neither falsity nor injury to official reputation, separately or in combination, is an adequate basis of libel action by a public official."

Thus, the prosecutors' ability to prove actual malice is of paramount importance for defamation law in particular or press freedom in general. Cases with intentional conduct to cause harm must be distinguished from cases caused by mistakes. "Freedom of the press also includes the freedom to make honest mistakes."[151]

In Case one the press defendant was forced to identify sources. Journalism is all about getting information and disseminating it to the public. Journalists use various sources to report on events. If they are forced to identify sources, it is going to be increasingly difficult to obtain information from those sources. The prosecutor or the plaintiff should carry the burden of proof. It is the plaintiff's duty to prove beyond a reasonable doubt that damage has occurred.

The press defendant (Case one) was accused of libel. The article was published in 2002, and the press defendant was accused in 2006; the appellate court gave the final verdict in 2007. Like in other areas, there is acute shortage of skilled man power in the justice system. The addition of a number of libel suits against the press will become a burden on an already overstretched legal system. This calls for alternative ways of addressing this problem. Therefore, instead of taking libel cases to court, it is better if the press is allowed to publish corrections or retractions. Arbitration of some sort as opposed to court action would correct the problem, and can be handled by press councils.

Licensing and registration: *Tarik*

Eyob Demeke, publisher and editor of *Tarik*, a privately owned Amharic weekly newspaper, was accused of "violation of the press law." According to the charges:

1   Eyob failed to print the name of the newspaper's deputy editor in the publication. The charges further indicated that the newspapers published from June 12 to July 26, 1999, did not carry the name of the newspaper's deputy editor.
2   He failed to renew his press license and continued to publish and disseminate the newspaper from September 12, 1998, to August 13, 1999.

As the file showed, Eyob explained to the court that he did not include the name of the newspaper's deputy editor because of the death of the editor. He did not renew the license because of policy change in the two government offices: Ministry of Industry and Tourism and Ministry of Information. According to Eyob, the ministry which was designated to handle the renewal of licenses was changed. For his defense, he brought the head of the Licensing and Control department in the Ministry of Information. The head testified that Eyob went to his office and wanted to renew his license. However, because of change of practice, he advised Eyob to go to the Ministry of Industry and Tourism, which was mandated to do this job. The whole process took a long time. Eyob reported that because of the long process and other personal reasons, he was forced to leave the newspaper business. So he requested that the court drop the case against him. Nevertheless, the court rejected his request and sentenced him to a 6000 birr (US$600) fine (4000 for the first charge and 2000 for the second charge).

Similarly, in 1999 CPJ reported that in the first week in December, the Ethiopian Ministry of Information and Culture suspended the publishing licenses of 12 private newspapers for not having the sum of 10 000 birr (US$1000) in their bank accounts. The newspapers affected were *Genanaw, Meyisaw, Tarik, Zeggabi, Kiker, Atlanta, Cantona, Fiker, Kal Kidane, Madonna, Rite,* and *Hikma*.[152]

These cases reveal two problems: the legitimacy of licensing and the problems with government-controlled licensing and registration systems. One may not need to have a license to exercise his or her natural right. Others might argue that media outlets should have licenses. Who should have control over licensing requirements? Should this responsibility be given to government bodies? If so, how can one be critical of a government that decides on the fate of a medium?

If the above mentioned 12 newspapers were suspended because of licensing requirements, how could one know that the issue at hand is a licensing issue and not abuse of power? Whatever the answer to this question, irresponsible reporting may invite government intervention. A system should be put in place to know who is doing what. However, as stated above, this should not be handled by a government. Licensing should be handled by press councils or other professional associations rather than government bodies.

National security

Case one

Dereje Biru, editor of *Tequami*, a privately owned Amharic weekly newspaper, was charged with reporting false information in two articles in the October 23, 1996 issue. The article apparently alleged that conflicts existed in two regions of the nation. According to the prosecutor, these articles incited war and violence.

After hearing prosecution and defense, the judges indicated that the articles might be exaggerated but did not incite war. The judges further stressed that the evidence presented by the prosecutor was insufficient to prove the case. As a result, the judges at the Federal High Court decided that the journalist was not guilty, and the case against him was dropped.

The prosecutor appealed to the Federal Supreme Court. Here, the prosecutor demanded proof that the alleged conflict occurred between the government army and armed groups. Dereje, on the other hand, insisted that it was the prosecutor who should bear the burden of proof. The Federal Supreme Court overturned the judgment of the High Court and found the journalist guilty of publishing articles that created disturbance and were incitement to war.

Case two

Lubaba Seid and Eyob Demeke, the editor and the publisher of *Tarik*, a privately owned Amharic weekly newspaper, were accused of publishing articles in the newspaper's August 9, 1996 issue reporting that an Oromo Peoples' Democratic Organization (OPDO) politician who replaced Samora Yenus in Eastern Oromiya had defected, and that the President's personal security guards had also defected. The prosecutor insisted that the press defendants published and disseminated false information that could disturb and confuse members of the defense force.

The prosecutor used as evidence a witness, a copy of the newspaper and Lubaba and Eyob's answers while in custody. Lubaba and Eyob argued that they had found the news in a foreign based newspaper "Ethio-News" and presented the translation of the original report.

The court asserted that it is up to the local newspaper to verify the credibility of the news and the source. The court further stated that it did not have jurisdiction or authority over newspapers published overseas. As a result, it is up to the editor to double check facts before publishing and disseminating information. Finally, the court sentenced the editor, Lubaba Seid, to a year imprisonment while dropping the charges against the publisher, Eyob Demeke.

Case one has two associated problems. First, who should bear the burden of proof: the prosecutor or the defendant? The prosecutor should have proved the falsity of the report. However, as it is presented in the court document, the judges at the Federal Supreme Court did not do this. It was reported that the court based its judgment on the content of the articles and the potential for inciting war and creating violence or disturbance.

Second, the judges based their ruling on their own interpretation of the articles. What the prosecutor brought before the court were the articles. The articles by themselves would not show that the alleged problems occurred. No other evidence was presented to strengthen the prosecutor's case alleging the falsity of the articles or the potential of the articles to cause alleged violence in the nation.

Inability to check and double-check for facts is one of the reasons for publishing false or inaccurate information. In addition to a lack of professional training and human and material resources to get first-hand information, the lack of willingness on the part of government officials to release information for the private press can cause exaggeration or sensational reporting. Denying access to information results in rumors – "Rumor thrives in the absence of solid, verifiable information. It becomes a substitute for news when institutionalized channels fail."[153]

In the second case, the fact that the press defendants claimed that they obtained the news from a foreign based newspaper cannot be a defense. The newspaper that publishes stories should make sure that reports are based on facts. Facts or "truth" may be a very good defense against claiming that certain reports and news are obtained from a different source. Obviously, cut and paste may not be a good practice for responsible and objective journalism.

An Ethiopian journalist depending on a foreign source for an event taking place in Ethiopia is difficult to understand. Journalists working for the private press face difficulty in obtaining information from government offices through the appropriate government channels. This bottleneck might force journalists to depend on other techniques to get information. However, cases such this may not need complicated techniques to check the facts.

In summary, the above cases show a trend toward abusing press laws by the government and abuse of press freedom by journalists. Neither action will help press freedom. Limiting press freedom affects the role a free press plays in the democratization process of the nation. The implications of the findings of this study are consistent with the conclusions of the Commission on Freedom of the Press: "Any power capable of protecting freedom is also capable of endangering it."[154]

Recommendations

Ethiopia is a nation with an ancient civilization. However, press freedom is in its infancy. Press freedom was nonexistent during Emperor Haile Selassie's era (1930–1974). People around the Emperor promoted a proverb which read: "*A king cannot be accused as the sky cannot be cultivated.*" As a result, the press did not have the power and the right to criticize government wrong doing. Press freedom was severely restricted by the emperor's successors, the Derg (1974–1991). The press served as a mouthpiece of the hardliner communist government. There was no privately owned media.

Freedom of expression and of the press took a different direction in Ethiopia during the present government. The government allowed publication by the private press. Formal censorship bodies were officially prohibited by the 1992 press law.

After this guarantee, independent newspapers flourished. However, the freedom did not last long, and freedom did not result in a responsible press. A study to assess postelection challenges to the free press in Ethiopia reported that nongovernmental publications that focus on social and political issues have reduced by 55% since May 2005. This has not helped the democratization process in the nation. How can such problems be addressed in a manner that will promote the democratic process and bring peace and stability to the nation?

This study has investigated existing laws and practices that affect journalism in order to suggest a viable legal protection for journalists to discharge their responsibilities in a free and responsible manner. The following are the major findings.

- Many press defendants were accused of disseminating "false, inaccurate or defamatory" statements.
- Many press defendants were accused of criminal defamation laws and were charged by prosecutors.
- The press defendants were found guilty of violating and abusing press freedom through unethical or irresponsible reporting.
- One needs to prove that there is intention or mental readiness in order to accuse somebody of defamation. In opposition to this view, the courts passed

Media Use and Abuse in Ethiopia

their decisions based on the content of the articles and testimonies by witnesses. Charging somebody because of what he or she publishes without considering other important factors (such as intention) is inconsistent with the constitution and national laws. Placing the burden of proof on the press defendant is another finding of this study.

- Cases involving the press may be handled and solved effectively by professional organizations. Indeed, press councils in many nations play a key role in promoting a free and responsible press. A press council may have multidimensional roles from arbitration cases involving the press to advising concerned government offices to take necessary measures to protect press freedom.
- Experiences in some states in the United States show that reporters are protected from state prosecutions by shield laws. The cases cited in this study showed otherwise. One of the press defendants was forced to identify his sources. Exposing sources will not promote critical and investigative journalism.
- One of the major problems for press freedom is laws framed with vague or broad meanings. Such laws are open for abuse.
- A press defendant was sentenced to 2000 birr (US$200) for failing to renew a press license. Similarly, the study showed that some 12 newspapers were shut down because of licensing. It is difficult to tell whether these actions are merely genuine measures to implement government policies or attack the press.

In summary, this study attempted to suggest legal protection for journalists in Ethiopia by comparing current practices vis-à-vis national and international provisions on press freedom. The study based itself on the principle that press freedom is the mother of all other rights: "when these rights weaken, other rights and democracy will suffer the same fate."[155] Thus, the effort to establish and develop a free and responsible press may be a step towards this end.

When people have the opportunity to express grievances freely, they are less likely to prefer violent ways of addressing differences. The press should be able to provide a forum and a channel of communication for people with different views. It is the fighting of ideas not fighting people that can bring Ethiopia out of its existing problems. "The contribution the media can make to healing sharp divisions is obvious, offering an alternative method of dealing with them. They encourage protagonists to sort out their differences in a peaceful way through argument rather than fighting. A newspaper column is better than a fistfight, or a bomb."[156]

Based on the findings of the study, I make the following recommendations.

1 *Making information accessible to the public*: Journalists do not need to be accused of disseminating "false information or inaccurate information to the public that created a sense of distrust in the people about the government." Making information accessible may prevent publication of inaccurate information. Whenever legal means of getting information are not possible, people rely on rumors and speculation. Rumors and speculation are not good for the public or government.

2 *Training*: As indicated, press freedom is in its infancy in Ethiopia. No strong program existed in Ethiopia until the establishment of a Graduate School of Journalism and Communications at Addis Ababa University. As a result, many of the working journalists have little or no training or education in journalism. Inadequate training or no education in journalism is one of the reasons for poor reporting.

3 *Criminal defamation laws*: Some irresponsible journalists use their right and freedom to blackmail individuals, and damage their reputations. Clearly, criminal defamation should not be used to insulate government officials through intimidating those who voice legitimate concerns about the actions or practices of public officials.

4 *Corrections or retractions*: In addition to some intentional and deliberate actions to blackmail the good names of individuals, mistakes can be made at any stage of gathering and disseminating information. Thus, instead of taking every libel case to court, it is better if the press is allowed to publish corrections or retractions. The press should be able to develop a tradition of publishing corrections. Allowing corrective measures would be more helpful for promoting accountability. Therefore, arbitration of some sort (as opposed to court action) would address the problem more effectively.

5 *Proof for actual malice*: The studies discussed here show that publication of false information is not a necessary condition for defamation. The court should be able to separate between cases with intentional conduct to cause harm and incidents caused by mistakes. Indeed, the court should be able to examine the press defendant's state of mind. In other words, the mental readiness of the journalist should be the basis of prosecuting a journalist. The literature and cases in this study showed that there are journalists who intentionally abuse press freedom for their own personal gains. The actions of these kinds of journalists would represent a "reckless disregard for truth." Mistakes can be made when a journalist is working under deadline pressure. Due to economic reasons, many newspapers cannot afford to employ an adequate number of journalists. As a result, many publications are run with a minimum staff. This means that a journalist is responsible for a number of assignments. This can be one of the reasons for making innocent mistakes.

6 *Time limit*: Some of the cases revealed that journalists were prosecuted because of articles they published some four or five years previously. A prosecutor should not be allowed to go back to four or five years and charge a journalist for publishing allegedly defamatory, false, or "dangerous" articles. The United States "statute of limitations" states that over time, memories fade and evidences are lost. This calls for a mechanism to limit deadlines over which one cannot file a legal suit.

7 *Establishing a press council*: A tendency exists to abuse laws pertaining to press freedom. The government may use laws to silence critical voices. The press abuses the freedom vested in it. "No civilized society can have mass media without some societal compulsions and moral obligations nor, without any restraints

and responsibilities."[157] Who should have control over this important institution? Allowing government to have control over this institution will erode press freedom. Leaving the press without some level of control is equally dangerous. Thus, a need exists for a mechanism to encourage the press to regulate itself by establishing an independent and strong press council.

8 *Shield laws:* Shield laws are crucial so that reporters do not have to disclose confidential sources. If journalists expose their sources, they will damage their reputations and may endanger their sources. Thus, shield laws should enable journalists to withhold information and sources. Facts or "truth" must be used as defense, not the exposing of sources. However, press councils and other professional associations should exert maximum effort to make sure that this privilege is not abused.

Notes

1   Street (2001); Sawant (2003).
2   Kruger (2007).
3   Central Statistics Authority (CSA) (2007).
4   Central Statistics Authority (CSA) (2007).
5   CIA in Gebremedhin (2006).
6   Aalen (2002).
7   Eshetu (2004).
8   Getachew (2003).
9   EU Final Report (2005).
10   EU Final Report (2005).
11   EU Final Report (2005).
12   Getachew (2003).
13   Constitution of Federal Democratic Republic of Ethiopia, Proclamation (1/1995).
14   Meiklejiohn (1960, p. 5).
15   Sunstein (1995, p. 121).
16   Meiklejiohn (1960, p. 21).
17   Smolla (1992, p. 30).
18   Ogbondah (2002).
19   The Commission on Freedom of the Press (1947).
20   The Commission on Freedom of the Press (1947).
21   Street (2001).
22   USAID (1999).
23   Street (2001, p. 232).
24   Street (2001, p. 232).
25   Street (2001, p. 232).
26   Getachew (2003); CPJ (2006).
27   Reporters without Borders (2005).
28   Alemaheyu (2003, p. 117).
29   Getachew (2003); Mekray (2007).
30   Ogbondah (2002).

31 Getachew (2003).
32 Getachew (2003).
33 Getachew (2003).
34 Getachew (2003, p. 568).
35 Gebremedhin (2006, p. 23).
36 Gebremedhin (2006, p. 23).
37 Mekray (2007).
38 Gebremedhin (2006, p. 27).
39 Eribo (1997, p. 52).
40 Kasoma (1997, p. 136).
41 Stein (1966, p. 38).
42 Sawant (2003, p. 17).
43 Pember (1999, p. 61); Stein (1966, p. 21).
44 Moynihhan (1998, p. 14).
45 Bush and Chamberlain (2000, p. 38).
46 Kumar and Jones (2005, p. 226).
47 Kruger (2007, p. 3).
48 Qualter (1985).
49 Qualter (1985).
50 Asante (1997, p. 3).
51 Ogbondah (2002, p. 62).
52 Sawant (2003).
53 Gamal Abdel Nasser in Ochs (1986, p. 17).
54 Johnson in McQuail (2005, pp. 176–177).
55 Johnson in McQuail (2005, pp. 176–177).
56 Djankov *et al.* (2003, p. 374).
57 Djankov (2003, p. 374).
58 Wilcox (1975, p. 71).
59 Wilcox (1975, p. 71).
60 Eribo (1997, p. 66).
61 Hindman (1997, p. 19).
62 The Commission on Freedom of the Press (1947, p. 4).
63 Lelyveld (1971, p. 166).
64 Bollinger in Hindman (1997, p. 8).
65 Hindman (1997, p. 18).
66 Hindman (1997, p. 18).
67 Hindman (1997, p. 19); Meiklejohn (1960).
68 Hindman (1997, p. 19).
69 Levy (1985, p. xii).
70 Berry *et al.* (1995).
71 Mizuno (2005, p. 148).
72 CPJ (2005).
73 Rao and Ting Lee (2005, p. 108).
74 Mizuno (2005, p. 150).
75 Cross in Uhm (2005, p. 134).
76 Getachew (2003, p. 562).
77 CPJ (2005).

78   Lening and Cohen (2005).
79   Sawant (2003).
80   Kruger (2007, p. 1).
81   Robert Leigh in Fengler (2003, p. 819).
82   Bertrand in Fengler (2003, p. 819).
83   Sawant (2003).
84   Anokwa (1997).
85   Eribo (1997, p. 57).
86   www.sanef.org.za (accessed August 2, 2010).
87   The working language of the nation
88   Getahun (2005).
89   Getachew (2003).
90   Getachew (2003, p. 566).
91   Getahun (2005).
92   Almaz in Getahun (2005, p. 52).
93   Getachew (2003).
94   Getachew (2003, p. 568).
95   Tedbabe (1998).
96   Tedbabe (1998).
97   CPJ (2005, p. 26).
98   Getachew (2003).
99   Martin in Asante (1997, p. 14).
100 Getachew (2003, p. 562).
101 Constitution of Federal Democratic Republic of Ethiopia, Proclamation 1/1995 (pp. 9–10).
102 Amare (2003); CPJ (2003).
103 Amare (2003); CPJ (2003).
104 Alemayehu (2003).
105 Ministry of Information (Draft Press Law (DPL) (2003, p. 33).
106 IPI (2007).
107 Berhan Hailu (2006).
108 Berhan Hailu (2006).
109 Hindman (1997, p. 150).
110 The Commission on Freedom of the Press (1947, p. 8).
111 Daily (1973, p. 3).
112 Burt (1998, p. 28).
113 Daily (1973, p. 143).
114 Daily (1973, p. 4).
115 Tribe (1973); Qualter (1985).
116 Qualter (1985, p. 146).
117 Daily (1973, p. 6).
118 Delgado and Stefancic (1997, p. 23).
119 Delgado and Stefancic (1997, p. 23).
120 Schoenfeld (2006).
121 Pember and Calvert (2005, pp. 70–72).
122 MacKinnon (1993, p. 9).
123 Qualter (1985, p. 146).

124   Asante (1996, p. 119).
125   McQuail (2005).
126   Wilcox (1975, p. 62).
127   Wilcox (1975, p. 62).
128   Wilcox (1975, p. 62).
129   www.rcfp.org/news/1999/0628f.html (accessed July 27, 2010).
130   Bezanson, Cranberg, and Soloski (1985, pp. 22–23).
131   Bezanson, Cranberg, and Soloski (1985, pp. 22–23).
132   Bezanson, Cranberg, and Soloski (1985, p. 1).
133   Article 19 (n.d.a).
134   Bezanson, Cranberg, and Soloski (1985, p. 11).
135   Emerson (1970).
136   Pember and Calvert (2005, p. 136).
137   Pember and Calvert (2005, p. 136).
138   Article 19 (2000, p. 7).
139   Article 19 (2000, p. 7).
140   Nelson (1973, p. 11).
141   Reporter (2007).
142   pers. comm. with the artist.
143   Tedbabe (1998).
144   Ogbondah (2002, p. 66).
145   Tedbabe (1998).
146   Bollinger in Hindman (1999).
147   Addis Admas (2007).
148   Addis Admas (2007).
149   pers. comm. with the investor.
150   Pember and Calvert (2005, pp. 69–70).
151   Moore (1992, p. 40).
152   Moore (1992, p. 40).
153   Qualter (1985, p. 158); Kruger (2007).
154   The Commission on Freedom of the Press (1947, p. 7).
155   Canton (2002).
156   Kruger (2007, p. 3).
157   Ray (n.d.).

References

Aalen, L. (2002) *Ethnic Federalism in a Dominant Party State: The Ethiopian Experience 1991–2000*, Michelsen Institute, Development Studies and Human Rights Bergen, www.cmi.no/publications/2002/rep/r2002-2.pdf (accessed July 30, 2010).

Addis, A. (2007) www.addisadmass.com/News/news_item.asp?NewsID=384 (accessed July 30, 2010).

Alemayehu G.M. (2003) A discussion on the draft Ethiopian Press Law. *The International Journal of Ethiopian* Studies, 103–120.

Amare Aregawi. 2005. (2005) www.developments.org.uk/articles/how-free-is-our-speech/ (accessed July 30, 2010).

Anokwa, K. (1997) Press performance under civilian and military regimes in Ghana: A reassessment of past and present knowledge, in *Press Freedom and Communication in Africa*, (eds F. Eribo and W. Jong-Ebot), Africa World Press, Inc, Trenton, pp. 3–28.

Article 19 (n.d.a) //www.rap21.org/article1398.html (accessed July 30, 2010).

Article 19 (2000) Defining Defamation: Principle on Freedom of Expression and Protection of Reputation, London, www.article19.org/pdfs/tools/editorial-def-campaigns.pdf (accessed July 30, 2010).

Article 19 World Report (1988) *Information, Freedom and Censorship*. Longman, Harlow, UK.

Asante, E.C. (1996) *The Press in Ghana: Problems and Prospects*, University Press of America, Inc, Lanham, MD.

Asante, E.C. (1997) *Press Freedom and Development: A Research Guide and Selected Bibliography*, Greenwood Press, London.

BBC (2001) Cleaning up the streets of Addis. http://news.bbc.co.uk/2/hi/africa/1319359.stm (accessed July 30, 2010).

Berhan Hailu (2006) www.ethiopianreporter.com/modules.php?name=News&file=article&sid=13933 (accessed July 30, 2010).

Berry E.W., Braman, S., Christains, C. *et al.*(1995) *Last Rights: Revisiting Four Theories of the Press*, University of Illinois Press, Urbana.

Bezanson, R.P., Cranberg, G., and Soloski, J. (1985) *Libel and the Press: Setting the Record Straight*, University of Minnesota, Minneapolis.

Burt, R. (1998) (Un)Censoring in details: The fetish of censorship in early modern past and the postmodern present, in *Censorship and Silencing: Practices of Cultural Regulation*, (ed. R.C. Post), Getty Research Institute for the History of Art and the Humanities, Los Angeles, pp. 17–41.

Bush, M., and Chamberlin, B.F. (2000) Access to electronic records in the States: How many are computer friendly, in *Access Denied: Freedom of Information in the Information Age*, (eds C.N. Davis and S. Splichal), Iowa State University Press, Iowa (Ames).

Canton, S.A. (2002) International organizations and the protection of press freedom (Andersen Lecture), www.wpfc.org/AL2002.html (accessed July 30, 2010).

Central Statistics Authority (CSA) (2007) http://www.csa.govs.et/text_files/national%20statistics%202006/Population.pdf (last accessed March 1, 2007.

Constitution of Federal Democratic Republic of Ethiopia, Proclamation (1995) *Negarit Gazette*, 1st Year, No.1., Addis Ababa.

CPJ (2003) www.cpj.org/attacks03/africa03/ethiopia.html (accessed July 30, 2010).

CPJ (2005) *Attacks on the Press in 2005 with a preface by Paul E. Steiger*, CPJ, New York.

CPJ (2006) www.cpj.org/attacks06/africa06/eth06.html (accessed July 30, 2010).

Daily, J.E. (1973) *The Anatomy of Censorship*, Marcle Dekker, Inc., New York.

Delgado, R., and Stefancic, J. (1997). *Must We Defend Nazis?: Hate Speech, Pornography, and the New First Amendment*, New York University Press, New York.

Djankov, S., McLiesh, C., Nenova, T. *et al.* (2003) Who owns the media? *Journal of Law and Economics*, 46 (2), 341–381.

Emerson, I.T. (1970) *The System of Freedom of Expression*, Random House, New York.

Eribo, F. (1997) Internal and external factors affecting press freedom in Nigeria, in *Press Freedom and Communication in Africa*, (eds F. Eribo and W. Jong-Ebot), Africa World Press, Inc, Trenton, pp. 51–74.

Eshetu C. (2004) *Underdevelopment in Ethiopia*, Organization for Social Science Research in Eastern and Southern Africa, Addis Ababa.

EU Final Report (2005) http://ec.europa.eu/external_relations/human_rights/eu_election_ass_observ/ethiopia/2005_final_report.pdf (last accessed December 19, 2006).

Fengler, S. (2003) Holding the news media accountable: A study of media reporters and media critics in the United States. *Journalism and Mass Communications Quarterly*, 80, (4), 818–832.

Gebremedhin, S. (2006) *Ethiopia: Research Findings and Conclusions*, BBC World Service Trust. London.

Getachew, M. (2003) Ethiopia Status of Media, in Johnston, D. H. (ed) (2003) *Encyclopedia of International Media and Communications*, Vol. I, (ed. D.H. Johnson) Elsevier, San Diego., pp. 561–569.

Getahun, A. (2005) Public access to Government Information in Ethiopia - with Particular Reference to PR Practices in Selected Public Institutions. MA thesis Addis Ababa University.

Hindman, E.B. (1997). *Rights Vs Responsibilities: The Supreme Court and the Media*, Greenwood Press, Westport.

IPI (2007) www.freemedia.at/cms/ipi/watchlist_detail.html?country=KW0155 (accessed July 30, 2010).

Kasoma, F.P. (1997) Communication and Press Freedom in Zambia, in *Press Freedom and Communication in Africa*, (eds F. Eribo and W. Jong-Ebot), Africa World Press, Inc, Trenton, pp. 135–156.

Kruger, F. (2007) Responsible media in a divided society. Media Challenges in a Society in Transition, United Nations Conference Centre, Addis Ababa, Ethiopia.

Kumar, J. M., and Jones, A. (2005) Government and the Press: Issues and Trends, in *The Press*, (eds G. Overholser and K.H. Jamieson), Oxford University Press, New York.

Lelyveld, A. (1971) I am against censorship, in *Censorship: For and Against*, Hart Publishing Company, Hart Publishing Company, pp. 164–177.

Lening, C., and Cohne, H. (2005) Journalists' Privilege to Withhold Information in Judicial and Other Proceedings: State Shield Statutes. Congressional Research Service, The Library of Congress, Washington DC.

Levy, W.L. (1985) *Emergence of the Free Press*, Oxford University Press, New York.

Mackinnon, C. (1993) *Only Words*, Harvard University Press, Cambridge.

McQuail, D. (2005) *McQuail's Mass Communication Theory*, 5th edn, Sage, London.

Meiklejohn, A. (1960) *Political Freedom: The Constitutional Powers of the People*, Greenwood Press, Westport, CT.

Mekray M. (2007) The right to get information. Panel discussion, Media challenges in a society in transition, United Nations Conference Centre, Addis Ababa, Ethiopia.

Ministry of Information (2003) *Draft Ethiopian Press Law*, Ministry of Information–Federal Democratic Republic of Ethiopia, Addis Ababa..

Mizuno, T. (2005) Federal government uses of the Japanese-language press from Pearl Harbor to mass incarceration, in *Journalism and Mass Communication Quarterly*, 82 (1), 148–166.

Moore, C.R. (1992) *The Political Reality of Freedom of the Press in Zambia*, University Press of America, Boston.

Moynihan, P.D. (1998) *Secrecy*, Yale University Press, New Haven, CT.

Nelson, J.L. (1973) *Libel: A Basic Program for Beginning Journalists*, Iowa State University Press, Ames.

Ochs, M. (1986) *The African Press*, The American University in Cairo, Cairo.

Ogbondah, W.C. (2002) Media laws in political transition, in *Media and Democracy in Africa*, (eds M. Lesslie and F.F. Ogundimu), Transaction Publishers, New Brunswick.

Pember, R.D. (1999) *Mass Media Law*, McGraw-Hill College, Boston.

Pember, R.D., and Calvert, C. (2005) *Mass Media Law*, McGraw Hill, Boston, MA.

Press Council of India. http://presscouncil.nic.in/home.htm (accessed July 30, 2010).

Qualter, T.H. (1985) *Opinion Control in the Democracies*, Macmillan, London.

Rao, S., and Ting Lee, S. (2005) Globalizing media ethics? An assessment of universal ethics among international political journalists. *Journal of Mass Media Ethics*, 20 (2&3), 9–120.

Ray, G.N. (n.d.) http://presscouncil.nic.in/home.htm (accessed July 30, 2010).

Reporter (2007) Ethiopian telecommunication held Ato Tesfaye and Co. accountable. www.ethiopianreporter.com/modules.php?name=News&file=article&sid=15656 (accessed July 30, 2010).

Sawant, B.P. (2003) Accountability in journalism, *Journal of Mass Media Ethics*, 18 (1), 16–28.

Schoenfeld, G. (2006) Commentary: Has the *New York Times* violated the espionage act? March, www.jonathanpollard.org/2006/030006.htm (accessed July 30, 2010).

Smolla A.R. (1992) *Free Speech in an Open Society*, Vintage, New York.

Stein, L.M. (1966) *Freedom of the Press: A Continuing Struggle*, Julian Messner, New York.

Street, J. (2001) *Mass Media, Politics and Democracy*, Palgrave, Houndsmill, UK.

Sunstein, C.R. (1995) *Democracy and the Problem of Free Speech*, The Free Press, New York.

Tedbabe, T. (1998) Developments and challenges of the privately owned press in Ethiopia. BA thesis, Addis Ababa University.

The Commission on Freedom of the Press (1947) *A Free and Responsible Press: A general report on Mass Communication: Newspapers, Radio, Motion Pictures, Magazines and Books*, The University of Chicago Press, Chicago.

Tribe, D. (1973) *Questions of Censorship*, George Allen & Unwin Ltd., London.

Uhm, K. (2005) The Cold War communication crisis: The right to know movement, in *Journalism and Mass Communication Quarterly*, 82 (1), 131–147.

USAID (1999) *The Role of Media in Democracy: A Strategic Approach*, Bureau for Global Programs, Field Support Research, Washington D.C.

Wilcox, L.D. (1975) *Mass Media in Black Africa: Philosophy and Control*, Praeger, New York.

Court Documents

Prosecutor Alemayehu Zemdkun (Government of Ethiopia) vs. Dereje Biru. Federal Supreme Court, File number/208/88; Date 06/09/1989 (Ethiopian Calendar).

Prosecutor (Government of Ethiopia) vs. Amare Aregawi. Federal High Court, 672/96; 242/96; File No 5-7018/672/96; Date 21/11/1997 (Ethiopian Calendar).

Prosecutor (Government of Ethiopia) vs. Lubaba Seid and Eyob Demeke. No name of the court and the file number; Date 25/7/1994 (Ethiopian Calendar).

Prosecutor Tarik Endale (Government of Ethiopia) vs. Eyob Demeke. Federal High Court, Case number/09918; Date 30/05/1998 (Ethiopian Calendar).

Prosecutor Minlik Yalew Woubshet (Government of Ethiopia) vs. Tesahelene Mengesha, editor of Mebruk. Federal High Court, Case number/15090 Date 25/8/1997 (Ethiopian Calendar).

Prosecutor Minlik Yalew Woubshet (Government of Ethiopia) vs. Wossenseged Gebre Kidan, editor-in-chief of Ethop, Federal High Court, case number/27870. Date 9/8/1998 (Ethiopian Calendar).

37

Collective Guilt as a Response to Evil
The Case of Arabs and Muslims in the Western Media

Rasha A. Abdulla and Mervat Abou Oaf

Islam is the fastest growing and probably most controversial of the three monotheistic religions. It is also the religion of over 90% of Arabs. Arabs and Muslims have long been the victims of negative, stereotypical portrayals by the Western media. This condition has been aggravated by the attacks of September 11, 2001, on the United States. Arabs and Muslims in the Middle East region are progressively a source of major news events as Iraq, Iran, Israel, the Palestinian territories, Saudi Arabia, oil, war, and terrorism, grab the attention of readers and viewers on the front pages of leading newspapers and prime time of major newscasts' headlines nationally, regionally and globally.

Even before September 11, Kai Hafez stated that:

> the media also portray many erroneous or one-sided images that misrepresent the West in the Islamic world and the Islamic world in the West. The large-scale dissemination of worldviews that are deeply rooted in the stereotypes and ideologies of religious and cultural conflict poses a serious threat to peace in the globalized world of the 21st century" (Hafez, 2000, p. 3).

Following the unfortunate criminal attacks of September 11, 2001, Arabs, Muslims, and Islam itself came to the forefront of the Western media, often with no differentiation of the three terms, and often in association with the word "terrorists." All four terms were used almost interchangeably. Many media outlets referred to the September 11 terrorists simply as "Muslims," which fueled the negative stereotyping of Islam and seemed to imply a sense of collective guilt or collective punishment by association.

This chapter investigates how biases and stereotypes are formed through the integrated influences of politics, money, media, and power. We examine the concepts of

---

The Handbook of Global Communication and Media Ethics, First Edition. Edited by Robert S. Fortner and P. Mark Fackler.
© 2011 Blackwell Publishing Ltd. Published 2011 by Blackwell Publishing Ltd.

collective guilt and collective punishment among other factors and roles that each plays against the ethical principles of fairness and objectivity. The main concern in this chapter is to challenge the collective media portrayal of Arabs and Muslims as evil-doers and illustrate how unethical and unfruitful such representation are against the West's own ethical benchmarks. It is much more useful for everyone to try to understand the other, appreciate diversity, and to learn to tolerate the other, however different they might appear to be. In the process, suppositions in reference to bias, stereotyping, truth, objectivity, fairness, power, collective guilt, and collective punishment are explored among other theories to investigate ethical principles as a reaction to the evil representations attached to Arabs and Muslims in the Western Media.

A Note on Operationalization: Arabs versus Muslims

Before considering and analyzing the literature, it is necessary to establish the differences between the terms "Arab" and "Muslim," which are used interchangeably in the media. Abdulla (2007) noted that Arabs constitute members of an ethnic group of people who inhabit the areas of North Africa and the Arabian Peninsula. The Arab population is estimated at around 300 million. Muslims are members of a group of about 1.5 billion people who choose to practice Islam as their religion. Therefore, the word "Arab" refers to an ethnicity while "Muslim" refers to a religion. Most Arabs (more than 90%) are Muslims. However, the majority of Muslims are not Arabs. The majority of Muslims come from Indonesia, India, Pakistan, Malaysia, and Afghanistan, all of which are non-Arab countries. The largest Muslim population in the world resides in Indonesia.

It should also be noted that there are vast differences between Arabs and non-Arab Muslims, and between Muslims of different Arab nations, and indeed, between Muslims within any given Arab nation. Treating "Arabs" or "Muslims" collectively is a vast misrepresentation of reality, which implies that these people are more or less the same. The lives of Muslims in Egypt are very different from those of Muslims in Saudi Arabia. Islam is practiced in Tunisia quite differently from Lebanon or Iran. Implying that there is a uniform way of practicing Islam that works for all 1.5 billion Muslims is simply naïve and unrealistic.

Why Is Islam a Threat?

McPhail (2006) in his book *Global Communication: Theories, Stakeholders, and Trends* argues that considerable technological advances have affected global communication, particularly with the advent of transnational and global broadcasting. McPhail elaborates that Western and other core nations' governments believe that most tyrants and terrorists originate in the Middle East and North Africa (MENA), and that all sorts of instabilities and threats against modern technological civilization comes from this region. He refers to "Jihadist" groups' attempt to fulfill Huntington's "Clash of

Civilizations" prophecy of rejection. Huntington argued that the main cause of conflict between peoples will be along cultural and religious lines:

> It is my hypothesis that the fundamental source of conflict in this new world will not be primarily ideological or primarily economic. The great divisions among humankind and the dominating source of conflict will be cultural. Nation states will remain the most powerful actors in world affairs, but the principal conflicts of global politics will occur between nations and groups of different civilizations. The clash of civilizations will dominate global politics. The fault lines between civilizations will be the battle lines of the future (Huntington, 1993).

McPhail (2006) argues that most peripheral countries are not satisfied with the cultural dominance of the West and believe they are being conquered by Western media, which affects many aspects of their cultures, norms, traditions, and their way of living. Islamic nations are no exception. Technological development is and will for the coming years be located in core nations and consequently the flow of information will continue to be one sided and peripheral nations will have to cope with the current Western trends. However, even Huntington says that the clash of civilizations will eventually come to an end as the Western countries and Islam will in due course, learn to coexist. Huntington (1993) wrote: "In the final analysis, however, all civilizations will have to learn to tolerate each other" (see also Huntington, 1993, 1996; McPhail, 2006).

McPhail (2006) further argues that the perception of Islam as a threat by the West has more than a few significant justifications. The hijackers of the September 11 attacks were Muslim; Osama bin Laden, their spiritual, financial, and strategic leader, hails from Saudi Arabia. Plots for the March 11, 2004, Madrid train bombing were initiated by Moroccan terrorists with support from Al Qaeda.

Additionally, organizations such as Hezbollah and Hamas support violence in the Palestinian territories and Israel. Such groups have their own print and broadcast means of access like Hezbollah's "Al Manar" satellite channel that has been constantly harsh on the United States and Israel. The Palestinian "Intifada" is also seen in the West as a source of instability in the region. Finally, there is Iran and its alleged nuclear program (McPhail, 2006).

On the other hand, it is only fair to address the other side of the previously mentioned allegations, which indicate the collective approach that the West takes in its approach to the region. Violence in the Middle East does not originate from the same source and is not caused by the same reasons. The historical political struggles of the Palestinian-Israeli conflict and the Iraqi war cannot compare with Bin Laden's terrorist acts. Lester (1997) states that is unethical and unprofessional for a foreign reporter and/or photojournalist to write a story and/or take a photo of an angry Palestinian during demonstrations expressing protest, and portray that person as a terrorist rather than investigate the underlying political origins of such reactions. Lester admits that Muslims and Arabs are constantly being positioned unjustly in such hostile and sometimes brutal representations.

Relevant Theoretical Notions

Five main ethical foundations

Aristotle's, Kant's, Mill's, Rawls' and Judeo-Christian philosophies

Louis Hodges came up with a classification of five categories of general ethical theories that are based on the principles of virtue, duty, utility, rights, and love. These five philosophical principles are generally accepted as essential in the application process of ethical decisions (Christians *et al.*, 2005). Aristotle's Golden Mean is the philosophy of "moderation and fairness." Moderation and temperance is regarded as the main virtue through which all other virtues (justice, courage, and wisdom) flow. "Moral virtue is a fixed quality of the will," says Aristotle, "consisting essentially in a middle state, as determined by the standard that a person of practical wisdom would apply" (cited in Christians *et al.*, 2005, p. 12). Christians *et al.* (2005) recommend this path for Palestinian-Israeli negotiations or for the CNN coverage of the war in Iraq.

The second ethical foundation hails from German philosopher Immanuel Kant (1724–1804), who developed a theory of "categorical imperative," where universal principles that one would want to apply across the world will be the bases for making sound ethical decisions. Universalization, or the ability to generalize the ethical principle, becomes the benchmark for the action. This, for example, stands in sharp contrast to many situations where Arabs and Muslims believe the West applies double standards.

The ethics of Kant gave way to what is now called deontology ethics, which depends to some extent, on ethical realism for it assumes the presence of ethical supremacy to make an action moral. In deontology, the nature of an act in itself determines its correctness or incorrectness regardless of the outcomes of the action. A deontologist would argue that the ends do not justify the means.

The third ethical foundation is credited to British philosophers John Stuart Mill (1806–1873) and Jeremy Bentham (1748–1832) with their "principle of utility," where the most ethical path would be one with the prevalent overall benefit for most beings. The benchmark would be what course of action would provide the greatest amount of good or happiness to the greatest number of people. This gave way to the ethics of consequentialism, where basically, unlike deontology, the ends do justify the means.

Peter Singer the utilitarian philosopher in *The Expanding Circle: Ethics and Sociobiology*, says that concern regarding other people's interests is essential for human existence. The principle foundation in the theory of utilitarianism promotes the notion that entails considering each person's interest equally while making decisions. If this is the case then the wellbeing of, for example, Muslims considering they are the "others" is essential for the welfare, security, and benefit of the rest whoever and wherever they are. Singer pointed out that *Expanding the Circle* was intended to basically establish conceivable justification for how some people believe in utilitarianism (cited in Festinger, 1957).

The forth ethical foundation refers to the "Veil of Ignorance" of American philosopher John Rawls, whereby the most ethical course of action is one taken with principles of fairness and equality in mind, and with no regards for one's status in society. Members of the society are judged with no consideration to particular characteristics, such as age, race, gender, religion, and socioeconomic status. It is interesting to note that, as will be demonstrated in this chapter, although of American origin, the principle of the Veil of Ignorance is rarely practiced in American media, particularly in regard to the coverage of Arabs and Muslims in news and/or entertainment programming.

The fifth ethical foundation represents what is referred to as the "Judeo-Christian" tradition, which is mainly based on the principle of love. A person is supposed to love others as they are, without trying to change them and with no particular respect for the self. It is also interesting to note that Islam has a sophisticated tradition of ethical teachings that is very similar to the Judeo-Christian tradition, but that is never brought to the attention of the Western media or publics. In fact, the mere labeling of an ethical principle based on love as the "Judeo-Christian" tradition implies that the third monotheistic religion, Islam, is devoid of or at least has no focus on that principal of love.

Cultivation theory

Although belonging to the tradition of mass communication theories rather than ethical theories, it is important at this point to briefly introduce George Gerbner's Cultivation Theory, since it interacts with other ethical principles illustrated here to cause what we believe is the current vast misrepresentation of Arabs and Muslims in the Western media.

Gerbner, Gross, Morgan and Signorielli (1980) argued that television has always been the most invasive mass medium worldwide. Television plays a unique role that no other medium can compete with, as

> the individual is introduced virtually at birth into (the television's) powerful flow of messages and images. The television set has become a key member of the family, the one who tells most of the stories most of the time. Its massive flow of stories showing what things are, how things work, and what to do about them has become the common socializer of our times. These stories form a coherent if mythical 'world' in every home" (Gerbner, Gross, Morgan and Signorielli, 1980).

Gerbner and his colleagues developed this theory to explain how and to what extent television viewing affects viewers' perceptions, attitudes and values. According to Gerbner and Gross (1976, p. 174), "Television is likely to remain for a long time the chief source of repetitive and ritualized symbol system cultivating the common consciousness of the most far-flung and heterogeneous mass publics in history." As a matter of fact it is evident that those who live in the virtual world of television cultivate perceptions and beliefs different from reality. This televised, socially constructed "reality" gives a seemingly pretty realistic picture of everything that is important in the world. The constant cultivation of such "realities" leads to a life where the viewer accepts the medium to be almost the number-one influence in his/her life (Gerbner and Gross, 1976).

Gerbner *et al.* (1980, p. 10) indicate that the concern here has to do with investigating the consequences of the continuous, omnipresent transmission of messages. They explain that audiences construct their views of the world in accordance with images and descriptions conveyed through television, which combine the virtual reality that television presents to real life situations in which we live, "and introduce theoretical developments dealing with the dynamics of the cultivation of general concepts of social reality (which we shall call 'mainstreaming') and of the amplification of issues particularly salient to certain groups of viewers (which we shall call 'resonance')."

Gerbner *et al.* (1980) explain further that intense television viewing builds up strong perceptions among people that the world is a dangerous place, in fact a "mean place" to live in. The theory suggests that substantial television viewing has an impact on viewers who respond to the world according to how it is portrayed on television rather than how it really is. Consequently, with a particular group of people, for example, Muslims, constantly portrayed over time as violent, barbaric, and dangerous, television viewers perceive that collective group of people as an imminent source of threat.

For viewers who watch a considerable amount of television, it becomes the main source of information and ideas. Viewers start to "live" in the virtual world of television, and their own ideas of social reality become very much in tune with what they see most persistently represented on the television screen. This is particularly true in the case of the representations of Arabs and Muslims, since television is in many cases *the only* source of information about these groups of people. Accordingly, images of Arabs and Muslims and representations of Islam and the Arab world conveyed through television have a major impact on Western audiences. With the excessive dramatization and frequent misrepresentation of such images in the aftermath of September 11, 2001, the media in the West cultivated negative images of Muslims and Arabs, and created an impact on viewers that is momentous and grave in many ways.

More Relevant Ethical Principles

Truth and objectivity

In the article "On Defining Truth," author Frank Deaver wrote:

> Communication of all sorts is passed off as 'truth,' when in fact it is a collection of varying 'degrees of truth, half-truth, and untruth.' The broad meaning of the word 'truth' is elaborated further via four identified ranges of expressions, the first regards full truthfulness and frankness, the second to intend to regard honesty but with care in employing data collected. The third range deals with the employment of falsity with no deliberate desire of dishonesty, and finally intentional malice where there exists a deliberate desire to mislead (Deaver, 1990).

Collective Guilt as a Response to Evil   741

Deaver (1990) explains that the ethics of journalism include news manipulation, truth, public interest, privacy, fantasy (a legitimate goal of media content), taste, conflict with the law, and finally stereotypes.

While "truth is the universal cornerstone of trustworthy value systems," objectivity could be seen as the process that people should follow to arrive at the truth (Bugeja, 2008, p. 99). While truth and objectivity may both be impossible to fully attain, such a notion should not be taken by individuals as an excuse to present half-truths or misrepresentations of reality. Merrill (1996) believes that objectivity and arriving at the facts incorporates components of epistemology and semantics. Words (or pictures) have different meanings; hence the choice of words or pictures will affect the final interpretation of meaning. That interpretation will however, also be affected by the context in which the words or pictures are presented, as well as by the relative understanding and personal environment of the receiver. For example, while studying for her PhD in the United States, the first author of this chapter repeatedly saw on US television images of Muslims in prayer in the midst of news stories concerning terrorism. In almost all these stories, there was absolutely no clear context for why the prayer scene might be included. The result is an untruthful association in the minds of the viewers between Muslim prayer and terrorism. Another example was a picture of Saddam Hussein in his military costume proudly drawing his sword that somehow found its way into every story about the war in Iraq. While the author is not at all supportive of Saddam Hussein's policies, she was unhappy that the Western viewers had no way of knowing that what they were seeing was actually an image of an Arab leader doing what is considered to be a celebratory dance movement on Iraq's National Day. Even more significant, was the emphasis of the media, backing and backed up by the Bush administration, on the presence of weapons of mass destruction in Iraq, and the alleged tie between Iraq and Al Qaeda, which were the primary reasons for the war.

Since the aftermath of the September 11 attacks, the Western media have been heavily cultivating a collective biased image of Arabs and Muslims as evil-doers who consequently are worthy of collective guilt and collective punishment. The fact that Arabs and Muslims are in agreement with the urgent necessity for security enforcement and anti-terrorism initiatives and the fact that they share the same fears and concerns regarding international terrorism does not undermine the Western world's outlook pertaining to their negative predispositions toward Arabs and Muslims. The latter groups are in turn frustrated for having to tolerate the burdens of discriminating policies and looks of accusations in the eyes of Western nationals.

Schanzer, Kurzman and Moosa (2010) state that "Muslim-American organizations and leaders have consistently condemned terrorist violence here and abroad since 9/11, arguing that such violence is strictly condemned by Islam ...these statements were not just for public consumption, but were supported by local Muslim religious and community leaders, who consistently condemned political violence in public sermons and private conversations" (Schanzer et al., 2010, p. 1). Instead of focusing on such realities, Western media channels centered their concerns on maintaining and perpetuating Western perceptions that terrorist threats have three potential sources all stemming from Arabs and Muslims. These were represented in Al-Qaeda itself, the extremist group living outside United States; members of Al-Qaeda who live inside the United States; and finally, those potential members who live inside the United States who might at some point initiate attacks, either on their own or as part of a group.

By selecting or priming certain news over others, by portraying certain images and not others, and by putting images in the wrong context or simply failing to provide an accurate context, the Western media have not shown a great deal of objectivity and have not been very successful in portraying a truthful image of Arabs and Muslims.

Fairness and balance

Bugeja (2008) argues that journalists should continually strive for fairness and balance through self examination and improvement. Objective reporters, he says, "commit to truth, especially to full disclosure.... Fair minded people also promote inclusivity; they do not discriminate because racism is a lie" (p. 239). For journalists to be fair, they have to admit their biases, accept responsibility for mistakes, and work hard to minimize both. The notions also include an assumption of covering both sides of a story, giving equal space/air time to different parties, and strive to provide a complete context for what's portrayed.

Again, most Western media systems fail to demonstrate fairness and balance when it comes to the representations of Arabs and Muslims. How many times do we see a non-terrorist, non-violent Arab or Muslim individual in a Hollywood production? How many times do we see a non-violent Arab or Muslim individual in an American sitcom? How many times do we see a non-violent representation of an Arab or Muslim individual in any context on Western media? Said Badria, an Egyptian-American actor who lives in California was interviewed on CNN saying, "I just want to be able to land a role where I don't have to say, 'In the name of Allah, I will kill you all!'" On The Axis of Evil comedy tour, which consists of three Muslim Americans of Egyptian, Iranian, and Palestinian origins, Maz Jobrani says, "I just want to see a Muslim of the news ... just baking a cookie! 'Hi, my name is Mohamed, and I'm just baking a cookie!'" It is so sad that the only faces of Arabs and Muslims seen on Western television appear to be those of terrorists.

As such, the Western media deny Arabs and Muslims the chance to be fairly represented. During that critical time immediately after the September 11 attacks, the views of the Arab and Muslim community whether in the United States or worldwide were severely underrepresented if not totally ignored. Many Muslims worldwide reported that were doubly sad, for the victims of the criminal attacks on the one hand, and for feeling that their religion has been "raped" by terrorists on the other. The official view of Arab governments, who unanimously condemned the attacks were also ignored by the Western media.

Generally speaking the Western media also ignore the many contributions of Arabs and Muslims to humanity throughout the ages. Arab and Muslim scholars

Collective Guilt as a Response to Evil   743

invented algebra (whose name comes from the Arabic word "Al Gabr," and sociology). They made significant contributions to the scientific fields of medicine, astronomy, philosophy, and geography. None of that is presented on the Western media, who instead prefer the hype created by the typical Arab or Muslim stereotype.

Bias and stereotyping

Stereotyping refers to putting particular labels or characteristics, often unfounded, on groups of people. Bias against a certain group of people inadvertently leads to negative stereotyping of that group. Stereotyping, by definition, is a collective process that does not take individual differences or diversity into account.

The Western media has done more than its fair share of negative stereotyping towards Arabs and Muslims. Kai Hafez (2000, p. 5) states that

> There is a strong tendency in Western mass media to characterize Islam as a fanatic and violent religion cutting-off hands, repressing women, and representing a clear antagonism towards Western ideas of freedom, human rights and democracy. Islam is equated with politics (a); Islamic politics is equated with fundamentalism (b); fundamentalism with terrorism (c); and political violence is interpreted without taking into consideration its social and political context (d).

Such stereotyping through continuously showing pictures of Arabs and Muslims as violent terrorists whether on news or entertainment programs results in creating a consistent, biased, and prejudiced portrait. Even if there is an element of truth in such a portrayal, overgeneralization is unethical under any circumstances.

Lester (1997, p. 69) argues that "it is not natural to stereotype. As with the printing term used to describe multiple stampings from a single mold, to stereotype is a short-hand way to describe a person with collective, rather than unique characteristics. … Consequently, media messages that stereotype individuals by their concentrations, frequencies, and omissions become a part of our long-term memory." These images then become part of our consciousness and professional ethics.

Arabs and Muslims in the Western Media

Long before the attacks of September 11, Arabs and Muslims have been misrepresented in the Western media. As early as the first years of the twentieth century, Arabs were portrayed as exotic Bedouins, with harems, sheikhs, and belly dancers. As a matter of fact, even popular children's cartoons that we all love and glorify carried such subliminal messages. The infamous song "Arabian Nights" from the movie "Aladdin" has the phrase "Where they cut off your ear if they don't like your face?" Where on Earth did that line come from!

Jack Shaheen has written prolifically about the misrepresentations of Arabs in the Western media, and particularly in American media, where Arabs have traditionally been portrayed as "billionaires, bombers, and belly dancers" (Shaheen, 1984, p. 4). "For years," Shaheen says, "I watched hordes of TV Arabs parade across the screen. It was like watching a disturbing experience, similar to walking into those mirrored rooms at amusement parks where all you see is distorted self-images" (p. 5).

Journalist Djelloul Marbrouk says the Arab in American television stands for "terrorism, hijack, intractability, sullenous, perverseness, cruelty, oil, sand, embargo, boycott, greed, bungling, comedic disunity, primitive torture, family feuds, and white slavery" (Shaheen, 1980, p. 1). Shaheen quotes *Newsweek* commenting on the image of the typical Arab on television, "He is swarthy and bearded, rich and filthy, dabbling in dope smuggling and white slavery; swaddled in white robes, he carries a curved knife, rides a camel and abuses young boys. He knows a thousand vile curses such as 'May the fleas of a diseased camel infect the hair of your first born'" (p. 2).

Shaheen provides many examples of programs, dating back to the 1970s, which portrayed a negative image of Arabs. These include Hollywood movies and productions such as Fantasy Island, Vegas, and Charlie's Angels to comic strips such as Brenda Starr and Dennis the Menace. He also provides examples of such negative coverage on reputed news shows such as "60 Minutes" and "20/20" as well as on regular news bulletins that typically associate Arabs and Muslims with terrorism.

Shaheen (1984) noted that "the stereotype (of Arabs) remains omnipresent, appearing in new programs and dated reruns" (p. 113). In an interview with a CBS Vice President, who confirmed the notion, the Vice President said he "had never seen a 'good Arab' on TV," and that Arabs are often shown as "warmongers and/ or covetous desert rulers" (p. 114). Along these same lines, Slade (1981) presented her own analysis of a poll of American attitudes and perceptions towards Arabs and concluded that Americans know little about Arab culture, history, or contributions to the world. She concluded that Americans commonly perceive of Arabs as "anti-American," "anti-Christian," "unfriendly," and "warlike."

In his seminal work on the portrayal of Arabs and Muslims in Hollywood movies, Shaheen (2001) took on the enormous task of analyzing close to 1000 movies showing Arab characters in American cinema. The results were published in his 574-page book *Reel Bad Arabs: How Hollywood Vilifies a People*. Out of all the movies he analyzed, Shaheen found that Hollywood has portrayed Arabs in a negative stereotype in over 900 movies. Only a dozen featured positive portrayals and about 50 movies featured "balanced" characters. This is a clear demonstration of the cultivation effect that Hollywood practices have on American audiences and the severe lack of sound ethical principles.

Over the past decade we have also started to become familiar with the word "Islamophobia." According to Christensen (2006a, 2006b) the spread of Islamophobia in the West is the result of distorted negative media portrayals, at least in part. He argued that news programs are frequently perceived as "serious" and "truthful" because of the association in people's minds between journalism and the principles of objectivity and fairness. He noted that Western news stories often show a mosque, a minaret, or a veiled woman regardless of the nature of the story and even if unrelated. "The combination of stereotypical images adds up to a whole that is, in many ways, greater than the sum of its parts" (Christensen, 2006b, p. 30). The images of praying Muslims on news stories depicting terrorism are a very dangerous example of this phenomenon.

Edward Said (1997) argued that the portrayals of Islam in the US media are characterized by "patent inaccuracy." This is because such images have always been influenced by a political agenda and sometimes hidden interests. He described the situation as "highly exaggerated stereotyping and belligerent hostility." According to Said,

> Malicious generalizations about Islam have become the last acceptable form of denigration of foreign culture in the West; What is said about the Muslim mind, or character, or religion, or culture as a whole cannot now be said in mainstream discussion about Africans, Jews, other Orientals, or Asians (p. xii).

If this has been the case before September 11, the situation became much worse after the attacks. The Western media failed to acknowledge the fact that all Arab countries condemned the criminal attacks. By and large, the mass media failed to differentiate between Arabs, Muslims, and terrorists, creating an association between terrorism and Islam in the eyes of the public. Eric Rouleau of *Le Monde*, expressed his dismay at the tendency to portray images of "Muslims praying, mosques or women in chadors to illustrate stories about extremism and terror" (cited in Pintak, 2006, p. 33–34). Pintak noted that after the events of September 11, "the U.S. media immediately fell back on the prevailing – and stereotyped – narrative about Arabs and Muslims and reverted to its historic tendency to present the world, in Henry Kissinger's words, as 'a morality play between good and evil'" (p. 39).

Fairness and Accuracy in Reporting (FAIR) noted that "many media pundits focused on one theme: retaliation. For some, it did not matter who bears the brunt of an American attack." For example, immediately following the attacks on September 11, former Secretary of State Lawrence Eagleburger said on CNN, "There is only one way to begin to deal with people like this, and that is you have to kill some of them even if they are not immediately directly involved in this thing" – a blatantly unethical statement.

On September 12, Steve Dunleavy wrote in the New York Post, "The response to this unimaginable 21st-century Pearl Harbor should be as simple as it is swift – kill the bastards! A gunshot between the eyes, blow them to smithereens, poison them if you have to. As for cities or countries that host these worms, bomb them into basketball courts" (FAIR, 2001).

On September 13, Bill O'Reilly, on his popular show the O'Reilly Factor on Fox News Channel, said, it "doesn't make any difference" who gets killed in the process of retaliation in response to the attacks. On the same day, syndicated columnist Ann Coulter wrote,

> This is no time to be precious about locating the exact individuals directly involved in this particular terrorist attack. ... We should invade their countries, kill their leaders

and convert them to Christianity. We weren't punctilious about locating and punishing only Hitler and his top officers. We carpet-bombed German cities; we killed civilians. That's war. And this is war (FAIR, 2001).

Perhaps most offensive to Muslims was the infamous statement made by Reverend Jerry Falwell on "60 Minutes," when he said, "I think (Muslim Prophet) Mohammed was a terrorist. I read enough of the history of his life written by both Muslims and non-Muslims, that he was a violent man, a man of war" (Falwell, 2002).

Statements such as this one coincided with and perhaps caused an increasing anti-Muslim sentiment. CNN reported that the anti-Islamic sentiment following September 11 was spreading all around the globe. Several mosques in Europe and Australia were petrol-bombed by individuals who believed they were "doing the US a favor." In South Shields, Northern England, graffiti on a wall near a mosque read in red paint, "Avenge U.S.A. Kill a Muslim now" (Jones, 2001).

At a meeting of the Global Policy Forum, Hans Giessmann of the University of Hamburg's Institute for Peace Research and Security Policy criticized the Western media for how it "fully attributed blame for the September attacks on 'Muslim terrorists' and stopped there." He added that "the media accepted the side effects of a stigmatization of religion, cultures, states, people and minorities and this paved the way for prejudices." There was an agreement among the journalists at the meeting that the media had failed to provide context for their pictures and stories. That, they said, would have "allowed readers, viewers and listeners to gain a clear understanding of the background issues and of the clash on interpretations in a war where the lines were blurred between reporting and propaganda in a controlled atmosphere" (Inbaraj, 2002).

Such trends in the American media coverage of the post-September 11 attacks were documented on several occasions. A content analysis of CBS newscasts carried out by the Center for Media and Public Affairs concluded that in covering the network was "most supportive" of the US war on Iraq. Individuals displaying anti-war sentiments only constituted of fewer than 10% of interviewees on *CBS Evening News with Dan Rather*. The study concluded that the CBS coverage was even more conservative than Fox News, which is seen as "the headquarters for patriotic fervor." Another study by the US Department of Defense analyzed the way American, European, and Middle Eastern newspapers covered the war on Iraq. The study concluded that the US media "primed its audience to support the war" while silencing any voices of opposition (cited in Pintak, 2006).

Gomaa (2002) conducted a content analysis of the image of Islam and Muslims during the 50 days following 9/11 in the newspapers of three countries: the United States, France, and Germany. She analyzed the *International Herald Tribune*, *Le Monde*, and *Frankfurter Allgemeine*. The results showed that although the *International Herald Tribune* focused on Osama Bin Laden as the main person responsible for the attacks (even before any evidence had arisen), the newspaper handled the whole situation in light of Huntington's (1993) clash of civilizations and portrayed it as a new Crusade between Islam and the Western world. The newspaper added that the Arab and Muslim countries are breeding a "culture of violence" as they have become a safe haven for terrorists. On the other hand, *Le Monde* stressed on the dangers of terrorism as a global issue rather than restricting it to Muslims, and made an effort to portray the nature of Islam as a religion of tolerance and peace. *Le Monde* focused on religious diversity and the importance of understanding and accepting the other, and acquainting oneself with foreign civilizations. The French newspaper stressed that the issue is not about the clash of civilizations, but rather a clash between extremists and moderates within each civilization and across ethnicities and religions worldwide. The paper argued that in this light, France should support the United States in a war against the terrorists who carried out these attacks on humanity but not in a war against Islam as a religion. Still, the study concluded that *Le Monde* also reported negatively on Arabs and Muslims almost 65% of the time. This percentage was up to 78% in *the International Herald Tribune*, and 86.5% in *Frankfurter Allgemeine*. The *International Herald Tribune* linked the origins of terrorism with the Arab and Muslim world 96% of the time.

Fadel (2002) conducted a content analysis of the Egyptian daily *Al Ahram* newspaper and the American daily *USA Today* during the three months following September 11. Interestingly, the study concluded that the two issues mentioned the most in association to Arab countries in both newspapers were terrorism and Islamic fundamentalism. However, while *Al Ahram* stressed the Arab world's condemnation of the attacks and fundamentalist views, *USA Today* ignored this fact and instead associated Arabs to Islamic fundamentalism, terrorism, and extremism worldwide. The study also reported that *USA Today* "adopted a clear line of linking violence and terrorism with resisting Israeli occupation in parts of Lebanon and the Palestinian territories."

Pintak (2006) argued that the severe bias in the American coverage of Arabs and Muslims after September 11 constituted what he called "jihad journalism." He added that the slanted coverage constituted "the hallmark of the post-9/11 era." Fruit (2001) called the biased coverage "a result of racist jingoism." He added, "This is shocking but not surprising in the face of the Anti-Islamic, xenophobic hysteria in the media and from our 'world-leaders.'"

Chomsky (2001) noted that the media institutions in the US represented "well-run propaganda systems" whose ability "to drive people to irrational, murderous, and suicidal behavior" should not be undermined. He therefore was not surprised that the media were acting the way they did, but urged viewers to oppose the idea of fighting terrorist crimes with more terror aimed at civilian Muslims (p. 69).

Concluding Remarks

In this chapter we aimed to shed some light on the misrepresentations of Arabs and Muslims in the Western, particular American, media. We started with a discussion of some of the relevant ethical philosophies and principles, and followed with examples on how or why these principles were relevant. We then went through a more extensive literature review and analysis of the media portrayals of Arabs and Muslims in the Western media, particularly after the September 11 attacks of 2001. Throughout, we tried to show how these biased stereotypical representations lacked the ethical principles of truth, objectivity, fairness, and balance, and instead helped in cultivating an inaccurate unfair image of the collective Arabs and Muslims as terrorists and evil-doers.

In his speech at Cairo University in 2009, President Obama spoke highly of Islam, saying, "Islam has always been a part of America's story." He added that Muslim-Americans have "fought in our wars, they have served in our government, they have stood for civil rights, they have started businesses, they have taught at our universities, they've excelled in our sports arenas, they've won Nobel Prizes, built our tallest building, and lit the Olympic Torch." These facts spoken by the US President should be what the Western media need to focus more on while minimizing the naïve stereotypical images that portray a group of 1.5 billion people as terrorists. Viewers undeniably acquire remarkable amounts of information from living in the mediated world where the cultivation effect provides beliefs, norms, and values of a virtual television community, which in most cases does not bear an accurate resemblance to our social reality.

A recent poll by the Gallup Center for Muslim Studies (2010) indicated that 43% of the American public has openly admitted to having anti-Muslim prejudice. That figure was higher among people who do not personally know a Muslim. Furthermore, almost one-third of the sample (31%) said their view of Islam was "not favorable at all," and over two-thirds of the sample was shown to have little or no knowledge of Islam. In its reaction to the study, the Council on American-Islamic Relations (CAIR) said that awareness and education about Islam were needed, particularly through an increase in educational outreach efforts by US Muslims (CAIR, 2010; Gallup, 2010).

On the other hand, another recent study conducted on Muslim-Americans in the US concluded that the Muslim-American population heavily opposes violence, and are keen to integrate within their American communities (Schanzer, Kurzman, and Moosa, 2010).

It is true that Arabs and Muslims must become heavily and actively involved in promoting a more accurate image of themselves, and in making louder their voices in condemning terrorism in all its forms. Arabs and Muslim have a responsibility to force themselves onto Western media institutions in any way they can as long as these institutions are not giving them their fair share of space/air time in the media. If Arabs and Muslims become louder in their denunciations of terrorism, the Western media might just have to listen. Arabs and Muslims must also become creative in using their own media systems, as well as the Internet, to spread a fair understanding of Islam and a more accurate image of themselves worldwide.

While it is true that Arabs and Muslims have a role to play in rectifying their image and fighting against the notions of collective guilt and collective punishment, media personnel and institutions have to take the responsibility of establishing

Collective Guilt as a Response to Evil 749

active internal codes of ethics, and actually adhering to these codes. News production is a business after all as is movie production. While it is acknowledged that most media organizations are driven by profit-oriented models, still, a minimum adherence to a universal code of ethics has to be enforced by the media institutions themselves as well as through demand from the public. It is in everyone's best interest, including media institutions if they look beyond the mere monetary profit, that the public be exposed to the truth or as much as can be reached of it. While we acknowledge again that the truth is not 100% attainable, and that the truth will mean different things to different people, at the very least, a conscious effort at arriving at some truths should be made. Universalization or at least utilitarian codes of ethics should be applied in this case.

It is only if and when reporters, photojournalists, producers, editors, and every other media personnel make the effort and take the time to accurately investigate and scrutinize Muslims' and Arabs' behavior and culture that perhaps an understanding would be initiated and people in the Western world would try to perceive underlying issues and frustrations.

It is also important to educate the public about the effects of concentrating media ownership in the hands of a few media mogul conglomerates. Diversity of the media is essential to allowing more voices to be heard, and thus breaking stereotypes. When media ownership is in the hands of a few, it becomes much easier to not adhere to universally accepted codes of ethics. The public should realize that it is in their best interest to become more media literate and more discriminatory in terms of using the media options available to them, including the Internet, to gain exposure to a greater variety of voices.

Finally, we reiterate that it is irrational, unreasonable, and rather naïve to hold 1.5 billion Muslims guilty of what was committed by a few terrorists in the name of Islam. The notions of collective guilt and collective punishment go against not only the basic principles of ethics but the basic principles of logic. It is imperative to demonstrate that human beings share common and positive traits far more than those that would segregate and isolate them. We all have basic needs, basic rights, and basic responsibilities. The commonalities in human beings, which bring us together, are far more than those which divide us. Adhering to universal ethical standards and holding ourselves and our communities accountable against these principles might help us realize that we are all only human after all.

References

Abdulla, R. (2007) Islam, jihad, and terrorism in post-9/11 Arabic discussion boards. *Journal of Computer-Mediated Communication*, 12 (3), http://jcmc.indiana.edu/vol12/issue3/abdulla.html (accessed August 2, 2010).

Bugeja, M. (2008) *Living Ethics across Media Platforms*, Oxford University Press, Oxford.

CAIR (The Council on American-Islamic Relations) (2010) *CAIR: Poll on Anti-Islam Bias Shows Need for U.S. Muslim Outreach*, PR Newswire, www.prnewswire.com/news-releases/

cair-poll-on-anti-islam-bias-shows-need-for-us-muslim-outreach-82282817.html(accessed August 2, 2010).

Chomsky, N. (2001) *9–11*, Seven Stories Press, New York.

Christensen, C. (2006a) God save us from the Islam clichés. *British Journalism Review*, 17 (1), 65–70.

Christensen, C. (2006b) Islam in the media: Cartoons and context. *Screen Education*, 43, 27–32.

Christians, C.G., Rotzoll, K., Fackler, M., McKee, K., and Woods, R. (2005) *Media Ethics: Cases and Moral Reasoning*, 7th edn. Allyn & Bacon, Boston, MA.

Deaver, F. (1990) On defining truth. *Journal of Mass Media Ethics*, 5 (3), 168–177.

Fadel, S. (2002) The image of the Arab countries in the daily Egyptian and American newspapers after 9/11: A comparative analytical study (in Arabic). *Proceedings of the Annual Scientific Convention of the Faculty of Communication*, Cairo University, Egypt, pp. 425–457.

FAIR (Fairness and Accuracy in Reporting) (2001) Media march to war, September 17, www.fair.org/press-releases/wtc-war-punditry.html (accessed August 2, 2010).

Falwell, J. (2002) Falwell brands Mohammed a terrorist.*CBS News*, October 4, www.cbsnews.com/stories/2003/06/05/60minutes/main557187.shtml (accessed August 2, 2010).

Festinger, L. (1957) *A Theory of Cognitive Dissonance*, Stanford University Press, Stanford, CA.

Fruit, S. (2001) Sikh man killed in Arizona as a result of racist jingoism. *Independent Media Center*, September 16, www.indymedia.org/front.php3?article_id=64396andgroup=webcast (last accessed June 20, 2009).

Gallup Center for Muslim Studies (2010) *Religious Perceptions in America: With an In-Depth Analysis of U.S. Attitudes Toward Muslims and Islam*, www.gallup.com/poll/125312/Religious-Prejudice-Stronger-Against-Muslims.aspx (accessed August 2, 2010).

Gerbner, G., and Gross, L.P. (1976) Living with television: The violence profile. *Journal of Communication*, 26 (2), 172–199.

Gerbner, G., Larry, G., Michael, M., and Signorielli, N. (1980) The "mainstreaming" of America: Violence profile no. 11. *Journal of Communication*, 30 (3), 10–29.

Gomaa, I. (2002) The image of Islam and Muslims in the Western press after 9/11: An analytical study of American, French, and German newspapers (in Arabic). *Proceedings of the Annual Scientific Convention of the Faculty of Communication*, Cairo University, Egypt, pp. 221–266.

Hafez, K. (2000) *The West and Islam in the Mass Media: Cornerstones for a New International Culture of Communication in the 21st Century*. ZEI Discussion Paper C 61, Center for European Integration Studies, Bonn, Germany, www.zei.de/download/zei_dp/dp_c61_hafez.pdf (accessed August 2, 2010).

Huntington, S. (1993) The clash of civilizations?, *Foreign Affairs*, www.foreignaffairs.com/articles/48950/samuel-p-huntington/the-clash-of-civilizations (accessed August 17, 2010).

Huntington, S. (1996) *The Clash of Civilizations and the Remaking Of World Order*, Simon and Schuster, New York.

Inbaraj, S. (2002) *Media: Post-Sep. 11 Reportage Adds to Divisions, Stereotypes*. Global Policy Forum, July 1, www.globalpolicy.org/wtc/media/2002/0701australia.htm (last accessed March 29, 2009).

Jones, G. (2001) Muslims targets in terror backlash. *CNN*, September 19, www.cnn.com/2001/WORLD/europe/09/19/gen.muslim.attacks/index.html (accessed August 2, 2010).

Lester, P. (1997) Images and stereotypes, in *Journalism Ethics: A Reference Handbook* (eds. E.D. Cohen and D. Elliott), (Contemporary Ethical Issues), ABC-CLIO, Santa Barbara, California, p. 69.

McPhail, T. (2006) *Global Communication: Theories, Stakeholders, and Trends*, 2nd ed., Blackwell, Oxford.

Merrill, J. (1996) *Journalism Ethics: Philosophical Foundations for News Media*, Bedford/St. Martin's, New York.

Pintak, L. (2006) *America, Islam, and the War of Ideas: Reflections in a Bloodshot Lens*, The American University in Cairo Press, Cairo.

Said, E. (1997) *Covering Islam: How the Media and the Experts Determine How we See the Rest of the World*, rev. edn, Vintage Books, New York.

Schanzer, D., Kurzman, C., and Moosa, E. (2010) *Anti-Terror Lessons of Muslim-Americans*, Project supported by the U.S. Department of Justice, www.sanford.duke.edu/news/Schanzer_Kurzman_Moosa_Anti-Terror_Lessons.pdf (accessed August 2, 2010).

Shaheen, J. (1980) The Arab stereotype on television, *The Link*, 13 (2), April/May, 1–13.

Shaheen, J. (1984) *The TV Arab*, Bowling Green University Press, Bowling Green, OH.

Shaheen, J. (2001) *Reel Bad Arabs: How Hollywood Vilifies a People*, Olive Branch Press, New York.

Slade, S. (1981) The image of the Arab in America: Analysis of a poll on American attitudes. *The Middle East Journal*, Spring, pp. 143–162.

38

Journalists as Witnesses to Violence and Suffering

Amy Richards and Jolyon Mitchell

Introduction

In this chapter we analyze how foreign correspondents bear witness to violence and suffering. For the frontline journalist this suffering is often close, all too easy to see, to hear, and to smell. By contrast for the Western viewer or reader this suffering can often be distant, sometimes thousands of miles away. Through the work of journalistic witnesses, and via various digital media, this distant suffering is commonly brought close, sometimes instantaneously, and often straight into the comfort and comparative security of the viewer's home. In order to see through the violence and suffering so commonly portrayed in various news media we investigate the complex and often ambiguous role of the frontline journalist working as a witness.

There are clearly different ways that journalists can bear witness: from vivid newspaper accounts of the bombing of Gaza City via radio reports of another burnt-out village in Darfur to photographs of decomposing bodies in one of Rwanda's killing churches. There is not space here to consider the range of internal influences and external pressures that help to shape news coverage of violence and distant suffering. In this essay we will, however, investigate some of the different reasons why journalists attempt to record such events. These journalistic descriptions are inevitably incomplete, overlooking violence closer to home or the actual causes of suffering.[1] Spectacular images can all too easily overwhelm narratives of explanation. These interpretations may even be incorrect, produced in the heat of a conflict or in the confusing dust following a disaster. Nevertheless, these partial accounts can shed light on corners of the world where violence is the most commonly spoken language and the resulting suffering has become part of people's daily diets. This may, of course, not be on the other side of the globe, but in the

---

The Handbook of Global Communication and Media Ethics, First Edition. Edited by Robert S. Fortner and P. Mark Fackler.
© 2011 Blackwell Publishing Ltd. Published 2011 by Blackwell Publishing Ltd.

journalist's home country or within easy reach by a short flight. As we shall see this comparative ease of access to violence and suffering has contributed to the transformation of the role of the journalist working abroad.

Central to the claim that a journalist is "bearing witness" is the fact that they are there, on-the-scene, as history unfolds. While the audience can be described as bearing witness through what they see or hear, our primary focus is on the role of the journalist who is actually present. Our suggestion is that a journalist bears witness for at least two separate groups of people: for their audiences and for those at the scene.

First, journalists bear witness on the frontline of wars and disasters because their audience cannot be there themselves. Journalists act as the stand-in or proxy eyes and ears for the public. One reason why the journalist goes to bear witness to violence and suffering is because their viewers, listeners, or readers cannot. Second, journalists bear witness by being there *with* and there *for* those who have suffered great injustice or trauma but do not have the means to give voice to their experience. In this way, journalists are the proxy voice for those who have suffered but do not have the means to testify before a wider audience that may be able to assist in righting the injustice or perhaps providing some relief from the suffering.

We will investigate these two interrelated roles, being there to bear witness for the public and being there to bear witness for the people on the ground. Stuart Allan and Barbie Zelizer suggest that it is crisis reporting that provides the starkest contrast with which to investigate everyday modes of journalistic practice.[2] In order to investigate the ethical dilemmas and challenges encountered by journalists bearing witness, we focus on bearing witness to war in the first part of this essay, and in the second part we consider bearing witness to genocide. We conclude with a discussion on the virtues of truthfulness and friendship involved in the journalistic claim to bearing witness. Through these discussions this essay makes a contribution to the ongoing discussion about the journalist working as a witness.[3]

The Foreign Correspondent as Witness

In Western journalism the foreign correspondent was traditionally a journalist native to the country of the news organization but living long-term in another country, acquiring fluency of language, developing knowledge about a country's history, functioning confidently in its culture, and building a network of contacts, often upon foundations laid by the previous correspondent.[4] Such practices of foreign correspondence provide a good example of what was involved in becoming a long-term journalistic witness. Changes in modern journalism, however, have altered the kind of witness provided by the journalists working abroad. With both technological changes and decreased attention to foreign news coverage, the practice of the correspondent spending years in a foreign country is becoming less common. News organizations now commonly send foreign correspondents from journalistic hubs, such as London, New York, or Tokyo, "parachuting" well-known journalists into foreign locations in the immediate aftermath of a major news story.[5]

In the age of steamboats and trains this was not possible, as it took days or months to reach most conflicts. In the age of jet travel and digital communication this practice is commonplace, with most wars accessible within a day's travel. The 1990s conflict in the Balkans, for example, was within a couple of hours by plane for most major European news agencies. Given the ease and speed of international travel the expert foreign correspondent has commonly been replaced by frontline reporters, used to bearing witness in many different settings.

Why do journalists spend their lives in this peripatetic fashion? In extensive interviews with frontline journalists who report on conflict, Howard Tumber and Frank Webster found that these reporters were drawn not only by the excitement of such assignments but also by the desire to "seek out the truth" and have a "front-row seat" at the making of history.[6] For many of these journalists they perceive their moral duty of "truth seeking" as a "vocation."[7] Allan and Zelizer believe that the journalistic practice of truth telling rests on the authority of "presence, on the moral duty to bear witness by being there." So actually "being there," even if it means travelling around the globe on a regular basis, matters. "Being there suggests that the violence, devastation, suffering, and death that inevitably constitute war's underside will somehow be rendered different – more amenable to response and perhaps less likely to recur – just because journalists are somewhere nearby."[8] Frontline journalism provides "visual authentication as well as personal testimonies, and thereby positions itself (and us the viewer) as 'bearing witness'."[9] Witness involves the physical significance of *being there*, or of someone being there in the name of the public. As we shall see, however, there are a number of constraints for journalists as they attempt to be present as witnesses in the face of war or genocide.

Witnessing War

Our first case study provides insight into ethical reasoning behind bearing witness to war. Here, we explore challenges to provide truthful and critical accounts for both the public and for those at the scene through issues relating to journalistic autonomy that arose at the start of the 2003 Iraq war.

"Independent" frontline journalism

Consider the experience of the BBC's World Affairs Editor, John Simpson, when covering the beginning of the 2003 Iraq war. Simpson recorded his experience of his second Gulf War in *The Wars against Saddam: Taking the Hard Road to Baghdad*.[10] In the first Gulf War, Simpson was frustrated by the US Pentagon's press management.[11] For Simpson, embedded journalism had the same ring to it as press pools.[12] Simpson had two central concerns after his press pool experience from the first Gulf War. First, the press pool system limited journalist access to military information. Simpson's second concern had to do with the limited contact with the civilian population of Iraq. Simpson did not want to work under similar constraints when covering his second Gulf War. He declined an embedded slot with coalition forces attacking Baghdad from the South. He chose instead to independently travel through Kurdish northern Iraq to reach Baghdad. Simpson and his BBC crew left from Turkey and traveled through Kirkuk, Mosul, and Tikrit before arriving in Baghdad. Simpson reasoned that retreating Iraqi soldiers and "shoot now, think later" American soldiers at check points would be his news team's greatest dangers.

Simpson and his news team consisted of cameramen, security adviser, producer, and local fixers. On the morning of April 6, Simpson discussed with Kamaran Abdurrazak Mohammed, his Kurdish translator, the risks of working with a non-embedded BBC crew, like "the lack of a flak-jacket", and asked Kamaran if his family knew the risky work he was doing. Kamaran answered, "No, they think I stay in the hotel and translate the newspapers. It is easier that way."[13] Later that day Simpson and his crew followed Kurdish and American Special Forces en route to Dibarjan. The troops sighted Iraqi tanks in the distance, stopped and called for American air strikes on the tanks. Simpson shouted, "Flak-jacket time." The BBC crew stopped at a crossroads behind the military troops and prepared the cameras to record the two incoming US Navy F-14s.

> By chance, there was a wrecked Iraqi tank lying right beside the crossroads; it must have been attacked and destroyed earlier in the day. It's not impossible that the presence of this tank, when an attack was being requested on another tank nearby, caused the disaster that followed.[14]

An American missile landed about 20 yards away from the crossroads where the convoy had pulled to the side, among them Simpson and his crew.

> Fourteen pieces of shrapnel hit me altogether, and I was knocked to the ground. Most were pretty small, like the ones that hit me in the face and head, but two the size of bullets were big enough to have killed me. One lodged in my left hip, the other stuck in the plastic plate of my flak jacket right over the spine.[15]

With head, legs and arms bleeding and a left eardrum "completely blown away," Simpson gathered himself and his colleagues near him and they started the process of broadcasting. Simpson soon discovered that Kamaran had been severely wounded. En route to hospital, Kamaran died of his wounds inflicted by American "friendly fire." All of Simpson's crew had been wounded to varying degrees, aside from Kamaran's mortal wounds, Simpson's wounds were the most severe and with long lasting effect: "the shrapnel in my hip will probably remain slightly painful for the rest of my life."[16] Upon returning to the United Kingdom, medical specialists advised that it was best not to remove the shrapnel, as his body will grow around the metal and it will become a part of him. Simpson named the shrapnel "George W. Bush". In his book, Simpson emphasizes that Kamaran's mortal injury, a severed artery in his leg caused by shrapnel, could not have been prevented by a flak-jacket.

What is evident in Simpson's book on the Iraq wars is that journalists and their crews are at great risk from friendly fire. In the first four weeks of the 2003 Iraq war, 16 journalists died, seven "were killed by American bombs, bullets and missiles."[17]

Journalists bearing witness to war is dangerous because *being there* is dangerous. The year 2007 was the most dangerous in over a decade for journalists' worldwide. The Committee to Protect Journalists reported that 65 journalists were killed in direct relation to their work in 2007, the highest death toll since 1994 when 66 journalists were killed amid conflicts in Algeria, Bosnia, and Rwanda.[18] With 32 deaths, Iraq was the deadliest location for reporters in 2007 and Iraq has been the deadliest location for journalists since the US-led invasion in 2003. Journalists bearing witness to war, as Simpson asserts, fulfill an important function in a liberal democratic society.[19] In order to provide a critical account of a war fought in the name of the public, journalists put themselves at grave risk to be at the scene.

Embedded journalism

The practice of being "embedded" has a long history: "from the earliest correspondents in the nineteenth century through to ... the Second World War and Vietnam" and most recently with the unprecedented numbers of embedded journalists in the Iraq war.[20] In 2003 the US Pentagon offered over 700 embedded slots to US and non-US journalists. The American taxpayers, rather than news organizations, paid the bill for the training, outfitting, transporting, sheltering, and feeding of the journalists.[21] Simpson, however, "didn't want to be beholden to the very people whose actions we were obliged to report on impartially."[22] He chose not to accept the free US Pentagon flight directly into Baghdad and, as we saw earlier, declined a ride embedded with coalition ground troops:

> It became quite difficult for all but the hardest-nosed reporters to be absolutely honest about the soldiers who fed them, transported them, gave them the power they needed for their equipment, and (when necessary) saved their lives from the enemy. That mere word, "enemy", shows how a mind-set was created ... If you are with one side in a war, your fortunes and those of the soldiers you are with are pretty tightly intertwined; deep down, you are praying that they won't fail.[23]

This is a common criticism of embedding: it allows the journalist to become too close to those he or she is scrutinizing.[24]

Could embedded journalism fulfill the watchdog function of Western journalism when the journalists are *embedded* with the very people they are meant to be scrutinizing? The US Pentagon claimed that the significance of embedded journalists was "to tell the factual story – good or bad",[25] but reporting in such a situation is in danger of being reduced to the *topos* of patriotism, standing against the "enemy" who is trying to take away "our way of life." Tumber and Webster conclude that embedded journalism in the opening of the 2003 war produced stories that promoted patriotism more than stories that encouraged deliberation.[26] Embedded

Journalists as Witnesses to Violence and Suffering   757

journalists admittedly reported feeling conflicting loyalties and commented on the one-dimensional nature of their reports. Impartial reporting is not easy when sharing lived experience, and is that much more difficult when the experience is in such an extreme, life-or-death situation. Tumber argues that reports quickly become "I was there" stories. Similarly, frontline correspondent Allan Little criticized the reporting done by "embeds." He argued that the journalist's job is that of scrutiny and the "hi, mom" reporting done by journalists of their host-soldiers was not scrutinizing anything.[27]

Journalists are reliant on multiple sources and in the case of being an "embed," military sources are the only sources available. The normal practice for journalists to gather information from multiple sources is severely limited when embedded with one battalion or when restricted to safe-zones in Baghdad. Such were Simpson's initial concerns. The journalist is not in a position to observe what the war is doing to the civilians. As the stand-in eyes and ears of the public, the embedded journalist is unable to provide witness to the consequences of the war in which their government is engaged. It was weeks before the embedded journalists had the opportunity to observe and interview the Iraqi people. The Project for Excellence in Journalism conducted a content analysis of US television coverage from the first week of the war produced by embeds: "The reports avoided graphic material; not one of the stories in the study showed pictures of people being hit by weapons fire."[28] The Cardiff School of Journalism had similar findings of reports filed by British embeds; the coverage was "full of action, but without the grisly consequences."[29] This was also Simpson's criticism in a report he filed from Baghdad at the end of the first Gulf War: "As for the human casualties, tens of thousands of them, or the brutal effect the war had on millions of others ... we didn't see so much of that."[30] Both Gulf Wars lacked detailed coverage of the suffering of the Iraqi people. At the start of both Gulf Wars, Western audiences largely witnessed war without consequences.

Rooftop journalism

Another barrier to being an effective witness was the fact that many journalists were holed-up in the Palestine Hotel because of the dangerous situation throughout most of Baghdad. Rooftop journalism was not just a consequence of the process of embedded journalism; rooftop journalism reflects the growing pressure for round-the-clock, real-time news coverage. The correspondents with the 24-hour news organizations were under pressure to produce live footage throughout the day and consequently earned the nickname "roof monkey."[31] The news organizations received live pictures of their correspondent standing on the hotel rooftop with bombs blasting in the background. Bill Neely of ITN described the scene:

> You have your hotel and up on the top you have your satellite dishes and cameras, and you have your journalist in front of the camera and they're just there all day long, talking to the camera – "And now we can go back to Baghdad live and talk to our

correspondent. What's happening there now?' And the correspondent will say, "Well, what's happening in Baghdad, is this ..." But they haven't left the roof. They're just getting their information from other people. ... You're just feeding a beast that's all-consuming, that wants instant information, instant judgements – what happened, how did it happen. It often takes a very long time to work out how something happened. But there you are, on the roof, [and] you've got to give answers. You can't keep saying, "Well, frankly, I don't know," otherwise you'd be out of a job.[32]

Neely argues that there has to be a place for the "journalism of discovery" and discovery takes time. He argues that as well as the roof monkey, there needs to be the journalist "on the ground ferreting away to get the story."[33]

In the experiment with "embedded journalism," what resulted was exciting visual coverage without much thick, contextual description about what was being witnessed.[34] Rooftop reporting is display rich, but provides very little contextual framing. As ITN reporter Neely pointed out "ferreting away" checking sources takes time and does not make for real-time or visually interesting footage. Moreover the "live exposure portrays the embedded war reporter as a human figure who is as concerned about *being* live as about staying alive."[35] This is the excitement of liveness and gives authority to the frontline reporter as bearing witness to actual war. In the midst of a conflict, this is true both for a journalist on a hotel rooftop as well as in a US tank. Physical and temporal proximity to conflict position the journalist as witness while live broadcast positions the distant audience at least as temporal witness.

Embedded and rooftop reporting of the start of the 2003 Iraq war produced an unprecedented view of modern war in action and reality-like television which resulted in increased audience ratings. The journalists and researchers discussed in this chapter believe that journalistic independence was regularly sacrificed. While Simpson's arrival in Iraq was more independent of military assistance than those journalists who chose to be embeds or who were flown directly into Baghdad, Simpson and other journalists on the scene interacting with Iraqi people found themselves to be involved in a dependence of another kind.

Frontline journalists and local fixers

Foreign correspondents are reliant on local fixers. Local fixers may perform many functions for the foreign journalist from translator to driver. Jerry Palmer and Victoria Fontan conducted interviews with 17 Western journalists and 14 local fixers operating in Iraq, identifying the most important attribute of fixers as the fixers' access to local contacts, in a context where "religious, tribal, political and personal affiliations are crucial in the creation of trust."[36] The researchers also reported that the Iraqi fixers' predominant frustration with Western journalists was that they asked questions in ways that the fixers found culturally offensive. Iraqi fixers experienced the burden of translating the Western journalists' questions in culturally acceptable ways before posing the questions to Iraqi citizens. The research on fixers conducted by Tumber and Webster as well as by Palmer and Fontan emphasized that word-for-word translation was not necessary, Western media agencies were not looking for professional interpreters where accuracy was of the highest value.[37] Rather, journalists wanted someone who could give quick summaries with background information. Journalists provide their local fixer with a brief of what they want for the news piece. Fixers first find the right person to interview and then the fixer translates for the interview. Due to the dangerous situation in Iraq, many fixers went without the foreign correspondent and conducted the interview on their own.[38]

Just because the local fixer is local, does not mean that the situation is without danger for the fixer. The tragic story of Kamaran Abdurrazak Mohammed, Simpson's local fixer, provides a sobering reminder. Frontline journalist Bill Neely of ITN reflects on the danger local fixers face:

> We are very aware that we come into these countries and stay for a while, and then we walk away and we move on to the next conflict. And the people that we work with, who help us, usually have to stay and suffer the consequences – of not just what has happened there but what we have done in publicizing this conflict … Then, when we leave, they're punished for it in some way. In Iraq, translators are killed for working not just with Coalition forces, but sometimes with journalists.[39]

Many fixers believe that the mortal risk involved in their work for the Western correspondent is worth it because they want justice for their people and country and believe that the light of Western publicity through the foreign correspondent can deliver that. Caroline Wyatt of the BBC describes the motives for the fixers and interviewees she worked with in Chechnya:

> The people who helped us there or who were interviewed by us got into trouble afterwards. But they knew in talking to us how dangerous it was … we said to people, "Are you sure you want to help us? Are you sure you want to be interviewed on camera? … Are you sure you want your real name put up?" And most of the time they said, "Yes, for sure. I don't care what happens because I want the world to know what's happening."[40]

As with embedded journalism, the using of local fixers brings up questions of impartiality. The local fixer can be partial toward a political party and purposefully mistranslate or omit material. The research shows that frontline journalists do not prioritize impartiality in their choosing of local fixers. The risk for journalists is that the fixers will shape their view of the situation by choosing interviewees and locations. Being there to bear witness again proves to be risky for the foreign correspondent, not just physical risk, but the risk of trusting strangers.

Up to this point we have observed that there are many forms of "being there": independent, embedded, or rooftop. Where journalists are located, whether inside a tank, on a rooftop or in a caravan driving across the desert, combined with whom they rely upon for their local information, all contributes to their ability to bear

760   *Amy Richards and Jolyon Mitchell*

witness. Bearing witness to a war being fought in the name of the public provided a vivid illustration with which we explored the role of the journalist as the proxy eyes and ears of the public. Our second case study, bearing witness to genocide, provides another extreme situation through which we will explore the role of the journalist as the proxy voice for the voiceless.

Witnessing Genocide

In the same way that Simpson's experience in Iraq allowed us to tease out some of the complexities of journalists bearing witness in the midst of war, in this section we use the work of another well-known BBC correspondent, Fergal Keane, to reflect upon the difficulties inherent in bearing witness to crimes against humanity. This is by no means a new practice. It is hard not to be haunted by Richard Dimbleby's 1945 radio report of what he saw at the Bergen-Belsen concentration camp, or John Pilger's photographic record of the Khmer Rouge's killing camps in Cambodia in 1979, or John Sweeney's exposing of the massacre by Bosnian Serbs of Muslim men and boys at Srebrenica in 1995. Keane's award-winning reports in the aftermath of the 1994 Rwandan genocide stand within this tradition of journalists who have borne witness to genocidal crimes against humanity.[41]

The then BBC Africa Correspondent, Fergal Keane was covering South Africa's first multiracial elections when his editors sent him to investigate the stories of atrocities in Rwanda following the assassination of President Habyarimana on April 6, 1994. Before then Keane was covering the turbulent run up to Mandela's election as South Africa's first postapartheid president. He had seen suffering, but what he witnessed in Rwanda had a profound impact upon him. Keane saw *limits* in the wars he had covered before Rwanda; he felt the atrocities committed in Rwanda had no limits. In the following discussion we consider not his memorable reports for BBC News and *Panorama*,[42] but his controversial decision to testify at the International Criminal Tribunal for Rwanda (ICTR). As we shall see this decision raises ethical questions about the responsibility of a journalist to bear witness to what they have seen in a legal context. We examine two contrasting examples. In one case Keane testified in favor of the accused and in the other against the accused.[43]

Witness for the defense and for the prosecution

Keane and his BBC television news team produced a story about the Hutu Mayor of Butare, Sylvain Nsabimana. The Mayor organized a convoy to remove Tutsi orphans out of Butare and to safety in Burundi.[44] When Nsabimana was arrested by the ICTR and charged with genocide, Nsabimana's lawyer asked Keane to testify on behalf of the man being charged with crimes against humanity. Keane had since read of the atrocities Nsabimana was accused of committing; nonetheless, Keane chose to testify

Journalists as Witnesses to Violence and Suffering 761

in the war crimes court as to the good act he witnessed. Keane's testimony at the ICTR testified to the veracity of the story he filed. He explains his position thus:

> We could only report what we saw him doing. ... I had seen Nsabimana do something that was ostensibly good. But I now knew about the circumstances in which he had taken power and I had read human rights reports which alleged he was an active participant in the slaughter of local Tutsis. Because I believe in the principles of international justice, and because the right to a fair defence should be an integral part of that system, I said I was willing to appear.[45]

It is illuminating to place this brief first account alongside Keane's decision to testify at the ICTR in the case against a second Hutu mayor, Sylvestre Gacumbitsi. Gacumbitsi was Mayor of Nyarubuye a town near the Tanzanian border. He "was the most powerful man in the district." For Keane, Gacumbitsi "would become a key figure in my Rwandan story, someone who would follow me past the borders of place and time, a sinister presence which frightened and angered me, and which I would one day have to return and confront."[46] In the chain of command, there may have been others more senior than Mayor Gacumbitsi who instigated the systematic killing of the Tutsi population, but according to Keane for the victims of his district, it was the arrest and conviction of their mayor that approximated anything near justice.

One of the reasons for this was that Mayor Gacumbitsi instructed the Tutsi people of his district to stay where they were and they would be safe. Days later he instructed them to gather at the local, Nyarubuye Catholic Church and school compound for a safe refuge. In his memoir, Keane retells the story told to him by many eyewitnesses:

> Sylvestre Gacumbitsi, along with local military and police officers, had sent orders for all the Hutu men in the district to gather together and march on Nyarubuye church. On 15 April, as many as 7,000 men crowded down the narrow lane towards the church. ... The marching men were all farmers who scraped a living from the overcrowded hills of south-east Rwanda. They were urged on by soldiers and policemen. ... The men outside had covered their faces with banana leaves, hiding their faces from their neighbours they were about to attack.[47]

> He [Gacumbitsi] gave orders to the police to open fire. ... Grenades were exploded among the densely packed crowd of Tutsis, splashing blood and flesh onto the walls. All of the survivors remember the terrible noise – the crashing of automatic rifle fire, the explosions, people screaming, babies dropped by their mothers howling. This went on for about twenty minutes. ... Then the order was given for the Hutu peasants to move in and kill. There were many Tutsis still alive, and Gacumbitsi and his cohorts wanted as many Hutus as possible to be complicit in the killing. It was the work of true Hutu patriots. That is what the architects of genocide called it: _work_. ... they hacked, slashed and bludgeoned their neighbours to death.[48]

A few survived this onslaught. Keane focuses on one of them: Valentina Iziribagwaya. She was still alive and pulled out of the church with other remaining survivors.

Gacumbitsi ordered the survivors to be killed. Valentina remembered, "He said they should kill us as they would kill a snake by hitting it on the head."[49] Two of Valentina's schoolmates were given charge to kill her; she pleaded with them by name to have mercy on her. They hit her on the shoulder with a club and then smashed her fingers into the ground and finally slashed her on the head with a machete knocking her unconscious. They left her for dead. Valentina regained consciousness and survived for 30 days among the dead. Rwandan Patriotic Front (RPF) soldiers eventually found her and brought her to a clinic where Keane first met her.

Keane was not in Rwanda when Gacumbitsi gathered the Tutsis of his district into the churchyard and then had them slaughtered. According to Gérard Prunier, the genocide claimed an estimated 640 000 people "in about six weeks between the second week of April and the third week of May."[50] Another 160 000 would be killed in the succeeding weeks. Up until mid-May, as we noted above, Keane was covering the elections in South Africa. His narrative coverage of what happened in the Rwandan town of Nyarubuye is pieced together from the multiple sources of Tutsi survivor testimony, Hutu farmers who observed from the hillsides, and his own visit to the churchyard weeks after the atrocities to witness for himself the decaying bodies in the tropical heat.

Sylvestre Gacumbitsi did not become a "key figure in [Keane's] Rwandan story"[51] because Keane was an eyewitness to the slaughter of Tutsis in the churchyard, rather Keane was an eyewitness to the suffering caused by Gacumbitsi, not to the actual violence. Keane was witness to the aftermath. Gacumbitsi was the name Keane heard again and again in his interviews with survivors at the clinic where he met Valentina. Upon hearing the survivor testimony, Keane and the BBC television crew went to Nyarubuye to see the churchyard. The reporter needed to corroborate survivor testimony with physical evidence. The RPF escorted the news team to the village. The suffering of those Keane interviewed and the churchyard of corpses he witnessed gave impetus to a somewhat audacious plan. Keane admits that it was his feeling of rage at what he saw that inspired him and his BBC crew to go after Gacumbitsi:

> I could never feel what the survivors felt about him; his role in their lives had been catastrophic, while I had been simply a witness. But I knew that if we could find him there was a chance of some justice for Valentina, and the murdered thousands of Nyarubuye. What we were seeing in Rwanda inspired rage. It would be wrong to say we felt a responsibility towards the dead. That is too neatly defined a way of putting it. … But here there was a chance to use our journalism to hold a killer to account. By that time we also knew that the country had been abandoned by the international community. The extremists knew this too. Wherever Gacumbitsi was hiding he would not be expecting a visit from a BBC television crew.[52]

Keane and his BBC crew heard that Gacumbitsi had fled to the refugee camp at Benaco in Tanzania. There were an estimated quarter of a million refugees in the Benaco camp. Gacumbitsi had managed to obtain a "community leader" role in the international camp and was in charge of distributing food to the refugees who had fled his district. In reflecting upon actually confronting Gacumbitsi face to face, Keane writes:

> I remember that I felt two emotions at that moment: a great deal of fear and boiling anger. And so I made a fierce effort of will to be calm. My questions could be firm, but I could not lose my temper. Apart from being unprofessional it could also prompt Gacumbitsi's supporters to attack. As I strode up and started to ask questions I kept the image of Valentina in my mind.[53]

Gacumbitsi responded coolly, denied everything, and suggested that Tutsis would indeed come up with such a story. Five years later, Keane faced Gacumbitsi again, this time at the United Nations International Criminal Tribunal for Rwanda. The evidence UN prosecutors wanted from Keane included the video footage of the aftermath of the massacre and his interview with Gacumbitsi, "our documentary had been influential in making sure that Gacumbitsi was placed on the priority list for arrest by the International Tribunal."[54] The recorded documentary and interviews were not sufficient for evidence, Keane's physical presence was necessary as an eyewitness to verify the footage.

The defense lawyer tried to prove that Keane's footage was propaganda from the Tutsis of the RPF given the fact that Keane and his crew were escorted to the massacre site by the opposition force.[55] This was not an unusual charge by the defense teams of people charged with crimes against humanity. At both the International Criminal Tribunal for the Former Yugoslavia (ICTFY) and the ICTR this charge was used when Western journalists were escorted to massacre sites. A year after Keane's testimony to the ICTR, "Gacumbitsi was convicted of genocide, crimes against humanity and rape and sentenced to thirty years' imprisonment."[56]

Keane's involvement in these two trials helps to highlight some of the challenges encountered by Western journalists reporting on genocide and choosing to testify in international criminal tribunals. There is a sense in which all reporters are engaged as active witnesses even when they are just reporting the facts. Keane is admittedly engaged in frontline reporting. He writes that his practice of journalism is motivated by a human rights agenda, the "concept of international justice" and the belief that, "the weak need protecting; the powerful need to be challenged."[57] This kind of journalism challenges the strongly held principle of reporter impartiality. Journalistic impartiality is strongly linked to the idea that in order to maintain objectivity, journalists must be detached from the subject of their reporting. We considered this concept in our earlier example questioning the impartiality of journalists embedded with coalition troops. Bearing witness to genocide poses new sets of questions to consider with regard to journalistic impartiality.

To bear witness or not to bear witness?

When, if ever, should journalists testify at international criminal tribunals? There is a range of views from those who believe that journalists should be granted the privilege of being able to disregard court subpoenas, to those who argue that journalists who witness crimes have a duty to testify. Keane clearly falls into this latter category. There is a noticeable American and British divide running along the continuum regarding testifying. This may partly be due to the United States' more rigid tradition of the "objectivity norm" and the specific appeal to "shield laws" to protect reporters from revealing sources.[58] Jonathan Randal of *The Washington Post* is a well-known case of a journalist who received a subpoena for the ITCFY and refused to testify. Randal was part of an appeal by over 30 international journalism organizations to the international court to create the privilege of a journalist's right to refuse to testify. Their aim was to establish that journalists first be seen as "independent observers rather than potential witnesses."[59] In response the Tribunal Appeals Chamber outlined a two-part test:

> First, the petitioning party must demonstrate that the evidence sought is of direct and important value in determining a core issue in the case. Second, it must demonstrate that the evidence sought cannot be reasonably obtained elsewhere.[60]

By contrast to Randal, Lindsey Hilsum, freelance reporter for the BBC, *The Guardian* and *The Observer*, was issued a subpoena and testified at the ICTR. Hilsum was one of the few Western correspondents in Rwanda when the Rwandan President was assassinated. She believed it was her obligation to testify at the ICTR about the "general situation" of Rwanda, but Hilsum felt she could not testify against any one "individual to whom I have had privileged access."[61] Hilsum argues that the opposition against journalists becoming legal witnesses is mostly an American criticism:

> They [Americans] say that if we act as witnesses in such tribunals, we lay ourselves open to charges of bias, cross the line between being observers and participants in a story, and endanger ourselves and fellow reporters trying to cover war crimes and other human rights abuses.[62]

Hilsum was also critical of the British newspaper journalist Ed Vulliamy, who not only testified against a specific Serbian individual but also attempted to cover the proceedings of the ICTFY for *The Guardian* before and after he took the stand. For Hilsum, this action was "a blurring of the line between the journalist as observer and as participant in the story."[63] In spite of this criticism Hilsum admits that she became a *participant* in covering the Rwandan genocide because she thought it was "the right thing to do."

> The normal rules of journalistic ethics are overwhelmed by murder on this scale. I was aware of crossing the line and becoming a participant rather than an observer, but I felt it was a moral duty to use my unique position to influence the historical record in the court. By accident of history, I happened to be there.[64]

Ed Vulliamy, of *The Guardian*, testified at the ICTFY twice and even inadvertently revealed a source. Nevertheless, Vulliamy was concerned with what kind of history is left on the records:

I decided this was a chance for some kind of reckoning for the only people I really cared about – the victims. I threw aside any pretence of neutrality and went to The Hague. I gave the prosecution in the Tadic case all my notebooks and I told them everything I knew.[65]

The duties that accompany the journalistic practice of foreign correspondents being there, Vulliamy argues, may include abandoning "neutrality" and "to reckon with what we witness and to urge others to do the same."[66]

The journalism of attachment

As can be seen from the proceeding discussions, journalists covering the genocide in Rwanda and ethnic cleansing in Bosnia in the early 1990s started asking related questions about the roles of objectivity and impartiality in reporting on crimes against humanity: How can we be *detached* about covering mass atrocities against civilians? How can we be *dispassionate* when we are walking among the rotting corpses of slaughtered innocent populations? How can we not become engaged? How far does being a witness to human atrocity carry with it an obligation to those who suffer?

The BBC reporter Martin Bell first coined the phrase "the journalism of attachment", which he defined as "a journalism that cares as well as knows; that is aware of its responsibilities; that will not stand neutrally between good and evil, right and wrong, the victim and the oppressor."[67] His experience reporting on Bosnia was essentially as an embed with the civilians of Sarajevo when it was under siege. Like embedded reporters, Bell was in physical solidarity with those on whom he reported, in this case the civilians of Sarajevo. This and related experiences in the Balkans led him to suggest that in "our anxiety not to offend and upset people, we were not only sanitizing war but even *prettifying* it".[68] In this context he argues that journalists must avoid "shading the truth", highlight the fact that "war is a bad taste business" and therefore not be afraid to show the bloody reality of the effects of war.[69] For Bell a journalism of attachment should not become an excuse for self-censorship or visual reticence.

Reporters advocating a "journalism of attachment" argue that in the coverage of ethnic cleansing or genocide, treating both sides as holding a reasonable position would be to "equate aggressor and victim."[70] The CNN reporter Christiane Amanpour, developed this point further:

I have come to believe that objectivity means giving all sides a fair hearing, but not treating all sides equally. Once you treat all sides the same in a case such as Bosnia, you are drawing a moral equivalence between victim and aggressor. And from here it is a short step to being neutral. And from here it's an even shorter step to becoming an accessory to all manners of evil.[71]

The logic here is rooted in her personal experience of covering the Bosnian conflict in the early 1990s. Both Amanpour and Bell acknowledge that for journalists, while there is no possibility of bearing witness neutrally from above, the validity of their singular and limited view from the ground was susceptible to manipulation.

Criticisms of the journalism of attachment

Some critics describe the journalism of attachment as "advocacy journalism," suggesting it is flawed in several ways. Two lines of criticism are particularly noteworthy. First, attachment to the civilians of one side may be at the expense of other civilian populations. This may result in overlooking atrocities committed by the side to which the journalist is "attached." Second, advocacy journalism is not as independent from government as it claims. Philip Hammond believed that the "journalism of attachment" was just as susceptible to becoming a tool of propaganda during war as impartial and detached journalism.

> Instead of truthful reporting, the agenda of advocacy journalism has sometimes made reporters highly selective, leading them to ignore inconvenient information ... And despite claims to be pursuing a moral, human rights agenda, the journalism of attachment has led to the celebration of violence against those perceived as undeserving victims.[72]

Hammond cites as examples the bombing of Serbian civilians during the Bosnian war and the emptying of the refugee camps sending the Hutus back into Rwanda where they were likely to become victims of revenge attacks by Tutsis. One reason why journalism of attachment is susceptible to such faults is because of what Hammond calls a simplistic reportage framing of "good versus evil morality."[73] As for Hammond's second criticism, questioning the actual independence of advocacy journalism, he found that advocacy journalism has frequently coincided with the perspectives and policies of powerful Western governments.

The debate between the journalism of attachment and the journalism of detachment is commonly framed in a polarized fashion, with advocates and proponents coming down forcefully on either side of the discussion. Nevertheless, journalists do move *from* observer *to* witness, from a level of detachment to engagement, whenever they embark on covering a story about violence or suffering. Even if they do not recognize it, they do make a moral judgment when they decide to show certain images and not others, when they select one local eyewitness, when they put themselves in a vulnerable position to cover a story or when they decide to testify at a war crimes tribunal. The physical risks journalists take in becoming witnesses to violence and suffering have been highlighted throughout this chapter, but journalists also put their psyches at risk and are susceptible to posttraumatic stress syndrome. War correspondent Ernie Pyle wrote in 1954 near the end of his life, "I've been immersed in it too long. My spirit is wobbly and my mind is confused. The hurt has become too great."[74] Given the many risks of getting the story wrong and getting hurt in the process, why do they do it?

Martha Gellhorn, after many successful years as a war correspondent, changed her mind about the answer to such a question. She realized that the success of her reporting was not based on galvanizing the public to do something. She was among the first journalists on the scene in Dachau following Germany's unconditional surrender in May 1945. Gellhorn began her career believing that her job was to motivate the public to do something; she came to disavow this reasoning and asserts that the role of the journalist is to bear accurate witness as an end in itself. She writes of the evolution of her motivation for reporting on conflicts, violence and suffering over a 60-year span:

> When I was young I believed in the perfectibility of man, and in progress, and thought of journalism as a guiding light. If people were told the truth, if dishonour and injustice were clearly shown to them, they would at once demand the saving action, punishment of wrong-doers, and care for the innocent. How people were to accomplish these reforms, I did not know. That was their job. A journalist's job was to bring news, to be eyes for their conscience. I think I must have imagined public opinion as a solid force, something like a tornado, always ready to blow on the side of the angels.[75]

Notice Gellhorn's change from the journalist as the public's conscience to the maintenance of trust between journalist and public as she continues:

> Now I have different ideas. I must always, before, have expected results. There was an obtainable end, called victory or defeat. One could hope for victory, despair over defeat. At this stage in my life I think that this is nonsense. Journalism is a means; and I now think that the act of keeping the record straight is valuable in itself. Serious, careful, honest journalism is essential, not because it is a guiding light but because it is a form of honourable behaviour, involving the reporter and the reader.[76]

Keeping the record straight is important for the journalist's relationship with the public, but it is also important for the journalist's role of speaking or recording for the victims of violence and suffering. While foreign correspondents may begin their coverage with a desire to be objective and impartial, representing the interests of their public, the evidence from this chapter shows how the relationship between the journalist and the victims of suffering become a powerful motivation for what Gellhorn describes as "keeping the record straight." In the end, an accurate record will better serve public deliberation and better serve those whose story the journalist retells.

Conclusion

Speaking on behalf of other people, the role of a proxy, as we have suggested in this chapter is among the roles performed by a frontline correspondent witnessing violence and suffering. The words *bearing witness* and the word proxy correspond with a sense of commitment and responsibility taken seriously. Philosopher Alasdair

MacIntyre suggests that the only people capable of systematically speaking for those unable to speak are "friends." A journalist has the ability to speak systematically for others, "that is, to assert, to question and to prescribe in the light of the other's conception of ... good."[77] The two frontline correspondents discussed in this chapter, John Simpson and Fergal Keane, through long and reputable journalistic careers have shown their friendship for victims of radical suffering who do not have a voice internationally let alone in their own countries. Simpson and Keane's friendships for the suffering have been both general and specific. For Simpson, he has befriended the Iraqi people as well as specific people from Iraq. Keane had been the BBC South Africa correspondent where he had developed important and deep relationships with South Africans over an extended period of time. When Keane was called away to Rwanda, he was quickly and very dramatically moved by the people of the Nyarubuye district in Rwanda, and particularly by a survivor named Valentina with whom a friendship continues to this day. Simpson's and Keane's distinctive performances of their journalism careers has given them the opportunity to amplify the voices of those who might not otherwise have been heard and even speak for those who are no longer able to speak for themselves. In this, they have performed the role of proxy not for a "generalized other," but for real people.

This is not to claim that all foreign correspondents are perfect proxies or even that Simpson and Keane have been infallible witnesses throughout their careers. They both acknowledge falling short of their own standards and learning how to improve their journalistic practice by taking correction from others. Simpson and Keane are exemplars because their repeat performances disciplined and refined their capabilities to enact the role of proxies, of even friends.[78] Given the nature of their backgrounds and roving jobs, there are clearly limitations to the kinds of friendships that frontline reporters are able to develop with the victims whose story they cover. Nevertheless, their interactions and temporary proximity to people who have experienced violence at first hand and are now suffering greatly clearly does have an impact upon their work.

Many journalistic memoirs reveal the contexts in which the individual journalist's practical moral reasoning developed and how they came to give voice to those who either had little access to the wider public sphere or could no longer speak for themselves. What was clear in Simpson's and Keane's memoirs, and in the reflective accounts produced by other frontline correspondents addressed throughout this essay, that when representing victims of violence and suffering the virtue of truthfulness was seen as the only way to do justice to their experience. Journalists recognize that they may be able to do little else than tell the story of the suffering people. Journalists' articles, photographs or video recordings may not result in any action that convicts the perpetrators or galvanizes the public to action, but reporting a truthful account of what happened still matters.

Alasdair MacIntyre pairs the ability to be a proxy, a friend who speaks for those unable to speak, with the virtue of truthfulness. Truthfulness includes the duty of justice for the one being represented as not to be truthful is an "act of injustice that deprives the other of what we owe to her or him."[79] Repeatedly journalists claimed

Journalists as Witnesses to Violence and Suffering 769

that frontline correspondents are recording history, they have "a sense of making history."[80] As Gellhorn reflected, the value of journalism is "the act of keeping the record straight"[81] the practice of working toward the truthful representation of other people's experience. In agreement with Gellhorn, the BBC journalist Allan Little admits:

> You want to be true to the people. You don't want to let them down.... How can I do justice to these people? I must get it right.... that is why I was there on the ground.[82]

Bearing witness as a foreign correspondent or frontline reporter involves the journalist being there and the risks associated with being there in extraordinary times of volatility, danger, and suffering. Journalists who judge the suffering of others to be injustice and who speak on behalf of these people increase their level of journalistic engagement *from* observation and reporting of the story *to* a practice of participation and making the story their own story. Bearing witness as a claim of journalistic practice involves entering into a story in which the journalist denounces the injustice experienced by those suffering.

As we have seen, the journalists' role of bearing witness to distant suffering often involves physical risk in being there in times of war and genocide. It also involves the risks of accurately representing others. Being there in extreme situations for the sake of the public and speaking on the behalf of others who have gravely suffered involves engagement in stories reported in a way that everyday journalism does not. Here, we have neither proposed that global crisis reporting should necessarily be done in the mode of journalism of attachment, nor that journalists have to testify at every war crimes tribunal. We have suggested rather that all journalism, involves some level of engagement and judgment in response to the events witnessed.

Notes

1   Mitchell (2009).
2   Allan and Zelizer (2004).
3   This discussion is taking place in both scholarly and journalistic circles. See for example: Mitchell (2007a), Seib (2002), Peters (2005), and Ellis (2000).
4   Hannerz (2004).
5   For a discussion on "parachute reporting," see Hannerz (2004, pp. 23–26). See also: Seib (2004), Pedelty (1995) and Hamilton and Jenner (2004).
6   Tumber and Webster (2006).
7   Tumber (2006, p. 445).
8   Allan and Zelizer (2004, p. 5).
9   Cottle and Rai (2006, p. 179).
10   Simpson (2003).
11   Simpson wrote *From the House of War: John Simpson in the Gulf* about his experiences during the first Gulf War (1991).

12 For further examples of embedded journalism see Katovsky and Carlson (2003).
13 Simpson (2003, p. 327).
14 Simpson (2003, p. 329).
15 Simpson (2003, p. 330–331).
16 Simpson (2003, p. 335).
17 Simpson (2003, p. 349).
18 The Committee to Protect Journalists is a New York-based non-profit and non-governmental organization founded to promote the protection of journalists and independent journalism. They have published the report *Journalists Killed in 2007* on www.cpj.org (accessed August 2, 2010).
19 Simpson (2003, p. 352).
20 Freedman (2004, pp. 67–68).
21 Seib (2004, p. 52).
22 Simpson (2003, p. 351).
23 Simpson (2003, p. 350).
24 Knightley (2003, p. 548).
25 Public Affairs Guidance on Embedding Media during Possible Future Operations/ Deployments in the U.S. Central Command's Area of Responsibility, United States Department of Defense, cited in Seib (2004, p. 52).
26 Tumber and Webster (2006).
27 Little (2007).
28 As reported in Seib (2004, p. 55).
29 As reported in Seib (2004, p. 56).
30 Simpson (2003).
31 Tumber and Webster (2006, p. 92).
32 Tumber and Webster (2006, p. 92–93).
33 Tumber and Webster (2006, p. 93).
34 Cottle and Rai (2006, p. 179).
35 Maier (2006, p. 98).
36 Palmer and Fontan (2007, p. 12).
37 Tumber and Webster (2006).
38 Palmer and Fontan (2007, p. 12).
39 Bill Neely quoted in Tumber and Webster (2003, p. 113).
40 Tumber and Webster (2003, p. 115).
41 For more on international and local coverage of the genocide see Mitchell (2007b).
42 For more from Keane see PBS's website *Ghosts of Rwanda*, and his interview (March 19, 2004) on his experience covering this story and his further reflections after the tenth anniversary: www.pbs.org/wgbh/pages/frontline/shows/ghosts/interviews/ keane.html (accessed August 17, 2010).
43 In the following two accounts of how Keane came to testify at the ICTR, we consider Keane's memoir in which he discusses how he came to be a witness for the ICTR (Keane, 2005). Keane wrote an earlier book on Rwanda giving an historical account of the lead up to the Rwanda genocide (1996).
44 While the mass violence followed within days after the April 6 assassination of the President in most of Rwanda, it was "slow" to reach Mayor Nsabimana's town because the head of the district was a Tutsi, Jean-Baptiste Habyarimana (no relation to the President). Angered by the "inaction" in the Butare district, "Interim Government President

Sindikubwabo … came down and gave an inflammatory speech, asking the people if they were 'sleeping' and urging them to violent deeds." On the April 20, the district head was replaced by an extremist, "and the killing started immediately" (Prunier, 1995, p. 244).

45 Keane (2005, p. 310).
46 Keane (2005, p. 318).
47 Keane (2005, p. 319).
48 Keane (2005, p. 320).
49 Keane (2005, p. 321).
50 Prunier (1995). Estimates range from half-a-million to one million victims. In his discussion of "How many were killed?" Prunier makes a strong case for their being about 850 000 victims.
51 Keane (2005, p. 318).
52 Keane (2005, p. 324).
53 Keane (2005, p. 326).
54 Keane (2005, p. 336).
55 Keane (2005, p. 344).
56 Keane (2005, p. 346).
57 Keane (2005, p. 365). The title of Keane's memoir, *All of these People*, is after a poem by Michael Longley. Keane felt Ulster writer Longley was, "one of the most sensitive chroniclers of the pain caused by the Troubles. It is his tribute to those who have inspired him; I carry a little photocopy of this poem wherever I travel in the world. *All of these people,/ alive or dead,/ are civilized*." (p. xv).
58 Schudson (2001).
59 Spellman (2005, p. 133).
60 *International Criminal Tribunal for the Former Yugoslavia, Trial Chamber, Prosecutor vs. Radoslav Brdjanin*, Decision on Motion of Jonathan Randal to Set Aside Confidential Subpoena to Give Evidence, June 7, 2002. As quoted in Spellman (2005, p. 134).
61 Hilsum (1997, pp. 32–33).
62 Hilsum (1997, p. 29).
63 Hilsum (1997, p. 33).
64 Hilsum (1997, p. 30).
65 Vulliamy (1999, p. 605).
66 Vulliamy (1999, p. 612).
67 Bell (1998, p. 19).
68 Bell (1995, p. 216).
69 Bell (1995, pp. 203–220).
70 Vulliamy (1999).
71 As quoted in Seib (2002, p. 53).
72 Hammond (2002, p. 180).
73 Hammond (2002, p. 178).
74 This remark by Ernie Pyle is cited in a pamphlet for journalists on how to deal with posttraumatic stress syndrome. Hight and Smyth (2003, p. 7).
75 Gellhorn, (1993, p. 373).
76 Gellhorn, (1993, p. 375).
77 MacIntyre (1999, p. 124).
78 For a more developed discussion on friendship and media violence see Mitchell (2007a, pp. 293–296).

79 MacIntyre (1999, p. 150).
80 Tumber (2006, p. 445).
81 Gellhorn, (1993, p. 375).
82 Little (2007).

References

Allan, S., and Zelizer, B. (eds) (2004), *Reporting War: Journalism in Wartime*, Routledge, New York.

Bell, M. (1995) *In Harm's Way*, Hamish Hamilton, London.

Bell, M. (1998) The journalism of attachment, in *Media Ethics*, (ed. M. Kieran), Routledge, London, pp. 15–22.

Cottle, S., and Rai, M. (2006) Between display and deliberation: Analyzing TV news as communicative architecture, *Media Culture and Society*, 28 (2), 179.

Ellis, J. (2000) *Seeing Things: Television in the Age of Uncertainty*, I.B. Tauris, London.

Freedman, D. (2004) Misreporting war has a long history, in *Tell Me Lies: Propaganda and Media Distortion in the Attack on Iraq*, (ed. David Miller), Pluto, London, pp. 63–69.

Gellhorn, M. (1993) *The Face of War*, rev edn, Granta, London.

Hamilton, J.M., and Jenner, E. (2004) Redefining foreign correspondence, *Journalism*, 5 (3), 301–321.

Hammond, P. (2002) Moral combat: Advocacy journalists and the new humanitarianism, in *Rethinking Human Rights: Critical Approaches to International Politics*, (ed. D. Chandler), Palgrave Macmillan, pp. 176–195.

Hannerz, U. (2004) *Foreign News: Exploring the World of Foreign Correspondents*, University of Chicago Press, Chicago.

Hight, J., and Smyth, F. (2003) *Tragedies and Journalists: A Guide for More Effective Coverage*, Dart Center for Journalism and Trauma, University of Washington, Seattle, WA.

Hilsum, L. (1997) Crossing the line to commitment, *British Journalism Review*, 8 (1), 29–33.

Katovsky, B., and Carlson, T. (eds) (2003) *Embedded: The Media at War in Iraq – An Oral History*, The Lyons Press, Guildford, CT.

Keane, F. (1996) *Season of Blood: A Rwandan Journey*, Harmondsworth, Penguin.

Keane, F. (2005) *All of These People: A Memoir*, Harper Perennial, London.

Knightley, P. (2003) *The War Correspondent as Hero, Propagandist and Myth-Maker from the Crimea to Iraq*, André Deutsch, London.

Little, A. (2007) The Remembrance Sunday debate, War, Journalism and History Conference, University of Edinburgh, November 11.

MacIntyre, A. (1999) *Dependent Rational Animals: Why Human Beings Need the Virtues*, Duckworth, London.

Maier, J. (2006) Being embedded – the Concept of "liveness" in journalism, *Journal of Visual Culture*, 5, 98.

Mitchell, J. (2007a) *Media Violence and Christian Ethics*, Cambridge University Press, Cambridge: Cambridge.

Mitchell, J. (2007b) Remembering the Rwandan genocide: Reconsidering the role of local and global media, *Global Media Journal*, Autumn, http://lass.calumet.purdue.edu/cca/gmj/index.htm (accessed August 17, 2010).

Mitchell, J. (2009) "Redescribing news: From Spectacular depictions of violence to unspectacular portrayals of HIV, in *Ethics and Evil in the Public Sphere: Media, Universal Values & Global Development* (eds M. Fackler and R. Fortner), University of Illinois Press, Urbana, pp. 29–46.

Palmer, J., and Fontan, V. (2007) Our ears and our eyes: Journalists and fixers in Iraq, *Journalism*, 8, 1, 12.

Pedelty, M. (1995) *War Stories: The Culture of Foreign Correspondents*, Routledge, New York.

Peters, J.D. (2005) *Courting the Abyss: Free Speech and the Liberal Tradition*, University of Chicago, Chicago.

Prunier, G. (1995) *The Rwanda Crisis: History of a Genocide*, Columbia University Press, New York.

Schudson, M. (2001) The objectivity norm in American journalism, *Journalism*, 2, (2), 149–170.

Seib, P. (2002) *The Global Journalist: News and Conscience in a World of Conflict*, Rowman & Littlefield, Boston, MA.

Seib, P. (2004) *Beyond the Front Lines: How the News Media Cover a World Shaped by War*, Palgrave-Macmillan, New York.

Simpson, J. (1991) *From the House of War: John Simpson in the Gulf*, Arrow, London.

Simpson, J. (2003) *The Wars against Saddam: Taking the Hard Road to Baghdad*, Macmillan, London.

Spellman, R.L. (2005) Journalist or witness? Reporters and war crimes tribunals, *Gazette: The International Journal for Communication Studies*, 67 (2), 123–139.

Tumber, H. (2006) The fear of living dangerously: Journalists who report on conflict, *International Relations*, 20, 445.

Tumber, H., and Webster, F. (2006) *Journalists under Fire: Information War and Journalistic Practice*, Sage, London.

Vulliamy, E. (1999) "Neutrality", and the Absence of reckoning: A journalist's account, *Journal of International Affairs*, 52 (2), 603–620.

39

Reporting on Religious Authority Complicit with Atrocity

Paul A. Soukup, S.J.

A popular accusation holds that churches or religious groups do bad things. Despite the logical fallacy – attributing to a religion the faults of individuals – the accusation still resonates in the popular imagination. From a journalist's perspective, religious involvement in such evil – for example, in the horrors that have recently marked our world – provide either the best or the worst reporting challenge. On the one hand, it gives the opportunity to highlight hypocrisy, to shock the audience, to bring often exempt groups to accountability, to call into question the honored or even revered status of religion and religious leadership, and to debate the social role of religion itself. On the other hand, such situations and their reporting may well lead to antireligious violence, create conflicted feelings about religion, give offense to some audience members, and foster misunderstandings about religion, culture, and religious history. More likely than not, journalists would quickly accept the challenge and report. Most readers would agree that indeed they should report.

From an ethical perspective, religious involvement in evil raises a host of issues for journalists (not to mention for the religious organizations and individuals themselves, though that lies beyond the scope of this work). Reporting on that religious involvement adds still more ethical issues, a number of them not immediately obvious.

Sad to relate, the participation of religious leaders in bad things happens more than people would like to admit and occurs in almost every part of the world. A partial list of religious involvement in, or complicity with, atrocity in living memory includes:

- The collaboration of Lutheran clergy with the Nazi movement in Germany in the 1930s and 1940s.
- The Shinto-connected militarism of World War II Japan and the ongoing reverence shown at the graves of war criminals at Yasukuni Jinja.

The Handbook of Global Communication and Media Ethics, First Edition. Edited by Robert S. Fortner and P. Mark Fackler.
© 2011 Blackwell Publishing Ltd. Published 2011 by Blackwell Publishing Ltd.

- The involvement of Orthodox and Islamic groups in the violent break-up of the former Yugoslavia.
- The Hindu-led destruction of the mosque at Ayodhya and the religious riots that followed across India.
- The rise of Islamic violence – from clergy imposed fatāwā on writers to the extremism inspired by conservative sects and movements.
- The role of Catholic clergy among the genocidaires in Rwanda in the early 1990s.
- The ongoing conflicts over land in Israel between Orthodox Jewish settlers, usually endorsed by their rabbis, and Palestinians.
- The cover-up of sexual abuse among Catholic clergy by the bishops and leadership of the Church.
- The role of clergy of many denominations at the US detention center at Guantanamo, even after allegations of the mistreatment of prisoners.

One or another researcher or reporter would probably add to this list, but the general point remains: members of all religious groups – and often the leading members of those groups – have behaved badly. The ethical challenge to journalists lies in the reporting challenge mentioned earlier. How should journalists respond when their reports touch on the moral foundations of society? Should churches have some kind of exemption from the scrutiny of the news? Should churches merit some kind of additional scrutiny? The larger ethical challenge has to do with why and how journalists act as they do.

Generally, journalists let various professional codes of behavior or codes of ethics guide them in these and other murky areas. Given the sensitivity of these questions, those codes may not provide enough guidance. However, communication ethics does matter here, as White states more generally, "communication ethics at its best defines how the actors in a communication system think that communication *should* be carried out in order to respond to the problems of human and social existence in that context" (2008, p. 2).

In that spirit, this essay will briefly discuss why religious groups fall under news examination, review some common journalistic codes, highlighting potential limitations, and then propose some other guides drawn from communication ethics that journalists might employ with religious stories. At each stage, further ethical issues emerge; these perhaps will help us – all actors in a communication system – reflect on how we think communication should occur.

Religious Groups and the News

By their very nature, religious organizations and their leadership play a public role in society. Many people would neither question that role nor the ways in which people function within it, with rationales from two highly divergent perspectives. Historically, the major world religions have shaped the cultures and moral understandings of almost every region in the world, with many states and regions at some time making no distinction between religion and state sovereignty. On the one hand, then, journalists from societies where religious groups still occupy a central role in social and cultural life often do not report bad news about religious groups out of a fear generated by a kind of lese majesté. Religion and religious leaders simply fall into a category beyond the scrutiny of the news media. On the other hand, the development of the idea of the separation of church and state and its promulgation in the West (in theory, in practice, or in both) and a growing secularism in democratic states has led to an expectation in the minds of Western-influenced journalists that a religious body should appear simply as separate, of little interest to the more serious concerns of politics or statecraft. These journalists – particularly political journalists – have come to regard religion as of little interest to their audiences and beyond their own expertise (Silk, 1995, pp. 3–10).

In fact, few journalistic courses or training programs demand any special knowledge of religion, with reporters themselves acknowledging their lack of knowledge (Soukup, 2002). Religious commentators have vocally criticized religion reporters on this score, terming some "religiously ignorant journalists" (Smith, 2004, quoted in Dart, 2005, p. xiii). Apart from a few specialists, those who do report on religion depend on their own religious background or on a small number of sources from the religious communities they cover. Some reporters build on their own, often rudimentary, religious education; others rely on quick briefings. Editors, too, often miss religious stories (Briggs, 1990) because of a common – or, at least, American – willingness to separate church and state or to regard religion as of little consequence. Like Stalin, ("The Pope! How many divisions has he got?" May 13, 1935, quoted in Churchill, 1948, vol. 1, ch. 8), they dismiss religion. As they view the world through a lens of political or economic or technological power, they find they do not have categories that allow them to understand religious groups.

In addition, journalists often lack the knowledge and familiarity with world cultures to help them understand, or at least to have a context for understanding, the role of religion across the world. Every religion, even the most global ones, exists deeply entwined with the particular cultures of its adherents, influencing those cultures and sometimes bearing the characteristics of those cultures – to the point that people find it hard to distinguish cultural and religious reality. Where journalists do not understand these situations, they most likely draw conclusions about religion from their own cultural or personal experience. While this may hold some value, it may also mislead them.

However, whatever their preparation, journalists must deal with religion. Religion and religious figures do play public roles and, as such, do influence society and do lead people to act, more often for good, but occasionally for ill. The danger for those who depend on the news media, of course, lies in how easily journalists and their editors may miss important stories, of good (like the American Civil Rights movement, begun in the churches of the South), of great international moment (like the Khomeini revolution in Iran), or of evil (like all those listed above). In each of the cases outlined above, where religious leaders failed, the news media failed along with them, missing the stories until they became simply too large to ignore and perhaps too large to fully comprehend.

In each of these cases, one could well argue that some kind of news coverage, some kind of public scrutiny would have helped both to foster public understanding and to keep the religious groups faithful to their own principles – and in the best world, to have prevented the atrocities. Where religious figures participate in atrocities, they betray (consciously or unconsciously, for whatever combination of reasons) their own goals and obligations. In retrospect, most would acknowledge their participation in such atrocities as evil. If one accepts the watchdog function of the communication sector, then journalists and others had a clear role to play and did not play it as well as they might have.

Such journalistic failure encompasses both the factual error – not reporting or not recognizing the story – and an ethical error – not doing what we have seen. White terms these the kinds of communication that they think "*should* be carried out in order to respond to the problems of human and social existence" (2008, p. 2). That journalistic failure has many causes. Among other things, the varying reasons for ignoring evils done under the name of religion point to two of the complicating factors of this ethical question: the role of cultural difference, particularly in terms of attitudes toward religion, religious authorities, and the social place of religion, and the level of knowledge that journalists bring to the task.

The perspective outlined here accepts the fact that people's religious beliefs and behaviors do play a role in society. The public consequence of even private belief places religious actions into the social position that everyone in society should expect to know what religious groups do. Insofar as these acts affect others, then those others and their representatives – even those from other religious groups – can examine and criticize the religious behaviors of every creed. The more difficult question, to which we shall return, remains whether such criticism takes place from within or from outside the religious world view of the religious group.

Just this initial examination of the role of religion and the role of journalists has identified four ethical issues: (1) The relation of religious groups to the news, as subjects for the news; (2) The role of the news media vis-à-vis society, as watchdog, as information source about the full range of social actors; (3) The preparation and training of journalists in terms of religion and culture; and (4) The duty of journalists to the religious groups, providing the public scrutiny that leads to accountability. Given the public and central role of religion in society, each issue has a clear response: the public accountability of religious groups; the duty of reporting all sectors of society; the competent preparation of journalists; and an obligation to take religion seriously, even from the outside.

Whatever their situation, journalists then have the initial role of publicizing the actions of religious groups. However, the limitations mentioned make it difficult to do so. In practice, journalists rely on codes of ethics.

Journalistic Codes

Codes of ethics and professional codes of conduct function as a kind of shorthand. They exist to guide people who may not have the time or freedom to reflect on their actions. A code, preferably short and easily understood, condenses the wisdom of practitioners and theorists so that an individual can act responsibly by following the code. When faced with religious complicity in atrocity, a journalist may well rely on a professional code of ethics to guide the preparation of the story.

Cooper *et al.*'s work (1989) offers two appendices of codes of ethics relevant to journalism and communication. While incomplete and "uneven" in their translations (p. 291) and perhaps somewhat dated, the codes still provide some idea of the ideals to which journalists around the world adhere. The first assemblage includes codes from Australia, Denmark, Finland, France, Great Britain, India, Israel, Japan, New Zealand, Nigeria, Norway, Pakistan, Peru, Poland, South Africa, South Korea, Sri Lanka, Turkey, the United States, and the then West Germany. The second, international codes, includes those of the International Federation of Journalists, UNESCO, the Federation of International Editors of Journals, and the common statement of working journalists.

Here follow some of the key principles (note that my summary here does not reflect the full and detailed codes of ethics, but only some of the key ideas):

- the respect for truth,
- the accuracy of information,
- the defense of the public's right to information,
- the freedom of the press, the freedom of speech,
- honesty in reporting and interpreting,
- reports based on evidence,
- objectivity or lack of bias in reports,
- the presentation of relevant contextual information,
- critical examination of sources, particularly those with interests in reporting,
- respect for human rights,
- respect for personal privacy, and
- the protection of confidentiality, whether of sources or of victims

A few of the codes – particularly from countries wracked by communal violence – include either the positive encouragement of respect for ethnic, racial, linguistic, or religious groups or the negative prohibition of the vilification of any group based on its ethnic, racial, linguistic, or religious identity. A number of the codes also add specifications for personal ethics: a prohibition of journalists' accepting favors or acting from self-interest, for example.

Individual countries or associations of journalists offer interpretations of each of these principles. As one might expect, the core values may well receive different emphases in different situations.

Given their nature, the international codes of ethics tend to take a more general approach as Merrill (1989) points out. While common ground exists, "a journalist's ethics stems from his own background and value system and is tied to his nation's political and social system. Such a recognition does not give much support to the idea of international codes of ethics" (p. 289). The international groups agree on the public's right to information, the right to open expression, the promotion of peace and understanding, "the journalist's dedication of objective reality," "the journalist's social responsibility," a "respect for privacy and human dignity," a "respect for public interest," a "respect for universal values and diversity of cultures," and "the elimination of war and other great evils confronting humanity" (Cooper et al., 1989, pp. 334–335). Similar to the items culled from the national codes above, these general principles also require local interpretation.

Just as the role of religion vis-à-vis journalism exists between the poles of taken-for-granted and non-interference, so too the role of journalistic ethics (as enshrined in these codes) exists between poles of universal and particular. In a discussion of communication ethics and universal values published some years after the work of Cooper and his colleagues, Christians and Traber (1997) note that communication ethics "has to respond to both rapid globalization of communications and the reassertion of local social-cultural identities" (p. viii). This compounds the difficulty of covering religion and religious involvement in atrocities: the particular may not immediately attend to the universal and the universal may not easily yield to an understanding rooted in the particular.

Here the codes of ethics fall distressingly silent. With the exception of those codes that caution journalists in terms of inciting communal violence, none of the codes provides any explicit guidance for covering religious groups. However, parts of existing codes could provide guidance on dealing with religious groups or individuals behaving badly. If we then choose key ethical principles from those lists for journalists faced with reporting the actions of religious authorities, we might have guidelines something like these:

- *Human rights.* Since all religious groups have endorsed the principles of human rights (with many of those principles growing out of religious values), journalists can use this concept in a twofold way as they approach religion, particularly religious individuals accused of atrocity. The journalists themselves must defend human rights and they must bind themselves to respect the human rights of those whose actions they report.
- *The defense of the public's right to information.* Here the journalist has the same obligation to make religious information and the actions of religious groups public as it does to make government information and action public. This also places an obligation on the journalist to learn about the various religious groups, their teachings, and their activities. If religion plays a public role, then the journalists should help make that role truly public.
- *Respect for truth and the accuracy of information.* This overarching principle includes several others: an honesty in reporting the events, statements, and

actions of religious groups and individuals; the use of reports based on evidence, with that evidence clearly presented and evaluated; the critical examination of sources, particularly those with interests (whether favorable or unfavorable) in the religious groups; and an objectivity or lack of bias in the presentation. This becomes particularly difficult for journalists who must recognize and acknowledge their own biases. Frequently journalists cannot separate their own religious perspective from their reporting, leading them either to overlook religious evil or to condemn what they perceive as evil in other cultures.

- *A respect for universal values and diversity of cultures.* Religion, of course, forms one of the chief kinds of cultural diversity and so it demands the presentation of relevant contextual information, particularly when one reports on what appears as evil done under the guise of religions behavior. Here the journalist must provide interpretation, but rigorously honest interpretation. As just noted, one should question one's own motives in reporting on religion, particularly when one adheres to that faith or opposes it.

- *Avoid self-interest.* While the typical warning against self-interest refers to the acceptance of gratuities or the fostering of one's political agenda, it also applies to reporting on religion, especially on stories that do not reflect well on religious institutions and leadership. Journalists and commentators who claim no religious affiliation face the temptation to use such stories to condemn religion in general; those who do identify with a given religious group may want use the stories to discredit a group they dislike or to put pressure on the leadership of their own group.

These five principles of journalism, already accepted in the various codes of ethics, provide a theoretical foundation for journalists' reporting on religion in general and, more particularly, on evil carried out in the name of religion or by religious leaders. The principles themselves, though, point to further underlying ethical issues: (1) The identification or definition of evil; (2) The role of context and culture in understanding evil, its causes, and the role of religious groups; (3) The role or justification of an outsider as critic of a religion or its leaders; and (4) The role of the journalist and the attitude of the journalist towards the issue. The first two of these go well beyond journalistic concerns and find only a partial answer in the general principle of human rights. Different cultures and religions define evil in different ways and different cultures expect varying religious responses to evil; for example, where Christianity may counsel forgiveness, another religion may seek justice through a kind of sanctioned vengeance, whether punishment by the state or the paying of reparations. Here the first two larger questions touch the third, the standing of one who would charge religious leaders, for example, of acting badly. Should such a charge take as its ground the tenets of the faith professed by the leaders? The more general requirements of human rights? What grants anyone the right of criticism? This, finally, brings the journalist into the picture. Any journalist revealing evil carried out by religious authority must at least bring a sense of self-knowledge to moderate an initial outrage. The journalist will also need to make

Reporting on Religious Authority Complicit with Atrocity   781

clear the grounding of any charges as well as the context in which both the questioned behavior and the critique take place.

What appeared fairly straightforward at the beginning – should journalists report on atrocity committed in the name of religion or by religious leaders? (Yes, of course!) – now appears much more difficult, in terms of how to do that reporting.

What To Do?

While journalists should report on religiously motivated atrocities, the greater ethical challenge lies in how they do so. Even following the principles sketched above, they still run the risk of misrepresenting religion through cultural or religious ignorance or bias. To guide those faced with such difficult tasks, here are some proposals.

First we must begin well before the reporting of evil. Better to create an environment where people avoid the temptation to act badly than to have to report evil after the fact. Religious leaders and groups need public help to see themselves in the light of their own values and teachings. Religiously interested journalists (perhaps those sharing the same religious values) and even people from outside the particular religion can provide a kind of mirror to help the religious leaders come to know themselves as others know them. What may seem an innocuous religious statement interpreted from within their own system may well lead to misinterpretation and misunderstanding and then trigger harm. What may seem like mere cultural or political accommodation may lead to an inability on the part of the religious leaders to take on (in the Judeo-Christian tradition) a prophetic role in condemning government-sponsored evils. Religious leaders need help to understand how they communicate and what they communicate. Religious leaders also need help in a globalized communication system to realize that they simultaneously address their own followers and millions of others who do not share their knowledge, understanding, values, or beliefs. For example, when Pope Benedict XVI spoke of Islam at Regensburg in 2006, his comments may have raised little surprise in the restricted circle of academic debate among scholars, but they led to widespread outrage outside that group. Here is where journalists can help both the religious groups and the wider public, giving one a sense of how they are perceived and the other a context for understanding. In taking on the role of public mirror, however, journalists and commentators cannot place themselves above religion. Their comment should find its foundation in universal values and the common good, particularly as espoused by the religious groups themselves. Those reporting on religion can also draw on the normative values, legislation, public policy, and moral philosophies in each culture. While these may go beyond a particular religion, they still reflect the cultural surroundings of the religious group, surroundings that the group itself may have helped to shape.

Second, journalists and commentators should remain true to their own role. They should report. Cautious of the danger of antireligious or anticlerical ideas, they should aim for clarity, avoid distortion, and strive for neutrality. Here the choice of stories matters as much as the framing of any given story. The journalists in a secular society must help others live as good citizens in that society and so should ask what religious information best helps their audience participate as informed citizens. Those in religious societies must similarly ask what religious information helps their audience as religious citizens. Tensions can exist between religion and public policy, between religion and government, between one religious group and another; and so the journalist should provide information to help people to understand the larger issues and even the religious values. On the other hand, a journalist should not take on the role of a propagandist nor that of a secular critic of religion. Religious groups do not need journalists and commentators to develop their theology, but society does need them to report on all the segments of that society, including the religious. For example, journalists have played a positive role in teaching a predominantly Christian United States about the beliefs and customs of Islam.

Third, journalists and commentators should develop both religious knowledge and self-knowledge. As already mentioned, journalists – particularly those faced with reporting evil done in the name of religion – must develop a religious literacy, finding expert sources who can provide information and interviewing members of the religious groups. What exactly has occurred? How does it conform to or violate the tenets of the religious group? What is the larger context of belief and action? For example, in reporting on the religious involvement in the break-up of the former Yugoslavia, journalists needed to place both Orthodox Christianity and the Islamic groups into the larger nationalistic and ethnic history of the Balkans. Clearly many of the religious leaders acted badly, but to what extent did they act from religious motives and to what extent from secular ones? All too often, in this and in other stories, the narrative structure of the reports pushed the journalists to favor one side or the other.

Journalists reporting on atrocities linked to religion should also keep in mind their own interests and attitudes to religion. They face a very strong temptation to carry out a critique of religion under the guise of uncovering the evils. Such strong feelings may also blind the journalists to their lack of preparation to report the story. For example, the journalists reporting on the sex abuse scandal within the Catholic Church often showed little knowledge or understanding of the past efforts of some of the Catholic bishops to address the issue; others relied on a small number of commentators who themselves had an interest in the story; and many let their (understandable) outrage color their attitudes towards Church practices like clerical celibacy.

Fourth, journalists and commentators should pay attention to the things that can inflame a story about bad behavior by religious leaders or groups. This caution refers less to conscious things than to the unconscious things, those taken for granted. Ethno- or religiocentrism falls into this category. In reporting on less familiar groups, one often takes refuge in what one knows. That habit makes it easier to stir up the passions of those disposed to agree with the journalist's perspective.

Reporting on Religious Authority Complicit with Atrocity

For example, news reports of the Taliban destruction of the Bamiyan statues of the Buddha in 2001 (Hirst, n.d.) led to widespread condemnation of the group for a kind of cultural barbarism, without much attempt to understand the religious motivations at work in Afghanistan. Similar prejudicial elements can enter with varieties of anticlericalism where any action taken by a religious leader can carry an antidemocratic charge. Linguistic choices matter here. Many times news reports in the United States describe foreign governments as "theocratic" or, with some skepticism, point out the influence of clergy in government. The linguistic aspect runs more deeply, too, since conflicting linguistic terms may manifest a prejudice against a religious practice. Here journalists would do well to choose neutral terminology. Finally, journalists reporting the evils carried out by religious leaders or in the name or religion should keep in mind the fallacy of attributing to a religion the faults of individuals. Even when a reporter knows this, the very story of an atrocity can easily become linked to a religious group, as when Islam receives the blame for the actions of militant nationalists in Iraq.

Conclusion

Yes, religious individuals do occasionally do bad things, abuse their power, exercise undue influence over their followers, and stir up passions. Occasionally religious leaders have no one within their own group to call them to accountability for such evil. Journalists have an obligation to report on such things and on religion, perhaps even more so when religious groups violate some commonly accepted norms of human rights or of their own creed or commandments. Journalists must however, also avoid personal prejudice and cultural blindness, based on their lack of knowledge of culture or religion. In such reporting, journalists must exercise caution in holding a religious group to values alien to it. The journalist should point out what the religious group believes and how its adherents have acted.

The journalist or commentator's task is not an easy one in these situations. As we have seen, the situations themselves raise important ethical questions that go beyond the reporting task. These include the relation of religious groups to the news; the role of the news media vis-à-vis society; the preparation and training of journalists; the duty of journalists to the religious groups; the identification or definition of evil and the role of context and culture in understanding evil; and the role or justification of an outsider as critic of a religion or its leaders. Alongside of these concerns, the journalist must also remain self-conscious of personal attitudes and motives towards the story and towards religion.

Every religious group acknowledges that it, and its leadership, serves a higher power or authority and that its members and leadership are accountable. Even if they assert that God alone can judge, they still participate in human society and must in public ways. Here the journalist's role intersects with the role of religion – not as judge but as witness.

References

Briggs, K.A. (1990) Why editors miss important religion stories, in *Reporting Religion: Facts & Faith*, (ed. B. J. Hubbard), Polebridge Press, Sonoma, CA, pp. 47–58.

Christians, C., and Traber, M. (eds) (1997) *Communication Ethics and Universal Values*, Sage, Thousand Oaks, CA.

Churchill, W. (1948) *The Second World War* (Vols. 1–6), Houghton Mifflin, Boston, MA.

Cooper, T.W., Christians, C.G., Plude, F.F. *et al.* (eds) (1989) *Communication Ethics and Global Change*, Longman, White Plains, NY.

Dart, J. (2005) Foreword, in *Quoting God: How Media Shape Ideas about Religion and Culture*, (ed. C.H. Badaracco), Baylor University Press, Waco, TX, pp. xiii–xv.

Hirst, K K. (n.d.) Destruction of the Bamiyan statues: Taliban vs. the Buddha, http://archaeology.about.com/od/heritagemanagement/a/buddha.htm (accessed August 17, 2010).

Merrill, J.C. (1989) Global commonalities for journalistic ethics: Idle dream or realistic goal?, in *Communication Ethics and Global Change*, (eds T.W. Cooper, C.G. Christians, F.F. Plude *et al.*), Longman, White Plains, NY, pp. 284–290.

Silk, M. (1995) *Unsecular Media: Making News of Religion in America*, University of Illinois Press, Urbana.

Smith, C. (2004) Religiously ignorant journalists. *Books & Culture*, January, 6–7.

Soukup, P.A. (2002) Media and religion, *Communication Research Trends*, 21 (2), 3–37.

White, R.A. (2008) Teaching communication ethics in the African context: A response to globalization. Unpublished paper.

40

The Ethics of Representation and the Internet

Boniface Omachonu Omatta

Introduction

There is no doubt that the Internet, more than any other media, has widened the information landscape in the global world. This holds true because of the unprecedented and emerging rapid connectivity from the widespread availability of Internet technology. The Internet remains a major medium through which information on world affairs (politics, economy, education, religion, culture, business, medicine, etc.) is disseminated. It is a bearer of messages that influence our dispositions and ways of thinking. With users being active participants in online activities, the Internet cannot be considered a passive venue for the dissemination of information. It not only shapes the everyday lives of users, but it is also constantly in the making. There is no doubt that networking through the Internet has proved indispensable. It is common to say that we live in a global village. The Internet globalizes the local and localizes the global in such a way that one can read about events happening elsewhere; and activities in one's backyard are circulated with dispatch beyond frontiers. It has become a medium that erases time and space. Various religious, marginal cultural, and diasporic groups are making their voices heard on the Internet, through *self*-representation; rather than outsider representation. In principle, freedom of self-representation, more than ever, is open to many. The importance of the Internet in our everyday lives cannot be over emphasized. CNN reported in mid-December 2008 on a survey in the United States in which people were asked to choose whether to give up the Internet or sex. The majority of people surveyed chose to give up sex. They said that Internet is better than sex. It has been widely reported in the American press that President Barack Obama successfully used the Internet for campaigning and fundraising during his election

The Handbook of Global Communication and Media Ethics, First Edition. Edited by Robert S. Fortner and P. Mark Fackler.
© 2011 Blackwell Publishing Ltd. Published 2011 by Blackwell Publishing Ltd.

bid. His use of the Internet was said to be unprecedented. However, in spite of the touted good tidings arising from the Internet, there are troubling concerns that call for attention. It appears that the producers of Internet programs are so given to commercialization that consideration of ethics suffers a major blow. The spirit of the neoliberal economy tends to overshadow ideals. There is an expressed anxiety, sometimes, on the incompetence of those behind materials displayed on the net. Also worrying is the imbalance in the flow of information between northern and southern nations. In this case, Africa is mentioned as lagging behind in providing information on the Internet to the rest of the world. These concerns are posers for the authenticity of representation in cyberspace. I argue in this work that discerning the issue of representation and authenticity on the Internet requires cyberliteracy; which means more than knowing just how to use the Internet. Problematizing the concept of authenticity reveals how issues of representation, especially cultural and religious, should be approached without giving in to naiveté. This is vital in tracking the revolution taking place through the Internet.

Internet Technology: An Unparalleled Revolution

Internet technology is grandly revolutionary. Users, though diverse in nature, actively create content for the medium and are transforming the technology and as well being transformed by it. However, the Internet is a double-edged sword that has both merits and demerits.

Like many others, I see the Internet as an unprecedented and immeasurable revolution that spreads with unimaginable speed. It is as epoch-changing as Gutenberg's printing press. However, it is also quite different from Gutenberg's revolution in writing and printing. Gutenberg has been credited with transcending orality through the art of writing and printing, but the pace of that revolution was slow and steady. According to Newby (2004, p. 45), it took many centuries for this revolution to be felt in all parts of the globe. However, the Internet, within a short period of time, and in varying degrees, has reached everywhere. The Internet is not only unique in the speed with which it spread. It has also changed the global equation in all walks of life be it democracy, economy, education, or religion. It is apropos here to quote directly from Dawson (2004, p. 385) thus:

> Media are not neutral or passive conduits for the transfer of information. They mold the message in ways that crucially influence the world views we construct. They adjust our self-conceptions, notions of human relations and community, and the nature of reality itself. Unlike previous media, however, the Internet has blossomed almost overnight, and its astonishing growth is proceeding at an accelerating pace.

Much is contained in this passage. Primarily, it acknowledges how the Internet is both bearer and the message. Users of the Internet cannot pretend neutrality. Human relationship is profoundly altered. Dawson (2004, p. 386) argues further that the Internet is very interactive, relatively less expensive to use and truly global in outreach. The interactivity engendered by the Internet is unsurpassed in the history of communication. Time and space are shrinking in its wake. In the mind of Mitra (2002, p. 27), people are spared long waits for information. This happens because the "traditional boundaries and hurdles to information availability simply evaporate" in the widened horizon of cyberspace. Even those confined by geography, like Al-Qaeda, can reach out to the world and create global events.

The walls hampering communication circulation are breaking down with the presence of Internet. An unforeseeable era of freedom of interaction and communication has come upon humanity. Dawson (2004, p. 389) describes this freedom as an "escape from the established restrictions" rampant in various societies. Any person with a little computer knowledge can launch a webpage. This freedom constantly defies regulations. Nevertheless, a lack of control of the web means that anything enlightening, humorous, or unsavory, can be discovered there. Many voices can and do surge forward about various issues; however rules for detecting valid or authentic material remain elusive. The challenge posed by the competing voices on the net is for that which is most appealing to a searcher at a particular time rather than what is true, useful, or authentic. This means that the apparent authentic voice, as Mitra calls it, may not be the truly authentic one. Mitra (2002, p. 28) says: "In cyberspace it is the discursive power of the speakers that becomes most important." Moreover, even when netizens are able to determine the real voice to trust, they must also pay attention to the fact that the speaker can tailor his/her message to appeal to prejudice or preconceptions. According to Mitra, "trustworthy voices bring the ideological baggage that implicates the speaking positions." Weighing representations and other materials on the Internet urgently calls for vigorous action.

The response of netizens to this call for urgency may not be uniform. They do not all share the same attitudes or dispositions. Dawson (2004, p. 393) relying on the work of Annette Markham, identifies three ways by which users relate to the Internet. The first group sees the Internet as a tool that is merely used. For the second group the Internet is more than a tool; it is a home or an environment where one lives with others. The third group is similar to the second, in which the Internet is integral and coterminous with one's life, but with this group, indispensability and inseparability of the Internet from human activities is underscored. Using these three categories of users, it is clear that the ability to judge the authenticity of representation online greatly depend on the group one belongs to.

The first category of users could be said to exhibit narrow mindedness by taking the Internet as a mere tool (see Karaflogka, 2002, p. 288; Scheifinger, 2008, p. 234). It makes it dangerous since users can easily fall prey to negative impacts of the online materials. As aforementioned, cyberspace is not neutral. If that is the fact, how can the Internet be a mere tool to be used? For instance, the second category of users would be very unlikely to bother about the dividing line between virtuality and reality. As a matter of fact, there is no demarcation between real and virtual for this group. Everything found on the Internet is real; hence the urgency we already advocated for would matter less to this group. Definitely, the concern of authenticity of representation makes no difference. I think Brody's warning of information naiveté could be useful for this class of users in their disposition towards the Internet. According Brody (2008, p. 1124) information naiveté is the willingness of netizens to accept everything online to be valid. This type of disposition is dangerous according to Brody (2008, p. 1125) because "the electronic information environment encourages the delivery of bits of information that have been removed from their contexts." Hackett (2006, p. 73) concurs: "As professors we are supposed to warn our students of the trivial, if not duplicitous, content of many websites." Hackett is a distinguished professor in the study of religion at the University of Tennessee in America and is very much concerned about information naiveté as she acknowledges that in cyberspace, a thin line exists between reality and virtuality. The undeniable actuality of the high possibility of trivial material being available online should discourage any form of information naiveté. The third group may be better equipped and enabled to evaluate the authenticity of online materials. Conceiving cyberspace as part and parcel of their lives, may motivate them to approach it with critical seriousness.

These three categories of netizens are not exhaustive. Mitra's (2002, 29) push beyond classification on how netizens behave on the Internet, is helpful here. First, Mitra agrees that neither pessimistic nor optimistic perspectives on the Internet are tenable. Pessimistic attitudes lead to information-rejection – with every representation in cyberspace considered untrustworthy. However, adopting an optimistic perspective seems to require a positive disposition to accord validity to any voice on the Internet that is confirmed as credible. According to Mitra, it is more realistic to strike a midpoint between pessimistic and optimistic perspectives, since neither of the two is fully realizable. I would even suggest that we go beyond classification of users. It could happen that a user of the Internet drifts between one perspective and the other. At one moment he behaves as if the Internet were a mere tool; at another time, as if it is more than a tool. Use actually occurs along a continuum of effort uses. Ultimately, it is important for netizens to be cyber-literate to discover the immensity and complexity of the Internet. The open possibility of the cyberspace is still nascent. The ability of Internet audiences to judge the authentic representation online needs enormous effort.

Problematizing the Concept of Authenticity

It is the intention here to veer into the problematic nature of the concept of authenticity. It is not to be taken for granted that its meaning is easily understood. For instance, does authenticity imply originality? Equally, how does originality remain unaffected and for how long? If changes occur in the original over the course of time, does it make what was authentic inauthentic?

The concept of authenticity subsists in fluidity. What it meant in one era changes over time, as does context. It is an indication that the concept itself is still in the making. Emphasis on authenticity appears to be recent. According to Starn

(2002, p. 8), the sharpened attention paid to the idea of authenticity emerged in the 1990s. For him, historically, there was no clear precedence in the construction of the concept of authenticity. What Starn referred to was the policy started by the World Heritage Group to determine monuments that would qualify for inclusion on the World Heritage list. He tried to show how difficult it was to arrive at the criteria for evaluating an authentic monument. As Starn (2002, p. 3) writes, "the concept of authenticity is fuzzy and an easy target for criticism." There were some monuments that were repaired in an attempt to preserve them. This mending process generated heated debate as to whether the amended monuments were still original. There no were quick solutions to the tension. The uneasy tension could make some suggest giving up the idea of authenticity.

In the mind of Adam Phillips, the idea of authenticity is difficult to pin point due to the contention surrounding it. Phillips (2007, p. 37) however, argues that the essentialistic understanding of authenticity may not be relevant anymore. There was a time then when authenticity was viewed in terms of valuable essences. Phillips (2007, p. 38) likens authenticity to the idea of phantom-limb effect, where "an absence acknowledged through an apparent presence – is clearly at work in the idea of authenticity." Phillips discredited what he was made to believe as child that he had a true and authentic self. To his dismay later on life, he discovered that there is nothing like a given authentic self. Phillips shows how the tone of authenticity has changed in the three examples used in "The authenticity issues." (Phillips, 2007). The first example was that of the poet John Clare who saw authenticity as ascription. The feeling of pleasure and pain in what he read during childhood had an impact on him because he allowed them authenticity. For Clare, authenticity is something one confers. The second example comes from John Banville's great novel *The Newton Letter* (1982), the story of a man who discovered his multiple personalities by falling in love with more than one woman at time. He came to realize that his authenticity consisted in dividedness of selves. Therefore, for him, authenticity is not something true or real – but rather giving up such possibilities. One's authenticity resides then in knowing that the real and authentic has no center. The third example came from Wendy Lesser, an American writer of a memoir *Room for Doubt*. She viewed authenticity as something that is accepted without doubt – in adopting the credulous mind of a child. Authenticity here is built on blind trust. The three examples Phillips selected reveal how fluid the concept of authenticity is.

The work of Chhabra (2005) *Defining Authenticity and Its Determinants: Toward an Authenticity Flow Model* further problematizes authenticity. This work explained how determination of the authenticity of Scottish goods sold by vendors in the United States and Canada depended more on the process of negotiation than on essentialist understanding. The different parties – producers, suppliers or vendors and receivers or tourists are all coopted in determining an authentic Scottish heritage product. Different ways of perceiving the authenticity of heritage sales are echoed by various authors mentioned by Chhabra (2005, p. 65). For Asplet and Cooper (2000), goods are taken to be authentic if they are locally made.

Authenticity according to Cohen (1988) is a social construction and serves as a critique of the essentialist view of MacCannell (1989). The authenticity of heritage material is also said to have been constantly distorted as the work of Hollinshead (1998) and Bhabha (1994) show. What Chhabra tries to demonstrate is that setting criteria for determining authentic heritage is not simple.

There is also a struggle among the population of Israel to define clearly what it means to be an authentic Jew. Jews belong to three major religious groups – orthodox, conservative, and liberal. The tendency is for one group to deny the others authenticity. With secularism where individuals have the freedom to follow the promptings of their hearts, there are bound to be multiple ways to act as a Jew. Charmé (2000) reflected on the challenges of how to know an authentic Jew. For him, different understandings of authenticity exist side by side and no single perspective can resolve the challenges. For instance, does being an authentic Jew entail loyalty to tradition or continuity with Jewish identity? The constitutive elements of Jewish tradition and identity are not givens. Therefore, there is no certified criteria to determine who is an authentic Jew.

Another work worth mentioning in laying out the problem of authenticity is by Tariq Mustafa (2008). Mustafa set out to take advantage of science to analyze the status of authenticity in matters of revelation. Mustafa sees authenticity of revelation based only on faith to be insufficient. The primary concern for him is detecting an authentic revelation from the multitude of claims to divine revelation. In order to be able to differentiate authentic revelation from false ones, Mustafa suggests several criteria. Some of his 15-point criteria are useful in this examination. For him, revelation should be consistent and free from contradictions; its appeal should be based on rational grounds and must not depend on blind faith; it should contain information that can be verified or rejected; the character, conduct, and behavior of the bearer of the message should be worthy of emulation. But the criteria themselves are not free of challenges. For instance, who determines whether a claimant to revelation is of questionable character or not? What are the grounds for setting these criteria? The issue of determining authenticity of revelation still looms large.

As Chidester (2005, p. 190) observes, authenticity of religion and religious practices is often contested. In fact, some bluntly declare the idea of religion to be merely human invention and hence not authentic. Yet, some religions are still seen as authentic while others are not. The determination of authenticity becomes more problematic too, in the presence of an avalanche of virtual religions that often mock the so called true religions. The fact that virtual religions exist as either a mockery or critical review of the established religions implies that all is not well with religion. The use of rationality during the Enlightenment to probe the reasonableness of Christian claims of revelation is tantamount to doubting the authenticity of religious practice in general. Although some cases of fraudulent activities in the name of religion are easily verified and discredited, not all cases can be.

Chidester (2005, p. 193) shows that religious authenticity consists of one religion declaring the other false, or declaring some internal claims within a religion to be heresies. The Roman Catholic Church in the medieval era excommunicated many on the basis of apparent heresies. The great reformation of Luther in the sixteenth century was also a critical indictment of Roman Catholic orthodoxy. Today, which Christian group among the myriad denominations could be said to be the authentic Christianity? This question applies to other world religions such as Islam, Hinduism, Buddhism, and traditional religions all of which are split into various voices claiming to be authentically speaking for a religion. Chidester (2005, p. 212) suggests that since so called fake religions all have serious impacts on the lives of people, they be allowed authenticity. For him, they are at worst real or authentic, even if fraudulent. Alberts (2008, p. 137) corroborates Chidester in according authenticity to apparently false religions. Alberts is convinced that "authenticity in religion is not a status to be determined" without question.

The many instances of the conundrum surrounding the idea of authenticity establish the difficulty experienced when considering the authenticity of representation on the Internet. The mediated nature of online material is indisputable. This mediatedness allows producers to remove things from their original context by way of abstraction. This can happen in such a way that what netizens see on the Internet is some steps removed from what it should be. A lot of simulations and imitations can occur with online materials. We have noted before that the Internet does not provide an easy way to determine authenticity. This difficulty doubles as netizens attempt to judge the authenticity of online representations because of the increasing virtuality of cyberspace. The ability to evaluate also depends on the kind of user one is. There are users whose ability to judge the authenticity of online representation is attenuated. We should also not forget that the line separating the authentic from the false is not clear either in online or offline representations.

Issues of Representation: Cultural and Religious

There is hardly any world discipline or activity that cannot be represented in cyberspace. We are aware that political advocates, commerce, healthcare providers, education, and business enterprises all use the Internet in sophisticated ways. Here we have chosen to examine cultural and religious representations. Whatever we say about these two areas however is also relevant to others. Our focus will be on how cultural and religious groups exploit the opportunity available on the Internet for making their voices heard globally. First, cultural representation.

One of the opportunities offered by the Internet is freedom of self-representation. Before the presence of cyberspace, several barriers prevented some cultural units from reaching out to the world (Mitra, 2002, p. 29). This is no longer the case. Marginalized voices are now heard on the Internet. Landzelius (2006a, p. 1) calls it homing on cyberspace. When we discuss cultural representation, we pay attention more to indigenous people whom Landzelius says have been isolated and denied access to the mainstream affairs of society. The same holds for diaspora of minority groups who live in communities where ruling cultural norms dominate that often exclude them from the centre of political and economic influence. These diasporic groups are able to find ways of being at home online thus avoiding the nostalgia of disconnection from their lands of origin.

The point at issue is not whether indigenous or diasporic groups make a home in cyberspace, but to what extent online homing is authentically a home. This is the aspect that appears problematic in indigenizing Internet technology. Normally, home is associated with a place and to be identified as belonging to a home implies being part of a place. This idea of home is now contradicted by online homing, which is not dependent on physical place. Invariably, the idea of home has been transformed. When we talk of indigenous cyberactivism (Landzelius, 2006a), we must recognize that it mainly happens in the high-tech countries of Europe and North America. That explains why most examples of natives on the Internet are from these countries. Illustrations of indigenous cyberactivism rarely come from African countries. Despite the global spread of the Internet, Africa features few if any examples.

We shall pinpoint some examples of indigenous cyberactivism from Landzelius (2006a, pp. 7ff), to demonstrate how indigenous people participate in mainstream affairs, thanks to cyberspace. The Navajo people in the southwestern part of United States of America can now engage in activities that were not possible before the advent of the Internet. With computer-mediated communications they were able to break barriers that excluded them for years. The environment in which they live is so rugged that it hampers physical connectivity. With electronic voting they now participate in electoral processes that were hitherto difficult. In Canada, too, there is a drive by the government to get every part of the country connected through cyberspace. The remotest places that are difficult to reach physically are provided with basic services – elearning, ejustice, ecommerce and ehealth, through the Internet. The first areas of Canada on its margins are drawn into the center through the Internet. Other instances of indigenous people gaining visibility and empowerment through the Internet are many. We mention only a few of them: the Zapatista group that put up strong electronic campaign of protest against the Mexican government; the Ngati Awa natives from New Zealand reclaiming their rightful place previously denied them. However, the virtuality of their representation on the Internet has both merits and demerits.

Diasporic groups use the Internet to register their presence and connectedness to their places of origin. It is a kind of speaking out on behalf of their distant members. Most diasporic cyber activities take place in industrialized nations by people who experience a form of nostalgia about estrangement from home. Sometimes the planners of the diasporic cyber-representation, in connection with their place of origin, have never had any physical contact with their homeland. The actuality of such people belonging to the claimed place of origin calls into question the real identity of some diasporic persons. Few diasporic instances can be given. There are two chat sites (*Planet Tonga* and *The Kava Bowl*), created by diasporic groups from of Pacific island of Tonga who claim to speak for the community. Franklin (2004, p. 5) gives the history of how Taholo Kami set up the Pacific Forum as an online meeting place for Tongans suffering from loneliness. The first challenge that arose was the issue of determining belongingness through language identity. Evidently, not all the diasporic members are fluent in (or even speak) their native language; thus it became a big issue to decide which language to use as a medium of communication. Nevertheless, through cyberspace youth, both at home and in the diaspora, opened their culture to the wider world. They gained empowerment through the chat site, although their activities were virtually constituted. There is also the example of second-generation Harari youth from Ethiopia whose parents departed for the West years ago. Some of these youth have not experienced what it means to be Ethiopian by actually living in Ethiopia. However, such youth, through cyberspace, claim Ethiopian identity and speak on behalf of their assumed homeland. Composing life or home online will definitely reconfigure the idea of locality and life offline. The Burundian Hutus and Tutsi exemplified the advantage of virtuality, in creating fora in cyberspace to initiate healing of wounds after their bitter war. Both diasporas and those at home participated online in building relationship that went beyond ethnic divides.

As Landzelius (2006b, p. 297) indicated, although cyberspace makes empowerment of the indigenous and diasporic people possible, it is not automatic and uniform. The result varies from instance to instance. What is undeniable is that many of the marginalized people are creating a home in cyberspace, and in so doing they are transforming the cyber-environment. Freedom in cyberspace has provided the means to put an end to marginalization and denial, and to provide entre into the mainstream.

Dominant institutions and nations also go online evidenced through different nations of the world creating websites. Volcic (2008) carried out significant work on how the former Yugoslav States took advantage of Internet technology to represent themselves to the world. The websites of these nations represent national territories, histories, products, and citizens as commodities to be marketed to the rest of the world. Volcic calls this branding a nation online for outsiders to experience. What is particularly import in this work is the possibility offered by cyberspace to these nations to self-represent rather than allowing outside representation to define them. Yet, such representation of a nation's self is influenced by the dynamics of the neoliberal economy of commodification. Branding a self-image to conform to the neoliberal environment raises serious doubts about whether such representation leaves behind the actual history and situation (Volcic, 2008, p. 396). In the end, it may be difficult to find valuable and historically true information on the websites of such nations that critically carry the past into the present. It is for this reason that some critical media scholars advise nations to go beyond commodification in their self-branding on the Internet. Volcic (2008, p. 197), mentioned scholars who are not comfortable with a nation's self-representation as commodified goods to be marketed. The implication is that when users go to these national websites they find an apparently real picture that is far removed from what is true. Thus, they may carry with them misleading impressions of these nations. National self-representation is inevitably connected to authenticity.

The presence of religion on the Internet defies tracking. Different religions and denominations have their websites where one can read about them. It is true that today, through the Internet, a great number of people are able to read about religion and discuss it with other people without restrictions. Dawson (2004) enumerates various religious activities that can be executed online. These range from searching scriptures with electronic indexes, viewing churches and religious centers, joining in rituals and meditation practices; watching religious videos, listening to religious music, sermons, prayers, and testimonies, and having discourses with religious leaders. With this undeniable global spread of computer mediated communication, individuals and groups can easily post their messages. Consequently, interactive responses are generated which in turn advance discussions to a higher level.

Ihejirika Chikwendu emphasizes the role of the different media types in religious conversion: for instance, his elaborate presentation of the Redeemed Christian Church of God's use of different media types for evangelization. He underscores a vital point when he affirms that the Internet offers more opportunities and accessibility to people patronizing the Redeemed Christian Ministry than either television programs or print media ever did. He avers: "With the provision of free email boxes, members have greater possibility of communicating among themselves and with the leaders of the church" (Chikwendu, 2004, p. 129). People can more quickly participate online in religious activities such as prayer and healing that take place at the church's church centers. The Redeemed Church is only singled out here as one of the many examples of religious use of the Internet. The Redeemed Church was founded in Nigeria by pastor Adeboye. It's website www.rccg.com contains much information about the Church. The interactive congeniality of the Internet is also underscored by Muhammed Haron (2004, p. 154) when writing on the role of the media in both religious and social change within the Muslim communities of South Africa.

Self-declared prophets, shamen, and gurus also create various sites to propagate their belief systems. The number of religious sites is so many that we are still counting. Dawson (2004, p. 387) lists some of them. Delocalization of religion also occurs via the Internet; a situation where the Internet becomes the point of contact for online religions. In fact, for such a religion, we cannot talk of a physical place of origin. There are also numerous virtual religions that utilize the cyberspace to register their presence. Chidester (2005, pp. 200ff) provided an extensive list of virtual religions.

Chidester carried out an extensive study of one set of religious beliefs in his work "Credo Mutwa, Zulu Shaman: The Invention and Appropriation of Indigenous Authenticity in African Folk Religion." He painstakingly reviewed the life and work of Mutwa in this study. According to Chidester, Mutwa was born in 1921 to a Christian father and a traditional religionist mother. The story claimed that when Mutwa became seriously ill, he turned to the religion of his mother for solutions. Mutwa later understood his illness to be an incident ushering him into his mission as an "indigenous healer, diviner and seer" (Chidester, 2004, p. 72). This singular event laid the foundation for Mutwa as an authentic representative of the indigenous

The Ethics of Representation and the Internet   795

religion of the Zulu. Mutwa consequently declared himself to be the witchdoctor of the Zulu. He claimed to have inherited this role from his maternal grandfather, who had cured his previous illness. According to Chidester's account (2006, p. 74), Mutwa became "officially known" as the high sanusi of the Zulu people. With this appropriated title, Mutwa presented himself as an authentic high sanusi who possessed "specialized indigenous knowledge that could be used in healing, divination, education, and social transformation" (Chidester, 2004, p. 76).

He continued his mission of propagating African Traditional Religion (ATR) far and wide within South Africa. His activities caught the attention of many observers at the time. In 1954 he got a job in a curio shop in Johannesburg that was devoted to providing African artifacts for tourists. Indeed, the reason for employing Mutwa at this centre was that the "employer, A. S. Watkinson, relied on him to authenticate these objects of African arts" (Chidester, 2004, p. 72). Relying on Mutwa for the authentication of these materials made sense because, Watkinson believed in him as an embodiment of the Zulu tradition. Mutwa later moved to Soweto to attend to another traditional African tourist centre.

Mutwa persuasively presented himself as an imaginative storyteller. These stories he claimed, were drawn from the authentic pool of Zulu traditional beliefs. These stories were so appealing that Watkinson sponsored a collection of them for publication (Mutwa, 1964, 1966). However, there were questions as to whether Mutwa's imaginative presentation of the Zulu tribal history and tradition was not at variance with what was commonly known. This question cast doubt on Mutwa's originality because the "extravagant and imaginative poetry and prose of these texts bore little if any relation to anything previously recorded in print about Zulu religion" (Chidester, 2004, p. 74).

Mutwa's motivating goal was to develop an indigenous African tradition in Zulu land that was totally different from foreign traditions. Most importantly for Mutwa this provided the South African Black race with the ability to maintain their authentic traditions through a separate life. In Mutwa's mind apartheid was a good opportunity for the Zulu people to preserve their original traditions from dilution that would ensue when it mixed with the white culture. Mutwa (1966, pp. 319–323; 1998, p. 13) says: "Apartheid is the high law of the Gods! It is the highest law of nature." For him "white men of South Africa are only too right when they wish to preserve their pure-bred racial identity." His message was negatively received by black South Africans. Even though Mutwa may have had a good mission to develop an authentic indigenous tradition in South Africa, the context of apartheid that he embraced did not convince his people. That may explain why Mutwa's enormous achievement through his writing and activities for many years as a high Zulu witchdoctor did not endear him to the black people of South Africa.

The terrain for Mutwa changed with the arrival of the Internet. His message began to be displayed on different websites allowing it to reach many new people. According to Chidester (2004, p. 76), "Credo Mutwa's indigenous authenticity had become global on the Internet" and hence "played an important role in a new global cultural village on the Internet." For instance, apart from the sponsorship

Mutwa received from the Ringing Rocks Foundation (established in Philadelphia in 1995), it has "promised Credo Mutwa a healing center in the cyberspace" (Chidester, 2004, p. 77).

Through the Internet Mutwa established himself as the authentic bearer of African indigenous knowledge. Consequently, according to Chidester, his authenticity was appropriated by many groups for their own projects. "For example, Credo Mutwa has been enthusiastically promoted by the African-American feminist Luisah Teish, who has her own website *Jambalaya Spirit*, celebrating feminist myths and rituals" (Chidester, 2004, p. 82). Undoubtedly then, the Internet has been inundated by the message of Mutwa as the authentic embodiment of indigenous religious and traditional knowledge. The enormous reach of cyberspace mediating Mutwa's activities gained him global notoriety, which invariably contributed to new popularity at home. Chidester noted that Mutwa's people in South Africa regarded his activities as false. They viewed his appropriation of indigenous authenticity of African folk religion as untrue. For them, whatever Mutwa did was no more than fake religion. Hence, the South African media portrayed Mutwa as "a fake, a fraud, and a charlatan," who did not represent an "authentic voice of indigenous African religion as he appears in cyberspace" (Chidester, 2004, p. 83). It is clear here that while Mutwa's appropriation of indigenous folk religion attracted condemnation in his homeland it gained him recognition on the global scene. According to Chidester (2004, p. 83), the reason for the global acceptance of Mutwa's authenticity was "[i]n the cyberspace, any line that might divide folk religion from fake religion has been blurred." In other words, the dichotomy between authenticity and fraud is too close to call in cyberspace. With this vital contribution, Chidester has opened a portal for addressing the divide between the authentic and the fraud.

When deliberating about how to champion ATR through the Internet in preparation for a conference in Nigeria 2008, I came across the website www.yorubareligion.org, I quickly sent it for comment to Ray Sesan Aina, who is a Yoruba person and a PhD student in theological ethics at the Katholieke Universiteit Leuven. He sent me an email with an evaluation of the information and claims appearing on the website. Part of the response reads:

> thanks for the info and the site. I have looked at it; and it has not dampened my skepticism which I expressed earlier today before I even checked the site. I admire the so-called high-priest's effort. Nevertheless, I think he is preying too much on oyinbo ignorance. For starters, one person cannot be a high priest [and there is even no 'high priest' in yoruba traditional religious system of belief; there is kekere awo – an initiate under tutelage – and there is agba awo – fully initiated and commissioned awo] for many deities to the point of mentioning ... It is an exaggeration to state on the website that his father initiated him into all the Yoruba irumole. There are 401 deities in the Yoruba pantheon and they do not command worship in all the places of Yorubaland. So how could his father have done this when he lived and died in Osogbo?

His response raises the authenticity issue of the claims of the high priest who created this site.

The Ethics of Representation and the Internet   797

Aina's response spurred me formulate questions and schedule an interview with Prince (Babalawo) Adigun Olosun at his base in Germany. The interview did finally take place at the IYA DUDU centre in Germany on June 8, 2008. The following are questions were used in the interview:

1   How was it possible, as indicated on your website, that you could be initiated into the cults of many deities?
2   Does the concept of high priest exist in Yoruba religion?
3   Has the Yoruba religion been officially recognized in Germany?
4   What is the desirability of Yoruba religion in Germany?
5   How has the Internet helped in promoting Yoruba religion globally?

Prince Olosun took his time to address my questions. First, he started with his own brief history. He said he was born a leader of Yoruba Traditional Religion (YTR). Born as a High Priest and to a well-known High Priest, Prince Iyanda Olayiwola-Olosun and Priestess, Anike Olayiwola-Olosun in YTR. He also lived with an Austrian woman, Susanne Wenger, who was a strong devotee of the religion. When he was born, as the tradition among YTR practitioners demands, his parents divined to know what nature had in store (his odu) for him. It was revealed that he was born a High Priest of Ifa, Ogun, Sango, Obatala, Osun, Oke, Ori, and Egbe, and so forth. It also indicated that he must receive a Western education to the highest level in order to prepare him for the modern challenges in YTR. His father then initiated him immediately to all the Irunmoles. His father also made sure that he would receive adequate knowledge to equip him in his future role as the High Priest of YTR.

He was subsequently able to study Ethnology, Education, History, Journalism, Media and Yoruba in Universities in Nigeria, Germany, and the United Kingdom in fulfillment of his destiny. He claimed also to be a trained Yoruba teacher and had worked in schools in Nigeria teaching Yoruba and had continued the same activities in Germany, Europe, and other parts of the world. According to him he published the first Yoruba religion language magazine "Akede Asa" in the early 1980s, and today he is still the publisher and editor-in-chief of *Ase* magazine. This magazine's aim is to simplify YTR for practitioners and nonpractitioners. *Ase* is presently published in German and in English.

After his brief introduction he addressed my questions. His answer to question one was that the cult of most of the deities is in Osogbo and environs. Besides that, he said, one does not need to go to the different shrines before he or she can be initiated. The presence of a priest is all that is required for an initiation. As a child, he said, his father initiated him into all the Irunmoles in the presence of the priest. In answering question two, he said that the idea of agbaowa (i.e., elder priest) could be regarded as high priest in Yoruba religion and that it was ifa that revealed that he would be a High Priest. He answered questions three and four together: that because of their famous activities and the desirability of YTR in Germany, it has now been officially recognized and accorded all legal status. Germany has become the international headquarters for (his own brand of) YTR.

He answered the fifth question with greater enthusiasm. He underscored the pertinence of the Internet in the promotion of YTR. According to him it was the realization of the indispensability of the Internet that spurred him to study media in the United Kingdom in 2001. He became the first person to open a website for YTR. As he said, without the Internet his religion could not have achieved as much it had. For him, the *Ase* magazine has less outreach than the Internet. The Internet allowed him to reach out to a wider audience and in some cases carry out online services such as divination, naming ceremonies, marriages, and so forth. Moreover, the website (www.yorubareligion.org) contains all necessary information about his religion. The opportunity provided by the Internet gave them the space and freedom to practice YTR. The limitation imposed by location and authority was reduced by the availability of the Internet. One can locate them online and obtain their services and teaching. They often refer to themselves as the ibile faith congregation online.

However, the achievement and progress made by Prince Olosun and his congregation online does not convince Aina. The part of Aina's email which says "it is an exaggeration to state on the website that his father initiated him into all the Yoruba irumole" questions the authenticity of the claims of the high priest. His criticism is in the line with the local condemnation of appropriation of indigenous religions authenticity. Perhaps Aina's response would change if he read the report of my interview with Prince Olosun. Meanwhile, YTR is globally recognized. Its teaching and practices are being accepted at the international level.

Afe Adogame underscores the global reach of African Traditional Religions (ATR) as a result of the Internet. For him, African indigenous religion's global spread cuts across racial lines. For instance, it is not only diasporic Africans that practice ATR; many non-African Americans have become priests and founders of neoindigenous African religions such as Ifa and Orisha religions in America. Interestingly, these priests easily "operate and communicate through their Internet websites with old and new clientele as well as with wider public" (Adogame, 2007, p. 531). According to Adogame, no other media gives African indigenous religion as much visibility as does the Internet, especially at the international level. However, one reality observed from the many websites on ATR, is that they are mainly created and run by people in diaspora. This may not be unconnected to Africa's lag in fully joining the information age, which could have more ethical implications there than for any other continent.

Cyberliteracy and Ethical Questions

Traditionally, literacy implies being able to read and write. Cyberliteracy, too, implies being able to use the Internet. However, I want to go further than that in using this term. I agree with Laura Gurak who reminds us of the expanded meaning of literacy. Gurak (2001, p. 9) quotes from Kathleen Welch (1999) in explaining that literacy is

> not only the ability to read and write but an activity of mind ... capable of recognizing and engaging substantive issues along with the ways that minds, sensibilities, and emotions are constructed by and within communities whose members communicate

The Ethics of Representation and the Internet   799

through specific technologies. In other words, literacy has to do with consciousness: how we know what we know and a recognition of the historical, ideological and technological forces that inevitably operate in all human beings.

This way of understanding literacy is very important in the area of the Internet. The complexity and intriguing reality of cyberspace calls everyone to abandon a minimalistic view of the Internet. It is no longer sufficient merely to know how to use the Internet. The reason for this kind of literacy definition is self-evident. It reveals enormous hidden entanglements that are not easily discernible in information technology itself. According to Gurak (2001, p. 12) there are "economic and political forces that are shaping information technologies" that users may not be aware of. These "invisible" forces direct these technologies to be in line with vested interests. They are thus not free from social, political, and economic undertones. The issue of who has control over information is at stake. In most cases, there is no privacy for personal information. Copyright regulations largely benefit the few corporations that lobby for protection. This restriction better serves the interest of lobbyists and corporations than individuals. Take for instance, the involvement of Microsoft in determining the growth and direction of cyberspace. Franklin (2004, p. 226) comments: "Corporate giants such as Microsoft "discovered" the commercial potential of the Internet as a mass market(ing) medium and have turned their significant economic and meaning-making resources to molding Internet technologies after their own image."

The commercialization of the Internet is one way for these corporations to decide the direction of the cyberspace. The Internet should not be oriented primarily as a commodity to sell. The vision planned for the Internet should be oriented to benefiting the public interest. The public must be cyberliterate to be aware of this. What cyberliteracy really means for users is the ability to know about the unwritten forces that bend technologies to yield the highest gains to a few interested parties rather than the public. Through cyberliteracy, users will develop critical approaches to the Internet by calling for active participation in giving direction to this technology. The vested interest groups would not be emboldened to give direction to the cyberspace by way of commercialization. However, several ethical questions emerge in the way cyberspace technology is operated.

The ethical challenges of information technologies are making great impact. Smith and Carbo (2008) bring to our notice the rising interest in information ethics. They discussed how the term appeared in public in the early-1980s. After a long period of development, there is now an *International Journal of Information Ethics* that deals with information related ethics. This work shows how urgent it has become to address ethical problems posed by information technologies, especially cyberspace. The journal basically points out that there are various ethical wrongs associated with information technologies. These wrongs include unjustified exploitation, misappropriation of indigenous knowledge, and incompetence. Mojica (2006, p. 204) also points out how nonexperts and incompetent people engage in creating material content for wikis that people access via Wikipedia. Control of the creators of information by vetting the qualification of those involved is long overdue. As Arnautu (2006, p. 24) maintains, information ethics touches human life so very deeply that it should be taken seriously.

Brody's notion of information naiveté is at the heart of ethical challenges facing cyberspace. She argues that information naiveté bedevils the creators as well as the recipients of information. According to Brody (2008, p. 1126) information naiveté has the tendency to move both creators and recipients of information to overconfidence. The danger for producers is that they fail to warn the public of the apparent limitations associated with Internet material. This can mislead those who access the information in the dark, trusting possibly untrustworthy material from the net and perhaps acting on it foolishly or otherwise inappropriately. Brody calls for some form of regulation to enable monitoring of the process of information production.

Another aspect that poses ethical problems is the lack of intercultural consideration in the creation of information. This disability finds expression in disequilibrium in information flow. As noted earlier information technologies are socially, culturally, politically, and economically oriented. Those who control these technologies run them from their own perspective. Information flow is mostly one directional – from North to South. One example that is often used is between the West and Africa. Capurro (2008, p. 1166) maintains that such values as *Ubuntu* could make a good contribution to ethical development for information. *Ubuntu* connotes the idea of belonging together; so that whatever one does aims to benefit every other person. In this spirit, the commercialization of information technologies that overlook the public interest is less likely. It would also mean that Africa could be part of the developing information society. We should also remember that the level of accessibility to the Internet varies from place to place. Arnold (2002, p. 341) notes that there, "is an issue of the Third and Fourth Worlds getting access to this powerful medium of the First-World technology." Without maximum accessibility to the technology in Africa, the possibility of making contributions that reflect cultural values will be limited. My personal experience in Nigeria indicates that Internet availability in individual homes is scarce. A person can hope to access the Internet at cyber cafes, but not without encountering difficulties.

Conclusion

The Internet is a central medium of communication. Its connective power has made it possible for users to avoid waiting for information. It connects people and things in a manner previously unknown in communication history. As it is not under strict regulatory policy, it provides maximum freedom for representation of material. However, unrestricted freedom can easily allow untrustworthy material to appear. Users are not always aware of the inherent possibility for representation of inauthentic material (admittedly the idea of authenticity remains elusive). It is therefore important for every user, as Gurak insists, to navigate the Internet with awareness. The capacities of users to judge the authenticity of representation without critical alertness is highly unlikely to occur without new methods to alert them or without an increase in cyberliteracy. Without the means to evaluate representation fully, the Internet will remain a double-edged sword that will deceive, misinform, and abuse.

References

Adogame, A. (2007) Sub-Saharan Africa, in *Religion, Globalization and Culture*, vol. 6, (ed. P. Beyer and L. Beaman), Brill, Leiden, Boston, pp. 527–547.

Alberts, T. (2008) Virtuality real: Fake religions and problems of authenticity in religion. *Culture and Religion*, 9 (2), 125–139.

Arnautu, R. (2006) Prolegomena to digital communication ethics. *JSRI*, 13, 23–31.

Arnold, P.P. (2002) Determining the place of religion: Native American traditions and the www. *Religion*, 32, 337–341.

Asplet, M. and Cooper, M. (2000) Cultural designs in New Zealand souvenir clothing: The question of authenticity. *Tourism Management*, 21, 301–312.

Bhabha, H. (1994) *The Location of Culture*, Routledge, London.

Brody, R. (2008) The problem of information naiveté. *Journal of the American Society for Information Technology*, 59 (7), 1124–1127.

Capurro, R. (2008) Information ethics for and from Africa. *Journal of the American Society for Information Science and Technology*, 59 (7), 1162–1170.

Charmé, S.Z. (2000) Varieties of authenticity in contemporary Jewish identity. *Jewish Social Studies*, 6 (2), 133–155.

Chhabra, D. (2005) Defining authenticity and its determinants: Toward an authenticity flow mode.. *Journal of Travel Research*, 44, 64–73.

Chidester, D. (2004) Credo Mutwa, Zulu Shaman: The invention and appropriation of indigenous authenticity in African Folk Religion, in *Religion, Politics, and Identity in a Changing South Africa*, (ed. D. Chidester, A. Tayob and W. Weisse), Waxmann, Munster, New York, Munchen, Berlin, pp. 69–87.

Chidester, D. (2005) Virtual religion, in *Authentic Fakes: Religion and American Popular Culture*, (ed. D. Chidester), University of California Press, Berkeley, Los Angeles, London, pp. 109–132.

Chidester, D. (2006) Authentic fakes: Religion and American popular culture. *Review in Religion and Theology*, 13 (4), 546–549.

Chikwendu, I.W. (2004) *An Audience Ethnography on the Role of the Mass Media in the Process of Conversion of Catholics to the Pentecostal Churches in Nigeria: Excerpts of the Doctoral Thesis in the Faculty of Social Sciences of the Pontifical Gregorian University*, Pontificia Universitate Gregoriana, Rome.

Cohen, E. (1988) Authenticity and commoditization in tourism. *Annals of Tourism Research*, 15 (3), 371–386.

Dawson, L.L. (2004) Religion and the Internet: Presence, problems and prospects, in *New Approaches to the Study of Religion: Regional, Critical and Historical Approaches*, (eds P. Antes, A.W. Geertz and R.R. Warne), Walter de Gruyter, Berlin, New York, pp. 385–403.

Franklin, M.I. (2004) *Postcolonial Politics, the Internet, and Everyday Life: Pacific Trasversals Online*, Routledge, New York.

Gurak, L.J. (2001) *Cyber Literacy: Navigating the Internet with Awareness*, Yale University Press, New Haven, London.

Hackett, R. (2006) Religion and the Internet. *Diogenes*, 211, 67–76.

Haron, M. (2004) The South African Muslims making (air) waves during the period of transformation, in *Religion, Politics, and Identity in a Changing South Africa*, (ed. D. Chidester), Waxmann, Munster, New York, Munchen, Berlin, pp. 125–159.

Hollinshead, K. (1998) Disney and commodity aesthetics: A critique of Fjellman's analysis of "Disney" and "historicide" of the past. *Current Issues in Tourism*, 1 (1).

Karaflogka, A. (2002) Religious discourse and cyberspace. *Religion*, 32, 279–291.

Landzelius, K. (2006a) Introduction: Native on the Net, in *Native on the Net: Indigenous and Diasporic Peoples in the Virtual Age*, (ed. K. Landzelius), Routledge, New York, pp. 1–42.

Landzelius, K. (2006b) Postcript: *Vox Populi* from the margins? in *Native on the Net: Indigenous and Diasporic Peoples in the Virtual Age*, (ed. K. Landzelius), Routledge, New York, pp. 293–304.

MacCannell, D. (1989) *The Tourist: A New Theory of the Leisure Class*, Schocken Books, New York.

Mitra, A. (2002) Trust, authenticity, and discursive power in cyberspace. *Communication of ACM*, 45 (3), 27–29.

Mojica, M. (2006) Technologies of delusion and subjectivity. *A Journal of Speculative Research*, 4 (3), 203–209.

Mustafa, T. (2008) Development of objective criteria to evaluate the authenticity of revelation. *Zygon*, 43 (3), 737–744.

Mutwa, C.V. (1964) *Indaba, My Children*, Blue Crane, Johannesburg.

Mutwa, C.V. (1966). *Africa Is My Witness*, Blue Crane, Johannesburg.

Mutwa, C.V. (1998) Foreword, in *South Africa, the 51st State*, (eds S. Ghersi and P. Major), Randburg, Fastdraft.

Newby, GD. (2004) The use of electronic media in the study of sacred texts, in *New Approaches to the Study of Religion: Regional, Critical and Historical Approaches*, (eds P. Antes, A.W. Geertz and R.R. Warne), Walter de Gruyter, Berlin, New York, pp. 45–58.

Phillips, A. (2007) The authenticity issue. *Raritan*, 27 (1), 37–45.

Scheifinger, H. (2008) Hinduism and cyberspace. *Religion*, 38, 233–249.

Smith, M.M., and Carbo, T. (2008) Global information ethics: Intercultural perspectives on past and future research. *Journal of American Society for Information Science and Technology*, 59 (7), 1111–1123.

Starn, R. (2002) Authenticity and historic preservation: Towards and authentic history. *History of the Human Sciences*, 15 (1), 1–16.

Volcic, Z. (2008) Former Yugoslavia on the World Wide Web: Commercialization and branding of nation-states. *The International Communication Gazette*, 70 (5), 395–413.

Welch, K. (1999) *Literacy is Electric Rhetoric: Classical Rhetoric, Oralism, and a New Literacy*, MIT Press, Cambridge, MA.

41

Authors, Authority, Ownership, and Ethics in Digital Media and News

Jarice Hanson

We are in a universe where there is more and more information, and less and less meaning.

(Baudrillard, 2007, p. 99)

Digital communications technologies make traditional media forms more portable and affordable and allow us to choose from a wider variety of content and sources of information, but while digital delivery of messages and the number of sources increase, traditional media industries try to survive economically. Digital media consumers can no longer assume that the same practices they have taken for granted in the past will result in messages that represent facts, or are true. Many of the newer digital media technologies and distribution systems allow a person to become publisher, producer, and content creator – all bypassing traditional hierarchies of control that insure quality. The elimination of the "middle men," where most factual information would be vetted, changes the equation among producers, content providers, and media consumers. In digital-speak, the term used to describe the process of user-generated media content that bypasses traditional "middle" processes is "disintermediation" (Cornog, 2008, p. 38).

From an economic perspective, the "old media" infrastructures (primarily advertising-based) such as print, radio, and broadcast television, are not the same ones that support digital media, in which transmission primarily occurs over the Internet, cell phones, portable digital devices, and related personal technologies. By examining factual information, and *news* in particular, it is possible to understand how the speed of message transmission and the forms of digital media technologies affect how the recipient accesses information, thinks about the information, and in the process, how public perception about news and truth contribute to what we know. In surveying the current landscape of digitally produced and consumed news, the

---

The Handbook of Global Communication and Media Ethics, First Edition. Edited by Robert S. Fortner and P. Mark Fackler.
© 2011 Blackwell Publishing Ltd. Published 2011 by Blackwell Publishing Ltd.

phrase "speed is the enemy of truth" (Rosenberg and Feldman, 2008, p. 28) becomes a metaphor for developing an understanding of the ethical meaning of news and how it functions in society. The ability of anyone to use digital technologies for multiple purposes, as well as for accessing news, anywhere, anytime, has changed the role of the traditional news organization and what is thought of as news. In the process, *how* we use media and ascribe *meaning* to the messages that are conveyed begins to suggest dynamic cultural changes when we think of the role these new media play in what we know, and how we know it.

In this chapter, three themes are developed to understand how the concept of news has changed since digital technologies have begun to undermine traditional news industries, and how cultural expressions of factual information have been changed by the use of the digital technologies. In particular, these themes include: (1) how the immediacy of digital information influences what is thought of as "news;" (2) how the ability of media users to be both producers and consumers of information challenges traditional concepts of authorship, authority, and truth; and (3) how the ability to manipulate digital information and images challenges traditional concepts of ownership.

The perspective from which this interpretation is developed includes *medium* theory and the contributions of McLuhan, Postman, Mumford and Innis, (scholars who wrote in the mid-twentieth century) who identified the unique characteristics of media form as a means of explaining how the public's thoughts, attitudes, and behaviors were influenced by mediated messages, and the works of twenty-first century scholars, most notably Levy who writes of "cyberculture" (2001), and Jenkins, who writes of "convergence culture" (2006). Embedded in the definition of each of these newer terms is a sense that digital technology and digital distribution forms of media have provided a new environment in which authors and consumers of messages, industries, laws, and ethical practices are viewed through a lens that reflects and refracts past practices, and in which the meaning of information can be viewed in a new light. The work of these theorists, along with examples of old and new media as industries and media users repurpose media habits, produce a new information ethic as the delivery form of media changes, and contemporary beliefs about authorship, authority, and ownership offer a new way in which we think of, and accept information that we call, "news."

Media Technology: Form and Content

At the risk of stating the obvious, news has always relied upon the most efficient means of getting information from one point to another in as timely a fashion as possible. In 1481, a letter reporting the death of a Turkish sultan took two years to reach England, and in 1841, it took three months and 20 days to get the information about President Harrison's death in the eastern part of the United States to Los Angeles (Stephens, 2007, p. 3). However, in 2009, within seconds of US Airways Flight 1549's emergency landing in the Hudson River, a passenger was

Ethics in Digital Media and News

able to send a text message and photo over his Twitter stream (Palser, 2009, p. 54). Technologies have always been used in the news gathering and news dissemination process, but the type of technology used has also influenced the relative importance that people give to information. Furthermore, every new form of news distribution improved the speed with which news could be presented – but at what cost to meaning and veracity?

Media historian Ben Bagdikian reminds us that media industries, (like all industries) have practitioners who represent high professional standards as well as those who demonstrate demagoguery and chicanery. Members of the media industries have participated in large part, in the constructions of the mythology surrounding their activities, sometimes "turning private myths into public virtues" (Bagdikian, 2004, p. 178). Even the *New York Times*, the newspaper widely considered as the "paper of record" in the United States has proudly advertised its own philosophy (and desire for a self-fulfilling promise) in its masthead, which reads, "all the news that's fit to print."

While this short essay cannot reflect the entire history of US or global journalism, typographic culture – particularly news in print, played an essential role in the development of the United States, and has been a critical agent influencing the intersection of publics, governments, and ideas, around the world. Colleges, universities, and journalism schools espouse the good practices of professional associations, such as the Society of Professional Journalists (SPJ) whose code of ethics encourages practicing journalists to be aware that: "Conscientious journalists from all media and specialties [must] strive to serve the public with thoroughness and honesty. Professional integrity is the cornerstone of a journalist's credibility" (SPJ, 2009b).

News and press values in the United States

While the same could not be said for every country of the world, the United States' commitment to freedom of the press, and freedom of speech, as written in the First Amendment to the Constitution, has contributed to a culture that values a free press in a democracy.

As the importance and availability of printed materials grew, as the nation did, the profession of journalism evolved. Publishers, journalists, editors, and production personnel, all specializing in their fields, sought to attain professional status, and developed professional standards. Professional unions evolved and established voluntary codes of ethics. Sigma Delta Chi, a fraternal group of professional journalists was established in 1909. By 1988, the name was changed to the Society of Professional Journalists, but the statement of purpose for the "perpetuation of a free press as the cornerstone of our nation and our liberty" remained the same (SPJ, 2009a). The American Society of Newspaper Editors (ASNE, 2009) formed its own professional association, complete with its own code of ethics to continue to strive for high standards of professionalism by editors who were responsible for the "gatekeeping" functions of news.

From the hey-day of the newspaper prominence in the United States (1880–1920), print was the dominant mode of informing the public, and delivering "news." The adoption of radio began to challenge print by means of transmitting messages with immediacy, and by the late 1940s, television brought the visual image into the home, as well as introducing a number of formats of news and information programs. In 2005, the Pew Research Center for People and the Press conducted a study of 3011 adults aged 18 or over, to see what each considered their primary source of news, the previous day. Of these adults 59% had received their news, on the previous day, from local TV; 47% from national TV; 38% from the local paper, and 23% from a national paper. In the same 2005 study, 23% reported that they received their news, on the previous day, via the Internet (Rainie, 2008, p. 2). Within two years, the Internet grew to become a source (though perhaps not the primary source) of news for 73% of the adult audience, due largely to the expansion of broadband technologies (Horrigan, 2008, p. 18).

News, as perfect or imperfect as it may be, remains an important feature in understanding how we as individuals, understand our government, and remains the best (perhaps the only) conveyor of government accountability to the public. Jeffrey Scheuer wrote of the American press: "Our system of self-government is based not just on laws but on informed and active citizens; and such citizens need timely, relevant, clear information – facts and their explanatory contexts – in order to reason, to debate, and to make intelligent decisions (Scheuer, 2008, p. vii)."

Television presented another unique medium for understanding news. Now, the televisual image, viewed in the comfortable, intimate surroundings of one's home competed for attention with children, chores, and other household activities. However, because of its convenience and the use of the close-up, which brought news anchors and reporters eye-to-eye with the public, television soon became the most pervasive form of bringing news to the public. Once again, professional television news organizations capitalized on the mythology of bringing the world of "truth" to consumers. ABC's "Eyewitness News" and the CBS logo of an unblinking eye, were examples of the metaphor that implied that what viewers could see, was indeed, truth. CBS' popular anchorman, Walter Cronkite, closed every network news program with the saying, "that's the way it is."

Marshall McLuhan, a leading theorist of the post-television era wrote a series of what he called "thought probes" that challenged audiences to think of how electronic forms of media overwhelmed the balance of our senses (McLuhan, 1964, pp. 36–45). Each medium, he claimed, amplified some of our senses over others, and our sensory responses to the way the medium was used influenced our concepts of time and space. McLuhan's ideas gave rise to what became known as medium theory, which put the unique communicative ability of the medium used for communication at the center of the debate of how messages were transformed and how audiences understood the meaning of messages in its mediated form, rather than by focusing on the content. One of McLuhan's most famous phrases is that the medium is the *message*, "because it is the medium that shapes and controls the scale and form of human association and action" (McLuhan, 1964, p. 23–24). Later, he expanded the idea to say that the medium is also the *massage* to explain how electronic media "is reshaping and restructuring patterns of social interdependence and every aspect of your [sic] personal life" (McLuhan and Fiore, 1967, back cover). McLuhan drew from the work of Lewis Mumford, who envisioned time as a cultural commodity (Mumford, 1934, p. 270) and Harold Innis, who viewed time as a social conundrum for which media could supply a solution, in the sense that as society grew, the more media (newspapers in his example) expanded content and distribution forms to fill the needs of consumers' available time (Innis, 1951, pp. 61–64). Mumford's and Innis' work led McLuhan to propose that each medium had its own time-binding characteristics (McLuhan, 1964, pp. 135–134), and that the concept of time would be altered, depending upon which medium a person chose to use. Television time, such as the half-hour news show, the 30-second commercial, and the seven-second sound bite, were all examples of what McLuhan claimed to be the artifacts of television's unique communicative characteristics. McLuhan's ideas concerning how media could influence our understanding of messages became a concept that was embraced by some, while others thought his ideas were sheer punditry, but the concept of the medium as capable of transforming the meaning of messages has been revived by the proliferation of digital media.

Fortunately, other theorists expanded upon the link between the unique characteristics of how a medium communicated, and the content. By the time Neil Postman authored *Amusing Ourselves to Death: Public Discourse in the Age of Show Business* (1985), ideas of how the medium influenced message meaning within culture became more widely accepted by members of academe and the public. Postman was both a critic of how new media created a market for old media to model itself on the new, and how that would distort the quality of the message.

While Innis had brilliantly chronicled the evolution of newspapers in North America and the way newspaper publishers, in their effort to fill the time of the many readers of news and entertainment, influenced public opinion (Innis, 1951, pp. 156–189), Postman wrote of how the "new" media were suggesting models that "old" media emulated, and that as a result, news stories were becoming shorter and more superficial. As examples, he discussed how the newspaper, *USA Today*, which debuted in September, 1982, used color pictures, short stories, a reliance on charts and graphs, extremely brief updates on sports, and was even sold in a kiosk that resembled a television set. "Journalists of a more traditional bent have criticized it for its superficiality and theatrics, but the paper's editors remain steadfast in their disregard of typographic standards" (Postman, 1985, pp. 111–112). He also criticized a local radio station in New York City that entreated its audience to "Give us twenty-two minutes and we'll give you the world" (Postman, 1985, p. 113) because he believed that the brevity of world news, packaged into a mere 22 minutes would undoubtedly provide little information, while leading audiences to assume that all of the news could fit into a 22 minute segment.

808   *Jarice Hanson*

Postman's ability to explain the cultural significance of the medium came from the concept of resonance, for which he credited Northrup Frye (1981, p. 218):

> Every medium of communication, I am claiming, has resonance, for resonance is metaphor writ large. Whatever the original and limited context of its use may have been, a medium has the power to fly far beyond that context into new and unexpected ones. Because of the way it directs us to organize our minds and integrate out experience of the world, it imposes itself on our consciousness and social institutions in myriad forms. It sometimes has the power to become implicated in our concepts of piety, or goodness, or beauty. And it is always implicated in the ways we define and regulate our ideas of truth (Postman, 1985, p. 18).

Postman continued his work beyond *Amusing Ourselves to Death*, but the middle of the 1980s were marked by a sea change in new media, and digital technologies began to enter the marketplace. Subscription television services, like Home Box Office (HBO) and direct to home satellite television delivery had become possible; video cassette recorders and the video tape rental market had developed; Apple and IBM each developed and marketed personal computers; the Sony Walkman had been introduced; cell phones (though still using analog signals in the 1980s) were starting to appear, and Internet Service Providers (ISPs) began to market access to the new distribution form of the Internet to the public. By 1990, those computers and ISPs around the world could be linked through the World Wide Web, using addresses that allowed virtually instant communication between person to person, and place to place. Many of these new technologies were inexpensive, and the content that they distributed was that of older media forms, or, to paraphrase McLuhan, the content of the new media, was that of the old media (McLuhan, 1964, p. 23). Postman viewed this evolution as a cultural shift. In thinking of the long history of typographic culture, steeped in practices and had a long history of social use and adaptation, he wrote; "Most of our modern ideas about the uses of intellect were formed by the printed word, as were our ideas about education, knowledge, truth and information … as typography moves to the periphery of our culture … the value of public discourse dangerously declines" (Postman, 1985, p. 29). Postman argued that news had lost its credibility, and that instead, our media were "amusing" us rather than providing a valuable function of stimulating our intellects and encouraging us to debate important issues of the day.

Digital Technology and Culture

Twenty years after Postman published *Amusing Ourselves to Death*, the proliferation of digital media exploded. Contemporary theorists may not always cite the medium theorists in the formation of their ideas, but the way they describe contemporary culture undoubtedly views the form of media as a critical aspect of understanding the meaning of messages. Two theorists in particular, examine digital culture with important conceptual ties to medium theory. Pierre Levy calls the current environment "cyberculture" (2001), and Henry Jenkins has referred to it as "convergence culture,"

Ethics in Digital Media and News

(2006). Embedded in the definition of each of these terms is a sense that digital technology and digital distribution forms of media have provided a new environment in which authors and consumers of messages, industries, laws, and ethical practices are viewed through a lens that reflects and refracts past practices, but in which the meaning of information can be viewed in a new light. While laws and cultural values pertaining to ownership of media content for "old" media were determined within the scope of the nations that supported them, digital media have the capacity to transcend regional borders, raising a new set of questions concerning authors, authority, and ownership of media content in our new, global digital culture.

Levy's logic toward understanding "cyberculture" demonstrates how any new distribution forms of information (like digital media) can become commodified and industrialized. While some meanings may retain preferred readings that cause most people to accept universal truths of meaning, a flood of information can also influence a sea of references for which individuals' interpretations may differ widely. Yet, he claims, they allow people to make judgments about the generalizability of the messages transmitted. "Always ambivalent, technologies project our emotions, intentions, and projects into the material world" (Levy, 2001, p. xv). Along with digital technology in cyberculture, blurring between authors, producers, readers, and consumers takes on a new form, while still privileging preferred meanings, depending on how well these different agents share responsibility for agreement on culturally-informed relevance.

Jenkins' notions of convergence culture also reflect on the fixity of universal meanings at the expense of changes in distribution form. He, however, finds the meaning of messages in the shared cultures to be the result of a "circulation of media content – across different media systems, competing media economies, and national borders" (Jenkins, 2006, p. 3). For Jenkins, the hybridization that occurs when technological forms come together is less important than the social interactions that result from the new relationships that are created at the intersections of persons, technologies, practices, and industries. With medium theory as the platform, and cyberculture and convergence culture as the metaphors to describe our current media environment, it is possible to identify both the unique characteristics of digital media and the power of the interpretation of messages for those who produce and consume digital messages.

The Immediacy of Digital News

Delivering what is thought of as "news" has always been inextricably tied to the timeliness of information and the cost of delivering that information. Many newspaper publishers have been driven to explore whether electronic news delivery can provide a sustaining economic future for the news industry, and all that do so have had to deal with changing both news form as well as content to fit the new digital medium.

By 2008, many print newspapers had created versions of electronic newspapers or news services, with Neilsen reporting that approximately 43% of the American public viewed an online newspaper in January, 2009 (Newspaper Association of America, 2009). The Pew Internet and American Life Project (Journalism.org,

2009) surveyed news consumers of all ages, and concluded that all ages had begun to migrate to digital news sources. Between 2001 and 2005; "Internet penetration rose from 58% of all adult Americans to 70%, and home broadband penetration grew from 20 million people (or 10% of adult Americans) to 74 million people (37% of adult Americans)" (Horrigan, 2006, p. 1).

News on the Internet may take on a variety of appearances as many traditional newspapers have modified versions of their newspapers to fit the form of Internet delivery, and have formatted electronic print and pictures to be displayed on a computer screen. Amateur writers have taken the form of web-logging, or blogging, to create personal writings that they post on the web, sometimes creating pages that look like news feeds and online news sources. In all of these cases, hyperlinks can lead a reader or "user" from story to story, and source to source, though people who produce Internet content know that the typical user will be willing to make (on average) six clicks before feeling "browsing fatigue" (Watts, 2003, p. 231).

The Form and Content of Digital News

The way people read stories on the web has attracted considerable attention from behaviorists, news professionals, and marketing personnel. In 1997, Nielsen and Coyne conducted eye-tracking research that showed that 79% of web users scanned stories on the web, while only 16% actually read the entire articles, word by word (Ruel and Paul, 2007, p. 1). Studies like Nielsen and Coyne's led researchers to presume that long-form journalism would not survive the migration to the Internet.

Wolf studied how the brain functions when reading, and believes that the type of information people seek (through any form of media) leads us to create patterns in our brains to help us make meaning (Wolf, 2007, p. 22); in the case of the web, she fears that the sheer amount of information can drive people to "frantic, chaotic gorging" on information (Meyer, 2008, p. 28), and Nicholas Carr has written that reading on the Internet could shift humans from "contemplative man" to "flickering man" because of the fragmentary nature of brief information produced on the Internet, and the need for the consumer to link between pages and make sense of the scanned messages (Carr, 2008, p. 58). Carr writes on the way skimming online print changes a person's mental habits. He cites Bruce Friedman, a blogger who writes about the use of computers in medicine, who claimed; "I now have almost totally lost the ability to read and absorb a longish article on the web or in print" (Carr, 2008, p. 58).

Another of the overwhelming problems of the ubiquity of news on the Internet is the problem of information overload. Nordenson has written:

> Before the digital era, information was limited by our means to contain it. Publishing was restricted by paper and delivery costs; broadcasting was circumscribed by available frequencies and airtime. The Internet, on the other hand, has unlimited capacity as

near-zero cost. There are more than 70 million blogs and 150 million Web sites today – a number that is expanding at a rate of approximately ten thousand an *hour* (emphasis original) (Nordenson, 2008, p. 30).

In addition to the way online news in consumed and the way people scan information the amount of information now available to us, raises both the concept of information overload, as well as what Meyer calls, "news fatigue" which may actually cause us to turn away from important information, or block it out. Meyer also reminds us that the amount of digital information available to us doubles every year. He writes:

> Overload – the amount people feel compelled to know combined with the volume of information they have to sift through in order to know it – is perhaps the largest factor in the increasingly distinct difference between how people read printed material and how they read online. Faced with the reality of having two eyes, one brain, and what the latest count estimates to be one trillion Web pages, many people forego immersive reading of a handful of sites in order to skim the surface of thousands (Meyer, 2008, p. 33).

Exactly what people seek on the Internet is also an important feature of the way online news is presented. Another Pew Internet and American Life Project report indicated that when it came to political news about the presidential race of 2008, 26% of the adult population of the United States consulted the Internet for news about the campaign, while 28% received their news from the newspaper. The majority of persons surveyed still reported television as the primary source of news for campaign information (approximately 78%), but what is most important about the use of the Internet for political information is that a third of online users (33%) reported that they sought out information that already confirmed their point of view (Smith, 2009, p. 1).

Selective perception, or the act of a person looking for sources that confirm their own attitudes and beliefs, is a long-held concept in the study of communication. Manjoo writes that the Internet as making it even easier to find ideas that suit one's own previously held ideas. He writes that online, there is

> a fundamental shift in the way Americans are thinking about the news. No longer are we merely holding opinions different from one another; we're also holding different facts ... At the same time that technology and globalization have pushed the world together, it is driving our minds apart (Manjoo, 2008, p. 59).

While the high cost of producing a newspaper insures that at best, a newspaper may come out once a day, online news sources can change whenever there is a need for the news organization to update the information. In terms of time, the Internet can provide information faster and more directly to a person's home, workplace, or laptop (anywhere, anytime) than any previous form of news delivery. What may be more important than speed and access however, is the way people use the medium.

Some newspapers, particularly quality papers like the *New York Times* produce electronic editions of their newspapers that resemble the traditional newspaper. Subscribers who use ebooks (Amazon's Kindle, and Sony's E-Book, for example) gain portability, but have the complete newspaper at their electronic disposal. However, even the *New York Times* has succumbed to an online news feed (*New York Times.com*) that is often targeted at younger readers, or those who browse for news and information online differently than if they used a traditional newspaper. For example, when the two versions of the front page of *The New York Times* are viewed side-by-side, the traditional paper has headlines and several paragraphs of a story on the front page, while the *New York Times.com* has headlines and a sentence or two that requires the reader to click to the rest of the story, while approximately one-third of the screen is dedicated to advertising.

Those services dedicated to producing news for Internet users, such as MSN.com, CNN.com, and Yahoo.com, have far less information that would fit the traditional category of "news," including foreign affairs, government actions, and local actualities, and focus far more on human interest features, gossip, and grotesqueries. These digital "news" sources change *what* is presented as "news" thereby altering the relationship between the news producers, and the news audience. If a consumer were looking for topical information, online news may be factual, may be truthful, and may be interesting, but it may not be useful in the sense of providing the link between agents for the maintenance of democratic checks and balances, or for stimulating civic participation.

Most online news sources and special online versions of newspapers organize content differently to traditional newspapers, with greater attention to gossip and celebrity news than public events or news that could inform serious public discourse. If a content analysis were to be conducted, online news services might suggest that many "news" stories are made up of gossip and feature information. A random screenshot of MSN.com's online news service revealed that the stories on the "front" page included: "10 Great Jobs for Spring," "Celebrity Baby Boom," "Cutting your Food Bills" and a video of a walrus mom cuddling her cub. Headlines for the "news" stories appeared on the right hand column in the lower section in three groups; "Is GM Bankruptcy Inevitable," Can Tiger Woods Rally at TPC," and a photo feature on former photography technologies that "We Want Back" (MSN.com, 2009). In this case, the immediacy and availability of information on a screen that appears to resemble a newspaper actually masquerades as news. If people assume that what they see on these pages is indeed news, it would appear that the only important news is an awareness of popular culture and self-help topics.

Citizen journalism

As a result of the economic crisis, many traditional newsrooms have seen a reduction in their staffs. One person operating a digital video camera, satellite dish, laptop and cell phone has become a more economic model of gathering foreign news

Ethics in Digital Media and News 813

for television sources (Dorroh, 2007, p. 12–13), and in newspaper newsrooms, among the first to be let go are the copy editors, who have traditionally been the "last line of defense against errors" (Keith, 2005, p. 930).

Among the drive for news organizations to seek inexpensive news content, is the development of citizen journalism, the term denoting a good deal of low-cost media filler that virtually anyone can produce with today's camcorders, digital cameras, or even cell phones. According to Steve Outing (2005), writing on the Poynter Institute's online website, *Poynter Online*, there are many interpretations of citizen journalism, ranging from newspapers that invite readers to comment on stories online, to individuals who blog on their own, with no professional standards toward fact-checking or editing their work, to the hybrid citizen and professional journalist collaboration in which the citizen, on the spot, might take a picture with a cell phone or camcorder, and feed the content to a professional news organization for publication. Certainly cell phone images taken by people during the London Underground bombings, showed extraordinary actual images of the effects of terrorism in July, 2005, and the two different actualities of students being tasered – first at UCLA, and later, at a John Kerry rally, were powerful expressions of news. In these cases, the ability of citizens to provide visual images can be very illuminating to a story, but questions arise when a person narrates the story from their first-person view, compared to a professional or organization that ensures that an interpretive context can be provided for the events surrounding the image.

The most extreme form of citizen journalism, according to Outing, is wiki journalism, in which the readers are also the editors of the material. For example, the online encyclopedia, Wikipedia, asks consumers to edit and add to entries. While Wikipedia is improving this process, a good deal of incorrect material is published before someone comes to correct or edit the entry. The theory behind wiki journalism is that the collective knowledge and intelligence of the participants will produce a piece that is credible, thorough, well-balanced, and appropriately vetted, but the time it takes for volunteer editors with knowledge of a subject to find an entry, offer editing or correcting services, and make the changes, the entry has already been seen and read by those who may believe what they see in its unedited presence.

Authors and Authority

In all of the examples above, it could be said that each form may have an appeal to a different audience with a different reason for searching for what they perceive of as "news." Authorship is an important feature of building trust when citizens seek knowledgeable sources for news, and journalists or news organizations in traditional media put their names on their stories, and represent the research and authority they have earned. If the name of the source appears to be credible, such as from a news source that has developed a reputation for authority, a news user can easily make an assumption that the information is truthful, factual, and in accordance with the principles of good journalistic practice. What if the media user has never heard of an author or examined her/his work before? Such is often the case of amateur news journalists who blog.

Blogging

Web logging, or blogging, is the act of writing specifically for self-publication on the Internet. While blogging may fit into the category of citizen journalism, it also has unique characteristics that may influence believability. The professional appearance of the blog, the language used, and the embedded hyperlinks that route a reader to additional information can be signifiers of professionalism – even if the blogger is not a professional journalist.

Andrew Sullivan, a popular blogger has written; "But as blogging evolves as a literary form, it is generating a new and quintessentially postmodern idiom that's enabling writers to express themselves in ways that have never been seen or understood before. Its truths are provisional, and its ethos collective and messy" (Sullivan, 2008, p. 106). He continues:

> We bloggers have scant opportunity to collect our thoughts, to wait until events have settled and a clear pattern emerges. We blog now – as news reaches us, as facts emerge … A reporter can wait – must wait – until every source has confirmed. … For bloggers, the deadline is always now. Blogging is therefore to writing what extreme sports are to athletics: more free-form, more accident-prone, less formal, more alive (Sullivan, 2008, p. 108).

The "messiness" Sullivan refers to, and the pressure of instant reporting of facts as they emerge, seems to fit the medium of the Internet, but the ability of a reader to respond immediately may also have a "chilling" effect on free speech.

> Reader comments posted on digital news sites are often heavy on invective, hurled from *noms d'Internet* that allow people to disregard traditional norms of civil discourse. For many of these anonymous snipers, the reported facts are not facts at all, but the unreliable product of paid liars, incompetents, toadies, and haters who dare to call themselves journalists (Johnston, 2008, p. 59).

In a study of blog readers and their perceived credibility, Johnson and Kaye found that people who blogged themselves, found other blogs more credible than traditional sources (Johnson and Kaye, 2004, p. 622). At face value, this would seem to suggest that bloggers understand the way in which bloggers communicate, and accept their obeisance to speed and timeliness, while acknowledging (if they are honest) that the information bloggers provide is often undocumented, fragmented, and potentially "accident prone" in Sullivan's words.

Ethics in Digital Media and News

Social networking and news

While social networking sites like *Facebook*, *MySpace*, and *LinkedIn* were developed specifically for the purpose of creating networks of people, one of the newest social media forms, *Twitter*, has combined the force of texting on cell phones with the distribution of email. Twitter starts each message with a simple question, "What Are You Doing?" Since its creation in 2006, the short messaging system (SMS) that functions as a "microblogging" system that allows participants to "tweet" each other in 140 characters of less, has turned into an instant news blast medium for members of the entertainment and news industries, as well as for personal uses. Celebrities and news anchors and reporters use Twitter and also build their base of reliable viewers/listeners. As a medium of news, Twitter performed admirably during the Southern California wildfires in October, 2007, when news groups used it to dispatch evacuation orders, shelter locations, and firefighter progress, to a number of people who had mobile technologies (Palser, 2009, p. 54) but when Twitter was used to dispatch information (often incomplete or inaccurate) about the outbreak of swine flu in April, 2009, the Center for Disease Control (CDC) feared that it could incite panic in the public (Sutter, 2009, p. 1)

These examples of bloggers and microblogging and how they perceive authorship and authority, and the abuses that can be perpetrated by users who are not committed to telling the truth are clear examples of medium theory, in which the unique characteristics of the medium's form influence the meaning of the message. Truth is not relevant if the technologies are thought of for their speed and instant messaging capabilities. The subsequent acceptance of the equality of the views of bloggers at the expense of traditional professional standards of measuring authorship and authority are indicators of the direction in which the shift to *prosumerism*, or producing and consuming, has steered our culture, and the use of social networking media to substitute for a news medium blurs the idea of what news is, with instant communication capability.

Trust: The Producer as Consumer

As digital technologies proliferate, and new services tempt audiences to participate in the collectivity (or network) they provide, the *disintermediation*, mentioned in the introduction, becomes the point at which trust would be determined. In traditional media industries, the trust the audience placed in the industry for factual information, professional standards, and quality news – was monitored at the author stage, and at the middle-stage of the message as it was prepared for transmission. Editors, fact-checkers, and the number of individuals who shaped and crafted news were the filters that applied their professional expertise to the message, and gave the media the authority to speak truthfully. In the age of digital news, which is produced so quickly, with little gatekeeping or even copy editing, "news and information is distinctly incoherent, individualized, and idiosyncratic, contingent on whatever choices we make as users" (Harper, 1998, p. 25). If this is true, is it ever possible to seek and find truth?

In 1980, Alvin Toffler coined the term *prosumer* to signify activities in which consumers produced for their own consumption (1980, p. 265). Today, Jenkins would expand upon the user's ability to navigate multiple roles in media production and consumption through the concept of *convergence*, but unlike some of the signified meanings of the term, Jenkins does not focus on convergence at the site of media forms that blend together (like printed news and news on the Internet), but rather, as the human being attempts to make sense of the new environment: "Convergence does not occur through media appliances, however sophisticated they may become. Convergence occurs within the brains of individual consumers, and through their social interactions with others (Jenkins, 2006, p. 3).

In the jumble of the constant flow of messages the context, or interpretative frame of news, is often lost in the process. What is most available (the stuff of popular culture) becomes the agenda, and the responsibility for verifying truth in online news falls upon the consumer of the news. The tension that is created is between the expert and the crowd (acclaimed as an important value that has captured popular imagination in the book, *The Wisdom of Crowds* (Surowiecki, 2004)). However, are crowds really wise, or is what stands for "wisdom" just collective agreement or collective attitude? Does frequency of appearance equate wisdom? "Experts are being nudged aside, by the aggregated opinions of consumers (or interested parties masquerading as consumers)" (Cornog, 2008, p. 39).

If critical standards are not given to us, can we expect the public to develop a critical sense to evaluate truth on their own? Can this happen especially, when the flow of messages is unrelenting? When the value of immediacy is elevated above the need for truth, do digital media actually mislead the public? While Neil Postman identified how all forms of media were leading us toward "amusing ourselves to death," we can see how the form of fake news, such as *The Daily Show with Jon Stewart* and *The Colbert Report* on Comedy Central have taken Postman's words to heart. The amusing nature of each of these fake news broadcasts seems like just another part and parcel of the style of television news in a media-saturated world. Both shows are satires of television news shows, but the comedians for whom the shows are named have to periodically remind audiences that the shows are comedy shows, and not news. The popularity of both of these cable television programs show that the public sometimes cannot tell the truth between program form, and program content. In the realm of popular culture Colbert's coining of the term *truthiness*, is a contemporary reality suggesting that real truth may not be possible but a "kind of a truth" can be a reasonable substitute for real truth.

Problems of Ownership

The concept of copyright as protection of "original works of authorship fixed in any tangible medium of expression" is a legal principal that has roots in the first US copyright law in 1790, and it is intended to protect the right of an author of original material to profit from (and earn a living from) the production of their

Ethics in Digital Media and News

own intellectual endeavors. Metaphorically, copyright gives control to the author of the work. However, in the online world of producers and consumers, services exist that act as huge repositories of pictures taken by amateurs that can easily be located, lifted, and published elsewhere with no credit to the owner, or no payment for use by commercial agencies. The ability to "steal" images on the Internet, and the digital manipulation of images are matters that challenge the issue of fair use in contemporary copyright law.

While previous examples in this chapter have focused primarily on typographic culture more than visual culture, the focus on digital imagery expands questions of news, truth, and ownership of intellectual property. By all means, the speed, access, and forwarding functions of digital information distribution give rise to "cut and paste" constructions of works in digital form that haunt questions of authorship and authority, but also lead toward legal definitions of plagiarism and unauthorized manipulation of digital information. Software, like *Photoshop* can create pictures that may amuse, but would defy logical explanation. While digital manipulation of photos is most often for amusement, they stretch the boundaries of preexisting critical standards, necessary to evaluate the plausibility of the artifact, such as the "Pregnant Bruce Willis Test" in a book illustrating fraudulent photos (Wheeler, 2002, p. 146).

Following the production/consumption argument, Alissa Quart has asked; "What will become of photojournalism in an age of bytes and amateurs?" (Quart, 2008, p. 14). When anyone posts images on *Facebook*, *Flickr*, or any one of the online services that make amateur photography available to the online public, can the profession of photojournalists survive? Quart says:

> Yet, paradoxically, visual culture is ever more important. It seems that everyone now takes photos and saves them and distributes them, and that all these rivulets supply a great sea of images for editors to use. This carries certain risks. If they are taking snapshots, amateur photographers are likely not developing a story, or developing the kind of intimacy with their subjects that brings revelation. So what's the actual photojournalistic value of all of these millions of images now available on Flickr and other photo-sharing archives – so many that they can seem like dead souls? (Quart, 2008, p. 14).

Due to the accessibility that the web provides, it is a common assumption that everything on the web is free, or available to anyone who wants to create a derivative work based on the seemingly "free" or available image.

Shortly after the election of President Barack Obama, the Associated Press (AP) threatened freelance artist Shepard Fairey with a lawsuit. Fairey, a graphic artist who produced the popular red, white, and blue campaign poster for featuring Obama looking upward, with the word "HOPE" providing the textual interpretation of the image, was featured on *Time* magazine, and seemed to appear everywhere, on T-shirts, posters, and even book covers, seemingly overnight. The original image had been taken from a 2006 photograph of Obama taken by freelance photographer Mannie Garcia, who was under contract to the Associated Press at that time. AP claimed ownership of the original material and demanded credit as the source and a portion of the royalties earned by use of the new graphic image. Fairey claimed the photograph, published widely in newspapers and on the web, should be considered under the provision of "fair use." The AP's threats prompted Fairey to file a lawsuit against them, claiming that his work significantly changed the meaning of the picture into what his lawyers called a "stunning, abstracted and idealized visual image that created powerful new meaning and conveys a radically different message (Kennedy, 2009, C1). While the courts are dealing with this issue and many others, provided by the availability of images on the Internet, it is possible to see how older laws (concerning ownership) can easily be challenged by digital media, digital software, and digital manipulation of images.

Digital Ethics

If digital technologies can be used personally, in the privacy of one's home, and in any manner one chooses, it is not surprising that many of the problems with digital media ownership involve material on the Internet that people assume, is "free" to be taken, and "free" to be used. Herrington has written; "Digitized information illustrates metaphorically and actually the implausibility of the exclusive ownership in intellectual products and casts doubt that authorship should produce ownership and, thus, exclusive control" (Herrington, 2001, p. 129). An inability to control the production and consumption of information, as well as the lack of attention to professional standards of practice, produce a situation in which authorship, authority, and ownership of digital media content is increasingly muddied. As Weinberger wrote; "If the Web is changing bedrock concepts such as space, time, perfection, social interaction, knowledge, matter, and morality … no wonder we're so damn confused" (Weinberger, 2001, p. 25).

When mixing traditionally professionally rendered news and information with amateur postings and self-publishing on the Internet, any belief in the truth of what one sees in text or image is problematized. For the average consumer of news, digital media may increase the number of sources to which they have access, and create an ability to link to additional points of view, but all of the "triggers" that associate information with authority and truth are slippery. The consumer may be led to believe that s/he is engaging in the activity of seeking news, when in reality s/he is engaged in seeking views that confirm her/his beliefs. At the same time, s/he is presented with more celebrity and gossip information than long-form news. The user is likely to engage in browsing behavior, rather than being drawn to a story by hierarchically organizing information to lead to a "truth" that is actively constructed in the reader's mind.

The meaning of the text and images have sliding signifiers and the medium's unique characteristics mislead a person who is browsing without a purpose, to filling time and assuming that the instant nature of digital media is in actuality, informing them of the news of the day. The ethical principles used in digital news gathering and dissemination *may* mirror those of traditional journalism, but the question will always remain, "how do you know?"

Digital news blurs boundaries of traditional practices and the practices of amateurs. The producer/consumer model opens the door to opportunities for creative expression, but at the same time, it opens doors to misrepresentation, hoaxes, and even lies (Hanson, 2007, p. 81). In extreme cases of the manipulation of personal information, so freely posted on social networking sites and elsewhere on the Internet, digitization opens the doors to identity theft and manipulation of one's personal information.

In a lapse of professional ethics, some journalists (professional and amateur) have taken to combing social networking sites for information about what interests people, but more dangerously, to use self-posted information to create "news" stories, look for friends of a person in the news, or to seek available pictures to illustrate stories (Spencer, 2007, p. 38). What signifies ownership, or even personal information, falls prey to questionable uses when digital information is manipulated for any purpose – professional or amateur.

One of the most challenging aspects about developing a sense of digital ethics, or ethics that influence our use of digital technologies is that information in digital form can be duplicated without prior authorization, while simultaneously having the characteristic of disappearing with the push of a button. Digital information is both permanent, and transitory. It is real, and it is ephemeral. It can be here today, and the computer one uses can be obsolete tomorrow, making it difficult, if not impossible to retrieve stored digital data. Additionally, in the context of news, information that binds us together may also tear us apart.

Conclusion

"The prosperity of a nation, geographical region, business, or individual depends on their ability to navigate the knowledge space. Power is now conferred through optimal management of knowledge, whether it involves technology, science, communication or our 'ethical' relationship with the other" (Levy, 1997, p. 1). For Levy, the availability of knowledge in cyberculture introduces new cultural arrangements that raise questions of how past practices influence our sense of self and others. For Jenkins, convergence culture creates a situation in which our minds put together the fragments of meaning, as we use different tools and technologies to mediate reality, as we navigate from medium to medium, and message to message. For both Levy and Jenkins, the challenge of living in contemporary culture is to learn what happens to the meaning of message and the value with which we hold information.

As we negotiate the change from long-held beliefs in the authority of typographic culture and the validity of unadulterated images, we may develop critical standards and practices that help us become better producers and consumers of media content. Or, we may fail in our attempt to understand information that comes at us so rapidly, over such portable media, and that presents us with fragments of information that the onus of construction, validation, and judgment of truth, is to be found in our minds. There is an irony to this picture. Prosumerism assumes action that the individual takes, but production/consumption of media messages may lull us into the seduction of the medium, rather than the message.

The economic difficulties encountered by traditional media industries, particularly those concerned with news gathering and dissemination, are real, and inescapable, but at the same time, historically, "news" has survived in other migrations from one form of media to another. The loss of gatekeepers whose role it was to authenticate facts, correct mistakes, and polish news messages unquestionably presents a problem for news that bows to the god of speed, rather than the god of accuracy and truth, but this problem is not new.

Will consumers eventually learn the literacy of digital media that presents stories in ways that require us to follow hyperlinks, and requires that we think critically about authors and their authority, and whether they own their stories and viewpoints? Will we learn the subtle clues embedded in digitally manipulated images that let us know if a picture has been digitally altered? Will we develop a healthy skepticism about stories and images that could conceivably be manipulated, such as hoaxes, or photofiction? Finally, what does what we think of as news, say about civil society?

"News" is plentiful, but what constitutes news is changing. Whether we learn from the experience of the past to develop critical standards, think of the medium as just important as the message, and whether we maintain First Amendment principles for the encouragement of professional standards that help us negotiate the relationships of government, the press, and digital media, remains to be seen. I would like to believe that we will find the meaning in the sea of information; I can't allow any other interpretation to enter my mind.

References

ASNE (American Society of Newspaper Editors) (2009) *A look at the formation of ASNE*, www.asne.org/index.cfm?ID=3460 (last accessed February 18, 2009).

Bagdikian, B.H. (2004) *The New Media Monopoly*, Beacon Press, Boston, MA.

Baudrillard, J. (2007) *In the Shadow of the Silent Majorities*, (trans. P. Foss, J. Johnston, Paul Patton *et al.*), MIT Press, Cambridge, MA.

Carr, N. (2008) Is Google making us stupid? *The Atlantic Monthly*, 302, 1 (July/August), 56–63.

Cornog, E. (2008) The ploughman and the professor. *Columbia Journalism Review*, (September/October), 38–41.

Dorroh, J. (2007) Armies of one, *American Journalism Review*, 29, 6, 12–13.

Frye, N. (1981) *The Great Code: The Bible and Literature*, Academic Press, Toronto.

Hanson, J. (2007) *24/7: How Cell Phones and the Internet Are Changing the Way We Live, Work, and Play*, Praeger, Westport, CT.

Harper, C. (1998) *And That's the Way It Will Be: News and Information in a Digital World*, New York University Press, New York.

Herrington, T.K. (2001) *Controlling Voices: Intellectual Property, Humanistic Studies, and the Internet*, Southern Illinois University Press, Carbondale, IL.

Horrigan, J.B. (2006) Online news. *Pew Internet and American Life Project*, March 22, www.pewinternet.org/~/media//Files/Reports/2006/PIP_News.and.Broadband.pdf (last accessed April 3, 2009).

Horrigan, J.B. (2008) Home broadband adoption. *Pew Internet and American Life Project*, July, www.pewinternet.org/~/media/Files/Reports/2008/PIP_Broadband_2008.pdf (last accessed March 2, 2009).

Innis, H.A. (1951) *The Bias of Communication*, University of Toronto Press, Toronto.

Jenkins, H. (2006) *Convergence Culture: Where Old and New Media Collide*, New York University Press, New York.

Johnston, D.C. (2008) My facts, your facts, *Columbia Journalism Review*, July/August, 59–60.

Johnson, T.J., and Kaye, B.K. (2004) Wag the blog: How reliance on traditional media and the internet influence credibility perceptions of weblogs among blog users, *Journalism and Mass Communication Quarterly*, 81 (3), 622–643.

Journalism.org (2009) Number of U.S. daily newspapers in 5-year increments. *Pew Research Center's Project on Excellence in Journalism*, www.journalism.org/node/1134 (accessed August 8, 2010).

Keith, S. (2005) Newspaper copy editors' perceptions of their ideal and real ethics roles. *Journalism and Mass Communication Quarterly*, 82 (4), 930–952.

Kennedy, R. (2009) Artist sues the AP over Obama image, *New York Times*, February 10, C1

Levy, P. (1997) *Collective Intelligence: Mankind's Emerging World in Cyberspace* (trans. R. Bonanno), Perseus Books, Cambridge, MA.

Levy, P. (2001) *Cyberculture* (trans. R. Bonanno), University of Minnesota Press, Minneapolis.

Manjoo, F. (2008) *True Enough: Learning to Live in A Post-Fact Society*, John Wiley and Sons, Inc., New York.

McLuhan, M. (1964) *Understanding Media: The Extensions of Man*, Signet, New York.

McLuhan, M., and Fiore, Q. (1967) *The Medium is the Massage*, Bantam, New York.

Meyer, M. (2008) Surface routines, *Columbia Journalism Review*, November/December, 33–34.

MSN.com (2009, May 10), www.msn.com (accessed August 8, 2010).

Mumford, L. (1934) *Technics and Civilization*, Harcourt, Brace & World, New York.

Newspaper Association of America (2009) Neilsen Online www.naa.org/TrendsandNumbers/Newspaper-Websites.aspx (accessed August 8, 2010).

Nordenson, B. (2008) Overload! *Columbia Journalism Review*, November/December, 30–32, 35–37, 40, 42.

Outing, S. (2005) The eleven layers of citizen journalism, *PoynterOnline*, June 15, www.poynter.org/content/content_view.asp?id=83126 (accessed August 8, 2010).

Palser, B. (2009) Hitting the tweet spot, *American Journalism Review*, April/May, 54.

Postman, N. (1985) *Amusing Ourselves to Death: Public Discourse in the Age of Show Business*, Penguin, New York.

Quart, A. (2008) Flickring out, *Columbia Journalism Review*, July/August, 14–17.

Rainie, L. (2008) Key news audiences now blend online and traditional sources. *Pew Research Center for People and the Press*, August 17, http://people-press.org/report/444/news-media (last accessed March 11, 2009).

Rosenberg, H., and Feldman, C.S. (2008) *No Time to Think: The Menace of Media Speed and the 24-hour News Cycle*, Continuum, New York.

Ruel, L., and Paul, N. (2007) Eyetracking points the way to effective news article design. *Knight Digital Media Center*, March 3, www.ojr.org/ojr/stories/070312ruel/ (accessed August 8, 2010).

Scheuer, J. (2008) Foreword, in *Press Critics Are the Fifth Estate*, (ed. A.S. Hayes), Praeger, Westport, CT, pp. vii–viii.

Smith, A. (2009) The Internet's role in Campaign 2008, *Pew Internet and American Life Project*, www.pewinternet.org/Reports/2009/6–The-Internets-Role-in-Campaign-2008.aspxect (last accessed April 3, 2009).

Spencer, J. (2007) Found in (my) space, *American Journalism Review*, 29 (5), 36–38.

SPJ (Society of Professional Journalists) (2009a) *History of the Society*, www.spj.org/spjhistory.asp (accessed August 2, 2010).

SPJ (Society of Professional Journalists) (2009b) *Code of Ethics*, www.spj.org/ethicscode.asp (accessed August 8, 2010).

Stephens, M. (2007) *A History of the News*, Oxford University Press, New York.

Sullivan, A. (2008) Why I blog. *The Atlantic Monthly*, 302, November (4), 106–113.

Surowiecki, J. (2004) *The Wisdom of Crowds*, Random House, New York.

Sutter, J.D. (2009) Swine flu creates controversy on Twitter, April 30, *CNN.com* www.cnn.com/2009/TECH/04/27/swine.flu.twitter/ (accessed August 8, 2010).

Toffler, A. (1980) *The Third Wave*, Bantam, New York.

Watts, D.J. (2003) *Six Degrees: The Science of a Connected Age*, W.W. Norton & Co., New York.

Weinberger, D. (2001) *Small Pieces Loosely Joined: A Unified Theory of the Web*, Perseus Books, Cambridge, MA.

Wheeler, T.H. (2002) *Phototruth or Photofiction? Ethics and Media Imagery in the Digital Age*, Lawrence Erlbaum Associates, Mahwah, NJ.

Wolf, M. (2007) *Proust and the Squid: The Story and Science of the Reading Brain*, Harper Perennial, New York.

42

Ethical Implications of Blogging

Bernhard Debatin

The New Media Landscape and the Ethics of Blogging

Over the past decade, blogging has become a highly popular and influential form of web content production, not least because of its ease of use and its multifunctional applicability. As a user-friendly Web 2.0 application, blogging has dramatically lowered the publication threshold of the Internet and enabled almost anybody to produce and publish content on the web. This has not only resulted in a surge of diary-like blogs, but also changed the quality of public discourse. As a new *media form*, an easily accessible platform for the delivery of information, blogging makes possible new forms of civic and grassroots journalism, advocacy-driven publishing, political opinion writing, media criticism, and last but not least novel approaches to news and investigative journalism. Blogs dealing with political and social issues, which will be the main focus of this article, have become serious competitors to conventional journalism and mainstream media. Though blogging has not singlehandedly caused the decline of newspapers, it has certainly contributed to the fundamental reshuffling of the news media business over the past decade. Blogs have become increasingly influential, with mega-events such as 9/11, the Iraq war, the 2004 Asian tsunami, and the 2005 Hurricane Katrina being frequently cited milestones in their ascendency. Often, blogs were the first media to provide eyewitness accounts, photos, and videos of these and other events, such as the terrorist attacks in Madrid (2004), London (2005), and Mumbai (2008). Bloggers have also exerted considerable pressure on political processes: Trent Lott's 2002 resignation as Senate majority leader after his racist comments at Strom Thurmond's 100th birthday party and Dan Rather's resignation in 2004 as CBS anchor after a flawed *60 Minutes* report on President Bush's National Guard service were heavily

The Handbook of Global Communication and Media Ethics, First Edition. Edited by Robert S. Fortner and P. Mark Fackler.
© 2011 Blackwell Publishing Ltd. Published 2011 by Blackwell Publishing Ltd.

influenced by bloggers. Similarly, human rights and democracy movements in various countries, such as Iraq, Iran, and China, were often based on blogging and other Internet applications (for further examples see Farrell and Drezner, 2008).

Blogging and online social media, such as wikis and social networking sites, have also resulted in the emergence of countless online communities on an almost unlimited number of topics and interests (In der Smitten, 2008). These online communities are well suited to serve as sounding boards for people's life-world experiences and problems – a central function of autonomous public spheres as described by Jürgen Habermas (1996). While this development has revitalized and enlarged the public sphere, it has also blurred the lines between journalistic and nonjournalistic work, between professional journalists and amateur writers (Debatin, 2007a). In the past, this distinction was predetermined by organizational and production barriers – the technical equipment needed to produce conventional print or broadcast content required large capital investments and centralized, closed media organizations. In other words, the access barriers were high enough that only a few specialized people – professional journalists – embedded in organizational routines and structures of the newsroom would produce journalistic content and serve as gatekeepers. Over time, this led to a highly differentiated and consolidated media system, in which relatively few globally operating corporations control the vast majority of the print and broadcast media (McChesney, 2004, ch. 5), often referred to and criticized as the mainstream media. The open architecture of the Internet and particularly of blogging provides easily available, inexpensive publication outlets, which not only challenge the established mainstream media, but also sever the connection between membership in a media organization and journalistic work – that is, gathering, filtering, framing, and publishing newsworthy information. Today, a simple post by an individual blogger can have the same impact as an article on the front page of the *New York Times*, and it may be just as well researched and written as the newspaper article. The lack of reliable organizational and professional criteria, together with the fact that – based on the First Amendment – journalism cannot require any formal training or certification, raises the question of who is a journalist in this new media environment.

As Cecilia Friend and Jane Singer (2007, pp. 35–47) have pointed out, the role of the journalist nowadays mostly depends on how much one adheres to generally accepted norms of journalism ethics and on whether one is *doing* journalism, following the standards of journalistic practice. Yet even though these two criteria seem straightforward, a lot of blogging takes place in a gray zone between informal personal observations, transmission of gossip, critical opinion writing, and actual reporting. Contrary to conventional journalism, the blogosphere and its various subcultures actually tolerate biased and opinionated writing. Bloggers are not as committed to objectivity as traditional journalists. Instead, transparency – disclosure of motives, sources, and affiliations – is regarded as the "golden rule of the blogosphere" (Lasica, 2005). Though transparency appears to be a good basic norm to ensure accountability and credibility, by no means does it cover all bases of possible

Ethical Implications of Blogging

ethical predicaments. There is, indeed, a widespread perception that blogging is prone to ethical transgressions. The list of potential ethical problems of blogging (see Perlmutter and Schoen, 2007) is long and typically includes:

- lack of fact-checking and editorial oversight;
- creation of tunnel vision and lack of systematic coverage of topics;
- circular and self-referential spin-doctoring;
- dissemination of hoaxes, lies, and rumors;
- trolling (inflammatory posting), libel, and character assassination;
- stalking, harassment, and invasion of privacy;
- plagiarism and violation of copyright;
- lack of accountability due to anonymity, pseudonymity, or false identity;
- undisclosed conflicts of interest and lack of independence; and
- deceptive and manipulative blogging practices by corporations and individuals.

Ethical violations like these, particularly if committed repeatedly, will hurt the credibility and overall reputation of a blog and its author(s), which serves as a reasonably effective mechanism of self-regulation because "reputation is the principal currency of cyberspace" (Lasica, 2005). However, this mechanism only works if a blogger is indeed interested in his or her reputation, if other bloggers react to violations, and if these violations are not tolerated or supported due to cultural, ideological, or religious orientations of specific blogging communities. In the end, however, ethical missteps tend to be noticed and criticized by other bloggers. David Perlmutter and Mary Schoen (2007, p. 44) point out, that the "fervent discussion within the blogosphere supports the fact that bloggers do think about the ethical implications of their writings," even though they usually do not subscribe to specific codes of blogging ethics. In their study of independent blogs, the authors found that only few bloggers had explicit or implicit ethics codes.

Actual blogging ethics codes, such as the widely known "weblog ethics" by veteran blogger Rebecca Blood (2002), emphasize truthful publishing, accurate sourcing, transparent correction of mistakes, permanence and integrity of content, disclosure of conflicts of interests, and identification of partisan, biased, or questionable sources. Such codes, however, are often criticized as redundant or too specific, because they just transfer ethical norms from professional journalism onto the much broader and disparate field of blogging (Kuhn, 2007). A good example for the latter is the *Cyberjournalist*'s code of blogging ethics. A modified version of the Society of Professional Journalists ethics code (SPJ, 1996), it states three main norms: (1) Be honest and fair, (2) minimize harm, and (3) be accountable (Dube, 2003). This criticism has led to the development of broader codes, such as Tim O'Reilly's (2007) "Blogger's Code of Conduct" – highlighting responsibility for posts, respectful conversation, effort to communicate privately before responding publicly, protection from unfair attacks, prohibition of anonymous comments, and ignoring trolls. Martin Kuhn's (2007) "Code of Blogging Ethics" emphasizes interactivity, freedom of expression, truth, transparency, and

826   *Bernhard Debatin*

the human element as main norms. However, Kuhn too, agrees that such codes might be mostly an academic exercise because "bloggers seem to be generally resistant to rules and codes established by others" (2007, p. 34). This resistance to formal ethical regulation of blogging, however, does not mean that there are no shared convictions and behaviors among bloggers (see Rosen, 2008). In addition to the above mentioned golden rule of transparency, the blogging community typically shares similar norms and values, practices and rituals, and activities and language (Lowrey, 2006, p. 479).

Formal Characteristics of Blogging and Their Ethical Implications

Blogging is not only a broad and disparate field of action but also a multifaceted and ambiguous term that invites misunderstandings and overbroad assumptions. The first and most basic terminological distinction that should be drawn is the difference between blogging as a specific media form and as a technologically mediated form of communicative action. As a *media form*, blogging is indifferent toward its actual content and usage, although the constraints of the form have an influence on the content. The inverse chronological order, a general form feature of blogging, highlights the most recent blog post and puts other entries in the background without regard to their importance, whereas the spatial organization of a newspaper's front page and the temporal organization of a newscast always reflect the journalistic relevance of the reported events. The chronological order also organizes blog posts consecutively regardless of the time span that lies between individual entries, which means that a long break from posting may be followed directly by a flurry of daily or even hourly entries. This is radically different from the temporal form of periodical media (newspapers, magazines, broadcast), where regular intervals define content production and publication schedules.

Another specific feature of blogging as a media form is that blogs usually allow readers to add their comments below each entry, thus creating a forum for dialogue among authors and their readers. The built-in dialogue orientation and the fact that bloggers frequently comment on content from other blogs and the Internet, have led to a commonly followed convention of providing a link to the commented source and to list blogs that the blogger frequently reads in the blogroll. This practice of consistent and unambiguous sourcing increases accountability to a level "not found in traditional media" (Blood, 2002, p. 158), and it is part of the transparency norm, which constitutes, as mentioned above, the most important ethical standard in blogging. Yet, the question of when to link is not uncontested. Contrary to scholarly writing, where every source has to be referenced properly, bloggers sometimes deny linking to a source they do not want to endorse to prevent giving it credibility and traffic. Linking to and quoting other blogs may also raise the issue of content theft and intellectual property, which raises questions about appropriate linking policies (VanFossen, 2007).

Additional formal characteristics of blogging are the visual organization of the front page, which usually follows a two or three column layout showing the most recent blog post prominently in the widest column, and the length of the posts, which is determined by the nature of the diary form as well as the pressure to update frequently and to adapt to the reader's assumed attention span. Although there is no general rule, blog posts tend to be relatively short and to the point, usually somewhere between 200 and 500 words (Brown, 2007). This means that blog posts often do not treat a topic in depth and instead mostly provide comments, aphorisms, or short remarks, which feeds into the common criticism that blogs are merely derivative and fail to provide original content unless it is based on first-person observation (Andrews, 2003). While normal blogging platforms do not restrict the length of post (and thus allow for in-depth pieces if needed), micro-blogging services like Twitter, Jaiku, or Plurk limit individual posts to 140 characters, the maximum number of letters that can be sent as a text message from a phone.[1] Microblogging is particularly suited for mobile telecommunication and works under completely different conditions than conventional blogging. A single tweet resembles more a status update line on a social networking site than an actual blog entry. It is often used as a filter or a quick pointer to other, more in-depth content. However, it does not provide the narrative and context of a typical blog post, which gives reason for concern that the constraints of mobile digital devices fragment meaning and decontextualize communication (see e.g., Swarts, 2006). This feeds into the more general criticism of a fragmented communications universe, in which personalized online news and the highly self-referential and politically divided blogosphere reinforce a trend towards a fragmented culture. As a result, people may develop tunnel vision, increasingly lose the basis for shared experience across social divisions, and forfeit the ability and motivation to listen to diverging points of view (Debatin, 2007a, pp. 67ff).

Blogging is a *form of communicative action* and thus generally aimed at creating some sort of understanding between the blogger and his or her reader through blog posts and comments to blog posts. As communicative action, blogging can also be assumed to be based on three implicit general validity claims – factual *truth*, *rightness* of social norms and values, and an actor's intended *truthfulness* (Habermas, 1984, ch. III). Any blog post with questionable validity claims may and usually will be criticized accordingly as factually untrue, normatively unacceptable, or inauthentic or dishonest. That is the point where communication switches to the discourse mode, an argument about the validity of claims and an exchange of (more or less) good reasons to justify or falsify these claims. In this respect, blogging is no different to any other form of communicative action, although it is particularly well suited to facilitate debate due to its comment function, which provides a built-in dialogue orientation. Ultimately, the credibility and overall reputation of a blog will depend largely on how well supported and justified its claims are (including the claim of truthfulness/authenticity, which cannot be justified discursively but only through consistency of an author's action, see Habermas, 1984, p. 41). Here, too, the transparency norm is decisive, not only with regard to revealing one's sources, but also with respect to disclosing one's intentions, interests, and affiliations as factors that influence the credibility of a validity claim.

As a technologically mediated form of communicative action in which the communication partners are not copresent in a shared temporal and spatial situation, blogging tends to reduce natural inhibitions, which in face-to-face communication guarantee a certain level of civility and decorum. It is a known issue of computer-mediated communication that the lack of nonverbal cues, the absence of the Other, and the anonymity of the online persona not only provide protection (Qian and Scott, 2007), but may also result in uninhibited behavior, deception, and flame wars (Avgerinakou, 2003). A general problem of any online communication, this issue was addressed at the advent of the World Wide Web with so-called netiquette, basic ethical and courtesy rules for Internet users (Johnson, 1997; Shea, 1994). However, most blogging codes of ethics do not deal with this issue, probably due to the fact, as Kuhn observed, that they tend to look more at the function of blogs than their form and thus at best formulate general standards of harm avoidance (see, e.g., Dube, 2003; Kuhn, 2007) and civility (e.g., O'Reilly, 2007). The terms of service and user policies on popular blogging platforms (such as blogger.com, wordpress.com, or livejournal.com) typically include language that at least implicitly addresses the issue of uninhibited behavior by prohibiting hate speech, violence, defamatory content, and misleadingly impersonating another person or company. Some platforms, such as LiveJournal, even explicitly recommend being polite and nice to others and "at least treat people the way you'd want to be treated. People who are nasty and aggressive online are at greater risk of being bullied or harassed themselves" (www.livejournal.com/site/safetytips.bml).

Types of Blogging and Their Ethical Implications

Blogging integrates a wide range of disparate activities and intentions. As a general publication platform, it can be employed by many different actors for all sorts of purposes and many kinds of textual or audiovisual communication. Due to their many different functions and dimensions, blogs can be classified into a multitude of typologies and taxonomies (see e.g., Domingo and Heinonen, 2008; Hartelius, 2005; Herring *et al.*, 2004; Lasica, 2003; and Shirky, 2003). These typologies are often based on specific aspects, such as:

- popularity (usually determined by the number of backtracking links to a blog);
- scope of topics (single-topic, related topics, open topic blogs);
- type of author (lay person, expert, journalist, advocate);
- author status (individual, group member, affiliated with an organization, official spokesperson, etc.);
- type of information (personal experience, fiction, advocacy, comment and criticism, news, watchdog/investigative, etc.);
- type of journalistic writing (citizen blog, audience blog, journalist blog, media blog);

Ethical Implications of Blogging

- societal function (politics, journalism, education, marketing, entertainment, etc.);
- degree of content control (moderated vs. unmoderated, open vs. fixed authorship, comment function enabled or disabled, etc.); and
- type of blogging platform (microblogs like Twitter, normal textblogs, photologs and multimedia bloges like Tumblr, pure video blogs [vlogs] or audio podcast blogs, blogs embedded in a broader social media platform such as MySpace).

From the viewpoint of ethical analysis, it is most promising to look at the communicative function and the individual or organizational context of blogging. Using the typology of David Karpf (2008), different blogging activities can be categorized into four functional groups with distinct communicative goals: (1) Classical blogs amplify the individual's voice; they serve mostly as personal diaries and chronologies of personal experience but they can also extend to individuals' political musings, such as the widely read *InstaPundit*. (2) Community blogs create an interest-driven social space and infrastructure; they serve as collaborative blogs, such as the community blogs at *Feministing* and diaries at *Daily Kos*, to enhance community interests and the coordination of social action. (3) Institutional blogs augment the organizational mission of established institutions; these are blogs by media organizations (for instance the *Dot Earth* blog of the *New York Times*), political parties, or corporations. They serve as a communicative extension of the institution and often also as a PR platform for it. (4) Finally, bridge blogs are hybrids that combine elements of institutional blogs with those of community blogs, such as the *Huffington Post*, a hybrid of traditional newsmedia and community blogging. As this new form of blogging is not yet well established, it is hard to say whether bridge blogs "represent the next frontier of online political engagement or ... may face intractable difficulties" (Karpf, 2008, p. 375) due to the contradiction between conventional media culture and community blogging values.

Ethically seen, the main distinction between these types runs along the difference between individual and group or organizational ethics: Individual bloggers in the category of classical blogs may follow their own ethical compass and merely react to criticism from fellow bloggers with credibility and reputation as the main regulatory forces. Here, criticism relies on implicit yet widely shared normative assumptions about the transparency, truthfulness, and authenticity of the author of a blog. In December 2009, Andrew Sullivan, who emphasizes that he is an honest one-man blogger, was severely criticized by other bloggers because he was using paid "underbloggers" in his *Daily Dish* blog. The critics had no issue with openly using underbloggers without attribution during times of Sullivan's absence. However, they disapproved of using them as ghostbloggers during normal times and accused him of hypocrisy, dishonesty, and depriving his staff of proper credit (Butler, 2009). As Amardeep Singh (2008) has shown, sincerity and authenticity of the author are crucial norms among experience-oriented bloggers, which is why fake blogs, deceptive identities, and plagiarized or made-up accounts of personal experiences are particularly frowned upon. To be sure, role playing, gender bending, and experimenting with online identities has long been a celebrated though contended activity on the Internet (Turkle, 1995) and is to be found among bloggers, as well – but malicious deception and fraudulent personas are not well tolerated in the blogosphere. It was bloggers who exposed the popular YouTube vlog *lonelygirl15* – ostensibly the authentic diary of a cute yet disturbed adolescent named Bree – as actually the product of a Beverly Hills Agency that launched the fake blog as a viral marketing campaign. Bree's fan community left angry and disappointed messages on her YouTube profile, accusing her of "taking advantage of her viewers' trust" (Pintado, 2006), while media commentators pointed more to the obvious fact that gullible Internet users and the hunger for originality and grounded authenticity made this possible. "In retrospect," remarked former VH1 Vice President Michael Hirschorn (2006, p. 114), "it was a thrilling hoax that was perfectly attuned to the cultural moment, playing in the interstices between authenticity and artifice, amateurism and professionalism." This shows that authenticity is both the currency for success and the critical yardstick for the credibility of an experience-based blog.

Individual bloggers quite frequently define comment policies to keep the conversation civil. Less common are terms of service agreements to keep bloggers from being sued for their content. On his *InstaPundit* blog, law professor Glenn Reynolds provides a byzantine tongue-in-cheek contract of adhesion (see http://pajamasmedia.com/instapundit/terms-of-use/). Usually however, there is not much formal normative language on these blogs. In contrast to this, bloggers in the community blogs category will be expected to adhere to overall community goals and standards that are often explicitly codified. Particularly political and issue-oriented blogging communities tend to create specific rules and regulations for their contributors, along with editing posts and moderating comments. For example, *Feministing* has an explicit user policy that defines the site's mission, membership and purpose of the community, and the comments policy. It states that "anti-feminist comments, blogs, and profiles are not permitted" and, more specifically, that comments containing "personal attacks, hate speech or offensive language will be deleted" (http://community.feministing.com/about/). The "posting rules" for *redstate.com*, a large conservative blogging community, explicitly prohibit profanity, personal attacks, harassing or demonizing individuals, disruptive behavior or off-topic remarks, and trolling or mobying (www.redstate.com/posting-rules/). Similar rules can be found in almost any blogging community. In some instances, such policies are quite detailed and resemble codes of politically correct speech (e.g., the "safe space" definitions on the *Shakesville* blog, http://shakespearessister. blogspot.com/2006/07/off-limits-humor.html). Some policies state the site owner's unlimited rights to ban members indiscriminately – "anyone the site owner does not like," as stated in the community guidelines of *RightNation.US* (www. rightnation.us/forums/index.php?act=Help&CODE=01 &HID=17).

Bloggers in the categories of institutional blogs and bridge blogs will more likely be bound by institutional policies. Such policies usually regulate three different kinds of organization-related blogging: First, members of the organization who are

Ethical Implications of Blogging

blogging on the organization's website in their professional function; second, members of the organization who maintain a personal blog outside the organization's site; and third, members of the community who are blogging on the organization's website. Regulations for the last group are often stipulated in "community rules" or "social media policies," whereas the former two are often lumped together in the institution's editorial policies or blog policies. Community rules are more general and usually address issues such as respect and decorum, personal attacks and harassment, privacy and personal information, offensive language and illegal content, spam and off-topic contributions, and proprietary information and copyright (see the collection of such policies at http://socialmediagovernance.com/policies.php). In addition to these general rules, editorial or blog policies usually delineate more specific issues related to the organization's culture and reputation. Most organizations reserve the right to review and remove content deemed inappropriate or otherwise objectionable, and they aim to establish high standards of accountability for the bloggers on their sites. A typical and very concise example of this is the ESPN (2007) employee blog policy, which states:

> Incomplete, inaccurate, inappropriate, threatening, harassing or poorly worded postings may be harmful to other employees, damage employee relationships, undermine ESPN's effort to encourage teamwork, violate ESPN policy or harm the Company, which may result in disciplinary action up to and including termination. Employees bear full responsibility for the material they post on personal blogs or other social media.

Media organizations are particularly concerned about maintaining journalistic standards on their blogs. Journalists' blogs on media websites are usually vetted through normal editorial routines, although only a few media organizations have explicit policies about this[2] while most seem to follow their established editorial routines and procedures without codifying them. The same is true for nonmedia organizations: relatively few institutions have actually codified their policies (Boudreaux, 2009).

Generally seen, ethics policies seem to be more explicit and more sophisticated in large, Internet-savvy organizations with a strong eye on their public appearance and reputation. The more that is at stake, the more likely it is that someone might lose his or her job because of blogging. Although no statistics exist, there are numerous reports of bloggers who got fired for blogging, usually because they supposedly violated some institutional policy and/or posted content that was regarded as inappropriate (Palan, 2008; Roberts, 2005; Wyld, 2008). Opening websites to user generated content, such as readers' blogs, poses similar problems. Conventional media organizations and other institutions find themselves in a bind between guarding their standards and tolerating offensive or otherwise subpar user-generated content. Though blogging has been embraced by countless news media, Dana Hull (2006) points out that there is "an inevitable clash of values between a newspaper, which has a journalistic reputation and brand name to

protect, and a swiftly changing medium that has grown in power and prestige precisely because it has flouted many of journalism's traditional rules." In the majority
of cases, media err on the side of caution and control users' posts closely, which is
why true bridge blogs are rare. However, this policy not only puts a strain on
resources – somebody has to monitor the blog posts – it is also faced with the
problem that rules and guidelines inevitably lag behind trends and development in
the digital world so that "the handiwork of the typically plodding task-force process of hammering out ethics codes will be horrendously outdated by the time it
emerges" (Hull, 2006.).

The difficulties with defining a working ethical position for blogging activities
on institutional websites are indicative of the transformation of basic characteristics
and assumptions of journalism itself. A prime force driving this transition are journalistic blogs, which are written by anyone who "commits journalism," anyone
who reports honestly and accurately about events (Lasica, 2002). Journalistic blogs
thus encompass individual citizen bloggers from outside the media, community
bloggers, and bloggers that are affiliated with the media or the political system.
Although journalistic blogs "may not strictly follow traditional journalistic routines
and conventions, [they] have the clear intention to collect, analyze, interpret or
comment on current events to wide audiences and in this way perform the very
same social function usually associated with institutionalized media" (Domingo
and Heinonen, 2008, p. 6).

The Political Blogosphere as Echo Chamber and Intelligent Megaphone

The fear of news media managers that blogs may taint their reputation is not
unfounded. The blogosphere is often referred to as an echo chamber that will
repeat and amplify any noise regardless of its content and truth value. Many of the
hot topics in the blogosphere are not so much based on careful fact checking, accurate reporting, and comprehensive coverage, but are more the result of a self-
reinforcing process in which somebody's unconfirmed claim is repeated and
reposted until it becomes a meme – a self-replicating and widely circulated idea or
piece of information (Dawkins, 1976, ch.11). The self-referential hypertext structure of the Internet facilitates the viral spread of such memes, many of which are
blatant rumors and urban legends (Balkin, 2003; Thieme, 1997). In addition, the
predominant form of blogging, commentary and aphorism, further supports and
accelerates the unvetted spread of gossip and rumor.

For example, the cable news service CNN learned the hard way how risky it can
be to allow unedited user-posts on their citizen journalism site *iReport* when a
blogger named Johntw posted on October 3, 2008, that Apple's Steve Jobs was
rushed to the ER after a severe heart attack (Blodget, 2008). Although the post
was only up for 20 minutes and showed all the signs of a rumor (a supposedly
"quite reliable" but anonymous source, no corroborating information), the story

Ethical Implications of Blogging

spread quickly, particularly through Twitter, and Apple's stock "took a major hit before bouncing back," triggering an investigation by the Securities and Exchange Commission (Blodget, 2008). CNN later called the report "fraudulent" and made it unavailable. Like many rumors, this one flew particularly well because there had already been a number of reports and rumors about Jobs' health, including an erroneously published obituary on the Bloomberg newswire (Tate, 2008). Late in 2008, new blog-based rumors about Jobs' health problems again significantly depressed Apple's stock and forced the company to release an official statement about his health status, which was rapidly eclipsed by a message hacked into the life feed of the MacWorld conference on January 6, 2009, claiming that Steve Jobs had died. Though debunked immediately, the rumor was quickly tweeted all over the place (Linkins, 2009). The power of the meme and its vast proliferation can also be seen on a webpage titled "Is Steve Jobs dead?" which was created by the independent Apple news blog *World of Apple*, displaying a lapidary "nope" (www. isstevejobsdead.com/). Reflecting on the questionable reliability of a simple statement like this, the source code of this webpage includes a disclaimer comment stating "This page is by no means a good method of seeing if Steve Jobs is dead." Processes like this exemplify how potentially any rumor may be echoed and amplified over and over again until it becomes a meme in public discourse.

Contrary to its appearance, however, the blogosphere is not just an unorganized chaos of chatter, gossip, and rumors. Particularly the political blogosphere follows its own logic of forming topics and opinions. The communicative processes of the blogosphere can be well demonstrated with the long tail model (Anderson, 2004; Shirky, 2003), which states that only a very few blogs have an extremely high number of readers, while the overwhelming majority of blogs have very few readers. This can be represented on a graph, which shows a curve in the form of a trumpet-shaped megaphone cut in half along the longitudinal axis. The long asymptotic end of the curve represents the "long tail," which is populated by millions of little or barely read blogs, while the opening of the bell consists of the few popular blogs (see Figure 42.1).

Bloggers usually acknowledge via trackback links that they posted on another blog's entry, and these trackbacks can be used as a measure for blog popularity. Services such as *Technorati* or *Blogpulse* count trackbacks to create a ranking of blogs called "blog authority." The rather small group of very high authority blogs is referred to A-list blogs, while the next group of high authority blogs is referred to as B-list blogs, and the middle and low authority blogs are C-list and D-list blogs (Ng, 2006). Although A-list blogs have the most exposure and tend to be highly influential, less popular blogs can exert quite some influence, as well, most notably when a topic bounces back and forth among them (Wallsten, 2007). The political blogosphere, in particular, is thus not a nondirectional, disorganized echo chamber but rather an intelligent megaphone that filters, focuses, and amplifies specific topics. In a snowball effect, these topics are transmitted from the less popular to the more popular blogs, become charged with newsworthiness, and are finally picked up by B-list and A-list bloggers. The more controversial or spectacular

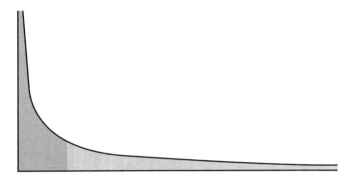

Figure 42.1 The long tail.
Source: Picture by Hay Kranen/PD

the issue, the more likely it is that this dynamic process will unfold. Amplification often receives an extra boost when blog posts get retweeted swiftly and reposted or linked to in online social networks. The intelligent megaphone works like a selective catalyst and amplifier. This contributes to a hierarchy, where well-established blogs function as opinion leaders, and other blogs both feed on them and provide them with thematic input. As a whole, the political blogosphere can be regarded as a highly sensitive sounding board that anticipates media and public agendas. Since both journalists and politicians read A-list and B-list blogs, some high profile blog topics have a decent chance to make it into the mass media: "Under specific circumstances – when key weblogs focus on a new or neglected issue – blogs can act as a focal point for the mainstream media and exert formidable agenda-setting power" (Drezner and Farrell, 2004, p. 34). Blogging can thus reverse the conventional agenda-setting mechanisms (Delwiche, 2005). Agenda setting used to be the privilege of conventional mass media (Luhmann, 1971; McCombs and Shaw, 1972), but in the era of networked online mass communication, the possibility of influencing public agendas is shifting more toward blogging citizens and amateur journalists (Domingo and Heinonen, 2008, p. 12). In terms of the theory of the public sphere, this means that the audience-generated agendas of blogs help revive and fulfill the public sphere's roles as a sensor and a sentinel for lifeworld issues (Debatin, 2007a).

Of course, the intelligent megaphone is bidirectional. Not only is there noise coming from it, one can also talk into it. This is exactly the case when media reports or political events become the subject of blogging and are then reflected back into the media. This is why it would be wrong to assume that blogging is merely a parasitic activity, simply feeding on the mainstream media; rather, it is a symbiotic two-way relationship, in which a "complex, bidirectional relationship between mainstream media coverage and blog discussion" arises (Wallsten, 2007, p. 581).

Politicians and professional journalists thus face a growing number of journalistic bloggers and online social networkers who influence the process of public opinion with microscopically small yet synergistically effective actions. Recent election campaigns in the United States clearly indicated this new type of microinfluence through user-generated content in social media (In der Smitten, 2008; Perlmutter,

2006). A study by the Pew Internet & American Life Project showed that a 55% majority of the voting-age population used the Internet to obtain information about the election process and "nearly one in five Internet users posted their thoughts, comments or questions about the campaign on a website, blog, social networking site or other online forum" (Smith, 2009, p. 12). Moreover, blogs and Twitter feeds were particularly used by politically interested Internet users, who "delved deeply into the long tail of political commentary in 2008" (Smith, 2009, p. 61). These users were also able to employ a large number of blog aggregators, trackers, and widgets to filter and focus information from blogs according to their interests. At the same time, many election controversies were fought out via blogs, Twitter, and online social networking sites (Gordon-Murnane, 2008). Never before had a presidential campaign been that prominently in the light of public scrutiny from bloggers. Particularly influential were watchdog blogs, such as *Factcheck.org*, which is run by the Annenberg Public Policy Center of the Pennsylvania University, or NPR's blog *Vox Politics*, as well as *Politico*, a news blog by former *Washington Post* journalists, and the independent political blog *Talking Points Memo*. These and similar blogs were highly popular, and they scrutinized almost every movement of the candidates, their statements, and their mishaps. They not only have a broad readership, they have also become an indispensible source for conventional journalists. According to a survey published in the *American Journalism Review*, 70% of all political reporters spend more than one hour per day reading blogs and other online sources (Lidman, 2008). Particularly popular among reporters are large aggregating blogs such as the *Huffington Post*, *Daily Kos*, and *Boing Boing*. Newspaper blogs such as *The Swamp* of the *Chicago Tribune* and political news blogs such as *Real Clear Politics* and *Talking Points Memo* are mentioned frequently as well.

The use of blogs and other social media to obtain and discuss political information is by no means restricted to the American populace: Zephyr Teachout (2009) has shown that the Internet as a truly global medium of mass, group, and interpersonal communication is increasingly allowing for extraterritorial electioneering, a process in which foreigners not only receive more information about domestic election campaigns, but also contribute to the debate. "Given the global impact of United States policy, twenty years from now massive efforts to influence United States elections – from outside its borders – will be routine," Teachout argues (2009, p. 164). She also points out that highly popular blogs like *Boing-Boing*, *Global Voices*, or *Daily Kos* encourage people from all over the world to contribute, and that the line between domestic and international blogs is increasingly blurred because blogs are organized topically and not by place (Teachout, 2009, p. 175–176). Since globalized electioneering both "enables and undermines self-government," it is difficult to assess its long-term effects and, according to Teachout, the only way to avoid manipulation from extraterritorial parties is "a deeper, societal commitment to education and good, reliable, information" (Teachout, 2009, p. 190).

All in all, political blogging seems to spawn a sort of collective intelligence through the selective processing of the "intelligent megaphone." Against the unparalleled decline of conventional newspapers, the blogosphere's exponential growth and its increasing popularity may provide a first glimpse into how the organization of societal knowledge and public discourses might look under conditions of highly networked online social media. To be sure, this does not make the Internet less fragmented. Obviously, the Internet as a whole and blogs in particular have no general gatekeepers, and there are no commonly shared criteria for how information is gathered and filtered on the Internet. Ethical guidelines for the blogosphere and other social media should therefore address not only the issue of competent and reliable content production, but also that of user competency and media literacy. The new social media jungle indeed presupposes active media literacy of its users, the ability to discern credibility, accuracy, and verisimilitude of web-based information. Thus, the gullible and naïve Internet consumer must be superseded by the critical and skilled online user who knows how to evaluate online sources and how to use filtering tools, tracking devices, and aggregators to navigate the digital information flood. This, ultimately, will not be a result of better or more detailed ethics codes, but of better education and the societal will to dedicate appropriate resources to it. A practical media ethics in the age of online social media starts with changes in the institutional goals and emphasis of the educational system.

A Normative Framework for Journalistic Blogging

Within a short period of just 10 years, political blogging has reached a level where it is slowly but steadily transforming politics and the media (Farrell and Drezner, 2008). This is not just a trend in the Western industrialized countries. For instance, blogs are increasingly influential in Asia, where "bloggers have become an important source of news outside of but also alongside of traditional mainstream media" (Katz and Lai, 2009, p. 105). Countries with oppressive political regimes, such as Iran or China, use sophisticated mechanisms to control and censor the content of their thriving blogospheres (Katz and Lai, 2009, p. 102; Loewenstein, 2008). Nevertheless, the Iranian political opposition has repeatedly been very successful in using blogging (and recently also Twitter) to organize political protest and create a platform for a lively public sphere: "What is certain is that the blogosphere offers new possibilities for Iranians seeking a virtual sphere wherein people can share their ideas, debate the diverse social and political aspects of their lives, and cleanse their minds and views of the media-saturated information disseminated by state-controlled media" (Ghanavizi, 2009, p. 150). Rather than initiating revolutionary change, grassroots bloggers contribute to a gradual cultural transition and to an increasingly open discussion of topics that used to be taboo. Though their impact may be at the level of incremental microinfluence, blogs can play an important role in the process of democratization – even in remote countries such as Kyrgyzstan (Kulikova and Perlmutter, 2007). At the same time, these blogs provide an important insider view to the rest of the world from countries whose official media are heavily censored and controlled by the authorities.

Ethical Implications of Blogging

It has to be mentioned, though, that blogs can also play a significant role in incendiary and violent processes. Controversial issues that trigger strong emotional reactions can easily become the focus of blogging activities; and in a globalized communication environment, any content that violates cultural sensitivities can set off a "butterfly effect" through swift and unforeseeable reactions in the blogosphere. When the Danish newspaper *Jyllands-Posten* published the infamous Mohammed cartoons, it was the discussion in Arab blogs, and not the mainstream media, that facilitated distribution of information in the Islamic world and thus inflamed and intensified the conflict. In many countries, this led to a "telemobilization" of the population and to violent protests and riots (Debatin, 2007b). In the pre-Internet world, the Mohammed cartoons would have hardly received any attention beyond the local or regional press. Today, however, with an increasingly connected world, a global flow of information, and worldwide migration processes, such local controversies can develop into intercultural conflicts of global dimensions.

Both aspects of blogging – its democratizing power and its incendiary effects – demonstrate its increasing influence on political processes and the media environment. It represents a transformation of the structural conditions of societal and political communication, driven by journalistic blogs. They are often the first to report extraordinary breaking news (such as terror attacks or natural catastrophes) and to comment on scandals and outrageous developments in society. They challenge conventional media with their muckraking attitude and their often relentless commentary that need not pay tribute to the established balance of power and economic or political sensitivities. Independence is therefore, together with transparency, an often-touted standard of blogging: "If there is one thing the blogger has, then, it is independence, particularly in the existential sense of being capable of defining oneself solely through one's actions – or words" (Singer, 2006, p. 9).

However, Cecilia Friend and Jane Singer (2007, p. 124) also point out that bloggers rarely disclose their own conflicts of interest, including where their paychecks come from, which may put their independence in question. Some bloggers have been criticized for their dependence on specific sponsors and advertisers, their affiliation with businesses, or their willingness to positively mention brands and products in their posts in exchange for compensation, a practice similar to product placement in movies and TV shows. Yet, fellow bloggers keep a close eye on such marketing practices and are quick to denounce them. Failed attempts by corporations to recruit bloggers in order to push their products, such as Dr Pepper/Seven Up and Mazda, or to create fake blogs for image marketing, such as the much ridiculed blog *Wal-Marting across America*, serve as cautionary tales: "Corporations should be very careful about entering the blogosphere, as already there have been prominent firms who have learned painful lessons about how not to engage in corporate blogging" (Wyld, 2008, p. 459). Recent regulations by the Federal Trade Commission now also prescribe that "bloggers who make an endorsement must disclose the material connections they share with the seller of the product or service" (FTC, 2009).

Most bloggers are their own master, therefore, accountability is not built into the routines of a blogger's action as it is in conventional journalism, where established professional practices, organizational routines, and institutional loyalties guarantee a certain level of accountability. Instead, it is imposed on the blogger through the criticism he or she may receive from other bloggers, mirroring the fact that the editing process in blogging is quasi inverted – following the maxim "publish first, edit later if you're getting criticized by your fellow bloggers."

This also has implications for the notion of truth. Conventional journalism ethics expects truth to be both the goal and result of the journalistic process: Comprehensive and accurate gathering of information from credible sources, as well as rigorous filtering and fact-checking from a detached position that separates facts from values, will lead to truthful and reliable reporting. This is usually represented in the objectivity norm (Schudson, 2001). In contrast to this, truth in blogging is more the result of a discursive process, an interaction of ideas that circulate and compete in the blogosphere. Although the more serious journalistic bloggers value accuracy just as much as conventional journalists do, they usually do not adhere to the ideal of detached objectivity and instead engage in citizen- and advocacy-oriented reporting (Domingo and Heinonen, 2008; Ward, 2009). While objectivity can be called a basic norm of professional journalism, journalistic blogging instead seems to follow a combination of three main norms, namely transparency, accuracy, and advocacy.

It can thus be argued that the actual practice of journalistic blogging is replacing the objectivity norm with a new normative constellation, the triangle of transparency, accuracy, and advocacy as shown in Figure 42.2. This normative constellation mirrors existing practice among bloggers and at the same time can serve as a normative framework to orient bloggers' activities. *Transparency* means openness about one's bias, intentions, standpoint, and preferences, and about the fluid, infinite character of stories. It is typically related to classical blogs of individual bloggers. *Accuracy* implies comprehensive, credible, and factual reporting that distinguishes reliable and credible information from mere gossip and rumor. It is most closely connected to news blogs. *Advocacy* stands for the fact that bloggers forgo the professional detachment of conventional journalists, are more connected to their audiences, and act as sensors and amplifiers of the lifeworld. Advocacy tends to be associated with citizen and community blogs.

The triangle of transparency, accuracy, and advocacy provides a normative framework for the analysis of journalistic blogs, combining values and practices of conventional journalism with the grassroots and community orientation of citizen journalism and the autonomy of the individual blogger. It can be used to evaluate and categorize journalistic blogs according to their specific emphasis. More importantly, it may serve as a yardstick for the ethical quality of a blog. Ideally, an ethically well done journalistic blog would occupy the intersection of transparency, accuracy, and advocacy. It would balance and integrate all three aspects evenly. It would be open about its bias, intents, and sources, it would be as accurate and comprehensive as possible in its factual claims, and it would provide informed

Figure 42.2 The new normative constellation.

advocacy and well supported opinion (as opposed to ideological rants and unreflected prejudice).

Accuracy, advocacy, and transparency are in fact blogging-specific instances of universal communication ethics as put forward in the three general validity claims of communicative action (Habermas, 1984, ch. III). Accuracy corresponds to the validity claim of factual truth concerning statements about the objective world. Advocacy corresponds to the validity claim of the rightness of norms and values in our social world. Transparency corresponds to the validity claim of truthfulness with regard to the sincerity and authenticity of an actor's intentions. Journalistic bloggers who adhere to this normative framework would thus have a thorough grounding in communicative ethics while at the same time also following basic blogging-specific norms. The triangle of transparency, accuracy, and advocacy can therefore be applied in a practical way as a normative framework for bloggers who want to follow standards of best practice for journalistic blogging. Although this does not amount to the prescriptive language of a rule-based ethics code, it has the advantage that it is grounded in a systematic and universal approach rather than a casuistic collection of norms. It thus provides a normative constellation of three basic benchmarks that allow the individual blogger to position and orient his or her communicative action as a blogger.

Summary and Conclusion: Toward an Ethical Blogosphere?

Although the ethicality of blogs is frequently questioned, they can and should be evaluated by general criteria of trustworthiness, veracity, and credibility just like any other media. The overall reliability of blogs can be determined by a number of interrelated quality criteria, including transparency, accuracy, independence, timeliness, sourcing, personal accountability, and long-term consistency and reputation. Compared to conventional journalism, the editing and fact checking process is inverted: publish first, edit later. Truth in blogging is thus the result of a collective self-correcting process through feedback and mutual criticism. Yet, since most bloggers are very interested in maintaining their reputation, they are usually thorough about editing and fact-checking before posting. Accountability is thus created through the mechanism of mutual criticism and the bloggers' interest in their own reputation. Individual bloggers who publish classical blogs, however, lack the organizational infrastructure needed to perform in-depth information gathering, fact checking, and editing.

Blogging is a media form, not a specific type of content or genre. As a publication platform, blogging can be used for many different purposes, including reporting events and commenting on them. While many blogs rely on the work of traditional media as their basis for commentary and opinion writing, they have many times served as primary sources of information and breaking news. Journalistic blogs exert a growing influence on both media and political processes and have given rise to a structural transformation of the media and political environment. Part of this transformation is a revitalization of the public sphere through grassroots blogging and a shift of agenda-setting power to bloggers. This happens especially when topics that are ignored by the mainstream media become amplified through a complex snowball effect in the "intelligent megaphone" of the blogosphere, often supported and accelerated by Twitter feeds and communications in online social networks. Conventional mass media and bloggers have thus entered into a symbiotic relationship.

With the increasing influence of bloggers comes growing responsibility. Ethics codes for bloggers have addressed the norms and standards of ethics, first and foremost transparency, but also norms derived from journalistic ethics, such as truth, fairness, honesty, harm avoidance, and independence. The downside of such ethics codes, however, is that they tend to be somewhat casuistic collections of rules and that they are usually rejected by bloggers as externally imposed.

As an alternative to rule-based ethics codes, this article proposes a rational reconstruction of the normative framework that is guiding journalistic bloggers. This framework consists of three basic benchmarks – accuracy, advocacy, and transparency – that are grounded in and correspond to the three validity claims – truth, rightness, and truthfulness – inherent to universal ethics of communicative action. This new normative constellation allows basic standards to be defined for journalistic blogging without the prescriptive, external approach of ethics codes. As the blogosphere is increasingly becoming an influential voice in public discourse, it can be expected that journalistic bloggers with a vested interest in their reputation and influence will position themselves in the intersection of the transparency, accuracy, and advocacy. If so, this will considerably enhance professionalism and strengthen ethics in the blogosphere.

Ethical Implications of Blogging   841

Notes

1   Though microblogging is not the focus of this article, it is relevant to the topic because of its interaction with and influence on blogging.
2   See for instance:
    - the *New York Times* policy at www.nytco.com/press/ethics.html#B5
    - the *Denver Post* policy at www.denverpost.com/ethics
    - the *San Antonio Express-News* policy at www.mysanantonio.com/about_us/express-news/Express-News_Ethics_Policy.html
(All accessed August 17, 2010).

References

Anderson, C. (2004) The long tail. *Wired*, October, 12.10, www.wired.com/wired/archive/12.10/tail.html (accessed August 2, 2010).

Andrews, P. (2003) Is blogging journalism? *Nieman Reports*, 57, 63–64.

Avgerinakou, A. (2003) "Flaming" in computer-mediated interactions, in *Rethinking Communicative Interaction: New Interdisciplinary Horizons*, (ed. C. Grant), Benjamins, Amsterdam, pp. 273–293.

Balkin, J.M. (2003) *Cultural Software: A Theory of Ideology*, Yale University Press, New Haven.

Blodget, H. (2008) Apple denies Steve Jobs heart attack report: It is not true. *The Business Insider – Silicon Alley Insider* (Blog), October 3, http://www.businessinsider.com/2008/10/apple-s-steve-jobs-rushed-to-er-after-heart-attack-says-cnn-citizen-journalist (accessed August 2, 2010).

Blood, R. (2002) *The Weblog Handbook: Practical Advice on Creating and Maintaining Your Blog*, Basic Books, New York.

Boudreaux, C. (2009) Analysis of social media policies: lessons and best practices, December 16, http://socialmediagovernance.com/downloads/Social-Media-Policy-Analysis.pdf (accessed on August 2, 2010).

Brown, S. (2007) How long is the ideal blog post? *Modern Life* (Blog) May 16, http://modernl.com/article/how-long-is-the-ideal-blog-post (accessed on August 2, 2010).

Butler, I. (2009) Andrew Sullivan explains his blog. *Parabasis* (Blog). December 21, http://parabasis.typepad.com/blog/2009/12/andrew-sullivan-explains-his-blog.html (accessed on August 2, 2010).

Dawkins, R. (1976) *The Selfish Gene*, Oxford University Press, Oxford.

Debatin, B. (2007a) The Internet as a new platform for expressing opinions and as a new public sphere, in *Handbook of Public Opinion Research*, (eds W. Donsbach and M.W. Traugott) Sage, London, pp. 64–72.

Debatin, B. (2007b) The cartoon debate and the pathologies of the global information society: An introduction, in *Der Karikaturenstreit und die Pressefreiheit / The Cartoon Debate and the Freedom of the Press*, (ed. B. Debatin), LIT, Berlin, pp. 13–21.

Delwiche, A. (2005) Agenda-setting, opinion leadership, and the world of web logs. *First Monday*, 10 (12–5), http://firstmonday.org/htbin/cgiwrap/bin/ojs/index.php/fm/article/view/1300/1220 (accessed August 2, 2010).

Domingo, D., and Heinonen, A. (2008) Weblogs and journalism: A typology to explore the blurring boundaries. *Nordicom Review*, 29 (1), pp. 3–15.

Drezner, D.W., and Farrell, H. (2004) Web of influence. *Foreign Policy*. Nov/Dec, pp. 32–40.

Dube, J. (2003) A blogger's code of ethics. *Cyberjournalist.net*, April 13, http://www.cyberjournalist.net/news/000215.php (accessed August 8, 2010).

ESPN (2007) Blog policy: Social media guidelines for ESPN employees. *ESPN Media Zone*, http://espnmediazone.com/documents/20090804_Blog_Policy.htm (last accessed November 12, 2009).

Farrell, H., and Drezner, D.W. (2008) The power and politics of blogs. *Public Choice*, 134, 15–30.

Friend, C., and Singer, J. B. (2007) *Online Journalism Ethics. Traditions and Transitions*, M.E. Sharpe, New York.

FTC (2009) *FTC Publishes Final Guides Governing Endorsements, Testimonials* (FTC Press Release), October 5, www.ftc.gov/opa/2009/10/endortest.shtm (accessed August 8, 2010).

Ghanavizi, N. (2009) Self-expression and the exchange of ideas: Iranians, the Internet and blogging. *antiTHESIS*, 19, 139–153.

Gordon-Murnane, L. (2008) The 51st State: The state of online. *Searcher*. Oct, 16 (9), 38–45.

Habermas, J. (1984) *The Theory of Communicative Action, Vol. 1: Reason and the Rationalization of Society*, (trans. T. McCarthy), original published 1981, Beacon Press, Boston, MA.

Habermas, J. (1996) *Between Facts and Norms*. (trans. W. Rehg), original published 1992, MIT Press, Cambridge, MA.

Hartelius, E.J. (2005) A content-based taxonomy of blogs and the formation of a virtual community. *Kaleidoscope: A Graduate Journal of Qualitative Communication Research*, 4, 71–91.

Herring, S.C., Scheidt, L.A., Bonus, S. *et al.* (2004) Bridging the gap: A genre analysis of weblogs. Proceedings of the 37th Annual Hawaii International Conference on System Sciences (HICSS'04), IEEE Press, Los Alamitos, www.blogninja.com/DDGDD04.doc (last accessed November 12, 2009).

Hirschorn, M. (2006) Thank you, YouTube. *The Atlantic Monthly*. November, 144–147.

Hull, D. (2006) Blogging between the lines. *American Journalism Review*. Dec 2006/Jan 2007. www.ajr.org/Article.asp?id=4230 (accessed August 8, 2010).

In der Smitten, S. (2008) Political potential and capabilities of online communities. *German Policy Studies/Politikfeldanalyse, 4* (4), 32–62.

Johnson, D.G. (1997) Ethics online. *Communications of the ACM, 40* (1), 60–65.

Karpf, D. (2008) Understanding blogspace. *Journal of Information Technology and Politics*, 5 (4), 369–385.

Katz, J.E., and Lai, C.-H. (2009) News blogging in cross-cultural contexts: A report on the struggle for voice. *Know Techn Pol*, 22, 95–107.

Kuhn, M. (2007) Interactivity and prioritizing the human: A code of blogging ethics. *Journal of Mass Media Ethics*, 22 (1), 18–36.

Kulikova, S.V., and Perlmutter, D. D. (2007) Blogging down the dictator? The Kyrgyz revolution and Samizdat websites. *The International Communication Gazette*, 69 (1), 29–50.

Lasica, J.D. (2002) When bloggers commit journalism. *Online Journalism Review.* September. 24, www.ojr.org/ojr/lasica/1032910520.php (accessed August 8, 2010).

Lasica, J.D. (2003) What is participatory journalism? *The Online Journalism Review*, August 7, www.ojr.org/ojr/workplace/1060217106.php (accessed August 8, 2010).

Lasica, J.D. (2005) The cost of ethics: Influence peddling in the blogosphere. *The Online Journalism Review*, February 17, www.ojr.org/ojr/stories/050217lasica/ (accessed August 8, 2010).

Lidman, M. (2008) Blog binge. *American Journalism Review*, August/September, www.ajr.org/Article.asp?id=4597 (last accessed December 20, 2009).

Linkins, J. (2009) Steve Jobs dead: How the MacWorld rumor spread. *Huffington Post* (Blog), January 6, www.huffingtonpost.com/2009/01/06/steve-jobs-dead-how-the-m_n_155639.html (accessed August 8, 2010).

Loewenstein, A. (2008) Bloggers of the world, let's shop! *The Australian*, August 23, 6.

Lowrey, W. (2006) Mapping the journalism blogging relationship. *Journalism*, 7 (4), 477–500

Luhmann, N. (1971) Öffentliche Meinung, in *Politische Planung. Aufsätze zur Soziologie von Politik und Verwaltung*, (ed. N. Luhman), Westdeutscher Verlag, Opladen, pp. 9–34.

McChesney, R.W. (2004) *The Problem of the Media: U.S. Communication Politics in the 21st Century*, Monthly Review Press, New York.

McCombs, M.E., and Shaw, D.L. (1972) The agenda-setting function of mass media. *Public Opinion Quarterly*, 36, 176–187.

Ng, T. (2006) Are you an A-list bloglebrity? *Kineda* (Blog), November 15, www.kineda.com/are-you-an-a-list-bloglebrity/ (accessed August 8, 2010).

O'Reilly, T. (2007) Draft blogger's code of conduct. *OReilly Radar* [Blog]. April, 8, 2007. http://radar.oreilly.com/archives/2007/04/draft-bloggers-1.html (last accessed December 21, 2009).

Palan, E. (2008) 7 people fired for blogging. *Mental Floss* (Blog), May 29, www.mentalfloss.com/blogs/archives/15329 (accessed August 8, 2010).

Perlmutter, D.D. (2006) Political Blogs: The New Iowa? *Chronicle of Higher Education*, 52 (38), May 26, B6–B8.

Perlmutter, D.D., and Schoen, M. (2007) If I break a rule, what do I do, fire myself? Ethics codes of independent blogs. *Journal of Mass Media Ethics*, 22 (1), 37–48.

Pintado, M. (2006) Lonelygirl15 Exposes the Net's Illogical Sense of Community. *Eureka Street*, 16 (13), September 18, http://eurekastreet.com.au/article.aspx?aeid=1762 (accessed on August 8, 2010).

Qian, H., and Scott, C. R. (2007) Anonymity and self-disclosure on weblogs. *Journal of Computer-Mediated Communication*, 12 (4), http://jcmc.indiana.edu/vol12/issue4/qian.html (accessed August 8, 2010).

Roberts, J. (2005) Fired for blogging: Blog-related firings prompt calls for better company policies. *CBS News*, March 7, www.cbsnews.com/stories/2005/03/07/tech/main678554.shtml (accessed August 8, 2010).

Rosen, J. (2008) If bloggers had no ethics blogging would have failed, but it didn't. So let's get a clue. *PRESSthink: Ghost of Democracy in the Media Machine* (Blog), September 18, http://journalism.nyu.edu/pubzone/weblogs/pressthink/2008/09/18/because_we_have.html (accessed August 8, 2010).

Schudson, M. (2001) The objectivity norm in American journalism. *Journalism*, 2 (2), 149–170.

Shea, V. (1994) *Netiquette*, Albion Books, San Francisco.

Shirky, C. (2003) Power laws, weblogs, and inequality. *Clay Shirky's Writings about the Internet: Economics and Culture, Media and Community, Open Source.* http://www.shirky.com/writings/powerlaw_weblog.html (accessed August 8, 2010).

Singer, J.B. (2006) The socially responsible existentialist: A normative emphasis for journalists in a new media environment. *Journalism Studies*, 7 (1), 2–18.

Singh, A. (2008) Anonymity, authorship, and blogger ethics. *Symploke*, 16 (1/2), 21–35.

Smith, A. (2009) *The Internet's Role in Campaign 2008. Pew Internet and American Life Project.*Washington,D.C.,April,www.pewinternet.org/~/media//Files/Reports/2009/The_Internets_Role_in_Campaign_2008.pdf (accessed August 8, 2010).

SPJ (1996) *Society of Professional Journalists: Code of Ethics*, www.spj.org/pdf/ethicscode.pdf (accessed August 8, 2010).

Swarts, J. (2006) Coherent fragments: The problem of mobility and genred information. *Written Communication*, 23 (2), 173–201.

Tate, R. (2008) Steve Jobs's obituary, as run by Bloomberg. *Valleywag* (Blog). August 27, http://gawker.com/5042795/steve-jobss-obituary-as-run-by-bloomberg (accessed August 8, 2010).

Teachout, Z. (2009) Extraterritorial electioneering and the globalization of American elections. *Berkeley Journal of International Law*, 27 (1), 162–191.

Thieme, R. (1997) Stalking the UFO meme. *Ctheory.net*. January 16, www.ctheory.net/articles.aspx?id=85 (accessed August 8, 2010).

Turkle, S. (1995) *Life on the Screen: Identity in the Age of the Internet*, Simon & Schuster: New York.

VanFossen, L. (2007) Link Etiquette: You Do Not Need Permission to Link. *Lorelle on WordPress* (Blog). http://lorelle.wordpress.com/2007/01/12/link-etiquette-you-do-not-need-permission-to-link/ (accessed August 8, 2010).

Ward, S. J.A. (2009) Truth and objectivity, in *The Handbook of Mass Media Ethics*, (eds L. Wilkins and C.G. Christians), Routledge, New York, pp. 71–83.

Wallsten, K. (2007) Agenda setting and the blogosphere: An analysis of the relationship between mainstream media and political blogs. *Review of Policy Research*, 24 (6), 567–587.

Wyld, D.C. (2008) Management 2.0: A primer on blogging for executives. *Management Research News*, 31 (6), May, 448–483.

43

Journalism Ethics in a Digital Network

Jane B. Singer

The core ethical principles important to professional journalists are quite resilient. Fundamental values such as truth-telling, universally emphasized as the hallmark of public service journalism, and independence from factional interests inform the production of journalistic content regardless of whether it eventually appears on a piece of paper or a television screen or a computer monitor.

Like a kaleidoscopic given a shake, the same pieces fit together to create a different pattern in a digital media environment. Bits that were less visible gain prominence; others combine in novel ways. This chapter considers the ethical principles that take on new configurations for online journalists. It also looks at how those principles might apply to people who are not journalists but who contribute to the shared space that constitutes the network. It concludes with a consideration of digital journalism ethics as an inherently collective enterprise.

Practitioner Ethics

The open publishing environment of the Internet has raised a question that would have seemed rhetorical a generation ago: Who is a journalist? More specifically, what distinguishes journalists from those who are not journalists? It cannot be access to a publishing platform because everyone now has that. It cannot be access to information sources because everyone now has that, too. Not everyone can write cogently, but a great many people who clearly are not journalists can. Although journalists are formally accredited in some countries, in many others they are not.

Journalists themselves typically point to attributes of the sociological construct of professionalism, a term used to characterize self-regulating occupations that hold special power and prestige and that are distinguished by a particular set of

---

The Handbook of Global Communication and Media Ethics, First Edition. Edited by Robert S. Fortner and P. Mark Fackler.
© 2011 Blackwell Publishing Ltd. Published 2011 by Blackwell Publishing Ltd.

knowledge, techniques, and public service norms (Larson, 1977). However, the claim that journalism is a profession has always been open to criticism, on grounds ranging from the implicit homogeneity of a professional label (Glasser, 1992) to its ability to infringe on individual autonomy (Merrill, 1974) to its potential abuse as an instrument of organizational control (Birkhead, 1986; Soloski, 1989) and more.

In fact, what journalists are generally referring to when they talk about journalism as a profession relates less to any formal definition of the term than to a set of widely recognized occupational values. Such values are multifaceted and operate at different levels, including the organizational and the ideological (Shoemaker and Reese, 1996), but ultimately, they all relate to safeguarding the credibility of the information provided by the journalist. Journalism as a public service enterprise gains credibility through the collective behavior of practitioners guided by these values (Weaver *et al.*, 2007).

The guidance is formalized by codification of the values, creating a readily accessible normative framework of professional "ethics" and operationalizing appropriate actions within that framework. Thus, the US Society of Professional Journalists (1996) turns the value of truth-telling into a normative principle by stating that journalists "seek truth and report it," then offers a list of behaviors that accord with the principle: Journalists should "test the accuracy of information from all sources," for instance, and "distinguish between advocacy and news reporting."

The values and the normative framework built around them, with its set of prescribed and proscribed behaviors, thus serve to define journalists to themselves as well as to others. The defining function is particularly useful in a network environment where other types of distinctions – for instance, those based on particular skills, privileges, or actions, such as creating and publishing information – are fuzzier. (As discussed below, this is not to say that nonjournalists cannot or should not be guided by the same values or behave in similar ethical ways. The norms and values serve as a tool for positive, rather than negative, identification: They highlight who is a journalist, but not necessarily who is not.)

At this rather high level, then, journalists' commitment to a set of professionally shared values provides a hallmark of, and a framework for, behavior that may be particularly desirable in a network open to all comers. At the same time, however, the Internet shakes things up so that the same values take on a different look. The rest of this section considers three core values of professional journalism – truth-telling, impartiality, and accountability – and examines how they are both extended and challenged online. There are other values, of course, but these serve to highlight some of the issues and effects of the networked environment. Quotes from journalists at the UK's *Guardian* newspaper, interviewed in late 2007 and early 2008 for a study on user-generated content and journalistic ethics, are included to illustrate the view from the newsroom. The *Guardian*'s award-winning website is among the most heavily used among British newspapers, with a global audience of more than 30 million unique users every month at the time of this writing.

Truth-telling

Telling the truth, fundamental to trust in all social relationships (Bok, 1989), is widely seen as a paramount journalistic virtue and seems to be a universal component of professional ethics codes (Cooper, 1990; Hafez, 2002; Laitila, 1995). Of course, innumerable unresolved arguments surround both the philosophical matter of what constitutes truth and the practical one of how best to go about pursuing and representing it. Does truthfulness reside in attributes of the process (such as honesty in gathering information), of the content (such as accuracy), or of the journalist (such as objectivity)? Perhaps it is simply the *desire* to discover and disseminate truth that constitutes the core of journalistic ethics (Merrill, 1997). Suffice to say that while the nature of truth is complicated, journalists everywhere see it as central to the enterprise in which they are, and ought to be, engaged.

A networked environment does not change the importance of truth-telling for the journalist. However, its characteristics do bring particular aspects to the fore. Take two attributes that have been notable since the first days of online news, the medium's immediacy and interactivity. When a government office building in Oklahoma City was bombed in April 1995, the relatively few news websites that existed at all were little more than repositories of "repurposed" content. Yet within minutes of the bombing, journalists were posting whatever information they could glean about the tragedy – and people who were not journalists were doing the same, from eyewitnesses to people offering emergency aid for victims (Allan, 2006). In 1995, that use of the then-new medium was noteworthy. Today, it is routine.

Journalists have recognized from the start that when a medium so easily facilitates immediacy, people will soon come to expect and even demand it – to the potential detriment of the profession's ethical bedrocks of accuracy and thus credibility. "In print, we've always had the luxury of, 'well, let's see if what we have immediately is actually true and the whole story and can be verified,'" a newspaper editor told me back in that same year of 1995. "The old adage was 'get it first, but first, get it right.' Now it's just 'get it first'" (Singer, 1997). For many, the issue has not gone away. More than 12 years later, *Guardian* journalists expressed the same concern: that the need to provide information quickly can take precedence over the need to ensure its accuracy. Accuracy remains a central tenet not only of credibility but also of responsibility and overall journalistic competence (Singer and Ashman, 2009).

Yet *Guardian* journalists also described an evolution in thinking about what constitutes truth online and how it is communicated – an evolution that again relates to those two core attributes of immediacy and interactivity. First, the medium's speed encourages those both inside and outside the profession to see journalism as the creation of an evolving product. Of course, that has always been the case. A story in today's newspaper can be corrected tomorrow; a piece on the midday news can be updated for the evening broadcast. However, the newspaper and the newscast were seen as packaged products, complete in two senses of the word: both finished and finite. A news website is neither; it is constantly changing and intricately interconnected with other material online. The same goes for individual stories the website contains. Journalists are coming to see the benefits in a fluidity that, a decade ago, was more likely to be seen as a danger. The speed of the medium does mean that inaccurate along with accurate information sometimes will be immediately disseminated – but it also means that the inaccurate information can be immediately corrected.

Guardian journalists highlighted the perception that this attribute makes the Internet different from a more traditional medium. "If you make a mistake, you can just go in and refresh it – it's not like it's out there in print forever," said one editor. "People expect it to be fluid, not like in print," another said. "People are a bit more forgiving of it's being in flux." A reporter described how a "little nugget of fact" emerged as an unverified rumor online and, over time, solidified into a story of what was happening amid an escalating crisis in Myanmar. "Clearly, something had happened, and it was interesting and valuable to show how that particular nugget had come out, that bit of information," he said.

Even more prominent in their reasoning was the effect of interactivity on truth-telling. The news story is no longer a bounded, packaged product; it is open to continual input from outside the newsroom, as well as to a continually expanding range of hyperlinked connections. This change has two primary effects on journalistic truth. One is that readers can easily spot (and, potentially, correct) anything in a story that is wrong; the other is that they also can contribute information to make it more fully right.

The knowledge that users instantly (and not necessarily politely) will point out any errors in a journalist's story serves as an added incentive to verify information before publishing it. "Whenever I write something, I think, 'is that bullet-proof?'" a *Guardian* writer and editor said. "I'm going to go and triple-check it because I know someone will shoot me down if I don't, and obviously that will destroy the credibility of anything else you say." A copy editor agreed that "when you have that thread of comments underneath, it makes you a lot more aware of checking everything and making sure it's right before it goes up." Even in the overtly give-and-take environment of a journalist's blog, "if you say something that is wrong, there's absolutely no way to get away with it," a *Guardian* blogger said. "There's always a fear of getting caught." Although the omnipresence of a vast, vigilant, and vocal set of fact-checkers makes journalists a little nervous, the professional norm of accuracy is strong enough to override most objections.

More broadly, an interactive environment means that a more thorough version of complex truth is possible than in the closed structures of traditional media formats. Journalists can provide significantly more information about any given story than print space or broadcast time allows. Indeed, the ability to convey not only the bare facts but the truth about those facts, emphasized by the Hutchins Commission more than 60 years ago as the responsibility of a free press in democratic societies (Commission on Freedom of the Press, 1947), has been exponentially enhanced. Links to archives and background information facilitate greater reach into the past; links to related stories, including material on external websites, provides greater reach into a multi-faceted present. In doing so, they enhance the

Journalism Ethics in a Digital Network

demonstrable veracity of the journalistic item, as discussed further below. "If it's a piece about a report, we'll try to link to the actual report. We'll link to new stories. If it's a speech and the actual text of the speech is available, or an audio or visual link of the speech is available, we'll link to that – so as much source material as possible," explained a *Guardian* copy editor.

Moreover, of course, the interactive nature of the medium means more people can contribute to a story, conveying a richer version than is possible in a print or television story containing voices that not only are far more limited but also are selected and edited by a journalist. This capacity for including many far-flung sources in building the account of a news event and then discussing its implications is one of the most significant effects on truth-telling created by the shift to a networked environment.

The idea that truth is enhanced by a diversity of perspectives is hardly a new one; it was eloquently proposed by John Milton back in the seventeenth century: "Let her and Falshood grapple; who ever knew Truth put to the wors, in a free and open encounter?" (Milton, 1644). For more than 350 years, however, that "free and open encounter" was mainly theoretical, at least in the context of the journalism that evolved over those same centuries. However, in a networked world, truth may be revealed not just from the top down, as in traditional mass media, but also from the bottom up: Instead of relying on the journalist to convey what he or she believes to be true, a potentially "truer" version of reality is created when lots of people contribute and defend (or fail to adequately defend) their ideas (Singer and Dorsher, forthcoming).

This shift to an interactive environment heralds a significant change for journalists individually and collectively; they lose a considerable amount of control over both the goods and the purveyors of those goods in this rather chaotic marketplace of ideas. Some relish the transition of journalism from a lecture to a conversation (Gillmor, 2004). The vast majority of contributors are "eloquent, intelligent, able to add to the debate," one *Guardian* editor and blogger said. "Journalism is increasingly a two-way thing. It's not a preacher/pulpit model, but it's a more collaborative thing ... Joining together (in) that collaborative process makes actually for a better end product often." Journalists also emphasized the value in providing a diversity of viewpoints; in fact, the Scott Trust, which publishes the *Guardian*, mandates that the paper provides a platform for free comment, where "the voice of opponents no less than that of friends has a right to be heard" (Guardian Media Group, 2007). "If somebody has lively, possibly controversial opinions, there can be a validity just in publishing that, even if it's a very idiosyncratic take on a subject," another editor said. "You're in a way just enabling a debate. You're not there to provide a line or to give people definitive answers."

Others found the loss of control more challenging, particularly when they saw user contributions as decreasing rather than enhancing the credibility of a story. "We're paid to know what we're talking about, and we're paid to be correct, and we're paid to be accurate and insightful," a third editor said. "In terms of what we know and how we come to know it, I think that's something we should be quite protective of," he added, explaining that users can and do offer "selective" interpretations and "claims that need no basis in fact." Another editor and blogger said that, "as journalists, we should know what we're talking about. We should be informed if not experts," but users do not need to be either of those. "It's putting journalists on a footing with people who aren't informed."

Truth-telling is a primary ethical concern of journalists but certainly not the only one. The rest of this section considers two other professional norms, impartiality and accountability.

Impartiality

The importance of offering a fair and even-handed consideration of both facts and viewpoints is central to the concept of journalism as something provided by people whose loyalty is to the public rather than to any particular faction (Kovach and Rosenstiel, 2001). This idea of nonpartisanship is associated with the ideal of objectivity, but with the key advantage of being both definable and attainable by actual human beings (Mindich, 2000). Neutrality, open-mindedness, and distance have been identified as crucial elements of impartiality; together, they are seen as enhancing the common good (BBC Trust, 2007).

Journalists use the norm of impartiality as a core rationale for preserving not only credibility but also their professional autonomy. "Journalists should be free of obligation to any interest other than the public's right to know," the US Society of Professional Journalists' ethics code states. It urges practitioners to safeguard their real and perceived impartiality by avoiding conflicts of interest, refusing gifts or favors that might compromise journalistic integrity, and so on. In Britain, where the print media are more overtly partisan, a prohibition on broadcaster advocacy is a cornerstone of public policy dating to the origins of the BBC in the 1920s (McNair, 2003), and the observance of impartiality is, in effect, a necessary condition of the right to broadcast for both commercial and public broadcasters (Harvey, 1998). Even in this context, however, impartiality is linked with autonomy, as expressed by a former BBC chairman: "Only as long as the nation as a whole believes the BBC is impartial and has no axe to grind will it give it the support which guarantees its independence, and therefore its ability when necessary to transmit challenging and uncomfortable programmes" (BBC, 1989, p. 5 cited in Harvey, 1998, p. 549).

Like truth-telling, the norm of impartiality remains important to journalism as it moves online. When anyone can publish information, it is a safe bet that many of those who do will have a vested interest in what they publish, leaving a crucial role for the impartial reporter to sort things out (Pavlik, 2000). In a traditional media environment, public relations messages had to pass through the journalist to reach the intended audience; they no longer do. Advertising no longer needs to be clearly identified as such, as it was within that structured, finite media package described above. Of course, individual "opinionators" of every conceivable allegiance or affiliation, overt or covert, can and do add to the online cacophony all day, every day. Journalists in this networked world continue to differentiate themselves through their professed allegiance to the public and independence from factional interests; typically, the only affiliation they offer is to their employer – which in turn seeks to use such hallmarks of credibility to stake out its own brand identity. The distinctions drawn by this normative emphasis are arguably of even greater value online, where the old structural cues are removed.

Yet unlike truth-telling, which remains central to the image of journalism in any medium, impartiality presents a more nuanced picture on the Internet. One reason is its connection with the notion of distance suggested above. Even in a traditional context, the value of professional distance is seen as somewhat less important than the related concepts of neutrality and open-mindeness (BBC Trust, 2007). Online, there may be still more problems because distance is not an idea that translates easily to a wholly integrated, interactive network. Boundaries of all sorts – among products, ideas, people, and social roles – are difficult to sustain. Physical distance is erased by the immediacy with which any message can span the globe; professional distance is at least challenged by interconnections among all sorts of information producers and the content they create. Moreover, the journalist who tries to stand metaphorically to one side can find himself, indeed, sidelined. Detachment is essentially isolating, and in a networked world, the one thing that has virtually no value is isolation (Singer and Dorsher, forthcoming).

At a more practical level, in a media world containing an exponentially expanded (and continually expanding) number of voices, there is increasing value of having a distinct and recognizable voice of one's own. In traditional media forms, columnists have long been encouraged to develop identifiable personalities, and those personalities often become branding devices for the media outlet that employs them. Most reporters, however, have been subsumed within the outlet's overall brand as a news provider. Online, the two roles come together, most obviously when journalists become bloggers. It is acceptable and often even expected for a j-blogger to have an opinion, or at least a clear persona, even if that blogger is also a reporter.

Journalist blogs, or "j-blogs," were one of the fastest-growing media trends of the 2000s. At the turn of the century, there were virtually none; by the second half of the decade, the websites of almost every large US newspaper included staff-written blogs, most of them loosely edited at best (Bivings Group, 2008; Project for Excellence, 2008). Not all reporters are happy at being lowered "into the foul-smelling muck of the blogworld" (Schultz and Sheffer, 2007, p. 71), but many seem to relish the freedom to explore new forms of expression. For instance, Robinson (2006) describes a newspaper reporter who blogged about her experiences embedded with US troops in Iraq – and wrestled with challenges to her professed professional role of detached and independent observer. Writing styles change, too, as blogging reporters "use traditional no-nos: Superlatives, first person, contractions, questions with no answers, answers with no questions" (p. 78). Robinson concludes that although journalists continue to view their blogs through the lens of existing occupational paradigms, the format is pushing them to define a new identity in which traditional lines of independence, among other norms, are blurred.

Journalists at the UK's *Guardian* also described a move away from unobtrusive neutrality and toward the creation and maintenance of an online voice, particularly in their blogs. "It's crucial to have an opinion when you're blogging," said one features blogger. "If we're talking to new bloggers, that's one thing we say: We want this to be an opinionated piece, not a news story or just relaying facts." Similarly, an editor described a blog as a place for "showing personality" and "being prepared to debate things." Another editor said that unlike an article, a blog must provide "something to engage with, a question that needs to be answered, or even an opinion that you know people are going to disagree with." In other words, one of the benefits of a blatant lack of impartiality is that it will draw users into a discussion or perhaps an argument – and thus boost traffic figures. An online writer described blogging as "recording your opinion" and hoping that "people will come because they like what you are interested in."

This is not to suggest that *Guardian* journalists were oblivious to the impact of j-blogs on traditional norms or values. As the expectation grows that reporters will also be bloggers, questions arise. "Will that affect their objectivity as a reporter if they're also writing comment pieces?" an online journalist asked, adding there was no consensus on the answer yet. "This is interesting territory for a brand like the *Guardian*, to editorialize content," to stress opinions and wit "rather than the actual reportage," an editor said. However, a lack of impartiality does not necessarily mean a lack of authority, said another online journalist. "You're surrounded by unqualified people who are also throwing in opinions. You need to show why your opinion is perhaps more important or better founded or ... more worthy of highlighting and bringing to public attention," she said. "Perhaps it's that it's an unusual opinion to hear or it's particularly controversial or it needs exploring in more depth."

That suggestion brings us to a third aspect of journalistic ethics that is taking on a novel configuration in the online environment. Journalists rarely explain why a story deserves space in the paper or time on the air. However, on the Internet, new forms of accountability come to the fore.

Accountability

Although accountability is not quite synonymous with responsibility – the latter has to do with defining proper conduct, while the former is more closely associated with compelling such conduct (Newton *et al.*, 2004) – the ideas are clearly connected. In an online environment, they also are linked with the more recently articulated concepts of transparency and openness, which in turn reconnect to the core value of truth and thus enhance credibility or trustworthiness (Singer, 2007). Accountability, openness, and transparency all involve being honest about the nature of what is known and how that knowledge has been generated (Kovach and Rosenstiel, 2001).

Indeed, some observers suggest that transparency is the paramount norm in an online environment, where the ongoing process of making news is so readily visible (Karlsson, 2008). "Net-native" communicators such as bloggers treat transparency as a central norm (Blood, 2002; Dube, 2003; Lasica, 2005), and prominent bloggers are especially likely to share information about themselves (Trammell and Keshelashvili, 2005). Kuhn's survey of bloggers indicated that they valued both truth and transparency, along with the promotion of free expression and interactivity, and he proposed a "code of blogging ethics" that incorporates the revelation of identity, affiliations, and source materials (Kuhn, 2007, pp. 33–34). These same values, however, also can be used to support the argument that such codes are unnecessary and even antithetical to the libertarian ethos of the blogosphere; in this view, the collective of contributors and readers will serve as a self-correcting mechanism more effectively than any formal code could do (Perlmutter and Schoen, 2007; Singer, 2006).

Journalists also have incorporated the notion of accountability within their own codified ethical guidelines – though not, it must be said, without some reluctance, stemming largely from the perception of a potential conflict between freedom and responsibility, discussed more below. Particularly in the US context of fiercely protected First Amendment rights to an unfettered press, calls for an acknowledgement that "the rights of editors and publishers to express themselves ... must be associated (with) a right of the public to be served with a substantial and honest basis of fact" (Hocking, 1947, p. 169) have been met largely with skepticism – and inertia. It took nearly half a century for the notion of accountability to be formalized in a US code of journalistic ethics (Society of Professional Journalists, 1996), and that only after considerable contentious debate (Black et al., 1999). Despite a desire to work for "the people," journalists tend to see formalized accountability to the public and to society at large as no less threatening than to the forces of the state or the market (Bardoel and d'Haenens, 2004).

The online environment does not introduce new formalities – on the contrary – but it does propagate a zeitgeist quite distinct from the one of a medium controlled by professional gatekeepers, bringing different normative aspects to the fore. The Internet changes the notion of information providers' responsibilities in two potentially opposite ways, one accommodating an absence of accountability and the other accommodating much greater accountability than before. On the one hand, anyone can publish anything in this ultimate free speech zone, with virtual impunity; moreover, the publisher can choose to remain anonymous, to ignore challenges or criticisms, and to deny errors. At the same time, the interactive nature of the medium encourages people who read something online to respond to it, making information production an open and interactive process (Singer, 2006).

Journalists are caught in the middle. They are on the receiving end of many of those responses, some of them quite harsh. Yet they cannot take full advantage of the medium's more liberating, but ethically problematic, qualities as an open publishing platform. They cannot publish anonymously nor with impunity; they cannot maintain credibility if they refuse to admit and address their mistakes; and ignoring criticism will only fuel charges of arrogance and aloofness. "Barriers are broken down," an online editor said. "Users do expect more journalists to step out from behind articles, defend and discuss them."

Indeed, *Guardian* journalists explicitly highlighted each of these ethical issues as differentiating them from website users – and as making them ultimately more accountable. "We are there, and we are accountable – people know who we are," one editor said. "There is no similar responsibility incumbent on the commenter." Another said putting a name to a published item enhances credibility, but at the same time, it means "you're there to be shot at." As highlighted above, accuracy was a paramount norm for these journalists (Singer and Ashman, 2009), and accountability demands that "if we make a mistake, we put our hands up," as an online writer said. "If you get something wrong, you need to admit it," an editor agreed. "The best way is to come clean as soon as you're found out."

Yet heightened, or at least more clearly visible, accountability also can suggest weakened journalistic authority (Lowrey and Anderson, 2005) and autonomy (Singer, 2007). Occupational authority relies on at least some degree of control over what is produced, and a network opens journalism up to jurisdictional encroachment (Lowrey, 2006) from all manner of information providers happily publishing within the same space – and challenging what journalists publish there, too. Moreover, while some challenges relate to accuracy of a particular bit of information, as discussed above, others deal more broadly with issues of news judgment or interpretation. Oversight of journalistic behavior has become a team sport rather than a professional perquisite.

Guardian journalists articulated interconnected concerns about challenges to their authority and autonomy in an open networked environment. While most acknowledged a theoretical value in the discourse, the reality proved challenging. User comments, especially nasty ones, can be "very off-putting, especially if you're used to just having your work out there in the newspaper, being unquestioned," one online journalist said. "It's something about the fact that you're sharing a space with these people who haven't sort of 'earned' it that I think is difficult for journalists to negotiate. Where does their authority come from?" said another online staffer. "If you're a journalist because you have a sense of responsibility to your readers and to your public, I think you're going to be quite open to encouraging feedback and creating more conversation. But I don't think that's something that journalists are trained for particularly," she added. "It's going to take a while for this sort of détente to take place."

The potential for user input to shape decisions about what journalists should write – that is, to influence their news judgment – was seen as an especially disturbing threat to professional autonomy. Some said traffic logs and comment counts were useful guides to user interests and ultimately a way of fulfilling a responsibility to audience members: "I could write endless things, but there's got to be a kind of reason for it and a demand for it and an audience for it," one online editor and writer said. However, many expressed misgivings about allowing "popularity" to dictate content decisions. "You've got to be careful here that you're not driven by agendas that are outside of the paper to tell you what the paper should be doing," one print editor said. "If you're going to start chasing hits or something, you're just going to end up writing about gratuitous remarks," an online writer said. "It appalls me, the idea of what you'd have to do for popularity." A print writer was even blunter: "It's called 'traffic whoring,'" he said.

Ultimately, though, the medium – with its unlimited space and unbounded connections – gives journalists a tool not only for greater accountability but also for enhanced authority. Showing how information evolves and where it comes from offers a valuable window into how a story comes together, an otherwise mysterious process that is too easily misunderstood. On live news blogs, one online reporter said, "You're allowed to learn with the readers" about where an event is occurring and who the key players are. "You show your own ignorance and your own understanding developing as the thing goes on, and that's sort of indulged." As mentioned previously, journalists now have a technically enabled capability to support their facts and back up their opinions rather than simply asking audiences to blindly trust them. They can build credibility by showing where their information comes from, explaining their rationales, providing background about their sources, soliciting additional input and feedback from readers, and more (Hayes *et al.*, 2007). "I can use links to verify statements that I wouldn't have space to spell out," a *Guardian* online writer said. "Especially if you're writing a comment piece, there's rarely space to air all of your opinions on a subject. So if someone says 'well, what about so-and-so?' you can then go 'well, actually yes, I do have an opinion on that, and this is what I think about it.'" In short, this unprecedented degree of information transparency is a tremendous journalistic resource, one foregrounded in an online environment and facilitated in new ways.

I have taken some time to consider the online evolution of these three core norms – truth-telling, impartiality and accountability – from the perspective of the professional journalist. However, the creation of online information is a collaborative project, which means the other collaborators also merit attention.

Audience Ethics

One of the most seriously understudied topics within the field of journalism studies is audience ethics. What little work has been done takes the output of professional journalists as its starting point. It focuses on responsibilities associated with the use of news products created and disseminated by professional journalists (Aucoin, 1996), particularly to the extent that those products contain the information that citizens of a democracy need to govern themselves wisely (Kovach and Rosenstiel, 2001). Although there has long been a recognition that the general public has a responsibility for the quality of mass communication (Rivers and Schramm, 1969), the underlying assumption has been one of a market logic, which construes the audience as a consumer of media content – ideally a discerning and even demanding consumer, but not a producer of that content. Ethical issues raised by the contributions to media spaces from "the people formerly known as the audience" (Rosen, 2006) have received virtually no attention. Those spaces include ones controlled by their users, such as social networking sites, and those controlled, albeit to a diminishing extent, by journalists, such as newspaper-affiliated websites. This section briefly summarizes this research, then outlines issues that merit additional consideration in the context of journalism in an open, networked media environment.

Despite the obvious fact that the notion of a profession necessarily implies a relationship between its members and its clients, almost all of a rather large body of work in the field of journalism ethics concentrates on the journalists themselves, leaving "the issues of freedom, quality and responsibility the sole concern of the professional" (Hamelink, 2000, p. 393). Yet even a professional-client relationship relies on mutual commitment to the professional's performance, which in turn implies some responsibility on the part of the client audience. Pinpointing exactly what this responsibility might entail, however, has not been easy, and statements about audience ethics tend to be rather broad. Funiok (2000), for instance, suggests that in all their actions and inactions, including media use, people are responsible to themselves, to others in their social environment, and to their natural environment. He emphasizes media literacy, suggesting that audiences can enhance media quality by demanding it and in fact have a responsibility to do so. Indeed, this audience capability is central to the functioning of media accountability systems such as press councils worldwide (Bertrand, 2000).

Saying that mass media audience members have responsibilities in the communication process implies that collective accountability is possible, that the audience is active, and that the audience has a role in creating the meaning of mass communication messages (Aucoin, 1996). The last two are givens on the Internet, unlike in traditional media formats, and scholars who have begun to consider audience ethics in an online environment have focused on this participatory aspect of the network. Silverstone (2004), for instance, argues for what he calls "media civics," a crucial component of twenty-first century citizenship and one that must "burst the bounds of both the nation state and the narcissistic limits of concern only with the individual and the self" (p. 379). He sees such media civics as contingent on the development of a morality of responsibility and participation, grounded in a critical engagement with media forms. A number of other scholars also have emphasized the political dimension of civic engagement with online media, again construing audience ethics in broad terms related primarily to contributions to a democratic polity or virtual public sphere (Dahlberg, 2001; Dahlgren, 2005; Papacharissi, 2002).

Important though such democratic functions are, there are many other aspects of audience ethics that beg for exploration in the context of the seamlessly interconnected space now inhabited by well over a billion people around the globe. In some ways, the issue of audience ethics is made more complicated by the global nature of the Internet, which encompasses cultures too diverse to allow a single version of online "netiquette" to prevail (Funiok, 2000). Yet despite cultural differences, there are at least three broad categories of audience ethics that merit consideration.

The first is the issue of media oversight, audience members' responsibility to demand a degree of quality in the product provided by journalists. As we have just seen, this holdover from a traditional media environment has received attention from ethicists. However, the Internet exponentially expands the number of media watchdogs – and their ability to make themselves heard, if not necessarily heeded. Many widely read bloggers, for example, carefully and continuously monitor what journalists report and how they report it, and they are not shy about calling attention to ethical problems, real or perceived. These cover a broad spectrum but commonly include hypocrisy, bias, inaccuracy, and inattention to potentially big stories (Singer, 2007). "For lazy columnists and defensive gatekeepers, it can seem as if the hounds from a mediocre hell have been unleashed," *Columbia Journalism Review* contributor Matt Welch wrote (2003) "Journalists finally have something approaching real peer review, in all its brutality."

As more media organizations have opened their articles and opinion pieces up to online comments, the opportunity to be brutal – or, of course, constructive – has become even easier to grab. It no longer requires any special thought, effort, or cost to criticize the media. Nor does it require collective action to be heard. Particularly with the forum for journalist-user interaction provided by comment threads, the ethical engagement by both parties is at a far more personal level than that between mass audience and mass media organization. This suggests a greater role for the classics of personal ethics, from treating fellow humans with respect to being fair and honest in discourse. It suggests that a willingness to listen is as important as a readiness to speak (Mindich, 2005) – and that goes for both members of the press and members of the public. It also suggests a greater degree of personal responsibility by both parties, who are participants in a newly reciprocal and relatively intimate relationship.

The second area of audience ethics that gains importance online involves what is commonly called "user-generated content": audience contributions to the shared communications space apart from media critique or commentary. If there is a move toward personal ethics as the role of media watchdog becomes more ubiquitous, ethics converge on more clearly professional norms as the role of information provider becomes similarly commonplace. These include the precepts considered above – truth-telling, impartiality, accountability – along with other broadly accepted (albeit not always honored) professional norms such as respect for privacy, avoidance of sensationalism, and refrain from ad hominem attacks. As suggested above, the Internet enables enormous strides toward a long-standing ethical goal of the media, that of enabling diverse voices to be heard and diverse views shared, with an emphasis on interaction and not simply inclusion (Witschge, 2008). However, the same openness and lack of formal oversight that make it wonderfully liberating also make it potentially debilitating. Some of what is published in this no-holds-barred environment is undeniably disturbing.

This is not to say that audience members should be guided by the overarching norms of public service that concern journalistic practitioners. Much of what is published online is likely to be of interest to only a small group of people – maybe only even to the person who published it – and that includes much of the "hyper-personal" content now hosted on media company websites such as my.telegraph.co.uk or lepost.fr. Such content raises few if any ethical concerns. It is, however, to suggest that a consideration of audience ethics should steer contributors away from content that is a *disservice* to the public. Deliberate misinformation and disinformation are a disservice to any civic entity. Material that is racist or sexist or some other species of "hate speech" is a disservice. Words or images that are needlessly hurtful or malicious are a disservice. The law allows journalists to publish most content that falls into these categories, but professional ethics generally preclude doing so. The law also affords nonjournalists the same rights. Audience ethics suggest benefits were we to adopt the same responsibilities, as well.

Such considerations take us to the third broad category of audience ethics: interactions among users of media spaces that have little or nothing to do with the information provider role just discussed. Basically, they talk among and about themselves and each other, and they use the media-provided platform to do it. Such a topic would seem to move us away from this chapter's focus on journalism ethics – were it not for the fact that preventing users from verbally abusing one another, in ways that are ethically and even legally problematic, constitutes a large chunk of the task of moderating comments posted on media websites. Journalists find themselves having to arbitrate disputes among users – an arbitration that typically involves simply hitting the "delete" key, thus removing the problem but also cutting off the conversation. In other words, media users who fail to use their freedom of speech responsibly lose the freedom by forcing someone else – the journalist – to shoulder the responsibility.

We return, then to the tension between freedom and responsibility that has long been familiar to journalists (Merrill, 1997). In the networked environment, it becomes especially crucial for audiences, too. To an even greater extent than journalists – who, after all, are members of a profession that advocates adherence to a set of codified guidelines – audience members must individually choose to conduct their social relationships ethically. There is no real penalty for not doing so. Their comment may be deleted; if their behavior is repeated and especially egregious, they may even be barred from a particular website – for the few moments it takes them to create a new user ID. The penalties may become more real, however, as media organizations increasingly adopt algorithm-based "reputation systems," which filter and display user contributions based on their prior activities, typically in a way that incorporates assessments from the community. With those emerging systems, we come back to the idea of collective audience ethics that this section started – but with a distinctively new twist.

In the meantime, none of these matters of audience ethics has been adequately explored by journalism scholars or ethicists, particularly in the contemporary media environment of a wide-open network. As for practitioners, they are still tentatively feeling their way around this newly shared space. For now, it seems that audience ethics point both inward and outward in overlapping ways. Journalists moderate user contributions, but users also serve as watchdogs on the watchdogs, holding journalists' feet to the fire in new and newly visible ways. Individual audience members ultimately are the strongest regulators of their own behavior, yet new collective opportunities are emerging for audiences to reward or even demand quality from one another as well as from the media. All in all, our kaleidoscope seems again to be displaying an image in which familiar pieces are fitting together to form new patterns of perception and action.

Collective Ethics

In some important ways, the Internet brings with it a shift toward personal ethics for both journalists and users, as we have seen. The media audience has become more massive, but at the same time, "mass communication" has become more fragmented, more atomized. Individual journalists interact directly with individual users. Journalist blogs highlight the views and amplify the voices of individual reporters or columnists, while simultaneously making them more personally accountable for what they write. The ease with which any person can hit the "send" button, instantly disseminating an item to every corner of the planet, carries with it an ethical responsibility to think twice before doing so. Conversely, control comes not from prepublication gatekeeping but from postpublication deletion of what we would rather not see.

From a broader perspective, ethics in a shared media space is a more inherently collaborative exercise than in a space controlled by journalists and essentially closed to outsiders. In this global network, isolation is virtually impossible; all communication and all communicators – every action and every actor – are interconnected. Every ethical decision we make has the potential to affect a truly vast range of stakeholders.

Moreover, freedom of the press has become coextensive with freedom of speech – a right of everyone, not just of society's designated scribes (Godwin, 2001). Perhaps more than in any other media space, then, freedom and responsibility must function in tandem in order to create ethically desirable and morally defensible outcomes. In an environment in which external controls are almost wholly absent, self-imposed constraints on freedom become crucial. This is certainly true for users, but it also applies to journalists whose professional norms and occupational roles are stretched in new directions by the online medium's immediacy, by emerging new formats for expressing their own voice, and by radically different relationships with people outside the newsroom.

This chapter points to the conclusion that journalists' overarching norm of public service, or of responsibility to citizens in a democratic society, distinguishes them from users, for whom it suffices ethically to avoid doing a public disservice. That distinction puts different weight on professional norms such as impartiality and accountability, and although truth-telling is fundamental to trust in any human relationship (Bok, 1989), journalists' role in society arguably makes truthfulness more fundamental to their ethical conduct.

Despite these distinctions, journalists and users must work together not only as information providers but also as ethical decision-makers in a publishing space that is now shared. The physical boundaries that separated them in a traditional media environment no longer exist. Many of the occupational boundaries also are blurring. Reporting and writing are increasingly collaborative exercises; so too are the tasks of analysis and interpretation. Journalists and users each oversee their own activities, as individuals and as members of their respective collectives, but they also oversee the activities of one another within the online space they cohabit. They both contribute to a vibrant and ever-expanding discourse. In short, they both are fundamental to a functioning democracy – which, after all, has always relied on the quality of the judgments made by its citizens.

References

Allan, S. (2006) *Online news: Journalism and the Internet*, London: Open University Press, Milton Keynes.

Aucoin, J. (1996) Implications of audience ethics for the mass communicator. *Journal of Mass Media Ethics*, 11 (2), 69–81.

Bardoel, J., and d'Haenens, L. (2004) Media meet the citizens: Beyond market mechanisms and government regulations. *Communication*, 19, 165–194.

BBC (1989) *Impartiality: Representing Reality*, BBC, London

BBC Trust (2007) *From seesaw to wagon wheel: Safeguarding impartiality in the 21st century*, June 18, www.bbc.co.uk/bbctrust/ assets/files/pdf/review_report_research/ impartiality_21century/report.pdf (last accessed January 24, 2009).

Bertrand, C.J. (2000) *Media Ethics and Accountability Systems*, Transaction Publishers, Piscataway, NJ.

Birkhead, D. (1986) News media ethics and the management of professionals. *Journal of Mass Media Ethics* 1 (2), 37–46.

Bivings Group (2008) The use of the Internet by America's newspapers. December18, www. bivings.com/thelab/presentations/ 2008study.pdf (last accessed January 24, 2009).

Black, J., Steele, B., and Barney, R. (1999) *Doing Ethics in Journalism: A Handbook with Case Studies*, 3rd edn, Allyn and Bacon, Needham Heights, MA.

Blood, R. (2002) *The Weblog Handbook: Practice Advice on Creating and Maintaining Your Blog*, Perseus Books Group, New York, www.rebeccablood.net/handbook/excerpts/ weblog_ethics.html (last accessed August 8, 2010).

Bok, S. (1989) *Lying: Moral Choice in Public and Private Life*, Vintage Books, New York.

Commission on Freedom of the Press (1947) *A Free and Responsible Press*, (ed. Robert D. Leigh), University of Chicago Press, Chicago.

Cooper, T.W. (1990) Comparative international media ethics. *Journal of Mass Media Ethics*, 5 (1), 3–14.

Dahlberg, L. (2001) Computer-mediated communication and the public sphere: A critical analysis. *Journal of Computer-Mediated Communication*, 7 (1), http://jcmc.indiana.edu/ vol7/issue1/dahlberg.html (accessed August 8, 2010).

Dahlgren, P. (2005) The Internet, public spheres, and political communication: Dispersion and deliberation. *Political Communication*, 22 (2),147–162.

Dube, J. (2003) A blogger's code of ethics. Cyberjournalist.net, April 15, www. cyberjournalist.net/news/000215.php (accessed August 8, 2010).

Funiok, R. (2000) Fundamental questions of audience ethics, in *Media Ethics: Opening Social Dialogue*, (ed. B. Pattyn), Peeters Publishers, Leuven, Belgium, pp. 403–422.

Gillmor, D. (2004) *We The Media: Grassroots Journalism by the People, for the People*. O'Reilly Media, Sebastapol, CA.

Glasser, T.L. (1992) Professionalism and the derision of diversity: The case of the education of journalists. *Journal of Communication*, 42 (2), 131–140.

Godwin, M. (2001) Who's a journalist – II: Welcome the new journalists on the Internet, in *What's Next? Problems and Prospects of Journalism*, (eds R.H. Giles and R.W. Snyder), Transaction Publishers, Piscataway, NJ, pp. 45–50.

Guardian Media Group (2007) The Scott Trust: The Scott Trust values. www.gmgplc.co.uk/ScottTrust/TheScottTrustvalues/tabid/194 /Default.aspx (last accessed January 8, 2009).

Hafez, K. (2002) Journalism ethics revisited: A comparison of ethics codes in Europe, North Africa, the Middle East, and Muslim Asia. *Political Communication*, 19, 225–250.

Hamelink, C.J. (2000) Ethics for media users, in *Media Ethics: Opening Social Dialogue*, (ed. B. Pattyn), Peeters Publishers, Leuven, Belgium, pp. 393–402.

Harvey, S. (1998) Doing it my way – broadcasting regulation in capitalist cultures: The case of "fairness" and "impartiality." *Media, Culture & Society*, October, 20 (4), 535–556.

Hayes, A.S., Singer, J.B., and Ceppos, J. (2006) Shifting roles, enduring values: The credible journalist in a digital age. *Journal of Mass Media Ethics*, 22 (4), 262–279.

Hocking, W.E. (1947) *Freedom of the Press: A Framework of Principle*, University of Chicago Press, Chicago.

Karlsson, M. B. (2008) Visibility of journalistic processes and the undermining of objectivity, May, International Communication Association, Montreal.

Kovach, B., and Rosenstiel, T. (2001) *The Elements of Journalism: What Newspeople should Know and the Public Should Expect*, Crown Books, New York.

Kuhn, M. (2007) Interactivity and Prioritizing the Human: A Code of Blogging Ethics, *Journal of Mass Media Ethics*, 22 (1), 18–36.

Laitila, T. (1995) Journalistic codes of ethics in Europe. *European Journal of Communication*, 10 (4), 527–544.

Larson, M.S. (1977) *The Rise of Professionalism: A Sociological Analysis*, University of California Press, Berkeley.

Lasica, J.D. (2005) The cost of ethics: Influence peddling in the blogosphere. *Online Journalism Review*, February 1, www.ojr.org/ojr/ stories/ 050217lasica/ (accessed August 8, 2010).

Lowrey, W. (2006) Mapping the journalism-blogging relationship, *Journalism*, 7 (4), 477–500.

Lowrey, W., and Anderson, W. (2005) The journalist behind the curtain: Participatory functions on the Internet and their impact on perceptions of the work of journalism. *Journal of Computer-Mediated Communication*, 10 (3), http://jcmc.indiana.edu/vol10/issue3/lowrey.html (accessed August 8, 2010).

McNair, B. (2003) *News and Journalism in the UK*, 4th edn. Routledge, London.

Merrill, J.C. (1997) *Journalism Ethics: Philosophical Foundations for News Media*, St.Martin's Press, New York.

Merrill, J.C. (1974) *The Imperative of Freedom: A Philosophy of Journalistic Autonomy*, Hastings House, New York.

Milton, J. (1644) Areopagitica: A speech to the Parliament of England for the liberty of unlicensed printing. Quote taken from digitized version of an 1819 edition; introduction by T. Holt White, p. 175, R. Hunter, printer, London, http://books.google.co.uk/books?id=YP5IAAAAIAAJ (accessed January 8, 2009).

Mindich, D.T.Z. (2000) *Just the Facts: How "Objectivity" Came to Define American Journalism*, NYU Press, New York.

Mindich, D.T.Z. (2005) *Tuned Out: Why Young People don't Follow the News*, Oxford University Press, New York.

Newton, L.H., Hodges, L., and Keith, S. (2004) Accountability in the professions: Accountability in journalism. *Journal of Mass Media Ethics*, 19 (3/4), 166–190.

Papacharissi, Z. (2002) The virtual sphere: The Internet as a public sphere. *New Media and Society*, 4 (1), 9–27.

Pavlik, J. (2000) The impact of technology on journalism. *Journalism Studies*, 1 (2), 229–237.

Perlmutter, D.D., and Schoen, M. (2007) "If I break a rule, what do I do, fire myself?" Ethics codes of independent blogs. *Journal of Mass Media Ethics*, 22 (1), 37–48.

Project for Excellence in Journalism (2008) The changing newspaper newsroom, *The State of the News Media 2008*, www.stateofthenewsmedia.org/2008/narrative_special_newsroom.php?cat=2andmedia=13 (accessed August 8, 2010).

Rivers, W.L., and Schramm, W. (1969) *Responsibility in Mass Communication*. Harper and Row, London.

Robinson, S. (2006) The mission of the j-blog: Recapturing journalistic authority online. *Journalism*, 7 (1), 65–83.

Rosen, J. (2006) The people formerly known as the audience. *PressThink*, June 27, http://journalism.nyu.edu/pubzone/weblogs/pressthink/2006/06/27/ppl_frmr.html (accessed August 8, 2010).

Schultz, B., and Sheffer, M. L. (2007) Sports journalists who blog cling to traditional values. *Newspaper Research Journal*, 28 (4), 62–76.

Shoemaker, P.J., and Reese, S.D. (1996) *Mediating the Message: Theories of Influences on Mass Media Content*, 2nd edn, Longman, New York.

Silverstone, R. (2004) Regulation, media literacy and media civics, in *E-merging Media: Communication and the Media Economy of the Future*, (eds A. Zerdick, A. Picot, K. Schrape, and J.-C. Burgelman), Springer, Heidelberg, pp. 367–379.

Singer, J.B. (1997) Still guarding the gate? The newspaper journalist's role in an on-line world. *Convergence: The International Journal of Research into New Media Technologies*, 3 (1), 72–89.

Singer, J.B. (2006) The socially responsible existentialist: A normative emphasis for journalists in a new media environment. *Journalism Studies*, 7 (1), 2–18.

Singer, J.B. (2007) Contested autonomy: Professional and popular claims on journalistic norms. *Journalism Studies*, 8 (1), 79–95.

Singer, J.B., and Ashman, I. (2009) "Comment is free, but facts are sacred": User-generated content and ethical constructs at the *Guardian*. *Journal of Mass Media Ethics*, 24 (1), 3–21.

Singer, J.B., and Dorsher, M. (forthcoming) Online ethics: Adjusting to new technologies and techniques, in *Controversies in Media Ethics*, (eds Gordon and J.M. Kittross), 3rd edn, Routledge, New York.

Society of Professional Journalists (1996) Code of ethics. http://spj.org/ethicscode.asp (accessed August 8, 2010).

Soloski, J. (1989) News reporting and professionalism: Some constraints on the reporting of the news. *Media, Culture and Society*, 11, 207–228.

Trammell, K.D., and Keshelashvili, A. (2005) Examining the new influencers: A self-presentation study of A-list blogs. *Journalism and Mass Communication Quarterly*, 82 (4), 968–982

Weaver, D.H., Beam, R.A., Brownlee, B.J. *et al.* (2007) *The American Journalist in the 21st Century*, Routledge, New York.

Welch, M. (2003) The new amateur journalists weigh in. *Columbia Journalism Review*, September/October, www.cjr.org/issues/2003/5/ blog-welch.asp (last accessed January 31, 2009).

Witschge, T. (2008) Examining online public discourse in context: A mixed method approach. *Javnost-The Public*, 15 (2), 75–92.

44

Now Look What You Made Me Do
Violence and Media Accountability

Peter Hulm

Everyone says there's too much violence on TV but secretly they want more.
(J.G. Ballard, 1994, p. 192)

Whose Violence?

Any number of financially and critically successful films and television dramas in the United States have ensured a warm reception by tapping, cynically, myopically or from obvious commercial motives, into the easily aroused general feeling that the media – and particularly newspapers – should be held socially accountable for their treatment of public issues. Identifiable villains include – to name two of the most famous – the press agent in *The Sweet Smell of Success* (1957) and the reporter in *Absence of Malice* (1981). Other films, such as *Citizen Kane* (1941), *Network* (1976) or *Broadcast News* (1987), draw much of their emotional force from the *frisson* to audiences of seeing an irresponsible use of the power inherent in operating a media business. Without the audience's predicted sense of shock, the plots would not make sense.

Hollywood films go notoriously for drama rather than credibility (Maltby, 1995, p. 344). As Richard Maltby points out, the incoherence enables viewers to escape the constraints of reality and for a time to enjoy the phantasmagorical operations of dream-work (outlined by Freud in *Traumdeutung/The Interpretation of Dreams*). Nevertheless, two long-term university lecturers have found these films plausible enough to present them for discussion in their courses on media ethics (Good and Dillon, 2002).

Societies themselves, particularly those with dubious claims to democracy, regularly hold journalists responsible for voicing uncomfortable truths. The New-York-based Committee to Protect Journalists (CPJ) reports that worldwide at least 792

The Handbook of Global Communication and Media Ethics, First Edition. Edited by Robert S. Fortner and P. Mark Fackler.
© 2011 Blackwell Publishing Ltd. Published 2011 by Blackwell Publishing Ltd.

journalists were killed on duty between January 1, 1992 and July 8, 2009, 71.8% were murdered and 86.5% of them were local correspondents. The perpetrators escaped with complete impunity in 88.7% of the killings (CPJ, 2009). Jacobo Timerman (1982) in Argentina lived to tell his tale of "the dirty war" – not least that different branches of the military were in dispute over who should control and kill prisoners. By contrast, Anna Politkovskaya, a Russian journalist, was shot dead in 2006 after years of courageous reporting from Chechnya (see http://www.annapolitkovskaya.com/).

Responsibility and the Facts

Democratic societies operating (ostensibly) under the rule of law tend to be more conflicted about how far journalistic responsibility extends.

- Is it okay to hang the Nazi rabble-rouser Julius Streicher, as the Nuremberg judges ordered after the end of World War II, but not to take action against Fox News for giving uncensored coverage to supporters of Vice-Presidential candidate Sarah Palin who shouted "Kill him!" at the mention of soon to be President (and campaign rival) Barack Obama?
- Is it fair to criticize the Qatar-based television station Al Jazeera, for its screen blindness to Palestinian terrorism while highlighting Israeli atrocities – but not take action against the *New York Times* for going along with the lies about Iraqi weapons of mass destruction?
- Are we content to see the imprisonment for life of the Rwanda radio journalists who repeatedly told Hutus to consider all Tutsis as their enemies in 1994, while allowing the man convicted of killing over 200 people aboard Pan Am flight 103 over Lockerbie, Scotland, to be released under an agreement that seemed designed to improve business relations between the United Kingdom and Libya?

Unfortunately, none of the assertions above bears close scrutiny. Even at the Nuremberg trials, other Nazi leaders kept their distance from Streicher as too stupid and brutish to deserve a place in the top echelon, as if their anti-Semitism was at a more intellectual level than his – and they included Herman Goering, the architect of Hitler's racist exterminations, while Streicher was condemned and hanged for his publishing activity.

The "kill him" story about Palin supporters emanated from one journalist, and the US Secret Service was unable to find any evidence for such an outburst, though cries of "liar" and "off with his head" were heard when Presidential candidate John McCain spoke of Obama's proposed policies (and described the Democrat as an honorable, decent opponent). The *Fox News* and *wizzbang* websites document the public record on this story.

Al-Jazeera bases its English language broadcasts on BBC standards of balance (many staff come from the British public broadcaster). The Palestinian National

866   *Peter Hulm*

Authority shut down the office in West Bank for its vigorous reporting. Al-Jazeera's facility for visitor comments on its website publishes the gamut of opinions about its performance. Not a bad record for any broadcaster.

By contrast, when the *New York Times* apologized on May 26, 2004 for its mistakes on misreporting, it said only that editing "was not as rigorous as it should have been." The terminology could have been interpreted as a move by the Democratic proprietors to undermine Republic arguments for prosecuting the war in Iraq.

As for the Rwanda radio journalists, the most thorough sociological examination of the 1994 massacres, by Scott Straus, concluded: "My evidence does not suggest that radio propaganda in and of itself caused most individuals to commit violence. Most men chose to participate in the killing after face-to-face mobilization and in a real situation of war and crisis. The evidence suggests that radio broadcasts had effects on particular perpetrator populations, in particular local elites and the most aggressive killers. But media effects alone did not drive most participation in the genocide" (Straus, 2008, p. 13)

With regard to Lockerbie, few UK stories of the release of the convicted bomber mentioned the long-standing controversy over the man's trial and conviction. A United Nations official observer had described the proceedings as "a spectacular miscarriage of justice" and in 2005 the prosecutor cast doubts on the reliability of the key witness (all documented and sourced on Wikipedia if the journalists had wanted to raise the issue). Instead, the broadcasters concentrated on the differences among victims' families about whether the man should be released.

The essential question here is not the inadequacies of the reporting but the plausibility of the tendentious phrasing; how many of these statements could pass without raising our suspicions as to their accuracy?

A 1998 survey by the Freedom Forum found that 88% of those polled believe reporters use unethical or illegal means to obtain their stories. The American Society of Newspaper Editors (ASNE) found in another 1998 poll that 80% of the population think that journalists sensationalize stories to sell more papers (Good and Dillon, 2002, p. xii). However, the examples just given, recording an elementary failure to distinguish between debatable "facts" and reliable information, surely require something more as explanation than the commercial motivation of venal news organizations.

The never-ending story of media violence

Television is the single most significant factor contributing to violence in America. (Ted Turner, President, Turner Broadcasting System in Carter and Weaver, 2003, p. 71)

The same cloud of puzzlement hangs over the issue of violence in the media and its effects, as well as its accountability. Despite numerous surveys pointing out the shortcomings of research results that point either way, the question returns incessantly, couched in whatever theoretical framework happens to be currently in

Violence and Media Accountability

fashion. Thus, in 1994 David Buckingham recorded: "At a conservative estimate, there have probably been over seven thousand accounts of research in the field [of television's impact on children, particularly violence] published since the introduction of television in the 1950s" (Buckingham, 1994, p. 103). He emphasized: "The levels of statistical significance are often low, for example, and the correlations disappear when all the potential variables are accounted for" (11994, p. 106).

In 2001 the American Academy of Pediatrics put the total at more than 3500 research studies, "all but 18" showing a positive relationship between media violence and violent behavior (FCC, 2007, p. 3). The 2001 assessment was strikingly similar to one given elsewhere in 1994 (3000), which had been challenged by a researcher who found only 250 "directly related to violence in the media" (FCC, 2007, p. 3).

The differences seem to have been over what constitutes a "study" (FCC, 2007, p. 3). Certainly, there seems to be some misreading of what sociologists mean when they describe a result as "significant." Michael Males pointed out that this does not mean the finding is important – only that it is "not likely to happen just by chance" (FCC, 2007, p. 10). However, the central concern must be the effects recorded.

The British cultural studies scholar Martin Barker declared in 2001: "The expression 'media violence' has to be one of the most commonly repeated, and one of the most ill-informed, of all time. ... Seventy years of research into this supposed topic have produced nothing worthy of note" (Barker, 2001, pp. 42, 43). No scientific work since then has established itself firmly with scholars, as distinct from lawmakers, to render this judgment obsolete.

A course book on media and violence that attempted to provide and even-handed discussion of the situation for the Open University (United Kingdom) said it was unwilling to dismiss all studies claiming negative effects of media violence but the authors had to conclude that research into essential questions related to audience reception was still needed. They bewailed a "dearth of studies" on how, for example, men and women separately react to film violence, which they judged as overwhelmingly and increasingly misogynistic (Carter and Weaver, 2003, p. 64).

At the same time, the field is replete with statistics that seem to assert important "truths":

- "By the time the average American child graduates from elementary school, he or she will have seen about 8,000 murders and about 100,000 other assorted acts of violence (e.g. assaults, rapes) on network television" (Bushman and Huesmann, 2001, p. 227).
- "By age 18, an American child will have seen upwards of 15,000 simulated murders and about 200,000 acts of violence" (FCC Commissioner Jonathan S. Adelstein, in FCC, 2007, p. 31).
- The key National Television Violence Study (1998) recorded that on US network and cable television about one-third of violent interactions were portrayed as justified, and more than one-half produced no visible harmful effects, while good guys tended not to be punished for their violence (Gunter et al., 2003, p. 5).

- After reviewing 271 studies, Paik and Comstock declared in 1994: "Approximately ten per cent of the variability in later criminal behavior can be attributed to television violence" (cited by Carter and Wheeler, 2003, p. 6).

Whether this extraordinarily precise assertion is true or not, it seems a very small result from the reported ubiquity of media violence in viewers' lives. The best interpretation a US survey could put on the decades of research was: "Although no reputable media scholar holds that media violence is the largest reason for violence in society, most accept that media violence is a small, but significant contributor to aggressive behavior" (Perse, 2001, p. 202).

In fact, in 2006, a US study found that television viewers overestimated the risk of youth violence while believing wrongly that punishment was more effective than rehabilitation in reducing such crime (Goidel *et al.*, 2006). White viewers also believed that sentencing was race neutral, while African-Americans held the realistic belief that they were much more likely to receive a harsher sentence than Whites for the same offence.

It is also a standard finding of television research that the more time people spend watching television the more likely they are to believe that violence is common and that people are at risk (Perse, 2001, p. 218). The problems of assessing TV effects are not just those of carrying out enough research.

The British sociologist David Buckingham observed: "US researchers have been keen to conclude that violence on television is a cause of aggression. Although, they have often been rather equivocal about exactly how significant a cause it is, ... researchers in the UK and in other English-speaking countries have often reached very different conclusions (Buckingham, 1994, p. 107). He added: "Even when reviewing the same studies, for example, British social psychologists have generally been much more skeptical than their American counterparts. What appears to underlie these different evaluations of the research are fundamental disagreements about what is to count as evidence, and indeed what is to count as a valid and meaningful research question" (Buckingham, 1994, p. 107).

The Third-person Effect

Given the methodological difficulties and doubtful premises of many of these studies, there seems no benefit to be gained from examining the claims in detail, since their differences rarely make them comparable, but it may be useful to point to some of the issues involved.

Perhaps the first point is that most of the direct research used to bolster arguments, for or against media effects, dates back before 2001, even that cited by the Federal Communication Commission in 2007, and this historic detail tends to be buried in the generalizations or a footnote.

Second, the effects of media violence on children have been "the most prominent preoccupation in this field," as Buckingham notes (1994, p. 108).

Violence and Media Accountability 869

The third is that "the dominant assumption in public debates is that children's relationship with the medium is a fundamentally negative and damaging element in their lives" (Buckingham, 1994, p. 104).

Some of this concern may be due what is known as the "third-person effect." People surveyed tend to see potential harm in media violence for others than themselves. The effect "has emerged as a particularly sensitive predictor of support for strict censorship of media," reported Barrie Gunter and his team (2003:7).

The problems of "hard science"

It is not a damning criticism of the research that it can speak of both "desensitization" and "arousal" effects from media violence, though a search for a single causal explanation of everything that is offensive in the behavior of the young is obviously wrong-headed. Attempts to give the research a "hard science" edge have also only served to highlight the difficulties of tackling the issues.

For example, the British psychologist and persistent critic of Freudian method, Hans Eyesenck, attempted in the 1970s to give a physical scientific response to the question of "desensitization" through media violence. Among the elementary distortions to which his report fell victim is his use of the term itself. In a survey of research he uses "skin conductance" (galvanic skin responses, recording increases in skin moisture) as an objective measure of sensitivity (Eyesenck and Nias, 1978, p. 281). Declines in galvanic skin response through repeated exposure to media violence were treated as "desensitization" to real violence. Children who watched either a "violent" *Peter Gunn* episode or a "neutral" *Green Acres* program then recognized fewer pictures as violent if they had seen *Peter Gunn*. In another experiment, children who watched a violent scene from *Hopalong Cassidy* were slower to call in adults when they saw a staged (videotaped) escalation of aggression between two children in another room. Eyesenck does not explain why girls were slower to call in help in all cases (Eyesenck and Nias, 1978, p. 253). One obvious explanation for "desensitization," that children watching media violence can learn to "frame" their viewing so that it is less arousing, is not considered.

Eyesenck's use of "desensitization" – via the media or watching comparatively mild aggressive behavior – is quite different from the desensitization practiced on Nazi Einsatzgruppen (killing squads) reported by Richard Rhodes. Basing his explanation on the violent-socialization theory of the American criminologist Lonnie Athens, he identifies four distinct stages in the Nazi desensitization process: (1)[physical] brutalization, (2) belligerency, (3) violent performances, and (4) virulency" (Rhodes, 2002, pp. 21, 22).

Even less of a schematic scenario was needed for experimenter Philip Zimbardo (2007) to turn Stanford students into brutal jailors and prisoner victims in less than one week. Zimbardo's reflections on his 1971 study that became known as the "Stanford Prison Experiment" put the blame on psychologists rather than media for failing to appreciate how much social and cultural factors define situations and legitimatize behavior" (Zimbardo, 2007, p. x, xi). Zimbardo later tried unsuccessfully to obtain clemency for a guard found guilty of abuses at the Abu Ghraib interrogation center in Iraq. Of course, his conclusion does not rule out media effects, but implies that the media, if they come into the picture, are largely channeling society's "economic, religious, historic and cultural" standards.

Stereotyping the child

Perhaps not surprisingly, US researchers have seemed less concerned than Eyesenck with providing a physical basis for their conclusions. Nevertheless, their findings are often cast against romanticized or stereotypical notions of the pretelevision child. However, age, gender and social class mean that "children can effectively occupy different 'media worlds' - ... which clearly undermines any easy generalizations about 'children' as a homogenous group" Buckingham points out (1994, p. 114). He continues "There appears to be an implicit view of the child as a 'deficit system': children at certain ages are seen to be unable to accomplish the 'logical' sequencing of visual images, to recall the 'essential' features of a narrative, or to 'correctly' distinguish between positive and negative characters – which of course implies that adults' responses to such things are taken as the norm" (1994, pp. 115–116). He also notes that a report by Susan Neuman (1991) refuted the idea that television displaced out-of-school reading (cited by Buckingham, 1994, p. 109).

The definition of media violence

Defining media violence itself is not just controversial but an essentially contested concept in sociological theory. In the United States the NTVS definition of television violence (NTVS, 1997) proved an important benchmark. It was:

> Any overt depiction of a credible threat of physical force or the actual use of such force intended to physically harm an animate being or group of beings. Violence also includes certain depictions of physically harmful consequences against an animate being or group that occur as a result of unseen violent means" (Gunter et al., 2003, p. 225).

This definition differed from the earlier influential work of George Gerbner and his colleagues, whose annual report on the status of violence on American network television included natural violent phenomena in its categories, on the grounds that program producers deliberately included such events to intensify the human drama (Gunter et al., 2003, p. 225).

"Violence directed by a human aggressor against an inanimate object was not counted" the survey notes (Gunter et al., 2003, p. 226). Which is one reason so many frustrated Hollywood characters are seen to take out their anger on the furniture around them (a postmodern explanation is that these are "evocatively nourishing objects" for our dreamtime phantasies, according to Christopher Bollas, in Phillips, 1994, p. 157).

The NTVS categorized media representations into four types thought to cause children to underestimate the seriousness of violence: unpunished violence, painless violence, happy violence (as in cartoons) and heroic violence, such as action by role models (Carter and Weaver, 2003, p. 3). Though these terms took over those from an earlier study (the *UCLA Television Violence Monitoring Report,* 1995), Carter and Weaver note that "not everyone will necessarily agree that the representations to which the researchers refer are violent" (such as threats rather than actual violence) and many media researchers "utterly reject" claims that such representations have an effect on adults or children's behavior (Carter and Weaver, 2003, p. 3).

A parallel UK study took over the basic definition of the NTVS, and found that in the mid-1990s, the four major British channels had violence in 28% of programs compared to the 44% found on the four main US networks by the NTVS (Gunter *et al.,* 2003, p. 227). By contrast the two satellite movie subscription channels recorded 80% in 1994–1995 and 84% in 1995–1996 (Gunter *et al.,* 2003, p. 230). Beyond this statistical recording, it is difficult to draw any policy conclusions, and no attempt is made to account for the differences in US and UK violent crime on the basis of these figures.

Cause and correlation

Whether considering television violence for behavioral, emotional, ideological, or attitudinal effects, researchers have rarely been able to overcome the methodological difficulties of proving causation from correlation. Until the cultural studies movement entered the field in the 1990s, cognitive and uses/gratifications students tended to treat television programs as having an objective meaning, while considering television viewing as a more purposive activity than most people would themselves have considered it (Buckingham, 1994, 114–115).

With its attempts to take full account of the varieties of the "ambiguity, 'openness' and contradiction, which many analyses of popular television have shown to be fundamental to its success," (Buckingham, 1993, p. 13) as well as the varieties of dynamic institutions and audiences, the cultural studies school not surprisingly has offered little fodder for journalistic generalizations or simple policy-making. The pioneering work of this school, *Demonstrations and Communication,* by James D. Halloran, Phillip Elliott, and Graham Murdock (1970) documented how a protest against US policy in Vietnam outside the American Embassy in London was treated by television in terms of its potential for violence and reported on that basis. Its own view of television as an instrument of establishment hegemony in political discourse gave it no reason to study further the causes of media bias, though journalists said they were simply following professional news standards.

Watersheds in the 1990s

Despite the failure of scientific researchers to confirm or disprove theories of media violence effects, 1994 was a watershed in UK legislation as much as the 1996 V-Chip ("parental control" technology) in the United States. In fact, the anxiety was directed more towards violence on film than on television. Today, as 10 years ago (Perse, 2001, p. 200), the most popular television programs and movies are not the most violent (unless you count *NCIS* and *Cold Case* as violent). However, a number (at least two) killings by young people associated by the media with violent videos available in the United Kingdom led a Member of Parliament to ask child psychologist Elizabeth Newson to prepare a short report on the dangers of "video nasties," as popular newspapers termed them. Endorsed by 25 other leading psychologists and pediatricians (Cumberbatch, 1994, p. 486), this led to changes in the UK's Criminal Justice Bill, imposing £20 000 fines on any distributor that allowed the circulation of films that had not received certification by the UK film control board.

Murders and videos

In response to the lawmaker's request, Newson contributed an unreferreed paper to *The Psychologist* in June 1994 that was to prove a key factor in changing the law. Reporting on the torture and murder of a two-year-old boy by two 12-year-olds (the Jamie Bulger case), along with similar brutal killings by children under the age of criminal responsibility, Newson noted that a number of social factors usually put forward as explanations for violent behavior did not apply to the killers. "What, then, can be seen as the 'different' factor that has entered the lives of countless children and adolescents in recent years?" she asks. "This has to be recognized as the easy availability to children of gross images of violence on video" (Newson, 1994, p. 273).

In the Bulger case, the press drew links with the US film *Child's Play 3*. The tabloid newspaper *The Sun* organized a public burning of the film on November 25, 1993.

Guy Cumberbatch looked more closely at the 1994 report in the *Journal of Mental Health* that year. Much of her report was based on accounts in the popular press. Cumberbatch observes: "Of course readers of the report might reasonably assume that a professor of child psychology might be expected to know more about the cases described than the average citizen. The attribution of motives such as 'sadistically', 'the expectation of deliberate and sustained violence', the implied familiarity in the use of 'Jamie' (instead of the preferred family name 'James') provide an illusory independent verification of press speculation" (1994, p. 487).

Fanciful links

Cumberbatch then turns to Newsom's use of the material available on violent videos. "Despite police evidence that there appeared to be no link with video violence in the James Bulger case, [press and policymaker] parallels with [the film] *Child's Play 3* were fancifully drawn." References to "evidence" of the effect of violent

Violence and Media Accountability

videos turned out to be a case of experts "now agreeing that they were wrong to underestimate the threat of violent videos" (Cumberbatch, 1994, p. 487).

"While Newson does not cite *Child's Play* in the context of the Bulger case, she later links it to a murder," Cumberbatch adds. "However, just as with the Bulger murder, police evidence that videos were not implicated is ignored by Newson.... The 'link' in the murder ... was not to a film but to the lyrics of a heavy metal band" (Cumberbatch, 1994, p. 487).

While proclaiming that she was simply keeping within her field of professional competence, Newson failed to recognize the discrepancies in the stories or the dangers of relying on popular media when appearing before a Parliamentary Home Affairs committee. Newson maintained that the video was implicated, and was corrected. She complained it had been "widely misreported" and commented that the impact "depended on whether that particular girl had seen the film and whether she was able to identify the film from the music" (Cumberbatch, 1994, p. 487). The Committee chair noted: "There were no videos in the houses that this young lady was held in, apparently." No correction or apology was made, however (Cumberbatch, 1994, p. 487).

Confused legislation

Cumberbatch observed that the same confusion existed in legislators' minds over an earlier killing, when Michael Ryan shot dead 16 people in the village of Hungerford on August 19, 1987. The press spoke of links with *Rambo* because of his use of a Kalashnikov assault rifle. Legislation was passed controlling semi-automatic firearms. However, there was no evidence that Ryan had ever seen any Sylvester Stallone films, and he killed more people with a pistol than with the rifle (Cumberbatch, 1994, p. 488).

Following this massacre, a BBC current affairs program investigated the evidence for links between videos and crime. It found six cases where the press claimed a clear link. "None of these cases stood up to even cursory examination," Cumberbatch reports (Cumberbatch, 1994, p. 488). The Director of the British Board of Film Classification told the Home Affairs Committee: "I do not know of particular cases in Britain where somebody has imitated a video and gone out and actually committed a serious crime as a result of what they have seen." Another researcher, David Smith, found 33 reports of similar crimes to the Bulger murder in the previous 150 years. Cumberbatch suggests: "This may well be an underestimate but serves to remind us that such events are not new and should not merit new explanations" (Cumberbatch, 1994, p. 489).

The V-Chip

Similar concerns about video nasties on television with the rise of cable television led to the "V-Chip" legislation – "v" refers to viewer control, according to the sponsor of this legislation, though many take it to refer to violence. All televisions with screens of 13 inches or more, sold in the United States from 2000, have to contain a control device to enable blocking of programs deemed inappropriate for specific ages. Signing the bill into law in 1996 President William Clinton, facing an election in which he wanted broad support across party lines, praised the legislation as giving parents power to protect their children from unsuitable content, side-stepping the First Amendment issues brought up by critics. However, the system does not block inappropriate commercials, which has led to protests (FCC, 2008), and only an estimated 15% of parents use the control (Kaiser Family Foundation telephone survey, 2004, cited in FCC, 2007, p. 14).

In these circumstances, it is not surprising that Elizabeth Perse's formulation that "media violence is a small, but significant contributor to aggressive behavior" should appear in the Federal Communication Commission report for 2007 in these terms: "We agree with the views of the Surgeon General and find that, on balance, research provides strong evidence that exposure to violence in the media can increase aggressive behavior in children, at least in the short term" (FCC, 2007, p. 3). The generalization gets its most extreme formulation in Craig Anderson's "No one is exempt from the deleterious effects of media violence" (Anderson et al,. 2003, cited in FCC, 2007, p. 5).

A skeptical reader, particularly from Europe, might also apply the results to television viewing of sports such as American football – where the aggression levels seem equally intense – and expect the V-Chip to block such programs. However, some backtracking appears in a footnote in the FCC 2007 report. This discloses that the Surgeon-General states in an appendix to the cited 2001 report: "[D]espite considerable advances in research, it is not yet possible to describe accurately how much exposure, of what types, for how long, at what ages, for what types of children, or in what types of settings, will predict violent behavior in adolescents and adults" (FCC, 2007, p. 11). The difficulty of proving causation from correlation remains.

Nor should it surprise anyone who has followed the variation between European and American attitudes on media violence that the low use of the V-Chip by parents is treated by Carter and Weaver as an indication that parents are less concerned by television violence than lawmakers while the FCC, while recognizing that "violent content is a protected form of speech under the First Amendment" (2007, p. 3), saw the failure of V-Chip controls to become widespread as a reason to simplify its rating system and use, and call for an extensive program of action including a summit on "Protecting America's Children" (FCC, 2008). European authorities, including the United Kingdom, use content-identification systems to rate programs, opt-in codes for satellite broadcasting, and "time channeling" for potentially disturbing elements but leave it to viewers to decide whether to watch. The FCC found both the V-Chip and a voluntary TV ratings system "of limited effectiveness" in achieving a reduction of media violence available to children (FCC, 2008, pp. 14, 15).

Some witnesses warned that time-channeling, used to regulate indecent broadcasting, could be ruled unconstitutional if applied to violent material. The FCC suggested that it could be introduced without falling foul of the First Amendment (FCC, 2007, p. 12). However, it warned, lawmakers would need to produce specific findings to support their views on "the nature of the harm inflicted by violent television content, how to define such content, and the ages of the children that the government is seeking to protect" (FCC, 2007, p. 12). This can hardly count as a vote of full confidence in previous research. The most vociferous Commissioner for tougher measures, Jonathan Adelstein, himself admitted "there are no easy answers and no panacea" (FCC, 2008, p. 2).

Film and video game violence

In art, you make what you want to see. (NASA Godard Space Station Center, *Footprints*, Science on a Sphere.)

For historians of film, the debates on television violence eerily recall those throughout the twentieth century about the control of movies, except that British authorities have shown themselves notoriously sensitive to film violence. Tongue in cheek, a British critic described the first Western film, Edwin Porter's *The Great Train Robbery* (1903), as including "the cinema's first example of truly gratuitous brutality" because of its unmotivated, shock-provoking scene of an outlaw staring into the audience as he fires his gun. More seriously, British film certifiers refused Sergei Eisenstein's *Battleship Potemkin* a permit for public exhibition until 1954 on the grounds of its violent content, and it was then restricted to audiences over 16 (Carter and Weaver, 2003, pp. 43, 47).

Censorship in America

It seems hardly worth repeating the history of the media violence debate over movies in the United States except to note some salient aspects relevant to the media's response to action to control violent representation. The first direct act of US film censorship took place in 1908 when Chicago police prevented a showing of *The James Boys in Missouri* because it "criminalized" American history (Carter and Weaver, 2003, p. 44). The same film led the Metropolitan Police in London to pressure the government to introduce a Cinematographic control bill in Britain. Ostensibly monitoring fire standards, local authorities used it to stop "immoral or indecent" films from exhibition (Carter and Weaver, 2003, p. 44).

In 1915, *Birth of the Nation*'s glorification of Ku Klux Klan violence led to it being banned in five states and 19 cities, and to a Supreme Court decision that movies could be subject to censorship and "could be regulated through prior censorship and be stopped before reaching their consumers in much the same way dangerous drugs or hazardous chemicals might" (Carter and Weaver, 2003, 45). Denied First Amendment rights, movie producers set up a National Association of Motion Picture Industries in 1916 to respond to complaints and set written standards for members. However, without powers to impose these standards, it proved ineffective, leading in 1930 to the restrictive self-imposed Hays Code, active from 1934 to1968. A major influence on the restrictions was the Payne Fund Studies, which concluded from much research that (later much criticized for biased methodology): "Motion pictures played a direct role in shaping the delinquent and criminal careers of substantial segments of those studied" (Carter and Weaver, 2003, p. 49).

"Honoring" the code

One reaction by movie producers was to make films that stayed within the Code by glorifying violent law enforcers: *G-Men* (1935), *Special Agent* (1935) and *Bullets or Ballots* (1936). This period also saw the rise of the psychotic villain and the *femme fatale*, each of whom received due punishment but not before the end of the film.

In 1953, a Supreme Court decision gave films First Amendment rights, effectively protected moviemakers from all charges except "obscenity" (which was always treated in the courts as relating to sex rather than violence). Britain at this time introduced a 16-or-older 'X' certificate for disturbing films.

Another key date was 1966, when the movie supervision board revised its content injunctions for the first time since 1934, removing specific stipulations on the depiction of violence and relied on filmmakers "discretion in showing the taking of human life" (Carter and Weaver, 2003, p. 54). A new classification, "Suggested for Mature Audiences" was also introduced.

Next year Arthur Penn released *Bonnie and Clyde*, with its slow-motion depiction of "overkill" by law officers against the two outlaws, and Robert Aldrich *The Dirty Dozen*, which showed a unit of US soldiers in World War II as "composed of murderers, rapists and other violent misfits" in one description. This led the industry to introduce an age-based coding system in November 1968. The next year saw the release of Sam Peckinpah's *The Wild Bunch*, with its climactic gun-battle also in gory slow motion. The way was open for Quentin Tarantino's cycle of hymns to violence.

From D.W. Griffiths (director of *Birth of a Nation*) to the film noir directors and the violent moviemakers of the late 1960s, the most controversial violent products have often come from the greatest of Hollywood creators, posing the most difficult challenge to the legislators: the 1952 Supreme Court case was over Roberto Rossellini's film *The Miracle*. Stanley Kubrick achieved a similar public stir by staging the gang rape and killing of an artist in *Clockwork Orange* (1971), and withheld it from distribution in the United Kingdom for 30 years after reports that it had inspired youth violence, though his widow later indicated that his action followed police advice on receiving death threats (documented on wikipedia).

Video games

Video game concerns have followed the same pattern, with psychologist Craig Anderson leading those convinced of effects from both television and games (FCC, 2007, p. 5). One hardly unexpected finding is that those who play no video games at all are most likely to be involved in violence (Kutner and Olsen, 2008, p. 18ff; techdirt, 2008). The UK censor in 2007 issued its first ban of a violent video game for 10 years, by the same Scottish firm that created the controversial *Grand Theft Auto* series. The board said giving *Manhunt 2* a certificate "would involve a range of unjustifiable harm risks to both adults and minors" (*Daily Record*, 2007, p. 23). Under UK rules it is not illegal to own a game bought abroad. The last game to be refused a certificate was *Carmageddon* in 1997 but the ban was later reversed.

Moral panics

All three forms of media suffer from what have been termed "moral panics," a phrase originating in the United Kingdom, used by Jock Young in a book on public concern about Mods and Rockers, two groups of teenagers (mainly men) with two distinctive styles of dress and transport (scooters vs. motorbikes), who were thought to be violently opposed to each other. In fact, their relations were often amicable, even friendly or indifferent. However, British media whipped up stories about their opposition.

The classic work used to discuss media-channeled symbolic working-out of what are seen as threatening issues, *Folk Devils and Moral Panics* (1972) by Stanley Cohen, does not forefront media in its definition of a moral panic: "a condition, episode, person or group of persons emerges to become defined as a threat to societal values and interests" (Cohen, 1972, p. 16). The issues, in his view, are not just driven by media agendas. Mass media can stimulate such panics simply by reporting the facts rather than campaigning, he points out (Cohen, 1972, p. 16).

The terminology is itself suspect, however, in its presupposition of a grounded moral concern and an emotional rather than rational stimulus. There is no reason to doubt assertions by bodies such as the FCC that many parents are concerned about the amount of violent programming available to children (FCC, 2007, p. 2).

Postmodernism to the rescue

> Death is the catastrophic knowledge, the truly forbidden thing, that everyone has to be protected from because no one can be (Adam Phillips, 1994, p. xx).

A survey of the issue of media violence thus confronts a reader with starkly opposed "scientific" views on the effects, except on the minor kind, legislation prompted by misunderstandings and "moral panics" with no basis in fact, laws and devices that admittedly fail to achieve their goals, media whose commitment to accuracy in reporting cannot be taken for granted, entertainment producers who are skilled at ducking under the net of regulation or challenge it in the name of art, the eternal recurrence of demands for control, and widespread parental anxiety about the impact on their children, even if none seems immediately visible. Is the media simply a scapegoat, a willing accomplice of evil forces, a power-seeker in the battle over commodified culture – and should it be held accountable for its products? If so, how?

The thesis of this paper is that only postmodern theory can provide a coherent understanding of the processes at work, and that if the media are implicated in the dissemination of violent images, they are not necessarily accountable. Changing their behavior will require more than simply adopting new practices.

The return to Lacan

The first step is to go back to Sigmund Freud via the controversial French psychoanalyst Jacques Lacan, and to Lacan via the cultural theorist Slavoj Žižek and his other interpreters. In what he termed "the return to Freud," Lacan provides a rereading of Freudian theory that brings to the center-stage some of his neglected writings, particularly "Screen Memories" (Freud, 1899), "The 'Uncanny'" (Freud, 1919a) and "'A Child is Being Beaten'" (Freud, 1919b). "Screen Memories" documents how we may fabricate memories and give these phantasies a pleasurable tinge to hide anxieties about repressed real events. "The 'Uncanny'" recounts how we can find ourselves repeating actions we cannot explain – in Freud's case continually finding himself back in a street of "painted ladies" when trying to find his way around a strange town. It also includes a moving footnote recounting how Freud one day rose from his seat in a railway carriage to see an old man doing the same, then realized he was seeing himself in a reflection. "'A Child is Being Beaten'" gives Freud's interpretation of what he thinks is happening in a particular fantization: "It is surprising how frequently people who come to be analysed for hysteria or an obsessional neurosis confess to having indulged in the phantasm," he wrote (1919b, p. 172), "Very probably it occurs even more often with other people who have not been obliged to come to this decision by manifest illness."

Lacan's rereading of Freud led him to elevate *Thanatos* (badly translated as the death drive) to a preeminent position, bringing psychoanalytical thought into line with the preeminent postmodern philosopher Martin Heidegger, for whom death was the unthinkable challenge to human thought (Homer, 2004). Lacan also brought order into Freud's varying ideas about the drive (*Trieb*, another difficult word to find anything more than the inadequate official English translation). In contrast to the instincts, which Freud saw as physical, the drives (as creations of phantasy) cannot be satisfied by their realization (Homer, 2004, p. 75).

This gives us a meaning for the apocalyptic writer J.G. Ballard's cryptic comment that though we complain there is too much violence in the media, we secretly want more. In Lacanian terms, the male appetite for violence is unending. We can never have enough. At the same time this need cannot be acknowledged. Women, as

Violence and Media Accountability

researchers have found (Perse, 2001, p. 200), do not find media violence appealing, perhaps because their capacity to give birth guarantees their future (at least in phantasy). Men have to live with the fact of their death and extinction, part of what Lacan termed the Real – the unspeakable truths of our existence to which we must find inadequate compensatory phantasies, such as the ego, the deceptively stable idea of ourselves we continually reassemble from fragmentary experience.

The obverse of pornography

We find the obverse of this situation in pornography, which is of equal public concern, an almost exclusively male preoccupation, and likewise finds no solution in legislation. Pornographic movies reenact the phantastic male fear that through the pleasures of sex, with its multiple variations, women block men from the simple act of reproduction. Feminists who complain that porn degrades women miss the point. Of course the woman has to be degraded into an instrument for men's desires, in order to stifle the fear that dare not speak its name. Otherwise male homosexual films would serve the purpose of excitation for the man viewing just as well. Chuck Palahniuk's novel *Snuff* (Palahniuk, 2008) derives its creative and comic energies from the disquieting idea that a porno movie resulted in the birth of a child.

In both violent and pornographic movies, the stability of the constructed ego is challenged. However, the violence stands in for something else: the fact of death. Interestingly, the definitions of violence used in the public debate do not distinguish between death and violence. Death is almost "the forbidden thing" from which we must be protected, as the psychotherapist Adam Phillips points out (1994, p. xx). He also observes: "The protection racket – like all protection rackets, and particularly the one arranged with oneself – leaves us radically unprotected."

This gives us a clue to the function of media violence in our phantasies. In "'A Child is Being Beaten'," Freud comes to the conclusion that "the original form of the unconscious male phantasy was...: '*I am loved by my father*'" (Freud, 1919b, pp. 194–195). In Lacanian terms, this can become a phantasmic celebration of survival (against the Real inevitability of death). The best way to become immortal, at least in phantasy, is to be the last person left alive – and the more violent the test, the more secure the satisfaction of the phantastic wish.

We can see the mechanism in operation in the films that fail to disguise their phantastic content (and often claim the defense of art as a result). *Bonnie and Clyde* and *The Wild Bunch* present us with artists who seem not quite in control of their phantasies. Forty years on, Tarantino is much more in synch with the dreamworld that video art explores, as French filmmaker Jean-Luc Godard was from the beginning. Godard's *Pierrot Le Fou* (1967) shows us Jean-Paul Belmondo wrapping explosives round his head in an almost playful, certainly parodic, suicide ("the only successful act" in Lacan's view). Suddenly Belmondo understands that the phantasy is real and attempts to stop it. Godard then pulls back and, almost consciously, celebrates his own (and our) survival when the character blows up before our eyes. The final scene of Tarantino's *Death Proof*, when two women stomp a serial killer to death, taps into the same responses. Women, of course, can laugh here at the phantasy being indulged.

The phantasy is not real

How is it then that a single viewing of *Rambo* or any of the pectoral dramas and chain-saw gorefests fails to console us? Why do we need to be reminded of the dreadful subject we cannot acknowledge? As Freud's "The 'Uncanny'" reminds us – and it seems no accident that Freud's abrupt self-reminder of his mortality is a footnote to this essay – we unconsciously seek out disturbing experiences that can stand in for what is really troubling us. The sexual tone to his lost wanderings is a red herring, as in pornography or Stanley Kubrick's *Eyes Wide Shut*, where the real story is that an unknown woman sacrifices herself in order that Tom Cruise may live, but the drama is cast in terms of sexual adventure.

Due to our insecurities, we need constant reassurance of our immortality. The categories of violence that the NTVS catalogues (unpunished violence, painless violence, happy violence, and heroic violence) can be seen as just ways to enable us to enjoy a varied diet without becoming bored, rather than different types with measurably different effects.

However, as Freud noted in the child-beating phantasy, the insatiable male appetite for reassurance of immortality is purely a phantasy and no predictor of a physical pleasure in violence: "It might…be expected that the sight of another child being beaten at school would also be a source of similar enjoyment [as in the phantasy]. But as a matter of fact this was never so" (Freud, 1919b, pp. 173–174). Patients usually spoke of a feeling of repugnance as well as excitation, and "in a few cases the real experience of the scenes of beating was felt to be intolerable."

The place of the child

For Lacan, who produced pioneering studies of the infant's construction of the ego in face of the Real ("The Mirror Image"), the extension of media violence into children's programming would have been no surprise, given the ubiquity of *Thanatos* in our imaginative lives. To transpose Karl Kraus's epigram on sex education: one can never learn too early how death is (to be) avoided.

British sociologists are often skeptical of adult claims of concern for children, and not just because of the "third-person" effect. For some, as noted by Carter and Weaver (2003, p. 75), it is seen as simply a way to assert adult control over children and create an artificial distinction between the two groups. For others it involves a construction of innocence that, for example, denies children political views or autonomy: the use of child soldiers in a cause is widely thought to discredit it (Alvarado *et al.*, 1987, p. 233).

Such symbolic manipulation opens the way for the consciousness industry to perform other profitable acrobatics with the imagination. "The construction of sexual innocence in children allows some media products to offer the exploitative *frisson* of portraying children involved in 'adult' sex and violence," write Alvarado *et al.* (1987, p. 232) in their school textbook. There is nothing radical about such products, they observe: "The pornographic representation of children does not challenge the cultural misrepresentations of childhood sexuality, but merely confirms children's passivity within the usual exploitative and voyeuristic male domination of pornography's visual regime" (Alvardo *et al.*, 1987, p. 232).

Nevertheless, the United Kingdom, notorious for its neglect of children's welfare (Garrett, 1997, p. 146), has prosecuted child pornography cases with a vigor that most observers found misplaced. A man who photographed his child and another playing naked after swimming (in the presence of the two mothers) had to wait 14 months for a jury to clear him of indecency. "The juridical intervention by the state was highly intrusive and also, arguably, indecent. It included interrogations over sexual acts that never took place, with the children reduced to tears while also being exposed to the sight of their parents being browbeaten by suspicious police officers," reports the journalist Laurence O'Toole (O'Toole, 1999, p. 217). He decided after investigating several other cases: "Worries over child sexual abuse and child pornography [have] led to the situation where nearly all images of children are sexualized and seen as open to doubt" (O'Toole, 1999, p. 238).

The British action was possible because the Protection of Children Act of 1978 permits any nude photograph of a person under 16 to be deemed indecent. "The bulk of *visible* police and judicial activity in the UK concerning child porn actually involves images of a non-pornographic nature – family snaps, naturist images and art-work," he found. For example, a woman television newsreader and her husband were arrested (though not charged), over photos of their daughter taking a bath (O'Toole, 1999, p. 225).

He contrasts "the public nature of porn" to "the elusive, secret reality of the sexual abuse of children that occurs mainly in private." Campaigner Linda Williams (1993) observes: "Because of this ... exhibitionist quality, it is often porn, and those who can be vilified through its use or production, rather than real sexual harassers, who end up being blamed and punished" (Williams, 1993, p. 53; also cited by O'Toole, 1999, p. 218).

Conspiracy theories

O'Toole found little evidence of child porn rings (two or three prosecuted a year) compared to the publicity given to such cases (mainly of downloading material to computers), and observes: "Panic over child porn ... can also be roused in order to make adult porn look guilty by association, as though watching a video of two adults having sex somehow connects the viewer with the darkest of abuses. ... The reality is that the adult entertainment industry employs only adults to produce porn entertainment for adults" (O'Toole, 1999, pp. 218–219).

O'Toole also condemns the conspiratorial tone given to the idea of child porn rings. "With conspiracy we tend to project outwards, giving a kind of shadowy presence to villainy while placing crimes against children in nasty, dark, 'other' situations, rather than in the place where children appear to be most at risk: in families, in children's homes, in foster families etc ... Conspiracy theories reflect the desire for easy answers and clean solutions, but they risk turning a society's attention away from the wider problem of abuse" (O'Toole, 1999, pp. 222–223).

The British record since 1999 is not good, including the arrest of a famous pop artist who was the first to bring child abuse within the family to the public stage (no further action was taken on his use of a credit card to enter a child porn site but he received no apology). The PCA was still being used for prosecutions after 2000 though an equally controversial Sexual Offences Act was passed in 2003 to replace all previous sexual offence laws.

Feed your phantasies

> The consumer "no more 'believes' in advertising than the child believes in Father Christmas, but this in no way impedes his capacity to embrace an internalized infantile situation, and to act accordingly" (Jean Baudrillard, 1968, p. 181).

Once the child is grown, what replaces the adult who protects? Lacan spoke of "the subject supposed to know," a reformulation of Freud's notion of transference (Homer, 2004, p. 123). The patient supposes the analyst knows everything that is hidden, and the analysis is only completed when the patient realizes that the doctor has no more special power or knowledge than the person being treated. Lacan's own controversial methods, such as breaking off sessions after only a few minutes, were designed to accelerate this process.

In televisual societies the media is the subject supposed to know, but it also has no reason to end the analysis. What it is supposed to know is the truth, but, as Baudrillard makes plain, it also supposed to know and feed our phantasies, which want to have no truck with truth. "The unconscious knows no negation," said Freud (Žižek, 2009, p. 86). Hence media are always caught within an aporia of duty when the two demands conflict.

Television, following film, has chosen to feed the phantasy, while newspapers have chosen phantasy but proclaim their commitment to truth and are in permanent decline having lost their credibility on both fronts (see the introductory section). The Internet has not yet found a formula (outside pornography) to present its phantasy products. Blogs and twittering mix the trivial with the important with no differentiation between them.

Sixty years of experience have taught news television that the best phantasy setup for its presentations is the mutually supportive middle-aged couple. The United Kingdom for its own cultural reasons, prefers the bickering couple to anchor its "lighter" news programs, just as its advertisements often feature couples who jeer at the other behind their backs, in place of pure delight through the possession of

Violence and Media Accountability

commodities in the United States. Both couples interact visually with the camera, however, rather than each other.

The news machine at work

We can see the effects of the "subject supposed to know" in the management of news. W. Lance Bennett reports that when an unemployed man set himself on fire in front of a television news crew in what he presented as an act of despair in protest against the Reagan administration's social and economic policies some 25 years ago, "this news story, with its highly unconventional form of political action and its equally radical message, was quickly replaced by official pronouncements from local authorities (none of whom were at the scene of the original event) that the man was not in his right mind. The news media then completed the repair operation on the momentary tear in the seamless web of cultural meaning by condemning the decision to report the story in the first place as bad journalism" (Bennett, 1997, p. 116).

This is a striking and egregious but not unusual occasion of media transformation of events. When Hurricane Katrina hit the Louisiana and Mississippi coast on August 29, 2005, media reports spoke of the disintegration of public order, rape and looting in New Orleans. The city's police commissioner was quoted in the *New York Times* as saying that in the convention center where refugees gathered: "The tourists are walking around there, and as soon as these individuals see them, they're being preyed on. They are beating, they are raping them in the streets." A month later he conceded: "We have no official reports to document any murder. Not one official report of rape or sexual assault" (Dwyer and Drew, 2005).

For Lacan's disciple Slavoj Žižek the intriguing aspect was how this fallacious presumption of lawlessness ran so long without investigation and had material effects: the rumors generated fears that "led the authorities to change troop deployments, they delayed medical evacuations, drove police officers to quit, grounded helicopters" (Dwyer and Drew, 2005). The real catastrophe, however, was "to a large extent due to human failure; the protective dams were not good enough, and the authorities were insufficiently prepared to meet the easily predictable humanitarian needs which followed" (Žižek, 2009, p. 80). Nevertheless, the media depicted the social catastrophe largely in terms of lawlessness by the poor (Blacks). This, he suggests, is because "poor blacks abandoned and left without the means of survival" (Žižek, 2009, p. 84) had become "subjects supposed to loot and rape" (Žižek, 2009, p. 83).

Lying in the guise of truth

Even if violence had erupted, the reaction would still have been grounded in racial prejudice, Žižek emphasizes. Lacan had said that even if a patient's wife is really sleeping with other men, the man's jealousy is to be treated as a pathological condition, and even if rich Jews did what the Nazis said, their anti-Semitism was pathological. "What made it pathological was the disavowed libidinal investment into the figure of the Jew ... , the spectral figure of mixed fascination and disgust. Exactly the same applies to the looting in New Orleans ... What motivated these stories was not facts but racist prejudice," Žižek writes (2009, p. 85). He terms this pathological condition "lying in the guise of truth" (Žižek, 2009, p. 85).

When this condition is given expression, official Christian and democratic discourse is "accompanied by a whole nest of obscene, brutal, racist, sexist fantasies, which can only be admitted in a censored form" (Žižek, 2009, p. 86). Thus William Bennett, the neoconservative author of *The Book of Virtues*, said on September 28, 2005 on his call-in program *Morning in America*: "If you wanted to reduce crime, you could, if that were your sole purpose, you could abort every black baby in this country, and your crime rate would go down. That would be an impossibly ridiculous and morally reprehensible thing to do, but your crime rate would go down." Two days later, Bennett defended himself with the statement: "I was putting a hypothetical proposition ... and then said about it, it was morally reprehensible to recommend abortion of an entire group of people" (*New York Times*, 2005).

As Freud's "Screen Memories" documented, such censorship can only operate if it is unacknowledged. For media this screen is professionalism.

The media supposed to know

> We like to blame someone. It makes us feel safe. (Pellington, 1999)

What does journalistic professionalism mean? On television, for instance, it means not analyzing the advertisements or statements that that surround and interrupt your programs, even if you have a segment (like Anderson Cooper on CNN) entitled "Keeping Them Honest." Similarly, the broadcasting organization is "supposed to know" whether violence or indecency is found in the advertisements it accepts, though the FCC notes continual abuses (FCC, 2007p. 21).

This displacement is a familiar psychological mechanism. It works both ways. The "real" person (the ego) can deny responsibility in favor of the subject supposed to know. At the same time, the subject supposed to know can relieve us from the responsibility of relating truth to phantasy. As Žižek (2009, pp. 82–83) remarks, a TV show filled with canned laughter makes us feel relieved even when we do not laugh. It is extremely unusual, not to say disturbing, for a person to question this framework. When a television reporter expresses shock or astonishment at what someone says, the person being interviewed is unlikely to ask back whether the journalist is faking the emotion, and is expected to react as it if is genuine (rather than fake a response). Movies, whose owners have their own motives for casting television (owned by other conglomerates) as fakery, sometimes expose this mechanism for dramatic surprise: *The China Syndrome* (1979), *Network, The Weatherman* (2005). A key element is their unbelievability – the viewer is expected to suspend disbelief while at the same time recognizing their sheer incredibility. HBO's series *The Wire* (Simon and Burns 2002–2008) offered a more sophisticated take on television's manipulations. In the fifth series, which highlighted media issues, the ambitious mayor of Baltimore expresses genuine outrage at the way in which cities treat the homeless, and is immediately told by

Violence and Media Accountability   885

his political adviser this indignation plays very well and can be used to promote him into the governor's mansion.

Some broadcasters have, on the real screen, broken out of their restraints. British television chat show host Clive Anderson, last seen chairing a game show, said once in the middle of his program: "We've got to stop for a bit now while people try to sell you things you don't want" (Cook, 1992/2001, p. 35). However, that was the only example that linguistics professor Guy Cook could find in researching advertising on television.

Framing the viewer

Lying in the guise of truth operates more subtly through the professional framing that television journalists give to their programs. Over 20 years ago, Barrie Gunter reported that news comprehension studies showed standard storytelling formats do not provide the optimal conditions for learning. Alternatives "have been demonstrated as producing better learning from news broadcast materials under laboratory conditions than did original broadcast versions of the same stories" (Gunter, 1987, p. 312). Nevertheless the old styles are still in vogue. If anything, the personalized news presentation is even less conducive to retaining information and "there is no conclusive evidence to support the thesis that film is necessarily more appreciated by the audience than other visual modes of presentation" (Gunter, 1987, p. 314). "Where effective communication of information is the ultimate goal, the impact of stills and graphics can be just as great" (Gunter, 1987, p. 314). When audio fails to match up with video even slightly, "the negative effect upon overall information gain could be considerable" (Gunter, 1987, p. 315). Summaries at the end of items (Gunter, 1987, p. 316) and quick changes of topic, common TV news techniques, can work against retention (Gunter, 1987, p. 317) unless carefully planned. "Good television" makes for bad communication.

All this presumes that news programs aim to offer information for viewers to retain. Journalists usually lack objective feedback about their audience's attitudes and do not want to learn what these might be (Gunter, 1987, pp. 308, 317). They have little direct contact with the audience (Gunter, 1987, p. 318). A study by Herbert Gans in 1979 indicates the results:

> When a network audience-research unit presented findings on how a sample of viewers evaluated a set of television news films, the journalists were appalled because the sample liked the films which the journalists deemed to be of low quality, and disliked the "good stories." In fact, the viewers' sample made its choices on the basis of film topics rather than film quality, preferring films about personally relevant topics to those about important national and international news. The journalists were so involved in judging the films from their own perspective, however, that they did not notice that the viewers' sample applied a very different one (Gunter, 1987, p. 320).

Later studies have confirmed this gap.

Journalists live continually with this dilemma. They proclaim their commitment to truth while operating on a commercial world that caters to phantasy. As a result, they find themselves regularly parroting a version of the favorite line of the domestic abuser: "Now look what you made me do." Tom Koch noted in 1990 that over 70% of the stories in the nation's principal newspapers were based on the statements and quotes of government officials (Koch, 1990, p. 175). "Objective truth is not the function of daily news," he argued. It operates at the level of generated myth, as delineated by Roland Barthes in his various writings. Myths are judged not by their accuracy but usefulness.

In public issues, such as violence and disasters, journalists promulgate a myth of concern and competence on the part of professionals and investigating officials. This "need bear no relation to the facts of a case, to the objective description of a specific event through the analysis of its parts. The narrative form assists officialdom to seem able and potent even where its sanctioned explanations are demonstrably fictitious," remarks Koch (1990, pp. 172–173).

Professional standards enable the reporter to practice displacement but as subjects supposed to know, they must fill the role of the questioning citizen in the same way as canned laughter on comedy shows fills in the responses for the real viewer. "Typically this does not require of officials either conscious censorship or active disinformation," Koch insists. "It is done automatically by editors and reporters themselves through a narrative form that assures that systematic faults will be transformed into isolated and thus unimportant events" (1990, pp. 172–173).

Treating such incidents as individual events provides the same psychological comfort as ascribing misfortune to an accident. Accidents, writes Adam Phillips, are "the best way, indeed, the only way of doing some things. Accidents [are] disowned intentions; other voices speak through our mistakes. ... The idea of accident – of the apparently unintended, the contingent – gives us access to otherwise unavailable desires or parts of the self. ... Without a notion of accident or contingency we would not be able sufficiently to disown them" (Phillips, 1994, p. 12).

The authorities who make journalists pay for voicing uncomfortable truths are refusing them the benefit of the accidental, and often suspect them of satisfying unacknowledged desires. Conversely, declares Žižek, creating a society built on truth, justice and fairness – whose rules John Rawls attempted to formulate in *A Theory of Justice* (1971) – would lead to uncontrollable resentment in much of the population. "In the Rawlsian model of a just society, social inequalities are tolerated only insofar as they also help those at the bottom of the social ladder, and insofar as they are based not on inherited hierarchies, but on natural inequalities, which are considered contingent, not merits. ... What Rawls doesn't see is how such a society would create conditions for an uncontrolled explosion of *resentment* in it," he comments." I would know that my lower status is fully 'justified' and would thus be deprived of the ploy of excusing my failure as the result of social injustice" (Žižek, 2009, p. 75).

From *The Front Page* (1931) to *The Wire*, the phantasy-feeding industries have attacked the truth-seeking organs as an expression of their resentment, usually suggesting the moral high ground is immorally achieved. The exceptions *All the President's Men* (1976) and *Goodnight, and Good Luck* (2005), come from the fringes of the movie world.

Mobilizing the living dead

The cultural critic Jean Baudrillard came to the conclusion in 1985 that: "What characterizes the mass media is that they are opposed to mediation, intransitive, that they fabricate noncommunication – if one accepts the definition of communication as an exchange, as the reciprocal space of speech and response, and thus of *responsibility*" (Baudrillard, 1985, p. 205).

The leading philosopher of political activism, Alain Badiou, has pointed to the way in which media practices fragment and dissolve the individual's effort to maintain an intelligible picture of the world: "Communication transmits a universe made up of disconnected images, remarks, statements and commentaries whose accepted principle is incoherence. Day after day communication undoes all relations and all principles, in an untenable juxtaposition that dissolves every relation between the elements it sweeps along in its flow. And what is perhaps even more distressing is that mass communication presents the world as a spectacle devoid of memory, a spectacle in which new images and new remarks cover, erase and consign to oblivion the very images and remarks that have just been shown and said" (Badiou, 1999, p. 41).

This oblivion arouses another anxiety for the audience which only the phantasy of violence can assuage. "For the millions of people without a history, and happy to be that way, it is necessary to deculpabilize their passivity," argues Jean Baudrillard (1970) in *La Société de Consommation* (meaning both *The Consumer Society* and *The Society of Perfect Pleasure/Consummation*). "This quietude of the private sphere must appear … constantly threatened, surrounded by a world whose destiny is catastrophic. The violence and inhumanity of the external world is necessary not only so that security is experienced more profoundly as such (in the economy of pleasure) but also so that at every moment it feels justified in being chosen as such" (my translation).

In the United States, Curtis White jokes that we are all now joining the living dead. "The frenzy of communication" in advanced societies operates, he says, as part of the consciousness industry's "pre-emptive efforts to saturate the field in which the imagination might do its work" (White, 2003). One of the few American television series to attempt to portray the impact of death in individual's lives, rather than cater to the phantasy of immortality, was Alan Ball's *Six Feet Under* (2001–2005). In the words of sociologists Avi Shoshana and Elly Teman (2006, p. 557): "The series hurls death provocatively in the viewer's face, each episode consciously serving as a 'memento mori' for its audience." In 2009 he launched his latest drama, *True Blood*. It deals with vampires.

References

Alvarado, M., Gutch, R., and Wollen, T. (1987) *Learning the Media: Introduction to Media Teaching*, Palgrave Macmillan, London.

Anderson, C.A., Berkowitz, L., Donnerstein, E. *et al.* (2003) The influence of media violence on youth. *Psychological Science in the Public Interest*, 4, 81–110.

Badiou, A. (1999) Philosophy and desire, in in *Infinite Thought: Truth and the Return of Philosophy*, (eds. Oliver Feltham and Justin Clemens, trans. Oliver Feltham and Justin Clemens), Continuum International Publishing Group Ltd., London/New York, pp. 39–57.

Ballard, J.G. (1994). *Essays for the New Millennium*, Picador, New York.

Barker, M. (2001) The Newson report: A case study in 'common sense' in *Ill Effects: The Media Violence Debate*, 2nd edn, (eds M. Barker and J. Petley), New York, Routledge, pp. 27–46.

Baudrillard, J. (1968) *La système des objets./The System of Objects*, Verso, London.

Baudrillard, J. (1970) *La Société de Consommation/Consumer Society*, Sage, New York.

Baudrillard, J. (1985) 'The Implosion of the Social in the Media, 1985, in *Jean Baudrillard: Selected Writings*, (ed. M. Poster), Stanford University Press, Stanford, CA, pp. 207–219.

Bennett, W.L. (1997) Cracking the news code. Some rules that journalists live by, in *Do Media Govern? Politicians, Voters, and Reporters in America*, (eds S. Iyengar and R. Reeves) Sage, Thousand Oak, CA, pp. 103–117.

Buckingham, D. (1993) *Children Talking Television: The Making of Television Literacy*, Routledge, New York.

Buckingham, D. (1994) Children and television: A critical overview of the research, in *Reader 4*, Leicester University Centre for Mass Communication Research, Leicester University, Leicester, pp. 103–127.

Bushman, B.J., and Huesmann, L.R. (2001) Effects of televised violence on aggression, in *Handbook of Children and the Media*, (eds D.G. Singer and J.L. Singer), Sage, Thousand Oaks, CA.

Carter, C., and Wheeler, C.K. (2003) *Critical Readings: Violence and the Media*, Open University Press, Milton Keynes, UK.

Cohen, S. (1972) *Folk Devils and Moral Panics*, Paladin, Boulder, CO.

Cook, G. (1992/2001) *The Discourse of Advertising*, Routledge, New York.

CPJ (Committee to Protect Journalists) (2009) Journalists killed, www.cpj.org/deadly/ (accessed August 8, 2010).

Cumberbatch, G. (1994) Legislating mythology: video violence and children. *Journal of Mental Health*, 3, 485–494.

Daily Record (2007) Brutal & Sadistic; UK Censors Ban Scottish Firm's Violent Video Game, June 20.

Dwyer, J., and Drew, C. (2005) Fear exceeded crime's reality in New Orleans. *New York Times*, September 29, www.nytimes.com/2005/09/29/national/nationalspecial/29crime.html (accessed August 25, 2010).

Eyesenck, H., and Nias, D.K.B. (1978) Desensitization, violence and the media, in *Media Studies: A Reader*, (eds P. Marris and S. Thornham) Edinburgh University Press, Edinburgh.

FCC (2007) *FCC 07–50*. Federal Communications Commission, USA.

FCC (2008) Commissioner Adelstein outlines an agenda to protect America's children. Federal Communications Commission, USA, June 11.

Freud, S. (1899/1953) Über Deckerinnerungen/Screen Memories, *Collected Papers V*, Hogarth, London.

Freud, S. (1919a/1953) The "uncanny," *Collected Papers IV*, Hogarth, London.

Freud, S. (1919b/1953) "A child is being beaten," *Collected Papers IV*, Hogarth, London.

Garrett, R. (1997) Gender, sex and the family, in *British Cultural Identities*, (eds. M. Storry and P. Childs), Routledge, London, pp. 129–162.

Goidel, K., Freeman, C.M., and Procopio, S.T. (2006) The impact of television violence and perceptions of juvenile crime. *Journal of Broadcasting and Electronic Media*, 50, 119.

Good, H., and Dillon, M.J. (2002) *Media Ethics Goes to the Movies*, Greenwood Press, New York.

Gunter, B. (1987) *Poor Reception*, Lawrence Erlbaum Associates, Mahwah, NJ.

Gunter, B., Harrison, J., and Wykes, M. (2003) *Violence on Television*. Lawrence Erlbaum Associates, Mahwah, NJ.

Halloran, J.D., Elliott, P., and Murdock, G. (1970) *Demonstrations and Communication. A Case Study*, Penguin, Harmondsworth, UK.

Homer, S. (2004). *Jacques Lacan*, Routledge, New York.

Koch, T. (1990) *The News as Myth: Fact and Context in Journalism*, Greenwood Press, New York.

Kutner, L., and Olson, C.K. (2008) *Grand Theft Childhood: The Surprising Truth about Violent Video Games and What Parents Can Do*, Simon & Schuster, New York.

Maltby, R. (1995) *Hollywood Cinema*, Blackwell, Malden, MA.

National Television Violence Study (1998) *National Television Violence Study*, vol. 3, Sage, Thousand Oaks, CA.

Neuman, S.B. (1991) *Literacy in the Television Age*. Ablex, Norwood, NJ.

New York Times (2005) White House condemns Bennett's remark, October 1, www.nytimes.com/2005/10/01/politics/01bennett.html?_r=1&sq=william%20bennett%20hypothetical&st=nyt&scp=2&pagewanted=print (accessed August 25, 2010).

Newson, E. (1994) Video violence and the protection of children. *The Psychologist*, 7 (6): 272–274.

NTVS (National Television Violence Study) (1997) *National Television Violence Study*, vol. 2, Sage, Thousand Oaks, CA.

O'Toole, L. (1999). *Pornocopia: Porn, Sex, Technology and Desire*, Serpent's Tail, London.

Palahniuk, C. (2008) *Snuff*, Doubleday, New York.

Paik, H., and Comstock, G. (1994) Effects of television violence on anti-social behavior: a meta-analysis. *Communication Research*, 21 (4), 516–546.

Pellington, M. (1999) *Arlington Road*. Script by Ehren Kruger.

Perse, E.M. (2001) *Media Effects and Society*, Lawrence Erlbaum Associates, Mahwah, NJ.

Phillips, A. (1994) *On Flirtation*, Harvard University Press, Cambridge, MA.

Rawls, J. (1971) *A Theory of Justice*, rev. edn 1999, Oxford University Press, Oxford.

Rhodes, R. (2002) *Masters of Death: The SS-Einsatzgruppen and the Invention of the Holocaust*, Vintage Books, London.

Shoshana, A., and Teman, E. (2006) Coming out of the coffin: 'Life-self' and 'death-self' in six feet under, *Symbolic Interaction*, 29, 4, 557–576, /www.scribd.com/doc/403594/Coming-Out-of-the-Coffin-LifeSelf-and-DeathSelf-in-Six-Feet-Under (accessed August 8, 2010).

Simon, D., and Burns, E. (2002–2008). *The Wire*, HBO.

Straus, S. (2008) *The Order of Genocide: Race, Power, and War in Rwanda*, Cornell University Press, Ithaca, NY.

techdirt (2008) www.techdirt.com/articles/20080418/005355882.shtml

Timerman, J. (1982) *Prisoner without a Name, Cell without a Number*, Penguin Books, Harmondsworth.

White, C. (2003) *The Middle Mind: Why Consumer Culture Is Turning Us Into the Living Dead*, HarperCollins, New York.

Williams, L. (1993) Second thoughts on hard core: American obscenity law and the scape-goating of deviance, in *Dirty Looks: Women, Pornography, Power*, (eds P. Church Gibson and R. Gibson), British Film Institute, London, pp. 46–61.

Zimbardo, P.G. (2007) *The Lucifer Effect: Understanding How Good People Turn Evil*, New York, Random House.

Žižek, S. (2009) *Violence*, Profile Books, London.

45

Protecting Children from Harmful Influences of Media through Formal and Nonformal Media Education

Asbjørn Simonnes and Gudmund Gjelsten

Media research today uses a holistic approach, combining old and new research theories. This interdisciplinary approach permits different perspectives to flow into one another, emphasizing not only social science in media research but opening up humanistic research with focus on values and attitudes. This convergence provides an understanding of media as an agent of socialization but with a critical awareness of the need to develop interpretative skills. Focus on the empowerment aspect of media literacy gives children the possibility of forming personal judgments and emphasizes critical autonomy. Teaching children viewing skills and interpretive competence helps them form personal judgments. Children need to understand more about communication in human experience in such a way that socialization, identity, and cultural integration give them an understanding of the role of media in their lives.

Using Media Literacy for Value Formation in Home and School

Media are altering our society and bringing new dimensions into our culture, challenging everyone to comprehend and make use of new possibilities. Kellner expands on this:

> I argue that we need multiple literacies for our multicultural society, that we need to develop new literacies to meet the challenge of new media and technologies, and that literacies of diverse sort – including a more fundamental importance for print literacy – are of crucial importance in restructuring education for a high-tech and multicultural society and global culture (Kellner, 2002, p. 34).

The Handbook of Global Communication and Media Ethics, First Edition. Edited by Robert S. Fortner and P. Mark Fackler.
© 2011 Blackwell Publishing Ltd. Published 2011 by Blackwell Publishing Ltd.

Literacy is a term most associated with the print media, and simply means the ability to read. Visual literacy includes film, television, and video. Computer literacy is about the ability to use and understand the computer world. W. James Potter argues that reading literacy, visual literacy, and computer literacy are not synonyms for media literacy, but merely components. He maintains that media literacy includes all these specialized abilities as well as something more general. Potter (2001) defines media literacy this way:

> Media literacy is a perspective we actively use when exposing ourselves to the media in order to interpret the meaning of the messages we encounter. We build our perspective from knowledge structures. To build our knowledge structures, we need tools and raw material. The tools are our skills. The raw material is information from the media and from the real world. Active use means that we are aware of the messages and are consciously interacting with them (p. 4).

> Information is an essential ingredient in knowledge structure. In gathering information, we are concerned with both its depth and breadth. This includes knowledge about the message conventions used by media producers, and knowledge about the media industries (p. 6).

When facing the challenge of pedagogical practice related to media literacy, we immediately see that both schools and homes are confronted with demanding tasks. Information and knowledge are central ingredients with regard to giving pupils the possibility to gain a thorough media literacy perspective. According to Potter, media literacy is a continuum and not a category, and therefore we all occupy some position on this media literacy continuum. People are positioned along that continuum based on the strength of their overall perspective on the media (Potter, 2001, pp. 7–8).

A real challenge is to get parents, teachers, and pupils motivated to travel the continuum of media literacy, knowing that media literacy is multidimensional: cognitive, emotive, aesthetic, and moral. While cognition deals with factual information, emotionality deals with hate and love, anger and happiness, frustration, and satisfaction. Some people have problems sensing the emotional level of a message, especially if these are more subtle emotions such as confusion, ambivalence, and wariness. Recent years have seen a strong focus on the question of emotional intelligence, including factors of self-awareness, self-discipline, and empathy (Goleman, 1997). Strengthening our ability to perceive the emotional level of a piece of information can be nurtured. Pupils and adults will benefit from that ability, especially with regard to developing relationships. In our data we have several examples of pupil's ability to perceive the emotional level of a media message, for example in their analysis of the film series Hotel Cæsar and Friends. Children are open to and actively searching for emotional experiences. In our findings this becomes clear in pupils' preferences in choosing programs for entertainment and excitement. The aesthetic dimension of information deals with how to produce messages, and helps us make judgments about different products of creative craftsmanship (Gjelsten and Simonnes, 2007).

The more information children and adults get from the aesthetic domain, the finer the discrimination that will be made between what is good and what is less good, and between art and artificiality. The aesthetic dimension of media literacy is an important quality for young people to develop in order to be selective in their media choice, and especially in their encounter with the commercialized mass media industry. The importance of training pupils and adults in an awareness of artistry and visual manipulation cannot be overestimated.

Finally, moral information focuses on a different domain of understanding, namely values. This type of information provides the basis for making judgments about right and wrong. Certainly it takes a highly media-literate person to perceive moral themes well (Potter, 2001, p. 9).

Potter observes that strong knowledge structures have information from all four domains. When one domain is missing, the result is a weaker knowledge structure. It is not enough to be highly analytical if you lack emotional information. A real pedagogical challenge is to help pupils understand that media messages have a surface meaning along with several deeper meanings. Potter (2001, p. 10) expands on this:

> People who are at a low level of media literacy are limited to accepting the surface meanings; thus the media are in control, because the media determine the meaning, and those meanings remain unchallenged – even unexamined. With only a limited perspective on the media, these people have smaller, more superficial, and less organized structures, which provide an inadequate perspective to use in interpreting the meaning of a media message. Thus, low-literacy people are much less able to identity inaccuracies; to sort through controversies; to appreciate irony or satire; or to develop a broad, yet personal view of the world.

This position will, of course, be challenged by uses-and-gratification studies, moving the perspective from the receiver as a passive respondent to an active participant in the communication process. Likewise, reception research theory sees communication as a meaning-creating process, being constructed in the encounter between media content and the receiver. Potter's intention, however, is to identify the fact that when a person operates at a high level of media literacy, then the person uses a set of highly developed interpretive skills to place a media message inside the context of well-elaborated knowledge structures. Such a person will normally be able to interpret any message along many different dimensions, providing the individual with more choices of meaning. This shows the importance of educating pupils in media literacy, giving them more options which translate into more power and more control over their beliefs and behaviors. A person who is aware of no choices is forced to accept unquestioningly the dominant themes, values, beliefs, and interpretations presented in the media (Potter, 2001, p. 10).

One big challenge for pedagogical practice then is to help pupils gain more control over the media. Homes and schools cannot change companies, but can educate concerning the impact of exposure to media. Teaching children the relation between intentional and functional education – about media exposure and effects – is very important in our media-dominated society. We are now at the core of the challenge in a visual environment. We must be able to recognize the full range of media effects and their influence. These media effects are subtle, as their effects take a long time to emerge and are hard to change (Potter, 2001, p. 11).

One major goal in our proposed strategy of strengthening media literacy in school and home is to help children and adults gain greater control over the media, by first developing interpretative skills. As Potter (2001, p. 11) puts it, "we can amplify the effects we want to have and discount those effects we want to avoid."

Another crucial goal must be to help people become critical viewers without destroying their joy of watching films and other media products. Many children do have a level of interpretive competence. A major task is to help people appreciate a movie. The more media literate a person is, the more dimensions of a film that person is able to appreciate.

Some people believe that every new piece of art is bad and every new medium is dangerous. We must underline the fact that young people need to be taught media literacy principles both in school and at home. When we have succeeded in teaching children how to see as much as possible in a given message, how to understand different levels of meaning, and how to be in charge of the processes of selection and to make meaning, this will give them understanding and control. By such a strategy we are pointing to some of the main principles in reception theory, which has its roots both in literary reception theory, cultural studies, and in uses-and-gratifications studies. When putting these principles into practice, both children and adults are more likely to get what they want from the message which enhances understanding, appreciation, and control (Potter, 2001, p. 12).

David Buckingham maintains that much of the positive potential of new media for children, including the computer world, rests in their educational role. Many authors agree on the importance of high-quality software with support from parents and a strong connection between home and school, if this potential is to be realized. As new technology becomes crucial to the lives of many children and adults, it is in a parallel manner important to provide media literacy skills for the same people in order to handle this new situation. A critical approach to new media and the computer world needs to take account of the social context in which children encounter new media. David Buckingham maintains that this may require a rethinking of the institutional contexts in the schools, and also of the relationships between schools, homes, and other sites of educational and cultural activity. Buckingham expands on this:

> Simply providing children with "information" is not enough: we have to enable them to develop the intellectual and cultural competencies that are required to select, interpret and utilize it. Despite the optimism of some advocates, children do not automatically know how to use new media technology, let alone evaluate what it provides (Buckingham, 2002, pp. 85–86).

This quotation underlines the necessity of providing media literacy education for pupils, teachers, and parents. In our research we have found that all three groups are

Protecting Children from Harmful Influences of Media 895

motivated to acquire more media literacy skills. It is not enough to supply school and home with new media technology. The process of acquiring knowledge and understanding of what this new technology brings into the schools and homes is important. We have to acknowledge that technology alone will not transform users into autonomous "cyberkids" of the popular imagination (Buckingham, 2002, p. 86).

We have in our research paid special attention to the value dimension in school and media. Our findings show that both 6th and 10th graders are conscious about the difference of values in school and media, without finding themselves in a difficult crossfire situation between them. James Brown maintains that

> "Critical viewing skills" is one major component of media literacy, referring to understanding of and competence with television, including its aesthetic, social, cultural, psychological, educational, economic, and regulatory aspects (Brown, 2001, p. 681).

A four year research project which constituted an attempt to discover how a group of children and young people aged 11–12 and 15–16 years experienced the dual value influence from school and media, was concluded in 2004. About 500 children from schools in seven municipalities within the county of Møre and Romsdal in Western Norway, participated. A short presentation of the project in the Yearbook of the International Clearinghouse on Children, Youth and Media, 2004 sums up the aim of the project:

> What dominating values do we find in the parallel school of the media? Are these values similar to or different from the set of values in the latest governmental planning document for the public school (grades 1–10), called L97? We focus especially on values and norms regarding relationships, attitudes, tolerance and problem solving.
>
> How do children and young people react to what they see and hear in "the parallel school of the media"? How do they consider the relationship between the values and attitudes existing in the established upbringing/education passed on to them in home and school, and the values and attitudes they encounter in the products of the "parallel school"?
>
> To what degree do children and young people experience being in a "crossfire" between the intentional school/upbringing and the "parallel school"? What challenges do the "parallel school" represent for pedagogical research today and in the future? And how do these challenges affect family life? (von Feilitzen, 2004, p. 100).

Without going into details of the findings in this research, we shall point to two obvious tendencies. Children and young people tend to underestimate the influences of the media, and they seem to overestimate their own ability to cope with the dual set of value inputs, from home and school on the one hand and from the media on the other.

Parents and teachers were much more concerned about negative influences from the media in competition with the value influences brought to the new generation from home and school.

How do we protect the children from harmful influences from media exposure? If this is to be done in a respectful way the answer is through *upbringing and education*. Education of children and parents in human communication must go hand in hand. However, in this connection we have to concentrate on the education of children about human communication and its particular purpose and functions.

So far we have focused on recent research on children and their use of media. Now we discuss some research that in a way builds an interesting bridge from research and theory into the field of education about human communication for children.

Children quickly understand basic codes of television visualization. They are neither naïve to meanings nor do they require technical media training. Media literacy, however, touches upon another dimension important for children and adults, which is to obtain critical autonomy and personal judgment.

One central role of the school is therefore to teach critical television-viewing skills, combined with developing a strategy of using new media constructively in intentional education. British and Canadian educators have often given impetus to many teachers of media analysis. Brown isolates key concepts and significant questions:

> Media messages are constructed (this involves choices and editing); messages are representations of reality (but how valid or accurate?); messages have social, economic, political, and aesthetic purposes and contexts (financed by megacorporations through advertising to audiences attracted by program content); individuals construct meaning in media messages through interpretation (viewers interpret the content through selective perception and "negotiating" meaning); and each form and genre of communication has unique characteristics. (Brown, 2001, p. 689

A real pedagogical challenge is to educate teachers about resources and how to use different material, and further stimulate them to create connections between their curricular goals and classroom practices. This has to happen through activating pupils both in media analysis and production, and thus empowering them to ask questions and to think for themselves.

On a global basis there have been many major conferences of scholars and educators exploring media education, and many underline the fact that media study helps build a bridge between theory and practice in school and at home. Brown elaborates on the purpose of media study:

> Many agree that media literacy per se ought not be an instrument for social change but, rather, a cognitive skill applying to broad areas of living, "promoting students' critical autonomy, described as the process of internalizing the tools of self-reflection, critical analysis and communication for one's own purposes and motives" (Brown, 2001, p. 693).

As in many other countries in Europe, we are in the initial phase of forming a teacher training education in Norway that develops teachers' understanding, attitudes and skills, using media literacy principles in their teaching and practice in the classroom.

Children and Television Advertising

Another challenge for families is the immediacy of stimuli and gratification in modern programming. Kubey and Donovan state: "The orientation toward immediate gratification so common to contemporary media and quick solutions to problems is in conflict with many of the basic commitments and slow, gradual processes necessary to sustain the family" (Kubey and Donovan, 2001, p. 331).

Many parents are puzzled by the messages sent into homes by television advertisers, presenting a strong commercial influence. As Kubey and Donovan (2001, p. 377) maintain that: "Commercial pressures in the mass media, along with the general speed of technological development, also result in an emphasis on 'the new'. Products, programs, fashions – things are better if they are new."

Several of our interviews with children revealed that pupils feel the influence of commercials on television. Children's exposure to television advertising is a by-product of their time spent before the screen. Dale Kunkel says when speaking about the content of commercials: "The most common theme or appeal (i.e., persuasive strategy) employed in advertising to children is associating the product with fun and happiness, rather than providing any factual product-related information" (Kunkel, 2001, p. 377).

Jean Kilbourne, one of America's best known authors on deconstructing television advertising, has expanded her analysis into several areas, such as the effect of advertising on our values, relationships, and commitment to civic life. One of her messages is that advertising works best because we do not think it works on us. Kilbourne maintains that the average American sees more than 3000 ads per day, and spends more than three years watching commercials. She says that ads encourage viewers to objectify each other and to believe that our most significant relationships are with products. Kilbourne expands on this:

> Ads turn lovers into things and things into lovers ... We are surrounded by hundreds, thousands, of messages every day that link our deepest emotions to products, that objectify people and trivialize our most heartfelt moments and relationships. Every emotion is used to sell us something. Our wish to protect our children is leveraged to make us buy an expensive car. A long marriage simply provides the occasion for a diamond necklace. A painful reunion between a father and his estranged daughter is drawn out and dramatized to sell us a phone system. Everything in the world – nature, animals, people – is just so much stuff to be consumed or to be used to sell us something (Kilbourne, 1999, pp. 11–13, 77).

A central aspect of advertising in the United States is that often sentimental images of children are being used to evoke deep feelings of love and protectiveness, which are then connected to a certain product. Kilbourne refers to an ad saying: "Can a shoe hug you like a tiny hand?" showing a woman cradling a child in her arms. Many ads that in the first part appear to be about the relationship between a parent and a child turn out to glorify the relationship between the parent and the product. Kilbourne maintains that the consumer culture always attempts to instill in viewers a longing for more of a given product, more goods and services, more money – rather than a longing for more authentic connection with people. She elaborates on this aspect:

> Advertising, a key component of our consumerist culture, constantly exhorts us to be in a never-ending state of excitement, never to tolerate boredom or disappointment, to focus on ourselves, never to delay gratification, to believe that passionate sex is more important than anything else in life, and always trade in old things for new. These messages are a kind of blueprint for how to destroy an intimate relationship. (Kilbourne, 1999, pp. 92–93)

When children encounter this kind of advertising, parents might find it difficult to explain to their children that a long-term relationship normally goes through periods of anger, boredom, and disillusionment. As Kilbourne expresses, "in a culture that surrounds us with images of lust and romance and very few models of long-term love, most of us grow up totally unprepared for life after infatuation" (Kilbourne, 1999, pp. 94–95). In the world of advertising, lovers grow cold, spouses grow old – but possessions stay with us and never change. In Kilbourne's opinion, it is a major task for parents to explain to their children that seeking the outcomes of a healthy relationship through products cannot work. They cannot make us happy or loved, and if we believe they can, we'll be disappointed, because products are only things and will never love us back (Kilbourne, 1999, pp. 94–95).

Dale Kunkel maintains that children must acquire two key information-processing skills to achieve mature comprehension of advertising messages:

> First, they must be able to discriminate at a perceptual level commercial from non-commercial content, and second, they must be able to attribute persuasive intent to advertising and to adjust their interpretation of commercial messages consistent with that knowledge. Each of these capabilities develops over time, largely as a function of cognitive growth and development rather than the accumulation of any particular amount of experience with media content (Kunkel, 2001, p. 378).

Many debates in Norwegian homes are about what impact advertising has on children. Our findings show that among the 10th grade age group there is often a negative attitude towards advertising, and this negative attitude toward commercials is not found at the same strength among the 6th graders of our sample. At the same time however, both age-groups admit being influenced by advertising (Simonnes, Gjelsten, and Kleven, 2004, pp. 123–125). This fact is noted by Kunkel in his article on children and television advertising:

> Research consistently indicates that children's attitudes toward commercials as a genre (as opposed to an individual advertisement for a given product) are negatively correlated with age; that is, the older a child is, the less likely he or she will hold a positive attitude toward television advertising. This is logical given that older children are more likely to comprehend the persuasive intent of advertising, which provides them with the foundation for recognizing the manipulation inherent in advertising messages (Kunkel, 2001, p. 381).

Protecting Children from Harmful Influences of Media

For parents to help their children understand the nature of and purpose of television advertising is a huge challenge. Children are more easily persuaded than older children and adults and therefore vulnerable to all kinds of advertising. Here parents might try some sort of "counter-advertising," and the most effective strategy seems to be trying to socialize children's consumer behavior, also in cooperation with the school. As Kunkel says, the huge economic stakes that are now associated with marketing to children, especially through the Internet, give both school and home a challenge:

> More recently, media literacy curricula in the schools have been employed to teach children to be "smarter" consumers of television advertising as well as programming. Yet neither of these mediators can accelerate young children's understanding of the advertising process beyond the limits of their cognitive capabilities at certain key points of their development (Kunkel, 2001, p. 389).

Several pupils admit that their friends try to get slim to look perfect. We are pointing to the role of the peers, showing that friends often mediate and increase an influence that has its origin in visual media. Both young children and adolescents are new and most often inexperienced consumers and thus prime targets for advertisers. They are in the process of learning their values and roles and also developing their self-concept. Most teenagers are sensitive to peer pressure and many find it difficult to resist or question the dominant culture messages perpetuated and reinforced by the commercialized mass media (Kilbourne, 1999, p. 129).

We have found that mass media are influential especially with regard to their expressions of the ideal body shape of girls and women. The message of the advertisers is often that this ideal is possible to achieve through self-sacrifice and self-effort, leaving many girls to spend much time and energy to achieve something that for many is unattainable. According to Jean Kilbourne, the messages many girls get through advertising is this:

> Primarily girls are told by advertisers that what is most important about them is their perfume, their clothing, their bodies, their beauty. ... Even very little girls are offered makeup and toys like Special Night Barbie, which shows them how to dress up for a night out. Girls of all ages get the message that they must be flawlessly beautiful and, above all these days, they must be thin (Kilbourne, 1999, p. 132).

There are numerous studies about ideal body shape. A study of 350 young men and women found that a preoccupation with one's appearance takes a toll on mental health. Women scored higher than men on what the researchers called "self-objectification." Kilbourne comments on this:

> This tendency to view one's body from the outside in – regarding physical attractiveness, sex appeal, measurements, and weight as more central to one's physical identity than health, strength, energy level, coordination, or fitness – has many harmful effects, including diminished mental performance, increased feelings of shame and anxiety, depression, sexual dysfunction, and the development of eating disorders (Kilbourne, 1999, p. 133).

Parents have an important obligation to talk with their children and especially their teenage girls about how advertising may create and feed an addictive mentality that is threatening the health of many young people. Of course, advertising does not create eating problems in a direct way, and we know that anorexia is a disease with a complicated aetiology. The problem is that both advertising and many pop-culture programs give an impetus about the ideal body shape that might create insecurity among girls. Therefore there is a great challenge to communicate with children and help them to achieve a healthy attitude toward the body and toward food.

To practice media literacy principles in the home in cooperation with the school and the church, is important in order to empower children and young people to be critical towards the fact that media have power to influence attitudes and increase desire for all kinds of products. Especially in the United States we often see a combination of unhealthy food advertisements, and a propagation of a thin ideal. This is less openly expressed in Norwegian commercials. This combination sends conflicting messages to children. Parents, teachers, and pastors need to talk to children and pupils about the risk of both obesity and other eating disorders. Children need a strong connection with at least one adult, at home or at school, thus building a good self-image in children's encounter with the commercialized mass media industry. With regard to advertising, there is a challenge for parents and others to communicate and connect with children in a deep and honest way.

Preserving Our Cultural Heritage and Creation of Identity

The global cultural influence includes news programs which often are the only perspective offered to world audiences. Recorded music and advertising comprise an important part of the world's cultural environment. The adoption of English as the world's second language has sent US pop culture all over the world for several decades. This free flow of information conferred a great advantage on US cultural industries. No foreign film industry, television production center, or publishing and news establishment seems to be able to compete on equal terms with the powerful US media-entertainment companies.

Through satellite communications and computerization, American pop culture has challenged teenagers all over the world to devote much of their time to mass-produced entertainment disseminated through media. Perhaps this industry's main purpose is to direct its attention to adolescents' psychological needs for identity, intimacy, and to find meaning through entertainment. The dominance of US pop culture gives a powerful communication message to adolescents. This ever-renewing demographic group with leisure time and money, being susceptible to the marketing wiles of the entertainment industry, listens with open hearts in their searching for answers. However, in the postmodern thinking we see the emphasis of how different cultural identities flow together focusing on the dialogue between them. Robert White says:

Protecting Children from Harmful Influences of Media   901

Contemporary societies have an enormous variety of specialized knowledge and occu-pational subcultures. Globalization puts once separate cultural identities in direct interaction. Every subculture has its own electronic channels (White, 2009, p. 59).

Is it possible to preserve community-formation in the face of the influence of glo-bal media and impact on local communities today? How will this mass media indus-try influence the moral value formation of children? Robert White suggests:

The cultural tendency to affirm one's unique personal and subcultural identity has led to the primacy of an "ethics of authenticity" (Taylor 1992b). The new tradition values types of communication in which identities are expressed and enhanced: the multipli-cation of channels, the proliferation of fanzines and zine culture (Atton 2002, 54–79), and the increased importance of audience ethnography and reception analysis. This paradigm calls for a new regulatory perspective that values opening up greater dialogue between cultural groups in communities (Horwitz 1989). (White, 2009, p. 60.)

Public broadcasting, inspired by responsibility to the public, seeks to enhance and preserve our cultural heritage of historical memory, religious values, literature, folklore, and civic commitment. Now when the dominant norm of culture through the public broadcasting systems has almost broken down, multiple channels have taken over to satisfy every taste. White elaborates:

In the liberal society, identities and values remain always in the private sphere and the public sphere is only the instrumental, utilitarian mutual help to achieve individual goals without any consensus regarding common values in the public sphere (White, 1996, pp. 14–15).

Here we are speaking about creating a moral dialogue, dealing with one's own identity but also the cultural identities of other groups. This encounter can clarify other cultural identities as other groups perceive, affirm, and value themselves. White says in this regard:

Although the interest in the cultural identity of other groups may be primarily defen-sive and apologetic, the need to persuade other groups to tolerate the existence of one's own identity implies that one must truly understand the motivations of others if one is to touch those motivations persuasively (White, 1996, p. 16).

Would it be possible to take progressive steps toward building mutual understand-ing and respect between people and cultures?

The public communicator should give an objective, true, and impartial account of events – it is vital in democratic decision making. Media institutions will always be faced with the choice of selectively reporting an event, and the criteria of these choices are most often embedded in the culture of a society and the subculture of the media. White says that "the major criteria for the liberal communication ethic are defined by the myth of modernization and what will contribute to the strengthening of the public economy of the nation state" (White, 1996, p.19). White contrasts this liberal position with the communitarian emphasis, where a sense of being treated unjustly arises out of an awareness of identity and one's human dignity. We might speak about an empathetically based communication. White elaborates on the need for such a communication:

> Communication is not simply a matter of greater technological power, as is so commonly promoted by those who say that communication problems will be solved by new technologies. Rather, good communication is a matter of mutual understanding (White, 2009, p. 64).

White underlines the need to build community confidence in cultural identities and to create structures of dialogue. This ideal of communication can be looked upon as much more "participatory," "dialogical," "horizontal," and "creative" than the old linear model of communication. White maintains that this new emphasis has certain priorities:

> The communitarian ethic of communication seeks to empower groups through affirmation of identity, but not in a way which seeks control and domination. The continual small actions of affirming and recognizing identities gradually builds toward a confident sense of cultural capital and awareness of the value of the group to the society (White, 1996, pp. 20–21)

With regard to the media literacy principles presented earlier in this article, we underline the importance of empowering children to form a solid platform for their ethical reasoning. To invest time in teaching children values that can affirm their identity will be the best investment for their adult lives. Coleman and Wilkins say:

> Any theory that claims to be "developmental" implies that people change as they age. In the case of moral development theory, the higher the age, the higher the quality of moral reasoning used. Thus, age and education are the primary determinants of moral development (Coleman and Wilkins 2009, p. 45).

Mark Fackler (2009, p. 305) says "communitarianism is the social strategy which distinguishes peace-loving virtues from greed hoarding impulses." In identity-shaping strategies in the home and in the school we have to be aware of the fact that children are vulnerable because they are seeking new knowledge and experience of the adult world. In the visual digital world of today we should therefore emphasize communication with children and adolescents that empowers them to be active actors in our society, adopting our best values in our culture. Mark Fackler says:

> The contemplative person understands that personhood is equivalent to soul-awareness, the maturity of moral judgment, expansion of sympathy, prioritizing of values, exercise of choice and courage, reflective self-sacrifice, the sense that one's life matters, that one cannot resign from moral accountability, that moral choice sets personal direction and creates a profile that one increasingly recognizes to be the self, the "I am" (Fackler, 2009, p. 313).

Protecting Children from Harmful Influences of Media   903

In our discourse of these values we want to underline the necessity of giving children a strategy of developing their moral judgment to maturity. The predisposition for this is a mutual dialogue where the young generation is challenged to give a response to the adult generation's communication of values. Mark Fackler elaborates:

> Communitarianism insists that the wisdom accumulated from centuries of reflection, and the orientation of conscience toward mutuality, are grand moral claims in a sustaining pattern of norms that offer the best middle-range account of moral obligation and accountability. That claim must be situated in an appeal to human dignity and directed toward life. Life must be prized, violence must be lost (Fackler, 2009, p. 314).

This statement brings us to the discussion of how children are able to handle the commercialized mass media industry that does not necessarily provide the wisdom accumulated from centuries of reflection, but rather might have a harmful effect on the children due to its violent content.

Children Faced with Possible Harmful Effect from Violent Media Production

In entertainment culture, the aggressive production of violent media content has for decades caused a debate that never seems to result in an agreement. However, many researchers such as Patrick Lee Plaisance acknowledge the depth of current knowledge:

> More than three decades of rigorous research has compellingly documented the negative effects of violent media content on certain populations and how exposure to such content appears to contribute to aggressive and antisocial behavior (Plaisance, 2009, p. 162).

Around the world, scholars are asking what consequence the consumption of action and violence on the screen might have for children's prosocial or aggressive behavior. Can the effects of mass media in society be looked upon as a health and social adjustment issue?

A new study adds evidence to previous findings that watching television violence increases aggression in the long run. This longitudinal study shows that the effects of children's viewing of television violence continue into adulthood, and increase aggressive behavior for both males and females (Huesmann *et al.*, 2003, pp. 201–221).

These authors refer to many psychological theories explaining the processes through which exposure to dramatic violence on television and in the movies could cause both short- and long-term increases in a child's aggressive and violent behavior.

The News Magazine from The International Clearinghouse on Children (ICCVOS), Youth and Media comments on this new major study:

> Long-term effects with children are, according to the authors, generally believed to be primarily due to long-term observational learning of cognitions (schemas about a hostile world, scripts for social problem solving that focus on aggression, normative beliefs that aggression is acceptable, and hostile attributional biases). Short term effects with adults and children are recognized as also due to priming, excitation transfer, or imitation of specific behaviors. Most researchers of aggression agree that severe aggressive and violent behavior seldom occurs unless there is a convergence of multiple predisposing and precipitating factors. Exposure to media violence is one such factor (ICCVOS, 2003, p. 6).

Some of the results from this research show that children's television-violence viewing, children's identification with aggressive TV characters, and children's understanding that TV violence is realistic, were significantly correlated with their adult aggression. Cecilia von Feilitzen in News from ICCVOS, elaborates on these findings:

> More viewing, greater identification, and stronger belief also predicted more adult aggression regardless of how aggressive participants were as children. The longitudinal relations primarily reflected the adult behavior of the highest TV-violence viewing children. The upper 20 percent of boys and girls on any of the three child TV-viewing variables scored significantly higher on aggression as adults than did the rest of the participants (von Feilitzen, 2003, p. 7).

Another important finding from this longitudinal research is that more aggressive children are more likely to watch media violence because it makes their own behavior seem more normal and accepted. Their subsequent viewing of violence then increases their aggressive scripts, schemas, and beliefs through observational learning. This makes subsequent aggression more likely. Von Feilitzen expands further on this scientific research:

> Although several parenting factors also correlate with aggression, the relations between watching TV violence and later aggression persist when the effects of socio-economic status, intellectual ability, and parenting factors are controlled. And even if watching TV violence is not the only factor predicting later aggression, there were few other factors shown to have larger effects (von Feilitzen, 2003, p. 7).

When some children seem to select out particular kinds of negative media experience and expose themselves to its patterns, they might retain many perceptual maps from which to interpret the world and make behavioral choices. Many children might render themselves vulnerable to media influence because of a lack of reflection both on a cognitive, emotional, aesthetic, and behavioral level. Von Feilitzen sums up the main results from five scholars carrying out media violence research:

In sum, the results of this initial, limited study of children's brain activations while viewing entertainment video violence suggests, according to the researchers, that the violence is arousing, engaging, and is treated by the brain as a real event that is threatening and worthy of being stored for long-term memory in an area of the brain that makes "recall" of the events almost instantaneous. Thus, the children stored away violent images in a manner that could be used to "guide" future behavior (von Feilitzen, 2003, p.7).

All these findings make it necessary for parents and other advocates for children to be alert and concerned about the potential negative impact of media. Many critics of media-effects research still point to the catharsis theory, defending the production of violence. Patrick Lee Plaisance (2009, p. 163) comments:

Defenders of the television and movie industries also have long argued that violent content, instead of stimulating imitative acts and aggressive tendencies, actually provides a cathartic outlet. In one characteristic comment, legendary film director Alfred Hitchcock said, "One of television's greatest contributions is that it brought murder into the home where it belongs. Seeing a murder on television can be good therapy. It can help work off one's antagonism" (Myers, 1999, p. 412). Extensive research, however, suggests that catharsis simply doesn't occur; there are dissenting views (Signorielli, 1990, Gunter, 1994), but the evidence "overwhelmingly shows that media violence has quite the opposite effect than that which is predicted by catharsis" (Strasburger and Wilson, 2003, p. 78).

This situation reinforces the need for parental control and monitoring in the home, because the effects on children and adolescents are cumulative. The media industry covers a variety of businesses, and therefore it is necessary to avoid a moralistic approach to media in general. Annet Aris and Jacques Bughin say:

Few industries are as divers, shifting and high-paced as the media industry. The industry is a unique crossbred of creativity and business, comprising a wide array of segments, enterprises and players – some of them dedicated strictly to economic value creation, others bordering on eccentricity (Aris and Bughin, 2009, p. 1).

When repeatedly exposed to the same messages and images, the attitudes and behaviors of young people might change. Therefore, parents, teachers, and pastors have to be aware of the fact that children's and adolescents' health and behavioral concerns may be associated with media use habits and choices. For parents, media education through practicing media literacy principles at home, in cooperation with the school, seems to be the most effective way of becoming selective, wise, and critical media consumers. Our world has changed in the past decades due to the overwhelming amount of media exposure, as John Calhoun Merrill says:

We live in a world of communication pollution. Propaganda, biased information, superficial journalism, vulgarizing streams of crime and sex, focus on celebrities ad nauseam, reputation-destroying stories, opinion camouflaged as fact, "spinning" assertions of expertise – all these, and more, tend to put global populations into a kind of drug-like stupor. A media-created world of puzzling shadows distracts the eyes and syncopated sounds of war and violence deafen the ears. The communication waters are polluted and little is being done to clean up the mess (Merrill, 2008, p. v).

In our research we have found that most children turn to their parents to know what is right and wrong. This is an important finding and gives us an impetus that parents still have an important role in the digital age. Marjorie J. Hogan gives a challenge in this regard:

> Parents can teach and model these insights for children and ensure that media education permeates every aspect of life in a family. Media education is a lifelong skill that will make all of us better media consumers, whether we are enjoying a movie, reading a newspaper, listening to a political ad, or surfing the Internet. Children who are media educated should enter adolescence and adulthood with healthy cynicism about media offerings. Is this movie worth the price of admission? Do I believe this political candidate's pledges? Why are young women's bodies used to promote this brand of beer? Parents can and should use every opportunity to bring media education into the family conversation (Hogan, 2001, pp. 666–667).

> Establishing guidelines for family media use tells children something important about parents' values and limits. Each family has to find its own guidelines, and the challenge is to have rules that maximize family time and optimize school performance (Hogan, 2001, p. 669).

The Internet with its growing capacity to exchange all kind of messages both in the form of sound, telephone calls, and still and moving pictures has opened up a new kind of communication that makes incalculable quantities of information instantly available.Kristen Campbell Eichhorn, Candice Thomas-Maddox and Melissa Bekelja Wanzer (2008, p. 369) ask:

> What are some of the pitfalls associated with Internet disclosure? Perhaps the biggest concern with online disclosure of information is safety. Not surprisingly, people differ in the amount and type of information they disclose on these Internet sites.

We know that sexual abuse of children happens today both in the real world and in the cyberworld, both in the so-called "developed world" and quickly developing into the "developing world." There is a great need for a coherent and coordinated strategy to do something about this huge problem. The great commercial market on the Internet provides many offers, including child pornography. "Zip" files and "sit" files are compacted data files that have become popular with various Internet providers (they can be used to transmit large amounts of child pornography).

Constructive Use of the Internet

There are hundreds of fun and exciting links that represent safe sites for children and youths. Some, such as Yahooligans (www.yahooligans.com), include lists of hundreds of webpages for children and teenagers. These pages are categorized by theme, such as sports, music. Mamamedia (www.mamamedia.com) presents a variety of fun and creative activities for children, together with a search tool which puts the user in contact with a collection of websites for children aged 10 years and younger. Kid's wave (www.safesurf.com/kidswave.htm) shows a limited list, organized according to age and content, and websites that have accepted the "SafeSurf" seal of approval. Finally, one should mention The American Library Association's Great Sites for Kids (www.ala.org./parentspage/greatsites/amazing.html),which lists hundreds of websites, from art and entertainment to science and technology, arranged by The Children and Technology Committee of the Association for Library Services to Children.

Confronted with the Internet, many realize that there are great opportunities to find massive amounts of information and knowledge that can contribute towards giving children and youths crucial help in succeeding educationally. Many also realize that the Internet contains material that can harm children and adolescents for the rest of their lives. The challenge faced by parents today is to guide their children through the many websites that: represent good sources of entertainment; provide knowledge; and can shape good values and attitudes. In the best situation, parents are informed and involved in a way that gives them occasion to participate with their children in these various processes. This type of participation requires time and effort, but is thought to be completely necessary in order to be able to communicate with children in a way which shapes the foundation for good social skills and the building of individual character. Currently there is an enormous amount of information and knowledge available on the Internet. Some sites provide this freely, while others require payment. Some of these that require payment can be worth it, especially if the subscription is used frequently. In conjunction with preparing schoolwork, parents and their children can together seek out appropriate websites. David Buckingham comments:

> The market in educational software needs to be understood in relation to broader tendencies in the media industries. The contemporary media environment is one of increasing commercial competition. There has been a concentration of ownership, both in production and distribution; and a degree of technological convergence, largely as a result of digitisation. Companies increasingly have to think on a global scale, and to develop properties that can be marketed across a range of media platforms (Buckingham, 2007, p. 35).

We should be on the lookout for questionable elements that can be harmful to children and youths. Through good parent-child contact and the installation of web filters, the risk of children becoming "hooked" on material that is inappropriate for youngsters can be reduced. Such filters are censoring programs that can be installed on the family's PC, and various filters have different definitions of what is considered to be undesirable material. Most of these filters censor material based on a list or words and expressions which are built into the program and such a list can ordinarily be personalized. In addition to Netscape Communicator and Internet Explorer browsers, there is also a range of software designed to filter out undesired material, such as, for example, Cyber Patrol (from The Learning Company) and KidDesk Internet Safe (from Edmark). The Norwegian net-filter, SOL Kvasirs Familiefilter, will not limit the use of either the Internet or a PC, but regulates the type of pages that are searchable and accessible. Cyber Patrol is considered to be a very restrictive word-based net-filter, where one can inhibit admittance to undesirable web pages, chat, and newsgroups. In the filters CyberSitter and Net Nanny, words and phrases that should be censored can be selected. The word-based filter, Net Nanny, shows a list of censored net-sites, something Surf Watch and CyberSitter do not do. If parents wish to find out which sites are being visited, it is possible to use a program for logging this information which is then available to view. A few sensor programs have this log function. By using these browser aids, a child will only gain access to the preselected websites, but no censoring product can successfully block all questionable elements.

The different IRC-chat groups provide a good opportunity for children and teenagers to share interests and develop new friendships. However, these chat groups can also become a place where people who wish to use children (such as pedophiles) assume false identities and "groom" other users. Among pedophiles, this is called "chicken hawking."

It is therefore important to help children and youths to stay away from emails with questionable and immoral elements, where subsequently child molesters present disturbing offers and requests.

Internet safety for young people is of paramount importance. Guidance on protection can be obtained from: www.cme.org and Save the Children (www. reddbarna.no).

The UN Convention on the Rights of the Child

Children's encounters with the media closely combine three major aspects of children's rights: access to provision, protection, and participation. The scientific coordinator of the UNESCO's International Clearing house on Children, Youth and Media, Cecilia von Feilitzen, says with regard to The Convention on the Rights of the Child:

> Basically, the issues of media education and children's participation are related to children's rights not only regarding the media but also in society – rights that are fundamental to increased democracy. According to the United Nations Convention on the Rights of the Child – in 1999 having been in force for ten years – the child shall have access to information and material from a diversity of national and international

Protecting Children from Harmful Influences of Media 909

sources, especially those aimed at the promotion of his or her social, spiritual and moral well-being (from article 17); the child shall have the right to freedom of expression (from article 13); and the child has the right to express her or his views in all matters affecting the child (from article 12) (von Feilitzen and Carlson, 1999, p. 15).

With regard to Article 17, we have also to bear in mind the provisions of Articles 13 and 18 in the Convention, that is, the right of the child to freedom of expression, and parents' primary responsibility for the upbringing of the child.

From our interviewees with 6th and 10th grade pupils, we found that most of these pupils turn to their homes for guidance about right and wrong. This gives the parents and the home a unique position in being able to help their children to experience that the interaction between the intentional and functional education that can create new possibilities for learning and identity formation among children. Professor Janne Haaland-Matlary says:

> The freedom of the child and the media are not limitless. The importance of the articles in the UN Convention on the Rights of the Child implies that I cannot shield my children from the media, but I need to be clear about what is good and what is wrong. The UN Convention on The Rights of the Child is a valuable instrument for empowering parents in their important task of guiding their children in a media saturated society. ... The super-power of international media corporations crosses all kind of borders in their relentless fight for commercial gains. Parents all over the world must unite, on the basis of the UN Declaration of Human Rights, in the fight for their rights to determine the values on which they will bring up their children (Simonnes and Gjelsten, 2002, pp. 41–43).

The UN Convention on the Rights of the Child thus actually supports both the child and the parents. Programs that are considered to be inappropriate for children shall be marked, either with a sound signal or in a visual manner.

Throughout this chapter we attempted to answer the question if and how children should be protected ethically in our digital world. It should be clear that children need protection. Our answer is that this can only happen through empowering children to focus on communication skills and media literacy principles. Such an emphasis will strengthen young people for a democratic lifestyle, and we have especially pointed to the responsibility schools and homes have in teaching these principles.

References

Aris, A., and Bughin, J. (2009) *Managing Media Companies. Harnessing Creative Value*, John Wiley and Sons, Inc., Glasgow.

Atton, C. (2002) *Alternative Media*, Sage, Thousand Oaks, CA.

Brown, J.A. (2001) Media literacy and critical television viewing in education, in *Handbook of Children and the Media*, (eds D.G. Singer and J.L. Singer), Sage, Thousand Oaks, CA, pp. 681–699.

Buckingham, D. (2002) The electronic generation: Children and new media, in *Handbook of New Media: Social Shaping and Consequences of ICTs*, (eds L.A. Lievrouw and S. Livingstone), Sage, London, pp. 77–89.

Buckingham, D. (2007) That's edutainment: New media, marketing and education in the home, in *Children, Media and Consumption*, (eds K.M. Ekström and B. Tufte), Göteborg University, Nordicom, pp. 33–45.

Coleman, R., and Wilkins, L. (2009) Moral development: A psychological approach to understanding ethical judgment, in *The Handbook of Mass Media Ethics*, (eds L.Wilkins and C.G. Christians), Routledge, New York and London, pp. 40–54.

Eichhorn, K.C., Thomas-Maddox, C., and Wanzer, M.B. (2008) From face to face to cyperspace, in *Interpersonal Communication. Building Rewarding Relationships*, (eds K.C. Eichhorn *et al.*), Kendall/Hunt Publishing Company, Iowa, p. 369.

Fackler, M. (2009) Communitarianism, in *The Handbook of Mass Media Ethics*, (eds L. Wilkins and C.G. Christians), Routledge, New York and London, pp.305–316

Gjelsten, G., and Simmones, A. (2007) *Skole og Media – Kommunikasjon og Pedagogikk*, Fagbokforlaget, Bergen.

Goleman, D. (1997) *Emotional Intelligence*. Bantam Books, New York, London, Sydney.

Gunter, B. (1994) The question of media violence, in *Media Effects: Advances in Theory and Research*, (eds J. Bryant and D. Zillman), Lawrence Erlbaum, Hillsdale, NJ, pp.

Hogan, M.J. (2001) Parents and other adults: Models and monitors of healthy media habits, in *Handbook of Children and the Media*, (eds D.G. Singer and J.L. Singer), Sage, Thousand Oaks, CA, pp. 663–680.

Horwitz, R.B. (1989) *The Irony of Regulatory Reform: The Deregulation of American Telecommunications*, Oxford University Press, New York.

Huesmann, R.L., Moise-Titus, J., Podolski, C.-L. *et al.* (2003) Longitudinal relations between children's exposure to TV violence and their aggressive and violent behaviour in young adulthood: 1977–1992, *Developmental Psychology*, 39 (2), 201–221.

ICCVOS (2003) *News magazine*, The International Clearinghouse on Children Youth and Media, Nordicom, Göteborg University, p. 6.

Kellner, D. (2002) New media and new literacies: Reconstructing education for the new millennium, in *Handbook of New Media: Social Shaping and Consequences of ICTs*, (eds L.A. Lievrouw and S. Livingstone), Sage, London, pp. 90–104.

Kilbourne, J. (1999) *Can't Buy my Love: How Advertising Changes the Way we Think and Feel*, Simon & Schuster, New York.

Kubey, R., and Donovan, B.W. (2001) Media and the family, in *Handbook of Children and the Media*, (eds D.G. Singer and J.L. Singer), Sage, Thousand Oaks, CA, pp. 323–340.

Kunkel, D (2001) *Sex on TV 2*, Henry J. Kaiser Family Foundation, University of California, Santa Barbara.

Merrill, J.C. (2008) Introduction, in *An Ethics Trajectory: Visions of Media Past, Present and Yet to Come*, (eds T.W. Cooper, C.G. Christians, and A.S. Babbili), University of Illinois Institute of Communications research, Urbana.

Myers, D.G. (1999) *Social Psychology*, 6th edn, McGraw-Hill, Boston, MA.

Plaisance, P.L. (2009) Violence, in *The Handbook of Mass Media Ethics*, (eds L. Wilkins and C.G. Christians), Routledge, New York and London, pp. 162–176.

Potter, J.W. (2001) *Media Literacy*, 2nd edn, Sage, Thousand Oaks, CA.

Signorielli, N. (1990) Children, television, and gender roles. Messages and impact. *Journal of Adolescent Health Care: Official Publication of the Society for Adolescent Medicine*, 11 (1), 50–58.

Simonnes, A., and Gjelsten, G. (2002) *Mass Media Communication and the Intentional Education in School and Family*, Volda University College and Møre Research, Volda, Norway.

Simonnes, A., Gjelsten, G., and Kleven, T.A. (2004) *The Child in the Interaction between Intentional and Functional Education*, Volda University College and Møre Research, Volda, Norway.

Strasburger, V.C., and Wilson, B.J. (2003) Children, adolescents and the media, *Communication Abstracts*, 26 (1), 3–151.

Taylor, C. (1992b) *The Ethics of Authenticity*, Harvard University Press, Cambridge, MA.

von Feilitzen, C. (2003) Media violence: Watching TV violence and aggressive behavior, *ICCVOS news magazine*, 1.

von Feilitzen, C. (2004) *Yearbook 2004*, The International Clearinghouse on Children Youth and Media, Nordicom, Göteborg University.

von Feilitzen, C., and Carlson, U. (1999) *Children and Media: Image, Education, Participation*, Nordicom/UNESCO, Göteborg.

White, R.A. (1996) *A communitarian ethic of communication in a postmodern age.*, Estudos Gerais da Arrábida. Conferéncias do Conceneto. Lisbon, Portugal, July.

White, R.A. (2009) Evolution of normative traditions, in *Normative Theories of the Media*, (eds C.G. Christians, L.T. Glasser and D. McQuail *et al.*), University of Illinois Press, Urbana and Chicago, pp. 37–64.

46

Ethics and International Propaganda

Philip M. Taylor

It can be argued that the field of communications studies owes its origins to the study of international propaganda. In the 1920s, a small group of American political scientists, notably Harold Lasswell and Walter Lippmann, became fascinated by the use of propaganda during the recent Great War, especially its role in persuading the United States to join the conflict on the Allied side in 1917. A decade later, Lasswell's *Propaganda in the Great War* was published as the first significant monograph of the field. It was in fact his PhD thesis awarded the previous year from the University of Chicago. In his later work, Lasswell combined psychology with political science, thus beginning the multidisciplinary approach to the study of communications and politics. Edward Bernays, often cited as the father of modern public relations, also wrote about propaganda and his views influenced politicians as far apart as Franklin Roosevelt and Adolph Hitler. Indeed, Hitler was so impressed with Allied propaganda techniques in the Great War that he himself dedicated two chapters in *Mein Kampf* to the topic. While best-selling books like Arthur Ponsonby's *Falsehood in Wartime* (1927) were exposing the huge image-reality gap between 1914–1918 and, in the process, associating propaganda with at best half-truths and, at worst, with downright lying, Hitler was to locate propaganda as a peacetime tool in his totalitarian form of government once he seized power in 1933. Whereas the word "propaganda" was originally devised by the Vatican to describe its organization for counter-Reformation in the seventeenth century, during the twentieth century it would thereafter acquire a pejorative meaning from which it was never able to recover.

The Handbook of Global Communication and Media Ethics, First Edition. Edited by Robert S. Fortner and P. Mark Fackler.
© 2011 Blackwell Publishing Ltd. Published 2011 by Blackwell Publishing Ltd.

Definitions

There is no universally accepted definition of propaganda. However, there are now essentially two distinct schools of thought about it. The first sees propaganda as a tool of manipulation and, as such, morally reprehensible. This "moralist school" owes its intellectual origins to the writings of Plato whose views from ancient Greece saw "rhetoric" as the art of persuasion and a tool for domination and "belief without knowledge."[1] Philosophy, for Plato, was a "love of truth" and thus distinct from rhetoric which was about persuading the multitude, not instructing or educating it on a path towards truth. In modern times, perhaps the most famous exponent of this school of thought was the French philosopher, Jacques Ellul, who, like Plato, recognized that people needed propaganda but that it was nonetheless a "menace" which threatened individual freedom of thought.[2] Ellul was no doubt influenced by recent European events that he had lived through, particularly World War II[3] and the apparent success of Nazi propaganda which had taken Germany to the heart of darkness. The Nazi philosophy of propaganda was encapsulated by the phrase, "The Big Lie." Adolf Hitler thought that "the truth" was irrelevant to its conduct. Rather he believed that if you repeated something over and over again, regardless of its veracity, people would believe it. Intellectuals were, in his view, immune from its influence. The enthusiasm for propaganda espoused by his fellow dictators, Mussolini, Franco, and Stalin, probably destroyed forever the reputation of propaganda as a value-neutral process of communication and ensured that its popular association would always be made with deceit and deception. The most eloquent contemporary proponent of this point of view is Stanley Cunningham.[4]

Nonetheless, a second school of thought, the "neutralist school," continues to provide an alternative point of view. The moralist school has a distinctive European influence although the neutralist school draws on more American influences; particularly Lasswell who famously wrote that propaganda was "no more moral or immoral than a pump handle."[5] This perspective draws more on Aristotle, Plato's student, who argued that it was not just what was being said that was important but how it was being said. Lasswell's famous definition of communication was "Who (says) What (to) Whom (in) What Channel (with) What Effect." If we add to this the question "Why" then we may be some way towards distinguishing propaganda from other forms of communications. The neutralist school sees propaganda as a mere process of communication where success or failure is irrelevant to its definition – that is the difference between effective and ineffective propaganda. Rather it is the intentions behind the process, the motives for undertaking the manipulation of language, symbols, and images, which should more appropriately attract moral scrutiny. This viewpoint thus sees propaganda as a planned process, although it does not preclude the possibility of accidental propaganda. It recognizes that manipulation is an inherent characteristic of humanity, or indeed all forms of life, from the perfume or aftershave that one wears to the blending into the background of a chameleon. It also leads to the possibility of propaganda for a good cause, although it again recognizes the historical abuse of propaganda by ruthless manipulators. As such, it accepts that propaganda can be used for "good" or "bad" purposes but only if the motivations are scrutinized in such moral terms. Members of this school would include Daniel Lerner, Leonard W. Doob, Lindley Fraser, and Terence Qualter.

The way nation states conduct propaganda internationally reflects the way they conduct politics at home. Although democracies fight shy of the word propaganda because of its historical associations with dictatorships, preferring instead "information activities" and a whole host of other euphemisms, they conduct propaganda in a value-neutral sense according to strict rules. Far from being a "big lie," democratic propaganda has to be conducted within the tradition of what President Franklin Roosevelt described as a "Strategy of Truth." We can therefore now see the emergence of two distinct models of propaganda – the democratic and the authoritarian. Democratic propaganda is guided by avoiding deliberate lies, by telling as much as the truth as can be told (within, for example, the confines of national security) and by its intentions to benefit the recipient as well as the source. The contemporary manifestation of this type of influence activity is perhaps best reflected by the conduct of public diplomacy. Totalitarian propaganda, by way of contrast, is designed to benefit the ruling elite at the expense of individual freedom of thought, and is accompanied by heavy censorship, and is in the business of telling people what to think rather than teaching them how to think. Hence the following definitions are now possible:

> *Propaganda* is the planned use of communications to manipulate words, images, symbols, and ideas that encourage a target audience to think and act *in a manner desired by the source.*

> *Democratic propaganda* is the planned use of communications to manipulate words, images, symbols, and ideas that encourage a target audience to think and/or behave in a manner desired by the source and in accordance with certain principles. It does not preclude the possibility that the target audience can also benefit from this process. To ensure credibility, it must be factually-based and avoid deliberate untruths. To ensure success, it must be desired by the target audience as a group of individuals rather than as a collective subordinate to the needs of the state. Its principal means to success is verifiable credibility where the means justify the ends.

> *Totalitarian propaganda* is the planned use of communications to manipulate words, images, symbols, and ideas that encourage a target audience to think and/or behave in a manner desired by the source and is characterized by certain values. These values have more to do with repetition than credibility; they are intolerant of alternative viewpoints and thus rely heavily upon censorship and a degree of coercion of reception, usually enforced by security services and surveillance. Its principal means to success is whatever needs to be done where the ends justify the means.

If there is an initial moral objection to the word "manipulation" then no form of propaganda is acceptable, although this perhaps belies the realities of everyday life

Ethics and International Propaganda   915

from the clothes one wears to the copy which a journalist edits. It would also apply moral opprobrium to advertising, public relations, marketing, and other forms of communication that are undertaken with the primary intention of benefiting the source, whether from a political, economic or cultural perspective.

The Internationalization of Propaganda

As the literature was growing from the 1920s onwards, the conduct of international propaganda was becoming more central to the practice of national and international affairs. In the United States, there was a massive isolationist backlash against being "duped" into the Great War by unscrupulous – usually British – propagandists and the American government refused to join the brainchild of its president, the League of Nations. Whether such charges were justified must remain open to doubt President Wilson had been reelected in 1916 on a "keep America out of the war" ticket and so the events between November 1916 and April 1917, when the United States did actually enter the war, must be most carefully scrutinized. The secret British organization that targeted American opinion from the start of the war in 1914, the War Propaganda Bureau at Wellington House in London, began its campaign really more with the intention of ensuring that the United States did not join the German side and that it remained neutral. As the war became locked in a stalemate and casualties mounted, especially with the Battle of the Somme, requiring the British to introduce conscription in 1916 for the first time in its history, the campaign shifted emphasis to encouraging intervention "to make the world safe for democracy." This looks odd to twenty-first century eyes given that women were not given the vote in Britain until after the war.

The six month period between the election and the US entry into the war was the period of the Zimmermann telegram. This intercepted telegram from the German foreign minister to his ambassador in Mexico proposed a deal whereby the Mexicans invaded the United States in return for territory including Texas. Given the iconoclastic significance of the Alamo for the American psyche, the British realized they had dynamite in their hands. The problem was that the still neutral Americans did not know that the British were intercepting not only German cable traffic but also their own traffic with Germany. The very first British action of the war had been to cut the direct German submarine cables across the Atlantic. A lucky discovery of German code books enabled the British intelligence services to break the German codes. Combined, all these factors brought intelligence and propaganda into a mutual relationship that survives to this day. The conundrum for the British was that if the British showed the Zimmermann telegram to the Americans in an attempt to prove German "barbarism," it would reveal to the Germans that their codes had been broken and would thus prompt them to change them, thereby removing a significant British advantage. However, it would also reveal to the Americans that they were reading trans Atlantic cable traffic including, as it turns out, American cables – hardly the actions of a friendly power which had recently suppressed an Irish uprising that had considerable opposition among the Irish-American community. But the fuse needed to be lit; it was too good an opportunity to miss. In the end, the British decided to show the Americans a cable that was sent via an indirect route that did not disclose British intercept operations between Germany and the United States. The problem then was how to convince the Americans that the cable was not a forgery. However, the plan worked. Coming after the 1915 Bryce Report into Alleged German atrocities in Belgium, the sinking of the passenger liner Lusitania by German U boats in the same year, and the killing of Nurse Edith Cavell in 1916, the cumulative "evidence" of German "barbarism" was such that the Zimmermann telegram proved to be the last straw and the Americans entered the war in April 1917 on the Allied side. Doubts about the veracity of all these events only emerged when the war was over.

International Radio Propaganda: The Early Years

The British, somewhat embarrassed by their new-found postwar reputation for international propaganda, decided that there was no role for it in peacetime and largely dismantled their wartime machinery in 1919. Only a small rump News Department was retained by the Foreign Office to deal with the press – the first press department of its kind in the British political system. This proved an ostrich-like reaction to what was actually happening elsewhere in the world. Just as the Americans had withdrawn from the international state system created by the Versailles Treaties, so the British withdrew from the tide of international propaganda that had been unleashed by the Great War. The transformation of radio in the 1920s, for example, from being a medium in Morse code for ship-to-ship or ship-to-shore communication into a voice and audio device for penetrating the walls of home dwellers, was a revolution every bit as significant then as the Internet is today. The new Soviet regime in Russia was particularly keen on using radio as both a medium of national unity and a tool for spreading revolutionary ideas abroad. In late 1922, Radio Moscow began transmission on 12 kilowatts – at that time the most powerful in the world and the world's first shortwave broadcasts began a few years later in 1927. Voice radio had the potential to overcome the vast illiteracy in the Soviet Union but radio receivers were still largely for public broadcasts via loudspeakers rather than home use. One of the first Russian stations called itself the "spoken Newspaper of the Russian Telegraph Agency" broadcasting political news at set times in factories or in village halls. However, external broadcasts directed especially at neighboring countries, cultivating support and promoting world-wide revolution, were particularly worrying for the British Empire in places like India. This issue became more and more serious as radio sets became more widely available, even prompting Anglo-Soviet accords attempting to limit their impact.

Perhaps this experience was a partial motivation for the British to establish their BBC Empire Service in 1932. Broadcasting in English on shortwave frequencies relayed by masts located in Britain's worldwide colonies London could keep its

Ethics and International Propaganda   917

imperial subjects in constant touch with the latest news from the capital. The motto which the BBC adopted then – and still holds today – reveals the hope that information could be a force for good was that "Nation Shall Speak Peace Unto Nation." However, by the 1930s, so-called "radio wars" were becoming more and more common. Once Hitler came to power in Germany in 1933, the new Nazi Ministry of Popular Enlightenment and Propaganda under Josef Goebbels saw radio as an ideal means of keeping in contact with those Germans separated geographically from their birthplace by the Versailles Treaties (the *auslandeutch*). The Nazis launched a new radio set, the People's Receiver (*Volksempfänger*) as a way of making news and entertainment in the home affordable for the average citizen – and of course as an electronic entry point into German families for propaganda purposes. Additionally the Nazis used radio to "soften up" their foreign opponents prior to political and later military attacks – a sort of verbal artillery barrage designed to intimidate and demoralize. Today, we would call this "psychological warfare." The first signs of this came prior to the Saar Plebiscite of 1935 and the increasingly intrusive nature of radio propaganda in the internal affairs of other states prompted the League of Nations in 1936 to introduce legislation attempting to outlaw its use in this way.

Essentially, the international community was becoming concerned that new communications technologies like radio were being used by extremist governments of both left and right persuasions to destabilize neighboring states by talking directly to the peoples of those neighboring states rather than through their governmental officials and diplomats. The Soviets had done this to foment revolutionary movements and the Nazis utilized radio as an instrument of their aggressive foreign policy – hardly nation speaking peace unto nation. In Fascist Italy, Mussolini also saw opportunities to destabilize British colonies in the Near and Middle East and in 1934 he established Radio Bari to broadcast in Arabic. With an uprising in Palestine under the British mandate from 1936 onwards, these broadcasts became so worrying that the Foreign Office decided to ask the BBC to begin their first foreign-language service in 1938 – in Arabic. These were followed by broadcasts in Spanish and Portuguese to counter Nazi propaganda in Latin America – a vital source of materials for raw rearmament. With Europe on the brink of war over the Munich crisis of September 1938, the BBC began broadcasts in German and other European languages.

The creation of what was to become the BBC World Service revealed the dilemmas inherent in the conduct of democratic propaganda. The Empire Service had started in 1932, broadcasting in English so that its colonies could keep in touch with events in Britain. However, broadcasting in foreign languages was much more controversial and in danger of easily being labeled with the by now wholly discredited word of "propaganda." Initially, the British Foreign Office wanted to do the Arabic foreign language broadcasts itself (from government owned transmitters in Cyprus). This was a case of a government department not trusting an independent media outlet disseminating its desired messages in support of its (foreign) policies. The BBC would demand editorial independence anyway. The problem was that if the Foreign Office carried out the broadcasting itself, its messages would simply be regarded as "British propaganda" because that was what nations like the Soviet

Union and Nazi Germany were clearly doing – and "propaganda" was by now so clearly associated with lying and with attempts to destabilize other countries. The Foreign Office was so concerned about other nations' attempts to do this in British colonies and other areas of national interest that it wanted to counter the negative things that were being said about Britain. It wanted to counter "the lies" with "the truth." In the end, a "gentleman's agreement" was made between the Foreign Office and the BBC whereby the latter would undertake the broadcasts on behalf of the former with a limited amount of editorial supervision. Clearly that didn't work as the very first BBC foreign language broadcast in Arabic contained some "bad news" about a British Army activity (the execution of a Palestinian). The Foreign Office was furious but in fact this type of editorial independence increased the credibility of the broadcasts. Thus began the BBC's evolution into what was to become the most trusted international broadcaster in the world. The BBC's desire to remain independent editorially from the government meant that it reserved the right to criticize the British government which financed it (from Foreign Office funds) and this, in turn, enhanced its credibility. The "gentleman's agreement" was to serve the British government well in future years, especially during the Suez crisis of 1956, although the symbiotic relationship came to be severely tested in the aftermath of the Iraq war of 2003 during the Hutton Enquiry.

All these developments seemed counter to a League of Nations convention that had been signed by most member states (but not the Germans) in 1936 trying to prevent international radio propaganda that was designed to destabilize the populations of foreign nations. It was more honored in the breach in the build up to World War II as it became clear that radio would become a new weapon of psychological warfare. Even the British were in breach of the convention when they covertly utilized Radio Luxembourg during the 1938 Munich Crisis to bypass Nazi information channels – the Nazis banned the listening of foreign radio programs – in an attempt to get the British version of events into the minds of the German populace. Thus began the separation of propaganda into "black," "white," and "grey" forms. White propaganda was messaging from a clearly identified source. It was overt. Black propaganda was from a disguised source, that is, it purported to come from a source which was not its real origin. Grey propaganda indicated no source whatsoever and could only be designated white or black when its true origin became known. – and with these designations came certain rules. White propaganda, for example, had to be what Nicholas Pronay would later describe as "propaganda with facts, because it was obvious where it was coming from, it had to tell "the truth." If it deliberately lied, and the lie was discovered, its credibility would be compromised (at least in so far as the democratic propaganda model is concerned). We should now perhaps start talking more about "credibility" than the truth – or perhaps "credible truths" would be better. Born of a lie, black propaganda – for as long as its real source remain disguised – could be much more liberal with its lies. These lies still had to be credible if they were to be believed and we shall see shortly how these credible lies worked during World War II. They were called "sibs" from the Latin *sibilare* (to whisper).

The New Literary Propaganda Boom

Inevitably, contemporary analysts watched these developments with considerable interest. Even novelists like Aldous Huxley wrote about them. Apart from his novel *Brave New World* in which he described how people are distracted by entertainment in order to divert them from the realities of their social and political circumstances, Huxley wrote several essays, the first of which was published in *Harper's* magazine in 1936 as "Notes on Propaganda" and a second on "Dictators Propaganda" published in *The Spectator* also in 1936. He later followed this up with a fascinating essay on "Propaganda in a Democratic State." His concluding remarks of that essay are still relevant today:

> A society, most of whose members spend a great part of their time, not on the spot, not here and now and in the calculable future, but somewhere else, in the irrelevant other worlds of sport and soap opera, of mythology and metaphysical fantasy, will find it hard to resist the encroachments of those who would manipulate and control it.
>
> In their propaganda today's dictators rely for the most part on repetition, suppression and rationalization – the repetition of catchwords which they wish to be accepted as true, the suppression of facts which they wish to be ignored, the arousal and rationalization of passions which may be used in the interests of the Party or the State. As the art and science of manipulation come to be better understood, the dictators of the future will doubtless learn to combine these techniques with the non-stop distractions which, in the West, are now threatening to drown in a sea of irrelevance the rational propaganda essential to the maintenance of individual liberty and the survival of democratic institutions (Huxley, 1958).

At the start of World War II, when the British recreated a Ministry of Information (MoI), its motto became to "tell the truth, nothing but the truth, and *as near as possible*, the whole truth" (my italics). Of course, this does not mean the whole truth was told but it did establish a pattern or rule for wartime British white propaganda and for democratic propaganda thereafter. The MoI, echoing Huxley, also recognized that film propaganda, for example, also had to be entertaining if it was to be successful.

World War II

The internationalization of propaganda reached its apogee in the second half of the twentieth century, beginning with World War II and then continued throughout the Cold War. The arrival of new technologies such as satellite television and the Internet obviously helped this, but the relationship between war and propaganda was inextricably sealed between 1939 and 1945. Indeed, the German pretext for invading Poland in September 1939 was made when two of its radio officials were killed, while most Britons learned they were at war with Germany via Neville

Chamberlain's broadcast to the nation on September 3, 1939. Americans, neutral until the Japanese attack on Pearl Harbor in December 1941, listened with fascination during the London Blitz of 1940 to Edward R. Murrow's radio bulletins about how "Britain can take it." The opening night of the war saw the RAF drop millions of leaflets over German towns reassuring the recipients that Britain was not fighting the German people, only the Nazi Party – although this policy was to change as the war dragged on, especially as Unconditional Surrender was declared to be the chief Allied war aim after the Casablanca conference of 1943. Even then, Churchill and Roosevelt declared that: "In our uncompromising policy we mean no harm to the common people of the Axis nations. But we do mean to impose punishment and retribution in full upon their guilty, barbaric leaders" (Army Information School, 1946).

World War II is often described as a Total War, one in which the entire resources of a nation – military, economic, cultural, and psychological - had to be mobilized in a war of national survival. In Total War, there was a need for Total Propaganda. One might say that all rules were off. Nonetheless, in their domestic white propaganda, the strategy of the (partial) truth was adhered to and even censorship was obvious – every British film was preceded on screen with a certificate that what was to follow had been passed by the British Board of Film Censors, while an MoI censor sat poised in every BBC news bulletin with his finger on a silent button in case the news reader strayed from the preapproved script. However, it was on the international front that the greatest propaganda war to date was fought. Nitrate films in 36mm cans could be easily stopped from entering a country, and the Nazis were able to ban all Hollywood films for this simple reason (although Hitler himself was a big fan and he watched them for his personal entertainment). Hence radio remained the principal instrument of international propaganda.

The problem for the British (and later the Americans once they entered the war) was how to get their messages into the minds of Germans, and then a German occupied European audience given the Nazi ban on foreign radio listening. This ban was enforced under penalty of death (by guillotine, an execution reserved specifically for this crime) and German boys and girls were under obligation to their Nazi youth organizations to report parents who transgressed. Following the British withdrawal from Dunkirk in 1940 and the subsequent Battle of Britain, surviving potential invasion was the greatest preoccupation of the new British Prime Minister, Winston Churchill. Once that was achieved and the Germans invaded Russia in June 1941, propaganda and espionage were the only nonkinetic weapons available to *attack* Germany, although the RAF bombing raids were to cause increasing kinetic damage (at enormous costs to their military personnel). To this end, Churchill wanted to "set Europe ablaze" and for this two organizations were created in 1941 – the Special Operations Executive (SOE) to conduct espionage and insert agents into occupied Europe, and the Political Warfare Executive (PWE) to conduct black propaganda because it was obvious that if the BBC conducted black propaganda, its usefulness as a credible source of information to the sizeable numbers of Europeans who risked breaking the Nazi foreign radio ban would be jeopardized.

Ethics and International Propaganda

The PWE was staffed by an extraordinary range of creative people. Among their many innovative and imaginative uses of the art and science of propaganda was the creation of covert radio stations under the code name of Research Units. These were radio transmissions that purported to originate from inside Germany and Occupied Europe when they in fact came from highly secret locations in southern England. Some were targeting enemy military personnel, for example using banned jazz music to attract German U boat crew listeners while others tried to inject sibs by a combination of rumors, information, and disinformation to unsettle both soldiers at the fighting fronts and civilians at home. As they appeared to be of German origin, civilians did not feel they would be breaking any law. It is not known how effective these transmissions were, but we do know that the Nazi Propaganda Minister was afraid of them as an alternative source of "information" to the tightly controlled Nazi media. Interestingly, Goebbels also tried broadcasting to British audiences – most notoriously through the Irishman William Joyce whose aristocratic sounding voice earned him the nickname "Lord Haw Haw" – but the British decided not to jam these broadcasts on the grounds that to censor them would be to show they were afraid of them. Just like the word "Information" in the British ministry (as compared to the word "Propaganda" in the German equivalent) covert censorship and propaganda were fast becoming what the totalitarian enemy practiced whereas "we" told the truth. Words were becoming weapons, together with images, and using the right ones to distance yourself from what you adversaries did was becoming more and more important as both sides tried to seize the moral high ground.

After the German invasion of the Soviet Union and the Japanese attack on Pearl Harbor that brought the Americans into the war, there was some coordination of Allied propaganda themes, especially in the realm of psychological warfare. The US government created the Office of War Information (OWI) for domestic propaganda and the Office of Special Services (OSS) for psychological warfare. The OWI famously produced a series of six "orientation films" called the *Why We Fight* series, which every new recruit to the US armed forces was required to watch. Directed by Hollywood Oscar winning Frank Capra, these films were labeled documentaries but their overarching theme was to "prove" a global coordinated worldwide conspiracy by the Axis powers of Germany, Italy, and Japan to secure world domination. This was perhaps the most effective channel through which to convince those new recruits that they should adhere to the Churchill-Roosevelt strategy of winning the war in Europe first before they sought revenge for Pearl Harbor. The Rome-Berlin-Tokyo Axis was depicted as a dark and demonic force labeled the "slave world" as distinct from the free world and this kind of rhetoric was picked up half a century later following the 9/11 terrorist attacks with President George W. Bush's "axis of evil." We know now that the Germans, Italians, and Japanese were nothing like as coordinated as the Allied propaganda theme suggested and that what they really had in common beyond a fascistic ideology was common enemies.

As the British and Americans, now allied with the Soviets, prepared for the invasion of Europe, they had to resist Moscow's demands for an invasion until they were properly ready. This caused tension but Britain was converted into a giant American aircraft carrier, that for now would help the Soviets by the "strategic bombing" of German towns and cities. This is another example of words mattering. The RAF and USAF bombing raids were conducted usually from a height of 20–30 000 feet and because of this the bombing was arguably not "strategic" and certainly not accurate. Meanwhile, the strategic commander for the Allied invasion was placed under US control and General Eisenhower established his headquarters, known as SHAEF (Strategic Headquarters Allied Expeditionary Force, the forerunner of NATO's SHAPE – Allied Powers Europe). As a result of British experience to date of propaganda and psychological warfare, a jointly staffed Psychological Warfare Division (PWD) was created within SHAEF to win the hearts and minds of the enemy soldiers and their population as the war drew to an end. This was becoming apparent following the German defeat at Stalingrad in 1943 and the Allied call for the Unconditional Surrender of Germany and her allies.

The war, of course, could only be won militarily but its psychological dimension was significant. This not only concerned the morale of civilians who had to endure persistent bombing raids and who were thus frontline soldiers themselves, but also increasingly tired conscripted soldiers, sailors, and airmen who faced a constant possibility of death. One might think that such a psychological state of mind might make them susceptible to propaganda themes concerning surrender, desertion, or defection. The problem facing German soldiers – and an explanation for why they only surrendered when they had absolutely no other choice – was that the declaration of Unconditional Surrender might leave them treated as war criminals. This predicament increased as the war came to an end with the discovery of the concentration camps which the Nazis had set up for the extermination of millions of people. Goebbels knew that the Allies had gifted him a propaganda coup through the declaration of Unconditional Surrender because it did what 10 years of his domestic propaganda had failed to do, namely to unite the German people behind the destiny of the Nazi Party. German soldiers, including teenagers, fought to the bitter end in the streets of Berlin as Allied, especially Soviet, forces moved in for the kill.

Where psychological warfare can claim some credit in World War II is in the deception campaign which accompanied the Normandy Landings. This was known as Operation Fortitude and it involved an elaborate plan to convince the Germans that the D-Day landing would take place at a date, time, and location other than the real plans. Apart from the millions of leaflets that were dropped by the British and Americans during the war – the Americans had a dedicated squadron, while the British used plane and balloon delivery – operation specific dissemination like Fortitude meant that deception and psychological warfare could smooth the military campaign, and this certainly worked to great effect prior to D-Day. Dropping leaflets, after all, was less deadly that dropping bombs and it could be argued that communicating with enemy soldiers to get them to stop fighting was morally more acceptable than killing them.

The Cold War

With the Axis defeated, the glue that welded the British and Americans to their communist wartime ally melted away. Disagreements over Soviet aspirations in liberated Eastern Europe and a mutual suspicion that had existed before the war drove the world into two competing blocs each led by a superpower that would see a war of words waged for almost the next 50 years. In 1948, this Iron Curtain which attempted to seal the peoples of east and west off from one another was firmly drawn, manifesting itself physically with the erection of the Berlin Wall in 1961. In the meantime, a supply crisis to Berlin – located inside what was now East Germany but itself divided into sections occupied by victorious Allies – a suppressed uprising in Hungary in 1956 and the acquiring of the atomic bomb thanks to Western spies providing the Soviets with its secrets – had polarized the world around two ideologies that were not only competing but also diametrically opposed. In the early 1950s the McCarthy witch hunts led by the US Senator of the same name seemed the more pertinent as China, a wartime ally, also fell to communist rule. A hot war broke out in Korea between 1950 and 1953 and the 1956 Suez Crisis threatened momentarily the Anglo-American alliance but as the bipolar world stuttered through these various crises, it was the ideological framework which set the tone for the international propaganda battle, essentially an extension of the wartime "free world vs. slave world" format.

The 1950s also saw technological advances in two important areas: television and rockets. Television had been invented before the war, suspended during it, and rolled out after it. In the decades that followed, it superseded radio in popularity – at least in the First World (the West). In the Second World (Russia and its satellites) it was rigorously controlled, reflecting the totalitarian nature of propaganda in those countries. As the European empires dissolved, creating a Third World, there developed a US-Soviet rivalry for client states. It was this struggle for allegiances that was accompanied by intense propaganda battles. The West had to convince the newly independent former colonies that the Western way of doing politics – democracy – was the best way forward, although many were so filled with resentment at past exploitation that they chose the alternative Soviet way. A nonaligned movement was formed in an attempt to stay out the East–West struggle and remain neutral but in order to develop their own economies they needed to modernize their communications and this left them vulnerable to outside influences. Radio and television signals spilled into neighboring countries and it was impossible to stop the influences contained in the programming which they carried.

Television was to remain a relatively localized medium until the 1960s and 1970s. The space race started in the 1950s was militarily designed to acquire intercontinental ballistic missiles that could carry nuclear warheads in the event of a nuclear war. It can be said that the Soviets won the first part of this race by being the first to get a man into space but lost the second part because the Americans got to the moon in 1969. In the meantime, satellites were being launched – again primarily for military purposes – but it was not long before these were made available to television companies which signaled the internationalization of television, really beginning with the 1964 Tokyo Olympic Games. A new age of propaganda had begun.

Most television programs made for democratic national audiences in any given country were not, of course, riddled with obvious propaganda. However, even entertainment programs contained insights into a value system and thus began what some historians have termed the cultural cold war. American programs from *I Love Lucy* in the 1950s to *Friends* in the 1990s, when exported, became windows into the value system which produced them, providing insights into attitudes towards freedom, women, and individuality. Hollywood films had also been doing this for some time which was why some authoritarian regimes afraid of the impact on their own populations of what insights these films might carry with them were banned. It was difficult to immunize the population of East Berlin from the spillages of West German television programming. While the Berlin Wall was a physical manifestation of the attempt to stop Easterners travelling to the West, nothing could stop the Levis advertisements or the sounds of The Beatles from penetrating the curtain.

The Soviets, afraid of these cultural influences every bit as much as political ones, banned and jammed. They banned "decadent" pop and, just as the Nazis had banned it before, jazz music. But still the sounds could be heard via what the KGB called "the voices." This was their nickname for the dozen or so Western radio stations created by Western governments targeted at people behind the Iron Curtain. The Voice of America, created in the aftermath of Pearl Harbor, was joined by Radio Liberty in Russia and Radio Free Europe for the peoples of "occupied" Europe. To oversee these stations, a United States Information Agency was created in 1953, at the height of the McCarthy communist hunting. Joined by the BBC World Service, whose wartime reputation as a source of trusted and reliable information was enhanced three years later by its critical news reporting of the British government's attempt to retake the Suez Canal, these "voices" were jammed by the Soviets until the late 1980s. Indeed the Soviets spent more money on jamming than they did on their own international broadcasting from stations like Radio Moscow.

Considerable debates surround the issue of whether the output of stations such as the BBC World Service constituted "propaganda." A simple answer is that it depends which side you are on. This is always the problem in international broadcasting issues. Even government owned international broadcasting stations that are staffed by journalists adhering to a tradition of journalistic independence are accused of disseminating official propaganda at the receiving end of the programming. The issues revolve not just around news but also views and the clues into how a free people lives and does politics. When the US government established Radio Marti (and later television) targeting the Cuban population, Castro certainly perceived this as Western propaganda designed to undermine his communist rule – and jammed the transmissions. Despite protestations that the American

Ethics and International Propaganda

government was merely providing news and information that was otherwise denied by an oppressive and censorious Castro regime, if you are on the receiving end and if you don't like what you are hearing – or are afraid of it – then it can be perceived as a form of psychological warfare. The Soviets certainly felt this way about Voice of America broadcasts during the 1956 Hungarian uprising, accusing the service – with some justification – of stirring up the trouble in the first place.

This is similar to another major debate that was to emerge running from the 1960s to the 1980s, namely that of cultural imperialism. With political independence, the former colonial powers began to feel they were still in many respects dependent upon their former colonial masters, not just economically but culturally as well. For example, as color television began to be introduced in Western countries during the late 1960s, they found a ready market for their old black and white systems in the Third World. Radio had initially been introduced in places like Libya because of the rising popularity of mainly music transmissions for the US servicemen stationed there after the war. Now there was an opportunity to buy relatively cheap, secondhand, black and white TV transmitters from those advanced countries converting to color. However, what was infrequently appreciated was the high cost of popular programming. Many countries simply could not afford the production costs but there was a ready solution in purchasing old black and white programs that were regarded as disposable once they had been broadcast in advanced countries. With this solution came the charge of cultural imperialism: external and often alien programming that threatened indigenous culture. Picked up by Marxist scholars – largely, it has to be said, as ammunition for beating up capitalism – this thesis was also applied to the flow of new from the north to the south. The flow was said to be unidirectional and because the concept of Western journalistic practice was mainly to report bad news – coups, earthquakes, famines, assassinations, and wars – Western news reports about the bad news in Africa were being rebroadcast in Africa and was debilitating in terms of morale. The chief international news agencies – Reuters, UPI, AP, and AFP – were singled out for particular criticism. The debate even reached UNESCO in the mid 1980s which called for a "New World Information and Communications Order" to redress the imbalances.

However valid these arguments might have been, the Americans and the British – the media at that time were largely Anglo-American – refused to accept the charges, arguing instead for the free flow of information as a market commodity. By the mid 1980s, two great champions of free-market deregulated capitalism – Ronald Reagan and Margaret Thatcher, had come to power in the United States and United Kingdom. They walked out of UNESCO. At least there was some hope for them in the form of a new type of Soviet leader in the form of Mikhail Gorbachev. Following the Soviet invasion of Afghanistan in 1979, Reagan had labeled the USSR as an "Evil Empire" and massively stepped up US efforts to win the war of words globally. He beefed up US public diplomacy – a phrase first coined in the 1960s as an acceptable alternative to "propaganda" – including radio broadcasts, deregulated other communications technologies including satellites, and he even expanded military psychological operations (PSYOP) that had gone into decline following the first defeat in American military history in Vietnam. As a former Hollywood actor, Reagan understood the power of communications and was nicknamed the "Great Communicator." The voices were about to get louder.

When, following a string of Soviet leadership deaths, Gorbachev came to power in 1985 he recognized the need for economic reform (perestroika) and, especially, openness (glasnost) as how this should be achieved. This was more the language of democracy and Thatcher informed Reagan after a meeting with Gorbachev that he "was a man we can do business with." However, following a week long Soviet news blackout about the explosion at Chernobyl in 1986, glasnost appeared to be another piece of disinformation, at which the Soviets were expert. Gorbachev thereafter stopped jamming the Western broadcasts and introduced a new initiative to reform the media, including investigative journalism. The degree to which such reforms contributed towards the collapse of the Soviet Union after 1989, combined with the increased access to Western news and views, must remain a matter of speculation. However, they cannot be ignored as contributory factors. As country after country in Eastern Europe threw off its communist straightjacket, it was all reported live on television, including the breaking down of the Berlin War.

The Post-Cold War Era

Although CNN had been founded in 1980 as the world's first 24/7 news channel, it burst into international prominence during the Gulf War of 1991. The event was significant because it demonstrated how international television news could be used as a medium of international propaganda. CNN itself was an independent news channel, based in Atlanta, free from any direct government controls. It even scooped the world on the opening night of the conflict because it had a crew in Baghdad who were able to report live (in audio only at that point) as the bombs began to fall. This was the first time that live reports happened from an enemy capital under fire by journalists who were from the country leading the bombing campaign. However, as the American led coalition set up its "Public Affairs" operation in Saudi Arabia, it was soon to become clear that, despite the Baghdad "loophole," military media management practices were to dominate the agenda of the world's media in covering the war.

The arrival of satellite television in the 1980s enabled the entire globe to watch the same event simultaneously. It was impossible to jam, and because many senior commanders in the US military blamed the television coverage of the Vietnam war for its defeat – a sort of "stab-in-the-back" thesis – the idea of unstoppable, 24/7, bad-news based news reporting was a potential nightmare. Following Iraq's invasion of neighboring Kuwait in July 1990, the Americans assembled a powerful military force and a 30 nation strong coalition in Saudi Arabia under UN resolutions to take "all necessary means" to expel Iraqi forces from the tiny oil-rich country. The Iraqi leader, Saddam Hussein, also believed in what had become known as the Vietnam Syndrome, namely the belief that you might not be able to

Ethics and International Propaganda

win militarily on the battlefield but you might stand a chance on the television screens of global public opinion. His decision to allow Western reporters to remain in Baghdad was unprecedented, and it was to launch a new era in the use of global media as a conduit for international propaganda largely through the media management techniques tried in the 1991 Gulf War.

One of the cleverest tricks used by the US military was to permit live press conferences from the Joint Information Bureau set up in Dhahran and populated with almost 1500 reporters. These attracted huge audiences, especially when the military's "star performer," General Norman "stormin" Schwarzkopf, appeared. He and his spokesmen would release video footage taken from the noses of precision guided cruise missiles showing how the accuracy of coalition targeting. These set the agenda for how the world watched the war on television. Saddam's gamble did not work as Baghdad was targeted only by a new breed of so-called "smart weapons" such as cruise missiles which used satellite technology to guide them precisely to their targets. An illusion was created of a smart, accurate and "clean" video-game war taking place in which death was largely absent. After Iraq was defeated and expelled from Kuwait after only six weeks of fighting, it came to light that these precision guided weapons constituted only around 10% of the coalition's ordinance. That meant that 90% of the bombs dropped on the Iraqi forces were old-fashioned "dumb" bombs that were just as inaccurate as the strategic bombing of World War II when dropped from 30 000 feet by Vietnam era B52 bombers. The US led coalition had won not just the real war but what was beginning to be called the information war. The defeat of Vietnam had been avenged and a means of using live media coverage for democratic propaganda purposes had been found.

If new communications technologies had revolutionized international politics in the 1980s – principally the arrival of satellites, computers, and even now defunct technologies like the fax-machine – they were to have even greater impact in the post-Cold War world in which the United States survived as the sole superpower. The invention of the World Wide Web in 1992 as the accessible front page of the Internet (developed during the Cold War as a means of maintaining defense communication in the event of a nuclear attack), combined with a digital revolution that miniaturized and made affordable everything from cameras to laptop computers was to have profound consequences for international propaganda. Moreover, following the founding of Al Jazeera in 1995, a Qatar-based 24/7 Arab news service that was the first to be relatively independent of its Arab government, broke the global Anglo-American media monopoly in the Middle East that had been so evident in the Gulf War of only three years earlier.

Academic thinkers began to talk of postmodern societies in which the struggle for control over information flows would be deciding political, economic, cultural, and even military outcomes. The military themselves talked of a revolution in military affairs whereby computers, satellite technology, and communications converged to change the nature of warfare. There was much said about the information "battlespace," of info-bombers, hacker warfare and cyberwarfare, a subordination of PSYOP to what was now being called Information Operations. In the meantime, US Public Diplomacy was being wound down as if US megapower needed no explanation because it was so obvious, culminating in the closure of the USIA in 1999. The military honed its Public Affairs activities that had served it so well in 1991 through the international crises of the 1990s in Somalia, the Balkans, and Haiti. These were new kinds of military interventions – "humanitarian" ones – made all the more necessary because of the 24/7 media coverage of the bad news in failed states that had become ideologically unhooked following the end of the Cold War. Some talked of a "CNN Effect" whereby such television coverage (now joined by new rolling news services such as BBC World, Sky News and even on the Internet by MNBC) had the power to drive the foreign policy-making process by showing the terrible things that were happening to the "innocent women and children" of time-honored propaganda usage as one international crisis followed another, culminating in genocide in places like Rwanda and Kosovo.

The use of the World Wide Web during the Kosovo crisis of 1999 by the Serbs who found themselves under aerial attack from NATO forces that claimed to be acting on humanitarian grounds to prevent genocide made it the first Internet war. It revealed how communications technologies had made international politics "asymmetric." Information power was a means of contesting military might. The Serbs knew that they could not defeat the combined military might of NATO but they might be able to cause the, largely American military campaign, some trouble on the information front – both in terms of "old media" and "new." It is a sort of extension of the Vietnam Syndrome, even though that it is a highly dubious assumption that wars can be won or lost in the information "space." The American military lost the Vietnam War, not journalism, for a variety of complex reasons. The Serb leader, Slobodan Milošević, like Saddam Hussein before him, nonetheless believed that wars could be influenced by the way their conduct was perceived through the media. This is based on several premises that could bear further academic research, namely that watching audiences would become antiwar if they saw its true horrors on the television screen in an age where censorship is near impossible. This perhaps exaggerates the power of the medium and underestimates the intelligence of the viewers. The second premise is that global and especially national audiences have become casualty averse, especially in democracies. A third premise is that television organizations do actually have the operational capability of *mediating* the realities of modern warfare, if they had the desire to do so.

The Post 9/11 World

These are significant issues, especially since the terrorist attacks on New York and Washington on September 11, 2001. Although barely noticed at the time, Al Qaeda that masterminded the attacks, had been using the Internet throughout the 1990s. Their first attempt to bring down the World Trade Centre had been in

1993 while their leader, Osama bin Laden, proclaimed his jihad against the United States in 1996 Bin Laden, a Saudi Arabian by birth, had been part of the Islamic religious mujahedeen resistance to the Soviet invasion of Afghanistan during the 1980s. With Soviet withdrawal in 1989, and then with the collapse of the Soviet Union soon after, he formed Al Qaeda ("the base") whose followers believed they had defeated a godless superpower. With the arrival of half a million "infidels" during the second half of 1990 into the holy land of Mecca, as the Americans prepared for Operation Desert Storm to drive Iraq from occupied Kuwait, he focused on the United States. Following some successful terrorist attacks against US embassies in Africa and a strike on the USS Cole in Yemen, Al Qaeda then went for "the heart of darkness" in a classic "propaganda of the deed."

Almost 3000 people died on 9/11. The twin towers were hit at New York's morning rush hour and the second tower strike was shown live to a global audience by a host of the city's traffic helicopters. In fact, the first tower strike was also captured on film – by a French film crew working on a documentary about the New York City Fire department – but this was not broadcast until much later in the day. After that first strike 16 minutes was enough to get the traffic helicopters on scene and so when live television pictures were beamed around the world of strike two and the subsequent collapse of both towers, the reaction of many people was that it was "like watching a movie." This was precisely the point. Although throughout the 1990s, Al Qaeda had been using the Internet to transform terrorism into an international phenomenon, linking recruits and sympathizers in an unprecedented way, the mass media remained the principal source of information for most people on the planet, and of these, television was the most trusted. Besides, although there is no universally agreed definition of terrorism, attacks like these are only partly designed to kill innocent people. Their main intention is publicity – or propaganda designed to generate fear and counter-reactions that will serve the terrorists' cause.

On 9/11, this worked. Within a month, the United States and United Kingdom attacked Afghanistan and by Christmas had captured Kabul from the Taliban who had seized the Afghan capital in 1995 and thereafter allowed bin Laden and his followers to create a number of terrorist bases for training purposes. The main challenge for the US PSYOP teams that accompanied the Western special forces was how to convince the locals that they were not repeating what the Soviets had done, that they were "liberators" rather than invaders, not least because no one there had seen the 9/11 attacks because the Taliban had banned television. Yet what began as a manhunt was soon to transform into a global "War on Terror" and a fresh ideological conflict of the twenty-first century of no less significance than the Cold War. It makes the decade from 1991 to 2001 look like the inter-ideological war years.

A new global propaganda war in the era of a fast expanding Internet began. The terrorists understood that they might not be able to defeat militarily the Western forces, but that was not their objective. Al Qaeda spokesmen over time revealed their ostensible objectives: the removal of all "infidel" troops (men and women) from Islamic lands, together with the "apostate" Muslim rulers who had allowed them to be stationed there; the subsequent establishment of an Islamic caliphate under Shari'a law; and the destruction of Western free market liberal capitalism that had "triumphed" at the end of the Cold War. The latter was why the World Trade Centre was attacked. The strike on the Pentagon was the symbolic attack on American military megapower. Despite considerable worldwide sympathy for the United States immediately after the 9/11 attacks, the next few years would see a remarkable rise in global anti-Americanism about the way the United States seemed to be waging the Global War on Terror.

The Americans reacted to the 9/11 propaganda of the deed not with counter-propaganda but with military force, first in Afghanistan and then, in 2003, in Iraq. This might have been understandable in light of the shock over the first attack on United States homeland soil since the British burned the White House in 1812, but it fundamentally missed the point about what 9/11 was all about. When President Bush foolishly called the military reaction a "crusade," he was playing into the hands of Al Qaeda because, for them, that was precisely what this was. These were the final battles of a 1000 year crusade against the infidel crusaders who had plundered their lands, first of science and technology and now oil. The President apologized, but it was too late. On the Internet, such remarks become permanent "facts" that enable conspiracy theorists to create an alternative reality, and there are many people who are prepared to swallow that real life version of what was depicted in the Hollywood movie, *The Matrix*. So, as we have seen from earlier periods, words really do matter.

Many mistakes were made in the subsequent years that fuelled Al Qaeda recruitment propaganda. The biggest was perhaps the war in Iraq because there was no proven connection between 9/11 and Saddam Hussein, even though at one point 70% of Americans believed there was. The war was sold to domestic and international audiences on grounds that Saddam had weapons of mass destruction, but none were found even after Baghdad fell to the "shock and awe" military capability of a coalition consisting of only four nations, and this time – unlike Desert Storm - with no Arab partners. The subsequent insurrection against the coalition "occupiers" tore Iraq apart for five more years and saw many incidents of "collateral damage" and, perhaps the most damaging of all, images of prisoner abuse by American soldiers in the prison at Abu Ghraib. Interestingly, those images were taken as trophy pictures by the soldiers themselves, not by journalists. This proved that the age of the "citizen journalist" had well and truly arrived. Cameras on cell phones were now ubiquitous and were capable of Internet access. As the first decade of the twentieth century unfolded, we entered the era of Web 2.0 which enabled individuals to interact, and not just passively receive information from the Internet. User generated content fuelled the phenomena of YouTube and Second Life while social networking sites such as Facebook created an entirely new global opportunity for international propaganda. Governments and the "old" media were no longer the primary controllers of the flow of information.

Ethics and International Propaganda

However, governments still felt they needed to set the agenda and, post-9/11, there was much debate about "why they hate us so much." The rise of anti-Americanism prompted a renewed debate about public diplomacy and the struggle for hearts and minds, particularly in the Islamic world. There were even calls for the recreation of the USIA. Joseph Nye's concept of soft power, which he had first formulated back in 1990, was seen by many to be an alternative reaction to the military deployment of hard power. Soft power, Nye argued, was a means to success in a nation's foreign policy by virtue of being so attractive that others would want to be like you. The problem was that this "to know us is to love us" philosophy did not always work, especially with committed fanatics willing to kill themselves for their cause. The 9/11 hijackers were largely Western educated Arabs (16 of the 19 were from Saudi Arabia) who knew the Western value system – and hated it.

Scholars of propaganda recognize that it is almost impossible to change the minds of dedicated believers. The most promising target audience is the uncommitted or undecided. Perhaps the old maxim that actions speak louder than words still holds true. The worldwide enthusiasm for the election of President Barack Obama in late 2008 would suggest that the rise of global anti-Americanism was more related to US policies in Iraq and Afghanistan than it was hostility towards the universal values of life, liberty, and the pursuit of happiness. Although the Global War on Terror had already been rebranded as "The Long War," President Obama changed the entire rhetoric of the propaganda war. Instead of public diplomacy or strategic communications as the preferred euphemisms of democratic propaganda, he talked in his Cairo speech of "global engagement." One of his very first actions as President was to give an interview on Al Arabiya television, all of which seemed to signify a break with not only past rhetoric but also with past foreign policy. Whether it is propaganda, however it is labeled, or policy that will prevail in the again rebranded "struggle against violent extremism," only time will tell.

Propaganda studies have been enriched by a wealth of scholarship but hampered by a reluctance in democratic societies to call a spade a spade. Even the new US Psychological Operations doctrine published in January 2010 redefines propaganda as something only an adversary undertakes.[6] Democratic governments are afraid of the word more because of its historical abuse rather than a conceptual understanding of what it actually is as a form of persuasion. As one British official put it in the 1920s, "it was a good word gone wrong."

Notes

1 Plato (n.d.).
2 Ellul (1965/1973).
3 He was a member of the French resistance to Nazi occupied France.
4 Cunningham (2002).
5 Seligman and Johnson (1937).
6 www.fas.org/irp/doddir/dod/jp3–13–2.pdf (accessed August 19, 2010).

References

Army Information School (1946) Pamphlet Number 4: *Pillars of Peace, Documents Pertaining to American Interest in Establishing a Lasting World Peace: January 1941–February 1946*. Book Department, Army Information School, Carlisle Barracks, PA.

Cunningham, S.B. (2002) *The Idea of Propaganda: A Reconstruction*, Praeger, Westport, CT.

Ellul, J. (1965/1973) *Propaganda, the formation of men's attitudes*, Vintage Books, New York.

Huxley, A. (1958) *Brave New World Revisited*, ch 4, www.huxley.net/bnw-revisited/index.html (accessed August 19, 2010).

Plato (n.d.) *The Republic*, http://classics.mit.edu/Plato/republic.html (accessed August 19, 2010).

Seligman, R.A., and Johnson, A. (1937) *Encyclopedia of the Social Sciences*, vol. II, Macmillan, New York.

47

Modernization and Its Discontents
Ethics, Development, and the Diffusion of Innovations

Robert S. Fortner

Introduction

The idea of modernization is one fraught with discontent. This is partly due to its inherent interdisciplinary character. It cannot be understood fully from the perspective of merely one discipline, but must invoke several, including political science, sociology, economics, communications, agriculture, anthropology, psychology, and art. One analysis (Rozman, 2005) claims that "disagreements about what modernization theory is and what has been learned from comparisons bedevil discussions between users and critics.... Although the theory exerted a huge impact on the disciplines of history, political science, and sociology, and on thinking about capitalism versus socialism, East Asia versus Western advanced capitalist countries, and more versus less developed countries, to many its legacy remains confusing, as does its connection to recent globalization theory. Even at the beginning of the twenty-first century, there is little agreement on what modernization theory is and how it has advanced social science analysis."

Modernization theory was entwined with issues of development and the media as a result of the work of two pioneers, Daniel Lerner (Lerner, 1958) and Wilbur Schramm (1964). Lerner (1958) was so convinced of the superiority of the US model for modernization that was the foundation of the theory that his study of the Middle East claimed that Islam was "absolutely defenseless" when it came to defending its traditions (pp. 45–48). For his part Schramm (1964) claimed that information was "one of the basic rights of mankind, and an indispensable requirement for the freedom and dignity of the world's people. Beyond that, it is a tool for accomplishing certain things the overwhelming majority of nations want" (p. 249).

The Handbook of Global Communication and Media Ethics, First Edition. Edited by Robert S. Fortner and P. Mark Fackler.
© 2011 Blackwell Publishing Ltd. Published 2011 by Blackwell Publishing Ltd.

But "both authors were working as US propagandists.... Both works explored the link between the mass media and national development in Third World countries, identifying the individual citizen's behaviors (such as the need for achievement, deferred gratification and empathy) as the primary cause of a nation's underdevelopment. Both view[ed] the mass media as the crucial conduit to the individuals actualizing their empathy and ultimately satisfying their needs and gratifications. Most importantly, both publications had a lasting influence on the formation and implementation of international development programs targeted at developing countries..., promoting a formula that would later be termed the dominant/modernization paradigm of development communication, and criticized by others as the dependency paradigm" (Bah, 2008, n.p.). Christopher Simpson's (1994) history of the relationship between communications research development and psychological warfare strategies makes the case that Lerner's studies in the Middle East contributed to the creation of "development theory" and that "combined propaganda, counter-insurgency warfare, and selective economic development of targeted regions was rapidly integrated into U. S. psychological warfare practice worldwide" (p. 85; see also Uche, 1994, p. 43; Frank, 1969; Ferraro, 1996).

Essentially development theory during the 1960s and 1970s was Cold War theory – driven by the fall of China to Mao in 1949 and Cuba to Castro in 1959, the Korean War, the Indochina civil war that eventually became the Vietnam debacle, the embrace of Communism in Egypt after the Suez Crisis – all of it seemed to confirm the "domino theory" first articulated by the Eisenhower/Nixon White House and subsequently endorsed by John F. Kennedy. (Ninkovich, 1994). Irving Lewis Horowitz (1965/1972) divided the planet into three worlds: first, second, and developing. These worlds were defined ideologically – capitalist-based democracies, state-dominated communist societies, and the developing world that emulated, or fused, the two alternative models. Development implied "a genuine break with tradition" (p. 24). However, this classical theory was criticized from a variety of directions and many claimed that it, rather than a theory of development, was a theory of dependency (see Frank, 1969; Ferraro, 1996; Yergin and Stanislaw, 2004; and Wallerstein, 1976, 2004). Perhaps the clearest statement of the ideological underpinnings of development theory came in the subtitle of W.W. Rostow's book (1990), *The Stages of Economic Growth*. The subtitle: *A Non-Communist Manifesto*.

Three recent books (Ekbladh, 2010; Gilman, 2003; Latham, 2000) have examined this history of modernization theory and its relationship with American foreign policy at the time. Their evaluations of the relationship and of the lasting impact of this theory, however, differ. Ekbladh begins his analysis by concentrating on the role of the perception of other countries within the West. "A crucial part of the perception of the 'backwardness' was the way these societies and cultures were viewed. A perceived lack of thrift, discipline, and promptness as well as traditional beliefs, indolence, and superstition prevented people in such places as Africa, India, and China from mastering modern technology. This perception regularly manifested itself in a belief... that these peoples were little more than children. Their inability to internalize the behaviors necessary for modern technologies to be effectively utilized made them appear to be lost in a state of arrested development" (Ekbladh, 2010, p. 19). "The assumption [of modernization theory] was that through the instruction and use of modern technologies the outlooks of people would be altered" (Ekbladh, 2010, p. 55; see also Stiglitz, 2002, p. 164). He credits Lerner's book, *The Passing of Traditional Society*, as achieving "near-canonical status" that reinvigorated a nearly 30-year-old assumption: "modernization was catalyzed by technology. The most powerful catalysts were mass communication technologies, particularly newspapers and radio. These media exposed people rooted in traditional structures to new opinions, attitudes, and ideas that created a greater empathy and association with others. This exposure also gave them new desires and aspirations and carried them away from older social structures" (Ekbladh, 2010, p. 173). Rostow saw Communism as an alternative means to achieve modernization, but in a "deformed" way (Ekbladh, 2010, p. 175). His "explicitly Cold War tract," (Ekbladh, 2010, p. 185) *The Stages of Economic Growth*, originally published in 1960, laid out the assumptions of modernization theory as it had developed since the 1950s and argued that the United States had to be involved in leading the modernization process (Ekbladh, 2010, p. 185). A variety of criticisms were leveled at the assumptions of these theorists in the 1960s and "discomfort with the implications of modern life made the prescriptions for widespread and dramatic social and psychological transformation that lay at the core of modernization less palatable" (Ekbladh, 2010, p. 237). As new ideas for "sustainable development" began to take hold, "'modernization' fell into disuse" (Ekbladh, 2010, p. 250), "increasingly seen as a label for a chauvinistic approach too dependen[t] on evolutionary universals" (Ekbladh, 2010, p. 250). In the 1970s the idea of appropriate technology replaced the old TVA-style massive investment project style thought to have the potential to raise entire societies to greater levels of modernization. The term itself "had been cast out of the international lexicon as strategic imperatives demanding its application had dissipated and its unintended consequences could not be ignored" (Ekbladh, 2010, p. 255).

Gilman's (2003) critique of modernization theory tracks with that of Ekbladh, but emphasizes some different dimensions of its development and application. He summarizes the story of modernization theory this way: "from the late 1950s through the 1960s, modernization theory dominated American social scientific thought regarding economic, political, and social change in the postcolonial world. Rooted in the contrast between 'traditional' and 'modern' societies, modernization theory posited the existence of a common and essential pattern of 'development,' defined progress in technology, military and bureaucratic institutions, and the political and social structure" (p. 3). But, Gilman argues, the approach was too simplistic. "If modernization theory was misguided in many ways, it also signified a necessary and serious attempt to grapple with the intellectual and policy issues that decolonization raised in the context of the cold war" (Gilman, 2003, p. 3). One main difference between Gilman's argument and that of Ekbladh, is that while Ekbladh saw modernization as the manifestation of conservatism in opposition to the "left," that is, communism, Gilman argues that it is best understood "as a manifestation of American postwar liberalism" (Gilman, 2003, p. 4). It included "technological advancement, urbanization, rising income, increased literacy, and the amplification of the mass media (Gilman, 2003, p. 5). It aimed toward "homogenization" in the American style (Gilman, 2003, p. 6). And, whereas Ekbladh emphasizes the polito-military struggles – such as those in Korea in the 1950s and Vietnam in the 1960s – as correctives to American expectations for modernization, and the death of the Soviet Empire as the end of a Cold War mentality, Gilman emphasizes that the failure of modernization theory should be understood to be the consequence of liberals' loss of faith. It was, to him, merely the inability "to sustain a transforming vision of the future in the absence of a classic progressive belief in the virtue of the people or the Enlightenment faith in the perfectibility of man" (Gilman, 2003, p. 19).

The assumption underlying the modernization efforts as envisioned by American social scientists, according to Gilman, was that if economic growth could be encouraged in "backward" countries, "the masses as a whole would benefit" (Gilman, 2003, p. 36). "The mission… was to 'modernize' the postcolonial world, to deliver its members to the secular heaven that the United States had pioneered. The aim was to spread the virtues of 'the American way of life,' an expansive phrase that included culture, technology, sociability, and piety" (Gilman, 2003, p. 69). A second assumption "was that development entailed a universal convergence on a monolithic 'modernity'" (Gilman, 2003, p. 100). In other words, eventually all countries would look alike – homogenization would occur (Gilman, 2003, p. 101). The end product, where this modernization and homogenization would lead, was an "ideal-typical baseline," that is, the West, for example, the United States (Gilman, 2003, p. 101). To accomplish this change, diffusion was implied (Gilman, 2003, p. 24) – diffusion of technology, democracy, social structure, even culture.

By the mid 1970s, Gilman says, modernization theory had collapsed: "What had died was the notion that there existed a singular and knowable path to a kind of materialist redemption or salvation in the form of modernity" (Gilman, 2003, p. 218). Finally, Gilman spends time (2003, pp. 225–240) outlining both the conservative and liberal objections to modernization theory that contributed to its demise, and then the postmodern critique (Chapter 7). The collective result of critique, of failed assumptions, and of the consequences of theory (such as the underpinnings of the Vietnam conflict), was "a deep sense of cynicism and pessimism about the future" (Gilman, 2003, p. 250).

Latham's (2000) principle concern is with the underlying ideology of modernization. He defines modernization as an ideology: "a conceptual framework that articulated a common collection of assumptions about the nature of American society and its ability to transform a world perceived as both materially and culturally deficient" (Latham, 2000, p. 5). This ideology was based on use of "value-free" social science that could discover universal laws "and apply them to produce knowledge independent of the viewpoint of the scientist…. Objective social analysis … could provide the fundamental tools necessary for shaping the world's future"

Modernization and Its Discontents   937

(Latham, 2000, pp. 48–49, referencing Talcott Parsons). "Liberal, capitalist modernization… was a universal process with a decidedly beneficial impact on the individual and society" (Latham, 2000, p. 53), the example of what could occur through modernization – the United States. As Latham explained,

> The essential qualities found only within Western civilizations had led to their prodigious advancement, but other societies could still look to that history for lessons to follow. Because deviations from the charted path would only delay a necessary and vital transformation, nationalistic resistance on the part of the developing society was xenophobic and irrational. The process was universal, but the catalysts of change were Western, and the West had the power to accelerate a desirable and ultimately inevitable process. … [These conclusions] were… held to be the product of objective, scientific analysis coupled with the fulfillment of disciplinary purpose, national mission, and patriotic, ethical duty (Latham, 2000, pp. 66–67).

Diffusion of Innovations

Not all aspects of the modernization thesis were abandoned, however. Everett Rogers (1969), for instance, used both Rostow's notion of "take-off" and the idea of diffusion in his work on modernization. Rogers (2003) defined diffusion as "the process by which (1) an innovation (2) is communicated through certain channels (3) over time (4) among the members of a social system" (p. 11). His model of the diffusion process included the "take-off" idea that Rostow had suggested.

Rogers (2003) argued that people went through a decision process about any innovation in which he or she is "motivated to reduce uncertainty about the advantages and disadvantages of an innovation" (Rogers, 2003, p. 172). This process had three phases: an awareness-knowledge phase in which information about an innovation was found to exist; a how-to knowledge phase in which information about how to use an innovation properly is obtained; and a principles-knowledge phase in which people discover information about how an innovation actually operates and what its underlying principles are (Rogers, 2003, p. 173).

Rogers' approach to modernization was influenced by the earlier scholarship in other important ways. First, he defined modernization as the change in individuals (1969, p. 14), placing himself squarely within the American political tradition. Second, he focused on the role of mass media in overcoming resistance to modernization, and the research he claimed, "indicates the crucial, integral role of mass media in modernization" (1969, p. 99). Third, he too was looking for universals and thought of modernization as a process that was equally applicable to all societies. The crucial issue (as it had been for Schramm) was that national governments were committed to this process – then it would become (as Lerner argued) invincible and the traditions that resisted it defenseless. He even told a personal story (Rogers, 1969, pp. 96–97) of a visit to an Indian village 30 miles from Delhi where he found a television set in a school. Although "alarmists" warned that "soon" it would be

938   *Robert S. Fortner*

difficult to find "virginal settings from which to obtain comparative data" to demonstrate the universals of modernization, he said, "this problem is not yet crucial."

Rogers' social science orientation and his commitment to a universal model of modernization led him to create an adopter model that provided the basis to compare individuals over time who adopted innovations and to determine the characteristics that influenced a person to adopt an innovation early or late. Using a slightly modified standard bell curve (with 2 standard deviations on one side and three on the other), he provided the basis to think of individuals as innovators (the first 2.5% to adopt an innovation), early adopters (the next 13.5%), early majority adopters (34%), late majority adopters (another 34%) and laggards (16%).

The advantage of Rogers' approach over earlier explanations of modernization was that it did not depend on any national commitments – as would be required, for instance, to build a dam, extend the electricity grid or improve the transportation infrastructure – and thus provided a means to understand the individual decisions that might be made in regard to investing in, or adopting, a single-user innovation. At the same time, however, the typology did not take account of the role of family or community relationships as an influence on adoption, or the fact that in many developing countries technologies would not be individually owned, but community "owned," that is, used within groups (see Sherry, 2002). So the typology continued to be driven by assumptions emerging from the individualistically-inclined culture of the West. Shelton Gunaratne (2009) argues that the concept of globalization itself has excluded non-Western cosmologies by depending on the "oligopoly of the social sciences" inherited from the modernization/development paradigm (pp. 60–61). Karin Wilkins (2007), writing about development communications, one of the strands of research that can be traced back to modernization and diffusion theories, writes: "By privileging national political and economic conditions at the expense of global, regional, and community dynamics, media development appears more squarely ensconced within modernization paradigms".

The danger, as Jeffrey James (2003) puts it, is that:

> It is precisely because of the importance… ascribed to technical change as a source of economic growth that our view of the way in which innovations are actually generated, appropriated and spread among different countries bears so heavily on what we think will be the dispersion over time of growth rates between rich and poor countries. On the one hand, there are some economists whose view of these technological relationships leads them to expect a convergence of per capita incomes between countries at different stages of development. On the other hand, if we take a different view of how technologies are generated, appropriated and diffused internationally, it is not difficult to conceive of a process of economic divergence, whereby the gap between rich and poor countries becomes larger rather than smaller over time.

It is also the case that depending on the transnational character of much modern communications and media technology to effect change assumes too much "power" for technology. It smacks of technological determinism. Beyond that is the existential reality of people's lives within individual countries, especially those who are

Modernization and Its Discontents

rural, poor, or otherwise on the margins of survival. The relevance of this? "This basic and extraordinary fact about human beings… we survive and flourish not by instinct, but by behavior that is learned, preserved, and transmitted…. [We] are nearly instinct-deficient: left to our own devices without even our most basic technological achievements, most of us couldn't survive for even several weeks. Lacking agricultural knowledge and the tools used to hunt, we would starve, if first we didn't freeze or become a modest meal for a wild beast. Lest our race be forced to begin discovering anew the most basic activities necessary for survival – how to cultivate crops, how to build shelters, how to communicate … – we transmit this knowledge through institutions and traditions. Indeed, there can be little doubt that the greatest technology of human origin and making is culture itself" (Deneen, 2008, p. 65). Later in his essay Deneen explains the practical implications of understanding this "extraordinary fact": "Everyone knows that if you have a problem with a computer, you go to the youngest person in the family for advice about how to repair it: ancestral knowledge replaced by constantly up-to-date. So, too, we professors are told that we need to adapt our teaching to the modern technologies used by our students, as if these won't in fact influence the teachings themselves. If all technologies ultimately replace themselves with something else, we are living in a time when our technologies are replacing the original and essential human technology of culture" (p. 70).[1]

This human technology of culture, with its traditions that have been crucial to survival, is based on what Walter Ong (1982) called memorable thoughts (p. 34). The necessity of such thought in survival situations is what saves lives. It is the substance of culture. The imposition of media technologies that obscure this reality, or that distract people from what is truly important to their wellbeing is thus not development but regression. The mere fact that such media become ever more technological capable, make connection more ubiquitous or provide access to data not seen before, is no testimony to its value in such situations. It is only the connectivity it provides to certain others – those who can actually improve the situation of a family or community – that can truly said to be developmental. Kang (2007) argues that "technology does not exist in the vacuum of culture" [sic] (1). What he means – as he goes on to explain – is that technology (in this case the Internet) is neither determinative of society nor essential to it – culture socially shapes the meaning of technology. This is a point emphasized by Lim (2007) in the Asian context. It is also the implication, I think, of Youngs and Allison's (2008) complaint that technology, in studies of globalization, is treated "exogenously" rather than "endogenously," that is external to change rather than integral to it. "Globalisation studies writ large have not adequately treated technological change as an intrinsic part of understanding what is happening in the world or given it a central place in addressing the whole meaning of the concept of globalization. This exogenous tendency identifies technologies as merely tools or instruments, means to ends, in other more important social processes. This tendency to locate technology outside the social dynamics is arguably a long-standing problem in social science that has limited analysis of social change in the past as much as in the present"

940   *Robert S. Fortner*

(p. 4). Nevertheless, the diffusion process continues to be instrumental in under-girding the study of the spread of communications technology (see Lunn and Suman, 2008), along with metaphors such as "the global village" (Shah, 2008).

Taking all these positions into account alters the focus of change. Technology is not an exogenous input into a society that is gradually adopted by individuals within it, but rather an object, or state of mind (Ellul's *la technique*) that responds within an existing tradition to a new possibility

In this model the sociocultural context of a society may be welcoming or resist-ant to change. Those societies that are interested in change must have access to a technology and affinity for what it offers. Access is affected by the existence of necessary infrastructure, attitudes of mind toward technology, the availability of funds for investment, the existence of time to use the technology, and so on. If availability, access, and affinity are all present, then people (either individually or corporately, within or without a particular community) may or may not explore the technology, based on a perceived value or lack thereof. Any technology with this perceived value may be provided to a community by intervention. This interven-tion may come as a result of familial diffusion from urban (where the technology is likely first to arrive) to rural through purchase and pass-through, or as a result of sharing among families or between generations. When this occurs, diffusion results within a community. The technology may then be shared across units within the community, as a radio or television set may become (at least virtually) a community asset. This diffusion, depending on the nature of the technology itself, may then alter tradition (and thus achieve "modernization" to a degree), or be absorbed within tradition (thus having little to no impact on the level of tradition vs. mod-ernization already present). In either case, the new reality becomes the socio-cultural context through which any subsequent technological intervention will be screened. The process is both dynamic and iterative (see Figure 47.1).

Ethical Issues in the Diffusion of Innovations

In the original days of modernization theory, there were assumptions that American and Western national security was at stake (See, Canon, 1980, p. 200). There were fears, especially after the defeat of Nationalist forces in China by Mao Tse Tung's army, that the developing world would fall domino by domino into the immoral forces of communism. Although the Cold War ended with the disintegration of the Soviet Union in 1991, it was soon replaced by concerns with the spread of nuclear weapons, the rise of Islamic fundamentalism, and then the so-called "war on ter-ror." A similar logic to that of the Cold War was employed as justification for con-fronting this new menace – the "axis of evil" was actively supporting the training of terrorists and the further spread of weapons of mass destruction. Similar rhe-torical strategies were also used, such as labeling and establishing the black-and-white nature of the conflict. "President Bush's declaration of the 'war on terror' with the famous statement 'either you're with us, or you're with the terrorists'

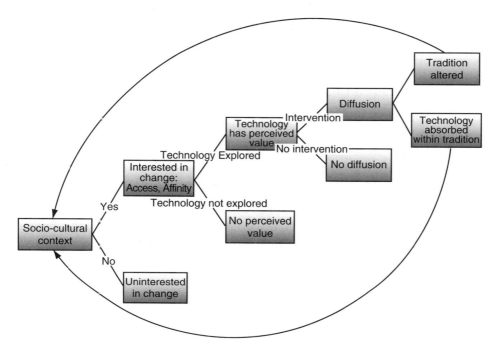

Figure 47.1 A decision-tree model of technology adoption within a specified socio-cultural context.

leaves no space for those disagreeing with the strategies and tactics adopted by either side. Such a binary, Manichaean distinction is also ill-suited to constructive political discourse" (Busch, 2006, p. 8).

What this means is that the foundation for providing development assistance has changed little since the original articulation of modernization theory, despite its loss of legitimacy in the 1970s. Priorities have changed, yes, but not the original impetus – to protect the United States through adroit application of development aid to at-risk countries. As one United Nations report (UNCTAD, 2009) put it, "actual or perceived threats to national security have become more numerous. Although the Cold War has ended, there are now many more local and regional conflicts, as well as terrorist attacks that can strike seemingly at random" (UNCTAD, 2009, p. xiv; see also Rosati, 2004).

The ethical difficulty created by this foundational logic is that "national security" concerns trump ethics hands down. The United States, as a result, has supported – even if reluctantly in some cases – ethically odious regimes who were defined as "bulwarks against communism," promulgated coups against democratically-elected governments (where such governments otherwise would have been defined as "good" due to their democratic foundation), or invaded various countries that were defined as significant to American security. This is however, merely one aspect of the failure of modernization and development theory to respond to long-standing democratic values.

Related to this are the ethical issues raised by both the Cold War, instability in the world (some created by the United States or its allies), and the war on terror in regard to internal policies. I suggest that the Bill of Rights, duly adopted by state ratification, established an ethical framework for US government relations with its citizens. This framework has often been violated in the interests of national security. As Jason Keiber (2006) has argued, "Simply asserting that the NSA [National Security Agency surveillance] program is necessary and respects civil liberties is not enough. In fact, downplaying the need for debate is dishonest and incommensurate with how Americans view civil liberties. Our struggle against terrorism appears to have no definite end. We must not allow the indefinite eavesdropping on Americans without requiring a court order or other oversight" (2006, p. 1).[2] An invitational discussion at the Brookings Institution (2003) contained this statement as part of its online report on the event: "Another speaker noted that during the Cold War, there were no rules about privacy; the definition of the enemy – and therefore the lengths to which government could go – kept expanding. It wasn't until Watergate that accountability and judicial oversight became important concepts" (see also Carafano, Gaziano and Kochems, 2005; Prieto, 2009). As the Center for National Security Studies' website (n.d), quoting James Madison to Thomas Jefferson on May 13, 1798, reminds us: "Perhaps it is a universal truth that the loss of liberty at home is to be charged to provisions against danger, real or pretended, from abroad." And, as Daniel Farber (2008) has said, "Threats to national security generally prompt incursions on civil liberties" (p. 1).

From an ethics perspective, I think these issues pitting national security against civil liberties or democratic traditions are the least interesting, however. The more difficult ones to unravel have to do with basic assumptions underlying approaches taken to modernization and development. What, at root, drives the decision to assist others? In the early modernization period, as well as in the later development and diffusion period, there were three unquestioned assumptions. First was the assumption that democracy and capitalism were morally superior to communism. This assumption was never defended; it was seen as self-evident.

Second, the need for development was assumed. It would occur, the theorists thought, one way or another, so it was preferable (and ethical) that it occur on the American model (ala TVA) rather than the state-control model of the Soviet Union. The fact that development under the Tennessee Valley Authority was itself a state-directed activity more Soviet than American in style was not an issue for theory. Also, the sort of development proposed through the period of the Cold War was based on a massive investment model – infrastructure was the focus: transportation, power grids, rehabilitation of sites for tourism, and the like. It was nation to nation development with only ancillary attention to the subsistence communities far removed from national capitals. This only began to change with the appropriate technology movement and the diffusion models that were introduced in the late 1970s.

Third was the assumption of universals. There was a universal path to modernization – it would happen everywhere following the same path. People would

Modernization and Its Discontents 943

universally respond to modernization – all individuals in a country where modernization began would fall into line over the course of time. This was especially true in diffusion theory where people would be categorized according to their orientation toward innovation but all (even the laggards) would eventually be onboard. Modernization/development was universally good, despite the changes that it might bring to community and family life, or preferences that might be perceived to exist as one tribe, area, or ethnic group modernized more quickly than others. Such differences might occur because there were more "innovators" in one group and "laggards" in another, but such labels were not merely analytical categories but also value or ethical judgments within a world where decisions to gain greater access to, and use of, technology was defined as a value for all to emulate. In other words, the trailing end of the bell curve was a value statement about the relative worth of those whom it purported merely to describe.

At least some fault for these assumptions must be laid at the feet of social science methodology. The methodologies used had two flaws. One was the individualistic bias of the methods – individuals were interviewed – sometimes many thousands of them – to assure a representative sample of the relevant national population (see Hallin and Mancini, 2004, p. 4). From these individual interviews would develop essentially a law of modernization, development, or diffusion that could then be applied to other similar cases. Unfortunately, seeking such a law of universal application to individuals gave short shrift to tradition (it was after all the starting point of modernization and would eventually be jettisoned as more individuals joined the throng of adopters), culture, religion, geography, and topography – as well as to psychological distance from dominant urban, political, or tribal constituencies. In other words, the methodology did not take into account the existential realities of day to day life among most of the people in the developing world who were outside elite circles. As Ellen Rose (2005) writes of the assumptions of "technology transfer" – a related concept to diffusion and development, "it is useful to consider the ideology that underlies many descriptions of the role of media and technology within traditional cultures: technology transfer. 'Technology transfer' refers to the process whereby a technique developed in one place is transferred wholesale to another place, the latter often a developing nation; but the term also refers to a way of conceptualizing and describing innovation and development that is characterized by a focus on tools and technological choices, and by a quest for theories, economic models, and conceptual frameworks to aid in quantifying the effects of technological innovations on the developing world." This approach, Rose says, has two deficits: deep roots in "a post-Enlightenment thoughtworld [sic] and value system" and a "tacit representation of the developing world as a passive receiver of Western innovation" (2005, pp. 4, 5).

Applying the universal law of modernization also required that, when it did not seem to work as well, that some reason for its failure be determined. The culprit was "culture." Some cultures were more accepting of the positive change offered by modernization (Weber's Calvinist Protestants) than were others. Despite Daniel Lerner's early claims (1958) about the inability of Islam to withstand the forces of modernization, the Middle East eventually was discovered to be quite resistant to change. So it's Islamic culture was to blame: "Using a comparative approach, often closely patterned on Western models of development, … analysts identified a process of modernization against which a country's progression could be charted. The model assumed many guises but tended to coalesce around certain characteristics, namely, rationalization, national integration, social stratification, economic change, and political autonomy…. It was assumed that as countries developed, their populations would shift toward the adoption of scientific knowledge and evolve from subsistence farming to commercial agricultural production and industrialization" (Deegan, 2005, p. 21). It "was assumed that modernization would eventually lead to democratization, even if… countries had first to go through an authoritarian phase to achieve rapid modernization…. [T]he historical evidence does not support a culturally deterministic explanation for failure in either modernization or democratization in the Muslim world and elsewhere" (Hunter, 2005, pp. 14,15; a slightly different interpretation of the role of culture can be found in Inglehart and Welzel, 2005, especially Chapter 2).

Culture is significant, however, when it comes to ethics. Given the ethics underlying the assumptions with which modernization and development theorists approached their tasks, it would even be fair to say that they were ethically imperialistic. They presumed certain ethics (such as those promoted by democratization, industrialization, and diffusion, increased communication, civil liberties, increased incomes and, with these, better education) not only in the theories themselves but in the aftermath of modernization efforts. Such ethics would, quite simply, exist. They were part of the package. But moral contents are variable (Salvatore, 2007, p. 87).

The implications of this, in Salvatore's analysis (2007), is that the morality that was part and parcel of culture prior to modernization (or the movement away from tradition, in Rostow's terms), became part of the public sphere of life (the "lifeworld"), while in the public sphere faith or morality became the basis for the development of "secular trust" (p. 216). "It comes as no surprise that as a result of the transformation the new private and public spheres were made to fit the capitalistic formations of the new era. However, the new approach obscured the diagnosis of modernity as intrinsically dynamic and conflict laden and produced transhistorical views of the public sphere and of its relations to the private sphere" (Salvatore, 2007, p. 217). Given the role of the state in assuring public order, it is no wonder that the ethical implications of modernization were obscured, both by the submersion of local communities and traditions into a lesser status that could easily be ignored when creating universal laws applicable to nations, and by the rationalization implied and necessitated by democratization if people were to become self-governing. Trueness to ones tradition, faith, values, and family ties were less necessary (or may even have been harmful) to the public trustworthiness needed in the homogenized public sphere.

Two later developments also hobbled whatever progress had been made in the modernization enterprise. First was globalization. At first blush globalization may

Modernization and Its Discontents 945

seem to simply build on the modernization/development thesis – it is diffusion writ large. However, globalization did not bring the utopia of a "global village" to the world. It actually entangled the media in the war on terror and changed the global media environment to defang much propaganda by opening what were once discrete markets into one free for all that no single nation could monopolize (see Buck-Morss, 2002, p. 17). It brought the trivialization and scintillation of sensationalist news, inane musical and "reality" contests, and high levels of commercialism to those who accessed it (see Parker, 1994, pp. 51–53). "What we really and urgently require is a globalization of moral responsibility" (Halloran, 1994, p. 182).

Second was the development of the digital divide, the situation in which the world currently exists, a world where those with access to rich information content become wealthier and those with little access to information continue to exist on the fringes. (See Kenny, 2002, on the problems of infrastructure development in rural areas, and Jin and Cheong, 2008, on the different definitions of the digital divide.) The center-periphery issues originally raised by Harold Innis continue to hold sway, with those with central control of the global information system consolidating their hold with increasingly expensive capital investments and distribution agreements, while those who have always lacked access by and large continuing to do so, or falling even further behind (see Picciotto, 2001; in India even with the use of information technologies to alleviate poverty, one study found that clients did not feel fully empowered by the arrival or use of these technologies, that distribution of access was uneven, and that the actual needs of people were not necessarily addressed by technology implementation strategies (Harris and Rajora, 2006, p. 3).

These two realities raise the question as to what ethics is truly possible as technology develops and becomes distributed. Is it ethical for those in wealthy urban enclaves to increase their capacity both to impart and receive information – thus meeting the standards of the international convention on the right to communicate – while those in poverty (even in proximity to such enclaves) and in distant rural areas of subsistence agriculture (where the majority of the world's population still resides) continue to languish outside the orbit of global information? But wait. If global information is, in fact, trivial and sensationalistic, does even that matter?

I want to approach the answer to these questions, which I take to be ethical at their root, from a different angle. The International Center for Media Studies (ICMS) has been conducting research in the developing world for several years. In August 2009, ICMS completed research in three areas of Indonesia (Aceh, Karawaci, and West Timor), and on Luzon Island, Philippines, both in and outside Manila and in the northern area of Banawe. We were curious as to if, and how, people were using technologies such as mobile telephones, radio, terrestrial television, satellite television, and the Internet. We came away from this research, not with a law by which development or diffusion should be governed or predicted to occur, but with a typology of uses to which people were putting technologies. We also came away with some of the variables, or factors, that seemed to affect the amount of use that was made of technology and the means by which technology was introduced into new communities.

First, the typology. We classified the respondents in our research into five groups, based on the number of technologies they used and the level of understanding they had of the technologies. Those who had the greatest level of use were technophiles. They used many different information and communication technologies and they had a complex understanding of what they could accomplish with each one and how to accomplish it. Next were those who used several technologies but who tended to do so in a limited way, using only some capabilities of each one. Those they did use they understood and could manipulate with some facility, but they did not fully explore the capabilities of each technology. We called them multiusers. Third was a group who had invested in a limited number of technologies and whose understanding of each one was also limited. These were lesser users. Fourth were those who only invested in, and used, a single technology. It might be only a mobile telephone, or only a radio, or only a television. They used this technology only for its most basic purpose – making voice calls, listening or watching media material. These were the uniusers. Finally were the nonusers. They were off the technology grid altogether, neither using nor understanding any of the available technologies. Due to the ethnographic nature of our research, we do not have predictions of the percentages of people in each group, and we make no representations about the movement (speed or demographic variables that influence) of people from one classification to another. However, we were able to identify what we believe to be basic determinants, or influences, on the uses made of information and communication technologies. These include: (1) economic ability – just how much income is available to an individual or family directly or indirectly (say, via, a relative working abroad) to invest in technology; (2) population density – those who lived in more densely-populated areas seemed to use more technologies than those in sparsely-populated areas. This is likely to be due to greater levels of availability, more reason to use them, and less expensive pricing due to competition; (3) social pressure – those in peer-cohort groups (such as students) tended to adopt technologies faster, understand them better, and use more of them; (4) exposure through education or occupation – those enrolled in schools or working in businesses where communication activities were necessary (email, fax, voice, text, etc.) tended to use, and understand, more technologies than others; (5) distance and relationship – the further people were from cities the less use they tended to make of these technologies, unless members of their family were distant from them and thus there were perceived good reasons to invest so as to stay in touch; (6) infrastructure – those nearer cities were more likely to be on electricity and wired information grids, facilitating the use of televisions, satellite dishes, and the Internet – or even to do the prosaic – charge a mobile telephone; (7) disaster – those who had lived through a disaster were more likely to use advanced technologies because of the intervention of the international relief and humanitarian community that imported or constructed infrastructure that was left in place after departing.

People, families, and entire communities were faced both with pressures toward use of these technologies and for not using them. Factors mentioned by people that encouraged their use within families were infrastructure (the better the more likely to be used), population density (more people, more use), exposure to technology and curiosity about it (tending to be the result of occupational or educational requirements cr observing others using it), access to education (the more education the more use, and especially the creation of nontraditional peer networks such as when students across castes, classes, tribes, or other traditional divisions were put together in school), and social pressure (if one's friends were using, it was more likely that one would also use). Factors that pulled the other direction, or discouraged use, were satisfaction with life (the more satisfied, the less use), reliance on traditional networks within communities for connection, economic ability (poverty discouraged use), age (younger people were more likely to use a technology within a family first), fear of the unknown (not knowing what a technology might provide – or fearing what it might provide – discouraged use), and nontechnological priorities (engagement in subsistence farming, obtaining electricity or clean water in the home, dealing with health and medical needs all discouraged use).

Also, when families were split up, with members leaving the home village to seek employment or join the military, the connections to those left behind were thin. These thin connections, along with the existence of younger people who were exposed to formal education, provided the incentive and often the means to bypass barriers to communication (lack of income, distance, satisfaction with life, fear of the unknown, etc.). Disasters, too, played a significant role. Not only did the arrival of international aid carry with it the seed of infrastructure development, but the disaster itself disrupted traditional ways of accomplishing tasks by destroying communities, decimating families (or worse), and providing new incentives for crossdivisional cooperation among people formerly at odds.

These apparent realities have been confirmed by other more generalizable research results from ICMS research in both East and West Africa, and in Nepal. Many of these observations considered factors such as the important roles of family income, distance from metropolitan centers, and the role of education play in determining the use of technology (see Fortner, 2008).

So what does all this have to do with communication and media ethics? There are a variety of important responses that must be made to this question.

First it is important to recognize that all the different manifestations of modernization/development/technology transfer/diffusion that have emerged since the 1950s have depended on the use of media as a change agent within countries that were in the process of change. Also, of course, any diffusion that occurs within any society depends on information being spread through communication. So in these respects both media and communication are essential to these processes. They cannot be separated. Everett Rogers (1974) makes this connection clear: "(1) … at present, the mass media play a major role in creating a climate for modernization among villagers, but are less important in diffusing technological innovations – although their potential for doing so is high; (2)… mass media channels are more effective when combined with interpersonal channels, as in media forums; and (3)… the traditional mass media, such as village theater and traveling storytellers, have an important potential for development purposes, especially when they are combined with the modern electronic and print media" (p. 44; see also Skuse, 2001, p. 2 and Economic Commission for Africa, 2003).

Beyond the ethical issues raised earlier, then – such as the distortions created in considering ethics by claims of national security or the assumption that through individualistically-oriented interviewing of people in developing countries universal laws can be developed to predict the future of diffusion or modernization – what other ethical concerns are raised by efforts to assist countries develop? The first issue concerns the use of data itself in analyses attempting to show "progress" from traditional society to modernity. For instance, a study by Chinn and Fairlie (2004) attempted to discover what factors were most significant in creating the global digital divide in computers and Internet penetration. The data used in this study came from the International Telecommunication Union, an organ of the United Nations that collects its information from relevant national compilations. It is not in a position to challenge state submitted claims. Those in the international research community are well aware of the often-questionable data published by the ITU and try to avoid it, preferring instead the data gathered in the field.

The ethical issue raised by such research is that it can inform decisions made by development organizations about investments that are assumed to speed up or facilitate development. Since there is a limited amount of assistance available for development, it is important that the analyses available and the implied advice they offer to assist funders to make the right investments be as accurate as possible. Otherwise even altruistically-driven investments can be wasted. People who might have been helped continue to languish. Justice for the poor and fairness in the allocation of resources are denied.

Another ethical issue is raised by the attention to technology as a catalyst for growth (and the development of a global civil society) that fails to account for the abilities of people in developing countries. Mobile telephones and computers become ever more complicated. The development of the Internet is premised on ever wider bandwidth available for broadband applications. The technological marvels introduced within the wealthy countries (Smartphones, the IPad, 3G capable laptops), if they are available at all in developing countries, are restricted to the wealthy few in metropolitan areas by and large. While this provides the basis for expanding the global civil society, it also divides the people in developing countries, with the information-rich increasingly interacting with colleagues abroad, while leaving their poorer brethren to fend for themselves. For instance, I have taken Africans to poor parts of their own countries where they were shocked by the situation of their countrymen. Yet these same people were accustomed to carrying on email conversations with those they knew in the West. In one study ICMS undertook in the Makassar language in Indonesia in 2008, it was not unusual to see young people in the city using a Blackberry while in rural areas where there was no electricity except by generator, people would listen to the radio together, or watch television in a neighbor's home, because the money was not available to them to invest in technology (including mobile telephones). People lived in different worlds.

Modernization and Its Discontents 949

In the interconnected world, then, if there is a right to communicate (as Article 19 of the UN Declaration on Human Rights suggests), it is a very uneven right. The inability of perhaps 2 billion people to exercise this right in any meaningful way creates, just as the internal digital divides create, a misshapen humanity – heavily muscled and powerful on one side and weak and atrophied on the other. Diffusion of technology and the development of media and interactive communication systems have not ameliorated this situation; in many respects they have exacerbated it – disentangling culture from the human condition in some cases and leaving all-too-human problems unaddressed for others. The solidarity that would be required for a people to demand that their basic needs be a priority for government has been weakened by unequal access. The delivery of new services via the Internet (such as telemedicine or tele-law) has been restricted to the few. The inequalities of opportunity, access to infrastructure, education, adequate nutrition and healthcare between urban and rural areas continues to imbalance societies as more and more people migrate to cities only to find themselves living in urban squalor rather than rural poverty and they remain largely apart from the glittering cities upon whose fringes they exist. In Africa the penetration of mobile telephones has skyrocketed, but most remain largely unused because people cannot afford to purchase the airtime to use them. In West Timor those with mobiles outside the cities restrict their use so that they do not have to trek so often to distant friends to recharge where there is electricity. In eastern Nepal where new private and community radio stations are slowly developing, most people still do not hear signals because of rough terrain and lack of radio sets. Television remains largely absent. Computers are restricted to cybercafés and then only when electricity is available. Mobile telephone towers are too far apart to provide reliable service. Kathmandu is a distant place, both physically and psychologically. There is no real right to communicate in such circumstances.

None of these ethical problems are easy to solve, even when people have the noblest intentions. However, considering them should be part of the conversation when development topics are on the table, when assumptions about the diffusion of technology are brought up. There is no "right to progress," and progress itself is problematic when foisted on skeptical or unwilling communities. If the people of this planet are to achieve completeness, telos, shalom, in the twenty-first century, then the love of humanity that might make that possibility real must proceed not by technological fixes, but by true understanding – a state we have yet to achieve.

Notes

1 Pfaffenberger (1992, p. 508) discusses the technology of culture as development that is not driven by the modernist assumptions of progress, but by a "sociotechnical system" based on activity "in which knowledge and behavior are reciprocally constituted by social, individual, and material phenomena."

2 Richard A. Posner (2001) argued shortly after 9/11 that civil liberties should be curtailed as a result of terrorism that targeted the United States, saying that the Bill of Rights was not a suicide pact. Clearly, then, there are ethical arguments to be made on both sides of this issue.

References

Bah, U. (2008) Daniel Lerner, Cold War propaganda and US development communication research: An historical critique. *Journal of Third World Studies*, (Spring) http://findarticles.com/p/articles/mi_qa3821/is_200806/ai_n25418589/ (accessed August 2, 2010).

Brookings Institution (2003) Balancing civil liberties and national security in the post-9/11 Era: The challenge of information sharing, June 5, www.brookings.edu/events/2003/0605technology.aspx (last accessed February 1, 2010).

Buck-Morss, S. (2002) A global public sphere? *Situation Analysis*, (1), October, 10–19.

Busch, A. (2006) GCSP policy brief No. 10: Ethics, civil liberties, globalization, and global security, September 28, Geneva Centre for Security Policy, Geneva, Switzerland.

Canon, D. (1980) Intelligence and ethics: The CIA's covert operations. *The Journal of Libertarian Studies*, 4 (2), 197–214.

Carafano, J.J., Gaziano, T., and Kochems, A. (2005) Domestic surveillance: Dual priorities, national security and civil liberties, must be met. December 21, The Heritage Foundation, www.heritage.org/Research/HomelandSecurity/wm950.cfm (accessed August 2, 2010).

Center for National Security Studies (n.d.) www.cnss.org (accessed August 2, 2010).

Chinn, M.D., and Fairlie, R.W. (2004) The determinants of the global digital divide: A cross-country analysis of computer and internet penetration, Center Discussion Paper No. 881, Economic Growth Center, Yale University.

Deegan, H. (2005) Culture and development, in *Modernization, Democracy, and Islam*, (eds S.T. Hunter and H.Malik), Praeger, Westport, CT, pp. 21–34.

Deneen, P.J. (2008) Technology, culture, and virtue. *The New Atlantis*, (Summer), 63–74.

Economic Commission for Africa (2003) Report on indicators of information and communications technologies and the impact of information and communications technology at the country level, April 10, Committee on Development Information, United Nations Economic and Social Council Addis Ababa, Ethiopia.

Ekbladh, D. (2010) *The Great American Mission: Modernization & the Construction of an American World Order*, Princeton University Press, Princeton, NJ.

Farber, D. (2008) Introduction, in *Security v. Liberty: Conflicts between Civil Liberties and National Security in American History* (ed. D. Farber), Russell Sage Foundation, New York, pp. 1–23.

Ferraro, V. (1996) Dependency theory: An introduction, www.mtholyoke.edu/acad/intrel/depend.htm (last accessed January 19, 2010).

Fortner, R.S. (2008) The impacts of technological adoption and religious radio programming on information flow and communication patterns in East Africa, New Media and Religious Transformations in Africa Conference, July, 10–12, Abuja, Nigeria.

Frank, A.G. (1969) *Capitalism and Underdevelopment in Latin America*, rev. edn, Monthly Review Press, New York.

Gilman, N. (2003) *Mandarins of the Future: Modernization Theory in Cold War America*, The Johns Hopkins University Press, Baltimore, MD.

Gunaratne, S.A. (2009) Globalization: A non-Western perspective: The bias of social science/communication oligopoly. *Communication, Culture & Critique*, 2, 60–82.

Hallin, D.C., and Mancini, P. (2004) Americanization, globalization and secularization: Understanding the convergence of media systems and political communication in the

U.S. and Western Europe, in *Comparing Political Communication: Theories, Cases, and Challenges*, (eds F. Esser and B. Pfetsch), Cambridge University Press, Cambridge, UK, pp. 25–44.

Halloran, J.D. (1994) Developments in communication and democracy: The contribution of research, in *The Global Political Economy of Communication*, (ed. E.A. Comor), St. Martin's Press, New York, pp. 165–185.

Harris, R., and Rajora, R. (2006) *Empowering the Poor: Information and Communications Technology for Governance and Poverty Reduction: A Study of Rural Development Projects in India*, UNDP Asia-Pacific Development Information Program, Bangkok.

Horowitz, I.L. (1965/1972) *Three Worlds of Development: The Theory and Practice of International Stratification*, Oxford University Press, New York.

Hunter, S.T. (2005) Introduction, in *Modernization, Democracy, and Islam*, (eds S.T. Hunter and H.Malik), Praeger, Westport, CT, pp. 1–20.

Inglehart, R., and Welzel, C. (2005) *Modernization, Cultural Change, and Democracy: The Human Development Sequence*, Cambridge University Press, Cambridge, UK.

James, J. (2003) *Bridging the Global Digital Divide*, Edward Elgar Publishing Limited, Northampton, MA.

Jin, J, and Cheorg, A.W.H. (2008) Measuring the digital divide: The exploration in Macao. *Observatorio (OBS*) Journal*, 6, 259–272.

Kang, I. (2007) Technology as culture: Social shaping of the Internet in Korea and Japan. Annual Meeting of the International Communication Association, May 23, San Francisco, CA.

Keiber, J. (2006) National security and civil liberties. *Director of Studies Strategy Report*, 2 (3) 1, Center for Strategic and International Studies, Washington, DC.

Kenny, C. (2002) Information and communication technologies for direct poverty alleviation: Costs and benefits. *Development Policy Review*, 20 (2), 141–157.

Latham, M.E. (2000) *Modernization as Ideology: American Social Science and Nation Building in the Kennedy Era*, University of North Carolina Press, Chapel Hill, NC.

Lerner, D. (1958) *The Passing of Traditional Society: Modernizing the Middle East*, Free Press, New York.

Lim, H.-C. (2007) Globalizing Asia: Towards a new development paradigm. *Globality Studies Journal*, 9 (August 10), 1–11.

Lunn, R.J., and Suman, M.W. (2008) A longitudinal examination of Internet Diffusion and adopter categories. *Observatorio (OBS*) Journal*, 6, 97–110.

Ninkovich, F.A. (1994) *Modernity and Power: A History of the Domino Theory in the Twentieth Century*, University of Chicago Press, Chicago, IL.

Ong, W. (1982) *Orality and Literacy: The Technologizing of the Word*, Methuen, New York.

Parker, I.C. (1994) Myth, telecommunication and the emerging global informational order: The political economy of transitions, in *The Global Political Economy of Communication*, (ed. E.A. Comor), St. Martin's Press, New York, pp. 37–60.

Pfaffenberger, B. (1992) Social anthropology of technology. *Annual Review of Anthropology*, 21, 491–516.

Picciotto, S. (2001) Democratizing globalism, in *The Market or the Public Domain: Global Governance and the Asymmetry of Power*, (ed. D. Drache) Routledge, New York, pp. 335–359.

Posner, R.A. (2001) Security versus civil liberties. *The Atlantic*. (December) www.theatlantic.com/doc/200112/posner (last accessed February 1, 2010).

Prieto, D.B. (2009) War about terror: Civil liberties and national security after 9/11: A CFR working paper, February, Council on Foreign Relations, New York.

Rogers, E.M. (1969) *Modernization among Peasants: The Impact of Communication*, Holt, Rinehart & Winston, New York.

Rogers, E.M. (1974) Communication in development. *The Annals of the American Academy of Political and Social Science*, 412, 44–54.

Rogers, E.M. (2003) *Diffusion of Innovations*, 5th edn, Free Press, New York.

Rosati, J.A. (2004) At odds with one another: The tension between civil liberties and national security in twentieth-century America, in *American National Security and Civil Liberties in an Era of Terrorism*, (eds D.B. Cohen and J.W. Wells), Palgrave Macmillan, New York, pp. 9–28.

Rose, E. (2005) The wiring of Bhutan: A test case for media ecology in the non-Western world. *Proceedings of the Media Ecology Association*, 6, 1–13.

Rostow, W.W. (1990) *The Stages of Economic Growth: A Non-Communist Manifesto*, 3rd end, Cambridge University Press, Cambridge, UK.

Rozman, G. (2005) Modernization theory. *New Dictionary of the History of Ideas*, The Gale Group Inc. *High Beam Research*, www.highbeam.com/doc/1G2–3424300497.html (accessed August 2, 2010).

Salvatore, A. (2007) *The Public Sphere: Liberal Modernity, Catholicism, Islam*, Palgrave Macmillan, New York.

Schramm, W.L. (1964) *Mass Media and National Development: The Role of Information in the Developing Countries*, Stanford University Press, Stanford, CA.

Shah, N. (2008) From *global village* to *global marketplace*: Metaphorical descriptions of the global Internet. *International Journal of Media and Cultural Politics*, 4 (1), 9–26.

Sherry, L. (2002) Sustainability of Innovations. *Journal of Interactive Learning Research*, 13 (3), 211–238.

Simpson, C. (1994) *The Science of Coercion*, Oxford University Press, New York.

Skuse, A. (2001) Information communication technologies, poverty and empowerment. Dissemination Note No. 3, Social Development Department, Department for International Development, London.

Stiglitz, J.E. (2002) Participation and development: Perspectives from the comprehensive development paradigm. *Review of Development Economics*, 6 (2), 163–182.

Uche, L.U. (1994) Some reflections on dependency theory. *Africa Media Review*, 8 (2), 39–55.

UNCTAD (2009) *The Protection of National Security in IIAs*, United Nations, New York.

Wallerstein, I. (1976) *The Modern World-System: Capitalist Agriculture and the Origins of the European World-Economy in the Sixteenth Century*, Academic Press, New York.

Wallerstein, I. (2004) *World-Systems Analysis: An Introduction*, Duke University Press, Durham, NC.

Wilkins, K. (2007) Retro-theory resurfacing: Positioning media development within development participation, Annual Meeting of the International Communication Association, May 23, San Francisco, CA, www.allacademic.com/meta/p170206_index.html (last accessed January 20, 2010).

Yergin, D., and Stanislaw, J. (2004) *Commanding Heights: The Battle between Government and the Marketplace that Is Remaking the Modern World*, Simon & Schuster, New York.

Youngs, G., and Allison, J.E. (2008) Globalisation, Communications and Political Action: Special Issue Introduction. *International Journal of Media and Cultural Politics*, 4 (1), 1–6.

48

Communication Technologies in the Arsenal of Al Qaeda and Taliban

*Why the West Is Not Winning
the War on Terror*

Haydar Badawi Sadig, Roshan Noorzai, and Hala Asmina Guta

Introduction: Exercising Virtual Global Trespassing While Residing in Caves

The last decade of the twentieth century witnessed major changes in the global political, economic, and social landscapes. The collapse of the former Soviet Union and the Berlin Wall, globalization, and global terrorism are hallmarks of a sharply altered twenty-first century. In our opinion, the sharp turn that took place at the threshold of this century, on September 11, 2001, is the culminating event which bears all the marks of the events preceding it, including the rise and fall of the Soviet Union and the massive military mobilization of US Armed Forces to eject Saddam Hussein from Kuwait. The reading of this turn as only a collision between Islam and the West is a shortsighted one. The attacks have more undercurrents and more far reaching imprints and implications on the global political and socioeconomic landscape that elude the attention of most observers.

In terms of international security, the possibility of war among great stateactor powers, which used to be the driver of international politics, has diminished. Instead, the threat comes from nonstate actors (Jervis, 2009). Muslim grievances just happened to be on the crossroads, at a tangential point, with the West. Muslim extremists, as nonstate actors, happened to be very adept at taking full advantage of what the present global advancements in communication and transportation technologies offer. Inheriting and effectively using the massive anger against imperialism and multinational corporations' greed, masquerading as US state policy and protecting the interest of "the American people," militant Muslim extremists became a real "Super" power, with minimal cost in treasure and blood. Putting the emphasis on the West versus Islam misses the point.

The Handbook of Global Communication and Media Ethics, First Edition. Edited by Robert S. Fortner and P. Mark Fackler.
© 2011 Blackwell Publishing Ltd. Published 2011 by Blackwell Publishing Ltd.

While it is fatal to ignore the hard-power logistics of Islamic extremism, it is now becoming increasingly clear that it is equally, if not more, fatal to put more emphasis and such huge resources on fighting the powerful windmills of Islamic extremism. True, in the twenty-first century, terrorism will continue to be the most serious challenge to the United States and Western interests (Cronin, 2002/2003). However, looking at this challenge from this prism alone isolates it from its larger global context and the contribution of the West itself in creating it.

The prevalent limited view of Western strategists that looks at Islamic extremism as a hard-power "military" threat, led the United States and its allies to use more massive hard-power to eradicate it. The futility of this approach stems from the fact that Western militaries are operating in a parallel world to the mostly virtual world in which the true strength of extremists grows exponentially. This parallel world is a world of soft-power, a world where communication is key, and where technology, mountainous terrain, cave-protection, and a powerful ideology are combined to empower people residing in caves to elude most sophisticated people and the most hard-powered states of the world. Using cave protection as defensive-offensive sanctuary is the most powerful, least expensive, and oldest form of hard-power no other form, no matter how advanced, can match. In this sense, as 9/11 has shown, a skyscraper becomes seriously vulnerable to the long hand of the destructive power residing in a cave thousands of miles away. In this sense, it is as if the powerful advantages of new communication technologies transformed the cave into the most powerful military tank that moves and shakes without actually moving and shaking. Those who operate from such a virtual defensive-offensive space can practice global- virtual trespassing, frequently eluding the most sophisticated means of traditional detection.

This essay presents a viewpoint, and then it describes what inspired it. A rudimentary examination of the use of information and communication technologies (ICTs) by al Qaeda and the Taliban is what promoted us to think critically, and deeply, about current counterterrorism approaches. This chapter does not claim to provide a full description of such a use. Nor does it claim to provide a fully developed and articulated evaluation of a phenomenon. What we hope to achieve is to articulately introduce the problem to the reader in the hopes of adding more relevant and urgent material to stir more debates to pave the way, through an ethics of communication approach, to rethink present counter-terrorism approaches. Our expectation is that this will be read in conjunction with other chapters in this volume to add to the mix a relevant perspective and pertinent material that may assist us in posing more urgent global communication ethics questions.

Our global communication environment is making virtual – global – trespassing easier than ever before. It emboldened more and more terror-communicators to defy state actors and all traditional limitations of space and time. Before we turn to the mostly descriptive part, we discuss why it is important to study the use of communication technology by Islamic extremists in this deeply troubled world of ours. The following section, describes the use of ICTs by militant Islamic extremist at the global and local levels. We discuss al Qaeda's use of the Internet at the global level as we pay a closer attention to the local level by investigating Taliban's use of ICTs in Afghanistan.

Al Qaeda and Taliban: Always a Step Ahead of the "Crusaders!"

Presently, the West operates not in the core world of extremism but in its periphery, its supportive source of power, its hardware capability, military, and otherwise. Initially, the United States and its allies were able to remove the Taliban from power and destroy the training camps of Al Qaeda in Afghanistan, an operation that took them only weeks. In subsequent years since then, however, these militant Islamic extremists were able to regroup and even expand to other parts of the world, using their status as "victims" of the "crusaders," as a powerful ideological tool to further expand the boundaries of their parallel world. This is what makes the emphasis on using military power, which is always subject to the limitation of time and space over other more important soft-power means to eradicate extremism more futile than ever. As nonstate actors become more adept at always being ahead of the game, it is least productive, and more destructive, to fight them with mostly traditional-state based approaches.

If the current state-actor approaches continue, extremists will always be ahead of the game. This is simply because they are better communicators of their message to their target audiences than state actors are. The traditional state in the West, in spite of its massive military, diplomacy, and publicity machines, at least presently, is no match to terror-communicators in using history, ideology, and technology, to augment their status as a superpower.

The collective mentality of Western state actors, as agents of imperial interests, perceiving the Western state as "too big to fail" and "we shall prevail," is the source of its real destruction. Former versions of al Qaeda and the Taliban, by historical happenstance, were hardened in the mountains and valleys of Afghanistan, by bloody engagement with the Soviet Union, itself a product of Western imperialism. In the process, they were hugely empowered by the United States, in its own aggressive imperial quests (through military, logistics, communication, and intelligence aid). Being at the heart of an historical crossroads of imperial conflict, with canny ability, al Qaeda and the Taliban deeply understood Western vulnerabilities and the significance of the opportunities this historical moment presents for them to be major players.

As terror-communicators, operating between the cracks of mammoth machines of hegemony, they now have a firm grip on the initiative in moving and shaking international security hard-power and soft-power alike. This firm grip on the initiative, without a doubt, will continue to make terror-communicators confuse and further weaken its adversaries with the least expensive, most cost-effective means if present counterterrorism approaches continue to be employed.

Terror-communicators have the upper hand in deciding where, whom, when, and how to hit, and more importantly how to frame and communicate why they do so.

In the process, they make everyone who boards a commercial flight take off their shoes before they do so, and have their bodies – their most sacred sanctuaries – searched and exposed to invasive scrutiny. As simple as these security measures may seem, they should not be seen just as mere inconveniences necessary sacrifices for collective and personal safety. They should be seen as real, tangible, and proof that terror-communicators are increasingly succeeding in changing our relationship with modernity – in this case flying in a modern machine.

This, perhaps, should challenge us to see terror-communication as a perverted new chaotic and most powerful form of postmodernism. Without acknowledging this, we will not resolve present day global security problems. Such massive influence on daily modern behavior in the United States by the Soviet Union, and vice versa, would have been a massive achievement against its adversaries. Being at the crossroads of these two state-actor superpowers, militant Muslim extremists seem to have understood Western mentality. They seem to have understood it in both its Soviet and European-American forms, using one against the other, ejecting the Soviet Union from Afghanistan, with the support of the United States, the ambitions and fears of which ultimately led to the creation of al Qaeda, the supreme entity of terror-communication. Islamic militants, as the new antagonist of the West, with very little cost, seem to be more successful than former superpowers in twisting the arms of their perceived enemies. Changing arrangements of daily activities of citizens of enemy states, like air travel procedures and check-ups when entering government buildings are constant reminders of this mischievous success.

When a single actor, trying to detonate a bomb from his underwear, leads the sole traditional superpower to doubt its ability to fight the enemy, aimlessly allocating additional huge resources nonetheless, the core of this superpower is in serious trouble. Umar Farouk Abdulmuttalib failed to detonate the device he planted in his underwear on board his flight to Detroit, but he achieved the actual goal of the act, which is to terrorize target audiences in a patient war of attrition where using the sensation of the drama-of-war is more important than winning the war itself. In a sensation hungry media environment, well understood by terrorists, media attention is what makes terrorists tick. They got it by recruiting, brainwashing, and exploiting the person in Umar Abdulmattalib, the underwear-bomber. In this sense, the underwear bomb story, in the mind of a terrorist, becomes more important than the person, more important than the detonation of bomb, and, perhaps, more important than the explosion of the plane. Without detonation, the purpose, which is maximum publicity of a terror-generating "staged" event, manufactured as much by sensation hungry Western media as by terrorists themselves, was served, and the mission accomplished. In this sense, violence becomes an ancillary to the terror-machine, not the machine itself. However, the West continues to deal with violence as violence, as though terrorist violence is the main device of ingenious terrorists. By continuing expensive and massive mobilizations of military forces, against an elusive enemy living and functioning in a parallel world of soft-power, the West effectively continues to allow itself to be the gift that keeps on giving. This, in the mind of a terrorist, is where the "West was won" even before the war officially started in Afghanistan.

Unless terrorism is seen as foremost a communication phenomenon (that uses staged violence to maximum publicity effect), the West will be wasting precious blood and treasure – of its own and of the Rest. If we are to create a major dent in the current approach, in hopes of fixing it, a major paradigm shift is warranted. Fighting terrorism in the new paradigm must be conceived as a joint venture between the West and the Rest, in which the human agency of counter-terrorism nonstate-actors must be at the core of action, with state-actors being enablers.

In such a new approach, all people are mobilized – using mechanisms thoroughly devised, through public debates led mostly by nonstate actors, with firm support from state-actors – to be effective and productive participants, in the fight against terrorism. As the recent economic troubles of the world tell us, the global interconnectedness of our new world makes it imperative for people the world over not to see ourselves as just nationstates, led by state-actors, and not to see our demographic and natural resources as just resources of our own "national" interest. In today's world, there is not a single "national" interest independent from, and not connected to, "international" security, economic environmental interests. Present day terrorism, as a nonstate successful communication phenomenon, is living proof that we should inject fields of global strategy thinking with new approaches. By continuing its failed counterterrorism strategies, the West, inadvertently and sadly, continues to aid and abet the "enemy" by the very acts it employs to "patriotically" fight it, while the most violent machine the world has known, the US military, increasingly looks like a wounded mammoth.

A new, and creatively destructive, approach enabled a minority of Muslim extremists, the leaders of whom presently dwell in caves, to present themselves and their constituents as powerless victims, whose land has been desecrated by invaders! while, in fact, they are so powerfully empowered by the advent of new technologies thus making the cave itself a powerful natural machine more powerful than any advanced US weapon. It is the ironic alliance of the protection of the most ancient sanctuary, the cave, and the protection of the most sophisticated of present day technologies that makes al Qaeda and Taliban elude the most powerful violent machine of the world. That is to say, the cave – the most private space – and the Internet – perhaps the most public one that can be accessed most privately – come together to make terrorism, at least for now, invincible in relation to present approaches of its enemies in fighting it.

For instance, al Qaeda was able to expand its influence and operations to a number of countries and evolve into a global fluid horizontal network of networks from its "base" in the caves of Afghanistan (al Qaeda in Arabic means "the base"). By the same token, the Taliban were able to reorganize and, in fact, evolve into one of the most sophisticated and effective insurgencies in contemporary history, as will be shown, mostly because of advancements in new technologies. They have not only challenged the presence of Western forces in Afghanistan, but they undermined most efforts to bring security and the rule of law in the war-torn country. This, while the corrupt government installed by the West, in pseudo-democratic fashion, continues to be itself another gift that keeps on giving and giving the Taliban.

In a complete reversal of policy, the United States is now actively considering talking with the Taliban to engage them in national transformation in Afghanistan, after almost a lost decade of a senseless and failed massive military mobilization. During this lost decade, what helped militant extremists survive, thrive, and operate successfully operate, and expand exponentially, was the rapid penetration of the Internet and mobile communication technologies. The Internet in particular, in tandem with new information and communication technologies in general, has, in totality, become the most cost-effective soft-death machine in the history to be used in the fight against an empire. The US military, the traditionally most effective and most expensive institution, but currently inept and most hard-death machine of the West, is currently in limbo as it continues to fight modern creative terror-manufacturing nonstate entities.

As eloquently put by Daniel Kimmage in a New York Times column, "Al Qaeda made its name in blood and pixels, with deadly attacks and an avalanche of electronic news media" (Kimmage, 2008a). Kimmage's words cannot capture the militant Islamic extremists groups' strategy of new media technologies use better. For Bin Laden and his supporters, the battle's weapons of war are not guns and bombs, but rather bytes and electronic images. Guns and bombs are just accessories, and not the main ones at that, the electronic media are! Kimmage pointed out that the number of extremist related website grew from 12 in 1997 to 4500 by 2005; this astonishing trend reveals the special emphasis the extremist place on communicating terror. To the extent the Internet has aided globalized communication and interaction; it has by the same measure put global security at levels greater levels of risk not yet quite comprehended.

Global Internet Use by the Militant Islamic Extremist

One of the major aims of any militant Islamic extremist group is to attract attention and publicize its action "and then, through the publicity it generates, to communicate a message" (Martin, 2009, p. 384). This trend of attracting attention is not limited to present global militant Islamic extremists groups but rather a historical trend. As argued by Wilkinson (1990) "the history of terrorism totally disproves [the] … claim that violence is speechless.…All serious terrorist campaigns are characterized by frenetic use of every available access to the mass media" (p. 26). Militant Islamic extremist groups' awareness of the role of mass media in publicizing its actions and spreading their ideology is not a trend that appeared with the September 11 attacks. In an interview with Bin Laden in March 1997,

Peter Arnett of CNN asked Bin Laden about his future plans, and Bin Laden briefly answered, "You'll see them and hear about them in the media, God willing" (Arnett, n.d.) This brief answer reveals how al Qaeda had thought about the media as a main battleground, since publicity and communicating terror messages are so integral to its operations. Just two weeks after the deadly attacks of the World Trade Center, Bin Laden appeared on Aljazeera urging Pakistanis to fight any assault on Afghanistan by "crusader Americans" (MEMRI, 2007). Before the end of the year, Bin Laden released four video messages to the world carried by mass media, mainly through Aljazeera network (which dubbed by some as the CNN of Arabs). Up to 2009, al Qaeda and its allies had produced more than 60 broadcast messages of Bin Laden and second-in-command Ayman Al-Zawahri since September 11, 2001(Reuters, 2009).

Militant Islamic extremist groups, as many other violent extremists groups throughout history, manipulate media channels to advance their political agenda. Ayman Al-Zawahiri, the second in command of al Qaeda, was reported in 2005 to have stated that the battle of al Qaeda is not only taking place on the ground and traditional battle fields, but over the waves, "we are in a battle, and that more than half of this battle is taking place in the battlefield of the media" (Aaron, 2008, p. 268). The battle is characterized by al Qaeda as "a battle for the hearts and minds" of the "Umma [Islamic Nation]" (Aaron, 2008, p. 268). The open space of the Internet has effectively become the main tool through which al Qaeda and other militant Islamic extremists maximize their power and impact.

The blossoming of virtual communities through the Internet and new communication technologies, in turn, brings a new reality to understanding the usages and effects of mass communication. As Kellner (2007) stated, the Internet "expands the realm for democratic participation and debate and creates new public spaces for political intervention" (p. 18). Likewise, it expands the arms of political and militant extremism. Unlike other mass communication media, where gate-keepers play a role in what message is to be broadcast, the Internet creates an open space with no gatekeepers. The Internet grants any user free and unhindered access to communicate to the masses, thus making the individual, both as sender and end user, in command and control. Cammaerts and Van Audenhove (2005) acknowledged that the significance of the Internet is also derived from the role it plays in facilitating the creation of a global public sphere that permeates and transcends the traditional state boundaries.

Radical social movements and political groups, especially militant Muslim extremists, once excluded from the mainstream media, found in the Internet a powerful cost-effective alternative forum. The importance and uniqueness of the Internet comes from the fact that "it makes more information available to a greater number of people, more easily and from a wider array of sources than any instrument of information and communication in history" (Kahn and Kellner, 2006, p. 704). Scott and Street (2001) pointed out four major characteristics that made the Internet very attractive and useful for social movements.

1   Mesomobilization: the Internet allows for coordination between movements' networks globally (network of networks).
2   Editorial control: The Internet provides social movements with editorial control over content and image.
3   Bypassing state control: The Internet allows for organizations to bypass state control and communicate in a secure environment.
4   Cost: The Internet allows for high impact with low or limited cost;

Using these characteristics, the following section will discuss how the Internet became an ideal means of communication for militant Islamic extremists groups.

Mesomobilization of the Internet

The Internet allows for coordination between movements' networks globally to form what can be called a network of networks. After the September 11 attacks, and the subsequent international counterterrorism efforts, militant Islamic extremist groups have moved from a hierarchical structure to more decentralized but networked structures. The Internet is crucial to maintaining these nonhierarchical structures and remains very effectively connected, which provides a "critical tool for terrorist functionality and viability" (Gary and Head, 2009, p. 397). Militant Islamic extremist groups who share similar political agenda exploit this feature of the Internet to communicate, coordinate, and exchange information while maintaining their animosity. In a study entitled "The Al-Qaeda Media Nexus," Kimmage (2008b) identified at least seven groups that can be identified as al Qaeda allies. These are: Islamic State of Iraq, Ansar al-Sunnah (Iraq), Taliban (Afghanistan), al Qaeda in the Islamic Maghrib (Morocco and Algeria), Young Mujahidin Movement (Somalia), Jaysh al-Islam (Ghaza), al Qaeda in the Arabian Peninsula (Saudi Arabia) as well as global al Qaeda. According to Kimmage, all these groups produce and distribute messages through the Internet. Each one of these groups has its own organizational structure which can be thought of as a standalone network. Yet, in terms of communication, the Internet allowed for mesomobilization and creation of a formation of a network of these networks. This network of networks is comprised of three key entities that connect these movements to the outside world through the Internet: Fajr, the Global Islamic Media Front, and Sahab. While the production of the message is centralized, the distribution is not centralized; "a shifting array of forums acts as the primary distribution channel. Forums that specialize in the distribution of jihadist media contain special sections featuring statements released by groups and media organizations" (Kimmage, 2008b, p. 4). This system of distribution reveals how the Islamic extremists made use of the Internet to create a connected network that transcends national boundaries. To use Weimann (2006) words, militant Islamic extremist groups are now "less structured, less organized, less local, yet [are] much more dangerous" (p. 21). Each of the three outlets, Fajr, the Global Islamic Media Front, and Sahab, produce content for different groups operating in different locations and then distribute them online through different forums and websites, creating a mesonetwork with more than one center. The main militant Islamic extremist network was traditionally known as al Qaeda. However, this notion is no longer valid. Al Qaeda is increasingly transforming to a network of networks of smaller militant groups. However, geographically dispersed, these networks are able to connect and network across national boundaries thereby keeping the global movement alive. The Internet is the main medium for their extremely active and very effective communication. The seven groups that Kimmage's study identified are located thousands of miles apart, yet were able to produce centralized messages and through the Internet distribute that message as they needed in different forums creating multiple outreach channels and thus, giving a boomerang effect. What makes it truly daunting to fight militant Islamic groups, which effectively employ mesomobilization, is that it makes identifying and getting hold of the center extremely difficult, if possible at all.

Editorial Control

Schmid and de Graaf's seminal study *Violence as Communication* explained how historically militant and violent insurgent groups have used their violent acts to gain access to mass media channels. As we stated earlier, violence become a means to getting the real prize, which is publicity. Insurgent terrorists, in contrast to state terrorism, vigorously seek publicity (Schmid and de Graaf, 1983). Frederick Hacker mentioned that terrorists attempt to "frighten and, by frightening, to dominate and control. They want to impress. They play to and for an audience, and solicit audience participation" (Hoffman, 2006a, p. 173). Similarly, Hoffman (2006b) pointed out that terrorism is a violent act to attract attention and to generate publicity to communicate a message. Mass media serve as the contested ground for publicity. Wolfsfeld (1997), in his "political contest" model, explained that where one side of the conflict is the state, a powerful state, and another side of war is a group, weaker, such as protesters, terrorists, riots, rebels, revolutionaries, the control over the message is contested but it is unequal. Insurgent groups, militant Islamic extremists in this case, often try to "promote their own frames of the conflict while the media attempt to construct a story that can be understood by their audience" (Wolfsfeld, 1997, p. 31). Wolfsfeld (1997) went further and discussed how the contest takes place and how the news stories are developed in an "unequal war." In this unequal war, the Internet also provides the global militant Islamic extremist groups with the advantage of control over the production of their messages. As expressed by Miller *et al.* (2008), "terrorism is a battle over awareness, ideas and values" (p. 23). While violence in itself provides militant Islamic extremist groups with access to news, it does not provide control over image. Traditionally social movements "tend to have their messages framed unfavorably and even ignored by the established media" (Heath and O'Hair, 2008, p. 24). The Internet revolutionized the concept of violence as communication in the sense that insurgent groups can use the media not only to attract attention and communicate a message, but also to justify and contextualize their acts to supporters and opponents alike.

Militant Islamic extremist groups still use violence as a means to communicate their message. In the statement of one of al Qaeda leaders, during the September 11 attacks, "the cameras of CNN and other Western Media dinosaurs undertook the task of filming the raid [9/11] and sowing fear in its aftermath. It didn't cost al Qaeda a cent," (Aaron, 2008, p. 270). This reveals that al Qaeda considered September 11 attacks as a big media event, not merely a military operation conducted by civilians. It was conceived and engineered as a propaganda event from beginning to end, with "free" sensation hungry mass media at the core. Yet, the Internet provides the militant Islamic extremists with an opportunity not only to depend on the mass media to package the message for them, in excellent video form, for instance, but also to control the framing and communication of the message to the world. Through the Internet, militant Islamic extremists can produce their own message and send it globally. This reality is best described by Michel Moutot, who is in charge of terrorism coverage at the press agency l'Agence France-Presse (AFP), when he said in an interview:

> Terrorists do not really need us anymore to convey their message. The "official" media have been replaced by the Internet which, in the end, is much easier to use, much quicker and much more effective. Terrorist groups now have their own websites where they can convey their propaganda and, for most of them, they advise their readers and followers not to trust the media which are now seen as the enemy (quoted in Terrorism and Media, 2008, p. 20).

In a publication entitled "Al-Jihad al-Elami: Ta'seel was ta'feel (Media Jihad: Authentication and Activation," an article on jihad media in Iraq, on the website *haqnews.com,* the author defined the aims of jihad media as to:

> provide the public with the realities of jihad and its purposes and its effects; to the transfer of news, facts and information about jihad in a proper and well-documented manner within and outside the Islamic nation (*Umma*); to respond to lies and rumors that have arisen around jihad to challenge it; to challenge those who perform it; and to motivate Muslims to support and perform jihad (Rawashdi, 2008, p. 31).

From the above paragraph, it is apparent that the militant Islamic extremist groups have gone beyond attracting attention by simply committing acts of violence. The Internet has provided them with the opportunity to frame their own message, to address supporters as well as the "enemy" public. In the Bin Laden video that was released on January 2009, the message addressed a wide array of audiences: from supporters calling them to jihad, to the West and to Arab leaders sending them threats of opening new fronts. The video on YouTube received more than half a million views and 4000 comments as of January 2010. The Internet medium allowed Bin Laden to frame his message, develop his argument and address opponents as

Why the West Is Not Winning the War on Terror

well as supporters, empowering him with the flexibility, access, and cost-effectiveness that would have been impossible through traditional mass media.

Bypassing State Control

One of the Internet's main features as a facilitator for global and transnational communication, writes Weimann (2006), is "the nature of the network – its international character and chaotic structure, its global reach, its simple access, and the anonymity it offers" (p. 21). The Internet provides militant Islamic extremist groups with the opportunity to build networks and still bypass state control. Militant Muslims use this feature of the Internet in more than getting the message out. They use it for recruiting supporters, soliciting technical help and mobilizing financial resources. The London train bombing of 2005 is a case in point of the extensive use of the Internet, not only for propaganda, but for training and operation planning (Aaron, 2008). All these activities would have been near impossible without the Internet, especially when taking into account the tight state controls that militant Islamic extremists operate under, and the massive intelligence activities to counteract their lethal activities.

Low Cost

The Internet provides militant Islamic extremists the opportunity to reach large pools of audiences, and exact a very high impact, at minimal costs. Al Suri, one of al Qaeda leaders, articulates the low cost of the Internet, in comparison with other means of mass communication, saying:

> Let us not forget the large scale publication expenses are exorbitantly high and exceed the budgets and capabilities of most organizations, not to mention the inconceivable option of disseminating a particular jihadist ideology. The answer to overcome that difficulty lies in the internet and the Satellite television stations that have and are visiting the critical mass of households, rich and poor (quoted in Aaron, 2008, p. 274).

This reveals how al Qaeda and its allies have exploited the cost-effectiveness of the Internet to execute their communication strategy. Now we turn to the Taliban, who are hugely enabled by ICTs to compete with mainstream media and to provide their own version of events.

Taliban and ICTs

Communication is the heart of the new insurgency in Afghanistan. Leaders of the Taliban, the main insurgent group, are well-aware of the importance of psychological warfare and they are "winning the war of words" (International Crisis

Group, 2008; Nathan, 2009). For their activities, the Taliban draw on the rich history and culture of resistance in the country. They hybridize it with new strategies and tools, acquired from the rich, modern, and very effective experiences of their ally, al Qaeda, and other insurgent groups in the region.

The use of new ICTs by the Taliban is the main component of their psychological warfare and operations. This is made possible further by the establishment of telecommunications infrastructures and diffusion of mobile technologies in the post-Taliban rule of Afghanistan, and in the whole region. Though the expansion of mass media and diffusion of ICTs are considered to be an important component of a democratic society, their use by warring parties also raises some serious ethical questions. Here we turn to discuss these issues in some detail.

Post-Taliban rule media/communication development

Prior to the September 11, 2001, Afghanistan was an almost totally disconnected nation. The country lacked basic transportation and communications infrastructures because of the destruction caused by decades of war. Furthermore, fundamentalist interpretations of Islam by the Mujahideen groups in the early 1990s, later cemented by the extremism of Taliban, hindered the expansion of media and communication technologies in the country. Under the Taliban, television, movies, music and even photos, were forbidden. They banned every form of communication except simple voice communication. The teledensity in Afghanistan was one of the lowest in the world. In 2001, out of the 33 000 landline phones available in the country, 12 000 lines were in Kabul, the capital of the country. These landlines were based on the old Soviet-made analogue system, and most of them were destroyed during the decades of violence (Noorzai, 2007).

Though in the last year or two of the Taliban's rule *Thuraya* satellite phones were in use in Afghanistan, they were limited in number and only used by a very few individuals, mainly drug smugglers, relief organizations, and warring parties. In terms of mass media, only state radio stations were operating, which were used for propaganda purposes by the Taliban. The Internet was used by some relief organizations; however, in 2001, the Taliban banned the Internet and ordered that no one, except Taliban's leadership, could access the Internet (Noorzai, 2007).

In the post-September 11 Afghanistan, one of the main achievements in the development and reconstruction process in the country has been the expansion of telecommunications infrastructure and penetration of mobile telephony. By January 2010, around 10.4 million mobile phone numbers were in use, and mobile signals covered the areas of the country where 80% of the population were living. In addition, the Afghan government, with the technical and financial support of the international community, is trying to provide broadband connectivity to major urban centers in Afghanistan and to connect the country with neighboring states and the world through fiber optics, wireless and other technologies (Ministry of Communication, 2010).

Rich history of mediated resistance

The Taliban consider themselves the heirs of Afghan Jihad against the Soviet Union and a legitimate force to fight against "foreign occupation." They adopted some of the strategies and tools used by Afghan resistance movements in the past. Besides using traditional and small media, the Taliban are also increasingly using new ICTs. The use of new technologies enabled the Taliban to be quick and efficient in their operation and communication of their messages to reach wider audiences, not only in geographical terms, but also by framing and packaging them in different formats and languages.

For their communications with local communities, the Taliban depend mainly on the use of traditional and small media. These include traditional and religious networks, night letters, folk poetry, posters, photos, tape cassettes, and so on. Historically, these channels were used as powerful weapons in the hands of resistance, which, by definition, is composed of nonstate actors. The advantage of small media is that they are participatory and decentralized in nature and not easily controlled by states and big corporations (Noorzai, 2006).

One of the most important of these channels has been *shabnama* or night letter. They are called night letters because they are posted or delivered at night, and those distributing them try to be anonymous. These night letters are hand-written on regular paper; however, in recent years, letter pads are also being used by the Taliban. Night letters are posted or delivered mainly at public places, such as the door or walls of Mosques or places where people gather. Though targeting the public, sometimes, these letters are also addressed to a person or a family.

Night letters have been used in Afghanistan to convey oppositional messages to the public, particularly in the areas where the insurgents do not have direct control (Noorzai, 2006). The Taliban use night letters for their announcements and communication with the local communities. This medium is also used to threaten a particular person or community. For instance, night letters were used by the Taliban to intimidate those locals working with the United States installed Afghan government and international forces into quitting their jobs.

Another channel used by the Taliban to convey their messages is tape cassettes. Since tape players are available in most houses and people are familiar with them, they have become a popular medium. These cassettes are recorded mainly in Pakistan. They are available in cassette shops in Pakistan. In Afghanistan, these cassettes cannot be accessed over the counter; however, they are distributed through effective private channels. Though cassettes have been used for conveying different messages, the Taliban use them mainly for motivational purposes. The genres used for the content of these cassettes are mainly poetry and songs. According to the Taliban's interpretation of Islam, all forms of instrumental music are considered to be un-Islamic. Therefore, Taliban's religious song, also called *tarana*, has only lyrics. Besides being commonly used by Islamic groups in the Middle East and other Islamic countries, they heavily borrow from forms of traditional Afghan poetry. They have deep cultural roots and are used as important channels for conveying resistance messages.

The audiences targeted by these cassettes include members of the Taliban, supporters and sympathizers. Topics and issues covered in these songs range from global/regional issues to very local topics. These songs have mainly religious and nationalistic themes supporting the Taliban's ideology and activities. New themes, such as considering execution of suicide attacks and supporting them as legitimate, are also poetically framed and packaged in these songs, generating powerful sentiments. Thus, the Taliban effectively uses historical and religious discourses in their songs to promote and legitimize their activities and violent actions.

Picture posters have also been used by the Taliban. However, this does not mean that all these communication tools, forms, and contents are conceived and disseminated by the Taliban alone. Other individuals and groups that are not associated with the Taliban may also use the same, or similar, messages and channels. Publicizing a picture of an Afghan woman being searched by a foreign soldier might not have anything to do with the Taliban (since this is a commonly protested act, even by supporters of Western presence). However, the Taliban may still get the credit for it because it has established itself as the most powerful terror-communicator. Also, footages of poets reading anti-American/Western and antigovernment poems are circulated, through mobile phones and the Internet, by ordinary Afghans who might not be supporting the Taliban.

The impact of the content packaged in traditional media easily finds its way to the Internet and all forms of mobile technology. Old media, in this sense, is no longer old. It is only old in genre, but form, content, and framing of messages, constantly adapt to the demands of the moment, the here and now, effectively building on history and tradition.

Taliban's use of old mass media

The Taliban publishes a number of magazines printed in Pakistan. The Taliban's magazines provide information on their organization, structure, and leadership (Nathan, 2009). Magazines became very popular during the civil war of the 1990s. As well as local individuals and groups, opposition entities were also publishing periodicals abroad targeting both local and Afghan Diaspora readerships. Though banned, these opposition publications are effectively distributed to the public, through well-lubricated and well-tested private channels. Hard copies of these magazines can be accessed in Pakistan. Using the Internet, the Taliban also provide soft copies of these magazines online.

In Afghanistan, radio is the main source of mass communication (Noorzai, 2006). Historically, the broadcasting outlets were controlled by the government. In addition, during the years of conflict, a number of transborder radio stations started broadcasting, targeting Afghan audiences. Under the Taliban, radio was the only broadcasting medium. Changing the name of Radio Kabul to Radio Shariat, the Taliban used the medium for their "Shari'a" propaganda and relied on radio to disseminate their policies.

After the fall of the rule of the Taliban, they attempted to establish mobile radio stations. As Nathan (2009) pointed out, these attempts, even if successful, would not have had a major impact (because Taliban's radio would have had operational as well as geographical limitations). However, the outburst of independent radio and television stations in post-September 11 Afghanistan has helped the Taliban to get their messages out. One of the main differences between independent and government-owned media is that independent media outlets are more able to provide a balanced account of the events. This means that for all security events the Taliban and their claims should be part of the story.

In order to get their message transmitted through independent and international media, the Taliban worked on their media relations. They appointed their own spokesmen. As many journalists say in Afghanistan, the Taliban are much better in their media relations than the international forces stationed there and the Afghan government (pers. com., August, 2009). The Taliban themselves call journalists or media organizations and tell them about events. They may call, send an SMS, or email (R. Samandar, pers. com., July 25, 2008).

One of the very important developments that enabled the Taliban not only to communicate easily and effectively with each other but also to compete and provide an alternative to the government/international version of news stories was the use of mobile technologies. Though the group is declared illegal and has no physical address, mobile technologies facilitate easy access and presence in all the media. Recently, with the availability of mobile technology capable of sending audio and video messages, the Taliban, particularly at the local level, started sending their messages and visuals directly to their audience. This gives the Taliban further freedom to communicate and address larger audiences. Even Taliban songs and ringtones are now easily circulated through mobile phones by supporters.

Technology: From Curse to Nurse

In post-Taliban rule, new communications technologies spread so fast that the Taliban found themselves forced to adopt them to reach a multitude of audiences with very little effort. A new technology which was seen as a "curse," a work of the devil, just a year ago, now becomes a nursery to old ideas to be poured in new bottles, to be nurtured and promoted in new forms and frames. The Taliban have started producing audio-visual materials and using DVDs. During their rule, they banned all forms of visuals and considered them un-Islamic. Now the producing and distributing of audio-visual materials has become an integral part of the Taliban's strategy in the post-September 11 era. DVDs are used for different purposes by the group. They are used to motivate, recruit, or simply communicate.

The content of these DVDs include Taliban's raids, violence, speeches, songs and other genres. Some of these DVDs contain terror acts, such as killing and slaughtering of government soldiers, who the Taliban call "spies" or "traitors." DVDs are also used to provide the media with footage of the fighting. Though DVDs are mainly produced in Pakistan, locally produced footage is also available (Nathan, 2009).

According to Nathan (2009), al Qaeda has its media production team for Afghanistan, called Al Sahab (the Clouds), that produces audio and video materials on Afghanistan. Taliban's DVDs are also readily available in Pakistani cities. Though these DVDs are banned in Afghanistan, they can easily be obtained privately.

"Anarchical Media"

The Taliban have had a presence online since 2005 (Nathan, 2009). By using the Internet, the Taliban are able to reach a huge array of audiences in ways and magnitude impossible to imagine previously. Besides providing content in Pashto and Dari, the two main local languages in Afghanistan, the Taliban also provide content in Urdu, Arabic, and English. This shows that the Taliban are operating through a global strategy designed for audiences at regional and international levels. As mentioned before, using different genre contents, in different forms, formerly abhorred by the Taliban, now makes them new devout converts before the altars of the information age.

Another advantage of using the Internet by the Taliban is that it empowers the Taliban to be available to their audiences 24 hours a day. However, sometimes their website cannot be accessed. To deal with this issue, the Taliban use multiple websites to provide the same content. Taliban's sites provide news, leadership statements, commentaries, radio programs, video clips, magazines, and links to other sites, songs and poetry.

Risks to the Taliban and the Public

Mobile telephony is not used by the Taliban alone to share information. For countermeasures, the international forces use jamming technologies and also use the phones for collecting information on the Taliban.[1] Mobile technology is an essential part of the Taliban operations (for instance, detonation of improvised explosive devices or IEDs, is an example of such operations).

Though the use of information and communication technologies has benefited the Taliban in their psychological warfare in military operations, and outreach, they also made them vulnerable. In a number of instances, the Taliban leaders were targeted by tracking the signals of their phones. The killings of Mullah Akhtar Mohammad Osmani and Mullah Dadullah Akhund, two high ranked Taliban leaders, was made possible by tracking the signals of their satellite phones.[2]

Mobile telephony may also create problems for the general population. People cannot travel to the areas under the threat of the Taliban with mobile phones having officials' names and numbers in their mobiles. The Taliban might accuse and kill local individuals if they possess information and communication technologies that in any way favorably link them to government officials. In August 2006, the Taliban killed a mother and her son for this reason.

Acknowledging the murder, the Taliban leader Dadullah mentioned that they killed these two because they had GPS and mobile technology, accusing them of being "spies" (Albone, 2006). Finally, the Taliban forced mobile telephony companies – by threatening them with targeting cell phone towers – to halt providing service at night in some parts of the country where the Taliban had presence. Thus, cell phone companies were forced to provide services only during the day (Shah, 2008). Since the international forces are monitoring communication over mobile phones, the Taliban have started using VoIP, such as Skype, to avoid being monitored or detected (Savvas, 2008). This clearly indicates their adaptability to new trends and technologies.

Conclusion: Some Ethical Considerations

The effective use of new communication technologies by militant Islamic extremists raises many ethical issues and questions to ponder. Chief among these issues is the utter disregard of these extremists to the sanctity and value of human life. For a Western mindset, manufacturing death to invite maximum publicity for a cause denies it any claim of legitimacy. Yet, in the mind of a Muslim Islamic terrorist, life in the hereafter is what matters. Sending oneself to Heaven and nonbelievers, including Muslims who do not share extreme interpretations of Islam, to Hell is a noble mission.

This leads many to think that denying Muslim extremists access to the Internet, and censorship of their websites and those suspected of being used by them are legitimate measures. While most people may not argue with such a view, the flexibility and the ease of starting that the Internet affords extremists, combined with the difficulty of identifying extremists before the act, make it an exercise in futility to be debating gains of security at the expense of freedom of expression and vice versa.

Many militant extremist groups claim that they have no option but to use violence because their voices are silenced. While the use of violence for publicity is criminal and unethical, this claim must be thoughtfully pondered. State violence in the Muslim world against nonstate entities and individuals, with complacency and tacit support from the West, lends the claim a powerful appeal. Even reformist and secularist Muslims find themselves supporting such a claim while abhorring the violence that results from it. As reformists and secularists themselves are frequently subjected to the ruthlessness of state violence, they become disarmed of any meaningful persuasive arguments against this claim. Such reformists and secularists thus become severely demoralized and ineffective in their war to win the hearts and minds of the public, especially the youths. Thus, they, in effect, they become painfully caught between two evils the violence of the state and the violence of the terrorists.

More importantly, reformists and secularists positions are further compromised and extremely complicated with the emphasis of the West on fighting violence-for-publicity with violence that detests, but fails to avoid, publicity. It is very difficult for a reformist to defend the acts of state actors, of the West and of their own. When images of bodies of school children killed by bombs of state actors permeate the Internet and satellite TV channels, reformists find themselves at a loss between two violent mindsets, unable to fight one or defend the other.

If terrorism is to be effectively eradicated, an alliance between peace-seeking nonstate actors, facilitated by state actors, of the West and the Rest, is warranted. The protection of the sanctity of the human life and dignity demands no less. However, a major shift from hard-powered military action to the soft-powered, albeit very lethal, communication world, in which terrorism thrives and multiplies, is a must. Such a shift would not necessarily take military action out of the equation. It will, nonetheless, seek to diminish it as nonstate actors, especially reformists, in the West and the Rest, empowered by state-actors, begin to take back the initiative in winning hearts and minds through civil debates supported by state actors.

The loss of treasure and blood and the huge opportunity cost the world incurs in pursuing the current official policy of state-based counterterrorism, is not only futile, but also unethical and criminal, simply because violence breads violence and ultimately results in unnecessary loss of life. Refraining from violence, funding, and providing logistic support for civil society agents of change, who are reform-minded peace communicators, together with addressing development issues, would achieved far more with far less than military action had achieved in the past decade in the fight of extremism.

As stated earlier, this chapter is a rudimentary attempt to point to what we think is the right direction toward a world in which extremism and terrorism are abhorred by all, including devout Muslims. By treading into this difficult terrain and exploring previously untapped areas, we think this chapter will help raise new questions, which – we hope – will ultimately lead us or others to new solutions. We are aware that some of the ideas presented here are still underdeveloped. Nonetheless, we are utterly committed to developing them to fruition as we engage our colleagues and readers in discussing them. As we do so, we hope to get as much feedback on our ideas as possible to help us further understand a problem that can only be resolved through engaging participatory approaches.

Notes

1 See Hyland (2009); Williams, Hickley, and Sims (2008); "Bombs Highlight Helicopter Shortage" (2009); Murray (2008).
2 See Smith (2006); Smith (2007).

References

Aaron, D. (2008) *In their own words: Voices of Jihad*, RAND Corporation, Santa Monica, CA.
Albone, T. (2006) Taliban kill mother and son accused of spying. *The Globe and Mail* (Canada), August 10, p. A12.

Al Rawashdi, A.R.S. (2008) al-Jihad al-Elami: Ta'seel was tafe'el (Jihad Media: Rooting and activating: Readings in jihad media in Iraq), http://haqnews.net/AllNews.aspx (last accessed December 30, 2009).

Arnett, P. (n.d.) Transcript of Osama Bin Laden interview by Peter Arnett, www.informationclearinghouse.info/article7204.htm (accessed August 25, 2010).

"Bombs Highlight Helicopter Shortage," (2009) *Daily Mail* (London), July 13.

Cammaerts, B., and Van Audenhove, L. (2005) Online Political debate, unbounded citizenship, and the problematic nature of a transnational public sphere. *Political Communication*, 22 (2), 179–196.

Cronin, A. (2002/2003) Behind the curve: Globalization and international terrorism. *International Security*, 27 (3), 30–58.

Gary, D., and Head, A. (2009) The importance of the Internet to the post-modern terrorist and its role as a form of safe haven. *European Journal of Scientific Research*, 25 (3), pp. 396–404.

Hoffman, B. (2006a) *Inside Terrorism*, Columbia University Press, New York.

Hoffman, B (2006b) Testimony presented to the House Permanent Select Committee on Intelligence on May 4, www.rand.org/pubs/testimonies/2006/RAND_CT262–1.pdf (accessed August 25, 2010).

Hyland, T. (2009) Low-tech attacks taking high toll on troops. *Sunday Age* (Melbourne), October 25, p. 13.

International Crisis Group (2008). Taliban Propaganda: Winning the War of Words? *International Crisis Group*, July, www.crisisgroup.org/home/index.cfm?id=5589 (accessed October 10, 2009).

Jervis, R. (2009) The era of leading power peace, in *International Politics: Enduing Concepts and Contemporary Issues*, (eds R.J. Art and R. Jervis), Pearson Education, Inc, Upper Saddle River, NJ.

Kahn, R., and Kellner, D. (2006) Oppositional politics and the Internet: A critical/reconstructive approach, in *Media and Cultural Studies: Key Works*, (eds M. Durham and D. Kellner), Blackwell, Malden, MA.

Kellner, D. (2007) Habermas, the public sphere, and democracy: A critical intervention, www.gseis.ucla.edu/faculty/kellner/essays/habermaspublicspheredemocracy.pdf (accessed August 25, 2010).

Kimmage, D. (2008a) Fight terror with YouTube, www.nytimes.com/2008/06/26/opinion/26kimmage.html (accessed August 25, 2010).

Kimmage, D. (2008b) *The Al-Qaeda Media Nexus: The Virtual Network behind the Global Message*. Radio Free Europe/Radio Liberty (RFE/RL), Washington DC.

Martin, G. (2009) *Understanding Terrorism: Challenges, Perspectives, and Issues*, Sage, Thousand Oaks, CA.

MEMRI (The Middle East Media Research Institute) (2007) Osama Bin Laden's video message to the American people, September 10, www.memritv.org/report/en/2364.htm (accessed August 31, 2010).

Miller, C.H., Matisitz, J., O'Hair, D. *et al.* (2008) The complexity of terrorism: Groups, semiotics, and the media, in *Terrorism: Communication and Rhetorical Perspectives* (eds O'Hair, H., Heath, R., Ayotte, K. *et al.*), Hampton Press, Cresskill, NJ, pp. 43–66.

Ministry of Communication (2010) Ministry of Communications and Information Technology Islamic Republic of Afghanistan, www.mcit.gov.af accessed on January 5, 2010.

Murray, J. (2008) Why do we send our troops out in flimsy vehicles to die on the Highway to Hell?; Soldiers' Land Rovers are not match for Taliban suicide bombers. *Sunday Express*, p. 16, May 25.

Nathan, J. (2009) Reading the Taliban, in *Decoding the New Taliban: Insights from the Afghan Field*, (ed. A. Giustozzi), C. Hurst & Co Publishers Ltd, London.

Noorzai, R. (2006) Communication and development in Afghanistan: A history of reforms and resistance. An unpublished master's thesis, Ohio University, Athens, US.

Noorzai, R. (2007) Balanced development: An ICT model for rural connectivity in Afghanistan. Communication and Development Studies Graduate Conference, Athens, OH.

Reuters (2009) Reuters alert net, www.alertnet.org/thenews/newsdesk/L07394110.htm (accessed August 25, 2010).

Savvas, A. (2008) *ComputerWeekly*, September 23, www.lexisnexis.com.proxy.library.ohiou. edu/hottopics/Inacademic (last accessed December 1, 2009).

Schmid, A., and de Graaf, J. (1982) *Violence as Communication: Insurgent Terrorism and the Western News Media*, Sage, London/ Beverly Hills.

Scott, A., and Street, J. (2001) From media politics to e-protest? The use of popular culture and new media in parties and social movements, in *Culture and Politics in the Information Age: A New Politics*, (ed. F. Webster), Routledge, London, pp. 32–51.

Shah, T. (2008) Taliban seek Cellphone Curfew and Threaten Wireless Firms. *The New York Times*, February 26, p. A4.

Smith, M. (2006) Taliban leader "killed" after RAF tracks phone. *The Sunday Times* (London), December 24, p. 2.

Smith, M. (2007) SBS behind Taliban leader's death. *The Sunday Times* (London), May 27, p. 21.

Terrorism and Media (2008) Working paper from COT Institute for safety, security and crisis management. Deliverable 6, Workpackage 4, www.transnationalterrorism.eu/ tekst/publications/WP4%20Del%206.pdf (accessed August 25, 2010).

Weimann, G. (2006) *Terror on the Internet: The New Arena, The New Challenges*, The United States Institute of Peace, Washington DC.

Wilkinson, P. (1990) Terrorism and propaganda, in *Terrorism and the Media: Dilemmas for Government, Journalist and the Public*, (eds Y. Alexander and R. Latter), Maxwell Macmillan Pergamon Publishing Corp, New York.

Williams, D., Hickley, M., and Sims, P. (2008) Why were they such an easy target for the Taliban bombers? *Daily Mail* (London), June 20, p. 6.

Wolfsfeld, G. (1997) *Media and Political Conflict: News from the Middle East*, Cambridge University Press, Cambridge.

49

The Ethics of a Very Public Sphere
Differential Soundscapes and the Discourse of the Streets

Robert S. Fortner

Countless dictators have fallen because they failed to detect the sounds of revolution soon enough. And probably an equal number have been hurled into power by bawling multitudes who couldn't even hear their own voices. The deaf can lead the deaf just as the blind can lead the blind.

(Schafer, 2003, p. 25)

Introduction

Scholarly attention to "soundscapes" or "acoustic ecology" has been increasing since the Canadian composer Murray Schafer first wrote about the concept in 1976. Despite the ephemerality of sound up to World War II when the first wire recorders were used, and thus the lack of past contemporary sounds to hear, enough people from the past wrote about the sounds of their environment, or complained about its quality (especially after the arrival of the industrial revolution with its steam engines and clattering machinery) that scholars have been able to reconstruct some of the soundscapes of human history.

Most of the work on soundscapes (outside the realm of recording, performance, and reproduction of music) has dealt with the acoustic dimensions of soundscapes – hence the synonym "acoustic ecology." Scholars have written about the uses of sound (such as church bells), the dimensions of sound (its amplitude, frequency, timbre, and attenuation), and the implications of these dimensions for the uses to which it was put, or to the satisfaction/disaffection with sound in particular environments. They have explored many different environments, including both natural and man-made. They have looked at the changes in one environment occasioned by the introduction of new sound – such as the sounds created by

The Handbook of Global Communication and Media Ethics, First Edition. Edited by Robert S. Fortner and P. Mark Fackler.
© 2011 Blackwell Publishing Ltd. Published 2011 by Blackwell Publishing Ltd.

increasing numbers of visitors to national parks – and at the meaning of sound in particular contexts, using examples from a variety of societies and contexts, both primitive and modern. The work has become richer and richer over time.

However, there has been little written about the implications of different soundscapes for the public sphere. Habermas's original concept of the public sphere arising in English coffee houses, French salons, and German literary societies was concerned with the class dimensions of public discourse, and the ability of like-minded bourgeoisie to discuss matters of common concern – trade, finance and other economic issues. The place (or the soundscape of the place) was not a truly relevant consideration – however difficult it might have been for people to carry on such conversations over the din of clattering cups, saucers and flatware in highly echoic space.

The soundscapes of current life are far different than those of the seventeenth and eighteenth century. Not only has technology introduced sound and noise that often make it difficult to carry on conversations in public space (from amplified music to the grind and squeal of steel wheels on tracks in city subways, along with the rumble heard above them mixed with the cacophony of automobile, truck, and bus traffic on the streets), it has also provided the means to create individual disparate soundscapes in public space and to enhance the ability to control soundscapes in group environments existing in both public and private (indoor) space.

To understand the ethical issues raised by current soundscapes seen as dimensions of a public sphere, it is necessary to sketch the dimensions of the sphere and the variations that exist within it. To begin, it is clear that no part of the public sphere, however defined, is anechoic. Human beings are unable to survive for long in a soundless environment. They thrive in an echoic environment: one replete with sound. The sound does not have to be loud, just there. It provides a means of orientation, an affirmation that life goes on. (One indication of this can be seen in Blesser and Salter, 2007, p. 18.) It is also the case, as Walter Ong (1982, p. 72) wrote, that because people hear sound from all around them (a 360° apprehension) they always are in the center of their own acoustic environment – unlike vision in which people are always on the fringe of the environment. Jim Cummings explains it this way: "Whatever beauty or complexity, pattern or structure we might see around us, the world would be stark beyond recognition if we could not hear all that lies beyond our sight, hidden around corners or behind the screens of people or trees" (2001). It is not merely the difference between being in the center of things versus being on the periphery. We perceive visually only what enters the aperture of the eye, but we not only hear sound with our ears, we feel it with our bodies – the corporeal itself resonates with the sounds within which we exist. "Resonance is the frequency at which an object begins to vibrate. Everything has a frequency that sets it in motion, from a bridge over a river, to a rock, to a crystal goblet. Our entire body is a symphony of sound, made of the different resonant frequencies of every organ, bone, and tissue" (Hale, 2007, p. 14).

In this respect, it is fair to say that people always exist within their own narrowly defined public sphere and thus multiple public spheres can coexist in the same

The Ethics of a Very Public Sphere

physical space. As sound attenuates as it becomes more distant from its source, because it may be amplified or de-amplified by its interaction with physical objects, because it reaches people in both direct and indirect manifestations, and because people's hearing and visceral response is not equally sensitive to the same frequencies or amplitudes, two people may be in close proximity to one another and yet experience varying apprehensions of their acoustic environment. The frequent questions, "did you hear that," or "did you feel that" is an indication of people's implicit understanding of these realities.

These questions imply something else as well. They imply that the other should have heard or felt the sound, that if he did not, he was not paying sufficient attention. So it is both a question and a criticism – "why didn't you say, why didn't you do, something, since you heard or felt (or should have heard or felt) it?" This is an entirely human response. Living in communities requires that those within them apprehend the same reality – that they recognize and respond to the same threats, that they have paid attention to the traditions and mores of the society of which they are members, that they know how to go along and get along with others within that environment. People within a social context, socially constructed by those within it themselves, demand that its cues be universally applicable to all who share it. Otherwise, social relations would be crippled. There must be both solidarity by the members of society and a sense that the common interpretations are the only interpretations. They must be inevitable within each specific context or they will fail.

What should people hear, physiologically speaking? Kendall Wrightson discusses soundscapes (n.d.) as having "keynotes" – what could be called "acoustic ambience," the background sounds of a place (the sounds of nature, the hammering of machinery in a factory, the rumble of streetcars, beeping of horns, etc. (what George Gershwin recreated to a degree in "An American in Paris")), "sound signals" – sounds intended to attract attention in the foreground of the scape and "soundmarks," the distinctive sonic attributes of a place or the sounds of its traditional activities (bells, the adhān, or natural sounds that define one place as against another. "[Murray] Schafer's terminology helps to express the idea that the sound of a particular locality (its keynotes, sound signals and soundmarks) can – like local architecture, customs and dress – express a community's identity to the extent that settlements can be recognised and characterised [sic] by their soundscapes" (Wrightson, n.d.).

Of course, these three elements of the soundscape are not mutually exclusive. The call to prayer (adhān), for instance, heard five times each day in countries with significant Muslim populations can both help define a place – and thus be a soundmark – and also be intended to attract attention over the din of urban life – and thus be a sound signal. Beyond its physical or aesthetic characteristics, the adhān also makes moral demands. It claims – as do church bells on a Sunday morning – that it is time to pray. Whatever activities a person is engaged in are now to be put aside or exchanged for communal prayer, oriented toward Mecca, in obedience to Allah.

I argue that this is a moral demand because the adhān purports to delimit a person's choice: one must put aside commerce, alms giving, conversation, benevolence, or any of a thousand other activities and replace that work with another in response to a superior claim. This demand is not only moral, but ethical, too. It is not merely a claim on individual choice, it is also a claim on the collective. Societies where the adhān is generally practiced expect people, although they may pray alone when necessary, to collect for group prayer – either in the mosque, prayer room, school, or along the street – to show the community's obedience.

The same argument can be made about church bells. Although their significance in western cities is probably far less than it was at one time, (See Smith, 2005, p. 22, referring to a report written about London in 1602) the ringing of the bells in smaller towns and villages may still carry the same moral and ethical expectations for people and communities as the adhān does today in many places. Even in cases where people have complained about such bells as "noise pollution," it may be the case that their objections are not aimed so much at the physicality of the bells as to their continual reminder of a faith that they have abandoned, or are only tangentially connected to (see Rose, 2001, p. 1). We might, then, consider such objections less aimed at aesthetics than at ethics – an ethic that reminds them of their own failings and of their distance from the "imagined community" within which they live[1] (see Schafer, 2003, pp. 26, 28.)

There are at least two important dimensions to the ethics of this very public sphere. One dimension describes central and basic issues: those that are primary in public space as they arise in places that have undergone only minimal alteration by human beings, or none at all. The second dimension describes the issues that emerge only as a result of modernization, or industrialization and technologicalization of urban space. Such ethics are not inherent, or primordial, to public space, but the result of human intervention and alteration of the landscape. In the first instance, the primary ethical issue is authority. In the second it is the interplay of imposition and escape from the soundscape, with consequent implications for appropriate conduct, public safety, and communal life. In each case it is control and identity, both individual and collective.

"Natural Space" and the Question of Authority

Our initial concern here is to recognize the phenomenology of sound, that is, how we experience the existence of sound in nonurban and nonindustrialized/technologicalized environments. In every environment, exterior or interior, sound is present. This is merely the result of what sound is – vibration. Every vibration has a frequency (pitch) and an amplitude (strength or loudness). Human beings can discern some frequencies but not all; they can hear some levels of loudness but not all. Some amplitudes are painful. Some frequencies that can be heard by the young become silent as people grow older. These are basic dimensions of the phenomenon

The Ethics of a Very Public Sphere 977

of sound. As every environment has sound with these characteristics, every environment also has a "noise floor." This is the amplitude level (which varies by frequency) that any sound must be above for it to be heard. It is probably self-evident, then, that the fewer "things" there are in an environment to create vibrations, the lower the noise floor of that place is, and thus the easier it is to hear individual sounds within that environment (provided they match human hearing range and at are perceptible amplitudes). In an anechoic chamber, for instance, people can hear their own heart pumping, blood whooshing through their arteries, and sometimes the buzz of their nervous system. These phenomena are normally masked by the noise floor of everyday life.

Another aspect of the phenomenon of sound is that we hear in 360°. That is, we are always in the center of our acoustic space. Sound surrounds us, we are centered within it, and – because we have biaural hearing (two ears) that are far enough apart for sound to arrive at each milliseconds apart, we can apprehend the source of a sound based on perceived directionality. Our experience of sound has both the quality of "surroundability" and "precise directionality" (Ihde, 2007, p. 78). As David Rothenberg puts it (2001, n.p.), "Sounds define us, hold us in, lead us away. They announce themselves to us, they call from all over the world. With only a little effort, the whole world can be heard as music."

Many scholars have noted or implied that we have paid scant attention to the phenomenon of sound because of the post-Enlightenment claim of the primacy of the visual (Attali, 1985; Bull and Back, 2003; Foucault, 1991). Sterne (2003, p. 2), argues that in addition to the Enlightenment, there was also an "Ensoniment," a disenchantment of understanding of sound. Despite this, however, Holl (2007, p. 57), discussing the physical environment of the city, says that "most, if not all of today's architecture is under the influence of a culture dominated by visual stimuli. We perceive the world through the simultaneous use of all senses but in modern societies the visual perception has been heavily and disproportionately favored." Stern also agrees with Holl's comment, however, remarking that "To take seriously the role of sound and hearing in modern life is to trouble the visualist definition of *modernity*" (2003, p. 3).

The first point to be made here in relation to this reality is a simple one: the public sphere, that imaginary place where human discourse occurs and civil society is created and maintained, is a multi-sensory environment. This public sphere may be dominated by one sense (visual in the modern age but auditory in oral culture), but no portion of this sphere functions with only one sense operating. The portion of this sphere occupied by members of deaf culture may lack the sound component, for instance, and thus visualize their comments to one another via sign, but sign itself requires a tactile sense (touch) to function, and the containing context is also one where smell and possibly taste will also function.

It is also fair to say that a single environment can be dominated by one sense at one time and a different one at another. For instance, what is obvious during the day can be cloaked at night. In the day sight may dominate, but at night sound may become more prominent as the defining sensory input. In a city the sight of skyscrapers may encourage the tourist to crane his neck skyward, but the sound of a fire engine may drag his sight back to the concrete reality of the street. Rain may obscure sight and snow may muffle sound. Our sensory environments are dynamic.

Sensory environments, however, are not necessarily chaotic because of their ever-changing sensory ecology. They can be peaceful or soothing. Or they can be cacophonic and nerve-rattling. They can present a bucolic serenity or a kaleidoscope of churning images and clamorous crescendos. Where is the authority in such soundscapes?

I argue here that authority adheres to the sounds that punctuate such soundscapes. Church bells punctuate, for instance, because they are not a continual presence like so many other sounds that are either omnipresent (traffic noise, for instance) or usual (the beating of rain on tin roofs, the whoosh of wind through trees). The freight train sound of a tornado is likewise a punctuating sound, or the loud crack of thunder. Both demand attention (See Ihde, 2007, p. 133). Both are warnings. Church bells, which at one time had the same effect as thunder in western society, have – as a result of the disenchantment of modern western life – become far easier to ignore or interpret within the cultural context as a signal that can safely be ignored. In some Islamic countries, such as many parts of Indonesia, this seems also the case with the adhān, while in others this call to prayer makes a more urgent claim.

Such a perspective sheds light on both the profound and the mundane – or trivial. In Standish, Michigan, for instance, a man who fell out of a canoe "let loose with a stream of profanities" in front of children, in violation of a 102-year-old anti-swearing law. ("Cursing Canoeist's Conviction Upheld," 2000) A sheriff's deputy overhead the profanity explosion (reportedly 3 minutes in length) on the Rifle River near a woman and two young children. ("Michigan Man to Stand Trial for Cursing in Front of Kids," 1999) Although the law under which Timothy Boomer was convicted was later overturned as a violation of the First Amendment (Simon, 2002), the novelty of the case came from the way that such an event punctuated the otherwise quiet scene of a woodsy river setting. It took on "authority" that challenged the expected in this case.

In another Michigan case the City of Dearborn limited Arabic Christian Perspective (ACP), a California-based group that attempts to convert Muslims to Christianity, to a designated area within the annual Arab Festival, rather than allowing 90 volunteer members of the group to walk freely through a four to five block area to pass out literature (Brand-Williams, 2009). In this case the American Arab Chamber of Commerce in Dearborn had altered the usual visual- and soundscapes of an area of Dearborn for its annual festival. It thus staked a claim to the area for a limited period of time and created a new environment. Within this environment the activities of ACP would have punctuated the temporary soundscape with a call to obey a different God. Although offered booth space with other Christian and Muslim groups at the festival, ACP claimed that its constitutional rights were infringed by such limits. ("Christian Group Can't Leaflet at Arab

The Ethics of a Very Public Sphere   979

Festival, Federal Judge Rules," 2009) The suit brought (and denied) was both a challenge to the authority of the City of Dearborn, and of Allah – the ostensible God of this festival.

In most circumstances what is at issue in the public square is significant. Clashes between protestors and military or police authority are the result of decisions to challenge the legitimacy of regimes in the public square. The rumbling of tanks in Tiananmen Square was a clear warning to protestors in 1989 that their civil disobedience could (and did) have serious consequences. The Iranians who took to the street in both 1979 and 2009 to challenge authority punctuated their protests with "Allahu Akbar," or "God is great" as both a show of defiance and a claim of legitimacy. In 2009 their shouts were eventually greeted with the roar of motorcycles as the Basij (a volunteer paramilitary force) moved in on protestors and street brawls ensued, including the torching of some of the cycles (see "'One shot dead' at Iran Protest," 2009).

Control and Identity, Individual and Collective

People have both individual and collective identities. In some societies these two aspects of identity are so intertwined that it can be difficult to prise them apart. In others one or the other of the two forms of identity can be the default orientation, with its opposite only a pale reflection. In some societies, too, people may feel that they have little option but to be a part of the collective identity, even if they have serious objections to it, or function within a kind of schizophrenic approach to society in which they practice compliance with the community while secretly living out their own individual identity. It would not be fair to generalize about one sort of society or another without serious research, but some individuals have commented on the relationship of these two identity-forms in their own experience. For instance, Natan Sharansky, formerly a Soviet dissident before he emigrated to Israel, wrote about his struggle with those who disagreed with his approach (2008, p. xviii): "To my critics, then and now, I had to make a choice: I could fight for universal values or for particularistic values. I could fight for human rights, democracy, and peace or I could fight for the rights of Jews, strengthen Jewish identity, and defend Israel. In this struggle, I would have to choose between the forces of freedom and the forces of identity, between being a man of the world and being a man of my people."

For Sharansky identity "is fundamentally about the links to others" (2008, p. 7). However, it is not difficult to imagine that for many people it is about separation from others; it is not connection *to*, but separation *from*. Each society will be helpful or destructive to one, or both, of these impulses.

Societies have a variety of tools at their disposal to function vis-à-vis identity impulses. They have a history, traditions, mythologies, political and legal systems, police powers – any or all of which they can call on in response to people's desires. Of course, the most famous of all examinations of the power of the state in regard to the individual is George Orwell's *1984*. However, societies do not have to be as draconian as Orwell suggested in his novel to have wide-ranging control over their citizens. Totalitarian states may appear to be the most obvious control environments, but societies that depended on the so-called "divine right of kings" prior to the revolutions of 1776, 1781, and 1848 were perhaps equally in control of possibilities for most of their subjects. Slaves were no less in subjugation to masters in ancient empires or the American South prior to their emancipation. Women argued for the voting franchise in hopes that it would lead to more ability to define themselves in society, although – at least in the US case – voting did not achieve all of what they had hoped. More freedom for women resulted, arguably, from their massive entrance into the labor force during World War II than from the right to vote.

These struggles had to play out, by definition, in the public arena. For them to succeed societies had to change dramatically. In some cases they did, in others not.

Societies exercise their police powers in a variety of ways to control soundscapes. In the Soviet Union, for instance, authorities continually jammed radio signals from the West in the attempt to prevent people from filling their personal soundscape with "propaganda." Many towns and cities were also outfitted with wired radio receivers (called "tochkas" in Russian) that could only receive official Soviet broadcasts. In most communist countries, massive parades were used, both as visual displays of military might, but also as aural displays – through the roar of jets above the crowds, amplified speeches from government officials, songs from mass choirs or required audience participation, and the sound of boots on tarmac. In the United States similar sound events, from the singing of the national anthem before baseball games to tapes played at military funerals, parades on Independence Day, and mass demonstrations and gatherings where amplified speeches are the centerpiece (e.g., Martin Luther King's "I Have a Dream Speech" on the steps of the Lincoln Memorial or Barak Obama's inauguration address on the steps of the Capitol Building, each at one end of the Washington mall). All such activities are means by which the collective identity of a people can be affirmed and maintained. It is not merely the passive visual that is the focus, but the physical participation (being there), and the shouting of slogans, affirmation through song, and the clapping, amens, and other ejaculations that accompany speeches, that involve people in the collective identity. The pomp and circumstance accompanying the funerals of celebrities (Michael Jackson, James Brown, Elvis Presley) and state persons (especially a slain President or military heroes) also serve the function of involvement. They use eulogies and music to celebrate and mourn; often there are salutes through gunfire to mark such occasions.

What happens when an individual who is within a given soundscape does not participate? The person who does not rise or sing the national anthem will be thought "unpatriotic." The person in a church service who does not know the tune of the hymn (or can't read music in some cases), will feel as though s/he doesn't "belong." In the more charismatic assembly, where sermons are routinely punctuated with audience responses, the uninitiated visitor is alienated. As long as involvement in such soundscapes is truly voluntary, of course, an individual can

The Ethics of a Very Public Sphere   981

avoid the discomfort of participation. When they are not, as is sometimes the case, a person is forced either to temporarily suspend the "self" to avoid stigma (see Goffman, 1963, pp. 3, 5, 66–67).

Church bells ringing on Sunday morning, the call to prayer, or even the air raid/tornado alert sirens that are used in American Midwestern cities are all means to remind people of who they are supposed to be. In societies where such signals are widely accepted (or at least not resisted), a failure to respond to them in the expected way can result in avoidance (shunning), reprimand, compulsion, or even violent reaction. In other cases, where such practices are less widely accepted, or where they are merely one option among several, there may be no negative reaction at all. When reaction does occur (as in the first case), the claim of the respondents suggests that the individual is not a part of the collective identity. His ostracism is self-induced. He is assumed to have chosen exclusion by refusal to seek inclusion. In the second case, although it may have no significance for his collective identity (he may still claim to be a Baptist, a Muslim, or a patriot), it can have consequences for his personal identity. Is he lying to himself as well as the community? Or is he being faithful to his own beliefs? In other words, as Charles Taylor (1991) puts it, is his behavior authentic to his self? "This is the powerful moral idea that has come down to us. It accords crucial moral importance to a kind of contact with myself, with my own inner nature, which it sees as in danger of being lost, partly through the pressures towards outward conformity" (p. 29).

Control of the Soundscape

Despite the various measures that government or institutions such as religious authorities may take to prod people into "correct behavior" and both individual and collective identities, people are not without resources to combat these efforts, or even to create their own soundscape in public space. Of course, in so doing they may actually be withdrawing from that space into their own cocoon. While this may eliminate the ethic of oppression that can come from the exercise of police power, tradition, or religious authority, it creates new ethical issues for any effort to engage individuals in collective enterprise or to inform citizens on public issues. The contention over public space created when rival demonstrations take to the streets often create more heat than light on significant issues.

- In Kabul the passage of a new family law that applied only to Shi'ite Muslims (about 10% of Afghans) resulted in small groups of protestors and supporters of the law gathering in front of a new mosque with rival banners: "We don't want Taliban law" and "Islamic justice." Protestors said the law legalized marital rape; supporters denied it. And another group of 200 male supporters also gathered and began throwing stones at the protestors (see Radio Free Europe/Radio Liberty, 2009). The shouting and stone throwing accomplished little to reconcile these differences.

- In China riots broke out when Uyghurs and Han Chinese confronted each other on the streets of Xingiang. Over 150 people were killed, police used tear gas and pressurized water to separate the two groups and photographs seen in the West showed protestors shouting at police behind their plastic shields. Much violence, little dialogue, no real results (see "Violence in Xingiang Persists," 2009). The massive protests in Tehran after the disputed presidential election also led to counter-demonstrations that were, in some cases, larger than the originals (AP, 2009).
- Rival protests between Buddhists and Muslims blocked roads in southern Thailand and by early 2007 "an Islamic separatist insurgency that flared up in January 2004 [had] led to the deaths of more than 2,000 people" (International Herald Tribune/AP, 2007).
- In London police "battled to separate rival groups on Wednesday. Nine men were arrested as hundreds of pro-Palestinian protestors clashed with supporters of the Israeli Government. Protestors fought police in angry scenes after the demonstration was held just yards from a rally in support of Israel's actions" (Lefley, 2009).

It is not merely in such street confrontations that people struggle to control the soundscape. The heckling of speakers by those who disagree with them (such as occurred when Iran's President Ahmadinejad spoke at Columbia University), or the sometimes raucous debates in the United Kingdom's House of Commons are well known. Even in smaller assemblies similar events can occur. "Despite repeated cries for a calmer debate, including one from a City Council representative..., it was wagging fists, name-calling, and raucous shouting matches that ruled the day at a hearing [about a possible charter school] last night in Harlem" (Green, 2009).

Individuals also increasingly have the technology to construct their own soundscape within the larger public soundscape that surrounds them. The struggle over loud boomboxes seems to have become passé as people have turned to the more private IPods and other MP3 players, but disputes over these devices, often carried on the shoulder by urban youth, were a part of the US landscape for several years. "Oh sure you remember the boom box. That has been the fad back in the 1980s. But it first was marketed and available for everyone back in the 1970s. Usually, people would bring them with them at the mall, in the park, at the beach, and anywhere else they would go. See, boom boxes blasted out the music and music is usually good to listen to especially if you are hanging out with friends. A party will never be a party without some good music. And because there were no mobile music gadgets back then, the boom box was the in thing" ("Bring Back the Boom Box," 2009). More recently the threshold of tolerance for loud music has been crossed by large speaker arrays in cars, supplemented by subwoofers, that can actually rock other people's vehicles at intersections.[2] As one blogger put it concerning such systems: "Quite frankly there is no need for a 10000 watt sound system. Communities and cities around the country are pimpin' the inconsiderate idiots who choose to blare their sound systems at dangerous, obnoxious and

The Ethics of a Very Public Sphere

disrespectful levels. I am sick and tired of the idiots with their "boombox" systems thumpin' down my street and on the main streets near me. I'm ready to start shooting their windows out. If you disrupt my sleep or my dinner or my watching television with your idioticly [sic] loud boombox systems, I feel I have every right to silence you. Cities and states need to ban these systems. There is no need for them. They are dangerous on our roads and disrupt peoples' lifestyles and sleep" (markkat9, 2007; see also Scott, 2001).

The arrival of the Walkman, followed by portable CD players, and then the MP3 (especially the iconic IPod), provided each owner with the opportunity to create an individual acoustic environment, more personal and private than anything before. Although the use of radios, tape and CD players, along with the use of air conditioning in cars had provided a form of this individual acoustic space, the control of the user (or of others who might be traveling with the user) was more limited. These spaces, too, could be more easily breached by the punctuating sounds of the wider soundscape as they depended on the use of speaker systems that merely inserted the desired soundscape into an imperfectly-controllable acoustic environment. The more personal systems, however, depended on the use of headphones or earbuds that not only provided the means to reproduce the desired prerecorded sound, but also effectively shut out the sounds of the larger soundscape.

This shifting control raises several ethical issues. For instance, the use of personal audio devices blurs the distinction between public and private. Is a person walking down a public street with earbuds in, and personal music blaring, in a public or a private place? Traditionally, different standards have applied to public versus private activities. If the line dividing private from public is blurred, what are the appropriate standards of conduct? Even the minimal level of civility that people in cities expect from others as they pass on a sidewalk can be violated by a person so lost in his own soundscape that he pays no attention to those around him. The warnings of approaching ambulances or fire trucks can be missed as they blare under the noise floor to the cranked-up IPod. The ability to respond to someone in distress can be foiled by immersion in a personal environment that crowds out recognition of the larger context. "[T]he culture heard is always a complex of orientations toward others, echoic of the other's expectations" (Carter, 2005, p. 57). Such behaviors raise a host of ethical questions about personal responsibility, community inclusion and engagement, care for others, and inadvertent endangerment by putting others at risk. Societies that define such behaviors as unacceptable are, in one sense, denying the authenticity of the private space within the public sphere. People ought to be paying attention. They owe it to others. "If interpersonal interaction is the presumptively primary or 'authentic' mode of communication, then sound reproduction is doomed to denigration as inauthentic, disorienting, and possibly even dangerous by virtue of its 'decontextualizing' sound from its 'proper' interpersonal context" (Sterne, 2003, p. 21).

Second, use of these devices promotes the individual at the expense of the community. When the community expects (rightly or wrongly) that the reminders of behavior it promotes will be attended to by its members, and some members choose to block out those reminders, it is a symbolic slap at the community standards envisioned. This slap does not have to be intentional for it to be harmful. The behavior presents an alternative possibility – a different way of life. It is therefore provocative. It may threaten religious or cultural traditions, the mythologies of the imagined community, the existing hierarchies and respectfulness assumed to define the nature of communal life. However, it is not usually an alternative that has resulted from sustained public engagement, debate, or experiment. It simply is – a symbolic swipe on the part of an individual. Although the individual has made a moral judgment ("this is what I want to do, now, however others see it" or "I'm not hurting anyone, so this is my choice") he has not necessarily done so consciously. His behavior "in many cases reflects a post-hoc justification or rationalization of previously held biases or beliefs" (Hauser, 2006, p. 25). This is the microlevel equivalent of two cultures – within the same society – a culture of the collective and of the individual. To return to Hauser, "If two cultures see the world through completely different moral lenses, then our ethical values are only relative to the details of the local culture, and free to vary. There are no absolutes, no truths, no universals" (2006, p. 40).

This may seem to some to be a trivial issue. After all, allowing a person the unfettered right to listen to his own music, or religious reading, or salacious novel, in the "privacy" of his own IPod is merely a recognition of difference between people's tastes, not a prescription for the destruction of society. Allowing such behavior merely admits to the existence – at a very low level – of pluralism.

The problem with this conclusion is that not all societies accept pluralism itself as a value. Those societies that do (probably most Western ones) have themselves already defined pluralism as a value and those of us who live within such societies are prone to judge other societies within a moral framework in which this value is significant. H. Tristran Engelhardt, Jr., (1989) reminds us of why this is a problem: "To identify the correct moral sense (or ranking of values), we need already to have a guiding moral sense (or ranking of values)." In other words, this is a tautology. To accomplish one thing requires a commitment to another thing which then defines the answer to the first thing – not really an impartial examination. Engelhardt goes on to argue that: "There is only one deliverance from nihilism, unconstrained relativism, and pluralism, when moral strangers (individuals who do not participate in a common moral vision) meet in a noncoercive [sic] society. If they cannot appeal to God or reason to provide a secular deliverance, then they must rely on what is implicit in the practice of secular ethics as the commitment to resolving moral controversies without a primary appeal to force: mutual respect in the process of negotiating points of collaboration." But this itself can be the problem in societies that are coercive – societies where the prevailing moral ethos depends on full cooperation, where it is against the law to convert to other ethical systems, and where the police power, when exercised, can be draconian and symbolically disfiguring. Both Christianity and Islam have adherents who believe in such a society. Both have practiced it at one time or another in their history (see Goldstein,

The Ethics of a Very Public Sphere 985

2008 and Ali, 2007). John Kekes suggests (1993, p. 19; see also Chapter 4) that understanding the differences between those who are willing to accept pluralism and those who are not may be irreconcilable: "Monists [those who deny pluralism] think that the conflicts can be resolved because it is possible to establish an authoritative system of values in which there is a highest value that will justifiably override lower ranked values and in which the standing of all values will be determined by their contribution to the highest-ranked value. Let us call this highest value 'overriding.' Pluralists deny that there is an authoritative system of values and, consequently, that there is any value that is always overriding. Pluralists think that all values are what we shall call 'conditional.'" J. Donald Moon (1993, p. 4) puts the issue in stark terms: "plurality may lead people to reach different and incompatible judgments, giving rise to conflicts that can threaten survival itself."

Third is the problem of interpreting the implications of such devices, and their use in the public square, for human rights. The Universal Declaration of Human Rights, adopted by the United Nations in 1948, declares in Article 19 that "everyone has the right to freedom of expression; this right includes freedom to hold opinions without interference and to seek, receive and impart information and ideas through any media and regardless of frontiers." Although this article seems iron clad, without exception, it is not always observed in practice. It seems to suggest that a person in his own sonic environment has the right to receive whatever information is encoded on his personal device without interference. This may well be where "rights" and "ethics" collide, especially when the ethical system in place in a given environment is seen to supersede such declarations. The operation of religious police in many Islamic countries, for instance, is justified by the need to protect Islam from blasphemy. State security police in other countries justify their activities with the necessity to protect the state from sedition.[3] In such societies it is difficult for an individual to claim that his rights are violated when he is forced to adhere to practices to which he may have conscientious objection, as the system provides no redress for such complaints. In other societies, even so-called "free" ones, the willingness to insult, shun, or even use violence against those with whom one disagrees (which happens all too-often in the United States), can lead people of certain races, ethnicities, religions, or sexual orientations to deny themselves expression in public for fear of triggering unpleasant or dangerous responses. Human rights in these situations are merely a largely unenforceable ideal, not a reality. Who, then, can tell what one's true identity is, an individually defined, when the society itself, either directly or indirectly, defines the type of identity that is acceptable?

Implications for the Soundscape and Public Sphere

Recognizing the significance of the aural environments, or soundscapes, of different societies, and the implications the differences have for participation in the public sphere, is an important step toward redressing the balance in our understanding of the use of space. In this sense any environment should "be considered as a reservoir of sound possibilities, an *instrumentarium* used to give substance and shape to human relations and everyday management of urban space" (Augoyard and Torgue, 2005, p 8). In any environment, too, the phenomenology of sound can differ – not merely as a result of the acoustical qualities of that environment that control sound directionality, echoic qualities (reverberation and absorption), the presence of frequencies and degrees of amplitude, but by the psychological perception of behavior in response to the sound that, in turn, is based on ethical and aesthetic commitments within the dominant community wherein the sound occurs. Societies make "sound" commitments. Some attempt to dampen it to reduce annoyance. Most celebrate it in various ways. People accept or resist the community's sound commitments. What at first may merely be experienced as the "sounds of things" gradually – through the legitimation or delegitimation of particular sounds, become different phenomena that can only be understood in one way. People who resist that definition violate the norms of society and may discover that they are sanctioned for it (see Ihde, 2007, pp. 85–86).

Every society also accords the soundscape with either legitimacy or suspicion. Hirschkind (2006) argues that after the death of Gamel Abd al-Nasser (1970) and the singer Abd al-Halim Hafiz (1972) "hearing lost its privileged relationship to the version of Egyptian national culture promoted by the state," and institutions that had previously organized its cultivation became suspect. "Associated with religious customs and knowledge that were now seen as obstacles to moderniza-tion, the aural traditions came to be viewed as morally and epistemologically untrustworthy, if not directly responsible for the rise of a violent militant movement carried out in the name of Islam" (2006, p. 54) In other cases (discussed earlier) it is the soundscape itself that carries legitimacy for sport, religion, or the state. People responding to this "sacred" soundscape thus take a position vis-à-vis the official legitimacy when they claim the right to control their aural environment.[4] People in urban environments, too, may try to take control of the aural aspects of that environment to combat its lack of perspective, although it is unclear how doing so via earbuds and MP3 players will compensate (see MacFarland, 1997, Chapter 7).

In Los Angeles, where Mexicanos were systematically excluded from the political power establishment, according to Raúl H. Villa (2000, p. 44), the creation of various self-help organizations in the early twentieth century resulted in a variety of parades, celebrations, and festivals within the community. "These nationalistic celebrations were cherished occasions in which *mexicanismo*, mediated through expressive cultural practices (music, dance, food, oratory, costuming etc.), was momentarily projected into and against a broader Anglo-metropolitan social space, overlaying a strong public persona upon the enforced anonymity that was ever more obscuring the civic identity of La Raza in the larger public sphere." Such activities are considered by many scholars to be counterpublic spheres, as they are in opposition to the majority or bourgeois public sphere originally discussed by Habermas, but they do not have to be seen using a negative descriptor. They are, rather than counterpublic spheres, spheres in which, if even for the briefest moment,

The Ethics of a Very Public Sphere

the public is engaged in discourse that pushes out or expands the dominant public conversation. This enriches the soundscape of the city and has provided many communities with ways of celebrating their own histories. This also provides the means by which those who have been significant contributors to the development of communities assert their claims on that history. Often city-wide or tourist events develop based on these celebrations, allowing for a mixture of elements from across the divides that otherwise tend to isolate particular communities, and thus carrying the promise of unity. In this respect the development of such events reaches for the communitarian ideal of solidarity within community.

This turns accusations of disruption on its head. It legitimizes the often difficult circumstances created for ordinary life by such events (street closings, rerouted traffic, congestion, parking problems, noise, and increased pollution for short periods) and, by definition, is invitational to all parties to join in.

The more problematic manifestations of such celebrations, such as the rampages of sports fans that vandalize automobiles and store fronts, and sometimes result in people's deaths, or the various marches, riots, and demonstrations that develop in response to injustice, fraud, or other inequities (real or perceived) create more difficulty for ethics. The inviolability of life and human dignity are accepted as universal values. However, these events can result in both of these universals being violated.

In Jürgen Habermas' original conception of the public sphere, regardless of the various criticisms that have been leveled at him by those who have objected to his narrow focus (thus omitting attention to women, labor unions and other nonbusiness-oriented publics), what characterized discourse was its attention to rational argument. The West had already, in Weber's terms, been "disenchanted," so the influence of religion had been significantly reduced in the public arena. The rise of science had given rise to an ascendant rationality as the basis for public debate. Habermas also omitted attention to another aspect of the wider public sphere, the aspect that is most relevant to this analysis. This is attention to the "masses." Warren Montag writes that this was due to Habermas' "fear of the masses." He argued (2000, p. 133) that Habermas' comment that "Laws passed under pressure of the street" indicated "that if any force other than the mere force of reason is brought to bear in the public sphere, rational debate ceases, the universal is lost and the necessarily violent rule of the particular is established, with the certainty that one particularism will soon be replaced by others."

Such fears may be justified if rationality is the only foundation of the public sphere. Of course this cannot be the case. To suggest this is to acknowledge the rightful control of all civil or military authority, no matter how despotic or cruel. It allows for continual – and legitimate – oppression of human rights, collective and personal identity, and even the protection of life and human dignity itself. It is often in the soundscapes created by protest, demonstration, even riot and insurrection, that such ethical dimensions of human life are asserted. Certainly such "particularisms" may lead to the loss of life (as it did in both Iran and China in mid-2009, but in these cases those who took to the streets in protest had reached

988   *Robert S. Fortner*

the end of their perceived ability to convince authority to relinquish what they perceived to be illegitimate power. The cries for release were simply not being heard – patience had not been rewarded. Playing "by the rules" had not resulted in equity. Should the cries of the oppressed remain unspoken in the demand for universality as Habermas suggests? Or should the soundscape of the street welcome the strains of raucous demands of protest? Habermas would deny that the shouts of the oppressed that reverberate from city walls in such protests are legitimate parts of the public sphere, as they are beyond the boundaries of reason (Montag, 2000, p. 141), but the corporeal action of the masses is sometimes all that can reasonably alert the globe of the oppression by powers whose interests would, in fact, be served by the "communicative action" that would silence alternative demands. Although the results of the invasion of the public sphere by such demands may sometimes lead to deaths (and thereby symbolize the oppression), or even to brutal and effective crackdowns that crush the regime's opponents, sometimes such protests are necessary. Sometimes the soundscape, ethically speaking, must reverberate with the cries of the oppressed.

Notes

1 The term "imagined community" is Benedict Anderson's (1991). The claim that church bells are noise pollution can be seen in a variety of web postings, including a forum provided by the Noise Abatement Society (www.noiseabatementsociety.com), to a story by Andrew Levy in the Daily Mail Online (2009), to advice given to clergy and church wardens by the Bristol Diocesan Advisory Committee for the Care of Churches (2002, June) and a reported fine of an Italian Catholic priest ("Italian Priest Fined," 2008).

2 Actually the problem of loudspeakers per se is not recent. In 1929, when New Yorkers were polled about the noises that bothered them most, 12% of them identified loudspeakers as one of their major noise complaints. "Acoustically aggrieved citizens had begun writing letters of complaint about the '*enfant terrible* of the present electrical age' as early as 1922, and in 1930 it was noted that the 'annoyance has increased since the powerful electro-dynamic loud-speakers became the vogue'" (Thompson, 2002, p. 151).

3 These two types of practices are not mutually exclusive. In Egypt, for instance, where Islam has essentially been "nationalized," sermons are vetted to assure that movement toward becoming a "modern Egyptian" is encouraged. This is because the state has incorporated religious institutions (See Hirschkind, 2006, pp. 46–48).

4 Although they are more interested in the visual aspects of media than its aural qualities, Alexander and Jacobs (1998, p. 29) make the point about the centrality of media for people's understanding of civil society that would equally apply to the soundscape.

References

Alexander, J.C., and Jacobs, R.N. (1998) Mass communication, ritual and civil society, in *Media, Ritual and Identity*, (eds T. Liebes and J. Curran), Routledge, New York, pp. 23–41.

Ali, A.H. (2007) The Role of Journalism Today: Speech at the National Press Club, New York, June 20, www.islam-watch.org/AyanHirsi/Role-of-Journalism-Today.htm (accessed August 25, 2010).

Anderson, B. (1991) *Imagined Communities: Reflections on the Origin and Spread of Nationalism*, rev edn, Verso, New York.

AP (2009) Iran election protests: Thousands swarm Tehran in rival demonstrations, June 17,www.chicagotribune.com/news/nationworld/chi-tc-nw-iran-box-0616–0617jun17, 0,925585.story, (last accessed July 8, 2009).

Attali, J. (1985) *The Spell of the Sensuous*, Random House, New York.

Augoyard, J.-F., and Torgue, H. (2005) *Sonic Experience: A Guide to Everyday Sounds*, (trans S. McCartney and D. Paquette), McGill-Queen's University Press, Montreal.

Blesser, B., and Salter, L.-R. (2007) *Spaces Speak, Are You Listening: Experiencing Aural Architecture?* The MIT Press, Cambridge, MA.

Brand-Williams, O. (2009) Christian group sues Dearborn over Arab festival access, June 17. *The Detroit News*, www.detnews.com (last accessed June 20, 2009).

Bring Back the Boom Box (2009) May 15, www.articlesbase.com/gadgets-and-gizmos-articles/ bring-back-the-boom-box-919472.html (accessed August 25, 2010).

Bristol Diocesan Advisory Committee for the Care of Churches (2002) Church Bells and the Law: Guidance Notes for Clergy and Wardens, June www.bristol.anglican.org/ admin/buildings/downloads/bells.pdf (accessed August 25, 2010).

Bull, M., and Back, L. (2003) Introduction: Into sound, in *The Auditory Culture Reader.* (eds M. Bull and L. Back), Berg, New York, pp. 1–18.

Carter, P. (2005) Ambiguous traces, mishearing, and auditory space, in *Hearing Cultures: Essays on Sound, Listening and Modernity*, (ed. V. Erlmann), Berg, New York, 43–63.

Christian Group Can't Leaflet at Arab Festival, Federal Judge Rules (2009) Associated Press, June 19, www.firstamendmentcenter.org (accessed August 25, 2010).

Cummings, J. (2001) Listen up: Opening our ears to acoustic ecology, *Soundscape Writings*, July/August, www.acousticecology.org/writings/listenup.html (accessed August 25, 2010).

Cursing Canoeist's Conviction Upheld (2000) *Los Angeles Times*, February 18, http:// articles.latimes.com/2000/feb/18/news/mn-256 (accessed August 25, 2010).

Engelhardt, H.T., Jr. (1989) Can ethics take pluralism seriously? *The Hastings Center Report*, 19, (5) 33ff.

Goffman, E. (1963) *Stigma: Notes on the Management of Spoiled Identity*, Touchstone, New York.

Goldstein, B. (2008) Text of Brooke Goldstein's Speech to UK Parliament, December 3, www.legal-project.org/article/132 (accessed August 25, 2010).

Green, E. (2009) A Divided House Spars over Charter Schools' Growth in Harlem, March 11, http://gothamschools.org/2009/02/11/a-divided-house-spars-over-charter-schools-growth-in-harlem/ (last accessed July 8, 2009).

Hale, S.E. (2007) *Sacred Space, Sacred Sound: The Acoustic Mysteries of Holy Places*, Quest Books, Wheaton, IL.

Hauser, M.D. (2006) *Moral Minds: The Nature of Right and Wrong*, Harper Perennial, New York.

Hirschkind, C. (2006) *The Ethical Soundscape: Cassette Sermons and Islamic Counterpublics*, Columbia University Press, New York.

Holl, S. (2007) Physical phenomena activate outer perception while mental phenomena activate inner perception, in *Resonance, Vol. 1: Essays on the Intersection of Music and*

990   *Robert S. Fortner*

Architecture, (eds M.W. Muecke and M.S. Zach), Culicidae Architectural Press, Ames, IA, pp. 56–59.

Ihde, D. (2007) *Listening and Voice: Phenomenologies of Sound*, 2nd edn, SUNY, Albany, NY.

International Herald Tribune/AP (2007) Muslims, Buddhists Stage Rival Demonstrations in Troubled Southern Thailand, March 1, http://pluralism.org/news/article.php?id=15390. (accessed August 25, 2010).

Italian Priest Fined $80,000 for Church Bells' 'Noise Pollution' (2008) *Christian Telegraph*, September 8, www.christiantelegraph.com/issue2935.html, (accessed August 25, 2010).

Kekes, J. (1993) *The Morality of Pluralism*, Princeton University Press, Princeton, NJ.

Lefley, J. (2009) Police count the cost of keeping apart rival demonstrations over the violence in Gaza, January 8, *MailOnline*, www.dailymail.co.uk/news/article-1108971/Police-count-cost-keeping-apart-rival-demonstrations-violence-Gaza.html (accessed August 25, 2010).

Levy, A. (2009) Church bells could be silenced after residents complain of 'deafening' noise, June 12 *MailOnline*. www.dailymail.co.uk (last accessed June 12, 2009).

MacFarland, D.T. (1997) *Future Radio Programming Strategies: Cultivating Listenership in the Digital Age*, Lawrence Erlbaum Associates, Mahwah, NJ.

markkat9 (2007) In Car Audio Boomboxes, November 20, http://boards.msn.com/Autosboards/threadid=474248 (last accessed July 8, 2009).

Michigan Man to Stand Trial for Cursing in Front of Kids (1999) *The Journal Record*, February 11, Oklahoma City, OK, http://findarticles.com/p/articles/mi_qn4182/is_19990211/ai_n10125757/ (accessed August 25, 2010).

Montag, W. (2000) The pressure of the street: Habermas's fear of the masses, *Masses, Classes, and the Public Sphere*, (eds M. Hill and W. Montag), Verso, New York, pp. 132–145.

Moon, J.D. (1993) *Constructing Community: Moral Pluralism and Tragic Conflicts*, Princeton University Press, Princeton, NJ.

"One Shot Dead" at Iran Protest. http:// Aljazeera.net. english.aljazeera.net/ news/middleeeast/2009/06/2009616165959764614.html (last accessed July 6, 2009).

Ong, W. (1982) *Orality and Literacy: The Technologizing of the Word*, Methuen, New York.

Radio Free Europe/Radio Liberty (2009) New Afghan law prompts rival demonstrations, April 15, www.unhcr.org/refworld/docid/49edb5f32a.html (accessed August 25, 2010).

Rose, M.S. (2001) Bring Back the Bells - And the Bell Tower, Too, *Adoremus Bulletin*, 7 (7), October, www.adoremus.org (last accessed October 9, 2008).

Rothenberg, D. (2001) Music in nature. *Alternatives Journal*, 27.

Schafer, M. (2003) Open ears, in *The Auditory Culture Reader*, (eds Michael Bull and Les Back), Berg, New York, pp. 25–39.

Scott, M.S. (2001) Loud car stereos, Guide No. 7, Center for Problem-Oriented Policing. www.popcenter.org/problems/loud_car_stereos/ (accessed August 25, 2010).

Sharansky, N. (2008) *Defending Identity: Its Indispensable Role in Protecting Democracy*, Public Affairs, New York.

Simon, S. (2002) 'Cussing canoeist' law overturned, *Los Angeles Times*, April 2, http://articles.latimes.com/2002/apr/02/news/mn-35828 (accessed August 25, 2010).

Smith, B.R. (2005) Listening to the wild blue yonder: The challenges of acoustic ecology, in *Hearing Cultures: Essays on Sound, Listening and Modernity*, (ed. Veit Erlmann), Berg, New York, pp. 21–41.

Sterne, J. (2003) *The Audible Past: Cultural Origins of Sound Reproduction*, Duke University Press, Durham, NC.

Taylor, C. (1991) *The Ethics of Authenticity*, Harvard University Press, Cambridge, MA.

Thompson, E. (2002) *The Soundscape of Modernity: Architectural Acoustics and the Culture of Listening in America, 1900–1933*, MIT Press, Cambridge, MA.

Universal Declaration of Human Rights (1948) www.un.org/en/ documents/udhr/ (last accessed July 9, 2009).

Villa, R.H. (2000) The right to the city in Los Angeles: Discourse and practice of a Chicano alternative public sphere, in *Masses, Classes, and the Public Sphere*, (eds M. Hill and W. Montana), Verso, New York, pp. 41–61.

Violence in Xinjiang Persists (2009) *Turkish Weekly*, www.turkishweedly.net/news/83667/ violence-in-xinjiang-persists.html, July 7, (last accessed July 8, 2009).

Wrightson, K. (n.d.) An introduction to acoustic ecology. http://cec.concordia.ca/ econtact/NAISA/introduction.html (accessed August 12, 2010).

Index

Accessibility of information 704

Accountability 531, 532, 702, 708, 717,
726, 777, 806, 824, 825, 826, 838,
846, 852, 853, 854, 855, 856, 857,
859, 866, 902, 903, 942

Accuracy 12, 161, 165, 215, 419, 490,
492, 527, 532, 663, 706, 717, 725,
745, 778, 779, 825, 836, 838,
839, 840, 846, 847, 848, 849,
857, 878, 886

Advertising/advertisers 182, 183, 184–5,
342, 357, 373, 406, 441, 447, 490,
507, 517, 518, 521, 527, 571, 627,
629, 639, 677, 681, 688, 703, 837,
850, 885, 897–900, 915

Advocacy 651, 846, 850

Aesthetic(s) 347, 348, 349, 356, 359,
368, 370, 491, 892, 893, 895, 896,
976. 986

Affiliation/assembly 398

Affirmative action 172, 408

Agency 243, 326, 327, 352, 368, 423,
610, 650
moral 174, 175, 178, 323, 325, 396,
417–19

Alienation 604, 980

Al-Jazeera 127, 222, 603, 630, 959

Alternative journalism 239

Anonymity of the Internet 238

Anonymous sources 691, 721, 725,
727, 832

Arbitration 721

Archetype 486, 487

Arendt, Hannah 21, 25, 32, 36, 110

Aristotle 3, 28, 101, 119, 125, 326, 417,
424, 509, 511, 738

Assisted suicide 236

Astrology 165–6

Atrocities 774

Audiences 359, 360

Authenticity 176, 401, 406, 463, 483,
503, 786, 787, 788–90, 791, 794–6,
800, 827, 829, 830, 839, 901, 983

Authoritarian/authoritarianism 313, 403,
559, 607, 679, 680, 714, 944

Authority/Authoritative 180, 321, 369,
678, 686, 804, 813, 815, 818, 820,
852, 854, 855, 976, 978, 985

Authorship 823–44

Balance 570, 634, 700, 742, 748, 865

Beneficence 187

Bias 162, 241, 570, 682, 683, 689, 690,
691, 703, 736, 743, 778, 825, 838,
857, 871

Blasphemy 263–97

The Handbook of Global Communication and Media Ethics, First Edition. Edited by Robert S. Fortner
and P. Mark Fackler.
© 2011 Blackwell Publishing Ltd. Published 2011 by Blackwell Publishing Ltd.

Blogging/blogosphere 217, 221, 229,
236, 239, 241, 242, 244, 248, 258,
304, 313, 371, 376, 381, 387, 470,
471, 472, 481, 484, 490, 495, 520,
692, 693, 810, 811, 813, 814,
823–44, 848, 850, 851, 852, 853,
857–8, 859, 982
Bollywood 577–601
Global nature 578
Bonhoeffer, Dietrich 10, 407, 509
Broadcast journalism/news 163, 167,
221, 226, 240, 253, 568
Broadcasting, religious 631
Buddhism 492, 501, 507, 554, 557, 558,
783, 791, 982
Business press 690–1

Cassette tapes 965–6
Caste 135, 162, 382, 383, 492, 493, 524,
558, 563, 583, 616, 947
Categorical imperative 138, 369, 409,
487, 488, 510, 738
Catholic, Catholicism 105–6, 140, 148,
617, 629, 781, 782, 791
Celebrity 255, 493, 496, 568, 569, 812,
815, 818, 905
Censorship 195, 197, 416, 518, 560,
562, 563, 605, 629, 663, 679, 682,
684–5, 686, 687, 688, 689, 693,
696, 713, 714, 715, 716, 836,
875–6, 886, 914, 920, 928
Character assassination 420
Child abuse/trafficking 166, 328
Christian/Christianity 579, 611, 618,
622, 701, 739, 744, 746, 780, 781,
782, 790, 791, 794, 884, 978, 984
Cinema 577–601, 744
Civil discourse 814
Civil rights/liberties 172, 253, 443, 512,
541, 606, 607, 704, 708, 716, 725,
776, 942, 944
Civil society 73, 98, 171, 378, 383, 385,
386, 387, 403, 489, 532, 629, 820,
970, 977
Global 378, 384, 389, 482, 948
Clash of Civilizations 736–7, 746, 747
Codes of ethics 157, 158, 160, 161, 162,
163, 323, 370, 439, 440, 442, 443,

446, 447, 449, 489, 529–30, 649,
655, 656, 659, 661, 710, 749, 775,
777, 778–9, 805, 825–6, 828, 836,
839, 840, 850, 853, 858
Coherence 491
Collective conscience/consciousness 265,
275, 283, 355, 522
Collective guilt 735–51
Colonialism 66, 88, 355, 630, 635
Commercialism/ization 305, 342, 344,
349, 358, 502, 564, 568, 569, 571,
786, 799, 866, 893, 903
Commission on Freedom of the
Press 489, 649, 707, 724, 848
Committee to Protect Journalists 563,
655, 703, 722, 864
Commodification of news 522
Common good 327–8, 330, 399, 406,
512, 850
Communication as catalyst 404
Communication rights 147, 383
Communicative action 827
Communitarianism 109, 113, 178, 180,
181, 234, 256–7, 393–414, 507,
508, 510, 512, 513, 650, 651, 902,
903, 987
Dialogic 399, 400–1, 403, 405, 406,
407, 408, 410
Community, imagined 389, 976
Community media 342–63, 519, 531–2,
566, 567, 627, 629
Compassion 184, 186–7, 317, 318, 319,
330, 334, 493
Conduct, appropriate 976
Confidentiality 254–5, 709, 778
Conflict of interest 492, 532, 825,
837, 850
Conflict resolution 605, 608
Confucius/Confucian(ism) 3, 188, 402,
554, 557, 558–9, 561, 562, 567,
568, 569, 573, 574
Consciousness industry 881, 887
Consequences 2, 420, 738
Consumerism 356, 358, 359, 518, 558
Contractualism 189
Convergence culture 804, 809, 816, 819
Copyright 416, 799, 816–17, 825
Coresponsibility 45, 47, 48

Corporate ownership of media 241, 257, 258, 306–12, 384, 386, 471, 472, 504–5, 517, 523, 524

Corruption 164, 251, 332, 336, 492, 503, 561, 565, 566, 571–2, 574, 626, 638, 641, 648, 649, 683, 684, 686, 687, 703, 705, 706, 707, 711, 717, 718

Cost-benefit analysis 313, 315

Credibility 244, 329, 330, 490, 682, 683, 723, 805, 813, 814, 825, 826, 827, 829, 836, 839, 846, 847, 848, 851, 852, 853–4, 855, 864, 918

Critique-as-ethics 369

Cultivation theory 739–40, 748

Cultural essentialism 356

Cultural flow 154, 900

Cultural imperialism 520, 521, 925

Cultural modernism 68–70, 72

Cultural peace 608

Cultural pluralism 5, 136

Cultural practices 163

Cultural violence 607, 608, 612, 615

Cyberactivism 792

Cyberbullying 423

Cyberculture 804, 809

Cyberethics 113

Cyber-immersion 484

Cyberliteracy 786, 788, 798–9, 800

Cyber-representation 792

Danish cartoon controversy 281–3, 562, 837

Datamining 305

Decentering of news production 470

Deception and trust 252, 386

Dehumanization 88, 462, 473, 474, 479, 607

Deliberative democracy 237–8, 328–9, 812

Demonization 203, 207, 462, 472

Dependency paradigm 934

Deregulation 346, 357, 516

Descriptive ethics 1, 15

Desensitization 869

Desktop publishing 164

Development ethics 317–41

Development journalism/ communication 228, 566, 567, 938

Development studies 610–1

Dharma 579, 580, 583, 585, 587, 598, 599

Dialogue 41, 137, 176, 178, 179, 181, 189, 328, 366, 383, 401–2, 489, 490, 531, 648, 673, 695, 826, 827, 902, 903, 982

Diaspora 792, 793, 798, 966

Digital divide 379–1, 531, 945, 948

Direct violence 605, 607, 608, 612, 613, 615

Discourse ethics 150, 396, 434, 493

Discrimination 135, 136, 407, 443, 449, 491

Disenchantment 62, 73, 987

Disenfranchised/ment 182, 188, 300, 315, 470, 634

Disinformation 202, 207, 858, 886, 921, 926

Dissent 503, 504

Diversity 56, 501, 503, 507, 552, 713, 743, 749, 779, 780

Documentary 149, 352, 406

Due diligence 493

Duty, obligation 2, 42, 171, 174, 177, 178, 179, 187, 313, 395, 439, 441, 462, 479, 487, 510, 542, 559

Editing 164

Editorial perspective 455, 635

Efficiency 16–17, 314

Egalitarian/egalitarianism/equality 189, 274, 278, 325, 334, 380, 381, 478, 504, 618, 620, 621

Empowerment 349, 793

Endorsements 837

Ends and means 660

Enlightenment 30, 80, 81, 82, 98, 100, 115, 369, 378, 379, 388, 393, 398, 401, 404, 409, 649, 650, 790, 936, 943, 977

Ensoniment 977

Environmental rights 144–5

E-papers 520

Ethical awareness 299, 825
  Choices/Predicaments 560, 664,
    667, 825
  Commitments 986
  Compass 829
  Demands 976
  Philosophies 747–8
  Reasoning 902
  Speech 662
  System 656
Ethics
  Audience 855–9
  Communication/ive 657, 839
  Consequentialist 434
  Deontological 313, 434, 440, 738
  Global 603
  Inadequacy of 655
  Information 799, 804
  Jewish 659
  Lack of 703
  Normative 506
  Of care 173, 176–7, 325, 326–7
  Postmodern 488
  Principles 446, 479, 490, 528,
    574, 649
  Standards 630, 640, 644, 649, 665,
    686, 692, 826
  Universal 708
Ethnic cleansing 388
Evil 774–84; *see also* Right and wrong
Excommunication 371, 791
Existentialism 21

Facebook 304, 314, 376, 423, 470, 481,
    815, 817, 930
Fair trial 491, 707
Fairness 115, 125, 162, 329, 399, 452,
    455, 458, 459, 460, 489, 492, 507,
    706, 708, 735, 738, 742, 744, 745,
    748, 825, 840, 857, 886, 948
False consciousness 122
Fanaticism 604, 620, 931
Feminism 171–92, 325, 396, 400, 487,
    606, 607, 830
Film producers 183
Flickr 817
Foucault, Michel 364–75

Frames, interpretive 611, 613, 615, 634,
    671, 962, 966
Fraud 791
Freedom of expression/speech 99, 104,
    113, 131, 244, 264, 265–6, 268,
    269, 274, 275, 280, 282, 284, 286,
    321, 398, 416, 427, 448, 449, 466,
    491, 495, 503, 517, 531, 678, 686,
    700, 701–2, 704, 706, 708, 709,
    710, 711, 713, 716, 778, 805,
    814, 825, 858, 859, 874, 909,
    969, 985
Freedom of information 441, 442, 787
Free press 162, 244, 441, 445, 495, 503,
    504, 528, 555, 560, 562, 563, 627,
    652, 665–6, 677, 678, 685, 686,
    688, 692, 693, 694, 696, 700–34,
    778, 805, 859
Fundamentalism 59

Gaming 86, 346, 484
Gatekeeper(s) 240, 820, 824, 836,
    857, 959
Gay rights 236
Genocide 388, 491, 602, 616, 671
Global flow of information 472, 736
Globalization 5, 41, 46–7, 49, 55, 57, 66,
    150, 151, 154, 156, 159, 162, 168,
    223, 343–4, 345, 346, 348, 359,
    360, 400, 471, 520, 522, 531, 534,
    583, 596, 779, 811, 901, 933, 938,
    939, 944–5, 953
Golden rule 11, 325, 383, 512
Good, the 21, 24–7, 28, 32, 35, 36,
    579, 917
Good and bad 259, 428
Google 314
Graphics 164
Great community 494
Gulf War 754, 757

Habermas, Jürgen 42, 47, 50–1, 150,
    358, 378, 384, 461, 464, 493, 824,
    974, 986, 987, 988
Happiness 25, 313, 511, 931
Hate speech 264, 268, 389, 416, 427,
    651, 671, 828

Hegemony 124, 128, 182, 189, 195,
  355, 466, 469, 520, 521, 602, 612,
  871, 955
Hidden cameras 522
Hinduism 557, 558, 578, 581, 582, 583,
  584, 585, 791
HIV / Aids 89, 162
Hollywood 744
Homophobia 174
Honesty 259, 452, 481, 482, 664, 778,
  825, 840, 847, 852, 857
Human
  condition 386, 402, 949
  consciousness 299
  dignity 1, 12–14, 83, 84, 85, 86, 87,
    88, 91, 135, 136, 137, 138, 146,
    147, 157, 171, 189, 234, 274, 318,
    319, 323, 324, 329, 330, 332, 333,
    334, 386, 397, 398, 403, 405, 406,
    410, 491, 492, 618, 665, 667, 779,
    902, 933, 970, 987
  nature 101, 105, 125, 129, 135, 511
  relationships 786
  rights 41, 49, 50, 81, 87–8, 93, 100,
    136, 140, 142, 146, 147, 151, 177,
    180, 188, 223, 263, 264, 265, 266,
    268, 274, 284, 328, 329, 330, 332,
    336, 379, 381, 385, 389, 397, 398,
    402, 409, 444, 448, 487, 491, 492,
    511, 541, 543, 544, 545, 546, 548,
    550, 552, 573, 607, 610, 621, 636,
    658, 667, 700, 706, 714, 743, 778,
    779, 780, 783, 824, 979, 985, 987
Humanism 25, 101, 102, 103, 121, 137,
  574, 650
Hyperreality 377

Identity/identity politics 35–6, 55, 56, 92,
  98, 173, 179, 343, 344, 345, 346–7,
  351, 352, 353, 355, 356, 359, 377,
  384, 399, 400, 410, 418, 507, 513,
  614, 615, 616, 618, 659, 778, 790,
  825, 830, 852, 853, 891, 900, 901,
  902, 909, 976, 979, 980, 985, 987
  Brand 851
Ideology 119–24, 125–6, 127–8, 129,
  131, 132, 194, 273, 276, 283, 383,

388–9, 397, 462, 463, 471, 477,
  495, 502, 511, 536, 596, 607, 610,
  613–14, 620, 637, 664, 679, 693,
  694, 695, 696, 709, 711, 712, 735,
  737, 936, 954, 955, 963, 965
Ignorance 418
Image as illusion 483
Impartiality 2, 174, 185, 215, 398, 445,
  460, 570, 846, 850–1, 852, 855,
  857, 859, 901
Impersonation 828
Independent sources 704
Individualism 92, 93, 98, 256, 257, 321,
  358, 378, 399, 435, 493, 558
Infanticide 165
Infomercial 571
Information
  Flow 737, 800, 837, 900, 925,
    927, 930
  Overload 810–11
  Power 928
  Society 150
  Space 302
  War 927
Infotainment 469–70
Institutional power 123
Instrumentalism 1, 15–16
Integrity 251, 259, 397, 419, 481, 482,
  528, 805, 825, 850
Interactivity 236, 237, 238, 314, 486,
  651, 694, 787, 825, 826, 838, 847,
  848, 851, 853, 857, 858
International television 159, 384
Internet 155, 173, 188, 220, 222, 229,
  235, 236, 237, 239, 244, 304, 305,
  346, 367, 376, 377, 379, 381, 385,
  387, 408, 415–33, 484, 485, 517,
  519–20, 530, 531, 536, 564, 570, 596,
  677, 685, 692, 693, 696, 748, 749,
  785–802, 803, 806, 808, 809, 811,
  814, 818, 819, 824, 825, 828, 830,
  831, 832, 835, 845, 846, 851, 853,
  856, 857, 899, 906, 907–8, 916, 919,
  927, 928, 929, 945, 948, 949, 953–72
  Empowering people 238, 243
  Hotlines 426–7
  Obfuscating reality 303, 483

War 928

Islam/Islamic 556, 557, 559, 568, 573, 604, 611, 614, 617, 618, 619, 622, 658, 735, 740, 745, 746, 746–7, 748, 781, 782, 783, 791, 931, 933, 943–4, 967, 978, 981, 982, 984, 985, 986
And global communication 60–2
And pluralism 57, 737
Extremists 953, 954, 958, 959, 960, 961, 969
Fundamentalism 556, 573, 605, 743, 747, 940. 964
Soul of 26£, 269

Islamic morals 562, 669, 741

Islamophobia 744

Jihad 615, 657, 658
Islamic 661, 662, 736
Journalism 747

Journalism/journalists 9, 124, 127, 128, 129, 130, 131, 148–9, 154, 155, 156, 157, 159, 161, 163, 165, 166, 168, 171, 176, 181, 182, 186, 234, 235, 240, 244, 248, 253, 256, 258, 304, 305, 313, 315, 357, 358, 365, 371, 373, 481, 483, 484, 486, 489, 526, 534, 535, 542, 549, 558, 561, 563, 564, 570, 571, 572, 573, 574, 631, 639, 651, 678, 689, 694, 695, 706, 713, 718, 724, 744, 746, 774–84, 805, 807, 823, 824, 828, 829, 840, 851, 858, 885, 915, 967
Activist 567, 838
Advocacy 766
Amateur 628, 638–9, 834
And exaggeration 208, 209
And public protest 199
Attacks on 703
Authentic 564–5, 573, 845, 846
Bad 883
Citizen 215, 220, 240, 244, 258, 481, 566, 570, 812–13, 814, 838, 930
Competence 847
Decline of 484–5, 693
Deference to military 201
Dissenting 561–2
Embedded 477

Envelope 571–2, 639
Expectations of 488, 679, 682, 700
Frontline 752–4, 756, 763–9
Graphic 568
International 630
Investigative 522, 647, 691, 725, 823, 926
Layered 216–18
Licensing 716, 721, 722
Motives 780
Of attachment 183
Online 219–20
Organization of 438–40, 441–2, 445
Protection of 704
Reputation 831
Self-regulation 446
Sources 241, 254, 256, 691, 709, 778, 780, 813, 825, 838
Standards 691, 831, 871
Tapelas 718
Television/broadcast 185, 485, 562, 806
Virtues 663
Women 198, 641, 689, 691
Yellow 693

Journalism ethics 155, 160, 166–7, 172, 173, 443, 683, 737, 832, 847

Justice/injustice 41, 115, 125, 136, 149, 177, 187, 305, 321, 332, 397, 409, 410, 439, 503, 508, 523, 526, 587, 606, 607, 618, 669, 708, 886, 948, 987

Kant, Emmanuel 29, 32, 36, 94, 136–7, 138, 146, 150, 151, 178, 223, 324, 369, 395, 409, 487, 488, 493, 510, 511, 738

Kierkegaard, Søren 31, 106, 376, 377

Knowledge space 819

Language of discourse 489–90

Least served/marginalized 140, 147, 162, 187

Libel 416, 702, 707, 716, 717, 718, 719, 720, 724, 726, 825

Liberalism 173, 264, 649, 692, 695, 901, 902, 936

Libertarianism 106, 112, 313, 708, 853
Life-world 384, 385
Literacy 107, 381, 386, 568, 628,
    891–2, 916
Loyalty 259
Lying 491, 686, 825

MacBride Commission 444, 925
Marginalization 793
    Of women 530, 531
Marketplace of ideas 237, 313, 704,
    708, 849
Mash-up 481
Media
    And morality 649, 883
    And peace 608, 626, 641, 642
    And sex 559
    And time 807
    As commodity 596, 597
    As scapegoat 197
    Attention 956
    Complaints against 631, 737
    Conglomerates 313, 749
    Consumer-oriented 526
    Context 627, 741, 742, 746, 813
    Control 561, 605, 613, 629,
        677, 678, 680, 684, 685–6,
        687, 689, 690, 694, 706,
        711, 836
    Coverage 551, 561, 562, 563, 565,
        568, 569, 570, 644
    Culture 829, 883
    Development 628–9, 630, 678
    Digital 803–22
    Disintermediation 803, 815
    Effects 608–10, 671, 866–9, 872, 893,
        903–4, 905
    Electronic 630, 631–2
    Ethics 157–8, 313, 358, 371
    Flow of information 704, 832
    Freedom 630, 687, 909
    Global 462, 465, 469, 473, 476, 477,
        504, 554, 555, 557, 566, 572,
        574, 835
    Jihadist 960, 963
    Incitement of violence 700, 722
    Independence 681, 683, 684, 690,
        692, 695, 696, 708, 712, 713, 714

Influence 686, 695, 700, 703, 895,
    900, 904
Institutions 608, 613, 749
Irresponsibility 639, 700, 708
Local 663, 690
Management 926, 927
Manipulation 202, 956
Mass 840, 936, 937, 962, 963, 964
Monopoly 445, 927
New 685, 894, 896, 928
Organizations 824, 834, 836, 840,
    926, 961
Outlets 691, 704, 712, 722
Power 525, 666, 672, 678, 681, 703
Profit-oriented 749
Public 663
Public-supported 692
Reach 652
Relations 967
Representations 735–51
Responsibility 700, 704, 713, 723,
    724, 847, 908–9
Role of 891
Role questioned 526, 678, 679
Sensitivity 527
Spectacle 200, 206, 461, 470, 483,
    484, 525, 887
State monopoly 631, 706
Structure 706
Technology 935, 964
Tribalization 638
Use of 677
Melodrama 578, 589–90, 594, 598
Metaethics 1, 2
Millennium Development Goals 140, 380
Modernity 376, 377, 378, 578, 598, 977
Modernization 901, 933–52, 976, 986
Moral
    Acceptability 922
    Action 494, 502, 664, 714
    Authenticity 981
    Character 559, 568, 660
    Choice 902, 903
    Commitment 371
    Controversy 984
    Demand 976
    Development 184, 902
    Dilemma 585, 685

Disarmament 436, 437
Discernment/insight 491, 505
Dissemination 659
Evil 175, 878
Failure 604
Ground/grounding 282, 323, 673
High ground 921
Imagination 405, 407, 408
Influences 557
Interconnectedness 318, 511
Language/dialog 176, 322, 331, 336,
    396, 403, 405, 407, 901
Legitimacy 329, 379
Lenses 984
Literacy 406–7, 651, 892
Panic 877
Principle(s)/order 135, 137, 157, 314,
    318, 372, 395, 449, 462, 510, 580,
    583, 651, 945, 984
Progress 511, 669
Reasoning 183, 189, 395, 449, 450,
    486, 487
Right of freedom 707
Subjectivity 366, 984
Support 712
Syntax 501
Universe 359–60, 569
Values/virtue 151, 174, 175, 320, 332,
    505, 618–19, 738
Moralism/moral obligation 4, 99, 101,
    102, 103, 174, 238, 259, 427, 445
Morality 4, 9, 236, 255, 273, 274, 300,
    315, 318, 366–7, 368, 384, 388,
    403, 406, 446, 483, 492, 558, 648,
    649, 655, 656, 669, 944
My Lai 198
MySpace 421–3, 815, 829
Myth/mythology 194, 196, 197, 202,
    207, 486, 487, 578–81, 585, 615,
    739, 805, 806, 886, 919, 979, 984

Narrative ethics 5
Negotiation of moral knowledge 180
Neutrality 782, 783, 786, 787, 850, 851,
    852; *See also* Bias
New World Information and
    Communication Order 520
News flow 107

Newspapers 159–60, 161, 364, 484, 517,
    535, 540, 542, 545, 549, 554–5,
    627, 633–4, 671, 693, 704, 712,
    722–23, 746, 806, 807, 809, 811,
    812, 813, 823, 826, 836, 847, 935
  On-line 809–10
Nietzsche, Friedrich 4, 30, 36
Nihilism 402, 984
Nonviolence 1, 11, 397, 405, 491, 492
Normative ethics/standards 1, 6, 150,
    151, 171, 174, 320, 365, 366, 372,
    395–6, 399, 401

Objectification 352
Objectivism 513
Objectivity 9–10, 124, 180, 215, 224, 226,
    227, 228, 230, 460, 488, 535, 541,
    542, 549, 552, 634, 651, 679, 681,
    682, 683, 689, 696, 706, 723, 735,
    736, 740, 741, 742, 744, 748, 778,
    824, 838, 847, 850, 852, 901, 937
  Multidimensional 216, 223–5, 226,
    228, 229, 230–1
  Pragmatic 224–5
Obscenity 268, 436
Offensiveness 455, 456–7, 458
Other, the 88, 180, 182, 186, 349, 356,
    371, 388, 397, 400, 462, 476, 479,
    481, 482, 495, 588, 613, 615,
    616–17, 618, 627, 975
Othering 613, 616, 618

Panopticon 364–75
Parachute reporting 753
Partisanship in news 241, 357, 358, 495,
    713, 850
Partisanship, political 239, 490, 825
Peace 13, 444, 445, 493, 502, 507, 508,
    603, 605, 606, 607, 622, 641, 642,
    665, 668, 672, 673, 706, 746, 779,
    902, 917, 979
  And democracy 607
  Cultural 608
  Journalism 11–12, 406, 626, 645–6,
    648, 649, 651
  Virtuous triangle 608
Photographs/photography 164, 421–53,
    469, 550, 817, 823, 964, 965, 982

Photojournalism/photojournalists 183,
187, 817–18
Delay of photos 201
Piracy 377
Plato 28, 119
Pleasure 25
Polarization 570–1
Polygamy 89
Pornography 81, 172, 389, 416,
424, 426, 427, 707, 715, 879,
881–2
Postmodernity 20, 22, 366, 488, 507,
511, 578, 877–9, 900, 936, 956
Power 125, 126, 139, 167, 173, 174,
177, 181, 185, 329, 332, 367, 368,
370, 371–2, 389, 505, 506, 569,
571, 605, 611, 613, 636, 657, 689,
735, 736, 845, 864, 938, 979, 980,
981, 984
Of language/words 670–1, 672
Pre-news 485
Press club 535, 542, 565, 566
Press conference 571
Press council 528–9, 710, 713, 721, 725,
726, 856
Privacy 1, 14–15, 79–97, 110, 162, 165,
416, 449, 482, 503, 532, 549, 568,
778, 779, 799, 825, 831, 857, 942
Product endorsements 571
Professionalism 9, 131, 365, 405, 440,
527, 563, 630, 680, 703, 709, 712,
713, 726, 737, 805, 813, 814, 818,
820, 830, 838, 845–6, 848, 855,
856, 857, 859, 884, 886
Propaganda 202, 208, 226, 437, 438,
442, 444, 445, 449, 502, 563, 566,
609, 634, 681, 682, 746, 747, 782,
866, 905, 906, 912–32, 934, 945,
962, 963, 964, 980
As psychological warfare 917, 918, 921,
922, 925, 963, 964, 968
Defined 914
Morality of 913–14
Total 920
Protestantism/Pentecostalism 140–1,
148–9, 617, 629
Protonorms 366, 397, 405, 487, 491
Public diplomacy 914, 925, 928, 931

Public interest 245, 387, 443, 448, 471,
485, 492, 493–4, 528, 529, 570,
702, 706, 713, 779, 799
Public journalism 110, 181
Public relations 183, 373, 441, 447–8,
490, 507, 712, 829, 850, 912, 915
Black 683
Public service broadcasting 354, 357, 358
Public sphere 173, 218, 236, 237, 240–1,
353, 355, 358, 377, 378, 415, 462,
472, 485, 490, 492, 493, 496, 517,
552, 652, 695, 824, 834, 836, 840,
901, 944, 974, 976, 977, 983,
985–6, 987, 988
Diasporic 385
Global 377, 378, 379, 383, 384, 385,
386, 387, 388, 389, 959
Virtual 836, 856
Publicity 82, 961
Pulitzer Prize 455

Racism 13, 67, 135, 172, 174, 182, 268,
278, 383, 405, 406, 407, 415, 443,
444, 742, 747, 883
Radio freedom 694–5
Rationalism/rationality 2, 136, 137, 251,
256, 329, 378, 384, 388, 393, 394,
403, 489, 509, 557, 790, 987
Rawls, John 42, 324, 327, 488, 493, 738,
886
Realism/reality 6, 484, 779, 787
Misrepresentation of 736, 741
Reification 123, 366
Relativism 1, 4, 5, 180, 333, 400, 506
Religion 5, 13, 30, 44, 58, 59, 66–7, 68,
69, 72, 92, 99, 126, 127, 135, 137,
138, 154, 162, 378, 379, 382, 388,
407, 442, 467, 468, 487, 488, 491,
562, 563, 570, 578, 586, 605, 607,
613, 616, 617, 622, 711, 737, 739,
742, 745, 746, 747, 774–84, 786,
965, 966, 981, 984, 986, 987
Virtual 790
Religious motivation 663, 664, 665, 985
Representation/misrepresentation 172,
173, 180, 352, 377, 482, 614, 785,
786, 787, 788, 791, 793, 800, 819
Reputation 825, 840

Resonance 808
Right and wrong/good and evil 5, 177,
    183, 405. 475, 567, 568, 579, 615,
    745, 893, 906, 909
Right to communicate 949
Right to know/information 704, 707,
    715, 778, 779, 850
Ritual 350, 352, 404

Sacred, the 578
Satanic Verses, The 267, 278, 279–81
Satellite television 188, 347, 381, 518,
    527, 529, 737, 871, 919, 924, 926
Scientific materialism 30, 31
Second Life 304, 377, 930
Self-censorship 555, 560, 562, 563, 566
Self-interest 326, 558, 574, 778, 780
Self-knowledge 782
Self-regulation 530, 710
Self-representation 791, 793
Sensationalism 478, 482, 495, 522–3,
    525, 555, 568, 648, 707, 708, 723,
    857, 945, 962
Sex discrimination/sexism 72, 174, 383,
    405, 406, 526
Sexting 83, 85, 86
Sexual harassment 185
Sexual orientation 284
Shield law(s) 254
Sincerity 259
SMS 640, 815, 967
    Polling 523
Social bonds as moral claims 404
Social capital 252–3
Social consciousness 352, 353
Social construction/reality 122, 127,
    352, 740, 790, 975
Social institutions 44
Social justice 1, 6–8, 135, 162, 166,
    168, 176, 223, 319, 322,
    324–5, 330, 334, 336, 388,
    492–3, 567, 659, 678
Social media 215, 836
Social networking 83, 86, 95, 237, 302,
    376, 381, 423, 470, 520, 815, 819,
    824, 835, 840, 856, 930
Social responsibility 98–118, 157, 178,
    253–4, 313, 379, 417, 418, 440,

442, 444, 445, 447, 495, 529, 707,
    708, 714, 779
Solidarity 179, 987
Soundscapes 973–91
Spam 831
Spin/spin-doctoring 825, 906
Standpoint theory 180, 182
State terrorism 203
Stereotypes/stereotyping 162, 172, 175,
    182, 252, 279, 282, 346, 474, 616,
    671, 710, 735, 736, 743–4, 745,
    748, 870
Story-telling 346, 347, 354, 739, 885
Suicide 420–1, 747
Surveillance 81, 364, 365, 367, 371,
    550, 914
Suspending disbelief 884
Symbolization 404, 607, 671, 739

Tabloidization of news 522, 532
Taboo 386
Talk radio 695, 696
Taoism 507, 554, 557, 558
Technicism 17
Technology transfer 943, 947
Television 473, 516, 518, 523, 525, 627,
    648, 680, 681, 687–8, 690, 694,
    695, 739, 803, 805, 806, 807, 811,
    816, 864–8, 882, 884, 899, 923,
    925, 926, 929, 945, 946, 948, 964
    Bridges 694
    Depoliticalization 688
    Local 484
    Networks 484–5
    News coverage 526, 671, 823, 871, 926
    Programmers 183
    Ratings 527
    Talk show 565, 694
    Visualization 896
Ten Commandments 579, 669
Terror, dissemination of 465
Terrorism 154, 416, 427, 461–80, 491,
    538, 541, 542, 543, 544, 545, 546,
    547, 548, 549, 550, 552, 562, 573,
    603–4, 617–18, 659, 661, 662, 663,
    665, 667, 671, 735, 737, 741, 744,
    745, 747, 748, 929, 940, 942, 953–72
Totalitarianism 398, 604, 679

Toutware 485
Tradition/ traditional 370, 790, 933, 934, 935, 939, 940, 943, 966
Transparency 130, 219, 239–40, 504, 508, 702, 706, 824, 825, 827, 829, 838, 839, 840, 852, 853, 855
Trust/distrust 329, 416, 567, 608, 626, 627, 652, 659, 787, 788, 815, 839, 852, 859, 929, 944
In journalists 247–62, 495, 528
Truth/truth telling/veracity 1, 8–9, 10, 110, 115, 121, 128, 161–2, 182, 218, 222, 226, 234, 237, 277, 299, 300, 315, 366, 369, 370, 371, 384, 386, 397, 405–6, 410, 445, 483, 488, 489, 490, 491, 503, 507, 557, 560, 565, 573, 580, 651, 666, 667, 683, 709, 714, 723, 727, 735, 740–1, 742, 744, 748, 749, 778, 779, 803, 804, 806, 808, 809, 812, 814, 815, 816, 817, 818, 820, 825, 827, 829, 832, 838, 839, 840, 845, 846, 847–50, 852, 855, 857, 859, 864, 883, 885, 886, 913, 918, 984
Twitter/tweeting 217, 220, 299, 304, 305, 376, 481, 805, 815, 827, 833, 834, 835, 836, 840

Ubuntu 627, 643, 644–5, 649, 650, 651, 652, 800
UNESCO 138, 437, 440, 442, 443, 444, 446, 530–2, 608, 778, 904, 908, 925
Universal Declaration of Human Rights 13, 49, 135–6, 137, 222, 379, 441, 661, 700, 701, 909, 949, 985
Universal principles/values 139, 151, 157–8, 318, 332–3, 389, 395, 449, 780, 979
Universal service 387
Universalism / Universalization 2, 8, 34, 41, 42, 43, 46, 54, 65, 109, 113, 121, 135, 136, 137, 138, 151, 155, 162, 174, 177, 179, 188, 279, 322, 330, 331, 365, 366, 369, 371, 379, 386, 393–414, 405, 478, 487, 489, 491, 492, 493, 495, 496, 507, 508, 621, 669, 700, 738, 749, 779, 839,

931, 935, 936, 937, 938, 942–3, 975, 984, 987, 988
Interactive 396
Utilitarianism 2, 180, 242–3, 245, 313, 488, 506, 738, 749

Values/value system 274, 284, 286, 299, 300, 321, 322, 323, 330, 343, 345, 354, 356, 359, 360, 383, 394, 405, 487, 559, 568, 650, 655, 660, 669, 670, 673, 695, 696, 714, 739, 741, 779, 781, 826, 827, 838, 839, 846, 852, 895, 897, 902, 903, 906, 907, 924, 931, 941, 943, 984, 985
Value-free 936
V-chip 872, 873–4
Veil of ignorance 739
Victimization 462, 472
Video games 877
Violence against women 328, 382
Virtual community 237, 300, 303
Virtual place/virtuality 302, 377, 787, 791, 792
Virtual reality/world 740
Virtue ethics 177, 186

War 328, 449, 468, 477
As entertainment 194–5
Images of 206
Reporting 183, 406
Whistle blower 495
Wi-fi 383, 387
Wikiality 242
Wikipedia 799, 813, 866
Women and water 140–1
Women's empowerment 525
Women's liberation movement 172
Wonder 20, 21–4, 37
World Health Organization (WHO) 145
World of Warcraft 377

Xenophobia 386, 501, 651, 747, 937

YouTube 220, 377, 470, 481, 830, 930, 962